Architect's Legal Handbook

Architect's Legal Handbook
The Law for Architects

Fifth edition

Anthony Speaight

Gregory Stone

Butterworth Architecture
London Boston Singapore Sydney Toronto Wellington

Butterworth Architecture
is an imprint of Butterworth–Heinemann

 PART OF REED INTERNATIONAL P.L.C.

First published in book form in 1973 by the Architectural Press Ltd

Second edition, 1978, Third edition 1982, Fourth edition 1985,
Reprinted 1987

Reprinted 1989 by Butterworth Architecture

© **Butterworth–Heinemann Ltd, 1990**
except Chapter 14 © Sir Desmond Heap; Chapter 17 © George
Stringer, 1971, Revisions © Michael Flint, 1982, 1984, 1990;
Chapter 20 © Peter Madge; Chapter 22 © Richard Dyton

British Library Cataloguing in Publication Data

AJ legal handbook: the law for architects—5th ed.
1. Architects—Legal status, Laws, etc.—Great Britain
I. Speaight, Anthony   II. Stone, Gregory
344.103′7872   KD2978

ISBN 0-750-61219-3

**Library of Congress Cataloging-in-Publication Data
applied for**

ISBN 0-750-61219-3

Composition by Genesis Typesetting, Laser Quay, Rochester, Kent
Printed in Great Britain at the University Press, Cambridge

Editors' Preface

This fifth edition marks a further stage in the development of this work from a collection of distinct articles into a single coherent guide to the law for architects.

The first edition of the *Handbook* was based on a series of articles commissioned by Peter Davey for the *Architect's Journal*. The idea took shape in Davey's mind while he was still a student working for his professional examinations. He realized that there was no up-to-date textbook on the law for architects, and that in consequence the questions were ill-put and the answers ill-informed. A structure was devised, and specialist contributors appointed, with the guidance of Evelyn Freeth, George Stringer, who was then legal Adviser to the RIBA, and George Burnet, legal adviser to the Royal Incorporation of Architects in Scotland. The articles were published during 1971 and 1972. In 1973 they appeared in book form under the title *Architects' Journal Legal Handbook*.

In successive editions the text was regularly updated to incorporate the unending stream of changes in the law. New sections and some completely new chapters were added. Over the years, too, the text became more closely integrated, as authors became familiar with the contributions from their colleagues.

This new edition contains more new material than any of its predecessors. There are entirely new chapters on International Work by Architects, on European Community Law affecting Architects, and Architects' Professional Indemnity Insurance. The growing confusion in the law of tort, especially concerning negligence and economic loss, led us to rearrange material and include fuller explanations of the principles of the law of contract and tort. The early chapters now guide readers from the origins and sources of the law, through the basic principles, and then to their application in architects' relations with their own clients and in their clients' contract with the contractor. One consequence of the new judicial climate is the growing popularity of collateral warranties or duty of care letters: the former chapter on the Architect's Appointment has been expanded to discuss this topic. Another change of recent years has been the availability to architects of the option of incorporation as a limited company: the chapter on Legal Organization of Architects' Offices, which formerly dealt mainly with partnership, now discusses limited companies as well.

Almost every field has seen important changes since the last edition. The chapter on Planning now prints the Town and Country Planning (Use Classes) Order 1987. Several amendment issues to the JCT form and the Scottish Building Contract are dealt with in the chapters on the standard forms of building contract. In the area of copyright there is a completely new statute, the Copyright, Designs and Patents Act 1988. The ripples of the House of Lords decision in *D & F Estates* v *Church Commissioners* reach many places. These are but a few examples of many changes.

There are too many people who have assisted us for us to acknowledge them individually. But we cannot leave the work without mentioning the valuable advice of Gina Wykeman of Kennedys on architects' contracts of engagement with their clients and collateral warranties.

Save when otherwise indicated, the law is as at 1st January 1990. In a few instances it has been possible to deal with changes already announced which will come into force at later dates: for example, the law on the European 'Works' Directive is stated as at 19th July 1990.

We do not seek to turn architects into lawyers. What we do hope is that the *Handbook* will continue that process whereby in recent years architects have become more aware of where legal pitfalls exist. Now that architects have the right of direct access to barristers for specialist advice, they are in a better position than ever before to inform both themselves and their clients of the legal implications of the work in which they are involved.

Anthony Speaight
Gregory Stone

Acknowledgements

Acknowledgement is given to the following bodies for permission to use sample documents and statutory publications:

Architects' Registration Council of the United Kingdom
British Property Federation
Building Employers' Confederation
Her Majesty's Stationery Office
Office for Official Publications of the European Communities
Royal Incorporation of Architects in Scotland
Royal Institute of British Architects
Scottish Building Contracts Committee

List of Contributors

Consultant Editors

Anthony Speaight – Barrister, of 12 King's Bench Walk, Temple; co-author of *The Law of Defective Premises* (1982); contributor to *Construction Disputes: Liability and the Expert Witness* (Butterworths, 1989); contributor of many articles on legal topics to the *Architects' Journal*; elected member of the General Council of the Bar

The present editors have been editors of the *Handbook* since its third edition published in 1982

Gregory Stone – educated in England and France, postgraduate work in Economics; first went into the City where he was Chief Economist for a merchant bank, then in 1976 qualified for the Bar where he was specialized in planning, administrative and local government law

---

Stephen Bickford–Smith, BA (Oxon) of the Midland and Oxford Circuit, Barrister, FCI Arb – practising Barrister in the Chambers of the Rt. Hon. Lord Rippon of Hexham PC QC at 2 Paper Buildings, Temple, London, EC4, where he has been in practice since 1974, specializing in construction, property and planning law; he is also an editor of *Emden's Construction Law* and consultant editor of Building Law Monthly

George Burnet – writer to the Signet; former secretary of the Scottish Building Contracts Committee from 1964–1987; legal adviser to the Royal Incorporation of Architects in Scotland from 1960 to date

Eileen Davie, LLB – Advocates Library, Parliament House, Edinburgh

Richard Dyton, LLB (Hons), AKC – obtained his law degree at Kings College, London; as a solicitor in the commercial department of Kennedys Solicitors, his experience includes advising in relation to international commercial contracts; in the field of construction law, he has a particular interest in providing contractual advice to architects and engineers

Patrick Elias, QC – Fellow of Pembroke College, Cambridge; lecturer in law at the University of Cambridge; author of *Trade disputes*; joint author of *Labour law: Cases and materials*; editor of the unfair dismissal section of *Harvey on labour relations and employment law*

Susanna Fischer – Barrister, member of the Middle Temple

Michael F. Flint – is the Chairman of Denton Hall Burgin & Warrens, having been a partner in that firm since 1960 except for a period of five years which he spent as an executive in the film industry; he is the author of *The User's Guide to Copyright*, the part author of *Intellectual Property – The New Law* by Flint, Thorne and Williams and of *Television by Satellite – Legal Aspects* edited by Stephen de Bate, and is a frequent contributor to legal journals on copyright and space law matters; he is also a member of the Council of the Common Law Institute of Intellectual Property

Andrew W. Foyle – partner of Lovell White Durrant, Member of the Institute of Arbitrators, the Society of Construction Law and of Committee T (Construction) of the Section on Business Law of the International Bar Association; both he and his firm have advised on numerous arbitrations involving all sides of the construction industry (employers, their professional advisers and contractors) and have also advised arbitrators on the conduct of arbitrations; he has spoken on the subject of arbitration at conferences organized by the Institute of Arbitrators and the International Chamber of Commerce

Kim Franklin, ACI Arb – Barrister, was called to the Bar in 1984 and practises in the field of construction disputes from the Middle Temple; she is a joint editor of *Construction Law Journal*, a contributing author of *Construction Disputes – Liability and the Expert Witness* and *The Architect: Liability*, a regular contributor to the *Architects' Journal* and gives lectures on building contract law and practice

Peter K. Franklin, MSc, FCIOB, MSFSE, MASI, MREHIS – Senior Building Adviser, Scottish Home and Health Department; he has been involved in building control legislation with the Scottish Office since 1966 as well as being a member of many BSI Committees; he lectures regularly on the subject to universities, colleges and professional institutions

J. F. Garner – Emeritus Professor of Public Law at Nottingham University; author of *Administrative Law, Control of Pollution Encyclopaedia, Law of Sewers and Drains* and *Countryside Law*

Andrew Geddes, MA (Oxon) – called to the Bar in 1972; he is a member of European Law Chambers specializing in EEC law with particular emphasis on competition law, product liability and the environment, on which he has written extensively in the specialist press and he is currently writing a book on Product Liability and Product Safety in the EEC; he was appointed a Recorder in February 1990

Charles Harpum, MA, LLB – Barrister of Lincoln's Inn, a Fellow of Downing College, Cambridge since 1977 and a Lecturer in Law at Cambridge University; he was called to the Bar by Lincoln's Inn in 1976; his academic interests are in land law, conveyancing, trusts and legal history

Sir Desmond Heap, LLM, Hon LLD, PPRTPI – Solicitor; formerly Comptroller and City Solicitor to the Corporation of London; currently consultant in private practice; author of *An Outline of Planning Law* (9th edn); general editor of *Encyclopaedia of Planning Law and Practice*; member of the editorial board of *Journal of Planning and Environmental Law*; past President of the Law Society and of the Royal Town Planning Institute; associate of the Royal Institute of Chartered Surveyors; Gold Medalist, RTPI, 1983; Gold Medal Award, Lincoln Institute of Law Policy, Cambridge, MA, USA, 1983

Peter Madge, LLM, FIRM, ACII, FCI Arb – qualified in law and insurance, has spent all his career in the insurance and risk management fields and is a consultant in legal liability, liability risk management and insurance; Principal of Peter Madge Risk Consultancies, prior to which he was a Director of Willis Faber where he was Managing Director of Corporate Liability and Managing Director of Willis Wright-

son Risk Management Services Limited; author of many books dealing with liability and construction insurance including *The Indemnity and Insurance Aspects of Building Contracts* and *A Concise Guide to the 1986 Insurance Clauses*; he has a close involvement with legal reform and its effect on insurance protection; acts as insurance consultant to the Royal Institute of British Architects and the Joint Contracts Tribunal

Roderick Males – architect and practice consultant; Director of Professional Training at the School of Architecture in the Victoria University of Manchester; lecturer and author on professional practice matters; member of various institutional groups and committees

Charles Manzoni, AMI MechE – Barrister at 12 King's Bench Walk; he is a qualified Mechanical Engineer and worked in industry for a number of years before going to the Bar; he specializes in law relating to the engineering industry as well as more general commercial matters

Dr A. R. Mowbray – lecturer in law at Nottingham University, editor of *Garner's Rights of Way* and author of various articles on administrative law

Dr Vincent Powell-Smith – author and construction law consultant; practising arbitrator; member of Gray's Inn; formerly lecturer in law at the University of Aston Management Centre, and visiting lecturer at the Birmingham School of Architecture and Cambridge University Department of Architecture; joint editor of *Construction Law Reports*; author of over 60 books including *The Building Regulations Explained and Illustrated* (8th edn, 1989); he has been legal correspondent of *Contract Journal* since 1974

Angus Stewart, QC, BA (Oxon), LLB (Edin) – 1971 visiting lecturer on *Nazi Architecture*, Sheffield Polytechnic; 1975 called to Scottish Bar; 1983–88 Standing Junior Counsel to the Department of the Environment in Scotland

Nicholas Vineall, MA (Cantab and Pittsburgh), Diph – Barrister and member of the Middle Temple; he specializes in employment, landlord and tenant and contract/commercial work; he went to the Bar after reading Natural Science at Cambridge University and holding a Harkness Fellowship at the University of Pittsburgh

George Young, BA, FInstAM – formerly partner and administrator in YRM; now deputy chairman of the Institute of Administrative Management; currently lecturing and examining in professional practice at schools of architecture and engaged as author and part editor of the new *RIBA Handbook of Management*

Contents

1

Introduction to English Law

ANTHONY SPEAIGHT*

1 The importance of law

Ignorantia juris non excusat

1.01 The well-worn maxim that ignorance of the law is no excuse applies with equal force to everyone, including architects. Everyone who offers a service to others and claims expertise to do what he offers has a responsibility to society in general and to his clients in particular to know the law.

Architects and the law

1.02 Architects and other professional people are under a special obligation to have a sound working knowledge of the law in every aspect of the services they give. The responsibility is a heavy one. In matters such as building law and regulations, planning legislation and building contracts, clients seem to expect near infallibility. Architects should always be capable of advising what action should be taken, when and in what circumstances, but readers must realize that architects must never assume the role of barristers or solicitors in offering advice in purely legal matters. At most they should do no more than express their considered opinions, which should be reinforced by knowledge and enlightened judgement. All architects should tell their clients to seek their own legal advice on matters that exceed the knowledge an architect can reasonably be expected to have.

The legal system – rules of society

1.03 People living in all types of community have one thing in common: mutually agreed rules of conduct appropriate to their way of life, with explicit consequences for failure to observe the rules. This is what law is about. The more varied the activities and the more complex the social structure, the greater is the need for everyone to be aware of the part he or she must play in formulating and observing the rules. In highly developed communities these rules have grown into a complex body of law. In England and Wales the law is continually developing and being modified as personal rights and social responsibilities are re-interpreted.

The English system of law

1.04 There is no single code of English law such as exists in many countries, though there is an increasing tendency towards codification, and the statute books already contain codes covering many areas of law. Roman law, on which most of the continental codes were based, failed to make a lasting impression in England; Roman laws, like their architecture,

*In the first edition, this chapter was written by Evelyn Freeth. It was later revised by Richard Gordon.

disappeared with the legions. Roman influence has survived to a much greater degree in Scotland, where, by the Act of Union of 1707, a largely independent system has been preserved. This accounts for many differences between English and Scottish law (see Scottish sections of this book, particularly Chapter 2).

2 Sources of law

2.01 English law may be conveniently divided into two main parts – unwritten and written – and there are several branches of these.

Common law

2.02 Common law – the unwritten law – includes the early customary laws assembled and formulated by judges, with modifications of the old law of equity (para 3.09). Common law therefore means all other than enacted law (para 2.06), and rules derived solely from custom and precedent are rules of common law. It is the unwritten law of the land because there is no official codification of it.

Judicial precedent

2.03 The basis of all legal argument and decision in the English courts is founded upon the application of rules announced in earlier decisions and is called *Stare decisis* (let the decision stand). From this has evolved the doctrine of judicial precedent, now a fundamental characteristic of common law.

2.04 Two factors contributed to the important position that the doctrine of judicial precedent holds today: the Judicature Acts (para 3.12) and the creation of the Council of Law Reporting, which is responsible for issuing authoritative reports which are scrutinized and revised by judges and which contain a summary of arguments by counsel and of the judgements given. It is essential for the operation of a system of law based on previous cases that well-authenticated records of arguments and decisions be available to all courts and everyone required to advise on the law.

Authority of a judgement

2.05 Legally, the most important part of a judgement is that where the judge explains the principles on which he has based his decision. A judgement is an authoritative lecture on a branch of the law; it includes a *ratio decidendi* (the statement of facts or grounds for the decision) and one or more *obiter dicta* (things said by the way, often not directly relevant to the

1

matters at issue). It is the *ratio decidendi* which creates precedents for the future. Such precedents are binding on every court with jurisdiction inferior to the court which gave the decision; even courts of equal or superior jurisdiction seldom fail to follow an earlier decision. Until recently both the Court of Appeal and the House of Lords regarded themselves as bound by their own decisions. The House of Lords has to some extent freed itself from this limitation but took the opportunity in *Davis* v *Johnson* [1978] 1 All ER 84 of stating that the Court of Appeal remains strictly bound by its own decisions.

Legislation

2.06 Legislation – the written or enacted law – comprises the statutes, acts and edicts of the sovereign and his advisers. Although historically enacted law is more recent than common law because Parliament has been in existence only since the thirteenth century, legislation by Acts of Parliament takes precedence over all other sources of law and is absolutely binding on all courts while it remains on the statute books. If an Act of Parliament conflicts with a common law rule, it is presumed that Parliament was aware of the fact and that there was a deliberate intention that it should do so.

2.07 All legislation must derive its authority directly or indirectly from Parliament; the only exception being that in cases of national emergency the Crown can still legislate by Royal Proclamation. In its statutes, Parliament usually lays down general principles, and in most legislation Parliament delegates authority for carrying out the provisions of statutes to non-parliamentary bodies. Subordinate legislation is required which may take the form of Orders in Council (made by the government of the day – in theory by the sovereign in Council), regulations, statutory instruments or orders made by government departments, and the byelaws of statutory undertakings and local authorities.

2.08 The courts are required to interpret Acts in accord with the wording employed. They may not question or even discuss the validity of the enactment. Rules have been established to help them interpret ambiguities: there is a presumption that Parliament in legislative matters does not make mistakes, but in general this principle does not apply to statutory instruments unless the governing Act says anything to the contrary. The courts may decide whether rules or orders are made within the powers delegated to the authorized body ordered to make them, or whether they are ultra vires (outside the body's power). Byelaws must not only be intra vires but also reasonable.

Branches

2.09 Of the branches of the law, those with the greatest general effect are civil law and criminal law; others are ecclesiastical (canon), military and naval, and administrative laws. These latter derive more than most from Roman law.

Civil law

2.10 Civil law is related to the rights, duties, and obligations of individual members of the community to each other, and it embraces all the law to do with family, property, contract, commerce, partnerships, insurance, copyright and the law of torts. The latter governs all actionable wrongs against persons and property – actions for damages, such as defamation, trespass, nuisance, negligence and a wide variety of other matters.

Criminal law

2.11 Criminal law deals with wrongful acts harmful to the community and punishable by the State. Except when

wrongful action may fall within the scope of both civil and criminal wrong, architects are usually concerned with civil law.

European Community law

2.12 Since 1 January 1973 there has been an additional source of law: that is the law of the European Community. By our accession treaty Her Majesty's Government undertook that the United Kingdom would accept the obligations of membership of the three original European Communities, that is the Coal and Steel Community, the Economic Community and the Atomic Energy Community. That commitment was honoured by the enactment of the European Communities Act 1972. Section 2(1) of the 1972 Act provided that all directly applicable provisions of the treaties establishing the European Communities should become part of English law; so, too, would all existing and future Community secondary legislation. Since the terms of the treaties are in the main in very general terms, most detailed Community policy is embodied in secondary legislation. Most major decisions are taken in the form of 'directives', which require member states to achieve stated results but leave it to the member state to choose the form and method of implementation. Other Community decisions, known as 'regulations', have direct effect.

In consequence, there is today an ever growing corpus of European Community decisions incorporated into English law. This topic is discussed more fully in Chapter 21.

3 Legal history

Origins of English law

3.01 The roots of English law lie deep in the foundations of English history. The seeds of custom and rules planted in Anglo-Saxon and earlier times have developed and grown gradually into a modern system of law. The Normans interfered little with common practices they found, and almost imperceptibly integrated them with their own mode of life. William I did not regard himself as a conqueror, but claimed to have come by invitation as the lawful successor of Edward the Confessor – whose laws he promised to re-establish and enforce.

Feudal system and land law

3.02 The Domesday Book (1086), assembled mainly by itinerant judges for taxation purposes, provided William I with a comprehensive social and economic survey of his newly acquired lands. The feudal system in England was more universally applied than it was on the Continent – a result perhaps of the thoroughness of the Domesday survey. Consequently, in England feudal law was not solely a law for the knights and bishops of the realm, nor of some parts of the country alone: it affected every person and every holding of land. It became part of the common law of England.

3.03 To the knowledge acquired from Domesday, the Normans applied their administrative skills; they established within the framework of the feudal system new rules for ownership of land, new obligations of loyalty to the adminstration under the Crown, and reorganized arrangements for control of the people and for hearing and judgement of their disputes. These were the true origins of our modern legal system.

3.04 Ultimate ownership of land in England is still, in theory, in the Crown. The lord as 'landowner' merely held an 'estate' or 'interest' in the land, directly or indirectly, as tenant from the king. A person holding an estate of the Crown could, in turn, grant it to another person, but the ownership still remained in the Crown. The tenant's 'interest' may have been

of long or short duration and as varied as the kinds of services that might be given in return for the 'estate'. In other words, many different estates and interests in land existed. Tenure and estate are distinct. 'Tenure' refers to the relation of the landlord to his overlord, at its highest level to the king. 'Estate' refers to the duration of his interest in the land, and has nothing whatever to do with the common use of the word.

Possession not ownership

3.05 English law as a result has never used the concept of ownership of land but instead has concentrated on the fact of 'possession', mainly because ownership can refer to so many things and is ill-fitted to anything so permanent and immovable as a piece of land. A man's title to land in England is based on his being able to prove that he has a better right to possession of it than anyone else who claims it.

Real and personal property

3.06 Law makes a distinction between 'real' and 'personal' property. The former are interests in land other than leasehold interests; the latter includes leasehold interests and applies to movable property (personal property and chattels).

A leasehold interest in land is classed as 'personal' rather than 'real' property because in early times it was not possible to recover a leasehold interest by 'real' actions for the return of the thing (*res*). In common law a disposessed owner of freehold land could bring an action for recovery of possession, and an order would be made for the return to him of his land. For the recovery of personal (tangible or movable) articles his remedy was limited to a personal action in which the defendant had the option of either returning the property or paying its value.

Beginnings of common law

3.07 Foundations of both the common law and the courts of justice were laid by Henry II (1154–1189). In his reign the 'king's justice' began to be adminstered not only in the King's Court – the *Curia Regis* – where the sovereign usually sat in person and which accompanied him on his travels about the country, but also by justices given commissions of assize directing them to administer the royal justice systematically in local courts throughout the whole kingdom. In these courts it was their duty to hear civil actions which previously had been referred to the central administration at Westminster. It was the judges of assize who created the common law. On

completion of their circuits and their return to Westminster they discussed their experiences and judgements given in the light of local customs and systems of law. Thus a single system common to all was evolved; judge-made in the sense that it was brought together and stated authoritatively by judges, but it grew from the people in that it was drawn directly from their ancient customs and practices.

3.08 Under the able guidance of Edward I (1272–1307) many reforms were made, notably in procedures and mainly in the interest of the subject as against the royal officials, and the law began to take its characteristic shape. Three great common law courts became established at Westminster:

1. The Kings' Bench, broadly for cases in which the Crown had interest.
2. Common pleas, for cases between subject and subject.
3. Exchequer, for those having a fiscal or financial aspect.

However, as adminstered in these courts, the common law was limited in its ability to meet every case. This led to the establishment of the principles of equity.

Equity

3.09 In the Middle Ages the common law courts failed to give redress in certain types of cases where redress was needed, either because the remedy the common law provided (i.e. damages) was unsuitable or because the law was defective in that no remedy existed. For instance, the common law did not recognize trusts and at that time there was no way of compelling a trustee to carry out his obligations. Therefore disappointed and disgruntled litigants exercised their rights of appeal to the king – the 'fountain of all justice'. In due course, the king, through his Chancellor (keeper of his conscience, because he was also a bishop and his confessor), set up a secial Court of Chancery to deal with them.

Rules of equity

3.10 During the early history of the Court of Chancery, equity had no binding rules. A Chancellor approached his task in a different manner to the common law judges; he gave judgement when he was satisfied in his own mind that a wrong had been done, and he would order that the wrong be made good. Thus the defendant could clear his own conscience at the same time. The remedy for refusal was invariably to be imprisoned until he came to see the error of his ways and agree with the court's ruling. It was not long before a set of general rules emerged in the Chancery Courts which hardened into law and became a regular part of the law of the land. There is, however, another and even more fundamental aspect of equity. Though it developed in the Court of Chancery as a body of law with defined rules, its ideal from earliest times was the simple belief in moral justice, fairness, and equality of treatment for all, based on the idea of natural justice as opposed to the strict letter of the law. Equity in that sense has remained to this day a basic principle of English justice.

Common law and equity in the nineteenth century

3.11 Up to the end of the fifteenth century the Chancellor had generally been a bishop, but after the Reformation the position came to be held by professional lawyers (of whom the first was Sir Thomas More) under whom the rules of equity became almost as rigid as those of common law; and the existence of separate courts administering the two different sets of rules led to serious delays and conflicts. By the end of the eighteenth century the courts and their procedures had reached an almost unbelievable state of confusion, mainly due to lack of coordination of the highly technical processes and overlapping jurisdiction. Charles Dickens describes without much exaggeration something of the troubles of a litigant in Chancery in the case of '*Jarndyce* v *Jarndyce*' (*Bleak House*).

Judicature Acts 1873–1875

3.12 Nineteenth century England was dominated by a spirit of reform, which extended from slavery to local government. The law and the courts did not escape reform, and the climax came with the passing of the Judicature Acts of 1873 (and much additional and amending legislation in the years that followed) whereby the whole court system was thoroughly reorganized and simplified, by the establishment of a single Supreme court. The Act also brought to an end the separation of common law and equity; they were not amalgamated and their rules remained the same, but henceforth the rules of both systems were to be applied by all courts. If they were in conflict, equity was to prevail.

The Supreme Court 1875–1971

3.13 The main object of the Judicature Act 1873 was an attempt to solve the problems of delay and procedural confusion in the existing court system by setting up a Supreme Court. This consisted of two main parts:

1. The High Court of Justice, with three Divisions, all courts of Common Law and Equity. As a matter of convenience cases concerned primarily with common law questions being heard in the Queen's Bench Division; those dealing with equitable problems in the Chancery Division; and the Probate, Divorce, and Admiralty Division with the three classes indicated by its title.
2. The Court of Appeal – hearing appeals from decisions of the High Court and most appeals from County Courts.

Modern reforms

3.14 In 1970, mainly as the result of recommendations by a Royal Commission on Assizes and Quarter Sessions under the chairmanship of Lord Beeching, Parliament made further reforms among the Chancery Division, the Queen's Bench Division, Commercial court, Admiralty Court, and the newly formed Family Division – the latter for dealing with guardianship, adoption, divorce and other matrimonial matters.

Courts Act 1971

3.15 The Courts Act 1971 then followed, with effect from January 1972, and the object of separating civil from criminal proceedings throughout the country and of promoting speedier trials. The Act established the Crown Court in all cities and main towns for hearing criminal cases in continuous session, leaving the High Court to deal with civil actions. The County Courts, Magistrates' Courts, and the Coroners' Courts remain unaffected by the new changes; but the Act abolished all Courts of Assize and Quarter Session and various other long-established courts of special jurisdiction, such as the Liverpool Court of Passage and the Tolzey and Pie Poudre Courts of Bristol and others whose usefulness had long been in decline.

3.16 Another episode of reform of the civil court structures appears to be upon us. The Civil Justice Review published in 1988 (Cm 394) recommended that the jurisdiction of the lower tier of civil courts, the County Courts, be enlarged from £5000 to £50000. This would leave the High Court handling claims for over £50000 and other cases of particular importance, complexity or difficulty. The Courts and Legal Services Bill, published just before this book went to press, if enacted in the terms of the Bill as published, will confer upon the Lord Chancellor effectively unlimited power to allocate to the County Courts such jurisdiction as he sees fit.

4 Construction cases within the present system

4.01 Most construction industry claims today are heard by Official Referees. Official Referees are judges nominated by the Lord Chancellor to hear 'Official Referees' business'. The definition of such business is a High Court case,

(a) which involves a prolonged examination of documents or accounts, or a technical scientific or local investigation such as could more conveniently be conducted by an official referee; or
(b) for which trial by an official referee is desirable in the interests of one or more of the parties on grounds of expedition, economy or convenience or otherwise. (Rules of the Supreme Court, Order 36, Rule 1)

In practice, however, any substantial building or engineering case is regarded as 'Official Referees' business', and little else figures as such. Therefore, for most practical purpose one can consider there to be a specialist construction division of the High Court. At present there are six full-time Official Referees in London; in addition a number of circuit judges based at important provincial centres have been nominated to handle Official Referees' business in their localities. An anomalous feature of the situation is that Official Referees have a lower status and lower pay than High Court judges, and yet they handle cases of a greater complexity than most High Court work. If their status were to be differentiated from that of ordinary High Court judges, it would be more logical to confer an elevated status upon them. In general Official Referees are extremely popular with court users: the heavy workload brought to their courts at the choice of litigants is the best possible testimony to the skill with which the present Official Referees conduct their work.

4.02 Another tribute to the work of the Official Referees is the fact that a number of innovations in procedure which they pioneered have been copied throughout the remainder of the civil court system. One such innovation was the requirement for prior disclosure of statements of witnesses of fact. Another innovation was a procedure whereby experts would meet to discuss the issues in the case at an 'off the record' meeting with a view to narrowing dispute and identifying the real issues. A third feature of the practice of Official Referee courts recently has been a far greater use of written submissions by advocates. At the time of writing a new chapter in civil procedure is being written by the introduction of a video camera and visual display units into the courtroom of one Official Referee: there seems little doubt that over the next few years they will lead to the introduction of information technology into the daily life of the courts.

4.03 An alternative method of dispute resolution, which is often used in construction cases, is arbitration. This topic is more fully discussed in Chapter 11. An arbitrator has jurisdiction to determine a dispute only if the parties agree. But such agreement is commonly included in contracts. Indeed, almost all standard forms of building or engineering contracts contain arbitration clauses. So, too, does the Memorandum of Agreement between architect and client published by the RIBA for use with the RIBA Architects Appointment (see Chapter 5). The importance of arbitration in the construction field became even greater with the Court of Appeal's decision in *Northern Health Authority* v *Crouch* [1984] 1 QB 644: it was held that where a contract defined parties' obligations with reference to certificates, and conferred on an arbitrator power to 'open up, review and revise' such certificates, only an arbitrator and not a judge could so modify certificates. The *Crouch* decision has created a number of difficulties. It is proposed in the Courts and Legal Services Bill that, if the parties consent, such powers may once again be exercised by a judge.

5 The scheme of this book

5.01 The general scheme of the new edition of this book is to take the reader from general principles to specific applications of such principles and specialized fields of the law. The book deals with Scottish law, as well as English law. For the Scottish reader there is a separate introductory chapter (Chapter 2) and separate chapters on Land Law (Chapter 8), Standard Building Contracts (Chapter 10), Statutory Authorities (Chapter 13), Construction Regulations (Chapter 16) and Professional Conduct (Chapter 24); in addition the chapters on copyright, arbitration and legal organization of architects' offices contain distinct Scottish sections.

5.02 For the English reader this introductory chapter is followed by chapters on the general principles of the two fields of the law which are of the greatest importance to architects, namely contract (Chapter 3) and tort (Chapter 4). The specific application of the law of contract to an architect's relationship with his own client is discussed in Chapter 5. Chapter 6 deals with the liability of the architect in contract and tort if, unhappily, a claim arises out his work for a client. Chapter 7 then introduces the general principles of a third area of English law, land law. With that basis laid one can proceed to the longest chapter, which is on Standard Building Contracts (Chapter 9). The treatment of arbitration, which normally arises out of a clause in a standard contract, follows in Chapter 11. The next group of chapters deal with the intervention of public authorities: Chapter 12 describes the authorities themselves, and then Chapters 14 and 15 deal, respectively, with the two crucial fields in which architects deal with public authorities, namely planning and construction regulations. The next group of chapters deals with aspects of the law of particular importance to architects in the running of their practices – copyright (Chapter 17); employment (Chapter 18); partnership law and company law (Chapter 19); and insurance (Chapter 20). Then there are two chapters dealing with the international dimension: Chapter 21 explains the impact on the construction field of European Community law, whilst Chapter 22 gives advice on legal aspects of work by British architects overseas. Finally, on the fringes of the law but at the heart of an architect's practice, the book deals with the rules of professional conduct.

2

Introduction to Scots Law

EILEEN P. DAVIE*

1 Law and Scotland

1.01 To many Scots, their legal system is an institution which expresses their individuality as a nation and is at least the equal of the more widespread English system of law. Despite the union of the Scottish and English legislative bodies in 1707 into the Parliament of Great Britain, the Treaty of Union preserved Scottish law and courts. As a result, Scots law is still in many respects entirely different from English, particularly in branches such as the law of property, constitutional and administrative law, and criminal law. But since 1707 much legislation has been enacted for the whole of the UK, and appeals have been permitted from the Scottish civil courts to the House of Lords, which since 1876 has always had at least one Scottish Law Lord and now, customarily, at least two. The current Lord Chancellor, Lord Mackay of Clashfern, is a former Scottish judge. Thus, much English law has been superimposed, sometimes unhappily, on what had previously been an entirely Scottish system.

2 Sources

2.01 Legislation, or enacted law, is still one of the principal sources of Scottish law. Considerations applicable to it are the same as for English law. Many of the Acts of the Scottish Parliament prior to 1707 are still in force, applying only to Scotland. Some UK legislation is not applicable to Scotland, while some is applicable there alone. In addition, membership of the European Economic Community binds the UK to give effect to European Community law properly made under the treaties.

2.02 The two other principal sources of modern Scottish law are to be found in judicial decisions and in the work of 'institutional' writers (para 2.09). Together these sources make up the common law, and form a body of law which has grown up over almost as long a perod as has English law and has been changed and added to by statute.

Feudal system

2.03 While primitive customary law has traces of Scots law, the first recognizable organized system of law derived from Norman feudalism, which was fully accepted in Scotland by the mid twelfth century. This system, embracing most aspects of organized society, was pyramidal. Theoretically all land belonged to the king, who granted areas to barons (his

vassals) in return for military and other services when required. Each baron was able to grant smaller areas of his land to his own vassals on a similar basis and so on down the scale. In time military service was replaced by a money payment called feu-duty, and although the feudal system still forms a theoretical basis of land tenure in Scotland, the owner being the vassal 'of a superior', it has been substantially reformed in the last twenty years. In 1970 provision was made enabling unreasonable, inappropriate, or unduly burdensome feudal conditions imposed by the superior to be varied or discharged. In 1974 machinery was created for redeeming existing feu-duties and prohibiting the creation of new feu-duties.

Sheriffs

2.04 At about the same time as the feudal system became accepted in Scotland, another institution was introduced which was to become of great importance in the administration of law: the office of sheriff. The sheriff was, and remains, an important administrative and judicial officer, and today the Sheriff Courts conduct the greatest part, by volume, of litigation. Actions for debt and damages can be raised there irrespective of the sums involved. Action for sums of up to £1 500 may only be raised in the Sheriff Court.

Dean of Guild Court

2.05 Another ancient legal institution, once familiar to architects, was the Dean of Guild Court, which exercised various functions in relation to buildings in burghs. The Dean of Guild Court has been abolished and its building control functions transferred to a local authority committee.

Fundamental institutions

2.06 The period prior to 1532 is of interest here only because by that date most of the fundamental institutions of Scottish law had come into existence. Lack of documentation in Scotland is the reason for much uncertainty; fewer records were kept there than in England, because Scotland was in a relatively backward and troubled state. The thirteenth and fourteenth centuries, however, saw the development of an early form of trial by jury, and the establishment of Sheriff Courts and the circuit courts.

2.07 In 1532 the College of Justice was founded with a court of 15 judges, the direct predecessors of the judges of the present Court of Session (para 3.01) which today comprises 24 judges. This was a major step towards establishing the present Scottish legal institutions.

*In the first edition, Donald MacFadyen QC and William Nimmo Smith QC wrote this chapter; in subsequent editions it was revised by Donald MacFadyen QC and Colin Harris.

Influence of Roman law

2.08 It is often said that Scots law is based on Roman law. While not immediately apparent today, this is still partly true, and is one of the principal causes of difference between Scottish and English private law. There are two reasons for this influence. First, prior to the reformation, much jurisdiction of private law was in the hands of ecclesiastical courts, which administered canon law with an ultimate appeal to the Papal Court at Rome; this formed the basis of matrimonial law and influenced other branches, such as the law of succession and the law of contract. Second, for many years Scotland was more in touch with other European countries than with England. Many Scots lawyers underwent part of the legal education abroad, particularly in Holland and, as a result, were influenced by study of Roman law in Continental universities.

Institutional writings

2.09 The year 1861 marked a turning-point in Scots law with the publication of Lord Stair's *Institutions*, a book which is the foundation of modern Scots private law. It is a systematic treatise, drawing together all the influences mentioned above. It was followed by a few other books by different authors, notably Eskine and Bell, which are together referred to as 'institutional writings'. They are highly regarded by the courts, and in some branches of law they may carry as much weight as previous judicial decisions.

2.10 Today's Scots lawyers in practice use for everyday reference statutes and statutory instruments, law reports (which are found either in the official series of Session Cases, started in 1820, or in the *Scots Law Times*), and a number of standard textbooks.

Equity in Scots law

2.11 The dichotomy in English law between common law and equity, which were administered by separate courts, was never a feature of Scots law. Scottish courts have long taken equitable principles into consideration, and equity is regarded as a principle which forms part of the law rather than as a force acting in opposition to it.

3 Courts and the legal profession

3.01 The House of Lords is the ultimate resort for appeals from the Court of Session, which is the supreme court of Scotland in civil matters. The Court of Session is made up of the Inner House and the Outer House (para 3.03). In the Inner House there are two divisions, equal in authority, each with four judges. The first division is presided over by the Lord President and the second division by the Lord Justice-Clerk. The work of each division is to hear appeals from decisions of lower courts, and to deal, as the court of first instance, with certain special cases and some types of petition (they do not hear cases where evidence must be taken).

3.02 Architects are more likely to be concerned, as a party or a witness, in two types of action: those arising from contract and those from delict (para 4.06), the name given in Scotland to what in England is called the law of torts. The hearing of evidence in such actions is either by way of a proof before a

single judge, or by way of jury trial before a judge and jury. A jury trial is principally limited to actions for damages for personal injuries.

3.03 Actions may be taken in the Outer House of the Court of Session or in the Sheriff Court; the location of a hearing is usually simply a matter of convenience. Court of Session judges who sit in the Outer House are called the Lords Ordinary. The decision of a Lord Ordinary may be appealed to one of the divisions of the Inner House and from there to the House of Lords. Sheriffs sit in local Sheriff Courts throughout Scotland. A Sheriff's decision may be appealed to either the Sheriff Principal of the Sheriffdom, and from him to one of the divisions of the Inner House of the Court of Session and so on, or direct from the Sheriff to one of the divisions of the Inner House.

Court procedure

3.04 Before a case comes to proof or jury trial there is a system of written pleading designed to make the parties – pursuer and defender (in England the plaintiff and defendant) – state the facts and principles of law on which they base their cases as clearly as possible, and points of difference between them are narrowed down. An action is started or raised by service on the defender of a summons (in the Court of Session) or an initial writ (in the Sheriff Court), setting out the pursuer's claim. Then follow various steps which must be taken within fixed periods. Defences are lodged on behalf of the defender, and for a time the parties are allowed to adjust their pleadings to meet what is said for the other side. Thereafter, a document called a 'closed record' is printed, containing the final version of the pleadings.

3.05 Before there is any proof or jury trial, there may be legal debate about the closed record, at which the sufficiency in law of the parties' pleadings may be called in question, with the result that some parts may be struck out, or even the whole action dismissed. At the proof or jury trial which follows, parties are restricted in the evidence to proving facts stated in the closed record. After the hearing of evidence for both parties, the speeches by their counsel or solicitors, the judge may, at a proof, give an immediate decision but more commonly makes avizandum (takes time to think and gives his decision later). At a jury trial, the jury, after being instructed or charged by the judge, retire to consider what they have heard and give their verdict unanimously or by a majority.

Legal profession

3.06 The structure of the legal profession in both Scotland and England is presently the subject of government reform. These reforms are wide ranging and in many areas the effect will only be measurable once they have become established practice. The most significant change for the profession is the proposed granting of rights of audience in the higher courts to solicitors. Until now the profession has been divided into two branches. By far the more numerous are solicitors, who deal directly with clients and see to all their legal affairs. All solicitors are members of the Law Society of Scotland, which is their statutory regulatory body. They may also belong to a professional society, such as the Writers to the Signet or the Solicitors in the Supreme Courts, and put the letters 'WS' or 'SSC' after their names. Whether they do or do not makes no practical difference to the work they undertake for clients.

3.07 The other branch of the profession consists of advocates divided into senior counsel (QCs) and junior counsel, who belong to the Faculty of Advocates, a collegiate professional body. They undertake work of broadly the same sort as that done by barristers in England, and specialize in arguing cases before courts and other tribunals and in giving opinions on matters of law. Until recently an advocate could only receive instructions indirectly from clients through their solicitors, however, again this aspect of the system is under review and instruction may be accepted in particular circumstances directly from professional bodies.

4 Branches of law

4.01 Differences among branches of English and Scottish law of interest to architects will be mentioned when particular topics are discussed later in this book. At this stage, only some of the more important differences among branches of law discussed in Chapter 1 are noted.

Contract

4.02 In Scots law the element of consideration essential to the formation of a binding contract in England is unnecessary. A contract is an agreement between parties which is intended to have legal effect. It is therefore perfectly possible to have a gratuitous contract, i.e. one in which all obligations rest on one side.

4.03 Sealed contracts have no place in Scots law, but certain contracts must be in writing to be properly constituted; the most important examples of these are contracts relating to heritable property (i.e. land and buildings), and leases and contracts of employment for more than one year.

Jus quaesitum tertio

4.04 In Scots law, parties to a contract may confer an enforceable right on a third party, but take no part in the formation of the contract. Provided appropriate circumstances obtain, a right known as a *jus quaesitum tertio* can be conferred on the third party, which enables the third party to enforce provisions in their favour agreed upon by the contracting parties. This is particularly important in relation to enforcement of building conditions. Where several feuars (vassals, para 2.03) hold land from the same superior, building conditions imposed in the fue contract may, in appropriate circumstances, be enforceable by one feuar against another; for example, alterations of particular kinds may be prevented.

Partnership

4.05 In contrast to the English position, a Scottish partnership is not in law simply a collection of individuals. The firm has a legal personality – i.e. an existence of its own – separate from those persons who compose it, and it can, for example, sue for debts owed to it in its own name. The separate existence of the firm does not, however, prevent the personal liability of the partners from being unlimited. Partnership law is dealt with in detail in Chapter 9.

Delict

4.06 The law of delict is that part of the law which deals with righting of legal wrongs, in the civil, as opposed to the criminal, sense. Broadly it is the Scottish equivalent of the English law of tort. The background and details of the Scots law of delict and the English law of torts are different in too many respects to mention here. They cover broadly the same ground, with the Scottish law concentrating more on general theory and less on specific wrongs than the corresponding English law. Although the wrong complained of may arise out of deliberate conduct, most actions based in delict arise out of negligence.

Property

4.07 Property law is perhaps the field in which Scots and English law diverge most widely, particularly in relation to the law of land ownership. Differences are so great and so fundamental that consideration of them is deferred to Chapter 8.

3

The English Law of Contract

NICHOLAS VINEALL

1 Introduction

1.01 The purpose of this chapter is to give an overview of the law of contract: to show both how it relates to other areas of the law, and to describe the general principles on which the English law of contract operates. Although most of the examples are from areas with which architects will be familiar, the principles they illustrate are for the most part general. Other sections of this book deal in detail with specific areas of the law of contract and their own special rules. The general rules described in this chapter may on occasion seem trite and hardly worth stating. Yet it is often with the most fundamental – and apparently simple – principles of law that the most difficult problems arise, and without understanding the framework of contract law, detailed knowledge of any particular standard form contract is of little use. This chapter condenses into a few pages material which if fully discussed would fill many long books. The treatment is necessarily selective and condensed.

2 Scope of the law of contract

2.01 The criminal law sets out limitations on people's behaviour, and punishes them when they do not conform to those rules. A criminal legal action is between the State (the Crown) and an individual. The civil law is quite different. It determines the liabilities which exist between parties in particular circumstances. The sanctions of the civil law are not (save in most unusual circumstances) punishments, but rather remedies – the law tries to put things 'back to rights'.

2.02 Two of the biggest areas of the civil law are contract and tort. In certain factual contexts they can overlap, and in recent years their overlap has caused the courts great problems, but they are conceptually quite distinct, and it is important to understand the distinction.

2.03 A plaintiff will sue a defendant in contract or tort when he objects to something the defendant has done or failed to do. Sometimes the plaintiff will not have spared a thought for the defendant – indeed may very well not know the defendant – before the objectionable act or omission occurs. For example: the defendant carelessly runs the plaintiff over; the defendant's bonfire smoke ruins the plaintiff's washing; the defendant tramples across the plaintiff's field; the defendant writes a scurrilous article about the plaintiff in the local paper. All these wrongs are torts (respectively negligence, nuisance, trespass and defamation), and the law of torts may impose a liability on the defendant. The law of torts is considered in Chapter 4.

2.04 On other occasions the plaintiff and defendant are parties to a contract, so that before the objectionable event occurs the parties have agreed what their legal obligations to one another shall be in certain defined circumstances. So, for instance, if the plaintiff gets the defendant plumber to install a new sink, and it leaks, or gets the defendant architect to design a house which falls down, or gets the defendant builder to build a house and it is not ready on time, the extent – if any – of the defendant's liability in contract will depend on the contract between them – and on nothing else. Of course, there may be liability in tort as well for the two are not mutually exclusive. But the conceptual distinction is quite clear.

3 What is a contract ?

3.01 A contract is a promise or a set of promises which the law will enforce: it is the legal relationship between the parties. Although one often talks of a 'written contract' it is not really the piece of paper which itself is the contract – the piece of paper merely records what the terms of the contract are.

Contracts under seal

3.02 Some contracts have to be made or evidenced in writing, and some contracts have to be made under seal. Either there is literally a wax seal at the end of the document where the parties sign, or there is some mark representing a seal. The commonest type of contract which must be made under seal is a contract for the sale of land (Law of Property Act 1925, section 40). But any contract may be made under seal, and the seal provides the consideration for the contract (see below). The most important consequence is that the limitation period for contracts under seal is twelve years instead of the usual six (see para 13.01).

Ingredients and recipe

3.03 There are basically three essential ingredients of any contract: intention to create legal relations, consideration, and agreement. The recipe is simple: offer and acceptance. Each of these aspects requires further consideration.

4 Intention to create legal relations

4.01 'If you save me my seat I'll buy you a drink.' 'OK.' Such a casual exchange has all the appearances of a contract, but if the thirsty seat saver tried to claim his dues through a court he would probably be disappointed, for the law will not enforce

a promise if the parties did not intend their promises to be legally binding. A moral obligation is not enough.

5 Consideration

5.01 A one-way promise – 'I'll paint your ceiling' – is not a contract, because there is no element of bargain. With the exception of contracts under seal English contract law demands that there must be 'consideration' to support any contract. Consideration in layman's terms is the other half of the bargain or the quid pro quo: in legal terms it has been defined like this:

> 'An act or forbearance of one party, or the promise thereof, is the price for which the promise of the other is bought, and the promise thus given for value is enforceable.' (*Dunlop* v *Selfridge* [1951] AC 847 at 855.)

There are a number of important rules about consideration.

1. Adequacy of consideration irrelevant

The value of the consideration can be quite disproportionate to the other half of the bargain which it supports. In *Midland Bank Trust Comany v Green* [1980] Ch 590, a farm worth £40 000 was sold by a husband to his wife for just £500. £500 was good consideration.

2. Consideration must move from the promisee

If A promises B he will build a wall in B's garden, and C agrees to pay A £1000 for building the wall, there is no contract, for the consideration of £1000 has not come from the person who benefited from the promise to build the wall. This doctrine is similar in some ways to the notion of privity of contract discussed below.

3. Consideration need not move to the promisor

On the other hand, if A, the builder of the wall, says to B that he wants him to pay £1000 to the Battersea Dogs Home, then B's promise to do so is good consideration.

4. Consideration must not be past

The general rule (there are some ways round it) is that an act which has already been performed cannot provide consideration to support a contract subsequently entered into. Suppose A gives B £1000 at Christmas, and at Easter B agrees to build a wall for B 'in consideration of the £1000. A cannot sue B if he does not build the wall, for there is no element of bargain, and no consideration supports the promise to build the wall.

5.02 Consideration rarely causes problems in contract law, because it is usually abundantly clear what the consideration is: very often in the contracts architects deal with the consideration for providing works or services will be the fee to be paid for them. But on the rare occasions when consideration is lacking the consequences can be fatal for the aggrieved party, who has no contract on which he can sue.

6 'Agreement'

6.01 The existence of agreement between the parties to a contract is in practice the most troublesome of the three essential imgredients.

6.02 The inverted commas around 'agreement' are intentional. The law of contract does not peer into the minds of contracting parties to see what they really intended to contract to do; it contents itself with taking an objective view and, on the basis of what the parties have said and done, and the surrounding context in which they did so, the courts decide what the parties should be taken to have intended. The court asks whether, in the eyes of the law, they should be considered to have been in agreement.

6.03 To perform this somewhat artificial task the courts use a set formula or analytical framework which can be thought of as the recipe which must be followed by parties to a contract. The recipe is simple: offer and acceptance.

George Cruikshank.

Offer

6.04 An offer is a promise, made by the offeror, to be bound by a contract if the offeree accepts the terms of the offer. The offer matures into a contract when it is accepted by the other party.

6.05 The offer can be made to just one person (the usual case) or it can be made to a group of people, or even to the world at large. The case of *Carlill* v *Carbolic Smoke Ball Company* [1892] 2 QB 484, [1893] 1 QB 256, is an example of an offer to all the world. The defendant company manufactured a device called a carbolic smoke ball, which was intended to prevent its users from catching flu. They advertised it with the promise that they would pay £100 to anybody who used the smoke ball three times a day as directed and still caught flu. The unfortunate plaintiff caught flu despite using the smoke ball, and not unnaturally felt she was entitled to the £100 offered. The Court of Appeal held that the company's advertisement constituted an offer to contract, and by purchasing the smoke ball the plaintiff had accepted the offer, so that a contract was created. Accordingly the plaintiff successfully extracted her £100 from the company.

6.06 Not all pre-contractual negotiations are offers to contract. In deals of any complexity there will often be a lot of exploratory negotiation before the shape of the final contract begins to emerge, and it is not until a late stage that there will be a formal offer to contract by one party to the other.

6.07 Easy to confuse with an offer to contract is an invitation to treat. An invitiation to treat is an offer to consider

accepting an offer to contract from the other party. Most advertisements 'offering' goods for sale, and also the goods lying on a supermarket shelf with their price labels, are merely invitations to treat. When the prospective purchaser proffers the appropriate sum to the cashier at the desk it is the customer who is making the offer, which can be accepted or rejected by the cashier. It will by now be obvious that the dividing line between an invitation to treat and an offer to contract can be very thin, but the distinction is important.

Acceptance

6.08 The acceptance of the offer can be by word – written or oral – or by conduct.

6.09 An acceptance must be unequivocal and it must be a complete acceptance of every term of the offer. 'I accept your terms but only if I can have 42 days to pay instead of 28' will not be an acceptance, for it purports to vary the terms of the offer. It is a counter-offer, which itself will have to be accepted by the seller. And such a counter-offer will destroy the original offer which it rejects, and which can therefore no longer be accepted. In the old case of *Hyde* v *Wrench* (1840) 3 Beav 334, the defendant Wrench offered to sell some land to the plaintiff for £1000. On 8 June Hyde said he would pay £950. On 27 June Wrench refused to sell for £950 and on 29 June Hyde said he would pay £1000 after all. Wrench refused to sell. It was held that there was no contract. Hyde's counter-offer on 8 June had destroyed the initial offer of £1000 and by 29 June it was too late for Hyde to change his mind.

Revocation and the postal rules

6.10 An offer can be withdrawn or revoked up until such time as it is accepted. An acceptance is of course final – otherwise people would constantly be pulling out of contracts because they had had afterthoughts. Since an offer can be both revoked by its maker and destroyed by a counter-offer, yet matures into a contract when it is accepted, it can be crucial to decide when these events occur.

6.11 An acceptance is generally effective when it is received by the offeror. But if the acceptance is made by posting a letter then the acceptance takes effect when the letter is posted. But revocation by post takes effect when the letter is received by the offeree. The working of these rules is neatly exemplified by the case of *Byrne* v *Van Tienhoven* (1880) 5 CPD 344. There the defendants made an offer to the plaintiffs by letter on 1 October. The letter was received on 11 October and immediately accepted by telegram. Meanwhile, on 8 October the defendants had thought better of their offer and sent a letter revoking it. The second letter did no reach the plaintiffs until 20 October. There was a binding contract because the acceptance took effect before the revocation. The result would have been the same even if the acceptance had been by letter and the letter had arrived with the defendants after 20 October.

Battle of the forms

6.12 These mostly Victorian rules about offer and acceptance may seem rather irrelevant to modern commercial transactions. But there is one context in which they regularly appear: the so-called 'battle of the forms' which takes place when two contracting parties both deal on their own standard terms of business, typically appearing on the reverse of their estimates, orders, invoices and other business stationery.

6.13 A vendor sends an estimate on his usual business form, with his standard terms and conditions on the reverse, and a note saying that all business is done on his standard terms. The purchaser sends back an order purporting to accept the estimate, but on the back of his acceptance are his standard terms, which are doubtless more favourable to him than the vendor's. The vendor sends the goods, and the purchaser pays for them. Is there a contract, and if there is, whose standard terms is it on?

6.14 The purchaser's 'acceptance' and order is not a true acceptance, because it does not accept all the terms of the vendor's offer, since it purports to substitute the pruchaser's standard terms. So the purchaser's order is in legal terms a counter-offer, and this is accepted – in this example – by the vendor's action in sending the goods.

6.15 If there are long drawn-out negotiations as to quantities, prices and so on, all on business stationery containing standard terms, the problems are compounded, and the result, best found by working backwards and identifying the last communication on standard terms, is rather artificial and is rather a matter of luck.

6.16 The courts have tried on occasion to substitute a rather less mechanical analysis of offer and acceptance, looking at the negotiations as a whole (see especially Lord Denning in *Butler Machine Tool Co Ltd* v *Ex-Cell-O Corporation (England) Ltd* [1979] 1 WLR 401 at 405) but this approach has not found widespread judicial acceptance, and it seems that whatever the artificiality of a strict analysis in terms of offer and acceptance it is difficult to find an alternative approach which is workable.

6.17 This topic leads on naturally to the next. Once it is established that a contract exists, what are its terms?

7 Terms of a contract
Express terms

7.01 The most obvious terms of a contract are those which the parties expressly agreed. In cases where there is an oral contract there may be conflicting evidence as to what actually was said and agreed, but with the written contracts with which architects will most often deal, construing the express terms is usually less problematic: just read the document evidencing the contract. The 'four corners rule' restricts attention to within the four corners of the document, and even if the written terms mis-state the intention of one of the parties – perhaps that party had not read the document carefully before signing it – he will be bound by what is recorded save in exceptional circumstances. This is another manifestation of the objective approach of English contract law discussed above.

7.02 It should be noted at this stage that things said or written prior to making a contract may affect the parties' legal obligations to one another even though they are not terms of the contract. This matter is discussed in the section on misrepresentation.

Implied terms

7.03 Implied terms are likely to catch out the unwary. There are three types of implied term: those implied by statute, those implied by custom, and those implied by the court.

Terms implied by the court

7.04 With unfortunate frequency constracting parties discover too late that their contract has failed to provide for the events which have happened. One party will wish that the contract had included a term imposing liability on the other in the circumstances that have turned out, and will try to persuade the court that such a term in his favour should be implied into the contract, saying, in effect, that the court

ought to read between the lines of the contract and find the term there.

7.05 There are some particular terms in particular types of contract which the courts will, as a matter of course, imply into contracts of a particular kind. For instance, a contract for the lease of a furnished property will be taken to include a term that it will be reasonably fit for habitation at the commencement of the tenancy.

7.06 More frequently there will be no authority on the particular type of term which it is sought to imply. The courts have developed an approach to these problems, based on an early formulation in the case of *The Moorcock* (1889) 14 PD 64. There the owner of the ship *The Moorcock* had contracted with the defendants to discharge his ship at their jetty on the Thames. Both parties must have realized that the ship would ground at low tide; in the event it not only grounded but, settling on a ridge of hard ground, it was damaged. The plaintiff owners said that the defendants should be taken to have given a warranty that they would take reasonable care to ensure that the river bottom was safe for the vessel – and the Court of Appeal agreed. Bowen LJ explained:

'the law [raises] an implication from the presumed intentions of the parties, with the object of giving to the transaction such efficacy as both parties must have intended it should have'.

This is called the 'business efficacy' test; but it is clear that the term must be *necessary* for business efficacy, rather than be simply a term which makes better sense of the contract if it is included than if it is not. In *Shirlow* v *Southern Foundries* [1939] 2 KB 206 at 227, Mackinnon LJ expressed the test in terms of the 'officious bystander' which provides a readily memorable – if not always easy applicable – formulation of the rule:

'Prima facie, that which in any contract is left to be implied and need not be expressed is something which is so obvious it goes without saying; so that, if while the parties were making their bargain an officious bystander were to suggest some express provision for it in their agreement, they would testily suppress him with a common, "Oh, of course".

The officious bystander test is obviously difficult to pass. *Both* parties must have taken the term as 'obvious'. The ploy of trying to persuade a court that a term should be read into the contract in favour of one party is tried much more often than it succeeds. The moral for architects as for any other contracting party, is that the proper time to define contractual terms is before the contract is made, not after things have gone wrong.

Terms implied by custom

7.07 The custom of a particular type of business is relevant in contruing the express terms of a contract and may on occasion be sufficient to imply into a contract a term which apparently is not there at all. In *Hutton* v *Warren* (1836) 1 M & W 466, a lease was held to include a term effecting the local custom that when the tenant's tenancy came to an end he would be entitled to a sum representing the seed and labour put into the arable land. There are other examples from the law of marine insurance, many of which are now crystallized in statute law, but

'An alleged custom can be incorporated into a contract only if there is nothing in the express or necessarily implied terms of the contract to prevent such inclusion and, further, that a custom will only be imported into a contract where it can be so imported consistently with the tenor of the document as a whole.' (*London Export* v *Jubilee Coffee* [1958] 2 All ER 411, at 420)

The place of terms implied by custom in the modern law is small; but custom as a guide in construing terms of a contract continues to be of some importance.

Terms implied by statute

7.08 For architects there are two very important statutes which may automatically incorporate terms into their contracts: the Sale of Goods Act 1979 and the Supply of Goods and Services Act 1982. The principal relevant sections of those Acts are fairly straightforward, but of course they have to be read in their context to see their precise effect (see Extracts 3.1 and 3.2).

Extract 3.1 Sale of Goods Act 1979

14.(1) Except as provided in this section and section 15 below and subject to any other enactment, there is no implied condition or warranty about the quality or fitness for purpose of goods supplied under a contract of sale.
(2) Where the seller sells goods in the course of a business, there is an implied condition that the goods supplied under the contract are of merchantable quality, except there is no such condition –
  (a) as regards defects specifically drawn to the buyer's attention before the contract is made; or
  (b) if the buyer examines the goods before the contract is made, as regards defects which the examination ought to reveal.
(3) Where the seller sells good in the course of a business and the buyer, expressly or by implication, makes known –
  (a) to the seller, or
  (b) where the purchase price or part of it is payable by instalments and the goods were previously sold by a credit-broker to the seller, to that credit-broker,
any particular purpose for which the goods supplied under the contract are reasonably fit for that purpose, whether or not that is a purpose for which such goods are commonly supplied, except where the circumstances show that the buyer does not rely, or that it is unreasonable for him to rely, on the skill or judgement of the seller or credit-broker.

Extract 3.2 Supply of Goods and Services Act 1982

12.(1) In this Act a "contract for the supply of a service" means, subject to subsection (2) below, a contract under which a person "the supplier" agrees to carry out a service.
(2) For the purposes of this Act, a contract of service or apprenticeship is not a contract for the supply of a service.

13. In a contract for the supply of a service where the supplier is acting in the course of a business, there is an implied term that the supplier will carry out the service with reasonable care and skill.

14.(1) Where, under a contract for the supply of a service by a supplier acting in the course of a business, the time for the service to be carried out is not fixed by the contract, left to be fixed in a manner agreed by the contract or determined by the course of dealing between the parties, there is an implied term that the supplier will carry out the service within a reasonable time.
(2) What is a reasonable time is a question of fact.

15.(1) Where, under a contract for the supply of a service, the consideration for the supply of a service is not determined by the contract, but left to be determined in a manner agreed by the contract or determined by the course of dealing between the parties, there is an implied term that the party contracting with the supplier will pay a reasonable charge.
(2) What is a reasonable charge is a question of fact.

7.09 The terms implied by SOGA and SOGASA can be exluded by express provision in the contract (SOGA, section 55 and SOGASA, section 16), although in both cases this is subject to the provisions of the Unfair Contract Terms Act 1977.

8 Exclusion clauses and UCTA

8.01 A contracting party, particularly a contracting party with a dominant position relative to the other, may try to include in the contract terms which are extremely advantageous to him in the event that he is in breach of some principal obligation under the contract. The commonest way to do this is to exclude or limit his liability in certain circumstances. A carrier might, for example, offer to carry goods on terms including a clause that in the event of loss or damage to the goods being carried his liability should be limited to £100 per each kilo weight of the goods carried. The consignor of a parcel of expensive jewellery would be little assisted by a finding that the carrier was liable for their loss if the damages he could recover were limited to £100 per kilo.

8.02 The Unfair Contracts Terms Act 1977 has an ambit more narrow than its title suggests, but it does impose a series of restrictions on the ability of contracting parties to exclude or limit their liability in cases of breach.

8.03 Section 2(1) of the Act precludes anybody from excluding or restricting their liability for death or personal injury arising from negligence by reference to any contract term or notice, and section 2(2) precludes any such limitation of liability for loss or damage of any kind resulting from negligence, save where the exclusion satisfies the requirement of reasonableness. The test of reasonableness is basically that the term should be fair and reasonable having regard to the circumstances which were known to the parties when the contract was made (section 11).

8.04 The Act also affects the ability of parties to exclude their liability for straightforward breach of contract whether or not negligence is involved, although the circumstances are more limited. One section from this important Act will serve to exemplify its operation.

> **3.**(1) This section applies as between contracting parties where one of them deals as consumer or on the other's written standard terms of business.
> (2) As against that party, the other cannot by reference to any contract term –
>   (a) when himself in breach of contract, exclude or restrict any liability of his in respect of the breach; or
>   (b) claim to be entitled –
>   (i) to render a contractual performance substantially different from that which was reasonably expected of him, or
>   (ii) in respect of the whole or any part of his contractual obligation, to render no performance at all,
> except in so far as (in any of the cases mentioned above in this subsection) the contract term satisfies the test of reasonableness.'

Even on a cursory inspection of this section its importance will be appreciated as will some of its limitations. As between two large commercial enterprises the section will have no effect since a party does not 'deal as a consumer' if he makes the contract in the course of a business (section 12). On the other hand, it is important to realize when dealing near the bottom of a contractual chain which ends up with the final consumer, that it may be impossible to transfer to the ultimate consumer the burden of exclusion clauses which the superior members of the contractual chain have been able to impose on the middlemen.

9 Standard term contracts

9.01 Many of the contracts with which architects are involved are standard form contracts. Chapter 9 deals at length with one such contract, the JCT Standard Form of Building Contract, and in other areas other standard form contracts are available. The use of such contracts has a number of advantages. A great deal of experience has gone into drafting these contracts so that many pitfalls of fuzzy or uncertain wording can be avoided. And where the words used are open to different interpretations it may well be that case law has definitively settled their meaning. In effect the user of a standard term contract enjoys the benefit of other people's earlier litigation in sorting out exactly what obligations the standard terms impose. The effects of well litigated and well-established terms and conditions also have an impact on third parties. Insurers in particular will know where they stand in relation to a contract on familiar terms and therefore the extra premiums inevitable on uncertain risks can be avoided.

9.02 One potential problem with STCs can be minimized if it is appreciated. Just as tinkering with a well-tuned engine can have catastrophic consequences, so 'home-made' modifications of STCs can have far-reaching effects. Many of the provisions and definitions used in STCs interlink, and modifying one clause may have unforeseen and far-reaching ramifications. If parties to an STC want to modify it because it does not seem to achieve exactly the cross-obligations they want to undertake, it is highly advisable to take specialist advice.

10 Misrepresentation

10.01 Pre-contractual negotiations often cover many subjects which are not dealt with by the terms (express or implied) of the eventual contract. In some circumstances things said or done before the contract is made can lead to liability.

Representations and misrepresentations

10.02 A representation is a statement of existing fact made by one party to the eventual contract (the misrepresentor) to the other (the misrepresentee) which induces the representee to enter into the contract. A misrepresentation is a representation which is false. Two elements of the definition need elaboration.

Statement of existing fact

10.03 The easiest way to grasp what is meant by a statement of existing fact is to see what is not included in the expression.

A promise to do something in the future is not a representation – such a statement is essentially the stuff of which contracts are made, and the place for promises is therefore in the contract itself.

An opinion which is honestly held and honestly expressed will not constitute an actionable misrepresentation. This is sometimes said to be because it is not a statement of fact and it is perhaps simplest to see this by realizing that it does not make sense to talk of an opinion being false or untrue, so that in any event it cannot be a misrepresentation. But a statement of opinion 'I believe such and such . . .' *can* be a representation and can therefore be a misrepresentation if the representor does not actually hold the belief, because, as Bowen LJ explained:

> 'The state of a man's mind is as much a fact as the state of his digestion. It is true that it is very difficult to prove what the state of a man's mind at a particular time is, but if it can be ascertained it is as much a fact as anything else. A misrepresentation as to the state of a man's mind is, therefore, a statement of fact.' (*Edgington* v *Fitzmaurice* (1885) 29 ChD 459 at 483.)

10.04 A somewhat more surprising line of authority holds that 'mere puff' does not constitute a representation: 'simplex

commendatio non obligat'. Hence describing land as 'uncommonly rich water meadow' was held not to constitute a representation in *Scott* v *Hanson* (1829) 1 Russ & M 128. But the courts today are rather less indulgent to exaggerated sales talk and if it can be established that effusive description of a vendor's product is actually untrue it seems that the courts would today be more likely to hold that to be a misrepresentation than would their nineteenth century predecessors.

10.05 Silence generally does not constitute a representation. A vendor is generally under no obligation to draw to the attention of his purchaser the defects in that which he is selling, and even tacit acquiescence in the purchaser's self-deception will not ususaly create any liability. However, there are cases in which silence can constitute a misrepresentation. If the representor makes some representation about a certain matter he must not leave out other aspects of the story so that what he says is misleading in toto: so although a total non-disclosure may not be a misrepresentation, partial non-disclosure may be.

Reliance

10.06 To create any liability the representee must show that the misrepresentation induced him to enter into the contract – the misrepresentation must have been material. Therefore if the misrepresentee knew that the representation was false, or if he was not aware of the representation at all, or if he knew of it but it did not affect his judgement, than he will have no grounds for relief. But the misrepresentation need not be the only, nor even indeed the principal, reason why the misrepresentee entered into the contract.

The three types of misrepresentation

10.07 If the representor making the misrepresentation made it knowing it was untrue, or without believing it was true, or recklessly, not caring whether it was true or false, then it is termed a fraudulent misrepresentation.

If, however, the representor made the false statement believing that it was true but had taken insufficient care to ensure that it was true, then it will be a negligent misstatement.

Finally, if the misrepresentor had taken reasonable care to ensure that it was true, and did believe that it was true, then it is merely an innocent misrepresentation.

Remedies for misrepresentation

10.08 This is a very difficult area of the law, and the finer details of the effects of the Misrepresentation Act 1967 are still not entirely clear. The summary which follows is extremely brief.

Principal remedy: rescission

10.9 The basic remedy for misrepresentation is rescission. The misrepresentee can in many circumstances oblige the misrepresentor to restore him to the position he would have been in had the contract never been made.

10.10 Rescission is not available if the misrepresentee has, with knowledge of the misrepresentation, affirmed the contract. A long lapse of time before the misrepresentee opts to rescind is often taken as affirmation. Rescission is not available if a third party has, since the contract was made, himself acquired for value an interest in the subject matter of the contract. Nor is it available, almost by definition, if it is impossible to restore the parties to the status quo before the contract was made.

10.11 The court now has a general power to grant damages in lieu of rescission (Misrepresentation Act 1967, section 2(2)), and may award damages to the victim of a negligent or innocent representation even where the misrepresentee would rather have the contract rescinded instead.

Damages

10.12 The victim of a fraudulent misrepresentation may sue for damages as well as claim rescission, and the measure of damages will be tortious.

10.13 The victim of a negligent misrepresentation may also recover damages (section 1) as well as rescission. It is not entirely clear how damages should be calculated.

10.14 In the case of an innocent misrepresentation there is no right to damages, but, as already explained, the court may in its discretion award damages in lieu of rescission.

The law of negligent misstatement

10.15 Misrepresentation alone is complicated. The matter is compounded by the availability of damages for the tort of negligent misstatement (rather than misrepresentation), which is discussed in Chapter 4. There will be many instances in which an actionable misrepresentation is also an actionable misstatement.

11 Performance and breach

11.01 All the topics considered so far have been concerned with matters up to and including the creation of a contract – matters generally of greater interest to lawyers than to men of business or to architects. But both lawyers and architects have a close interest in whether or not a party fulfils its obligations under a contract and, if it does not, what can be done about it.

The right to sue on partial performance of a complete contract

11.02 Many contracts take the general form of A paying B to perform some work or to provide some service. It is unusual for the party performing the work or providing the service to do nothing at all; the usual case will be that much of the work is done according to the contract, but some part of the work remains incomplete, undone, or improperly performed. This situation needs to be considered from both sides. We begin with examining whether the incomplete performer can sue his paymaster if no money is forthcoming.

11.03 The general rule of contract law is that a party must perform precisely what he contracted to do. The consequence is that in order to make the other liable in any way under the contract all of that party's obligations must be performed. If the contract is divided up into clearly severable parts each will be treated for these purposes as a separate contract, and virtually all building contracts will of course make provision for stage payments. Nevertheless it is important to be aware of the general rule which applies to a contract where one lump sum is provided for all the works. Non-performance (as opposed to misperformance) of some part will disentitle the partial performer from payment.

11.04 An example is *Bolton* v *Mahadeva* [1972] 1 WLR 1009. There the plaintiff agreed to instal a hot water system for the defendant for a lump sum payment of £560. The radiators emitted fumes and the system did not heat the house properly. Curing the defects would cost £174. The defendant was held not liable to pay the plaintiff anything.

11.05 There is an important exception to this rule, even for entire contracts. If the party performing the works has 'substantially performed' his obligations then he is entitled to the contract sum subject only to a counter-claim for those parts remaining unperformed. In *Hoenig* v *Isaacs* [1952] 2 All ER 176, there was a lump-sum contract for the decoration and furnishing of the defendant's flat for the price of £750. When the plaintiff left, one wardrobe door needed replacing and one shelf was too short, and would have to be remade. The Court of Appeal held that although 'near the border-line' on the facts, the plaintiff had substantially performed his contractual obligations and was therefore able to recover his £750, subject only to the deduction of £56, being the cost of the necessary repairs.

Remedies against the incomplete performer

11.06 The flip-side of the situation of suing on an incompletely performed contract is suing the incomplete performer. Obviously incomplete performance or misperformance gives to the other party, who has so far performed his obligations as they fall due, a right to damages to put him in the position he would have been in had the contract been performed. But in some circumstances another remedy will be available to the aggrieved party, for he will be able to hold himself absolved from any further performance of his obligations under the contract.

11.07 This right to treat the contract as at an end arises in three situations.

Breach of a contractual condition

11.08 The first situation is if the term which the non or misperforming party has breached is a contractual condition rather than merely a warranty. It used to be thought that all contractual terms were either conditions or warranties. Whether a term was one or the other might be determined by statute, by precedent, or might have to be decided by the court by looking at the contract in the light of the surrounding circumstances. If the term was a condition then any breach of it, however minor, would allow the aggrieved party to treat the contract as at an end. The modern tendency is to adopt a more realistic approach and to escape from the straitjacket dichotomy of conditions and warranties. In *Hong Kong Fir Shipping Co Ltd* v *Kawasaki Kisen Kaisha Ltd* [1962] 2 QB 26, at 70 Lord Diplock explained that

> 'There are, however, many contractual terms of a more complex character which cannot be categorised as being "conditions" or "warranties" . . . Of such undertakings all that can be predicated is that some breaches will and others will not give rise to an event which will deprive the party in default of substantially the whole benefit which it was intended he should obtain from the contract; and the legal consequences of the breach of any such undertaking, unless provided for expressly in the contract, depend on the nature of the event to which the breach gives rise and do not follow automatically from a prior classification of the undertaking as a "condition" or "warranty".'

These terms which are neither conditions nor warranties have been unhelpfully named 'innominate terms' and although their existence decreases the importance of this first type of circumstance in which an aggrieved party can treat its contractual obligations as at an end, it is nevertheless still open for the contracting parties expressly to make a contractual term a condition, in which case any breach of it allows this remedy in addition to a claim for damages.

Repudiatory breach

11.09 If the breach 'goes to the root of the contract' or deprives the party of substantially the whole benefit the contract was intended to confer on him, then he will be entitled to treat the contract as at an end.

Renunciation

11.10 If one party evinces an intention not to continue to perform his side of the contract then the other party may again treat the contract as at an end.

Election

11.11 In all three of the circumstances described above the innocent party has a choice as to whether or not to treat himself as discharged. He may prefer to press for performance of the contract so far as the other pary is able to perform it, and to restrict himself to his remedy in damages. But once made the election cannot unilaterally be changed, unless the matter which gave rise to it is a continuing state of affairs which therefore continues to provide the remedy afresh.

11.12 The rule that the innocent party may, if he prefers, elect to press for performance following (for instance) a renunciation can have a bizarre result. In *White and Carter (Councils)* v *McGregor* [1962] AC 413 the plaintiff company supplied litter bins to local councils. The councils did not pay for the bins, but they allowed them to carry advertising, and the plaintiffs made their money from the companies whose advertisements their bins carried. The defendant company agreed to hire space on the plaintiffs' bins for three years. Later the same day they changed their mind and said that they were not going to be bound by the contract. The plaintiffs could have accepted that renunciation, but, perhaps short of work and wanting to keep busy, opted to carry on with the contract, which they proceeded to do for the next three years. They sued successfully for the full contract price: there was no obligation on them to treat the contract as at an end and they were not obliged to sue for damages only.

12 Privity of contract and agency

Privity of contract

12.02 As was explained in the opening section of this chapter, the distinguishing feature of contract law is that it defines the rights and obligations of two parties between whom there is a contract. A person who is not a party to a contract cannot gain any benefit by suing on it, nor can he suffer any detriment by being sued on it. This principle – which is simplicity itself – is all that is meant by the expression 'privity of contract'. But although the basic notion is straightforward, its application is not always so simple, for it is not always obvious who the parties to a contract are. The law of agency provides the framework within which that question is decided.

The two aspects of agency in contract law

12.02 For A to act as an agent for P his principal, is for A to act as P's representative. A's words or actions will create legal rights and liabilities for A who is therefore bound by what A does. It is just as if P had said or done those things himself. The agent's actions might have consequences for P in contract, or tort, or some other area of the law, but in this chapter it is naturally only with contractual liabilities that we are concerned. In general, if A, as P's agent, properly contracts with C, then the resulting contract is a contract between P and C. A is not privy to the contract, and can neither sue or be sued upon it.

12.03 There are two sets of legal obligations which are of interest. The first is those between the principal and his agent. That relationship of agency may, but need not, itself be the subject of a contract – the contract of agency. For

instance, A may be rewarded by a percentage commission on any of P's business which he places with C. If A does not receive his commission he may wish to sue P, and he will do so under their contract of agency. That is a matter between P and A, and of no interest to C. It is governed by the rules for contracts of agency. These rules, just a specialized subset of the rules of contract generally, will not be further discussed here.

12.04 The second set of legal questions raised by an agency concerns how the relationship is created, whether and how it is that A's actions bind his principal, and whether A is ever left with any personal liability of his own. We begin by considering the first of these issues.

Creation of agency

12.05 There are three important ways in which an agency may be created.

1. By express appointment

This is of course the commonest way to create an agency. Generally no formalities are necessary: the appointment may be oral or in writing. To take an example, the employees of a trading company are frequently expressly appointed by their contract of emplyment to act as the agents of the company and to place and receive orders on its behalf.

2. By estoppel

If P by his words or conduct leads C to believe that A is his agent, and C deals with A on that basis, A cannot escape the contract by saying that, in fact, A was not his agent. In these circumstances P will be stopped, or 'estopped', from making that assertion.

3. By ratification

If A, not in fact being P's agent, purports to contract with C on P's behalf, and P then discovers the contract, likes the look of it and ratifies and adopts it, then, ex post facto, A is P's agent for the purposes of that contract. The precise working of the rules of ratification are rather involved.

Authorization

12.06 The effect of an agent's words or actions will depend crucially on whether or not he was authorized by his principal to say or do them. The agent's authority will usually be an actual authority, that is to say an authority which he has expressly or impliedly been granted by his principal. But the scope of the agent's authority may, most importantly, be enlarged by the addition of his ostensible authority.

12.07 Ostensible authority is another manifestation of the operation of estoppel. If P represents to C that his agent A has an authority wider than, in fact, has been expressly or impliedly granted by P to A, and in reliance on that representation C contracts with P through A, then P will be stopped ('estopped') from denying that the scope of A's authority was wide enough to include the contract that has been made.

The liabilities of principal and agent

12.08 We now consider the liabilities of both principal and agent with the contracting third party C, and the discussion is divided into those cases in which the agent is authorized to enter into the transaction, and those in which he is not so authorized.

The agent acts within the scope of his authority

12.09 This division has three subdivisions, depending on how much the contracting party C knows about the principal. The agent may tell C that P exists, and name him. Or he may tell C that he has a principal, but not name him. Or – still less communicative – he may not tell C that he has a principal at all, so that as far as C is concerned he is contracting with A direct.

1. Principal is named

This is in a sense the paradigm example of agency in action. A drops out of the picture altogether, the contract is between P and C and A can neither sue nor be sued on the P–C contract.

2. Existence of principal disclosed, but not his identity

The general rule is the same as in case 1.

3. Neither name nor existence of principal disclosed to C

This case is described as the case of the undisclosed principal. The rule here is somewhat counter-intuitive: both the agent and the principal may sue on the contract, and C may sue the agent, and, if and when he discovers his identity, the principal.

The agent acts outside the scope of his authority

12.10 The position as regards the principal is clear. The principal is not party to any contract, and can neither sue nor be sued upon it. This of course would have to be the case, for really in these circumstances there is no agency operating at all. But it is important to remember that ostensible authority may fix a principal with liability when the agent is acting outside his express or implied authority.

12.11 The position of the agent is more complex. We first consider the position of the agent as far as benefits under the contract are concerned – whether the agent can sue upon the contract. If the agent purported to contract as agent for a named principal, then the agent cannot sue on the contract. On the other hand, if the name of the principal is not disclosed the agent can sue upon the contract as if it were his own.

12.12 Turning now to the liability of an unauthorized agent to be sued by C, the position depends on what the agent thought was the true position between himself and P. If A knows all along that he does not have P's authority to enter into the contract, then C can sue A, although for the tort of deceit, rather than under the contract.

12.13 If on the other hand A genuinely thought that he was authorized by P to enter into the contract, he cannot be sued by P for deceit – after all, he has not been deceitful, merely mistaken. But C has an alternative means of enforcing his contract. A court will infer the existence of a collateral contract by A (as principal) with C, under which A warranted that he had P's authority to contract. This is a quite separate contract to the non-existent contract which C thought he was entering into with P, but from C's point of view it is just as good, for now C can sue A instead.

13 Limitation under the Limitation Act 1980

13.01 Armed with the information derived from this chapter a prospective plaintiff should have some idea of what his contract is, whether it has been breached, what he can do about it, and who he should sue. There is one more point to consider.

13.02 An action for breach of contract must generally be commenced within six years. Time begins to run – the six years starts – when the contract is breached. This may mean that the plaintiff can sue before any real physical damage has been experienced. Suppose the defendant is an architect who has, in breach of contract, designed foundations for a building which are inadequate, and it is clear that in ten to twenty years' time the building will fall down if remedial works are not carried out. The plaintiff can sue straight away. Of course, although no physical damage has yet occurred there has been economic loss because the defendant has got out of the contract a building worth much less than what he paid for it, and it is obviously right that he should be able to sue straight away.

13.03 The exception to this rule is that a plaintiff may sue on a contract contained in a deed up to twelve years after the contract was breached. It is for this reason that building contracts – which may take more than six years from inception to completion – are frequently made under deed.

13.04 The law on limitation periods is to be found in the Limitation Act 1980. The law on limitation periods for suing on a tort is different and more complicated, and is explained in Chapter 4.

4

The Law of Tort

CHARLES MANZONI

1 Introduction

1.01 It is difficult in a chapter of this nature to define adequately the law of tort. A definition was given by Winfield earlier this century which stated that 'Tortious liability arises from the breach of a duty primarily fixed by Law; this duty is towards persons generally and its breach is redressible by an action for unliquidated damages' (Winfield (1931)). However, without a great deal of further explanation which is beyond the scope of this book that definition lacks the desired clarity. It is perhaps more appropriate to investigate the aims of the law of tort rather than attempt to a strict definition.

1.02 In general terms it can be said that tort is concerned with the allocation or prevention of losses which are bound to occur within our society. In a society of people it is bound to be the case that conflict of interests will occur and people will be thrown into relationships which they had no choice but to enter. For example, if A walks down the street and is knocked down by a motor car driven by B, A has no relationship with B other than by virtue of the fact that B was driving at the time. They are thrown together by force of circumstance and are therefore unable to dictate the terms of their relationship. Accordingly it is the law which must govern and this is the province of the law of tort.

1.03 The law of tort covers a very broad spectrum of matters: A knocking B down with a motor car, a tree on C's land causing damage to a building on D's land, E writing untrue and libellous stories about F and G giving bad professional advice to H. The principles which apply to each area are necessarily different in their detail but, one hopes, are all founded on the same basic premise of correcting the wrong suffered by one person which has been caused by another. That is not to say, however, that every loss which is suffered will have a redress in law. If A starts a business similar to B's in the same area in which B previously had a monopoly it is clear that, subject to A's business being of an equal quality and efficiency, B will suffer loss. Indeed, it was probably the very intention of A to cause such loss to B but there will be no redress in the law of tort. It has been said that the law cannot even go so far as to provide support to all people who are the victims of morally reprehensible behaviour: In *Donaghue* v *Stevenson* [1932] AC 562, 580 Lord Atkin commented that

> 'Acts or Omissions which any moral code would censure cannot in a practical world be treated so as to give a right to every person injured by them to demand relief. In this way rules of law arise which limit the range of complaints and the extent of their remedy.'

The law of tort is therefore concerned with identifying when and where and how liability can attach to re-allocate the burden of losses suffered. This chapter, although headed the law of tort, will only deal with some of the areas of tort that relate to architects; some of the relationships which are governed by tort will not be covered (for instance, defamation) and so the reader should not think that after reading this chapter he has an exhaustive knowledge of the law of tort. The categories of situation for which redress may or may not be available are never closed and can change very rapidly. Accordingly all one can do is to know the basics and keep abreast of the developments and in the light of that knowledge analyse every factual situation separately.

1.04 There is one further matter about which the reader may like to think. In the majority of cases the law of tort is concerned purely with allocating risk and, by that allocation, determining who should pay for damage. The aim is that the person suffering the loss should be fully recompensed and any person at fault should pay. In recent years a system of insurance has evolved which effectively takes the liability to pay away from the person at fault. There are many forms of this insurance: the welfare state, mutual clubs, commercial insurance, and it should be asked how much further the system should be developed. Is the law of tort the most effective way of giving recompense or would some global scheme of no fault insurance provide a better solution?

From the general concepts attention is now focused on particular aspects of the law of tort.

2 Nuisance

2.01 Nuisance is traditionally concerned with the protection of the environment, although in today's parlance that phrase would limit it to 'green' issues rather than traditional nuisances. It is perhaps better to say that it relates to the protection of the environment and the protection of a man's use of his own land and land over which there is a public right of way. Nuisance is concerned with such matters as pollution by oil, noxious fumes, interference with leisure activities and interference with support of adjoining land. It is based entirely on the principles of the common law; that is to say, nuisance itself is not governed by statute but has been developed by the courts over the years. However, more recently there has developed a large body of statute law which is concerned with the protection of the environment and the public as a whole. These statutes generally do not provide a civil remedy to members of the public, and their enforcement rests often with bodies set up specifically. The most frequently sought remedy in nuisance is an injunction to prevent the acts complained of and it is likely that the most effective way to obtain such remedy is to make a complaint to the relevant public body, thereby passing both the burden and cost to them.

2.02 Nuisance is divided into two types: public and private. Public nuisance affects members of the public in general, for example pollution by oil or the emission of noxious fumes. It is a crime to cause such nuisance and it is not actionable by the public generally. The reason for this is obvious. If everybody was able to sue the oil carrier who spilt oil onto the beach, because it spoilt their enjoyment of the use of the beach, there would be a multiplicity of actions, all perhaps with varying results, the courts would become log jammed and the costs would be disproportionately high. The carrier is liable to a criminal prosecution, which is considered to be a sufficient deterrent and punishment. Further, if appropriate, the Attorney-General has the right to bring a civil action for an injunction to prevent the nuisance from continuing or re-occurring; such an action is called a relator action.

2.03 This is the case even if a member of the public has incurred cost in removing the nuisance. If the highway is temporarily blocked by a local authority in such a way that it constitutes a nuisance and a member of the public incurs cost in removing the obstruction he will be unable to recover that cost (*Winterbottom* v *Lord Derby* (1867) LR 2 Ex 316). However, if that person has suffered some special damage over and above that suffered by members of the public as a whole he is able to bring an action in nuisance to recover that damage. Where noxious fumes are released by an oil refinery it constitutes a public nuisance which is actionable only under a relator action. If Mrs Smith lives next door to the refinery and has hung her washing out to dry on the day the fumes are released it may well be that it is damaged irrecoverably by the fumes. This would be an example of special damage that would vest a cause of action in public nuisance on Mrs Smith.

2.04 Private nuisance can be described as 'unlawful interference with a person's use or enjoyment of land or some right over or in connection with it'. The word 'unlawful' in that description is important because it is not every interference with use or enjoyment that will constitute a nuisance. There are many everyday acts which do interfere with use or enjoyment but which are not nuisances. The courts constantly have to tread the middle ground between the two conflicting interests of the land occupiers. The act complained of will generally only become a nuisance if it is unreasonable, and in deciding whether something is unreasonable a large number of factors are taken into account.

2.05 An important consideration in this respect is the conduct of the defendant. This raises the question of whether there need be fault on behalf of the defendant in order to establish nuisance. If so, what degree of fault is required and is the test to be the same as it is for negligence? The answer is not easy, for many of the cases are expressed in unclear terms. A distinction should be drawn between the types of remedy sought. If an injunction is all the plaintiff wants then it is more likely to issue without fault on behalf of the defendant than if damages are sought. Something may be an unlawful interference through no fault of the defendant, but nevertheless the courts will put a stop to it if the thing in itself is unreasonable. However, they are always reluctant to order a defendant to pay damages in the absence of fault. When looking at the degree of fault required the best judgement to use is that of Lord Reid in *The Wagon Mound (No. 2)* (1967) 1 AC 617:

'It is quite true that negligence is not an essential element in nuisance. Nuisance is a term used to cover a wide variety of tortious acts or omissions and in many negligence in the narrow sense is not essential. An occupier may incur liability for the emission of noxious fumes or noise although he has used the utmost care in building and using his premises. The amount of fumes or noise which he can lawfully emit is a question of degree and he or his advisers may have miscalculated what can be justified. Or he may

deliberately obstruct the highway adjoining his premises to a greater degree than is permissible, hoping that no one will object. On the other hand, the emission of fumes or noise or the obstruction of the adjoining highway may often be the result of pure negligence on his part: there are many cases (e.g. *Dollman* v *Hillman*) where precisely the same facts will establish liability both in nuisance and in negligence. And although negligence may not be necessary, fault of some kind is almost always necessary and fault generally involves foreseeability, e.g. in cases like *Sedleigh-Denfield* v *O'Callaghan* the fault is in failing to abate the nuisance the existence of which the defender is or ought to be aware as likely to cause damage to his neighbour.'

So what other factors are taken into account?

The extent of the harm and the nature of the locality

2.06 If there has been damage to property then there is an actionable nuisance. If, however, the complaint is one of interference with use or enjoyment of land, then one must look at how severe the interference is and whether it is to be expected in that particular area. In *St Helens Smelting Co* v *Tipping* (1865) 11 HLC 642 it was said: 'If a man lives in a town it is necessary that he should subject himself to the consequences of those operations of trade which may be carried on in his immediate locality.' Or in the famous words of another judge: 'What would be a nuisance in Belgrave Square would not necessarily be so in Bermondsey.'

The public utility of the defendant's conduct

2.07 Nuisance is inevitably concerned with striking a balance between the conflicting interests arising in society. It therefore is bound to have some regard for the benefit to the community as a whole that is conferred by the defendant's activity; thus everybody must accept the intrusive noise of the emergency services' sirens on the occasions when it occurs. However, there is a point above which the courts will not go. When the interference to the plaintiff reaches this point the courts will prevent the nuisance regardless of the effect on society as a whole. The law will not ask one man to suffer in what is perceived by some to be in the interests of society. Thus in *Bellew* v *Cement Co* [1948] Ir R 61 the courts closed down the only cement factory in Ireland at a time during the Second World War when cement was at a premium because it constituted a nuisance to the person living next door.

The undue sensibility of the plaintiff

2.08 When deciding whether something constitutes a nuisance the courts will not have regard to the particular sensitiviy of the plaintiff. In that regard the test is objective: would the act complained of affect a normal healthy person? The case of *Robinson* v *Kilvert* (1889) 41 Ch D 88 illustrates the point. The plaintiff kept sensitive brown paper on the ground floor of a building. The defendant occupied the cellar and, because of the nature of his business, kept it at a higher temperature than usual. This high temperature heated the floor of the ground floor and discoloured the sensitive paper, thereby diminishing its value. It was accepted that the actual temperature of the floor did not affect the workmen of the plaintiff and would have had no effect on ordinary paper. On this basis the defendant was held not liable in nuisance.

2.09 If, however, a nuisance can be established then damages will extend to take into account the extra sensitivity of the plaintiff (*McKinnon Industries* v *Walker* [1951] 3 DLR 577). Thus if it had been the case that the heat would have damaged ordinary paper and this constituted a nuisance then the plaintiff would have been able to recover the cost of his extra-sensitive paper notwithstanding the fact that it was more expensive than ordinary paper.

The temporary nature of the injury

2.10 This is a particularly important consideration in building cases. If the alledged nuisance is of a very temporary nature then it is likely to be given a much more sympathetic hearing by the courts. The injury must be 'of a substantial nature, not fleeting or evanescent' (*Benjamin* v *Storr* (1874) LR 9 CP 400). The temporary nature is therefore a consideration but is not conclusive. If the injury in itself is serious it may be sufficient to establish a nuisance notwithstanding that it is only temporary.

Malice of the defendant

2.11 If a defendant deliberately bangs on his wall, shouts, screams and generally makes a noise in order to annoy his next door neighbour, is that a nuisance? This was the case in *Christie* v *Davey* [1893] 1 Ch 316 and it was held that it did constitute a nuisance because the acts were done deliberately. The judge expressly stated that if the acts had been done totally innocently, without malice or intention to annoy, he would have taken an entirely different view.

2.12 This attitude must of course be right. The law of nuisance treads the middle ground between the conflicting interests of two land owners. It confers on one a privilege to interfere with the enjoyment of the other for the purpose of furthering his own enjoyment. If his sole intention is interference with the plaintiff's enjoyment of land the privilege must be lost, one of its essential ingredients is missing, and the courts should not uphold his right to interfere. The rule in *Christie* v *Davey* has now been adopted and followed in *Hollywood Silver Fox Farm Ltd* v *Emmett* [1936] 2 KB 468 which found the defendant liable in nuisance for firing shotguns deliberately to upset the breeding habits of the silver fox. He would probably not have been liable had the guns been fired for some other, legitimate, purpose.

3 The rule in *Rylands* v *Fletcher*

3.01 The rule in *Rylands* v *Fletcher* certainly has origins in the tort of nuisance but has developed into a separate, although connected, tort of its own. The law is stated by Blackburn J (1866) LR 1 Ex 265, 279–280 in the case itself in the following manner:

> 'We think that the true rule of law is, that the person who for his own purposes brings on his lands and collects and keeps there anything likely to do mischief if it escapes must keep it in at his peril and if he does not do so is prima facie answerable for all the damage which is a natural consequence of its escape.'

This broad principle of the rule has been applied to many situations and things which can escape: fire, gas, oil, explosions, electricity, vibrations and poisonous vegetation, but the scope of the rule has been limited by the qualification that the use of the land which gave rise to the escape must be 'non-natural user'. The reason for the qualification is that the rule is otherwise one of strict liability and requires no fault on behalf of the defendant to render him liable for what are potentially enormous damages. So what is 'non-natural user'?

3.02 It has been suggested that the courts understand 'natural' to mean 'that which is ordinary and usual, even though it may be artificial'. The most oft used definition of non-natural user is that given in *Richards* v *Lothian* [1913] AC 163: 'It must be some special use bringing with it increased danger to others and must not merely be the ordinary use of the land or such a use as is proper for the general benefit of the community.' In general terms there appears to be a balance being struck between the magnitude of risk, which can be measured in terms of the seriousness of

any injury being caused and the chance of such injury occurring, and the desirability or necessity of the activity from the point of view of both the defendant and the public as a whole.

3.03 In this way the rule can be deflected from one of strict liability to being one which involves foreseeability of harm as an essential ingredient together with the unreasonable risk of creating the possibility for that harm. The courts are therefore creating a device through which they can determine liability along the lines of their views of public policy. This brings the rule in *Rylands* v *Fletcher* more into line with the law of negligence than it does with any form of strict liability.

3.04 Even with this important restriction to the rule it is vital to know of the defences available rather than simply rely upon the hope that one's use of the land would be considered as natural. The most obvious defence would be if the plaintiff had consented to your keeping the escaping materials on your land. Such consent can be express or implied by conduct, and its existence or not will depend entirely on the circumstances of each individual case. Secondly, there is the defence of common benefit. This is arguably the same as consent, but is usually treated separately. In a block of flats there is often one central tank to contain hot water. It is for the benefit of every person occupying the flats, and if it leaks it would be a defence to the application of *Rylands* v *Fletcher* to plead common benefit.

3.05 If the escape is caused by the acts of two particular people then the rule will not apply. The first is God. An act of God is a complete defence and *Rylands* v *Fletcher* will not apply. The second is an independent and unforeseeable stranger. The onus, of course, is on the defendant to establish the intervention of the stranger and also that he (the defendant) was in no way negligent in his protection of the goods or his anticipation of the acts of the stranger.

3.06 There are also statutory exceptions to the rule in order to excuse bodies such as the water board from strict liability under the rule in the event of leak from any of their reservoirs.

4 Breach of statutory duty

4.01 Where a statute imposes a duty on a certain person or group of persons there is obviously a liability on those persons for breach of that duty up to whatever penalty is prescribed by statute. There is also a liability in tort to those persons injured by the breach provided that certain requirements are met. The rules as to liability are strict and the statutes are construed tightly; there are at least four aspects which must be considered.

The duty must be owed to the plaintiff

4.02 Various statutes limit the classes of person to whom the duty is owed because the statute is enacted for the purpose of protecting and benefiting those people only. If the plaintiff does not fall within the class or classes of person for whose protection the statute provides then he is unable to take advantage of the protection.

The injury must be of the kind which the statute is intended to prevent

4.03 This rule is amply illustrated by the case of *Gorris* v *Scott* 1874 LR 9 Exch 125. Statute provided that a shipowner was to provide pens for cattle and sheep when they were on his ship so as to lessen the chance of disease. The shipowner failed to do so and during a storm one night all the cattle from the deck of his ship were washed overboard. The cattle owner

sued, arguing breach of the duty to provide the pens; had pens been provided then the cattle would not have been lost. It was held that there was no liability on the shipowner because the intention of the statute was to avoid disease and not to protect from the perils of the sea. The loss actually suffered was therefore not covered by the statute.

There must have been a breach of the statutory obligations

4.04 The obligations under a statute are often very finely defined. For instance, requirements for health and safety under the Factories Act are only requirements for workplaces which fall within the definition in that Act of a factory. If something is slightly out of that definition then the safety requirements do not apply and there can be no action for breach of statutory duty in respect of any failure to meet the safety requirements. In addition it may be that the scope of the duty owed is very tightly defined. In the case of *John Summers and Sons Ltd* v *Frost* [1955] AC 740 a grinding wheel operator was injured whilst using the wheel. His thumb came into contract with it through the gap in the protection through which the tools were applied to the wheel. The factories Act provided that 'every dangerous part of any machinery . . . shall be securely fenced'. It was held on a strict interpretation of the Act that the part of the wheel on which the plaintiff injured his thumb was not securely fenced and accordingly the defendant was in breach of his statutory duty. It was no answer to argue that had it been securely fenced the wheel could not have been used. The statute was to be construed strictly and the defendant was in breach. Other statutes militate against the harshness of this decision by using such clauses as 'so far as is reasonably practical'.

The breach of duty must have caused damage

4.05 This may seem a trite proposition but in fact raises difficult questions of causation which are beyond the scope of this chapter. Suffice it to say that the breach of duty and the damage must be sufficiently proximate so as to establish a direct causal link between the two. The question is only raised here to indicate that it is one which must be considered rather than to give the rules by which the answer can be obtained.

Breach of the Building Regulations

4.06 The broad position under the Building Regulations is that there is no civil liability for breach. There is provision in the enabling statute for an action in damages to lie but the section has not been brought into force by Parliament and it appears that until that section comes into force the position will remain that there is no civil suit available for breach of the Building Regulations.

In the light of recent cases it seems unlikely that the section will be enacted. Lord Wilberforce in the famous case of *Anns* v *Merton London Borough Council* [1978] AC 728 hinted that the builder may indeed have such a liability. He said: '. . . since it is the duty of the builder to comply with by-laws, I would agree that an action could be brought against him in effect, for breach of statutory duty by any person for whose benefit or protection the by-law was made'. However, by virtue of the English system of precedent, his words are not directly binding on all courts; they are to be treated with great respect but only as persuasive authority. His argument was not followed in 1981 by a judge of first instance in *Warlock* v *Saws and Rushmor Borough Council* [1981] NLS 1054, and in what is now considered the authority on the point Judge Newy QC, Official Referee, followed a previous and opposite line of authority emanating from the Court of Appeal in *Taylor Woodrow Construction (Midlands) Ltd* v *Charcon Structures Limited* (unreported, 1962). He said:

'The Act was plainly intended to protect owners and occupiers of buildings, but they were not without remedies at common law, as in respect of almost all matters covered by the by-laws they could bring actions for negligence. Possibly the only exceptions are by-laws dealing with size of windows and space about buildings.

The local authority's liability in *Anns* was not for breach of statutory duty, but for negligence in the exercise of statutory powers. The builders in that case would probably have been liable in negligence.

In my opinion building by-laws did not give rise to liability in damages, but I trust that before long there will be a specific decision of the Court of Appeal on the subject.'

The author is unaware of any Court of Appeal decision on the point and, until such time as there is one, this judgement in *Perry* v *Tendring District Council* 30 BLR 118 remains authority for the propostion that there is no liability for breach of the Building Regulations.

5 The Defective Premises Act 1972

5.01 Section 1 of the Defective Premises Act provides:

'**Duty to build dwellings properly** (1) – A person taking on work for or in connection with the provision of a dwelling (whether the dwelling is provided by the erection or by the conversion or enlargement of a building) owes a duty –
(a) if the dwelling is provided to the order of any person, to that person; and
(b) without prejudice to paragraph (a) above, to every person who acquires an interest (whether legal or equitable) in the dwelling;
to see that the work which he takes on is done in a workmanlike or, as the case may be, professional manner, with proper materials and so that as regards that work the dwelling will be fit for habitation when completed.'

It imposes a statutory duty on builders, sub-contractors, architects and others who take on work for or in connection with the provision of a dwelling. It also, by a further subsection of section 1, places the same duty on developers, local authorities and others who arrange for such work to be done. The scope of the duty is to ensure that the building is erected in a workmanlike manner with proper materials such that it will be fit for human habitation. The duty cannot be excluded by agreement and can be imposed upon persons who are not necessarily parties to the building contracts, e.g. the architects. The duty is owed to any person who acquires an interest in the dwelling whether or not he was party to the original building contract.

5.02 However, until 1979 the provisions of section 1 were of little importance because the majority of new houses were registered under the NHBC scheme and were excluded by virtue of that scheme being an approved scheme under section 2 of the Act. The last NHBC scheme to be recognized under section 2 was the 1979 edition in force on 28 March 1979. Since that date NHBC have declined to obtain approval of the Secretary of State for amendments to the scheme and consequently all schemes after 28 March 1979 are not approved. This has the consequence that any house registered on a scheme after this date is covered by the provisions of the Defective Premises Act 1972 and all those taking on work for the provision of such a dwelling house will be under the statutory duty provided for by section 1.

6 Trespass

6.01 Any entry upon the land of another without the other's permission or without some legal right to enter constitutes the tort of trespass to land. This is so whether the entry is temporary or permanent, the incursion large or small. It may

be committed by placing or throwing objects upon the land. It is usually committed at ground level, but may also be committed below or above ground level; an occupier of property is treated as having possession of the space under his property, and also above it up to any height that building works are likely to project over. It is no defence that the trespasser intended no harm or did not know that he was trespassing; he must not violate an occupier's property rights.

6.02 As far as architects and building contractors are concerned, even the slightest infringements are actionable, however innocent the situation. For example, it is trespass for a surveying assistant to set foot on adjoining property without authority, or, in the case of building operations, to allow any soil disturbance, or anything to overhang or fall onto or be thrown over the land. Land and property owners are generally suspicious of 'surveyors' and irritated by nearby 'works', so the greatest care must be exercised to see that irritation does not lead to legal action.

6.03 As the law stands, there is no right to go upon the neighbour's property, in the absence of his permission or of an easement, to carry out repairs. This is so even if it is impossible to do the repairs without going upon the adjoining property. Thus where someone needed to erect scaffolding on neighbouring land in order to mend his wall, and the neighbour did not reply to his letters requesting permission,

he was liable in an action for trespass to land when he went ahead (*John Trenberth Ltd* v *National Westminster Bank* (1979) 253 EG 151).

6.04 Despite the frequency of notices which say 'Trespassers will be prosecuted', it is only a civil wrong, not a crime, to trespass. A trespass is only a crime if something more accompanies it – if, for example, the trespasser breaks down fences in order to trespass, which could be the offence of criminal damage contrary to the Criminal Damage Act 1971; though even here, there is a defence to a criminal charge (though not to a civil action) if the trespasser believed he had a right to do what he did.

7 Negligence

7.01 Negligence can be described as the breach of a legal duty to take care which results in damage to the plaintiff. There are three essential ingredients. A legal duty to exercise the requisite skill and care, a breach of that duty and consequent damage. The next few paragraphs will investigate each of those constituents of the tort and then there will follow a review of the courts' changing attitude to negligence in the recent past, particularly in relation to the recovery of economic loss.

The legal duty to take care

7.02 Although there were early attempts to define when and where and how a duty arose, the most important statement of the law comes from the case of *Donaghue* v *Stevenson* [1932] AC 562, 580, which concerns a snail in a bottle of ginger beer. The manufacturer of the beer sold it in an opaque bottle to a café owner. He resold it to a lady who had bought it for her friend Mrs Donaghue. The bottle contained a decomposed snail which gave Mrs Donaghue a great shock and made her seriously ill when she discovered it. She had no contract with either the café owner or the manufacturer and so was forced to sue the manufacturer in tort. The law is stated by Lord Atkin in a passage in which he sets out the whole basis of the duty of care owed:

'In English Law there must be, and is, some general conception of relations giving rise to a duty of care, of which the particular cases found in the books are instances. The liability for negligence, whether you style it such or treat it as in other systems as a species of "culpa", is no doubt based upon a general public sentiment of moral wrongdoing for which the offender must pay. But acts or omissions which any moral code would censure cannot in a practical world be treated so as to give a right to every person injured by them to demand relief. In this way rules of law arise which limit the range of complainants and the extent of their remedy. The rule that you are to love your neighbour becomes, in law, you must not injure your neigbour; and the lawyer's question, Who is my neighbour? receives a restricted reply. You must take reasonable care to avoid acts or omissions which you can reasonably foresee would be likely to injure your neighbour. Who, then, in law is my neighbour? The answer seems to be – persons who are so closely and directly affected by my act that I ought reasonably to have them in contemplation as being so affected when I am directing my mind to the acts or omissions which are called in question.'

Since that time this passage has been approved many times by the courts and it can now be recognized as being a statement of legal principle on which the whole of the law of negligence rests.

7.03 The duty was further defined and explained by Lord Wilberforce in *Anns* v *Merton London Borough Council* [1978] AC 728, 751 and the passage can be read in response to the question 'who is my neighbour in 1978?'

'Through the trilogy of cases in this House – *Donaghue* v *Stevenson* [1932] AC 562, *Hedley Byrne & Co Limited* v *Heller & Partners Limited* [1964] AC 465 and *Dorset Yacht Co Limited* v *Home Office* [1970] AC 1004, the position has now been reached that in order to establish that a duty of care arises in a particular situation, it is not necessary to bring the facts of that situation within those of previous situations in which a duty of care has been held to exist. Rather the question has to be approached in two stages. First one has to ask whether, as between the alleged wrongdoer and the person who has suffered damage there is a sufficient relationship of proximity or neighbourhood such that, in the reasonable contemplation of the former, carelessness on his part may be likely to cause damage to the latter – in which case a prime facie duty of care arises. Secondly, if the first question is answered affirmatively, it is necessary to consider whether there are any considerations which ought to negative, or to reduce or limit the scope of the duty or the class of person to whom it is owed or the damages to which a breach of it may give rise.'

This two stage test of Lord Wilberforce was really a very wide application of the principle set down in *Donaghue* v *Stevenson* and opened the gates for many people to attempt to establish liability through negligence. There are many situations that will affect many people: it is more often than not that one should be in the reasonable comtemplation of the other. In such circumstances a duty will arise unless there are considerations which negative it. These considerations are rarely ones of a factual nature but are considerations of what the courts consider to be public policy. It is in relatively few circumstances that such considerations will carry sufficient force to negative the prime facie duty and accordingly the net of negligence has been cast very widely by Lord Wilberforce.

7.04 For a number of years the passage cited above was the litmus test of a duty of care, but the courts became more and more concerned about the wide scope of the tests. The words of Lord Wilberforce had shadows cast upon them by very senior judges, and the test was qualified by the introduction of a 'just and reasonable' test: Is it just and reasonable in all the circumstances that the duty should be owed? So the question of 'To whom do I owe a duty in 1989?' is answered by deciding whether three requirements are satisfied. They are set out by Bingham LJ in *Caparo Industries* v *Dickman* [1989] 2 WLR 316, 321:

'The first [requirement] is foreseeability . . . The second requirement is more elusive. It is usually described as proximity, which means not simple physical proximity but extends to "such close and direct relations that the act complained of directly affects a person whom the person alleged to be bound to take care would know would be directly affected by his careless act" (*Donaghue* v *Stevenson*) . . . The third requirement . . . is that the court should find it just and reasonable to impose such a duty.'

In the words of Australian Judge Weintraub CJ in *Goldberg* v *Housing Authority for the City of Newark* (1962) 186A. 2d 291, 293 which were approved by Bingham LJ:

'Whether a duty exists is ultimately a question of fairness. The inquiry involves a weighing of the relationship of the parties, the nature of the risk and the public interest in the proposed solution.'

Breach of the duty

7.05 Having established a duty the next step is to establish a beach of that duty. 'Negligence is the omission to do something which a reasonable man, guided upon those considerations which ordinarily regulate the conduct of human affairs, would do, or doing something which a prudent and reasonable man would not do' (*Blyth* v *Birmingham Waterworks Company* (1856) 11 Ex 781). But who is the reasonable man? He has been described as the 'man on the top deck of the Clapham omnibus' or 'the man who takes the magazines at home, and in the evening pushes the lawn mower in his shirt sleeves'. The reasonable man is expected to know the law and regulate his conduct by it. Where a person holds himself out as being of a particular skill, trade or profession he has to attain the standards reasonably to be expected from a competent member of that trade or profession. There is no lower standard of care for the apprentice. In *Nettleship* v *Weston* [1971] 2 QB 691 the defendant was a learner driver and had injured the plaintiff during a driving lesson. She argued in defence that, as a learner, she owed a lower duty of care than a fully qualified driver and accordingly was not in breach of that lower duty when she hit the accelerator rather than the brake. It was held that she owed the same duty as a reasonably competent, fully qualified driver and she was liable for the damage caused.

7.06 What is reasonable will vary according to the circumstances, and even according to the personality of the judge. But it is an objective test because the standard to be reached is that of the hypothetical reasonable man. It is to be expected that the judge is able to lift himself above his own feelings and place himself in the shoes of such a man. The reasonable man in a profession is expected to keep generally up to date with

developments in his field, e.g. by reading the relevant journals, but is not expected to have the same knowledge of specialist areas as those on the forefront of research and development.

7.07 In deciding whether a particular act breaches the standards of the reasonable man the courts will have regard to two main factors: the likelihood of injury occurring and the seriousness of the injury that is being risked (which shows the need for foreseeability of the injury). Two cases neatly illustrate this point. In *Boulton* v *Stone* the plaintiff was walking along a path on one side of which was a 6 foot fence protecting a cricket pitch. The height from the pitch to the top of the fence was 15 feet. The plaintiff was hit by a ball which had been hit for six over the fence by a visiting batsman. It was held that the cricket club were not liable in negligence. There was only a small risk that batsmen would hit the ball so far and in any event the injury potentially to be suffered by any person hit by a ball would be minor.

7.08 In *The Wagon Mound (No. 2)* [1967] AC 617, crude oil spilled from a ship into a harbour in Australia. The risk of its catching fire was apparently very small and it was agreed that the welding sparks from a welder on the dockside were highly unlikely to cause a fire. However, a spark from the welder fell onto a piece of flammable material floating on the oil and this was just the exceptional circumstance required to start a fire. The damage done was substantial. It was held that, notwithstanding that the risk was very samll, given the foreseeable extent of the injury that was risked, the defendants were negligent in allowing the risk to continue unabated.

Damage must result as a breach of the duty

7.09 This concept was mentioned in relation to breach of statutory duty and is the same in relation to negligence. It is a matter beyond the scope of this chapter but is raised simply to warn of its existence.

Economic loss

7.10 What is termed economic loss deserves special consideration because it heralds special treatment by the court. Cases such as *Donaghue* v *Stevenson* relate to the physical injury to persons or property, and it was thought for a long time that damage which was purely economic in nature was not recoverable under the principles of *Donaghue* v *Stevenson*. The first attack on this idea was made in 1964 in *Hedley Byrne & Co Ltd* v *Heller and Partners* [1964] AC 465. The case concerned a statement by a bank to the plaintiff about the financial integrity and creditworthiness of a third party. The plaintiff relied on this statement and, as it was wrong, suffered loss. They sued the bank, who claimed that the loss was irrecoverable as purely economic. Although the bank were held not liable it was established that where there was a voluntary responsibility by the maker of a statement for its accuracy and there was reliance on that satement by the defendant, then economic loss could be recoverable on proof of negligence in making the statement. The rule is called neglïgent mis-statement and is of direct relevance to archïtects giving professional advice. If no express disclaimer of responsibility is made a person will be liable for the consequences of a statement which he makes in circumstances where he is deemed to have assumed the responsibility.

7.11 The matter arose again in various building cases in the 1970s and the courts found various ways of saying that the damage suffered was not in fact economic loss whereas in reality, of course, it was. In 1977 in *Batty* v *Metropolitan Realisations Ltd* [1978] QB 554 it was made clear that economic loss was recoverable and *Junior Books Ltd* v *Veitchi & Co Ltd* [1982] 3 WLR was the case that had the

potential to open the floodgates of economic loss litigation. However, at this point the tide began to turn and the courts started to retract from the principle that economic loss was recoverable. In *Muirhead* v *Industrial Tank Specialists Ltd* [1986] QB 507 Junior Books was said to turn on its own facts and to be of almost no further relevance. Then there was probably the low water mark for economic loss claims in the case of *D & F Estates* v *Church Commissioners for England* [1988] 3 WLR 368. The claim was one in tort against the builders for defective plastering which they had carried out. The question was whether the builders, even if they had been negligent, could be held liable for the cost of repars to the plaster itself. It was held that, in the absence of a contractual relationship between the parties, the cost of repairing a defect in a chattel or structure, which was discovered before the defect had caused personal injury or physical damage to other property, was not recoverable in negligence by a remote buyer or hirer or lessee of the chattel or structure from the manufacturer of the chattel or the builder of the structure responsible for causing the defect, because the cost of repair was pure economic loss which was not recoverable in tort. It followed that since the cost of repairing the plaster was economic loss the builders would not be liable for the cost of the remedial work. In other words economic loss, or the cost of repair of damage to the 'thing itself' caused by defective work or design was not recoverable in negligence.

7.12 This decision must be of some comfort to both builders and professionals involved in the building trade, but there are problems and possible exceptions to the apparently strict rule and so care must be taken in its interpretation. The first exception is that set out by Lord Oliver at the end of his judgement. He held that where the negligence has damaged the thing itself it is possible to recover damages under the principles in *Anns* v *Merton*, but such damages are limited to expenses necessarily involved in averting a danger to health and safety. The exact scope of this exception is unknown because *Anns* v *Merton* is becoming of more dubious authority as time progresses, and Lord Bridge in *D & F Estates* expressed the opinion that unless damage to health and safety has in fact occurred, once the damger is discovered, putting right the defects to avert the danger is purely economic loss and therefore not recoverable. However, it would appear that Lord Oliver is correct. There is support for his opinion in the speech of Lord Brandon in *Junior Books* v *Veitchi* [1983] AC 520 at 550, and it has been followed by Judge Newey QC in *Portsea Island Mutual Cooperative Society* v *Michael Brashier Associates* [1989] CILL 50. In that case the judge held that the plaintiffs could recover the cost of removing brick slips which were in danger of falling and injuring somebody, but could not recover the cost of replacing the brick slips as that would be economic loss and irrecoverable under *D & F Estates*.

7.13 The second exception is that of the complex structure. It is a new concept in the law and its scope is uncertain. It was set out by Lord Bridge in the following way:

> 'However, I can see that it may well be arguable that in the case of complex structures, as indeed possibly in the case of complex chattels, one element of the structure should be regarded for the purpose of the application of the principles under discussion as distinct from another element, so that damage to one part of the structure caused by a hidden defect in another part may qualify to be treated as damage to "other property", and whether the argument should prevail may depend on the circumstances of the case.'

Again, Judge Newey QC has been prepared to follow the route opened up by this passage and hold in *Frost* v *Moody Homes* in March 1989 that foundations are separate property to the superstructure of a house. This distinction was also implicit in the judgement of Judge Peter Bowsher QC, Official Referee in *Warner* v *Basildon Developement*

Corporation [1989] CILL 484, although he did not expressly decide the point. This is as far as judicial enquiry into this concept goes and so it remains distinctly vague with its boundaries unexplored.

7.14 The third, and perhaps most important, exception to the rule is the possibility that *D & F Estates* does not apply to professional men. The judgement is couched in terms of actions by builders and does not easily fit advice given by professionals such as architects and engineers. What if the statements made by such people were to be governed by the rules laid down in *Hedley Byrne* v *Heller* rather than the rules laid down in *D & F Estates*? In such circumstances an architect would remain liable for economic loss arising from his negligence in design or supervision notwithstanding that the builder would not be liable in respect of negligent workmanship relating to that same thing. It may appear to be a strange result but it is not beyond the realms of possibility. There are already two conflicting decisions of the courts. In *Robert Leonard Estates* v *Robert Walpole, Campion and Partners* (unreported, 1989) Judge Lewis Hawser QC held that the principles of *Hedley Byrne* v *Heller* still applied to an engineer in so far as a developer could recover economic loss in tort in circumstances where the developer and engineer were previously known to each other. In *Portsea Island* v *Brashier* Judge Newey QC applied the principles laid down in *D & F Estates* to the architects and held them liable only for the removal of the danger to health and safety. The decisions conflict although they can be distinguished, and it is suggested that the decision of Judge Newey is probably the correct view in most circumstances. It would therefore appear that the liability of architects and engineers will be interpreted in accordance with the strict rule of *D & F Estates*. Some comfort can be drawn from this but the decision of Judge Lewis Hawser should always be kept in mind as a warning.

7.15 The conclusion to this review of negligence must be that if there is damage to property or person there is little difficulty in recovering damages provided the three requirements of duty (as set out in *Caparo Industries* v *Dickman*), breach and damage can be satisfied, but where the loss is purely economic there appears little chance of recovery. However, professional people should remain alert to the possiblity of suit under *Hedley Byrne* v *Heller* even though those principles may be further eroded by the course of future litigation.

8 Limitation

8.01 It is important that where a person has a cause of action against another he does not ignore it, because if he ignores it for too long it will die and he will be unable to obtain redress for the wrong he has suffered. There are arguments on both sides of the question of whether this should be so. First, the defendant argues that he should not be subject to old and stale claims about matters in which he may have discarded the documentation, or in which witnesses are dead or otherwise unavailable and he is thereby deprived of a defence. On the other hand why should it be that a plaintiff who has really suffered some wrong should be denied redress for that very wrong?

There are two main sources of statute which govern this area: the Limitation Act 1980 and the Latent Damage Act 1986.

The Limitation Act 1980

8.02 Section 2 of this Act provides that actions based in tort shall be commenced within six years of the date of accrual of the cause of action. If it is started outside this time the defendant must raise the defence at the outset of proceedings, otherwise he will lose it as a defence. In the case of personal

injury the time limit is reduced to three years. There are, however, two ways around these limits. First, in the case of personal injury the court is given a discretion to exclude any time limits if it feels in the circumstances it would be equitable to do so. Secondly, by section 32 of the Act in a case where there has been fraud by the defendant or the facts which give rise to the cause of action have been deliberately concealed by the defendant, or the action is for relief from the consequences of a mistake, the limitation period (of six years) will not run until the plaintiff has discovered or, with reasonable diligence, could have discovered, the fraud, concealment or mistake. This is of particular importance when, in the course of building works, negligent design or workmanship is covered up by the natural process of construction. In *King* v *Victor Parsons* [1973] 1 WLR 29 it was held that what was required was some behaviour by the defendant such that 'it would be "against conscience" for him to avail himself of the lapse of time'. Applying this case in *William Hill Organisation* v *Bernard Sunley and Sons* 22 BCR 1, it has been held that simply carrying on with the normal course of building work and thereby covering up negligence was not unconscionable unless there were additional circumstances, for instance if the defendant knew that by continuing the work he was covering up his own negligence.

8.03 By section 2 the period runs from the date of accrual of the cause of action. In most cases this does not cause a problem. In a car accident the negligent act occurs and damage happens seconds afterwards. But in the case of buildings, and particularly actions against architects, matters are not so easy. A design may be made one year, built five years later and defects discovered five years after that. If it was the design at fault, when does the cause of action accrue? This has been the subject of much litigation, the history of which is too complex to examine in detail here. Basically, it was held in *Anns* v *Merton* that the cause of action accrues when the damage occurs to the building. But this still did not solve the problem because it was argued further that one could not have a cause of action until it was reasonably discoverable. If damage occurred in year one but it was damage to the foundations of a building which was not reasonably discoverable until year eight, a plaintiff's cause of action would expire before he knew it had accrued. The matter came before the House of Lords in *Pirelli General Cable Works* v *Oscar Faber* [1983] AC 1, when they were not unaware of the problems faced by architects and the like in keeping files, records and, indeed, people almost indefinitely in the constant fear that some latent defect in some old building would suddenly become discoverable and render them liable to a suit. With these problems in mind they held that limitation now ran from the date at which the damage actually occurred, irrespective of when it became discoverable. The law is now settled, at least on this point, but argument still rages as to when damage actually occurred. Of course, the argument has most force when it is said that the damage occurred more than six years before it was discoverable – but how does anybody know that if at that time it was not discoverable? The argument would have continued unabated, providing much income for lawyers and expert witnesses, had it not been for parliamentary intervention in the form of the Latent Damage Act 1986. The Act has certain transitional provisions which mean that the old law still applies in many cases but in time it will become widely applicable and, it is hoped, solve many of the problems.

The Latent Damage Act 1986

8.04 In simple terms the Act introduces three dates at which the limitation period may expire. The first is 15 years from the negligent act by the defendant. This is the long stop provision and no action for damages in negligence can be brought after the expiry of 15 years from the date of the breach of duty. However, there may be an earlier expiry of the limitation

period because the Act says it will expire on whichever is the later of the following two dates (provided they are both within the 15 year long stop):

- six years from the accrual of the cause of action, which date is fixed by *Pirelli* to be the date damage occurred, or
- three years from the date at which the damage was discovered or could reasonably have been discovered.

The new time limits apply only to claims in the tort of negligence and do not apply to personal injury claims. Nor do they apply to cases involving deliberate concealment, which are still governed by section 32 of the Limitation Act 1980. The final, additional function of the Act is to pass any cause of action vested in an owner of property on to subsequent owners of the same property and thereby enable them to sue as if they had been the original owners.

8.05 It is to be hoped that the Latent Damage Act will solve many of the problems currently encountered, but this whole area of the law is not straightforward and has undergone rapid change in recent years. The Act is not drafted as clearly as it might have been, and so there will almost certainly be much argument on how the Act should apply.

9 Liability of local authorities in respect of negligence in building control

9.01 The principles applicable in respect of liability of a local authority were very clearly set out by Slade LJ in the case *Investors in Industry Commercial Properties Ltd v South Bedfordshire District Council* [1986] 2 WLR 937, 959. It is best to set them out as enunciated by Slade LJ, unabridged and unaltered.

'We can see no difference in principle, and it has not been submitted that there is any material difference, between the powers to secure or enforce compliance with building regulations which have been conferred on a local authority by the Public Health Act 1936 and those conferred on it by pragraph 15 of Part III of Schedule 9 to the [London Government Act 1963]. We will refer to all these powers collectively as "supervisory powers" and venture to think that the following five propositions of law can be derived from the *Anns* case [1978] AC 728 and the *Peabody* case [1985] AC 210 when considered together, in the light of the overruling of *Acrecrest Limited* v *W. S. Hattrell & Partners* [1983] QB 260. (1) The purpose for which the legislature has conferred the supervisory powers over building operations on local authorities is to protect the occupiers of buildings built in the local authority's area and also members of the public generally against dangers to health or personal safety. It is not to safeguard the building developer himself against economic loss incurred in the course of a building project, or indeed anyone else against purely economic loss. (2) In view of the statutory purpose of these supervisory powers (though this point does not arise for decision in the present case) it may well be that on the basis of the *Anns* case [1978] AC 728 a local authority, in exercising their statutory powers, will be held to owe a duty to a subsequent occupier other than the original building owner to take reasonable care to ensure that the building is erected in accordance with the building regulations, so as not to cause danger to health or personal safety of the occupier. (3) Where this duty of care had been broken and, as a result, the condition of the property gives rise to danger to the health or safety of persons present on the premises, an occupier to whom the duty is owed may be at liberty to restore the property to a condition in which such danger is eliminated, and having done so, to recover the amount of any such necessary expenditure from the local authority. Whether or not he will have such right of recovery must depend on the particular facts of the case. (4) On the basis of the *Peabody* case [1985] AC 210, however, a local authority, in exercising these supervisory powers, will normally owe no duty to an original building owner, because it is normally incumbent on the building owner himself to ensure that the building is erected in accordance with the relevant building regulations, and it cannot have been the intention of the legislature that, save perhaps in exceptional circumstances, a local authority could owe a duty to a person who is in such breach. (5) A fortiori, again on the basis of the *Peabody* case, a local authority in exercising these supervisory powers, will normally owe no duty to an original building owner who has had the benefit of the advice of architects, engineers and contractors and has relied on it. In such circumstances it will normally be neither reasonable nor just to impose on the local authority to indemnify the building owner against liability resulting from such reliance.'

10 Contribution

10.01 Having looked at the various torts for which one can recover damages, or indeed for which one can be found liable, it is now important to mention that more than one person can be liable in respect of the same tort. The plaintiff himself can be found liable in some respect and the court will assess the part that his contributory negligence played in causing the damage complained of. For example, in the case of *Froom* v *Butcher* [1976] QB 286 it was held that one person travelling in a car without wearing a seat belt who was injured by the negligence of another person was guilty of contributory negligence to the tune of 15%. Full damages were therefore assessed but the plaintiff was entitled to recover only 85% of that sum. The level of contributory negligence can be anything from 0% to 100% and will be assessed by the court on the basis of what is just and equitable.

10.02 It may also be the case that the plaintiff has been injured by the tortious actions of more than one person simultaneously. In this case he is able to pursue either or both people for the full extent of his damage notwithstanding the 'contribution' which each person's breach of duty made to the actual damage suffered. This is the concept of joint and several liability. The decision of which person to sue is often made on such pragmatic grounds as which one can be found or which one is insured. It should be noted that the plaintiff cannot execute judgement for more than the total amount due.

10.03 This concept requires that the joint tortfeasors should be able to balance between them what is the correct contribution that each is to make to the judgement debt according to the level of contribution which each made to the damage. Indeed, the idea of contribution should not be limited to joint tortfeasors (as it used to be before 1978) and should be spread wide open so that any person liable for a judgement debt should be able to recover a contribution from any other person liable for the same debt, whether both or either liability rests in tort, contract, breach of trust or any other cause of action.

10.04 This idea was encapsulated by section 1 of the Civil Liability (Contribution) Act 1978:

'Subject to the following provisions of this section, any person liable in respect of any damage suffered by another person may recover contribution from any other person liable in respect of the same damage (whether jointly with him or otherwise).'

There are provisions within the Act to allow for contribution even when a defendant settles the matter out of court and the contribution to be made is to be assessed so that it is fair and reasonable in all the circumstances.

10.05 In this way Parliament has allowed for simplicity of proceedings in court without the unfair rule of joint and several liability. If a plaintiff chooses to pursue only one defendant, that defendant is able to pursue other wrongdoers for a just and equitable contribution to the judgement.

Addendum

Since the main text of this chapter was written and sent to print the House of Lords have handed down judgment in the case of *Murphy* v *Brentwood District Council* [1990] 2 All ER 908. This is one of the most significant cases in the law of tort to be decided in recent years and its true implications will be emerging for a long time.

The most fundamental point about the case is that it overrules the previous House of Lords decision of *Ann* v *Merton London Borough* [1977] 2 All ER 492. This obviously means that a local authority is no longer liable in negligence for acts which it undertakes pursuant to its duties under the Public Health Acts, but the case also has wider implications. The two stage test mentioned in *Anns* is no longer viable to decide whether there is a duty of care or not. It is now said that '. . . the law should develop novel categories of negligence incrementally and by analogy with established categories rather than by a massive extension of a prime facie duty of care . . .'. It would appear from this that new situations of liability in negligence will be harder to establish.

The case also discusses the effects of *D & F Estates* v *Church Commissioners*. It has implications on the three exceptions mentioned in the above chapter.

Public health and safety

The difference between Lord Bridge and Lord Oliver in *D & F Estates* has apparently been reconciled. It is now the law that once a dangerous defect has been discovered it ceases to be dangerous because it can be rectified. Accordingly the cost of rendering it non-dangerous is purely economic loss and is not recoverable. Lord Bridge's view has prevailed, subject to the exception he set out in *Murphy*: if the defect gives a potential source of danger to persons on neighbouring land or on the highway, then the building owner should be able to recover the cost of obviating that danger.

Remember the case of *Portsea Island Co-op* v *Michael Brashnir* where the plaintiff recovered the cost of removing defective brick slips? If the building was set out in the middle of the Co-op's land then such cost would not be recoverable. If one edge of the building was abutting the highway the Co-op would recover the cost of removing the brick slips from that wall only. The decision thus has implications as to where an architect should position his buildings so as to minimize the liability of both himself and the builder.

Complex structure theory

Their Lordships have attempted to lay to rest the exception of the complex structure. Lord Bridge (who first enunciated the theory) analyses various decisions of foreign jurisdictions which bear on the point and summarizes that '. . . the complex structure theory offers no escape from the conclusion that damage to a house itself which is atributable to a defect in the structure of the house is not recoverable in tort . . .'. Thus damage to a wall caused by defective foundations will be economic loss and irrecoverable. However Lord Bridge also drew the 'critical distinction' between 'part of a complex structure which is said to be a danger only because it does not perform its proper function in sustaining the other parts and some distinct item incorporated in the structure which positively malfunctions so as to inflict positive damage on the structure in which it is incorporated'. In the light of this it is can be said that they have shut the complex structure theory out by the front door but allowed its close relative in by the back.

'Professional man' exception

This is not mentioned directly in the decision but Lord Keith is of the view that the *Pirelli* v *Oscar Faber* case and *Junior Books* v *Veitelii Co Ltd* were decided along the lines of *Hedley Byrne* v *Heller*. This emphasizes that negligent mis-statement is, and remains, a viable cause of action against professionals on building sites. The case does not assist on how easy it is to establish the requisite reliance or, in other words, how wide the duty can be cast. It may be that it is only owed to the immediate client of the architect, but warning bells should be ringing and the case of *Robert Leonard Estates* v *Robert Walpole* should be remembered. On the other hand their Lordships were of the view that Parliament had placed sufficient statutory duties, by way of the Defective Premises Act 1972, on those involved in building that the Courts would be usurping the role of the legislature if they took any liabilities further than that Act. Accordingly it can be argued that the liability of professionals should not be extended further by way of *Hedley Byrne* v *Heller* principles.

Whilst the main effect of this case was not unexpected it is still a good example of how one case can change the common law. It remains to be seen how far the implications in their Lordships' speeches will be taken by subsequent litigation and how the apparent dilemma will be resolved, but in the meantime the foregoing chapter should be read subject to the above comments.

5

Architect's Appointment and Collateral Warranties

A. RODERICK MALES

1 The appointment

1.01 An architect has many factors to consider when considering a commission, and it is important that he should fully appreciate their implications before entering into a legal commitment to undertake the work.

He must be satisfied that the client has the authority and resources to commission the work; he must appreciate the background to the proposal and understand its scope at least in outline; and he must be aware of any other consultants who have been, or are likely to be, associated with the project.

The architect must be satisfied that he has the experience and competence to undertake the work; that the office has the necessary finance, staff, and resources; and that the proposal will not conflict with the RIBA Code of Professional Conduct, the ARCUK statement of Conduct and Discipline, other commissions in the practice, or the policy in the practice.

The preliminary negotiations between the parties may involve exchange of business references, and where the architect and employer are previously unknown to each other more detailed enquiries may be necessary.

It is becoming increasingly common for architects to be invited to enter into collateral agreements with funding bodies or other third parties as a condition of the appointment. The significance of these agreements is discussed below.

1.02 Any appointment offered to an architect must be considered in relation to the requirements of the ARCUK statement concerning conduct and discipline (Chapter 23), and if the architect is a member of the RIBA or other professional institution, also its code of conduct. The architect must be able to demonstrate that he has acted properly in obtaining the commission and is able to carry out the work properly and in accordance with the codes. An employer may not be conscious of the constraints on the profession, and it is the responsibility of the architect to ensure that he is made aware of them wherever necessary.

The architect must consider his position in relation to other architects who may have been involved with the same scheme. An employer is free to offer the commission to whomever he wishes, to obtain alternative schemes from different architects, and to make whatever arrangements for professional services he considers to be necessary. However, the architect must ensure that he has acted, and continues to act, properly and fairly in his dealings with other architects. In particular he must be able to show that he has not attempted to supplant another architect nor has offered any improper inducements in order to obtain the commission.

An architect who is approached by a potential client in connection with a project with which another architect has already been concerned has a duty to inform the first architect. The first architect has no power to prevent the second architect from proceeding with the work, but it is ethically desirable and commercially prudent that he should be informed.

1.03 The need to consider the position of other architects is particularly important in large, complex projects involving various consultant architects providing different but related services, especially if the nature of the services changes during the duration of the work.

The scope of services and relations between consultant architects and executive architects are grounds for potential difficulty in developing and changing circumstances. All parties must be very careful to ensure that their terms of reference are fully understood throughout the project.

1.04 Occasionally difficulties may arise where the client wishes to make a single all-in appointment for all the necessary professional consultants. Standard conditions of services and remunerations of various institutions vary in detail and it is necessary for the consultants concerned to agree upon a unified basis before making an offer to a potential client.

2 Agreement of appointment

2.01 Although in law a verbal agreement may be accepted as the basis of a contract of engagement between architect and employer, the risks inherent in such an arrangement are obvious, and a formal procedure of appointment should always be adopted. Such a procedure creates a clearly identifiable legal basis for the commission and establishes a sound business approach to the relationship between architect and employer. The appointment may be made by either an informal exchange of letters or an exchange of a formal memorandum of agreement, in each case supported by appropriate supplementary material such as conditions of engagement.

The exchange of letters is frequently used but is not recommended. Informal letters of appointment are liable to misinterpretation and misunderstanding and are often the source of difficulties and disagreements between the parties.

2.02 Various institutions publish standard forms of agreement and their use is strongly recommended. These forms are generally self-explanatory. The RIBA Memorandum of Agreement and Schedule of Services and Fees, is particularly useful. It is available in both the standard works form and the minor works form.

2.03 Where a standard form of agreement is not used, it is suggested that the following matters should be clearly identified in any exchange of letters between the parties:

1. The date of the agreement.
2. The name and address of the employer.
3. The name and address of the architect.
4. The title and address of the project.
5. The formal agreement to the appointment of the architect.
6. The basis of remuneration for the architect.
7. The form and scope of services to be provided by the architect.
8. The appointment procedure for a quantity surveyor, other consultants, and the clerk of works as appropriate.
9. The procedure to be followed in the event of the architect's incapacity.
10. The procedure for the termination of the agreement.
11. The procedure for resolving disputes between parties.

The basis of remuneration and the scope of services may be further defined in other documents to which reference should be made in the agreement.

Occasionally, employers may wish to use their own forms of agreement. These should be comparted with the standard forms issued by the RIBA and advice sought in the case of serious differences.

2.04 The authority of the architect is strictly limited to the terms of his appointment, that is, as shown in any form of agreement and conditions of engagement. It is in the interests of the employer, the architect, the quantity surveyor, and other independent consultants that these terms should be fully and clearly understood.

2.05 Where a commission arises out of a recognized competition, the competition conditions usually form the conditions of the appointment. Difficulties develop occasionally when the subsequent building is substantially different from that originally envisaged and where there has been a material change in the conditions.

The subsequent appointment of other consultants following a competition may also be a cause of some difficulty.

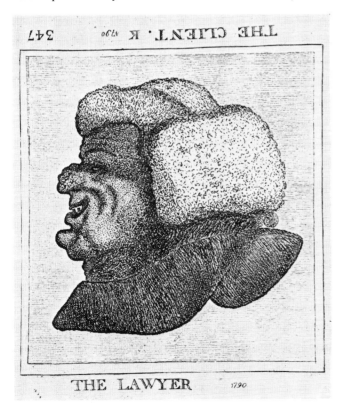

THE LAWYER *1790*

2.06 Forms of memoranda of appointment should be signed by both parties, each keeping a copy, before the beginning of the work, and the signatures should be formally witnessed. The forms may be sealed if either party should so desire. The normal formalities would be involved, and, of course, the architect would have to consider his extended responsibilities carefully.

2.07 The architect's contract of engagement is usually personal to himself or the partnership. He cannot delegate his duties completely. He is under no obligation to carry out all the works personally or to go into every detail himself. The extent to which he may be prepared to delegate his duties to an assistant is a matter of competence, confidence, reliability, and experience of the assistant and the principal. The architect is becoming increasingly dependent on the skill and labour of others within his office and elsewhere, but he remains responsible to his client within the terms of his appointment, and continues to be responsible for the acts and defaults of his subordinates. The subordinates in turn are responsible to their principal and could be held liable to their employers for results of their acts.

Where the business is conducted as an unlimited or a limited company, the relationships will depend upon the form of contract involved. However, the ethical responsibilities between the parties remains, and liability in tort continues.

3 Termination

3.01 The contract of engagement between the architect and his employer may be terminated by either party on reasonable notice. Reasons for the termination need not be stated, but in the event of dispute over outstanding fees or payments, the cause of the termination would be of importance to an arbitrator or a court in determining an award.

In the event of the termination of the contract, any outstanding fees for work properly carried out become due to the architect, but it is unlikely that the employer could be held responsible for any loss of anticipated profits on work not yet carried out.

3.02 Difficulties sometimes arise in connection with the use of material prepared before termination of the engagement. The standard form of memoranda of agreement usually defines the rights of the parties in such circumstances. In the absence of any statement concerning the use of material following the termination of an engagement, it is generally assumed that if the work was substantially advanced at the time of termination it would be unreasonable for the employer not to be entitled to complete the project. It is usually accepted that the employer is entitled to a licence to use the drawings to complete the work effectively. The copyright, of course, remains with the architect unless some other agreement is made.

3.03 In the event of the death or the incapacity of the architect, it is usually held that the employer is entitled to the use of the drawings and other documents to complete the work. Provision for the procedure to be adopted in such circumstances should be included in the standard form of agreement. The death of either party to a personal contract generally dissolves the contract, but it is usually possible with agreement, for a third party to assume responsibility for the completion of the contract.

Agreements of appointments between companies and partnerships, rather than between individuals, avoid the occasional embarrassing technical difficulties and delays that occur in the transfer of responsibility to others in the event of death.

3.04 In the event of the bankruptcy of either party, the contract can usually be continued, subject to the agreement of a receiver and assurances about fees and monies which may be due or become due.

4 Ownership

4.01 Ownership of drawings and other documents is often a source of debate. Correspondence and other documents exchanged between the architect and others in connection with the approval of plans, the running of the project, or the administration of the contract by the architect in his role as an agent technically belong to the employer, although it is unusual for all these documents to be transferred to the employer. Other material prepared in the architect's professional capacity belong to the architect, and this accounts for the greater part of the documentation prepared in the course of a project.

5 Conditions of engagement

Part 1   Architect's services

This part describes Preliminary and Basic Services which an architect will normally provide.

PRELIMINARY SERVICES

Work stage A: Inception

Brief	1.1	Discuss the client's requirements including timescale and any financial limits; assess these and give general advice on how to proceed; agree the architect's services.
Information to be provided by the client	1.2	Obtain from the client information on ownership and any lessors and lessees of the site, any existing buildings on the site, boundary fences and other enclosures, and any known easements, encroachments, underground services, rights of way, rights of support and other relevant matters.
Site appraisal	1.3	Visit the site and carry out an initial appraisal.
Advice on other consultants' services	1.4	Advise on the need for other consultants' services and on the scope of these services.
Design work by specialist firms	1.5	Advise on the need for specialist contractors, sub-contractors and suppliers to design and execute part of the works to comply with the architect's requirements.
Site staff	1.6	Advise on the need for site staff.
Timetable and fee basis	1.7	Prepare where required an outline timetable and fee basis for further services for the client's approval.

Work stage B: Feasibility

Feasibility studies	1.8	Carry out such studies as may be necessary to determine the feasibility of the client's requirements; review with the client alternative design and construction approaches and cost implications; advise on the need to obtain planning permissions, approvals under building acts or regulations, and other similar statutory requirements.

BASIC SERVICES

Work stage C: Outline proposals

Outline proposals	1.9	With other consultants where appointed, analyse the client's requirements; prepare outline proposals and an approximation of the construction cost for the client's preliminary approval.

Work stage D: Scheme design

Scheme design	1.10	With other consultants where appointed, develop a scheme design from the outline proposals taking into account amendments requested by the client; prepare a cost estimate; where applicable give an indication of possible start and completion dates for the building contract. The scheme design will illustrate the size and character of the project in sufficient detail to enable the client to agree the spatial arrangements, materials and appearance.
Changes in scheme design	1.11	With other consultants where appointed, advise the client of the implications of any subsequent changes on the cost of the project and on the overall programme.
Planning application	1.12	Make where required application for planning permission. The permission itself is beyond the architect's control and no guarantee that it will be granted can be given.

Work stage E: Detail design

Detail design	1.13	With other consultants where appointed, develop the scheme design; obtain the client's approval of the type of construction, quality of materials and standard of workmanship; co-ordinate any design work done by consultants, specialist contractors, sub-contractors and suppliers; obtain quotations and other information in connection with specialist work.
Cost checks and changes in detail design	1.14	With other consultants where appointed, carry out cost checks as necessary; advise the client of the consequences of any subsequent changes on the cost and programme.
Statutory approvals	1.15	Make and negotiate where required applications for approvals under building acts, regulations or other statutory requirements.

Work stages F and G: Production information and bills of quantities

Production information	1.16	With other consultants where appointed, prepare production information including drawings, schedules and specification of materials and workmanship; provide information for bills of quantities, if any, to be prepared; all information complete in sufficient detail to enable a contractor to prepare a tender.

Work stage H: Tender action

Other contracts	1.17	Arrange, where relevant, for other contracts to be let prior to the contractor commencing work.
Tender lists	1.18	Advise on and obtain the client's approval to a list of tenderers.
Tender action and appraisal	1.19	Invite tenders from approved contractors; appraise and advise on tenders submitted. Alternatively, arrange for a price to be negotiated with a contractor.

Work stage J: Project planning

Project planning	1.20	Advise the client on the appointment of the contractor and on the responsibilities of the client, contractor and architect under the terms of the building contract; where required prepare the building contract and arrange for it to be signed by the client and the contractor; provide production information as required by the building contract.

Work stage K: Operations on site

Contract administration	1.21	Administer the terms of the building contract during operations on site.
Inspections	1.22	Visit the site as appropriate to inspect generally the progress and quality of the work.
Financial appraisal	1.23	With other consultants where appointed, make where required periodic financial reports to the client including the effect of any variations on the construction cost.

Work stage L: Completion

Completion	1.24	Administer the terms of the building contract relating to the completion of the works.
Guidance on maintenance	1.25	Give general guidance on maintenance.
Record drawings	1.26	Provide the client with a set of drawings showing the building and the main lines of drainage; arrange for drawings of the services installations to be provided.

Part 2   Other services

This part describes services which may be provided by the architect to augment the Preliminary and Basic Services described in Part 1 or which may be the subject of a separate appointment. The list of services so described is not exhaustive.

Surveys and investigations

Building sites	2.1	Advise on the selection and suitability of sites; conduct negotiations concerned with sites and buildings.
Measured surveys	2.2	Make measured surveys, take levels and prepare plans of sites and buildings.
Soil investigations	2.3	Provide services in connection with soil and other similar investigations.
Condition of premises	2.4	Make inspections, prepare reports or give general advice on the condition of premises.
Schedules of dilapidations	2.5	Prepare schedules of dilapidations; negotiate them on behalf of landlords or tenants.
Structural surveys	2.6	Make structural surveys to ascertain whether there are defects in the walls, roof, floors, drains or other parts of a building which may materially affect its safety, life and value.
Building failures	2.7	Investigate building failures; arrange and supervise exploratory work by contractors or specialists.
Repairs and restoration work	2.8	Take particulars on site; prepare specifications and/or schedules for repairs and restoration work, and inspect their execution.
Problems in existing buildings	2.9	Investigate and advise on problems in existing buildings such as fire protection, floor loadings, sound insulation, or change of use.
Energy surveys	2.10	Advise on the efficient use of energy in new and existing buildings.
Cost in use	2.11	Carry out life cycle analyses of buildings to determine their cost in use.
Valuations	2.12	Make an inspection and valuation for mortgage or other purposes.

Development services

Special drawings and models	2.13	Prepare special drawings, models or technical information for the use of the client or for applications under planning, building act, building regulation or other statutory requirements, or for negotiations with ground landlords, adjoining owners, public authorities, licensing authorities, mortgagors and others; prepare plans for conveyancing, land registry and other legal purposes.
Development plans	2.14	Prepare development plans for a large building or complex of buildings; prepare a layout only, or prepare a layout for a greater area than that which is to be developed immediately.
Estate plans	2.15	Prepare layouts for housing, industrial or other estates showing the siting of buildings and other works such as roads and sewers.
Road and sewers	2.16	Prepare drawings and specification of materials and workmanship for the construction of housing, industrial or other estate roads and sewers.
Demolitions	2.17	Provide services in connection with demolition works.
Environmental studies	2.18	Provide services in connection with environmental studies.

Design services

Furniture and fittings	2.19	Design or advise on the selection of furniture and fittings; inspect the making up of such furnishings.
Shopfitting and other works of special quality	2.20	Advise on and prepare detailed designs for works of special quality such as shopfitting or exhibition design, either independently or within the shell of an existing building.

Works of art	2.21	Advise on the commissioning or selection of works of art; supervise their installation.
Acoustical investigations	2.22	Carry out specialist acoustical investigations.
Special constructional research	2.23	Carry out special constructional research in connection with a scheme design, including the design, construction or testing of prototype buildings or models.
Building systems and components	2.24	Develop a building system or mass-produced building components; examine and advise on existing building systems; monitor the testing of prototype buildings and models.

Cost estimating and financial advisory services

Cost plans and cash flow requirements	2.25	Carry out cost planning for a building project, including the cost of associated design services, site development, landscaping, furniture and equipment; advise on cash flow requirements for design cost, construction cost, and cost in use.
Schedules of rates and quantities	2.26	Prepare schedules of rates or schedules of quantities for tendering purposes; value work executed where no quantity surveyor is appointed. Fees for this work are recommended to be in accordance with the Professional Charges of the Royal Institution of Chartered Surveyors.
Cost of replacement	2.27	Carry out inspections and surveys; prepare estimates for the replacement and reinstatement of buildings and plant; submit and negotiate claims following damage by fire or other causes.
Grant applications	2.28	Provide information; make applications for and conduct negotiations in connection with local authority, government or other grants.

Negotiations

Planning applications exceptional negotiations	2.29	Conduct exceptional negotiations with a planning authority.
Planning appeals	2.30	Prepare and submit an appeal under planning acts; advise on other work in connection with planning appeals.
Building regulations exceptional negotiations	2.31	Conduct exceptional negotiations for approvals under building acts or regulations; negotiate waivers or relaxations.
Royal Fine Art Commission	2.32	Make submissions to the Royal Fine Art Commission and other non-statutory bodies.
Landlords' approvals	2.33	Submit plans of proposed building works for approval of landlords, mortgagors, freeholders or others.
Rights of owners and lessees	2.34	Advise on the rights and responsibilities of owners or lessees including rights of light, rights of support, and rights of way; provide information; undertake any negotiations.
Party walls	2.35	Provide services in connection with party wall negotiations.
Litigation and arbitration	2.36	Prepare and give evidence; settle proofs; confer with solicitors and counsel; attend court and arbitrations; appear before other tribunals; act as arbitrator.

Administration and management of building projects

Site staff	2.37	Provide site staff for frequent or constant inspection of the works.
Project management	2.38	Provide management from inception to completion: prepare briefs; appoint and co-ordinate consultants, construction managers, agents and contractors; monitor time, cost and agreed targets; monitor progress of the works; hand over the building on completion; equip, commission and set up any operational organisations.
Design and build contracts	2.39	Provide services to the client, whether employer or contractor, in carrying out duties under a design and build contract.
Separate trades contracts	2.40	Provide services in connection with separate trades contracts; agree a programme of work; act as co-ordinator for the duration of the contracts.
Direct labour	2.41	Provide services in connection with labour employed directly by the client; agree a programme of work; co-ordinate the supply of labour and materials; provide general supervision; agree the final account.
As built' drawings	2.42	Provide specially prepared drawings of a building 'as built'.
Maintenance manuals	2.43	Compile maintenance and operational manuals; incorporate information prepared by other consultants, specialist contractors, sub-contractors and suppliers.
Maintenance programme	2.44	Prepare a programme for the maintenance of a building; arrange maintenance contracts.

Services normally provided by consultants

Consultants' services	2.45	Provide such services as:

a Quantity surveying
b Structural engineering
c Mechanical engineering
d Electrical engineering
e Landscape and garden design
f Civil engineering
g Town planning
h Furniture design
j Graphic design
k Industrial design
l Interior design

Where consultants' services are provided from within the architect's own office or by consultants in association with the architect it is recommended that fees be in accordance with the scales of charges of the relevant professional body.

Consultancy services

Consultant architect	2.46	Provide services as a consultant architect on a regular or intermittent basis.

Part 3   Conditions of appointment

This part describes the conditions which normally apply to an architect's appointment. If different or additional conditions are to apply, they should be set out in the Schedule of Services and Fees or letter of appointment.

Duty of care	3.1	The architect will exercise reasonable skill and care in conformity with the normal standards of the architect's profession.

Architect's authority

Authority	3.2	The architect will act on behalf of the client in the matters set out or implied in the architect's appointment; the architect will obtain the authority of the client before initiating any service or work stage.
Variation of service	3.3	The architect shall not make any material alteration, addition to or omission from the approved design without the knowledge and consent of the client, except if found necessary during construction for constructional reasons in which case the architect shall inform the client without delay.
Variation of cost or time	3.4	The architect will inform the client if the total authorised expenditure or the building contract period is likely to be materially varied.

Consultants

Nomination of consultants	3.5	Consultants may be nominated by either the client or the architect, subject to acceptance by each party.
Consultants employed by client	3.6	Where the client employs the consultants, either directly or through the agency of the architect, the client will hold each consultant, and not the architect, responsible for the competence, general inspection and performance of the work entrusted to that consultant; provided that in relation to the execution of such work under the contract between the client and the contractor nothing in this clause shall affect any responsibility of the architect for issuing instructions or for other functions ascribed to the architect under that contract.
Co-ordination of consultants' services	3.7	The architect will have the authority to co-ordinate and integrate into the overall design the services provided by any consultant, however employed.

Contractors, sub-contractors and suppliers

Design work by specialist contractors, sub-contractors and suppliers	3.8	A specialist contractor, sub-contractor or supplier who is to be employed by the client to design any part of the works may be nominated by either the architect or the client, subject to acceptance by each party. The client will hold such contractor, sub-contractor or supplier, and not the architect, responsible for the competence, proper execution and performance of the work thereby entrusted to that contractor, sub-contractor or supplier. The architect will have the authority to co-ordinate and integrate such work into the overall design.
Responsibility of the contractor	3.9	The client will employ a contractor under a separate agreement to undertake construction or other works. The client will hold the contractor, and not the architect, responsible for the contractor's operational methods and for the proper execution of the works.

Site inspection

Inspection	3.10	The architect will visit the site at intervals appropriate to the stage of construction to inspect the progress and quality of the works and to determine that they are being executed generally in accordance with the contract documents. The architect will not be required to make frequent or constant inspections.
Site staff Clerk of works	3.11	Where frequent or constant inspection is required a clerk or clerks of works will be employed. They may be employed either by the client or by the architect and will in either event be under the architect's direction and control.
Site staff Resident architect	3.12	Where frequent or constant inspection by the architect is agreed to be necessary, a resident architect may be appointed by the architect on a part or full time basis.

Client's instructions

Information from the client	3.13	The client will provide the architect with such information and make such decisions as are necessary for the proper performance of the agreed service.
Client's representative	3.14	The client, if a firm or other body of persons, will, when requested by the architect, nominate a responsible representative through whom all instructions will be given.

Copyright

Copyright	3.15	Copyright in all documents and drawings prepared by the architect and in any works executed from those documents and drawings shall, unless otherwise agreed, remain the property of the architect.
Copyright entitlement	3.16	The client, unless otherwise agreed, will be entitled to reproduce the architect's design by proceeding to execute the project provided that:

   – the entitlement applies only to the site or part of the site to which the design relates; and

   – the architect has completed work stage D or has provided detail design and production information in work stages E, F and G; and

   – any fees due to the architect have been paid or tendered.

This entitlement will also apply to the maintenance, repair and renewal of the works.

Entitlement restrictions	3.17	Where an architect has not completed work stage D, or where the client and the architect have agreed that clause 3.16 shall not apply, the client may not reproduce the design by proceeding to execute the project without the consent of the architect and payment of any additional fee that may be agreed in exchange for the architect's consent.
Limited services	3.18	The architect shall not unreasonably withhold his consent under clause 3.17 but where his services are limited to making and negotiating planning applications he may withhold his consent unless otherwise determined by an arbitrator appointed in accordance with clause 3.26.

Assignment

Assignment	3.19	Neither the architect nor the client may assign the whole or any part of his duties without the other's written consent.

Suspension and termination

Suspension of services Force majeure	3.20	The architect will give immediate notice in writing to the client of any situation arising from force majeure which makes it impracticable to carry out any of the agreed services, and agree with the client a suitable course of action.
Suspension of services: Client	3.21	The client may suspend the performance of any or all of the agreed services by giving reasonable notice in writing to the architect.
Resumption of services	3.22	If the architect has not been given instructions to resume any suspended service within six months from the date of suspension the architect will make written request for such instructions which must be given in writing. If these have not been received within 30 days of the date of such request the architect will have the right to treat the appointment as terminated upon the expiry of the 30 days.
Termination	3.23	The architect's appointment may be terminated by either party on the expiry of reasonable notice given in writing.
Death or incapacity of architect	3.24	Should the architect through death or incapacity be unable to provide the agreed services, the appointment will thereby be terminated. In such an event the client may, on payment or tender of all outstanding fees and expenses, make full use of reports, drawings or other documents prepared by the architect in accordance with and for use under the agreement, but only for the purpose for which they were prepared.

Settlement of disputes

3.25   A difference or dispute arising on the application of the Architect's Appointment to fees charged by a member may, by agreement between the parties, be referred to the RIBA, RIAS or RSUA for an opinion provided that:

– the member's appointment is based on this document and has been agreed and confirmed in writing; and

– the opinion is sought on a joint statement of undisputed facts; and

– the parties undertake to accept the opinion as final and binding upon them.

3.26   Any other difference or dispute arising out of the appointment and any difference or dispute arising on the fees charged which cannot be resolved in accordance with clause 3.25 shall be referred to arbitration by a person to be agreed between the parties or, failing agreement within 14 days after either party has given to the other a written request to concur in the appointment of an arbitrator, a person to be nominated at the request of either party by the President of the Chartered Institute of Arbitrators, provided that in a difference or dispute arising out of provisions relating to copyright, clauses 3.15 to 3.18 above, the arbitrator shall, unless otherwise agreed, be an architect.

or

Alternative for Scotland   3.26S   *In Scotland, any other difference or dispute arising out of the appointment and any difference or dispute arising on the fees charged which cannot be resolved in accordance with clause 3.25 shall be referred to arbitration by a person to be agreed between the parties or, failing agreement within 14 days after either party has given to the other a written request to concur in the appointment of an arbiter, a person to be nominated at the request of either party by the Dean of the Faculty of Advocates, provided that in a difference or dispute arising out of provisions relating to copyright, clauses 3.15 to 3.18 above, the arbiter shall, unless otherwise agreed, be an architect.*

By agreement   3.27   Nothing herein shall prevent the parties agreeing to settle any difference or dispute arising out of the appointment without recourse to arbitration.

Governing laws

England and Wales   3.28   The application of these conditions shall be governed by the laws of England and Wales.

or

Alternative for Scotland   3.28S   *The application of these conditions shall be governed by the laws of Scotland.*

or

Alternative for Northern Ireland   3.28NI   *The application of these conditions shall be governed by the laws of Northern Ireland.*

Part 4

Recommended fees and expenses

This part describes the recommended and not mandatory methods of calculating fees for the architect's services and expenses. Fees may be based on a percentage of the total construction cost or on time expended, or may be a lump sum. This part should be read in conjunction with Parts 1, 2 and 3.

Percentage fees

New works   4.1   The percentage fee scales shown in Figure 1 (graph) are for use where the architect's appointment is for the Basic Services described in Part 1 for new works having a total construction cost between £20,000 and £5,000,000. Where the total construction cost is less than £20,000 or more than £5,000,000 client and architect should agree an appropriate fee basis at the time of appointment.

Percentage fees   4.2   Percentage fees are based on the total construction cost of the works; on the issue of the final certificate fees should be recalculated on the actual total construction cost.

Total construction cost   4.3   Total construction cost is defined as the cost, as certified by the architect, of all works including site works executed under the architect's direction, subject to the following:

a   The total construction cost includes the cost of all work designed by consultants and co-ordinated by the architect, irrespective of whether such work is carried out under separate building contracts for which the architect may not be responsible. The architect will be informed of the cost of any such separate contracts.

b   The total construction cost does not include specialist sub-contractors' design fees for work on which consultants would otherwise have been employed. Where such fees are not known, the architect will estimate a reduction from the total construction cost.

c   For the purpose of calculating the appropriate fee, the total construction cost:

– includes the actual or estimated cost of any work executed which is excluded from the contract but otherwise designed by the architect;

– is not subject to any deductions made in respect of work not in accordance with the building contract.

d   The total construction cost includes the cost of built-in furniture and equipment. Where the cost of any special equipment is excluded from the total construction cost, the architect may charge additionally for work in connection with such items.

e   Where any material, labour or carriage is supplied by a client who is not the contractor, the cost will be estimated by the architect as if it were supplied by the contractor, and included in the total cost.

f   Where the client is the contractor, a statement of the ascertained gross cost of the works may be used in calculating the total construction cost of the works. In the absence of such a statement, the architect's own estimate will be used. In both a statement of the ascertained gross cost and an architect's estimate there will be included an allowance for the contractor's profit and overheads.

Classification of buildings   4.4   Buildings are divided into five classes for fee calculation purposes. For guidance only the building types most likely to fall into each class are shown in Figure 3.

Repetition

Repetition   4.5   The classification of buildings in Figure 3 takes account of reduced design work arising from the nature of the building.

Repeated buildings   4.6   Where a building is repeated for the same client the recommended fee for the superstructure may be reduced on all except the first three of any houses of the same design and on all except the first of all other building types of the same design.

Identical compartments   4.7   Where a single building incorporates a number of identical compartments such as floors or complete structural bays the recommended fee may be reduced on all identical compartments in excess of ten.

Fee reduction   4.8   Reductions should be made by waiving the fee for work stages E, F and G where a complete design can be re-used without modification other than the handing of a plan.

Time charge fees

Time charges: Principals and technical staff   4.9   Time charges are based on hourly rates for principals and other technical staff. In assessing the hourly rate all relevant factors should be considered, including the complexity of the work, the qualifications, experience and responsibility of the architect, and the character of any negotiations. Hourly rates for principals shall be agreed. The hourly rate for technical staff should be not less than 18 pence per £100 of gross annual income.

Technical staff   4.10   Technical staff are defined as architectural and other professional and technical staff, where the architect is responsible for deducting PAYE and National Insurance contributions from those persons' salaries on behalf of the Inland Revenue.

Gross annual income   4.11   Gross annual income includes bonus payments plus the employer's share of contributions towards National Insurance, pension and private medical schemes and other emoluments such as car and accommodation allowances.

Agency staff   4.12   Where staff are provided by an agency hourly rates shall be agreed.

Site staff   4.13   Where site staff are employed by the architect hourly rates shall be agreed.

Secretarial and administrative staff   4.14   Unless otherwise agreed no separate time charges will be made for secretarial staff or staff engaged on general accountancy or administrative duties.

Architect's records   4.15   The architect will maintain records of time spent on services performed on a time basis. The architect will make such records available to the client on reasonable request.

Lump sum fees

Lump sum fee   4.16   The architect may agree with the client to charge a lump sum fee for any of the services described in Parts 1 and 2 in appropriate circumstances, for example where:

– the client's requirements are provided in a form such that the architect is not obliged to undertake any additional preparatory work;

– the full extent of the service can be determined when the architect is appointed; and

– the architect's service can be completed within an agreed period.

Works to existing buildings

Alterations or extensions   4.17   The percentage fee scales shown in Figure 2 (graph) are for use where the architect's appointment is for the Basic Services described in Part 1 for alterations or extensions to an existing building having a total construction cost of between £20,000 and £5,000,000. Where the total construction cost is less than £20,000 or more than £5,000,000 client and architect should agree an appropriate fee basis at the time of the appointment.

Extensions substantially independent   4.18   Where extensions to existing buildings are substantially independent, percentage fees should be as Figure 1 for new works, but the fee for those sections of the works which marry existing buildings to the new should be charged separately as Figure 2 applicable to an independent commission of similar value.

Repair and restoration work   4.19   Where the architect's appointment is for repair and restoration work fees should be on a time basis; alternatively a percentage fee may be agreed.

Historic or listed buildings   4.20   Where the architect's appointment is in connection with works to a building of architectural or historic interest, or to a building in a conservation area, higher fees may be charged.

Compounding of fees

Compounding of fees   4.21   By agreement the percentage or lump sum fee may be compounded to cover all or any part of the architect's services and expenses.

Interim payments

Fee instalments   4.22   Fees and expenses should be paid in instalments either at regular intervals or on completion of work stages of the Basic Services (Part 1).

Fee apportionment   4.23A   Where interim payment of percentage or lump sum fees is related to completion of work stages of the Basic Services the recommended apportionment is as follows:

Work stage	Proportion of fee	Cumulative total
C	15%	15%
D	20%	35%
E	20%	55%
F G	20%	75%
H J K L	25%	100%

Fees in respect of work stages E to L should be paid in instalments proportionate to the work completed or the value of the works certified from time to time. Interim payments should be based on the current estimated cost of the works.

The apportionment of fees is a means of assessing interim payments and does not necessarily reflect the amount of work completed in any work stage. By agreement an adjustment in the apportionment may be made.

Interest   4.23B   Any sums remaining unpaid at the expiry of 30 days from the date of submission of the fee account shall bear interest thereafter, such interest to accrue from day to day at the rate of 2% per annum above the current base rate of the architect's principal bank.

Partial services

Partial services   4.24   The architect may be required to provide part only of the Basic Services (Part 1). In such cases the architect will be entitled to a commensurate fee.

Work done by client   4.25   Where work is to be done by or on behalf of the client, resulting in the omission of part of work stages C to L, or a sponsored constructional method is to be used, a commensurate reduction in the recommended percentage fee may be agreed. In assessing the reduction, due account should be taken of the need for the architect to become thoroughly familiar with the work done by others, and a familiarisation fee will be charged for this work.

Partial service fee basis   4.26   All percentage fees for partial services should be based on the architect's current estimate of the total construction cost of the works. Such estimates may be based on an accepted tender or, subject to the following, on the lowest of unaccepted tenders. Where partial services are provided in respect of works for which the executed cost is not known and no tender has been accepted, percentage fees should be based either on the architect's estimated total construction cost or on the most recent cost limit agreed with the client, whichever is the lower.

Alternative fee arrangements   4.27   Fees for partial services may alternatively be on a time or lump sum basis.

Suspension, resumption and termination

Fees on suspension or termination

4.28 On suspension or termination of the architect's appointment the architect will be entitled to fees for all work completed at that time. Fees will be charged on a partial service basis.

Reimbursement during suspension

4.29 During such period of suspension the architect will be reimbursed by the client for all expenses and disbursements necessarily incurred under the appointment.

Fees on resumption

4.30 On the resumption of a suspended service within six months, previous payments will be regarded solely as payments on account towards the total fee.

Reimbursement on termination

4.31 Where the architect's appointment is terminated by the client the architect will be reimbursed by the client for all expenses and disbursements necessarily incurred in connection with work then in progress and arising as a result of the termination.

Expenses and disbursements

Expenses and disbursements

4.32 In addition to the fees charged the architect will be reimbursed for all expenses and disbursements properly incurred in connection with the appointment, including the following:

a Printing, reproduction or purchase costs of all documents, drawings, maps, models, photographs, and other records, including all those used in communication between architect, client, consultants and contractors, and for enquiries to contractors, sub-contractors and suppliers, notwithstanding any obligation on the part of the architect to supply such documents to those concerned, except that contractors will pay for any prints additional to those to which they are entitled under the contract.

b Hotel and travelling expenses, including mileage allowance for cars at rates stated in the Schedule of Services and Fees and other similar disbursements.

c All payments made on behalf of the client, such as expenses incurred in advertising for tenders and resident site staff including the time and expenses of interviewers and reasonable expenses for interviewees.

d Fees and other charges for specialist professional advice, including legal advice, which have been incurred by the architect with the specific authority of the client.

e The cost of postage, telephone charges, telex messages, telegrams, cables, facsimiles, air-freight and courier services.

f Rental and hire charges for specialised equipment, including computers, where required and agreed by the client.

g Where work charged on a percentage fee is at such a distance that an exceptional amount of time is spent travelling, additional charges may be made.

Records

4.33 The architect will maintain records of all such expenses and disbursements and will make these records available to the client on reasonable request.

Compounding of expenses

4.34 Expenses and disbursements may by agreement be estimated or standardised in whole or in part, or compounded for an increase in the percentage or lump sum fee.

Payment of statutory fees

4.35 The client will pay all fees in respect of applications under planning and building acts and other statutory requirements.

Variations

Variation of fees

4.36 Where the scope of the architect's services is varied fees may be adjusted accordingly.

Extra work and expense

4.37 Where the architect is involved in extra work and expense for reasons beyond the architect's control and for which the architect would not otherwise be remunerated additional fees are due. Any of the following is likely to involve the architect in extra work and expense:

a The need to revise reports, drawings, specifications or other documents due to changes in interpretation or enactment or revisions of laws, statutory or other regulations.

b Changes in the client's instructions, or delay by the client in providing information.

c Consideration of notices, applications or claims by the contractor under a building contract; delays in the building contract operations; delays resulting from defects or deficiencies in the work of the contractor, sub-contractors or suppliers; default, bankruptcy or liquidation of the contractor, sub-contractors or suppliers.

d Any other cause beyond the architect's control.

Value Added Tax

Value Added Tax

4.38 The amount of any Value Added Tax on the services and expenses of the architect arising under the Finance Act 1972 will be chargeable to the client in addition to the architect's fees and expenses.

Figure 1: Recommended percentage fee scales: New works

Total construction cost: July 1987

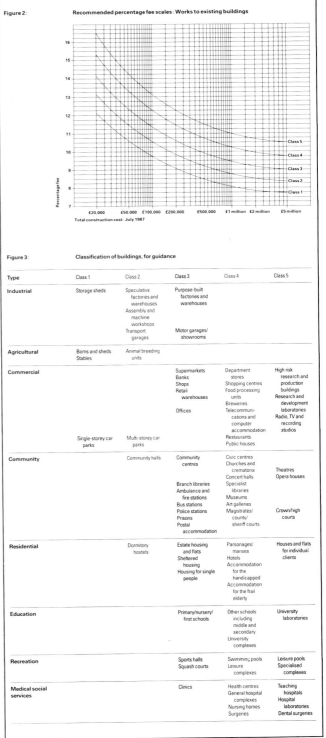

Figure 2: Recommended percentage fee scales: Works to existing buildings

Total construction cost: July 1987

Figure 3: Classification of buildings, for guidance

Type	Class 1	Class 2	Class 3	Class 4	Class 5
Industrial	Storage sheds	Speculative factories and warehouses Assembly and machine workshops Transport garages	Purpose-built factories and warehouses Motor garages/ showrooms		
Agricultural	Barns and sheds Stables	Animal breeding units			
Commercial			Supermarkets Banks Shops Retail warehouses Offices	Department stores Shopping centres Food processing units Breweries Telecommunications and computer accommodation Restaurants Public houses	High risk research and production buildings Research and development laboratories Radio, TV and recording studios
	Single-storey car parks	Multi-storey car parks			
Community		Community halls	Community centres Branch libraries Ambulance and fire stations Bus stations Police stations Prisons Postal accommodation	Civic centres Churches and crematoria Concert halls Specialist libraries Museums Art galleries Magistrates/ county/ sheriff courts	Theatres Opera houses Crown/high courts
Residential		Dormitory hostels	Estate housing and flats Sheltered housing Housing for single people	Parsonages/ manses Hotels Accommodation for the handicapped Accommodation for the frail elderly	Houses and flats for individual clients
Education			Primary/nursery/ first schools	Other schools including middle and secondary University complexes	University laboratories
Recreation			Sports halls Squash courts	Swimming pools Leisure complexes	Leisure pools Specialised complexes
Medical social services			Clinics	Health centres General hospital complexes Nursing homes Surgeries	Teaching hospitals Hospital laboratories Dental surgeries

5.01 The RIBA publishes its recommended conditions for the engagement of an architect in the form of the *Architects Appointment* which is updated from time to time. These conditions are not mandatory but in the interests of both architects and their clients the use of these model conditions is strongly recommended. Where it is proposed that other arrangements should apply it is suggested that the alternative conditions should be carefully compared with those of the *Architects Appointment*.

The ARCUK statement Conduct and Discipline makes no reference to the fees or charges of an architect, and leaves fees to be negotiated between architects and their clients.

5.02 The *Architects Appointment* is devised in order to enable the architect and the client to achieve a clear understanding of the services required by the client, the conditions concerning the provision of these services, and the basis of the fees and charges to be paid for these services.

The document, which is indispensable, comprises four sections: Part 1 describing the preliminary and basic services which an architect would normally provide; Part 2 describing services which may be provided to augment the preliminary and basic services or which may be subject to a separate appointment; Part 3 describing the conditions which normally apply to an architect's appointment; and Part 4 describing the recommended methods of calculating fees on the basis of a percentage of the total construction costs or the time expended or as a lump sum. Part 4 also includes a draft memorandum of agreement between the client and his architect together with a schedule of services and fees to be completed by the parties.

The requirements of the documents are clearly defined and it is essential that the document itself be carefully studied.

A modified version of the Architects Appointment is available for use with Small Works.

5.03 Critics of published conditions of engagement have rightly complained that the terms are not readily understood by lay clients, particularly in such matters as interpretation of additional services and reduction of fees for repetitive work. The architect has a clear responsibility to explain the scale to his client at the outset. It should not be assumed that an architect has discharged his duty simply by issuing a copy of the conditions to his client.

5.04 Prospective clients frequently require an estimate of the anticipated total fees likely to be involved in projects. Difficulties may arise where fees are forecast on the basis of a premature estimate of the likely total cost of the building work. As in all cases of financial forecast, it is important that care should be taken and clients should be advised of the nature of the estimate being made.

Difficulties may also arise where time charges are to be made and the forecast of the likely period of work is given.

5.05 Any value added tax (VAT) chargeable on the services of the architect is chargeable to the client at the appropriate rate current at the time. Clients who are taxable persons under the Finance Act 1972 are able to recover such input tax from the Customs and Excise Department.

5.06 Architects carrying out work overseas in situations where RIBA or other conditions do not apply are advised to uphold any local scales of charges. If there are no locally recognized scales, the architect, of course, would have to devise his own.

5.07 It is by no means uncommon for the client's brief or requirements to change during the course of a commission. Where this has happened, or is likely to happen, it is essential that the architect brings to the attention of the client any implications there may be for the conditions of the architect's appointment. Failure to draw attention to possible changes in the nature or range of service required and the basis of payment can have embarrassing consequences for both the client and the architect.

5.08 Frequently potential clients wish to impose particular conditions on the architect's engagement. The implications of these conditions need to be carefully assessed and where there is a substantial extension to the liability or duties of the architect appropriate additional reimbursement should be negotiated. Extensions of liability outside those of an existing professional indemnity policy should be discussed with the architect's broker or insurers. Public bodies and large commercial clients may require the architect to undertake to maintain professional indemnity insurance for six years following completion of the works; the architect must insist that the undertaking is subject to the reasonable availability of insurance cover.

5.09 The RIBA has now issued a variant of the Architects Appointment for use in connection with Historic Buildings and a supplement for use in connection with Community Architect Services.

6 Speculative work and tendering for architects' services

6.01 Two characteristics of the increasingly commercial and competitive environment in which architects now have to operate have had a profound effect on architects' negotiations with their clients, i.e. speculative work and competitive fee tendering. Speculative work in which the architect undertakes work at risk on the basis that payment will only be made in the event of the work proceeding is now widespread, especially in commercial and development work. Competitive fee tendering has become commonplace with official and quasi-official bodies being obliged to obtain competitive tenders for substantial projects, and private clients becoming aware of the possibilities of competitive tendering.

6.02 The extent to which an architect is prepared to undertake speculative work must depend upon many factors such as the policy of the practice, the architect's knowledge of the potential client, the nature of the proposed project, the likelihood of its success, the architect's existing commitments, the capacity of the office now and in the foreseeable future, the possible income and profit from the commission if it proceeds, the extent of competition for the work and so on. But regardless of these conditions and the fact that the architect is not to be paid initially, it is important that there should be a formal agreement between the architect and the client defining the extent of the service to be provided by the architect and the commitment of the client to the architect in the event of the project proceeding. In the event of the project proceeding it is usual for the architect to be reimbursed for the initial work undertaken at risk.

6.03 The cost of speculative work undertaken at risk by an architect may be substantial and it is important that the practice should budget for non-fee earning speculative work, as part of its overheads, fixing a limit to the amount it does, and maintaining strict record of time and costs. Where teams of design and other consultants are involved in joint submissions on a speculative basis it is becoming usual for the costs to be shared.

6.04 Architects should be particularly wary of invitations to prepare design solutions in conjunction with competitive fee tenders often on the basis of scant information – only rarely would such an invitation be acceptable. Architects should also endeavour to discover details of others invited to submit fee tenders and refuse to participate in competitive fee bidding in which the number of tenderers or the form of competition is unreasonable.

6.05 As the range of possible sources of design and procurement routes widens it is understandable that clients should increasingly make detailed enquiries about services and charges before making formal appointments. The basis of comparison is often inadequate and architects should endeavour to ensure that clients appreciate the nature of the service being offered and not make an appointment on the basis of fee alone. Potential clients are often unaware of fundamental differences between, say, conventional design services and design by a contractor's organization; more

subtle differences in design services are certain to elude them unless they are carefully explained by the architect. The fee is determined by the service required and the cost of providing that service; unless this is known a fee quotation can be little more than a guess.

6.06 Dissatisfaction with the approach of some large commercial organizations seeking competitive fee bids has resulted in the publication of RIBA's guidance note *Tendering for architects' services*.

7 Collateral warranties

Form of Agreement for
Collateral Warranty

This form is for use where a warranty is to be given to a company providing finance for the proposed development.

This Agreement

is made the_____day of_____19_____

Between

(1) _____
(Insert name of the consultant)

of whose registered office is situate at_____

_____('the Consultant');

(2) _____
(insert name of the consultant's client)

whose registered office is situated at_____

_____('the Client'); and

(3) _____
(insert name of the financier)

whose registered office is at_____

_____('the Company')

Whereas

A   The Company has entered into an agreement ('the Finance Agreement') with the Client for the provision of certain finance in connection with the carrying out of

_____
(insert description of the works)

at_____('the Development')
(insert address of the development)

B   By a contract ('the Appointment') dated_____(insert date of appointment) the Client has appointed the Consultant as architects consulting structural mechanical engineers quantity surveyors in connection with the Development

C   The Client has entered or may enter into a building contract ('the Building Contract')

with_____
(insert name of building contractor or 'a building contractor to be selected by the Client')

for the construction of the Development.

Now it is hereby agreed

In consideration of the payment of ten pounds (£10) by the Company to the Consultant, receipt of which the Consultant hereby acknowledges

1   The Consultant warrants that he she has exercised and will continue to exercise reasonable skill and care in the performance of his her duties to the Client under the Appointment provided that the Consultant shall have no greater liability to the Company by virtue of this Agreement than he she would have had if the Company had been named as the 'Client' under the Appointment.

Delete 2 where the Consultant is the quantity surveyor

2   The Consultant further warrants that he she has exercised and will continue to exercise reasonable skill and care to see that unless authorised by the Client none of the following has been or will be specified by the Consultant for use in the construction of those parts of the Development to which the Appointment relates

(a) high alumina cement in structural elements;

(b) wood wool slabs in permanent formwork to concrete or in structural elements;

(c) calcium chloride in admixtures for use in reinforced concrete;

(d) asbestos products;

(e) aggregates for use in reinforced concrete which do not comply with British Standard Specification 882: 1983, aggregates for use in concrete which do not comply with the provisions of British Standard Specification 8110: 1985.

3   The Company has no authority to issue any direction or instruction to the Consultant in relation to performance of the Consultant's duties under the Appointment unless and until the Company has given notice under Clause 5 or 6.

4   The Company acknowledges that the Client has paid all fees and expenses due and owing to the Consultant under the Appointment up to the date of this Agreement. The Company has no liability to the Consultant in respect of fees and expenses under the Appointment unless and until the Company has given notice under Clauses 5 and 6.

5   The Consultant agrees that in the event of the termination of the Finance Agreement by the Company the Consultant will if so required by notice in writing given by the Company and subject to Clause 7 accept the instructions of the Company or its appointee to the exclusion of the Client in respect of the carrying out and completion of the Development upon the terms and conditions of the Appointment. The Client acknowledges that the Consultant shall be entitled to rely on a notice given to the Consultant by the Company under this Clause 5 as conclusive evidence for the purposes of this Agreement of the termination of the Finance Agreement by the Company.

6   The Consultant further agrees that he she will not without first giving the Company not less than twenty-one days previous notice in writing exercise any right he she may have to terminate the Appointment or to treat the same as having been repudiated by the Client or to discontinue the performance of any duties to be performed by the Consultant pursuant thereto. The Consultant's right to terminate the Appointment or treat the same as having been repudiated or discontinue performance shall cease if within such period of notice and subject to Clause 7 the Company shall give notice in writing to the Consultant requiring the Consultant to accept the instructions of the Company or its appointee to the exclusion of the Client in respect of the carrying out and completion of the Development upon the terms and conditions of the Appointment.

7   Provided always that any notice given by the Company under Clause 5 or 6 shall state that the Company or its appointee accepts liability for payment of the fees payable to the Consultant under the Appointment and for performance of the Client's obligations under the Appointment including payment of any fees outstanding at the date of such notice.

8   The copyright in all drawings reports specifications bills of quantities calculations and other similar documents provided by the Consultant in connection with the Development shall remain vested in the Consultant but the Company and its appointee shall have a licence to copy and use such drawings and other documents and to reproduce the designs contained in them for any purpose related to the Development including but without limitation the construction completion maintenance letting promotion advertisement reinstatement and repair of the Development. The Company and its appointee shall have a licence to copy and use such drawings and other documents for the extension of the Development but such use shall not include a licence to reproduce the design contained in them for any extension of the Development. The Consultant shall not be liable for any such use by the company or its appointee of any drawings and other documents for any purpose other than that for which the same were prepared and provided by the Consultant.

9   The Consultant shall maintain professional indemnity insurance in the amount of not less than

_____pounds (£_____) for any one occurrence or series of occurrences arising out of any one event for a period

of_____years from the date of practical completion of the Development for the purposes of the Building Contract provided always that such insurance is available in the market at commercially reasonable rates. The Consultant shall immediately inform the Company if such insurance ceases to be available at commercially reasonable rates. As and when he she is reasonably requested to do so by the Company or its appointee under Clause 5 or 6 the Consultant shall produce for inspection documentary evidence that his her professional indemnity insurance is being maintained.

10   The Client has agreed to be a party to this Agreement for the purposes of acknowledging that the Consultant shall not be in breach of the Contract by complying with the obligations imposed on him her by Clauses 5 and 6.

11   Any notice to be given by the Consultant hereunder shall be deemed to be duly given if it is delivered by hand at or sent by registered post to the Company at its registered office and any notice to be given by the Company hereunder shall be deemed to be duly given if it is addressed to 'The Senior Partner' and delivered by hand or sent by registered post to the above mentioned address of the Consultant or other business address of the Consultant for the time being and in the case of any such notice the same shall if sent by registered post be deemed to have been received forty-eight hours after being posted.

12   This Agreement may be assigned to one further Company prior to practical completion and within three years hereof subject to the express consent of the Consultant, which shall not be unreasonably withheld, and subject to the payment of all fees due to the Consultant with credit for payments made. No further assignment will be permitted.

As Witness

the hands of the parties the day and year first before written

Consultant   _____

_____

_____

Client   _____

_____

Company   _____

_____

7.01 At the time of appointment the architect may be invited by the client to enter into an agreement with a third party such as a funding institution. These agreements are known as 'collateral warranties' or 'collateral agreement' and occasionally as 'duty of care agreements'. The agreement between the architect and the third party exists in parallel with the agreement between the architect and the client. It makes the architect contractually liable to the third party. In the absence of such an agreement an aggrieved third party can only take an action in tort against the architect; with the agreement in effect an action for breach of contract becomes possible. Actions in tort may be difficult to sustain; the outcome may be uncertain; and since the recent decision of the House of Lords in *D & F Estates* v *Church Commissioners* [1988] 3 WLR 368, damages for consequential economic loss are unlikely. For these and possibly other reasons the use of collateral warranties has become widespread.

7.02 As a consequence of their increasing use and the proliferation of different forms and conditions the RIBA prepared its model *Form of Agreement for Collateral Warranty (for use where a warranty is to be given to a company providing finance)* in 1988. The British Property Federation also prepared its own form. Discussions concerning the use of these particular forms continue: they have yet to gain universal acceptance, and most forms in use have been prepared individually by the legal advisers of various funding institutions. Initially the warranties were devised as means of protecting the interests of funding institutions but their application has now spread into use by other third parties such as tenants who may also have financial interest in a project. In a large and complex project there may be several forms of agreement in force; care needs to be taken to ensure that these forms are consistent and compatible.

7.03 The third party is usually seeking the warranty in order to obtain the potential benefits of the architect's professional indemnity insurance policy. The extent to which the underwriters of the architect's professional indemnity policy would be willing to meet a claim brought under the form of warranty would depend upon the conditions of the policy. It is essential that an architect faced with an invitation to enter into a warranty should consult his broker or insurers before signing the agreement.

7.04 The conditions of a proposed form of agreement between an architect and a third party should be very carefully studied and legal advice should be sought before entering into the agreement. The architect should ensure that the conditions of the agreement do not extend the liability of the architect beyond those of the agreement with the client; that the architect's liability to the third party does not exceed that of the client's own liability to the third party; that the architect is not made liable for the acts of commission or omission of the contractor; and that the architect is not expected to assume responsibility for other independent and directly appointed consultants and specialists.

7.05 The conditions of warranties frequently include the architect's assurance that such deleterious materials as high alumina cement and asbestos will not be used. It is important that the conditions state that the architect cannot be held responsible for the inadvertent or concealed use of these materials by the contractor.

7.06 The implications of warranty conditions concerning the rights of third parties to take over the appointment of the architect in the event of the client's default, subject to the payment of fees due, and the use of drawings and documents need to be very carefully assessed.

7.07 The form of collateral warranty may be 'under hand' or in the nature of a deed executed 'under seal', the period of liability being respectively six years or twelve years. It is not essential that the architect's appointment and the collateral warranty should both be either 'under hand' or 'under seal' but the architect must be aware that a warranty 'under seal' would incur a liability of twelve years, regardless of the six year liability of an 'under hand' architect's appointment. The use of warranties by tenants and others may have other implications for liability periods, the point at which liability periods begin to run, and the possible dates at which causes of action may accrue may be significant. (See Chapters 7 and 8.)

6

Architects' Liability

KIM FRANKLIN*

1 Introduction

1.01 This chapter is about liability to pay damages when things go wrong. 'Damages' are sums of money payable to compensate for harm done. The person seeking compensation may set off his claim for damages against the architect's claim for fees, or he may take the architect to court if he owes the architect no fees or if the damages claimed exceed the amount of any fees owing.

Different sources of liability

1.02 It will be necessary to examine the basic principles of liability for breach of contact, the tort of negligence, and the various statutory extensions to both of these.

2 Liability for breach of contact

Contractual obligations

2.01 The meaning of 'contract' generally has been explained in Chapter 3. Specific features of contracts between architects and their clients have been discussed in Chapter 5. The contract between an architect and his employer, which is the main concern of this chapter, is an arrangement under which an architect makes various binding promises to his employer in return for the employer's promise to pay his fees. The architect's promises are both express and implied. His *express* promises will be to do any number of a range of things, varying from job to job: to survey the site and the subsoil, to produce drawings, to advise on building regulations and planning, to select a contractor to do the works, to recommend a form of contract for the engagement of the builder, to supervise the works, to issue certificates, and so on. The express promises can be made orally in the course of a telephone or other conversation. Alternatively they can be made in writing, for example in correspondence. Rather than discuss or write down all the express promises made by the architect and his client, the RIBA standard terms of engagement set out in the blue book *Architect's Appointment* can be incorporated into the contract if they are expressly referred to. If no reference is made to these terms, however, they cannot be implied into the contract (*Re Sidney Kaye, Eric Firmin & Partners* (1973) 4 BLR 1). The courts also deem the architect to make various *implied* promises supplementary to the express ones: first and foremost, an implied promise to use reasonable care in all he does. Thus the architect undertakes to do a careful survey, to draw up competent plans within a reasonable time, to take care in his selection of a builder, and so on.

*This chapter in its original form in the third edition was written by John R. Spencer, Fellow of Selwyn College, Cambridge.

Breach of contract

2.02 The leading textbook of contract law defines a breach of contract as follows: 'A breach of contract is committed when a party without lawful excuse refuses or fails to perform, performs defectively or incapacitates himself from performing the contract', Treitel (*The Law of Contract* (1987), Steven and Sons, London). So if an architect neglects to do what he undertook to do, or bungles it, he commits a breach of contract which makes him liable to the person who engaged him. His liability may wipe out his claim for fees, but it is not limited to the amount of his fees. Liability for breach of contract includes liability for *consequential loss*, in so far as this is of a reasonably foreseeable type. Consequential loss means loss over and above the money wasted on fees for bad work. For example, if an architect produces incompetent plans which specify inadequate foundations, and the owner of the building later has to spend on underpinning large sums of money greatly in excess of the architect's fees, the cost of underpinning may be recoverable as damages for consequential loss.

The level of an architect's contractual duties

2.03 In broad terms, contractual duties are of two main types: duties of care, and strict duties (*alias* duties of result). A duty of care is a duty to make reasonable efforts to produce the desired result. A strict duty is a guarantee that the desired result will be produced, making the promiser liable if the result is not obtained, even if the failure to produce it cannot be shown to be his fault. A builder's contractual duties to his employer are strict duties in a number of respects: for example, he guarantees the quality of his materials, and if it is a house he is building, that it will be fit for habitation when completed. An architect's duties, on the other hand, are generally duties of care, not duties of result: he is contractually liable only if he failed to take reasonable care. His liability may, however, be strict in two situations.

Contractual liability for delegates

2.04 The first is if he delegates parts of his work to someone else. If he does so, he guarantees due care on the part of the delegatee. This means that if an architect engages an independent structural engineer to do part of his measurements and calculations, the architect is liable for the consequences of the structural engineer's carelessness, even though the architect may not have been careless in his choice or supervision of the engineer. The architect's contractual duty is not merely a duty of care, but a duty to ensure that care is taken. (It should be stressed, however, that this principle only applies to the case where the architect has delegated *his* work. It does not make him liable for absence of

due care on the part of the builder who is carrying out the plans: the builder is not doing the architect's job.)

Where someone is hired to solve a particular problem

2.05 The second case where liability may be strict is if an architect – or more usually a specialist engineer – is brought in to solve a particular problem. For example, in *Greaves (Construction) Ltd* v *Baynham Meikle* [1975] 3 All ER 99, a firm of consultant structural engineers was called in to design a warehouse, the first floor of which could withstand the weight of fork-lift trucks carrying heavy drums of oil. The floor proved inadequate. The engineers were held not merely to have assumed a duty of care, but to have guaranteed their work would do what was required. It is not always easy to say whether a duty of result has been assumed in the absence of an express term in the contract covering the matter. In an Australian case, it was held that an architect who was engaged to plan a building which could be erected for a specified figure had undertaken a duty of care, not a duty of result: if he had not been careless, he was not liable if the building cost more to erect (*Nemer* v *Whitford* (1982) 31 SASR 475). To avoid uncertainty about the level of duty, it is therefore wise to specify the level of duty at the outset.

Exclusion of liability by contract

2.06 As has just been mentioned, the terms of an architect's contract can raise his duty from a duty of care to a duty of result. It was once equally possible for express terms in the contract to lower his duties as well, even to the extent of absolving him from all duty to take reasonable care. Since the Unfair Contract Terms Act 1977, however, this has become largely impossible, because this Act largely invalidates attempts to exclude 'business liability' for negligence. Contractual terms which purport to exclude liability for negligence in the business context are completely invalid in so far as they exclude liability for negligence causing personal injury or death; where other loss is concerned, such clauses are only valid to the extent that the person relying on them can convince the court that they are fair and reasonable according to criteria set out in the Act: the relative bargaining strength of the parties, whether the client received some benefit in return for agreement to this term, how prominently the term was drawn to his attention, etc.

Liability in the tort of negligence

2.07 The general nature of tortious liability has already been explained (Chapter 4). The tort of negligence imposes a broadly based liability on those who cause foreseeable harm to others by their negligent acts and, sometimes, negligent omissions as well. Such liability is for careless conduct in general, and does not depend on the existence of any contract. It may, however, arise in the course of performing a contract; for example, a service engineer who has a contract

with a landlord to service a lift in a block of flats will be liable in the tort of negligence to a passenger in the lift who is injured when the engineer negligently reassembles the mechanism so that the lift plunges to the bottom of the shaft. Whereas contractural liability is owed exclusively to the other party to the contract – in the case of an architect, his client – tortious liability makes the contracting party liable to other people as well. Herein lies its importance and its potential for growth: in recent years the courts have steadily increased the range of people who can sue architects, builders, building inspectors, and others concerned in construction work in the tort of negligence for the careless performance of their contractual obligations. Whether an architect is liable to his client in tort for negligence as well as for breach of contract is examined later (para 4.05).

3 Liability for carelessness in contract and in tort

Carelessness – the meaning of 'reasonable care'

3.01 Both the law of contract and the tort of negligence require an architect to exercise reasonable care. So the question at once arises: What is reasonable care? In the case of an ordinary citizen who is sued for negligence in the course of performing some everyday act, such as driving a car or running his home so as to avoid accidents to visitors, the standard of care is the standard of the 'reasonable man' – often popularly styled 'the man on the Clapham omnibus'. Where the case concerns a professional man with some special skill or comptence, it is obviously futile to apply the standard of the man on the Clapham omnibus, because the latter lacks the special skill. In cases of professional negligence, the standard is that of the ordinary skilled man exercising and professing to have that special skill. As Lord Tindall said in *Lanphier* v *Phipos* (1838) 8 C & P 475:

> 'Every person who enters into a learned profession undertakes to bring to the exercise of it a reasonable degree of care and skill. He does not undertake, if he is an attorney, that at all events you shall gain your case, nor does a surgeon undertake that he will perform a cure; nor does he undertake to use the highest possible skill. There may be persons who have higher education and greater advantages than he has, but he undertakes to bring a fair, reasonable and competent degree of skill.'

The question whether the architect has used a reasonable and proper amount of care and skill is one of fact, and it appears to rest on the consideration whether other persons following the same profession, and being men of experience and skill, would or would not have acted in the same way as the architect in question. Ultimately, the question whether the architect has failed to exercise due care depends on all the facts in evidence in the case, and there is a limit to the guidance that can be obtained from previous court decisions on possibly different facts. Some guidance can certainly be gleaned from reported decisions, and some help may be gained from the cases in the following sections, in which one of the points at issue was sometimes whether reasonable care had been taken. But no one should lose sight of the real question, which is 'Would a reasonable architect have done this?', not 'Is there a reported case a bit like this one?'

The scope of the duty of care owed to the client in contract

3.02 It is, however, a question of law rather than a question of fact what aspects of an architect's work are capable of giving rise to liability if he carries them out without reasonable care as discussed in the last paragraph. Can he be liable for negligent legal advice? Can he be liable for negligently certifying work which has not been properly

done? These are questions of law, and the answer to them is 'yes'. As will appear, there are nowadays few, if any, aspects of an architect's work for which he cannot in principle be held liable, to his client at least, if he fails to take reasonable care. In the examples that follow, it is the architect's contractual liability to his client which is under consideration; how far he is also liable in the tort of negligence to other people as well is discussed later (paras 3.06–3.09).

Negligent surveys

3.03 An architect can be held liable for failing to make an adequate examination of the site for a building. Particular care should be taken in all matters relating to foundations. Extensive tests may be required, particularly if the ground is made up or gives rise to other difficulties. In *Eames London Estates Ltd v North Hertfordshire DC* (1981) 259 EG 491 the foundations of an industrial building built on made up ground proved inadequate. Extensive repairs were required. The architect was found to be negligent for specifying the loading for piers without ascertaining for himself the ground's bearing capacity and for ignoring a query as to the adequacy of the excavations for foundations raised at the time. If the job of ascertaining the nature of the site is beyond the architect then he should advise the client to engage a specialist to make the necessary investigations.

The architect must take account not only of subsoil but also of other things, such as the effect of planting or felling trees, the rights of neighbours or planning restrictions, which may affect the building. In *Re St Thomas a Becket, Framfield* [1989] 1 WLR 689, architects were blamed for supervising works to the church without ascertaining whether there was ecclesiastical authority for the execution of those works before they were begun. If such enquiries have not been made, the architect would be wise to warn the client.

Incompetent design

3.04 An architect may be liable to the client if errors or omissions are made in the plans, drawings or specification. Liability cannot be escaped on the grounds that the design was delegated to another. If the design is outside of the expertise of the architect he should inform the client. The architect is under a continuing duty to check the design up to completion of the works. Design includes the choice of materials for the building, its 'buildability' and its 'supervisability'.

Inadequate supervision

3.05 The architect is obliged to administer and supervise the works to ensure that the standard is that originally contemplated. Reasonable supervision does not require the architect to stand over the contractor and monitor every detail. He is, however, expected to oversee the principal parts of the works, especially if they are subsequently to be hidden from view, and other aspects sufficient to certify that the works have been executed in accordance with the contract.

Negligent financial advice

3.06 An architect can also be liable if he causes his client damage by negligent advice on likely building costs. In *Nye Saunders & Partners v Bristow* AE (1987) BLR 92 CA the architects were asked to estimate the cost of renovating a country house owned by the successful helicopter millionaire, within a budget of £250,000. In February 1974 the architects gave an estimate of £238,000. In August the estimate was revised and a new figure of £440,000 given. Bristow, saying that he had been misled, terminated the architects' engagement and refused to pay fees totalling £15,000. The architects were found to be negligent for failing to point out that the estimate was based on prices current in February during a time of very high inflation. Similarly in *Aubrey Jacobus & Partners v Gerrard* (1981) 984 BLR 37 the court held that if an architect bases his estimate on current building costs and makes it plain that he has done so, that ought to be sufficient.

Negligent legal advice

3.07 Architects are expected to have some knowledge of the law as it affects their business, and they can be liable for the consequences to their client if they do not. For example, a surveyor was engaged by a client to negotiate a claim for compensation from the local authority for land belonging to the client which had been compulsorily purchased. A recent decision of the Court of Appeal, which was quite well publicized, had condemned the basis upon which compensation had previously been calculated, and substituted a new basis more favourable to the client. The surveyor was held liable when, in ignorance of the decision, he negotiated a low figure calculated on the old rules (*Weedon v Hindwood Clarke and Esplin* (1974) 234 EG 121). But an architect is not required to have the deep legal knowledge of a QC who is a specialist in planning law, and he is not negligent if he accepts the advice of the planning department of his local authority in so far as this is not obviously wrong. Thus where an architect was told by the local planning department that an Office Development Permit was needed only if the floor area of the office part of the proposed development exceeded the specified size, and that the floor area of ancillary buildings could be disregarded for those purposes – a view of the law which was condemned as incorrect by the judge in the law suit which followed – he was not negligent to act on this advice at the time (*B. L. Holdings Ltd v Robert J. Wood & Partners* (1979) 12 BLR 3).

Negligence in certifying payments

3.08 When an architect certifies that payments are due under a building contract, he often has to judge between the claims of the builder and the complaints of the client. Because of this, it was formerly held that he was, when issuing certificates, in the same position as an arbitrator or a judge – immune from all liability for negligence on grounds of public policy. This view was overturned by the House of Lords in *Sutcliffe v Thackrah* (1974) AC 727, holding that the client can sue the architect if he negligently overcertifies. Before the case reached the House of Lords, Judge Stabb QC considered the proper approach to be adopted by an architect in issuing interim certificates ((1971) 18 BLR 149). Thus, although a prolonged or detailed inspection at an interim stage is impractical, more than a glance round is expected. If the contract provides for certificates to give the valuation of work properly executed, the architect should satisfy himself as to the quality of the work before requiring the employer to make payment in respect of it. Where a quantity surveyor is also engaged, the architect should keep him informed of any defective work so that it can be excluded from interim valuations. In *Arenson v Arenson* [1977] AC 405, the House of Lords suggested that just as an architect was liable to the employer if he negligently over certified, he may be liable to the contractor if he negligently certified that less money was payable than was in fact due and thereby starved the contractor of money. Some doubt has been cast on this view by the case of *Pacific Associates v Baxter* (1988) 44 BLR 33 (see para 3.12).

The scope of the architect's liability in the tort of negligence

Personal injuries

3.09 There is no doubt that an architect may be liable for negligence which causes foreseeable personal injury to any foreseeable victim. This was established in *Clay v A. J.*

Crump & Sons Ltd [1964] 1 QB 533. An architect supervising demolition and rebuilding instructed the demolition contractor to leave temporarily standing a wall which closed off one boundary to the site. He accepted the demolition contractor's word that the wall was safe, and did not check himself, although he visited the site. Had he looked, he would have seen that it was tottering unstably above a 6ft trench cut under its foundations. The architect, together with the demolition contractor and the builder, was held liable when the wall collapsed and injured one of the builder's men. It should be remembered when considering whether an architect was negligent, however, that his main function is to see that his client gets value for money, and that the safety of the builder's employees is mainly a matter for the builder himself. Thus an architect is not negligent if, unlike the architect in *Clay* v *Crump*, he orders something to be done which involves danger only if it is done the wrong way. Thus an architect was not negligent when he ordered a chase to be cut in a wall, and the builder chose to do it without shoring the wall up, so that it fell and injured a workman (*Clayton* v *Woodman & Son Ltd* [1962] 1 WLR 585).

Liability to subsequent purchasers for defects in the building

3.10 An architect may be liable to subsequent purchasers of a building for defects arising out of his design or supervision of its construction. The law of negligence in this area has been the subject of significant change over the last decade or so. This change has been likened both to a rising tide followed by a marked ebb and a military advance followed by an orderly retreat dissolving into a chaotic rout (Garland J, 24 February 1989 Seminar for Official Referees Business and Richard Fernyhough QC, lecture 1988). Cases such as *Dutton* v *Bognore Regis UDC* [1972] 1 QB 373 and *Anns* v *Merton BC* [1978] AC 728 considerably widened the circumstances in which purchasers of properties, who were not party to any contract with the contractors or construction professionals, could nevertheless claim against them in tort if the building proved defective: thus the tide of negligence rose. Recently, however, the circumstances in which contractors and professionals can be liable for such defects have been restricted by cases such as *Peabody Donation Func* v *Sir Lindsay Parkinson* [1985] 1 AC 210, *D & F Estates* v *Church Commissioners* [1989] 1 AC 177; and the law of negligence has retreated.

3.11 One of the more important restrictions relates to the difference between actual physical damage to a building such as cracking, flooding or decay and the cost, called economic loss, of repairing defects that have not caused any damage. In *London Congregational Union* v *Harriss* [1985] 1 All ER 335, the Court of Appeal held that no claim could arise in negligence until there was actual physical damage to the building. In that case the design of the drains was defective and it was only a matter of time before the church flooded. Even so, the church was unable to recover the cost of replacing the drains before such damage occurred as it was economic loss. As a result of the *D & F Estates* case the scope for claims for negligence has been reduced further. The House of Lords held that if the damage complained of was actual physical damage to the very item the architect was asked to design, for example a garden wall, then the cost of repairing that damage was irrecoverable as it was economic loss. It was only if the damaged state of the garden wall had caused injury or damaged other property, for example by falling on the gardener and lawnmower, that damages for negligence could be recovered. The House of Lords said, however, that a garden wall was a single structure: a building could be considered to be a complex structure. An action for negligence may be brought if one element of the complex structure was defective and in turn caused actual physical damage to another element. In *Portsea Island Co-operative* v

Michael Brasier [1989] CILL 520, architects designed and supervised the construction of a supermarket. Brickslips started to fall off the walls and they had to be removed to make the building safe to customers and staff. The court considered that although the cost of removing the brickslips was economic loss it was recoverable from the architects since it was necessary to make the walls safe. Portsea Co-op would not be able to recover the cost of replacing the cladding to the walls.

Another restriction to a purchaser's ability to sue for negligence was the courts' insistence that the damage complained of must have occurred during the ownership of the plaintiff. In the case of *Perry* v *Tendring DC* [1984] 3 Con LR, the judge held that if an owner suffers damage to his property without being aware of it – if, for example, the foundations settle, and the owner sells the property before significant cracks develop – the subsequent owner would be precluded from suing in negligence any person concerned in the building's construction unless the original owner's right to sue were assigned to the new owner. This problem area of the law has been simplified somewhat by the Latent Damage Act 1986 and now in certain circumstances a subsequent purchaser gains the right to sue in respect of any negligence to which the damage to the property is attributable. If the subsequent purchaser had reason to suspect that the foundations were inadequate, and turned down the opportunity to have a survey which would have revealed the troubles to come, he will be regarded by the courts as the author of his own misfortunes and thereby disentitled to sue (*Stewart* v *East Cambridgeshire District Council* (1979) 252 EG 1105).

In the ordinary course of things, however, if a purchaser fails to have a full structural survey carried out on premises that subsequently prove defective, such omission may be seen to contribute to the purchaser's losses only, and then not to any great degree. Further, the House of Lords in *Smith* v *Bush* and *Harris Wyre Forest DC* [1989] 2 WLR 790 held that a valuer instructed by, for example, a building society, to carry out a valuation of a modest house for the purpose of deciding whether to grant a mortgage, could be liable to the purchaser if he were negligent in his survey of the house, especially if he knew that the purchaser would rely upon his valuation without an independent survey.

Liability to the builder for economic loss

3.12 It was once the case that there could be no liability in the tort of negligence for misrepresentation causing purely economic loss; the only person who could sue for such negligent misrepresentation was the other party to a contract – that is to say, the architect's client, not the builder. Then in *Hedley Byrne & Co Ltd* v *Heller & Partners Ltd* [1964] AC 465, the House of Lords decided that the author of a negligent misrepresentation could in principle be liable in tort to someone with whom he had no contractual relations, provided that some 'special relationship' existed between them. This opened up the possibility of the courts finding such a 'special relationship' between an architect and the builder, with resulting liability if the architect's negligent advice caused the builder economic loss. The imposition of such liability was considered in *Pacific Associates* v *Baxter* (1988) 44 BLR 33. In that case contractors entered into a contract with the Ruler of Dubai for the dredging of a lagoon in the Persian Gulf. The work was delayed and the contractors claimed additional expenses. Their claim was rejected by the engineers. When the contractors referred their claim to arbitration, the Ruler paid them £10m in settlement. The contractors sued the engineers for £45m being the unrecovered balance of their claim against the Ruler. The Court of Appeal held that the engineers were not liable to the contractors because the contractors had entered into a contract with the Ruler which excluded liability on the part of the engineers and provided for disputes to be resolved by arbitration. Because of these special factors it is far from

clear whether this case resolves the question of the liability of the certifier, be he architect or engineer, to the contractor in all cases.

4 Liability in contract and in a tort compared and contrasted

4.01 Liability in contract is narrower than liability in tort in one most important respect: it exists only towards the other party to the contract. English law recognizes the doctrine of *privity of contract*, which means that the rights and duties arising under a contract are limited to the contracting parties. Thus where an architect is engaged by a client, only the client can sue the architect for breach of contract; 'strangers to the contract' must base their claim in tort. By way of exception to privity of contract, it is sometimes possible for the benefit of a contract to be *assigned*; that is to say, various legal formalities are performed by which someone other than the original contracting party is substituted as the recipient of the benefits which the other party is bound to confer. Besides the need for appropriate legal formalities to make it effective, there are important limits on assignment. Thus there can be no valid assignment of a right to personal services, which means that the client may not without the architect's consent require him to carry on supervising the site for some other employer. It used to be said that there can be no valid assignment of a right to sue for damages for a breach of contract which has already occurred; thus a client could not, on selling a complete but defective house, assign to the purchaser his claims for breach of contract against the architect. However, a recent Court of Appeal decision indicates that where property is sold, a right to claim damages in respect of that property may now be assigned with it (*Trendtex Trading Corporation* v *Crèdit Suisse* [1980] 3 All ER 721).

4.02 Contractual liability, although narrower than tort liability in that it lies in favour of fewer persons, is usually more stringent when it does arise. As we have seen, an architect sometimes by contract assumes a duty higher than a duty to take reasonable care: first, he may sometimes guarantee his solution to a problem, and second, in contract he not only undertakes to take reasonable care himself, but also guarantees reasonable care by those to whom he delegates performance of parts of the work (para 2.04). In tort, an employer is vicariously liable as well, but for the negligent acts of a narrower range of people. In tort, he is liable only for the acts of those whom the law quaintly terms his 'servants' – who are, by and large, his full-time salaried employees. In contract, on the other hand, he assumes responsibility not only for the negligence of his employees, but also for that of 'independent contractors' – consultants and suchlike who are independent of his business, whom he calls in at a fee to do part of what he has undertaken to his client to do.

4.03 Contractual liability is also more stringent than liability in tort as economic loss can be recovered in claims in contract whereas claims in tort, with the exception of claims for negligent misrepresentation resulting in economic loss, require actual physical damage to the person or property of the plaintiff.

4.04 There is, however, one respect in which contractual liability is less stringent than liability in tort, which is that the rules about the time within which an action must be brought work more favourably to the defendant in contract claims than in tort.

4.05 From what has been said, it is clear that a claim in contract normally has, from the plaintiff's point of view, a number of advantages over a claim in tort, but there are certain situations in which a claim in tort is stronger. This raises a difficult question: Can the architect's client, to whom the architect is liable in contract, ignore the contract and base his claim on the tort of negligence if in the circumstances of the particular case the rules of tortious liability would suit him better? This point has been considerably affected by the retreat of the laws of negligence referred to above. The answer used to be 'yes', as the scope for bringing claims in negligence was broadened. Recent decisions of the courts have re-established the dominant role of the contract. In *Tai Hing Cotton Mill Ltd* v *Liu Chong Hing Bank Ltd* [1986] 1 AC 80, the House of Lords said that the law was not to search for a liability in negligence where the parties were in a contractual relationship and that the parties' obligations in negligence cannot be any greater than those to be found in their contract. Subsequently in *Greater Nottingham Co-operative Society* v *Cementation Ltd* [1988] 3 WLR 396, the Court of Appeal held that the existence of a direct but limited contract was inconsistent with any assumption of responsibility beyond that which was expressly undertaken by that contract. These decisions indicate that where the parties have entered into a contract, it will be the express and implied terms of that contract which set the boundaries of any liability for negligence. If the law of negligence continues in its retreat the position may be that where there is a contract there can be no liability in tort.

5 Statutory liability

The Defective Premises Act 1972, section 1

5.01 This provides:

'A person taking on work for or in connection with the provision of a swelling (whether the dwelling is provided by the erection or by the conversion or enlargement of a building) owes a duty –
(a) If the dwelling is provided to the order of any person, to that person; and
(b) without prejudice to paragraph (a) above, to every person who acquires an interest (whether legal or equitable) in the dwelling:
to see that the work which he takes on is done in a workmanlike or, as the case may be, professional manner, with proper materials and so that as regards that work the dwelling will be fit for habitation when completed.'

The scope of the duty

5.02 Architects undoubtedly count as persons 'taking on work for or in connection with the provision of a dwelling', although builders and their sub-contractors are the persons whom Parliament mainly had in mind. Under this statute, an architect owes a duty not merely to take reasonable care, but also '*to see that the work which he takes on is done*' in a careful manner. The level of his duty is thus like that of his duty in contract: he must take care himself, and he also must guarantee care is taken by those to whom he delegates parts of his work. The duty is elaborated in subsections 2 and 3 in ways more relevant to builders than to architects. These subsections say that when a person takes on work consisting of following instructions furnished by another, he fulfils his duty under the Act in so far as he carries the instructions out; however, a person in this position may incur liability for failure to warn of defects in those instructions, presumably if he spots some obvious defect in the instructions which he realizes no one else has noticed, and says nothing about it. And a person does not escape liability as one who is merely carrying out instructions if it was he who originally suggested what he should be instructed to do. The duty under the Act is owed to the person to whose order the dwelling is provided, and to every other person 'who acquires an interest (whether legal or equitable) in the dwelling'. This means that the duty

runs with the land in favour of subsequent owners, landlords, tenants, and mortgagees.

Limitations on the duty – relationship with duties in contract and tort

5.03 In a number of ways, the duty imposed by the Defective Premises Act 1972, section 1 is narrow. It applies only to *dwellings*; thus there is no liability under these provisions for defective work on factories, offices, and warehouses. The duties it creates are owed solely to those to whom the statute says it is owed. Section 2 excludes actions for breach of the duty created by section 1 in respect of houses covered by an 'approved scheme'. The scheme principally envisaged by this section was the 10 year protection scheme of the National House Building Council. Importantly however, the last NHBC scheme to be approved was their 1979 scheme. The 1985 scheme is not approved. Thus owners of houses covered by this and subsequent schemes can still claim against builders and construction professionals under section 1.

Until recently the Defective Premises Act was not relied upon by owners of defective homes because the duties imposed by the courts on the builders and construction professionals in contract and tort completely outflanked those created by Parliament by statute. As a result of the retreat of the law of negligence, however, the Defective Premises Act has regained prominence. In the *D & F Estates* case the House of Lords made particular reference to this Act. As a result plaintiffs are likely to seize upon its provisions in an attempt to obtain a remedy now denied them by law of negligence.

Liability for breach of the Building Regulations

5.04 Section 38 of the Building Act 1984 says that a breach of duty imposed by the Building Regulations, shall so far as it causes damage, be actionable except where the regulations say otherwise. The Act elsewhere says that this provision shall come into force when the Secretary of State – meaning in practice the Department of the Environment – shall determine. It has not been brought into force. In fact, it is further from being in force now than when it was first enacted, because it has been brought into force so far as was needed to empower the Minister to make new Building Regulations, for breach of which civil liability will be excluded, and the Department of the Environment says that it has no plans to make the section effective.

The Supply of Goods and Services Act 1982

5.05 Part II of the Act relates to contracts for the supply of services and this includes services provided by an architect for an employer. Section 13 says that in such a contract there is an implied term that the architect will carry out the service with reasonable skill and care. Section 14 says that if no time has been fixed by the contract in which the service is to be carried out, there is an implied term that the architect will carry it out in a reasonable time.

6 Measure of damages

Principles of calculation

6.01 The basis of calculating damages is theoretically different in contract and in tort. In contract, damages are supposed to put the plaintiff in the position he would have been in if the defendant had kept his promise. In tort, damages are supposed to put the plaintiff in the position he would have been in if the tortious act had never taken place. Looked at another way, the fundamental principle governing the measure of damages is that the plaintiff must be put so far as money can do it in the position he would have occupied if the architect had properly discharged his duty. For some time

these different principles made little difference to the damages awarded in the usual sort of case against architects, that is, in which someone complains that because of the architect's lack of reasonable care his building is defective. Whether the claim was brought in contract or tort the damages recovered would be the cost of rectifying the defects in the building. Once again, however, the recent changes in the law of negligence and especially the *D & F Estates* case, have emphasized the difference between the two types of claim. If, in breach of contract, an architect designs a building that is defective, the plaintiff can recover the cost of rectifying all those defects resulting from the defective design: that is, putting the building into the condition it would have been in had the architect discharged his duty. If the plaintiff brings his claim in negligence, however, he must show that there is actual physical damage, not merely defects and he must show that damage was caused by one part to another part of a complex structure. Thus, if there is no damage, or the damage is to a simple structure or one part of a complex structure only he cannot recover. An exception was made in the *Portsea Co-op* case for the cost incurred in making a dangerous wall safe by removing the defective brickslips. Similar principles would apply to the calculation of damages under the Defective Premises Act 1972, section 1, except that as the duty created under this section applies only to dwellings, losses of commercial rents will not be recoverable. Of course, a plaintiff who can sue a defendant relying on more than one cause of action gets only one set of damages. Damages can also be recovered for inconvenience, distress and annoyance, if for example, the plaintiff has been kept out his house whilst building works take much longer than they should have, or whilst extensive remedial works are executed. Other consequential losses are only recoverable in so far as they were reasonably foreseeable.

Where the damage is too remote

6.02 Two important limitations on the extent of damages should be noted. The first is that the plaintiff is under a *duty to mitigate his loss*. This means that he must behave reasonably to keep the damage as small as possible, and if he fails to do this, he cannot recover for the loss he could have avoided. Thus someone who complains of a defective roof on his house must get it mended as soon as possible. He is not allowed to let the rain wreck his ceilings and his furniture while he sues the architect or builder, and then add the cost of these to the bill. The second is that a defendant is not liable to pay for damage of a kind which is not a reasonably foreseeable consequence of his negligence. Thus if a businessman lost the chance of an enormously profitable contract with an Arab oil sheik as the unforeseeable consequence of the closure of his office on the vital day because of a structural defect, he could not sue for that loss. However, if the general *type* of damage is foreseeable, the defendant is liable even if the *extent* of the damage is not. Thus in one case, an architect negligently failed to take account of the effect of the removal of some fruit trees on the behaviour of the clay subsoil when he calculated the depth of the foundations of a block of flats. Some slight damage from 'heave' was a foreseeable result. Unforeseeably, a row of mature elms was felled nearby as well, and the damage from heave – nearly all of which would have been prevented by adequate foundations – was far worse than could have been anticipated. The architect was held liable to the full extent of the damage (*Acrecrest Ltd* v *W. S. Hattrell & Partners* (1979) 252 EG 1107).

The date of assessment

6.03 Formerly, the plaintiff was awarded the cost of reinstatement at the time when the damage occurred. In times of inflation and rising building costs, this rule was very good for defendants who were builders or architects: the

longer they could avoid payment, the less in real terms they had to pay. In *Dodd Properties (Kent) Ltd* v *Canterbury City Council* [1980] 1 All ER 928, this rule was reversed. The defendant damaged the plaintiff's property in 1970; he disputed liability, and was eventually held liable at a trial in 1978. The Court of Appeal held the plaintiff was entitled to the cost of repairs at the time when he could first reasonably have been expected to do them. As it would have caused the plaintiff financial problems to have done the repairs out of his own pocket, and he would not have bothered to do them at all unless the defendant was made to pay for them, the plaintiff was quite reasonable to wait until 1978 before he did the repairs, and was entitled to their cost at that time.

Apportionment

6.04 Large building projects involve many different parties with different functions and skills. Damage or defects in the building may be the result of breaches of duty by more than one participant. Similarly, several parties may be responsible for the same defects but to a different extent. For example, the contractor may be in breach of contract for executing bad workmanship and the architect liable for failing to supervise the works properly and notice the contractor's breach. In such cases responsibility may be apportioned between the various defendants. In *Equitable Debenture Assets Corpn* v *Moss* [1984] 2 Con LR 1 the plaintiff's claim related to defective design of curtain walling and bad workmanship to the parapet walling. The specialist design sub-contractors were held 75% liable for the curtain walling and the architects 25%. The apportionment in respect of the parapet walling was 80% to the subcontractors, 15% to the main contractors and 5% to the architects.

7 When liability is barred by lapse of time

Limitation Act 1980

7.01 Section 2 of this Act provides that certain types of action, of which claims against architects and builders for negligence are one, shall not be brought 'after the expiration of six years from the date on which the cause of action accrued'. The vital question is: When does a cause of action 'accrue'? In general, a cause of action accrues when facts first exist upon which the plaintiff has the right to sue. When this is depends on whether the claim is based on a breach of contract or on tort. A person can first sue for a breach of contract when the breach of contract occurs; he does not have to wait until he suffers damage as a result. In the case of an architect who is sued for a negligent breach of contract, he can be sued from when he acts negligently: if he fails adequately to supervise the laying of drains or foundations, he can be sued then and there. So six years from then, the cause of action against him in contract expires. It matters not that, during those six years, his client was unaware of the negligence because no flooding or cracking had yet occurred – unless, exceptionally, the architect had resorted to fraud to prevent his negligence being discovered. If the flooding or cracking occurs after the six years from the negligent supervision, as far as the law of contract is concerned, that is just the client's bad luck. In tort, on the other hand, no one can be sued until damage is suffered, which means that the cause of action does not accrue until then. Thus in tort, time runs, in the case of a

defective building, from when the damage to it occurs. In *Pirelli General Cable Works* v *Oscar Faber* [1983] AC 1 the House of Lords ruled that the limitation period ran from the date when the damage occurred. In that case, a factory chimney had cracked at the top because of negligent design, the cracks not being reasonably discoverable until some two years after they had occurred. The House of Lords ruled that time ran from when the cracks happened, which meant that the defence of limitation succeeded. The time limit within which actions in negligence for defective buildings can be brought have been revised by the Latent Damage Act 1986. Under that Act negligence claims become barred either six years from the date when damage occurred, or three years from the date when the plaintiff discovered the damage, whichever is the later. Actions in either case are subject to a 'long stop' of fifteen years from the date of the negligence complained of.

7.02 It has already been mentioned that a plaintiff who contracted with an architect is normally at liberty to sue him in tort rather than in contract in order to gain the benefit of the more extended limitation period. He may not always be able to do this, however. In *William Hill Organisation* v *Bernard Sunley & Sons Ltd* (1983) 22 BLR 1 an owner sued a builder with whom he had contracted to fix decorative cladding to a wall, which was now falling off. The contractual limitation had expired, so he tried to sue in tort for negligence. He failed. The builder's method of fixing could only be said to have been negligent in so far as he had disregarded a term in the contract expressly requiring him to use a different method, and the Court of Appeal held that where negligence could only be shown by reference to the terms of the contract, the plaintiff was bound by the contractual period of limitation.

Defective Premises Act 1972 section 1 – limitation period

7.03 According to section 1(5):

'Any cause of action in respect of a breach of duty imposed by this section shall be deemed . . . to have accrued at the time when the dwelling was completed, but if after that time a person who has done work for or in connection with the provision of the dwelling does further work to rectify the work he has already done, any such cause of action in respect of that the further work shall be deemed . . . to have accrued at the time the further work was finished'.

Thus the period for bringing claims is, by and large, six years from the completion of the house.

The issue of a writ

7.04 A claim is not statute barred if a law suit is begun within the limitation period; that is to say, if the plaintiff issues a writ against the defendant within that time. It should be noticed, however, that the Courts and Legal Services Bill, if enacted in the terms of its published draft, will provide that a writ must be *served*, as opposed to merely *issued*, within the limitation period. The claim is not time barred because the case is not finally tried within the limitation period. Once begun, actions can drag on for years. A procedure exists, however, whereby the defendant can have an action struck out if, after starting it, the plaintiff unreasonably fails to get on with it.

7

English Land Law

CHARLES HARPUM*

1 Conveyancing

1.01 This study is intended to give an impression of those aspects of land law that are relevant to architects, either in their professional capacity as they design buildings for clients, or in their personal capacity as tenants of their offices. It is necessary to distinguish land law as such from conveyancing. Land law is concerned with the rights in or over land which a landowner has and the rights which others have over his land. The law of conveyancing is concerned with the creation and transfer of rights in and over land, usually, but not necessarily, pursuant to a contract. An architect need not concern himself with the intricacies of conveyancing. A certain amount must, however, be said about title to land in England and the methods that exist to protect rights in and over land.

*In the first edition, this chapter was written by George Stringer. In the second edition, it was revised by Evelyn Freeth.

1.02 Many of the concepts that underlie English land law are ancient, and this is reflected in much of the curious terminology which is associated with the subject. The law was greatly simplified and restructured in 1925 by a series of important statutes. These form the foundation of the modern law.

1.03 Title to land in England is either unregistered or registered. In time all land will be registered, and unregistered conveyancing will disappear. Unregistered conveyancing, which may be described as 'title deed' conveyancing, is the traditional method. A landowner will be either a freeholder or a leaseholder. On the sale of the freehold, or upon an assignment of a lease, the vendor's proof of title is found in the title deeds to the property, and the purchaser's solicitor will investigate these title deeds to satisfy himself

that the vendor does indeed have title to the land. Until 1969, it was necessary for the purchaser's solicitor to peruse all dealings with the land back to the first conveyance of it more than 30 years old. That conveyance is known as 'the root of title'. Since 1969 it has been necessary to go back only to the first root of title that is more than 15 years old (Law of Property Act 1969, section 23).

1.04 Rights over unregistered land are either 'legal. or 'equitable'. It is unnecessary to explain why some rights are legal and some equitable. The distinction is historical in origin, but now as a result of statutory intervention, the dichotomy is governed largely by considerations of conveyancing expediency. Legal estates and rights are binding on all the world, regardless of whether a purchaser of land knows of them or not. The only legal *estates* that can now exist are freeholds and leaseholds. Most easements and many mortgages are legal rights. Equitable rights, by contrast, are good against all the world except a purchaser in good faith of a legal estate or interest in land for value and without notice of the right. Notice is actual, constructive, or imputed:

1. A purchase has *actual notice* of those encumbrances of which he is aware, and of what are called 'land charges' (see para 1.05).
2. A purchaser has *constructive notice* of those matters which would have come to his attention if he had made those enquiries which a reasonable purchaser would have made. A reasonable purchaser will do two things: (a) inspect the title deeds back to a good root of title, and (b) inspect the land itself, making enquiries, for example, of any person whom he finds in occupation of it.
3. A purchaser has *imputed notice* of all those matters which his agent (such as his solicitor) knows or discovers while acting as agent in that transaction, or which the agent ought reasonably to have discovered.

1.05 Many equitable encumbrances on land are registrable at the Land Registry as land charges under the Land Charges Act 1972 (replacing the Land Charges Act 1925). Some of the most important from an architect's point of view are:

1. Estate contracts, i.e. contracts for the sale of land or of any interest in land, including contracts to grant leases, options to purchase (i.e. a standing offer by a landowner to sell), and rights of pre-emption (i.e. rights of first refusal).
2. Restrictive covenants (fully explained in para 4.01), except those found in a lease and those entered into before 1926.
3. Certain types of easement, such as those not granted by deed or those which endure only for the life of a given person.

Registration of such an encumbrance constitutes actual notice of it to all persons for all purposes. If the encumbrance is registrable but not registered, it will be void against a purchaser of the land regardless of whether he knows of it. This will be so even if the sum paid by the purchaser is only a fraction of the true value of the property (*Midland Bank Trust Co Ltd* v *Green* [1981] Ac 513). Land charge registration suffers from a serious defect: registration of the charge is not made against the land itself, but against the name of the landowner for the time being. In order to search the Land Charges Register, it is therefore necessary to discover the names of the persons who have owned the land from time to time. This is done by looking at the title deeds. However, it is only possible to examine the deeds back to a good root of title, which may now be only 15 years old. Land charges have been registrable since 1925. It is often impossible, therefore, to discover the names of all the landowners back to 1925. Because registration of the land charge constitutes actual notice, a purchaser will still be bound by it, even though he could not discover the name of the landowner against whom it was registered and could not

therefore search the Register. Under the Law of Property Act 1969, compensation is payable for any loss suffered because of land charges registered against landowners whose names lie behind the root of title. It should be noted that any person may search the Land Charges Register, and that an Official Certificate of Search is conclusive in favour of a purchaser, actual or intending. Thus, if for any reason, a Certificate of Search fails to reveal a registered land charge, the purchaser will take free of it, provided that he searched against the correct name.

1.06 Registered land is quite different:

1. The actual title to the land is itself registered, eliminating the need for title deeds. Details of many encumbrances will also appear on the Register, and such encumbrances are registered against the land and *not* against the name of the landowner at the time the encumbrance was created. Transfer of the land is effected by registering the purchaser as the new proprietor. Freeholds and many but not all leaseholds may be registered.
2. The Register is, subject to certain exceptions, conclusive as to the state of the title to the land, and the doctrine of notice has no application to registered land. If for any reason the Register is not a true reflection of the title, it may, in certain circumstances, be rectified. Any person suffering loss as a result may be entitled to compensation out of public funds. Because the Register is conclusive, if an erroneous Certificate of Search is issued which omits a registered encumbrance, a purchaser will still be bound by it, but will be entitled to compensation.
3. A purchaser of registered land will take the following steps:
   (a) obtain the authority of the vendor to enable him to inspect the Register. At present the Register is not public and cannot be inspected by anyone. A vendor must, however, give his authority to an intending purchaser. When the Land Registration Act 1988 comes into force, this will change. Subject to certain conditions, any member of the public will be able to inspect the Register.
   (b) Inspect the Register.
   (c) Inspect the land itself, because the Register is not conclusive on all matters. Certain rights – called overriding interests – may not appear on the Register. These include many easements, leases of 21 years or less, squatters' rights, local land charges (para 1.08), and the rights of persons in actual occupation. This last category can be a trap for the unwary. A person may protect any right of a proprietary nature simply by virtue of his actual occupation, even though such a right is in fact capable of protection by an entry on the Register: *Williams & Glyn's Bank Ltd* v *Boland* [1981] AC 487.

1.07 It will be clear from this that the registered land system considerably facilitates and expedites conveyancing and provides a more efficient method of protecting encumbrances than is found in unregistered conveyancing. The whole of England and Wales will shortly become areas of compulsory registration. This means that in such areas, if a landowner wishes to sell his land and the title to that land has not as yet been registered, the Chief Land Registrar will take the title deeds, investigate the title, and then enter it on the Register. Thereafter, the Register replaces the title deeds.

1.08 Whether the land is registered or unregistered, there are certain rights which are registrable quite separately at a register kept by all local authorities. These are called local land charges, and they are regulated by the Local Land Charges Act 1975, which came into force in 1977. These charges are registered by reference to the land which they affect and not against the name of the landowner. Registration of such charges constitutes actual notice of it to all persons for all purposes. A charge is, however,

enforceable even if not registered, but a purchaser of land burdened by an unregistered charge will be entitled to compensation from the local authority. Local land charges are numerous and of considerable importance. They include:

1. Preservation instructions as to ancient monuments.
2. Lists of buildings of special architectural or historic interest.
3. Planning restrictions.
4. Drainage schemes.
5. Charges under the Public Health and Highway Acts.

1.09 An architect will be well advised to find out from the client what encumbrances if any affect the client's property. It is particularly important that he discovers the existence of any restrictive covenants, and of local land charges, because these may constrict the architect in his plans.

2 The extent of land

2.01 'Land' in English law includes not only the soil but also:

1. Any buildings, parts of buildings, or similar structures.
2. Anything permanently attached to the soil ('fixtures', see para 5.03).
3. Rights under the land. It has never been definitely settled how far down the rights of a landowner extend, though it is commonly said that they extend down to the centre of the earth. Certainly they go down as far as the limits of economic exploitation. A landowner is therefore entitled to the minerals under his land, though all gold, silver and petroleum are vested in the Crown, and coal is vested in the British Coal Corporation.
4. Rights above the land 'to such height as is necessary for the ordinary use and enjoyment of [a landowner's] land and the structures upon it' (*Baron Bernstein* v *Skyviews & General Ltd* [1978] QB 479, 488).
5. Easements (such as rights of way or rights to light) and profits (such as a right to fish on another's land).

2.02 Any unjustifiable intrusion by one person upon the land in the possession of another is a trespass – a tort. It is likewise a trespass to place anything on or in the land in the possession of another (for example, by driving a nail into his wall, or propping a ladder against his house). It is a popular misconception that to be actionable as a tort, the trespass must involve damage to the plaintiff's property. Even if no damage is done, the court may restrain the trespass by injunction. It was thought until recently that the court must suspend the injunction if no harm was suffered, but the better view is that the injunction will be immediate (*Anchor Brewhouse Developments Ltd* v *Berkley House (Dockland Developments) Ltd* [1987] 2 EGLR 173, not following *Woollerton and Wilson Ltd* v *Richard Costain Ltd* [1970] 1 WLR 411). In both those cases, the trespass arose out of building works on land adjacent to that of the plaintiff. If construction work is likely to necessitate an incursion on to neighbouring land in some way – for example, to erect scaffolding, or because a crane jib will swing over that land – then the client must come to an arrangement with the landowner. This will usually take the form of a contractual licence (para 2.03). But if a permanent incursion is contemplated – for example, by the eaves of a building – it may be better to negotiate an easement – of 'eavesdrop' in this particular example. (On easements, see para 3.01.)

2.03 Something can conveniently be said at this point about licences. A licence is permission to do something which would otherwise be unlawful. A licence to enter upon land therefore makes lawful what would otherwise be a trespass. There are several types of licence, of which only two need be considered here. First, there is a bare licence, that is, permission to enter land, given quite gratuitously without any consideration. It is

revocable at any time by the licensor, and on such revocation, the licensee becomes a trespasser, though he is entitled to a reasonable time to enable him to leave the land. The second type of licence that is relevant is the contractual licence. This is a licence that is granted for some consideration. Often a residential contractual licence closely resembles a lease. If the arrangement confers exclusive possession on the grantee for a fixed period, it will create a lease and not a licence: *Street* v *Mountford* [1985] AC 809. The typical hallmark of a contractual licence is the provision of services (such as cleaning) by the licensor. Whether a contractual licence can be revoked depends upon the construction of the contract in question. If a licence is either expressly or by necessary implication irrevocable, the licensor will be unable to prevent the licensee from going on to the land, because a court will prevent any purported revocation of the licence either by the grant of an injunction or in appropriate circumstances, by a decree of specific performance (*Verrall* v *Great Yarmouth Borough Council* [1981] QB 202).

2.04 If a landowner has an easement over adjacent land – such as a right of way – any interference with it will not constitute a trespass but a nuisance. Not every interference will amount to a nuisance. If the easement is a positive one (e.g. a right of way), the interference will constitute a nuisance only if it prevents the practical and substantial enjoyment of the easement. If the easement is negative (e.g. a right of light), the interference will be actionable only if it substantially interferes with the enjoyment of the right. (On positive and negative easements, see para 3.03.)

Boundaries

2.05 A boundary has been defined as 'an imaginary line which marks the confines or line of division of two contiguous parcels of land' (*Halsbury's Laws of England* (4th edn) vol 4, para 831). Boundaries are fixed in one of three ways: (1) by proved acts of the respective owners; (2) by statutes or by orders of the authorities having jurisdiction; or (3) in the absence of either of these, by legal presumption.

Proved acts of the parties

1. The parties may expressly agree on the boundaries.
2. The boundaries may be defined by the title deeds. These may in turn refer to a plan or to an Ordnance Survey map. Ordnance Survey maps do not purport to fix private boundaries, and it is the practice of the Survey to draw the boundary line down the middle of a boundary feature (e.g. down the middle of a ditch) regardless of where the boundary line actually runs. If the title deeds do refer to an Ordnance Survey map, however, then that map *will* be conclusive (*Fisher* v *Winch* [1939] 1 KB 666). In the case of registered land, the plans used by the Land Registry are based on the Ordnance Survey maps, but the boundaries on them are regarded as general and are not intended to be fixed precisely by the plan. A little used procedure exists by which the boundary may be defined exactly, and where this has been done the plan on the Register *is* definitive.
3. A boundary may be proved by showing twelve or more years' undisturbed possession.

Orders

Establishment of boundaries by orders of authorities is now largely historical. Under the Enclosure Acts, the Tithe Acts, and certain Agricultural Acts, awards were made, defining boundaries precisely. In rural areas such an award may help in determining a boundary. A boundary may be fixed by judicial decision, for example, in an action for trespass or for the recovery of land.

Legal presumption

In the absence of clear definition by either of the above methods, certain rebuttable presumptions apply:

Hedges and ditches

It is presumed that a man excavating a ditch will not dig into his neighbour's land, but that he will dig it at the very edge of his own property, making a bank on his side of the ditch with the soil that he removes. On top of that bank a hedge is usually planted. He is, therefore, owner of both the hedge and the ditch. This presumption applies only where the ditch is known to be artificial.

Fences

It is said that there is a presumption that a wooden fence belongs to the owner of the land on whose side the posts are placed, on the basis that a landowner will use his land to the fullest extent. This presumption is, however, unsupported by authority and must be regarded as uncertain.

Highways

The boundary between lands separated by a highway or a private right of way is presumed to be the middle line of the highway or private right of way. There is no such presumption with railways. The bed of a railway will be the property of British Rail.

The seashore

The boundary line between the seashore and the adjoining land is (unless usage to the contrary is proved) the line of the median high tide between the ordinary spring and neap tide (*Attorney General* v *Chambers* (1854) 4 De GM & G 206 at 218). Prima facie the seashore belongs to the Crown.

Rivers and streams

If a river or stream is tidal, the soil of the bed of the river or stream belongs to the Crown, or the Duchies of Cornwall or Lancaster, where appropriate. As a general rule, the boundary between the bed of a tidal stream and adjoining land is the line of medium high water mark. If the river or stream is non-tidal, it is assumed that adjoining owners own land to the middle of the watercourse.

Walls

If the division between two properties is a wall and the exact line of the boundary is not known, in determining the ownership of the wall, certain presumptions apply. Party walls outside London and Bristol (for the situation in London and Bristol, see Chapter 15) are subject to rights at common law. The usual, but by no means necessary, presumption is that the party wall is divided longitudinally into two strips, one belonging to each of the neighbouring owners, but where each half is subject to a right of support in favour of the other. If one owner removes his building, he is obliged to waterproof the exposed party wall. (See Chapter 15 for the complicated procedures necessary when changes to party walls are contemplated in London.) Extensions can bear only on the half of the wall belonging to the owner of the building being extended, unless the consent of the adjoining owner is obtained; this cannot be enforced as it can in London (Chapter 15).

3 Easements

3.01 Easements are rights which one owner of land may acquire over the land of another. They should be disting-uished from profits, i.e. rights to take something off another's land, for example, to cut grass or peat, or to shoot or fish; natural rights, for example, rights of support of land (but not of buildings; a right of support for a building is an easement); public rights, for example, rights of way over a highway; restrictive covenants (para 4.01); and licences (para 2.03).

3.02 The essentials of an easement are:

1. There must be a dominant and a servient tenement (a tenement being a plot of land held by a freeholder or leaseholder).
2. The easement must benefit the dominant tenement to which it will enure. The servient tenement is subjected to the burden of the easement. Although the two plots need not be contiguous, they must be sufficiently close for the dominant tenement to be benefited by the easement.
3. The two tenements must not be owned and occupied by the same person.
4. The easement claimed must be capable of forming the subject matter of a grant. Although there are well-defined categories of easements – rights of way, rights to light, rights of support – the list is not closed. Within the last 30 years, the following rights have been held to be capable of existing as easements: to use a neighbour's lavatory; to use an airfield; to use a letter-box; to use paths in a park for pleasure and not simply for getting from one place to another. Against this, certain rights cannot exist as easements; a right to a view; to privacy; to a general flow of air; to have a property protected from the weather; an exclusive right to use boats on a canal.

3.03 Easements may be either positive or negative. A positive easement is one which enables the dominant owner to do some act upon the dominant tenement, for example, a right of way. A negative easement merely allows the dominant owner to prevent the servient owner from doing something on his land, for example, a right to light, which restricts the servient owner's ability to build on athe servient tenement. Some easements do not readily fall into either category, for example, a right of support for a building.

3.04 Easements may be acquired in one of four ways:

1. By express grant or reservation. A landowner may by deed expressly grant an easement over his land in favour of a neighbouring landowner. Equally, if a landowner is selling off part of his land, he may expressly reserve in his favour in the conveyance an easement over the part that he is selling.
2. By implied reservation or grant. A landowner sells off part of his land and retains the rest. He fails to reserve expressly any easements over the part sold. The only easements that will be implied in his favour over that part will be easements of necessity and perhaps easements necessary to give effect to the common intentions of the parties. An easement of necessity in this context means an easement without which the vendor's retained land cannot be used at all. For example, if he retains land to which there is no access (often called a land-locked close), an easement of necessity will be impliedly reserved over the land that he has sold. If a purchaser buys land from a vendor (the vendor again retaining certain land), the following easements will be implied in the purchaser's favour over the land retained by the vendor:
   (a) Easements of necessity, which in this context mean easements without which the grantee cannot enjoy the land *for the purposes for which it was intended*.
   (b) Easements necessary to give effect to the common intentions of the parties.
   (c) Easements within the rule in *Wheeldon* v *Burrows* (1879) 12 ChD 31. This is best explained by an example. A landowner owns two adjacent plots. A and B. He does certain acts over B for the benefit of A which would be an

easement if A and B were separately owned. This is called a 'quasi-easement'. When he sells off plot A, retaining plot B, the purchaser of plot A will acquire an easement to do those acts over plot B which the common owner had hitherto done if the quasi-easement was 'continuous and apparent', that is, discernible on a careful inspection of the land; necessary for the reasonable enjoyment of plot A; and had been and was at the time of the grant used by the grantor for the benefit of plot A.

3. Under the statutory 'general words'. By section 62 of the Law of Property Act 1925, there will pass on every conveyance (unless a contrary intention is shown) all 'liberties, privileges, easements, rights and advantages whatsoever appertaining to or reputed to appertain to the land'.

It has been held by the House of Lords that this section will not pass quasi-easements. This is because a landowner does not have 'rights or 'easements' over his own land. What he does on his own land, he does as owner (*Sovmots v The Secretary of State* [1979] AC 144).

The section will convert merely permissive user into a full easement. For example, A, a freeholder, permits B, a tenant of part of A's land, to drive over A's land. A then sells and conveys to B the land of which he has hitherto been only a leaseholder. On the conveyance B acquires a full easement to drive over A's land (*International Tea Stores Co v Hobbs* [1903] 2 Ch 165).

4. By prescription. Long user *nec vi, nec clam, nec precario* – without force, secrecy, or permission – can give rights to easements. An easement by prescription can only be claimed by one freehold owner against another, and, with certain exceptions, user must be shown to have been continuous. There are three methods of acquiring easements by prescription:
   (a) at common law;
   (b) under the doctrine of lost modern grant; and
   (c) under the Prescription Act 1832.

At common law an easement could be acquired by prescription only if it could be proved to have been used from time immemorial (i.e. from 1189). In fact, user for 20 years before the claim was made would normally be accepted, but a claim could always be defeated by showing, for example, that a right of light claimed for a building could not have existed since 1189 if the building had been constructed in 1500.

The doctrine of lost modern grant was invented because of the ease with which it was possible to defeat a claim to prescription at common law. Where the origin of an alleged easement cannot otherwise be accounted for, then provided that there has been upwards of 20 years' user of the right, the court will presume that the right was lawfully granted and that the grant has been lost. This presumption can be rebutted only by evidence that the existence of such a grant was impossible. The evidence necessary to persuade a court to infer a lost modern grant must be stronger than that required to prove common law prescription. A claim to an easement by lost modern grant will not be precluded just because the party claiming the right exercised it under the mistaken belief that he had permission to do so: *Bridle v Ruby* [1989] QB 169. The doctrine of lost modern grant can be invoked only if common law prescription is for some reason excluded.

The Prescription Act 1832 laid down prescriptive periods in general and for rights of light in particular (the latter are discussed in para 3.08). The Act provides that uninterrupted user for 20 years before some action by the dominant owner for confirmation of a right of easement or by the servient owner for a declaration that a right does not exist means that the claim cannot be defeated merely by showing that it cannot have existed since 1189. The Act further provides that user without interruption for 40 years before action confirms an absolute and indefeasible easement. In both cases user must be of right, i.e. *nec vi, nec clam, nec precario*. 'Interruption' is

important because if an owner wishes to establish an easement by prescription, he must not acquiesce to interruption of his right for one year by the owner of the property on which he wishes to establish the easement. Acquiescence to interruption does not necessarily imply agreement; the owner who wishes to establish the easement may simply not notice an interruption. Any period during which the owner of the land on which the easement is claimed could not give consent to establishing an easement (e.g. because he was an infant or a lunatic) must be added to the 20-year period. Any period in excess of three years during which the servient tenement is leased must be added to the 40-year period.

Estinguishment of easements

3.05 Apart from an express release by deed, the most important method of extinguishing an easement is by the dominant and servient tenements coming into the same ownership and possession.

Types of easement

Rights of way

3.06 A right of way, whether acquired expressly, impliedly, or by prescription, may be limited as to both frequency and type of use, e.g. a right obtained for passage by horse and cart in the nineteenth century will not extend to passage for many caravans if the dominant tenement has become a caravan site.

Rights of support

3.07 Although the natural right of support for land by other land has been distinguished from an easement (para 3.01), it is possible for one building to acquire an easement of support against another after a period of 20 years. The only remedy against this would be for the owner of the supporting building to seek a declaration during the 20 years that the supported building has no right to support. It should be noted that where two detached buildings adjoin on separate plots an easement cannot be acquired requiring a person who removes his abutting wall to weatherproof the exposed flank wall of the remaining building (but if the wall is a party wall, other rules apply; para 2.05).

Rights of light

3.08 To a considerable extent the law relating to rights of light has been rendered of secondary importance by daylighting regulations under planning legislation (Chapter 11), but a knowledge of the law is still required. There is no right to light generally, but only in respect of some definite opening, such as a window or skylight. The owner of the decominant tenement has a right only to such amount of light as is necessary for 'ordinary purposes'. Many years' user of an exceptional amount of light does not prevent an adjoining owner from building so as to reduce light; this was held in a case where an architect claimed that he had enjoyed and needed more light for his office than for ordinary office purposes (*Ambler v Gordon* [1905] 1 KB 417).

The decision whether or not enough light is left for ordinary purposes must, therefore, depend on personal observation, and on all the scientific methods now available for measuring light. The so-called 45° rule from the centre of a window can do no more than help the judge make up his mind. It should also be noted that if light could be obtained from an existing but blocked skylight, then this must be counted as an available alternative source.

3.09 Under the Prescription Act 1832, as amended by the Rights of Light Act 1959, it was provided that an absolute right of light could be obtained only after 20 years' uninterrupted user. Because of the possibility of prescriptive

rights being acquired over bomb-damaged sites, the 1959 Act provided a temporary extension of the period to 27 years for actions alleging infringement beginning before that date. The 1959 Act also provided for registration as a local land charge (para 1.08) of a theoretical wall of stated dimensions in such a position as would prevent an adjoining owner from claiming a prescriptive right of light because the owner of the servient tenement did not erect a permanent structure to the registered dimensions. This useful provision avoids the cumbersome procedure by which screens and hoardings had to be erected by the person seeking to prevent a right of light being acquired over his land; in any case such hoardings would now be subject to planning control (Chapter 14).

4 Restrictive covenants

4.01 A restrictive covenant is a covenant which restricts an owner of the servient tenement in some way in his use and enjoyment of his land. The covenant must be made for the benefit of the dominant land belonging to the covenantee. Typical examples are covenants not to build above a given height or in a given place, or covenants restricting the user of the land to given purposes. Although to some extent superseded by planning controls, restrictive covenants still have a valuable role to play, particularly in preserving the character of housing estates. The essentials of a restrictive covenant are:

1. That it is in substance negative.
2. That it is made between the covenantor and the covenantee for the benefit of the covenantee's land.
3. That the parties intend the burden of the covenant to run with the covenantor's land so as to bind not only the covenantor but also his successors in title.

4.02 A restrictive convenant is an equitable interest and therefore requires registration as a land chanrge in unregistered land unless the covenant is contained in a lease when registration is not required. In registered land a restrictive covenant is protected by registering a notice or caution on the Register. If a restrictive covenant complies with the requirements listed in para 4.01 and is properly protected, it will bind the covenantor's successors in title. The usual remedy for infringement of a restrictive covenant is an injunction to restrain further breaches, but the court may give damages either in addition to or in lieu of an injunction.

The rules on the passing of the benefit of restrictive covenants are complex and need not be considered here.

4.03 Architects should request that their clients obtain confirmation that there are no restrictive covenants applying to a site that could affect the proposed design of a building or indeed whether a building could be constructed at all. An architect must proceed with caution. Although the point has never been tested in court, an architect who continued to act for a client in designing a building that was known by both of them to contravene a restrictive covenant, might be liable jointly with his client for the tort of conspiracy, i.e. of agreeing to do an unlawful act.

Discharge of restrictive covenants

4.04 Many restrictive covenants imposed in former years are no longer of real benefit to the owners of adjoining lands and may indeed be anti-social or in conflict with reasonable redevelopment proposals. Power is given to the Lands Tribunal by section 84 of the Law of Property Act 1925, as amended by section 28 of the Law of Property Act 1969, for the discharge or modification of any covenant if the Tribunal is satisfied that, *inter alia*, changes in the neighbourhood make the covenant obsolete or that the restriction does not now secure practical advantages of substantial value to the person entitled to its benefit or is contrary to public policy (i.e. planning policy). Compensation may be awarded in lieu of the covenant.

5 Landlord and tenant covenants

5.01 The vast majority of leases with which architects are concerned on behalf of their clients, particularly of trade and business premises, are the subject of formal agreements defining precisely the respective rights and obligations of the parties. Whether the architect's client is a tenant who wishes to rebuild, alter, or repair premises, or a landlord who requires evidence to recover damages from a tenant who has failed to observe a covenant for repair, regard must be had first to the express terms of the lease, and the client's solicitor should be asked to advise on the meaning and extent of the terms. The following general remarks, except where otherwise stated, introduce the law only in so far as the lease has not stated to the contrary.

Doctrine of waste

5.02 'Waste' consists of an act or omission which causes or is likely to cause a lasting alteration to the nature of the land and premises to the prejudice of the landlord. A tenant of land for more than one year is, apart from statute and any terms of the lease, liable for voluntary waste (any positive act such as pulling down or altering the premises) and permissive waste (allowing the premises to fall into disrepair). In practice, a lease will always contain repairing covenants. Normally the landlord is responsible for external repairs and the tenant for internal repairs. In any event, in respect of a lease of a dwelling house for less than seven years, the landlord is obliged to keep the exterior in repair and to keep in repair and working order all installations relating to heating and the supply of services: Housing Act 1985, section 11. There is a third type of waste: ameliorating waste – some change which will improve the value of the reversion. The courts are very unlikely to restrain the commission of this form of waste.

Fixtures

5.03 Prima facie anything that is attached to the land becomes part of the land and therefore the property of the landowner. If, therefore, a tenant attaches something to the land that has been leased to him, it will, presumptively, become the property of the landlord. However, two questions arise: Is the addition in truth a fixture, or does it remain a chattel? Even if it is a fixture, is it one which a tenant may remove?

1. Fixture or chattel? In deciding whether something attached to the land is a fixture or chattel, two matters are considered:
   (a) How is the thing attached to the land? Is it attached so that it can be removed readily without damaging the fabric? If so, it may still be regarded as a chattel, and therefore the property of the tenant.
   (b) Why is the thing attached? This is now the more important test (*Berkeley v Poulett* (1976) 241 EG 911). If the thing is attached to the land simply because it cannot otherwise be enjoyed as a chattel (e.g. a tapestry fixed to a wall), then it remains a chattel. If the thing is attached in order to improve the land permanently, then it is a fixture.
2. Tenant's fixtures. Even if the thing is a fixture, a tenant who has attached it may be able to remove it. In the case of non-agricultural holdings, the tenant may remove trade, domestic and ornamental fixtures before the expiry of the tenancy. He must make good any damage to the premises occasioned by the removal of fixtures. If the tenancy is of agricultural land, the tenant can remove *all* fixtures which he has attached within two months of the lease expiring. The landlord has the option to purchase them if he wishes.

Alterations and improvements

5.04 In the absence of any term in the lease regulating the matter, the tenant should obtain the landlord's consent to any alterations. This is because any alteration to the premises will constitute waste (voluntary or ameliorating). It is common for a lease to contain an express condition that no alterations shall be made without the landlord's consent. It is provided by the Landlord and Tenant Act 1927, section 19 that such consent shall not be unreasonably withheld where the alteration constitutes an improvement. Whether a proposed alteration is an improvement is a question of fact to be considered from the tenant's point of view. It should be noted that it is the tenant's responsibility to prove that the landlord's consent is being unreasonably withheld, that the landlord may object on aesthetic, artistic, and even sentimental grounds, and that although the Act forbids the taking of any premium as a condition of giving consent, the landlord may reasonably require the tenant to pay the landlord's legal and other expenses (including architects' and surveyors' fees) plus a reasonable amount for any diminution in the value not only of the leased premises but also of any adjoining premises of the landlord.

Repairing covenants

Surveys

5.05 Architects are frequently asked to prepare a schedule of dilapidations at the beginning of a tenancy, during the course of, or at the end of the lease. The importance of initial schedules is that in the absence of any covenant to do works as a condition of the grant of the lease, any repairing covenant must be construed with reference to the original condition of the premises. Different phrases may be used, but generally the tenant's obligation is to 'repair, keep in repair and deliver the premises in repair at the end of the term'. Repair may include the replacement or renewal of parts but not renewal of the whole or substantially the whole of the premises.

5.06 A term to 'keep and deliver up premises in good and tenantable repair' is used almost exclusively in leases of houses and flats, and in such cases (unless the amount of the rent brings the premises within the restrictions of the Housing Acts with the statutory implications that the premises were and will be kept fit for human habitation) the covenant could include an obligation to put the premises into repair as well as to keep them in repair. That repair must be such 'as having regard to the age, character and locality of the premises would make it reasonably fit for occupation by another reasonably minded tenant of the same class' (*Proudfoot* v *Hart* (1890) 25 QBD 42, 55). The standard of repair is neither increased by an improvement, nor decreased by a deterioration in the class of tenants (*Lord Calthorpe* v *McOscar* [1924] 1 KB 716).

5.07 It is the tenant's responsibility to prove that a bad state of repair is within the exception of 'fair wear and tear'. In general terms the phrase means that the tenant is not responsible for damage resulting from exposure to the natural elements or reasonable use. Although not liable for direct damage the tenant could be liable for consequential damages – e.g. he might not be liable for repair of tiles slipping from a roof after a storm, but he would be liable for damage to the interior of the premises from flooding resulting from his failure to take steps to prevent rain entering.

Enforcement of repairing covenants

5.08 Under the Leasehold Property (Repairs) Act 1938, as extended by the Landlord and Tenant Act 1954, a landlord cannot forfeit the lease or even begin an action for damages in respect of a tenant's failure to observe a repairing covenant unless he has first served on the tenant a notice under section 146 of the Law of Property Act 1925 clearly specifying the breach. If the tenant serves a counter-notice within 28 days the landlord cannot take any action without the consent of the court. Architects are frequently asked to produce a schedule of defects to accompany such a notice (see also para 5.11).

Consents

5.09 It is emphasized that what has been stated is always subject to the express wording of the lease and also to the many statutory provisions for the protection of tenants of certain types of premises, particularly houses. Architects should remember that a client's tenancy may come at the end of a long line of underleases, and the consents of superior landlords may be required for any work which the client has requested.

Mortgages

5.10 It is not proposed to discuss this subject in detail, but architects should remember that alteration to premises will alter the value of the mortgagee's security. For this reason most mortgages contain covenants requiring the mortgagee's consent to works. As with leases, there may be several mortgagees having different priorities of charge on the premises, and the architect should ask the client whether the property is mortgaged, and if it is request him to obtain any necessary consents.

Architect's responsibilities for surveys

Dilapidations

5.11 If asked to prepare a schedule of dilapidations, an archiect should first find out from his client's solicitor the terms of the lease, so that he is clear as to which portions of the building come within the repairing covenant. These are the only portions he need examine. As tenant's fixtures are removable by the tenant, only dilapidations to landlord's fixtures need usually be catalogued, but because of the difficulties of assessing ownership of fixtures, it is often wise to examine dilapidations on anything that is at all doubtful.

5.12 Estimates of cost of making good dilapidations are often required. Unless an architect has much experience of this kind of work, it is advisable to involve a quantity surveyor. When lessor and lessee cannot agree about the extent of damages or the extent of responsibility for making them good, their dispute may have to be resolved in the courts. In such cases the schedule of dilapidations becomes evidence, and it is therefore important that it is very clearly drawn. When making a survey for a schedule the possibility that matters might come to court should be borne in mind.

Where the parties agree to appoint an architect or surveyor to prepare a schedule of dilapidations, then, by analogy with the cases on valuations, if no reasons for the schedule are given and it was made honestly and in good faith, it cannot be set aside, even though it turns out to be mistaken: *Campbell* v *Edwards* [1976] 1 WLR 403. If reasons are given for the schedule and they are fundamentally erroneous, it may be set aside: *Burgess* v *Purchase & Sons (Farms) Ltd* [1983] Ch 216.

Surveys of property to be purchased

5.13 Architects are often asked to inspect property for clients who intend to purchase or lease. An examination of the property is required, bearing in mind the proposed use and taking into account all defects and dilapidations. Useful guides to technical points to be noted in such a survey are given in *Architectural Practice and Procedure* and in *Guide to Domestic Building Surveys*.

5.14 It is important to note that if defects are not observed, the architect may be held to be negligent. For example, where a surveyor failed to report that the timbers of a house were badly affected by death watch beetle and worm, he was held liable in negligence to the purchaser of that property (*Phillips v Ward* [1956] 1 WLR 471). The measure of damages in such a case is the difference between the market value of the property with the defect and the purchase price. It is *not* the difference between the market value with the defect and the value of the property as it would have been if it had been as described (*Perry* v *Sidney Phillips & Son* [1982] 1 WLR 1297).

Hidden defects

5.15 It is often wise, particularly when investigating old property, to open up and inspect hidden portions of the building. If this is not done, the limitations of the investigation should be clearly pointed out ot the client, and he should be asked to take a decision as to whether the expense of opening up is worth while. He must of course be informed of the probability or otherwise of e.g. rot. If rot is discovered and it was not mentioned in the survey and the architect did not recommend opening up to check, he is almost certainly negligent.

6 Business tenancies – architects' offices

6.01 This review of business tenancies can be in routine only, and it is written from the point of view of architects as tenants of office premises. Two preliminary matters which recent cases involving architect tenants have shown to be of importance concern landlords' rights of forfeiture and rights of assignment.

1. An architect should be careful if a lease offered includes an absolute right of forfeiture in the event of bankruptcy, as he will find that he cannot raise finance from either a building society or a bank on the security of such a lease.
2. Care should be taken to check the wording of covenants empowering assignment or subletting, not only in the immediate lease offered (where the landlord may have only a right of reasonable objection) but also in any sueprior lease (where the superior landlord may have reserved an absolute right of refusal without reasonable cause). Consent may be obtained from the immediate landlord but refused by the superior landlord.

Protection of business tenants

6.02 Part II of the Landlord and Tenant Act 1954, as amended by Part I of the Law of Property Act 1969, provides a substantial measure of protection to occupiers of business premises by providing in effect that the tenant may continue in occupancy indefinitely, unless the landlord satisfies the court that a new tenancy ought not to be granted for certain defined statutory reasons (para 6.03). If the tenant receives notice of determination (not less than six nor more than twelve months' notice) expiring not earlier than the existing tenancy would otherwise have ended, he may within two months of receipt serve a counter-notice on the landlord that he is unwilling to leave and then apply to the court for a new tenancy.

6.03 There are seven reasons which might prevent the grant of a new tenancy, the first three of which, if proved, prevent the grant absolutely, the latter four being left to the discretion of the court.

1. If, on termination of the existing tenancy, the landlord intends to demolish or reconstruct the premises and could not reasonably do so without possession of the whole. (Since the 1969 Act, this does not prevent a new tenancy of the whole or part of the premises if the landlord will be able to do the work without seriously 'interfering' with the tenant's business.)
2. If the landlord proves that he intends to occupy the premises for his own business or as a residence. (Since 1969 the landlord may successfully resist if he intends the premises to be occupied by a company in which he has a controlling interest.)
3. If the landlord proves the premises are part of a larger holding for which he could obtain a substantially larger rent than for the individual parts.
4. If the tenant fails to keep the premises in repair.
5. If there are persistent delays in paying rent.
6. If there are breaches of covenant.
7. If the landlord is willing to provide suitable alternative accommodation on reasonable terms.

Compensation

6.04 If the court cannot grant a new tenancy for any of the first three reasons above, the tenant will be entitled to compensation of the rateable value or twice the rateable value where the tenant and his predecessors in the same business have occupied for 14 years or more.

New tenancy

6.05 The length of a new tenancy (but not exceeding 14 years), the rent, and other terms are fixed by the court.

8

Scottish Land Law

ANGUS STEWART QC*

1 Introduction

1.01 The term 'property' is used in Scots law to denote both a right and the subject of a right. The right can be described as the right of using and disposing of a thing as one's own. This may be subject to many different statutory, contractual, or other restrictions. Property as the subject of the right is classified either as heritable or movable. Heritable property is property which by its nature is immovable, for example, land or buildings, while movable property consists of things such as furniture or motor cars, which by their nature can be moved.

Heritable and movable property

1.02 Movable property may become heritable through attachment to heritable property. Building materials are movable until they are incorporated in the building, when they become part of the heritage. Articles such as light fittings, a central heating system, or machinery, which are installed in a building, become part of the heritable property if they are sufficiently attached to or connected with the building. The question whether or not movable property has become heritable in this way, i.e. has become a 'fixture', depends on the whole circumstances and has given rise to a large body of case law. The important point in deciding this is generally the degree of attachment to the heritage (whether, for example, the thing in question can be removed without damage to itself or the heritage). Things may also be heritable because they are essential accessories of the heritage as, for example, the keys of a house, or unattached articles essential for the operation of fixed machinery. Articles such as pictures or fitted carpets are not regarded as fixtures, since they are only lightly attached. Fitted cupboards, and gas or electric fires which are built in, would be.

1.03 In certain circumstances heritable property may become movable. Examples are minerals removed from the land, or standing timber which is felled.

1.04 Whether property is heritable or movable may be of considerable importance in, among others, questions of valuation for rating and in interpretation of contracts for the sale of heritage, where it is necessary to know what is included in the sale. Houses, for example, are often sold 'complete with fixtures and fittings'. Felled timber or harvested crops would not in the absence of express provision in the contract be included in a sale of land.

Corporeal and incorporeal

1.05 Heritable and movable property are both further classified as corporeal or incorporeal property, the former being tangible, the latter consisting of intangible rights. Examples of incorporeal property are servitude rights (para 3.08), such as rights of wayleave for pipes, or certain security rights in heritage, which are heritable, and patent or copyright rights (Chapter 17), which are movable.

2 Corporeal heritable property and feudal law

2.01 For centuries a valid title to heritage in Scotland has been obtained only by having the disposition, contract, or other deed publicly recorded. Traditionally, deeds have been recorded in the Register of Sasines. If a deed recorded in the Register appears good and has been followed by possession for ten years, the title cannot be challenged. As from 1980, under the Land Registration (Scotland) Act 1979, the traditional system will be replaced, in one area after another, by a new system of registration of titles in the Land Register for Scotland. In general, an entry in the title sheet made up by the Keeper will represent an unchallengeable entitlement to the registered interest, be it a right of ownership, of security or wayleave, and so on. Entries in the title sheet will be conclusive of the location and extent of the property and of all interests affecting it. The technical content of deeds will be reduced and conveyancing simplified. Registered titles will be backed by a State guarantee. In exceptional circumstances the Keeper may decline to guarantee a title. Possession for ten years after registration will make such a title unchallengeable.

2.02 The terminology and technicalities of Scots land law still owe something to the feudal system of land holding. Under feudal law, all rights to land derive from the Crown, the paramount feudal 'superior'. Historically, grants of land were made by the Crown to its 'vassals' in return for military or other services. A Crown vassal might in turn make land grants for services and in turn stand in the position of superior to his vassals.

Feuing

2.03 The Crown is still in theory the paramount superior of all land, although the practical importance of this is probably limited to the fact that certain types of property, such as the foreshore, are assumed to be vested in the Crown. Most privately owned land and buildings are held on a feu. However, the distinctive feudal element of the system of holding has been modified and now greatly attenuated by a number of statutes.

*In the first edition, this chapter was written by Andrew Grotian.

2.04 Today the vassal who holds property on feu may have to pay a feu-duty. Frequently this is purely nominal. Provided he pays his feu-duty his successors (whether they succeed on his death or through a purchase of his interest) hold the land in perpetuity. The vassal may sell his interest in the land, or part of it, or feu the whole or parts to other person, himself retaining an interest as mid-superior. If he sells or feus parts he may still be liable to his superior for the whole feu-duty. But he may make an arrangement with him to allocate the feu-duty so that each part of the land is liable for a proportion only. If he does not do so, each part and each proprietor is liable for the whole. Under the Conveyancing and Feudal Reform (Scotland) Act 1970, he can now compel the superior to come to such an arrangement.

2.05 The Land Tenure Reform (Scotland) Act 1974, although it has not abolished feu-duties outright, has done much to pave the way for their eventual disappearance by (1) banning the creation of new feu-duties, (2) making it compulsory to redeem existing feu-duties when properties are sold (the purchaser makes a lump sum payment which is fixed according to a statutory formula), and (3) allowing the vassal to insist on redemption, in return for a lump sum payment, at other times. The Act also introduces elaborate provisions to prevent superiors from frustrating the purpose of the reform by exacting other kinds of periodic payment, for example by creating long leases for dwelling houses. It may happen that several houses, for example in one tenement, together make up a single feu burdened by a single feu-duty which has not

been formally allocated among the individual flats. In such a case the provisions for redemption do not apply. But as has already been mentioned, the 1970 Act allows any single proprietor to insist on allocation; and once the feu-duty has been allocated, the provisions of the 1974 Act will apply.

Restrictions on ownership by vassals

2.06 Although in many respects the vassal is in the position of absolute owner of the land, his right of ownership may be subject to many conditions and restrictions contained in his title. The disposition of the property may, for example, regulate the number and type of buildings the vassal may erect, and the use to which the property may be put. It may require the vassal to keep any buildings in good repair, insure them with an approved company, and rebuild them within a certain time in the event of their destruction. It may also require the vassal to contribute to the cost of building or maintaining roads serving the feu. These are examples of conditions which, if properly framed in a feudal title, can be enforced by the superior against all vassals in perpetuity. When ground is feued for building it is practice to impose a deadline for the completion of the building with a condition that if the deadline is not met ownership will revert to the grantor. Before starting to design, architects should suggest to their clients that the feudal title of the property be examined to check for conditions. The client's solicitor will do this.

Pre-emption

2.07 The superior may also insert a clause of pre-emption, stipulating that if the vassal wishes to sell he must first offer the property to the superior, either at a fixed price or, more commonly, at a price which he has been offered and for which he would sell if the superior does not exercise his right. Such a right is now exercisable on the occasion of the first sale only and must be exercised within 21 days of the vassal's offer to the superior.

2.08 Not any and every condition is enforceable by the superior, however. The superior must have an interest to enforce the condition, which in fact is fairly readily assumed, and the condition must be precise in its terms so that the vassal will be able to ascertain, through reading the condition, what is required of him. There is a presumption that the vassal is free to do as he wishes with his property, and when a condition is being interpreted he will always receive the benefit of the doubt if there is any ambiguity.

Jus quaesitum tertio

2.09 Some feuing conditions are enforceable by persons other than the superior; this right is called *jus quaesitium tertio* (Chapter 2, para 4.04). If, for example, a superior feus out lots of land on which buildings are to be erected according to a uniform plan, one feuar may in certain circumstances object to another feuar breaching the feuing conditions. The breach must affect him directly in some way, for instance, by damaging his amenity. If it is stated in the title that certain things may be done only with the permission of the superior, however, other vassals may not object to these things if the superior's permission is obtained. Otherwise the fact that a superior acquiesces in a breach of the conditions is of no consequence in a question between vassals.

Altering and discharging conditions

2.10 A superior may alter or discharge feuing conditions, though, if other vassals have a right to object to a breach, their consent must be obtained. In return for waiving conditions, the superior may demand a lump payment or, indeed, any other consideration he thinks he can obtain but

not, since the 1974 Act, any increase in feu-duty or other periodic payment or the imposition of such a payment. The situation where desirable development could be obstructed by superiors led to statutory reform in the shape of the Conveyancing and Feudal Reform (Scotland) Act 1970. Under sections 1 and 2 of the Act the Lands Tribunal has power to vary or discharge any 'land obligations' (including feuing conditions and rights such as servitudes) which for a variety of reasons have become unreasonable, or unduly burdensome compared with any benefit they might bring, or the existence of which impedes some reasonable use of the land. This includes powers formerly held by a sheriff (Chapter 2) under the Housing (Scotland) Act 1966 to allow the division of a single dwelling house into two or more dwellings in breach of the feuing conditions, and the sheriff's power has thus ended. The Lands Tribunal has power to order payment of compensation and to add or substitute different provisions. It is of course still open to the parties to come to a private arrangement, and there may be situations in which such an arrangement is more convenient than an application to the Tribunal.

Leases

2.11 A proprietor may lease his property to another, the basis of the contract being that the tenant has the right to occupy and make use of the property in return for payment of rent. There are numerous statutory provisions regulating leases of various kinds, mainly by restricting rents or providing some degree of security of tenure for the tenant. It is not proposed to deal with this subject in the present chapter in any detail.

Business tenancies

2.12 It should be noted, however, that the statutory provisions relating to security of tenure in business tenancies which apply in England (Chapter 3) do not extend to Scotland. Thus the architect in Scotland who rents his office premises relies wholly on his contract with his landlord for security of tenure, there being no corresponding Scottish legislation.

Surveys

2.13 The responsibilities of Scottish architects with regard to surveys are the same as for English architects (Chapter 3).

Non-feudal feuure

2.14 A distinctive system of non-feudal ownership survives here and there in the Northern Isles. It is known as udal tenure. Udal owners hold their land outright of no superior and the ultimate superiority of the Crown is not acknowledged. Udal titles include foreshore. The validity of a udal title depends on possession rather than recording. In other parts of Scotland these are isolated instances of non-feudal tenures and tenures whose origins pre-date the feudal system. Parish churches and lands are said to be held of no superior. Compulsory purchase or other statutory acquisition of feudal lands is said to eliminate all mid-superiorities but not the ultimate superiority of the Crown.

3 Other restrictions of corporeal heritable property

3.01 Apart from any restrictions in his title, numerous other restrictions, both statutory and otherwise, may affect the proprietor of heritable property.

Statutory restrictions

3.02 It is not proposed to enter into the statutory restrictions in detail, but obvious examples of these are the Town and Country Planning Acts and the numerous statutes and regulations governing compulsory purchase (Chapter 14). In addition various bodies have power to enter land or premises compulsorily (Chapter 13). A number of uses are not permitted except under licence (sale of alcohol, gaming, sex shops, etc.). The Public Health (Scotland) Acts prohibit the carrying on of a large number of activities, defined as statutory nuisances, on various kinds of property. A proprietor is also subject to building regulations administered by the appropriate local authority in respect of any building operations he may wish to carry out (Chapter 16). A statutory right to continue in occupation of the family home is given to the spouse of the owner or tenant by the Matrimonial Homes (Family Protection) Scotland Act 1981. The right can be enforced against third parties who should protect their interest by getting the protected spouse's consent to any transaction in accordance with the statutory formalities. Unless 'de-crofted', croft land and buildings continue subject to the statutory crofting regime even after purchase by the crofting tenant.

3.03 In addition the occupier of premises is obliged under the Occupiers' Liability (Scotland) Act 1960 to take reasonable care to see that persons entering the premises (which include land and other types of property) do not suffer injury owing to the state of the premises. His failure to do so may result in his being liable.

Common structures

3.04 In his use of his property the proprietor may also have to take into account the interests of his neighbours in a variety of ways. Where there is a common gable or dividing wall between two properties, either proprietor may object to the other carrying out operations which may be injurious to it, since it is common property. Where the property is a flatted or tenement building in which each house is owned separately, each proprietor has a common interest in the property outwith his own, so far as necessary for his support and shelter. Thus although the external walls of each property belong to individual proprietors, they may not interfere with them in such a way as to endanger the other properties. Similarly each proprietor is sole owner of his floors and ceilings, down to the mid-point of the joists, but must not interfere with them in such a way as to weaken his neighbour's floor or ceiling. The roof of a tenement property belongs to the owner of the top storey, but all proprietors in the building have a common interest in seeing that it is properly maintained, and they may compel the owner to keep it in repair and to refrain from damaging it. Common stairs and passages are the common property of all to whose premises they form an access, and all are obliged to maintain them. If alterations to common property or the roof are contemplated it is often (though not always) necessary to obtain the consent of all proprietors. Clients should be advised to consult their solicitors who can check the feudal titles and, if necessary, attempt to obtain consents.

3.05 These rules apply to all tenement property in Scotland, unless, as frequently happens, there is express provision to the contrary in the titles (see paras 2.06 ff), in which case the provisions in the titles prevail over the common law rules. A check on the feudal titles by the client's solicitor should reveal feuing conditions which may affect design.

3.06 It often happens that there are difficulties in getting all proprietors in a tenement building to agree to mutual repairs. There may be difficulty in deciding, without legal advice, whether a particular repair is a mutual responsibility or in agreeing how the cost of the repair should be allocated. Local authorities have statutory powers to carry out repairs and charge the cost to all proprietors in proportion to the rateable value of their properties. The local authority should be applied to in the case of deadlock among the proprietors. Under the Civic Government (Scotland) Act 1982 district and islands councils have powers to light common stairs and passage and to require common areas to be kept clean and properly decorated. Fire authorities have power to deal with fire hazards in common areas.

Natural rights

3.07 A proprietor may also have to take account of servitude rights and natural rights of his neighbours or others. Natural rights arise independently of any separate contract or title, through ownership of the land. They include right of support of land. Thus a proprietor may not quarry up to the boundary of his land if this would lead to subsidence of his neighbour's land. He is not entitled to interfere with a stream flowing through his land in such a way as to change its natural flow as it comes to his neighbour's land, since all the riparian proprietors have a common interest in the stream and may object if they are deprived of its natural flow. He may not carry on operations on his property which constitute a 'nuisance', i.e. which interfere with his neighbour's right to the comfortable enjoyment of his property. What is or is not a nuisance at common law depends on the nature of the neighbourhood, but it may consist of excessive noise or foul smells. If a nuisance has existed without challenge for a period of 20 years or more, however, it cannot be objected to.

Servitudes

3.08 A servitude, in contrast to a natural right, is founded on agreement, whether express or implied. A servitude may be positive or negative; a positive servitude entitles the person who has right to the servitude to do certain things, such as obtaining access to his property over his neighbour's; a negative servitude entitles one proprietor to insist that another refrain from certain acts, for example, erecting buildings over a certain height. Property may be subject to many different kinds of servitude, including servitudes of support, stillicide (which entitles the proprietor of property to let rainwater from his own house fall on his neighbour's ground), and light, affecting mainly urban property, and servitudes of way or access, pasturage, and drawing or conducting water, affecting land.

Express or implied servitudes

3.09 Servitudes may be constituted either by express agreement, which may be followed by recording in the Register of Sasines so that the servitude appears in the title, or by implied agreement. For example, where A sells part of his land to B and the only means of access is over A's land, there is an implied agreement that B has a servitude right of access over A's land. Positive servitudes may also be constituted by uninterrupted use for a period of 20 years, and may lapse if not exercised for that period. Negative servitudes lapse only if a breach is allowed to continue for 20 years without interruption.

Defeating acquisition of implied servitudes

3.10 Servitudes roughly correspond to easements in England. Methods of preventing easements being obtained by prescription (i.e. long use) are discussed in Chapter 3, but these are not applicable in Scotland to servitudes. However, many of the matters which are subjects of servitudes, including support, stillicide, and light, are within the provisions of the Scottish Building Regulations (Chapter 16), which are much more comprehensive and detailed than the English ones. In

most cases, the regulations prevent new buildings being designed so that their proprietors acquire onerous servitudes by implication over their neighbours. properties.

Rights of way

3.11 Land may be subject to a public right of way, which is a right for members of the public to pass by a definite route over land from one public place to another. Such a right is almost invariably constituted by use for a period of 20 years, and lapses if not used for that period.

3.12 The Prescription and Limitation (Scotland) Act 1973 now gives in one statute the various periods of occupation or use required to set up rights over land, from ownership to rights of way, and conversely the periods of non-use which will defeat claims, for example, of servitude.

4 Sale of land and buildings

4.01 The law does not recognize verbal agreements for the sale of land or buildings. Agreements for the sale of heritage must be in writing and signed. If not handwritten by the signatories they must be 'adopted as holograph' or properly witnessed. Agreements once completed in normal Scottish form are binding and cannot be withdrawn from unilaterally. But such agreements do not of themselves effect a transfer of the property. Property is transferred when the title is delivered and recorded. Purchasers should normally not alter or spend money on property until they have a title. Since the title supersedes the sale agreement, purchasers' legal advisers should ensure that all sale conditions which are meant to have continuing effect are either incorporated in the title or otherwise kept in force.

4.02 The contract of sale is concluded and is binding on the purchaser and the seller when a written offer to purchase has been accepted in writing. It is too late thereafter for the purchaser to complain about the structural state of the property or that it is less extensive than he believed or is subject to feudal conditions that prevent his using it in the way he intended.

4.03 Normally missives of sale are concluded by solicitors acting for the parties. Prospective purchasers would be well advised not to sign agreements prepared by house builders or developers without taking legal advice.

5 Incorporeal heritable property

5.01 This type of property consists, broadly speaking, of rights over heritage. Servitudes are one example, and rights to leases and feu-duties are others. Security rights over land are another, as, for example, the right of a building society over property on the security of which it has granted a mortgage (Chapter 3).

6 Corporeal movable property

6.01 Ownership of movable property does not depend, as does that of heritage, on possession of a documentary title. The possessor of an article is presumed to be the owner in the absence of proof to the contrary. A person is the legal possessor of an article even if he has placed it in the hands of some other person who is his agent or servant, or whom he places in the position of custodier of the property for some reason. Thus a person taking a car to a garage for repair puts the garage in the position of custodier and does not in the eyes of the law lose possession of his car. Accordingly he continues to be the presumed owner. Similarly if an article is on hire, the legal possessor is the person who hires it out and not the person to whom it is hired. Conversely property in movables does not pass by mere agreement. There must be some element of delivery to and possession by the transferee. This aspect of Scots law has important practical implications, e.g. in relation to the effectiveness of clauses in building contracts purporting to transfer ownership of plant and materials.

7 Incorporeal movable property

7.01 This type of property consists of rights which are not, generally speaking, directly connected with heritage. Shares in a limited company and a partner's interest in his firm (Chapter 19) are both movable, even though the company or firm may own heritage. Other examples are rights to debts or rights under contracts. Trade names and trade-marks are further legal examples, as are rights to designs and copyright (Chapter 17).

9

Standard building contracts in England

STEPHEN BICKFORD-SMITH*

Introduction to the Standard Form of Contract

1 Meaning of terms

1.01 The Standard Form of Building Contract, published by the Joint Contracts Tribunal (JCT), represents the latest stage in the evolution of a form of contract originally issued by the RIBA, and hence still in some quarters erroneously called the 'RIBA Form of Contract'. This form was originally produced by the RIBA alone in the nineteenth century, but in 1909 agreement was reached on the form between the RIBA and the precursor of the NFBTE. In 1931 the JCT was established, consisting at that time of the RIBA and the NEBTE, now known as the Building Employers Confederation (BEC), with the object of publishing and where necessary amending the form of contract. Since then, the JCT has published new editions of the Standard Form in 1939, 1950, 1957, 1963, and 1980.

1.02 During this period the JCT has expanded to include in addition to its original constituent bodies the RICS, the Association of Consulting Engineers, the major local authority associations, the two principal organizations representing specialist sub-contractors (the Federation of Associations of Specialists and Sub-contractors and the Committee of Associations of Specialist Engineering Contractors), and the British Property Federation. The JCT is now therefore broad-based and comprehensive.

1.03 In 1964 there appeared an official report entitled 'The Placing and Management of Contracts for Building of Civil Engineering Works' ('the Banwell Report'). This report recommended inter alia that the conditions on which sub-contractors tender and enter into contracts should be standardized. Accordingly, in 1966 the JCT obtained authority from its constituent members to assume responsibility for the production of standard forms of sub-contract; at the same time (again on a recommendation contained in the Banwell Report) the FASS and CASEC were invited to become members of the JCT. In 1980 there appeared for the first time a Standard Form of Nominated Sub-contract bearing the imprimatur of the JCT, together with associated nominated sub-contract documentation.

*In the previous editions, this chapter was written by Donald Keating QC. In the preparation of the commentary in this edition, considerable use has been made by permission of Mr Keating's text from the second edition. For the fourth edition, the text was revised by David Chappell.

2 Documents currently published by the JCT

2.01 The JCT currently publishes the following forms of contract and associated documents.

1. The Standard Form of Building Contract in the following variants:
   (a) local authorities edition with quantities;
   (b) local authorities edition with approximate quantities;
   (c) local authorities edition without quantities;
   (d) private edition with quantities;
   (e) private edition with approximate quantities; and
   (f) private edition without quantities.
2. Standard Form of Nominated Sub-contract Tender and Agreement (NSC/1).
3. Standard Form of Employer/Nominated Sub-contractor Agreement (NSC/2).
4. Standard Form of Nomination for Sub-contractor where NSC/1 has been used (NSC/3).
5. Standard Form of Nominated Sub-contract for those sub-contractors who have
   (a) tendered on NSC/1;
   (b) executed agreement on form NSC/2;
   (c) been nominated under form NSC/3.
   This Standard Form of Nominated Sub-contract is known as NSC/4.
6. Form NSC/2a, which is a variant of NSC/2 adapted for use where tender NSC/1 has not been used.
7. Form NSC/4a, which is a variant of NSC/4 for use where tender NSC/1 has not been used.
8. Standard Form of Tender by Nominated Supplier (TNS/1) and Warranty (TNS/2).
9. Standard Form with Contractor's Design.
10. Fixed Fee Form of Prime Cost Contract.
11. Intermediate Form of Building Contract (IFC 84).
12. Agreement for Minor Building Works.
14. Sectional Completion Supplement.
15. Renovation Grant Works Form of Agreement (with architect).
16. Renovation Grant Works Form of Agreement (without architect).
17. Practice Notes.
18. Minor Works Supplement.
19. Contractor's Designed Portion Supplement (for use with the Standard Form of Contract with quantities revision).
20. Formula rules for use with Standard Form of Building Contract.
21. Formula rules for use with Standard Form of Sub-contract.
22. Formula rules for use with Standard Form of Contract with Contractor's Design.

The 1980 JCT form permits the use of domestic (i.e. non-nominated sub-contractors in certain circumstances. The

JCT publishes no standard form of non-nominated sub-contract but the BEC does publish one, known as DOM/1.

A number of amendments have ben made to the JCT forms since their original publication. Space does not permit reference to all of these. Prospective areas should check that the text of the form they propose to use contains all relevant amendments.

The sections which follow deal with the Standard Form of Main Contract, incorporating all amendments up to amendment 8 (April 1989), and the commentary deals with this and the Standard Form of Sub-contract NSC/4 together with associated documents. The other JCT forms are discussed at the end of this chapter.

3 Nature of the Standard Form

3.01 The 1980 Standard Form of Main Contract is the direct successor of the 1963 Form, but with some major changes of the form and content. In form, one major change has been the adoption of a system of subordinate decimal numbering in the interest of clarity (though one must not, for example, confuse clause 35.18.1.2 with clause 35.1.8.12 or even clause 3.5.18.12!).

3.02 A second change of format involved placing the arbitration clause (previously at the end of the conditions) at the beginning of the contract in the Articles of Agreement. The Conditions of Contract themselves are now divided into three parts: Part 1, general matters; Part 2, dealing with nominated sub-contractors and nominated suppliers; and Part 3, covering fluctuations.

3.03 The main changes in substance from the 1963 edition are:

1. The greatly expanded provisions relating to nominated sub-contractors and suppliers contained in Part 2.
2. The redrafting of the arbitration clause now contained in the articles, so as to introduce a third-party procedure.
3. The expansion of the definition of variations.
4. New provisions relating to extensions of time.
5. New provisions relating to loss and expense.

These and other provisions of the Standard Form are discussed in more detail in the commentary which follows (see The Standard Form of Building Contract, 1980 edition).

3.04 The various forms relating to nominated sub-contractors are intended for use with the Standard Form of Main

Contract; very broadly the Standard Form of Sub-contract is the successor of the 'green form' of sub-contract previously issued by the NEBTE, now the BEC. This form, together with its associated documentation, is considered more fully in the commentary which follows.

3.05 There are virtually no differences of substance between the private and local authority variants of the Standard Form of Main Contract; such divergences as there are are designed to bring the local authorities' variants into line with local authority law and practice. In the *with quantities* versions, a bill of quantities forms part of the contract documentation, and the rates contained in the bills of quantities are used for pricing variations and omissions to the contract. In principle the contract is a 'fixed price' contract, i.e. one in which the contractor takes the risk that the work may prove more costly or extensive than he had foreseen. It should, however, be noted that the effect of the relevant contract provisions (discussed in the commentary) is that the employer guarantees that the bills have been accurately prepared, and therefore the contractor is entitled to extra payment if the bills of quantities do not fully or accurately describe the work included in the contract. The *without quantities* variants incorporate, instead of bills of quantities, a specification describing the work, and a Schedule of Rates which is used for the valuation of variations. Again, the contract is a fixed price one. The *with approximate quantities* variant is a *remeasurement* contract rather than a fixed price one. In this variant a bill of quantities is prepared, showing the approximate amount of work which is estimated to be required. When the work is completed it is remeasured, and the contract sum recalculated by reference to the amount of work actually done in accordance with the bill rates. These variants are suitable for situations where it is impossible or impracticable to estimate with accuracy the amount of work required in advance.

3.06 All variants of the Standard Form are 'entire' contracts in law, i.e. ones in which the contractor is bound substantially to complete the contract work prior to receiving payment of the price, although payment is made by way of interim certificates on account of the contract sum as work proceeds.

3.07 Because the Standard Form takes effect by agreement and not by statute, it can be amended in any way the parties choose, but care should be taken when attempting any amendment less unintended ambiguities and inconsistencies are introduced. Further, any amendment to be effective must be in or referred to in the document itself and not merely in the contract bills (or specification where applicable). In the case of *Gleesons* v *London Borough of Hillingdon* (1970) 215/EG 165, the conditions were not amended, and in the appendix completion was stated to be 24 months after possession. The contract bills provided for completion in stages from 12 to 24 months. It was held that having regard to what is now clause 2 the bills must be ignored so that liquidated damages were not recoverable until the completion date specified in the appendix had passed. The special Sectional Completion Supplement is available for dealing with this specific situation. See also *Bramall and Ogden Ltd* v *Sheffield City Council* (1983) 29/BLR 73.

4 The commentary

The commentary covers both the Standard Form of Main Contract, 1980 edition (local authorities with quantities version) and the Nominated Sub-contract NSC/4, together with asociated documents related to nominated sub-contractors and suppliers. There is also a section dealing with the variant form of Nominated Sub-contract NSC/4a, although this is not set out *extenso*. Space does not permit the commentary to provide anything more than an introduction

to the Standard Form of Main Contract and of Sub-contract and their associated documents, together with a discussion of the more important problems which experience has shown arise with their use. The differences among the variant forms of the Main Contract are noted briefly in relation to each clause. The abbreviation 'MF' stands for 'main form', i.e. the Standard Form of Main Contract, and 'SCF' stands for 'sub-contract form', i.e. the Standard Form of Nominated Sub-contracts known in JCT nomenclature as NSC/4. The various other documents are referred to by their JCT reference numbers, which are set out above. Unless specifically stated otherwise, any reference to a clause means that clause of the conditions of the document concerned, and not of the articles.

The Standard Form of Building Contract, 1980 edition

5 Articles of agreement

5.01 The articles begin by naming the parties, the architect, and the quantity surveyor, and record certain matters in the recitals. Articles 1 and 2 define the basic obligations of the parties: that of the contractor is to carry out and complete the works shown upon or described by or by reference to the contract document (defined in clause 2.1 of the conditions). The employer agrees to pay the contractor the contract sum at the times and in the manner specified in the conditions. The employer is under an implied duty to appoint an architect, and, if he ceases to act, to appoint another *Croudace* v *London Borough of Lambeth* (1986) 33 BLR 20.

5.02 Article 3A defines the architect, and is only applicable where the person concerned is entitled to use the name 'architect' under and in accordance with the Architects Registration Acts 1931–1969. Article 3B is for use where the person charged with the duties normally performed by the architect under the contract is not entitled to call himself 'architect' within these Acts. Article 4 defines the quantity surveyor. The private edition does not have article 3B or footnote [e]. There is, therefore, no provision for a 'Supervising Officer' and the contractor may make reasonable objection to the appointment of another architect and (under article 4) to the appointment of another quantity surveyor.

Articles of Agreement

made the _____ day of _____ 19____

between _____

_____

(hereinafter called 'the Employer') of the one part and

_____

_____

of (or whose registered office is situated at) _____

_____

(hereinafter called 'the Contractor') [a] of the other part

Whereas

First　the Employer is desirous of (b) _____

_____

_____

(hereinafter called 'the Works') at

_____

_____

and has caused Drawings and Bills of Quantities showing and describing the work to be done to be prepared by or under the direction of

_____

_____

_____

Footnotes [a] Where the Contractor is not a limited liability　　[b] State nature of intended works.
company incorporated under the Companies Acts, see
Footnote [v] to clause 35·13·5·4·4.

Second the Contractor has supplied the Employer with a fully priced copy of the said Bills of Quantities (which copy is hereinafter referred to as 'the Contract Bills');

Third the said Drawings numbered _____

_____

(hereinafter referred to as 'the Contract Drawings') and the Contract Bills have been signed by or on behalf of the parties hereto;

Fourth the status of the Employer, for the purposes of the statutory tax deduction scheme under the Finance (No. 2) Act, 1975, as at the Date of Tender is stated in the Appendix.

Now it is hereby agreed as follows

Article 1
For the consideration hereinafter mentioned the Contractor will upon and subject to the Contract Documents carry out and complete the Works shown upon, described by or referred to in those Documents.

Article 2
The Employer will pay to the Contractor the sum of _____

_____

_____ (£ _____)
(hereinafter referred to as 'the Contract Sum') or such other sum as shall become payable hereunder at the times and in the manner specified in the Conditions.

Article 3A　[c] [d]
The term 'the Architect' in the Conditions shall mean the said

_____

of _____

_____

or, in the event of his death or ceasing to be the Architect for the purpose of this Contract, such other person as the Employer shall nominate for that purpose, *not being a person to whom the Contractor shall object for reasons considered to be sufficient by an Arbitrator appointed in accordance with article 5.* [e] Provided always that no person subsequently appointed to be the Architect under this Contract shall be entitled to disregard or overrule any certificate or opinion or decision or approval or instruction given or expressed by the Architect for the time being.

Article 3B [c] [d]
The term 'the Supervising Officer' in the Conditions shall mean the said

_____

_____

of _____

_____

or, in the event of his death or ceasing to be the Supervising Officer for the purpose of this Contract, such other person as the Employer shall nominate for that purpose, *not being a person to whom the Contractor shall object for reasons considered to be sufficient by an Arbitrator appointed in accordance with article 5.* [e] Provided always that no person subsequently appointed to be the Supervising Officer under this Contract shall be entitled to disregard or overrule any certificate or opinion or decision or approval or instruction given or expressed by the Supervising Officer for the time being.

Article 4 [d]
The Term 'the Quantity Surveyor' in the Conditions shall mean

_____

of _____

_____

or, in the event of his death or ceasing to be the Quantity Surveyor for the purpose of this Contract, such other person as the Employer shall nominate for that purpose, *not being a person to whom the Contractor shall object for reasons considered to be sufficient by an Arbitrator appointed in accordance with article 5.* [e]

Footnotes [c] Article 3A is applicable where the person concerned is entitled to the use of the name 'Architect' under and in accordance with the Architects Registration Acts, 1931 to 1969. Article 3B is applicable in all other cases. Therefore complete whichever is appropriate and delete the alternative. Where article 3A is completed the expression 'Supervising Officer' shall be deemed to have been deleted throughout the Conditions. Where article 3B is completed the expression 'Architect' shall be deemed to have been deleted throughout the Conditions.

[d] In cases where the Works are to be carried out under the direction of officials of the Local Authority, insert the names of such officials as are to perform the respective functions of the 'Architect/Supervising Officer' and the 'Quantity Surveyor' under this contract.

Footnote [e] Strike out words in italics in cases where 'the Architect', 'the Supervising Officer' or 'the Quantity Surveyor' is an official of the Local Authority.

Article 5
5·1　In case any dispute or difference shall arise between the Employer or the Architect/Supervising Officer on his behalf and the Contractor, either during the progress or after the completion or abandonment of the Works, as to

5·1　1　the construction of this Contract, or

5·1　2　any matter or thing of whatsoever nature arising hereunder or in connection herewith including any matter or thing left by this Contract to the discretion of the Architect/Supervising Officer or the withholding by the Architect/Supervising Officer of any certificate to which the Contractor may claim to be entitled or the adjustment of the Contract Sum under clause 30·6·2 or the rights and liabilities of the parties under clauses 27, 28, 32 or 33 or unreasonable withholding of consent or agreement by the Employer or the Architect/Supervising Officer on his behalf or by the Contractor, but

5·1　3　excluding any dispute or difference under clause 19A, under clause 31 to the extent provided in clause 31·9 and under clause 3 of the VAT Agreement,

then such dispute or difference shall be and is hereby referred to the arbitration and final decision of a person to be agreed between the parties to act as Arbitrator, or, failing agreement within 14 days after either party has given to the other a written request to concur in the appointment of an Arbitrator, a person to be appointed on the request of either party by the President or a Vice-President for the time being of the Royal Institute of British Architects.

5·1　4　Provided that if the dispute or difference to be referred to arbitration under this Contract raises issues which are substantially the same as or connected with issues raised in a related dispute between

the Employer and a Nominated Sub-Contractor under Agreement NSC/2 or NSC/2a as applicable or

the Contractor and any Nominated Sub-Contractor under Sub-Contract NSC/4 or NSC/4a as applicable or

the Contractor and/or the Employer and any Nominated Supplier whose contract of sale with the Contractor provides for the matters referred to in clause 36·4·8,

and if the related dispute has already been referred for determination to an Arbitrator, the Employer and Contractor hereby agree that the dispute or difference under this Contract shall be referred to the Arbitrator appointed to determine the related dispute; and such Arbitrator shall have power to make such directions and all necessary awards in the same way as if the procedure of the High Court as to joining one or more defendants or joining co-defendants or third parties was available to the parties and to him;

5·1　5　Save that the Employer or the Contractor may require the dispute or difference under this Contract to be referred to a different Arbitrator (to be appointed under this Contract) if either of them reasonably considers that the Arbitrator appointed to determine the related dispute is not appropriately qualified to determine the dispute or difference under this Contract.

5·1　6　Articles 5·1·4 and 5·1·5 shall apply unless in the Appendix the words ''Articles 5·1·4 and 5·1·5 apply'' have been deleted.

5·2　Such reference, except

1　on article 3 or article 4; or

2　on the questions
whether or not the issue of an instruction is empowered by the Conditions; or whether or not a certificate has been improperly withheld; or whether a certificate is not in accordance with the Conditions; or whether a determination under clause 22C·4·3·1 will be just and equitable or

3　on any dispute or difference under clause 4·1 in regard to a reasonable objection by the Contractor, and clauses 25, 32 and 33,

under clause 18·1 or clause 23·3·2 in regard to and withholding of consent by the Contractor

shall not be opened until after Practical Completion or alleged Practical Completion of the Works or termination or alleged termination of the Contractor's employment under this Contract or abandonment of the Works, unless with the written consent of the Employer or the Architect/Supervising Officer on his behalf and the Contractor.

5·3　Subject to the provisions of clauses 4·2, 30·9, 38·4·3, 39·5·3 and 40·5 the Arbitrator shall, without prejudice to the generality of his powers, have power to direct such measurements and/or valuations as may in his opinion be desirable in order to determine the rights of the parties and to ascertain and award any sum which ought to have been the subject of or included in any certificate and to open up, review and revise any certificate, opinion, decision, requirement or notice and to determine all matters in dispute which shall be submitted to him in the same manner as if no such certificate, opinion, decision, requirement or notice had been given.

---

5 4   The award of such Arbitrator shall be final and binding on the parties.

5 5   Whatever the nationality, residence or domicile of the Employer, the Contractor, any sub-contractor or supplier or the Arbitrator, and wherever the Works or any part thereof are situated, the law of England shall be the proper law of this Contract and in particular (but not so as to derogate from the generality of the foregoing) the provisions of the Arbitration Acts 1950 (notwithstanding anything in S.34 thereof) to 1979 shall apply to any arbitration under this Contract wherever the same, or any part of it, shall be conducted.[f]

Footnote [f] Where the parties do not wish the proper law of the Contract to be the law of England and/or do not wish the provisions of the Arbitration Acts 1950 to 1979 to apply to any arbitration under the Contract held under the procedural law of Scotland (or other country) appropriate amendments to article 5 5 should be made.

Attestation [g]

[g] This page should be completed with the appropriate attestation clause.

The arbitration provisions

5.03 Article 5 contains the provisions governing arbitration of disputes which arise out of the contract. Article 5.1 defines the arbitrator's jurisdiction in very wide terms: it extends, for example, to a review of all decisions of the architect.

In *Northern Regional Health Authority* v *Derek Crouch Construction* (1984) QB 644, 26 BLR 1, it was held that the court did not have the same powers as conferred on an arbitrator under article S.3. Accordingly, disputes of this nature must be referred to arbitration.

In *Ashville Investments Ltd* v *Elmer Contractors Ltd* (1987) 37 BLR 55 it was held that claims for rectifications and for innocent and negligent misrepresentation fell within this clause.

5.04 Clause 35(2) of the 1963 JCT Form is reproduced in article 5.2. However, there are a number of departures from the former wording, which are as follows:

1. The contractor can now request immediate arbitration (as opposed to waiting until after practical completion) on the question whether he is entitled to make reasonable objection to an instruction relating to the variation of restrictions on methods of working etc. imposed by the employer (see article 5.2.3, and conditions clauses 4.1.1 and 13.1.2).
2. He likewise has a right to request immediate arbitration on the question whether he is entitled to an extension of time for completion of the works (see article 5.2.3 and conditions clause 25).

5.05 Clause 35(3) of the 1963 JCT Form is reproduced in article 5.3, and clause 35(4) in article 5.4. Article 5.5 reproduces 1963 JCT Form clause 35(5).

5.06 Article 5.1.4, read subject to articles 5.1.5 and 5.1.6, represents an attempt to introduce a form of 'third-party' procedure, similar to that possible in normal litigation. Article 5.1.4 provides that if a dispute or difference arises between the employer and the contractor:

1. there has already been referred to arbitration as dispute between
   (a) the employer and a nominated sub-contractor;
   (b) the contractor and any nominated sub-contractor;
   (c) the contractor or employer and any nominated supplier; and
2. if the dispute which arises between the employer and the contractor raises issues which are substantially the same as or connected with issues raised in the existing arbitration the matter is to be referred to the arbitrator dealing with the existing dispute.

As far as nominated suppliers are concerned, under clause 36.4 it is provided that the architect shall nominate as a supplier only a person who will enter into a contract for sale with the contractor, providing inter alia (by clause 36.4.8) that if any dispute arises between the contractor and the nominated supplier which raises issues which are substantially the same as or are connected with issues raised in a related dispute between the employer and the contractor, then where articles 5.1.4 and 5.1.5 apply, such dispute or difference shall be referred to the arbitrator appointed or to be appointed pursuant to article 5 who shall have power to make such directions and all necessary awards in the same way as if the procedure of the High Court as to joining one or more defendants or joining co-defendants or third parties was available to the parties and to him and in any case the award of such arbitrator shall be final and binding on the parties. Therefore, where the terms of a nominated supplier's contract with the contractor contain provisions corresponding to clause 36.4.8, any dispute between the contractor and the nominated supplier raising issues which are substantially the same as or are connected with issues in a related dispute between the employer and the contractor are to be referred to the arbitrator seized of the dispute between the employer and the contractor.

However, neither clause 36.4.8 nor article 5 govern the mechanism for invitation of arbitration between the main contractor and nominated supplier where reference to an existing arbitrator is not required under the former. The provisions of the Standard Form of Tender by Nominated Supplier (TNS/1) and Warranty by a Nominated Supplier (TNS/2), especially clause 1.2 of TNS/1 and clause 4.2 of TNS/2 (para 46.10), should also be noted in this connection.

Under the concluding words of article 5.1.4, the arbitrator is to have power to make all directions and all necessary awards in the same way as if the procedure of the High Court as to joining one or more defendants or joining co-defendants or third parties was available to the parties and to him. The intention is that a form of 'third-party' procedure should be available, modelled on that laid down principally in Order 16 of the Rules of the Supreme Court 1965.

The provisions of article 5.1.4 are more limited than those of the Rules of the Supreme Court, since an arbitration agreement can be binding only on the parties thereto. It is thought that article 5.1.4 will be of considerable help, particularly in more complex disputes relating to such matters as delay, where responsibility may have to be apportioned among a large number of nominated sub-contractors, the contractor, and possibly the employer or his architect. In such cases it will be possible by agreement (for that is the practical effect) for all the parties potentially liable in respect of the delay to be brought before the same tribunal, to make claims against such other parties as are appropriate, and for liability to be apportioned equitably among them.

The machinery of article 5.1.4 contemplates reference of a dispute to the arbitrator appointed to determine the related dispute which *ex-hypothesi* has already arisen. It is not clear whether the arbitration relating to the related dispute must still be on foot, or whether article 5.1.4 applies even where the arbitrator in the related dispute has already made his final award when the new dispute arises. Nor is it clear whether it is possible to refer the new dispute to the arbitrator dealing with the related dispute where the related dispute arbitration has reached a very advanced stage.

Presumably the question whether a dispute is to be referred to an arbitrator dealing with an existing dispute must be determined as at the time the reference to arbitration falls to be made, so that if at that time the existing arbitration does not raise issues connected with the fresh dispute which has arisen, that dispute is not to be referred to the arbitrator dealing with the existing dispute, even though subsequently the issues in the existing arbitration are widened so as to include some which are substantially the same as or are connected with the fresh dispute.

It is not clear who is to decide whether the criteria for referring the dispute to an arbitrator dealing with an existing dispute are satisfied, cf *Higgs & Hill Building Ltd* v *Campbell Dennis Ltd* (1982) 28 BLR 47.

5.07 Article 5.1.5 entitles either the employer or the contractor to object to their dispute being referred to the arbitrator appointed to determine the related dispute if he is not appropriately qualified to determine the new dispute. It is not clear who is to decide whether the objection is reasonable.

5.08 Article 5.2 provides that arbitration is not to be commenced until after practical completion or alleged practical completion or after termination or alleged termination of the contractor's employment, or abandonment of the works without the parties' written consent save in certain circumstances.

Excluded disputes

5.09 Under article 5.1.3 (which had no counterpart in the 1963 JCT Contract) there are excluded from the arbitration provisions disputes relating to fair wages, the statutory tax deduction scheme, and the VAT agreement. The object of these exclusions is clear: statute provides alternative methods of resolving disputes relating to these matters, which would bind the parties irrespective of the arbitrator's decision.

Part 1 Conditions

6 Clause 1: Interpretation, definitions, etc.

6.01 This clause calls for very little comment. Its purpose is to provide a helpful list of definitions of the main terms used in the contract. Note that a 'person' may be an individual, firm (partnership) or body corporate. It is therefore possible for the architect, under clause 8.5, to issue an instruction for the exclusion from the works of an entire firm of, say, sub-contractors if he has sufficient reason.

Part 1: General

1 **Interpretation, definitions etc.**

1·1   Unless otherwise specifically stated a reference in the Articles of Agreement, the Conditions or the Appendix to any clause means that clause of the Conditions.

1·2   The Articles of Agreement, the Conditions and the Appendix are to be read as a whole and the effect or operation of any article or clause in the Conditions or item in or entry in the Appendix must therefore unless otherwise specifically stated be read subject to any relevant qualification or modification in any other article or any of the clauses in the Conditions or item in or entry in the Appendix.

1·3   Unless the context otherwise requires or the Articles or the Conditions or an item in or entry in the Appendix specifically otherwise provides, the following words and phrases in the Articles of Agreement, the Conditions and the Appendix shall have the meanings given below or as ascribed in the article, clause or Appendix item to which reference is made:

Word or phrase	Meaning
All Risks Insurance:	see **clause 22·2**.
Appendix:	the Appendix to the Conditions as completed by the parties.
Arbitrator:	the person appointed under **clause 41** to be the Arbitrator.
Articles or Articles of Agreement:	the Articles of Agreement to which the Conditions are annexed, and references to any recital are to the recitals set out before the Articles.
Architect:	the person entitled to the use of the name "Architect" and named in **article 3** or any successor duly appointed under **article 3** or otherwise agreed as the person to be the Architect.
Base Date:	the date stated in the Appendix.
Certificate of Completion of Making Good Defects:	see **clause 17·4**.
Completion Date:	the Date for Completion as fixed and stated in the Appendix or any date fixed under either **clause 25** or **33·1·3**.
Conditions:	the clauses 1 to 37 and clause 41 and either clause 38 or 39 or 40, and the Supplemental Provisions ("the VAT Agreement") annexed to the Articles of Agreement.

Word or phrase	Meaning
Contractor:	the person named as Contractor in the Articles of Agreement.
Contract Bills:	the Bills of Quantities referred to in the **First recital** which have been priced by the Contractor and signed by or on behalf of the parties to this Contract.
Contract Documents:	see **clause 2·1**.
Contract Drawings:	the Drawings referred to in the **First recital** which have been signed by or on behalf of the parties to this Contract.
Contract Sum:	the sum named in **article 2** but subject to **clause 15·2**.
Date for Completion:	the date fixed and stated in the Appendix.
Date of Possession:	the date stated in the Appendix under the reference to **clause 23·1**.
Defects Liability Period:	the period named in the Appendix under the reference to **clause 17·2**.
Domestic Sub-Contractor:	see **clause 19·2**.
Employer:	the person named as Employer in the Articles of Agreement.
Excepted Risks:	ionising radiations or contamination by radioactivity from any nuclear fuel or from any nuclear waste from the combustion of nuclear fuel, radioactive toxic explosive or other hazardous properties of any explosive nuclear assembly or nuclear component thereof, pressure waves caused by aircraft or other aerial devices travelling at sonic or supersonic speeds.
Final Certificate:	the certificate to which **clause 30·8** refers.
Interim Certificate:	any one of the certificates to which **clauses 30·1** and **30·7** and the entry in the **Appendix** under the reference to **clause 30·1·3** refers.
Joint Names Policy:	a policy of insurance which includes the Contractor and the Employer as the insured.
Nominated Sub-Contractor:	see **clause 35·1**.
Nominated Sub-Contract Documents: Tender NSC/1 Agreement NSC/2 Agreement NSC/2a Nomination NSC/3 Sub-Contract NSC/4 Sub-Contract NSC/4a	see **clause 35·3**.
Nominated Supplier:	see **clause 36·1·1**.
Numbered Documents:	any Document referred to in the first recital in any Sub-Contract with a Nominated Sub-Contractor.
Period of Final Measurement and Valuation:	the period named in the **Appendix** under the reference to **clause 30·6·1·2**.
Period of Interim Certificates:	the period named in the **Appendix** under the reference to **clause 30·1·3**.
person:	an individual, firm (partnership) or body corporate.
Practical Completion:	see **clause 17·1**.
Quantity Surveyor:	the person named in **article 4** or any successor duly appointed under **article 4** or otherwise agreed as the person to be the Quantity Surveyor.
Relevant Event:	any one of the events set out in **clause 25·4**.
Retention:	see **clause 30·2**.
Retention Percentage:	see **clause 30·4·1·1** and any entry in the Appendix under the reference to **clause 30·4·1·1**.
Site Materials:	see **clause 22·2**.
Specified Perils:	fire, lightning, explosion, storm, tempest, flood, bursting or overflowing of water tanks, apparatus or pipes, earthquake, aircraft and other aerial devices or articles dropped therefrom, riot and civil commotion, but excluding Excepted Risks.
Statutory Requirements:	see **clause 6·1·1**.
Sub-Contract:	the sub-contractual rights and obligations of the Contractor and a Nominated Sub-Contractor as set out in the Sub-Contract Documents as defined in Sub-Contract NSC/4 or NSC/4a.
Valuation:	see **clause 13·4·1·1**.
Variation:	see **clause 13·1**.
VAT Agreement:	see **clause 15·1**.
Works:	the works briefly described in the **First recital** and shown and described in the Contract Drawings and in the Contract Bills.

1·4   Notwithstanding any obligation of the Architect to the Employer and whether or not the Employer appoints a clerk of works, the Contractor shall remain wholly responsible for carrying out and completing the Works in all respects in accordance with clause 2·1, whether or not the Architect or the clerk of works, if appointed, at any time goes on to the Works or to any workshop or other place where work is being prepared to inspect the same or otherwise, or the Architect includes the value of any work, materials or goods in a certificate for payment, save as provided in clause 30·9·1·1 with regard to the conclusiveness of the Final Certificate.

7 Clause 2: Contractor's obligations

7.01 The contractor has to carry out and complete the contract works, but he is both entitled to the benefit of the conditions and subject to the obligations which they impose upon him.

7.02 Clause 2.1 provides that where and to the extent that approval of the quality of materials or of the standards of workmanship is a matter for the opinion of the architect, such policy and standards shall be to the reasonable satisfaction of the architect. Under clause 30.9.1.1 the effect of the final certificate is conclusive evidence that where the quality of materials or the standard of workmanship are to be to the reasonable satisfaction of the architect, the same are to such satisfaction. Whether or not materials or workmanship come within the class of work subject to the reasonable satisfaction of the architect requires consideration of the contract document, in particular of the contract bills. As examples consider: 'finish to the architect's approval' and 'to the standards of BSS no. – (with no reference to the architect)'. The first example comes, it is suggested, within clause 30.9.1.1, whereas the second does not.

2		Contractor's obligations
2·1		The Contractor shall upon and subject to the Conditions carry out and complete the Works shown upon the Contract Drawings and described by or referred to in the Contract Bills and in the Articles of Agreement, the Conditions and the Appendix (which Drawings, Bills, Articles of Agreement, Conditions and Appendix are in this Contract referred to collectively as 'the Contract Documents') in compliance therewith, using materials and workmanship of the quality and standards therein specified, provided that where and to the extent that approval of the quality of materials or of the standards of workmanship is a matter for the opinion of the Architect, such quality and standards shall be to the reasonable satisfaction of the Architect.
2·2	·1	Nothing contained in the Contract Bills shall override or modify the application or interpretation of that which is contained in the Articles of Agreement, the Conditions or the Appendix.
2·2	·2	Subject always to clause 2·2·1 :
	·2 ·1	the Contract Bills, unless otherwise specifically stated therein in respect of any specified item or items, are to have been prepared in accordance with the Standard Method of Measurement of Building Works, 6th Edition published by the Royal Institution of Chartered Surveyors and the Building Employers Confederation;
	·2 ·2	if in the Contract Bills there is any departure from the method of preparation referred to in clause 2·2·2·1 or any error in description or in quantity or omission of items, then such departure or error or omission shall not vitiate this Contract but the departure or error or omission shall be corrected and such correction shall be treated as if it were a Variation required by an instruction of the Architect under clause 13·2.
2·3		If the Contractor shall find any discrepancy in or divergence between any two or more of the following documents, including a divergence between parts of any one of them or between documents of the same description, namely:
2·3	·1	the Contract Drawings,
2·3	·2	the Contract Bills,
2·3	·3	any instruction issued by the Architect under the Conditions (save insofar as any such instruction requires a Variation in accordance with the provisions of clause 13·2) and
2·3	·4	any drawings or documents issued by the Architect under clause 5·3·1·1, 5·4 or 7,
2·3	·5	the Numbered Documents.
		he shall immediately give to the Architect a written notice specifying the discrepancy or divergence, and the Architect shall issue instructions in regard thereto.

The position of the architect

7.03 The architect is the employer's agent with authority to exercise those powers conferred on him by the contract. As such, he is both entitled and obliged to protect the employer's interests. Formerly, the courts took the view that because of the grave disadvantages which would be suffered by the contractor if the architect failed to certify properly or otherwise exercise in a proper manner duties given to him by the contract, the architect was to some extent in an independent 'quasi-judicial' position, and immune from actions for negligence by either party when performing functions requiring the exercise of his independent professional judgement and the application of his mind fairly and impartially between the parties. However, in *Sutcliffe* v *Thackrah* [1974] AC 727, it was held that an architect was

liable to his employer for negligently over-certifying on interim certificates, and the House of Lords said that the architect enjoyed no such 'quasi-judicial' immunity.

The architect must at all times seek to perform as exactly as possible his duties under the contract. Thus, for example, it is wrong to permit a contractor to carry out work to a standard lower than that required by the contract because the architect discovers that the contractor has tendered low. It is also wrong to insist on a standard of work higher than the contract standard because the employer demands it. Architects are reminded that quite apart from what the courts have explained as their role under the Building Contract, Rule 1.4 of the RIBA Code of Professional Conduct requires all members and students of the RIBA to act impartially in all matters of dispute between the building owner and the contractor and to interpret the conditions of the Building Contract with entire fairness as between the parties.

7.04 This duty to act fairly is often extremely difficult for a client to appreciate, but is essential to the correct functioning of the contract. The foregoing does not mean that the architect may not consult with the employer on matters within the sphere of his independent duty, but obliges the architect when he comes to make his decision to make up his own mind, doing the best to decide what the parties must have intended according to the contract document and circumstances obtaining at the time of entering into the contract. He should then certify or give his decision accordingly whether or not he thinks it will please the employer. It is in this way that the architect must act in an independent manner.

Method of work

7.05 It is not the architect's function to direct the contractor in the way he shall carry out the works, save where the conditions expressly give him this power (see clause 13). But the contractor must carry out works included in the bills, and these sometimes include temporary works, e.g. form work or other force work.

Liability for design

7.06 Although the position in law is not entirely clear, it is generally accepted that provided the contractor carries out the work strictly in accordance with the contract documents, he is not responsible if such works prove to be unsuitable for the purpose which the employer or the architect had in mind. But the contractor may have certain duties relating to design. The contract bills may include such duties; compliance with the Building Regulations (see clause 6) often involves some design considerations, and further it is probably the contractor's implied duty to bring to the architect's attention obvious errors in the architect's design of which the contractor had actual knowledge. In any event he has an express duty to give notice to the architect of any discrepancy or divergence which he finds (see clause 2.3 and, for statutory requirements, clause 6.1.2).

7.07 Clause 2.2.1 provides that nothing in the bills shall override or modify the interpretation of the articles, conditions, or appendix. Thus if a provision in the bills conflicts with anything in these latter documents, the latter prevails as a matter of interpretation (see *Gleesons* v *Hillingdon* (1970) 215 EG 165, *English Industrial Estates* v *George Wimpey* [1973] 1 Lloyds Reports 118, and *Henry Boot Construction Limited* v *Central Lancashire New Town Development Corporation* (1980) 15 BLR 1).

7.08 Under clause 2.2.2.1 unless otherwise expressly stated in respect of any specified item or items, the contract bills are deemed to have been prepared in accordance with the principles of the *Standard Method of Measurement*, 6th edition (SMM). If they have not been so prepared, there is an

error which must be corrected and the correction is deemed to be a variation required by the architect. Clause A2.1 of SMM 6 expressly requires bills fully and accurately to describe the work. Thus, for example, if there is no provision in the contract bills for excavation in rock but in carrying out the work it becomes clear that such excavation is necessary, then it seems the bills must be read as if they included an item for excavation in rock – see SMM item D13 – and the contractor will become entitled to extra payment (cf *Bryant & Son Limited* v *Birmingham Hospital Saturday Fund* [1938] 1 All ER 503.

8 Clause 3: Contract sum – additions or deductions – adjustment – interim certificate

8.01 This clause makes it clear that where adjustments are made in the contract sum, as soon as the adjustment has been quantified whether in whole or in part it is to be taken into account in computing the next interim certificate, not left until the final certificate.

3	Contract Sum – additions or deductions – adjustment – Interim Certificates
	Where in the Conditions it is provided that an amount is to be added to or deducted from the Contract Sum or dealt with by adjustment of the Contract Sum then as soon as such amount is ascertained in whole or in part such amount shall be taken into account in the computation of the next Interim Certificate following such whole or partial ascertainment.

9 Clause 4: Architect's/supervising officer's instructions

9.01 The contractor must comply with the architect's instructions. Failure to comply gives rise to the rights under this clause to have work carried out by others, and in some circumstances can result in the employer having the right to determine the contractor's employment (see clause 27.1.3).

4	Architect's instructions
4·1 ·1	The Contractor shall forthwith comply with all instructions issued to him by the Architect in regard to any matter in respect of which the Architect is expressly empowered by the Conditions to issue instructions; save that where such instruction is one requiring a Variation within the meaning of clause 13·1·2 the Contractor need not comply to the extent that he makes reasonable objection in writing to the Architect to such compliance.
4·1 ·2	If within 7 days after receipt of a written notice from the Architect requiring compliance with an instruction the Contractor does not comply therewith, then the Employer may employ and pay other persons to execute any work whatsoever which may be necessary to give effect to such instruction; and all costs incurred in connection with such employment may be deducted by him from any monies due or to become due to the Contractor under this Contract or may be recoverable from the Contractor by the Employer as a debt.
4·2	Upon receipt of what purports to be an instruction issued to him by the Architect the Contractor may request the Architect to specify in writing the provision of the Conditions which empowers the issue of the said instruction. The Architect shall forthwith comply with any such request, and if the Contractor shall thereafter comply with the said instruction (neither party before such compliance having given to the other a written request to concur in the appointment of an Arbitrator under clause 41 in order that it may be decided whether the provision specified by the Architect empowers the issue of the said instruction), then the issue of the same shall be deemed for all the purposes of this Contract to have been empowered by the provision of the Conditions specified by the Architect in answer to the Contractor's request.
4·3 ·1	All instructions issued by the Architect shall be issued in writing.
4·3 ·2	If the Architect purports to issue an instruction otherwise than in writing it shall be of no immediate effect, but shall be confirmed in writing by the Contractor to the Architect within 7 days, and if not dissented from in writing by the Architect to the Contractor within 7 days from receipt of the Contractor's confirmation shall take effect as from the expiration of the latter said 7 days. Provided always:
·2 ·1	that if the Architect within 7 days of giving such an instruction otherwise than in writing shall himself confirm the same in writing, then the Contractor shall not be obliged to confirm as aforesaid, and the said instruction shall take effect as from the date of the Architect's confirmation; and
·2 ·2	that if neither the Contractor nor the Architect shall confirm such an instruction in the manner and at the time aforesaid but the Contractor shall nevertheless comply with the same, then the Architect may confirm the same in writing at any time prior to the issue of the Final Certificate, and the said instruction shall thereupon be deemed to have taken effect on the date on which it was issued otherwise than in writing by the Architect.

Power to issue instructions

9.02 The architect can only issue instructions where express power is given. The most important instances are:

1. Clause 2.3.4 (discrepancies in documents).
2. Clause 6.1.3 (statutory requirement).
3. Clause 7 (levels).
4. Clause 8.3 (inspections and tests).
5. Clause 8.4 (removal of work materials or goods).
6. Clause 8.5 (exclusions of persons from the works).
7. Clause 13.2 (variations).
8. Clause 13.3 (instructions on provisional sums).
9. Clause 17.2 (defects, shrinkages, or other faults).
10. Clause 17.3 (rectification of defects).
11. Clause 22C.2.3.2 (removal of debris).
12. Clause 23.2 (postponement of work).
13. Clause 32.2 (protective work on outbreak of hostilities).
14. Clause 33.1.2 (war damage).
15. Clause 34.2 (antiquities).
16. Clause 35.10.2 (nomination of nominated sub-contractors).
17. Clause 35.24.4.1 (notice specifying default of nominated sub-contractor).
18. Clause 35.24.5 (nomination of new sub-contractor).
19. Clause 36.2 (nominating a supplier).

Under clause 4.2, the contractor may request the architect to specify in writing the provision of the conditions which empowers the issue of the instruction. If the architect does this and the contractor then obeys the instruction, it is to be deemed to be empowered by the provision in the contract specified in the architect's answer. Failing this, there is provision for arbitration which (by virtue of article 5.2.2) need not await practical completion.

Form of instructions

9.03 Under article 4.3.1, instructions are to be in writing, but note the elaborate provisions in clause 4.3.2 for confirmation in writing if the architect purports to issue an oral instruction.

Site meeting minutes

9.04 Sometimes the architect and contractor expressly agree that such minutes are to operate as the confirmation of oral instructions contemplated by clause 4.3. If there was no express agreement as to the status of the minutes, it must be decided in each case whether it was intended they should act as written confirmation. Significant factors would be the authorship of the minutes and whether they are accepted by all parties as a true record.

10 Clause 5: Contract documents – other documents – issue of certificates

10.01 This clause is concerned with that aspect of contract administration relating to the custody and issue of the contract and other documents. The provisions of clause 5.3.1.2 should be particularly noted: this requires the contractor to supply the architect with two copies of his master programme for the execution of the works and to update it to take account of extensions of time granted under clause 25 or clause 33 (relating to outbreak of hostilities). However, under clause 5.3.2, this master programme will not impose any obligation beyond those imposed by the contract documents.

5		Contract Documents – other documents – issue of certificates

5·1 The Contract Drawings and the Contract Bills shall remain in the custody of the Architect or the Quantity Surveyor so as to be available at all reasonable times for the inspection of the Employer and of the Contractor.

5·2 Immediately after the execution of this Contract the Architect without charge to the Contractor shall provide him (unless he shall have been previously so provided) with:

5·2 ·1 one copy certified on behalf of the Employer of the Contract Documents;

5·2 ·2 two further copies of the Contract Drawings; and

5·2 ·3 two copies of the unpriced Bills of Quantities.

5·3 ·1 So soon as is possible after the execution of this Contract:

·1 ·1 the Architect without charge to the Contractor shall provide him (unless he shall have been previously so provided) with 2 copies of any descriptive schedules or other like documents necessary for use in carrying out the Works; and

·1 ·2 the Contractor without charge to the Employer shall provide the Architect (unless he shall have been previously so provided) with 2 copies of his master programme for the execution of the Works and within 14 days of any decision by the Architect under clause 25·3·1 or 33·1·3 with 2 copies of any amendments and revisions to take account of that decision. [h]

5·3 ·2 Nothing contained in the descriptive schedules or other like documents referred to in clause 5·3·1·1 (nor in the master programme for the execution of the Works or any amendment to that programme or revision therein referred to in clause 5·3·1·2) shall impose any obligation beyond those imposed by the Contract Documents. [i]

5·4 As and when from time to time may be necessary the Architect without charge to the Contractor shall provide him with 2 copies of such further drawings or details as are reasonably necessary either to explain and amplify the Contract Drawings or to enable the Contractor to carry out and complete the Works in accordance with the Conditions.

5·5 The Contractor shall keep one copy of the Contract Drawings, one copy of the unpriced Bills of Quantities, one copy of the descriptive schedules or other like documents referred to in clause 5·3·1·1, one copy of the master programme referred to in clause 5·3·1·2 (unless clause 5·3·1·2 has been deleted) and one copy of the drawings and details referred to in clause 5·4 upon the Works so as to be available to the Architect or his representative at all reasonable times.

5·6 Upon final payment under clause 30·8 the Contractor shall if so requested by the Architect forthwith return to him all drawings, details, descriptive schedules and other documents of a like nature which bear the name of the Architect.

5·7 None of the documents mentioned in clause 5 shall be used by the Contractor for any purpose other than this Contract, and neither the Employer, the Architect nor the Quantity Surveyor shall divulge or use except for the purposes of this Contract any of the rates or prices in the Contract Bills.

5·8 Except where otherwise specifically so provided any certificate to be issued by the Architect under the Conditions shall be issued to the Employer, and immediately upon the issue of any such certificate the Architect shall send a duplicate copy thereof to the Contractor.

[h] To be deleted if no master programme is required.	[i] Words in parentheses to be deleted if no master programme is required.

Issue of certificates

10.02 Certificates are to be issued to the employer with a copy to the contractor.

11 Clause 6: Statutory obligations, notices, fees and charges

11.01 This clause imposes heavy obligations. The contractor has both to comply with and give statutory notices and also comply with relevant statutory requirements, including the Building Regulations 1985 which, outside London, now replace the local byelaws formerly in operation. Within inner London the construction of buildings is still regulated by the London Building Acts and the London Building Constructional Byelaws (but see section 70 of the Health and Safety etc. at Work Act 1974).

6		Statutory obligations, notices, fees and charges

6·1 ·1 Subject to clause 6·1·5 the Contractor shall comply with, and give all notices required by, any Act of Parliament, any instrument, rule or order made under any Act of Parliament, or any regulation or byelaw of any local authority or of any statutory undertaker which has any jurisdiction with regard to the Works or with whose systems the same are or will be connected (all requirements to be so complied with being referred to in the Conditions as 'the Statutory Requirements').

6·1 ·2 If the Contractor shall find any divergence between the Statutory Requirements and all or any of the documents referred to in clause 2·3 or between the Statutory Requirements and any instruction of the Architect requiring a Variation issued in accordance with clause 13·2, he shall immediately give to the Architect a written notice specifying the divergence.

6·1 ·3 If the Contractor gives notice under clause 6·1·2 or if the Architect shall otherwise discover or receive notice of a divergence between the Statutory Requirements and all or any of the documents referred to in clause 2·3 or between the Statutory Requirements and any instruction requiring a Variation issued in accordance with clause 13·2, the Architect shall within 7 days of the discovery or receipt of a notice issue instructions in relation to the divergence. If and insofar as the instructions require the Works to be varied, they shall be treated as if they were Architect's instructions requiring a Variation issued in accordance with clause 13·2.

6·1 ·4 ·1 If in any emergency compliance with clause 6·1·1 requires the Contractor to supply materials or execute work before receiving instructions under clause 6·1·3 the Contractor shall supply such limited materials and execute such limited work as are reasonably necessary to secure immediate compliance with the Statutory Requirements.

·4 ·2 The Contractor shall forthwith inform the Architect of the emergency and of the steps that he is taking under clause 6·1·4·1.

·4 ·3 Work executed and materials supplied by the Contractor under clause 6·1·4·1 shall be treated as if they had been executed and supplied pursuant to an Architect's instruction requiring a Variation issued in accordance with clause 13·2 provided that the emergency arose because of a divergence between the Statutory Requirements and all or any of the documents referred to in clause 2·3 or between the Statutory Requirements and any instruction requiring a Variation issued in accordance with clause 13·2, and the Contractor has complied with clause 6·1·4·2.

6·1 ·5 Provided that the Contractor complies with clause 6·1·2, the Contractor shall not be liable to the Employer under this Contract if the Works do not comply with the Statutory Requirements where and to the extent that such non-compliance of the Works results from the Contractor having carried out work in accordance with the documents referred to in clause 2·3 or with any instruction requiring a Variation issued by the Architect in accordance with clause 13·2.

6·2 The Contractor shall pay and indemnify the Employer against liability in respect of any fees or charges (including any rates or taxes) legally demandable under any Act of Parliament, any instrument, rule or order made under any Act of Parliament, or any regulation or byelaw of any local authority or of any statutory undertaker in respect of the Works. The amount of any such fees or charges (including any rates or taxes other than value added tax) shall be added to the Contract Sum unless they:

6·2 ·1 arise in respect of work executed or materials or goods supplied by a local authority or statutory undertaker as a Nominated Sub-Contractor or as a Nominated Supplier; or

6·2 ·2 are priced in the Contract Bills; or

6·2 ·3 are stated by way of a provisional sum in the Contract Bills.

6·3 The provisions of clauses 19 and 35 shall not apply to the execution of part of the Works by a local authority or a statutory undertaker executing such work solely in pursuance of its statutory obligations and such bodies shall not be sub-contractors within the terms of this Contract.

11.02 Under section 71 of the Health and Safety etc. at Work Act 1974 'subject to the provisions of this section, breach of duty imposed by building regulations shall so far as it causes damage be actionable except insofar as the regulations provide otherwise'. This provision has not yet been brought into force but a contractor probably also owes a duty at common law to take reasonable care to comply with the Building Regulations (see *Anns* v *Merton London Borough Council* [1978] AC 728). However, where the architect's design does not comply with the regulations, the contractor may be entitled to an indemnity against any claim for breach of this clause, thus effectively relieving him of liability – see *EDAC* v *William Moss* (1984) Const LJ 1.

Breach of these duties, in addition to giving rise to the possibility of criminal proceedings, makes the contractor liable in damages to the employer. The architect may also be liable to the employer and in some circumstances to the contractor (see *Townsend (Builders) Limited* v *Cinema News Etc Limited* [1959] 1 WLR 119).

11.03 Note the contractor's duty to give notice of a variation required by compliance with Building Regulations and the like.

11.04 Under clause 6.1.3 provided the contractor gives notice of any divergence between the statutory requirements and the contract documents or an architect's instructions, he is entitled to treat any resulting architect's instruction requiring a variation as an instruction requiring a variation under clause 13.2.

11.05 Clause 6.3 expressly excludes work carried out by local authorities or statutory undertakers in pursuance of their statutory obligations from the provisions of clauses 19 and 35 relating respectively to domestic and nominated sub-contractors. It is important to note that this applies only where the work is being carried out by the local authority or

statutory undertaker 'solely in pursuance of its statutory obligations' and would not apply where, for example, an electricity board were carrying out works as sub-contractors in the normal way (cf *Henry Boot Construction Limited* v *Central Lancashire New Town Development Corporation* (1980) 15 BLR 1).

12 Clause 7: Levels and setting out of the works

12.01 The words 'unless the architect . . . shall otherwise instruct . . .' are uncertain in meaning. They may mean that the architect has the power to engage others to correct the contractor's errors, deducting the cost from the contract sum; or to accept the errors and assess a suitable reduction in the contract sum; or to order the employer to pay for the contractor's error. It is suggested that this last action would only be taken in very unusual circumstances. The normal practice would be for the contractor to correct his own errors or, at least, bear the cost.

7	Levels and setting out of the Works
	The Architect shall determine any levels which may be required for the execution of the Works, and shall provide the Contractor by way of accurately dimensioned drawings with such information as shall enable the Contractor to set out the Works at ground level. The Contractor shall be responsible for, and shall, at no cost to the Employer, amend any errors arising from his own inaccurate setting out. With the consent of the Employer the Architect may instruct that such errors shall not be amended and an appropriate deduction for such errors not required to be amended shall be made from the Contract Sum.

13 Clause 8: Materials, goods and workmanship to conform to description, testing and inspection

13.01 This clause defines the kinds and standards of materials and workmanship which the contract requires and gives the architect certain important powers. The wording makes clear that the contractor cannot be required to provide that which may have become unobtainable since the date of tender. However, it would seem that he is not obliged to suggest any alternative. Although the contract is silent on this point, it would usually fall to the architect to issue an instruction requiring a variation under clause 13.2. So far as the contract bills do not describe standards, the contractor must carry out the work in accordance with the standards implied by law. These are that he must do the work with all proper skill and care (or as it is sometimes expressed, in a good and workmanlike manner) and supply materials which, firstly, are reasonably fit for the purpose for which they will be used, and, secondly, are of good quality.

8	Materials, goods and workmanship to conform to description, testing and inspection
8·1	·1 All materials and goods shall, so far as procurable, be of the kinds and standards described in the Contract Bills, provided that materials and goods shall be to the reasonable satisfaction of the Architect where and to the extent that this is required in accordance with clause 2·1.
8·1	·2 All workmanship shall be of the standards described in the Contract Bills, or, to the extent that no such standards are described in the Contract Bills, shall be of a standard appropriate to the Works, provided that workmanship shall be to the reasonable satisfaction of the Architect where and to the extent that this is required in accordance with clause 2·1.
8·2	·1 The Contractor shall upon the request of the Architect provide him with vouchers to prove that the materials and goods comply with clause 8·1.
8·2	·2 In respect of any materials, goods or workmanship, as comprised in executed work, which are to be to the reasonable satisfaction of the Architect in accordance with clause 2·1, the Architect shall express any dissatisfaction within a reasonable time from the execution of the unsatisfactory work.

8·3	The Architect may issue instructions requiring the Contractor to open up for inspection any work covered up or to arrange for or carry out any test of any materials or goods (whether or not already incorporated in the Works) or of any executed work, and the cost of such opening up or testing (together with the cost of making good in consequence thereof) shall be added to the Contract Sum unless provided for in the Contract Bills or unless the inspection or test shows that the materials, goods or work are not in accordance with this Contract.
8·4	If any work, materials or goods are not in accordance with this Contract the Architect, without prejudice to the generality of his powers, may:
8·4	·1 issue instructions in regard to the removal from the site of all or any of such work, materials or goods; and/or
8·4	·2 after consultation with the Contractor (who shall immediately consult with any relevant Nominated Sub-Contractor) and with the agreement of the Employer, allow all or any of such work, materials or goods to remain and confirm this in writing to the Contractor (which shall not be construed as a Variation) and where so allowed and confirmed an appropriate deduction shall be made in the adjustment of the Contract Sum; and/or
8·4	·3 after consultation with the Contractor (who shall immediately consult with any relevant Nominated Sub-Contractor) issue such instructions requiring a Variation as are reasonably necessary as a consequence of such an instruction under clause 8·4·1 or such confirmation under clause 8·4·2 and to the extent that such instructions are so necessary and notwithstanding clauses 13·4, 25 and 26 no addition to the Contract Sum shall be made and no extension of time shall be given; and/or
8·4	·4 having had due regard to the Code of Practice appended to these Conditions *(following clause 37)*, issue such instructions under clause 8·3 to open up for inspection or to test as are reasonable in all the circumstances to establish to the reasonable satisfaction of the Architect the likelihood or extent, as appropriate to the circumstances, of any further similar non-compliance. To the extent that such instructions are so reasonable, whatever the results of the opening up for inspection or test, and notwithstanding clauses 8·3 and 26 no addition to the Contract Sum shall be made. Clause 25·4·5·2 shall apply unless as stated therein the inspection or test showed that the work, materials or goods were not in accordance with this Contract.
8·5	The Architect may (but not unreasonably or vexatiously) issue instructions requiring the exclusion from the Works of any person employed thereon.

Exclusion of the usual implied obligations

13.02 The implied obligations referred to above can be excluded if the circumstances show that the parties did not intend them to apply. Thus:

1. There is no obligation as to fitness for a particular purpose if that purpose was not made known to the contractor at the time of making the contract.
2. There is no obligation as to fitness for purpose of materials where there was no reliance upon the skill and judgement of the contractor in the choice of those materials. Thus, say an architect, without reliance on a contractor, specified for use on a roof 'Somerset 13' tiles, then the contractor is not liable if Somerset 13 tiles of good quality are not fit for use on that roof. The contractor is, however, liable if the tiles fail because, for example, they laminate owing to some latent defect of quality even though the defect could not have been detected by the exercise of proper skill and care on his part (see *Young and Marten* v *McManus Childs Limited* [1968] 2 All ER 1169, and *Norta Wallpapers* v *John Sisk* [1978] 1 IR 114 (an Irish case); *Comyn Ching & Co (London) Ltd* v *Oriental Tube Co Ltd* (1979) 17 BLR 47.
3. There is no obligation as to latent defects of quality of materials where the circumstances show that the parties do not intend the contractor to accept such obligations. Thus it seems (though the point is not clear) that in the example just cited the contractor would not have been liable for the latent defects in the tiles if the employer (or the architect on his behalf) had required the contractor to purchase them from the supplier who, to the knowledge of the parties, would only supply them upon terms which substantially limited the contractor's remedies against the supplier in respect of such defects (see *Young and Marten* (above) and *Gloucestershire County Council* v *Richardson* [1969] 2 All ER 1181).
4. In the case of a nominated supplier whose sale contract restricts, limits, or excludes liability to the contractor, and the architect specifically has approved such restriction, limitation, or exclusion, the employer's rights against the contractor are restricted, limited, or excluded to the same extent – see clause 36.5.1.

Position of employer

13.03 If there is no breach of an express or implied term, the employer normally has no remedy against the contractor or sub-contractor or supplier under the terms of the contract. This is a situation which should be avoided if possible. If the contractor will not accept liability, one way of protecting the employer is to obtain a warranty direct from the supplier or sub-contractor concerned. The JCT issue a Standard Form of Employer/Nominated Sub-contractor Agreement (NSC/2), and a Standard Form of Tender by Nominated Supplier (TNS/1) which contains such 'direct warranties' (paras 43.01 ff and 46.01 ff).

13.04 Alternatively or in addition to duties owed by virtue of contract, a contractor, sub-contractor, or supplier may owe a duty to an employer in tort to take reasonable care in the design and construction of the work he carries out or the materials he supplied, as the case may be (see *Junior Books* v *Veitchi Co Ltd* [1982] 3 WLR 477).

Effect of price on standards

13.05 The question whether the price is low or high should be ignored when considering the required standard unless the parties have expressly or by implication agreed the prices to be considered. But it seems that the architect can accept a lower standard than usual where the parties have agreed at the time of the contract that the price is low and that the contractor is to 'build down to a price'. A suitable term should be included in the contract documents to make the intentions of the parties clear.

Effect of proposed use of works on standards

13.06 Where the use is known to the contractor at the time of contract it can, probably, be taken into account in considering the requisite standard where the bills are silent. But it is better to have express agreement of possible matters of dispute, e.g. as to tolerances and how far they are cumulative.

Clause 8.3: Testing

13.07 The architect is not bound to order tests under this clause before saying that he is not reasonably satisfied. If he orders tests, and the work, materials, or goods are found to be satisfactory the contractor has rights to an extension of time (clause 25.4.5.2), payment of loss and expense (clause 26.2.2), and the costs of the tests. But it is thought that where tests of parts of a class of work – e.g. piling – show that the whole must be rejected, the contractor is not entitled to payment for tests in respect of those parts – e.g. individual piles – which pass the test or to the other rights set out above.

Clause 8.4: Removal

13.08 The architect must order *removal from site* of defective work. It is not sufficient merely to order correction (see *Holland Hannen & Cubitts (Northern) Ltd* v *Welsh Health Technical Services Organisation* (1981) 18 BLR 80). There is no provision for re-execution, because upon the removal of the unsatisfactory work, materials, or goods, the contractor's duty to complete remains and no further instruction is required. For the architect's remedies for non-compliance with an instruction, see clauses 4.1.2, 27.1.3, and 30.2.1.1. Defects which appear after practical completion are dealt with under clause 17.

Without quantities variant

13.09 References in clause 8 to the contract bills should be read as references to the specification.

14 Clause 9: Royalties and patent rights

> **9   Royalties and patent rights**
>
> **9·1**   All royalties or other sums payable in respect of the supply and use in carrying out the Works as described by or referred to in the Contract Bills of any patented articles, processes or inventions shall be deemed to have been included in the Contract Sum, and the Contractor shall indemnify the Employer from and against all claims, proceedings, damage, costs and expense which may be brought or made against the Employer or to which he may be put by reason of the Contractor infringing or being held to have infringed any patent rights in relation to any such articles, processes or inventions.
>
> **9·2**   Provided that where in compliance with Architect's instructions the Contractor shall supply and use in carrying out the Works any patented articles, processes or inventions, the Contractor shall not be liable in respect of any infringement or alleged infringement of any patent rights in relation to any such articles, processes or inventions and all royalties damages or other monies which the Contractor may be liable to pay to the persons entitled to such patent rights shall be added to the Contract Sum.

15 Clause 10: Person in charge

15.01 The person in charge is the contractor's agent to receive instructions. To avoid confusion he should be named.

> **10   Person-in-charge**
>
> The Contractor shall constantly keep upon the Works a competent person-in-charge and any instructions given to him by the Architect or directions given to him by the clerk of works in accordance with clause 12 shall be deemed to have been issued to the Contractor.

16 Clause 11: Access for architect/supervising officer to the works

16.01 In the absence of express provision doubts might arise as to the architect's right of access to site, since the contractor is entitled as against the employer to free and uninterrupted possession of the site during the progress of the works.

The provisions relating to domestic and nominated sub-contractors do not, of course, directly affect the obligations of the sub-contractors, but the contractor would be liable in damages to the employer if he could establish damage flowing from failure by the contractor to ensure that the appropriate terms were included in the sub-contracts.

> **11   Access for Architect to the Works**
>
> The Architect and his representatives shall at all reasonable times have access to the Works and to the workshops or other places of the Contractor where work is being prepared for this Contract, and when work is to be so prepared in workshops or other places of a Domestic Sub-Contractor or a Nominated Sub-Contractor the Contractor shall by a term in the sub-contract so far as possible secure a similar right of access to those workshops or places for the Architect and his representatives and shall do all things reasonably necessary to make such right effective. Access in accordance with clause 11 may be subject to such reasonable restrictions of the Contractor or any Domestic Sub-Contractor or any Nominated Sub-Contractor as are necessary to protect any proprietary right of the Contractor or of any Domestic or Nominated Sub-Contractor in the work referred to in clause 11.

17 Clause 12: Clerk of works

17.01 The clerk of works is to act 'solely as inspector'. He is not the architect's agent to give instructions, and it is a source of confusion and dispute if he purports to do so. The clause provides for the position if the clerk of works gives 'directions'. They are to be of no effect unless converted into architect's instructions by the architect within two working days. Such directions can lead to uncertainty on the part of the contractor. It is suggested that the clerk of works be ·discouraged from giving directions in ordinary circumstances. If directions are given, it at least reduces the possible problems if they are in writing and the architect immediately confirms, amends, or rejects them.

In *Kensington and Chelsea and Westminster Area Health Authority* v *Wettern Composites* (1984) 31 BLR 57 it was held

that the employer was vicariously liable for the negligence of the Clerk of Works, and that responsibility for his acts was not borne by the architect, even though he was acting under the direction and control of the architect.

12　Clerk of works

The Employer shall be entitled to appoint a clerk of works whose duty shall be to act solely as inspector on behalf of the Employer under the directions of the Architect and the Contractor shall afford every reasonable facility for the performance of that duty. If any direction is given to the Contractor by the clerk of works the same shall be of no effect unless given in regard to a matter in respect of which the Architect is expressly empowered by the Conditions to issue instructions and unless confirmed in writing by the Architect within 2 working days of such direction being given. If any such direction is so given and confirmed then as from the date of issue of that confirmation it shall be deemed to be an Architect's instruction.

Work done before confirmation of directions

17.02 The architect can, if such work is a variation, subsequently sanction it in writing under clause 13.2. This may be particularly appropriate where the contractor has carried out extra work in an emergency upon the direction of the clerk of works.

Resident architect

17.03 A person so entitled is sometimes appointed to the site of a large contract. His position should be sharply distinguished from that of the clerk of works and should be defined in a communication to the contractor stating clearly how far, if at all, he is not to have all the powers to issue architect's instructions given by the terms of the contract.

18　Clause 13: Variations and provisional sums

18.01 This clause is essentially concerned with three matters:

1. Defining what constitutes a variation.
2. Defining the method in which variations are to be ordered.
3. Laying down the rules for valuing variations.

13　Variations and provisional sums

13·1 The term "Variation" as used in the Conditions means:

13·1　·1 the alteration or modification of the design, quality or quantity of the Works as shown upon the Contract Drawings and described by or referred to in the Contract Bills; including

　·1　·1 the addition, omission or substitution of any work,

　·1　·2 the alteration of the kind or standard of any of the materials or goods to be used in the Works,

　·1　·3 the removal from the site of any work executed or materials or goods brought thereon by the Contractor for the purposes of the Works other than work materials or goods which are not in accordance with this Contract;

13·1　·2 the imposition by the Employer of any obligations or restrictions in regard to the matters set out in clauses 13·1·2·1 to 13·1·2·4 or the addition to or alteration or omission of any such obligations or restrictions so imposed or imposed by the Employer in the Contract Bills in regard to:

　·2　·1 access to the site or use of any specific parts of the site;

　·2　·2 limitations of working space;

　·2　·3 limitations of working hours;

　·2　·4 the execution or completion of the work in any specific order;

but excludes

13·1　·3 nomination of a Sub-Contractor to supply and fix materials or goods or to execute work of which the measured quantities have been set out and priced by the Contractor in the Contract Bills for supply and fixing or execution by the Contractor.

13·2 The Architect may, subject to the Contractor's right of reasonable objection set out in clause 4·1·1, issue instructions requiring a Variation and he may sanction in writing any Variation made by the Contractor otherwise than pursuant to an instruction of the Architect. No Variation required by the Architect or subsequently sanctioned by him shall vitiate this Contract.

13·3 The Architect shall issue instructions in regard to:

13·3　·1 the expenditure of provisional sums included in the Contract Bills; [j] and

13·3　·2 the expenditure of provisional sums included in a Sub-Contract.

13·4　·1　·1 Subject to clause 13·4·1·2 all Variations required by the Architect or subsequently sanctioned by him in writing and all work executed by the Contractor in accordance with instructions by the Architect as to the expenditure of provisional sums which are included in the Contract Bills shall be valued by the Quantity Surveyor and such Valuation (in the Conditions called "the Valuation") shall, unless otherwise agreed by the Employer and the Contractor, be made in accordance with the provisions of clause 13·5.

　·1　·2 The valuation of Variations to the Sub-Contract Works executed by a Nominated Sub-Contractor in accordance with instructions of the Architect and of all instructions issued under clause 13·3·2 shall (unless otherwise agreed by the Contractor and the Nominated Sub-Contractor concerned with the approval of the Employer) be made in accordance with the relevant provisions of Sub-Contract NSC/4 or NSC/4a as applicable.

13·4　·2 Where under the instruction of the Architect as to the expenditure of a provisional sum a prime cost sum arises and the Contractor under clause 35·2 tenders for the work covered by that prime cost sum and that tender is accepted by or on behalf of the Employer, that work shall be valued in accordance with the accepted tender of the Contractor and shall not be included in the Valuation of the instruction of the Architect in regard to the expenditure of the provisional sum.

13·5　·1 To the extent that the Valuation relates to the execution of additional or substituted work which can properly be valued by measurement such work shall be measured and shall be valued in accordance with the following rules:

　·1　·1 where the work is of similar character to, is executed under similar conditions as, and does not significantly change the quantity of, work set out in the Contract Bills the rates and prices for the work so set out shall determine the Valuation;

　·1　·2 where the work is of similar character to work set out in the Contract Bills but is not executed under similar conditions thereto and/or significantly changes the quantity thereof, the rates and prices for the work so set out shall be the basis for determining the valuation and the valuation shall include a fair allowance for such difference in conditions and/or quantity;

　·1　·3 where the work is not of similar character to work set out in the Contract Bills the work shall be valued at fair rates and prices.

13·5　·2 To the extent that the Valuation relates to the omission of work set out in the Contract Bills the rates and prices for such work therein set out shall determine the valuation of the work omitted.

13·5　·3 In any valuation of work under clauses 13·5·1 and 13·5·2:

　·3　·1 measurement shall be in accordance with the same principles as those governing the preparation of the Contract Bills as referred to in clause 2·2·2·1;

　·3　·2 allowance shall be made for any percentage or lump sum adjustments in the Contract Bills; and

　·3　·3 allowance, where appropriate, shall be made for any addition to or reduction of preliminary items of the type referred to in the Standard Method of Measurement, 6th Edition, Section B (Preliminaries).

13·5　·4 To the extent that the Valuation relates to the execution of additional or substituted work which cannot properly be valued by measurement the Valuation shall comprise:

　·4　·1 the prime cost of such work (calculated in accordance with the 'Definition of Prime Cost of Daywork carried out under a Building Contract' issued by the Royal Institution of Chartered Surveyors and the Building Employers Confederation which was current at the Base Date) together with percentage additions to each section of the prime cost at the rates set out by the Contractor in the Contract Bills; or

　·4　·2 where the work is within the province of any specialist trade and the said Institution and the appropriate [k] body representing the employers in that trade have agreed and issued a definition of prime cost of daywork, the prime cost of such work calculated in accordance with that definition which was current at the Base Date together with percentage additions on the prime cost at the rates set out by the Contractor in the Contract Bills.

Provided that in any case vouchers specifying the time daily spent upon the work, the workmen's names, the plant and the materials employed shall be delivered for verification to the Architect or his authorised representative not later than the end of the week following that in which the work has been executed.

13·5　·5 If compliance with any instruction requiring a Variation or any instruction as to the expenditure of a provisional sum substantially changes the conditions under which any other work is executed, then such other work shall be treated as if it had been the subject of an instruction of the Architect requiring a Variation under clause 13·2 which shall be valued in accordance with the provisions of clause 13.

13·5　·6 To the extent that the Valuation does not relate to the execution of additional or substituted work or the omission of work or to the extent that the valuation of any work or liabilities directly associated with a Variation cannot reasonably be effected in the Valuation by the application of clauses 13·5·1 to ·5 a fair valuation thereof shall be made.

Provided that no allowance shall be made under clause 13·5 for any effect upon the regular progress of the Works or for any other direct loss and/or expense for which the Contractor would be reimbursed by payment under any other provision in the Conditions.

13·6 Where it is necessary to measure work for the purpose of the Valuation the Quantity Surveyor shall give to the Contractor an opportunity of being present at the time of such measurement and of taking such notes and measurements as the Contractor may require.

13·7 Effect shall be given to a Valuation under clause 13·5 by addition to or deduction from the Contract Sum.

---

[j] If the Architect nominates a Sub-Contractor or Supplier by any instructions under clause 13·3·1, then the provisions of Part 2 of the Conditions apply to such nominations.

[k] There are three Definitions to which clause 13·5·4·2 refers namely those agreed between the Royal Institution and the Electrical Contractors Association, the Royal Institution and the Electrical Contractors Association of Scotland and the Royal Institution and the Heating and Ventilating Contractors Association.

Definition of variation

18.02 Clause 13.1 defines variation in wide terms. Not only does it include alterations in the work itself (clause 13.1.1), but also by clause 13.1.2 alterations in obligations or restrictions imposed by the employer in the contract bills in regard to such matters as site access, working space, working hours, and work sequence. The architect would appear to have no power to vary such obligations or restrictions if they are not already set out in the contract bills. But, by clause 13.1.3 variation is to exclude nomination of the sub-contractors to supply and fix materials or goods or to execute work of which the measured quantities ahve been set out and priced by the contractor in the contract bills for supply and fixing or execution by the contractor. Thus the employer is not entitled to vary the work by ordering the omission of work and nominating a sub-contractor to carry it out.

Disputes frequently arise between employer and contractor as to whether work constitutes a variation, and such disputes are frequently referred to arbitration. The architect's decision as to what constitutes and does not constitute variations is subject to review by the arbitrator appointed under article 5. Under article 5.2.3 there is provision for arbitration before practical completion in relation to objections raised by the contractor arising out of variations ordered under clause 13.1.2.

The same instruction may amount both to another order and to a postponement of work within clause 23 (see *M Harrison & Co v Leeds City Council* [1980] 14 BLR 118).

Deemed variations

18.03 This term is frequently used to denote an occurrence which entitles (or is alleged to entitle) the contractor to extra payment even though the requirements of clause 13 have not been complied with. These are of two principal kinds: firstly, the bills of quantities may be inaccurate and fail to record correctly the quantity of work actually required. In these circumstances, the contractor is entitled to extra payment under clause 2.2.2.2, since the standard method of measurement referred to in clause 2.2.2.1 requires bills of quantities to fully and accurately describe the work. Secondly, misstatements or inaccuracies in the bills of quantities (or specification in the without quantities variant) may constitute an actionable misrepresentation for which the contractor is entitled to damages under the Misrepresentation Act 1967.

Limitation on architect's powers

18.04 Despite the apparent width of the architect's powers to order variations, it is generally thought he cannot order variations of such extent or nature as to change the nature of the works as originally contemplated. Further, the architect's powers are limited to those given by the conditions, which he has no power to vary or waive. Thus he cannot without the contractor's agreement require work that is the subject matter of a prime cost sum (see clause 35) to be carried out by the contractor, and (see clause 13.1.3) cannot omit work in order to have it carried out by another contractor or nominated sub-contractor (see *Commissioner for Main Roads v Reed & Stuart Pty* (1974) 48 ALJR 461). He cannot, it is thought, order variations after practical completion. He is, however, entitled to vary work to be carried out by nominated sub-contractors.

Prime cost and provisional sums

18.05 The distinction between prime cost and provisional sums, referred to in clause 13.3, is that a provisional sum represents a sum which is included to meet unforeseen contingencies (which may not arise), whereas prime cost sums are pre-estimates of expenditure which it is known will have to be incurred when the contract is entered into. The definitions are set out in more detail in the *Standard Method of Measurement*.

Procedure

18.06 Clause 13.2 lays down the procedure for variations, which requires the issue of an architect's instruction. There is provision for subsequent sanctioning by the architect of varied work, and although the architect's decision is subject to review by an arbitrator, in principle in the absence of an architect's instruction, the contractor is not entitled to extra payment. Merely permitting the contractor to alter the proposed method of construction at the contractor's request does not ordinarily amount to a variation, although the particular circumstances must always be considered (see *Simplex Concrete Piles* v *Borough of St Pancras* (1958) 14 BLR 80).

Without quantities variant

18.07 In the without quantities variant the specification replaces the contract bills in the definition of a variation.

Valuation rules

18.08 Clause 13.5 lays down the rules for valuing provisional work and variations, except for nominated sub-contractors' variations and work contained in the contractor's tender for prime cost work (under clause 35.2). Clause 13.5.1 deals with the situation where additional or substituted work is capable of measurement. This task of measurement is to be carried out by the quantity surveyor, who is to value the work in accordance with the rules laid down in clauses 13.5.1.1, 13.5.1.2, and 13.5.1.3, whichever are appropriate.

Under clause 13.5.2 where bill work is omitted, the amount of the omission is to be determined by the bill rates and prices. Clause 13.5.3 makes it clear that measurement of variations is to be carried out in accordance with the *Standard Method of Measurement*, that allowance shall be given for any percentage of lump sum adjustment, and that preliminary items must also be subject to adjustment. Preliminary items defined in Section B of the *Standard Method of Measurement* consist broadly of overhead items which the contractor will incur, such as plant, site establishment, etc.

Where work is incapable of measurement, clause 13.5.4 requires it to be valued at day work rates.

Clause 13.5.5 deals with what might be termed indirect variations, where a variation which directly affects one aspect of the work also has indirect effects on another aspect. For example, the architect may require work to be carried out in a different sequence from that envisaged, which results in certain finishing trades being obliged to work in parts of the building which are not fully watertight. The contractor would be entitled to be paid extra under clause 13.5.5.

Clause 13.5.6 provides a 'fall back' way of valuing a variation where none of the other methods can be applied to produce a fair result. The proviso to clause 13.5.6 is intended to make it clear that claims for loss and expense are not to be included in the build up of any variations. The policy of the 1980 JCT Form is to divorce completely claims for variations from claims for loss and expense (formerly, under the 1963 JCT Form they were to some extent confused, having regard to clauses 11(6) and 24(1) of that form). This divorce is in line with the recommendations of the Banwell Report, see para 1.03. But, since the loss and expense is excluded only if the contractor 'would be reimbursed under any other provision', there might well be circumstances where the intended divorce will not be complete.

Sub-contract work

18.09 Under clause 13.4.1 variations to nominated sub-contract works are to be valued in accordance with the provisions of the nominated sub-contract (see clause 16 of

Sub-contract NSC/4). Where the contractor tenders for provisional work which has become the subject of a prime cost sum and that tender is accepted, any variation is to be valued in accordance with the contractor's tender for that work.

Disputes about valuations

18.10 The rule of valuation contained in clause 13.5.1.3 (work not of similar character to work set out in the contract bills) is in practice probably the most difficult of application. It is necessary to decide whether it applies and then if it does how to apply it. It seems that one must look at the position at the time of acceptance of the tender and consider the character of the work then priced and the conditions after which the parties must have contemplated it would be carried out. If the character of the various works or the conditions under which they were carried out differ, then this rule applies. It is thought that the following may be examples of its application: material change in quantities; winter working instead of summer working; wet instead of dry; high instead of low; confined working space instead of ample working space. If it is decided the rule applies, the next question is its effect, which must vary according to circumstances. In some cases no or very little change from bill rates may constitute a 'fair valuation'. Indeed, the wording of this sub-clause is so wide that payment of less than bill rates might be justified. Note, however, that a claim under clause 13.5.1.3 must be sharply differentiated from a claim for loss and expense (see above).

Daywork

18.11 Clause 13.5.4.2 contains a proviso requiring submission of what are known as 'daywork sheets'. It is thought that these are a condition precedent to the contractor's right to payment under clause 13.5.4, and therefore the practice is for the contractor to ask the clerk of works to sign the daywork sheets as correct. This does not, however, preclude arguments subsequently being raised on the part of the employer that even though the daywork sheets are factually correct, the work the operatives in question were carrying out at the relevant time does not constitute a variation, e.g. if they were remedying previously executed defective work.

Role of quantity surveyor

18.12 Subject to any special agreement the quantity surveyor carries out the valuation in accordance with the rules laid down in this clause, but the architect is not bound to follow the quantity surveyor's valuation. The responsibility for valuation ultimately rests with the architect, who may in a particular case take the view that the quantity surveyor has failed to apply the rules laid down correctly in principle. He may, for example, consider that varied work should have been valued at bill rates, whereas the quantity surveyor has valued it at 'fair' rates. In these circumstances the architect is entitled and bound to overrule the quantity surveyor (*R B Burden Ltd* v *Swansea Corporation* (1957) 3 All ER 243).

The quantity surveyor has no authority vary the terms of the contract: *John Laing Construction Ltd* v *County and District Properties Ltd* (1982) 23 BLR 1.

Without quantities variant

18.13 In the without quantities variant, the Schedule of Rates which the contractor must provide is the starting document for the valuation of variations. The Schedule of Rates forms the basis for the contractor's tender, although it need only be provided after the contract is entered into. It is generally considered prudent to insist on the availability of the Schedule of Rates before the contract is signed, to obviate subsequent disputes as to the correctness of the rates in the Schedule.

Errors in the bills

18.14 The contractor may have made errors in pricing his tender on the basis of the bills of quantities, either by totalling figures incorrectly or by inserting a rate for a particular item which is manifestly excessive or too low. In so far as the total contract figure is wrong, the parties are precluded from disputing it by the wording of clause 14. Where a particular item is priced manifestly too low, contractors sometimes argue that if work the subject of the uneconomically low rate becomes the subject of variation it should be valued at an economic rate and not at the bill rate. It is submitted that in the absence of any claim for rectification being sustainable an architect would be in breach of his duty to his employer were he to agree to this course without the employer's express agreement (see also the *Code of Procedure for Single Stage Selective Tendering 1977* and the *Code of Procedure for Two Stage Selective Tendering*).

19 Clause 14: Contract sum

19.01 Unless there is a case for rectification the parties are bound by any errors incorporated into the contract sum. Rectification is available either where the document fails to record the mutual intentions of the parties or where it fails to record accurately the intention of one party only, where the other with knowledge of the other party's error has nevertheless stood by and allowed the other to sign the agreement (see *Bates* v *Wyndhams* [1981] 1 All ER 1077).

14	Contract Sum
14·1	The quality and quantity of the work included in the Contract Sum shall be deemed to be that which is set out in the Contract Bills.
14·2	The Contract Sum shall not be adjusted or altered in any way whatsoever otherwise than in accordance with the express provisions of the Conditions, and subject to clause 2·2·2·2 any error whether of arithmetic or not in the computation of the Contract Sum shall be deemed to have been accepted by the parties hereto.

20 Clause 15: Value added tax – supplementary provisions

20.01 The impact of value added tax is regulated by the 'supplementary provisions' (the VAT agreement), which is bound into the form as published by the JCT immediately following the Appendix. It is clear from this clause that the contractor's price is to be VAT exclusive.

15	Value added tax – supplemental provisions
15·1	In clause 15 and in the supplemental provisions pursuant hereto (hereinafter called the "VAT Agreement") 'tax' means the value added tax introduced by the Finance Act 1972 which is under the care and management of the Commissioners of Customs and Excise (hereinafter and in the VAT Agreement called 'the Commissioners').
15·2	Any reference in the Conditions to 'Contract Sum' shall be regarded as such Sum exclusive of any tax and recovery by the Contractor from the Employer of tax properly chargeable by the Commissioners on the Contractor under or by virtue of the Finance Act 1972 or any amendment or re-enactment thereof on the supply of goods and services under this Contract shall be under the provisions of clause 15 and of the VAT Agreement.
15·3	To the extent that after the Base Date the supply of goods and services to the Employer becomes exempt from the tax there shall be paid to the Contractor an amount equal to the loss of credit (input tax) on the supply to the Contractor of goods and services which contribute exclusively to the Works.

21 Clause 16: Materials and goods unfixed or off-site

21.01 This clause should be read with clause 30.2. The position as to materials and goods intended for the works is as follows:

1. As soon as brought to or adjacent to the works, they must not be removed without the architect's consent (clause 16.1).
2. When paid for, property passes to the employer (clause 16.1).
3. When incorporated into the works, property passes to the owner of the land by operation of law whether the goods are paid for or not.

21.02 The decision whether to certify for the value of goods and materials 'off-site' is at the discretion of the architect under clause 30.3. If off-site materials are certified for, the property passes to the employer (clause 16.2). The employer has no interest in or right to retain the contractor's plant and equipment unless and until the contractor's employment has been determined under clause 27.

---

16   Materials and goods unfixed or off-site

16·1   Unfixed materials and goods delivered to, placed on or adjacent to the Works and intended therefor shall not be removed except for use upon the Works unless the Architect has consented in writing to such removal which consent shall not be unreasonably withheld. Where the value of any such materials or goods has in accordance with clause 30·2 been included in any Interim Certificate under which the amount properly due to the Contractor has been paid by the Employer, such materials and goods shall become the property of the Employer, but, subject to clause 22B or 22C (if applicable), the Contractor shall remain responsible for loss or damage to the same.

16·2   Where the value of any materials or goods intended for the Works and stored off-site has in accordance with clause 30·3 been included in any Interim Certificate under which the amount properly due to the Contractor has been paid by the Employer, such materials and goods shall become the property of the Employer and thereafter the Contractor shall not, except for use upon the Works, remove or cause or permit the same to be moved or removed from the premises where they are, but the Contractor shall nevertheless be responsible for any loss thereof or damage thereto and for the cost of storage, handling and insurance of the same until such time as they are delivered to and placed on or adjacent to the Works whereupon the provisions of clause 16·1 (except the words 'Where the value' to the words 'the property of the Employer, but,') shall apply thereto.

---

22 Clause 17: Practical completion and defects liability

22.01 This clause provides for a certificate of practical completion followed by the delivery of a Schedule of Defects usually at the end of but in any event not later than 14 days after the expiration of the defects liability period (specified in the Appendix). Instructions may be issued from time to time to make good particular defects appearing in the defects liability period, after which a certificate of completion of making good defects is issued. The contractor is not required to make good damage caused by frost occurring after practical completion, unless the architect certifies otherwise.

---

17   Practical Completion and Defects Liability

17·1   When in the opinion of the Architect Practical Completion of the Works is achieved, he shall forthwith issue a certificate to that effect and Practical Completion of the Works shall be deemed for all the purposes of this Contract to have taken place on the day named in such certificate.

17·2   Any defects, shrinkages or other faults which shall appear within the Defects Liability Period and which are due to materials or workmanship not in accordance with this Contract or to frost occurring before Practical Completion of the Works, shall be specified by the Architect in a schedule of defects which he shall deliver to the Contractor as an instruction of the Architect not later than 14 days after the expiration of the said Defects Liability Period, and within a reasonable time after receipt of such schedule the defects, shrinkages, and other faults therein specified shall be made good by the Contractor at no cost to the Employer unless the Architect with the consent of the Employer shall otherwise instruct; and if the Architect does so otherwise instruct then an appropriate deduction in respect of any such defects, shrinkages or other faults not made good shall be made from the Contract Sum.

17·3   Notwithstanding clause 17·2 the Architect may whenever he considers it necessary so to do, issue instructions requiring any defect, shrinkage or other fault which shall appear within the Defects Liability Period and which is due to materials or workmanship not in accordance with this Contract or to frost occurring before Practical Completion of the Works, to be made good, and the Contractor shall within a reasonable time after receipt of such instructions comply with the same at no cost to the Employer unless the Architect with the consent of the Employer shall otherwise instruct; and if the Architect does so otherwise instruct then an appropriate deduction in respect of any such defects, shrinkages or other faults not made good shall be made from the Contract Sum. Provided that no such instructions shall be issued after delivery of a schedule of defects or after 14 days from the expiration of the Defects Liability Period.

17·4   When in the opinion of the Architect any defects, shrinkages or other faults which he may have required to be made good under clauses 17·2 and 17·3 shall have been made good he shall issue a certificate to that effect, and completion of making good defects shall be deemed for all the purposes of this Contract to have taken place on the day named in such certificate (the "Certificate of Completion of Making Good Defects").

17·5   In no case shall the Contractor be required to make good at his own cost any damage by frost which may appear after Practical Completion, unless the Architect shall certify that such damage is due to injury which took place before Practical Completion.

Meaning of practical completion

22.02 The term 'practical completion' is not defined in the contract, but it has been said (by Lord Dilhorne in *Westminster City Council* v *Jarvis Limited* [1970] 1 All ER 943 at 948) that it does not mean the stage when the work 'was almost but not entirely finished' but 'the completion of all the construction works that has to be done'. Such completion is subject to defects which may thereafter appear and require action under clause 17. In the same case in the Court of Appeal, Salmon LJ said: 'I take these words to mean completion for all practical purposes, i.e. for the purpose of allowing [the employer] to take possession of the works and use them as intended. If 'completion' in clause 21 [clause 23 of the 1980 JCT Form] means completion down to the last detail, however trivial and unimportant, then clause 22 [clause 24 of the 1980 Form] would be a penalty clause and as such unenforceable'. Neither explanation is binding as to the meaning of the words for the purposes of considering whether the contractor has reached the stage of practical completion. It is, however, suggested that the architect can issue his certificate despite minor defects if

1. He is reasonably satisfied the works accord with the contract.
2. There is adequate retention.
3. The employer will not suffer loss due to disturbance or otherwise.
4. He obtains a written acknowledgement of the existence of the defect and an undertaking to put it right from the contractor. If the defects are other than trivial, the views of the employer should first be obtained.

Form of certificate

22.03 This is not prescribed by the contract, but it should be clear and definite. The RIBA issues forms.

Effect of certificate of practical completion

22.04 The practical completion certificate fixes the commencement of the defects liability period (as defined in the Appendix) and the period of final measurement laid down by clause 30. It gives rise to the right to the release of the first half of the retention percentage (clause 30.4.1); it is the time for the release of the obligation to insure under clause 22A.1 where this clause applies. It is the end of the contractor's liability for damage to the works arising as an incident of his obligation to complete. It marks the end of liability for liquidated damages under clause 24 and the end of liability for frost damage under clause 17.2. Regular interim certificates cease to be issued. The restrictions on the opening of certain references to arbitration end. The review period for extensions of time begins.

The employer's remedies for defective work are not limited to those contained in the clause (i.e. requiring the contractor to make good defects and non-release of retention). He may additionally sue for damages for breach of contract – *HW Nevill (Sunblest) Ltd* v *Wm Press & Son Ltd* (1981) 20 BLR 78.

Meaning of defects

22.05 For contractor's obligation as to standards of workmanship, materials, and goods, see clauses 2 and 8, and the notes thereto. Defects are, generally, work, materials and goods which are not in conformity with the contract documents.

The contractor is not obliged to remedy work left defective by a nominated sub-contractor – *Fairclough* v *Rhuddlan Borough Council* (1985) 30 BLR 26.

Effect of site inspections

22.06 It is, in general, no excuse for a contractor to say that the architect or the clerk of works ought to have observed bad work on site inspections. See clause 30 for the effect of the final certificate.

Frost damage

22.07 The contractor is not responsible for frost damage after practical completion unless the architect certifies that the damage is due to injury which took place befgore practical completion.

Instructions under 17.3 making good defects

22.08 This clause enables the architect in a proper case to issue instructions before the Schedule under clause 17.2, but he should only do so when he 'considers it necessary so to do'. One of the matters to be taken into account in considering whether it is necessary to issue such instructions is probably whether it is reasonable to leave the defect unremedied until after the issue of the Schedule.

The meaning of the words 'and (unless the Architect shall otherwise instruct . . .) entirely at his own costs . . .' is not certain. They apparently give the architect power to instruct that the employer will pay for making good (see clause 30.6.2.10). This would be a most unusual occurrence. It is submitted that they are intended to give the architect power to accept, with the employer's consent, certain defects and reduce the contract sum accordingly (see clause 30.6.2.5).

Architect's remedies

22.09 For breach of an instruction to make good defects a notice under clause 4.1.2 can be given, and if it is not complied with, others can be employed to do the work necessary and the cost deducted from the retention percentage. Further, until defects have been made good, the architect need not and should not issue his certificate under clause 17.4 so that the second half of the retention percentage is not released, and issue of the final certificate with the protection it usually affords to the contractor (see clause 30) may be delayed. It is not clear whether the power of determination under clause 27 can be exercised after practical completion. The remedies just set out ought to be sufficient to make it unnecessary to attempt to rely on clause 27.

Irremediable breach

22.10 The architect may include a defect in an instruction or the Schedule, but then find on representation by the contractor that it cannot be remedied except at a cost which is unreasonable in comparison with the loss of the employer and the nature of the defect. In such circumstances he has, it is thought, discretion to issue his certificate under clause 17.4 to make a reduction of the amount certified for payment in respect of the works not properly carried out, being the amount by which the works are reduced in value by reason of the unremedied defect. But where the approval of the quality of any material or the standards of any workmanship is a matter for his opinion, he would be wise to consider carefully the implications of issuing a final certificate (see clauses 2.1 and 30.9).

Defects appearing after the expiry of the defects liability period

22.11 If defects appear after the issue of the certificate under clause 17.4, the architect can no longer issue instructions under clause 17, but the appearance of the defect is the disclosure of a breach of contract by the contractor. The employer is entitled to damages, and the architect should

adjust any further certificate to reflect the effect on the value of the works. In accordance with common law rules as to mitigation of damages, the contractor, if it is reasonable to do so, should be given the opportunity of rectifying the defects. An unqualified final certificate should not be issued if the defects are unremedied (see clause 30.9).

Practical completion of part

22.12 Clause 18 makes provision for 'partial' practical completion where the employer takes possession of part of the work before completion of the work as a whole. Therefore, the procedure laid down under clause 17 may be applied a number of times during the course of the contract.

23 Clause 18: Partial possession by employer

23.01 This clause provides for the situation where before the works are completed the employer, with the consent of the contractor, takes possession of part or parts and provides for the application to each part of provisions as to practical completion, defects, insurance, and retention percentage analogous to those which apply to the whole and for proportionate reduction of any liquidated damages payable. The appropriate Appendix entry must be completed so as to allow the proper operation of clause 18.1.5, otherwise liquidated damages will not be enforceable. In *Bramall & Ogden Ltd* v *Sheffield City Council* [1983] 29 BLR 73 a case on JCT 63, the Appendix was completed so as to allow a sum in damages for each uncompleted dwelling. This was held to be inconsistent with clause 16(e) (equivalent to JCT 80 clause 18.1.5). If possession is given in sections, the architect must apply this clause and has no power without the consent of the parties to issue a certificate of practical completion for an average date of completion.

18	Partial possession by Employer
18·1	If at any time or times before the date of issue by the Architect of the certificate of Practical Completion the Employer wishes to take possession of any part or parts of the Works and the consent of the Contractor (which consent shall not be unreasonably withheld) has been obtained, then notwithstanding anything expressed or implied elsewhere in this Contract, the Employer may take possession thereof. The Architect shall thereupon issue to the Contractor on behalf of the Employer a written statement identifying the part or parts of the Works taken into possession and giving the date when the Employer took possession (in clauses 18, 20·3, 22·3·1 and 22C·1 referred to as 'the relevant part' and 'the relevant date' respectively).
18·1 ·1	For the purposes of clauses 17·2, 17·3, 17·5 and 30·4·1·2 Practical Completion of the relevant part shall be deemed to have occurred and the Defects Liability Period in respect of the relevant part shall be deemed to have commenced on the relevant date.
18·1 ·2	When in the opinion of the Architect any defects, shrinkages or other faults in the relevant part which he may have required to be made good under clause 17·2 or clause 17·3 shall have been made good he shall issue a certificate to that effect.
18·1 ·3	As from the relevant date the obligation of the Contractor under clause 22A or of the Employer under clause 22B·1 or clause 22C·2 whichever is applicable to insure shall terminate in respect of the relevant part but not further or otherwise; and where clause 22C applies the obligation of the Employer to insure under clause 22C·1 shall from the relevant date include the relevant part.
·4	In lieu of any sum to be paid or allowed by the Contractor under clause 24 in respect of any period during which the Works may remain incomplete occurring after the relevant date there shall be paid or allowed such sum as bears the same ratio to the sum which would be paid or allowed apart from the provisions of clause 18 as the Contract Sum less the amount contained therein in respect of the relevant part bears to the Contract Sum.

Duty to complete in sections

23.02 This clause does not impose such a duty; equally, if the contractor is delayed and therefore subject to liquidated damages, he is not entitled to any contra-credit for having completed some of the work *before* the contractual completion date. If sectional completion is required, the JCT Sectional Completion Supplement should be employed.

Use, but not possession

23.03 Neither the Standard Form nor the Section Completion Supplement makes provision for the situation where the

employer without taking possession of a part, requires use of it for storage purposes, for example. If such an arrangement is desired, specific amendments to the form of contract must be made (see *English Industrial Estates* v *George Wimpey* [1973] 1 Lloyds Reports 118).

24 Clause 19: Assignment and sub-contracts

24.01 At law, a party may assign the *benefit* of a contract on giving notice of the assignment to the other party, but may not assign the *burden* without the other party's consent. This clause prohibits either party making any assignment without the consent of the other.

19		Assignment and Sub-Contracts
19·1	·1	Neither the Employer nor the Contractor shall, without the written consent of the other, assign this Contract.
19·1	·2	Where clause 19·1·2 is stated in the Appendix to apply then, in the event of transfer by the Employer of his freehold or leasehold interest in, or of a grant by the Employer of a leasehold interest in, the whole of the premises comprising the Works, the Employer may at any time after Practical Completion of the Works assign to any such transferee or lessee the right to bring proceedings in the name of the Employer (whether by arbitration or litigation) to enforce any of the terms of this contract made for the benefit of the Employer hereunder. The assignee shall be estopped from disputing any enforceable agreements reached between the Employer and the Contractor and which arise out of and relate to this Contract (whether or not they are or appear to be a derogation from the right assigned) and made prior to the date of any assignment.
19·2		The Contractor shall not without the written consent of the Architect (which consent shall not be unreasonably withheld) sub-let any portion of the Works. A person to whom the Contractor sub-lets any portion of the Works other than a Nominated Sub-Contractor is in this Contract referred to as a ''Domestic Sub-Contractor''.
19·3	·1	Where the Contract Bills provide that certain work measured or otherwise described in those Bills and priced by the Contractor must be carried out by persons named in a list in or annexed to the Contract Bills, and selected therefrom by and at the sole discretion of the Contractor the provisions of clause 19·3 shall apply in respect of that list.
19·3	·2 ·1	The list referred to in clause 19·3·1 must comprise not less than three persons. Either the Employer (or the Architect on his behalf) or the Contractor shall be entitled with the consent of the other, which consent shall not be unreasonably withheld, to add [I] additional persons to the list at any time prior to the execution of a binding sub-contract agreement.
	·2 ·2	If at any time prior to the execution of a binding sub-contract agreement and for whatever reason less than three persons named in the list are able and willing to carry out the relevant work then either the Employer and the Contractor shall by agreement (which agreement shall not be unreasonably withheld) add [I] the names of other persons so that the list comprises not less than three such persons or the work shall be carried out by the Contractor who may sub-let to a Domestic Sub-Contractor in accordance with clause 19·2.
19·3	·3	A person selected by the Contractor under clause 19·3 from the aforesaid list shall be a Domestic Sub-Contractor.
19·4		It shall be a condition in any sub-letting to which clause 19·2 or 19·3 refers that:
19·4	·1	the employment of the Domestic Sub-Contractor under the sub-contract shall determine immediately upon the determination (for any reason) of the Contractor's employment under this Contract; and
19·4	·2	the Sub-Contract shall provide that
	·2 ·1	Subject to clause 16·1 of these Conditions (in clauses 19·4·2·2 to ·4 called 'the Main Contract Conditions'), unfixed materials and goods delivered to, placed on or adjacent to the Works by the Sub-Contractor and intended therefor shall not be removed except for use on the Works unless the Contractor has consented in writing to such removal, which consent shall not be unreasonably withheld.
	·2 ·2	Where, in accordance with clause 30·2 of the Main Contract Conditions, the value of any such materials or goods shall have been included in any Interim Certificate under which the amount properly due to the Contractor shall have been discharged by the Employer in favour of the Contractor, such materials or goods shall be and become the property of the Employer and the Sub-Contractor shall not deny that such materials or goods are and have become the property of the Employer.
	·2 ·3	Provided that if the Main Contractor shall pay the Sub-Contractor for any such materials or goods before the value therefor has, in accordance with clause 30·2 of the Main Contract Conditions, been included in any Interim Certificate under which the amount properly due to the Contractor has been discharged by the Employer in favour of the Contractor, such materials or goods shall upon such payment by the Main Contractor be and become the property of the Main Contractor.
	·2 ·4	The operation of clause 19·4·2·1 to ·3 hereof shall be without prejudice to any property in any materials or goods passing to the Contractor as provided in clause 30·3·5 of the Main Contract Conditions (off-site materials or goods).
19·5	·1	The provisions of this Contract relating to Nominated Sub-Contractors are set out in Part 2 of the Conditions.
19·5	·2	Subject to clause 35·2 the Contractor is not himself required, unless otherwise agreed, to supply and fix materials or goods or to execute work which is to be carried out by a Nominated Sub-Contractor.

[I] Any such addition must be initialled by or on behalf of the parties

---

24.02 In addition, clauses 19.2, 19.3, and 19.4 make specific provision for 'domestic sub-contractors', i.e. sub-contractors to whom the contractor delegates part of the work who are not *nominated* pursuant to clause 35 in Part 2 of the Conditions (see para 39). Clause 19.2 begins by imposing a general prohibition on subletting any portion of the works without the consent of the architect, whose consent shall not be unreasonably withheld. The person to whom a portion of the work is so sublet other than a nominated sub-contractor is called a domestic sub-contractor.

Lists of domestic sub-contractors

24.03 Clause 19.3 makes further provision for domestic sub-contractors, without, however, derogating from the principle that any sub-contractor other than a nominated sub-contractor is a domestic sub-contractor. Clause 19.3.1 provides that the bills *may* in respect of any work measured or described in the bills provide that that work is to be carried out by persons named in a list contained in or annexed to the contract bills and selected therefrom at the sole discretion of the contractor. This recognizes a practice which has been adopted by some employers. Clause 19.3.2.1 provides that this list must comprise not less than three persons, and is subject to amendment by either the employer or the contractor with the consent of the other so as to add further names to the list at any time prior to the execution of a binding sub-contract. Clause 19.3.2.2 makes provision for the situation if at any time prior to the sub-contract being entered into less than three persons on the list are prepared to carry out the work in question either further names are to be added to the list or the work is to be carried out by the contractor who may, if he wishes, sublet to a domestic sub-contractor under clause 19.2 (subject to the architect's approval).

24.04 Note that this procedure is only available where the work is measured or described in the bills *and* priced by the contractor. Thus it can never apply where the work in question is the subject of a provisional or prime cost sum or where for some other reason the work is not included in the bills.

24.05 Clause 19.4.1 provides, perhaps unnecessarily, that any domestic sub-contract is subject to a condition that the domestic sub-contractor's employment shall determine if the contractor's employment under the main contract is determined. Since domestic sub-contractors will not, of course, be parties to this contract, any rights they may have in fact against the main contractor on such determination would not be affected by this clause. In the High Court decision (*Dawber Williamson Roofing Ltd* v *Humberside County Council* (1979) 14 BLR 70) the sub-contractor remained owner of materials because the main contractor in liquidation had not paid for them, thus causing the employer to have to pay a second time. An amendment (no. 1:1984) has been issued by the JCT so that where an employer has paid a certificate including the value of such materials delivered to site, the sub-contractor will not deny that property in such materials has passed to the employer. Corresponding amendments (no. 2) have been issued for NSC/4 and NSC/4a (see also para 67.09).

24.06 Clause 19.5.2 makes it clear that apart from the provisions of clause 35.2 the contractor is not himself required to carry out work for which provision is made for execution by a nominated sub-contractor. This confirms the position as laid down in *North West Metropolitan Hospital Board* v *T A Bickerton & Son Limited* [1970] 1 WLR 607, where it was held that where a nominated sub-contractor failed to perform, it was the duty of the employer to renominate a further nominated sub-contractor.

25 Clause 19A: Fair wages

25.01 This clause does not appear in the private variant. Original clause 19A.3 was deleted by Amendment 2: 1986 and subsequent sub-clauses renumbered.

19A   Fair Wages

19A 1   1 The Contractor shall pay rates of wages and observe hours and conditions of labour not less favourable than those established for the trade or industry in the district where the work is carried out by machinery of negotiation or arbitration to which the parties are organisations of employers and trade unions representative respectively of substantial proportions of the employers and workers engaged in the trade or industry in the district

19A 1   2 In the absence of any rates of wages, hours or conditions of labour so established the Contractor shall pay rates of wages and observe hours and conditions of labour which are not less favourable than the general level of wages, hours and conditions observed by other employers whose general circumstances in the trade or industry in which the Contractor is engaged are similar

19A 2 The Contractor shall in respect of all persons employed by him (whether in carrying out this Contract or otherwise) in every factory, workshop or other place occupied or used by him for the carrying out of this Contract (including the Works) comply with the general conditions required by clause 19A. The Contractor hereby warrants that to the best of his knowledge and belief he has complied with the general conditions required by clause 19A for at least 3 months prior to the date of his tender for this Contract

19A 3 The Contractor shall recognise the freedom of his workpeople to be members of trade unions

19A 4 The Contractor shall at all times during the continuance of this Contract display, for the information of his workpeople, in every factory, workshop or place occupied or used by him for the carrying out of this Contract (including the Works) a copy of clause 19A. Where rates of wages, hours or conditions of work have been established either by negotiation or arbitration as described in clause 19A 1 1 or by any agreement commonly recognised by employers and workers in the district a copy of the award agreement or other document specifying or recording such rates hours or conditions shall also be exhibited by the Contractor or made available by him for inspection in any such place as aforesaid

19A 5 The Contractor shall be responsible for the observance of clause 19A by sub-contractors employed in the carrying out of this Contract, and shall if required notify the Employer of the names and addresses of all such sub-contractors

19A 6 The Contractor shall keep proper wages books and time sheets showing the wages paid to and the time worked by the workpeople in his employ in and about the carrying out of this Contract, and such wages books and time sheets shall be produced whenever required for the inspection of any officer authorised by the Employer

19A 7 If the Employer shall have reasonable ground for believing that the requirements of any of the preceding provisions of clause 19A are not being observed, he or the Architect/Supervising Officer on his behalf shall be entitled to require proof of the rates of wages paid and hours and conditions observed by the Contractor and sub-contractors in carrying out the Works

---

26 Clause 20: Injury to persons and property and employer's indemnity

Contractor's liability under clause 20.1 in respect of personal injury

26.01 This clause is printed as substituted by Amendment 2: 1986. This is in very wide terms, and it is thought that the burden of proving negligence on the employer's part could rest on the contractor.

---

20   Injury to persons and property and indemnity to Employer

20 1 The Contractor shall be liable for, and shall indemnify the Employer against, any expense, liability, loss, claim or proceedings whatsoever arising under any statute or at common law in respect of personal injury to or the death of any person whomsoever arising out of or in the course of or caused by the carrying out of the Works, except to the extent that the same is due to any act or neglect of the Employer or of any person for whom the Employer is responsible including the persons employed or otherwise engaged by the Employer to whom clause 29 refers.

20 2 The Contractor shall, subject to clause 20 3 and, where applicable, clause 22C 1, be liable for, and shall indemnify the Employer against, any expense, liability, loss, claim or proceedings in respect of any injury or damage whatsoever to any property real or personal in so far as such injury or damage arises out of or in the course of or by reason of the carrying out of the Works, and to the extent that the same is due to any negligence, breach of statutory duty, omission or default of the Contractor, his servants or agents or of any person employed or engaged upon or in connection with the Works or any part thereof, his servants or agents, other than the Employer or any person employed, engaged or authorised by him or by any local authority or statutory undertaker executing work solely in pursuance of its statutory rights or obligations.

20 3   1 Subject to clause 20 3 2 the reference in clause 20 2 to 'property real or personal' does not include the Works, work executed and/or Site Materials up to and including the date of issue of the certificate of Practical Completion or up to and including the date of determination of the employment of the Contractor (whether or not the validity of that determination is disputed) under clause 27 or clause 28 or clause 28A or, where clause 22C applies, under clause 27 or clause 28 or clause 28A or clause 22C 4 3, whichever is the earlier.

20 3   2 If clause 18 has been operated then, in respect of the relevant part, and as from the relevant date such relevant part shall not be regarded as 'the Works' or 'work executed' for the purpose of clause 20 3 1.

Contractor's liability under clause 20.2 in respect of property

26.02 This is very wide, although the employer must prove a causal connection between the injury and the execution of the works, and a default on the part of the contractor. Subject to the exceptions, if clauses 22B or 22C apply, the contractor is liable under this clause for: claims by third parties whose property is damaged; claims by the employer in respect of his own property; and, it seems, damage to the works. However, this clause is not wide enough to cover the situation where the work is defectively executed as a result of the contractor's negligence (see *City of Manchester* v *Fram Gerrard* 6 BLR 70).

In addition to his liability under clause 20.2, the contractor must as an incident of his duty to complete make good any damage to the works such as that due to vandalism or theft occurring before practical completion and not caused by the employer's negligence or default or within the risks accepted by the employer where clause 22B or 22C is used. The contractor's plant, equipment, and unfixed goods and materials are at his risk. Goods and materials when certified for remain at his risk.

Where by nature of clause 20.3 the contractor is not responsible for damage, the employer may be unable to recover damages likewise from a sub-contractor who caused the damage in question – *Norwich City Council* v *Harvey* (1987) 39 BLR 75.

Employer and contractor liable to third party

26.03 In *A M F International* v *Magnet Bowling* [1968] 1 WLR 1028, both employer and contractor were held liable to a third party for damage to the third party's property; it was held the employer could not recover under the indemnity in what is now clause 20.2 because the indemnity did not apply where, as was the case, the third party's loss arose partly as a result of the employer's negligence. The employer succeeded in recovering from the contractor the sum he had to pay the third party because the damage arose from the contractor's failure to comply with items in the bills requiring the diversion of storm water and the protection of the works.

27 Clause 21: Insurance against injury to persons and property

27.01 Clause 21 imposes on the contractor certain duties to insure. Clause 21.1 relates to employers' liability insurance, in respect of death or injury to the employees of the contractor or any sub-contractor. Clause 21.2 relates to damage to third party property caused by the actual execution of the works, subject to certain exceptions, including inter alia damage caused by the contractor's own negligence.

Clause 22: Insurance of the works against clause 22 perils

27.02 Clause 22 provides for all-risks insutance of the works. There are three alterations, two (22A & B) relate to new works, and one (22c) relates to works to existing buildings. In practice insurance brokers and companies provide standard form policies with wording corresponding to the alterations considered by clause 22.

28 Clause 23: Date of possession, completion and postponement

28.01 This clause should be read with clause 24 (damages for non-completion) and clause 25 (extension of time).

23	Date of Possession, completion and postponement

23.1 **.1** On the Date of Possession possession of the site shall be given to the Contractor who shall thereupon begin the Works, regularly and diligently proceed with the same and shall complete the same on or before the Completion Date.

23.1 **.2** Where clause 23.1.2 is stated in the Appendix to apply the Employer may defer the giving of possession for a period not exceeding six weeks or such lesser period stated in the Appendix calculated from the Date of Possession.

23.2 The Architect may issue instructions in regard to the postponement of any work to be executed under the provisions of this Contract.

23.3 **.1** For the purposes of the Works insurances the Contractor shall retain possession of the site and the Works up to and including the date of issue of the certificate of Practical Completion, and, subject to clause 18, the Employer shall not be entitled to take possession of any part or parts of the Works until that date.

23.3 **.2** Notwithstanding the provisions of clause 23.3.1 the Employer may, with the consent in writing of the Contractor, use or occupy the site or the Works or part thereof whether for the purposes of storage of his goods or otherwise before the date of issue of the certificate of Practical Completion by the Architect. Before the Contractor shall give his consent to such use or occupation the Contractor or the Employer shall notify the insurers under clause 22A or clause 22B or clause 22C.2 to .4 whichever may be applicable and obtain confirmation that such use or occupation will not prejudice the insurance. Subject to such confirmation the consent of the Contractor shall not be unreasonably withheld.

23.3 **.3** Where clause 22A.2 or clause 22A.3 applies and the insurers in giving the confirmation referred to in clause 23.3.2 have made it a condition of such confirmation that an additional premium is required the Contractor shall notify the Employer of the amount of the additional premium. If the Employer continues to require use or occupation under clause 23.3.2 the additional premium required shall be added to the Contract Sum and the Contractor shall provide the Employer, if so requested, with the additional premium receipt therefor.

24	Damages for non-completion

24.1 If the Contractor fails to complete the Works by the Completion Date then the Architect shall issue a certificate to that effect.

24.2 **.1** Subject to the issue of a certificate under clause 24.1 the Contractor shall, as the Employer may require in writing not later than the date of the Final Certificate, pay or allow to the Employer the whole or such part as may be specified in writing by the Employer of a sum calculated at the rate stated in the Appendix as liquidated and ascertained damages for the period between the Completion Date and the date of Practical Completion and the Employer may deduct the same from any monies due or to become due to the Contractor under this Contract (including any balance stated as due to the Contractor in the Final Certificate) or the Employer may recover the same from the Contractor as a debt.

24.2 **.2** If, under clause 25.3.3, the Architect fixes a later Completion Date the Employer shall pay or repay to the Contractor any amounts recovered allowed or paid under clause 24.2.1 for the period up to such later Completion Date.

28.02 If 'possession of the site' cannnot be given on the date for possession, the employer is in serious breach of contract and the contractor is entitled to claim damages. In addition, the employer would be unable to deduct liquidated damages for non-completion on the due date. There is no contractual provision enabling the architect to award an extension of time in such circumstances, and the provision enabling the architect to postpone the 'work' gives him no power to postpone possession of the site. The best that can be done is to reach an agreement between the contractor and the employer to alter the dates for possession and completion.

28.03 The words 'complete the same' mean completion to the stage of practical completion (see clause 17).

Postponement

28.04 Note the contractor's right to extension of time (clause 25.4.5.1) and to claim loss and expense (clause 26.2.5), and if the whole of the works are suspended for the period of delay stated in the Appendix, to determination (clause 28.1.3). For circumstances when a variation order may also amount to a postponement of work, see *M Harrison & Co* v *Leeds City Council* (1980) 14 BLR 118.

29 Clause 24: Damages for non-completion

29.01 This clause gives the employer the right to deduct or claim liquidated damages if the contractor fails to achieve practical completion by the date of completion extended as may be necessary under clause 25 and the architect has given his certificate under this clause. The certificate is, it seems, required in order to ensure that the architect has properly considered any notices of delay under clause 25 and has granted all extensions of time to which the contractor is entitled. Under clause 25 provision is made for reassessment of extension of time throughout the contract period, and therefore clause 24.2 makes provision for the situation where, after liquidated damages have been deducted, a later completion date is fixed than that on the basis of which liquidated damages were deducted. In these circumstances, the employer is obliged to pay or repay to the contractor amounts for the period up to such later completion date (see also para 23.01).

29.02 The issue of a certificate under clause 24.1 is a condition precedent to the employer's right to deduct liquidated damages (see *Ramac Construction* v *Lesser* [1975] 2 Lloyds Reports 430). A form of certificate of non-completion is available from RIBA publications Ltd.

Advantage of liquidated damages

29.03 If there is no provision for liquidated damages, ascertainment of damage suffered for non-completion can involve the parties in long and costly proceedings. Where the parties have made and agreed upon a genuine pre-estimate of damages, such proceedings are avoided. The rate agreed, termed here 'liquidated and ascertained damages', will be given effect to by the courts without enquiring into the actual loss suffered.

Liquidated damages and penalties distinguished

29.04 The contractor can, however, have the agreed rate of liquidated damages set aside and make the employer prove and be limited to his actual loss if the rate was a penalty. If the amount fixed for liquidated damages does not represent a genuine attempt by the parties to pre-estimate the loss likely to be incurred through delay, but was in truth designed 'in terrorem' against the contractor and is so high that it cannot represent a genuine pre-estimate of the employer's loss, it will be held to be a penalty.

Delay partly employer's fault

29.05 At common law an employer partly responsible for delay could not rely on a liquidated damages clause. However, under clause 25 extensions of time may be granted in respect of relevant events which include delay caused by the employer's fault, and provided such extensions are properly granted the right to liquidated damages is preserved. However, failure to grant proper extensions of time in respect of such relevant events as arise through the employer's fault will disentitle him from claiming liquidated damages. In *Percy Bilton Limited* v *Greater London Council* [1982] 2 All ER, 623, HL it was held that delay caused by the bankruptcy of a nominated sub-contractor (for which no provision for extension is made by clause 25) did not arise through any fault by the employer, so as to disentitle him from claiming liquidated damaged. Failure to give possession of the site on the due date could result in the right to liquidated damages being lost, as this is not a ground for extension under clause 25, but is a fault of the employer: *Rapid Building Group Ltd* v *Ealing Family Housing Association Ltd* (1984) 29 BLR 5.

Procedure

29.06 The employer has a discretion whether to deduct liquidated damages. In practice, though not required by the contract, it is convenient for the architect to set out his calculation of the employer's right to liquidated damages and send a copy to each party when giving his certificate. Under

the 1963 JCT Form, it has been held that no certificate under clause 22 of that Form (replaced by clause 24) could be issued after the issue of the final certificate (*Fairweather* v *Asden Securities* (1979) 12 BLR 40). It is thought the position is the same under the 1980 Form.

30 Clause 25: Extension of time

30.01 Clause 25 makes provisions for extensions of time through delay caused by 'relevant events' as defined in clause 25.4.

When it becomes reasonably apparent that the progress of the works is being or is likely to be delayed, the contractor is obliged forthwith to give written notice to the architect of the material circumstances, including

1. The cause or causes of the delay.
2. Identifying in such notice any event which in his opinion is a relevant event.

---

25 Extension of time [p]

25·1 In clause 25 any reference to delay, notice or extension of time includes further delay, further notice or further extension of time.

25·2 **·1 ·1** If and whenever it becomes reasonably apparent that the progress of the Works is being or is likely to be delayed the Contractor shall forthwith give written notice to the Architect of the material circumstances including the cause or causes of the delay and identify in such notice any event which in his opinion is a Relevant Event.

·1 ·2 Where the material circumstances of which written notice has been given under clause 25·2·1·1 include reference to a Nominated Sub-Contractor, the Contractor shall forthwith send a copy of such written notice to the Nominated Sub-Contractor concerned.

25·2 ·2 In respect of each and every Relevant Event identified in the notice given in accordance with clause 25·2·1·1 the Contractor shall, if practicable in such notice, or otherwise in writing as soon as possible after such notice:

·2 ·1 give particulars of the expected effects thereof; and

·2 ·2 estimate the extent, if any, of the expected delay in the completion of the Works beyond the Completion Date resulting therefrom whether or not concurrently with delay resulting from any other Relevant Event and shall give such particulars and estimate to any Nominated Sub-Contractor to whom a copy of any written notice has been given under clause 25·2·1·2.

25·2 ·3 The Contractor shall give such further written notices to the Architect, and send a copy to any Nominated Sub-Contractor to whom a copy of any written notice has been given under clause 25·2·1·2, as may be reasonably necessary or as the Architect may reasonably require for keeping up-to-date the particulars and estimate referred to in clauses 25·2·2·1 and 25·2·2·2 including any material change in such particulars or estimate.

25·3 ·1 If, in the opinion of the Architect, upon receipt of any notice, particulars and estimate under clauses 25·2·1·1 and 25·2·2,

·1 ·1 any of the events which are stated by the Contractor to be the cause of the delay is a Relevant Event and

·1 ·2 the completion of the Works is likely to be delayed thereby beyond the Completion Date

the Architect shall in writing to the Contractor give an extension of time by fixing such later date as the Completion Date as he then estimates to be fair and reasonable. The Architect shall, in fixing such new Completion Date, state:

·1 ·3 which of the Relevant Events he has taken into account and

·1 ·4 the extent, if any, to which he has had regard to any instruction under clause 13·2 requiring as a Variation the omission of any work issued since the fixing of the previous Completion Date,

and shall, if reasonably practicable having regard to the sufficiency of the aforesaid notice, particulars and estimates, fix such new Completion Date not later than 12 weeks from receipt of the notice and of reasonably sufficient particulars and estimate, or, where the period between receipt thereof and the Completion Date is less than 12 weeks, not later than the Completion Date.

If, in the opinion of the Architect, upon receipt of any such notice, particulars and estimate, it is not fair and reasonable to fix a later date as a new Completion Date, the Architect shall if reasonably practicable having regard to the sufficiency of the aforesaid notice, particulars and estimate so notify the Contractor in writing not later than 12 weeks from receipt of the notice, particulars and estimate, or, where the period between receipt thereof and the Completion Date is less than 12 weeks, not later than the Completion Date.

25·3 ·2 After the first exercise by the Architect of his duty under clause 25·3·1 the Architect may in writing fix a Completion Date earlier than that previously fixed under clause 25 if in his opinion the fixing of such earlier Completion Date is fair and reasonable having regard to the omission of any work or obligation instructed or sanctioned by the Architect under clause 13 after the last occasion on which the Architect fixed a new Completion Date.

25·3 ·3 After the Completion Date, if this occurs before the date of Practical Completion, the Architect may, and not later than the expiry of 12 weeks after the date of Practical Completion, shall in writing to the Contractor either

·3 ·1 fix a Completion Date later than that previously fixed if in his opinion the fixing of such later Completion Date is fair and reasonable having regard to any of the Relevant Events, whether upon reviewing a previous decision or otherwise and whether or not the Relevant Event has been specifically notified by the Contractor under clause 25·2·1·1; or

·3 ·2 fix a Completion Date earlier than that previously fixed under clause 25 if in his opinion the fixing of such earlier Completion Date is fair and reasonable having regard to the omission of any work or obligation instructed or sanctioned by the Architect under clause 13 after the last occasion on which the Architect fixed a new Completion Date; or

·3 ·3 confirm to the Contractor the Completion Date previously fixed.

25·3 ·4 Provided always

·4 ·1 the Contractor shall use constantly his best endeavours to prevent delay in the progress of the Works, howsoever caused, and to prevent the completion of the Works being delayed or further delayed beyond the Completion Date;

·4 ·2 the Contractor shall do all that may reasonably be required to the satisfaction of the Architect to proceed with the Works.

25·3 ·5 The Architect shall notify in writing to every Nominated Sub-Contractor each decision of the Architect under clause 25·3 fixing a Completion Date.

25·3 ·6 No decision of the Architect under clause 25·3 shall fix a Completion Date earlier than the Date for Completion stated in the Appendix.

25·4 The following are the Relevant Events referred to in clause 25:

25·4 ·1 force majeure;

25·4 ·2 exceptionally adverse weather conditions;

25·4 ·3 loss or damage occasioned by any one or more of the Specified Perils;

25·4 ·4 civil commotion, local combination of workmen, strike or lock-out affecting any of the trades employed upon the Works or any of the trades engaged in the preparation, manufacture or transportation of any of the goods or materials required for the Works;

25·4 ·5 compliance with the Architect's instructions

·5 ·1 under clauses 2·3, 13·2, 13·3, 23·2, 34, 35 or 36; or

·5 ·2 in regard to the opening up for inspection of any work covered up or the testing of any of the work, materials or goods in accordance with clause 8·3 (including making good in consequence of such opening up or testing) unless the inspection or test showed that the work, materials or goods were not in accordance with this Contract;

25·4 ·6 the Contractor not having received in due time necessary instructions, drawings, details or levels from the Architect for which he specifically applied in writing provided that such application was made on a date which having regard to the Completion Date was neither unreasonably distant from nor unreasonably close to the date on which it was necessary for him to receive the same;

25·4 ·7 delay on the part of Nominated Sub-Contractors or Nominated Suppliers which the Contractor has taken all practicable steps to avoid or reduce;

25·4 ·8 ·1 the execution of work not forming part of this Contract by the Employer himself or by persons employed or otherwise engaged by the Employer as referred to in clause 29 or the failure to execute such work;

·8 ·2 the supply by the Employer of materials and goods which the Employer has agreed to provide for the Works or the failure so to supply;

25·4 ·9 the exercise after the Base Date by the United Kingdom Government of any statutory power which directly affects the execution of the Works by restricting the availability or use of labour which is essential to the proper carrying out of the Works or preventing the Contractor from, or delaying the Contractor in, securing such goods or materials or such fuel or energy as are essential to the proper carrying out of the Works;

25·4 ·10 ·1 the Contractor's inability for reasons beyond his control and which he could not reasonably have foreseen at the Base Date to secure such labour as is essential to the proper carrying out of the Works; or

·10 ·2 the Contractor's inability for reasons beyond his control and which he could not reasonably have foreseen at the Base Date to secure such goods or materials as are essential to the proper carrying out of the Works;

25·4 ·11 the carrying out by a local authority or statutory undertaker of work in pursuance of its statutory obligations in relation to the Works, or the failure to carry out such work;

25·4 ·12 failure of the Employer to give in due time ingress to or egress from the site of the Works or any part thereof through or over any land, buildings, way or passage adjoining or connected with the site and in the possession and control of the Employer, in accordance with the Contract Bills and/or the Contract Drawings, after receipt by the Architect of such notice, if any, as the Contractor is required to give, or failure of the Employer to give such ingress or egress as otherwise agreed between the Architect and the Contractor;

25·4 ·13 where clause 23·1·2 is stated in the Appendix to apply, the deferment by the Employer of giving possession of the site under clause 23·1·2.

[p] See clauses 38·4·7, 39·5·7 and 40·7 (restriction of fluctuations or price adjustment during period where Contractor is in default over completion).

30.02 Clause 25.2.2 requires the contractor in his notice or as soon as possible thereafter to give particulars of the expected effects of the cause of delay and an estimate of the extent, if any, of the expected delay in completion of the works beyond the completion date resulting therefrom whether or not concurrently with the delay resulting from any other relevant event.

Position of sub-contractors

30.03 Where any notice by the contractor makes reference to a nominated sub-contractor, the contractor must serve a copy

of the notice on the nominated sub-contractor, and he must also serve the further details required by clause 25.2.2 on that nominated sub-contractor. This is designed to protect the position of a nominated sub-contractor on whom the main contractor is seeking to cast blame for the delay which is occurring.

The contract clearly contemplates that the contractor is to give full particulars and all details of the alleged cause of delay, even if it is the contractor's own fault, and the effect it is likely to have on the progress of the works, and clearly more than one such notice and details may be served by the contractor during the course of the contract.

Architect's action

30.04 On receipt of the contractor's notice, particulars, and estimate, the architect must first decide whether the contractor is entitled to an extension of time in principle (i.e. whether the delay is caused by a relevant event) and secondly, whether the occurrence of the relevant event will, in fact, cause delay beyond the completion date. Having decided these two points, the architect grants an extension of time in writing by fixing a new completion date. His notice must state which of the relevant events he has taken into account and the extent, if any, to which he has had regard to any instruction under clause 13.2 requiring as a variation the omission of any work issued since the fixing of the previous completion date (clause 25.3.1.4). He is not bound, however, to allocate the extension period between the relevant events, e.g. by awarding so many weeks for adverse weather, some variations, etc. He must take this action not later than twelve weeks from receipt of the notice and of reasonably sufficient particulars and estimate or (where there are fewer than twelve weeks to completion) not later than the completion date.

30.05 Under clause 25.3.2, if the architect has already exercised his power to grant an extension he may fix a completion date earlier than the previously extended completion date if he thinks it fair and reasonable, having regard to variations requiring the omission of work which have been issued after the last occasion on which an extension of time was granted. This is, however, subject to the proviso that (under clause 25.3.6) no completion date can be fixed earlier than the date for completion stated in the Appendix. Thus the architect is entitled to reduce a previously granted extension of time if work is subsequently ordered to be omitted, thereby reducing the amount of the contractor's commitments and justifying an earlier completion date. RIBA Publications Ltd publish a form of 'Notification of Revision to Completion Date'. Its use is not mandatory, however.

Duties of architect after practical completion

30.06 When practical completion has occurred, provision is made for the architect to review the position as regards extensions of time finally. He may fix a later completion date than that previously fixed and take into account all relevant events whether or not specifically notified by the contractor. Or he may fix an earlier completion date, having regard to omissions which have occurred since the last occasion when an extension of time was granted. Alternatively, he may simply confirm the previously fixed completion date.

The relevant events
Clause 25.4.1

30.07 The meaning of the term 'force majeure' is difficult to state exactly, but very broadly the words extend to special circumstances quite outside the control of the contractor and not dealt with elsewhere in the contract. Interference by government and the effect of epidemics are examples of events which are probably within this clause. Financial difficulties experienced by the contractor are equally clearly not within this definition.

Clause 25.4.2

30.08 Exceptionally adverse weather conditions require quite unusual severity: it will frequently be necessary to establish this with the aid of weather charts covering a considerable period. Note that the definition includes exceptional extremes of heat and dryness, as well as the more normal English weather; such extremes of heat and dryness can, of course, have a serious effect on progress.

Clause 25.4.3

30.09 These contingencies are very wide, and in some instances may be due to an act of negligence on the part of the contractor, at any rate in their underlying causes.

Clause 25.4.6

30.10 The phrase 'neither unreasonably distant from' refers to drawings, etc. If these were in fact late and the contractor has failed to make a specific application at the time required, the architect should not refuse to consider whether to make an extension but can, it is thought, take into account the effect, if any, of such failure when considering the amount of any extension. It was held in *Percy Bilton Limited* v *Greater London Council* that delay by the employer of the previous nominated sub-contractor fell within the predecessor of this sub-clause.

Clause 25.4.7

30.11 Where this sub-clause applies, neither the nominated sub-contractor or nominated supplier nor the contractor has to pay liquidated damages. The extension must be granted whatever the cause of the delay, including the making good of his own bad work by a nominated sub-contractor before completion of his sub-contract work (see *Westminster City Council* v *Jarvis Ltd* [1970] 1 All ER 943). But where defects are discovered in the sub-contract works after the nominated sub-contractor has purported to complete the works and the works have been accepted by the architect and contractor, there is no right to an extension even where the work has been accepted with some suspicions (ibid). The employer's interests in respect of loss caused by delay on the part of nominated sub-contractors and nominated suppliers can be protected by obtaining warranties of timely completion from them. These forms of direct warranty (TNS/1 in the case of nominated suppliers, NSC/2 in the case of nominated sub-contractors) are discussed in paras 46 and 43.

Clause 25.4.8

30.12 In *Henry Boot Construction Limited* v *Central Lancashire New Town Development Corporation* (1980) 15 BLR 1, it was held that work carried out by statutory undertakers under contracts with the employer fell within this sub-clause rather than clause 25.4.11, even though the work was referred to in the bills of quantities as work in respect of which direct payment would be made by the employer and the amounts deducted from the final account.

Clause 25.4.10

30.13 Although the wording of this sub-clause is on the face of it wide, it is thought that it is not of as great assistance to

contractors as it may first appear: the requirement is of the contractor's 'inability for reasons beyond his control' to procure the necessary labour or materials. Merely because it has become more difficult (because, for example, labour rates have risen, and therefore it is necessary for the contractor to pay uneconomically high prices for labour or materials having regard to his tender) would not come within this sub-clause.

Clause 25.4.11

30.14 This covers delay caused by local authorities and statutory undertakers in performing their statutory obligations; the contractor having no choice but to employ these local authorities or statutory undertakers, it is thought unjust he should be penalized for their delay. But this does not apply where they are carrying out work as sub-contractors extending beyond their statutory obligations (see *Henry Boot Construction Limited* v *Central Lancashire New Town Development Corporation* (1980) 15 BLR 1 discussed above).

Clause 25.4.12

30.15 This clause only applies if the employer is in possession and control of the land in question, which must adjoin the site, and fails to give access after any required notice given by the contractor. Alternatively, it would apply in respect of special arrangements between the architect, presumably acting with the consent of the employer, and the contractor. This latter situation may cover agreed wayleaves, etc.

Danger in amending clause 25

30.16 If clause 25 is amended, clause 29.5.8.1 provides in effect that fluctuations are not to be 'frozen' as at the completion date, but the contractor is entitled to claim fluctuations even though the completion date has passed. Therefore, if clause 25 is amended, clause 29.5.8.1 should also be changed.

31 Clause 26: Loss and expense caused by matters materially affecting regular progress of the works

Nature of clause 26

31.01 Clause 26 entitles the contractor to claim direct loss and/or expense due to the regular progress of the works or any part thereof being materially affected by the list of matters contained in clause 26.2. Under clause 26.6 the provisions of clause 26 are without prejudice to any other rights and remedies which the contractor may possess, and therefore the provisions of clause 26 do not preclude any claim by the contractor for damages for breach of contract, negligence, misrepresentation, etc.

The word 'direct' excludes thereby claims for consequential loss (see *Cawoods* v *Croudace* [1978] 2 Lloyds Reports 55). It is thought that in general the computation of the amount of direct loss and/or expense is to follow the lines for computation for ordinary damages for breach of contract, although, of course, a claim under clause 26 is not a claim for breach of contract as such. See *Wright Ltd* v *PH & T (Holdings) Ltd* (1980) 13 BLR 26.

In *Minter* v *Welsh Health Technical Services Organization* 13 BLR 1, it was held that under the 1963 JCT Form clause 24(1) the contractor could claim as part of his direct loss and/or expense the amount of finance changes incurred by him in respect of the amount of such loss and expense.

---

26 Loss and expense caused by matters materially affecting regular progress of the Works

26·1 If the Contractor makes written application to the Architect stating that he has incurred or is likely to incur direct loss and/or expense in the execution of this Contract for which he would not be reimbursed by a payment under any other provision in this Contract due to deferment of giving possession of the site under clause 23·1·2 where clause 23·1·2 is stated in the Appendix to be applicable or because the regular progress of the Works or of any part thereof has been or is likely to be materially affected by any one or more of the matters referred to in clause 26·2; and if and as soon as the Architect is of the opinion that the direct loss and/or expense has been or is likely to be incurred due to any such deferment of giving possession or that the regular progress of the Works or of any part thereof has been or is likely to be so materially affected as set out in the application of the Contractor then the Architect from time to time thereafter shall ascertain, or shall instruct the Quantity Surveyor to ascertain, the amount of such loss and/or expense which has been or is being incurred by the Contractor; provided always that:

26·1 ·1 the Contractor's application shall be made as soon as it has become, or should reasonably have become, apparent to him that the regular progress of the Works or of any part thereof has been or was likely to be affected as aforesaid, and

26·1 ·2 the Contractor shall in support of his application submit to the Architect upon request such information as should reasonably enable the Architect to form an opinion as aforesaid, and

26·1 ·3 the Contractor shall submit to the Architect or to the Quantity Surveyor upon request such details of such loss and/or expense as are reasonably necessary for such ascertainment as aforesaid.

26·2 The following are the matters referred to in clause 26·1:

26·2 ·1 the Contractor not having received in due time necessary instructions, drawings, details or levels from the Architect for which he specifically applied in writing provided that such application was made on a date which having regard to the Completion Date was neither unreasonably distant from nor unreasonably close to the date on which it was necessary for him to receive the same;

26·2 ·2 the opening up for inspection of any work covered up or the testing of any of the work, materials or goods in accordance with clause 8·3 (including making good in consequence of such opening up or testing), unless the inspection or test showed that the work, materials or goods were not in accordance with this Contract;

26·2 ·3 any discrepancy in or divergence between the Contract Drawings and/or the Contract Bills and/or the Numbered Documents;

26·2 ·4 ·1 the execution of work not forming part of this Contract by the Employer himself or by persons employed or otherwise engaged by the Employer as referred to in clause 29 or the failure to execute such work;

·4 ·2 the supply by the Employer of materials and goods which the Employer has agreed to provide for the Works or the failure so to supply;

26·2 ·5 Architect's instructions under clause 23·2 issued in regard to the postponement of any work to be executed under the provisions of this Contract;

26·2 ·6 failure of the Employer to give in due time ingress to or egress from the site of the Works, or any part thereof through or over any land, buildings, way or passage adjoining or connected with the site and in the possession and control of the Employer, in accordance with the Contract Bills and/or the Contract Drawings, after receipt by the Architect of such notice, if any, as the Contractor is required to give, or failure of the Employer to give such ingress or egress as otherwise agreed between the Architect and the Contractor;

26·2 ·7 Architect's instructions issued under clause 13·2 requiring a Variation or under clause 13·3 in regard to the expenditure of provisional sums (other than work to which clause 13·4·2 refers).

26·3 If and to the extent that it is necessary for ascertainment under clause 26·1 of loss and/or expense the Architect shall state in writing to the Contractor what extension of time, if any, has been made under clause 25 in respect of the Relevant Event or Events referred to in clause 25·4·5·1 (so far as that clause refers to clauses 2·3, 13·2, 13·3 and 23·2) and in clauses 25·4·5·2, 25·4·6, 25·4·8 and 25·4·12.

26·4 ·1 The Contractor upon receipt of a written application properly made by a Nominated Sub-Contractor under clause 13·1 of Sub-Contract NSC/4 or NSC/4a as applicable shall pass to the Architect a copy of that written application. If and as soon as the Architect is of the opinion that the loss and/or expense to which the said clause 13·1 refers has been incurred or is likely to be incurred due to any deferment of the giving of possession where clause 23·1·2 is stated in the Appendix to apply or that the regular progress of the Sub-Contract Works or of any part thereof has been or is likely to be materially affected as referred to in clause 13·1 of Sub-Contract NSC/4 or NSC/4a and as set out in the application of the Nominated Sub-Contractor then the Architect shall himself ascertain, or shall instruct the Quantity Surveyor to ascertain, the amount of loss and/or expense to which the said clause 13·1 refers.

26·4 ·2 If and to the extent that it is necessary for the ascertainment of such loss and/or expense the Architect shall state in writing to the Contractor with a copy to the Nominated Sub-Contractor concerned what was the length of the revision of the period or periods for completion of the Sub-Contract Works or of any part thereof to which he gave consent in respect of the Relevant Event or Events set out in clause 11·2·5·5·1 (so far as that clause refers to clauses 2·3, 13·2, 13·3 and 23·2 of the Main Contract Conditions), 11·2·5·5·2, 11·2·5·6, 11·2·5·8 and 11·2·5·12 of Sub-Contract NSC/4 or NSC/4a as applicable.

26·5 Any amount from time to time ascertained under clause 26 shall be added to the Contract Sum.

26·6 The provisions of clause 26 are without prejudice to any other rights and remedies which the Contractor may possess.

Notice

31.02 Clause 26.1 requires the giving of a notice stating that the contractor has incurred or is likely to incur such loss and expense. Once such notice has been given, the loss and expense must be ascertained from time to time by the architect or quantity surveyor. Only one such notice need be given (reversing the position under the previous JCT Form)

(see *Minter* v *Welsh Health Technical Services Organization*). Under clause 26.1 the application must be made as soon as it has become or should reasonably have become apparent to the contractor that regular progress is being affected. The contractor must submit information in support of his application, and must on request supply a breakdown of the loss and/or expense (see clause 26.1.3). It is thought that the requirement of a notice is a condition precedent to the contractor's rights under this clause.

Note that all that is required is that 'regular progress of the works' is 'materially affected'. This does not require that progress be delayed, or that the whole of the works be affected. It could apply, for example, where the contractor is obliged to bring extra operatives on site, or where there is a loss of productivity of certain trade. Note, however, that there is a strict divorce in the conditions between claims under clause 26 and claims under clause 13 (see the proviso to clause 13.5.6).

Claims generally

31.03 The term 'claim' has no exact meaning, but for present purposes it may be considered any claim for payment by the contractor in respect of the original contract work arising other than under clause 30. Any such claims fall under one of the following categories:

1. A right to payment arising under a clause of the contract.
2. A claim for damages ordinarily for breach of contract.
3. A claim under neither 1 nor 2.

If a claim comes within 1, the architect follows whatever procedure the contract prescribes according to the clause relied on by the contractor. The architect need not consult the employer, although he may do so if he thinks it desirable. If the claim falls within 2, the architect should consult the employer and should not include any sum in a certificate in respect of such a claim without the employer's agreement, for the contract gives him no power to certify in respect of the claim for damages. If the claim falls within 3, the contractor has no right to payment. The architect cannot certify save on the employer's direction, and any payment will be made *ex gratia*.

Provisions relating to nominated sub-contractors

31.04 Clause 26.4 contains provisions where a nominated sub-contractor claims loss and expense under clause 13.1 of Sub-contract NSC/4. The contractor is under an obligation to pass such application on to the architect, who then reaches a decision on it and instructs the quantity surveyor to ascertain the amount of loss and expense (or carries out this function himself). To the extent that it is necessary to ascertain such loss and expense, the architect shall state in writing to the contractor the length of the revision of the period or periods for completion of the sub-contract works to which he gave consent in respect of the relevant event or events set out in clauses 11.2.5.5.1 (so far as that clause refers to clauses 2.3, 13.2, 13.3, and at 23.2 of the Main Contract conditions), 11.2.5.5.2, 11.2.5.6, 11.2.5.8, and 11.2.5.12 of Sub-contract NSC/4. This applies to such matters as discrepancies in sub-contract documents, variations, expenditure of provisional sums, postponement, exceptionally adverse weather conditions, delayed instructions, delay caused by employer carrying out work not forming part of the Main Contract, and delay in giving access etc. to the sub-contractor.

32 Clause 27: Determination by employer

32.01 This clause makes provisions for the following matters:

1. Discretionary determination by the employer in event of certain defaults by the contractor.

2. Automatic determination of the contractor's employment in the event of bankruptcy or liquidation.
3. The financial position of the parties following determination of the contractor's employment.

---

27   Determination by Employer

27·1 Without prejudice to any other rights or remedies which the Employer may possess, if the Contractor shall make default in any one or more of the following respects, that is to say:

27·1 ·1 if without reasonable cause he wholly suspends the carrying out of the Works before completion thereof; or

27·1 ·2 if he fails to proceed regularly and diligently with the Works; or

27·1 ·3 if he refuses or neglects to comply with a written notice from the Architect requiring him to remove defective work or improper materials or goods and by such refusal or neglect the Works are materially affected; or

27·1 ·4 if he fails to comply with the provisions of clause 19,

then the Architect may give to him a notice by registered post or recorded delivery specifying the default. If the Contractor either shall continue such default for 14 days after receipt of such notice or shall at any time thereafter repeat such default (whether previously repeated or not), then the Employer may within 10 days after such continuance or repetition by notice by registered post or recorded delivery forthwith determine the employment of the Contractor under this Contract; provided that such notice shall not be given unreasonably or vexatiously.

27·2 In the event of the Contractor becoming bankrupt or making a composition or arrangement with his creditors or having a proposal in respect of his company for a voluntary arrangement for a composition of debts or scheme or arrangement approved in accordance with the Insolvency Act 1986, or having an application made under the Insolvency Act 1986 in respect of his company to the court for the appointment of an administrator, or having a winding up order made or (except for the purposes of amalgamation or reconstruction) a resolution for voluntary winding up passed or having a provisional liquidator, receiver or manager of his business or undertaking duly appointed, or having an administrative receiver, as defined in the Insolvency Act 1986, appointed, or having possession taken, by or on behalf of the holders of any debentures secured by a floating charge, of any property comprised in or subject to the floating charge, the employment of the Contractor under this Contract shall be forthwith automatically determined but the said employment may be reinstated and continued if the Employer and the Contractor, his trustee in bankruptcy, liquidator, provisional liquidator, receiver or manager as the case may be shall so agree.

27·3 The Employer shall be entitled to determine the employment of the Contractor under this or any other contract, if the Contractor shall have offered or given or agreed to give to any person any gift or consideration of any kind as an inducement or reward for doing or forbearing to do or for having done or forborne to do any action in relation to the obtaining or execution of this or any other contract with the Employer, or for showing or forbearing to show favour or disfavour to any person in relation to this or any other contract with the Employer, or if the like acts shall have been done by any person employed by the Contractor or acting on his behalf (whether with or without the knowledge of the Contractor), or if in relation to this or any other contract with the Employer the Contractor or any person employed by him or acting on his behalf shall have committed an offence under the Prevention of Corruption Acts 1889 to 1916.

27·4 In the event of the employment of the Contractor under this Contract being determined under clauses 27·1 or 27·2 and so long as it has not been reinstated and continued, the following shall be the respective rights and duties of the Employer and the Contractor:

27·4 ·1 the Employer may employ and pay other persons to carry out and complete the Works and he or they may enter upon the Works and use all temporary buildings, plant, tools, equipment, goods and materials intended for, delivered to and placed on or adjacent to the Works, and may purchase all materials and goods necessary for the carrying out and completion of the Works;

27·4 ·2 ·1 except where the determination occurs by reason of the bankruptcy of the Contractor or of him having a winding up order made or (other than for the purposes of amalgamation or reconstruction) a resolution for voluntary winding up passed, the Contractor shall if so required by the Employer or by the Architect on behalf of the Employer within 14 days of the date of determination, assign to the Employer without payment the benefit of any agreement for the supply of materials or goods and/or for the execution of any work for the purposes of this Contract but on the terms that a supplier or sub-contractor shall be entitled to make any reasonable objection to any further assignment thereof by the Employer;

·2 ·2 unless the exception to the operation of clause 27·4·2·1 applies the Employer may pay any supplier or sub-contractor for any materials or goods delivered or works executed for the purposes of this Contract (whether before or after the date of determination) in so far as the price thereof has not already been paid by the Contractor. The Employer's rights under this clause are in addition to his obligation or discretion as the case may be to pay Nominated Sub-Contractors as provided in clause 35·13·5 and payments made under clause 27·4·2 may be deducted from any sum due or to become due to the Contractor or shall be recoverable from the Contractor by the Employer as a debt;

27·4 ·3 the Contractor shall as and when required in writing by the Architect so to do (but not before) remove from the Works any temporary buildings, plant, tools, equipment, goods and materials belonging to or hired by him. If within a reasonable time after any such requirement has been made the Contractor has not complied therewith, then the Employer may (but without being responsible for any loss or damage) remove and sell any such property of the Contractor, holding the proceeds less all costs incurred to the credit of the Contractor;

27·4 ·4 the Contractor shall allow or pay to the Employer in the manner hereinafter appearing the amount of any direct loss and/or damage caused to the Employer by the determination. Until after completion of the Works under clause 27·4·1 the Employer shall not be bound by any provision of this Contract to make any further payment to the Contractor, but upon such completion and the verification within a reasonable time of the accounts therefor the Architect shall certify the amount of expenses properly incurred by the Employer and the amount of any direct loss and/or damage caused to the Employer by the determination and, if such amounts when added to the monies paid to the Contractor before the date of determination exceed the total amount which would have been payable on due completion in accordance with this Contract, the difference shall be a debt payable to the Employer by the Contractor; and if the said amounts when added to the said monies be less than the said total amount, the difference shall be a debt payable by the Employer to the Contractor.

Determination on notice

32.02 The employer is entitled to determine the contractor's employment in the circumstances specified in clause 27.1, subject to the giving of the notices requires by this clause. It is thought that these requirements must be strictly complied with if the employer is not to be in breach of contract.

32.03 At common law, a party is entitled to treat a contract as repudiated if the other party so conducts himself as to show no intention to go on with the contract (see *Universal Cargo Carriers* v *Citati* [1957] 2 QB 401). The employer in the event of a breach of contract by the contractor amounting to repudiation is entitled to treat the contract as at an end at common law. The purpose of clause 27 is to confer on him additional and alternative rights to determine the contractor's employment without having to prove the contractor has repudiated the contract. However, having regard to the proviso at the end of clause 27.1.4 requiring that notice be not given unreasonably or vexatiously, there is sometimes uncertainty as to whether circumstances exist justifying determination of the contractor's employment. See *J M Hill & Sons Ltd* v *London Borough of Camden* (1980) 18 BLR 31, CA; see also *John Jarvis Ltd* v *Rochdale Housing Association Ltd* (1986) 36 BLR 48, CA, on the corresponding provisions in clause 28.

32.04 Under clause 27.3 the employer is entitled to determine the contractor's employment in the event of any corrupt practices by the contractor, and in this case the requirements of clause 27.1 do not have to be complied with. This provision is not present in the private edition, nor is the provision (clause 27.1.4) for determination due to failure to comply with clause 19A.

Bankruptcy

32.05 In contra-distinction to the previous form of determination, the employment of the contractor determines automatically on his bankruptcy, subject to the option of reinstatement.

Rights of parties after determination

32.06 Clause 27.4 governs the rights of the parties after determination. Briefly, the position is that:

1. The employer is entitled to get the work completed by others and to take an assignment of contracts for supply of materials and sub-contracts (except where the determination occurs by reason of the contractor's bankruptcy).
2. The employer is entitled to make direct payment to suppliers or sub-contractors, again except where determination occurs by reason of the contractor's bankruptcy.
3. The contractor is obliged to remove all temporary plant etc.

Typically, the employer will obtain a new contractor to carry out and complete the work. Under clause 27.4.4, the employer is not bound to make any further payments to the contractor whose employment has been determined until completion of the work. Thereafter, an account is taken by the architect: if the employer has in fact got the work completed for less than he would have had to pay to the contractor, the contractor is in principle entitled to be paid the difference, but if (as is far more likely) the work has cost more than the contractor would have charged, the contractor is obliged to pay the difference to the employer. In addition, the architect must certify the amount of direct loss and/or damage caused to the employer by the determination, which is to be taken into account in carrying out the foregoing computation.

33 Clause 28: Determination by contractor

33.01 This clause is to be compared with clause 27, and entitles the contractor to determine his own employment in certain events. Clause 28.1.1 provides for non-payment of a certificate; clause 28.1.2 deals with obstruction of certificates; clause 28.1.3 deals with suspension of the work.

28	Determination by Contractor

28·1 Without prejudice to any other rights and remedies which the Contractor may possess, if

28·1 ·1 the Employer does not pay the amount properly due to the Contractor on any certificate (otherwise than as a result of the operation of the VAT Agreement) within 14 days from the issue of that certificate and continues such default for 7 days after receipt by registered post or recorded delivery of a notice from the Contractor stating that notice of determination under clause 28 will be served if payment is not made within 7 days from receipt thereof; or

28·1 ·2 the Employer interferes with or obstructs the issue of any certificate due under this Contract; or

28·1 ·3 the carrying out of the whole or substantially the whole of the uncompleted Works (other than the execution of work required under clause 17) is suspended for a continuous period of the length named in the Appendix by reason of:

·3 ·1 Architect's instructions issued under clause 2·3, 13·2 or 23·2 unless caused by reason of some negligence or default of the Contractor, his servants or agents or of any person employed or engaged upon or in connection with the Works or any part thereof, his servants or agents other than a Nominated Sub-Contractor or the Employer or any person employed, engaged or authorised by the Employer or by any local authority or statutory undertaker executing work solely in pursuance of its statutory obligations; or

·3 ·2 the Contractor not having received in due time necessary instructions, drawings, details or levels from the Architect for which he specifically applied in writing provided that such application was made on a date which having regard to the Completion Date was neither unreasonably distant from nor unreasonably close to the date on which it was necessary for him to receive the same; or

·3 ·3 delay in the execution of work not forming part of this Contract by the Employer himself or by persons employed or otherwise engaged by the Employer as referred to in clause 29 or the failure to execute such work or delay in the supply by the Employer of materials and goods which the Employer has agreed to provide for the Works or the failure so to supply; or

·3 ·4 the opening up for inspection of any work covered up or the testing of any of the work, materials or goods in accordance with clause 8·3 (including making good in consequence of such opening up or testing), unless the inspection or test showed that the work, materials or goods were not in accordance with this Contract;

·3 ·5 failure of the Employer to give in due time ingress to or egress from the site of the Works or any part thereof through or over any land, buildings, way or passage adjoining or connected with the site and in the possession and control of the Employer, in accordance with the Contract Bills or the Contract Drawings, after receipt by the Architect of such notice, if any, as the Contractor is required to give, or failure of the Employer to give such ingress or egress as otherwise agreed between the Architect and the Contractor.

28·1 ·4 the Employer becomes bankrupt or makes a composition or arrangement with his creditors or has a proposal in respect of his company for a voluntary arrangement for a composition of debts or scheme of arrangement approved in accordance with the Insolvency Act 1986, or has an application made under the Insolvency Act 1986 in respect of his company to the Court for the appointment of an administrator, or has a winding-up order made or (except for the purposes of an amalgamation or reconstruction) has a resolution for voluntary winding-up passed or a provisional liquidator, receiver or manager of his business or undertaking is duly appointed, or has an administrative receiver, as defined in the Insolvency Act 1986, appointed, or possession is taken, by or on behalf of the holders of any debentures secured by a floating charge, of any property comprised in or subject to the floating charge;

then the Contractor may thereupon by notice by registered post or recorded delivery to the Employer or Architect forthwith determine the employment of the Contractor under this Contract; provided that such notice shall not be given unreasonably or vexatiously.

28·2 Upon such determination, then without prejudice to the accrued rights or remedies of either party or to any liability of the classes mentioned in clause 20 which may accrue either before the Contractor or any sub-contractors shall have removed his or their temporary buildings, plant, tools, equipment, goods or materials or by reason of his or their so removing the same, the following shall be the respective rights and liabilities of the Contractor and the Employer:

28·2 ·1 the Contractor shall with all reasonable dispatch and in such manner and with such precautions as will prevent injury, death or damage of the classes in respect of which before the date of determination he was liable to indemnify the Employer under clause 20 remove from the site all his temporary buildings, plant, tools, equipment, goods and materials and shall give facilities for his sub-contractors to do the same, but subject always to the provisions of clause 28·2·2·4;

28·2 ·2 after taking into account amounts previously paid under this Contract the Contractor shall be paid by the Employer

·2 ·1 the total value of work completed at the date of determination, such value to be computed as if it were a valuation in respect of the amounts to be stated as due in an Interim Certificate issued under clause 30·1 but after taking account of any amounts referred to in clauses 28·2·2·3 to ·6;

·2 ·2 the total value of work begun and executed but not completed at the date of determination, the value being ascertained in accordance with clause 13·5 as if such work were a Variation required by the Architect under clause 13·2 but after taking account of any amounts referred to in clauses 28·2·2·3 to ·6;

·2 ·3 any sum ascertained in respect of direct loss and/or expense under clauses 26 and 34·3 (whether ascertained before or after the date of determination);

·2 ·4 the cost of materials or goods properly ordered for the Works for which the Contractor shall have paid or for which the Contractor is legally bound to pay, and on such payment by the Employer any materials or goods so paid for shall become the property of the Employer;

Non-payment of certificates

33.02 The contract does not deal in express terms with the position where the employer does not pay the amount of a certificate by reason of a bona fide counter-claim for defective work, for example, or by reason of some matter arising under some express provision of the contract. It is thought that a purported determination under this sub-clause would not be valid or would ordinarily be held to be unreasonable or vexatious if based solely upon a deduction which the employer was entitled to make, or bona fide considered himself entitled to make.

Obstruction of certificates

33.03 This includes preventing the architect from performing his duties or directing the architect as to the amount for which he is to give his certificate or as to the decision he should arrive at on matters which are within the sphere of his independent duty.

Suspension of work

33.04 See the Appendix for this period. Care must be taken to ensure that the periods in the Appendix are reasonably sufficient.

In *John Jarvis Ltd* v *Rochdale Housing Association Ltd* (1986) 36 BLR 48, CA, it was held that the words 'unless caused by some negligence or default of the contractor' do not include nominated sub-contractors. Therefore the main contractor is entitled to determine his employment if the work is suspended by reason of the default of a nominated sub-contractor.

33.05 In the same case it was held that notice under clause 28.1.3 is not given 'unreasonably or vexatiously' unless a reasonable contractor ins the same circumstances would have thought it unreasonable or vexatious to give the notice.

33.06 The private edition provides for the contractor to determine if the employer becomes insolvent.

34 Clause 29: Works by employer or persons employed or engaged by employer

34.01 This clause governs the position where the employer wishes to carry out certain work himself (or via persons employed by him) while the contractor is engaged on the works. Where this work is described in the bills the contractor is obliged to permit the employer to carry the work out, but where it is not the contractor is required to give his consent, which must not, however, be unreasonably withheld. Clause 29.3 makes it clear that there is no relationship between the contractor and persons so employed. (For the meaning of 'work not forming part of this contract' see *Henry Boot Construction Limited* v *Central Lancashire New Town Development Corporation* (1980) 15 BLR 1).

35 Clause 30: Certificates and payments

35.01 This clause provides for:

1. Interim certificates (clause 30.1).
2. Rules for ascertainment of amounts due in interim certificates (clause 30.2).
3. Rules for valuing off-site materials or goods (clause 30.3).
4. Rules for ascertainment of retention (clause 30.4).
5. Rules on treatment of retention (clause 30.5).
6. Final adjustment of contract sum (clause 30.6).
7. Final adjustment of nominated sub-contract sums (clause 30.7).
8. Issue of an effect of final certificate (clauses 30.8 and 30.9).

·1 ·3 the total value of any materials or goods other than those to which clause 30·2·1·2 refers where the Architect in the exercise of his discretion under clause 30·3 has decided that such total value shall be included in the amount stated as due in an Interim Certificate;

·1 ·4 the amounts referred to in clause 21·4·1 of Sub-Contract NSC/4 or NSC/4a as applicable in respect of each Nominated Sub-Contractor;

·1 ·5 the profit of the Contractor upon the total of the amounts referred to in clauses 30·2·1·4 and 30·2·2·5 less the total of the amount referred to in clause 30·2·3·2 at the rates included in the Contract Bills, or, in the cases where the nomination arises from an instruction as to the expenditure of a provisional sum, at rates related thereto, or if none, at reasonable rates.

30·2 ·2 There shall be included the following which are not subject to Retention:

·2 ·1 any amounts to be included in Interim Certificates in accordance with clause 3 as a result of payments made or costs incurred by the Contractor under clauses 6·2, 8·3, 9·2, 21·2·3, 22B·2 and 22C·3;

·2 ·2 any amounts ascertained under clause 26·1 or 34·3 or in respect of any restoration, replacement or repair of loss or damage and removal and disposal of debris which in clauses 22B·3·5 and 22C·4·4·2 are treated as if they were a Variation;

·2 ·3 any amount to which clause 35·17 refers;

·2 ·4 any amount payable to the Contractor under clause 38 or 39, if applicable;

·2 ·5 the amounts referred to in clause 21·4·2 of Sub-Contract NSC/4 or NSC/4a as applicable in respect of each Nominated Sub-Contractor.

30·2 ·3 There shall be deducted the following which are not subject to Retention:

·3 ·1 any amount deductible under clause 7 or 8·4·2 or 17·2 or 17·3 or any amount allowable by the Contractor to the Employer under clause 38 or 39, if applicable;

·3 ·2 any amount referred to in clause 21·4·3 of Sub-Contract NSC/4 or NSC/4a as applicable in respect of each Nominated Sub-Contractor.

30·3 The amount stated as due in an Interim Certificate may in the discretion of the Architect include the value of any materials or goods before delivery thereof to or adjacent to the Works (in clause 30·3 referred to as "the materials") provided that:

30·3 ·1 the materials are intended for incorporation in the Works;

30·3 ·2 nothing remains to be done to the materials to complete the same up to the point of their incorporation in the Works;

30·3 ·3 the materials have been and are set apart at the premises where they have been manufactured or assembled or are stored, and have been clearly and visibly marked, individually or in sets, either by letters or figures or by reference to a pre-determined code, so as to identify:

·3 ·1 the Employer, where they are stored on the premises of the Contractor, and in any other case the person to whose order they are held; and

·3 ·2 their destination as the Works;

30·3 ·4 where the materials were ordered from a supplier by the Contractor or by any sub-contractor, the contract for their supply is in writing and expressly provides that the property therein shall pass unconditionally to the Contractor or the sub-contractor (as the case may be) not later than the happening of the events set out in clauses 30·3·2 and 30·3·3;

30·3 ·5 where the materials were ordered from a supplier by any sub-contractor, the relevant sub-contract between the Contractor and the sub-contractor is in writing and expressly provides that on the property in the materials passing to the sub-contractor the same shall immediately thereon pass to the Contractor;

30·3 ·6 where the materials were manufactured or assembled by any sub-contractor, the sub-contract is in writing and expressly provides that the property in the materials shall pass unconditionally to the Contractor not later than the happening of the events set out in clauses 30·3·2 and 30·3·3;

30·3 ·7 the materials are in accordance with this Contract;

30·3 ·8 the Contractor provides the Architect with reasonable proof that the property in the materials is in him and that the appropriate conditions set out in clauses 30·3·1 to ·7 have been complied with;

30·3 ·9 the Contractor provides the Architect with reasonable proof that the materials are insured against loss or damage for their full value under a policy of insurance protecting the interests of the Employer and the Contractor in respect of the Specified Perils, during the period commencing with the transfer of property in the materials to the Contractor until they are delivered to, or adjacent to, the Works.

30·4 ·1 The Retention which the Employer may deduct and retain as referred to in clause 30·2 shall be such percentage of the total amount included under clause 30·2·1 in any Interim Certificate as arises from the operation of the following rules:

·1 ·1 the percentage (in the Conditions and Appendix called "the Retention Percentage") deductible under clause 30·4·1·2 shall be 5 per cent (unless a lower rate shall have been agreed between the parties and specified in the Appendix as the Retention Percentage); and the percentage deductible under clause 30·4·1·3 shall be one half of the Retention Percentage; [s]

·1 ·2 [t] the Retention Percentage may be deducted from so much of the said total amount as relates to:

work which has not reached Practical Completion (as referred to in clauses 17·1, 18·1·1 or 35·16); and

amounts in respect of the value of materials and goods included under clauses 30·2·1·2, 30·2·1·3 and 30·2·1·4 (so far as that clause relates to materials and goods as referred to in clause 21·4·1 of Sub-Contract NSC/4 or NSC/4a as applicable);

[s] Where the Employer at the tender stage estimates the Contract Sum to be £500,000 or over, the Retention Percentage should not be more than 3 per cent.

·1 ·3 [t] half the Retention Percentage may be deducted from so much of the said total amount as relates to work which has reached Practical Completion (as referred to in clauses 17·1, 18·1·1 or 35·16) but in respect of which a Certificate of Completion of Making Good Defects under clause 17·4 or a certificate under clause 18·1·2 or an Interim Certificate under clause 35·17, has not been issued.

30·4 ·2 The Retention deducted from the value of work executed by the Contractor or any Nominated Sub-Contractor, and from the value of materials and goods intended for incorporation in the Works, but not so incorporated, and specified in the statements issued under clause 30·5·2·1, is hereinafter referred to as the "Contractor's retention" and the "Nominated Sub-Contract retention" respectively.

30·5 The Retention shall be subject to the following rules:

30·5 ·1 the Employer's interest in the Retention is fiduciary as trustee for the Contractor and for any Nominated Sub-Contractor (but without obligation to invest);

30·5 ·2 ·1 at the date of each Interim Certificate the Architect shall prepare, or instruct the Quantity Surveyor to prepare, a statement specifying the Contractor's retention and the Nominated Sub-Contract retention for each Nominated Sub-Contractor deducted in arriving at the amount stated as due in such Interim Certificate;

·2 ·2 such statement shall be issued by the Architect to the Employer, to the Contractor and to each Nominated Sub-Contractor whose work is referred to in the statement.

30·5 ·3 The Employer shall, to the extent that the Employer exercises his right under clause 30·4, if the Contractor or any Nominated Sub-Contractor so requests, at the date of payment under each Interim Certificate place the Retention in a separate banking account (so designated as to identify the amount as the Retention held by the Employer on trust as provided in clause 30·5·1) and certify to the Architect with a copy to the Contractor that such amount has been so placed. The Employer shall be entitled to the full beneficial interest in any interest accruing in the separate banking account and shall be under no duty to account for any such interest to the Contractor or any sub-contractor.

30·5 ·4 Where the Employer exercises the right to deduct referred to in clause 30·1·1·2 against any Retention he shall inform the Contractor of the amount of that deduction from either the Contractor's retention or the Nominated Sub-Contract retention of any Nominated Sub-Contractor by reference to the latest statement issued under clause 30·5·2·1.

30·6 ·1 ·1 Not later than 6 months after Practical Completion of the Works the Contractor shall provide the Architect, or if so instructed by the Architect, the Quantity Surveyor, with all documents necessary for the purposes of the adjustment of the Contract Sum including all documents relating to the accounts of Nominated Sub-Contractors and Nominated Suppliers.

·1 ·2 Not later than 3 months after receipt by the Architect or by the Quantity Surveyor of the documents referred to in clause 30·6·1·1

·2 ·1 the Architect, or, if the Architect has so instructed, the Quantity Surveyor shall ascertain (unless previously ascertained) any loss and/or expense under clauses 26·1, 26·4·1 and 34·3, and

·2 ·2 the Quantity Surveyor shall prepare a statement of all adjustments to be made to the Contract Sum as referred to in clause 30·6·2 other than any to which clause 30·6·1·2·1 applies

and the Architect shall forthwith send a copy of any ascertainment to which clause 30·6·1·2·1 refers and of the statement prepared in compliance with clause 30·6·1·2·2 to the Contractor and the relevant extract therefrom to each Nominated Sub-Contractor.

30·6 ·2 The Contract Sum shall be adjusted as follows:

There shall be deducted:

·2 ·1 all prime cost sums, all amounts in respect of sub-contractors named as referred to in clause 35·1, the certified value of any work by a Nominated Sub-Contractor, whose employment has been determined in accordance with clause 35·24, which was not in accordance with the relevant Sub-Contract but which has been paid or otherwise discharged by the Employer, and any Contractor's profit thereon included in the Contract Bills;

·2 ·2 all provisional sums and the value of all work described as provisional included in the Contract Bills;

·2 ·3 the amount of the valuation under clause 13·5·2 of items omitted in accordance with a Variation required by the Architect under clause 13·2, or subsequently sanctioned by him in writing, together with the amount included in the Contract Bills for any other work as referred to in clause 13·5·5 which is to be valued under clause 13·5;

·2 ·4 any amount deducted or deductible under clause 7 or 8·4·2 or 17·2 or 17·3 or any amount allowed or allowable to the Employer under clause 38, 39 or 40, whichever is applicable;

·2 ·5 any other amount which is required by this Contract to be deducted from the Contract Sum;

There shall be added:

·2 ·6 the amounts of the Nominated Sub-Contract Sums or Tender Sums for all Nominated Sub-Contractors as finally adjusted or ascertained under all relevant provisions of Sub-Contract NSC/4 or NSC/4a as applicable;

·2 ·7 the tender sum (or such other sum as is appropriate in accordance with the terms of the tender as accepted by or on behalf of the Employer) for any work for which a tender made under clause 35·2 has been accepted;

·2 ·8 any amounts properly chargeable to the Employer in accordance with the nomination instruction of the Architect in respect of materials or goods supplied by Nominated Suppliers; such amounts shall include the discount for cash of 5 per cent referred to in clause 36 but shall exclude any value added tax which is treated, or is capable of being treated, as input tax (as referred to in the Finance Act 1972) by the Contractor;

·2 ·9 the profit of the Contractor upon the amounts referred to in clauses 30·6·2·6, 30·6·2·7 and 30·6·2·8 at the rates included in the Contract Bills or in the cases where

[t] By the operation of clauses 30·4·1·2 and 30·4·1·3 the Contractor will have released to him by the Employer upon payment of the next Interim Certificate after Practical Completion of the whole or part of the Works approximately one half of the Retention on the whole or the appropriate part; and upon payment of the next Interim Certificate after the expiration of the Defects Liability Period named in the Appendix, or after the issue of the Certificate of Completion of Making Good Defects, whichever is the later, the balance of the Retention on the whole or the appropriate part. When Retention is so included in Interim Certificates it becomes a 'sum due' to the Contractor and therefore subject to the rights of the Employer to deduct therefrom in accordance with the rights of the Employer so to deduct as set out in the Conditions.

the nomination arises from an instruction as to the expenditure of a provisional sum at rates related thereto or if none at reasonable rates;

·2 ·10 any amounts paid or payable by the Employer to the Contractor as a result of payments made or costs incurred by the Contractor under clauses 6·2, 8·3, 9·2 and 21·2·3;

·2 ·11 the amount of the Valuation under clause 13·5 of any Variation, including the valuation of other work, as referred to in clause 13·5·5, other than the amount of the valuation of any omission under clause 13·5·2;

·2 ·12 the amount of the Valuation of work executed by, or the amount of any disbursements by, the Contractor in accordance with instructions of the Architect as to the expenditure of provisional sums included in the Contract Bills and of all work described as provisional included in the Contract Bills;

·2 ·13 any amount ascertained under clause 26·1 or 34·3;

·2 ·14 any amount paid by the Contractor under clause 22B or clause 22C which the Contractor is entitled to have added to the Contract Sum;

·2 ·15 any amount paid or payable to the Contractor under clause 38, 39 or 40, whichever is applicable;

·2 ·16 any other amount which is required by this Contract to be added to the Contract Sum.

30·7 So soon as is practicable but not less than 28 days before the date of issue of the Final Certificate referred to in clause 30·8 and notwithstanding that a period of one month may not have elapsed since the issue of the previous Interim Certificate, the Architect shall issue an Interim Certificate the gross valuation for which shall include the amounts of the sub-contract sums for all Nominated Sub-Contracts as finally adjusted or ascertained under all relevant provisions of Sub-Contract NSC/4 or NSC/4a as applicable.

30·8 The Architect shall issue the Final Certificate (and inform each Nominated Sub-Contractor of the date of its issue) not later than 2 months after whichever of the following occurs last:

the end of the Defects Liability Period;

the date of issue of the Certificate of Completion of Making Good Defects under clause 17·4;

the date on which the Architect sent a copy to the Contractor of any ascertainment to which clause 30·6·1·2·1 refers and of the statement prepared in compliance with clause 30·6·1·2·2.

The Final Certificate shall state:

30·8 ·1 the sum of the amounts already stated as due in Interim Certificates, and

30·8 ·2 the Contract Sum adjusted as necessary in accordance with clause 30·6·2

and the difference (if any) between the two sums shall (without prejudice to the rights of the Contractor in respect of any Interim Certificates which have not been paid by the Employer) be expressed in the said Certificate as a balance due to the Contractor from the Employer or to the Employer from the Contractor as the case may be, and subject to any deductions authorised by the Conditions, the said balance shall as from the 28th day after the date of the said Certificate be a debt payable as the case may be by the Employer to the Contractor or by the Contractor to the Employer.

30·9 ·1 Except as provided in clauses 30·9·2 and 30·9·3 (and save in respect of fraud), the Final Certificate shall have effect in any proceedings arising out of or in connection with this Contract (whether by arbitration under article 5 or otherwise) as

·1 ·1 conclusive evidence that where and to the extent that the quality of materials or the standard of workmanship are to be to the reasonable satisfaction of the Architect the same are to such satisfaction, and

·1 ·2 conclusive evidence that any necessary effect has been given to all the terms of this Contract which require that an amount is to be added to or deducted from the Contract Sum or an adjustment is to be made of the Contract Sum save where there has been any accidental inclusion or exclusion of any work, materials, goods or figure in any computation or any arithmetical error in any computation, in which event the Final Certificate shall have effect as conclusive evidence as to all other computations, and

·1 ·3 conclusive evidence that all and only such extensions of time, if any, as are due under clause 25 have been given, and

·1 ·4 conclusive evidence that the reimbursement of direct loss and/or expense, if any, to the Contractor pursuant to clause 26·1 is in final settlement of all and any claims which the Contractor has or may have arising out of the occurrence of any of the matters referred to in clause 26·2 whether such claim be for breach of contract, duty of care, statutory duty or otherwise.

30·9 ·2 If any arbitration or other proceedings have been commenced by either party before the Final Certificate has been issued the Final Certificate shall have effect as conclusive evidence as provided in clause 30·9·1 after either:

·2 ·1 such proceedings have been concluded, whereupon the Final Certificate shall be subject to the terms of any award or judgment in or settlement of such proceedings, or

·2 ·2 a period of 12 months during which neither party has taken any further step in such proceedings, whereupon the Final Certificate shall be subject to any terms agreed in partial settlement,

whichever shall be the earlier.

30·9 ·3 If any arbitration or other proceedings have been commenced by either party within 28 days after the Final Certificate has been issued, the Final Certificate shall have effect as conclusive evidence as provided in clause 30·9·1 save only in respect of all matters to which those proceedings relate.

30·10 Save as aforesaid no certificate of the Architect shall of itself be conclusive evidence that any works, materials or goods to which it relates are in accordance with this Contract.

Interim certificates

35.02 The architect is under a duty to issue certificates showing the amount due from time to time; if he certifies an excessive amount, he may be liable to his employer in damages (see *Sutcliffe* v *Thackrah* [1974] AC 727). Certificates are payable within 14 days of issue, but under clause 30.1.1.2, the employer is entitled to make a deduction from interim certificates, including retention money included in such certificates, subject to a restriction in relation to retention payable to a nominated sub-contractor. The employer is obliged to give reasons for such deduction (see clause 30.1.1.3).

Amounts due in interim certificates

35.03 The amount to be included in interim certificates is defined by clauses 30.2.1 and 30.2.2, dealing respectively with matters which are and are not subject to retention. The principal item in clause 30.2.1 is (clause 30.2.1.1) the total value of work properly executed by the contractor. This means that the amounts certified should take into account adjustments for variation, price fluctuations, and defects (cf the words 'properly executed'). RIBA Publications Ltd publish forms of interim certificate and direction, and a statement of retention.

35.04 Clause 30.2.2 deals with matters which are not subject to retention. The distinction between matters which are and are not subject to retention is, broadly, that retention is to be deducted where the contractor has some responsibility for the matters in question so that the employer's interests have to be protected by making the deduction, whereas those matters not subject to retention are those where the employer's interests do not require any such protection: thus amounts of direct loss and/or expense payable to the contractor and included in interim certificates are not subject to retention, for example (see clause 30.2.2.2).

35.05 Clause 30.1.2 requires that valuations be carried out by the quantity surveyor, although the architect must be astute to ensure that the quantity surveyor adopts the correct principles when making such valuations.

Valuation of off-site materials

35.06 Clause 30.3 confers on the architect a discretion to certify for payment in respect of goods and materials not on the site. If goods and materials are not on the site, the employer has less protection in the event of the contractor's insolvency and certain other circumstances than if they are on the site. It is suggested that instead of the code allowed by clause 30.3.3, it is better to use plain language such as 'SOLD the property of ——— [the employer] for use at ——— [the works]'.

35.07 Architects must be extremely careful in deciding whether to exercise their power to certify for off-site materials or goods: in general, it is suggested that this power should not be exercised in respect of what might be termed 'ordinary' goods or materials, such as bricks, timber, concrete, etc. It may, however, prove of assistance where some particularly large or costly purpose-made component is required for the work, which the contractor would otherwise be obliged to incur the expense of purchasing a considerable time before it can be incorporated in the works and certified for payment otherwise, e.g. a large purpose-made central heating boiler. It is unlikely that such a component could readily be adapted for use elsewhere, and thus the risk in certifying for payment in respect of such an item is relatively small. The subject is covered in JCT Practice Note 5.

Set-off

35.08 There are conflicting views regarding the employer's right to set-off against monies due to the contractor on interim certificates, the amount of any counter-claim he has in respect of such matters as defects in the work. It is widely held that *Gilbert-Ash (Northern) Ltd* v *Modern Engineering (Bristol) Ltd* [1974] AC 689 supports the right to set-off, but in that case there was an express provision allowing such deduction. The later *Mottram Consultants Ltd* v *Bernard Sunley & Sons Ltd* [1975] 2 Lloyds Reports 197 suggests that set-off can only be allowed if an express term is included. However, the employer cannot withhold payment on the ground of a counter-claim having been made against the contractor by a nominated sub-contractor (see *George E Taylor* v *Percy Trentham* (1980) 16 BLR 15).

Retention

35.09 The purpose of retention is to provide the employer with security for the contractor's due performance of his obligations in relation to the quality of the work. The percentage of retention is 5% on work which has not reached practical completion (clause 30.4.1.1), and 2½% on work which has reached practical completion. When the certificate of making good defects is issued, it has the effect of releasing the retention in respection of the works or that part of them to which that certificate relates. See also JCT Practice Note 18.

Rules on treatment of retention

35.10 Under clause 30.5.1, the employer is a trustee of the contractor and any nominated sub-contractor in relation to retention. In the private variant clause 30.5.3, an obligation is imposed on the employer to pay the retention money into a separate bank account at the contractor's request (this is thought not to be necessary in the case of local authorities). The intention is that the retention money should, in effect, be set aside as a separate fund to be used only for the purpose of providing the employer with security against the making good of defects, and the purpose of making the employer a trustee is to protect the retention money against his liquidation. However, the court will not grant an injunction compelling the employer to set aside the retention money in a separate func where the employer has a claim against the contractor for a greater amount – *Henry Boot Building Ltd* v *The Croyden Hotel and Leisure Co Ltd* (1985) 36 BLR 41.

35.11 In *Re Arthur Sanders Limited* [1981] 17 BLR 125, it was held that where the contractor has gone into liquidation, its liquidator was entitled to recover from the employer a sum representing the amount of retention due to a nominated sub-contractor notwithstanding that the liquidator conceded that the employer was entitled to withhold that part of the retention which related to the value of the contractor's own work.

In that case, the reason given by the employer for withholding the retention was that the contractor owed the employer money in respect of damages sustained by the employer as a result of the contractor's default on another contract. It is, however, doubtful whether the employer is entitled to withhold retention money due to a contractor on the grounds that the employer has a claim against the contractor in relation to some other contract, since the employer's only right against retention money is restricted to claims arising out of the failure by the contractor to execute correctly the work covered by the contract in question (cf *National Westminster Bank* v *Halesowen Pressworks and Assemblies Ltd* [1972] AC 785).

Final adjustment of contract sum

35.12 Clause 30.6 provides a detailed guide as to how the final account is to be prepared. Subject to the architect's decision on matters of principle, this will be prepared by the quantity surveyor. In the private edition, clause 30.6.2.14 deals with payment to the contractor if he has to insure the works following the employer's default.

Final adjustment of sub-contract sum

35.13 Clause 30.7 relates to the final adjustment or ascertainment of nominated sub-contract sums. This must be carried out not less than 28 days before the date of issue of the final certificate.

Final certificate

35.14 The responsibility for issuing this certificate is a heavy one, and the architect should not issue it unless he is satisfied that the contract has been fully complied with. It must be issued within a period stated in the Appendix – if no period is stated it is three months (it is fixed at three months in the private edition) – from the latest of the following events:

1. The end of the defects liability period.
2. Completion of making good defects.
3. Receipt by the architect or the quantity surveyor of the documents referred to in clause 30.6.1.1.

The form of the final certificate is governed by clauses 39.8.1 and 30.8.2. Note that the final certificate may show a balance in favour of the employer if monies have been overpaid in earlier certificates. It is not necessary to hold back payment from earlier certificates merely to keep something in reserve for the purposes of the final certificate, although it is often considered prudent. RIBA Publications Ltd publish a form of Final Certificate.

Effect of final certificate

35.15 The final certificate is not merely the last certificate; it is, if properly issued in accordance with the contract, a document of considerable legal importance. Subject to certain qualifications it is conclusive evidence that where the quality of materials or the standards of workmanship are to be to the reasonable satisfaction of the architect, they are to such satisfaction, and that any necessary effect has been given to all the terms of the contract which require an adjustment to be made of the contract sum. For the exact effect of the qualifications refer to clause 30.9, and in summary they are:

1. Where proceedings have been commenced by either party before the issue of the final certificate, the conclusiveness of the certificate becomes limited as set out in clause 30.9.2.
2. Where proceedings have been commenced by either party within 14 days of its issue, the final certificate is then conclusive save only in respect of all matters to which the proceedings relate (see clause 30.9.3).
3. Fraud (clause 30.9.1).
4. Mathematical error (clause 30.9.1.2).

Matters not within the final certificate

35.16 It is submitted that questions of extension of time under clause 25 and the architect's certificate under clause 24 are not within the range of matters upon which the final certificate is conclusive. Further, the certificate cannot deal with any claim for damages made by the contractor or with claims for consequential losses by the employer.

However, following *H Fairweather Ltd* v *Asden Securities Ltd* (1978) 12 BLR 40, a certificate under clause 24 could not be issued after the final certificate.

36 Clause 31: Finance (No. 2) Act 1975 – statutory tax deduction scheme

---

31 Finance (No.2) Act 1975 – statutory tax deduction scheme

31·1 In this Condition 'the Act' means the Finance (No.2) Act 1975; 'the Regulations' means the Income Tax (Sub-Contractors in the Construction Industry) Regulations 1975 S.I. No.1960; '''contractor''' means a person who is a contractor for the purposes of the Act and the Regulations; 'evidence' means such evidence as is required by the Regulations to be produced to a 'contractor' for the verification of a 'sub-contractor's' tax certificate; 'statutory deduction' means the deduction referred to in S.69(4) of the Act or such other deduction as may be in force at the relevant time; '''sub-contractor''' means a person who is a sub-contractor for the purposes of the Act and the Regulations; 'tax certificate' is a certificate issuable under S.70 of the Act.

31·2 ·1 Clauses 31·3 to ·9 shall not apply if, in the Appendix, the Employer is stated not to be a 'contractor'.

31·2 ·2 If in the Appendix the words ''is a 'contractor''' are deleted, nevertheless if, at any time up to the issue and payment of the Final Certificate, the Employer becomes such a 'contractor', the Employer shall so inform the Contractor and the provisions of clause 31 shall immediately thereupon become operative.

31·3 ·1 Not later than 21 days before the first payment under this Contract is due to the Contractor or after clause 31·2·2 has become operative the Contractor shall:

either

·1 ·1 provide the Employer with the evidence that the Contractor is entitled to be paid without the statutory deduction;

or

·1 ·2 inform the Employer in writing, and send a duplicate copy to the Architect, that he is not entitled to be paid without the statutory deduction.

31·3 ·2 If the Employer is not satisfied with the validity of the evidence submitted in accordance with clause 31·3·1·1, he shall within 14 days of the Contractor submitting such evidence notify the Contractor in writing that he intends to make the statutory deduction from payments due under this Contract to the Contractor who is a 'sub-contractor' and give his reasons for that decision. The Employer shall at the same time comply with clause 31·6·1.

31·4 ·1 Where clause 31·3·1·2 applies, the Contractor shall immediately inform the Employer if he obtains a tax certificate and thereupon clause 31·3·1·1 shall apply.

31·4 ·2 If the period for which the tax certificate has been issued to the Contractor expires before the final payment is made to the Contractor under this Contract the Contractor shall not later than 28 days before the date of expiry:

either

·2 ·1 provide the Employer with evidence that the Contractor from the said date of expiry is entitled to be paid for a further period without the statutory deduction in which case the provisions of clause 31·3·2 shall apply if the Employer is not satisfied with the evidence;

or

·2 ·2 inform the Employer in writing that he will not be entitled to be paid without the statutory deduction after the said date of expiry.

31·4 ·3 The Contractor shall immediately inform the Employer in writing if his current tax certificate is cancelled and give the date of such cancellation.

31·5 The Employer shall, as a 'contractor' in accordance with the Regulations, send promptly to the Inland Revenue any voucher which, in compliance with the Contractor's obligations as a 'sub-contractor' under the Regulations, the Contractor gives to the Employer.

31·6 ·1 If at any time the Employer is of the opinion (whether because of the information given under clause 31·3·1·2 or of the expiry or cancellation of the Contractor's tax certificate or otherwise) that he will be required by the Act to make a statutory deduction from any payment due to be made the Employer shall immediately so notify the Contractor in writing and require the Contractor to state not later than 7 days before each future payment becomes due (or within 10 days of such notification if that is later) the amount to be included in such payment which represents the direct cost to the Contractor and any other person of materials used or to be used in carrying out the Works.

31·6 ·2 Where the Contractor complies with clause 31·6·1 he shall indemnify the Employer against loss or expense caused to the Employer by any incorrect statement of the amount of direct cost referred to in clause 31·6·1.

31·6 ·3 Where the Contractor does not comply with clause 31·6·1 the Employer shall be entitled to make a fair estimate of the amount of direct cost referred to in clause 31·6·1.

31·7 Where any error or omission has occurred in calculating or making the statutory deduction the Employer shall correct that error or omission by repayment to, or by deduction from payments to, the Contractor as the case may be subject only to any statutory obligation on the Employer not to make such correction.

31·8 If compliance with clause 31 involves the Employer or the Contractor in not complying with any other of the Conditions, then the provisions of clause 31 shall prevail.

31·9 The provisions of article 5 shall apply to any dispute or difference between the Employer or the Architect on his behalf and the Contractor as to the operation of clause 31 except where the Act or the Regulations or any other Act of Parliament or statutory instrument, rule or order made under an Act of Parliament provide for some other method of resolving such dispute or difference.

---

37 Clause 32: Outbreak of hostilities
Clause 33: War damage

37.01 Clauses 32 and 33 regulate the position in circumstances which might otherwise bring the contract to an end by the operation of the doctrine of frustration of contracts.

---

32 Outbreak of hostilities [u]

32·1 If during the currency of this Contract there shall be an outbreak of hostilities (whether war is declared or not) in which the United Kingdom shall be involved on a scale involving the general mobilisation of the armed forces of the Crown, then either the Employer or the Contractor may at any time by notice by registered post or recorded delivery to the other, forthwith determine the employment of the Contractor under this Contract:

Provided that such notice shall not be given

32·1 ·1 before the expiration of 28 days from the date on which the order is given for general mobilisation as aforesaid, or

32·1 ·2 after Practical Completion of the Works unless the Works or any part thereof shall have sustained war damage as defined in clause 33·4.

32·2 The Architect may within 14 days after notice under clause 32·1 shall have been given or received by the Employer issue instructions to the Contractor requiring the execution of such protective work as shall be specified therein and/or the continuation of the Works up to points of stoppage to be specified therein, and the Contractor shall comply with such instructions as if the notice of determination had not been given.

Provided that if the Contractor shall for reasons beyond his control be prevented from completing the work to which the said instructions relate within 3 months from the date on which the instructions were issued, he may abandon such work.

32·3 Upon the expiration of 14 days from the date on which a notice of determination shall have been given or received by the Employer under clause 32·1 or where works are required by the Architect under clause 32·2 upon completion or abandonment as the case may be of any such works, the provisions of clause 28·2 (except clause 28·2·2·6) shall apply and the Contractor shall also be paid by the Employer the value of any work executed pursuant to instructions given under clause 32·2, the value being ascertained in accordance with clause 13·5 as if such work were a Variation required by an instruction of the Architect under clause 13·2.

---

33 War damage

33·1 In the event of the Works or any part thereof or any unfixed materials or goods intended for, delivered to and placed on or adjacent to the Works sustaining war damage as defined in clause 33·4 then notwithstanding anything expressed or implied elsewhere in this Contract:

33·1 ·1 the occurrence of such war damage shall be disregarded in computing any amounts payable to the Contractor under or by virtue of this Contract;

33·1 ·2 the Architect may issue instructions requiring the Contractor to remove and/or dispose of any debris and/or damaged work and/or to execute such protective work as shall be specified;

33·1 ·3 the Contractor shall reinstate or make good such war damage and shall proceed with the carrying out and completion of the Works, and the Architect shall in writing fix such later Completion Date as, in his opinion, is fair and reasonable;

33·1 ·4 the removal and disposal of debris or damaged work, the execution of protective works and the reinstatement and making good of such war damage shall be treated as if it were a Variation required by an instruction of the Architect under clause 13·2.

33·2 If at any time after the occurrence of war damage as aforesaid either party serves notice of determination under clause 32, the expression 'protective work' as used in clause 32 should in such case be deemed to include any matters in respect of which the Architect can issue instructions under clause 33·1·2 and any instructions issued under clause 33·1·2 prior to the date on which notice of determination is given or received by the Employer and which shall not then have been completely complied with shall be deemed to have been given under clause 32·2.

33·3 The Employer shall be entitled to any compensation which may at any time become payable out of monies provided by Parliament in respect of war damage sustained by the Works or any part thereof or any unfixed materials or goods intended for the Works which shall at any time have become the property of the Employer.

33·4 The expression 'war damage' as used in clause 33 means war damage as defined by S.2 of the War Damage Act 1943 or any amendment or re-enactment thereof.

---

[u] The parties hereto in the event of the outbreak of hostilities may at any time by agreement between them make such further or other arrangements as they may think fit to meet the circumstances

---

38 Clause 34: Antiquities

38.01 The words 'direct loss and expense' bear the same meaning as in clause 26, as to which see the discussion in the notes to that clause.

---

34 Antiquities

34·1 All fossils, antiquities and other objects of interest or value which may be found on the site or in excavating the same during the progress of the Works shall become the property of the Employer and upon discovery of such an object the Contractor shall forthwith:

34·1 ·1 use his best endeavours not to disturb the object and shall cease work if and insofar as the continuance of work would endanger the object or prevent or impede its excavation or its removal;

34·1 ·2 take all steps which may be necessary to preserve the object in the exact position and condition in which it was found; and

34·1 ·3 inform the Architect or the clerk of works of the discovery and precise location of the object.

34·2 The Architect shall issue instructions in regard to what is to be done concerning an object reported by the Contractor under clause 34·1, and (without prejudice to the generality of his power) such instructions may require the Contractor to permit the examination, excavation or

removal of the object by a third party. Any such third party shall for the purposes of clause 20 be deemed to be a person for whom the Employer is responsible and not to be a sub-contractor.

34·3 ·1 If in the opinion of the Architect compliance with the provisions of clause 34·1 or with an instruction issued under clause 34·2 has involved the Contractor in direct loss and/or expense for which he would not be reimbursed by a payment made under any other provision of this Contract the Architect shall himself ascertain or shall instruct the Quantity Surveyor to ascertain the amount of such loss or expense.

34·3 ·2 If and to the extent that it is necessary for the ascertainment of such loss and/or expense the Architect shall state in writing to the Contractor what extension of time, if any, has been made under clause 25 in respect of the Relevant Event referred to in clause 25·4·5·1 so far as that clause refers to clause 34.

34·3 ·3 Any amount from time to time so ascertained shall be added to the Contract Sum.

Part 2 Nominated sub-contractors and suppliers

39 Clause 35: Nominated sub-contractors
General introduction

39.01 This clause is one of the most elaborate in the whole contract (very considerably longer than clause 27 in the 1963 JCT Form). It marks the growing importance of nominated sub-contractors in the building industry: frequently work carried out by nominated sub-contractors forms a high proportion of the value of the contract as a whole, and they play an especially large role in such areas as foundation construction and mechanical and electrical services.

---

35   GENERAL

35·1   Where

35·1 ·1 in the Contract Bills; or

35·1 ·2 in any instruction of the Architect under clause 13·3 on the expenditure of a provisional sum included in the Contract Bills; or

35·1 ·3 in any instruction of the Architect under clause 13·2 requiring a Variation to the extent, but not further or otherwise,

  ·3 ·1 that it consists of work additional to that shown upon the Contract Drawings and described by or referred to in the Contract Bills and

  ·3 ·2 that any supply and fixing of materials or goods or any execution of work by a Nominated Sub-Contractor in connection with such additional work is of a similar kind to any supply and fixing of materials or the execution of work for which the Contract Bills provided that the Architect would nominate a sub-contractor; or

35·1 ·4 by agreement (which agreement shall not be unreasonably withheld) between the Contractor and the Architect on behalf of the Employer

the Architect has, whether by the use of a prime cost sum or by naming a sub-contractor, reserved to himself the final selection and approval of the sub-contractor to the Contractor who shall supply and fix any materials or goods or execute work, the sub-contractor so named or to be selected and approved shall be nominated in accordance with the provisions of clause 35 and a sub-contractor so nominated shall be a Nominated Sub-Contractor for all the purposes of this Contract. The provisions of clause 35·1 shall apply notwithstanding the provisions of Section B·9·1 of the Standard Method of Measurement, 6th Edition.

35·2 ·1 Where the Contractor in the ordinary course of his business directly carries out works included in the Contract Bills and to which clause 35 applies, and where items of such works are set out in the Appendix and the Architect is prepared to receive tenders from the Contractor for such items, then the Contractor shall be permitted to tender for the same or any of them but without prejudice to the Employer's right to reject the lowest or any tender. If the Contractor's tender is accepted, he shall not sub-let the work to a Domestic Sub-Contractor without the consent of the Architect. Provided that where an item for which the Architect intends to nominate a Sub-Contractor is included in Architect's instructions issued under clause 13·3 it shall be deemed for the purposes of clause 35·2·1 to have been included in the Contract Bills and the item of work to which it relates shall likewise be deemed to have been set out in the Appendix.

35·2 ·2 It shall be a condition of any tender accepted under clause 35·2 that clause 13 shall apply in respect of the items of work included in the tender as if for the reference therein to the Contract Drawings and the Contract Bills there were references to the equivalent documents included in or referred to in the tender submitted under clause 35·2.

35·2 ·3 None of the provisions of clause 35 other than clause 35·2 shall apply to works for which a tender of the Contractor is accepted under clause 35·2.

35·3   The following documents relating to Nominated Sub-Contractors (identified as under) are issued by the Joint Contracts Tribunal for the Standard Form of Building Contract and are referred to in the Conditions and in those documents:

Name of document	Identification No.
The JCT Standard Form of Nominated Sub-Contract Tender and Agreement	Tender NSC/1
The JCT Standard Form of Employer/Nominated Sub-Contractor Agreement	Agreement NSC/2
Agreement NSC/2 adapted for use where Tender NSC/1 has not been used	Agreement NSC/2a
The Standard Form for Nomination of a Sub-Contractor where NSC/1 has been used	Nomination NSC/3
The JCT Standard Form of Sub-Contract for Sub-Contractors who have tendered on Tender NSC/1 and executed Agreement NSC/2 and been nominated by Nomination NSC/3 under the Standard Form of Building Contract (clause 35·10·2)	Sub-Contract NSC/4
Sub-Contract NSC/4 adapted for use where Tender NSC/1 has not been used.	Sub-Contract NSC/4a

PROCEDURE FOR NOMINATION OF A SUB-CONTRACTOR

35·4 ·1 No person against whom the Contractor makes a reasonable objection shall be a Nominated Sub-Contractor.

35·4 ·2 Where the Tender NSC/1 and Agreement NSC/2 are used the Contractor shall make any such reasonable objection at the earliest practicable moment but in any case not later than the date when in accordance with clause 35·10·1 he sends the Tender NSC/1 to the Architect.

35·4 ·3 Where the Tender NSC/1 and Agreement NSC/2 are not used so that the provisions of clauses 35·11 and 35·12 apply the Contractor shall make any such reasonable objection at the earliest practicable moment but in any case not later than 7 days from receipt by him of the instruction of the Architect under clause 35·11 nominating the sub-contractor.

35·5 ·1 ·1 Tender NSC/1 and Agreement NSC/2 shall be used in respect of any part of the Works for which a sub-contractor will be nominated by the Architect unless clause 35·5·1·2 is operated.

  ·1 ·2 The Contract Bills, or any instruction under clause 13·2 requiring a Variation (including an instruction under clause 35·5·2) or under clause 13·3 on the expenditure of a provisional sum, may state that clauses 35·11 and 35·12 (Tender NSC/1 and Agreement NSC/2 not used) shall apply to any part of the Works for which a sub-contractor will be nominated by the Architect; and where so stated the Contract Bills or the instruction shall also state whether or not the proposed sub-contractor has tendered, or has been or will be asked to tender on the basis that Agreement NSC/2a will be used.

35·5 ·2 In respect of any part of the Works for which a sub-contractor will be nominated, the Architect may issue an instruction substituting for the use of Tender NSC/1 and Agreement NSC/2, the application of the provisions of clauses 35·11 and 35·12 or substituting the use of Tender NSC/1 and Agreement NSC/2 for the application of clauses 35·11 and 35·12. Any such instruction shall be treated as if it were a Variation required by an instruction of the Architect under clause 13·2. No such instruction may be issued after the Architect has issued a preliminary notice of nomination under clause 35·7·1 or a nomination instruction under clause 35·11 in regard to any such part of the Works for which a sub-contractor will be nominated, save in any case where clause 35·23 or 35·24 is applicable.

Use of Tender NSC/1 and Agreement NSC/2

35·6   Unless clauses 35·11 and 35·12 apply only persons who have tendered on Tender NSC/1 and entered into Agreement NSC/2 may be nominated.

35·7 ·1 Where under clause 35·6 a proposed sub-contractor has tendered on Tender NSC/1 and entered into Agreement NSC/2 the Architect, before being empowered to issue an instruction as referred to in clause 35·10·2 nominating such proposed sub-contractor, shall send to the Contractor the tender of the proposed sub-contractor set out on the Tender NSC/1 duly completed, a copy of Agreement NSC/2 and a preliminary notice of nomination instructing the Contractor forthwith to settle with the proposed sub-contractor any of the Particular Conditions in Schedule 2 of the Tender NSC/1 which remain to be agreed.

35·7 ·2 Upon receipt of the preliminary notice of nomination the Contractor shall forthwith proceed to settle with the proposed sub-contractor any of the Particular Conditions in Schedule 2 of the Tender NSC/1 which remain to be agreed.

35·8   If the Contractor is unable within 10 working days from receipt of the preliminary notice of nomination to reach agreement with the proposed sub-contractor the Contractor shall continue to comply with clause 35·7 but inform the Architect in writing of the reasons for the inability to reach such agreement; and the Architect shall issue such instructions as may be necessary.

35·9   If the proposed sub-contractor named in the Tender NSC/1 informs the Contractor that he is withdrawing his offer set out in that Tender the Contractor shall immediately inform the Architect in writing and shall take no further action under clause 35·7 until the further instructions of the Architect are received.

35·10 ·1 Immediately upon settlement with the proposed sub-contractor under clause 35·7·2 the Contractor shall send the duly completed Tender NSC/1 (including the Particular Conditions at Schedule 2) to the Architect.

35·10 ·2 Upon receipt thereof but not otherwise the Architect shall forthwith issue an instruction to the Contractor (with a copy to the proposed sub-contractor) on Nomination NSC/3 nominating the proposed sub-contractor to supply and fix the materials or goods or to execute the work referred to in that Tender.

Tender NSC/1 and Agreement NSC/2 not used

35·11   Where clause 35·5·1·2 has been operated:

35·11 ·1 the Employer shall enter into Agreement NSC/2a with the proposed sub-contractor (unless the tender of the proposed sub-contractor referred to in clause 35·5·1·2 has been requested and submitted and approved on behalf of the Employer on the basis that Agreement NSC/2a shall not be entered into) and

35·11 ·2 the Architect shall issue an instruction to the Contractor (with a copy to the proposed sub-contractor) nominating the proposed sub-contractor to supply and fix the materials or goods or to execute the work.

35·12 The Contractor shall proceed so as to conclude a sub-contract on Sub-Contract NSC/4a with the proposed sub-contractor within 14 days of the nomination instruction under clause 35·11.

PAYMENT OF NOMINATED SUB-CONTRACTOR

35·13 ·1 The Architect shall on the issue of each Interim Certificate:

·1 ·1 direct the Contractor as to the amount of each interim or final payment to Nominated Sub-Contractors which is included in the amount stated as due in Interim Certificates and the amount of such interim or final payment shall be computed by the Architect in accordance with the relevant provisions of Sub-Contract NSC/4 or NSC/4a as applicable; and

·1 ·2 forthwith inform each Nominated Sub-Contractor of the amount of any interim or final payment directed in accordance with clause 35·13·1·1.

35·13 ·2 Each payment directed under clause 35·13·1·1 shall be duly discharged by the Contractor in accordance with Sub-Contract NSC/4 or NSC/4a as applicable.

35·13 ·3 Before the issue of each Interim Certificate (other than the first Interim Certificate) and of the Final Certificate the Contractor shall provide the Architect with reasonable proof of the discharge referred to in clause 35·13·2.

35·13 ·4 If the Contractor is unable to provide the reasonable proof referred to in clause 35·13·2 because of some failure or omission of the Nominated Sub-Contractor to provide any document or other evidence to the Contractor which the Contractor may reasonably require and the Architect is reasonably satisfied that this is the sole reason why reasonable proof is not furnished by the Contractor, the provisions of clause 35·13·5 shall not apply and the provisions of clause 35·13·3 shall be regarded as having been satisfied.

35·13 ·5 ·1 The Employer may, but where the Employer and the Nominated Sub-Contractor have executed Agreement NSC/2 or NSC/2a, shall, operate clauses 35·13·5·3 and ·4.

·5 ·2 If the Contractor fails to provide reasonable proof under clause 35·13·3, the Architect shall issue a certificate to that effect stating the amount in respect of which the Contractor has failed to provide such proof, and the Architect shall issue a copy of the certificate to the Nominated Sub-Contractor concerned.

·5 ·3 Provided that the Architect has issued the certificate under clause 35·13·5·2 and subject to clause 35·13·5·4, the amount of any future payment otherwise due to the Contractor under this Contract (after deducting any amounts due to the Employer from the Contractor under this Contract) shall be reduced by any amounts due to Nominated Sub-Contractors which the Contractor has failed to discharge (together with the amount of any value added tax which would have been due to the Nominated Sub-Contractor) and the Employer shall himself pay the same to the Nominated Sub-Contractor concerned. Provided that the Employer shall in no circumstances be obliged to pay amounts to Nominated Sub-Contractors in excess of amounts available for reduction as aforesaid.

·5 ·4 The operation of clause 35·13·5·3 shall be subject to the following:

·4 ·1 where the Contractor would otherwise be entitled to payment of an amount stated as due in an Interim Certificate under clause 30, the reduction and payment to the Nominated Sub-Contractor referred to in clause 35·13·5·3 shall be made at the same time as the Employer pays the Contractor any balance due under clause 30 or, if there is no such balance, not later than the expiry of the period of 14 days within which the Contractor would otherwise be entitled to payment;

·4 ·2 where the sum due to the Contractor is the Retention or any part thereof, the reduction and payment to the Nominated Sub-Contractor referred to in clause 35·13·5·3 shall not exceed any part of the Contractor's retention (as defined in clause 30·4·2) which would otherwise be due for payment to the Contractor;

·4 ·3 where the Employer has to pay 2 or more Nominated Sub-Contractors but the amount due or to become due to the Contractor is insufficient to enable the Employer to pay the Nominated Sub-Contractors in full, the Employer shall apply the amount available pro rata to the amounts from time to time remaining undischarged by the Contractor or adopt such other method of apportionment as may appear to the Employer to be fair and reasonable having regard to all the relevant circumstances;

·5 ·4 ·4 clause 35·13·5·3 shall cease to have effect absolutely if at the date when the reduction and payment to the Nominated Sub-Contractor referred to in clause 35·13·5·3 would otherwise be made there is in existence

either a Petition which has been presented to the Court for the winding up of the Contractor,

or a resolution properly passed for the winding up of the Contractor other than for the purposes of amalgamation or reconstruction

whichever shall have first occurred. [v]

35·13 ·6 Where, in accordance with clause 2·2 of Agreement NSC/2 or clause 1·2 of Agreement NSC/2a, the Employer, before the issue of an instruction nominating a Sub-Contractor, has paid to him an amount in respect of design work and/or materials or goods and/or fabrication which is/are included in the subject of the Sub-Contract Sum or Tender Sum:

·6 ·1 the Employer shall send to the Contractor the written statement of the Nominated Sub-Contractor of the amount to be credited to the Contractor, and

·6 ·2 the Employer may make deductions up to the amount of such credit from the amounts stated as due to the Contractor in any of the Interim Certificates which include amounts of interim or final payment to the Nominated Sub-Contractor; provided that the amount so deducted from that stated as due in any one Interim Certificate shall not exceed the amount of payment to the Nominated Sub-Contractor included therein as directed by the Architect.

[v] Where the Contractor is a person subject to bankruptcy law and not the law relating to the insolvency of a company, clause 35·13·5·4·4 will require amendment to refer to the events on the happening of which bankruptcy occurs. (See also Footnote [a].)

EXTENSION OF PERIOD OR PERIODS FOR COMPLETION OF NOMINATED SUB-CONTRACT WORKS

35·14 ·1 The Contractor shall not grant to any Nominated Sub-Contractor any extension of the period or periods within which the sub-contract works (or where the sub-contract works are to be completed in parts any part thereof) are to be completed except in accordance with the relevant provisions of Sub-Contract NSC/4 or NSC/4a as applicable which requires the written consent of the Architect to any such grant.

35·14 ·2 The Architect shall operate the relevant provisions of Sub-Contract NSC/4 or NSC/4a as applicable upon receiving any notice particulars and estimate and a request from the Contractor and any Nominated Sub-Contractor for his written consent to an extension of the period or periods for the completion of the sub-contract works or any part thereof as referred to in clause 11·2·2 of Sub-Contract NSC/4 or NSC/4a as applicable.

FAILURE TO COMPLETE NOMINATED SUB-CONTRACT WORKS

35·15 ·1 If any Nominated Sub-Contractor fails to complete the sub-contract works (or where the sub-contract works are to be completed in parts any part thereof) within the period specified in the Sub-Contract or within any extended time granted by the Contractor with the written consent of the Architect, and the Contractor so notifies the Architect with a copy to the Nominated Sub-Contractor, then, provided that the Architect is satisfied that clause 35·14 has been properly applied, the Architect shall so certify in writing to the Contractor. Immediately upon the issue of such a certificate the Architect shall send a duplicate thereof to the Nominated Sub-Contractor.

35·15 ·2 The certificate of the Architect under clause 35·15·1 shall be issued not later than 2 months from the date of notification to the Architect that the Nominated Sub-Contractor has failed to complete the Sub-Contract Works or any part thereof.

PRACTICAL COMPLETION OF NOMINATED SUB-CONTRACT WORKS

35·16 When in the opinion of the Architect practical completion of the works executed by a Nominated Sub-Contractor is achieved he shall forthwith issue a certificate to that effect and practical completion of such works for the purposes of clauses 35·16 to 35·19 or clause 18 shall be deemed to have taken place on the day named in such certificate, a duplicate copy of which shall be sent by the Architect to the Nominated Sub-Contractor.

EARLY FINAL PAYMENT OF NOMINATED SUB-CONTRACTORS

35·17 Where the Agreement NSC/2 or NSC/2a has been entered into and provided that clause 5 of agreement NSC/2 or clause 4 of agreement NSC/2a remain in force unamended, then at any time after the day named in the certificate issued under clause 35·16 the Architect may, and on the expiry of 12 months from the aforesaid day shall, issue an Interim Certificate the gross valuation for which shall include the amount of the relevant Sub-Contract Sum or Ascertained Final Sub-Contract Sum as finally adjusted or ascertained under the relevant provisions of Sub-Contract NSC/4 or NSC/4a as applicable; provided always that the Nominated Sub-Contractor:

35·17 ·1 has in the opinion of the Architect and the Contractor remedied any defects, shrinkages or other faults which have appeared and which the Nominated Sub-Contractor is bound to remedy under the Sub-Contract; and

35·17 ·2 has sent through the Contractor to the Architect or the Quantity Surveyor all documents necessary for the final adjustment of the Sub-Contract Sum or the computation of the Ascertained Final Sub-Contract Sum referred to in clause 35·17.

35·18 Upon due discharge by the Contractor to the Nominated Sub-Contractor ("the original sub-contractor") of the amount certified under clause 35·17 then:

35·18 ·1 ·1 if the original sub-contractor fails to rectify any defect, shrinkage or other fault in the sub-contract works which he is bound to remedy under the Sub-Contract and which appears before the issue of the Final Certificate under clause 30·8 the Architect shall in accordance with clause 35·24·4 issue an instruction nominating a person ("the substituted sub-contractor") to carry out such rectification work and all the provisions relating to Nominated Sub-Contractors in clause 35 shall apply to such further nomination;

·1 ·2 the Employer shall take such steps as may be reasonable to recover, under the Agreement NSC/2 or NSC/2a as applicable, from the original sub-contractor a sum equal to the sub-contract price of the substituted sub-contractor. The Contractor shall pay or allow to the Employer any difference between the amount so recovered by the Employer and the sub-contract price of the substituted sub-contractor provided that, before the further nomination has been made, the Contractor has agreed (which agreement shall not be unreasonably withheld) to the sub-contract price to be charged by the substituted sub-contractor.

35·18 ·2 Nothing in clause 35·18 shall override or modify the provisions of clause 35·21.

35·19 Notwithstanding any final payment to a Nominated Sub-Contractor under the provisions of clause 35:

35·19 ·1 until the date of Practical Completion of the Works or the date when the Employer takes possession of the Works, whichever first occurs, the Contractor shall be responsible for loss or damage to the Works, materials and goods for which a payment to which clause 35·17 refers has been made to the same extent but not further or otherwise than he is responsible for that part of the Works for which a payment as aforesaid has not been made;

35·19 ·2 the provisions of clause 22A or 22B or 22C whichever is applicable shall remain in full force and effect.

POSITION OF EMPLOYER IN RELATION TO NOMINATED SUB-CONTRACTOR

35·20 Neither the existence nor the exercise of the powers in clause 35 nor anything else contained in the Conditions shall render the Employer in any way liable to any Nominated Sub-Contractor except by way and in the terms of the Agreement NSC/2 or NSC/2a as applicable.

CLAUSE 2 OF AGREEMENT NSC/2 OR CLAUSE 1 OF AGREEMENT NSC/2a – POSITION OF CONTRACTOR

35·21 Whether or not a Nominated Sub-Contractor is responsible to the Employer in the terms set out in clause 2 of the Agreement NSC/2 or clause 1 of the Agreement NSC/2a the Contractor shall not be responsible to the Employer in respect of any nominated sub-contract works for anything to which such terms relate. Nothing in clause 35·21 shall be construed so as to affect the obligations of the Contractor under this Contract in regard to the supply of workmanship, materials and goods.

RESTRICTIONS IN CONTRACTS OF SALE ETC. – LIMITATION OF LIABILITY OF NOMINATED SUB-CONTRACTORS

35·22 Where any liability of the Nominated Sub-Contractor to the Contractor is limited under the provisions of clause 2·3 of Sub-Contract NSC/4 or NSC/4a as applicable the liability of the Contractor to the Employer shall be limited to the same extent.

POSITION WHERE PROPOSED NOMINATION DOES NOT PROCEED FURTHER

35·23 The Architect shall either issue an instruction under clause 13·2 requiring as a Variation the omission of the work for which the Architect intended to nominate a proposed sub-contractor or select another person to be nominated as a sub-contractor under the provisions of clause 35 if:

35·23 ·1 the Contractor under clause 35·4 sustains a reasonable objection to a proposed sub-contractor; or

35·23 ·2 where clauses 35·6 to 35·10 apply (use of Tender NSC/1), the proposed sub-contractor does not within a reasonable time settle and agree the Particular Conditions in Schedule 2 of the Tender NSC/1 when so requested by the Contractor on receipt of the Architect's preliminary notice of nomination under clause 35·7·1; or

35·23 ·3 where clauses 35·11 and 35·12 apply (use of Sub-Contract NSC/4a), the proposed nominated sub-contractor without good cause fails within a reasonable time to enter into the Sub-Contract NSC/4a.

CIRCUMSTANCES WHERE RE-NOMINATION NECESSARY

35·24 If in respect of any Nominated Sub-Contract:

35·24 ·1 the Contractor informs the Architect that in the opinion of the Contractor the Nominated Sub-Contractor has made default in respect of any one or more of the matters referred to in clause 29·1·1 to ·1·4 of Sub-Contract NSC/4 or NSC/4a as applicable; and the Contractor has passed to the Architect any observations of the Sub-Contractor in regard to the matters on which the Contractor considers the Sub-Contractor is in default; and the Architect is reasonably of the opinion that the Sub-Contractor has made default; or

35·24 ·2 the Nominated Sub-Contractor becomes bankrupt or makes a composition or arrangement with his creditors or has a proposal in respect of his company for a voluntary arrangement for a composition of debts or scheme of arrangement approved in accordance with the Insolvency Act 1986 or has an application made under the Insolvency Act 1986 in respect of his company to the Court for the appointment of an administrator or has a winding up order made or (except for the purposes of amalgamation or reconstruction) passes a resolution for voluntary winding up or a provisional liquidator or receiver or manager of the business or undertaking is duly appointed or has an administrative receiver, as defined in the Insolvency Act 1986, appointed or possession is taken, by or on behalf of the holders of any debentures secured by a floating charge, of any property comprised in or subject to the floating charge; or

35·24 ·3 the Nominated Sub-Contractor determines his employment under clause 30 of Sub-Contract NSC/4 or NSC/4a as applicable; or

35·24 ·4 the Contractor has been required by the Employer to determine the employment of the Sub-Contractor under clause 29·3 of Sub-Contract NSC/4 or NSC/4a as applicable and has so determined that employment; or

35·24 ·5 work properly executed or materials or goods properly fixed or supplied by the Nominated Sub-Contractor have to be taken down and/or re-executed or re-fixed or re-supplied ('work to be re-executed') as a result of compliance by the Contractor or by any other Nominated Sub-Contractor with any instruction or other exercise of a power of the Architect under clauses 7 or 8·4 or 17·2 or 17·3 and the Nominated Sub-Contractor cannot be required under the Sub-Contract and does not agree to carry out the work to be re-executed;

then:

34·24 ·6 Where clause 35·24·1 applies:

·6 ·1 the Architect shall issue an instruction to the Contractor to give to the Sub-Contractor the notice specifying the default to which clause 29·1 of Sub-Contract NSC/4 or NSC/4a as applicable refers; and may in that instruction state that the Contractor must obtain a further instruction of the Architect before determining the employment of the Sub-Contractor under clause 29·1 of Sub-Contract NSC/4 or NSC/4a as applicable; and

·6 ·2 the Contractor shall inform the Architect whether, following the giving of that notice for which the Architect has issued an instruction under clause 35·24·6·1, the employment of the Sub-Contractor has been determined by the Contractor under clause 29·1 of Sub-Contract NSC/4 or NSC/4a as applicable; or where the further instruction referred to in clause 35·24·6·1 has been given by the Architect the Contractor shall confirm that the employment of the Sub-Contractor has been determined; then

·6 ·3 if the Contractor informs, or confirms to the Architect that the employment of the Sub-Contractor has been so determined the Architect shall make such further nomination of a Sub-Contractor in accordance with clause 35 as may be necessary to supply and fix the materials or goods or to execute the work and to make good or re-supply or re-execute any work executed by or any materials or goods supplied by the Sub-Contractor whose employment has been determined which were not in accordance with the relevant Sub-Contract; provided that where the employment of the Nominated Sub-Contractor has been determined for the reasons referred to in clause 29·1·3 of Sub-Contract NSC/4 or NSC/4a as applicable, the Contractor shall agree (which agreement shall not be unreasonably withheld) the price to be charged by the substituted Sub-Contractor as provided in clause 35·18·1.

35·24 ·7 Where clause 35·24·2 or clause 35·24·4 apply, the Architect shall make such further nomination of a Sub-Contractor in accordance with clause 35 as may be necessary to supply and fix the materials or goods or to execute the work and to make good or re-supply or re-execute as necessary any work executed by or any materials or goods supplied by the Sub-Contractor whose employment has been determined which were not in accordance with the relevant Sub-Contract; provided that where a receiver or manager or administrative receiver or administrator of the business of the Nominated Sub-Contractor is appointed the Architect may postpone the duty to make a further nomination as provided in clause 35·24·7 if there are reasonable grounds for supposing that the receiver or manager or administrative receiver or administrator is prepared to continue to carry out or fulfil the relevant Sub-Contract in a way that will not prejudice the interests of the Employer, the Contractor or any Sub-Contractor whether Nominated or Domestic engaged, or to be engaged, upon or in connection with the Works.

35·24 ·8 ·1 Where clause 35·24·3 applies the Architect shall make such further nomination of a Sub-Contractor in accordance with clause 35 as may be necessary to supply and fix the materials or goods or to execute the work and to make good or re-supply or re-execute as necessary any work executed by or any materials or goods supplied by the Sub-Contractor who has determined his employment which were not in accordance with the relevant Sub-Contract.

·8 ·2 Where clause 35·24·5 applies the Architect shall make such further nomination of a Sub-Contractor in accordance with clause 35 as may be necessary to carry out the work to be re-executed referred to in clause 35·24·5.

35·24 ·9 The amount properly payable to the Nominated Sub-Contractor under the Sub-Contract resulting from such further nomination under clause 35·24·6·3 or 35·24·7 shall be included in the amount stated as due in Interim Certificates and added to the Contract Sum. Where clauses 35·24·3 and 35·24·8·1 apply any extra amount, payable by the Employer in respect of the Sub-Contractor nominated under the further nomination over the price of the Nominated Sub-Contractor who has validly determined his employment under his Sub-Contract, and where clauses 35·24·5 and 35·24·8·2 apply the amount payable by the Employer, resulting from such further nomination may at the time or any time after such amount is certified in respect of the Sub-Contractor nominated under the further nomination be deducted by the Employer from monies due or to become due to the Contractor under this Contract or may be recoverable from the Contractor by the Employer as a debt.

35·24 ·10 The Architect shall make the further nomination of a Sub-Contractor as referred to in clauses 35·24·6·3, 35·24·7, 35·24·8·1 and 35·24·8·2 within a reasonable time, having regard to all the circumstances, after the obligation to make such further nomination has arisen.

DETERMINATION OR DETERMINATION OF EMPLOYMENT OF NOMINATED SUB-CONTRACTOR – ARCHITECT'S INSTRUCTIONS

35·25 The Contractor shall not determine any Nominated Sub-Contract by virtue of any right to which he may be or may become entitled without an instruction from the Architect so to do.

35·26 Where the employment of the Nominated Sub-Contractor is determined under clause 29 of Sub-Contract NSC/4 or NSC/4a as applicable the Architect shall direct the Contractor as to any amount included in the amount stated as due in an Interim Certificate in respect of the value of work executed or materials or goods supplied by the Nominated Sub-Contractor in accordance with clause 29·4 of that Sub-Contract.

39.02 This clause is primarily concerned with the following areas:

1. Ways of nomination.
2. Procedure for nomination.
3. Payment of nominated sub-contractor.
4. Extensions of time.
5. Failure to complete nominated sub-contract works and the consequences thereof.
6. Practical completion of nominated sub-contract works.
7. Final payment to nominated sub-contractor.
8. Renomination.

Ways of nomination

39.03 There are now eight ways in which a sub-contractor can be nominated: the nomination can arise either by the use of a prime cost sum or by naming a sub-contractor, and then in one of the four ways set out in clauses 35.1.1 to 35.1.4.

39.04 Under clause 35.2 the contractor is given a right depending on the architect's discretion to tender for work which it is proposed to be carried out by a nominated sub-contractor where 'in the ordinary course of his business' he 'directly carries out works' of the type envisaged to be carried out by the nominated sub-contractor.

Procedure

39.05 Clause 35.3 sets out the documents issued by the JCT in regard to nominated sub-contractors. These are commented on in paras 42, 43, 44, 45, and the sections on NSC/4 and NSC/4a.

Basic method and alternative method

39.06 There are two methods of nomination, called the basic method and the alternative method. The basic method involves essentially use of Tender NSC/1, Agreement NSC/2, Nomination NSC/3, and Sub-contract NSC/4. The alternative method involves use of Agreement NSC/2a and Sub-contract MSC/4a alone, and arises where Tender NSC/1 is not to be used.

39.07 Under clause 35.5.1.2, it is possible for the contract bills or instruction requiring the expenditure of a provisional sum to state whether the basic or the alternative method is to be used. If the alternative method is to be used, it is further to be stated whether the proposed sub-contractor has tendered or has been or will be asked to be tendered on the basis that Agreement NSC/2a will be used. Further, under clause 35.5.2, it is possible for the architect to instruct that the alternative method be used instead of the basic method.

Basic method procedure

39.08 This is governed by clauses 35.6 to 35.10. One of the features of the new procedure is an attempt to ensure that in so far as possible, agreement is reached between contractor and proposed nominated sub-contractor before the sub-contract is entered into as to such matters as sub-contract programme, the period required for working drawings, the notice required to commence work on site, and the period required for execution of the sub-contract works. These are matters contained in Schedule 2 to Tender NSC/1.

39.09 The sequence of events should ideally be as follows: the proposed nominated sub-contractor tenders on Tender NSC/1 and enters into Agreement NSC/2. The architect then sends to the contractor the Tender (which is in form NSC/1) and a copy of the Agreement NSC/2 with a 'preliminary notice of nomination' instructing the contractor forthwith to settle with the proposed sub-contractor any of the particular conditions in Schedule 2 of Tender NSC/1 which remain to be agreed.

39.10 Thereafter the contractor is to endeavour to agree these outstanding terms; if he becomes unable to do so he should inform the architect, who must then issue 'such instruction as may be necessary'. If the proposed sub-contractor withdraws, the contractor must notify the architect and take no further action until further instructions are received from the architect.

39.11 If agreement is reached on the outstanding terms, the contractor is to send a copy of the duly completed Tender NSC/1 to the architect, who then nominates the sub-contractor on form NSC/3.

Alternative method procedure

39.12 Here the procedure is far simpler, in that the employer enters into an agreement in form NSC/2a with the proposed sub-contractor (unless the tender is invited on the basis that NSC/2a will not be entered into). Thereafter, the nomination proceeds without any endeavour to agree the matters contained in Schedule 2 to NSC/1. The contractor is then obliged to enter into a sub-contract with the nominated sub-contractor in form NSC/4a.

Advantages of basic and alternative methods

39.13 The basic method of nomination is more complex, but has the advantage that provided the contractor and sub-contractor agree on the matters contained in Schedule 2 to NSC/1, difficulties are less likely to arise among contractor, sub-contractor, and employer during the execution of the works. In general, it is suggested that the basic method be employed where the sub-contract work is particularly important or complex, but the alternative method should be employed in more straightforward cases.

Contractor's right of objection

39.14 The contractor has a right of 'reasonable objection' to any proposed nominated sub-contractor (see clause 35.4.1). It is thought, however, that the contractor should not be entitled to use this right so as to endeavour to place himself in a better position for tendering for the work himself under clause 35.2.

Payment of nominated sub-contractor

39.15 The nominated sub-contractor is entitled to payment of sums stated as due to him in interim certificates issued to the contractor. The liability of the contractor to pay the nominated sub-contractor does not arise until the certificate has been issued (see clause 35.13.2, and cf Sub-contract NSC/4 para 21.3.1.1). There is provision for the architect to inform the nominated sub-contractor of the amount directed to be paid to him in any interim certificate (see clause 35.13.1.2).

39.16 Under clause 35.13.3, the contractor is obliged to provide the architect with reasonable proof of payment of sums previously certified to the nominated sub-contractor before the issue of the next interim certificate; failure to provide such proof entitles the employer to make direct payment to the sub-contractor of any amount which the contractor has failed to pass on to the nominated sub-contractor. Before doing this, however, the architect is obliged to issue a certificate (clause 35.13.5.2) stating the amount in respect of which the contractor has failed to provide proof of payment to the nominated sub-contractor. This amount is then deducted from money which would otherwise be due to the contractor and paid direct to the nominated sub-contractor (clause 35.13.5.3). The detailed machinery for operating clause 35.13.5.3 is set out in clause 35.13.5.4.

Architects should be astute to ensure that:

1. Nominated sub-contractors are informed of the amount shown as due to them in interim certificates issued to the contractor.
2. Proof is required from the contractor that nominated sub-contractors have been paid sums previously shown as due to them in interim certificates before issuing a new certificate.
3. If necessary, clause 35.15.5.3 is operated and direct payment made to the nominated sub-contractors concerned.

39.17 Under clause 35.13.4, the contractor is relieved from the obligation to furnish reasonable proof of payment if this is due to some failure or omission of the nominated sub-contractor.

39.18 Under clause 35.13.5.4.4, the right to make direct payments ceases on the liquidation of the contractor.

Extensions of time

39.19 Extensions of time for the sub-contract works can only be granted with the consent of the architect under the relevant terms of Sub-contract NSC/4 (see clause 11.2 of that sub-contract). Clause 35.14 makes it clear that the contractor cannot give an extension of time to the sub-contractor on his own without the architect's consent. Under clause 35.14.2, the architect is obliged to operate the relevant provisions of NSC/4 or NSC/4a as applicable upon receipt of the notice,

particulars, and estimate, the procedure for which is laid down in clause 11.2 or NSC/4 or NSC/4a, where applicable.

Failure to complete nominated sub-contract works

39.20 If the nominated sub-contractor fails to complete the sub-contract works within the sub-contract period or any extended time granted by the contractor with the architect's consent, and the architect is satisfied that clause 35.14 has been properly applied, then the architect must certify to that effect (see clause 35.15.1). This certificate is important since under NSC/4 clause 12.2, the contractor is entitled to damages equivalent to any loss or damage suffered by him as a result of the sub-contractor's failure to complete, but this right is subject to the issue of the certificate under this clause of the Main Contract as a condition precedent (see *Brightside Kilpatrick Engineering* v *Mitchell Construction (1973) Limited* [1975] 2 Lloyds Reports 493).

Practical completion of nominated sub-contract works

39.21 Each nominated sub-contract is the subject of a separate certificate of practical completion, under clause 35.16. This then brings into operation the machinery for:

Final payment of nominated sub-contractors

39.22 Where a certificate of practical completion of nominated sub-contract works has been issued, the architect may (and must within twelve months) issue an interim certificate including the amount of the relevant sub-contract sum or ascertained final sub-contract sum as finally adjusted under the relevant provisions of the nominated sub-contract, provided that the sub-contractor has made good defects and provided all documents necessary for the final adjustment of the sub-contract sum to take place (see clause 35.17.2).

39.23 This procedure is conditional (under clause 35.17) on Agreement NSC/2 or NSC/2a being entered into, and clause 5 thereof being unamended (clause 5 of NSC/2 imposes on the nominated sub-contractor an obligation to indemnify the employer against failure by the nominated sub-contractor to remedy defects occurring between final payment to the nominated sub-contractor and the issue of the final certificate relating to the work as a whole). The purpose of making this a condition precedent is to protect the employer's rights in the event of the nominated sub-contractor failing to remedy such defects.

39.24 Clearly, if nominated sub-contractors are to receive final payment before the works as a whole are complete, provision has to be made for the situation where defects occur in the nominated sub-contract works prior to final certificate but after final payment to the nominated sub-contractor. Under clause 35.18, if the nominated sub-contractor fails to remedy such defects, the architect is to employ a substituted sub-contractor to make them good, who is to be regarded as a nominated sub-contractor under clause 35.

39.25 The primary liability for defective work, including defective work carried out by nominated sub-contractors, rests with the contractor, but in this particular case under clause 35.18.1.2, the employer agrees with the contractor first to seek to pursue his remedies against the nominated sub-contractor under NSC/2 or NSC/2a in respect of the failure to make good the defects and to take such steps as may be reasonable to recover the cost of these. Thereafter, the employer is entitled to look to the contractor for reimbursement, provided the contractor has agreed (which agreement is not to be unreasonably withheld) to the sub-contract prices charged by the substituted sub-contractor.

39.26 Under clause 35.19, the contractor remains responsible for the sub-contract works where final payment has been made until practical completion. Thus damage which occurs to these parts of the works are at the contractor's risk during this period, as are the contractor's own works.

JCT Practice Note 12 deals with Direct Payment and Final Payment to Nominated Sub-contractors.

Renomination

39.27 Under clause 27 of the 1963 JCT Form, it was held that where a nominated sub-contractor failed to complete his work the employer was under a duty to nominate a new nominated sub-contractor (see *North West Metropolitan Hospital Board* v *T A Bickerton & Son Limited* [1970] 1 WLR 607). Another case under JCT 63 (*Fairclough Building Ltd* v *Rhuddlan Borough Council* (1985) 30 BLR 26, CA), established that the architect had a duty to renominate a firm, not only to complete the sub-contract works but also, to carry out any necessary remedial work. The contractor is entitled to an extension of time if the renomination does not match the original programme. This remains the position under the 1980 JCT Form.

The duty to renominate may arise in three circumstances:

1. Where the contractor informs the architect that in the contractor's opinion the nominated sub-contractor has made default in respect of any one or more of the matters referred to in clauses 29.1.1 to 1.4 of NSC/4 or NSC/4a, and the contractor has passed to the architect any observations of the sub-contractor in regard to the matters in question, and the architect is reasonably of the opinion that the sub-contractor has made default.
2. Where the nominated sub-contractor becomes bankrupt (clause 35.24.2).
3. Where the nominated sub-contractor determines his employment under clause 30 of NSC/4 or NSC/4a.

39.28 Where 1 above applies, prior to determination provision is made by clause 35.24.4 for the following procedure to be adopted: the architect first instructs the contractor to give a notice to the sub-contractor specifying the default; the architect may instruct the contractor to include in that notice a statement that the contractor requires a further instruction of the architect before determining the sub-contractor's employment. Then the contractor informs the architect whether he has determined the sub-contractor's employment; where the further instruction from the architect is required and has been given, the contractor is to confirm that the employment of the sub-contractor has been determined. Thereafter, the architect is obliged to nominate a new sub-contractor. Where the sub-contractor's employment has been determined for failure to remove defective work or to remedy defects, the contractor is to be given the opportunity to agree a price to be charged by the substituted sub-contractor.

39.29 Where 2 above applies, the architect is obliged to nominate a new sub-contractor, subject to a right to postpone this if there are reasonable grounds for supposing that the receiver or manager of the sub-contractor is prepared to continue to carry out the work. This clearly may be advantageous in some circumstances.

39.30 Where 3 above applies, the architect is to nominate a new sub-contractor, but the extra cost of employing the new sub-contractor is to be deducted from money otherwise payable to the contractor.

39.31 The contractor is not entitled to determine a nominated sub-contractor's employment without an architect's instruction, and accordingly in all cases the procedure for determining a nominated sub-contractor's employment is as

laid down in clause 35.24. Architects must be careful to ensure that where it is sought to determine the sub-contractor's employment under clause 35.24.1, they fully investigate the circumstances before issuing an instruction to determine the sub-contractor's employment. In particular, they must ensure that they receive all representations which the sub-contractor wishes to make as to his alleged default. Where the sub-contractor's employment is determined, the architect shall direct the contractor as to any amount included in the amount stated as due in an interim certificate in respect of the value of work executed or materials or goods supplied by the nominated sub-contractor in accordance with clause 29.4 of that sub-contract. Clause 29.4 of Sub-contract NSC/4 entitles the architect to certify in respect of amount of expenses properly incurred by the employer and the amount of direct loss and/or damage caused to the employer by the determination of the sub-contract; when the sub-contractor's employment is determined, the employer is entitled to deduct from sums otherwise payable to the sub-contractor the amount of any damage suffered by him from sums that would otherwise become payable to the sub-contractor, and this provision obliges the main contractor to give effect to that deduction.

39.32 Architects must take special care therefore to ensure that the direct warranty form NSC/2 or NSC/2a where applicable is in all cases entered into between the employer and the nominated sub-contractor. It would clearly be highly undesirable for NSC/2a not to be used, even though clause 35.11.1 contemplates the possibility of it not being so.

Position where proposed nomination does not proceed further

39.33 Clause 35.23 makes provision for the situation where no binding sub-contract is finally entered into either because of an objection by the contractor, failure to agree the matters in Schedule 2 of NSC/1, or failure (where the alternative method is used) of the sub-contractor to enter into Sub-contract NSC/4a. In these circumstances the architect may nominate a new sub-contractor.

JCT Practice Note 13 deals with 'abortive' nomination and re-nomination.

40   Clause 36: Nominated suppliers

40.01 There are four ways in which a supplier may be nominated, as set out in clauses 36.1.1 to 1.4. The first three (clauses 36.1.1 to 36.1.1.1 to 36.1.1.3) all have as their hallmark the inclusion of a prime cost or provisional sum in the bills. The fourth, contained in clause 36.1.1.4, deals with the situation where a variation occurs and the architect specifies materials or goods for which there is a sole supplier, in which case those goods are to be made the subject of a prime cost sum, and the sole supplier is deemed to have been nominated as a nominated supplier by the architect. Clause 36.1.2 makes it clear that apart from this situation, no nominated supplier situation arises unless goods are the subject of a prime cost sum, even though there is a 'sole supplier' as defined by clause 36.1.1.3.

36·1   ·1   In the Conditions "Nominated Supplier" means a supplier to the Contractor who is nominated by the Architect in one of the following ways to supply materials or goods which are to be fixed by the Contractor:

   ·1   ·1   where a prime cost sum is included in the Contract Bills in respect of those materials or goods and the supplier is either named in the Contract Bills or subsequently named by the Architect in an instruction issued under clause 36·2;

   ·1   ·2   where a provisional sum is included in the Contract Bills and in any instruction by the Architect in regard to the expenditure of such sum the supply of materials or goods is made the subject of a prime cost sum and the supplier is named by the Architect in that instruction or in an instruction issued under clause 36·2;

   ·1   ·3   where a provisional sum is included in the Contract Bills and in any instruction by the Architect in regard to the expenditure of such a sum materials or goods are specified for which there is a sole source of supply in that there is only one supplier from whom the Contractor can obtain them, in which case the supply of materials or goods shall be made the subject of a prime cost sum in the instructions issued by the Architect in regard to the expenditure of the provisional sum and the sole supplier shall be deemed to have been nominated by the Architect;

   ·1   ·4   where the Architect requires under clause 13·2, or subsequently sanctions, a Variation and specifies materials or goods for which there is a sole supplier as referred to in clause 36·1·1·3, in which case the supply of the materials or goods shall be made the subject of a prime cost sum in the instruction or written sanction issued by the Architect under clause 13·2 and the sole supplier shall be deemed to have been nominated by the Architect.

36·1   ·2   In the Conditions the expression "Nominated Supplier" shall not apply to a supplier of materials or goods which are specified in the Contract Bills to be fixed by the Contractor unless such materials or goods are the subject of a prime cost sum in the Contract Bills, notwithstanding that the supplier has been named in the Contract Bills or that there is a sole supplier of such materials or goods as defined in clause 36·1·1·3.

36·2   The Architect shall issue instructions for the purpose of nominating a supplier for any materials or goods in respect of which a prime cost sum is included in the Contract Bills or arises under clause 36·1.

36·3   ·1   For the purposes of clause 30·6·2·8 the amounts "properly chargeable to the Employer in accordance with the nomination instruction of the Architect" shall include the total amount paid or payable in respect of the materials or goods less any discount other than the discount referred to in clause 36·4·4, properly so chargeable to the Employer and shall include where applicable:

   ·1   ·1   any tax (other than any value added tax which is treated, or is capable of being treated, as input tax (as referred to in the Finance Act 1972) by the Contractor) or duty not otherwise recoverable under this Contract by whomsoever payable which is payable under or by virtue of any Act of Parliament on the import, purchase, sale, appropriation, processing, alteration, adapting for sale or use of the materials or goods to be supplied; and

   ·1   ·2   the net cost of appropriate packing, carriage and delivery after allowing for any credit for return of any packing to the supplier; and

   ·1   ·3   the amount of any price adjustment properly paid or payable to, or allowed or allowable by the supplier less any discount other than a cash discount for payment in full within 30 days of the end of the month during which delivery is made.

36·3   ·2   Where in the opinion of the Architect the Contractor properly incurs expense, which would not be reimbursed under clause 36·3·1 or otherwise under this Contract, in obtaining the materials or goods from the Nominated Supplier such expense shall be added to the Contract Sum.

36·4   Save where the Architect and the Contractor shall otherwise agree, the Architect shall only nominate as a supplier a person who will enter into a contract of sale with the Contractor which provides, inter alia:

36·4   ·1   that the materials or goods to be supplied shall be of the quality and standard specified provided that where and to the extent that approval of the quality of materials or of the standards of workmanship is a matter for the opinion of the Architect, such quality and standards shall be to the reasonable satisfaction of the Architect;

36·4   ·2   that the Nominated Supplier shall make good by replacement or otherwise any defects in the materials or goods supplied which appear up to and including the last day of the Defects Liability Period under this Contract and shall bear any expenses reasonably incurred by the Contractor as a direct consequence of such defects provided that:

   ·2   ·1   where the materials or goods have been used or fixed such defects are not such that reasonable examination by the Contractor ought to have revealed them before using or fixing;

   ·2   ·2   such defects are due solely to defective workmanship or material in the materials or goods supplied and shall not have been caused by improper storage by the Contractor or by misuse or by any act or neglect of either the Contractor, the Architect or the Employer or by any person or persons for whom they may be responsible or by any other person for whom the Nominated Supplier is not responsible;

36·4   ·3   that delivery of the materials or goods supplied shall be commenced, carried out and completed in accordance with a delivery programme to be agreed between the Contractor and the Nominated Supplier including, to the extent agreed, the following grounds on which that programme may be varied:

   force majeure; or

   civil commotion, local combination of workmen, strike or lock-out; or

   any instruction of the Architect under clause 13·2 (Variations) or clause 13·3 (provisional sums); or

   failure of the Architect to supply to the Nominated Supplier within due time any necessary information for which he has specifically applied in writing on a date which was neither unreasonably distant from nor unreasonably close to the date on which it was necessary for him to receive the same; or

   exceptionally adverse weather conditions

or, if no such programme is agreed, delivery shall be commenced, carried out and completed in accordance with the reasonable directions of the Contractor.

36·4   ·4   that the Nominated Supplier shall allow the Contractor a discount for cash of 5 per cent on all payments if the Contractor makes payment in full within 30 days of the end of the month during which delivery is made;

36·4   ·5   that the Nominated Supplier shall not be obliged to make any delivery of materials or goods (except any which may have been paid for in full less only any discount for cash) after the determination (for any reason) of the Contractor's employment under this Contract;

36·4   ·6   that full discharge by the Contractor in respect of payments for materials or goods supplied by the Nominated Supplier shall be effected within 30 days of the end of the month during which delivery is made less only a discount for cash of 5 per cent if so paid;

36·4   ·7   that the ownership of materials or goods shall pass to the Contractor upon delivery by the Nominated Supplier to or to the order of the Contractor, whether or not payment has been made in full;

36·4 ·8 ·1 that in any dispute or difference between the Contractor and the Nominated Supplier which is referred to arbitration the Contractor and the Nominated Supplier agree and consent pursuant to Sections 1 (3)(a) and 2(1)(b) of the Arbitration Act 1979 that either the Contractor or the Nominated Supplier

– may appeal to the High Court on any question of law arising out of an award made in the arbitration and

– may apply to the High Court to determine any question of law arising in the course of the arbitration;

and that the Contractor and the Nominated Supplier agree that the High Court should have jurisdiction to determine any such questions of law;

·8 ·2 that if any dispute or difference between the Contractor and the Nominated Supplier raises issues which are substantially the same as or are connected with issues raised in a related dispute between the Employer and the Contractor under this contract then, where clauses 41·2·1 and 41·2·2 apply, such dispute or difference shall be referred to the Arbitrator to be appointed pursuant to clause 41; that the Arbitrator shall have power to make such directions and all necessary awards in the same way as in the procedure of the High Court as to joining one or more defendants or joining co-defendants or third parties was available to the parties; that the agreement and consent referred to in clause 36·4·8·1 on appeals or applications to the High Court on any question of law shall apply to any question of law arising out of the awards of such arbitrator in respect of all related disputes referred to him or arising in the course of the reference of all the related disputes referred to him; and that in any case, subject to the agreement referred to in clause 36·4·8·1, the award of such Arbitrator shall be final and binding on the parties.

36·4 ·9 that no provision in the contract of sale shall override, modify or affect in any way whatsoever the provisions in the contract of sale which are included therein to give effect to clauses 36·4·1 to 36·4·9 inclusive.

36·5 ·1 Subject to clauses 36·5·2 and 36·5·3, where the said contract of sale between the Contractor and the Nominated Supplier in any way restricts, limits or excludes the liability of the Nominated Supplier to the Contractor in respect of materials or goods supplied or to be supplied, and the Architect has specifically approved in writing the said restrictions, limitations or exclusions, the liability of the Contractor to the Employer in respect of the said materials or goods shall be restricted, limited or excluded to the same extent.

36·5 ·2 The Contractor shall not be obliged to enter into a contract with the Nominated Supplier until the Architect has specifically approved in writing the said restrictions, limitations or exclusions.

36·5 ·3 Nothing in clause 36·5 shall be construed as enabling the Architect to nominate a supplier otherwise than in accordance with the provisions stated in clause 36·4.

Clause 36.1.1.3: Sole supplier

40.02 The meaning of these words is unclear: if there is only one supplier of the goods in the whole country, that would constitute probably a sole supplier, but where there is more than one, it would presumably be a question of fact and degree as to whether the contractor could obtain the material in question from only one of those suppliers. Presumably the number of suppliers and their physical proximity to the work would be the factors in deciding whether there is a sole supplier.

40.03 Clause 36.3 lays down rules for ascertaining the amount to be set against prime cost sums in respect of nominated suppliers' materials. In addition, under clause 36.3.2, the contractor is entitled to recover expenses properly incurred and which he would not have incurred had he not obtained the materials or goods from the nominated supplier. This would include, for example, extra travelling costs in the case where a supplier is nominated whose distance from the works was more than an alternative source of supply of the same or similar materials.

Terms of nominated supplier's contracts

40.04 Under clause 36.4, the architect is not (save by agreement with the contractor) to nominate a supplier whose terms of sale do not conform to certain criteria. These cover such matters as standard of materials, replacement of defective materials, delivery times, discount, passing of property on delivery, and submission to the arbitration provisions in article 5 of the contract.

Contractor's liability for goods supplied by nominated supplier

40.05 Nomination itself ordinarily shows that there has been no reliance on the contractor's skill and judgement so that the contractor is not liable if the goods of the nominated supplier of good quality are unfit for their intended purpose. Clause 36.5.1 exempts the contractor from liability to the employer

in respect of defects in goods supplied by a nominated supplier to the extent that the contract between the contractor and the nominated supplier contains similar exemptions, provided they have been specifically approved by the architect. Even without such a provision it is unlikely that the contractor would be held responsible to the employer if the goods supplied by the nominated supplier failed to answer to their purpose (see *Young and Marten* v *McManus Childs*, [1968] 2 All ER 1181). The employer's interests *vis-à-vis* the nominated supplier are to be protected by the direct warranty Tender TNS/1, and it is of the utmost importance that the architect ensure that this form of direct warranty is entered into in all cases where nominated suppliers are involved.

Part 3 Fluctuations

41 Clauses 37 to 40

41.01 Clause 37.1 identifies three different bases, namely those set out in clauses 38, 39, and 40, by reference to which fluctuations are to be calculated. Clause 37.2 provides that clause 38 shall apply where neither clause 39 nor 40 is identified in the Appendix.

37 ·1 Fluctuations shall be dealt with in accordance with whichever of the following alternatives [w]
clause 38; or
clause 39; or
clause 40 [y]
is identified in the Appendix. The provisions so identified shall be [x] deemed to be incorporated with the Conditions as executed by the parties hereto.

37 ·2 Clause 38 shall apply where neither clause 39 nor 40 is identified in the Appendix.

Clause 38: Contributions, levy and tax fluctuations
Clause 39: Labour and materials cost and tax fluctuations
Clause 40: Use of price adjustment formulae

These clauses are published separately in 'Fluctuation clauses for use with the Private Edition With, Without and With Approximate Quantities'.

[w] Clause 39 should be used where the parties have agreed to allow the labour and materials cost and tax fluctuations to which clause 39·1 to ·3 refers. Alternatively, clause 40 should be used where the parties have agreed that fluctuations shall be dealt with by adjustment of the Contract Sum under the Price Adjustment Formulae for Building Contracts.

[x] Notwithstanding the provisions of clause 37·1 on deemed incorporation the parties may nevertheless wish to incorporate the agreed alternative fluctuation provisions in the executed Contract.

[y] Clause 40 is used where the parties have agreed that fluctuations shall be dealt with by adjustment of the Contract Sum under the Price Adjustment Formulae for Building Contracts.

Supplemental Provisions (the VAT Agreement)

The following are the supplemental provisions (the VAT Agreement) referred to in clause 15·1 of the Conditions:

1 The Employer shall pay to the Contractor in the manner hereinafter set out any tax properly chargeable by the Commissioners on the Contractor on the supply to the Employer of any goods and services by the Contractor under this Contract. Supplies of goods and services under this Contract are supplies under a contract providing for periodical payment for such supplies within the meaning of Regulation 26 of the Value Added Tax (General) Regulations 1985 or any amendment or re-enactment thereof.

1A·1 Where it is stated in the Appendix pursuant to clause 15·2 of the Conditions that Clause 1A of this Agreement applies clauses 1·1 to 2·2 inclusive hereof shall not apply unless and until any notice issued under clause 1A·4 hereof becomes effective or unless the Contractor fails to give the written notice required under clause 1A·2. Where Clause 1A applies clauses 1 and 1·3 to 8 of this Agreement remain in full force and effect.

1A·2 Not later than 7 days before the date for the issue of the first Interim Certificate the Contractor shall give written notice to the Employer, with a copy to the Architect, of the rate of tax chargeable on the supply of goods and services for which Interim Certificates and the Final Certificate are to be issued. If the rate of tax so notified is varied under statute the Contractor shall, not later than 7 days after the date when such varied rate comes into effect, send to the Employer, with a copy to the Architect, the necessary amendment to the rate given in his written notice and that notice shall then take effect as so amended.

1A·3 For the purpose of complying with the VAT Agreement for the recovery by the Contractor, as stated in clause 15·2 of the Conditions, from the Employer of tax properly chargeable by the Commissioners on the Contractor, an amount calculated at the rate given in the aforesaid written notice (or, where relevant, amended written notice) shall be shown on each Interim Certificate issued by the Architect and, unless the procedure set out in clause 1·3 hereof shall have been completed, on the Final Certificate issued by the Architect. Such amount shall be paid by the Employer to the Contractor or by the Contractor to the Employer as the case may be within the period for payment of certificates set out in clause 30·1·1·1 (Interim Certificates) or clause 30·8 (Final Certificate) as applicable.

1A·4 Either the Employer or the Contractor may give written notice to the other, with a copy to the Architect, stating that with effect from the date of the notice clause 1A shall no longer apply. From that date the provisions of clause 1·1 to 1·2·2 inclusive hereof shall apply in place of clause 1A hereof.

1·1 Unless clause 1A applies the Contractor shall not later than the date for the issue of each Interim Certificate and, unless the procedure set out in clause 1·3 of this Agreement shall have been completed, for the issue of the Final Certificate give to the Employer a written provisional assessment of the respective values (less any Retention Percentage applicable thereto) of those supplies of goods and services for which the Certificate is being issued and which will be chargeable, at the relevant time of supply under Regulation 26 of the Value Added Tax (General) Regulations 1985 on the Contractor at

1·1 ·1 a zero rate of tax (Category (i)) and

1·1 ·2 any rate or rates of tax other than zero (Category (ii)).

The Contractor shall also specify the rate or rates of tax which are chargeable on those supplies included in Category (ii), and shall state the grounds on which he considers such supplies are so chargeable.

1·2 ·1 Upon receipt of such written provisional assessment the Employer, unless he has reasonable grounds for objection to that assessment, shall calculate the amount of tax due by applying the rate or rates of tax specified by the Contractor to the amount of the assessed value of those supplies included in Category (ii) of such assessment, and remit the calculated amount of such tax, together with the amount of the Certificate issued by the Architect, to the Contractor within the period for payment of certificates set out in clause 30·1·1·1 of the Conditions.

1·2 ·2 If the Employer has reasonable grounds for objection to the provisional assessment he shall within 3 working days of receipt of that asessment so notify the Contractor in writing setting out those grounds. The Contractor shall within 3 working days of receipt of the written notification of the Employer reply in writing to the Employer either that he withdraws the assessment in which case the Employer is released from his obligation under clause 1·2·1 of this Agreement or that he confirms the assessment. If the Contractor so confirms then the Contractor may treat any amount received from the Employer in respect of the value which the Contractor has stated to be chargeable on him at a rate or rates of tax other than zero as being inclusive of tax and issue an authenticated receipt under clause 1·4 of this Agreement.

1·3 ·1 Where clause 1A is operated clause 1·3 only applies if no amount of tax pursuant to clause 1A·3 has been shown on the Final Certificate issued by the Architect. After the issue of the Certificate of Completion of Making Good Defects under clause 17·4 of the Conditions the Contractor shall as soon as he can finally so ascertain prepare a written final statement of the respective values of all supplies of goods and services for which certificates have been or will be issued which are chargeable on the Contractor at

·1 ·1 a zero rate (Category (i)) and

·1 ·2 any rate or rates of tax other than zero (Category (ii))

and shall issue such final statement to the Employer.

The Contractor shall also specify the rate or rates of tax which are chargeable on the value of those supplies included in Category (ii) and shall state the grounds on which he considers such supplies are so chargeable.

The Contractor shall also state the total amount of tax already received by the Contractor for which a receipt or receipts under clause 1·4 of this Agreement have been issued.

1·3 ·2 The statement under clause 1·3·1 of this Agreement may be issued either before or after the issue of the Final Certificate under clause 30·8 of the Conditions.

1·3 ·3 Upon receipt of the written final statement the Employer shall, subject to clause 3 of this Agreement, calculate the final amount of tax due by applying the rate or rates of tax specified by the Contractor to the value of those supplies included in Category (ii) of the statement and deducting therefrom the total amount of tax already received by the Contractor specified in the statement, and shall pay the balance of such tax to the Contractor within 28 days from receipt of the statement.

1·3 ·4 If the Employer finds that the total amount of tax specified in the final statement as already paid by him exceeds the amount of tax calculated under clause 1·3·3 of this Agreement the Employer shall so notify the Contractor who shall refund such excess to the Employer within 28 days of receipt of the notification, together with a receipt under clause 1·4 of this Agreement showing the correction of the amounts for which a receipt or receipts have previously been issued by the Contractor.

1·4 Upon receipt of any amount paid under certificates of the Architect and any tax properly paid under the provisions of clause 1 or clause 1A of this Agreement the Contractor shall issue to the Employer a receipt of the kind referred to in Regulation 12(4) of the Value Added Tax (General) Regulations 1985 containing the particulars required under Regulation 13(1) of the aforesaid Regulations or any amendment or re-enactment thereof to be contained in a tax invoice.

2·1 If, when the Employer is obliged to make payment under clause 1·2 or 1·3 of this Agreement he is empowered under clause 24 of the Conditions to deduct any sum calculated at the rate stated in the Appendix as liquidated and ascertained damages from sums due or to become due to the Contractor under this Contract he shall disregard any such deduction in calculating the tax due on the value of goods and services supplied to which he is obliged to add tax under clause 1·2 or 1·3 of this Agreement.

2·2 The Contractor when ascertaining the respective values of any supplies of goods and services for which certificates have been or will be issued under the Conditions in order to prepare the final statement referred to in clause 1·3 of this Agreement shall disregard when stating such values any deduction by the Employer of any sum calculated at the rate stated in the Appendix as liquidated and ascertained damages under clause 24 of the Conditions.

2·3 Where clause 1A is operated the Employer shall pay the tax to which that clause refers notwithstanding any deduction which the Employer may be empowered to make under clause 24 of the Conditions from the amount certified by the Architect in an Interim Certificate or from any balance certified by the Architect as due to the Contractor under the Final Certificate.

3·1 If the Employer disagrees with the final statement issued by the Contractor under clause 1·3 of this Agreement he may but before any payment or refund becomes due under clause 1·3·3 or 1·3·4 of this Agreement request the Contractor to obtain the decision of the Commissioners on the tax properly chargeable on the Contractor for all supplies of goods and services under this Contract and the Contractor shall forthwith request the Commissioners for such decision. If the Employer disagrees with such decision then, provided the Employer indemnifies and at the option of the Contractor secures the Contractor against all costs and other expenses, the Contractor shall in accordance with the instructions of the Employer make all such appeals against the decision of the Commissioners as the Employer shall request. The Contractor shall account for any costs awarded in his favour in any appeals to which clause 3 of this Agreement applies.

3·2 Where, before any appeal from the decision of the Commissioners can proceed, the full amount of the tax alleged to be chargeable on the Contractor on the supply of goods and services under the Conditions must be paid or accounted for by the Contractor, the Employer shall pay to the Contractor the full amount of tax needed to comply with any such obligation.

3·3 Within 28 days of the final adjudication of an appeal (or of the date of the decision of the Commissioners if the Employer does not request the Contractor to refer such decision to appeal) the Employer or the Contractor, as the case may be, shall pay or refund to the other in accordance with such final adjudication any tax underpaid or overpaid, as the case may be, under the provisions of this Agreement and the provisions of clause 1·3·4 of this Agreement shall apply in regard to the provision of authenticated receipts.

4 Upon receipt by the Contractor from the Employer or by the Employer from the Contractor, as the case may be, of any payment under clause 1·3·3 or 1·3·4 of this Agreement or where clause 1A of this Agreement is operated of any payment of the amount of tax shown upon the Final Certificate issued by the Architect, or upon final adjudication of any appeal made in accordance with the provisions of clause 3 of this Agreement and any resultant payment or refund under clause 3·3 of this Agreement, the Employer shall be discharged from any further liability to pay tax to the Contractor in accordance with the VAT Agreement. Provided always that if after the date of discharge under clause 4 of this Agreement the Commissioners decide to correct the tax due from the Contractor on the supply to the Employer of any goods and services by the Contractor under this Contract the amount of any such correction shall be an additional payment by the Employer to the Contractor or by the Contractor to the Employer, as the case may be. The provisions of clause 3 of this Agreement in regard to disagreement with any decision of the Commissioners shall apply to any decision referred to in this proviso.

5 If any dispute or difference is referred to an Arbitrator appointed under article 5 or to a court then insofar as any payment awarded in such arbitration or court proceedings varies the amount certified for payment for goods or services supplied by the Contractor to the Employer under this Contract or is an amount which ought to have been so certified but was not so certified then the provisions of this Agreement shall so far as relevant and applicable apply to any such payments.

6 The provisions of article 5 shall not apply to any matters to be dealt with under clause 3 of this Agreement.

7 Notwithstanding any provisions to the contrary elsewhere in the Conditions the Employer shall not be obliged to make any further payment to the Contractor under the Conditions if the Contractor is in default in providing the receipt referred to in clause 1·4 of this Agreement. Provided that clause 7 of this Agreement shall only apply where:

7 ·1 the Employer can show that he requires such receipt to validate any claim for credit for tax paid or payable under this Agreement which the Employer is entitled to make to the Commissioners, and

7 ·2 the Employer has

paid tax in accordance with the provisional assessment of the Contractor under clause 1 of this Agreement unless he has sustained a reasonable objection under clause 1·2 of this Agreement; or

paid tax in accordance with clause 1A of this Agreement.

8 Where clause 27·4 of the Conditions becomes operative there shall be added to the amount allowable or payable to the Employer in addition to the amounts certified by the Architect any additional tax that the Employer has had to pay by reason of determination under clause 27 of the Conditions as compared with the tax the Employer would have paid if the determination had not occurred.

If the copy of the amended VAT Agreement is used to amend a Local Authorities version of the Standard Form the term 'the Architect/the Contract Administrator' shall be deemed to be substituted for the term the 'Architect'.

41.02 Clause 38 allows fluctuations in prices arising from changes in the matters specified in clause 38.1.1, namely rates of contribution, levy, or tax payable by the contractor. These cover such matters as national insurance contributions. VAT is dealt with specifically by the VAT agreement and is not within clause 38. Apart from changes in tax rates, no other price changes are taken into account where the parties contract on the basis that fluctuations are to be governed by clause 38.

38 CONTRIBUTION, LEVY AND TAX FLUCTUATIONS

38·1 The Contract Sum shall be deemed to have been calculated in the manner set out below and shall be subject to adjustment in the events specified hereunder:

38·1 ·1 The prices contained in the Contract Bills are based upon the types and rates of contribution, levy and tax payable by a person in his capacity as an employer and which at the Date of Tender are payable by the Contractor. A type and rate so payable are in clause 38·1·2 referred to as a 'tender type' and a 'tender rate'.

38·1 ·2 If any of the tender rates other than a rate of levy payable by virtue of the Industrial Training Act 1964, is increased or decreased, or if a tender type ceases to be payable, or if a new type of contribution, levy or tax which is payable by a person in his capacity as an employer becomes payable after the Date of Tender, then in any such case the net amount of the difference between what the Contractor actually pays or will pay in respect of

·2 ·1 workpeople engaged upon or in connection with the Works either on or adjacent to the site, and

·2 ·2 workpeople directly employed by the Contractor who are engaged upon the production of materials or goods for use in or in connection with the Works and who operate neither on nor adjacent to the site and to the extent that they are so engaged

or because of his employment of such workpeople and what he would have paid had the alteration, cessation or new type of contribution, levy or tax not become effective, shall, as the case may be, be paid to or allowed by the Contractor.

38·1 ·3 There shall be added, to the net amount paid to or allowed by the Contractor under clause 38·1·2, in respect of each person employed by the Contractor who is engaged upon or in connection with the Works either on or adjacent to the site and who is not within the definition of 'workpeople' in clause 38·6·3 the same amount as is payable or allowable in respect of a craftsman under clause 38·1·2 or such proportion of that amount as reflects the time (measured in whole working days) that each such person is so employed.

38·1 ·4 For the purposes of clause 38·1·3:

no period less than 2 whole working days in any week shall be taken into account and periods less than a whole working day shall not be aggregated to amount to a whole working day;

the phrase "the same amount as is payable or allowable in respect of a craftsman" shall refer to the amount in respect of a craftsman employed by the Contractor (or by any Domestic Sub-Contractor under a sub-contract to which clause 38·3 refers) under the rules or decisions or agreements of the National Joint Council for the Building Industry or other wage-fixing body and, where the aforesaid rules or decisions or agreements provide for more than one rate of wage emolument or other expense for a craftsman, shall refer to the amount in respect of a craftsman employed as aforesaid to whom the highest rate is applicable; and

the phrase "employed by the Contractor" shall mean an employment to which the Income Tax (Employment) Regulations 1973 (the PAYE Regulations) under S.204 of the Income and Corporation Taxes Act 1970, apply.

38·1 ·5 The prices contained in the Contract Bills are based upon the types and rates of refund of the contributions, levies and taxes payable by a person in his capacity as an employer and upon the types and rates of premium receivable by a person in his capacity as an employer being in each case types and rates which at the Date of Tender are receivable by the Contractor. Such a type and such a rate are in clause 38·1·6 referred to as a 'tender type' and a 'tender rate'.

38·1 ·6 If any of the tender rates is increased or decreased or if a tender type ceases to be payable or if a new type of refund of any contribution, levy or tax payable by a person in his capacity as an employer becomes receivable or if a new type of premium receivable by a person in his capacity as an employer becomes receivable after the Date of Tender, then in any such case the net amount of the difference between what the Contractor actually receives or will receive in respect of workpeople as referred to in clauses 38·1·2·1 and 38·1·2·2 or because of his employment of such workpeople and what he would have received had the alteration, cessation or new type of refund or premium not become effective, shall, as the case may be, be paid to or allowed by the Contractor.

38·1 ·7 The references in clauses 38·1·5 and 38·1·6 to premiums shall be construed as meaning all payments howsoever they are described which are made under or by virtue of an Act of Parliament to a person in his capacity as an employer and which affect the cost to an employer of having persons in his employment.

38·1 ·8 Where employer's contributions are payable by the Contractor in respect of workpeople as referred to in clauses 38·1·2·1 and 38·1·2·2 whose employment is contracted-out employment within the meaning of the Social Security Pensions Act 1975 the Contractor shall for the purpose of recovery or allowance under clause 38·1 be deemed to pay employer's contributions as if that employment were not contracted-out employment.

38·1 ·9 The reference in clause 38·1 to contributions, levies and taxes shall be construed as meaning all impositions payable by a person in his capacity as an employer howsoever they are described and whoever the recipient which are imposed under or by virtue of an Act of Parliament and which affect the cost to an employer of having persons in his employment.

38·2 The Contract Sum shall be deemed to have been calculated in the manner set out below and shall be subject to adjustment in the events specified hereunder:

38·2 ·1 The prices contained in the Contract Bills are based upon the types and rates of duty if any and tax if any (other than any value added tax which is treated, or is capable of being treated, as input tax (as referred to in the Finance Act 1972) by the Contractor) by whomsoever payable which at the Date of Tender are payable on the import, purchase, sale, appropriation, processing or use of the materials, goods, electricity and, where so specifically stated in the Contract Bills, fuels, specified in the list attached thereto under or by virtue of any Act of Parliament. A type and a rate so payable are in clause 38·2·2 referred to as a 'tender type' and a 'tender rate'.

38·2 ·2 If in relation to any materials or goods specified as aforesaid, or any electricity or fuels specified as aforesaid and consumed on site for the execution of the Works including temporary site installations for those Works, a tender rate is increased or decreased, or a tender type ceases to be payable or a new type of duty or tax (other than any value added tax which is treated, or is capable of being treated as input tax (as referred to in the Finance Act 1972) by the Contractor) becomes payable on the import, purchase, sale, appropriation, processing or use of those materials, goods, electricity or fuels, after the Date of Tender then in any such case the net amount of the difference between what the Contractor actually pays in respect of those materials, goods, electricity or fuels and what he would have paid in respect of them had the alteration, cessation or imposition not occurred, shall, as the case may be, be paid to or allowed by the Contractor. In clause 38·2 the expression 'a new type of duty or tax' includes an additional duty or tax and a duty or tax imposed in regard to specified materials, goods, electricity or fuels in respect of which no duty or tax whatever was previously payable (other than any value added tax which is treated, or is capable of being treated, as input tax (as referred to in the Finance Act 1972) by the Contractor).

38·3 Fluctuations – work sub-let – Domestic Sub-Contractors

38·3 ·1 If the Contractor is obliged by clause 19·3, or shall decide subject to clause 19·2, to sub-let any portion of the Works to a Domestic Sub-Contractor he shall incorporate in the sub-contract provisions to the like effect as the provisions of

clause 38 (excluding clause 38·3) including the percentage stated in the Appendix pursuant to clause 38·7

which are applicable for the purposes of this Contract.

38·3 ·2 If the price payable under such a sub-contract as referred to in clause 38·3·1 is increased above or decreased below the price in such sub-contract by reason of the operation of the said incorporated provisions, then the net amount of such increase or decrease shall, as the case may be, be paid to or allowed by the Contractor under this Contract.

38·4 to ·6 Provisions relating to clause 38

38·4 ·1 The Contractor shall give a written notice to the Architect/Supervising Officer of the occurrence of any of the events referred to in such of the following provisions as are applicable for the purposes of this Contract:

·1 ·1 clause 38·1·2;

·1 ·2 clause 38·1·6;

·1 ·3 clause 38·2·2;

·1 ·4 clause 38·3·2.

38·4 ·2 Any notice required to be given under clause 38·4·1 shall be given within a reasonable time after the occurrence of the event to which the notice relates, and the giving of a written notice in that time shall be a condition precedent to any payment being made to the Contractor in respect of the event in question.

38·4 ·3 The Quantity Surveyor and the Contractor may agree what shall be deemed for all the purposes of this Contract to be the net amount payable to or allowable by the Contractor in respect of the occurrence of any event such as is referred to in any of the provisions listed in clause 38·4·1.

38·4 ·4 Any amount which from time to time becomes payable to or allowable by the Contractor by virtue of clause 38·1 and ·2 or 38·3 shall, as the case may be, be added to or deducted from:

·4 ·1 the Contract Sum; and

·4 ·2 any amounts payable to the Contractor and which are calculated in accordance with either clauses 28·2·2·1 or 28·2·2·2.

The addition or deduction to which clause 38·4·4 refers shall be subject to the provisions of clauses 38·4·5 to ·4·7.

38·4 ·5 As soon as is reasonably practicable the Contractor shall provide such evidence and computations as the Architect/Supervising Officer or the Quantity Surveyor may reasonably require to enable the amount payable to or allowable by the Contractor by virtue of clause 38·1 and ·2 or 38·3 to be ascertained; and in the case of amounts payable to or allowable by the Contractor under clause 38·1·3 (or clause 38·3 for amounts payable to or allowable by the Domestic Sub-Contractor under provisions in the sub-contract to the like effect as clauses 38·1·3 and 38·1·4) – employees other than workpeople – such evidence shall include a certificate signed by or on behalf of the Contractor each week certifying the validity of the evidence reasonably required to ascertain such amounts.

38·4 ·6 No addition to or deduction from the Contract Sum made by virtue of clause 38·4·4 shall alter in any way the amount of profit of the Contractor included in that Sum.

38·4 ·7 Subject to the provisions of clause 38·4·8 no amount shall be added or deducted in the computation of the amount stated as due in an Interim Certificate or in the Final Certificate in respect of amounts otherwise payable to or allowable by the Contractor by virtue of clause 38·1 and ·2 or 38·3 if the event (as referred to in the provisions listed in clause 38·4·1) in respect of which the payment or allowance would be made occurs after the Completion Date.

38·4 ·8 Clause 38·4·7 shall not be applied unless:

·8 ·1 the printed text of clause 25 is unamended and forms part of the Conditions; and

·8 ·2 the Architect/Supervising Officer has, in respect of every written notification by the Contractor under clause 25, fixed or confirmed in writing such Completion Date as he considers to be in accordance with clause 25.

38·5 Clauses 38·1 to ·3 shall not apply in respect of:

38·5 ·1 work for which the Contractor is allowed daywork rates under clause 13·5·4;

38·5 ·2 work executed or materials or goods supplied by any Nominated Sub-Contractor or Nominated Supplier (fluctuations in relation to Nominated Sub-Contractors and Nominated Suppliers shall be dealt with under any provision in relation thereto which may be included in the appropriate sub-contract or contract of sale);

38·5 ·3 work executed by the Contractor for which a tender made under clause 35·2 has been accepted (fluctuations in relation to such work shall be dealt with under any provision in the accepted tender of the Contractor);

38·5 ·4 changes in the rate of value added tax charged on the supply of goods or services by the Contractor to the Employer under this Contract.

38·6 In clause 38:

38·6 ·1 the expression 'the Date of Tender' means the date 10 days before the date fixed for the receipt of tenders by the Employer;

38·6 ·2 the expressions 'materials' and 'goods' include timber used in formwork but do not include other consumable stores, plant and machinery (save that electricity and, where specifically so stated in the Contract Bills, fuels are dealt with in clause 38·2);

38·6 ·3 the expression 'workpeople' means persons whose rates of wages and other emoluments (including holiday credits) are governed by the rules or decisions or agreements of the National Joint Council for the Building Industry or some other wage-fixing body for trades associated with the building industry;

38·6 ·4 the expression 'wage-fixing body' shall mean a body which lays down recognised terms and conditions of workers within the meaning of the Employment Protection Act 1975, Schedule 11, paragraph 2(a).

38·7 Percentage addition to fluctuation payments or allowances

38·7 ·1 There shall be added to the amount paid or allowed by the Contractor under:

·1 ·1 clause 38·1·2,

·1 ·2 clause 38·1·3,

·1 ·3 clause 38·1·6,

·1 ·4 clause 38·2·2

the percentage stated in the Appendix.

41.03 Clause 39 and clause 40 both provide for what are known as 'full' fluctuations entitling the contractor to recover extra costs of labour and materials as from a date specified in the contract. The system under clause 39 is as follows:

---

39 LABOUR AND MATERIALS COST AND TAX FLUCTUATIONS

39·1 The Contract Sum shall be deemed to have been calculated in the manner set out below and shall be subject to adjustment in the events specified hereunder

39·1 ·1 The prices (including the cost of employer's liability insurance and of third party insurance) contained in the Contract Bills are based upon the rates of wages and the other emoluments and expenses (including holiday credits) which will be payable by the Contractor to or in respect of

·1 ·1 workpeople engaged upon or in connection with the Works either on or adjacent to the site, and

·1 ·2 workpeople directly employed by the Contractor who are engaged upon the production of materials or goods for use in or in connection with the Works and who operate neither on nor adjacent to the site and to the extent that they are so engaged

in accordance with

·1 ·3 the rules or decisions of the National Joint Council for the Building Industry or other wage-fixing body which will be applicable to the Works and which have been promulgated at the Date of Tender; and

·1 ·4 any incentive scheme and/or productivity agreement under the provisions of Rule 1·16 or any successor to this Rule (Productivity Incentive Schemes and/or Productivity Agreements) of the Rules of the National Joint Council for the Building Industry (including the General Principles covering Incentive Schemes and/or Productivity Agreements published by the aforesaid Council to which Rule 1·16 or any successor to this Rule refers) or provisions on incentive schemes and/or productivity agreements contained in the rules or decisions of some other wage-fixing body; and

·1 ·5 the terms of the Building and Civil Engineering Annual and Public Holidays Agreements (or the terms of agreements to similar effect in respect of workpeople whose rates of wages and other emoluments and expenses (including holiday credits) are in accordance with the rules or decisions of a wage-fixing body other than the National Joint Council for the Building Industry) which will be applicable to the Works and which have been promulgated at the Date of Tender;

and upon the rates or amounts of any contribution, levy or tax which will be payable by the Contractor in his capacity as an employer in respect of, or calculated by reference to, the rates of wages and other emoluments and expenses (including holiday credits) referred to herein.

39·1 ·2 If any of the said rates of wages or other emoluments and expenses (including holiday credits) are increased or decreased by reason of any alteration in the said rules, decisions or agreements promulgated after the Date of Tender, then the net amount of the increase or decrease in wages or other emoluments and expenses (including holiday credits) together with the net amount of any consequential increase or decrease in the cost of employer's liability insurance, of third party insurance, and of any contribution, levy or tax payable by a person in his capacity as an employer shall, as the case may be, be paid to or allowed by the Contractor.

39·1 ·3 There shall be added, to the net amount paid to or allowed by the Contractor under clause 39·1·2, in respect of each person employed by the Contractor who is engaged upon or in connection with the Works either on or adjacent to the site and who is not within the definition of 'workpeople' in clause 39·7·3 the same amount as is payable or allowable in respect of a craftsman under clause 39·1·2 or such proportion of that amount as reflects the time (measured in whole working days) that each such person is so employed.

39·1 ·4 For the purposes of clauses 39·1·3 and 39·2·3:

no period less than 2 whole days in any week shall be taken into account and periods less than a whole working day shall not be aggregated to amount to a whole working day;

the phrase 'the same amount as is payable or allowable in respect of a craftsman' shall refer to the amount in respect of a craftsman employed by the Contractor (or by any Domestic Sub-Contractor under a sub-contract to which clause 39·4 refers) under the rules or decisions or agreements of the National Joint Council for the Building Industry or other wage-fixing body and, where the aforesaid rules or decisions or agreements provide for more than one rate of wage, emolument or other expenses for a craftsman, shall refer to the amount in respect of a craftsman employed as aforesaid to whom the highest rate is applicable, and

the phrase 'employed by the Contractor' shall mean an employment to which the Income Tax (Employment) Regulations 1973 (the PAYE Regulations) under S.204 of the Income and Corporation Taxes Act 1970, apply.

39·1 ·5 The prices contained in the Contract Bills are based upon:

the transport charges referred to in a basic transport charges list submitted by the Contractor and attached to the Contract Bills and incurred by the Contractor in respect of workpeople engaged in either of the capacities referred to in clauses 39·1·1·1 and 39·1·1·2; or

upon the reimbursement of fares which will be reimbursable by the Contractor to workpeople engaged in either of the capacities referred to in clauses 39·1·1·1 and 39·1·1·2 in accordance with the rules or decisions of the National Joint Council for the Building Industry which will be applicable to the Works and which have been promulgated at the Date of Tender or, in the case of workpeople so engaged whose rates of wages and other emoluments and expenses are governed by the rules or decisions of some wage-fixing body other than the National Joint Council for the Building Industry, in accordance with the rules or decisions of such other body which will be applicable and which have been promulgated as aforesaid.

39·1 ·6 If:

·6 ·1 the amount of transport charges referred to in the basic transport charges list is increased or decreased after the Date of Tender; or

·6 ·2 the reimbursement of fares is increased or decreased by reason of any alteration in the said rules or decisions promulgated after the Date of Tender or by any actual increase or decrease in fares which takes effect after the Date of Tender,

then the net amount of that increase or decrease shall, as the case may be, be paid to or allowed by the Contractor.

39·2 The Contract Sum shall be deemed to have been calculated in the manner set out below and shall be subject to adjustment in the events specified hereunder:

39·2 ·1 The prices contained in the Contract Bills are based upon the types and rates of contribution, levy and tax payable by a person in his capacity as an employer and which at the Date of Tender are payable by the Contractor. A type and a rate so payable are in clause 39·2·2 referred to as a 'tender type' and a 'tender rate'.

39·2 ·2 If any of the tender rates other than a rate of levy payable by virtue of the Industrial Training Act 1964, is increased or decreased or if a tender type ceases to be payable, or if a new type of contribution, levy or tax which is payable by a person in his capacity as an employer becomes payable after the Date of Tender, then in any such case the net amount of the difference between what the Contractor actually pays or will pay in respect of workpeople as referred to in clauses 39·1·1·1 and 39·1·1·2 or because of his employment of such workpeople and what he would have paid had the alteration, cessation or new type of contribution, levy or tax not become effective, shall, as the case may be, be paid to or allowed by the Contractor.

39·2 ·3 There shall be added, to the net amount paid to or allowed by the Contractor under clause 39·2·2, in respect of each person employed by the Contractor who is engaged upon or in connection with the Works either on or adjacent to the site and who is not within the definition of ''workpeople'' in clause 39·7·3, the same amount as is payable or allowable in respect of a craftsman under clause 39·2·2 or such proportion of that amount as reflects the time (measured in whole working days) that each such person is so employed. The provisions of clause 39·1·4 shall apply to clause 39·2·3

39·2 ·4 The prices contained in the Contract Bills are based upon the type and rates of refund of the contributions, levies and taxes payable by a person in his capacity as an employer and upon the types and rates of premium receivable by a person in his capacity as an employer being in each case types and rates which at the Date of Tender are receivable by the Contractor. Such a type and such a rate are, in clause 39·2·5 referred to as a 'tender type' and a 'tender rate'.

39·2 ·5 If any of the tender rates is increased or decreased or if a tender type ceases to be payable or if a new type of refund of any contribution, levy or tax payable by a person in his capacity as an employer becomes receivable or if a new type of premium receivable by a person in his capacity as an employer becomes receivable after the Date of Tender, then in any such case the net amount of the difference between what the Contractor actually receives or will receive in respect of workpeople as referred to in clause 39·1·1·1 and 39·1·1·2 or because of his employment of such workpeople, and what he would have received had the alteration, cessation or new type of refund or premium not become effective, shall, as the case may be, be paid to or allowed by the Contractor.

39·2 ·6 The reference in clauses 39·2·4 and 39·2·5 to premiums shall be construed as meaning all payments howsoever they are described which are made under or by virtue of an Act of Parliament to a person in his capacity as an employer and which affect the cost to an employer of having persons in his employment

39·2 ·7 Where employer's contributions are payable by the Contractor in respect of workpeople as referred to in clauses 39·1·1·1 and 39·1·1·2 whose employment is contracted-out employment within the meaning of the Social Security Pensions Act 1975, the Contractor shall, subject to the proviso hereto, for the purpose of recovery or allowance under clause 39 be deemed to pay employer's contributions as if that employment were not contracted-out employment, provided that clause 39·2·7 shall not apply where the occupational pension scheme, by reference to membership of which the employment of workpeople is contracted-out employment, is established by the rules of the National Joint Council for the Building Industry or of some wage-fixing body other than the National Joint Council for the Building Industry so that contributions to such occupational pension scheme are within the payment and allowance provisions of clause 39·1

39·2 ·8 The reference in clauses 39·2·1 to 39·2·5 and 39·2·7 to contributions, levies and taxes shall be construed as meaning all impositions payable by a person in his capacity as an employer howsoever they are described and whoever the recipient which are imposed under or by virtue of an Act of Parliament and which affect the cost to an employer of having persons in his employment

39·3 The Contract Sum shall be deemed to have been calculated in the manner set out below and shall be subject to adjustment in the events specified hereunder

39·3 ·1 The prices contained in the Contract Bills are based upon the market prices of the materials, goods, electricity and, where specifically so stated in the Contract Bills, fuels, specified in a list submitted by the Contractor and attached to the Contract Bills, which were current at the Date of Tender. Such prices are hereinafter referred to as 'basic prices' and the prices set out by the Contractor on the said list shall be deemed to be the basic prices of the specified materials, goods, electricity and fuels.

39·3 ·2 If after the Date of Tender the market price of any of the materials or goods specified as aforesaid increases or decreases, or the market price of any electricity or fuels specified as aforesaid and consumed on site for the execution of the Works (including temporary site installations for those Works) increases or decreases, then the net amount of the difference between the basic price thereof and the market price payable by the Contractor and current when the materials, goods, electricity or fuels are bought shall, as the case may be, be paid to or allowed by the Contractor

39·3 ·3 The references in clauses 39·3·1 and 39·3·2 to 'market prices' shall be construed as including any duty or tax (other than value added tax which is treated, or is capable of being treated as input tax (as referred to in the Finance Act 1972) by the Contractor) by whomsoever payable which is payable under or by virtue of any Act of Parliament on the import, purchase, sale, appropriation, processing or use of the materials, goods, electricity or fuels specified as aforesaid.

39·4 Fluctuations – work sub-let – Domestic Sub-Contractors

39·4 ·1 If the Contractor is obliged by clause 19·3, or shall decide subject to clause 19·2, to sub-let any portion of the Works to a Domestic Sub-Contractor he shall incorporate in the sub-contract provisions to the like effect as the provisions of

clause 39 (excluding clause 39·4) including the percentage stated in the Appendix pursuant to clause 39·8

which are applicable for the purposes of this Contract

39·4 ·2 If the price payable under such a sub-contract as referred to in clause 39·4·1 is increased above or decreased below the price in such sub-contract by reason of the operation of the said incorporated provisions, then the net amount of such increase or decrease shall, as the case may be, be paid to or allowed by the Contractor under this Contract

39·5 to ·7 Provisions relating to clause 39

39·5 ·1 The Contractor shall give a written notice to the Architect/Supervising Officer of the occurrence of any of the events referred to in such of the following provisions as are applicable for the purposes of this Contract

·1 ·1 clause 39·1·2;

·1 ·2 clause 39·1·6;

·1 ·3 clause 39·2·2;

·1 ·4 clause 39·2·5;

·1 ·5 clause 39·3·2;

·1 ·6 clause 39·4·2.

39·5 ·2 Any notice required to be given by clause 39·5·1 shall be given within a reasonable time after the occurrence of the event to which the notice relates and the giving of written notice in that time shall be a condition precedent to any payment being made to the Contractor in respect of the event in question.

39·5 ·3 The Quantity Surveyor and the Contractor may agree what shall be deemed for all the purposes of this Contract to be the net amount payable to or allowable by the Contractor in respect of the occurrence of any event such as is referred to in any of the provisions listed in clause 39·5·1.

39·5 ·4 Any amount which from time to time becomes payable to or allowable by the Contractor by virtue of clauses 39·1 to ·3 or 39·4 shall,as the case may be,be added to or deducted from:

·4 ·1 the Contract Sum; and

·4 ·2 any amounts payable to the Contractor and which are calculated in accordance with either clauses 28·2·2·1 or 28·2·2·2.

The addition or deduction to which clause 39·5·4 refers shall be subject to the provisions of clauses 39·5·5 to ·5·7.

39·5 ·5 As soon as is reasonably practicable the Contractor shall provide such evidence and computations as the Architect/Supervising Officer or the Quantity Surveyor may reasonably require to enable the amount payable to or allowable by the Contractor by virtue of clauses 39·1 to ·3 or 39·4 to be ascertained; and in the case of amounts payable to or allowable by the Contractor under clause 39·1·3 (or clause 39·4 for amounts payable to or allowable by the Domestic Sub-Contractor under provisions in the sub-contract to the like effect as clauses 39·1·3 and 39·1·4) – employees other than workpeople – such evidence shall include a certificate signed by or on behalf of the Contractor each week certifying the validity of the evidence reasonably required to ascertain such amounts.

39·5 ·6 No addition to or deduction from the Contract Sum made by virtue of clause 39·5·4 shall alter in any way the amount of profit of the Contractor included in that Sum.

39·5 ·7 Subject to the provisions of clause 39·5·8 no amount shall be added or deducted in the computation of the amount stated as due in an Interim Certificate or in the Final Certificate in respect of amounts otherwise payable to or allowable by the Contractor by virtue of clause 39·1 to ·3 or clause 39·4 if the event (as referred to in the provisions listed in clause 39·5·1) in respect of which the payment or allowance would be made occurs after the Completion Date.

39·5 ·8 Clause 39·5·7 shall not be applied unless:

·8 ·1 the printed text of clause 25 is unamended and forms part of the Conditions; and

·8 ·2 the Architect/Supervising Officer has, in respect of every written notification by the Contractor under clause 25, fixed or confirmed in writing such Completion Date as he considers to be in accordance with clause 25.

39·6 Clauses 39·1 to ·4 shall not apply in respect of:

39·6 ·1 work for which the Contractor is allowed daywork rates under clause 13·5·4;

39·6 ·2 work executed or materials or goods supplied by any Nominated Sub-Contractor or Nominated Supplier (fluctuations in relation to Nominated Sub-Contractors and Nominated Suppliers shall be dealt with under any provision in relation thereto which may be included in the appropriate sub-contract or contract of sale);

39·6 ·3 work executed by the Contractor for which a tender made under clause 35·2 has been accepted (fluctuations in relation to such works shall be dealt with under any provision in the accepted tender of the Contractor);

39·6 ·4 changes in the rate of value added tax charged on the supply of goods or services by the Contractor to the Employer under this Contract.

39·7 In clause 39:

39·7 ·1 the expression 'the Date of Tender' means the date 10 days before the date fixed for the receipt of tenders by the Employer;

39·7 ·2 the expressions 'materials' and 'goods' include timber used in formwork but do not include other consumable stores, plant and machinery (save that electricity and, where specifically so stated in the Contract Bills, fuels are dealt with in clause 39·3);

39·7 ·3 the expression 'workpeople' means persons whose rates of wages and other emoluments (including holiday credits) are governed by the rules or decisions or agreements of the National Joint Council for the Building Industry or some other wage-fixing body for trades associated with the building industry;

39·7 ·4 the expression 'wage-fixing body' shall mean a body which lays down recognised terms and conditions of workers within the meaning of the Employment Protection Act 1975, Schedule 11, paragraph 2 (a).

39·8 **Percentage addition to fluctuation payments or allowances**

39·8 ·1 There shall be added to the amount paid or allowed by the Contractor under

·1 ·1 clause 39·1·2,
·1 ·2 clause 39·1·3,
·1 ·3 clause 39·1·6,
·1 ·4 clause 39·2·2,
·1 ·5 clause 39·2·5,
·1 ·6 clause 39·3·2

the percentage stated in the Appendix.

Use of Price Adjustment Formulae

40·1 ·1 ·1 The Contract Sum shall be adjusted in accordance with the provisions of clause 40 and the Formula Rules current at the Date of Tender issued for use with clause 40 by the Joint Contracts Tribunal for the Standard Form of Building Contract (hereinafter called 'the Formula Rules').

·1 ·2 Any adjustment under clause 40 shall be to sums exclusive of value added tax and nothing in this clause shall affect in any way the operation of clause 15 and the VAT Agreement.

40·1 ·2 The Definitions in rule 3 of the Formula Rules shall apply to clause 40.

40·1 ·3 The adjustment referred to in clause 40 shall be effected (after taking into account any Non-Adjustable Element) in all certificates for payment issued under the provisions of the Conditions.

40·1 ·4 If any correction of amounts of adjustment under clause 40 included in previous certificates is required following any operation of rule 5 of the Formula Rules such correction shall be given effect in the next certificate for payment to be issued.

40·2 Interim valuations shall be made before the issue of each Interim Certificate and accordingly the words 'whenever the Architect/Supervising Officer considers them to be necessary' shall be deemed to have been deleted in clause 30·1·2.

40·3 For any article to which rule 4 (ii) of the Formula Rules applies the Contractor shall insert in a list attached to the Contract Bills the market price of the article in sterling (that is the price delivered to the site) current at the Date of Tender. If after that Date the market price of the article inserted in the aforesaid list increases or decreases then the net amount of the difference between the cost of purchasing at the market price inserted in the aforesaid list and the market price payable by the Contractor and current when the article is bought shall, as the case may be, be paid to or allowed by the Contractor. The reference to 'market price' in clause 40·3 shall be construed as including any duty or tax (other than any value added tax which is treated, or is capable of being treated, as input tax (as defined in the Finance Act 1972) by the Contractor) by whomsoever payable under or by virtue of any Act of Parliament on the import, purchase, sale, appropriation or use of the article specified as aforesaid.

40·4 ·1 Where the supply and fixing of any goods or the execution of any work is to be carried out by a sub-contractor nominated by the Architect/Supervising Officer the Sub-Contract between the Contractor and the Nominated Sub-Contractor shall provide if required for adjustment to be made of the Sub-Contract Sum or of amounts ascertained under clause 17 of Sub-Contract NSC/4 or NSC/4a as applicable by the operation of clause 34 of Sub-Contract NSC/4 or NSC/4a as applicable by reference to whichever of the following has been tendered upon by the Sub-Contractor and approved in writing by the Architect/Supervising Officer prior to the issue of the nomination instruction:

·1 ·1 in the case of electrical installations, heating and ventilating and air conditioning installations, lift installations, structural steelwork installations, and in the case of catering equipment installations, the relevant specialist formula (see the Formula Rules, rule 50, rule 54, rule 58, rule 63 and rule 69 for the text of the relevant specialist formula);

·1 ·2 where none of the specialist formulae applies, the Formula in Part I of Section 2 of the Formula Rules and one or more of the Work Categories set out in Appendix A to the Formula Rules;

·1 ·3 where neither clause 40·4·1·1 nor 40·4·1·2 applies, some other method.

40·4 ·2 If the Contractor shall decide to sub-let any portion of the Works he shall, unless the Contractor and Domestic Sub-Contractor otherwise agree, incorporate in the sub-contract provisions for formula adjustment of the sub-contract sum namely:

·2 ·1 in the case of electrical installations, heating and ventilating and air conditioning installations, lift installations, structural steelwork installations and in the case of catering equipment installations, the relevant specialist formula;

·2 ·2 where none of the specialist formulae applies, the Formula in Part I of Section 2 of the Formula Rules and one or more of the Work Categories set out in Appendix A to the Formula Rules appropriate to such sub-contract works.

40·5 The Quantity Surveyor and the Contractor may agree any alteration to the methods and procedures for ascertaining the amount of formula adjustment to be made under clause 40 and the amounts ascertained after the operation of such agreement shall be deemed for all the purposes of this Contract to be the amount of formula adjustment payable to or allowable by the Contractor in respect of the provisions of clause 40. Provided always:

40·5 ·1 that no alteration to the methods and procedures shall be agreed as aforesaid unless it is reasonably expected that the amount of formula adjustment so ascertained will be the same or approximately the same as that ascertained in accordance with Part I or Part II of Section 2 of the Formula Rules whichever Part is stated to be applicable in the Contract Bills; and

40·5 ·2 that any agreement under clause 40·5 shall not have any effect on the determination of any adjustment payable by the Contractor to any sub-contractor to whom clause 40·4 refers.

40·6 ·1 If at any time prior to the issue of the Final Certificate under clause 30·8 formula adjustment is not possible because of delay in, or cessation of, the publication of the Monthly Bulletins, adjustment of the Contract Sum shall be made in each Interim Certificate during such period of delay on a fair and reasonable basis.

40·6 ·2 If publication of the Monthly Bulletins is recommenced at any time prior to the issue of the Final Certificate under clause 30·8 the provisions of clause 40 and the Formula Rules shall apply for each Valuation Period as if no delay or cessation as aforesaid had occurred and the adjustment under clause 40 and the Formula Rules shall be substituted for any adjustment under clause 40·6·1.

40·6 ·3 During any period of delay or cessation as aforesaid the Contractor and Employer shall operate such parts of clause 40 and the Formula Rules as will enable the amount of formula adjustment due to be readily calculated upon recommencement of publication of the Monthly Bulletins.

40·7 ·1 ·1 If the Contractor fails to complete the Works by the Completion Date, formula adjustment of the Contract Sum under clause 40 shall be effected in all Interim Certificates issued after the aforesaid Completion Date by reference to the Index Numbers applicable to the Valuation Period in which the aforesaid Completion Date falls.

·1 ·2 If for any reason the adjustment included in the amount certified in any Interim Certificate which is or has been issued after the aforesaid Completion Date is not in accordance with clause 40·7·1·1, such adjustment shall be corrected to comply with that clause.

40·7 ·2 Clause 40·7·1 shall not be applied unless:

·2 ·1 the printed text of clause 25 is unamended and forms part of the Conditions; and

·2 ·2 the Architect/Supervising Officer has, in respect of every written notification by the Contractor under clause 25, fixed or confirmed in writing such Completion Date as he considers to be in accordance with clause 25.

41.04 In respect of labour costs, extra costs as a result of awards by the National Joint Council for the Building Industry are recoverable – this also applies to reimbursement of travelling charges (see clause 39.1.5).

41.05 Tax increases are recoverable under clause 38. JCT Practice Note 17 gives guidance on the choice of Fluctuations Provisions. NJCC Procedure Note 7 contains information about clauses 38.7 and 39.8.

41.06 Material increases are recoverable based on the increases over a price list to be submitted by the contractor and attached to the contract bills current at the date of tender. This forms a list of basic prices, and if an increase above the basic prices occurs, the contractor is entitled to reimbursement.

41.07 Under clause 40, adjustment of prices takes place in accordance with the formula rules issued by the Joint Contracts Tribunal, that were current at the date of tender. Monthly bulletins are issued by the Joint Contracts Tribunal giving details of price changes, and the contract sum falls to be adjusted in accordance with these.

Fluctuations where contractor is guilty of delay

41.08 In principle, the contractor is not entitled to price increases under the fluctuations clauses where these price increases arise during a period after the contractual completion date: this provides an added incentive to the contractor to meet the completion date. This is subject, however, to no amendments being made to clause 25, and to the architect having in respect of every written notification by the contractor under clause 25 fixed or confirmed in writing a completion date in accordance with that clause (see clause 38.4.8, clause 39.5.8, and clause 40.7.2). It is therefore incumbent on the architect to ensure that clause 25 is properly administered, and that no amendments have been made to clause 25, or alternatively that the appropriate parts of the fluctuations clauses are amended so as to delete the provision removing the 'freeze' on fluctuations if clause 25 is amended.

41.09 In *J Murphy & Sons* v *Southwark London Borough Council* (1982) 22 BLR 41, CA, it was held that under the predecessor of what is now clause 39 the contractor was not entitled to recover increases in rates of wages, etc., payable to work people who were self-employed, since their wages were not 'governed by' the rules or decisions or agreements of the National Joint Council for the Building Industry within what is now clause 39.7.3. However, this anomaly has been rectified in the 1980 JCT Form by the wording of clause 39.1.3.

THE SUB-CONTRACT DOCUMENTS: NSC/1, NSC/2, NSC/2a, NSC/3

The sub-contract documents issued under the aegis of the JCT came into existence as a result of that body obtaining authority from its constituent members to prepare a standard form of sub-contract (see para 1.03). The procedure for nomination of nominated sub-contractors and nominated suppliers is laid down in MF clauses 35 and 36.

42 JCT Standard Form of Nominated Sub-contract Tender and Agreement (Tender NSC/1)

42.01 The procedure for nominating a sub-contractor is initiated by the architect. He will invite tenders normally from a number of contractors whom he considers capable of performing the nominated sub-contract works. The decision which tender, if any, should be accepted rests with the architect, who then nominates the successful tenderer and instructs the main contractor to enter into a sub-contract with the successful tenderer, who thereby becomes the nominated sub-contractor.

42.02 NSC/1 serves three purposes: firstly, it contains an offer by the person invited to tender for the nominated sub-contract works, which is to be submitted in response to the architect's invitation to tender. Secondly (in Schedule 1), it contains information as to the terms of the Main Contract and as to the terms of the sub-contract which the successful tenderer will be required to enter into; this part will be completed by the architect before inviting tenders, and NSC/1 with Schedule 1 completed will be sent to those invited to tender. Thirdly, NSC/1 forms an essential part of the machinery whereby main contractor and proposed nominated sub-contractor endeavour to agree such matters as programme and access for the sub-contract works, as envisaged in MF clause 35.7.

42.03 The first part of NSC/1 constitutes an offer by the person invited to carry out the sub-contract works to carry them out in accordance with the tender documents at a stated price. The tender is to be submitted to the employer and the main contractor (assuming his identity is known at the time the tender is invited). If his identity is not known, the tender may be withdrawn within 14 days of the main contractor's identity becoming known (stipulation 2).

42.04 The stipulations further provide that the tenderer is not to be bound by the employer/sub-contractor Agreement NSC/2 until both that and NSC/1 have been signed or sealed by the employer. Stipulation 3 entitles the sub-contractor to withdraw if there is failure to agree on the terms contained in Schedule 2. Under MF clause 35.8, the contractor is obliged to inform the architect of the reasons for inability to reach agreement on such terms, and the architect has power to issue such instructions as may be necessary. However, clearly such instructions could not bind the tenderer for the nominated sub-contract works, and presumably the power contained in clause 35.8 entitles the architect simply to order a variation so as to resolve, if possible, a difficulty arising between the main contractor and proposed sub-contractor. Stipulation 4 entitles the sub-contractor to withdraw if no nomination is made under MF clause 35.10 within a specified period (to be completed by the tenderer).

42.05 Although tenders for nominated sub-contract works can be invited before the identity of the main contractor is known, clearly it is not possible to actually nominate a sub-contractor until the identity of the main contractor is known, and indeed up to that time no tender for nominated sub-contract works is binding.

42.06 Stipulation 5 generously provides that where the proposed nominated sub-contractor withdraws his tender this is to be without charge to the employer. This merely restates the position at law: possibly the purpose of the provision is to make it clear that an indication by the employer that a particular person is the successful tenderer for nominated sub-contract works and that a nomination will be issued in due course is not to be regarded as a letter of intent imposing some obligation on the employer (cf *Turriff* v *Regalia Knitting Mills* [1972] EGD 257). There is an exception where the architect has, prior to nominating the sub-contractor under MF clause 35.10.2, instructed the proposed sub-contractor to proceed with the design or proper ordering or fabrication of any materials or goods for the sub-contract works, in accordance with clause 2.2.1 of Agreement NSC/2 (see para 43).

Schedule 1

42.07 Schedule 1 sets out the particulars of the Main Contract and the sub-contract which the proposed tenderer will have to enter if his tender is accepted. The purpose of this Schedule is to give the proposed tenderer the fullest possible information as to the terms of the Main Contract (which may

materially affect the conditions under which the sub-contract work is carried out) and the terms of the sub-contract. This will, of course, always be in form NSC/4, but Schedule 1, paragraph 2 makes it clear which of the alternative fluctuations provisions in that contract apply. An amendment sheet has been issued to bring the tender into line with the Sectional Completion Supplements now incorporated into NSC/4 and NSC/4a.

Schedule 1: Particulars of Main Contract and Sub-Contract

Names and addresses of:

Employer: Tel. No:

†Architect/Supervising Officer/
Contract Administrator: Tel. No:

Quantity Surveyor: Tel. No:

Main Contractor: Tel. No:

1. Sub-Contract Conditions: Sub-Contract NSC/4, appropriate to the Standard Form of Building Contract edition identified in item 5 of this Schedule, unamended: 19   edition (incorporating Amendments numbered ....). To be executed forthwith after Architect's/Supervising Officer's/Contract Administrator's nomination on Nomination NSC/3.[e]

2. Sub-Contract Fluctuations: NSC/4 [f] Clause 35 (see also Appendix A)
or Clause 36 (see also Appendix A)
35·7 or 36·8...........%
or Clause 37 (see also Appendix B)

3. Main Contract Appendix and entries therein: [f1] (see item 10 pages 4 and 5) Where relevant will apply to the Sub-Contract unless otherwise specifically stated here. The entry relating to clause 37 of the Main Contract Conditions is for information of the Sub-Contractor only.

4. Main Contract Works: [g]

5. Form of Main Contract Conditions: Standard Form of Building Contract, 1980 edition.

Local Authorities/Private version WITH/WITH APPROXIMATE/WITHOUT Quantities (incorporating Amendments numbered.................) [h]

Sectional Completion Supplement [f1]

6. Inspection of Main Contract: The unpriced *Bills of Quantities/Bills of Approximate Quantities/Specification (which incorporate the general conditions and preliminaries of the Main Contract) and the Contract Drawings may be inspected by appointment at: [i]

*Delete as applicable.
†Note: The expression 'Supervising Officer' or 'Contract Administrator' is applicable where the nomination instruction will be issued under the Local Authorities versions of the Standard Form of Building Contract and by a person who is not entitled to the use of the name 'Architect' under and in accordance with the Architects (Registration) Acts 1931 to 1969. 'Supervising Officer' is used in those versions which **do not** incorporate Amendment 4 | issued July 1987 and 'Contract Administrator' those which **do** incorporate Amendment 4. If so, the expression 'Architect' shall be deemed to have been deleted throughout this Tender including the Schedules and in Agreement NSC/2. Where the person who will issue the nomination instruction is entitled to the use of the name 'Architect' the expression 'Supervising Officer' or 'Contract Administrator' shall be deemed to have been deleted.

7. Execution of Main Contract: *is/is to be
*under hand/under seal

8. Main Contract Conditions – alternative etc. provisions: Architect/Supervising Officer/Contract Administrator:
*Article 3A/Article 3B

WITHOUT Quantities versions only: *Article 4A/Article 4B

master programme: Clause 5·3·1·2 *deleted/not deleted

Works insurance: *Clause 22A   22B   22C·2 to·4

Insurance – liability of Employer   Clause 21·2·1   Insurance *may be required/is not required

Amount of indemnity for any one occurrence or series of occurrences arising out of one event

£...............

9. Main Contract Conditions – any changes from printed Standard Form identified in item 5:

10. Main Contract: Appendix and entries therein (as amended by Amendment 2 November 1986 and by Amendment 4 issued July 1987 to JCT 80) [f1]

	Clause etc.	
Statutory tax deduction scheme – Finance (No.2) Act 1975	Fourth recital and 31	Employer at Base Date is/is not a 'contractor' for the purposes of the Act and the Regulations.
†Settlement of disputes – Arbitration	Article 5·1 Articles 5·1·4 and 5·1·5 apply (see Articles 5·1·6)	
††Base Date	1·3	
Date of Completion	1·3 [j]	
Defects Liability Period (if none other stated is 6 months from the day named in the Certificate of Practical Completion of the Works)	17·2	
††Assignment by Employer of benefits after Practical Completion	19·1·2	Clause 19·1·2 applies/does not apply

*Delete as applicable.

†Delete if Main Contract incorporates Amendment 4: July 1987.

††Delete if Main Contract does **not** incorporate Amendment 4: July 1987.

10. Main Contract: Appendix *continued*

	Clause etc.	
Insurance cover for any one occurrence or series of occurrences arising out of one event	21·1·1	£
Insurance – liability of Employer	21·2·1	Insurance may be required/is not required Amount of indemnity of any one occurrence or series of occurrences arising out of one event £
Insurance of the Works – alternative clauses	22·1	Clause 22A/Clause 22B/Clause 22C applies
Percentage to cover professional fees	22A 22B·1 22C·2	
Annual renewal date of insurance as supplied by Contractor	22A·3·1	
Insurance for Employer's loss of liquidated damages – clause 25·4·3	22D	Insurance may be required/is not required
	22D·2	Period of time
Date of Possession	23·1·1	
††Deferment of the Date of Possession	23·1·2 25·4·13 26·1	Clause 23·1·2 applies/does not apply Period of deferment if it is to be less than 6 weeks is
Liquidated and ascertained damages	24·2	at the rate of ______ per ______
†Period of delay: (i) by reason of loss or damage caused by any one of the Specified Perils	28·1·3 28·1·3·2	
†(ii) for any other reason	28·1·3·1 28·1·3·3 to ·3·7	
††Period of delay:	28·1·3	
††Period of delay:	28A·1·1 28A·1·3	
††Period of delay:	28A·1·2	
Period of Interim Certificates (if none stated is one month)	30·1·3	
†Period of Final Measurement and Valuation (if none stated is 6 months from the day named in the Certificate of Practical Completion of the Works)	30·6·1·2	
†Period for issue of Final Certificate (if none stated is 3 months)	30·8	
Retention Percentage (if less than 5 per cent)	30·4·1·1	
Work reserved for Nominated Sub-Contractors for which the Contractor desires to tender	35·2	
Fluctuations: (if alternative required is not shown clause 38 shall apply)	37	clause 38 clause 39 clause 40
Percentage addition	38·7 or 39·8	
Formula Rules	40·1·1·1	
	rule 3	Base Month ______ 19___
	rule 3	Non-Adjustable Element [k] ______ % (not to exceed 10%)
	rules 10 and 30(i)	Part I/Part II of Section 2 of the Formula Rules is to apply
††Settlement of disputes – Arbitration – appointor (if no appointor is selected the appointor shall be the President or a Vice-President, Royal Institute of British Architects)	41·1	President or a Vice-President: Royal Institute of British Architects Royal Institution of Chartered Surveyors Chartered Institute of Arbitrators
††Settlement of disputes – Arbitration	41·2	Clauses 41·2·1 and 41·2·2 apply (See clause 41·2·3)

11. Order of Works Employer's requirements affecting the order of the Main Contract Works (if any).

12. Location and type of access.

13. Obligations or restrictions by the Employer not covered by Main Contract Conditions:
(e.g. in Preliminaries in the Contract Bills) [l]

14. Other relevant information: (if any)

Signed by or on behalf of the Sub-Contractor Information noted ______

†Delete if Main Contract incorporates Amendment 4: July 1987. ††Delete if Main Contract does **not** incorporate Amendment 4: July 1987.

Fluctuations

See Tender NSC/1 page 3, item 2

Notes:
Complete column (1) where Sub-Contract NSC/4, clause 35 applies.
Complete columns (1)-(4) where Sub-Contract NSC/4, clause 36 etc. applies.

The †Date of Tender/††Base Date [n] for the purposes of Sub-Contract NSC/4, clauses 35/36.
is ______

(1) Materials, goods, electricity and fuels [o]	(2) Rate (or appropriate standard price list description)	(3) Discounts	(4) Unit to which rate applies

Signed by or on behalf of the Sub-Contractor

Date

Note: Architect/Supervising Officer/Contract Administrator and Sub-Contractor to complete this Appendix as appropriate where Sub-Contract NSC/4, clause 37 applies.

1. 37·1 – Sub-Contract/Works Contract Formula Rules dated December 1987
*Part I/Part III of these Rules applies
2. 37·3·3 and ·3·4 – Non-Adjustable Element [p] ______ % (not to exceed 10%)
3. 37·4 – List of Market Prices
4. Sub-Contract/Works Contract Formula Rules
rule 3 (Definition of Balance of Adjustable Work)
Any measured work not allocated to a Work Category

Base Month (rule 3) ______

Base Date (rule 3) ______

rule 8 Method of dealing with 'Fix-only' work

rule 11(a) or 11(b) Part I only: the Work Categories applicable to the Sub-Contract Works

rule 43 Part III only: Weightings of labour and materials – Electrical Installations or Heating, Ventilating and Air Conditioning Installations or Sprinkler Installations [q]

	Labour	Materials
Electrical	______%	______%
Heating, Ventilating and Air Conditioning [r]	______%	______%
Sprinkler Installations	______%	______%

rule 55a The separate materials index for sprinkler installations
*will/will not apply

rule 61a Adjustment shall be effected for Lift Installations:
*upon completion of manufacture of all fabricated components
*upon delivery to site of all fabricated components

rule 64 Part III only: Structural Steelwork Installations:
(i) Average price per tonne of steel delivered to fabricator's work
£ ______

(ii) Average price per tonne for erection of steelwork
£ ______

rule 70a Catering Equipment Installations:
apportionment of the value of each item between
(i) materials and shop fabrication £ ______
(ii) supply of factor items £ ______
(iii) site installations £ ______

Signed by or on behalf of the Sub-Contractor

Date

*Delete as applicable.

†Delete if Main Contract incorporates Amendment 4: July 1987. ††Delete if Main Contract does **not** incorporate Amendment 4: July 1987.

42.08 Schedule 1, paragraph 11 relates to the employer's requirements affecting the order of the main contract works (if any). Presumably it is envisaged that there will here be reproduced any requirements in the bills or other contract documents relating to these matters.

42.09 An architect must clearly be astute to ensure that this part of NSC/1 is completed correctly; however, under the fourth recital to NSC/2, 'nothing contained in this agreement nor anything contained in the tender is intended to render the Architect . . . in any way liable to the sub-contractor in relation to matters in the said agreement and tender'.

42.10 Apart from this exemption clause, it is thought that the architect could be liable to the contractor for negligence on

the principle laid down in *Hedley Byrne* v *Heller & partners* [1964] AC 465, if he negligently made statements in completing NSC/1 which were incorrect and caused economic loss to the sub-contractor, although the architect's obligation would not be one of utmost good faith, but merely to take reasonable care to make disclosure of information in his possession which he ought reasonably to have considered necessary to enable the sub-contractor to form a proper view of the scope of the works. Alternatively, the statements in NSC/1 might constitute a collateral contract whereby the employer guaranteed that the site conditions, etc., would be as stated in NSC/1 and for which liability in damages might arise. The exemption clause may give some protection against such liability, although the precise extent of this protection is highly doubtful having regard to the provisions of the Unfair Contract Terms Act 1977 and the rules relating to the construction of exemption clauses at law. Therefore, the architect must be extremely careful to ensure that the information contained in NSC/1 is as full and accurate as possible; where it is not possible to give full details, it is suggested the proposed sub-contractor should be warned expressly of this fact.

Fluctuations

42.11 The relevant part of Schedule 1, Appendices A and B are to be completed depending upon which of the methods of fluctuations provided for in clauses 35 to 37 of NSC/4 is to be used. SCF clause 35 relates to partial fluctuations (i.e. those caused by changes in rates of contribution, levy, or tax) and clause 36 to 'full' fluctuations. Clause 37 relates to full fluctuations in accordance with the formula rules issued by the JCT.

Schedule 2

42.12 Under MF clause 35.7, once the sub-contractor had tendered on NSC/1 and entered into Agreement NSC/2, the main contractor prior to nomination of the sub-contractor is to be instructed forthwith to settle with the proposed sub-contractor any of the particular conditions in Schedule 2 which remain to be agreed. If these negotiations fail, the proposed sub-contractor may withdraw, and if they are successful the architect, once agreement is reached, nominates the proposed sub-contractor (MF clause 35.10.2).

Schedule 2: Particular Conditions

Note: When the Contractor receives Tender NSC/1 together with the Architect's/Supervising Officer's/Contract Administrator's preliminary notice of nomination under clause 35·7·1 of the Main Contract Conditions then the Contractor has to settle and complete any of the particular conditions which remain to be completed in this Schedule in agreement with the proposed Sub-Contractor. The completed Schedule should take account not only of the preliminary indications of the Sub-Contractor stated therein, but also of any particular conditions or requirements of the Contractor which he may wish to raise with the Sub-Contractor.

1.A Any stipulation as to the period, periods when Sub-Contract Works can be carried out on site: [s]

to be between _____ and _____

Period required by Architect to approve drawings after submission _____

1.B Preliminary programme details [t] (having regard to the information provided in the invitation to tender)

Periods required:

(1) for submission of all further sub-contractors drawings etc. (co-ordination, installation, shop or builders' work, or other as appropriate) [u]

(2) for execution of Sub-Contract Works: off-site _____

on-site _____

Notice required to commence work on site _____

1.C Agreed programme details (including sub-contract completion date: see also Sub Contract NSC/4, clause 11·1) [v]

2. Order of Works to follow the requirements, if any, stated in Schedule 1, item 11 [w]

3.A   Attendance proposals (other than †general attendance). [x]

(a) Special scaffolding or scaffolding additional to the Contractor's standing scaffolding.

(b) The provision of temporary access roads and hardstandings in connection with structural steelwork, precast concrete components, piling, heavy items of plant and the like.

(c) Unloading, distributing, hoisting and placing in position giving in the case of significant items the weight and/or size. (To be at the risk of the Sub-Contractor).

(d) The provision of covered storage and accommodation including lighting and power thereto.

(e) Power supplies giving the maximum load.

(f) Maintenance of specific temperature or humidity levels.

(g) Any other attendance not included under (a) to (f) or as †general attendance under Sub-Contract NSC/4, paragraph 27·1·1.

3.B   [y]

4.   Insurance [z]

5.A Employment of Labour – Special Conditions or Agreements [aa]

5.B Employment of Labour – Special Conditions or Agreements [bb]

6.   The Adjudicator is: [cc]

The Trustee – Stakeholder is: [cc]

7.   Finance (No. 2 Act 1975 – Statutory Tax Deduction Scheme) [dd]

1. The Contractor* is/is not entitled to be paid by the Employer without the statutory deduction referred to in the above Act or such other deduction as may be in force;

2. The Sub-Contractor* is/is not entitled to be paid by the Contractor without the above-mentioned statutory deduction or such other deduction;

3. The evidence to be produced to the Contractor for the verification of the Sub-Contractor's tax certificate (expiry date   19   ) will be:

8.   Value Added Tax – Sub-Contract NSC/4 Clause 19A/19B [ee] (alternative VAT provisions) will apply.

9.A Any other matters (including any limitation on working hours). [ff]

9.B [gg]

10. Any matters agreed by the Architect/Supervising Officer/Contract Administrator and Sub-Contractor before preliminary notice of nomination. [s]

11. Sub-Contract NSC/4 Edition as identified in Schedule 1, Item 1 to be executed under hand/under seal [ee] forthwith after Architect's/Supervising Officer's/Contract Administrator's nomination on Nomination NSC/3.

The above Particular Conditions are agreed

Signed by or on behalf of   Date
the Sub-Contractor

Signed by or on behalf
of the Main Contractor   Date

†Note: For general attendance see clause 27·1·1 of Sub-Contract NSC/4 which states: "General attendance shall be provided by the Contractor free of charge to the Sub-Contractor and shall be deemed to include only use of the Contractor's temporary roads, pavings and paths, standing scaffolding, standing power operated hoisting plant, the provision of temporary lighting and water supplies, clearing away rubbish, provision of space for the Sub-Contractor's own offices and for the storage of his plant and materials and the use of messrooms, sanitary accommodation and welfare materials." See SMM, 6 edn., B 9.2.

42.13 The procedure for completing Schedule 2 will normally be as follows: the architect will complete items 1 A and 10 when sending out NSC/1 to the proposed sub-contractor for tender. The sub-contractor, when returning NSC/1, will complete item 3A showing his proposals for attendance. Thereafter, the document will be transmitted by the architect to the contractor, who will then agree with the nominated sub-contractor the remaining outstanding matters (in so far as not yet agreed).

42.14 The purpose of the machinery contained in Schedule 2 is so far as possible to ensure that before a nomination is made of a proposed sub-contractor full agreement is reached among architect, contractor, and sub-contractor as to the precise details of such matters as programme and attendances relating to the sub-contract works, and thereby to obviate later difficulties, misunderstandings, and attendant claims.

Basic and alternative methods

42.15 NSC/1 is employed only where the basic method of nomination (as defined in MF clause 35.11) is used. Where the alternative method is employed, NSC/1 is not used.

43 JCT Standard Form of Employer/Nominated Sub-contractor Agreement (Agreement NSC/2)

General

43.01 At common law there is no direct contractual relationship between an employer and a sub-contractor. The employer's contract is with the main contractor, who is solely responsible as against the employer for the performance of the work and solely entitled to payment from him. Agreement NSC/2, however, constitutes a direct contract between the employer and the nominated sub-contractor covering a number of matters. Its provisions should be read in conjunction with MF clause 35.

JCT

JCT Standard Form of Employer/Nominated Sub-Contractor Agreement

Agreement between a Sub-Contractor to be nominated for Sub-Contract Work in accordance with clauses 35·6 to 35·10 of the Standard Form of Building Contract for a main contract and the Employer referred to in the main contract.

Main Contract Works: ____________________

Location: ____________________

Sub-Contract Works: ____________________

This Agreement

The date to be inserted here must be the date when the Tender NSC/1 is signed as 'approved' by the Architect/the Contract Administrator on behalf of the Employer

is made the __________ day of __________ 19 ______

between ____________________

of or whose registered office is situated at ____________________

____

(hereinafter called 'the Employer') and

____

of or whose registered office is situated at ____________________

____

(hereinafter called 'the Sub-Contractor')

Whereas

First — the Sub-Contractor has submitted a tender on Tender NSC/1 (hereinafter called 'the Tender') on the terms and conditions in that Tender to carry out Works (referred to above and hereinafter called 'the Sub-Contract Works') as part of the Main Contract Works referred to above to be or being carried out on the terms and conditions relating thereto referred to in Schedule 1 of the Tender (hereinafter called 'the Main Contract');

Second — the Employer has appointed

____

to be the Architect/the Contract Administrator for the purposes of the Main Contract and this Agreement (hereinafter called 'the Architect/the Contract Administrator' which expression as used in this Agreement shall include his successors validly appointed under the Main Contract or otherwise before the Main Contract is operative);

Third — the Architect/the Contract Administrator on behalf of the Employer has approved the Tender and intends that after agreement between the Contractor and Sub-Contractor on the Particular Conditions in Schedule 2 thereof an instruction on Nomination NSC/3 shall be issued to the Contractor for the Main Contract (hereinafter called 'the Main Contractor') nominating the Sub-Contractor to carry out and complete the Sub-Contract Works on the terms and conditions of the Tender;

Fourth — nothing contained in this Agreement nor anything contained in the Tender is intended to render the Architect/the Contract Administrator in any way liable to the Sub-Contractor in relation to matters in the said Agreement and Tender.

Now it is hereby agreed

Completion of Tender Sub-Contractor's obligations

1·1 The Sub-Contractor shall, after the Architect/the Contract Administrator has issued his preliminary notice of nomination under clause 35·7·1 of the Main Contract Conditions, forthwith seek to settle with the Main Contractor the Particular Conditions in Schedule 2 of the Tender.

1·2 The Sub-Contractor shall, upon reaching agreement with the Main Contractor on the Particular Conditions in Schedule 2 of the Tender and after that Schedule is signed by or on behalf of the Sub-Contractor and the Main Contractor, immediately through the Main Contractor so inform the Architect/the Contract Administrator.

Design, materials, performance specification

2·1 The Sub-Contractor warrants that he has exercised and will exercise all reasonable skill and care in

·1 the design of the Sub-Contract Works insofar as the Sub-Contract Works have been or will be designed by the Sub-Contractor; and

·2 the selection of materials and goods for the Sub-Contract Works insofar as such materials and goods have been or will be selected by the Sub-Contractor; and

·3 the satisfaction of any performance specification or requirement insofar as such performance specification or requirement is included or referred to in the description of the Sub-Contract Works included in or annexed to the Tender.

Nothing in clause 2·1 shall be construed so as to affect the obligations of the Sub-Contractor under Sub-Contract NSC/4 in regard to the supply under the Sub-Contract of workmanship, materials and goods.

2·2 ·1 If, after the date of this Agreement and before the issue by the Architect/the Contract Administrator of the instruction on Nomination NSC/3 under clause 35·10·2 of the Main Contract Conditions, the Architect/the Contract Administrator instructs in writing that the Sub-Contractor should proceed with

·1 the designing of, or

·2 the purchase under a contract of sale of materials or goods or the fabrication of components for

the Sub-Contract Works the Sub-Contractor shall forthwith comply with the instruction and the Employer shall make payment or reimbursement for such compliance in accordance with clauses 2·2·2 to 2·2·4.

·2 No payment or reimbursement referred to in clauses 2·2·3 and 2·2·4 shall be made after the issue of Nomination NSC/3 under clause 35·10·2 of the Main Contract Conditions except in respect of any design work properly carried out and/or materials or goods properly ordered under a contract of sale or components properly fabricated in compliance with an instruction under clause 2·2·1 but which are not used for the Sub-Contract Works by reason of some written decision against such use given by the Architect/the Contract Administrator before the issue of Nomination NSC/3 of the Main Contract Conditions.

·3 The Employer shall pay the Sub-Contractor the amount of any expense reasonably and properly incurred by the Sub-Contractor in carrying out work in the designing of the Sub-Contract Works and upon such payment the Employer may use that work for the purpose of the Sub-Contract Works but not further or otherwise.

·4 The Employer shall pay the Sub-Contractor for any component properly fabricated and shall reimburse the Sub-Contractor for any amounts properly due and paid by the Sub-Contractor under the contract of sale for materials or goods properly purchased by the Sub-Contractor for the Sub-Contract Works and upon such payment or reimbursement the materials and goods shall become the property of the Employer.

·5 If any payment or reimbursement has been made by the Employer under clauses 2·2·3 and 2·2·4 and the Sub-Contractor is subsequently nominated in Nomination NSC/3 issued under clause 35·10·2 of the Main Contract Conditions to execute the Sub-Contract Works the Sub-Contractor shall allow to the Main Contractor or, where clause 35·13·6 of the Main Contract Conditions is operated, to the Employer full credit for such payment or reimbursement in the discharge of the amount due in respect of the Sub-Contract Works and the Sub-Contractor shall provide the Employer with a written statement, in duplicate, of the amount so credited. Provided that no credit shall be so allowed in respect of payments or reimbursements made by the Employer for design work properly carried out and/or materials or goods properly purchased under a contract of sale and/or components properly fabricated in compliance with an instruction under clause 2·2·1 but which are not used by reason of some written decision against such use by the Architect/the Contract Administrator before the issue of Nomination NSC/3 under clause 35·10·2 of the Main Contract Conditions.

Delay in supply of information and in performance by Sub-Contractor

3·1 The Sub-Contractor will not be liable under clauses 3·2, 3·3 or 3·4 until the Architect/the Contract Administrator has issued his instruction on Nomination NSC/3 under clause 35·10·2 of the Main Contract Conditions nor in respect of any revised period of time for delay in carrying out or completing the Sub-Contract Works which the Sub-Contractor has been granted under clause 11·2 of Sub-Contract NSC/4.

3·2 The Sub-Contractor shall so supply the Architect/the Contract Administrator with information (including drawings) in accordance with the agreed programme details or at such time as the Architect/the Contract Administrator may reasonably require so that the Architect/the Contract Administrator will not be delayed in issuing necessary instructions or drawings under the Main Contract, for which delay the Main Contractor may have a valid claim to an extension of time for completion of the Main Contract Works by reason of the Relevant Event in clause 25·4·6 or a valid claim for direct loss and/or expense under clause 26·2·1 of the Main Contract Conditions.

3·3 The Sub-Contractor shall so perform his obligations under the Sub-Contract that the Architect/the Contract Administrator will not by reason of any default by the Sub-Contractor be under a duty to issue an instruction to determine the employment of the Sub-Contractor under clause 35·24 of the Main Contract Conditions provided that any suspension by the Sub-Contractor of further execution of the Sub-Contract Works under clause 21·8 of Sub-Contract NSC/4 shall not be regarded as a 'default by the Sub-Contractor' as referred to in clause 3·3.

3·4 The Sub-Contractor shall so perform the Sub-Contract that the Contractor will not become entitled to an extension of time for completion of the Main Contract Works by reason of the Relevant Event in clause 25·4·7 of the Main Contract Conditions.

Architect's direction on value of Sub-Contract Work in Interim Certificates information to Sub-Contractor

4 The Architect/The Contract Administrator shall operate the provisions of [**a**] clause 35·13·1 of the Main Contract Conditions.

Employer's duty – final payment for Sub-Contract Works

5·1 The Architect/The Contract Administrator shall operate the provisions in [**b**] clauses 35·17 to 35·19 of the Main Contract Conditions.

Discharge of final payment to Sub-Contractor – Sub-Contractor's obligations

5·2 After due discharge by the Contractor of a final payment under clause 35·17 of the Main Contract Conditions the Sub-Contractor shall rectify at his own cost (or if he fails so to rectify, shall be liable to the Employer for the costs referred to in clause 35·18 of the Main Contract Conditions) any omission, fault or defect in the Sub-Contract Works which the Sub-Contractor is bound to rectify under Sub-Contract NSC/4 after written notification thereof by the Architect/the Contract Administrator at any time before the issue of the Final Certificate under clause 30·8 of the Main Contract Conditions.

Footnotes

[**a**] Note: Clause 35·13·1 requires that the Architect/the Contract Administrator, upon directing the Main Contractor as to the amount included in any Interim Certificates in respect of the value of the Nominated Sub-Contract Works issued under clause 30 of the Main Contract Conditions, shall forthwith inform the Sub-Contractor in writing of that amount.

[**b**] Note: Clause 35·17 deals with final payment by the Employer for Sub-Contract Works prior to the issue of the Final Certificate under the Main Contract Conditions.

5·3 After the issue of the Final Certificate under the Main Contract Conditions the Sub-Contractor shall in addition to such other responsibilities, if any, as he has under this Agreement, have the like responsibility to the Main Contractor and to the Employer for the Sub-Contract Works as the Main Contractor has to the Employer under the terms of the Main Contract relating to the obligations of the Contractor after the issue of the Final Certificate.

Architect's instructions - duty to make a further nomination - liability of Sub-Contractor

6 Where the Architect/the Contract Administrator has been under a duty under clause 35·24 of the Main Contract Conditions except as a result of the operation of clause 35·24·6 to issue an instruction to the Main Contractor making a further nomination in respect of the Sub-Contract Works, the Sub-Contractor shall indemnify the Employer against any direct loss and/or expense resulting from the exercise by the Architect/the Contract Administrator of that duty.

Architect's certificate of non-discharge by Contractor - payment to Sub-Contractor by Employer

7·1 The Architect/The Contract Administrator and the Employer shall operate the provisions in regard to the payment of the Sub-Contractor in clause 35·13 of the Main Contract Conditions.

7·2 If, after paying any amount to the Sub-Contractor under clause 35·13·5·3 of the Main Contract Conditions, the Employer produces reasonable proof that there was in existence at the time of such payment a petition or resolution to which clause 35·13·5·4·4 of the Main Contract Conditions refers, the Sub-Contractor shall repay on demand such amount.

Conditions in contracts for purchase of goods and materials - Sub-Contractor's duty

8 Where [**c**] clause 2·3 of Sub-Contract NSC/4 applies, the Sub-Contractor shall forthwith supply to the Contractor details of any restriction, limitation or exclusion to which that clause refers as soon as such details are known to the Sub-Contractor.

Assignment

8A Where clause 19·1·2 of the Main Contract applies then, in the event of transfer by the Employer of his freehold or leasehold interest in, or of a grant by the Employer of a leasehold interest in, the whole of the premises comprising the Works, the Employer may at any time after Practical Completion of the Works assign to any such transferee or lessee the right to bring proceedings in the name of the Employer (whether by arbitration or litigation) to enforce any of the terms of this Agreement made for the benefit of the Employer hereunder. The assignee shall be estopped from disputing any enforceable agreements reached between the Employer and the Sub-Contractor and which arise out of and relate to this Agreement (whether or not they are or appear to be a derogation from the rights assigned) and made prior to the date of any assignment.

Conflict between Tender and Agreement

9 If any conflict appears between the terms of the Tender and this Agreement, the terms of this Agreement shall prevail.

Arbitration

10·1 In case any dispute or difference shall arise between the Employer or the Architect/the Contract Administrator on his behalf and the Sub-Contractor, either during the progress or after the completion or abandonment of the Sub-Contract Works, as to the construction of this Agreement, or as to any matter or thing of whatsoever nature arising out of this Agreement or in connection therewith, then such dispute or difference shall be and is hereby referred to the arbitration and final decision of a person to be agreed between the parties, or, failing agreement within 14 days after either party has given to the other a written request to concur in the appointment of an Arbitrator, a person to be appointed on the request of either party by the President or a Vice President for the time being of the Royal Institute of British Architects.

10·2 ·1 Provided that if the dispute or difference to be referred to arbitration under this Agreement raises issues which are substantially the same as or connected with issues raised in a related dispute between the Employer and the contractor under the Main Contract or between the Sub-Contractor and the Contractor under Sub-Contract NSC/4 or NSC/4a or between the Employer and any other Nominated Sub-Contractor under Agreement NSC/2 or NSC/2a or between the Employer and any Nominated Supplier whose contract of sale with the Main Contractor provides for the matters referred to in clause 36·4·8 of the Main Contract Conditions, and if the related dispute has already been referred for determination to an Arbitrator, the Employer and the Sub-Contractor hereby agree that the dispute or difference under this Agreement shall be referred to the Arbitrator appointed to determine the related dispute; such Arbitrator shall have power to make such directions and all necessary awards in the same way as if the procedure of the High Court as to joining one or more defendants or joining co-defendants or third parties was available to the parties and to him; and the agreement and consent referred to in clause 10·5 on appeals or applications to the High Court on any question of law shall apply to any question of law arising out of the awards of such arbitrator in respect of all related disputes referred to him or arising in the course of the reference of all the related disputes referred to him.

10·2 ·2 Save that the Employer or the Sub-Contractor may require the dispute or difference under this Agreement to be referred to a different Arbitrator (to be appointed under this Agreement) if either of them reasonably considers that the Arbitrator appointed to determine the related dispute is not appropriately qualified to determine the dispute or difference under this Agreement.

10·2 ·3 Clauses 10·2·1 and 10·2·2 shall apply unless in the Appendix to the Main Contract Conditions the words 'clauses 41·2·1 and 41·2·2 apply' have been deleted.

10·3 Such reference shall not be opened until after Practical Completion or alleged Practical Completion of the Main Contract Works or termination or alleged termination of the Contractor's employment under the Main Contract or abandonment of the Main Contract Works, unless with the written consent of the Employer or the Architect/the Contract Administrator on his behalf and the Sub-Contractor.

10·4 Subject to clause 10·5 the award of such Arbitrator shall be final and binding on the parties.

10·5 The parties hereby agree and consent pursuant to Sections 1(3)(a) and 2(1)(b) of the Arbitration Act 1979, that either party

·1 may appeal to the High Court on any question of law arising out of an award made in an arbitration under this Arbitration Agreement and

·2 may apply to the High Court to determine any question of law arising in the course of the reference;

and the parties agree that the High Court should have jurisdiction to determine any question of law.

10·6[**d**] Whatever the nationality, residence or domicile of the Employer, the Contractor, any Sub-Contractor or supplier or the Arbitrator, and wherever the Works or any part thereof are situated, the law of England shall be the proper law of this Agreement and in particular (but not so as to derogate from the generality of the foregoing) the provisions of the Arbitration Acts 1950 (not withstanding anything in S·34 thereof) to 1979 shall apply to any arbitration under clause 10 wherever the same, or any part of it, shall be conducted.

Signed by or on behalf of the Sub-Contractor [**e1**] ______________________

in the presence of:

Signed by or on behalf of the Employer [**e1**] ______________________

in the presence of:

Signed, sealed and delivered by [**e2**]/The Common seal of [**e3**]: ______________________

in the presence of [**e2**]/was hereunto affixed in the presence of [**e3**]:

Signed, sealed and delivered by [**e2**]/The common seal of [**e3**]: ______________________

in the presence of [**e2**]/was hereunto affixed in the presence of [**e3**]:

Footnote

[**c**] Note: Clause 2·3 deals with specified supplies and restrictions etc. in the contracts of sale for such supplies.

[**d**] Where the parties do not wish the proper law of the contract to be the law of England and/or do not wish the provisions of the Arbitration Acts 1950 to 1979 to apply to any arbitration under the Contract held under the procedural law of Scotland (or other country) appropriate amendments to Clause 10·5 should be made.

[**e1**] For use if Agreement is executed under hand.

[**e2**] For use if executed under seal by an individual or firm or unincorporated body.

[**e3**] For use if executed under seal by a company or other body corporate.

43.02 It is of utmost importance that the architect ensure that NSC/2 (or NSC/2a where the alternative method of nomination is employed) is employed whenever a sub-contractor is to be nominated. This is particularly important, since under MF clasue 35.21, the contractor is not responsible to the employer in relation to defects in the nominated sub-contract works for which the sub-contractor is directly liable to the employer under clause 2 of NSC/2 whether or not any nominated sub-contractor is *in fact* responsible to the employer under NSC/2 or NSC/2a.

Further, the employer's right to make deductions from payments to the contractor in respect of defects in the nominated sub-contract works is conditional (under MF clause 35.18.1.2) on the employer taking steps under NSC/2 or NSC/2a as appropriate first.

43.03 It is important to note that NSC/2 only binds the proposed sub-contractor where both the employer has signed NSC/1 and the employer and sub-contractor have signed NSC/2 (see NSC/1 cause 1). Architects must be extremely careful to ensure the procedure is properly operated.

43.04 The agreement is made between the employer and the sub-contractor, and begins with a number of recitals. It is envisaged that NSC/2 will not be signed until the architect approves the tender submitted by the sub-contractor on form NSC/1. It must be borne in mind that the signing of NSC/2 does not of itself mean that a sub-contract will be concluded between the employer and the proposed sub-contractor, since the proposed sub-contractor may still withdraw in the circumstances specified in the stipulations contained in NSC/1. These are:

1. Where the original tender was submitted when the identity of the main contractor was unknown, in which case the proposed sub-contractor can withdraw within 14 days of the main contractor's identity becoming known.
2. In the event of failure to agree the matters contained in Schedule 2 to NSC/1.
3. In the event of a nomination not being made within a specified period.

The effect of the fourth recital is discussed in para 42.09.

Clause 2

43.05 Clause 2.1 contains warranties by the sub-contractor as to the fitness of his design, quality of materials, and fitness for specified purpose. If a fault occurs which is not caused by the sub-contractor's negligence (e.g. an undiscoverable defect in a batch of material) he is not liable to the employer.

Clause 2.2

43.06 This enables the architect to order the sub-contractor to start design or fabrication work before a formal nomination, and is very useful where there are long lead-in times for specialist mechanical and electrical services, for example.

Clause 3

43.07 Under MF clauses 25 and 26, the contractor may claim from the employer an extension of time and loss of expense if delay or disturbance to the regular progress of the work is caused by a nominated sub-contractor. Under clause 3 the sub-contractor warrants to the employer that he will carry out his work in a way that will not give rise to a claim under these clauses of the Main Contract, thereby enabling the employer, in effect, to reclaim from the sub-contractor any amount he has to pay to the main contractor under MF clauses 25 and 26 arising out of default of the sub-contractor. Further, the sub-contractor agrees not to carry out his work in such a way that it will be necessary to determine his employment under

MF clause 34.24. However, it is made clear in the proviso to clause 3.3 that where the sub-contractor is entitled to suspend execution of the works under SCF clause 21.8, he is not liable under this clause.

43.08 Under clause 3.4 the sub-contractor agrees so to perform his sub-contract that the contractor will not become entitled to an extension of time under MF clause 25.4.7. This is curiously drafted, since it does not seem to be confined to delay caused by the particular sub-contractor in question, nor to relevant events for which the nominated sub-contractor is not himself entitled to an extension. Probably the court would imply these two restrictions.

Clause 4

43.09 The architect agrees to give the sub-contractor information as to the amounts contained in interim certificates as due to the nominated sub-contractor.

Clause 5

43.10 Under MF clauses 35.17 to 35.19, each nominated sub-contractor's work may be the subject of a separate final certificate, and clause 5 contains provisions incidental to those provisions of the Main Contract. The sub-contractor agrees to rectify defects occurring before the issue of the final certificate relating to the work as a whole, and under clause 5.3, the sub-contractor's responsibilities to the main contractor and to the employer after the issue of the final certificate relating to the works as a whole are to be co-extensive with the responsibilities of the main contractor to the employer under clause 30.9 of the Main Contract.

Clause 6

43.11 Where the sub-contractor has his employment determined under clause 35.24 for one of the reasons specified in SCF clause 29.1, the employer becomes under a duty to nominate a new sub-contractor to complete the work; almost inevitably the cost of completing the work with the aid of another sub-contractor will be higher than the amount which would have been paid to the original nominated sub-contractor had he continued with the work, and clause 6 obliges the original nominated sub-contractor to indemnify the employer against this loss. There is an exception where the sub-contractor was entitled to determine his employment under SCF clause 30 where the main contractor without reasonable cause wholly suspends the main contract works before completion, or without reasonable cause fails to proceed with the main contract works so that the reasonable progress of the sub-contract works is seriously affected.

Clause 7

43.12 The architect and the employer agree to operate the 'direct payment' provisions of MF clause 35 where the contractor fails to make payment to the nominated sub-contractor. The provision for repayment in clause 7.2 accords with the scheme of the 'direct payment' clause whereby it ceases to have effect on the bankruptcy of the main contractor. The reason for this is that it is doubtful whether a clause entitling the employer to make direct payment to sub-contractors after the bankruptcy of the main contractor would bind the contractor's liquidator, and therefore the employer might have to make payments for the work done by the nominated sub-contractor to the contractor's liquidator irrespective of the fact that payment has already been made to the sub-contractor in respect of the same work.

Clause 10

43.13 Clause 10.2.1 is designed to give effect to the 'third-party' procedure introduced for arbitration under the

JCT Forms, and which as between employer and main contractor is set out in MF article 5, to which reference should be made.

44 JCT Standard Form of Employer/ Nominated Sub-contractor Agreement (Agreement NSC/2a)

44.01 This agreement is substantially in the same form as NSC/2, but it is to be used where the alternative method of nomination envisaged by MF clauses 35.11 and 35.12 is used. For the advantages and disadvantages of the basic and alternative methods of nomination see para 39.13.

45 JCT Standard Form of Nomination of Sub-contractor where Tender NSC/1 has been used (Nomination NSC/3)

45.01 This document forms the last stage in the nomination process, and is issued under MF clause 35.10.2 where the basic method of nomination is used and clause 35.11.2 where the alternative method is employed. Where the basic method is used, a binding contract on form NSC/4 and incorporating the matters agreed between contractor and sub-contractor under MF clause 35.7 comes into existence. Where the alternative method is used, the contractor under clause 35.12 is to proceed so as to conclude a sub-contract in form NSC/4a within 14 days of the nomination.

46 JCT Standard Form of Tender by Nominated Supplier (TNS/1) and Warranty by a Nominated Supplier (TNS/2)

46.01 These two documents are considered together since the Warranty TNS/2 forms Schedule 3 to TNS/1 and is to be used in conjunction with it, unless clause 3 of TNS/1 is deleted.

JCT Standard Form of Tender by Nominated Supplier

For use in connection with the Standard Form of Building Contract (SFBC) issued by the Joint Contracts Tribunal, 1980 edition, current revision

Job Title
(name and brief location of Works)

Employer *

Main Contractor *
(if known)

Tender for *
(abbreviated description)

Name of Tenderer

To be returned to *

Lump sum price *£

(words)

and/or Schedule of rates (attached)

1 We confirm that we will be under a contract with the Main Contractor:

  .1 to supply the materials or goods described or referred to in **Schedule 1** for the price and/or at the rate set out above; and

  .2 in accordance with the other terms set out in that Schedule, as a Nominated Supplier in accordance with the terms of SFBC clause 36·3 to ·5 (as set out in **Schedule 2**) and our conditions of sale in so far as they do not conflict with the terms of SFBC clause 36·3 to ·5

provided:

  .3 the Architect/Supervising Officer has issued the relevant nomination instruction (a copy of which has been sent to us by the Architect/Supervising Officer); and

  .4 agreement on delivery between us and the Main Contractor has been reached as recorded in **Schedule 1** Part 6 (see SFBC clause 36·4·3); and

  .5 we have thereafter received an order from the Main Contractor accepting this tender.

2   We agree that this Tender shall be open for acceptance by an order from the Main Contractor within   (d) of the date of this Tender. Provided that where the Main Contractor has not been named above we reserve the right to withdraw this Tender within 14 days of having been notified, by or on behalf of the Employer named above, of the name of the Main Contractor.

3(a)   Subject to our right to withdraw this Tender as set out in paragraph 2 we hereby declare that we accept the Warranty Agreement in the terms set out in **Schedule 3** hereto on condition that no provision in that Warranty Agreement shall take effect unless and until

          a copy to us of the instruction nominating us,
          the order of the Main Contractor accepting this Tender, and
          a copy of the Warranty Agreement signed by the Employer

        have been received by us.

        For and on behalf of

        Address
        Signature   Date

(a) To be completed by or on behalf of the Architect/Supervising Officer

(b) To be completed by the supplier: see also Schedule 1 item 7

(c) By SFBC clause 36·4·9 none of the provisions in the contract of sale can override, modify or affect in any way the provisions incorporated from SFBC clause 36·4 in that contract of sale. Nominated Suppliers should therefore take steps to ensure that their sale conditions do not incorporate any provisions which purport to override, modify or affect in any way the provisions incorporated from SFBC clause 36·4

(d) May be completed by or on behalf of the Architect/Supervising Officer, if not so completed, to be completed by the supplier

(e) To be struck out by or on behalf of the Architect/Supervising Officer if no Warranty Agreement is required

Schedule 1

1.   Description, quantity and quality of materials or goods:

      1A

      1B

      1C

Note: 1A to be completed by or on behalf of the Architect/Supervising Officer setting out his requirements. If the supplier is unable to comply with 1A he is to state in 1B what modifications he proposes, and the Architect/Supervising Officer is to state in 1C if such modifications are acceptable.

2.   Access to Works:

      2A

      2B

Note: 2A to be completed by or on behalf of the Architect/Supervising Officer. The supplier in 2B either confirms that the access in 2A is acceptable or states what modifications etc. to the access he requires or if 2A has not been completed, completes 2B.

3.   Provisions, if any, for returnable packings:

4.   Completion Date of Main Contract (or anticipated Completion Date if Main Contract not let):

Note: To be completed by or on behalf of the Architect/Supervising Officer.

5.   Defects Liability Period of the Main Contract   months.

Note: To be completed by or on behalf of the Architect/Supervising Officer.

6A Anticipated commencement and completion dates for the nominated supply after any necessary approval of drawings (subject to SFBC clause 36·4·3, which provides that delivery shall be commenced, carried out and completed in accordance with any delivery programme agreed between the Contractor and supplier or in the absence of such programme in accordance with the reasonable directions of the Contractor):

6B ·1   Supplier's proposed delivery programme to comply with 6A:

     ·2   If 6B·1 not completed, delivery programme shall be to the reasonable directions of the Contractor.

6C Delivery programme as agreed between the supplier and the Contractor, if different from 6B:

Note: 6A to be completed by or on behalf of the Architect/Supervising Officer. The supplier to complete 6B·1 to take account of 6A; but the completion of 6B·1 is subject to the terms of 6C which may need to be used when the Contractor and supplier are settling item 6.

7.   Provisions, if any, for fluctuations in price or rates:

      7A

      7B

      7C

Note: 7A to be completed by or on behalf of the Architect/Supervising Officer. If the supplier is unable to comply with 7A he is to state in 7B what modifications to the provisions in 7A he requires, and the Architect/Supervising Officer is to state in 7C if such modifications are acceptable.

8.   SFBC clause 25 (extensions of time) applies to the Main Contract without modification except as stated below:

The liquidated and ascertained damages (SFBC clause 2·4·2 and Appendix entry) under the Main Contract are at the rate of £ _____ per _____

Note: To be completed by or on behalf of the Architect/Supervising Officer.

9.   Contract of sale with Contractor to be under hand/under seal.

Note: Alternative not to be used to be deleted by the supplier subject to agreement on the method of execution of the sale contract with the Main Contractor.

Schedule 2

JCT Standard Form of Building Contract

Clause 36·3 to ·8 provides as follows:

Ascertainment of costs to be set against prime cost sum

36·3   ·1   For the purposes of clause 30·6·2·8 the amounts "properly chargeable to the Employer in accordance with the nomination instruction of the Architect/Supervising Officer" shall include the total amount paid or payable in respect of the materials or goods less any discount other than the discount referred to in clause 36·4·4·, properly so chargeable to the Employer and shall include where applicable:

        ·1·1   any tax (other than any value added tax which is treated, or is capable of being treated, as input tax (as referred to in the Finance Act 1972) by the Contractor) or duty not otherwise recoverable under this Contract by whomsoever payable which is payable under or by virtue of any Act of Parliament on the import, purchase, sale, appropriation, processing, alteration, adapting for sale or use of the materials or goods to be supplied; and

        ·1·2   the net cost of appropriate packing carriage and delivery after allowing for any credit for return of any packing to the supplier; and

        ·1·3   the amount of any price adjustment properly paid or payable to, or allowed or allowable by the supplier less any discount other than a cash discount for payment in full within 30 days of the end of the month during which delivery is made.

        ·2   Where in the opinion of the Architect/Supervising Officer the Contractor properly incurs expense, which would not be reimbursed under clause 36·3·1 or otherwise under this Contract, in obtaining the materials or goods from the Nominated Supplier such expense shall be added to the Contract Sum.

Sale contract provisions – Architect's/Supervising Officer's right to nominate supplier

36·4   Save where the Architect/Supervising Officer and the Contractor shall otherwise agree, the Architect/Supervising Officer shall only nominate as a supplier a person who will enter into a contract of sale with the Contractor which provides, inter alia:

        ·1   that the materials or goods to be supplied shall be of the quality and standard specified provided that where and to the extent that approval of the quality of materials or of the standards of workmanship is a matter for the opinion of the Architect/Supervising Officer, such quality and standards shall be to the reasonable satisfaction of the Architect/Supervising Officer;

        ·2   that the Nominated Supplier shall make good by replacement or otherwise any defects in the materials or goods supplied which appear up to and including the last day of the Defects Liability Period under this Contract and shall bear any expenses reasonably incurred by the Contractor as a direct consequence of such defects provided that:

            ·2·1   where the materials or goods have been used or fixed such defects are not such that reasonable examination by the Contractor ought to have revealed them before using or fixing;

            ·2·2   such defects are due solely to defective workmanship or material in the materials or goods supplied and shall not have been caused by improper storage by the Contractor or by misuse or by any act or neglect of either the Contractor, the Architect/Supervising Officer or the Employer or by any person or persons for whom they may be responsible or by any other person for whom the Nominated Supplier is not responsible;

        ·3   that delivery of the materials or goods supplied shall be commenced, carried out and completed in accordance with any delivery programme agreed between the Contractor and the Nominated Supplier or in the absence of such programme in accordance with the reasonable directions of the Contractor;

        ·4   that the Nominated Supplier shall allow the Contractor a discount for cash of 5 per cent on all payments if the Contractor makes payment in full within 30 days of the end of the month during which delivery is made;

        ·5   that the Nominated Supplier shall not be obliged to make any delivery of materials or goods (except any which may have been paid for in full less only any discount for cash) after the determination (for any reason) of the Contractor's employment under this Contract;

        ·6   that full discharge by the Contractor in respect of payments for materials or goods supplied by the Nominated Supplier shall be effected within 30 days of the end of the month during which delivery is made less only a discount for cash of 5 per cent if so paid;

        ·7   that the ownership of materials or goods shall pass to the Contractor upon delivery by the Nominated Supplier to or to the order of the Contractor, whether or not payment has been made in full;

        ·8   that if any dispute or difference between the Contractor and Nominated Supplier raises issues which are substantially the same as or connected with issues raised in a related dispute between the Employer and the Contractor under this Contract then, where ●articles 5·1·4 and 5·1·5 apply, such dispute or difference shall be referred to the Arbitrator appointed or to be appointed pursuant to article 5 who shall have power to make such directions and all necessary awards in the same way as if the procedure of the High Court as to joining one or more defendants or joining co-defendants or third parties was available to the parties and to him and in any case the award of such Arbitrator shall be final and binding on the parties:

·9 that no provision in the contract of sale shall override modify or affect in any way whatsoever the provisions in the contract of sale which are included therein to give effect to clauses 36·4·1 to 36·4·9 inclusive.

36·5 ·1 Subject to clauses 36·5·2 and 36·5·3, where the said contract of sale between the Contractor and the Nominated Supplier in any way restricts, limits or excludes the liability of the Nominated Supplier to the Contractor in respect of materials or goods supplied or to be supplied, and the Architect/Supervising Officer has specifically approved in writing the said restrictions, limitations or exclusions, the liability of the Contractor to the Employer in respect of the said materials or goods shall be restricted, limited or excluded to the same extent.

·2 The Contractor shall not be obliged to enter into a contract with the Nominated Supplier until the Architect/Supervising Officer has specifically approved in writing the said restrictions, limitations or exclusions.

·3 Nothing in clause 36·5 shall be construed as enabling the Architect/ Supervising Officer to nominate a supplier otherwise than in accordance with the provisions stated in clause 36·4.

*The Architect/Supervising Officer should state whether in the Appendix to the SFBC the words "Articles 5·1·4 and 5·1·5" have been struck out; if so then clause 36·4·8 will not apply to the Nominated Supplier.

46.02 At common law there would be no direct contractual relationship between the employer and a supplier of materials for incorporation in the works unless the employer purchased them directly.

46.03 Under MF clause 36, there is provision for nomination of suppliers or materials to be purchased by the contractor for incorporation in the works. The objects of this form of tender and warranty are supplemental to the provisions of clause 36. The provisions for nomination of suppliers are considerably less complex than those relating to nominated sub-contractors, and the use of TNS/1 and TNS/2 is not obligatory. Nevertheless, it is highly desirable that these forms should be used, on account of the protection they give to the employer against defects in the goods supplied by the nominated supplier and other defaults on his part.

46.04 Under clause 1, the nominated supplier confirms that he will be under a contract to the main contractors to supply the goods described in Schedule 1 at the price set out in his tender. Further, he covenants that his terms of sale will not conflict with MF clauses 36.3 to 36.5. Without such a direct covenant, the provisions of these clauses of the Main Contract would not be directly binding on the nominated supplier in the absence of privity of contract between the employer and him. This is a valuable provision, because in certain circumstances where a nominated supplier's terms excluded liability, the contractor might also be under no liability in respect of the matters covered by the exclusion clause not only under MF clause 35.8 but also at common law (see *Gloucestershire County Council* v *Richardson* [1968] 2 All ER 1181).

46.05 Under clause 2, the nominated supplier is entitled to withdraw if his tender has been given at a time when the main contractor is unknown, within 14 days of the identity of the main contractor becoming known (cf NSC/1 stipulation 2).

46.06 Clause 3 incorporates the direct warranties contained in TNS/2. The architect must be careful to ensure that the requirements of this clause are satisfied so that the direct warranties take effect.

Schedule 3: Warranty by a Nominated Supplier

To the Employer:
named in our Tender dated

For:
(abbreviated description of goods/materials)

To be supplied to:
(job title)

---

1 Subject to the conditions stated in the above mentioned Tender (that no provision in this Warranty Agreement shall take effect unless and until the instruction nominating us, the order of the Main Contractor accepting the Tender and a copy of this Warranty Agreement signed by the Employer have been received by us) WE WARRANT in consideration of our being nominated in respect of the supply of the goods and/or materials to be supplied by us as a Nominated Supplier under the Standard Form of Building Contract referred to in the Tender and in accordance with the description, quantity and quality of the materials or goods and with the other terms and details set out in the Tender ('the supply') that:

1·1 We have exercised and will exercise all reasonable skill and care in:

1·1 1 the design of the supply insofar as the supply has been or will be designed by us; and

2 the selection of materials and goods for the supply insofar as such supply has been or will be selected by us; and

3 the satisfaction of any performance specification or requirement insofar as such performance specification or requirement is included or referred to in the Tender as part of the description of the supply.

1·2 We will:

1·2 1 save insofar as we are delayed by

1·1 force majeure; or

1·2 civil commotion, local combination of workmen, strike or lock-out; or

1·3 any instruction of the Architect/Supervising Officer under SFBC clause 13·2 (Variations) or clause 13·3 (provisional sums); or

1·4 failure of the Architect/Supervising Officer to supply to us within due time any necessary information for which we have specifically applied in writing on a date which was neither unreasonably distant from nor unreasonably close to the date on which it was necessary for us to receive the same

so supply the Architect/Supervising Officer with such information as the Architect/Supervising Officer may reasonably require; and

2 so supply the Contractor with such information as the Contractor may reasonably require in accordance with the arrangements in our contract of sale with the Contractor; and

3 so commence and complete delivery of the supply in accordance with the arrangements in our contract of sale with the Contractor

that the Contractor shall not become entitled to an extension of time under SFBC clauses 25·4·6 or 25·4·7 of the Main Contract Conditions nor become entitled to be paid for direct loss and/or expense ascertained under SFBC clause 26·1 for the matters referred to in clause 26·2·1 of the Main Contract Conditions; and we will indemnify you to the extent but not further or otherwise that the Architect/Supervising Officer is obliged to give an extension of time so that the Employer is unable to recover damages under the Main Contract for delays in completion, and/or pay an amount in respect of direct loss and/or expense as aforesaid because of any failure by us under clause 1·2·1 or 1·2·2 hereof.

2 We have noted the amount of the liquidated and ascertained damages under the Main Contract, as stated in TNS Schedule 1, item 8.

3 Nothing in the Tender is intended to or shall exclude or limit our liability for breach of the warranties set out above.

4·1 If at any time any dispute or difference shall arise between the Employer or the Architect/Supervising Officer on his behalf and ourselves as to the construction of this Agreement or as to any matter or thing of whatsoever nature arising out of this Agreement or in connection therewith, then such dispute shall be and is hereby referred to the arbitration and final decision of a person to be agreed between the parties hereto, or, failing agreement within 14 days after either party has given to the other a written request to concur in the appointment of an arbitrator, a person to be appointed on the request of either party by the President or a Vice-President for the time being of the Royal Institute of British Architects.

4·2 ·1 Provided that if the dispute or difference to be referred to arbitration under this Agreement raises issues which are substantially the same as or connected with issues raised in a related dispute between the Employer and the Contractor under the Main Contract or between a Nominated Sub-Contractor and the Contractor under Agreement NSC/4 or NSC/4a or between the Employer and any Nominated Sub-Contractor under Agreement NSC/2 or NSC/2a, or between the Employer and any other Nominated Supplier, and if the related dispute has also been referred for determination to an arbitrator, the Employer and ourselves hereby agree that the dispute or difference under this Agreement shall be referred to the arbitrator appointed to determine the related dispute; and such arbitrator shall have power to make such directions and all necessary awards in the same way as if the procedure of the High Court as to joining one or more of the defendants or joining co-defendants or third parties was available to the parties and to him.

·2 Save that the Employer or ourselves may require the dispute or difference under this Agreement to be referred to a different arbitrator (to be appointed under this Agreement) if either of us reasonably considers that the arbitrator appointed to determine the related dispute is not properly qualified to determine the dispute or difference under this Agreement.

4·3 Paragraphs 4·2·1 and 4·2·2 hereof shall apply unless in the Appendix to the Main Contract Conditions the words 'Articles 5·1·4 and 5·1·5 apply' have been deleted.

4·4 The award of such arbitrator shall be final and binding on the parties.

Signature of Supplier:

Signature of Employer:

46.07 The nominated supplier is under an obligation to use all reasonable skill and care in

1. Design in so far as he is responsible for it.
2. Selection of materials selected by him.
3. Satisfaction of any performance specification forming part of the description.

These warranties correspond with those assumed by nominated sub-contractors under NSC/2. They are less favourable to the employer than the terms which would be implied by law against a seller of goods in favour of a buyer under section 14 of the Sale of Goods Act 1979, in that the obligation of the supplier is only to use reasonable skill and care in the design

and selection of materials and in ensuring that they satisfy the performance specification. At common law between buyer and seller the obligations of the seller would be independent of fault. Because clause 1 *defines* as opposed to *limits* the supplier's obligation, it is thought that it would not constitute an exemption clause so as to be subject to the Unfair Contract Terms Act 1977.

46.08 Clause 1.2 in effect comprises a warranty by the nominated supplier that he will not default so that the main contractor is entitled to an extension of time under clause 25 or to claim loss and expense under clause 26. Although the wording of clause 1.2 does not in terms limit the references to MF clauses 25.4.6, 25.4.7, 26.1, and 26.2.1 in such a way as to make it clear that they are limited to matters arising out of the default of this nominated supplier, such limitation is doubtless to be implied.

46.09 Under clause 3 the nominated supplier is fixed with express notice of the amount of liquidated damages: presumably the purpose of this is so that the nominated supplier has express notice of the likely amount of the loss which the employer will sustain if the nominated supplier is in default of his obligations under clause 1.2, so ensuring that the amount of such liquidated damages could be recoverable from the nominated supplier by way of damages for breach of his obligations under the rule in *Hadley* v *Baxendale* (1854) 9 Ex 341.

46.10 Clause 4 gives effect to the JCT Scheme for Arbitration of related sisputes, and must be read subject to MF article 5 and SCF article 3. Under MF clause 36.4.8, it is envisaged that the contract between the nominated supplier and the main contractor will contain a provision that if a dispute arises between them raising issues substantially the same or connected with issues raised in a related dispute between the employer and the contractor under the Main Contract, the dispute between the main contractor and the nominated supplier is to be decided by the arbitrator already appointed to determine the dispute under the Main Contract. As noted above (para 5.06) there is no provision directly regulating the appointment of an arbitrator to decide disputes between main contractor and nominated supplier where no existing related dispute has arisen. Clause 4.2.1 should be read together with MF article 5.1.4 and clause 36.4.8.

JCT NOMINATED SUB-CONTRACT NSC/4

47 Nature of the sub-contract form

47.01 The JCT Form of Sub-contract NSC/4 represents the first form of sub-contract ever produced by the JCT, and it is expressly designed for use with the main form following the procedure under MF clause 35. Its origin, however, owes much to the 'green form' of sub-contract drafted by the NFBTE and FASS for use with the 1963 JCT Main Contract. The considerable length and complexity of the sub-contract form arises principally becuase of inherent difficulties in the concept of nomination of sub-contractors. The firm has undergone various amendments. The version printed here incorporates all amendments up to amendment 8 issued April 1989.

48 Articles of Agreement

48.01 This part of the form names the parties and records certain matters in the recitals (beginning 'WHEREAS').

Articles of Sub-Contract Agreement

made the _____ day of _____ 19 ____

Between _____

_____

of (or whose registered office is situated at)

_____

_____

(hereinafter called "the Contractor") of the one part and

_____

_____

of (or whose registered office is situated at)

_____

_____

(hereinafter called "the Sub-Contractor") of the other part.

Whereas

First   the Sub-Contractor has submitted a tender on Tender NSC/1 for works (hereinafter called "the Sub-Contract Works") referred to on page 1 thereof and described in numbered documents annexed thereto (hereinafter called the "Numbered Documents") and which are to be executed as part of works (hereinafter called "the Works") referred to in Schedule 1 of the tender and being carried out by the Contractor under a contract as described by or referred to in Schedule 1 of the tender (hereinafter called "the Main Contract") with

(name of Employer) _____

_____

(hereinafter called "the Employer");

Second   the tender on Tender NSC/1 has been duly completed and signed which tender (comprising page 1 and the numbered documents and the completed Schedules 1 and 2 thereof) is hereinafter called "the Tender";

Third   the Contractor has retained the original of the Tender and the Sub-Contractor and the Employer each have a certified copy of the Tender and a further certified copy is appended hereto;

Fourth   the Sub-Contractor has been given notice of the provisions of the Main Contract as set out or referred to in Schedule 1 of the Tender except the detailed prices of the Contractor included in schedules and bills of quantities;

Fifth   the Contractor and the Sub-Contractor by a signature on page 1 of the Tender have agreed that the provisions of Sub-Contract NSC/4 shall apply unamended to the Sub-Contract for the Sub-Contract Works;

Sixth   the Architect has nominated the Sub-Contractor in Nomination NSC/3;

Seventh: at the date of the Sub-Contract

(A) the Sub-Contractor is/is not [a] the user of a current sub-contractor's tax certificate under the provisions of the Finance (No.2) Act 1975 (hereinafter called "the Act") in one of the forms specified in Regulation 15 of the Income Tax (Sub-Contractors in the Construction Industry) Regulations, 1975 and the Schedule thereto (hereinafter called "the Regulations") or any re-enactment or amendment thereof;

(B) the Contractor is/is not [a] the user of a current sub-contractor's tax certificate under the Act and the Regulations;

(C) the Employer under the Main Contract is/is not [a] a "contractor" within the meaning of the Act and the Regulations.

Now it is hereby agreed as follows

Article 1

1·1   In accordance with the Tender the Sub-Contractor will carry out and complete the Sub-Contract Works.

Article 2

2·1   Where a Sub-Contract Sum is stated on page 1 of the Tender the Contractor will pay to the Sub-Contractor that Sub-Contract Sum or such other sum as shall become payable in accordance with the Sub-Contract.

[a] Delete whichever alternative is not applicable; such deletion must follow the way in which the Tender, Schedule 1, item 10 and Schedule 2, item 7 have been completed unless the position as set out in the Tender has changed by the time NSC/4 is executed; in such circumstances the Seventh recital should be correctly completed and the Tender corrected so that the Seventh recital and the Tender are not in conflict.

2·2 Where a Tender Sum is stated on page 1 of the Tender the Contractor will pay to the Sub-Contractor such sum or sums as shall become payable in accordance with the Sub-Contract and the total of such sums is in Sub-Contract NSC/4 called "the Ascertained Final Sub-Contract Sum".

Article 3

3·1 If any dispute or difference, except a dispute or difference under clause 20A or clause 20B to the extent provided in clause 20A·8 or 20B·6, shall arise between the Contractor and Sub-Contractor, whether arising during the execution or after the completion or abandonment of the Sub-Contract Works or after the determination of the employment of the Sub-Contractor under Sub-Contract NSC/4 (whether by breach or in any other manner) it shall be and is hereby referred to arbitration in accordance with clause 38.

(A) Signed by or on behalf of the Contractor
in the presence of: **[b]** _____

Signed by or on behalf of the Sub-Contractor
in the presence of: **[b]** _____

(B) The Common Seal of the Contractor
was hereunto affixed
in the presence of: **[c]**   (C.S.)

The Common Seal of the Sub-Contractor
was hereunto affixed
in the presence of: **[c]**   (C.S.)

[b] Delete if Tender, Schedule 2, item 11 states that Sub-Contract NSC/4 is to be executed under seal and execute as provided in (B).

[c] Delete if Tender, Schedule 2, item 11 states that Sub-Contract NSC/4 is to be executed under hand and execute as provided in (A).

Article 1

48.02 The sub-contract works are defined in clause 1.3.

Article 3

This should be read in conjunction with clause 38.

For discussion of problems associated with the similar provisions of the NFBTE (now BEC) domestic form of sub-contract, clause 27, see *Higgs and Hill Building Ltd* v *Campbell Dennis Ltd* (1982) 28 BLR 47 and *Multi-Construction (Southern) Ltd* v *Stent Foundations Ltd* (1988) 41 BLR 98. See also *Hyundai Engineering and Construction Active Building* (1988) 45 BLR 62.

Conditions

49 Clause 1: Interpretation, definitions, etc.

49.01 This clause contains a helpful list of definitions; it also defines 'a variation', in terms not dissimilar to those contained in MF clause 13.1. The reason for the two alternatives arises because under clause 15 the method of ascertaining the price for the work depends on whether the sub-contract is on a 'lump sum' basis or a 'remeasurement' basis, in which case the contract price is ascertained on the basis of the remeasurement. Where a contract is on a remeasurement basis, its very nature contemplates that the quantities may not be the same as those on which the tender figure is based, and therefore it is inappropriate to regard an alteration in the quantities as a variation. Amendment no. 1 (April 1983) has been issued to insert a new sub-clause 1.4 to take account of the Section Completion Supplement.

The Sub-Contract Conditions Annexed to the Articles of Sub-Contract Agreement

1 **Interpretation, definitions etc.**

1·1 Unless otherwise specifically stated a reference in the Articles of Agreement or the Sub-Contract Conditions to any clause means that clause in the Sub-Contract Conditions.

1·2 Sub-Contract NSC/4 is to be read as a whole and the effect or operation of any recital, article or clause in Sub-Contract NSC/4 must therefore unless otherwise specifically stated be read subject to any relevant qualification or modification in any other recital, article or clause in Sub-Contract NSC/4.

1·3 Unless the context otherwise requires or Sub-Contract NSC/4 specifically otherwise provides, the following words and phrases shall have the meanings given below or as ascribed in the article, clause or other provision to which reference is made;

Word or phrase	Meaning
Agreement NSC/2:	the Employer/Nominated Sub-Contractor Agreement referred to in the Main Contract Conditions, **clause 35·3**.
Arbitrator:	the person appointed under **clause 38** to be the Arbitrator.
Architect:	the person named as the Architect/Contract Administrator in the **Tender, Schedule 1** or any successor appointed or otherwise agreed under the Main Contract Conditions.
Article or Articles of Sub-Contract Agreement:	the Articles of Sub-Contract Agreement in Sub-Contract NSC/4 to which the Sub-Contract Conditions are annexed and references to any recital are to the recitals set out before the Articles.
Ascertained Final Sub-Contract Sum:	see **article 2·2** and **clause 15·2**.
Base Date:	the date set out in the **Tender, Schedule 1, Appendix [A]** or **[B]** whichever is applicable.
Completion Date:	the Completion Date for the Main Contract as defined in **clause 1·3** of the Main Contract Conditions.
Contractor:	the person named as the Main Contractor in the **Tender, Schedule 1**.
Contract Bills:	the Bills of Quantities referred to in the Main Contract Conditions, **first recital** and **clause 1·3**.
Contract Drawings:	the drawings referred to in the Main Contract Conditions, **first recital** and **clause 1·3**.
Date for Completion:	the date stated in the completed Appendix of the Main Contract Conditions set out in the **Tender, Schedule 1, item 10**.
Employer:	the person with whom the Contractor has entered into the Main Contract.
Excepted Risks:	ionising radiations or contamination by radioactivity from any nuclear fuel or from any nuclear waste from the combustion of nuclear fuel, radioactive toxic explosive or other hazardous properties of any explosive nuclear assembly or nuclear component thereof, pressure waves caused by aircraft or other aerial devices travelling at sonic or supersonic speeds.
Joint Names Policy:	a policy of insurance which includes the Contractor and the Employer as the insured.
Main Contract:	the contract between the Contractor and the Employer as described by or referred to in the **Tender, Schedule 1**.
Main Contract Conditions:	the Articles of Agreement, Conditions and completed Appendix of the edition of the Standard Form of Building Contract identified in the **Tender, Schedule 1, items 5 and 10**.
Numbered Documents:	the documents referred to in the **First Recital**.
person:	an individual, firm (partnership) or body corporate.
Quantity Surveyor:	the person named as the Quantity Surveyor in the **Tender Schedule 1** or any successor appointed or otherwise agreed under the Main Contract Conditions.
Relevant Event:	see **clause 11·2·5**.
Site Materials:	all unfixed materials and goods delivered to, placed on or adjacent to the Works and intended for incorporation therein.
Specified Perils:	fire, lightning, explosion, storm, tempest, flood, bursting or overflowing of water tanks, apparatus or pipes, earthquake, aircraft and other aerial devices or articles dropped therefrom, riot and civil commotion but excluding Excepted Risks.
Sub-Contract:	the contractual rights and obligations of the Contractor and Sub-Contractor as set out in the Sub-Contract Documents.
Sub-Contract Conditions:	the Conditions in Sub-Contract NSC/4.
Sub-Contract Documents:	see **clause 2·1·1**.
Sub-Contract NSC/4:	the document referred to in the **Tender, Schedule 1, item 1**, comprising the Articles of Sub-Contract Agreement, the Sub-Contract Conditions annexed thereto and the Tender appended thereto.
Sub-Contract Sum:	the sum referred to in **clause 15·1**.
Sub-Contract Works:	the works referred to in the **Tender, page 1**, and described in the Numbered Documents annexed thereto to be executed as part of the Works.
Sub-Contractor:	the person named as the Sub-Contractor in the Tender and/or in the Articles of Sub-Contract Agreement.
Tender:	the duly completed and signed Tender NSC/1 (see **second recital** and **clause 2·1·1**).
Tender Sum:	the sum referred to in **clause 15·2**.

Terminal Dates:	see **clause 6·1·2**.
Variation:	where **clause 15·1** applies the term "Variation" means any of the following changes which are required by an instruction of the Architect:
	·1 the alteration or modification of the design, quality or quantity of the Sub-Contract Works as shown in the Sub-Contract Documents including:
	·1 the addition, omission or substitution or any work;
	·2 the alteration of the kind or standard of any of the materials or goods to be used in the Sub-Contract Works;
	·3 the removal from the site of any work, materials or goods executed or brought thereon by the Sub-Contractor for the purposes of the Sub-Contract Works other than work, materials or goods which are not in accordance with the Sub-Contract.
	·2 the imposition by the Employer of any obligations or restrictions in regard to the matters set out in paragraphs ·2·1 to ·2·4 or the addition to or alteration or omission of any such obligations or restrictions so imposed or imposed by the Employer as set out or referred to in the **Tender, Schedule 1, item 13** in regard to:
	·1 access to the site or use of any specific parts of the site;
	·2 limitations of working space;
	·3 limitations of working hours;
	·4 the execution or completion of the work in any specific order.
	where **clause 15·2** applies the term "Variation" has the same meaning but in lines 4 and 5 of this definition **delete** "design, quality or quantity" **insert** "design or quality".
Works:	the main contract works referred to in the **Tender, Schedule 1, item 4** including the Sub-Contract Works.

1·4 Where in the Tender, Schedule 1, item 5 it is stated that the Sectional Completion Supplement (JCT Practice Note 1) applies to the Main Contract Conditions and the "Appendix (Sectional Completion Supplement)" and entries therein have been set out in the Tender, Schedule 1, item 10, Sub-Contract NSC/4 shall be deemed to incorporate the modifications set out in the NSC/4 Sectional Completion Supplement at pages 46.1 and 46.2 of this Sub-Contract.

50 Clause 2: Sub-contract documents

50.01 The sub-contract documents are defined in clause 2 of the sub-contract and include the following:

1. The Tender NSC/1 including page 1 on a numbered document annexed thereto and the completed Schedules 1 and 2 and any documents annexed thereto *or referred to therein.*
2. Sub-contract NSC/4.

It is specifically provided (clause 2.1.2) that nothing contained in any descriptive Schedule or other like document issued in connection with and for use in carrying out the sub-contract works shall impose any obligation beyond those imposed by the sub-contract documents.

2	**Sub-Contract Documents**
2·1	·1 The Tender (comprising page 1 and the Numbered Documents annexed thereto and the completed Schedules 1 and 2 and any documents annexed thereto or referred to therein) and the Sub-Contract NSC/4 shall constitute the Sub-Contract Documents.
2·1	·2 Nothing contained in any descriptive schedule or other like document issued in connection with and for use in carrying out the Sub-Contract Works shall impose any obligation beyond those imposed by the Sub-Contract Documents.
2·2	If any conflict appears between the terms of Sub-Contract NSC/4 and any other Sub-Contract Documents apart from the terms of the Main Contract as described by or referred to in the Tender, Schedule 1 the terms of Sub-Contract NSC/4 shall prevail. If any conflict appears between the terms of the Main Contract as described by or referred to in the Tender, Schedule 1 and the other Sub-Contract Documents, the terms of the Main Contract as so described or referred to shall prevail.
2·3	·1 If in the Sub-Contract Documents the Sub-Contractor is required to enter into a sub-sub-contract or a contract of sale with a person or persons other than the Contractor, then clauses 2·3·2 to 2·3·4 shall apply.
2·3	·2 If the said sub-sub-contract or contract of sale in any way restricts, limits or excludes the liability of the sub-sub-contractor or supplier in respect of work or services carried out or the goods or materials supplied then the Sub-Contractor shall forthwith inform the Contractor in writing of the restriction, limitation or exclusion who shall thereupon send a copy of such information to the Architect.
2·3	·3 Where the Contractor, and the Architect through the Contractor, have specifically approved in writing the said restriction, limitation or exclusion, the liability of the Sub-Contractor to the Contractor in respect of the said work, services, materials or goods shall be restricted, limited or excluded to the same extent as the liability of the sub-sub-contractor or supplier to the Sub-Contractor is restricted, limited or excluded.
2·3	·4 The Sub-Contractor shall not be obliged to enter into a sub-sub-contract or a contract of sale as aforesaid until the specific written approval referred to above has been obtained.

50.02 Clause 2.2 deals with the situation where there is a conflict between the sub-contract documents. It is provided that:

1. If there is a conflict between NSC/4 and any other contract document *apart* from the terms of the Main Contract as described by or referred to in NSC/1 Schedule 1, the terms of NSC/4 prevail.
2. In the case of a conflict between Schedule 1 of NSC/1 and the other sub-contract documents, the terms of the Main Contract as described in that Schedule are to prevail.

Thus the Main Contract (as described in Schedule 1 to NSC/1) is paramount, but in case of any conflict other than with the terms of the Main Contract as described in Schedule 1 to NSC/1, the terms of the Sub-contract NSC/4 prevail.

50.03 Note that in NSC/4a (where the alternative method of nomination is used) this provision is amended: in the alternative method, no Tender NSC/1 is used, and the details reserved for Schedule 1 to NSC/1 are put in the Appendix to NSC/4a. Therefore, the references which appear in NSC/4 to the Schedule 1 to NSC/1 are altered to references to the Appendix to NSC/4a in NSC/4a. The contents of NSC/1 have already been dealt with (see para 42). Particular regard should be had to item 1A (period during which sub-contract work is to be carried out), item 1B (programme), item 3A (attendance), and item 9A (other matters) including any limitation on working hours.

50.04 There seems no provision for the situation where details of the Main Contract are, in fact, incorrectly filled in in Schedule 1 to NSC/1, and presumably therefore the only remedy open to either party would be an action for rectification. It is not clear whether the words of clause 2.2 operate so as to incorporate all provisions of the Main Contract whatsoever or only to incorporate those provisions specifically referred to in Schedule 1 of NSC/1 or described therein.

50.05 Under clause 2.3, where the sub-contract documents require the sub-contractor to enter into a sub-sub-contract or a contract of sale with a person other than the contractor and that sub-contract or sale contract excludes or limits the liability of the sub-sub-contractor or supplier, the obligations of the sub-contractor may similarly be limited *vis-à-vis* the main contractor – and similarly between the main contractor and the employer (see MF clause 35.22). It is submitted that in general the sub-contractor will owe the contractor the normal duties implied by law as to quality of work, fitness of materials, and fitness for purpose of the completed work save in so far as these may be excluded either expressly or by necessary implication.

50.06 Note that there is no provision in the JCT documentation for nominated sub-sub-contractors or sub-suppliers.

51 Clause 3: Sub-contract sum – additions or deductions – computation of ascertained final sub-contract sum

51.01 This clause should be read together with clauses 15, 16, 17, 21 and MF clause 30.

| 3 | **Sub-Contract Sum – additions or deductions – computation of Ascertained Final Sub-Contract Sum** |
| | Where in Sub-Contract NSC/4 it is provided that an amount is to be added to or subtracted from the Sub-Contract Sum or dealt with by adjustment of the Sub-Contract Sum or included in the computation of the Ascertained Final Sub-Contract Sum, then as soon as such amount is ascertained in whole or in part such ascertained amount shall be taken into account in the computation of the interim payment next following such whole or partial ascertainment. |

52 Clause 4: Execution of the sub-contract works – instructions of architect – directions of contractor

52.01 Clause 4.1.1 defines the basic obligation of the sub-contractor in regard to carrying out the work. The provision lays heavy emphasis on incorporation by reference from NSC/1 which makes provision for annexation of such documents as drawings, specifications, bills, Schedule of Rates, etc. Presumably it is anticipated that these documents will contain provisions expressly laying down the standard of work; in the absence of such express provisions there will be implied terms that the work will be carried out in a good and workmanlike manner, with proper materials, and so as to be fit for its purpose, unless the context otherwise requires.

4 Execution of the Sub-Contract Works – instructions of Architect – directions of Contractor

4·1 ·1 The Sub-Contractor shall carry out and complete the Sub-Contract Works in compliance with the Sub-Contract Documents and in conformity with all reasonable directions and requirements of the Contractor (so far as they may apply) regulating for the time being the due carrying out of the Works.

4·1 ·2 All materials and goods shall, so far as procurable, be of the kinds and standards described in the Sub-Contract Documents provided that where and to the extent that approval of the quality and standards of materials and goods is a matter for the opinion of the Architect such quality and standards shall be to the reasonable satisfaction of the Architect.

4·1 ·3 All workmanship shall be of the standards described in the Sub-Contract Documents, or, to the extent that no such standards are specified in the Sub-Contract Documents, shall be of a standard appropriate to the Sub-Contract Works provided that where and to the extent that approval of workmanship is a matter for the opinion of the Architect such workmanship shall be to the reasonable satisfaction of the Architect.

4·1 ·4 The Sub-Contractor shall continually keep upon the Sub-Contract Works while such Sub-Contract Works are being executed a competent person-in-charge and any instruction of the Architect given to him by the Contractor, or any direction given to him by the Contractor, shall be deemed to have been issued to the Sub-Contractor.

4·1 ·5 If the Sub-Contractor shall find any discrepancy in, or divergence between any two or more of, the documents referred to in clause 2·3 of the Main Contract Conditions, including a divergence between parts of any one of them or between documents of the same description, he shall immediately give to the Contractor a written notice specifying the discrepancy or divergence, and the Contractor shall forthwith send that notice to the Architect and request instructions under clause 2·3 of the Main Contract Conditions.

4·2 The Contractor shall forthwith issue to the Sub-Contractor any written instruction of the Architect issued under the Main Contract affecting the Sub-Contract Works (including the ordering of any Variation therein); and may issue any reasonable direction in writing to the Sub-Contractor in regard to the Sub-Contract Works.

4·3 ·1 The Sub-Contractor shall forthwith comply with any instruction or direction referred to in clause 4·2 save that where such instruction is one requiring a Variation within the definition of "Variation" clause 1·3, paragraph ·2, the Sub-Contractor need not comply to the extent that he makes reasonable objection in writing to such compliance. Upon receipt by the Contractor of any written objection by the Sub-Contractor, the Contractor shall thereupon submit that objection to the Architect.

4·3 ·2 ·1 Where any work, materials or goods are not in accordance with this Sub-Contract ('non-complying work') and the provisions of clause 8·4 of the Main Contract Conditions ('Main Contract 8·4') are operated in respect of such non-complying work clauses 4·3·3, 4·3·4, 4·3·5 and 4·3·7 shall apply.

·2 ·2 Where the Architect consults with the Contractor as required by Main Contract 8·4 the Contractor shall immediately, as required by Main Contract 8·4·2 and 8·4·3, consult with the Sub-Contractor and report the outcome of such consultation to the Architect in writing with a copy of that report to the Sub-Contractor.

4·3 ·3 The Sub-Contractor shall comply

·3 ·1 with any instructions under Main Contract 8·4·1 issued to the Sub-Contractor by the Contractor pursuant to clause 4·2; and

·3 ·2 with any instructions under Main Contract 8·4·3 issued to the Sub-Contractor by the Contractor pursuant to clause 4·2 requiring a Variation to the extent that they are reasonably necessary as a consequence of an instruction under Main Contract 8·4·1; and to the extent that such instructions are so necessary and notwithstanding clause 16 *(valuation of Variations and provisional sum work)* and clause 17 *(valuation of all work comprising the Sub-Contract Works)*, clause 11·2 *(extension of Sub-Contract time)* and clause 13·1 *(matters affecting regular progress – direct loss and/or expense)* no adjustment shall be made to the Sub-Contract Sum or be included in the computation of the Ascertained Final Sub-Contract Sum and no extension of time shall be given.

4·3 ·4 ·1 Where the Architect under Main Contract 8·4·2 allows all or any non-complying work to remain the Contractor shall so inform the Sub-Contractor in writing and an appropriate deduction shall be made from the Sub-Contract Sum or in the computation of the Ascertained Final Sub-Contract Sum.

·4 ·2 The Sub-Contractor shall comply with any instructions under Main Contract 8·4·3 issued to the Sub-Contractor by the Contractor pursuant to clause 4·2 requiring a Variation to the extent that they are reasonably necessary as a consequence of the Architect allowing all or any non-complying work to remain; and to the extent that such instructions are so necessary and notwithstanding clause 16 *(valuation of Variations and provisional sum work)* and clause 17 *(valuation of all work comprising the Sub-Contract Works)*, clause 11·2 *(extension of Sub-Contract time)* and clause 13·1 *(matters affecting regular progress – direct loss and/or expense)* no adjustment shall be made to the Sub-Contract Sum or be included in the computation of the Ascertained Final Sub-Contract Sum and no extension of time shall be given.

4·3 ·5 Where there is non-complying work the Sub-Contractor shall comply with such instructions issued by the Architect pursuant to Main Contract 8·4·4 and issued to the Sub-Contractor by the Contractor pursuant to clause 4·2 to open up for inspection or to test as are reasonable in all the circumstances to establish to the reasonable satisfaction of the Architect the likelihood or extent, as appropriate to the circumstances, of any further similar non-compliance. To the extent that such instructions are so reasonable, whatever the results of the opening up for inspection or test and notwithstanding clause 8·3 of the Main Contract Conditions and clause 13·1 *(matters affecting regular progress – direct loss and/or expense)*, no addition shall be made to the Sub-Contract Sum nor shall any monies be included in the computation of the Ascertained Final Sub-Contract Sum in respect of such instructions. Clause 11·2·5·5·2 shall apply unless as stated therein the inspection or test showed that the work, materials or goods were not in accordance with this Sub-Contract.

4·3 ·6 ·1 Where compliance by the Contractor or by any other Nominated Sub-Contractor with any instruction or other exercise of a power of the Architect under Main Contract 8·4 necessarily results in work properly executed or materials or goods properly fixed or supplied under this Sub-Contract having to be taken down and/or re-executed or re-fixed or re-supplied, the Sub-Contractor shall, in accordance with directions, so take down and/or re-execute or re-fix or re-supply if the direction so to do is issued at any time before the date of practical completion of the Sub-Contract Works (as referred to in clause 14·2). A copy of such directions shall be sent forthwith by the Contractor to the Nominated Sub-Contractor in respect of whose non-complying work the Architect issued instructions or allowed non-complying work to remain under Main Contract 8·4.

·6 ·2 The Sub-Contractor shall be paid by the Contractor on the basis of a fair valuation for any taking down and/or re-execution or re-fixing or re-supply directed under clause 4·3·6·1 and which has been carried out by the Sub-Contractor and the provisions of clause 11·2 *(extension of Sub-Contract time)* and clause 13·2 *(matters affecting regular progress – direct loss and/or expense)* shall apply in respect of any compliance with directions to which clause 4·3·6·1 refers. The payment to which clause 4·3·6·2 refers shall be made by the Contractor within 14 days after the end of the month during which the taking down and/or re-execution or re-fixing or re-supply was carried out.

4·3 ·7 The Sub-Contractor shall indemnify the Contractor in respect of any liability, and reimburse the Contractor for any costs, which the Contractor has incurred as a direct result of compliance by the Sub-Contractor with clauses 4·3·3 and/or 4·3·4 and/or 4·3·5 or arising out of the operation of clause 4·3·6 in other Nominated Sub-Contracts but only to the extent that such operation is a direct result of the provisions of Main Contract 8·4 being operated in respect of non-complying work.

4·4 If the Architect or Contractor purports to give any instruction or direction referred to in clause 4·2 otherwise than in writing to the Sub-Contractor or his person-in-charge then such instruction or direction shall be of no immediate effect but shall be confirmed in writing by the Sub-Contractor to the Contractor within 7 days and if not dissented from in writing by the Contractor within 7 days from the receipt of the Sub-Contractor's confirmation shall take effect as from the expiration of the latter said 7 days. Provided always:

4·4 ·1 that if the Contractor within 7 days of such instruction or direction otherwise than in writing having been given shall himself confirm the same in writing, then the Sub-Contractor shall not be obliged to confirm as aforesaid and the said instruction or direction shall take effect as from the date of the Contractor's confirmation; and

·2 if neither the Contractor nor the Sub-Contractor shall confirm such an instruction or direction in the manner and at the time aforesaid but the Sub-Contractor shall nevertheless comply with the same, then the Contractor may confirm the same in writing (and must if the Architect has confirmed in writing in similar circumstances under the Main Contract) at any time prior to the final payment of the Sub-Contractor in accordance with Sub-Contract NSC/4 and the said instruction or direction shall thereupon be deemed to have taken effect on the date on which it was issued.

4·5 If within 7 days after receipt of a written notice from the Contractor requiring compliance with a direction of the Contractor the Sub-Contractor does not begin to comply therewith, then the Contractor may, if so permitted by the Architect, employ and pay other persons to comply with such direction and all costs incurred in connection with such employment may be deducted from any monies due or to become due to the Sub-Contractor under the Sub-Contract or shall be recoverable from the Sub-Contract as a debt.

4·6 Upon receipt of what purports to be an instruction of the Architect issued in writing by the Contractor to the Sub-Contractor, the Sub-Contractor may require the Contractor to request the Architect to specify in writing the provision of the Main Contract which empowers the issue of the said instruction. The Contractor shall forthwith comply with any such requirement and deliver to the Sub-Contractor a copy of the Architect's answer to the Contractor's request. If the Sub-Contractor shall thereafter comply with the said instruction then the issue of the same shall be deemed for all the purposes of the Sub-Contract to have been empowered by the provision of the Main Contract specified by the Architect in answer to the Contractor's request. Provided always that if before compliance the Sub-Contractor shall have made a written requirement to the Contractor to request the Employer to concur in the appointment of an Arbitrator under the Main Contract Conditions in order that it may be decided whether the provision specified by the Architect empowers the issue of the said instruction then, subject to the Sub-Contractor giving the Contractor such indemnity and security as the Contractor may reasonably require, the Contractor shall allow the Sub-Contractor to use the Contractor's name and if necessary will join with the Sub-Contractor in abitration proceedings at the instigation of the Sub-Contractor to decide the matter as aforesaid.

Variations

52.02 A distinction is drawn between 'instructions' from the architect and 'directions' from the contractor: the sub-contractor is obliged to comply with both, save that where the instruction is one requiring a variation relating to obligations or restrictions in regard to site access, limitations of working space, limitations of working hours, or the execution or completion of work in any specific order the sub-contractor has a right of reasonable objection. It will be recalled that a similar right of reasonable objection is conferred on the main contractor *vis-à-vis* the employer by MF clause 13.1.2 and MF clause 4.1.1. Architects must ensure that the requirements of clause 4.4 are complied with as regards the form of instruction, disobedience with which entitles the architect to exercise the powers conferred by clause 4.5.

52.03 Clause 4.6 provides the machinery whereby the sub-contractor can question the authority for a particular architect's instruction. If the sub-contractor wishes to, he can use the contractor's name in arbitration proceedings under the Main Contract to challenge the validity of the instruction.

53 Clause 5: Sub-contractor's liability under incorporated provisions of the Main Contract

53.01 Clause 5.1.1 provides that the sub-contractor shall observe, perform, and comply with all the provisions of the

Main Contract as described by or referred to in the tender Schedule 1 on the part of the contractor to be observed, performed, and complied with so far as they relate and apply to the sub-contract works or any portion of the same. Without prejudice to that general statement the sub-contractor is specifically bound to comply with the provisions of the Main Contract relating to statutory obligations, levels and setting out of the works, royalties and patent rights, unfixed materials, outbreak of hostilities, war damage, and antiquities. In addition by clause 5.1.2, the sub-contractor is obliged to indemnify the contractor against any breach or non-observance or non-performance by the sub-contractor of the provisions of the Main Contract referred to in clause 5.1.1 and any act or omission of the sub-contract which involves the contractor in any liabilities to the employer under the provisions of the Main Contract referred to in that sub-clause.

5 **Sub-Contractor's liability under incorporated provisions of the Main Contract**

5·1 The Sub-Contractor shall:

5·1 ·1 observe, perform and comply with all the provisions of the Main Contract as described by or referred to in the Tender, Schedule 1 on the part of the Contractor to be observed, performed and complied with so far as they relate and apply to the Sub-Contract Works (or any portion of the same). Without prejudice to the generality of the foregoing, the Sub-Contractor shall observe, perform, and comply with the following provisions of the Main Contract Conditions: clauses 6, 7, 9, 16, 32, 33 and 34; and

5·1 ·2 indemnify and save harmless the Contractor against and from:

·2 ·1 any breach, non-observance or non-performance by the Sub-Contractor or his servants or agents of any of the provisions of the Main Contract referred to in clause 5·1·1; and

·2 ·2 any act or omission of the Sub-Contractor or his servants or agents which involves the Contractor in any liability to the Employer under the provisions of the Main Contract referred to in clause 5·1·1.

5·2 Nothing contained in the Sub-Contract Documents shall be construed so as to impose any liability on the Sub-Contractor in respect of any act or omission or default on the part of the Employer, the Contractor, his other sub-contractors or their respective servants or agents nor (except by way of and in the terms of the Agreement NSC/2) create any privity of contract between the Sub-Contractor and the Employer or any other sub-contractor.

53.02 This provision is not easy to interpret. It is not clear whether the words 'the provisions of the main contract referred to in clause 5.1.1', which occur in clause 5.1.2, refer to the specific provisions innumerated in the former or to all terms of the Main Contract which are on a true construction incorporated in the sub-contract. For cases on incorporation by reference in this way see *Chandler Brothers* v *Boswell* [1936] 3 All ER 179, *Geary-Walker & Co* v *Lawrence & Son* (1906) 2 Hudson's BC 4th edn 382, and *Dunlop and Rankin* v *Hendall Steel Structures* [1957] 3 All ER 344.

54 Clause 6: Injury to persons and property – indemnity to contractor

54.01 These clauses oblige the sub-contractor to indemnify the contractor against personal injury or death caused by the carrying out of the sub-contract works *unless* caused by the contractor or the employer, and to indemnify the contractor in respect of damage to property real or personal caused by the sub-contract works *provided* that the same is due to any negligence, omission, or default of the sub-contractor. Unless the sub-contractor can prove negligence on the part of the contractor or the employer, he is liable to indemnify in respect of personal injury or death; however, in so far as damage to property is concerned, the contractor must prove negligence on the part of the sub-contractor. Clause 7 imposes a correlative obligation to insure.

6 **Injury to persons and property – indemnity to Contractor**

6·1 ·1 In clauses 6 to 10 inclusive the phrase in column 1 shall have the meaning set out in column 2:

Column 1	Column 2
the Contractor or any person for whom the Contractor is responsible	the Contractor, his servants or agents or any person employed or engaged upon or in connection with the Works or any part thereof his servants or agents (other than the Sub-Contractor or any person for whom the Sub-Contractor is responsible), or any other person who may properly be on the site upon or in connection with the Works or any part thereof, his servants or agents; but such persons shall not include the Employer or any person employed, engaged or authorised by him or by any local authority or statutory undertaker executing work solely in pursuance of its statutory rights or obligations;
the Sub-Contractor or any person for whom the Sub-Contractor is responsible	the Sub-Contractor, his servants or agents, or any person employed or engaged by the Sub-Contractor upon or in connection with the Sub-Contract Works or any part thereof, his servants or agents or any other person who may properly be on the site upon or in connection with the Sub-Contract Works or any part thereof, his servants or agents; but such persons shall not include the Contractor or any person for whom the Contractor is responsible nor the Employer or any person employed, engaged or authorised by him or by any local authority or statutory undertaker executing work solely in pursuance of its statutory rights or obligations.

6·1 ·2 The term "Terminal Dates" shall mean the dates identified in clause 6·4.

6·2 The Sub-Contractor shall be liable for, and shall indemnify the Contractor against, any expense, liability, loss, claim or proceedings whatsoever arising under any statute or at common law in respect of personal injury to or the death of any person whomsoever arising out of or in the course of or caused by the carrying out of the Sub-Contract Works except to the extent that the same is due to any act or neglect, breach of statutory duty, omission or default of the Contractor or any person for whom the Contractor is responsible or of the Employer or any person for whom the Employer is responsible including the persons employed or otherwise engaged by the Employer to whom clause 29 of the Main Contract Conditions refers or of any local authority or statutory undertaker executing work solely in pursuance of its statutory rights or obligations.

6·3 The Sub-Contractor shall, subject to clause 6·4 and where applicable clause 8C·1·1, be liable for, and shall indemnify the Contractor against, any expense, liability, loss, claim or proceedings in respect of any injury or damage whatsoever to any property real or personal including the Works in so far as such injury or damage arises out of or in the course of or by reason of the carrying out of the Sub-Contract Works, and to the extent that the same is due to any negligence, breach of statutory duty, omission or default of the Sub-Contractor or any person for whom the Sub-Contractor is responsible.

6·4 The liability and indemnity to the Contractor referred to in clause 6·3 shall not include any liability or indemnity in respect of injury or damage to the Works and/or Site Materials (nor, where clause 8C applies, injury or damage to the existing structures and the contents thereof owned by the Employer or for which the Employer is responsible) by one or more of the Specified Perils, whether or not caused by the negligence, breach of statutory duty, omission or default of the Sub-Contractor or any person for whom the Sub-Contractor is responsible, for the period up to and including whichever of the following is the earlier date:

the date of issue of the certificate of practical completion of the Sub-Contract Works (as referred to in clause 14·2) or

the date of determination of the employment of the Contractor (whether or not the validity of that determination is contested) under clause 22C·4·3 (where applicable) or clause 27 or clause 28 of the Main Contract Conditions.

7 **Insurance against injury to persons or property**

7·1 Without prejudice to his obligation to indemnify the Contractor under clause 6, the Sub-Contractor shall take out and maintain insurance which shall comply with clause 7·2 in respect of claims arising out of his liability referred to in clauses 6·2 and 6·3 as modified by clause 6·4, except that the obligation of the Sub-Contractor to take out and maintain insurance in respect of his liability for injury or damage to property as stated in clause 6·3 shall not extend to taking out and maintaining insurance for injury and damage to the Sub-Contract Works by a risk other than a Specified Peril up to and including whichever is the earlier of the Terminal Dates. **[d]**

7·2 The insurance in respect of claims for personal injury to, or the death of any person under a contract of service or apprenticeship with the Sub-Contractor and arising out of and in the course of such person's employment, shall comply with the Employer's Liability (Compulsory Insurance) Act, 1969, and any statutory orders made thereunder or any amendment or re-enactment thereof. For all other claims to which clause 7·1 applies the insurance cover shall be not less than **[e]** the sum stated in the Sub-Contract Documents for any one occurrence or series of occurrences arising out of one event.

7·3 Notwithstanding the provisions of clauses 6·2, 6·3 and 7·1 the Sub-Contractor shall not be liable either to indemnify the Contractor or to insure against any personal injury to or the death of any person or any damage, loss or injury caused to the Works, work executed, Site Materials, the site or any property by the effect of an Excepted Risk.

[d] The Sub-Contractor has the benefit of the main contract works insurance for loss or damage by the Specified Perils to the Sub-Contract Works but not for other risks e.g. subsidence, impact, theft or vandalism. The insurance to which clause 7·1 refers in respect of injury or damage to property is a third party or public liability policy; such policy will not however give cover for any property such as the Sub-Contract Works while they are in the custody and control of the Sub-Contractor. For this reason the obligation to insure under clause 7·1 is modified by this sentence. As the Sub-Contractor is liable for those other risks if they cause loss or damage to the Sub-Contract Works he may well consider that he needs to take out a works insurance to provide such cover which he does not get under the main contract works insurance. See also footnote **[f]**.

[e] The Sub-Contractor may, if he wishes, insure for a sum greater than that stated in the Sub-Contract Documents.

55 Clause 8

55.01 These clauses 8–8c should be read with MF clauses 22A–C. They contain provisions which are designed to ensure that the sub-contractor's liability is limited to those matters which are neither specified perils nor due to the fault of the contractor or the employer.

8 **Loss or damage to the Works and to the Sub-Contract Works**

8·1 Clause 8A shall apply where it is stated in the Sub-Contract Documents that clause 22A shall apply to the Main Contract; clause 8B shall apply where it is stated in those Documents that clause 22B shall apply to the Main Contract; clause 8C shall apply where it is stated in those Documents that clause 22C shall apply to the Main Contract.

8·2 The exception set out in clause 8A·2·1 or clause 8B·2·1 or clause 8C·2·1 whichever is applicable shall extend to any loss or damage for which either the Employer or the Contractor as Joint Insured under the Joint Names Policy referred to in clause 22A or clause 22B or clause 22C·2 of the Main Contract Conditions does not make a claim under that Policy or to the extent that no claim under that Policy can be made because of a condition therein that the insured shall bear the first part of any claim for loss or damage.

8·3 Nothing in clause 8A or clause 8B or clause 8C whichever is applicable shall in any way modify the Sub-Contractor's obligations in regard to defects in the Sub-Contract Works as set out in clauses 14·3 and 14·4.

8·4 Where the Sub-Contractor is, pursuant to clause 22·3 of the Main Contract Conditions, recognised as an insured under the Joint Names Policy referred to in clause 22A or clause 22B or clause 22C of the Main Contract Conditions, whichever is applicable to the Main Contract, the Sub-Contractor shall not object to the payment by the insurers under such Joint Names Policy to the Employer of any relevant insurance monies.

8·5 The occurrence of loss or damage affecting the Sub-Contract Works occasioned by one or more of the Specified Perils shall be disregarded in computing any amounts payable to the Sub-Contractor under or by virtue of this Sub-Contract.

[f]8A   Sub-Contract Works in New Buildings – Main Contract Conditions Clause 22A

8A·1 The Contractor shall, prior to the commencement of the Sub-Contract Works, ensure that the Joint Names Policy referred to in clause 22A of the Main Contract Conditions shall be so issued or so endorsed that, in respect of loss or damage by the Specified Perils to the Works and Site Materials insured thereunder, the Sub-Contractor is either recognised as an insured under the Joint Names Policy or the insurers waive any rights of subrogation they may have against the Sub-Contractor; and that this recognition or waiver shall continue up to and including whichever is the earlier of the Terminal Dates.

8A·2 ·1 Before whichever is the earlier of the Terminal Dates the Sub-Contractor shall (subject to clause 8A·2·2) be responsible for the cost of restoration of Sub-Contract work lost or damaged, replacement or repair of Sub-Contract Site Materials and removal and disposal of any debris arising therefrom in accordance with clause 8A·3 except to the extent that the loss or damage to the Sub-Contract Works or Sub-Contract Site Materials is due to:

one or more of the Specified Perils (whether or not caused by the negligence, breach of statutory duty, omission or default of the Sub-Contractor or any person for whom the Sub-Contractor is responsible) or

any negligence, breach of statutory duty, omission or default of the Contractor or any person for whom the Contractor is responsible or of the Employer or any person engaged, employed or authorised by him or by any local authority or statutory undertaker executing work solely in pursuance of its statutory rights or obligations.

·2 Where during the progress of the Sub-Contract Works sub-contract materials or goods have been fully, finally and properly incorporated into the Works before practical completion of the Sub-Contract Works, the Sub-Contractor shall be responsible, in respect of loss or damage to sub-contract work comprising the materials or goods so incorporated caused by the occurrence of a peril other than a Specified Peril, for the cost of restoration of such work lost or damaged and removal and disposal of any debris arising therefrom in accordance with clause 8A·3 but only to the extent that such loss or damage is caused by the negligence, breach of statutory duty, omission or default of the Sub-Contractor or any person for whom the Sub-Contractor is responsible.

8A·3 If before the earlier of the Terminal Dates any loss or damage affecting the Sub-Contract Works or Sub-Contract Site Materials is occasioned, whether by one or more of the Specified Perils or otherwise, then, upon discovering the loss or damage, the Sub-Contractor shall forthwith give notice in writing to the Contractor of the extent, nature and location thereof. The Sub-Contractor shall, in accordance with any instructions of the Architect or directions of the Contractor, with due diligence restore Sub-Contract work lost or damaged, replace or repair any Sub-Contract Site Materials which have been lost or damaged, remove and dispose of any debris arising therefrom and proceed with the carrying out and completion of the Sub-Contract Works.

8A·4 Where under clause 8A·2 the Sub-Contractor is not responsible for the cost of compliance with clause 8A·3, such compliance shall be treated as if it were a Variation required by an instruction of the Architect to which clause 4·2 refers and valued under clause 16 or clause 17 whichever is applicable. The amount of the valuation under clause 16 shall not be added to the Sub-Contract Sum and the amount of the valuation under clause 17 shall not be included in the gross valuation referred to in clause 21·4 but such amounts shall be paid by the Contractor to the Sub-Contractor or recoverable by the Sub-Contractor from the Contractor as a debt.

8A·5 On or after the earlier of the Terminal Dates the Sub-Contractor shall not be responsible for loss or damage to the Sub-Contract Works except to the extent of any loss or damage caused thereto by the negligence, breach of statutory duty, omission or default of the Sub-Contractor or any person for whom the Sub-Contractor is responsible.

[f]8B   Sub-Contract Works in new buildings – Main Contract Conditions clause 22B

8B·1 The Contractor shall, prior to the commencement of the Sub-Contract Works, ensure that the Employer arranges that the Joint Names Policy referred to in clause 22B·1 of the Main Contract Conditions shall be so issued or so endorsed that, in respect of loss or damage by the Specified Perils to the Works and Site Materials insured thereunder, the Sub-Contractor is either recognised as an insured under the Joint Names Policy or the insurers waive any rights of subrogation they may have against the Sub-Contractor; and that this recognition or waiver shall continue up to and including whichever is the earlier of the Terminal Dates.

8B·2 ·1 Before whichever is the earlier of the Terminal Dates the Sub-Contractor shall (subject to clause 8B·2·2) be responsible for the cost of restoration of Sub-Contract work lost or damaged, replacement or repair of Sub-Contract Site Materials and removal and disposal of any debris arising therefrom in accordance with clause 8B·3 except to the extent that the loss or damage to the Sub-Contract Works or Sub-Contract Site Materials is due to:

one or more of the Specified Perils (whether or not caused by the negligence, breach of statutory duty, omission or default of the Sub-Contractor or any person for whom the Sub-Contractor is responsible) or

any negligence, breach of statutory duty, omission or default of the Contractor or any person for whom the Contractor is responsible or of the Employer or any person employed, engaged or authorised by him or by any local authority or statutory undertaker executing work solely in pursuance of its statutory rights or obligations.

·2 Where during the progress of the Sub-Contract Works sub-contract materials or goods have been fully, finally and properly incorporated into the Works before practical completion of the Sub-Contract Works, the Sub-Contractor shall be responsible, in respect of loss or damage to sub-contract work comprising the materials or goods so incorporated caused by the occurrence of a peril other than a Specified Peril, for the cost of restoration of such work lost or damaged and removal and disposal of any debris arising therefrom in accordance with clause 8B·3 but only to the extent that such loss or damage is caused by the negligence, breach of statutory duty, omission or default of the Sub-Contractor or any person for whom the Sub-Contractor is responsible.

8B·3 If before the earlier of the Terminal Dates any loss or damage affecting the Sub-Contract Works or Sub-Contract Site Materials is occasioned, whether by one or more of the Specified Perils or otherwise, then, upon discovering the loss or damage, the Sub-Contractor shall forthwith give notice in writing to the Contractor of the extent, nature and location thereof. The Sub-Contractor shall, in accordance with any instructions of the Architect or directions of the Contractor, with due diligence restore Sub-Contract work lost or damaged, replace or repair any Sub-Contract Site Materials which have been lost or damaged, remove and dispose of any debris arising therefrom and proceed with the carrying out and completion of the Sub-Contract Works.

[f] The Sub-Contractor should consider whether he should take out insurance to cover any risks for which he is not covered under clause 8B e.g. impact, subsidence, theft, vandalism.

8B·4 Where under clause 8B·2 the Sub-Contractor is not responsible for the cost of compliance with clause 8B·3, such compliance shall be treated as if it were a Variation required by an instruction of the Architect to which clause 4·2 refers and valued under clause 16 or clause 17 whichever is applicable.

8B·5 On or after the earlier of the Terminal Dates the Sub-Contractor shall not be responsible for loss or damage to the Sub-Contract Works except to the extent of any loss or damage caused thereto by the negligence, breach of statutory duty, omission or default of the Sub-Contractor or any person for whom the Sub-Contractor is responsible.

[f] 8C   Sub-Contract Works in existing structures – Main Contract Conditions clause 22C

8C·1 The Contractor shall, prior to the commencement of the Sub-Contract Works, ensure

·1 that the Employer arranges that the Joint Names Policy referred to in clause 22C·1 of the Main Contract Conditions shall be so issued or so endorsed that, in respect of loss or damage by the Specified Perils to the existing structures and the contents thereof owned by the Employer or for which the Employer is responsible and which are insured thereunder, the Sub-Contractor is either recognised as an insured under the Joint Names Policy or the insurers waive any rights of subrogation they may have against the Sub-Contractor; and

·2 that the Employer arranges that the Joint Names Policy referred to in clause 22C·2 of the Main Contract Conditions shall be so issued or so endorsed that, in respect of loss or damage by the Specified Perils to the Works and Site Materials insured thereunder, the Sub-Contractor is either recognised as an insured under the Joint Names Policy or the insurers waive any rights of subrogation they may have against the Sub-Contractor; and

·3 that the recognition or waiver referred to in clauses 8C·1·1 and 8C·1·2 shall continue up to and including whichever is the earlier of the Terminal Dates.

8C·2 ·1 Before whichever is the earlier of the Terminal Dates the Sub-Contractor shall (subject to clause 8C·2·2) be responsible for the cost of restoration of Sub-Contract work lost or damaged, replacement or repair of Sub-Contract Site Materials and removal and disposal of any debris arising therefrom in accordance with clause 8C·3·3 except to the extent that the loss or damage to the Sub-Contract Works or Sub-Contract Site Materials is due to:

one or more of the Specified Perils (whether or not caused by the negligence, breach of statutory duty, omission or default of the Sub-Contractor or any person for whom the Sub-Contractor is responsible) or

any negligence, breach of statutory duty, omission or default of the Contractor or any person for whom the Contractor is responsible or of the Employer or any person employed, engaged or authorised by him or by any local authority or statutory undertaker executing work solely in pursuance of its statutory rights or obligations.

·2 Where during the progress of the Sub-Contract Works sub-contract materials or goods have been fully, finally and properly incorporated into the Works before practical completion of the Sub-Contract Works, the Sub-Contractor shall be responsible, in respect of loss or damage to sub-contract work comprising the materials or goods so incorporated caused by the occurrence of a peril other than a Specified Peril, for the cost of restoration of such work lost or damaged and removal and disposal of any debris arising therefrom in accordance with clause 8C·3·3 but only to the extent that such loss or damage is caused by the negligence, breach of statutory duty, omission or default of the Sub-Contractor or any person for whom the Sub-Contractor is responsible.

8C·3 ·1 If before the earlier of the Terminal Dates any loss or damage affecting the Sub-Contract Works or Sub-Contract Site Materials is occasioned, whether by one or more of the Specified Perils or otherwise, then, upon discovering the loss or damage, the Sub-Contractor shall forthwith give notice in writing to the Contractor of the extent, nature and location thereof.

·2 If the occurrence of such loss or damage or any other loss or damage gives rise to a determination of the employment of the Contractor under clause 22C·4 of the Main Contract Conditions clause 31·2 shall apply as if the employment of the Contractor had been determined under clause 28 of the Main Contract Conditions but subject to the exception in regard to the application of clause 28·2·2·6 of the Main Contract Conditions referred to in clause 22C·4·3·2 of the Main Contract Conditions.

·3 If the employment of the Main Contractor is not determined under clause 22C·4 of the Main Contract Conditions the Sub-Contractor shall, in accordance with any instructions of the Architect or directions of the Contractor, with due diligence restore Sub-Contract work lost or damaged, replace or repair any Sub-Contract Site Materials which have been lost or damaged, remove and dispose of any debris arising therefrom and proceed with the carrying out and completion of the Sub-Contract Works.

8C·4 Where under clause 8C·2 the Sub-Contractor is not responsible for the cost of compliance with clause 8C·3·3 such compliance shall be treated as if it were a Variation required by an instruction of the Architect to which clause 4·2 refers and valued under clause 16 or clause 17 whichever is applicable.

8C·5 On or after the earlier of the Terminal Dates the Sub-Contractor shall not be responsible for loss or damage to the Sub-Contract Works except to the extent of any loss or damage caused thereto by the negligence, breach of statutory duty, omission or default of the Sub-Contractor or any person for whom the Sub-Contractor is responsible.

[f] The Sub-Contractor should consider whether he should take out insurance to cover any risks for which he is not covered under clause 8C·1·2 e.g. impact, subsidence, theft, vandalism.

55.02 The provisions for waiver of subrogation against the sub-contractor are inserted to prevent the insurer who has indemnified the employer or main contractor against a specified peril seeking to claim in respect of such loss against the sub-contractor. This reflects the position established by case law, that a sub-contractor is not liable in tort to the employer for loss covered by insurance effected under the main contract – *Surrey Heath BC* v *Lovell Construction* (1988) 42 BLR 25.

56 Clause 9: Policies of insurance

9 **Policies of Insurance – production – payment of premiums**

9·1 The Sub-Contractor shall, as and when reasonably required to do so by the Contractor, produce documentary evidence showing that the insurance required under clause 7 has been taken out and is being maintained by the Sub-Contractor. On any occasion the Contractor may, but not unreasonably or vexatiously, require the Sub-Contractor to produce the relevant policy or policies and premium receipts therefor.

9·2 If the Sub-Contractor defaults in insuring as provided in clause 7 the Contractor may himself take out insurance against any liability or expense which he may incur arising out of such default and the premium for such insurance shall be paid by the Sub-Contractor to the Contractor or recoverable by the Contractor from the Sub-Contractor as a debt.

9·3 Except where the Main Contract Conditions include clause 22B or clause 22C of the Local Authorities version of the Standard Form **[g]** the Contractor shall, as and when reasonably required to do so by the Sub-Contractor, produce documentary evidence of compliance by the Contractor with the provisions of clause 8A·1 or clause 8B·1 or clause 8C·1 whichever is applicable and the Sub-Contractor may on any occasion, but not unreasonably or vexatiously, require the Contractor to produce the relevant policy or policies and premium receipts therefor.

9·4 If the Contractor defaults in compliance with clause 9·3 the Sub-Contractor may himself take out insurance against any liability or expense which he may incur arising out of such default and the premium for such insurance shall be paid by the Contractor to the Sub-Contractor or recoverable by the Sub-Contractor from the Contractor as a debt.

[g] This exception is included because the Local Authorities version of the Standard Form does not provide any right for the Contractor to require the Employer to produce any documentary evidence or relevant policy or policies and premium receipts.

57 Clause 10

10 **Sub-Contractor's plant etc. – responsibility of Contractor**

The Contractor shall only be responsible for any loss or damage to the plant, tools, equipment or other property belonging to or provided by the Sub-Contractor, his servants or agents and to any materials or goods of the Sub-Contractor which are not Sub-Contract Site Materials to the extent that such loss or damage is due to any negligence, breach of statutory duty, omission or default of the Contractor or any person for whom the Contractor is responsible.

58 Clause 11: Sub-contractor's obligation – carrying out and completion of sub-contract works – extension of sub-contract time

11 **Sub-Contractor's obligation – carrying out and completion of Sub-Contract Works – extension of Sub-Contract time [h]**

11·1 The Sub-Contractor shall carry out and complete the Sub-Contract Works in accordance with the agreed programme details in the Tender, Schedule 2, item 1C, and reasonably in accordance with the progress of the Works but subject to receipt of the notice to commence work on site as detailed in the Tender, Schedule 2, item 1C, and to the operation of clause 11·2.

11·2 ·1 ·1 If and whenever it becomes reasonably apparent that the commencement, progress or completion of the Sub-Contract Works or any part thereof is being or is likely to be delayed, the Sub-Contractor shall forthwith give written notice to the Contractor of the material circumstances including the cause or causes of the delay and identify in such notice any matter which in his opinion comes within clause 11·2·2·1. The Contractor shall forthwith inform the Architect of any written notice by the Sub-Contractor and submit to the Architect any written representations made to him by the Sub-Contractor as to such cause as aforesaid.

·1 ·2 In respect of each and every matter which comes within clause 11·2·2·1, and identified in the notice given in accordance with clause 11·2·1·1, the Sub-Contractor shall, if practicable in such notice, or otherwise in writing as soon as possible after such notice:

·1 ·2 ·1 give particulars of the expected effects thereof; and

·1 ·2 ·2 estimate the extent, if any, of the expected delay in the completion of the Sub-Contract Works or any part thereof beyond the expiry of the period or periods stated in the Tender, Schedule 2, item 1C, or beyond the expiry of any extended period or periods previously fixed under clause 11 which results therefrom whether or not concurrently with delay resulting from any other matter which comes within clause 11·2·2·1; and

·1 ·2 ·3 the Sub-Contractor shall give such further written notices to the Contractor as may be reasonably necessary or as the Contractor may reasonably require for keeping up-to-date the particulars and estimate referred to in clause 11·2·1·2·1 and ·2 including any material change in such particulars or estimate.

·1 ·3 The Contractor shall submit to the Architect the particulars and estimate referred to in clause 11·2·1·2·1 and ·2 and the further notices referred to in clause 11·2·1·2·3 to the extent that such particulars and estimate have not been included in the notice given in accordance with clause 11·2·1·1 and shall, if so requested by the Sub-Contractor join with the Sub-Contractor in requesting the consent of the Architect under clause 35·14 of the Main Contract Conditions.

11·2 ·2 If on receipt of any notice, particulars and estimate under clause 11·2·1 and of a request by the Contractor and the Sub-Contractor for his consent under clause 35·14 of the Main Contract Conditions the Architect is of the opinion that:

[h] See clauses 35·4·7, 36·5·8 and 37·7 (restriction of fluctuations or price adjustments where Sub-Contractor is in default over completion).

·2 ·1 any of the matters which are stated by the Sub-Contractor to be the cause of the delay is an act, omission or default of the Contractor, his servants or agents or his sub-contractors, their servants or agents (other than the Sub-Contractor, his servants or agents) or the occurrence of a Relevant Event; and

·2 ·2 the completion of the Sub-Contract Works or any part thereof is likely to be delayed thereby beyond the period or periods stated in the Tender, Schedule 2, item 1C, or any revised such period or periods

then the Contractor shall, with the written consent of the Architect, give in writing to the Sub-Contractor an extension of time by fixing such revised or further revised period or periods for the completion of the Sub-Contract Works or any part thereof as the Architect in his written consent then estimates to be fair and reasonable. The Contractor shall, in agreement with the Architect, when fixing such revised period or periods state:

·2 ·3 which of the matters, including any of the Relevant Events, referred to in clause 11·2·2·1 they have taken into account; and

·2 ·4 the extent, if any, to which the Architect, in giving his written consent, has had regard to any instructions under clause 13 of the Main Contract Conditions requiring the omission of any work or obligation or restriction since the previous fixing of any such revised period or periods for the completion of the Sub-Contract Works or any part thereof,

and shall, if reasonably practicable having regard to the sufficiency of the aforesaid notice, particulars and estimate, fix such revised period or periods not later than 12 weeks from the receipt by the Contractor of the notice and of reasonably sufficient particulars and estimates, or, where the time between receipt thereof and the expiry of the period or periods for the completion of the Sub-Contract Works or any part thereof is less than 12 weeks, not later than the expiry of the aforesaid period or periods.

If, upon receipt of the aforesaid notice, particulars and estimate and request of the Contractor and the Sub-Contractor, the Architect is of the opinion that he is unable to give his written consent to any revision or further revision of the period or periods for completion of the Sub-Contract Works or any part thereof, the Architect shall so inform the Contractor who shall inform the Sub-Contractor of the opinion of the Architect not later than 12 weeks from the receipt by the Contractor of the aforesaid notice, particulars and estimate and request by the Sub-Contractor or, where the period of time between such receipt and the expiry of the period or periods for the completion of the Sub-Contract Works is less than 12 weeks, not later than the expiry of the aforesaid period or periods.

11·2 ·3 After the first exercise by the Contractor of the duty under clause 11·2·2, the Contractor, with the written consent of the Architect, may in writing to the Sub-Contractor fix a period or periods for completion of the Sub-Contract Works or any part thereof shorter than that previously fixed under clause 11·2·2 if, in the opinion of the Architect, the fixing of such shorter period or periods is fair and reasonable having regard to any instructions issued under clause 13 of the Main Contract Conditions requiring the omission of any work or obligation or restriction where such issue is after the last occasion on which the Contractor with the consent of the Architect made a revision of the aforesaid period or periods.

11·2 ·4 If the expiry of the period when the Sub-Contract Works should have been completed in accordance with the agreed programme details in the Tender, Schedule 2, item 1C, as revised by any operation of the provisions of clause 11, occurs before the date of practical completion of the Sub-Contract Works certified under clause 35·16 of the Main Contract Conditions the Contractor with the consent of the Architect, may

and

not later than the expiry of 12 weeks after the aforesaid date of practical completion of the Sub-Contract Works, the Contractor, with the consent of the Architect, shall

either:

·1 fix such a period or periods for completion of the Sub-Contract Works or any part thereof longer than that previously fixed under clause 11·2 as the Architect in his written consent considers to be fair and reasonable having regard to any of the matters referred to in clause 11·2·2·1 whether upon reviewing a previous decision or otherwise and whether or not the matters referred to in clause 11·2·2·1 have been specifically notified by the Sub-Contractor under clause 11·2·1; or

·2 fix such a period or periods for completion of the Sub-Contract Works or any part thereof shorter than that previously fixed under clause 11·2 as the Architect in his written consent considers to be fair and reasonable having regard to any instruction issued under clause 13·2 of the Main Contract Conditions requiring as a Variation the omission of any work where such issue is after the last occasion on which the Contractor made a revision of the aforesaid period or periods; or

·3 confirm to the Sub-Contractor the period or periods for the completion of the Sub-Contract Works perviously fixed.

Provided always the Sub-Contractor shall use constantly his best endeavours to prevent delay in the progress of the Sub-Contract Works, howsoever caused, and to prevent any such delay resulting in the completion of the Sub-Contract Works being delayed or further delayed beyond the period or periods for completion; and the Sub-Contractor shall do all that may reasonably be required to the satisfaction of the Architect and the Contractor to proceed with the Sub-Contract Works.

11·2 ·5 The following are the Relevant Events referred to in clause 11·2·2·1:

·5 ·1 force majeure;

·5 ·2 exceptionally adverse weather conditions;

·5 ·3 loss or damage occasioned by any one or more of the Specified Perils;

·5 ·4 civil commotion, local combination of workmen, strike or lock-out affecting any of the trades employed upon the Works or any of the trades engaged in the preparation, manufacture or transportation of any of the goods or materials required for the Works;

·5 ·5 compliance by the Contractor and/or Sub-Contractor with the Architect's instructions:

·5 ·5 ·1 under clauses 2·3, 13·2, 13·3, 23·2, 34, 35 or 36 of the Main Contract Conditions, or

·5 ·5 ·2 in regard to the opening up for inspection of any work covered up or the testing of any of the work, materials or goods in accordance with clause 8·3 of the Main Contract Conditions (including making good in consequence of such opening up or testing) unless the inspection or test showed that the work, materials or goods were not in accordance with the Main Contract or the Sub-Contract as the case may be;

·5 ·6 the Contractor, or the Sub-Contractor through the Contractor, not having received in due time necessary instructions, drawings, details or levels from the Architect for which the Contractor or the Sub-Contractor, through the Contractor, specifically applied in writing provided that such application was made on a date which having regard to the Completion Date or the period or periods for the completion of the Sub-Contract Works was neither unreasonably distant from nor unreasonably close to the date on which it was necessary for the Contractor or the Sub-Contractor to receive the same;

·5 ·7 delay on the part of Nominated Sub-Contractors (other than the Sub-Contractor) or of Nominated Suppliers in respect of the Works which the Contractor has taken all practicable steps to avoid or reduce;

<table>
<tr><td>

·5 ·8 ·1 the execution of work not forming part of the Main Contract by the Employer himself or by persons employed or otherwise engaged by the Employer as referred to in clause 29 of the Main Contract Conditions or the failure to execute such work;

·5 ·8 ·2 the supply by the Employer of materials and goods which the Employer has agreed to provide for the Works or the failure so to supply;

·5 ·9 the exercise after the Base Date by the United Kingdom Government of any statutory power which directly affects the execution of the Works by restricting the availability or use of labour which is essential to the proper carrying out of the Works, or preventing the Contractor or Sub-Contractor from, or delaying the Contractor or Sub-Contractor in, securing such goods or materials or such fuel or energy as are essential to the proper carrying out of the Works;

·5 ·10 ·1 the Contractor's or Sub-Contractor's inability for reasons beyond his control and which he could not reasonably have foreseen at the Base Date for the purposes of the Main Contract or the Sub-Contract as the case may be to secure such labour as is essential to the proper carrying out of the Works; or

·5 ·10 ·2 the Contractor's or Sub-Contractor's inability for reasons beyond his control and which he could not reasonably have foreseen at the Base Date for the purposes of the Main Contract or the Sub-Contract as the case may be to secure such goods or materials as are essential to the proper carrying out of the Works;

·5 ·11 the carrying out by a local authority or statutory undertaker of work in pursuance of its statutory obligations in relation to the Works, or the failure to carry out such work;

·5 ·12 failure of the Employer to give in due time ingress to or egress from the site of the Works or any part thereof through or over any land, buildings, way or passage adjoining or connected with the site and in the possession and control of the Employer, in accordance with the Contract Bills and/or the Contract Drawings, after receipt by the Architect of such notice, if any, as the Contractor is required to give, or failure of the Employer to give such ingress or egress as otherwise agreed between the Architect and the Contractor;

·5 ·13 the valid exercise by the Sub-Contractor of the right in clause 21·8 to suspend the further execution of the Sub-Contract Works;

·5 ·14 Where it is stated in the Tender, Schedule 1, item 10 that clause 23·1·2 of the Main Contract Conditions applies to the Main Contract, any deferment by the Employer in giving possession of the site of the Works to the Contractor.

11·3 If the Sub-Contractor shall feel aggrieved by:

a failure of the Architect to give the written consent referred to in clause 11·2·2; and/or

a failure of the Architect to give the written consent referred to in clause 11·2·2 within the period allowed in that clause; and/or

the terms of any written consent referred to in clause 11·2·2

then, subject to the Sub-Contractor giving the Contractor such indemnity and security as the Contractor may reasonably require, the Contractor shall allow the Sub-Contractor to use the Contractor's name and if necessary will join with the Sub-Contractor in arbitration proceedings at the instigation of the Sub-Contractor to decide the matter as aforesaid.

</td></tr>
</table>

Clause 12: Failure of sub-contractor to complete on time

58.01 These two clauses are most logically considered together.

<table>
<tr><td>

12   Failure of Sub-Contractor to complete on time

12·1 If the Sub-Contractor fails to complete the Sub-Contract Works (or any part thereof) within the period or periods for completion or any revised period or periods as provided in clause 11·2·2, the Contractor shall so notify the Architect and give to the Sub-Contractor a copy of such notification.

12·2 The Sub-Contractor shall pay or allow to the Contractor a sum equivalent to any loss or damage suffered or incurred by the Contractor and caused by the failure of the Sub-Contractor as aforesaid. Provided that the Contractor shall not be entitled so to claim unless the Architect in accordance with clause 35·15 of the Main Contract Conditions shall have issued to the Contractor (with a copy to the Sub-Contractor) a certificate in writing certifying any failure notified under clause 12·1.

</td></tr>
</table>

58.02 In considering these clauses it is necessary also to have regard to NSC/1 and NSC/2 in order fully to understand the scheme provided by the sub-contract as regards time for completion of the sub-contract works.

58.03 In NSC/1 Schedule 2 a number of items relevant to the obligation as to sub-contract period are contained. These particular conditions are to be completed in small part by the architect, in part and initially by the sub-contractor, and finally and in agreement with the sub-contractor by the contractor. The procedure is dealt with more fully in the commentary to NSC/1.

NSC/1 Schedule 2, item 1A deals with stipulations as to when sub-contract work can be carried out on site and the period required by the architect for approval of drawings:

these are completed by the architect before sending out NSC/1. Further, under NSC/1 Schedule 2, item 1B provision is made for the sub-contract tenderer to enter his requirements as to drawings, work off site, and work on site. Under item 1C an agreed programme is to be worked out between contractor and sub-contractor, and the order of works likewise is to be agreed.

Relevant provisions of NSC/2

58.04 Clause 1 of NSC/2 requires the proposed sub-contractor to follow the procedures to settle the details in NSC/1 Schedule 2, and clause 3.4 thereof obliges the sub-contractor so to perform the sub-contract that the contractor will not become entitled to an extension of time due to delay on his part.

58.05 Under article 1 of NSC/4 the sub-contractor will carry out and complete the sub-contract works 'in accordance with the tender': further, by clause 11.1 the sub-contractor is under an obligation to proceed in accordance with the programme agreed to proceed in accordance with the programme agreed between himself and the contractor as envisaged by NSC/1 Schedule 1, item 1C and MF clause 35.7.

58.06 It follows that the sub-contractor's timetable will be regulated *vis-à-vis* both the employer and the contractor by what has been agreed between the contractor and the sub-contractor pursuant to the procedure laid down by clause 35.7 of the Main Contract as regards the matters set out in Schedule 2 to NSC/1. Typically there will be an agreed programme for the sub-contract works.

Duties relating to extensions of time

58.07 Under clause 11.2.1.1, the sub-contractor is obliged forthwith to give written notice to the contractor, who shall forthwith inform the architect if the delay occurs or is likely to occur in the commencement, progress, or completion of the sub-contract works.

In regard to each and every such cause of delay specified in clause 11.2.2.1, the sub-contractor either in his notice of delay or in writing thereafter as soon as possible must give particulars of the likely effect of the delay, estimate the length of delay, and give further notices to keep the position up to date when necessary (see clauses 11.2.1.2.2 and 11.2.1.3.3).

58.08 Under clause 11.2.1.3, the contractor is obliged to requesting consent to granting an extension of time for the sub-contractor. This is in accordance with MF clause 35.14, which prohibits the contractor from granting an extension of time to the sub-contractor except in accordance with the provisions of the sub-contractor, which in turn require the architect's written consent.

Action by architect

58.09 Where the architect is of the opinion that the delay is caused by a default of the contractor or a 'relevant event' and completion is likely to be delayed, then the contractor shall with the written consent of the architect give an extension of time such as the architect estimates to be fair and reasonable (see clauses 11.2.2.1 and 11.2.2.2).

58.10 The contractor in agreement with the architect is obliged to state when fixing the extension which matters (including relevant events) have been taken into account and the extent to which the architect has had regard to any variation requiring an omission issued since the previous time for completion was fixed (see clauses 11.2.2.3 and 11.2.2.4). Such period for completion must be fixed not later than twelve weeks from receipt by the contractor of the notice, particulars, and estimate referred to in clause 11.2.1, but in

any event not later than the date already fixed for completion.

58.11 In the event of a variation being ordered resulting in omission of work after the last revision of the period for completion, the contractor may, with the written consent of the architect, fix a period for completion shorter than that previously fixed if the architect thinks this is fair and reasonable, under clause 11.2.3.

58.12 Not later than twelve weeks after the date of practical completion of the sub-contract works (see MF clause 35.16) or the date of practical completion of the main contract works (whichever occurs first), the contractor with the written consent of the architect shall either

1. fix a longer period, or
2. fix a shorter period (but only where a variation requiring an omission has occurred since the last revision of the completion date and if the architect considers it fair and reasonable to do so), or
3. confirm the period previously fixed for the completion of the sub-contract works (see clauses 11.2.4.1 to 11.2.4.3). The sub-contractor must use his best endeavours to avoid delay under clause 11.2.

Relevant events

58.13 Relevant events are defined in clause 11.2.5 and are similar to those in the Main Contract clause 25 (but delay by nominated sub-contractors is restricted to delay caused by *other* nominated sub-contractors).

In addition, under clause 11.2.5.13, the sub-contractor is entitled to an extension of time if he validly exercises his right conferred by clause 21.8 to suspend the further execution of the works for non-payment by the contractor.

If the sub-contractor is dissatisfied by the failure of the architect to give written consent in accordance with clause 11.2.2, or to give written consent to the proposed extension, the sub-contractor may use the contractor's name and join in proceedings in arbitration subject to the provisions of clause 11.3. Note that 'the period allowed in that clause' in clause 11.3 relates to the twelve-week period within which the *contractor* is obliged to give an extension under clause 11.2.2.4.

Damages for delay

58.14 If the sub-contractor delays in completing, the contractor is obliged to inform the architect (with a copy to the sub-contractor). Under MF clause 35.15.2, provision is made for the architect to certify within two months from being notified that the sub-contractor has not completed to time. Under clause 12.2, subject to such certificate, the sub-contractor is to pay or allow to the contractor a sum equivalent to any loss or damage suffered or incurred by the contractor as a result of the delay. It is clear from the case of *Brightside Kilpatrick Engineering* v *Mitchell Construction (1973) Limited* [1975] 2 Lloyds Reports 493, that the issue of such a certificate is a condition precedent to the right of the contractor to claim this loss or damage.

59 Clause 13: Matters affecting regular progress – direct loss and/or expense – contractor's and sub-contractor's rights

59.01 Clause 13.1 gives the sub-contractor rights broadly analogous to those given to the main contractor under MF clause 26. Clause 13.1 provides that if the sub-contractor makes written application to the contractor stating that he has incurred or is likely to incur direct loss and/or expense in the

execution of the sub-contract for which he would not be reimbursed by payment under any other provision of the sub-contract by reason of the regular progress of the sub-contract works or any part thereof having been or being likely to be materially affected by any one or more of the matters referred to in clause 13.1.2, the contractor shall require the architect to operate clause 26.4 of the Main Contract conditions so that the amount of that direct loss and/or expenses if any, may be ascertained.

The circumstances that give rise to a claim under clause 13.1 are based on material effect on the progress of the works. It should be noted that an extension of time under clause 11 is not a condition precedent to a claim for direct loss and expense: presumably, however, if an extension of time has been given for any of the matters in respect of which direct loss and expense are claimable, this will assist the sub-contractor.

---

13   Matters affecting regular progress – direct loss and/or expense – Contractor's and Sub-Contractor's rights

13·1   ·1   If the Sub-Contractor makes written application to the Contractor stating that he has incurred or is likely to incur direct loss and/or expense in the execution of the Sub-Contract for which he would not be reimbursed by a payment under any other provision in the Sub-Contract due to deferment of giving to the Contractor possession of the site of the Works where it is stated in the Tender, Schedule 1, item 10 that clause 23·1·2 of the Main Contract Conditions applies to the Main Contract or by reason of the regular progress of the Sub-Contract Works or of any part thereof having been or being likely to be materially affected by any one or more of the matters referred to in clause 13·1·2 the Contractor shall require the Architect to operate clause 26·4 of the Main Contract Conditions so that the amount of that direct loss and/or expense, if any, may be ascertained. Provided always that:

·1   ·1   the Sub-Contractor's application shall be made as soon as it has become, or should reasonably have become, apparent to him that the regular progress of the Sub-Contract Works or of any part thereof has been or was likely to be affected as aforesaid; and

·1   ·2   the Sub-Contractor shall submit to the Contractor such information in support of his application as is requested by the Architect to obtain from the Sub-Contractor in order reasonably to enable the Architect to operate clause 26·4 of the Main Contract Conditions; and

·1   ·3   the Sub-Contractor shall submit to the Contractor such details of such loss and/or expense as the Contractor is requested by the Architect or the Quantity Surveyor to obtain from the Sub-Contractor in order reasonably to enable the ascertainment of that loss and/or expense under clause 26·4 of the Main Contract Conditions.

13·1   ·2   The following are the matters referred to in clause 13·1·1.

·2   ·1   the Contractor, or the Sub-Contractor through the Contractor, not having received in due time necessary instructions, drawings, details or levels from the Architect for which the Contractor, or the Sub-Contractor through the Contractor, specifically applied in writing provided that such application was made on a date which having regard to the Completion Date or the period or periods for completion of the Sub-Contract Works was neither unreasonably distant from nor unreasonably close to the date on which it was necessary for the Contractor or the Sub-Contractor to receive the same; or

·2   ·2   the opening up for inspection of any work covered up or the testing of any of the work, materials or goods in accordance with clause 8·3 of the Main Contract Conditions (including making good in consequence of such opening up or testing), unless the inspection or test showed that the work, materials or goods were not in accordance with the Main Contract or the Sub-Contract as the case may be; or

·2   ·3   any discrepancy in or divergence between the Contract Drawings and/or the Contract Bills and/or the Numbered Documents; or

·2   ·4   the execution of work not forming part of the Main Contract by the Employer himself or by persons employed or otherwise engaged by the Employer as referred to in clause 29 of the Main Contract Conditions or the failure to execute such work or the supply by the Employer of materials and goods which the Employer has agreed to provide for the Works or the failure so to supply; or

·2   ·5   Architect's instructions issued in regard to the postponement of any work to be executed under the provisions of the Main Contract or the Sub-Contract; or

·2   ·6   failure of the Employer to give in due time ingress to or egress from the site of the Works, or any part thereof through or over any land, buildings, way or passage adjoining or connected with the site and in the possession and control of the Employer, in accordance with the Contract Bills and/or the Contract Drawings, after receipt by the Architect of such notice, if any, as the Contractor is required to give to the Employer to give such ingress or egress as otherwise agreed between the Architect and the Contractor; or

·2   ·7   Architect's instructions issued under clause 13·2 of the Main Contract Conditions requiring a Variation or under clause 13·3 of the Main Contract Conditions in regard to the expenditure of provisional sums (other than work to which clause 13·4·2 of the Main Contract Conditions refers).

13·1   ·3   Any amount from time to time ascertained as a result of the operation of clause 13·1·1 shall be added to the Sub-Contract Sum or included in the calculation of the Ascertained Final Sub-Contract Sum.

13·1   ·4   The Sub-Contractor shall comply with all directions of the Contractor which are reasonably necessary to enable the ascertainment which results from the operation of clause 13·1·1 to be carried out.

13·2   If the regular progress of the Sub-Contract Works (including any part thereof which is sub-sub-contracted) is materially affected by any act, omission or default of the Contractor, his servants or agents, or any sub-contractor, his servants or agents or sub-sub-contractor (other than the Sub-Contractor, his servants or agents or sub-sub-contractors) employed by the Contractor on the Works, the Sub-Contractor shall within a reasonable time of such material effect becoming apparent give written notice thereof to the Contractor and the agreed amount of any direct loss and/or expense thereby caused to the Sub-Contractor shall be recoverable from the Contractor as a debt.

13·3   If the regular progress of the Works (including any part thereof which is sub-contracted) is materially affected by any act, omission or default of the Sub-Contractor, his servants or agents,

59.02 There are several matters listed in clause 13.1.2 as matters affecting regular progress which give rise to a claim. These are:

1. The contractor or the sub-contractor through the contractor not having received in due time necessary instructions, drawings, details, or levels from the architect which the contractor or the sub-contractor through the contractor specifically applied in writing, provided that such application was made on a date which having regard to the completion date or the period or periods for completion of the sub-contract works was neither unreasonably distant from nor unreasonably close to the date on which it was necessary for the contractor or the sub-contractor to receive the same.

    It should be noted that this covers not only late receipt of information by the sub-contractor, but also late receipt by the main contractor of information causing disruption to the sub-contract works.

    Note also that under NSC/2 clause 3.2, the sub-contractor agrees with the employer to supply information so that no delay occurs in the architect's issuing instructions or drawings under the Main Contract in circumstances giving rise to a claim for extension or for loss of expense under the Main Contract.
2. Opening up for inspection of any work. It should be noted that again this applies to the main contractor's work as well as the sub-contract work. It should be noted in passing that there is no equivalent in NSC/4 to MF clause 8.3, and it therefore seems that all opening up and testing is to be carried out by the main contractor.
3. Discrepancies or divergence between contract drawings and/or bills. This refers to the Main Contract drawings and bills, and no express provision seems to be made for discrepancies between the sub-contract drawings and bills.
4. Execution of work not forming part of the Main Contract by the employer as referred to in clause 29 of the Main Contract conditions or the failure to execute such work. Reference should be made to MF clause 29, which obliges the main contractor to permit the employer or those engaged by him to carry out work.
5. Architect's instructions postponing main contract or sub-contract work. Note MF clause 23.2. In fact, that clause of the Main Contract seems on its face only applies to work carried out under the Main Contract ('to be executed under the provisions of this contract'), but presumably is to be interpreted as authorizing postponement both of main contractor's and sub-contractor's work.
6. Failure of employer to give ingress or egress. Architects must be careful to ensure that it will be possible to give ingress and egress at the times provided for in the Main Contract and sub-contract. This may involve securing rights of way or licences from adjoining landowners in order to ensure that no obstruction occurs. Note that the employer is not responsible for failure to give ingress or egress over land which is not in his possession and control. Thus, works to the highway which blocked the access would not provide grounds for a claim for loss and expense (see also SCF clause 11.2.5.12 and MF clause 25.4.12).
7. Architect's instructions issued under clause 13.2 of the Main Contract requiring a variation or under clause 13.3 of the Main Contract in regard to the expenditure of provisional sums (other than where a prime cost sum arises

and the contractor carries out the work under MF clause 35.2).

Procedure

59.03 The prime requirement is that the sub-contractor must make a written application to the main contractor as soon as it has become apparent or should reasonably become apparent to the sub-contractor that regular progress has been or was likely to be affected.

    It is thought that failure to make the application timeously would afford the contractor and the employer a complete defence to a claim under this clause.

59.04 On receipt of the notice, the main contractor is obliged to require the architect to operate clause 26.4 of the Main Contract. This obliges the contractor to pass to the architect the copy of the sub-contractor's written application, and the architect or quantity surveyor then ascertains the amount due. MF clause 26.4 further states that if it is necessary for such ascertainment, the architect is obliged to state in writing the length of the extensions he has given for the completion of the sub-contract works in relation to stated specific relevant events – these are identical with the relevant events set out in SCF clause 13.

59.05 The sub-contractor has to submit such information as is required and details of the loss and expense; he must comply with all directions of the main contractor reasonably necessary to enable ascertainment to take place.

Payment of loss and expense

59.06 Initially this is made by interim certificate under clause 21.4, which also states that $\frac{1}{39}$ is to be added thereto (i.e. main contractor's discount). The amount is not subject to retention. Finally, the amount of the claim is added when the sub-contract sum is calculated in accordance with clause 15.

Claims against contractor

59.07 Under clause 13.2, the sub-contractor may claim against the main contractor for disturbance to the regular progress of the works caused by the main contractor or any sub-contractor of his. Again, notice must be given within the reasonable time of the effect of the act, omission, or default becoming apparent. When the amount of such loss and/or expense is agreed, it does not get adjusted with the sub-contract sum or included in the ascertained final contract sum, but it is recoverable as a debt from the contractor.

Claims by main contractor

59.08 These are dealt with by clause 13.3. Again, the contractor is obliged to give notice within a reasonable time, and the amount agreed may be either deducted by the main contractor for monies due or becoming due to the sub-contractor or recovered as a debt.

60 Clause 14: Practical completion of sub-contract works – liability for defects

60.01 This clause must be read with MF clauses 18 and 35.16. When the sub-contractor thinks the work has been practically completed, he notifies the contractor, who must thereupon inform the architect. The architect then issues a certificate of practical completion of the sub-contract works under MF clause 35.16. Alternatively, if the employer takes possession of the sub-contract works under MF clause 18, practical completion is deemed to have taken place at that time.

---

14   Practical completion of Sub-Contract Works – liability for defects

14·1   If the Sub-Contractor notifies the Contractor in writing of the date when in the opinion of the Sub-Contractor the Sub-Contract Works will have reached practical completion the Contractor shall immediately pass to the Architect any such notification together with any observations thereon by the Contractor (a copy of which observations must immediately be sent by the Contractor to the Sub-Contractor).

14·2   Practical completion of the Sub-Contract Works shall be deemed to have taken place on the day named in the certificate of practical completion of the Sub-Contract Works issued by the Architect under clause 35·16 of the Main Contract Conditions or as provided in clause 18·1·1 of the Main Contract Conditions.

14·3   Subject to clause 18 of the Main Contract Conditions but without prejudice to the obligation of the Sub-Contractor to accept a similar liability to any liability of the Contractor under the Main Contract to remedy defects in the Sub-Contract Works, the Sub-Contractor shall be liable to make good at his own cost and in accordance with any instruction of the Architect or direction of the Contractor all defects, shrinkages and other faults in the Sub-Contract Works or in any part thereof considered necessary by reason of such defects, shrinkages or other faults being due to materials or workmanship not in accordance with the Sub-Contract or due to frost occurring before the date of practical completion of the Sub-Contract Works.

14·4   Where under clause 17·2 or clause 17·3 of the Main Contract Conditions an appropriate deduction from the Contract Sum is made then to the extent that such deduction is relevant to the Sub-Contract Works a pro rata share of such appropriate deduction shall be borne by the Sub-Contractor; and such share may be deducted from any monies due or to become due to the Sub-Contractor or may be recoverable by the Contractor from the Sub-Contractor as a debt.

14·5   The Sub-Contractor upon practical completion of the Sub-Contract Works shall properly clear up and leave the Sub-Contract Works, and all areas made available to him for the purpose of executing them and, so far as used by him for that purpose, clean and tidy to the reasonable satisfaction of the Contractor.

60.02 Practical completion involves not completion down to the last detail but completion for all practical purposes (see *Westminster City Council* v *Jarvis Limited* [1971] 1 All ER 943).

61 Clause 15: Price for sub-contract works

61.01 Where the sub-contract tender was on a lump sum basis, the sub-contract sum is defined by clause 15.1. Where the sub-contract was on the remeasurement basis, the total amount due to the sub-contractor arising out of the remeasurement is called the ascertained final sub-contract sum.

---

15   Price for Sub-Contract Works

15·1   Where in the Tender the Sub-Contractor has quoted a VAT-exclusive Sub-Contract Sum the price for the Sub-Contract Works shall be the Sub-Contract Sum or such other sum as shall become payable in accordance with the Sub-Contract.

15·2   Where in the Tender the Sub-Contractor has quoted a VAT-exclusive Tender Sum subject to complete re-measurement the price for the Sub-Contract Works shall be such sum or sums as shall become payable in accordance with the Sub-Contract and the total of such sum or sums shall be the Ascertained Final Sub-Contract Sum.

61.02 A lump sum contract in this context means one where the contract price for the job is fixed, subject only to changes required by variations. A remeasurement contract is one where the price for the job is not fixed, but the contractor is paid according to the amount of work actually done, as ascertained by remeasurement. This does not, however, affect the contractor's obligation to complete the work (see *Ibmac* v *Marshall* [1968] EGD 218 (QBD) and 611 (CA)).

62 Clause 16: Valuation of variations and provisional sum work

62.01 This clause only applies where the sub-contract is a fixed price sub-contract, where remeasurement is required the rules are laid down in clause 17.

---

16   Valuation of Variations and provisional sum work

16·1   Where clause 15·1 applies, all Variations (including any sanctioned by the Architect in writing) and all work executed by the Sub-Contractor in accordance with the instructions of the Architect as to the expenditure of provisional sums included in the Sub-Contract Documents, shall be valued by the Quantity Surveyor and such valuation (in clause 16 called "the Valuation") shall (unless otherwise agreed by the Contractor and Sub-Contractor and approved by the Employer) be made in accordance with the provisions of clause 16·3.

16·2   Where the Sub-Contractor has included in the Tender a schedule of rates or prices for measured work and/or a schedule of daywork prices, such rates or prices shall be used in determining the Valuation in substitution for any rates or prices or Daywork Definitions which would otherwise be applicable under the relevant provisions of clause 16·3.

16·3   ·1   To the extent that the Valuation relates to the execution of additional or substituted work which can properly be valued by measurement such work shall be measured and shall be valued in accordance with the following rules:

   ·1   ·1   where the work is of similar character to, is executed under similar conditions as, and does not significantly change the quantity of, work set out in bills of quantities and/or other documents comprised in the Sub-Contract Documents the rates and prices for the work so set out shall determine the Valuation;

   ·1   ·2   where the work is of similar character to work set out in bills of quantities and/or other documents comprised in the Sub-Contract Documents but is not executed under similar conditions thereto and/or significantly changes the quantity thereof, the rates and prices for the work so set out shall be the basis for determining the Valuation and the Valuation shall include a fair allowance for such difference in conditions and/or quantity;

   ·1   ·3   where the work is not of similar character to work set out in bills of quantities and/or other documents comprised in the Sub-Contract Documents the work shall be valued at fair rates and prices.

16·3   ·2   To the extent that the Valuation relates to the omission of work set out in bills of quantities and/or other documents comprised in the Sub-Contract Documents the rates and prices for such work therein set out shall determine the Valuation of the work omitted.

16·3   ·3   In any Valuation of work under clauses 16·3·1 and 16·3·2:

   ·3   ·1   where bills of quantities are a Sub-Contract Document measurement shall be in accordance with the same principles as those governing the preparation of those bills of quantities as referred to in clause 18;

   ·3   ·2   allowance shall be made for any percentage or lump sum adjustments in bills of quantities and/or other documents comprised in the Sub-Contract Documents; and

   ·3   ·3   allowance, where appropriate, shall be made for any addition to or reduction of preliminary items of the type referred to in the Standard Method of Measurement 6th Edition, Section B (Preliminaries).

16·3   ·4   To the extent that the Valuation relates to the execution of work which cannot properly be valued by measurement the Valuation shall comprise the prime cost of such work calculated in accordance with the Definition or Definitions of Prime Cost of Daywork identified on page 1 of the Tender together with percentage additions to each section of the prime cost at the rates set out by the Sub-Contractor in the Tender.

   Provided that in any case vouchers specifying the time daily spent upon the work, the workmen's names, the plant and the materials employed shall be delivered for verification to the Contractor for transmission to the Architect or his authorised representative not later than the end of the week following that in which the work has been executed.

16·3   ·5   To the extent that the Valuation does not relate to the execution of additional or substituted work or the omission of work or to the extent that the valuation of any work or liabilities directly associated with a Variation cannot reasonably be effected in the Valuation by the application of clauses 16·3·1 to ·4 a fair valuation thereof shall be made.

   Provided that no allowance shall be made under clause 16·3 for any effect upon the regular progress of the Sub-Contract Works or for any other direct loss and/or expense for which the Sub-Contractor would be reimbursed by payment under any other provision in the Sub-Contract.

16·4   Where it is necessary to measure work for the purpose of the Valuation the Contractor shall give to the Sub-Contractor an opportunity of being present at the time of such measurement and of taking such notes and measurements as the Sub-Contractor may require.

16·5   If compliance with any instruction requiring a Variation under clause 13·2 of the Main Contract Conditions or any instruction as to the expenditure of a provisional sum under clause 13·3 of the Main Contract Conditions substantially changes the conditions under which any part or parts of the Sub-Contract Works which are not the subject of the aforementioned instruction is executed, then such part or parts shall be treated as if it had been the subject of an instruction of the Architect requiring a Variation under clause 13·2 of the Main Contract Conditions which shall be valued in accordance with the provisions of clause 16.

16·6   Effect shall be given to a Valuation under clause 16·3 by addition to or deduction from the Sub-Contract Sum.

62.02 Valuation is to be carried out by the quantity surveyor: clause 16 lays down detailed rules for valuation of these variations. Clause 16.2 provides that where the tender included a Schedule of Rates, variations are to be valued by reference to these and not to daywork rates, which would otherwise form the basis of valuation.

Where it is impossible to measure the work satisfactorily, the sub-contractor is entitled to be paid daywork rates subject to daywork sheets being provided not later than the end of the week following that in which the work was executed. Architects should refuse to pay for daywork not substantiated in this way.

62.03 Note the proviso to clause 16.3, designed to make it clear that no claim for loss and expense, which is reimbursable under any other sub-contract provision, is to be included in a valuation under clause 16.

63 Clause 17: Valuation of all work comprising sub-contract work

63.01 Where the sub-contract is subject to remeasurement so as to produce the ascertained final sub-contract sum under

clause 15.2, clause 17 lays down the method of remeasurement. Essentially, the rules are the same as those for valuing variations under clause 16.

17 **Valuation of all work comprising the Sub-Contract Works**

17·1 Where clause 15·2 applies all work executed by the Sub-Contractor in accordance with the Sub-Contract Documents and the instructions of the Architect, including any instruction requiring a Variation or in regard to the expenditure of a provisional sum included in the Sub-Contract Documents, shall be valued by the Quantity Surveyor and such valuation (in clause 17 called "the Valuation") shall (unless otherwise agreed by the Contractor and Sub-Contractor and approved by the Employer) be made in accordance with the provisions of clause 17·4.

17·2 Where it is necessary to measure work for the purpose of the Valuation the Contractor shall give to the Sub-Contractor an opportunity of being present at the time of such measurement and of taking such notes and measurements as the Sub-Contractor may require.

17·3 Where the Sub-Contractor has included in the Tender a schedule of rates or prices for measured work and/or a schedule of daywork prices, such rates or prices shall be used in determining the Valuation in substitution for any rates or prices or Daywork Definitions which would otherwise be applicable under the relevant provisions of clause 17·4.

17·4 ·1 To the extent that the Valuation relates to the execution of work which can properly be valued by measurement such work shall be measured and shall be valued in accordance with the following rules:

·1 ·1 where the work is of similar character to, is executed under similar conditions as, and does not significantly change the quantity of, work set out in bills of quantities and/or other documents comprised in the Sub-Contract Documents the rates and prices for the work so set out shall determine the Valuation;

·1 ·2 where the work is of similar character to work set out in bills of quantities and/or other documents comprised in the Sub-Contract Documents but is not executed under similar conditions thereto and/or significantly changes the quantity thereof, the rates and prices for the work so set out shall be the basis for determining the Valuation and the Valuation shall include a fair allowance for such difference in conditions and/or quantity;

·1 ·3 where the work is not of similar character to work set out in bills of quantities and/or other documents comprised in the Sub-Contract Documents the work shall be valued at fair rates and prices.

17·4 ·2 In any valuation of work under clause 17·4·1:

·2 ·1 where bills of quantities are a Sub-Contract Document measurement shall be in accordance with the same principles as those governing the preparation of those bills of quantities as referred to in clause 18;

·2 ·2 allowance shall be made for any percentage or lump sum adjustments in bills of quantities and/or other documents comprised in the Sub-Contract Documents; and

·2 ·3 any amounts priced in the Preliminaries section of the Sub-Contract Documents adjusted, where appropriate, to take into account any instructions of the Architect requiring a Variation or in regard to the expenditure of a provisional sum included in the Sub-Contract Documents, shall be included.

17·4 ·3 To the extent that the Valuation relates to the execution of work which cannot properly be valued by measurement the Valuation shall comprise the prime cost of such work calculated in accordance with the Definition or Definitions of Prime Cost of Daywork identified on page 1 of the Tender together with percentage additions to each section of the prime cost at the rates set out by the Sub-Contractor in the Tender.

Provided that in any case vouchers specifying the time daily spent upon the work, the workmen's names, the plant and the materials employed shall be delivered for verification to the Contractor for transmission to the Architect or his authorised representative not later than the end of the week following that in which the work has been executed.

17·4 ·4 If compliance with any instruction of the Architect requiring a Variation under clause 13·2 of the Main Contract Conditions or any instruction as to the expenditure of a provisional sum under clause 13·3 of the Main Contract Conditions or any instruction as a result of which work included in the Tender is not executed substantially changes the conditions under which any part or parts of the Sub-Contract Works which are not the subject of the aforementioned instruction is executed, then such part or parts shall be valued in accordance with the provisions of clause 17·4·1·2.

17·4 ·5 To the extent that the Valuation of any instruction of the Architect requiring a Variation or any instruction as to the expenditure of a provisional sum does not relate to the execution of work or to the extent that the valuation of any work or liabilities directly associated with such Variation cannot reasonably be effected in the Valuation by the application of clause 17·4·1 to ·4 a fair valuation thereof shall be made.

Provided that no allowance shall be made under clause 17·4 for any effect upon the regular progress of the Sub-Contract Works or for any other direct loss and/or expense for which the Sub-Contractor would be reimbursed by payment under any other provision in the Sub-Contract.

64 Clause 18: Bills of quantities – standard method of measurement

64.01 This clause provides that where bills of quantities are a sub-contract document, they are deemed to have been prepared in accordance with the *Standard Method of Measurement of Building Works*, 6th edition. If they are not so prepared, any discrepancy is to be corrected by way of variation. Further, clause 18.1.1.3 specifically provides that the quality and quantity of the work included in the sub-contract sum or tender sum shall be deemed to be that which is set out in the bills of quantities.

18 **Bills of quantities – Standard Method of Measurement**

18·1 Subject always to clause 2·2, if bills of quantities are a Sub-Contract Document:

18·1 ·1 such bills, unless otherwise specifically stated in respect of any specified item or items, are to have been prepared in accordance with the Standard Method of Measurement of Building Works, 6th Edition published by the Royal Institution of Chartered Surveyors and the National Federation of Building Trades Employers;

·2 if in the bills of quantities there is any departure from the method of preparation referred to in clause 18·1·1 or any error in description or in quantity or omission of items, then such departure or error shall not vitiate the Sub-Contract but the departure or error shall be corrected and such correction shall be treated as if it were a Variation required by an instruction of the Architect under clause 13·2 of the Main Contract Conditions;

·3 the quality and quantity of the work included in the Sub-Contract Sum or Tender Sum shall be deemed to be that which is set out in the bills of quantities.

65 Clause 19A: Value added tax Clause 19B: Value added tax – special arrangement – VAT (General) Regulations 1972, regulations 8(3) and 21

65.01 Clauses 19A and 19B are alternatives; clause 19B can be used only where the contractor has under regulation 8(3) of the Value Added Tax (General) Regulations 1972 been allowed to prepare the tax document in substitution for an authenticated receipt issued by the sub-contractor under regulation 21(2), with the sub-contractor's agreement. The tender in NSC/1 Schedule 1 item 1 states whether clause 19A or clause 19B applies. The clauses in their present form were substituted by Amendment 8.

65.02 Both clauses 19A and 19B make it clear that the sub-contract sum is VAT exclusive.

19A **Value added tax**

19A·1 1 In this clause 'tax' means the value added tax introduced by the Finance Act 1972, which is under the care and management of the Commissioners of Customs and Excise (hereinafter called 'the Commissioners')

19A·1 2 To the extent that after the Base Date the supply of goods and services to the Contractor becomes exempt from the tax there shall be paid to the Sub-Contractor an amount equal to the loss of credit (input tax) on the supply to the Sub-Contractor of goods and services which contribute exclusively to the Sub-Contract Works

19A·2 Any reference in the Sub-Contract to 'Sub-Contract Sum', 'Tender Sum' or 'Ascertained Final Sub-Contract Sum' shall be regarded as such Sum exclusive of any tax and recovery by the Sub-Contractor from the Contractor of tax properly chargeable by the Commissioners on the Sub-Contractor under or by virtue of the Finance Act 1972, or any amendment or re-enactment thereof on the supply of goods and services under the Sub-Contract shall be under the provisions of clause 19A Clause 19A 5 shall only apply where so stated in the Tender, Schedule 2, item 8 (NSC/4) in Appendix, part 5A (NSC/4a)

19A·3 Supplies of goods and services under the Sub-Contract are supplies under a contract providing for periodical payment for such supplies within the meaning of Regulation 26 of the Value Added Tax (General) Regulations 1985 or any amendment thereof

19A·4 The Contractor shall pay to the Sub-Contractor in the manner set out in clause 19A any tax chargeable by the Commissioners on the Sub-Contractor on the supply to the Contractor of any goods and services by the Sub-Contractor under the Sub-Contract

19A·5 [h.1] 1 Where it is stated in the Tender Schedule 2, Item 8 (NSC/4) in the Appendix, part 5A (NSC/4a) that clause 19A 5 applies, clauses 19A 6 1 and 19A 6 2 shall not apply unless the Sub-Contractor fails to give the written notice required under clause 19A 5 2 Where clause 19A 5 applies, clauses 19A 1 1, 19A 1 2, 19A 2, 19A 3, 19A 4 and 19A 7 to 10A 10 remain in full force and effect

19A·5 2 Not later than 14 days before the first payment under the Sub-Contract is due to the Sub-Contractor, the Sub-Contractor shall give written notice to the Contractor of the rate of tax chargeable on the supply of goods and services for which interim and final payments are to be made If the rate of tax so notified is varied under statute the Sub-Contractor shall, not later than 7 days after the date when such varied rate comes into effect, send to the Contractor the necessary amendment to the rate given in his written notice and that notice shall then take effect as so amended

19A·5 3 For the purpose of complying with clause 19A 2 for the recovery by the Sub-Contractor from the Contractor of tax properly chargeable by the Commissioners on the Sub-Contractor, an amount calculated at the rate given in the aforesaid written notice (or, where relevant, amended written notice) shall be added to the amount of each interim payment and of the final payment to which clause 21 refers

19A·5 4 Either the Contractor or the Sub-Contractor may give written notice to the other stating that with effect from the date of the notice, clause 19A 5 shall no longer apply From that date the provisions of clauses 19A 6 1 and 19A 6 2 shall apply in place of clause 19A 5

19A·6 1 Unless clause 19A 5 applies the Sub-Contractor shall, not later than 7 days before the date when payment is due to the Sub-Contractor under clause 21 3, give to the Contractor a written provisional assessment of the respective values (less the Retention and cash discount referred to in clause 21 3) of those supplies of goods and services for which payment is due as aforesaid and which will be chargeable at the relevant time of supply under the aforesaid Regulation 26 on the Sub-Contractor at

a zero rate of tax (category one)
and
any rate or rates of tax other than zero (category two)

The Sub-Contractor shall also also specify the rate or rates of tax which are chargeable on those supplies included in category two and shall state the grounds on which he considers such supplies are so chargeable

19A·6 2 The Sub-Contractor shall in relation to any amount payable in accordance with the provisions of clause 21 calculate, by applying the rate or rates of tax specified by the Sub-Contractor as applicable to the sub-contract supply, the tax properly chargeable on such supply and remit such tax to the Sub-Contractor within the period prescribed by clause 21 3 for the payment of the amount in relation to which the tax was calculated

19A·7 Upon receipt of the amounts referred to in clause 21 3 and in either clause 19A 5 3 or clause 19A 6 2 whichever is applicable the Sub-Contractor shall immediately issue to the Contractor a receipt as referred to in Regulation 12(4) of the Value Added Tax (General) Regulations 1985 containing the particulars required under Regulation 13(1) of the Value Added Tax (General) Regulations 1985 or any amendment thereof

Footnote: [h.1] Clause 19A 5 can only apply where the Sub-Contractor is satisfied at the date the Sub-Contract is entered into that his output tax on ***all*** supplies to the Contractor under the Sub-Contract will be at either a positive or a zero rate of tax Some supplies by the Contractor to the Employer are zero rated by a certificate in statutory form Only the person holding the certificate, usually the Contractor, may zero rate his supply Sub-contract supplies for a main contract zero rated by certificate are standard rated: see the VAT leaflet 708 revised 1989

19A·8 If the Sub-Contractor disallows any cash discount claimed by the Contractor under clause 21 3 and the Contractor pays the amount of such discount to the Sub-Contractor the provisions of either clause 19A 5 3 or clause 19A 6 2 whichever is applicable shall not apply to such payment.

19A·9 If for any reason the amount paid under either clause 19A 5 3 or clause 19A 6 2 whichever is applicable is not the amount of tax properly chargeable on the Sub-Contractor by the Commissioners, the Sub-Contractor shall notify the Contractor and the Contractor shall forthwith make any adjustment that may be necessary.

19A·10 Not withstanding any provisions to the Contrary elsewhere in the Sub-Contract, the Contractor, if he has not received from the Sub-Contractor, within 21 days of a payment to which clause 19A refers, any receipt or receipts due under clause 19A 7 may so notify the Sub-Contractor in writing and shall be entitled in that notice to state that he will withhold further payments to the Sub-Contractor unless the receipt or receipts outstanding as specified in the aforesaid written notice have been received before the next payment becomes due. If any payment to the Sub-Contractor is withheld in accordance with clause 19A 10, such payment shall be released to the Sub-Contractor immediately upon receipt by the Contractor of the outstanding receipt or receipts as specified in the aforesaid written notice. Clause 19A 10 does not entitle the Contractor to withhold any payment due to the Sub-Contractor on any ground other than that specified in clause 19A 10.

[i]19B **Value added tax – Special Arrangement – Value Added Tax Act 1983 S 5 (4) – VAT (General) Regulations 1985, Regulations 12(3) and 26**

19B·1 ·1 In this clause 'tax' means the value added tax introduced by the Finance Act 1972, which is under the care and management of the Commissioners of Customs and Excise (hereinafter called 'the Commissioners').

19B·1 ·2 To the extent that after the Base Date the supply of goods and services to the Contractor becomes exempt from the tax there shall be paid to the Sub-Contractor an amount equal to the loss of credit (input tax) on the supply to the Sub-Contractor of goods and services which contribute exclusively to the Sub-Contract Works.

19B·2 Any reference in the Sub-Contract to 'Sub-Contract Sum', 'Tender Sum' or 'Ascertained Final Sub-Contract Sum' shall be regarded as such Sum exclusive of any tax and recovery by the Sub-Contractor from the Contractor of tax properly chargeable by the Commissioners on the Sub-Contractor under or by virtue of the Finance Act 1972, or any amendment or re-enactment thereof on the supply of goods and services under the Sub-Contract shall be under the provisions of clause 19B. Clause 19B 5 shall only apply where so stated in the Tender, Schedule 2, item 8 (NSC/4) in the Appendix, part 5A (NSC/4a).

19B·3 Supplies of goods and services under the Sub-Contract are supplies under a contract providing for periodical payment for such supplies within the meaning of Regulation 26 of the Value Added Tax (General) Regulations 1985 or any amendment thereof.

19B·4 The Contractor shall pay to the Sub-Contractor in the manner set out in clause 19B any tax chargeable by the Commissioners on the Sub-Contractor on the supply to the Contractor of any goods and services by the Sub-Contractor under the Sub-Contract.

19B·5 ·1 Where it is stated in the Tender Schedule 2, item 8 (NSC/4) in the Appendix part 5A (NSC/4a) that clause 19B 5
[i.1] applies, clauses 19B 6 1 and 19B 6 2 shall not apply unless and until any notice issued under clause 19B 5 4 becomes effective or unless the Sub-Contractor fails to give the written notice required under clause 19B 5 2. Where clause 19B 5 applies, clauses 19B 1 1, 19B 1 2, 19B 3, 19B 4, 19B 7 1 to 7 3 and 19B 8 to 19B 10 remain in full force and effect.

19B·5 ·2 Not later than 14 days before the first payment under the Sub-Contract is due to the Sub-Contractor, the Sub-Contractor shall give written notice to the Contractor of the rate of tax chargeable on the supply of goods and services for which interim and final payments are to be made. If the rate of tax so notified is varied under statute the Sub-Contractor shall, not later than 7 days after the date when such varied rate comes into effect, send to the Contractor the necessary amendment to the rate given in his written notice and that notice shall then take effect as so amended.

19B·5 ·3 For the purpose of complying with clause 19B 2 for the recovery by the Sub-Contractor from the Contractor of tax properly chargeable by the Commissioners on the Sub-Contractor, an amount calculated at the rate given in the aforesaid written notice (or, where relevant, amended written notice) shall be added to the amount of each interim payment and of the final payment to which clause 21 refers.

19B·5 ·4 Either the Contractor or the Sub-Contractor may give written notice to the other stating that with effect from the date of the notice clause 19B 5 shall no longer apply. From that date the provisions of clauses 19B 6 1 and 19B 6 2 shall apply in place of clause 19B 5.

19B·6 ·1 Unless clause 19B 5 applies the Sub-Contractor shall, not later than 7 days before the date when payment is due to the Sub-Contractor under clause 21 3, give to the Contractor a written provisional assessment of the respective values (less the Retention and cash discount referred to in clause 21 3) of those supplies of goods and services for which payment is due as aforesaid and which will be chargeable at the relevant time of supply under the aforesaid Regulation 26 on the Sub-Contractor at

a zero rate of tax (category one)
and
any rate or rates of tax other than zero (category two)

The Sub-Contractor shall also also specify the rate or rates of tax which are chargeable on those supplies included in category two and shall state the grounds on which he considers such supplies are so chargeable.

19B·6 ·2 The Sub-Contractor shall in relation to any amount payable in accordance with the provisions of clause 21 calculate, by applying the rate or rates of tax specified by the Sub-Contractor as applicable to the sub-contract supply the tax properly chargeable on such supply, and remit such tax to the Sub-Contractor within the period prescribed by clause 21 3 for the payment of the amount in relation to which the tax was calculated.

19B·7 ·1 The Contractor shall together with the payment under clause 21 3 and the payment of tax under clause 19B 5 3 or clause 19B 6 2, whichever is applicable issue to the Sub-Contractor a document approved by the Commissioners under Regulations 12(3) and 26 of the Value Added Tax (General) Regulations 1985 and shall not insert in this document any date or other writing which purports to represent for any purposes whatsoever the time of supply in respect of which the Sub-Contractor becomes liable for tax (output tax) on the relevant supplies of goods and services to the Contractor. Without prejudice to the above obligation of the Contractor in relation to the time of supply by the Sub-Contractor, the Contractor shall insert in this document the date of despatch of the document to the Sub-Contractor. Provided always that the payment including tax referred to in the document (or reconciled with the actual payment received by the Sub-Contractor in accordance with clause 19B 7 3) has been received, the Sub-Contractor shall insert on this document in a space left thereon for this purpose by the Contractor the date of receipt of the document by the Sub-Contractor. If such payment has not been received the Sub-Contractor shall immediately reject the document and explain to the Contractor the reasons for such rejection.

19B·7 ·2 If the Sub-Contractor disallows any cash discount claimed by the Contractor under clause 21 3 and the Contractor pays the amount of such discount to the Sub-Contractor the provisions of clause 19B 5 3 or clause 19B 6 2 whichever is applicable and clause 19B 7 1 shall not apply.

19B·7 ·3 If the payment received is different from that stated in the document issued by the Contractor to the Sub-Contractor, the Contractor shall issue with that document a reconciliation statement.

19B·8 If:

19B·8 ·1 at any time the Commissioners withdraw the approval referred to in clause 19B 7 1 (in which event the Contractor shall immediately so inform the Sub-Contractor in writing); or

19B·8 ·2 the Sub-Contractor withdraws his consent to the procedure referred to in clause 19B 7 1 and so notifies the Commissioners and the Contractor in writing

then clause 19A (as amended by Amendment 8 issued April 1989) shall be deemed to be incorporated in the Sub-Contract Conditions in respect of payment and tax thereon for any supplies of goods and services remaining to be supplied and/or paid for under the Sub-Contract.

19B·9 Subject to clause 19B 8 the Sub-Contractor shall at no time in respect of supplies and goods and services under the Sub-Contract issue a document which is or purports to be an authenticated receipt within the meaning of Regulation 12(4) of the Value Added Tax (General) Regulations 1985.

19B·10 It is hereby agreed and declared that in issuing any documents referred to in clause 19B the Contractor is not acting as agent for the Sub-Contractor.

Footnote: [i] Clause 19B can ***only*** be used where the Contractor under the Value Added Tax (General) Regulations 1985, Regulations 12(3) and 26 has been allowed to prepare the tax documents in substitution for an authenticated receipt issued by the Sub-Contractor under Regulation 12(4) of the above Regulations, and the Sub-Contractor has consented to the use of this method. The Tender, Schedule 2, item 8 (NSC/4) the Appendix, part 5A (NSC/4a) states whether clause 19A or 19B applies.

Footnote: [i.1] Clause 19B 5 can only apply where the Sub-Contractor is satisfied at the date the Sub-Contract is entered into that his output tax on ***all*** supplies to the Contractor under the Sub-Contract will be at either a positive or a zero rate of tax. Some supplies by the Contractor to the Employer are zero rated by a certificate in statutory form. Only the person holding the certificate, usually the Contractor, may zero rate his supply. Sub-contract supplies for a main contract zero rated by certificate are standard rated: see the VAT leaflet 708 revised 1989.

66 Clause 20A: Finance (No. 2) Act 1975 – tax deduction scheme

Clause 20B: Finance (No. 2) Act 1975 – tax deduction scheme – sub-contractor not user of a current tax certificate

20A **Finance (No. 2) Act 1975 – Tax Deduction Scheme [j] [k]**

20A·1 In clause 20A and in clause 20B the Act means the Finance (No. 2) Act 1975 and the Regulations means the Income Tax (Sub-Contractors in the Construction Industry) Regulations 1975 S.I. No. 1960 or any re-enactment or amendment thereof.

20A·2 ·1 Subject to clause 20A·2·2:

either

20A·2 ·1 ·1 the Sub-Contractor, not later than 21 days before the first payment is due to the Sub-Contractor, shall produce to the Contractor his current tax certificate issued to him under S.70 of the Act and the Contractor shall within 7 days of the date of such production confirm to the Sub-Contractor in writing such production and his satisfaction or non-satisfaction under Regulation 21(1) (a) of the Regulations;

or

·1 ·2 at the sole option of the Sub-Contractor where the Sub-Contractor is a company which is the user of a tax certificate in the form numbered 714C in the Schedule to the Regulations, the Sub-Contractor, not later than 21 days before the first payment is due to the Sub-Contractor, shall lodge with the Contractor a document, as referred to in Regulation 22(1) (c) of the Regulations, referable to his current tax certificate, and the Contractor shall within 7 days of such production confirm to the Sub-Contractor in writing such production and that he has or has not reason to doubt the correctness of the information shown on the document under Regulation 22(1).

20A·2 ·2 Clause 20A·2·1 shall not apply where the Sub-Contractor has previously produced to the Contractor either the tax certificate referred to in clause 20A·2·1·1 or the document referred to in clause 20A·2·1·2 and the Contractor has previously expressed in writing to the Sub-Contractor either his satisfaction as referred to in Regulation 21(1) (a) of the Regulations or that he has no reason to doubt the correctness of the information shown on the document under Regulation 22(1), whichever is applicable.

20A·2 ·3 Where under clause 20A·2·1·2 the Sub-Contractor has produced to the Contractor the document referred to therein the Sub-Contractor shall notify the Contractor in writing of any change in the nominated bank account or accounts specified in that document.

20A·2 ·4 Where either production of the tax certificate and notification of satisfaction under clause 20A·2·1 or lodgement of the document and admission that the Contractor has no reason to doubt under clause 20A·2·1·2 have been made, payment under the Sub-Contract shall, subject to clause 20A·4, be made without the statutory deduction referred to in S.69 (4) of the Act.

20A·3 ·1 The Sub-Contractor shall immediately inform the Contractor in writing if the tax certificate produced by him or referred to in the document produced by him is withdrawn or cancelled and give the date of such withdrawal or cancellation.

20A·3 ·2 The Contractor shall immediately inform the Sub-Contractor of any change in the position stated in the Seventh recital (B) (or in the Tender, Schedule 2,item 7) in regard to the user by the Contractor of a sub-contractor's tax certificate or in the position stated in the Seventh recital (C) (or in the Tender, Schedule 1, item 10) as to whether the Employer is or is not a 'contractor' within the meaning of the Act and the Regulations.

20A·4 ·1 Where the tax certificate produced to the Contractor is in one of the forms numbered 714I or 714P in the Schedule to the Regulations the Sub-Contractor shall immediately upon receipt of any payment from which the deduction referred to in S.69 (4) of the Act has not been made issue to the Contractor a voucher as required by Regulation 23(1) of the Regulations in the form numbered 715 in the aforesaid Schedule.

20A·4 ·2 Where the tax certificate produced to the Contractor is in the form numbered 714S in the Regulations, not later than 7 days before any payment under this Sub-Contract becomes due the Sub-Contractor shall inform the Contractor in writing of the amount to be included in such payment which represents the direct cost to the Sub-Contractor of materials used or to be used by the Sub-Contractor and give to the Contractor a special voucher as required by the Regulations in the form numbered 715S. Where the remainder of the payment as indicated by the voucher exceeds for payment during any one week £150 the Contractor will in accordance with the Regulations deduct the statutory rate of deduction for the time being in force from any excess.

20A·4 ·3 The Contractor shall immediately on receipt pass the voucher referred to in clause 20A·4·1 or clause 20A·4·2 as applicable to the Inland Revenue.

20A·5 ·1 If at any time before a payment is due under the Sub-Contract the Contractor is required by the Act and the Regulations (whether by reason of expiry, withdrawal or cancellation of the Sub-Contractor's tax certificate or otherwise) to make the deduction referred to in S.69 (4) of the Act the Contractor shall immediately notify the Sub-Contractor in writing and require him to state not later than 7 days before such payment becomes due (or, if the said notification is less than 7 days before the payment becomes due, within 10 days of such notification) the amount to be included in such payment which represents the direct cost to the Sub-Contractor of materials used or to be used by the Sub-Contractor.

20A·5 ·2 Where the Sub-Contractor complies with clause 20A·5·1 he shall indemnify the Contractor against any loss or expense caused to the Contractor by any incorrect statement of the amount of direct cost referred to in clause 20A·5·1.

20A·5 ·3 Where the Sub-Contractor does not comply with clause 20A·5·1 the Contractor shall be entitled to make a fair estimate of the amount of direct cost referred to in clause 20A·5·1 and calculate the deduction to be made under S.69 (4) of the Act by taking into account the amount of that fair estimate.

20A·6 Where any error or omission has occurred in calculating or making the deduction referred to in S.69 (4) of the Act the Contractor shall correct that error or omission by repayment to, or by further deduction from payments to, the Sub-Contractor as the case may be, subject only to any statutory obligation on the Contractor not to make such correction.

20A·7 If compliance with clause 20A involves the Contractor or the Sub-Contractor in not complying with any other provisions of the Sub-Contract, then the provisions of clause 20A shall prevail.

20A·8 The provisions of Article 3 shall apply to any dispute or difference as to the operation of clause 20A except where the Act or the Regulations or any other Act of Parliament or statutory instrument rule or order made under an Act of Parliament provide for some other method of resolving such dispute or difference.

[j] For use where in the Seventh recital (A) the words "is not" have been deleted; see also Tender, Schedule 2, item 7. Clause 20B should be deleted where clause 20A applies

[k] Where the Contractor operates with the permission of Inland Revenue the system of dealing with the Tax Deduction Scheme known as "self-vouchering", clause 20A is not applicable; and the Contractor and Nominated Sub-Contractor must make appropriate sub-contractual arrangements; see also Tender, Schedule 2, item 7.

20B Finance (No. 2) Act 1975 – Tax Deduction Scheme – Sub-Contractor not user of a current tax certificate [l]

20B·1 ·1 Not later than 7 days before any payment under this Sub-Contract becomes due the Sub-Contractor shall inform the Contractor in writing of the amount to be included in such payment which represents the direct cost to the Sub-Contractor of materials used or to be used by the Sub-Contractor in order that the deduction referred to in S.69 (4) of the Act can be made from that payment.

20B·1 ·2 Where the Sub-Contractor complies with clause 20B·1·1 he shall indemnify the Contractor against any loss or expense caused to the Contractor by any incorrect statement of the amount of direct cost referred to in clause 20B·1·1.

20B·1 ·3 Where the Sub-Contractor does not comply with clause 20B·1·1 the Contractor shall be entitled to make a fair estimate of the amount of direct cost referred to in clause 20B·1·1 and calculate the deduction to be made under S.69 (4) of the Act by taking into account the amount of that fair estimate.

20B·2 Where any error or omission has occurred in calculating or making the deduction referred to in S.69 (4) of the Act, the Contractor shall correct that error or omission by repayment to, or by further deduction from payments to, the Sub-Contractor as the case may be, subject only to any statutory obligation on the Contractor not to make such correction.

20B·3 The Contractor shall immediately inform the Sub-Contractor of any change in the position stated in the Seventh recital (B) (or in the Tender, Schedule 2, item 7) in regard to the user by the Contractor of a sub-contractor's tax certificate or in the position stated in the Seventh recital (C) (or in the Tender, Schedule 1, item 10) as to whether the Employer is or is not a 'contractor' within the meaning of the Act and the Regulations.

20B·4 If compliance with clause 20B involves the Contractor or the Sub-Contractor in not complying with any other provisions of the Sub-Contract, then the provisions of clause 20B shall prevail.

20B·5 If at any time up to and including the date when the last payment under the Sub-Contract is due to the Sub-Contractor the Sub-Contractor becomes the user of a current sub-contractor's tax certificate under the Act and Regulations, the Sub-Contractor shall immediately notify the Contractor in writing and clause 20A·2 to ·8 of the Sub-Contract Conditions shall be reinstated from the date of such notification as if it had not been deleted and shall come into effect in substitution for clause 20B with the following amendment:

clauses 20A·2·1·1 and 20A·2·1·2 –

delete 'first payment'
insert 'first or next payment'

20B·6 The provisions of Article 3 shall apply to any dispute or difference as to the operation of clause 20B except where the Act or the Regulations or any other Act of Parliament or statutory instrument, rule or order made under an Act of Parliament provide for some other method or resolving such dispute or difference.

[l] For use where in the Seventh recital (A) the word "is" has been deleted; see also Tender, Schedule 2, item 7. Clause 20A·2 to ·8 should be deleted where clause 20B applies.

67 Clause 21: Payment of sub-contractor

67.01 Reference should be made initially to article 2. Article 2.1 contains a contractor's undertaking to pay sub-contract sum, and article 2.2 contains an undertaking to pay on the basis stated in the tender.

21 Payment of Sub-Contractor

21·1 Interim payments and final payment shall be made to the Sub-Contractor in accordance with the provisions of clause 21.

21·2 ·1 Notwithstanding the requirement that the Architect shall issue Interim Certificates under clause 30 of the Main Contract Conditions, the Contractor shall, if so requested by the Sub-Contractor, make application to the Architect as to the matters referred to in clauses 30·2·1·4, 30·2·2·5 and 30·2·3·2 of the Main Contract Conditions.

21·2 ·2 The Contractor shall include in or annex to any application under clause 21·2·1 any written representations of the Sub-Contractor which the Sub-Contractor wishes the Architect to consider including those referred to in clause 37·3·2.

21·2 ·3 The Sub-Contractor shall observe any relevant conditions in clause 30·3 of the Main Contract Conditions before the Architect is empowered to include the value of any off-site materials or goods in Interim Certificates.

21·2 ·4 ·1 Subject to clause 16·1 of the Main Contract Conditions, unfixed materials and goods delivered to, placed on or adjacent to the Works by the Sub-Contractor and intended therefor shall not be removed except for use on the Works unless the Contractor has consented in writing to such removal, which consent shall not be unreasonably withheld.

·4 ·2 Where, in accordance with clause 30·2 of the Main Contract Conditions, the value of any such materials or goods shall have been included in any Interim Certificate under which the amount properly due to the Contractor shall have been discharged by the Employer in favour of the Contractor, such materials or goods shall be and become the property of the Employer and the Sub-Contractor shall not deny that such materials or goods are and have become the property of the Employer. Provided always that the Architect shall in accordance with clause 35·13·1·2 of the Main Contract Conditions have informed the Sub-Contractor of the amount of any interim or final payment directed by the Architect in the Interim Certificate to which clause 21·2·4·2 refers.

·4 ·3 Provided also that if the Contractor shall pay the Sub-Contractor for any such materials or goods before the value therefor has, in accordance with clause 30·2 of the Main Contract Conditions, been included in any Interim Certificate under which the amount properly due to the Contractor has been discharged by the Employer in favour of the Contractor, such materials or goods shall upon such payment by the Contractor be and become the property of the Contractor.

·4 ·4 The operation of clauses 21·2·4·1 to 21·2·4·3 shall be without prejudice to any property in any materials or goods passing to the Contractor as provided in clause 30·3·5 of the Main Contract Conditions *(off-site materials or goods)*.

21·3 ·1 ·1 Within 17 days of the date of issue of an Interim Certificate (including the Interim Certificate referred to in clause 35·17 or clause 30·7 of the Main Contract Conditions) the Contractor shall notify to the Sub-Contractor the amount of the interim or final payment in respect of the Sub-Contract Works which, in accordance with clause 35·13·1 of the Main Contract Conditions, is included in the amount stated as due in the Interim Certificate. The Contractor shall duly discharge his obligation under clause 35·13·2 of the Main Contract Conditions and the Sub-Contract to make that payment within the aforementioned 17 days but less a cash discount of 2½ per cent if discharge is so effected. Immediately upon discharge by the Contractor as aforesaid the Sub-Contractor shall supply the Contractor with written proof of such discharge so as to enable the Contractor to provide the Architect with the "reasonable proof" referred to in clause 35·13·3 of the Main Contract Conditions. **[m]**

·1 ·2 Where the Employer has exercised any right under the Main Contract to deduct from monies due to the Contractor and such deduction is in respect of some act or default of the Sub-Contractor, his servants or agents the amount of such deduction may be deducted by the Contractor from any monies due or to become due under the Sub-Contract or may be recoverable by the Contractor from the Sub-Contractor as a debt.

21·3 ·2 ·1 The Contractor shall only be under an obligation duly to discharge any amount certified in an Interim Certificate issued under clause 35·17 of the Main Contract Conditions provided the Sub-Contractor shall have entered into Agreement NSC/2 including clause 5 of that Agreement unamended in any way and such Agreement is in full force and effect;

·2 ·2 Where the Contractor is under an obligation duly to discharge any amount certified in an Interim Certificate issued under clause 35·17 of the Main Contract Conditions the Sub-Contractor upon such discharge hereby agrees to indemnify the Contractor in respect of any omission, fault or defect in the Sub-Contract Works caused by the Sub-Contractor, his servants or agents for which the Contractor may at any time become liable to the Employer but subject always to the terms of clause 35·19·1 of the Main Contract Conditions.

21·3 ·3 Where, in accordance with clause 2·2 of Agreement NSC/2, the Employer, before the issue of an instruction nominating the Sub-Contractor, has paid to him an amount in respect of design work and/or materials or goods and/or fabrication which is/are included in the subject of the Sub-Contract Sum or Tender Sum and the Employer has made a deduction from the amount due to the Contractor in an Interim Certificate in accordance with clause 35·13·6 of the Main Contract Conditions, then, to the extent of the amount deducted by the Employer, the Contractor shall be deemed to have discharged the interim or final payment to the Sub-Contractor directed by the Architect as being included in the amount due in that Interim Certificate.

21·4 Subject to any agreement between the Sub-Contractor and the Architect as to stage payments, the amount of an interim payment to the Sub-Contractor which is included in the amount stated as due in an Interim Certificate and to which the provisions of clause 35·13 of the Main Contract Conditions apply shall be the gross valuation as referred to in clause 21·4 less

an amount equal to any amount which may be deducted and retained by the Employer as provided in clause 30·2 of the Main Contract Conditions (referred to in the Main Contract Conditions as "the Retention") in respect of the Sub-Contract Works; and

the total amount in respect of the Sub-Contract Works included in the total amount stated as due in Interim Certificates previously issued under the Main Contract Conditions.

The gross valuation shall be the total of the amounts referred to in clauses 21·4·1, and 21·4·2 less the total amount referred to in clause 21·4·3 as applied up to and including a date not more than 7 days before the date of the Interim Certificate as follows:

21·4 ·1 ·1 the total value of the sub-contract work properly executed by the Sub-Contractor including any work so executed to which clause 16·1 refers but excluding any restoration, replacement or repair of loss or damage and removal and disposal of debris which in clauses 8B·4 and 8C·4 are treated as if they were a Variation, together with, where applicable, any adjustment of that total value under clause 37;

·1 ·2 the total value of the materials and goods delivered to or adjacent to the Works for incorporation therein by the Sub-Contractor but not so incorporated provided that the value of such materials and goods shall only be included as and from such times as they are reasonably, properly and not prematurely so delivered and are adequately protected against weather and other casualties;

·1 ·3 the total value of any materials or goods other than those to which clause 21·4·1·2 refers where the Architect in the exercise of his discretion under clause 30·3 of the Main Contract Conditions has decided that such total value shall be included in the amount stated as due in an Interim Certificate.

21·4 ·2 ·1 any amount to be included in Interim Certificates in accordance with clause 3 as a result of payments made or costs incurred by the Sub-Contractor under clause 6 or 7 of the Main Contract Conditions as referred to in clause 5·1·1, and under clause 14·4;

·2 ·2 any amount ascertained as a result of the application of clause 13·1 or in respect of any restoration, replacement or repair of loss or damage and removal and disposal of debris which in clauses 8B·4 and 8C·4 are treated as if they were a Variation;

·2 ·3 any amount payable to the Sub-Contractor under clause 35 or 36, whichever is applicable;

·2 ·4 an amount equal to one thirty-ninth of the amounts referred to in clauses 21·4·2·1, 21·4·2·2 and 21·4·2·3.

21·4 ·3 any amount deductible under clause 4·3·4·1 or 14·4 or any amount allowable by the Sub-Contractor to the Contractor under clause 35 or 36, whichever is applicable together with an amount equal to one thirty-ninth of that amount.

21·5 The Retention which the Employer may deduct and retain as referred to in clause 30·2 of the Main Contract Conditions and clause 21·4 is such percentage of the total amount included under clauses 21·4·1·1 to 21·4·1·3 in any Interim Certificate as arises from the operation of the rules set out in clause 30·4 of the Main Contract Conditions.

21·6 The Retention is subject to the rules set out in clause 30·5 of the Main Contract Conditions.

21·7 If the Sub-Contractor shall feel aggrieved by any amount certified by the Architect or by his failure to certify, then subject to the Sub-Contractor giving to the Contractor such indemnity and security as the Contractor shall reasonably require, the Contractor shall allow the Sub-Contractor to use the Contractor's name and if necessary will join with the Sub-Contractor in arbitration proceedings at the instigation of the Sub-Contractor in respect of the said matters complained of by the Sub-Contractor.

[m] Attention is directed to clause 23 and also to clause 20A or 20B which may be relevant to the due discharge by the Contractor to which clause 21·3·1·1 refers.

21·8 ·1 If:

·1 ·1 subject to clause 23 the Contractor shall fail to discharge his obligation to make any payment to the Sub-Contractor as hereinbefore provided; and

·1 ·2 the Employer has

either for any reason not operated the provisions of clause 35·13·5 of the Main Contract Conditions

or has operated those provisions but for any reason has not paid the Sub-Contractor direct the whole amount which the Contractor has failed to discharge,

within 35 days from the date of issue of the Interim Certificate in respect of which the Contractor has so failed to make proper discharge of his obligation in regard to payment of the Sub-Contractor,

then provided the Sub-Contractor shall have given 14 days' notice in writing to the Contractor and the Employer of his intention to suspend the further execution of the Sub-Contract Works, the Sub-Contractor may (but without prejudice to any other right or remedy) suspend the further execution of the Sub-Contract Works until such discharge or until such direct payment is made whichever first occurs.

21·8 ·2 Such period of suspension shall not be deemed a delay for which the Sub-Contractor is liable under the Sub-Contract. The Contractor shall be liable to the Sub-Contractor for any loss, damage or expense caused to the Sub-Contractor by any suspension of the Sub-Contract Works under the provisions of clause 21·8·1. The right of the Sub-Contractor under clause 21·8·1 shall not be exercised unreasonably or vexatiously.

21·9 ·1 The Contractor's interest in the Sub-Contractor's retention (as identified in the statement issued under clause 30·5·2 of the Main Contract Conditions and referred to in clause 21·6) is fiduciary as trustee for the Sub-Contractor (but without obligation to invest) and if the Contractor attempts or purports to mortgage or otherwise charge such interest or his interest in the whole of the amount retained as aforesaid (otherwise than by floating charge if the Contractor is a limited company) the Contractor shall thereupon immediately set aside in a separate bank account and become a trustee for the Sub-Contractor of a sum equivalent to the Sub-Contractor's retention as identified in the aforesaid statement; provided that upon payment of the same to the Sub-Contractor the amount due to the Sub-Contractor upon final payment under the Sub-Contract shall be reduced accordingly by the amount so paid.

21·9 ·2 If any of the Sub-Contractor's retention is withheld by the Contractor after the period within which such retention should be discharged by the Contractor, the Contractor shall immediately upon the expiry of the aforesaid period place any such unpaid retention money in a separate trust account so identified as to make clear that the Contractor is the trustee for the Sub-Contractor of all such undischarged retention.

21·10 ·1 ·1 Where clause 15·1 applies not later than 6 months after practical completion of the Sub-Contract Works the Sub-Contractor shall send to the Contractor or, if so instructed by him, to the Architect or the Quantity Surveyor, all documents necessary for the purpose of the adjustment of the Sub-Contract Sum.

·1 ·2 Not later than 3 months after receipt by the Contractor (or, if so instructed under clause 21·10·1·1, after receipt by the Architect or the Quantity Surveyor) of the documents referred to in clause 21·10·1·1 a statement of all adjustments to the Sub-Contract Sum to which clause 21·10·2 refers shall be prepared by the Architect or, if the Architect has so instructed, by the Quantity Surveyor and the Architect shall forthwith send a copy of the statement to the Contractor and the Sub-Contractor which shall be before the Architect certifies final payment for the Sub-Contract Works under clause 35·17 or clause 30·7 of the Main Contract Conditions.

21·10 ·2 The Sub-Contract Sum shall be adjusted as follows.

There shall be deducted:

·2 ·1 all provisional sums and the value of all work described as provisional included in the Sub-Contract Documents;

·2 ·2 the amount of the valuation under clause 16·3·2 of items omitted in accordance with a Variation required by an instruction of the Architect or subsequently sanctioned by him in writing together with the amount of any other work included in the Sub-Contract Documents as referred to in clause 16·3·5 which is to be valued under clause 16·3;

·2 ·3 any amount deducted or deductible under clause 4·3·4·1 or 14·4 or any amount allowed to the Contractor under clause 35, 36 or 37, whichever is applicable, together with (except where clause 37 is applicable) an amount equal to one thirty-ninth of that amount;

·2 ·4 any other amount which is required by the Sub-Contract Documents to be deducted from the Sub-Contract Sum.

There shall be added:

·2 ·5 any amount paid or payable by the Contractor to the Sub-Contractor as a result of payments made or costs incurred by the Sub-Contractor under clause 6 or 7 of the Main Contract Conditions as referred to in clause 5·1·1 and under clause 14·4;

·2 ·6 the amount of the valuation under clause 16·3 of any Variation including the valuation of other work, as referred to in clause 16·3·5, under clause 16·3 other than the amount of the valuation of any omission under clause 16·3·2;

·2 ·7 the amount of the valuation of work executed by, or the amount of any disbursements made by, the Sub-Contractor in accordance with the instructions of the Architect as to the expenditure of provisional sums included in the Sub-Contract Documents, and of all work described as provisional included in the Sub-Contract Documents;

·2 ·8 any amount ascertained as a result of the application of clause 13·1;

·2 ·9 any amount paid or payable to the Sub-Contractor under clause 35, 36 or 37, whichever is applicable;

·2 ·10 any other amount which is required by the Sub-Contract to be added to the Sub-Contract Sum;

·2 ·11 an amount equal to one thirty-ninth of the amounts referred to in clauses 21·10·2·5, 21·10·2·8 and, where clause 35 or 36 applies, of the amount referred to in clause 21·10·2·9.

21·11 ·1 Where clause 15·2 applies, not later than 6 months after practical completion of the Sub-Contract Works the Sub-Contractor shall send to the Contractor or, if so instructed by him, to the Architect or the Quantity Surveyor, all documents necessary for the purpose of computing the Ascertained Final Sub-Contract Sum. Not later than 3 months after receipt by the Contractor (or, if so instructed under clause 21·11·1, after receipt by the Architect or the Quantity Surveyor) of the aforesaid documents a statement of the computation of the Ascertained Final Sub-Contract Sum to which clause 21·11·2 refers shall be prepared by the Architect or, if the Architect has so instructed, by the Quantity Surveyor, and the Architect shall forthwith send a copy of the statement to the Contractor and the Sub-Contractor which shall be before the Architect certifies final payment for the Sub-Contract Works under clause 35·17 or clause 30·7 of the Main Contract Conditions.

21·11 ·2 The Ascertained Final Sub-Contract Sum shall be the aggregate of the following:

·2 ·1 any amount paid or payable by the Contractor to the Sub-Contractor as a result of payments made or costs incurred by the Sub-Contractor under clause 6 or 7 of the Main Contract Conditions as referred to in clause 5·1·1 and under clause 14·4;

·2 ·2 the amount of the Valuation under clause 17;

·2 ·3 any amount ascertained as a result of the application of clause 13·1;

·2 ·4 any amount deducted or deductible under clause 4·3·4·1 or 14·4 or any amount paid or payable to or allowed or allowable by the Sub-Contractor under clause 35, 36 or 37, whichever is applicable;

·2 ·5 any other amount which is required to be included or taken into account in computing the Ascertained Final Sub-Contract Sum;

·2 ·6 an amount equal to one thirty-ninth of the amounts referred to in clauses 21·11·2·1, 21·11·2·3 and 21·11·2·4 (so far as clause 21·11·2·4 refers to clauses 35 and 36).

21·12 ·1 Except as provided in clauses 21·12·2 and 21·12·3 (and save in respect of fraud) the Final Certificate issued under clause 30·8 of the Main Contract Conditions shall have effect in any proceedings arising out of or in connection with this Sub-Contract (whether by arbitration under Article 3 or otherwise) as

·1 conclusive evidence that where and to the extent that the quality of materials or goods or the standard of workmanship are to be to the reasonable satisfaction of the Architect the same are to such satisfaction, and

·2 conclusive evidence that any necessary effect has been given to all the terms of this Sub-Contract which require that an amount is to be added to or subtracted from the Sub-Contract Sum or included in the calculation of the Ascertained Final Sub-Contract Sum save where there has been any accidential inclusion or exclusion of any work, materials, goods or figure in any computation or any arithmetical error in any computation in which event the Final Certificate shall have effect as conclusive evidence as to all other computations, and

·3 conclusive evidence that all and only such extensions of time, if any, as are due under clause 11 have been given, and

·4 conclusive evidence that the reimbursement of direct loss and/or expense, if any, to the Sub-Contractor pursuant to clause 13·1 is in final settlement of all or any claims which the Sub-Contractor has or may have arising out of the occurrence of any of the matters referred to in clause 13·1·2 whether such claim be for breach of contract, duty of care, statutory duty or otherwise.

21·12 ·2 If any arbitration or other proceedings have been commenced by either party (or by the Employer and to which the Sub-Contractor is a party) before the Final Certificate under clause 30·8 of the Main Contract Conditions has been issued the Final Certificate shall have effect as conclusive evidence as provided in clause 21·12·1 after either:

·1 such proceedings have been concluded, whereupon the Final Certificate shall be subject to the terms of any award or judgment in or settlement of such proceedings, or

·2 a period of 12 months during which no party has taken any further steps in such proceedings, whereupon the Final Certificate shall be subject to any terms agreed in partial settlement

whichever shall be the earlier.

21·12 ·3 If any arbitration or other proceedings have been commenced by either party (or by the Employer and to which the Sub-Contractor is a party) within 21 days after the Final Certificate under clause 30·8 of the Main Contract Conditions has been issued, the Final Certificate shall have effect as conclusive evidence as provided in clause 21·12·1 save only in respect of all matters to which those proceedings relate.

67.02 It is also necessary to refer to MF clause 30.1.3, which provides that interim certificates are to be issued at the period of interim certificates specified in the Appendix up to and including *the end of the period during which the certificate of practical completion is issued.*

This ensures that a certificate is issued at or just after practical completion so as to, in effect, release half the retention held and also so as to ensure that the basic formula that applies to that payment (if 'formula' fluctuations, as to which see FCS clause 27) is in use rather than the special formulae for payments which occur later.

67.03 Further certificates are to be issued as and when further amounts are ascertained to be payable and also

1. after the expiration of the defects liability period, or
2. upon the issue of the certificate of completion of making good defects (whichever is the later).

This has the effect of releasing the balance of retention.

67.04 Under MF clause 30.7, not later than 28 days prior to the issue of the final certificate an interim certificate is to be issued dealing with the *final amount* related to nominated sub-contractors.

67.05 The provision in NSC/2 clause 2.2 should also be noted. This entitles the sub-contractor to payment for work carried out in advance of nomination on NSC/3 if no nomination results. If nomination does result, there is

provision for credit for the amount paid in advance of nomination.

67.06 Note also NSC/2 clause 4, which gives the nominated sub-contractor a direct right against the employer to ensure that the architect informs the contractor as to the amounts included in respect of the nominated sub-contractor's work in interim certificates as issued in accordance with clause 35.13.1 of the main form.

67.07 Also, NSC/2 clause 5.1 gives the nominated sub-contractor a direct right against the employer to ensure that the early final payment provision of MF clause 35.17 is operated (assuming NSC/2 or NSC/2a has been entered into).

67.08 It should also be remembered that under clause 7.1 of NSC/2, the nominated sub-contractor has a direct right against the employer to ensure that the provisions of MF clause 35.13 are applied, relating to direct payment on failure by the main contractor to make such payment. This is subject to the sub-contractor's obligation to make repayment in the event of the contractor's liquidation (see NSC/2 clause 7.2).

67.09 Against this background, the specific provisions of clause 21 can now be considered. The position is as follows:

1. The architect must issue interim certificates under MF clause 30, including amounts due to nominated sub-contractors.
2. The contractor must, if the nominated sub-contractor so requests, make application to the architect as to the amounts due to the nominated sub-contractor.
3. There is provision for the sub-contractor to comply with the provisions of the main form relating to payment for off-site materials (clause 21.2.3).
4. The sub-contractor will not deny the employer's ownership of on-site materials for which payment has been included in a certificate to the main contractor (see Amendment no. 2, 1984 and discussion in para 24.05).
5. The contractor must within 17 days of the interim certificate notify the sub-contractor of the amount included for him and discharge his obligation to pay.
6. The sub-contractor must immediately thereupon supply proof of such discharge.
7. As regards early final payment to the sub-contractor, the contractor is only liable to discharge the amount certified in such interim certificate for final payment provided NSC/2 with clause 5 thereof unamended is in full force and effect.
8. Where discharge takes place under MF clsue 35.17, the sub-contractor agrees to indemnify the contractor in relation to omission, default, or defect in the sub-contract works caused by the sub-contractor.
9. Provision is made, if the sub-contractor feels aggrieved by the amount certified, for him to commence arbitration in the contractor's name under clause 21.7.

Calculation of amount due

67.10 The rules for calculation are set out in clause 21.4. The items to be included are

1. Work properly executed.
2. Materials on-site.
3. Materials off-site subject to the architect's discretion and compliance with MF clause 30.3.
4. Fees and charges etc. and amount properly to be added for setting out and defects where the cost of these is not to be borne by the sub-contractor.
5. Loss and expense ascertained under clause 13.1.
6. Fluctuation.

One thirty-ninth of the last three items.
Downward fluctuation plus $^1/_{39}$ and retention fall to be deducted.

The amounts to be included are amounts up to and including a date not more than seven days before the date of the interim certificate.

Retention deductions and adjustments

67.11 MF clause 30.2 deals with retention. MF clause 30.2.1 defines those matters subject to retention, and MF clause 30.2.2 those matters which are not. Reference should be made to the relevant provisions of MF clause 30 and notes.

67.12 Under clause 21.9.1, the contractor's interest in the sub-contractor's retention is a fiduciary one: if the contractor attempts to mortgage such interest, an obligation arises immediately to set the retention aside in a separate bank account; if the contractor withholds the sub-contractor's retention beyond the date for discharge, it must likewise be paid into a separate trust account (clause 21.9.2). Clauses 21.10 and 21.11 make provision for final adjustment of the sub-contract sum and for computation of the ascertained sub-contract sum. In both cases, before the architect certifies final payment, the sub-contractor must be supplied with a copy of the computations. As far as deductions are concerned, the provisions of clause 21.3.1.2 should be noted. Presumably what is contemplated is deductions made in respect of defective work (although no provision in the Main Contract gives an express right to make deductions in respect of this). It is difficult to reconcile this provision fully with the provisions of clause 23 (para 69).

67.13 Further, clause 21.10.2 sets out the permissible deductions including 'downward' fluctuations (clause 21.10.2.3).

Right to suspend works

67.14 Under clause 21.8, the sub-contractor is entitled to suspend the work if

1. The contractor does not make payment to the sub-contractor.
2. The employer fails to make direct payment to the sub-contractor where the contractor has failed to make payment, in accordance with MF clause 35.13.5.

The sub-contractor is entitled to suspend work in these circumstances but not to terminate the contract; he is not to be liable for any delay caused thereby, and the contractor is obliged to compensate the sub-contractor for any loss or expense caused by the suspension.

67.15 It is provided that the sub-contractor's rights are not to be exercised unreasonably or vexatiously. It is difficult to be sure of the precise ambit of these words: do they mean that the sub-contractor may not exercise his right for purely trivial or technical reasons, or do they mean that he must not exercise his right unless the failure by the contractor or the employer has been very substantial? The architect should ensure that no cause is given to the sub-contractor to suspend work because of the employer's failure to operate the direct payment provisions of the Main Contract.

67.16 In addition to this express right to suspend work, the sub-contractor does, of course, have a right conferred by the general law to treat the sub-contract as repudiated if the contractor acts in a way evincing an intention no longer to apply by the terms of the sub-contract.

68   Clause 22: Benefits under Main Contract

68.01 It is doubtful whether this clause is likely to be of great importance. But it may be of utility where the sub-contractor wishes to challenge a decision of the architect (e.g. under

clause 26). Under this clause the sub-contractor could presumably initiate proceedings in arbitration under the Main Contract. The sub-contractor is impliedly entitled to necessary assistance and co-operation from the main contractor in enforcing his rights – *Lorne Stewart Ltd* v *William Sindall plc* (1986) 35 BLR 109.

---

22   Benefits under Main Contract

The Contractor will so far as he lawfully can at the request and cost, if any, of the Sub-Contractor obtain for him any rights or benefits of the Main Contract so far as the same are applicable to the Sub-Contract Works but not further or otherwise.

---

69 Clause 23: Contractor's right to set-off

69.01 Set-off involves the situation where A has a claim against B and B has a claim against A which may or may not be related to the subject matter of A's claim and may or may not exceed A's claim.

---

23   Contractor's right to set-off

23·1   The Contractor shall be entitled to deduct from any money (including any Sub-Contractor's retention, notwithstanding the fiduciary obligation of the Contractor under clause 21·9·1) otherwise due under the Sub-Contract any amount agreed by the Sub-Contractor as due to the Contractor, or finally awarded in arbitration or litigation in favour of the Contractor and which arises out of or under the Sub-Contract.

23·2   ·1   Subject to clause 23·2·2, where the Contractor has a claim for loss and/or expense and/or damage which he has suffered or incurred by reason of any breach of, or failure to observe the provisions of, the Sub-Contract by the Sub-Contractor (whether or not the Contractor may have further claims for loss and/or expense and/or damage by reason of any such breach or failure) the Contractor shall be entitled to set-off the amount of such loss and/or expense and/or damage so suffered or incurred against any money otherwise due under the Sub-Contract from the Contractor to the Sub-Contractor including any Sub-Contractor's retention notwithstanding the fiduciary obligation of the Contractor under clause 21·9·1. No loss and/or expense and/or damage suffered or incurred by the Contractor which relates to any delay in completion by the Sub-Contractor may be set-off under clause 23·2 unless the certificate of the Architect has been issued in accordance with clause 12·2 to the Contractor with a duplicate copy to the Sub-Contractor.

          ·2   No set-off under clause 23·2·1 may be made unless

                  such set-off has been quantified in detail and with reasonable accuracy by the Contractor;

                  and

                  the Contractor has given to the Sub-Contractor notice in writing specifying his intention to set-off the amount so quantified together with the details referred to above and the grounds on which such set-off is claimed to be made. Such notice shall be given not less than 3 days before the date of issue of the Interim Certificate which includes, in the amount stated as due, an amount in respect of the Sub-Contractor and from which latter amount the Contractor intends to make the set-off

                  provided that such written notice shall not be binding insofar as the Contractor may amend it in preparing his pleadings for any arbitration pursuant to the notice of arbitration referred to in clause 24·1·1.

23·3   Any amount set off under the provisions of clause 23·2 is without prejudice to the rights of the Contractor or Sub-Contractor in any subsequent negotiations, arbitration proceedings or litigation to seek to vary the amount claimed and set off by the Contractor under clause 23·2.

23·4   The rights of the parties to the Sub-Contract in respect of set-off are fully set out in Sub-Contract NSC/4 and no other rights whatsoever shall be implied as terms of the Sub-Contract relating to set-off.

69.02 Originally at common law no account was taken of mutual claims, and if A sued B, B would have to bring a separate action to enforce hsi right against A.

69.03 In *Gilbert-Ash* v *Modcern Engineering* [1974] AC 689, it was held that unless a contract expressly excluded the normal right of set-off for damages for defects in relation to claims based on the price of work and materials, that right of set-off continued unimpaired (see also *The Aries* [1977] 1 All ER 398). But see also the comments in para 35.08.

The new JCT sub-contract does, however, restrict the common law right of set-off. See *Chatbrown Ltd* v *Alfred McAlpine Construction (Southern) Ltd* (1986) 35 BLR 44.

69.04 Thus one has the position that before setting off a claim for unliquidated damages, the main contractor must

1. In the case of a delay only obtain an architect's certificate.
2. In any case quantify the claim in detail and with reasonable accuracy.
3. Give the requisite notice under clause 23.2.3. See *BWP Architectural Ltd* v *Beaver Building Systems Ltd* (1988) 42 BLR 86.

70 Clause 24: Contractor's claims not agreed by the sub-contractor – appointment of adjudicator

70.01 The adjudicator's role arises where the main contractor has given to the sub-contractor notice of his intention to deduct from money due to the sub-contractor a sum which is neither agreed by the sub-contractor as being due nor finally quantified in arbitration or litigation (under clause 23.2.3). Assuming notice has been given, the sub-contractor, if he does not agree with this notice, may under clause 24.1 send to the contractor by registered post or recorded delivery a written statement setting out the reasons for such disagreement and particulars of any counter-claim against the contractor arising out of the sub-contract to which the sub-contractor considered he is entitled, provided always that he shall have quantified such counter-claim in detail and with reasonable accuracy. This statement is not to bind him, however, in subsequent arbitration or litigation (cf clause 23.2.3).

---

24   Contractor's claims not agreed by the Sub-Contractor– appointment of Adjudicator

24·1   ·1   If the Sub-Contractor, at the date of the written notice of the Contractor issued under clause 23·2·3, disagrees the amount (or any part thereof) specified in that notice which the Contractor intends to set off, the Sub-Contractor may, within 14 days of receipt by him of such notice, send to the Contractor by registered post or recorded delivery a written statement setting out the reasons for such disagreement and particulars of any counterclaim against the Contractor arising out of the Sub-Contract to which the Sub-Contractor considers he is entitled, provided always that he shall have quantified such counterclaim in detail and with reasonable accuracy (which statement and counterclaim if any, shall not however be binding insofar as the Sub-Contractor may amend it in preparing his pleadings for any arbitration pursuant to the notice of arbitration referred to in clause 24·1·1·1) and shall at the same time:

                  ·1   ·1   give notice of arbitration under Article 3 to the Contractor; and

                  ·1   ·2   request action by the Adjudicator in accordance with the right given in clause 24·1·2 (and immediately inform the Contractor of such request) and send to the Adjudicator by registered post or recorded delivery a copy of the aforesaid statement and the written notice of the Contractor to which that statement relates and the aforesaid counterclaim (if any) and brief particulars [n] of the Sub-Contract sufficient to identify for the Adjudicator the terms thereof and where relevant a copy of the certificate of the Architect referred to in clause 12·2.

24·1   ·2   Subject to the provisions of clause 24 and of clauses 21·3 and 23 the Sub-Contractor shall be entitled to request the Adjudicator named in the Tender, Schedule 2, item 6 to act as the Adjudicator to decide those matters referable to the Adjudicator under the provisions of clause 24. If

                  an Adjudicator is not named in the Sub-Contract Documents; or

                  the Adjudicator so named is deceased or is otherwise unable or unwilling to act as the Adjudicator

                  the Adjudicator shall be a person appointed by the Sub-Contractor from the list of Adjudicators maintained by the Building Employers Confederation [o]. Provided that no person shall be appointed, or if appointed shall act, as Adjudicator who has any interest in the Sub-Contract or the Main Contract of which the Sub-Contract is part or in other contracts or sub-contracts in which the Contractor or the Sub-Contractor is engaged unless the Contractor, Sub-Contractor and the Adjudicator so interested otherwise agree in writing within a reasonable time of the Adjudicator's interest becoming apparent.

24·2   Upon receipt of the aforesaid statement the Contractor may within 14 days from the date of such receipt send to the Adjudicator by registered post or recorded delivery a written statement with a copy to the Sub-Contractor setting out brief particulars of his defence to any counterclaim by the Sub-Contractor.

24·3   ·1   If

                  no statement by the Contractor under clause 24·2 has been received by the Adjudicator within the time limit set out in clause 24·2, then within 7 days of expiry of that time limit, or

                  a statement by the Contractor under clause 24·2 has been received within that time limit, then within 7 days of receipt by the Adjudicator of such statement,

                  the Adjudicator without requiring any further statements than those submitted to him under clause 24·1 and where relevant clause 24·2 (save only such further written statements as may appear to the Adjudicator to be necessary to clarify or explain any ambiguity in the written statements of either the Contractor or the Sub-Contractor) and without hearing the Contractor or Sub-Contractor in person, shall, subject to clause 24·3·2, in his absolute discretion and, without giving reasons, decide, in respect of the amount notified by the Contractor under clause 23·2·3, whether the whole or any part of such amount shall be dealt with as follows:

                  ·1   ·1   shall be retained by the Contractor; or

                  ·1   ·2   shall, pending arbitration, be deposited by the Contractor for security with the Trustee-Stakeholder named in the Sub-Contract Documents, or if no Trustee-Stakeholder is so named, with the Trustee-Stakeholder, being a deposit-taking Bank, selected by the Adjudicator; or

                  ·1   ·3   shall be paid by the Contractor to the Sub-Contractor; or

                  ·1   ·4   any combination of the courses of action set out in clauses 24·3·1·1, 24·3·1·2 and 24·3·1·3.

[n] if such brief particulars do not, in the Adjudicator's view, sufficiently identify the terms of the Sub-Contract he has power under clause 24·3·1, lines 8 – 10, to obtain further particulars.   [o] While the Building Employers Confederation (BEC) takes all reasonable care to ensure that the persons entered in the list are appropriately qualified to settle sub-contract disputes of the kind referable to an Adjudicator the BEC offers no guarantee of any kind as to the competence of those listed to discharge the duties of an Adjudicator.

The Adjudicator's decision shall be binding upon the Contractor and the Sub-Contractor until the matters upon which he has given his decision have been settled by agreement or determined by an Arbitrator or the court.

24·3 ·2 The Adjudicator shall reach such decision under clause 24·3·1 as he considers to be fair, reasonable and necessary in all the circumstances of the dispute as set out in the statements referred to in clauses 24·1 to ·3, and such decision shall deal with the whole amount set off by the Contractor under clause 23·2.

24·3 ·3 The Adjudicator shall immediately notify in writing the Contractor and the Sub-Contractor of his decision under clause 24·3·1.

24·4 ·1 Where any decision of the Adjudicator notified under clause 24·3·3 requires the Contractor to deposit an amount with the Trustee-Stakeholder, the Contractor shall thereupon pay such amount to the Trustee-Stakeholder to hold upon the terms hereinafter expressed provided that the Contractor shall not be obliged to pay a sum greater than the amount due from the Contractor under clause 21·3 in respect of which the Contractor has exercised the right of set-off referred to in clause 23·2.

24·4 ·2 Where any decision of the Adjudicator notified under clause 24·3·3 requires the Contractor to pay an amount to the Sub-Contractor, such amount shall be paid by the Contractor immediately upon receipt of the decision of the Adjudicator but subject to the same proviso as set out in clause 24·4·1.

24·5 ·1 The Trustee-Stakeholder shall hold any sum received under the provisions of clauses 24·3 and 24·4 in trust for the Contractor and Sub-Contractor until such time as:

·1 ·1 the Arbitrator appointed pursuant to the notice of arbitration given by the Sub-Contractor under clause 24·1·1·1; or

·1 ·2 the Contractor and Sub-Contractor in a joint letter signed by each of them or on their behalf,

shall otherwise direct and shall, in either of the above cases, forthwith dispose of the said sums as may be directed by the Arbitrator, or failing any direction by the Arbitrator, as the Contractor and Sub-Contractor shall jointly determine. The Trustee-Stakeholder shall deposit the sum received in a deposit account in the name of the Trustee-Stakeholder but shall add the interest to the sum deposited. The Trustee-Stakeholder shall be entitled to deduct his reasonable and proper charges from the sum deposited (including any interest added thereto). The Sub-Contractor shall notify the Trustee-Stakeholder of the name and address of the Adjudicator and Arbitrator referred to in clause 24.

24·5 ·2 Where the Trustee-Stakeholder is a deposit-taking Bank then sums so received by it under the provisions of clauses 24·3 and 24·4 may, notwithstanding the trust imposed, be held by the Trustee-Stakeholder as an ordinary bank deposit to the credit of an account of the Bank as a Trustee-Stakeholder re the Contractor and Sub-Contractor referred to herein; and in respect of such deposit the Trustee-Stakeholder shall pay such usual interest which shall accrue to and form part of the deposit subject to the right of the Trustee-Stakeholder to deduct its reasonable and proper charges and any tax in respect of such interest from the sum deposited.

24·6 The Arbitrator appointed pursuant to the notice of arbitration given under clause 24·1·1·1 may be in his absolute discretion at any time before his final award on the application of either party vary or cancel the decision of the Adjudicator given under clause 24·3 if it appears just and reasonable to him so to do.

24·7 Any action taken by the Contractor under clause 23·2 and by the Sub-Contractor in respect of any counterclaim under clause 24·1·1 is without prejudice to similar action by the Contractor or Sub-Contractor as the case may be if and when further sums become due to the Sub-Contractor.

24·8 The fee of the Adjudicator shall be paid by the Sub-Contractor but the Arbitrator appointed pursuant to the notice of arbitration under clause 24·1·1·1 shall in his final award settle the responsibility of the Contractor or Sub-Contractor or both for payment of the fee or any part thereof and where relevant for the charges of the Trustee-Stakeholder or any part thereof.

70.02 At the same time as serving his counter-notice (if it may be so called), the sub-contractor must give notice of arbitration and request action by the adjudicators.

The role of the adjudicator

70.03 The role of the adjudicator is to give an interim ruling on the disputed set-off pending the setting in motion of the arbitration procedure. Under clause 24.3, he can order the amount of the set-off claimed

1. To be retained by the contractor.
2. To be deposited by the contractor as security with the trustee stakeholder named in the Tender NSC/1 Schedule 2, item 6.
3. Order payment of the amount of the set-off by the contractor to the sub-contractor.
4. Make any combination of such orders.

His decision is binding until the dispute has been settled by an arbitration or the court. Under clause 24.3.2, he is obliged to reach 'such decisions as he considered to be fair and reasonable and necessary in all the circumstances of the dispute'.

70.04 The adjudicator must act on the basis of only the notice and the counter-notice (with any clarification called for by him) and must not hear the parties in person (clause 24.3.1). The aim is to provide for an interim decision and not to have a full-blown arbitration.

Presumably the provisions of clause 24 can be operated on more than one occasion, but it is not clear whether further successive notices of arbitration need be given.

Role of the arbitrator

70.05 Where the adjudicator is involved, the sub-contractor must give notice of arbitration (clause 24.1.1). Under clause 24.6, the arbitrator appointed to that notice 'may in his absolute discretion at any time before his final award on the application by the party vary or cancel the decision of the adjudicator under clause 24.3 if it appears just and reasonable to him so to do'.

Fees

70.06 The fees of the adjudicator are to be paid by the sub-contractor, but the arbitrator has power to direct by whom his fees and the charges of the trustee stakeholder are to be paid.

71 Clause 25: Right of access of contractor and architect

71.01 This right of access extends not only to access on-site, but also to places where work is being prepared for use in the sub-contract works, e.g. the sub-contractor's own factory.

25 **Right of Access of Contractor and Architect**

The Contractor and the Architect and all persons duly authorised by either of them shall, but subject to such reasonable restrictions of the Sub-Contractor as are necessary to protect any proprietary right of the Sub-Contractor, at all reasonable times have access to any work which is being prepared for or will be utilised in the Sub-Contract Works unless the Architect shall certify in writing that the Sub-Contractor has reasonable grounds for refusing such access.

72 Clause 26: Assignment – sub-letting

72.01 At common law the benefit of a contract can be assigned without the other party's consent, although the rule is different in the case of the burden. Sub-contracting is permissible again only with the contractor's and the architect's consent.

26 **Assignment – sub-letting**

26·1 The Sub-Contractor shall not without the written consent of the Architect and Contractor assign the Sub-Contract.

26·2 The Sub-Contractor shall not without the written consent of the Architect and Contractor (which consents shall not be unreasonably withheld) sub-let any portion of the Sub-Contract Works. In case of any difference of opinion on this issue between the Architect and the Contractor the opinion of the Architect shall prevail.

73 Clause 27: General attendance – other attendance etc.

73.01 The contractor has overall control of the site, and therefore will be responsible for items of 'general attendance' as defined in clause 27.1.1. Clearly, it is sensible that the sub-contractor should be entitled to use these, and to have space to erect his own offices etc. NSC/1 Schedule 2, item 3 makes provision for specific items of attendance to be provided by the contractor to the sub-contractor (see clause 27.2).

---

27   General attendance – other attendance etc.

27·1   ·1   General attendance shall be provided by the Contractor free of charge to the Sub-Contractor and shall be deemed to include only the use of the Contractor's temporary roads, pavings and paths, standing scaffolding, standing power operated hoisting plant, the provision of temporary lighting and water supplies, clearing away rubbish, provision of space for the Sub-Contractor's own offices and for the storage of his plant and materials and the use of mess rooms, sanitary accommodation and welfare facilities.

27·1   ·2   Without prejudice to the obligations set out in clause 27·1·1 the Sub-Contractor shall from time to time during the execution of the Sub-Contract Works clear away to a place provided on the site all rubbish resulting from his execution of the Sub-Contract Works and shall keep access to those Works clear at all times.

27·2   The Contractor shall provide, free of charge to the Sub-Contractor, the other items of attendance detailed in the Tender, Schedule 2, item 3.

27·3   Subject to clauses 27·1 and 27·2 the Sub-Contractor shall at his own expense provide, erect, maintain and subsequently remove all necessary workshops, sheds or other temporary buildings for his employees and workmen at or from such places on the site as the Contractor, subject to any reasonable objection by the Sub-Contractor, shall appoint and the Contractor agrees to give all reasonable facilities to the Sub-Contractor for such erection.

27·4   The Contractor, the Sub-Contractor, their employees and workmen respectively in common with all other persons having a like right shall for the purposes of the Works (but not further or otherwise) be entitled to use any erected scaffolding belonging to or provided by the Contractor or the Sub-Contractor as the case may be while it remains so erected upon the site. Provided that such user shall be on the express condition that no warranty or other liability on the part of the Contractor or the Sub-Contractor as the case may be or of their other sub-contractors shall be created or implied under the Sub-Contract in regard to the fitness, condition or suitability of the said scaffolding.

---

74 Clause 28: Contractor and sub-contractor not to make wrongful use of or interfere with the property of the other

---

28   Contractor and Sub-Contractor not to make wrongful use or interfere with the property of the other

The Contractor and the Sub-Contractor respectively and their respective servants or agents or sub-contractors shall not wrongfully use or interfere with the plant, ways, scaffolding, temporary works, appliances or other property belonging to or provided by the other of them or be guilty of any breach or infringement of any Act of Parliament or bye-law, regulations, order or rule made under the same or by any local or other public or competent authority; provided that nothing herein contained shall prejudice or limit the rights of the Contractor or of the Sub-Contractor in the carrying out of their respective statutory duties or contractual duties under the Sub-Contract or under the Main Contract.

---

75 Clause 29: Determination of the employment of the sub-contractor by the contractor

75.01 Two types of determination are envisaged by this clause:

1. Automatic determination of the sub-contractor's employment under the sub-contract on sub-contractor's bankruptcy under clause 29.2. This is straightforward.
2. Determination by reason of sub-contractor's default under clause 29.1.

In relation to the latter, it is important to note that the decision to determine the sub-contractor's employment rests not with the main contractor but with the architect, and reference should be made to MF clause 35.24.4.1 and the notes thereto. The procedure is:

1. Sub-contractor makes default in one of the respects specified in clause 29.1.
2. Contractor informs architect.
3. Contractor sends architect any written observations of the sub-contractor in regard to the matters on which the contractor considers the sub-contractor is in default.
4. Architect is reasonably of opinion that sub-contractor has made default.

In these circumstances *then*

1. Architect issues instructions to contractor to give sub-contractor notice specifying default to which clause 29.1 refers. This instruction may state that the contractor must obtain a further instruction before determining sub-contractor's employment.

2. Contractor then informs architect whether following that notice employment of sub-contractor has been determined. If a further instruction is required (as specified in the original instruction), the contractor must inform the architect whether after this instruction the employment of the sub-contractor has been determined (MF clause 35.24.4.2).
3. In event of contractor informing architect that sub-contractor's employment has been determined, a further sub-contractor is nominated, provided that where the employment of the nominated sub-contractor has been determined under clause 29.1.3, the main contractor is to be given an opportunity to agree the price to be charged by the substituted sub-contractor for rectifying the defective work (MF clause 25.24.4.3).

Where the nominated sub-contractor is in receivership, MF clause 35.24.5 enables the architect to continue his employment where appropriate.

---

29   Determination of the employment of the Sub-Contractor by the Contractor

29·1   Without prejudice to any rights or remedies which the Contractor may possess, if the Sub-Contractor shall make default in any one or more of the following respects that is to say:

29·1   ·1   if without reasonable cause he wholly suspends the carrying out of the Sub-Contract Works before completion thereof; or

·2   if without reasonable cause he fails to proceed with the Sub-Contract Works in the manner provided in clause 11·1; or

·3   if he refuses or neglects after notice in writing from the Contractor to remove defective work or improper materials or goods and by such refusal or neglect the Works are materially affected, or wrongfully fails to rectify defects, shrinkages or other faults in the Sub-Contract Works, which rectification is in accordance with his obligations under the Sub-Contract; or

·4   if he fails to comply with the provisions of either clause 26 or clause 32;

then the Contractor shall so inform the Architect and send to the Architect any written observation of the Sub-Contractor in regard to the default or defaults of which the Contractor is informing the Architect. If so instructed by the Architect under clause 35·24·4·1 of the Main Contract Conditions the Contractor shall issue a notice to the Sub-Contractor by registered post or recorded delivery specifying the default (and send a copy thereof by registered post or recorded delivery to the Architect). If the Sub-Contractor shall either continue such default for 14 days after receipt of such notice or shall at any time thereafter repeat such default (whether previously repeated or not), then the Contractor may (but subject where relevant to the further instruction of the Architect to which clause 35·24·4·1 of the Main Contract Conditions refers) within 10 days after such continuance or repetition by notice by registered post or recorded delivery forthwith determine the employment of the Sub-Contractor under the Sub-Contract; provided that such notice shall not be given unreasonably or vexatiously.

29·2   In the event of the Sub-Contractor becoming bankrupt or making a composition or arrangement with his creditors or having a proposal in respect of his company for a voluntary arrangement for a composition of debts or scheme of arrangement approved in accordance with the Insolvency Act 1986, or having an application made under the Insolvency Act 1986 in respect of his company to the court for the appointment of an administrator, or having a winding up order made or (other than for the purposes of amalgamation or reconstruction) having a resolution for voluntary winding up passed, or having a provisional liquidator, receiver or manager of his business or undertaking duly appointed or, having an administrative receiver, as defined in the Insolvency Act 1986, appointed, or having possession taken by or on behalf of the holders of any debentures secured by a floating charge, of any property comprised in or subject to the floating charge, the employment of the Sub-Contractor under the Sub-Contract shall forthwith automatically be determined. Such determination shall be without prejudice to any other rights or remedies of the Contractor.

29·3   If the Sub-Contractor or any person employed by the Sub-Contractor or acting on his behalf (whether with or without the knowledge of the Sub-Contractor)

·1   shall have offered or given or agreed to give to any person any gift or consideration of any kind as an inducement or reward for doing or forbearing to do or for having done or forborne to do any action in relation to the obtaining or execution of this or any other sub-contract with the Contractor where the Employer is the same Employer as named in the First recital, or for showing or forbearing to show any favour or disfavour to any person in relation to this or any other sub-contract where the Employer is the same Employer as named in the First recital; or

·2   in relation to this or any other sub-contract with the Contractor where the Employer is the same Employer as named in the First recital, shall have committed any offence under the Prevention of Corruption Acts, 1889 to 1916 or where the Employer is a local authority shall have given any fee or reward the receipt of which is an offence under sub-section (2) of Section 117 of the Local Government Act 1972 or any re-enactment thereof

then, if the Employer so requires, the Contractor shall determine the employment of the Sub-Contractor under this Sub-Contract or any other sub-contract referred to in clause 29·3.

29·4   In the event of the employment of the Sub-Contractor under the Sub-Contract being determined under clause 29·1 or 29·2 or 29·3 the following shall be the respective rights and duties of the Contractor and the Sub-Contractor:

29·4   ·1   when the Employer through the Architect nominates a person to carry out and complete the Sub-Contract Works such person may enter upon the Sub-Contract Works and use all temporary buildings, plant, tools, equipment, goods and materials intended for, delivered to and placed on or adjacent to the Works, and may purchase all materials and goods necessary for the carrying out and completion of the Sub-Contract Works;

29·4   ·2   ·1   except where the determination occurs by reason of the bankruptcy of the Sub-Contractor or of him having a winding up order made or (other than for the purposes of amalgamation or reconstruction) a resolution for voluntary winding up passed, the Sub-Contractor shall if so required by the Employer or by the Architect on behalf of the Employer and with the consent of the Contractor within 14 days of the date of determination, assign to the Contractor without payment the benefit of any agreement for the supply of materials or goods and/or for the execution of any work for the purposes of the Sub-Contract but on the terms that the supplier or sub-sub-contractor shall be entitled to make any reasonable objection to any further assignment thereof by the Contractor;

·2   ·2   unless the exception to the operation of clause 29·3·2·1 applies the Contractor, if so directed by the Architect, shall pay any supplier or sub-sub-contractor for any materials or goods delivered or works executed for the purposes of the Sub-Contract (whether before or after the determination) insofar as the price thereof has not already been paid by the Sub-Contractor;

29·4   ·3   the Sub-Contractor shall as and when required by a direction of the Contractor or by an instruction of the Architect so to do (but not before) remove from the Works any temporary buildings, plant, tools, equipment, goods and materials belonging to or hired by him. If within a reasonable time after any such requirement has been made the Sub-Contractor has not complied therewith, then the Contractor may (but without being responsible for any loss or damage) remove and sell any such property of the Sub-Contractor holding the proceeds less all costs incurred to the credit of the Sub-Contractor.

29·5   The Sub-Contractor shall allow or pay to the Contractor in the manner hereinafter appearing the amount of any direct loss and/or damage caused to the Contractor by the determination. Until after completion of the Sub-Contract Works under clause 29·3·1 the Contractor shall not be bound by any provision of the Sub-Contract to make any further payment to the Sub-Contractor. Upon such completion the Sub-Contractor may apply to the Contractor who shall pass such application to the Architect who shall ascertain or instruct the Quantity Surveyor to ascertain the amount of expenses properly incurred by the Employer and the amount of direct loss and/or damage caused to the Employer by the determination; and shall issue an Interim Certificate certifying the value of any work executed or goods and materials supplied by the Sub-Contractor to the extent that their value has not been included in previous Interim Certificates; in paying that Certificate the Employer may deduct the amount of the expenses and direct loss and/or damage of the Employer as aforesaid. The Contractor in discharging his obligation to pay the Sub-Contractor such amount may deduct therefrom a cash discount of 2½ per cent and, without prejudice to any other rights of the Contractor, the amount of any direct loss and/or damage caused to the Contractor by the determination.

Financial consequences and procedure

75.02 These are dealt with by clauses 29.3 and 29.4. The sub-contractor must on direction by the contractor or architect's instruction remove himself and his equipment etc. from site; he can be compelled (provided determination has not occurred as a result of his liquidation) to assign the benefit of any contract for the supply of material or for the execution of any work in relation to the sub-contract. The contractor is under no obligation to make further payment to the sub-contractor until completion. The sub-contractor is obliged to pay the contractor the amount of any loss and expense arising out of the determination; the architect or quantity surveyor are to determine the amount of expenses and loss caused to the employer by the determination. An interim certificate is then issued certifying the value of the sub-contractor's work (less what was previously certified) subject to deduction in respect of the amount of the employer's direct loss and expenses.

Position at common law

75.03 The point must be made again that a failure to proceed on the part of the sub-contractor could amount to repudiation of the sub-contract at common law, entitling the contractor to treat the sub-contract as at an end quite apart from the rights conferred by this clause.

Unjustified exercise of power of determination

75.04 Where the determination of the sub-contractor's employment under the sub-contract was not justified, it seems on principle that the contractor will be liable in damages to the sub-contractor for wrongful determination; it is possible that the architect might also be liable for inducing breach of the sub-contract, in that the contractor is not entitled to determine without an architect's instruction. It is by no means clear, however, whether the contractor would be guilty of wrongfully repudiating the sub-contract if he genuinely believed he was entitled to exercise the contractual power of determination, having regard to the decision in *Woodar* v *Wimpey* [1980] 1 All ER 571.

76 Clause 30: Determination of employment under the sub-contract by the sub-contractor

76.01 This right given to the sub-contractor must be distinguished from his right to suspend work under clause 21.8. The procedure is for the sub-contractor, assuming the circumstances mentioned in clause 30.1.1.1 or 30.1.1.2 arise, to serve a notice on the contractor specifying the default. If the default continues or is subsequently repeated, the

sub-contractor may determine his employment, provided that the notice of determination not be given 'unreasonably or vexatiously'. It is thought that the requirement that the notice be given by registered post or recorded delivery is not a condition precedent to the validity of the sub-contractor's right to determine, provided some equally effective means of communication is used.

30   **Determination of employment under the Sub-Contract by the Sub-Contractor**

30·1   Without prejudice to any other rights or remedies which the Sub-Contractor may possess if the Contractor shall make default (for which default a remedy under any other provisions of the Sub-Contract would not adequately recompense the Sub-Contactor) in any of the following respects:

30·1   ·1   ·1   if without reasonable cause he wholly suspends the Works before completion; or

·1   ·2   if without reasonable cause he fails to proceed with the Works so that the reasonable progress of the Sub-Contract Works is seriously affected;

then the Sub-Contractor may issue to the Contractor a notice by registered post or recorded delivery (a copy of which must be sent at the same time to the Architect by registered post or recorded delivery) specifying the default. If the Contractor shall continue such default for 14 days after receipt of such notice or if the Contractor shall at any time thereafter repeat such default (whether previously repeated or not) the Sub-Contractor may thereupon by notice by registered post or recorded delivery determine the employment of the Sub-Contractor; provided that such notice shall not be given unreasonably or vexatiously.

30·2   Upon such determination, then without prejudice to the accrued rights or remedies of either party or to any liability of the classes mentioned in clause 6 which may accrue before the Sub-Contractor shall have removed his temporary buildings, plant, tools, equipment, goods or materials or by reason of his so removing the same, the respective rights and duties of the Sub-Contractor and Contractor shall be as follows:

30·2   ·1   the Sub-Contractor shall with all reasonable dispatch and in such manner and with such precautions as will prevent injury, death or damage of the classes in respect of which he is liable to indemnify the Contractor under clause 6 remove from the site all his temporary buildings, plant, tools, equipment, goods or materials subject to the provisions of clause 30·2·2·4;

30·2   ·2   after taking into account amounts previously paid under the Sub-Contract the Sub-Contractor shall be paid by the Contractor:

·2   ·1   the total value of work completed at the date of determination, such value to be ascertained in accordance with clause 21;

·2   ·2   the total value of work begun and executed but not completed at the date of determination, such value to be ascertained either under clause 16 as if it were a Valuation of a Variation (where clause 15·1 applies) or under clause 17 (where clause 15·2 applies);

·2   ·3   any sum ascertained in respect of direct loss and/or expense under clause 13·1 (whether ascertained before or after the date of determination);

·2   ·4   the cost of materials or goods properly ordered for the Sub-Contract Works (but not incorporated therein) for which the Sub-Contractor shall have paid or is legally bound to accept delivery and on such payment by the Contractor any materials or goods so paid for shall become the property of the Contractor;

·2   ·5   the reasonable cost of removal under clause 30·2·1;

·2   ·6   any direct loss and/or expense caused to the Sub-Contractor by the determination.

76.02 The financial effects of determination under clause 30 are dealt with by clause 30.2. Under clause 30.2.2.1, the sub-contractor is entitled to the total value of the work completed. In addition he is entitled to

1. The value of work incomplete.
2. The amount of any direct loss and expense.
3. The cost of materials ordered for the works and which cannot be returned.
4. The reasonable cost of removing from site.
5. The amount of loss and expense caused by the determination.

Note that the value of work in clauses 30.2.2.1 and 30.2.2.2 means the value of the work taking into account any defects (cf *Lintest Builders* v *Roberts* 10 BLR 120).

77 Clause 31: Determination of the main contractor's employment under the Main Contract

77.01 This clause deals with two situations in which the main contractor's employment under the Main Contract may be determined

1. Determination under MF clause 27 on default or bankruptcy.
2. Determination under MF clause 28 for non-payment or obstruction of certificates or continuous suspension of the works for a period of the length named in the Appendix to the Main Contract.

---

31   Determination of the Contractor's employment under the Main Contract

31·1   If the employment of the Contractor is determined under clause 27 of the Main Contract Conditions, then the employment of the Sub-Contractor under the Sub-Contract shall thereupon also determine and the provisions of clause 30·2 shall thereafter apply.

31·2   ·1   If the employment of the Contractor is determined under clause 28 or clause 28A of the Main Contract Conditions then the employment of the Sub-Contractor under the Sub-Contract shall thereupon also determine. The entitlement of the Sub-Contractor to payment shall be the proportion fairly and reasonably attributable to the Sub-Contract Works of the amounts paid by the Employer under clause 28·2·2·1 to ·5 of the Main Contract Conditions inclusive together with, where the determination is under clause 28 any amounts paid in respect of the Sub-Contractor under clause 28·2·2·6 of the Main Contract Conditions provided the Sub-Contractor shall have supplied to the Contractor all evidence reasonably necessary to establish the direct loss and/or damage caused to the Sub-Contractor by the determination as referred to in clause 28·2·2·6 of the Main Contract Conditions.

31·2   ·2   Nothing in clause 31·2·1 shall affect the entitlement of the Sub-Contractor to the proper operation of clause 21 in respect of the amount, included in the amount stated as due therein, in respect of the Sub-Contract Works in an Interim Certificate of the Architect whose date of issue was prior to the date of determination of the employment of the Contractor under clause 28 of the Main Contract Conditions.

Where determination is under clause 27 of the Main Contract, the sub-contractor is entitled to be paid on the basis of clause 30.2 and is treated as if he had justifiably determined his own employment. Where the determination is under clause 28, the contractor is, of course, entitled to be paid (under MF clause 28.2)

1. The value of completed and uncompleted work.
2. The amount of any direct loss and expense.
3. The cost of materials ordered for the works.
4. The reasonable cost of removal.
5. Any direct loss and/or damage caused to the contractor or to any nominated sub-contractor by the determination.

It will be observed that this list roughly corresponds with the list set out in SCF clause 30.2. Accordingly, clause 31.2 provides, in effect, that the sub-contractor is entitled to his share of the benefits given to the main contractor where determination occurs under MF clause 28 in respect of both the value of work etc., and any direct loss and/or expense caused by the determination.

78   Clause 32: Fair wages

---

32   Fair Wages

The following provisions shall apply where clause 19A is included in the Main Contract Conditions.

32·1   ·1   The Sub-Contractor shall pay rates of wages and observe hours and conditions of labour not less favourable than those established for the trade or industry in the district where the work is carried out by machinery of negotiation or arbitration to which the parties are organisations of employers and trade unions representative respectively of substantial proportions of the employers and workers engaged in the trade or industry in the district.

32·1   ·2   In the absence of any rates of wages, hours or conditions of labour so established the Sub-Contractor shall pay rates of wages and observe hours and conditions of labour which are not less favourable than the general level of wages, hours and conditions observed by other employers whose general circumstances in the trade or industry in which the Sub-Contractor is engaged are similar.

32·2   The Sub-Contractor shall in respect of all persons employed by him (whether in carrying out the Sub-Contract or otherwise) in every factory, workshop or other place occupied or used by him for the carrying out of the Sub-Contract (including the Sub-Contract Works) comply with the general conditions required by clause 32. The Sub-Contractor hereby warrants that to the best of his knowledge and belief he has complied with the general conditions required by clause 32 for at least 3 months prior to the date of his tender for the Sub-Contract.

32·3   The Sub-Contractor shall recognise the freedom of his workpeople to be members of trade unions.

32·4   The Sub-Contractor shall at all times during the continuance of the Sub-Contract display, for the information of his workpeople, in every factory, workshop or place occupied or used by him for the carrying out of the Sub-Contract (including the Sub-Contract Works) a copy of clause 32. Where rates of wages, hours or conditions of work have been established either by negotiation or arbitration as described in clause 32·1·1 or by any agreement commonly recognised by employers and workers in the district, a copy of the award, agreement or other document specifying or recording such rates, hours or conditions shall also be exhibited by the Sub-Contractor or made available by him for inspection in any such place as aforesaid.

32·5   The Sub-Contractor shall be responsible for the observance of clause 32 by sub-sub-contractors employed in the carrying out of the Sub-Contract, and shall if required notify the Contractor and Employer of the names and addresses of all such sub-sub-contractors.

32·6   The Sub-Contractor shall keep proper wages books and time sheets showing the wages paid to and the time worked by the workpeople in his employ in and about the carrying out of the Sub-Contract, and such wages books and time sheets shall be produced whenever required for the inspection of any officer authorised by the Contractor and Employer.

32·7   If the Contractor and Employer shall have reasonable ground for believing that the requirements of any of the provisions of clause 32 are not being observed, the Contractor, the Employer or the Architect on behalf of the Employer shall be entitled to require proof of the rates of wages paid and hours and conditions observed by the Sub-Contractor and sub-sub-contractors in carrying out the Sub-Contract Works.

---

79   Clause 33: Strikes – loss or expense

79.01   This clause makes it clear that no claim is to be made by either contractor or sub-contractor if the work is affected by strike action, subject to the contractor's obligation in clause 33.1.2 and the sub-contractor's obligation in clause 33.1.3.

79.02   Presumably (though this is not spelt out) the incidents of a strike will not entitle the parties to exercise their rights under clause 29 or clause 30, since a strike would not be a factor normally within the control of either party. However, a strike might amount to 'force majeure' under MF clause 28.1.3.1, and thereby give rise to determination under SCF clause 31.2.1, where it resulted in total prevention of work on-site over a prolonged period. Alternatively, such a strike might cause the contractor to be frustrated, leading to its being treated as discharged under the Law Reform (Frustrated Contract) Act 1943.

---

33   Strikes – loss or expense

33·1   If the Works or the Sub-Contract Works are affected by a local combination of workmen, strike or lockout affecting any of the trades employed upon the Works or any of the trades engaged in the preparation, manufacture or transportation of any of the goods or materials required for the Works:

33·1   ·1   neither the Contractor nor the Sub-Contractor shall be entitled to make any claim upon the other for any loss and/or expense resulting from such action as aforesaid;

33·1   ·2   the Contractor shall take all reasonably practicable steps to keep the site open and available for the use of the Sub-Contractor;

33·1   ·3   the Sub-Contractor shall take all reasonably practicable steps to continue with the Sub-Contract Works.

33·2   Nothing in clause 33 shall affect any other right of the Contractor or Sub-Contractor under the Sub-Contract if such action as aforesaid occurs.

---

80   Clause 34: Choice of fluctuation provisions – Tender, Schedule 1, Item 2

---

34   Choice of fluctuation provisions – Tender, Schedule 1, item 2 [p]

34·1   Fluctuations shall be dealt with in accordance with whichever of the following alternatives:

    clause 35, or
    clause 36, or
    clause 37

is stated in the Tender, Schedule 1, item 2 as being applicable to the Sub-Contract. The provisions so stated shall be deemed to be incorporated with Sub-Contract NSC/4 as executed by the parties thereto. [q]

34·2   Clause 35 shall be used where neither clause 36 nor 37 is stated in the Tender, Schedule 1, item 2 as applicable to the Sub-Contract.

[p] Clause 36 should be used where the parties have agreed to allow the labour and materials cost and tax fluctuations to which clauses 36·1 to ·3 refer. Alternatively clause 37 should be used where the parties have agreed that the Sub-Contract Sum or the Tender Sum shall be adjusted by the formula method under the JCT Sub-Contract/Works Contract Formula Rules.

[q] Notwithstanding the provisions of clause 34·1 on deemed incorporation the parties may nevertheless wish to incorporate the agreed alternative fluctuation provisions in the executed Sub-Contract.

Clause 35: Contribution, levy and tax fluctuations

---

35   Contribution, levy and tax fluctuations

35·1   The Sub-Contract Sum or Tender Sum as the case may be shall be deemed to have been calculated in the manner set out below and shall be subject to adjustment in the events specified hereunder:

35·1   ·1   The prices contained in the Sub-Contract Sum or the Tender Sum are based upon the types and rates of contribution, levy and tax payable by a person in his capacity as an employer and which at the Date of Tender are payable by the Sub-Contractor. A type and rate so payable are in clause 35·1·2 referred to as a 'tender type' and a 'tender rate'.

35·1   ·2   If any of the tender rates other than a rate of levy payable by virtue of the Industrial Training Act 1964, is increased or decreased, or if a tender type ceases to be payable, or if a new type of contribution, levy or tax which is payable by a person in his capacity as an employer becomes payable after the Date of Tender, then in any such case the net amount of the difference between what the Sub-Contractor actually pays or will pay in respect of

·1   workpeople engaged upon or in connection with the Sub-Contract Works either on or adjacent to the site, and

2   2   workpeople directly employed by the Sub-Contractor who are engaged upon the production of materials or goods for use in or in connection with the Sub-Contract Works and who operate neither on nor adjacent to the site and to the extent that they are so engaged

or because of his employment of such workpeople and what he would have paid had the alteration, cessation or new type of contribution, levy or tax not become effective, shall, as the case may be, be paid to or allowed by the Sub-Contractor.

35·1 ·3 There shall be added, to the net amount paid to or allowed by the Sub-Contractor under clause 35·1·2, in respect of each person employed by the Sub-Contractor who is engaged upon or in connection with the Sub-Contract Works either on or adjacent to the site and who is not within the definition of 'workpeople' in clause 35·6·3 the same amount as is payable or allowable in respect of a craftsman under clause 35·1·2 or such proportion of that amount as reflects the time (measured in whole working days) that each such person is so employed.

35·1 ·4 For the purposes of clause 35·1·3:

no period less than 2 whole working days in any week shall be taken into account and periods less than a whole working day shall not be aggregated to amount to a whole working day;

the phrase "the same amount as is payable or allowable in respect of a craftsman" shall refer to the amount in respect of a craftsman employed by the Sub-Contractor (or by any sub-sub-contractor under a sub-sub-contract to which clause 35·3 refers) under the rules or decisions or agreements of the National Joint Council for the Building Industry or other wage-fixing body and, where the aforesaid rules or decisions or agreements provide for more than one rate of wage emolument or other expense for a craftsman, shall refer to the amount in respect of a craftsman employed as aforesaid to whom the highest rate is applicable; and

the phrase "employed by the Sub-Contractor" shall mean an employment to which the Income Tax (Employment) Regulations 1973 (the PAYE Regulations) under S.204 of the Income and Corporation Taxes Act 1970, apply.

35·1 ·5 The prices contained in the Sub-Contract Sum or the Tender Sum are based upon the types and rates of refund of the contributions, levies and taxes payable by a person in his capacity as an employer and upon the types and rates of premium receivable by a person in his capacity as an employer being in each case types and rates which at the Date of Tender are receivable by the Sub-Contractor. Such a type and such a rate are in clause 35·1·6 referred to as a 'tender type' and a 'tender rate'.

35·1 ·6 If any of the tender rates is increased or decreased or if a tender type ceases to be payable or if a new type of refund of any contribution, levy or tax payable by a person is his capacity as an employer becomes receivable, or if a new type of premium receivable by a person in his capacity as an employer becomes receivable after the Date of Tender, then in any such case the net amount of the difference between what the Sub-Contractor actually receives or will receive in respect of workpeople as referred to in clauses 35·1·2·1 and 35·1·2·2 or because of his employment of such workpeople and what he would have received had the alteration, cessation or new type of refund or premium not become effective, shall, as the case may be, be paid to or allowed by the Sub-Contracor.

35·1 ·7 The references in clauses 35·1·5 and 35·1·6 to premiums shall be construed as meaning all payments howsoever they are described which are made under or by virtue of an Act of Parliament to a person in his capacity as an employer and which affect the cost to an employer of having persons in his employment.

35·1 ·8 Where employer's contributions are payable by the Sub-Contractor in respect of workpeople as referred to in clauses 35·1·2·1 and 35·1·2·2 whose employment is contracted-out employment within the meaning of the Social Security Pensions Act 1975, the Sub-contractor shall for the purpose of recovery or allowance under clause 35·1 be deemed to pay employer's contributions as if that employment were not contracted-out employment.

35·1 ·9 The references in clause 35·1 to contributions, levies and taxes shall be construed as meaning all impositions payable by a person in his capacity as an employer howsoever they are described and whoever the recipient which are imposed under or by virtue of an Act of Parliament and which affect the cost to an employer of having persons in his employment.

35·2 The Sub-Contract Sum or the Tender Sum as the case may be shall be deemed to have been calculated in the manner set out below and shall be subject to adjustment in the events specified hereunder:

35·2 ·1 The prices contained in the Sub-Contract Sum or the Tender Sum are based upon the types and rates of duty if any and tax if any (other than value added tax which is treated, or is capable of being treated, as input tax (as referred to in the Finance Act 1972) by the Sub-Contractor) by whomsoever payable which at the Date of Tender are payable on the import, purchase, sale, appropriation, processing or use of the materials, goods, electricity and, where so specifically stated by the Employer in the Tender, Schedule 1, Appendix (A), fuels, specified in the list included in or attached to the aforesaid Appendix, under or by virtue of any Act of Parliament. A type and a rate so payable are in clause 35·2·2 referred to as a 'tender type' and a 'tender rate'.

35·2 ·2 If in relation to any materials or goods specified as aforesaid, or any electricity or fuels specified as aforesaid and consumed on site for the execution of the Sub-Contract Works including temporary site installations for those Sub-Contract Works, a tender rate is increased or decreased, or a tender type ceases to be payable or a new type of duty or tax (other than value added tax which is treated, or is capable of being treated as input tax (as referred to in the Finance Act 1972) by the Sub-Contractor) becomes payable on the import, purchase, sale, appropriation, processing or use of those materials, goods, electricity or fuels, after the Date of Tender, then in any such case the net amount of the difference between what the Sub-Contractor actually pays in respect of those materials, goods, electricity or fuels and what he would have paid in respect of them had the alteration, cessation or imposition not occurred, shall, as the case may be, be paid to or allowed by the Sub-Contractor. In clause 35·2·2 the expression 'a new type of duty or tax' includes an additional duty or tax and a duty or tax imposed in regard to specified materials, goods, electricity or fuels in respect of which no duty or tax whatever was previously payable (other than any value added tax which is treated, or is capable of being treated, as input tax (as referred to in the Finance Act 1972) by the Sub-Contractor).

35·3 Fluctuations – work sub-let to sub-sub-contractors

35·3 ·1 If the Sub-Contractor shall decide subject to clause 26·2 to sub-let any portion of the Sub-Contract Works he shall incorporate in the sub-sub-contract provisions to the like effect as the provisions of

clause 35 (excluding clause 35·3) including the percentage stated in the Tender, Schedule 1, item 2 pursuant to clause 35·7

which are applicable for the purposes of the Sub-Contract.

35·3 ·2 If the price payable under such a sub-sub-contract as referred to in clause 35·3·1 is decreased below or increased above the price in such sub-sub-contract by reason of the operation of the said incorporated provisions, then the net amount of such decrease or increase shall, as the case may be, be allowed by or paid to the Sub-Contractor under the Sub-Contract.

35·4 to ·6 Provisions relating to clause 35

35·4 ·1 The Sub-Contractor shall give a written notice to the Contractor of the occurrence of any of the events referred to in such of the following provisions as are applicable for the purposes of the Sub-Contract:

35·4 ·1 ·1 clause 35·1·2;

·1 ·2 clause 35·1·6;

·1 ·3 clause 35·2·2;

·1 ·4 clause 35·3·2.

35·4 ·2 Any notice required to be given by clause 35·4·1 shall be given within a reasonable time after the occurrence of the event to which the notice relates, and the giving of a written notice in that time shall be a condition precedent to any payment being made to the Sub-Contractor in respect of the event in question.

35·4 ·3 The Contractor and the Sub-Contractor may agree with the Quantity Surveyor what shall be deemed for all the purposes of the Sub-Contract to be the net amount payable to or allowable by the Sub-Contractor in respect of the occurrence of any event such as is referred to in any of the provisions listed in clause 35·4·1.

35·4 ·4 Any amount which from time to time becomes payable to or allowable by the Sub-Contractor by virtue of clauses 35·1 and ·2 or 35·3 shall, as the case may be, be added to or deducted from

35·4 ·4 ·1 the Sub-Contract Sum; and

·4 ·2 any amounts payable to the Sub-Contractor and which are calculated in accordance with clause 30·2·2·1 or 30·2·2·2,

or included in the calculation of the Ascertained Final Sub-Contract Sum. The addition or deduction to which clause 35·4·4 refers shall be subject to the provisions of clauses 35·4·5 to ·4·7.

35·4 ·5 As soon as is reasonably practicable the Sub-Contractor shall provide such evidence and computations as the Contractor and the Architect or the Quantity Surveyor may reasonably require to enable the amount payable to or allowable by the Sub-Contractor by vitue of clauses 35·1 and ·2 or 35·3 to be ascertained, and in the case of amounts payable to or allowable by the Sub-Contractor under clause 35·4·1·3 (or clause 35·3 for amounts payable to or allowable by the Sub-Contractor under provisions in the sub-sub-contract to the like effect as clauses 35·1·3 and 35·1·4) – employees other than workpeople – such evidence shall include a certificate signed by or on behalf of the Sub-Contractor each week certifying the validity of the evidence reasonably required to ascertain such amounts.

35·4 ·6 No addition to or deduction from the Sub-Contract Sum or inclusion in the calculation of the Ascertained Final Sub-Contract Sum made by virtue of clause 35·4·4 shall alter in any way the amount of profit of the Sub-Contractor included in that Sum.

35·4 ·7 Subject to the provisions of clause 35·4·8 no amount shall be added or deducted in the computation of the amount stated as due in an Interim Certificate in respect of amounts otherwise payable to or allowable by the Sub-Contractor by virtue of clauses 35·1 and ·2 or 35·3 if the event (as referred to in the provisions listed in clause 35·4·1) in respect of which the payment or allowance would be made occurs after the date of the failure by the Sub-Contractor to complete as certified by the Architect as referred to in clause 12·2.

35·4 ·8 Clause 35·4·7 shall not be applied unless

35·4 ·8 ·1 the printed text of clauses 11·2 and 11·3 is unamended and forms part of the Sub-Contract Conditions; and

·8 ·2 the Architect has in respect of every written request by the Contractor and Sub-Contractor under clause 11·2·2, consented or not consented in writing to such revision of the period or periods for completion of the Sub-Contract Works as he considered to be in accordance with clause 11·2 and with clause 35·14 of the Main Contract Conditions.

35·5 Clauses 35·1 to ·3 shall not apply in respect of:

35·5 ·1 work for which the Sub-Contractor is allowed daywork rates under clause 16·3·4 or 17·4·3;

35·5 ·2 changes in the rate of value added tax charged on the supply of goods or services by the Sub-Contractor to the Contractor under the Sub-Contract.

35·6 In clause 35:

35·6 ·1 the expression 'the Date of Tender' means the date inserted in the Tender, Schedule 1, Appendix (A);

35·6 ·2 the expressions 'materials' and 'goods' include timber used in formwork but do not include other consumable stores, plant and machinery (save that electricity and, where specifically so stated in the Tender, Schedule 1, Appendix (A), fuels are dealt with in clause 35·2);

35·6 ·3 the expression 'workpeople' means persons whose rates of wages and other emoluments (including holiday credits) are governed by the rules or decisions or agreements of the National Joint Council for the Building Industry or some other wage-fixing body for trades associated with the building industry;

35·6 ·4 the expression 'wage-fixing body' shall mean a body which lays down recognised terms and conditions of workers within the meaning of the Employment Protection Act 1975 Schedule 11, paragraph 2(a).

35·7 Percentage addition to fluctuation payments or allowances

35·7 ·1 There shall be added to the amount paid to or allowed by the Sub-Contractor under:

35·7 ·1 ·1 clause 35·1·2;

·1 ·2 clause 35·1·3;

·1 ·3 clause 35·1·6;

·1 ·4 clause 35·2·2;

the percentage stated in the Tender, Schedule 1, item 2.

Clause 36: Labour and materials cost and tax fluctuations

36 Labour and materials cost and tax fluctuations

36·1 The Sub-Contract Sum or the Tender Sum as the case may be shall be deemed to have been calculated in the manner set out below and shall be subject to adjustment in the events specified hereunder:

36·1 ·1 The prices contained in the Sub-Contract Sum or Tender Sum (including the cost of employer's liability insurance and of third party insurance) are based upon the rates of wages and the other emoluments and expenses (including holiday credits) which will be payable by the Sub-Contractor to or in respect of

36·1 ·1 ·1 workpeople engaged upon or in connection with the Sub-Contract Works either on or adjacent to the site, and

·1 ·2 workpeople directly employed by the Sub-Contractor who are engaged upon the production of materials or goods for use in or in connection with the Sub-Contract Works and who operate neither on nor adjacent to the site and to the extent that they are so engaged

in accordance with:

·1 ·3 the rules or decisions of the National Joint Council for the Building Industry or other wage-fixing body which will be applicable to the Sub-Contract Works and which have been promulgated at the Date of Tender; and

·1 ·4 any incentive scheme and/or productivity agreement under the provisions of Rule 1·16 or any successor to this Rule (Productivity Incentive Schemes and/or Productivity Agreement) of the Rules of the National Joint Council for the Building Industry (including the General Principles covering Incentive Schemes and/or Productivity Agreements published by the aforesaid Council to which Rule 1·16 or any successor to this Rule refers) or provisions on incentive schemes and/or productivity agreements contained in the rules or decisions of some other wage-fixing body; and

·1 ·5 the terms of the Building and Civil Engineering Annual and Public Holidays Agreements (or the terms of agreements to similar effect in respect of workpeople whose rates of wages and other emoluments and expenses (including holiday credits) are in accordance with the rules or decisions of a wage-fixing body other than the National Joint Council for the Building Industry) which will be applicable to the Sub-Contract Works and which have been promulgated at the Date of Tender;

and upon the rates or amounts of any contribution, levy or tax which will be payable by the Sub-Contractor in his capacity as an employer in respect of, or calculated by reference to, the rates of wages and other emoluments and expenses (including holiday credits) referred to herein.

36·1 ·2 If any of the said rates of wages or other emoluments and expenses (including holiday credits) are increased or decreased by reason of any alteration in the said rules, decisions or agreements promulgated after the Date of Tender, then the net amount of the increase or decrease in wages and other emoluments and expenses (including holiday credits) together with the net amount of any consequential increase or decrease in the cost of employer's liability insurance, of third party insurance, and of any contribution, levy or tax payable by a person in his capacity as an employer shall, as the case may be, be paid to or allowed by the Sub-Contractor.

36·1 ·3 There shall be added to the net amount paid to or allowed by the Sub-Contractor under clause 36·1·2, in respect of each person employed by the Sub-Contractor who is engaged upon or in connection with the Sub-Contract Works either on or adjacent to the site and who is not within the definition of 'workpeople' in clause 36·7·3 the same amount as is payable or allowable in respect of a craftsman under clause 36·1·2 or such proportion of that amount as reflects the time (measured in whole working days) that each such person is so employed.

36·1 ·4 For the purposes of clauses 36·1·3 and 36·2·3:

no period less than 2 whole working days in any week shall be taken into account and periods less than a whole working day shall not be aggregated to amount to a whole working day;

the phrase 'the same amount as is payable or allowable in respect of a craftsman' shall refer to the amount in respect of a craftsman employed by the Sub-Contractor (or by any sub-sub-contractor under a sub-sub-contract to which clause 36·4 refers) under the rules or decisions or agreements of the National Joint Council for the Building Industry or other wage-fixing body and, where the aforesaid rules or decisions or agreements provide for more than one rate of wage, emolument or other expense for a craftsman, shall refer to the amount in respect of a craftsman employed as aforesaid to whom the highest rate is applicable; and

the phrase 'employed by the Sub-Contractor' shall mean an employment to which the Income Tax (Employment) Regulations 1973 (the PAYE Regulations) under S.204 of the Income and Corporation Taxes Act 1970, apply.

36·1 ·5 The prices contained in the Sub-Contract Sum or the Tender Sum are based upon:

the transport charges referred to in the basic transport charges list submitted by the Sub-Contractor and attached to the Tender, Schedule 1, Appendix (A) incurred by the Sub-Contractor in respect of workpeople engaged in either of the capacities referred to in clauses 36·1·1·1 and 36·1·1·2; or

the reimbursements of fares which will be reimbursable by the Sub-Contractor to workpeople engaged in either of the capacities referred to in clauses 36·1·1·1 and 36·1·1·2 in accordance with the rules or decisions of the National Joint Council for the Building Industry which will be applicable to the Sub-Contract Works and which have been promulgated at the Date of Tender or, in the case of workpeople so engaged whose rates of wages and other emoluments and expenses are governed by the rules or decisions of some wage-fixing body other than the National Joint Council for the Building Industry, in accordance with the rules or decisions of such other body which will be applicable and which have been promulgated as aforesaid.

36·1 ·6 If:

36·1 ·6 ·1 the amount of transport charges as referred to in the basic transport list is increased or decreased after the Date of Tender; or

·6 ·2 the reimbursement of fares is increased or decreased by reason of any alteration in the said rules or decisions promulgated after the Date of Tender or by an actual increase or decrease in fares which takes effect after the Date of Tender

then the net amount of that increase or decrease shall, as the case may be, be paid to or allowed by the Sub-Contractor.

36·2 The Sub-Contract Sum or the Tender Sum as the case may be shall be deemed to be calculated in the manner set out below subject to adjustment in the events specified hereunder:

36·2 ·1 The prices contained in the Sub-Contract Sum or the Tender Sum are based upon the types and rates of contribution, levy and tax payable by a person in his capacity as an employer and which at the Date of Tender are payable by the Sub-Contractor. A type and rate so payable are, in clause 36·2·2, referred to as a 'tender type' and a 'tender rate'.

36·2 ·2 If any of the tender rates other than a rate of levy payable by virtue of the Industrial Training Act 1964, is increased or decreased or if a tender types ceases to be payable, or if a new type of contribution, levy or tax which is payable by a person in his capacity as an employer becomes payable after the Date of Tender, then in any such case the net amount of the difference between what the Sub-Contractor actually pays or will pay in respect of workpeople as referred to in clauses 36·1·1·1 and 36·1·1·2 or because of his employment of such workpeople, and what he would have paid had the alteration, cessation or new type of contribution, levy or tax not become effective, shall, as the case may be, be paid to or allowed by the Sub-Contractor.

36·2 ·3 There shall be aded, to the net amount paid to or allowed by the Sub-Contractor under clase 36·2·2, in respect of each person employed by the Sub-Contractor who is engaged upon or in connection with the Sub-Contract Works either on or adjacent to the site and who is not within the definition of "workpeople" in clause 36·7·3 the same amount as is payable or allowable in respect of a craftsman under clause 36·2·2 or such proportion of that amount as reflects the time (measured in whole working days) that each such person is so employed. The provisions of clause 36·1·4 shall apply to clause 36·2·3.

36·2 ·4 The prices contained in the Sub-Contract Sum or the Tender Sum are based upon the type and rates of refund of the contributions, levies and taxes payable by a person in his capacity as an employer and upon the types and rates of premium receivable by a person in his capacity as an employer being in each case types and rates which at the Date of Tender are receivable by the Sub-Contractor. Such a type and such a rate are, in clause 36·2·5 referred to as a 'tender type' and a 'tender rate'.

36·2 ·5 If any of the tender rates is increased or decreased or if a tender type ceases to be payable or if a new type of refund of any contribution, levy or tax payable by a person in his capacity as an employer becomes receivable or if a new type of premium receivable by a person in his capacity as an employer becomes receivable after the Date of Tender, then in any such case the net amount of the difference between what the Sub-Contractor actually receives or will receive in respect of workpeople as referred to in clauses 36·1·1·1 and 36·1·1·2 or because of his employment of such workpeople, and what he would have received had the alteration, cessation or new type of refund or premium not become effective, shall, as the case may be, be paid to or allowed by the Sub-Contractor.

36·2 ·6 The reference in clauses 36·2·4 and 36·2·5 to premiums shall be construed as meaning all payments howsoever they are described which are made under or by virtue of an Act of Parliament to a person in his capacity as an employer and which affect the cost to an employer of having persons in his employment.

36·2 ·7 Where employer's contributions are payable by the Sub-Contractor in respect of workpeople as referred to in clauses 36·1·1·1 and 36·1·1·2 whose employment is contracted-out employment within the meaning of the Social Security Pensions Act 1975, the Sub-Contractor shall, subject to the proviso hereto, for the purpose of recovery or allowance under clause 36·2 be deemed to pay employer's contributions as if that employment were not contracted-out employment; provided that clause 36·2·7 shall not apply where the occupational pension scheme, by reference to membership of which the employment of workpeople is contracted-out employment, is established by the rules of the National Joint Council for the Building Industry or of some other wage-fixing body so that contributions to such occupational pension scheme are within the payment and allowance provisions of clause 36·1.

36·2 ·8 The reference in clauses 36·2·1 to 36·2·5 and 36·2·7 to contributions, levies and taxes shall be construed as meaning all impositions payable by a person in his capacity as an employer howsoever they are described and whoever the recipient which are imposed under or by virtue of an Act of Parliament and which affect the cost to an employer of having persons in his employment.

36·3 The Sub-Contract Sum or the Tender Sum as the case may be shall be deemed to have been calculated in the manner set out below and shall be subject to adjustment in the events specified hereunder:

36·3 ·1 The prices contained in the Sub-Contract Sum or the Tender Sum are based upon the market prices of the materials, goods, electricity and, where specifically so stated by the Employer in the Tender, Schedule 1, Appendix (A), fuels, specified ina list submitted by the Sub-Contractor and included in or attached to the Tender, which were current at the Date of Tender. Such prices are hereinafter referred to as 'basic prices', and the prices set out by the Sub-Contractor on the said list shall be deemed to be the basic prices of the specified materials, goods, electricity and fuels.

36·3 ·2 If after the Date of Tender the market price of any of the materials or goods specified as aforesaid increases or decreases, or the market price of any electricity or fuels specified as aforesaid and consumed on site for the execution of the Sub-Contract Works (including temporary site installations for these Sub-Contract Works) increases or decreases, then the net amount of the difference between the basic price thereof and the market price payable by the Sub-Contractor and current when the materials, goods, electricity or fuels are bought shall, as the case may be, be paid to or allowed by the Sub-Contractor.

36·3 ·3 The references in clauses 36·3·1 and 36·3·2 to 'market prices' shall be construed as including any duty or tax (other than value added tax which is treated, or is capable of being treated as input tax (as referred to in the Finance Act 1972) by the Sub-Contractor) by whomsoever payable which is payable under or by virtue of any Act of Parliament on the import, purchase,sale, appropriation, processing or use of the materials, goods, electricity or fuels specified as aforesaid.

36·4 Fluctuations – work sub-let to sub-sub-contractors

36·4 ·1 If the Sub-Contractor shall decide, subject to clause 26·2, to sub-let any portion of the Sub-Contract Works he shall incorporate in the sub-sub-contract provisions to the like effect as the provisions of

clause 36 (excluding clause 36·4) including the percentage stated in the Tender, Schedule 1, item 2 pursuant to clause 36·8

which are applicable for the purposes of the Sub-Contract.

36·4 2 If the price payable under such a sub-sub-contract as referred to in clause 36·4·1 is decreased below or increased above the price in such sub-sub-contract by reason of the operation of the said incorporated provisions, then the net amount of such decrease or increase shall, as the case may be, be allowed by or paid to the Sub-Contractor under the Sub-Contract.

36·5 to 7 **Provisions relating to clause 36**

36·5 1 The Sub-Contractor shall give a written notice to the Contractor of the occurrence of any of the events referred to in such of the following provisions as are applicable for the purposes of the Sub-Contract:

36·5 ·1 ·1 clause 36·1·2;

    ·1 ·2 clause 36·1·6;

    ·1 ·3 clause 36·2·2;

    ·1 ·4 clause 36·2·5;

    ·1 ·5 clause 36·3·2;

    ·1 ·6 clause 36·4·2;

36·5 2 Any notice required to be given by clause 36·5·1 shall be given within a reasonable time after the occurrence of the event to which the notice relates, and the giving of a written notice in that time shall be a condition precedent to any payment being made to the Sub-Contractor in respect of the event in question.

36·5 3 The Contractor and the Sub-Contractor may agree with the Quantity Surveyor what shall be deemed for all the purposes of the Sub-Contract to be the net amount payable to or allowable by the Sub-Contractor in respect of the occurrence of any event such as is referred to in any of the provisions listed in clause 36·5·1.

36·5 4 Any amount which from time to time becomes payable to or allowable by the Sub-Contractor by virtue of clauses 36·1 to ·3 or 36·4 shall, as the case may be, be added to or deducted from:

36·5 4 ·1 the Sub-Contract Sum; and

    ·4 ·2 any amounts payable to the Sub-Contractor and which are calculated in accordance with clauses 30·2·2·1 or 30·2·2·2

or included in the calculation of the Ascertained Final Sub-Contract Sum.

The addition or deduction to which clause 36·5·4 refers shall be subject to the provisions of clauses 36·5·5 to ·5·7.

36·5 5 As soon as is reasonably practicable the Sub-Contractor shall provide such evidence and computations as the Contractor and the Architect or the Quantity Surveyor may reasonably require to enable the amount payable to or allowable by the Sub-Contractor by virtue of clauses 36·1 to ·3 or 36·4 to be ascertained; and in the case of amounts payable to or allowable by the Sub-Contractor under clause 36·1·3 (or clause 36·4 for amounts payable to or allowable by the sub-sub-contractor under provisions in the sub-sub-contract to the like effect in clauses 36·1·3 and 36·1·4) – employees other than workpeople – such evidence shall include a certificate signed by or on behalf of the Sub-Contractor each week certifying the validity of the evidence reasonably required to ascertain such amounts.

36·5 6 No addition to or deduction from the Sub-Contract Sum or inclusion in the calculation of the Ascertained Final Sub-Contract Sum made by virtue of clause 36·5·4 shall alter in any way the amount of profit of the Sub-Contractor included in that Sum.

36·5 7 Subject to the provisions of clause 36·5·8 no amount shall be added or deducted in the computation of the amount stated as due in an Interim Certificate in respect of amounts otherwise payable to or allowable by the Sub-Contractor by virtue of clauses 36·1 to ·3 or 36·4 if the event (as referred to in the provisions listed in clause 36·5·1) in respect of which the payment or allowance would be made occurs after the date of the failure by the Sub-Contractor to complete as certified by the Architect as referred to in clause 12·2.

36·5 8 Clause 36·5·7 shall not be applied unless:

36·5 8 ·1 the printed text of clauses 11·2 and 11·3 is unamended and forms part of the Sub-Contract Conditions; and

    8 ·2 the Architect has, in respect of every request by the Contractor and Sub-Contractor under clause 11·2·2, consented or not consented in writing to such revisions of the period or periods for completion of the Sub-Contract Works as he considered to be in accordance with clause 11·2 and with clause 35·14 of the Main Contract Conditions.

36·6 Clauses 36·1 to ·4 shall not apply in respect of:

36·6 ·1 work for which the Sub-Contractor is allowed daywork rates under clause 16·3·4 or 17·4·3;

36·6 ·2 changes in the rate of value added tax charged on the supply of goods or services by the Sub-Contractor to the Contractor under the Sub-Contract.

36·7 In clause 36:

36·7 ·1 the expression 'the Date of Tender' means the date inserted in the Tender, Schedule 1, Appendix (A);

36·7 ·2 the expression 'materials' and 'goods' include timber used in formwork but do not include other consumable stores, plant and machinery (save that electricity and, where specifically so stated in the Tender, Schedule 1, Appendix (A), fuels are dealt with in clause 36·3);

36·7 ·3 the expression 'workpeople' means persons whose rates of wages and other emoluments (including holiday credits) are governed by the rules or decisions or agreements of the National Joint Council for the Building Industry or some other wage-fixing body for trades associated with the building industry;

36·7 ·4 the expression 'wage-fixing body' shall mean a body which lays down recognised terms and conditions of workers within the meaning of the Employment Protection Act 1975, Schedule 11, paragraph 2(a).

36·8 **Percentage addition to fluctuation payments or allowances**

36·8 ·1 There shall be added to the amount paid to or allowed by the Sub-Contractor under:

36·8 ·1 ·1 clause 36·1·2;

    ·1 ·2 clause 36·1·3;

    ·1 ·3 clause 36·1·6;

    ·1 ·4 clause 36·2·2;

    ·1 ·5 clause 36·2·5;

    ·1 ·6 clause 36·3·2;

the percentage stated in the Tender, Schedule 1, item 2.

Clause 37: Formula adjustment

37 **Formula adjustment**

37·1 The Sub-Contract Sums or amounts ascertained under clause 17 as the case may be shall be adjusted in accordance with the following provisions of clause 37 and the 'Nominated Sub-Contract Formula Rules' identified in the Tender, Schedule 1, Appendix (B), that is to say:

37·1 ·1 where the Sub-Contract is for the supply and fixing of materials or goods or the execution of work to which one or more of the Work Categories referred to in Section 2, Part I of the Nominated Sub-Contract Formula Rules applies, adjustment shall be under the formulae (but subject to rule 7) in that Part of the Rules.

37·1 2 where the Sub-Contract is for the supply and fixing of materials or goods or the execution of works to which one of the formulae set out in Section 2, Part III of the Nominated Sub-Contract Formula Rules applies, adjustment shall be under the relevant formulae in that Part of the Rules.

37·2 1 Any adjustment under clause 37 shall be to sums exclusive of value added tax and nothing in clause 37 shall affect in any way the operation of clauses 19A or 19B (value added tax).

37·2 2 The Definitions in rule 3 of the Nominated Sub-Contract Formula Rules shall apply to clause 37.

37·2 3 Where clause 40 of the Main Contract Conditions does not apply to the Main Contract but clause 37 applies to adjustment of the Sub-Contract Sum or to amounts ascertained under clause 17, valuations shall be made for the purposes of calculating formula adjustment due under clause 37.

37·3 1 The Contractor shall ensure that the adjustment referred to in clause 37 shall be effected in all Interim Certificates to which clause 21 applies.

37·3 2 The Sub-Contractor shall be entitled, through the Contractor, to make to the Architect any representations on the value of the work to which formula adjustment is to be made. The Contractor shall forthwith pass such representations to the Architect.

37·3 3 Where any Non-Adjustable Element applies to formula adjustment under the Main Contract, the amount of the Non-Adjustable Element recorded in the Tender, Schedule 1, Appendix (B) shall apply to the amount of adjustment under clause 37.

37·3 4 Where clause 40 of the Main Contract Conditions does not apply to the Main Contract but clause 37 applies to the Sub-Contract and it has been agreed that a Non-Adjustable Element shall apply, the amount of the Non-Adjustable Element shall be inserted in the Tender, Schedule 1, Appendix (B) provided that clause 37·3·4 shall only apply where the Main Contract Conditions are those set out in the Local Authorities Edition of the Standard Form of Building Contract identified in the Tender, Schedule 1, item 5.

37·4 For any article to which rule 4 (ii) of the Nominated Sub-Contract Formula Rules applies the Sub-Contractor shall insert in the Tender, Schedule 1, Appendix (B) the market price of the article in sterling (that is the price delivered to the site) current at the Date of Tender. If after the Date of Tender the market price of the article inserted in the aforesaid Appendix (B) increases or decreases then the net amount of the difference between the cost of purchasing at the market price inserted in the aforesaid Appendix (B) and the market price payable by the Sub-Contractor and current when the article is bought shall, as the case may be, be paid to or allowed by the Sub-Contractor. The reference to 'market price' in clause 37·4 shall be construed as including any duty or tax (other than any value added tax which is treated, or is capable of being treated, as input tax (as defined in the Finance Act 1972) by the Sub-Contractor) by whomsoever payable under or by virtue of any Act of Parliament on the import, purchase, sale, appropriation or use of the articles specified as aforesaid.

37·5 The Contractor on behalf of and with the consent of the Sub-Contractor may agree with the Quantity Surveyor any alteration to the methods and procedures for ascertaining the amount of formula adjustment to be made under the formulae to which clause 37 refers and the amounts ascertained in accordance with and from the effective date of such agreement shall be deemed for all the purposes of the Sub-Contract to be the amount of formula adjustment payable to or allowable by the Sub-Contractor in respect of the provisions of clause 37. Provided always that no alterations to the methods and procedures shall be agreed as aforesaid unless it is reasonably expected that the amount of formula adjustment will be the same or approximately the same as that ascertained in accordance with Section 2, Part I or Part III of the Nominated Sub-Contract Formula Rules whichever Part is stated in the Tender, Schedule 1, Appendix (B) to be applicable.

37·6 1 If at any time prior to the final payment of the Sub-Contractor under clause 21, formula adjustment is not possible because of delay in, or cessation of, the publication of the Monthly Bulletins, adjustment of the Sub-Contract Sum shall be made in each interim Payment during such period of delay on a fair and reasonable basis.

37·6 2 If publication of the Monthly Bulletins is recommenced at any time prior to the final payment of the Sub-Contractor under clause 21 the provisions of clause 37 and the Nominated Sub-Contract Formula Rules shall operate and the adjustment under clause 37 and the aforesaid Rules shall be substituted for any adjustment under clause 37·6·1.

37·6 3 During any period of delay or cessation as aforesaid the Employer, the Contractor and the Sub-Contractor shall operate such parts of clause 37 and the aforesaid Rules as will enable the amount of formula adjustment to be readily calculated upon recommencement of publication of the Monthly Bulletins.

37·7 1 If the Sub-Contractor fails to complete the Sub-Contract Works within the period or periods specified in the Tender, Schedule 2, item 1C or within any revised period or

periods fixed in accordance with clause 11 2, formula adjustment under clause 37 shall be effected in the computation of the amount due in Interim Certificates issued after the expiry of the aforesaid period or periods (or any revision thereof) by reference to the Index Numbers applicable to the Valuation Period in which the aforesaid date of expiry (or any revision thereof) falls.

37 7   **2**   Clause 37 7 1 shall not be applied unless the Architect has, in respect of every request by the Contractor and Sub-Contractor under clause 11 2 2 consented or not consented in writing to such revision of the period or periods for completion of the Sub-Contract Works as he considered to be in accordance with clause 11 2 and with clause 35 14 of the Main Contract Conditions.

37 7   **3**   Clause 37 7 1 shall be applied only if the printed text of clauses 11 2 and 11 3 is unamended and forms part of the Sub-Contract Conditions.

80.01 These clauses deal with three types of fluctuation provision: clause 35 deals with fluctuations in contribution taxes and levies, clause 36 with full fluctuations, and clause 37 with fluctuations according to the JCT formula rules. The appropriate alternative will be included in the sub-contractor's Tender NSC/1.

Clauses 35 and 36

80.02 These can be considered together: in relation to labour increases the date of tender means the date in Schedule 1 of NSC/1. Work people means persons whose rates of wages and other emoluments including holiday credits are governed by the rules or decisions of the National Joint Council for the Building Industry or other wage-fixing body for trades associated with the building industry, and a wage-fixing body is one which lays down recognized terms and conditions of workers within the meaning of the Employment Act 1975. Recovery is to include for those engaged upon or in connection with the sub-contract works either on or adjacent to the site including those not on or adjacent to the site who are engaged upon the production of materials or goods for the sub-contract works. Tender rates are to allow for incentive bonus schemes in accordance with the arrangements of the relevant wage-fixing body schemes, and hence any increases in wage rates are reflected in the bonus payment and will be recoverable (this reverses *William Sindal* v *North West Thames Regional Health Authority* 74 LGR 440). Further, it should be noted that fluctuations in wages paid to those employed on or adjacent to the site but who are not within the definition of work people shall, providing they are fixed by an approved wage-fixing body, be recoverable as if such people were craftsmen. This removes the difficulty shown by the decision in *J Murphy & Sons* v *Southwark Borough Council* in connection with clause 31A of the 1963 JCT Form.

80.03 Fuel increases are recoverable, and increases in transport charges or fares may be recovered. The sub-contractor is required to provide evidence and computations as required by the contractor, architect, or quantity surveyor to support fluctuations, and in the case of those who are not work people but who are going to be allowed as craftsmen a weekly certificate signed by the sub-contractor validating the days claimed.

Clause 37

80.04 This provides for fluctuations in accordance with the JCT formula rules.

Limits on fluctuations

80.05 Fluctuations are to be 'frozen' as at the date the architect issues a certificate stating that the sub-contract works ought to have been completed, and this means that if, for example, the labour rate has increased by 10p per hour after the date when the sub-contract works ought to have been completed, the cost of the increase will not be recoverable.

80.06 A Sectional Completion Supplement has been added (April 1983) as a permanent part of this sub-contract to follow clause 37, but it will only come into operation under the terms of new sub-clause 1.4 (see *para 49.01*).

Clause 38

The arbitration provisions in this sub-contract are comprehensive and provide for 'related dispute' arbitration by an arbitrator appointed under the Main Contract, as to which see the notes to article 3. The JCT arbitration rules are to be followed in any arbitration under the sub-contract.

38   **Settlement of disputes – Arbitration**

38·1   If a dispute or difference as referred to in Article 3 arises in regard to any matter or thing of whatsoever nature arising out of this Sub-Contract or in connection therewith, then either party shall give to the other notice in writing of such dispute or difference and such dispute or difference shall be referred to the arbitration and final decision of a person to be agreed between the parties to act as Arbitrator, or, failing such agreement within 14 days after either party has given to the other a written request to concur in the appointment of an Arbitrator, a person to be appointed on the request of either party by the person named in the Tender, Schedule 2.

38·2   **·1**   Provided that if the dispute or difference to be referred to arbitration under this Sub-Contract raises issues which are substantially the same as or connected with issues raised in a related dispute between

the Contractor and the Employer under the Main Contract, or

the Sub-Contractor and the Employer under Agreement NSC/2, or

the Contractor and any other nominated sub-contractor under Sub-Contract NSC/4 or NSC/4a as applicable, or

the Contractor and any Nominated Supplier whose contract of sale with the Contractor provides for the matters referred to in clause 36·4·8 of the Main Contract Conditions

and if the related dispute has already been referred for determination to an Arbitrator, the Contractor and the Sub-Contractor hereby agree that the dispute or difference under this Sub-Contract shall be referred to the Arbitrator appointed to determine the related dispute; such Arbitrator shall have power to make such directions and all necessary awards in the same way as if the procedure of the High Court as to joining one or more defendants or joining co-defendants or third parties was available to the parties and to him; and the agreement and consent referred to in clause 38·7 on appeals or applications to the High Court on any question of law shall apply to any question of law arising out of the awards of such Arbitrator in respect of all related disputes referred to him or arising in the course of the reference of all the related disputes referred to him.

38·2   **·2**   Save that the Contractor or the Sub-Contractor may require the dispute or difference under this Sub-Contract to be referred to a different Arbitrator (to be appointed under this Sub-Contract) if either of them reasonably considers that the Arbitrator appointed to determine the related dispute is not appropriately qualified to determine the dispute or difference under this Sub-Contract.

38·2   **·3**   Clauses 38·2·1 and 38·2·2 apply unless in the Tender, Schedule 1, item 10 the words 'clauses 41·2·1 and 41·2·2 apply' have been deleted.

38·3   Such Arbitrator shall not without the written consent of the Contractor and the Sub-Contractor enter on the arbitration until after the practical completion or abandonment of the Works, except to arbitrate:

38·3   **·1**   whether a payment has been improperly withheld or is not in accordance with the Sub-Contract; or

38·3   **·2**   whether practical completion of the Sub-Contract Works shall be deemed to have taken place under clause 14·2; or

38·3   **·3**   in respect of a claim by the Contractor or counterclaim by the Sub-Contractor to which the provisions of clause 24 apply in which case the Arbitrator shall exercise his powers given to him in clause 24; or

38·3   **·4**   any matters in dispute under clause 4·3·1 in regard to reasonable objection by the Sub-Contractor or under clauses 4·3·2 to 4·3·7 inclusive or under clauses 11·2 and 11·3 as to extension of time.

38·4   In any such arbitration as is provided for in clause 38 any decision of the Architect which is final and binding on the Contractor under the Main Contract shall also be and be deemed to be final and binding between and upon the Contractor and the Sub-Contractor.

38·5   Subject to the provisions of clauses 4·6, 21·12, 35·4·3, 36·5·3, 37·5 and clause 30 of the Main Contract Conditions the Arbitrator shall, without prejudice to the generality of his powers, have power to direct such measurements and/or valuations as may in his opinion be desirable in order to determine the rights of the parties and to ascertain and award any sum which ought to have been the subject of or included in any certificate and to open up, review and revise any certificate, opinion, decision (except a decision of the Architect to issue instructions pursuant to clause 8·4·1 of the Main Contract Conditions and which instructions were issued to the Sub-Contractor as referred to in clause 4·3·3·1), requirement or notice and to determine all matters in dispute which shall be submitted to him in the same manner as if no such certificate, opinion, decision, requirement or notice had been given.

38·6   Subject to clause 38·7 the award of such Arbitrator shall be final and binding on the parties.

38·7   The parties hereby agree and consent pursuant to Sections 1(3)(a) and 2(1)(b) of the Arbitration Act 1979 that either party

38·7   **·1**   may appeal to the High Court on any question of law arising out of an award made in an arbitration under this Arbitration Agreement and

38·7   **·2**   may apply to the High Court to determine any question of law arising in the course of the reference;

and the parties agree that the High Court should have jurisdiction to determine any such questions of law.

38·8   Whatever the nationality, residence or domicile of the Employer, the Contractor, the Sub-Contractor, and any sub-contractor or supplier or the Arbitrator, and wherever the Works or Sub-Contract Works, or any parts thereof, are situated, the law of England shall be the proper law applicable to the Sub-Contract and in particular (but not so as to derogate from the generality of the foregoing) the provisions of the Arbitration Acts 1950 (notwithstanding

81 Collateral warranties

81.01 The concept of a collateral warranty is of a contractual arrangement which is supplementary to some other contract, not necessarily between the same two parties. In practice the subject of collateral warranties is important for architects in two contexts: firstly, there is the question of collateral warranties to be obtained by the employer from suppliers and sub-contractors who have no direct contractual relationship with the employer. Secondly, and more immediately important from the architect's point of view, there is the question of collateral warranties sought from the architect in favour of third parties such as funding institutions who are backing the development by the employer.

81.02 Dealing first with the practice of obtaining warranties in favour of the employer from sub-contractors and suppliers, the general rule at common law is that there is no contract relationship between the employer and a sub-contractor (whether nominated or not) or a supplier who supplies material to the contractor, although in exceptional cases such a collateral warranty may arise – see *Shanklin Pier v Detel Products* [1951] 2 All ER 471. The practice has, however, grown up of extracting such warranties. From the employer's point of view there are two main advantages in obtaining such warranties. Firstly and most straightforwardly, the employer will have a direct claim against the sub-contractor or supplier for defects in the goods or services against the person actually responsible for supplying them. This is particularly important now that it has been established that the tort of negligence will not generally give the employer a remedy in these circumstances, as defects in such goods and services are normally regarded in contemplation of the law as economic loss, which is not compensatable in negligence. Secondly, the employer can by claiming on the collateral warranty avoid complications caused by the terms of the contract between himself and the contractor. For example, the main contract may give the contractor a right to claim an extension of time in the event of default by a nominated sub-contractor. An appropriate form of collateral warranty can cast responsbility for the loss this causes to the employer on the sub-contractor, as indeed is provided for in the form of agreement between employer and nominated sub-contractor under the JCT contract, NSC/2. Further, it may well be that under the form of main contract the contractor is not responsible for materials selected by the employer without relying on the contractor's skill and judgement. Under the collateral warranty, however, claims can be made directly against the sub-contractor or supplier concerned.

81.03 The responsibility of the architect in regard to collateral warranties should be firstly to advise his client of the desirability of obtaining such warranties whenever possible, certainly in regard to more important components of the work. Secondly, he should ensure that where the forms of contract he advises the employer to use provide for the procedure involving collateral warranties, as is the case, for example, under JCT 80, with Form NSC/2 and TNS/2 (in the case of nominated suppliers), these forms of collateral warranty are properly executed and are in order.

81.04 Funding institutions frequently seek collateral warranties from architects. The effects of such collateral warranties when given is that the architect assumes a duty of care not only towards the employer but also towards the funding institution, so that if, for example, defects appear in the building once it has been purchased by the funding institution the architect can be made liable to compensate.

81.05 Although many architects object to entering into such forms of collateral warranty it seems inevitable that their use will become more widespread given the difficulties in pursuing claims in negligence, economic loss against a defendant with whom the plaintiff has no contractual relationship, and given the fact that many large developments are funded by institutions who wish to be sure that their investment is safe.

81.06 An architect's approach to the question of collateral warranties must therefore be dictated by circumstances. When initially approached by a prospective client it would be sensible for him to enquire whether he will be likely to be asked to provide collateral warranties in favour of third parties. He can legitimately object to being asked to provide such warranties subsequently if he is not put on notice of this requirement. Secondly, he should consider whether to levy a substantial charge for the provision of such a warranty. Such charge should reflect the risk the architect undertakes, and also the fact that many forms of warranty specifically require the architect to maintain insurance against the risk of negligence claims arising out of the project in question for a specified period. This may well prove expensive. These may justify quite a substantial extra fee, and the architect should consider whether to ask for a provision to be inserted in the conditions of engagement entitling him specifically to charge for such warranties.

81.07 With regard to insurance further, the architect should remember that the provision of a collateral warranty will almost certainly be a material matter affecting the risk, of which he must inform his professional indemnity insurers. Failing this there is the possibility that the insurers might repudiate liability leaving the architect uninsured.

81.08 With regard to the terms of the collateral warranty, care must be taken to see that the architect is not by the terms of the warranty put under a higher duty than that owed to his employer. For example, he ought not give any absolute guarantee as to the performance of the building, nor ought he to be responsible for matters where the employer has taken the risk, for example where on the architect's advice the employer has engaged a specialist consultant to deal with a particular aspect of the design.

81.09 RIBA Publications Limited publish a form of agreement for collateral warranty (W/F). This form strikes a reasonable balance between the funding institution and the architect. Other standard forms of collateral warranty may appear in the future, but their growth has been inhibited by the general reluctance of professional institutions to commit their members to extensive and long-lasting liabilities.

82 Other standard forms

82.01 Architects are frequently called upon to advise their clients on what contractual arrangements will best achieve the client's objective. The ever-changing and expanding pattern of building and civil engineering works today frequently involve the architect either directly or in association with professional colleagues in related fields in what were traditionally regarded as civil engineering projects and which are usually outside his own experience. Nowhere is evidence of this more pronounced than in arrangements within the

construction industry as a whole for competitive contracting and sub-contracting of works. Architects cannot afford to remain unaware of these developments.

82.02 In the section which follows brief guidance is given to some of the more important standard forms in use in the UK building industry at the present time. The proliferation of standard forms, however, means that it is not possible to cover all of them. In respect of standard forms which are not dealt with in this work, the reader should consult Emden's *Construction Law* (Butterworths), which contains the full text of all standard forms currently in use in the UK building industry, and other important material, such as the RIBA Conditions of Engagement and Form of Collateral Warranty. Emden's *Construction Law* is regularly updated. JCT Practice Note 20 gives guidance as to which JCT form of contract is most suitable to a given project.

82.03 Where the architect is invited to comment on a form of contract, it is suggested that he ought to start on a preliminary basis from the following checklist, and see how the form of contract proposed measures up to it:

1. Is the price fixed, and if so for what period? If the price is subject to fluctuations, in what circumstances can it be increased?
2. What are the contractor's obligations as to the standard and quality of the work? Are they adequately defined, or are they vague? If the standards and quality of work are defined by reference to other documents, what steps need be taken to insert in those other documents (e.g. bills of quantities) sufficiently clear obligations on the contractor?
3. What are the contractor's rights to sub-contract work? In respect of sub-contracted work
   (a) What are the employer's rights against contractor and sub-contractor in respect of defects in the sub-contract work?
   (b) Is the contractor entitled to claim extensions of time or further payment by reason of defaults of the sub-contractor?

(c) How onerous are the architect's duties in regard to sub-contractors, for example nomination and renomination.
   (d) Is the sub-contract documentation satisfactory?
4. What provisions are made for extensions of time? How effective are the sanctions on the contractor for late completion, and what provision is made for liquidated damages?
5. What provision is made in the contract for contractor's claims against the employer, e.g. for late architect's instructions and other matters?
6. What arrangements are proposed for payment to the contractor?
7. What safeguards are there to the employer in regard to payment matters, including
   (a) making direct payments to sub-contractors who have not been paid by the contractor;
   (b) withholding payment in respect of defective and incomplete work – does the contract exclude all normal rights of set-off?
   (c) contractual rights of determination;
   (d) dispute resolutions.
8. What is the role of the architect, and can he properly discharge it?

82.04 The foregoing is simply a guide to the more important aspects of modern contractual machinery. Generally it is suggested that architects should be cautious about recommending the employer to use a form other than one of the standard forms in use in the industry. The decision to draft a tailor-made form, and the drafting of such a form, are matters requiring specialist legal expertise and advice. The expense of this, coupled with the general reluctance within the industry to contract on forms other than standardized ones means that only the most substantial undertakings consider it worth while to draft their own forms and have the necessary economic power to impose them.

83 JCT Fixed Form of Prime Cost Contract

83.01 The first Edition of the fixed fee form of prime cost contract was issued in March 1967. Since then it has been the subject of a number of amendments and reprints.

83.02 The broad idea behind this form of contract is that the contractor is paid the cost of the work plus a fixed fee of an amount agreed between the parties before the contract is signed. From the contractor's point of view he knows that he will be paid the actual cost of the work plus his fee, and thus takes no risk. From the employer's point of view he benefits from any savings in the cost of the work, but on the other hand runs the risk of cost overruns.

Main characteristics

83.03 The contract envisages a specification and drawings, though the latter are not mandatory. In practice the specification may be in outline only. The appointment of an architect and quantity surveyor are required.

83.04 The contractor's basic obligations are contained in clauses 3 and 7 – he is to carry out and complete the works in accordance with the specification and agreement, and provide the labour, materials and other things required for the contract.

83.05 The contractor can sub-let parts of the work with the architect's consent, subject to reasonable conditions. Clause 23 deals with the question of nominated sub-contractors, and clause 24 covers nominated suppliers.

83.06 Payment is dealt with by clause 27. Interim valuations are made whenever the architect considers them to be necessary. Payment is to be made of the prime cost of the work less certain deductions, including retention. There is the usual provision for release of retention following practical completion, and for the issue of a final certificate which has conclusive effect.

83.07 Clauses 21 and 22 deal with determination by the employer and the contractor respectively. The grounds are similar to those in JCT 80.

Advantages

83.08 The fixed fee form of prime cost contract has the advantage from the contractor's point of view that he knows he will be reimbursed the amount it actually costs him to carry out the work plus the amount of the fee. This may also be an advantage to the employer, particularly if his plans for the project have not been fully prepared but he is anxious to make an early start on the work. The wide power to order variations means that the work can be designed while it is being built.

Disadvantages

83.09 These are the obverse of the advantages. The ultimate price is uncertain, and it may also be difficult to get competitive tenders if the contract documents are limited. Some care is required in negotiating the actual prime cost with the contractor. This places a heavy burden on the quantity surveyor.

Situation where contracts suitable

83.10 This form of contract should not be used for a normal fully designed project where it is desired to obtain proper competitive tenders and important for the employer to know in advance what the likely cost outturn is. However it can usefully be used for large projects the scope of which can be ascertained with reasonable accuracy, and where the employer's main interest is in making a speedy start, and where he has a competent professional team capable of providing the contractor with the necessary flow of information and negotiating the prime cost of the work actually carried out. Thus, for example, it may be thought appropriate where it is proposed to construct or refurbish a large retail store or hotel, where fast completion is a high priority, and where much of the design of details can be carried out as the project proceeds, and where the expected cash flow of the completed project will more than compensate for the financial risks of any likely anticipated cost over-run.

84 JCT Management Contract 1987 Edition

84.01 This is a form of management contract issued by the JCT. The essential concept is that the employer makes a contract with the management contractor who organizes the execution of the works by works contractors. The management contract itself is in a standard form known as Man/Con. The contracts between the management contractor and various work contractors are in two parts, Works Contract/1 (WK/CON1) and Works Contract/2 (WK/CON2). Works contract/1 is in three sections namely:

Section 1: Invitation to tender.
Section 2: Tender.
Section 3: Articles of Agreement.

Works Contract/2 comprises the works contract condition and is incorporated by reference in Works Contract/1, Section 3.

84.02 There are also the following documents which require to be used:

1. Standard Form of Employer/Works Contractor Agreement (WK/CON3).
2. Management Contract Phase Completion Supplement (MC/PCS).
3. Works Contract Phased Completion Supplement (WC/PCS).
4. Practice Note MC/1.
5. Commentaries MC/2.
6. JCT Sub-Contract/Works Contract Formula Rules (87/FR/SC).

The formula rules are applicable also to certain other forms of sub-contract.

The management contract has been amended by Amendment 1 issued in July 1988.

Main characteristics

84.03 The management contract envisages that the employer has appointed a 'professional team' who have prepared drawings and a specification for the project ('project drawings' and 'project specification'). The general obligation of the management contractor is to co-operate with the professional team and to provide the services specified in the Third Schedule. This covers a number of building management functions. A contract administrator is to be appointed. The obligations of the management contractor are to manage the works contract. By clause 1.7 the management contractor remains responsible to the employer for breaches of the works contracts. The standards of materials, goods and workmanship required are set out in clauses 3.8–3.12.

84.04 Where a works contractor is in breach of the works contract somewhat complex provisions in clause 3.21 apply. The management contractor is entitled to seek reimbursement from the employer save where the management contractor has himself caused the problem, as set out in clause 3.22.

84.05 Payment is dealt with in section 4 of the management contract. Payment is to be made on interim certificates, in respect of costs of the work, and the fee due to the management contractor provision is made for adjustment of the management contractor's fee.

84.06 Section 7 deals with determination in the event of default by the management contractor and the employer. By clause 7.10 the employer has an absolute right to determine the management contractor's employment, subject to the management contractor's right to compensation and an indemnity against claims by works contractors.

Advantages

84.07 A management contractor has the advantage to the employer that he can look to one management contractor to co-ordinate the works of a large number of separate specialist contractors. The fee structure can provide an incentive to the management contractor to ensure that the works are carried out rapidly and efficiently. From the management contractor's point of view he takes little risk, and commits no resources of his own beyond management skills.

Disadvantages

84.08 Commitment to the management contractor will arise before the full cost of the project is known, and indeed before tenders are invited for many, possibly all, items. The employer may find himself indemnifying the management contractor in respect of large numbers of claims by works contractors if the project does not run to time, and it is the

employer's responsibility to have a design team. Thus it is in general not possible for the employer to rely on the management contractor for the design of the project.

Situations where contract suitable

84.09 Management contract and the works contracts are, it is suggested, suitable for special situations where the importance to the employer of the management skills of a management contractor and the necessity of co-ordinating different works contractors properly outweigh the risks and expense. The management contract would be appropriate, for example, where a very large office or commercial development was being constructed to a size and complexity requiring the use of a large number of different contractors.

85 JCT Standard Form of Contract with Contractor's Design

85.01 As its name implies, the contractor is under this form obliged to design the work, in accordance with the employer's requirements. No particular form of design is proposed, but it is clearly envisaged that documents such as bills of quantities, drawings, measurements and calculations should be used.

The form was revised in 1986.

Main characteristics

85.02 The contract documents are the employer's requirements, the contractor's proposals, and a contract sum analysis. The contract is a lump sum contract, subject to that sum being varied such variations being valued in accordance with the contract sum analysis.

85.03 The contractor's obligations are contained in clause 2. By clause 2.5 the contractor undertakes a duty of care in regard to the design of the works to the standard of an appropriate professional designer. By clause 4 the employer is entitled to give instructions. The form does not expressly envisage that the employer will engage an architect. Clause 8 deals with the quality of materials and goods, etc. Clause 10 obliges the contractor to keep a competent person in charge of the works and clause 11 gives the employer's agent the right of access to the works.

85.04 Clause 12 deals with the situation where the employer wishes to change his requirements, and valuation rules are prescribed.

85.05 Clause 18 deals with assignment and sub-contracts. There is no provision for nomination of sub-contractors, but the contractor can sub-let portions of the work with the employer's consent.

85.06 The dates of possession, completion and postponement are dealt with in clauses 23 to 25. The contractor may claim extensions of time in the event of relevant events as defined by clause 25.4. These grounds on which extensions can be claimed are extensive. In certain circumstances the contractor can claim loss and expense under clause 26. One somewhat unusual ground on which the contractor can claim loss and expanse is delay in the receipt of any permission or approval for the purposes of development control requirements necessary for the works to be carried out or proceed (clause 26.2.2). Thus delays in obtaining planning permission for example are at the risk of the employer.

85.07 Determination by the employer is dealt with by clause 27 and determination by the contractor is dealt with by clause 28. These grounds are similar to the grounds in the corresponding clauses of the JCT 1980 Form Main Contract.

Advantages

85.08 In theory at least the employer is relieved of the necessity of engaging a design team. From the contractor's point of view the form offers the advantage of simplicity unless risk of uncertainty bought about by the problems of dealing with the employer's architect, and the administrative burdens this entails. He can design in the way most satisfactory to him.

Disadvantages

85.09 The employer is inadequately protected against design defects, since the contractor undertakes only an obligation to use reasonable care in the design, i.e. the same duty as required from an independent architect. But if the employer had engaged an independent architect that architect would in terms of design be endeavouring to meet closely the employer's requirements and protect his interests. In practice it may not be easy for the employer to exercise adequate control over the works unless he goes to the expense of employing his own independent advisers in any event, in which case some of the alleged advantages of simplicity, etc. will have been lost.

Situations where contract suitable

85.10 In general it is suggested this form could be employed where the employer wants a building of a fairly common type involving no great structural or architectural complexity, for example a warehouse or a standard office type building.

86 Intermediate Form of Contract IFC/84

86.01 This form was introduced as its title implies in 1984 as a response to growing disenchantment in the industry and building related professions with JCT 80. This disenchantment had manifested itself in a stubborn adherence to JCT 63. Essentially IFC/84 represents a reversion in many respects to JCT 63, with, however, the difference that there is no provision for nominated sub-contractors. Having said that, there is provision for 'naming' of sub-contractors to be selected from an approved list, and there is a standard form of sub-contract for such named sub-contractors (NAM/SC). Thus in practice the essential idea of nomination has to some extent been retained.

IFC/84 stands in terms of complexity somewhere between JCT 80 and the minor works form.

86.02 Apart from IFC/84 and the sub-contract for named sub-contractors NAM/SC the following documentation is relevant:

1. Practice Note IN/1.
2. RIBA/CASEC Employer/Specialist Agreement Reference ESA1 to be used with the new sub-contract.
3. Sectional Completion Supplement.
4. Domestic Sub-Contract Form IN/SC issued by the Building Employers Confederation.
5. Tender and Agreement for Named Sub-Contractors NAM/T.
6. Sub-Contract Formula Rules for Named Sub-Contractors NAM/SC/FR.
7. Fluctuations Clauses and Formula Rules SUPP/IFC84.

The intermediate form of building contract is subject to six amendments issued between 1986 and 1989.

Main characteristics

86.03 The contract is a lump sum fixed price contract subject to fluctuations which may be either a full price adjustment formula or limited to tax fluctuations. These provisions are

set out in clauses 4.9 and 4.10 and the Appendix, Sections C and D. The contractor's basic obligations are set out in article 1, and clauses 1.1 and 1.2. The contract documents must include contract drawings, and may include a specification, schedule of work or bill of quantities. Some price document is required in order to value variations and fluctuations. Provision is made for the appointment of a quantity surveyor.

86.04 The contractor is also obliged to comply with statutory requirements by clause 5 of the contract. By clause 5.3 the contractor is exempted from liability for non-compliance with the statutory requirements where this arises from him having carried out work in accordance with the contract documents or any instructions from the architect or contract administrator. This, it is thought, reflects the position at common law – see *Edac v William Moss* [1985] 2 Const LJ 131.

86.05 Payment is governed by clause 4. The payment provisions are conventional, with interim certificates subject to retention, and provision for release of that retention on practical completion and the issue of the final certificate.

86.06 The contractor is obliged to complete the works by the completion date under clause 2 of the contract. Liquidated damages are payable subject to a certificate of non-completion in the event of delay. Extensions of time are provided for in clause 2.3, and once again these follow conventional JCT 1963 practice. The contractor has a right to claim extra payment for disturbance of the regular progress of the works under clause 4.11, in respect of the matters set out in clause 4.12. Once again these claims for loss and expense are based on grounds that will be familiar to those who use JCT 63. The grounds include delayed instructions, failure to supply materials and goods which the employer has agreed to supply for the works, instructions postponing the work and instructions relating to the expenditure of provisional sums.

86.07 Power to vary the work is contained in clause 3.6 of the contract, and the valuation rules are in clause 3.7.

86.08 As regards sub-contracting, there is no provision for nominated sub-contractors but non-named sub-contractors may be appointed under clause 3.2 subject to certain conditions. Clause 3.3 covers the appointment of named persons as sub-contractors. In order for the naming provisions to apply it must be stated in the specification/ schedules of work/contract bills that work described therein for pricing by the contractor is to be executed by a named person. If it is not possible to procure the named person to carry out the work then appropriate instructions must be given, and the work is treated as though it were covered by a provisional sum.

86.09 Unlike the situation which pertains to nominated sub-contractors under both JCT 63 and JCT 80, where the named person defaults it is possible for the architect to instruct the contractor to carry out or complete the necessary work himself – clause 3.3.3(b).

86.10 Determination of the contract is dealt with in clause 7. No particular remarks are called for here, as the provisions are broadly similar to those appertaining under JCT 80.

Advantages

86.11 The contract gives the architect control of the works on behalf of the employer, without involving the considerable procedural complexities of JCT 80. The form is clearly laid out and easy to understand. Matters such as extensions of time, variations, etc., are dealt with in sufficient detail to ensure smooth administration.

Disadvantages

86.12 The provision for 'naming' of sub-contractors is a potential source of complication, and represents a not always straightforward compromise between eliminating nominated sub-contractors altogether and the elaborate nomination provisions in JCT 80. Although the form is more simple than JCT 80 there are still quite heavy burdens on the architect, and scope for claims by unscrupulous contractors.

Situations where contract suitable

86.13 The endorsement on the back of the contract suggests it would be suitable where the building works are

1. of a simple content involving normally recognized basic trades and skills of the industry;
2. without any building service installations of a complex nature or other specialist work of a similar nature; and
3. adequately specified or specified and billed as appropriate prior to the invitation of tenders.

In practice IFC/84 has proved popular. The sentiment in the industry and among the professions seems to be that it strikes a good balance between the parties, and has achieved greater simplicity coupled with clarity than JCT 80. It is the ideal form for the medium-sized project where normal tendering procedures will be gone through, provided the building will be fully designed and involves no exceptional complexities.

87 JCT Agreement for Minor Building Works

87.01 This agreement published in 1980 supersedes a form of agreement produced by the RIBA. It is, as its name implies, intended for minor building works. The 1988 version incorporates all amendments up to MW/4 (1987).

Main characteristics

87.02 The form is a fixed price lump sum contract, for works to be supervised by an architect engaged by the employer. The employer must provide either drawings, a specification, or a schedule or a combination of any of these as required to describe the works.

87.03 The contractor's basic obligations are to carry out the work in accordance with the contract documents. No provision is made for nominated sub-contractors. Payment is to be made by way of progress payments where requested by the contractor, i.e. the provisions for interim certificates in JCT 80 are not imported. However, such payments are subject to retention, and there is procedure whereby penultimate and final certificates are issued in clause 4. The contract is a fixed price contract subject to clause 4.5 dealing with contribution, levy and tax changes.

87.04 In the event of delay liquidated damages are payable. There is no provision for certification of delay. The employer may deduct liquidated damages from monies due to the contractor or recover them from the contractor as a debt.

87.05 Extensions of time may be granted if delay is caused by reason beyond the control of the contractor. No definition is given as to these reasons.

87.06 Variations are valued on a fair and reasonable basis using where relevant the prices in the specification schedules or schedules of rates.

87.07 No provisions are made for partial possession, or claims by the contractor for loss and expense.

Advantages

87.08 Simplicity and ease of administration are the key notes.

Disadvantages

87.09 In such a simplification process a number of matters are left undefined. For example, extensions of time and valuation of variations are dealt with only in the most sketchy manner.

Situations where contract suitable

87.10 There was a tendency to use the Minor Works Form simply because it offered an alternative to JCT 80. With the advent of IFC/84 this is no longer a valid reason for choosing the Minor Works Form. It is suggested that the Minor Works Form should be used only for relatively simple projects which are unlikely to run for a long time or require the employment of particular specialist sub-contractors. The rather sketchy guidance given by the Minor Works Form on a number of crucial aspects of contract administration would be such that relations between the employer and the contractor could easily break down if disputes involving large sums of money arose, for example in regard to extensions of time.

88 ICE Form – for civil engineering work

88.01 The standard form prepared and issued by the Institution of Civil Engineers 5th Edition, reprinted January 1986, is appropriate for civil engineering works. This form of contract bears no resemblance to the JCT forms as it is drafted to conform to civil engineering practice. The use of this form would not be appropriate to the type of project in which architects are generally engaged, to which many of the clauses in the form, such as clause 12 (relating to physical conditions or artificial obstructions which could not have been reasonably foreseen by an experienced contractor) would not be readily applicable. The form envisages remeasurement of the work.

89 ACA Forms of Contract

89.01 In 1982 the Association of Consultant Architects produced a form of building agreement. The 2nd Edition is dated 1984. The production of the form was prompted to some extent by dissatisfaction with JCT 80. The ACA intended to produce a form which was simpler and more explicit in the duties it cast on the contractor. Certainly the form is generally drafted more in the employer's favour than is JCT 80, for example. However, partly for that reason the form has not achieved widespread acceptance in the industry, and appears to be little used. For this reason it is not necessary to give an account of its provisions here.

10

Building Contracts in Scotland

GEORGE BURNET

1 Introduction

1.01 The Standard Form of Building Contract published by the Joint Contracts Tribunal (JCT) has for the last 27 years, as amended by the Scottish supplement, been the accepted set of contract conditions for building contracts in Scotland.

1.02 The Scottish supplement to the Standard Form is published by the Scottish Building Contract Committee (SBCC), which was set up in 1964 and with, initially, similar representation to that of the Joint Contracts Tribunal; subsequently the Association of Scottish Chambers of Commerce and the Confederation of British Industry joined.

The 1963 edition of the Standard Form was the first edition for which a Scottish supplement was published, and a revision was issued almost every year by the SBCC to match the revisions issued by the JCT until the publication of the 1980 edition of the Standard Form by the JCT. This edition contained a number of important amendments as compared with the 1963 edition, but the major change related to the procedure for nomination of a sub-contractor and the publication by the Tribunal of a Standard Form of Sub-contract for a Nominated Sub-contractor, which is fully described in Chapter 9.

1.03 The publication of the 1980 edition of the Standard Form necessitated the preparation of a Scottish supplement to that edition together with preparation of the series of documents for completing nomination of a sub-contractor and a Scottish supplement to the Standard Form of Contract for a Nominated Sub-contractor. In spite of the issue of a formal contract it is still possible in Scotland to enter into a contract by an exchange of letters, and indeed this old established custom is still adhered to in many cases, particularly in local authority contracts. Whether this is wise is a matter of opinion; certainly the SBCC recommend the use of the formal Building Contract in all but the smallest of contracts. The principal advantage of doing so is that the parties will know that all matters which have to be included have been dealt with, whereas if a contract is set up in an informal way, it is only too easy to overlook one of the many details. Furthermore, today, when contracts are for very large sums of money, and the employer is taking on some very onerous obligations, it is right that the importance of these should be emphasized in a formal contract; with the introduction of the new nominated sub-contractor procedure, under which employers are required to sign certain documents, the reluctance to sign a formal document for the main contract is difficult to understand. The small amount of

additional time and trouble which this takes is well worth while, and brings home the importance of the obligations which the employer is taking on.

1.04 Possibly the most important reason for signing a formal contract is to ensure, where work is being carried out in Scotland, that Scots law applies to the contract and to any arbitration following thereon. The Standard Form contains a clause ensuring that not only does English law apply to arbitrations but also becomes the proper law of the contract, and it is not sufficient to include a reference to Scots law as the proper law of the contract in the contract bills. Such a statement must be contained in the document creating the contract between the employer and the contractor, and the appropriate clause is found in the formal Scottish Building Contract.

1.05 The Scottish Supplement to the 1980 edition of the Standard Form (JCT 80) is known generically as 'the Scottish Building Contract' and it consists of:

1. The formal Building Contract between the Employer and the Contractor.
2. Appendix No. I containing the Scottish Supplement.
3. Appendix No. II containing an Abstract of Conditions similar to the appendix in JCT 80.

When first issued there was only one version which could be adapted for use in either Local Authority or Private Contracts With or Without Quantities, but with the proliferation of different types of contract issued by the JCT over the last ten years or so, there are now no less than six editions of the Scottish Building Contract as follows:

1. With Quantities – either Local Authority or Private.
2. Without Quantities – either Local Authority or Private.
3. With Approximate Quantities – either Local Authority or Private.
4. Sectional Completion – either Local Authority or Private.
5. With Contractor's Design where an Architect/Contract Administrator has not been appointed.
6. Contractor's Designed Portion.

At the time of publication the latest revision of all six is January 1988, with the exception of the With Quantities Design edition which was revised in April 1989. To aid visual identification each edition is printed in paper of a different colour.

2 The Building Contract

2.01 The contents of the Building Contract are virtually the same in all six editions and it is important to note the new treatment of the arbitration clause. As in earlier editions it is still found in clause 4 but only to the extent that the employer and the contractor agree to refer disputes to arbitration in accordance with clause 41 of Appendix I which contains the detailed arrangements for arbitration. Originally the arbitration clause was the last clause 35 of JCT 80, then after some five or six years it was transferred to the Articles of Agreement (in England) and the Building Contract (in Scotland) and now it appears in both the Contract and Appendix No. I.

2.02 Clause 6 is the same as in earlier editions, namely 'Both parties consent to registration hereof for preservation and execution'. This gives the parties to the contract a useful additional course of action outside any course open to them in terms of the Contract Conditions, and furthermore it is open only to parties contracting under Scots law.

2.03 The clause provides that once the Building Contract has been registered in the Books of Council and Session (which is an official register located in Meadowbank House, London

Signed by the above named Contractor at

on the _____ day of _____ 19 ____ before these

witnesses

_____ witness

_____ address

_____

_____

_____ occupation

_____ Contractor

_____ witness   (Attention is drawn to the note at the foot of this page)

_____ address

_____

_____

_____ occupation

N.B. – This document is set out as for execution by individuals or firms. Where Limited Companies or Local Authorities are involved amendment will be necessary and the appropriate officials should be consulted or legal advice taken.

In addition, both parties sign on pages 8 and 10.

Road, Edinburgh) and an extract obtained, the extract can be handed to a Sheriff Officer or Messenger-at-Arms and used as an equivalent to a court decree on which diligence (i.e. proceedings for recovery of money) for the sum due to the contractor or to the employer, as the case may be, can proceed.

2.04 The Building Contract registered as above is then ready for use, but three requirements must be fulfilled:

1. The parties concerned must be clearly identifiable. In the case of the Building Contract there is no doubt on this score, since the parties concerned are the employer and the contractor.
2. The sum of money payable must be clearly identifiable. Again in the case of a Building Contract where there is a sum of money due to a contractor, the sum concerned would be the amount brought out, for example, in an architect's certificate.
3. The date from which the sum is owed must be capable of being fixed. The date would be 14 days from the issue of an architect's certificate.

2.05 This little-known facility is rarely, if ever, employed by the parties to a Building Contract, but it is perhaps surprising that contractors do not see fit to make use of it when an employer delays in paying a certificate.

2.06 The final clause in the Building Contract is known as 'the testing clause' and attention is drawn to the note at the bottom of p. 3 in the following terms:

'This document is set out for execution by individuals or firms. Where Limited Companies or Local Authorities are involved amendment will be necessary and the appropriate officials should be consulted or legal advice taken.'

This note is added because a limited company executes formal documents in accordance with the provisions of its Memorandum and Articles of Association, which may vary from one company to another, and a local authority in accordance with its standing orders, which may likewise be different.

2.07 Finally, it is worth mentioning that the process of executing a document 'under Seal' which extends the length of time under which parties are bound by it, is not applicable to Scotland.

2.08 The habit of the JCT to issue frequent amendments to JCT 80 (often forced upon them by government legislation or court decisions) undoubtedly causes much confusion and at times irritation, especially when, as is invariably the case, the amendments appear in a separate Amendment Sheet and

may not be incorporated into the printed document for some considerable time.

2.09 To date no less than eight amendments have been issued, some making substantial changes to JCT 80 and the SBCC has a very hard task in trying to ensure that these are properly and competently incorporated into the Scottish Building Contract. The January 1988 Revision refers in clause 2.2. of the Building Contract to JCT Amendments 1 to 5, but JCT Amendments 6, 7 and 8 require to be incorporated into the Scottish Building Contract by means of a separate published SBCC Amendment Sheet no. 1 (issued in April 1989) which msut be signed by both the employer and the contractor and securely attached to the Scottish Building Contract thereafter.

3   The Scottish supplement – Appendix I

Part 1: General

Clause 1: Interpretation, definitions, etc.

3.01 The 1980 edition of the Standard Form contains an interpretation and definition clause (see Chapter 9). This has been adopted in the Scottish supplement subject to the amendments shown and with the addition of a small number of further definitions, all of which are self-explanatory. It might perhaps be convenient at this stage to mention that the series of documents produced by the SBCC for the process of nomination of a sub-contractor have retained the titles and numbering of the English documents with the addition of the word 'Scot' after the appropriate number.

Clause 5: Contract documents – other documents

3.02 This amendment makes clear whether the contractor is to be required to comply with the new requirement for a

master programme or progress schedule which has been introduced into the 1980 edition of the Standard Form.

Clause 14: Contract sum

3.03 The words added to clause 14.2 ensure that an employer is not debarred from deducting liquidate damages following on the decision in the *Robert Paterson* v *Household Supplies* case (para 3.16).

Clause 16: Materials and goods unfixed or off-site

3.04 Two amendments have been made to clause 16 of the Standard Form: an addition to the end of 16.1, and a provision deleting 16.2 (para 3.14).

Clause 19: Assignations and sub-contracts

3.05 This amendment introduced in the January 1988 Revision deletes clause 19.1.2 of JCT 80 added by JCT Amendment 4 – the terminology of which was not applicable to Scotland. The new clause introduces into Scotland a similar provision by which an employer who disposes of his interest in the works after practical completion may assign his rights to initiate proceedings to that person. Clauses 19.4.2.1, .2, .3 and .4 are also deleted.

Clause 27: Determination by employer

3.06 The amendment made to this clause is similar to previous editions, but it should be noted in the amended clause 27.2.2 reference is now made to the Insolvency Act 1986 and the appointment of an administrator or an administrative receiver as defined in that Act.

3.07 An amendment has also been made to clause 27.4.3 to meet the requirements of Scots law: there has been added the words 'so far as belonging to the Contractor'. This makes it clear that the employer is entitled only in the event of the bankruptcy of the main contractor to sell property (i.e. temporary plant buildings, tools, equipment, goods, and materials) which actually belong to the contractor.

Clause 28: Determination by contractor

3.08 This amendment which applies only to Private Editions again reflects the terms of the Insolvency Act 1986.

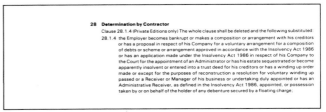

Clause 30: Certificates and payments

3.09 A number of important amendments have been made to clause 30 of the Standard From where these deal with the architect's discretionary power to certify payment for off-site goods and materials because of the differences between Scots law and English law. It should be noted that the Scottish supplement provides for the total deletion of clause 30.2.1.3 as contained in the 1980 edition of the Standard Form.

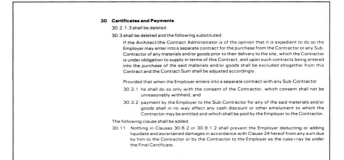

3.10 Under English law it is understood that provided the stringent provisions of clause 30.2.1.3 are followed, the right of property in off-site materials and goods is satisfactorily transferred from the main contractor to the employer. This is not the position under Scots law because, except in a contract of sale or purchase (which a building contract is not), the right of property in an article does not necessarily pass from A to B simply because A has paid B for it.

3.11 Recognizing the need to have a similar provision in the Scottish supplement, the problem has been solved in Scotland by taking the specific off-site materials and goods out of the Building Contract and transferring them into a contract of sale. Two special documents are available in Scotland to effect this: a contract of sale between an employer and a main contractor, and a contract of sale among an employer, a main contractor, and a sub-contractor. These two contracts are the means by which the transaction dealing with off-site goods and materials is taken out of the Building Contract, with the result that the contract sum in the Building Contract is reduced by the amount paid for them, and the architect issues a variation order to this effect.

3.12 There are a number of important points to note in connection with both contracts of sale:

1. The conditions listed in the instructions attached to the contract must be carefully complied with, particularly

those regarding the contract between the main contractor and the sub-contractor or supplier. These instructions are in fact identical to those contained in clause 30.2.1.3 of the Standard Form.

2. The architect must, as has been said before, reduce the contract sum by means of a variation order, the reduction being equivalent to the total cost of the materials and goods being purchased. The purchase price is paid for in two instalments – 95%, normally, at the time of the purchase and 5%, normally, at the end of the defects liability period – and it is essential that a receipt for the price is obtained from the contractor or sub-contractor, as the case may be.

3. The materials and goods concerned must be fully described in the contract.

4. A separate contract is required for each purchase separated by a period of time, although several items can be included in each contract.

3.13 The risk an employer runs in paying a contractor or sub-contractor for materials and goods before they have been delivered to the site arises in the event of the bankruptcy of either the contractor or the sub-contractor. If, for example, a main contractor went bankrupt, unless the right of property had been legally transferred to the employer, the liquidator could successfully resist any attempt by the employer to claim these goods as his own, even though the employer had paid for them.

3.14 Clause 30.3 of the Scottish supplement gives the architect the power to recommend the employer to enter into a separate contract with either a contractor or a sub-contractor for the purchase of certain materials and goods prior to their delivery to the site, although there is no obligation on the employer to do so if he does not wish it. In this connection should be noted the amendment made to clause 16.1 which deals with the main contractor's continuing responsibility for the insurance of off-site materials and goods after their purchase.

3.15 When the employer wishes to enter into a contract of purchase with a sub-contractor, it should be carefully noted that by clause 30.3.1 of the Scottish supplement he may do so only with the consent of the main contractor, which shall not be unreasonably withheld, and that by clause 30.3.2 payment by the employer to the sub-contractor for any of the materials and goods does not affect any cash discount or other emolument to which the main contractor is entitled.

3.16 The second amendment made to clause 30 – the addition of a new clause 30.11, which confirms the employer's right to deduct or add liquidate damages from any sums due by him to the contractor or by the contractor to the employer under a final certificate – has been added because of the decision in the Scottish case of *Robert Paterson* v *Household Supplies*, which seemed to suggest that unless specific reference was made to the damages in the final certificate, the employer's right to deduct them was lost.

Part 2: Nominated sub-contractors and nominated suppliers

3.17 As will be seen from Chapter 9, para 3.02 the 1980 edition of the Standard Form is in three parts – Part 1 dealing with the main contract, Part 2 containing all the provisions appropriate to the nomination of a sub-contractor or supplier, and Part 3 fluctuations. The same procedure has been adopted in the 1980 Scottish supplement, although a Part 4 has been added (para 3.26).

3.18 The amendments required for Scottish contracts to either clause 35 or clause 36 are relatively few, and dealing first with clause 35 (nominated sub-contractors) they are as follows:

Clause 35: Nominated sub-contractors

3.19 Clause 35.3 has been deleted, and a reference to the corresponding Scottish documents substituted.

3.20 Clause 35.13.5.4.4 has been deleted and the alternative clause is similar to early editions although the reference in the fourth line to the contractor being 'apparently insolvent' should be noted. This is to comply with the new bankruptcy laws.

3.21 The amendments to clauses 35.13.6 and 35.17 are necessary owing to different clause numbers in NSC/2/Scot and NSC/2a/Scot.

3.22 Clause 35.24.2 has been deleted, and the substituted clause in the Scottish supplement uses Scottish legal phraseology.

3.23 Finally, clause 35.27 has been added requiring a nominated sub-contractor to recognize an assignation by the contractor in favour of the employer in terms of clause 27.4.2.1. This additional clause is required to clarify the situation and to conform with the requirements of Scots law.

Clause 36: Nominated suppliers

3.24 The two amendments made to this section are as follows:

1. Clause 36.4.8 has been deleted, and the clause now provides that if the dispute between the contractor and the nominated supplier is substantially the same as a dispute under the Building Contract, then it should be referred to the arbiter appointed by clause 4 of the Building Contract.

2. The second amendment is the addition of clause 36.6, which like clause 35.27 requires the nominated supplier to recognize an assignation by the contractor in favour of the employer.

```
36  Nominated Suppliers
    36.4.8 shall be deleted and the following substituted:
        that if any dispute or difference between the Contractor and the Nominated Supplier is
        substantially the same as a matter which is in dispute under this Contract then such dispute
        or difference shall be referred to an Arbiter appointed or to be appointed under Clause 41 and
        the award of such Arbiter shall be final and binding on the parties.
    The following clause shall be added:
    36.6  Determination of employment of Contractor
        The Nominated Supplier shall recognise an Assignation by the Contractor in favour of the
        Employer in terms of Clause 27.4.2.1.
```

Part 3: Fluctuations

3.25 It is not necessary to make any amendments to this part in the Scottish supplement, but attention is drawn to the appropriate entry in Appendix II, page 8, by which the applicable fluctuation clause is identified.

Part 4: Settlement of disputes – arbitration

3.26 Part 4 of early editions of the Scottish Building Contract was only introduced for those who chose to create the contract between the employer and the contractor by an exchange of letters (cf para 1.03) so that they could incorporate it into their contract by reference, but in the January 1988 Revision, Part 4 contains the full arbitration clause 41, replacing the corresponding English clause of JCT 80.

```
PART 4 – SETTLEMENT OF DISPUTES – ARBITRATION
41 shall be deleted and the following substituted therefor:
41   In the event of any dispute or difference between the Employer and the Contractor arising during
     the progress of the Works or after completion or abandonment thereof in regard to any matter or
     thing whatsoever arising out of this Contract or in connection therewith (but excluding any such
     dispute or difference arising under Clause 31 to the extent provided in Clause 31.9 and under
     Clause 3 of the VAT Agreement) the said dispute or difference shall be and is hereby referred to
     the arbitration of such person as the parties may agree to appoint as Arbiter or failing agreement
     within 14 days after either party has given to the other written notice to concur in the appointment
     of an Arbiter as may be appointed by the person named in the Appendix No II Abstract of Conditions:
     Arbitration proceedings shall be deemed to have been instituted on the date on which the said
     written notice has been given.
     41.1  No arbitration shall commence without the written consent of the parties until after deter-
           mination or alleged determination of the Contractor's employment or until after Practical
           Completion or alleged Practical Completion or abandonment of the Works unless it relates to
           41.1.1  the nominations of an Architect/Contract Administrator or Quantity Surveyor to a
                   vacant appointment
           41.1.2  whether or not the issue of an instruction is empowered by the said Conditions
           41.1.3  whether or not a certificate has been improperly withheld or is not in accordance
                   with the said Conditions
           41.1.4  Clauses 4.1, 18.1 or 23.3.2 (so far as these relate to the Contractor's withholding
                   of consent), 8.4, 25, 32 and 33.
           41.1.5  whether a determination under Clause 22C.4.3.1 will be just and equitable.
     41.2  If the dispute or difference is substantially the same as or is connected with a dispute or
           difference between
           41.2.1  the Employer and a Nominated Sub-Contractor under Agreement NSC/2/Scot or
                   NSC/2a/Scot, or
           41.2.2  the Contractor and any Nominated Sub-Contractor
           41.2.3  the Contractor and/or the Employer and any Nominated Sub-Supplier whose contract
                   with the Contractor contains the like provisions as in Clause 36.4.8.
           the Employer and Contractor hereby agree that such dispute or difference shall be referred
           to an Arbiter appointed or to be appointed to determine the related dispute or difference:
           Provided that either party may require the appointment of a different Arbiter if he reasonably
           considers the Arbiter in the related dispute is not suitably qualified to determine the dispute
           or difference under this Contract
     41.3  Subject to the provisions of Clauses 4.2, 30.9, 38.4.3, 39.5.3 and 40.5 the Arbiter shall
           have power to
           41.3.1  direct such measurements and/or valuations as may in his opinion be desirable in
                   order to determine the rights of the parties
           41.3.2  ascertain and amend any sum which ought to have been referred to or included in
                   any certificate
           41.3.3  open up review and revise any certificate opinion decision requirement or notice
                   (except where Clause 8.4 is relevant, a decision of the Architect/the Contract
                   Administrator) to issue instructions pursuant to Clause 8.4.1)
           41.3.4  determine all matters in dispute which shall be submitted to him in the same manner
                   as if no such certificate opinion decision requirement or notice had been given
           41.3.5  award compensation or damages and expenses to or against any of the parties to
                   the arbitration.
     41.4  The Law of Scotland shall apply to all arbitrations in terms of this clause and the award of
           the Arbiter shall be final and binding on the parties subject to the provisions of Section 3 of
           the Administration of Justice (Scotland) Act 1972.
     41.5  The Arbiter shall be entitled to appoint a Clerk to assist him in accordance with normal arbit-
           ration practice, to issue interim, part and final awards as well as proposed findings, to
           remuneration and reimbursement of his outlays, and to find the parties jointly and severally
           liable therefor, and to decern; and to dispense with a Deed of Submission.

PART 5 – PROPER LAW
(This part has been added for convenience so that it may be included by reference in the Contract
Document when the formal Scottish Building Contract is not being executed.)
42   This Contract shall be regarded as a Scottish Contract and shall be construed and the rights of
     parties and all matters arising hereunder determined in all respects according to the Law of Scotland.
```

3.27 There are some important changes in the current arbitration clause as compared with earlier versions:

1. In place of the traditional arrangement that the arbiter, failing agreement by the parties, should be appointed by the Sheriff of the Sheriffdom in which the works are being carried out, the arbiter is now in these circumstances appointed by one of either the Sheriff, the Dean of the Faculty of Advocates or the Chairman or Vice-Chairman of the SBCC as may be indicated in the Abstract of

Conditions comprising Appendix no. II. Failing such indication the appointee is the Chairman or Vice-Chairman of the SBCC. In July 1988 the JCT issued Arbitration Rules which are obligatory for parties conducting arbitrations under JCT 80. These Rules were not adopted by the SBCC but instead the SBCC has created an arbitration appointment service in conjunction with which it has published a series of forms aimed at facilitating the appointment of an arbiter. These forms are as follows:

1. ARB.1 – Notice to Consent in the Appointment of an Arbiter.
2. ARB.2 – Application to the Chairman, SBCC for the Appointment of an Arbiter.
3. ARB.3 – Form of Notice of Unilateral Application for the Appointment of an Arbiter.
4. ARB.4 – Form of Notice of Appointment.
5. ARB.5 – Form of Objection to Nomination.
6. ARB.6 – Notice of Decision following Objection to nominated Arbiter.
7. ARB.7 – Form of Application to declare Office of Arbiter vacant.
8. ARB.8 – Form of Intimation of Notice of Application to declare the Office of Arbiter vacant.
9. ARB.9 – Notice of Decision following Application to Declare the Office of Arbiter vacant.
10. ARB.10 – Notice of Hearing.

2. New grounds for the appointment of an arbiter have been aded in clauses 41.1.4 and 41.1.5.
3. A new clause 41.5 has been added giving the arbiter power, for example to appoint a clerk, to find the parties jointly and severally liable and to dispense with a Deed of Submission. In practice any properly drawn Deed of Submission will contain all the powers given to the arbiter under this clause and as the majority of arbitrations entered into in terms of the Scottish Building Contract will be initiated by a Deed of Submission, this clause may well be seldom invoked.

Part 5: Proper law

This is a new Part added in the January 1988 Revision and repeats clause 5 of the Building Contract for the convenience of those who do not choose to use it.

4 The Scottish supplement – Appendix II

4.01 This appendix is similar to the appendix annexed to JCT 80 with the exception of the final entry dealing with the method of appointment of an arbiter to which reference has already been made (cf para 3.27) and which obviously is unique to Scotland.

```
                                                    APPENDIX No. II

                                             ABSTRACT OF CONDITIONS
                                          Clause
¹Delete as required     Statutory tax deduction scheme –   31      Employer at Base Date is a 'contractor'¹/is not a
                        Finance (No. 2) Act 1975                    'contractor' for the purposes of the Act and the
                                                                    Regulations

                        Base Date                          1.3     _____

                        Defects Liability Period (if none  17.2    _____
                        other stated is 12 months from the
                        day named in the Certificate of
                        Practical Completion of the Works)

                        Assignation by Employer of         19.1.2  Clause 19.1.2 applies¹/does not apply
                        benefits after Practical Completion

                        Insurance cover for any one occur- 21.1.1  £_____
                        rence or series of occurrences
                        arising out of one event

²If the indemnity is to be for an  Insurance – Liability of Employer  21.2.1  Insurance may be ¹/is not required.
aggregate amount and not for any
one occurrence or series of                                          Amount of indemnity for any one occurrence or
occurrences the entry should make                                    series of occurrences arising out of one event²
this clear
                                                                     £_____
```

		Clause	
	Insurance of the Works – Alternative clauses	22.1	Clause 22A¹/22B¹/22C applies
¹No percentage should be inserted if those concerned are all Employees of a Local Authority, but the sum assured should cover the cost of professional services	Percentage to cover Professional fees	22A¹/22B.1¹ 22C.2	_____ %¹
	Annual renewal date of insurance as supplied by the Contractor	22A.3.1	
	Insurance for Employer's loss of liquidate and ascertained damages – Clause 25.4.3	22D	Insurance may be ¹/is not required
		22D.2	Period of time_____
	Date of Possession	23.1.1	
	Date for Completion	1.3	
	Deferment of Date of Possession	23.1.2 25.4.13	Clause 23.1.2 applies¹/does not apply
		26.1	Period of deferment if it is to be less than 6 weeks is
¹It is suggested the periods should be 28.1.3 one month; 28A.1.1 and 28A.1.3 three months. It is essential that periods be inserted since otherwise no period of delay would be prescribed	Liquidate and Ascertained Damages	24.2	at the rate of £_____ per_____
	Period of delay	28.1.3	¹
	Period of delay	28A.1.1 28A.1.3	¹
	Period of delay	28A.1.2	¹
	Period of Interim Certificates (if none stated is one month)	30.1.3	
	Retention Percentage (if less than five per cent)	30.4.1.1	
	Work reserved for Nominated Sub-Contractors for which the Contractor desires to tender	35.2	
¹Delete as required	Fluctuations (if alternative required is not shown Clause 38 shall apply)	37	Clause 38¹/Clause 39¹/Clause 40
	Percentage addition	38.7 or 39.8	_____ %
	Formula Rules (September 1980) Rule 3	40.1.1.1 Base Month	_____19___
¹Not to exceed 10%	Rule 3		¹Non-Adjustable Element_____ % (Local Authorities Edition only)
	Rules 10 and 30(i)		Part I¹/Part II of Section 2 of the Formula Rules is to apply.
	Settlement of disputes – Arbitration if no appointor is selected the appointor shall be the Chairman or Vice-Chairman, The Scottish Building Contract Committee	41	The Chairman or Vice-Chairman of the Scottish Building Contract Committee/The Dean of the Faculty of Advocates/The Sheriff of the Sheriffdom in which the Works are situated.

_____ Employer _____ Contractor

5 Different editions of the Standard Form

5.01 The above comments apply equally to the With Quantities Edition and the Without Quantities Edition except for the reference in the Building Contract for the latter to the method by which the contract sum has been calculated, i.e. by pricing the Specification/Schedule of Works or by a Contract Sum Analysis.

5.02 The same pattern is followed in the other four editions but note that in the case of the With Contractor's Design edition the name of the Employer's agent for the purposes of the contract requires to be inserted in clause 3 of the Building Contract since in this type of contract an architect is not engaged by the employer.

6 Nominated sub-contracts

6.01 In 1980 the Scottish Building Contract Committee published for use with nominated sub-contracts a series of documents corresponding to those issued by the Tribunal; those for use when the 'basic' method of nomination is employed (see Chapter 9) are Tender NSC/1/Scot, Agreement NSC/2/Scot, Nomination NSC/3/Scot, and Sub-contract NSC/4/Scot. When the 'alternative' method is used, the documents are Tender NSC/1a/Scot, and NSC/2a/Scot, Nomination NSC/3a/Scot, and Sub-contract NSC/4a/Scot. In all cases these documents fulfil the same role as their English counterparts with differences in style to conform with Scottish procedure.

Tender NSC/1/Scot

6.02 This is the basic Scottish document consisting of the sub-contractor's offer or tender – which can be either a lump sum or a tender sum subject to remeasurement on completion – on pages 1 and 2; Schedule 1 on pages 3 to 7 containing particulars of the main contract and the fluctuation provisions; and Schedule 2 on pages 8 to 11 containing the detailed matters which have to be agreed on between the main contractor and the sub-contractor. It is these matters which in the past, under the old haphazard arrangement for completing nomination, tended to cause problems; now that they have to be settled before nomination is finalized, it is hoped they will be resolved less painfully.

Standard Form of Nominated Sub-Contract Tender for use in Scotland

Main Contract Works:

Location:

Sub-Contract Works:

To: The Employer and Main Contractor

We_____

of_____

hereby offer subject to the conditions overleaf to carry out and complete as a Nominated Sub-Contractor the Sub-Contract Works referred to above for

*Delete as applicable

*The VAT exclusive sum of £_____ (hereinafter referred to as 'the Sub-Contract Sum')

OR

†For use where the Sub-Contract Works are to be completely remeasured and valued

*The VAT exclusive tender sum† of £_____ (hereinafter referred to as 'the Sub-Contract Tender Sum')

(Any VAT payable will be dealt with in accordance with the Sub-Contract referred to in (2) below).

in accordance with

(1) The drawings*/specifications*/bills of quantities*/schedule of rates annexed hereto numbered_____ (the 'Numbered Documents') signed by ourselves and the Architect/the Contract Administrator.

(2) The Scottish Building Sub-Contract known as NSC/4/Scot (January 1988 revision) together with the amendments and modifications contained in the Appendix thereto, to the Standard Conditions of Contract for Nominated Sub-Contractors known as NSC/4.

(3) The particulars of the Main Contract contained in Schedule 1 hereto.

(4) The Particular Conditions set out in Schedule 2 hereto after agreement of the same with the Main Contractor.

(5) The following day work percentages (Sub-Contract NSC/4 Clauses 16.3.4 or 17.4.3) are

Applicable Definition	Labour	Materials	Plant
1. R.I.C.S./N.F.B.T.E.	___%	___%	___%
2. R.I.C.S./E.C.A./E.C.A. of S	___%	___%	___%
3. R.I.C.S./H.V.C.A	___%	___%	___%

We confirm that the Sub-Contract Sum or Sub-Contract Tender Sum and the above percentages take into account the 2½% cash discount allowable to the Main Contractor.

_____ Date

Sub-Contractor

The foregoing offer is approved on the terms and conditions set out above

_____ Date

(Approved by the Architect/the Contract Administrator on behalf of the Employer)

The foregoing offer is accepted on the terms and conditions set out above

_____ Date

(Accepted by the Main Contractor subject to receipt of a nomination instruction).

Conditions referred to on Page 1

1. We agree to be bound by the Agreement between ourselves and the Employer (NSC/2/Scot), which we have executed simultaneously with this tender, after the Architect/the Contract Administrator has approved our tender on behalf of the Employer by signature overleaf.

2. If the identity of the Main Contractor is not known to us at the date of this tender we reserve the right within 14 days of written notification by the Architect/the Contract Administrator of such identification to withdraw this tender notwithstanding prior approval by or on behalf of the Employer.

3. We reserve the right to withdraw this tender if we are unable to agree the Particular Conditions set out in Schedule 2 hereto with the Main Contractor.

*Sub-Contractor to insert acceptance period

4. Without prejudice to 2 and 3 above this tender shall be deemed to have been withdrawn if the nomination instruction is not issued by the Architect/the Contract Administrator within *_____ weeks from the date hereof or such other later date as may be notified by us in writing to the Architect/the Contract Administrator.

5. Any withdrawal under 2, 3 or 4 above shall be free of cost to the Employer except for any sums that may be due to us in accordance with the Agreement NSC/2/Scot referred to in 1 above.

Schedule 1:
Particulars of the Main Contract and Sub-Contract

Employer:

Architect/Contract Administrator:

Quantity Surveyor:

Main Contractor:

1. **Sub-Contract Conditions** — NSC/4 as modified and amended by Scottish Building Sub-Contract NSC/4/Scot (revised January 1988) all as appropriate to the Standard Form of Building Contract referred to in item 5 hereof (Scottish Building Sub-Contract NSC/4/Scot is to be executed forthwith after issue of the Architect/the Contract Administrator's Nomination NSC/3/Scot).

2. **Sub-Contract Fluctuations** — NSC/4
*Clause 35 (see Appendix (A)): Clause 35.7_____%
*Clause 36 (see Appendix (A)): Clause 36.8_____%
*Clause 37 (see Appendix (B)).

Delete as applicable

3. **Main Contract Appendix II & entries therein (see item 10)** — Where relevant these will apply to the Sub-Contract unless otherwise specifically stated here. The entry relating to Clause 37 of the Main Contract is for information of the Sub-Contractor only.

4. **Title and address of Main Contract Works**

5. **Form of Main Contract Conditions** — Scottish Building Contract and Scottish Supplement (1980 Edition) revised January 1988 to the Standard Form of Building Contract 1980 Edition With Quantities*/Without Quantities*/Sectional Completion*/With Approximate Quantities

Delete as appropriate

6. **Inspection of Main Contract** — The unpriced Bills of Quantities*/Bills of Approximate Quantities*/Contract Specification (which incorporate the general conditions and preliminaries of the Main Contract) and the Contract Drawings may be inspected at

Delete as applicable

7. **Execution of Main Contract** — *This item which indicates whether the Main Contract is or is not executed under Seal is not applicable to Scotland but it is retained to maintain the same numerical sequence as in NSC/1/Schedule 1 published by the J.C.T. for use in England.*

8. **Main Contract Conditions alternative provisions** — Scottish Building Contract Clause 3. Works insurance: Insurance: | Architect*/Contract Administrator Clause 22A*/22B*/22C.2 to .4 Clause 21.2.1 Insurance may be */is not required. Amount of demnity for any one occurrence or series of occurrences arising out of one event £

Delete as applicable

9. **Main Contract Conditions – insert here any amendments or additions to Form of Main Contract referred to in item 5 above**

Delete as applicable

When in Schedule 1 item 5 it is stated that Sectional Completion of the Main Contract Works is to apply, Appendix II of the Scottish Building Contract Sectional Completion Edition must be substituted at item 10

10. **Main Contract: †Appendix II and entries therein**

		Clause	
Statutory tax deduction scheme – Finance (No. 2) Act 1975		31	Employer at Base Date is a 'contractor'*/is not a 'contractor' for the purposes of the Act and the Regulations
Base Date		1.3	
Defects Liability Period (if none other stated is 12 months from the day named in the Certificate of Practical Completion of the Works)		17.2	
Assignation by Employer of benefits after Practical Completion		19.2	Clause 19.1.2 applies*/does not apply
Insurance cover for any one occurrence or series of occurrences arising out of one event		21.1.1	£
Insurance – Liability of Employer		21.2.1	Insurance may be*/is not required. Amount of idemnity for any one occurrence or series of occurrences arising out of one event £
Insurance of the Works – Alternative clauses		22.1	Clause 22A*/22B*/22C applies
Percentage to cover Professional fees		22A/22B./22C.2	%
Annual renewal date of insurance as supplied by the Contractor		22A.3.1	
Insurance for Employer's loss of liquidate and ascertained damages – Clause 25.4.3		22D	Insurance may be*/is not required
		22D.2	Period of time
Date of Possession		23.1.1	
Date for Completion		1.3	
Deferment of Date of Possession		23.1.2 25.4.13	Clause 23.1.2 applies*/does not apply
		26.1	Period of deferment if it is to be less than 6 weeks is
Liquidate and Ascertained Damages		24.2	At the rate of £_____per_____
Period of delay		28.1.3	
Period of delay		28A.1.1 28A.1.3	
Period of Delay		28A.1.2	
Period of Interim Certificates (if none stated is one month)		30.1.3	
Retention Percentage (if less than five per cent)		30.4.1.1	%
Work reserved for Nominated Sub-Contractors for which the Contractor desires to tender		35.2	
Fluctuations		37	Clause 38*/Clause 39*/Clause 40
Percentage addition		38.7 or 39.8	%
Formula Rules (September 1980) Rule 3		40.1.1.1	Base month_____19___
Rule 3			*Non-Adjustable Element _____% (Local Authorities Edition only)

Not to exceed 10%

		Clause	
	Rule 10 and 30(i)		Part I*/Part II of Section 2 of the Formula Rules is to apply.
	Settlement of disputes – Arbitration	41	The Chairman or Vice-Chairman of the Scottish Building Contract Committee*/The Dean of the Faculty of Advocates*/The Sheriff of the Sheriffdom in which the Works are situated

Delete as applicable

11. **Order of Works** — Employer's requirements affecting the order of the Main Contract Works (if any).

12. **Location and type of access**

13.* **Obligations or restrictions imposed by Employer not covered by Main Contract Conditions (e.g. in the Preliminaries in the Contract Bills)**

If extensive this information could be given by a copy of the Preliminaries Bill of the Main Contract Bills

14.* **Other relevant information (if any)**

We have noted the foregoing information

_____ Sub-Contractor.

Fluctuations (see Page 3 item 2)

N.B. – This Appendix should be completed by the Sub-Contractor where Sub-Contract NSC/4 Clauses 35 or 36 apply, attaching further sheets if necessary, which if Clause 36.1.5 is to apply should include the Sub-Contractor's basic transport charges.

Where Clause 35 applies only column 1 need be completed.

Where Clause 36 applies columns 1 to 4 must be completed.

The Base Date for the purpose of Clauses 35 and 36 is_____19___

1. Materials, Goods, Electricity and *Fuels	2. Rate (or approximate standard price list description)	3. Discounts	4. Unit to which rate applies

To be deleted by the Architect/Contract Administrator if fuels not to be included

_____ Date_____ 19___

Sub-Contractor

Fluctuations (see Page 3 item 2)

N.B. – This Appendix should be completed by the Sub-Contractor when Sub-Contract NSC/4 Clause 37 applies.

(i) 37.1 – Nominated Sub-Contract Formula Rules are those dated_____19___ Part I*/Part III of these Rules applies.

Delete as applicable

(ii) 37.3.3 and 37.3.4 *Non-Adjustable Element_____% (Local Authority versions only).

Not to exceed 10%

(iii) 37.4 – List of Market Prices for articles manufactured outside the United Kingdom (use separate sheet if required).

(iv) Nominated Sub-Contract Formula Rules.

Rule 3. (Definition of Balance of Adjustable Work).
Any measured work not allocated to a Work Category.

Base Month_____19___

Base Date_____19___

Rule 8.
Method of dealing with 'Fix only' work. Rule 8(i)*/8(ii)*/8(iii) applies.

Delet as applicable

Rule 11(a).
Part I only: the Work Categories applicable to the Sub-Contract Works.

If both specialist engineering formulae apply to the Sub-Contract the percentages for use with each formula should be inserted and clearly identified

*The weightings for sprinkler installations may be inserted where different weightings are required

*Delete as applicable

Rule 43.
Part III only: Weightings of labour and materials – Electrical Installations or Heating, Ventilating and Air Conditioning Installations.

	Labour	Materials
Electrical	_____ %	_____ %
*Heating, Ventilating and Air Conditioning	_____ %	_____ %
Sprinklers	_____ %	_____ %

Rule 61a.
Adjustment shall be effected *upon completion of manufacure of all fabricated components.
*upon delivery to site of all fabricated components.

Rule 64.
Part III only: Structural Steelwork Installations:

(i) Average price per tonne of steel delivered to fabricator's works £ _____

(ii) Average price per tonne for erection of steelwork £ _____

Rule 70a.
Catering Equipment Installation;
Apportionment of the values of each item between

(i) Materials and shop fabrication £ _____

(ii) Supply of factor items £ _____

(iii) Site installations £ _____

_____ Date _____ 19 ___
Sub-Contractor.

Schedule 2: Particular Conditions

Note: When the Contractor receives Tender NSC/1/Scot together with the Architect/the Contract Administrator's preliminary notice of nomination under Clause 35.7.1 of the Main Contract Conditions then the Contractor has to agree this Schedule with the proposed Sub-Contractor.

To be completed by the Architect/Contract Administrator before issue

1.A. Any stipulations as to the period/periods when Sub-Contract Works are to be carried out on site; to be between _____

and _____

Period required by the Architect/the Contractor Administrator to examine any drawings submitted to him _____ weeks

The Sub-Contractor will set out here (or on attached sheet if necessary) details of the carrying out of the Sub-Contract Works as a preliminary indication to the Architect, Contract Administrator and Contractor. Adapt as necessary where in Schedule 1, item 5, it is stated that Sectional Completion applies to the Main Contract Conditions

*Not including any period for examination

1.B. Preliminary programme
(having regard to the information provided in the invitation to tender).

Period required:

*for preparation of further design work and/or drawings _____ weeks

*for preparation of working drawings or installation drawings _____ weeks

*for preparation of shop drawings (if required) _____ weeks

for execution of the Sub-Contract Works off site _____ weeks

on-site _____ weeks

Notice required to commence work on site _____ weeks

Agreed details on the programme for carrying out the Sub-Contract Works (which must include the subjects set out in 1.A and 1B) must be inserted here or on an attached sheet initialled by the Contractor and Sub-Contractor. The programme details must take account of any Sectional Completion of the Main Contract Works where in Schedule 1, item 5 it is stated that Sectional Completion applies to the Main Contract Conditions. The details of 1.A and 1.B (and any sheet attached thereto) must then be deleted and the deletion initialled by the Contractor and the Sub-Contractor

1.C Agreed programme details (including sub-contract completion date: see Sub-Contract NSC/4 Clause 11.1).

2. Order of Works – to follow the requirements, if any, stated in Schedule 1, item 11.

The Sub-Contractor will set out here or on an attached sheet as a preliminary indication to the Architect/the Contract Administrator and Contractor the special attendances which he will require to be supplied free of charge by the Contractor

3.A. Attendance proposals (other than *general attendance)

(a) Special scaffolding or scaffolding additional to the Contractor's standing scaffolding.

(b) The provision of temporary access roads and hardstandings in connection with structural steelwork, precast concrete components, piling, heavy items of plant and the like.

(c) Unloading, distributing, hoisting and placing in position giving in the case of significant items the weight and/or size (to be at the risk of the Sub-Contractor).

(d) The provision of covered storage and accommodation including lighting and power thereto.

(e) Power supplies giving the maximum load.

(f) Maintenance of specific temperature or humidity levels.

*(g) Any other attendance not included under (a) to (f) or as general attendance under Sub-Contract NSC/4 Clause 27.1.1.

*Note: *For general attendance see Clause 27.1.1 of Sub-Contract NSC/4 which states:*

'General attendance shall be provided by the Contractor free of charge to the Sub-Contractor and shall be deemed to include only use of the Contractor's temporary roads, pavings and paths standing scaffolding, standing power operated hoisting plant, the provision of temporary lighting and water supplies, clearing away rubbish, provision of space for the Sub-Contractor's own offices and for the storage of his plant and materials and the use of mess rooms; sanitary accommodation and welfare facilities: see S.M.M. 6th Edition B.9.2.

The Contractor will set out in agreement with the Sub-Contractor any alterations to any of the details of the attendance set out in 3A above

3.B. Agreed special attendances.

The Contractor to complete in agreement with the Sub-Contractor. The item must include any limits of indemnity which are required in respect of insurance to be taken out by the Sub-Contractor

4. Insurance.

Any special conditions or agreements affecting the employment of labour should be inserted in 5A by the Sub-Contractor and in 5B by the Contractor after agreement with the Sub-Contractor; thereafter delete 5A

5.A. Employment of Labour – Special Conditions or Agreements.

5.B. Employment of Labour – Special Conditions or Agreements.

6. This item which deals with the appointment of an Adjudicator and Trustee Stakeholder is not applicable to Scotland but it is retained to maintain the same numerical sequence as in NSC/1/Schedule 2 published by the J.C.T. for use in England.

To be completed by the Contractor after agreement with the Sub-Contractor
*Delete as applicable

7. Finance (No. 2) Act 1975 – Statutory Tax Deduction Scheme.

1. The Contractor is */is not entitled to be paid by the Employer without the statutory deduction referred to in the above Act or any amendment or re-enactment thereof or such other deduction as may be in force;

2. The Sub-Contractor is/is not entitled to be paid by the Contractor without the above-mentioned statutory deduction or such other deduction;

3. The evidence to be produced to the Contractor for the verification of the Sub-Contractor's tax certificate (expiry date 19) will be:

*Delete as applicable

8. Value Added Tax – Sub-Contract NSC/4.
Clause 19A*/19B (alternative provisions) will apply.

The Sub-Contractor will set out here or on an attached sheet any matter he wishes to agree with the Contractor

9.A. Any other matters (including any limitation on working hours).

To be completed by the Contractor after agreement with the Sub-Contractor. Thereafter 9A should be deleted and initialled by the Contractor and Sub-Contractor

9.B.

10. Any other matters agreed by the Architect/the Contract Administrator and Sub-Contractor before preliminary notice of nomination.

*To be deleted as appropriate by the Architect/Contract Administrator
If no appointor is selected the appointor shall be the Chairman or Vice-Chairman, The Scottish Building Contract Committee

11. Settlement of disputes – Arbitration – Appointor
The Chairman or Vice-Chairman of the Scottish Building Contract Committee */ The Dean of the Faculty of Advocates */The Sheriff of the Sheriffdom in which the Works are situated.

The above Particular Conditions are agreed

_____ Date _____ 19 ___
Signed by or on behalf of the Sub-Contractor.

_____ Date _____ 19 ___
Signed by or on behalf of the Main Contractor.

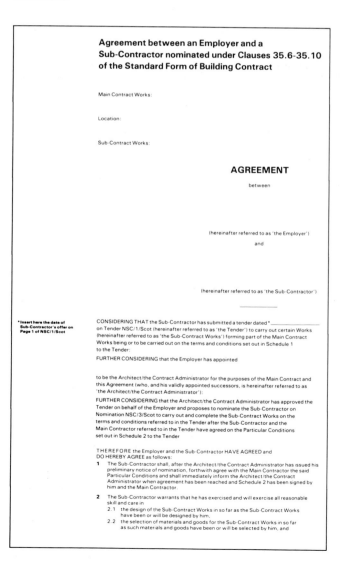

Instructions for Use

Stage

1 Architect issues a principal and one copy to proposed Nominated Sub-contractor (NSC) having first completed those parts of the document which require completion by him (i.e. Schedule 1 and relevant part of Appendix (A) if applicable: Item 1A of Schedule 2). Retains photocopies for his own use.

(Other documents required: Agreement NSC/2/Scot also sent to NSC).

2 NSC completes those parts of the document which require completion by him i.e. Page 1 Appendix (A) or (B) and relevant parts of Schedule 2). Signs document on Pages 1 and 5 and 6 or 7 and thereafter returns principal to the Architect.

(Other documents required: NSC signs Agreement NSC/2/Scot and returns it to Architect).

3 Architect signs Page 1 and then sends principal and one copy to Main Contractor with instructions to agree Schedule 2 with NSC.

(Other documents required: Employer signs NSC/2/Scot and photocopy sent by Architect to NSC).

4 After reaching agreement with NSC, Main Contractor completes relevant parts of Schedule 2 which is then signed by Main Contractor and NSC on Page 11. Main Contractor also signs document on page 1 and then returns principal to Architect.

5 Architect makes two photocopies of completed document. Retains one for his own use. Sends the other to NSC and the principal to the Main Contractor.

(Other documents required: Architect issues Nomination NSC/3/Scot to Main Contractor with copy to NSC. Sends copy of Agreement NSC/2/Scot to Main Contractor).

NB

As compared with the original the following alterations have been made.

November 1984 Revision.

P1 Provision for numbering drawings in (i).

P4 Note added re Sectional Completion.

P6 Note added referring to basic transport charges.

P7 Textual amendment to (iii).

P8 Textual amendment to 1A.

April 1987 Revision.

P3 Item 8. Text amended to apply to new insurance clauses issued January 1987.

P4 Main Contract Appendix amended to apply to new insurance clauses issued January 1987.

January 1988 Revision.

Adapted for January 1988 revisions to Main Contracts and NSC/4/Scot.

Supervising Officer changed to Contract Administrator. Revised Main Contract Appendix II incorporated. Choice of appointing authority for Arbiter to be made.

---

other to the nominated sub-contractor at the same time as he returns the principal to the main contractor.

Agreement NSC/2/Scot

6.05 This document, like its English counterpart, sets up a clear contractual relationship between the employer and the nominated sub-contractor for the first time. In exchange for certain guarantees or warranties given by the nominated sub-contractor, the employer undertakes that he will ensure that the architect complies with certain provisions of the main contract which in the main authorize direct payment to the nominated sub-contractor in certain circumstances. Although the format of the document is different from its English counterpart and the wording employed comes more naturally to Scottish ears and tongues, the obligations and rights which the employer and the nominated sub-contractor are taking on or giving to each other are the same as in the Tribunal's document. It should be noted, however, that when originally published the warranty given by the sub-contractor in Agreement NSC/2/Scot (clause 2) was restricted, so that the sub-contractor's guarantee in respect of the design of the sub-contract works was limited to the performance specification or requirement set out in the description of the sub-contract works included in his tender. Later editions of Agreement NSC/2/Scot have, however, amended this, so that the design warranty given by the sub-contractor is no longer restricted in this way, and the provisions of clause 2 are now identical with the corresponding clause in the English document.

6.03 There are slight differences in phraseology between the Scottish and English documents, but there is nothing in Tender NSC/1/Scot which alters the respective rights and/or duties of the three parties to the contract, namely the employer, the main contractor, and the sub-contractor. Users of the Scottish document, however, should note that in Schedule 2, items 6 and 11 of the English document do not apply, but the numbers have been retained to keep the same sequence in both documents.

6.04 On the back page of Tender NSC/1/Scot have been printed detailed instructions for using the document which vary slightly from the English procedure and which can be summarized as follows:

1. The architect sends the principal and a copy to the proposed nominated sub-contractor, having completed Schedule 1 and those parts of Appendix A which are noted in the appendix as having to be completed by him.
2. The nominated sub-contractor inserts on the first two pages the details of his tender or offer (noting in particular to insert in paragraph 4 on page 2 the number of weeks for which he is prepared to allow his offer to lie on the table); completes Appendix A or Appendix B, as appropriate, of Schedule 1 and the relevant parts of Schedule 2; and returns the principal to the architect, having signed the document three times on pages 1 and 5 and on either page 6 or 7, depending upon the method of calculating fluctuations. The nominated sub-contractor should retain the copy he received from the architect for his own use and of course should insert on it the additional information he has added to the principal.
3. The architect then signs the principal on page 1 as having approved the offer and sends the principal and a copy to the main contractor with instructions that he should immediately agree the provisions of Schedule 2 with the nominated sub-contractor. It should be noted that in the process of negotiation between the main contractor and the nominated sub-contractor, some of the requirements initially indicated by the nominated sub-contractor may be varied, and there is provision in Schedule 2 for the ultimate agreement to be substituted for the nominated sub-contractor's original requirements.
4. When agreement has been reached (within the period of ten days as provided for in the Standard Form clause 35.8) both the main contractor and the sub-contractor sign Schedule 2 on page 11, and the main contractor returns the principal to the architect.
5. Finally, the architect makes two copies of the completed document, retaining one for his own use and sending the

---

Agreement between an Employer and a Sub-Contractor nominated under Clauses 35.6-35.10 of the Standard Form of Building Contract

Main Contract Works:

Location:

Sub-Contract Works:

AGREEMENT

between

(hereinafter referred to as 'the Employer')

and

(hereinafter referred to as 'the Sub-Contractor')

*Insert here the date of Sub-Contractor's offer on Page 1 of NSC/1/Scot

CONSIDERING THAT the Sub-Contractor has submitted a tender dated *_____ on Tender NSC/1/Scot (hereinafter referred to as 'the Tender') to carry out certain Works (hereinafter referred to as 'the Sub-Contract Works') forming part of the Main Contract Works being or to be carried out on the terms and conditions set out in Schedule 1 to the Tender:

FURTHER CONSIDERING that the Employer has appointed

to be the Architect/the Contract Administrator for the purposes of the Main Contract and this Agreement (who, and his validly appointed successors, is hereinafter referred to as 'the Architect/the Contract Administrator'):

FURTHER CONSIDERING that the Architect/the Contract Administrator has approved the Tender on behalf of the Employer and proposes to nominate the Sub-Contractor on Nomination NSC/3/Scot to carry out and complete the Sub-Contract Works on the terms and conditions referred to in the Tender after the Sub-Contractor and the Main Contractor referred to in the Tender have agreed on the Particular Conditions set out in Schedule 2 to the Tender

THEREFORE the Employer and the Sub-Contractor HAVE AGREED and DO HEREBY AGREE as follows:

1 The Sub-Contractor shall, after the Architect/the Contract Administrator has issued his preliminary notice of nomination, forthwith agree with the Main Contractor the said Particular Conditions and shall immediately inform the Architect/the Contract Administrator when agreement has been reached and Schedule 2 has been signed by him and the Main Contractor.

2 The Sub-Contractor warrants that he has exercised and will exercise all reasonable skill and care in
   2.1 the design of the Sub-Contract Works in so far as the Sub-Contract Works have been or will be designed by him,
   2.2 the selection of materials and goods for the Sub-Contract Works in so far as such materials and goods have been or will be selected by him, and

2.3 the satisfaction of any performance specification or requirement in so far as such performance specification or requirement is included or referred to in the description of the Sub-Contract Works included in or annexed to the Tender.

Nothing in Clause 2 shall be construed so as to affect the obligations of the Sub-Contractor under Building Sub-Contract NSC/4/Scot in regard to the supply under that Sub-Contract of workmanship, materials and goods.

3 3.1 If, after execution of this Agreement and before the issue by the Architect/the Contract Administrator of the Nomination NSC/3/Scot, the Architect/the Contract Administrator instructs the Sub-Contractor in writing to proceed with the designing of, or the purchase under a contract of sale of materials or goods or the fabrication of components for the Sub-Contract Works then the Sub-Contractor shall forthwith comply with the instruction and the Employer shall make payment or reimbursement for such compliance in accordance with Clauses 3.2 to 3.4.

3.2 No payment or reimbursement referred to in Clauses 3.3 and 3.4 shall be made after the issue of Nomination NSC/3/Scot except in respect of any design work properly carried out and/or materials or goods properly ordered under a contract of sale or components properly fabricated in compliance with an instruction under Clause 3.1 but which are not used for the Sub-Contract Works by reason of some written decision against such use given by the Architect/the Contract Administrator before the issue of Nomination NSC/3/Scot.

3.3 The Employer shall pay the Sub-Contractor the amount of any expense reasonably and properly incurred by the Sub-Contractor in carrying out work in the designing of the Sub-Contract Works and upon such payment the Employer may use that work for the purpose of the Sub-Contract Works but not further or otherwise.

3.4 The Employer shall pay the Sub-Contractor for any component properly fabricated and shall reimburse the Sub-Contractor for any amounts properly due and paid by the Sub-Contractor under the contract of sale for materials or goods properly purchased by the Sub-Contractor for the Sub-Contract Works and upon such payment or reimbursement the materials and goods shall become the property of the Employer.

3.5 If any payment or reimbursement has been made by the Employer under Clauses 3.2 to 3.4 and the Sub-Contractor is subsequently nominated in Nomination NSC/3/Scot to execute the Sub-Contract Works, the Sub-Contractor shall allow to the Main Contractor or, where Clause 35.13.6 of the Main Contract Conditions is operated, to the Employer full credit for such payment or reimbursement in the discharge of the amount due in respect of the Sub-Contract Works and the Sub-Contractor shall provide the Employer with a written statement, in duplicate, of the amount so credited. Provided that no credit shall be so allowed in respect of payments or reimbursements made by the Employer for design work properly carried out and/or materials or goods properly purchased under a contract of sale and/or components properly fabricated in compliance with an instruction under Clause 3.1 but which are not used by reason of some written decision against such use by the Architect/the Contract Administrator before the issue of Nomination NSC/3/Scot.

4 The Sub-Contractor shall supply the Architect/the Contract Administrator with such information (including drawings) in accordance with the agreed programme details or at such time as the Architect/the Contract Administrator may reasonably require so that the Architect/the Contract Administrator shall not be delayed in issuing necessary instructions or drawings under the Main Contract for which delay the Main Contractor might have a valid claim for an extension of time for the completion of the Main Contract Works under Clause 25.4.6 or a valid claim for direct loss and expense under Clause 26.2.1 of the Main Contract Conditions.

5 The Sub-Contractor shall perform the Sub-Contract so that the Architect/the Contract Administrator will not by reason of any default of the Sub-Contractor be required to issue an instruction to determine the employment of the Sub-Contractor under the Main Contract: provided that any suspension by the Sub-Contractor of further execution of the Sub-Contract Works under Clause 21.8 of Sub-Contract Conditions NSC/4 shall not be regarded as coming within this clause.

6 The Sub-Contractor shall perform the Sub-Contract so that the Contractor will not become entitled to an extension of time for completion of the Main Contract Works.

7 The Employer agrees that the Sub-Contractor will not be liable under Clauses 4, 5 and 6 hereof until the Architect/the Contract Administrator has issued Nomination NSC/3/Scot.

8 The Employer shall ensure that the Architect/the Contract Administrator will operate the provisions of Clauses 35.13.1* and 35.17† to 35.19 of the Main Contract Conditions.

8.1 After final payment to the Sub-Contractor under Clause 35.17 of the Main Contract Conditions the Sub-Contractor shall rectify at his own cost (or if he fails to do so shall be liable to the Employer for the costs referred to in Clause 35.18 of the Main Contract Conditions) any omission, fault or defect in the Sub-Contract Works which the Sub-Contractor is bound in accordance with the Sub-Contract to rectify, after written notification of the same by the Architect/the Contract Administrator at any time prior to the issue of the Final Certificate under the Main Contract.

8.2 After issue of said Final Certificate the Sub-Contractor shall in addition to such other responsibilities if any, as he has under this Agreement, have the same responsibility to the Contractor and to the Employer for the Sub-Contract Works as the Contractor has to the Employer under the Main Contract after the issue of the Final Certificate.

***Clause 35.13.1 requires the Architect/the Contract Administrator when directing the Contractor as to the amount included in an Interim Certificate in respect of the value of the Nominated Sub-Contract Works issued under Clause 30 of the Main Contract Conditions forthwith to inform the Sub-Contractor in writing of that amount**

†Clause 35.17 deals with final payment by the Employer for the Sub-Contract Works prior to the issue of the Final Certificate under the Main Contract Conditions

9 Where the Architect/the Contract Administrator has been required under Clause 35.24 of the Main Contract Conditions to make a further nomination in respect of the Sub-Contract Works, the Sub-Contractor shall indemnify the Employer for any direct loss and/or expense resulting therefrom, except where Clause 35.24.6 of the Main Contract Conditions applies.

10 The Employer shall operate, and shall ensure that the Architect/the Contract Administrator shall operate, the provisions in regard to the payment of the Sub-Contractor contained in Clause 35.13 of the Main Contract Conditions.

10.1 If, after paying any amount to the Sub-Contractor under Clause 35.13.5.3 of the Main Contract Conditions, the Employer produces reasonable proof that there was in existence at the time of such payment a petition or resolution to which Clause 35.13.5.4.4 of the Main Contract Conditions refers, the Sub-Contractor shall repay such amount on demand.

11 Where Clause 2.3* of Sub-Contract Conditions NSC/4 applies the Sub-Contractor shall forthwith give the Contractor details of any restriction, limitation or exclusion to which that clause refers as soon as such details are known to the Sub-Contractor.

***Clause 2.3 deals with specified supplies and restrictions, etc. in the contracts of sale for such supplies**

11a Where Clause 19.1.2 of the Main Contract Conditions applies then, in the event of the Employer alienating by sale or lease or otherwise disposing of his interest in the Works, the Employer may at any time after the issue of the Certificate of Practical Completion of the Works assign to the person acquiring his interest in the Works, his right, title and interest to bring proceedings in the name of the Employer (whether in court or arbitration proceedings) to enforce any of the rights of the Employer arising under or by reason of breach of this Agreement.

12 If any conflict appears between the terms of the Tender and this Agreement, the terms of this Agreement shall prevail.

13 In the event of any dispute or difference of opinion arising regarding any term of this Agreement or as to any matter or thing arising hereunder or in connection herewith, the same shall be and is hereby referred to the decision of an Arbiter mutually agreed on, or failing such agreement within fourteen days after either party has given written notice to the other to concur in the appointment of an Arbiter by the Chairman or Vice-Chairman of the Scottish Building Contract Committee.

13.1 The Arbiter shall without prejudice to the generality of his powers have power to make such orders and directions as may in his opinion be necessary to determine the rights of the parties and to open up, review and revise any directions, requirements or notices given by either party to the other, and to determine all matters in dispute as if no such direction, requirement or notice had been given.

13.2 The Law of Scotland shall apply to all arbitrations under these presents, and the award of the Arbiter shall be final and binding on parties, subject always to the provisions of Section 3 of the Administration of Justice (Scotland) Act 1972.

13.3 The Arbiter shall be entitled to appoint a Clerk to assist him in accordance with normal arbitration practice, to issue interim, part and final awards as well as proposed findings, to remuneration and reimbursement of his outlays, and to find the parties jointly and severally liable therefor, and to decern: and to dispense with a Deed of Submission.

14 This Agreement shall be construed and the rights of the Employer and the Sub-Contractor and all matters arising hereunder shall be determined according to the Law of Scotland:

IN WITNESS WHEREOF these presents are executed as follows:

Signed by the above named Employer at

on the ______ day of ______ 19 ______ before these witnesses

______ witness

______ address

______

______

______ occupation

______ Employer.
(Attention is drawn to the note at the foot of this page)

______ witness

______ address

______

______

______ occupation

Signed by the above named Sub-Contractor at

on the ______ day of ______ 19 ______ before these witnesses

______ witness

______ address

______

______

______ occupation

______ Sub-Contractor.
(Attention is drawn to the note at the foot of this page)

______ witness

______ address

______

______

______ occupation

N.B. – This document is set out for execution by individuals or firms: Where Limited Companies or Local Authorities are involved amendment will be necessary and the appropriate officials should be consulted or legal advice taken.

6.06 Finally, in connection with this document it should be noted that as an integral part of the process of nomination, when the basic method is employed, it should be sent by the architect to the potential nominated sub-contractor at the same time as he sends the latter the Tender NSC/1/Scot, and the latter is required to return it to the architect at the same time as he sends back to him Tender NSC/1/Scot containing his offer. Once it has been signed by the employer, a copy of the completed agreement is then sent to the nominated sub-contractor to retain.

Nomination NSC/3/Scot

6.07 This one-page document is issued by the architect to the main contractor after the latter and the nominated sub-contractor have reached agreement on the particular conditions set out in Schedule 2 of Tender NSC/1/Scot. It is the formal instruction from the architect to the main contractor requiring him to enter into a Standard Form of Sub-contract with the nominated sub-contractor.

Standard Form for Nomination of Sub-Contractors for use in Scotland
(where Tender NSC/1/Scot has been used)

To (Main Contractor)

Main Contract Works

Sub-Contract Works

Page(s) number of Bills
or Specification

Name and address of
Nominated Sub-Contractor

Further to   (1)   My/Our preliminary notice of nomination dated_____
and (2)   The Tender NSC/1/Scot and Schedules thereto completed by the
Sub-Contractor referred to above and approved by me/us on
behalf of the Employer

I/we hereby nominate the Sub-Contractor referred to above under Clause 35.10.2
of the Main Contract.

_____
Architect/Supervising Officer

Date_____

Issued to	Main Contractor	Q.S.	Nominated Sub-Contractor	Clerk of Works	Consulting Engineer	A/S.O. file
	☐	☐	☐	☐	☐	☐

Copyright SBCC, 27 Melville Street, Edinburgh EH3 7JF   February 1980

Sub-contract NSC/4/Scot

6.08 This document is based on the JCT Sub-contract NSC/4 and takes the form of a contract known as a Building Sub-contract between the contractor and sub-contractor and a Scottish Supplement to the Conditions of Sub-contract NSC/4. The principal features of these are as follows:

Building sub-contract

6.09 It should be noted that clause 1 of the sub-contract requires to be completed in accordance with the method of tendering adopted by the nominated sub-contractor when submitting his tender under Tender NSC/1/Scot, i.e. a lump sum offer or a tender sum which requires to be remeasured on completion of the work. There is an addition printed in italics to clause 2 of the Building Sub-contract which applies only where sectional completion is to apply to the main contract and the sub-contract works form part of a section or sections.

Scottish Building Sub-Contract NSC/4/Scot
(Revised January 1988)

For use in Scotland for Sub-Contractors who have tendered on Tender NSC/1/Scot, executed Agreement NSC/2/Scot and have been nominated by Nomination NSC/3/Scot, under the Standard Form of Building Contract Clause 35.10.2

Main Contract Works:

Location:

Sub-Contract Works:

BUILDING SUB-CONTRACT

between

(hereinafter referred to as 'the Contractor')

and

(hereinafter referred to as 'the Sub-Contractor')

CONSIDERING THAT the Sub-Contractor has submitted a tender on Tender NSC/1/Scot offering to carry out and complete certain Sub-Contract Works forming part of a Main Contract being carried out by the Contractor, all as the said Sub-Contract Works and Main Contract are described in the said Tender:

FURTHER CONSIDERING that the said Tender (comprising page 1 and the Numbered Documents annexed thereto and the Completed Schedules 1 and 2 thereof) has been approved by the Architect/the Contract Administrator therein referred to and accepted by the Contractor (and the original has been retained by the Contractor and copies by the Employer in the Main Contract and the Sub-Contractor):

FURTHER CONSIDERING that the Sub-Contractor has been given notice of the provisions of the Main Contract except the detailed prices of the Contractor included in schedules and bills of quantities:

FURTHER CONSIDERING that the Sub-Contractor has been nominated by the Architect/the Contract Administrator on Nomination NSC/3/Scot to carry out the Sub-Contract Works:

FURTHER CONSIDERING that at the date of this Building Sub-Contract

* *Delete as applicable*

(a) the Sub-Contractor is *is not the user of a current Sub-Contractor's Tax Certificate under the provisions of the Finance (No. 2) Act 1975 or any amendment or re-enactment thereof in one of the forms specified in Regulation 15 of the Income Tax (Sub-Contractors in the Construction Industry) Regulations 1975 or any amendment thereof and the Schedule thereto:

(b) the Contractor is *is not the user of a current Sub-Contractor's Tax Certificate under the said Act and Regulations; and

(c) the Employer under the Main Contract is *is not 'a Contractor' within the meaning of the said Act and Regulations:

THEREFORE the Contractor and the Sub-Contractor HAVE AGREED AND DO HEREBY AGREE

* *Complete in accordance with Tender NSC/1/Scot page 1*

1   The Sub-Contractor will carry out and complete the Sub-Contract Works for *the Sub-Contract Sum stated in the said Tender or such other sum as shall become payable in accordance with his Building Sub-Contract.

OR

*the Sub-Contract Tender Sum stated in the said Tender as finally ascertained in accordance with this

2   The Sub-Contract Works shall be carried out and completed in accordance with, and the rights and duties of the Contractor and Sub-Contractor shall be regulated by the Conditions of the Standard Form of Sub-Contract for Sub-Contractors nominated under the Standard Form of Building Contract (known as Sub-Contract NSC/4) including and incorporating Amendments 2 (January 1984), 3 (November 1986), 4 (July 1987) and 5 (January 1988) all as issued by the Joint Contracts Tribunal which are held to be incorporated in and form part of this Sub-Contract subject only to the amendments and modifications contained in the Scottish Supplement forming Appendix No. I hereto. *

* *The words in italics should be deleted unless Sectional Completion of the Main Contract Works applies*

and where Sectional Completion of the Main Contract Works is to apply so that the Sub-Contract Works form part of a Section or Sections of the Main Contract Works, to the further amendments and modifications in Appendix No. II hereto.

3   If any dispute or difference, except a dispute or difference under Clause 20A or Clause 20B of the above mentioned Conditions to the extent provided in Clause 20A.8 or 20B.6, shall arise between the Contractor and Sub-Contractor, arising during the execution or after the completion or abandonment of the Sub-Contract Works or after the determination of the employment of the Sub-Contractor under Scottish Building Sub-Contract NSC/4/Scot (whether by breach or in any other manner) it shall be and is hereby referred to arbitration in accordance with Clause 38.

4   Both parties agree that this Sub-Contract shall be regarded as a Scottish Contract and shall be construed and the rights of parties and all matters arising hereunder determined in all respects according to the Law of Scotland.

5   Both parties consent to registration hereof for preservation and execution:

IN WITNESS WHEREOF these presents are executed as follows:

Signed by the above named Contractor at

on the   day of   19   before these

witnesses

_____witness

_____address

_____occupation

                                                _____Contractor
                                                (Attention is drawn to the note
                                                at the foot of this page)

_____witness

_____address

_____occupation

Signed by the above named Sub-Contractor at

on the   day of   19   before these

witnesses

_____witness

_____address

_____occupation

                                                _____Sub-Contractor
                                                (Attention is drawn to the note
                                                at the foot of this page)

_____witness

_____address

_____occupation

N.B. – This document is set out as for execution by individuals or firms. Where Limited Companies are involved amendment will be necessary and the appropriate officials should be consulted or legal advice taken.

Both parties sign here and on page 6 and where Sectional Completion applies, also on page 8.

Scottish supplement

Clause 1: Interpretation, definitions, etc.

6.10 The interpretation and definition clause contained in Sub-contract NSC/4 is adopted subject to the amendments and the additional definitions set out in clauses 1.3 and 1.4.

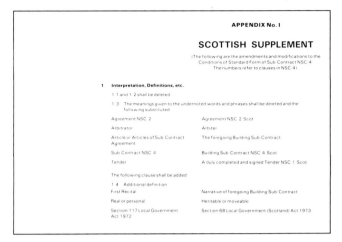

Clause 19A and 19B: Value added tax

6.11 This clause should be completed to indicate which of the alternative methods of dealing with VAT is being employed.

Clause 20A and 20B: Finance (No. 2) Act 1977

6.12 This clause also contains alternative provisions which have to be completed correctly depending upon whether the sub-contractor has or has not got a current sub-contractor's tax certificate.

The amendments to clauses 20A.3.2/20B.3 and 20A.8/20B.6 are required because of the different way in which the Scottish documents are set out from those published by the Tribunal.

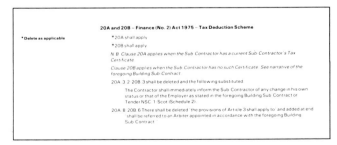

Clause 21: Payment of sub-contractor

6.13 Important amendments have been made to this clause in so far as it deals with payment for off-site goods and materials belonging to nominated sub-contractors. The new clause 21.4.4 corresponds to clause 30.3 of the Scottish supplement to the main form, and when this clause is invoked, the separate contract of sale between the main contractor and sub-contractor referred to in Chapter 9 must be employed. The last sentence in clause 21.4.4 is important and should be

carefully noted, since it preserves the main contractor's right to benefit from cash discounts or other emoluments to which he would be entitled had the provisions of this clause not been invoked.

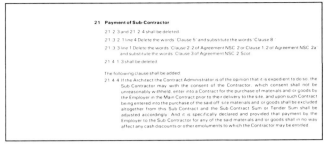

Clause 24: Contractor's claims not agreed by the sub-contractor – appointment of adjudicator

6.14 The amendments which have been made to clause 24 reflect the differences between Scots and English procedures, but the principal intention remains the same, i.e. to provide machinery for the appointment of an adjudicator to resolve claims and counter-claims between a main contractor and a nominated sub-contractor.

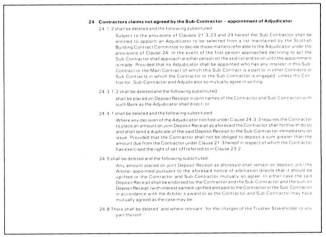

6.15 The substituted clause 24.1.2 states that the adjudicator is to be selected from the list maintained by the Scottish Building Contract Committee, which is different from the procedure adopted in England, where the adjudicator's name is inserted in the sub-contract. The SBCC maintains a list of people willing to act as adjudicators located in different parts of the country, and this list is obtainable on demand from the committee.

6.16 The amendments made to clauses 24.3.1.2, 24.4.1, and 24.5 are required because of the procedure in Scotland which directs that the sum awarded by the adjudicator is to be placed on joint deposit receipt with a bank selected by the adjudicator. The ability to place money on what in Scotland is known as deposit receipt is not available in English banks, but is a facility peculiar to banks in Scotland frequently utilized on occasions such as this. Having received the money, the bank will issue a receipt which runs in the name of both the contractor and the sub-contractor concerned, and the money cannot be uplifted until the deposit receipt has been signed by both parties, as indicated by the substituted clause 24.5.

6.17 The final amendment to this clause is the deletion of the provision of part of clause 24.8 dealing with payment of

charges due to the trustee stakeholder which are clearly not incurred in Scotland.

Clause 29: Determination of the employment of the sub-contractor by the contractor

6.18 This amendment should be read in conjunction with the comments on clause 27.2 of the main contract and provides for optional determination of the sub-contractor's contract by the main contractor if a provisional liquidator, interim liquidator or interim trustee is appointed to control the affairs of the sub-contractor.

6.19 The amendment to clause 29.43 is identical to the amendment made to clause 27.4.3 of the Building Contract and the comment on that clause is also relevant.

Clause 31: Determination of the main contractor's employment under the main contract

6.20 Clause 31.3 has been added to this clause requiring the sub-contractor to recognize an assignation by the contractor in favour of the employer. This corresponds to clause 35.27 added to the Building Contract. Again the notes on that clause should be read in conjunction with this clause.

Clause 38: Settlement of disputes – arbitration

6.21 As in the January 1988 edition of the Scottish Building Contract the arbitration clause now appears in the Scottish Supplement as a substituted clause 38. It is similar to the arbitration clause 41 in the main contract but it should be noted that the arbiter, failing agreement, is to be appointed by the person named in Item 11, Schedule 2 of Tender NSC/1/Scot who is in fact one of either the Chairman or Vice-Chairman of the SBCC, the Dean of the Faculty of Advocates or the Sheriff of the Sheriffdom in which the works are being carried out. There are also amendments printed in italics which apply only when Sectional Completion has been stipulated.

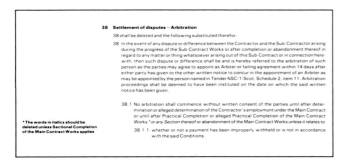

Clause 39: Proper law

6.22 This clause, which is identical to clause 4 of the Building Contract is new, but the intention is not clear. In the main contract it is necessary when that contract is created by an exchange of letters, but it is impossible to create a sub-contract by such procedure so the clause seems superfluous.

Appendix II

6.23 This new Appendix printed in italics contains the amendments required to adapt the form for use with a Section Completion Contract and is only applicable to that type of contract.

11.2.1.2.2 Add after 'Sub-Contract Works' the words 'in the relevant Section'

11.2.2 Add after 'Sub-Contract Works' the words 'in the relevant Section'

Add after 'revised period or periods for completion of the Sub-Contract Works' the words 'in the relevant Section'

Add after 'the expiry of the period or periods for the completion of the Sub-Contract Works' the words 'in the relevant Section'

11.2.3 Add after 'Sub-Contract Works' the words 'in any Section'

11.2.4 Add after 'Sub-Contract Works' the words 'in each Section'

11.2.4.1 Add after 'Sub-Contract Works' the words 'in the relevant Section'

11.2.4.2 Add after 'Sub-Contract Works' the words 'in the relevant Section'

11.2.4 Add to Proviso after 'completion of the Sub-Contract Works' the words 'in each Section'

11.2.5.6 Add after 'Sub-Contract Works' the words 'in any Section'

12 Failure of Sub-Contractor to complete on time

12.1 Add after 'Sub-Contract Works' the words 'in any Section'

13 Matters affecting regular progress

13.1.1 Add after 'Sub-Contract Works' the words 'in any Section'

13.1.2.1 Add after 'Sub-Contract Works' the words 'in any Section'

13.2 Add after 'Sub-Contract Works' the words 'in any Section'

14 Contract completion of Sub-Contract Works in each Section

14.1 Add after 'Sub-Contract Works' the words 'in a Section'

14.2 Add after 'Sub-Contract Works' in two places the words 'in a Section'

14.3 Add after 'faults in Sub-Contract Works' the words 'in any Section of'

Add after 'completion of the Sub-Contract Works' the words 'in the relevant Section'

14.5 Add after 'Practical completion of the Sub-Contract Works' the words 'in each Section'

Add after 'leave the Sub-Contract Works' the words 'in that Section'

The following clause shall be added

14.6 Practical completion of the Sub-Contract Works in all Sections shall be deemed to have taken place on the day named in the Certificate of Practical Completion of the Sub-Contract Works in all Sections issued by the Architect under clause 35.16 of the Main Contract Conditions

21 Payment of Sub-Contractor

21.10.1.1 Add after 'Sub-Contract Works' the words '(or where relevant the Sub-Contract Works in any Section)'

35 Fluctuations

35.4.7 Add after 'Sub-Contractor to complete' the words 'the Sub-Contract Works in any Section'

35.4.8.1 Add after 'clauses 11.2 and 11.3' the words 'as modified by this Appendix'

35.4.8.2 Add after 'Sub-Contract Works' the words 'in the relevant Section'

36 Fluctuations

36.5.7 Add after 'Sub-Contractor to complete' the words 'the Sub-Contract Works in any Section'

36.5.8.1 Add after 'clauses 11.2 and 11.3' the words 'as modified by this Appendix'

36.5.8.2 Add after 'Sub-Contract Works' the words 'in the relevant Section'

37 Fluctuations

37.7.1 Add after 'Sub-Contract Works' the words 'in any Section'

Add after 'any revised period or periods' the words 'in relation thereto'

Add after 'clause 37' the words 'relevant to that Section'

37.7.2 Add after 'Sub-Contract Works' the words 'in the relevant Section'

37.7.3 Add after 'clauses 11.2 and 11.3' the words 'as modified by this Appendix'

_____ Contractor _____ Sub-Contractor

7 The alternative method of nomination

7.01 Reference was made earlier in this chapter to an alternative method of nomination available to employers and architects under JCT 80. The documents used in Scotland for the alternative are distinguished from those for use with the Basic Method by the addition of an 'a' after the identifying number and they are all printed on yellow paper to aid identification. When originally published they did not include a Tender document but in March 1989 an optional Form of Tender was published by the JCT and the SBCC and is recommended as ensuring that the same information is given to each Tenderer.

Tender NSC/1a/Scot

7.02 This differs substantially in format from Tender NSC/1/Scot and is divided into two sections:

1. Section 1: The Invitation to Tender on pages 1–10. This comprises a description of the works for which a tender is required and gives full details of the main contract.
2. Section 2: The Tender by the Sub-contractor on pages 11–17. This contains the sub-contractor's tender and gives

details which he requires to agree with the main contractor.

There seems to be no particular reason why the two forms of tender should be so different in style and with comparatively little amendment Tender NSC/1a/Scot could readily be used with the Basic Method of Nomination when the Basic Method is being followed.

Standard Form of Nominated Sub-Contract Tender for use in Scotland in conjunction with Clauses 35.11 and 35.12 of the Conditions of the Standard Form of Building Contract

Notes on completion		
(a) Architect/Contract Administrator to insert same description as Main Contract	(a)	Main Contract Works and Location:
		Particulars of Sub-Contract Works:
*Delete as applicable		
(b) Architect/Contract Administrator to complete this section	(b)	**Section 1 – Invitation to tender**
(c) Insert full name and address of Tendering Sub-Contractor	(c)	To:
		You are invited to tender
(d) Alternative for use where the Sub-Contact Works are to be completely re-measured and valued	(d)	*a VAT – exclusive Sub-Contract Sum *a VAT – exclusive Tender Sum for the Sub-Contract Works referred to above by completing Section 2 and returning the whole form to:
(e) Insert the name and address of the person to whom NSC/1a/Scot should be returned by the Sub-Contractor after he has completed Section 2: this should normally be the Architect/Contract Administrator	(e)	not later than _____ 19___ Your tender must be in accordance with all the information set out in Section 1 (including item 17 – fluctuations) except where changes are specifically provided for in Section 2 and should be held open for the period as required by the stipulations on page 15. You will */will not be required to enter into the Agreement between an Employer and a Sub-Contractor nominated under Clauses 35.11 and 35.12 of the Standard Form of Building Contract (Agreement NSC/2a/Scot).
*Delete as applicable		Numbered Documents enclosed with this invitation (which will be annexed to Sub Contract NSC/4a/Scot – drawings */specification */bill of quantities */schedule of rates (to be listed here and attached).
(f) Signature of Architect/Contract Administrator	(f)	Signed_____ Name_____ Date_____ 19___

Particulars of the Main Contract

*Delete as applicable
(g) Insert the same description as in the Main Contract

(g) Main Contract Works and Location:

Job reference:

(h) The expression 'the Contract Administrator' is applicable where the nomination instruction will be issued under the Local Authorities versions of the Standard Form of Building Contract and by a person who is not entitled to the use of the name 'Architect' under and in accordance with the Architects (Registration) Acts 1931 to 1969. If so, the expression 'Architect' shall be deemed to have been deleted through out this Tender NSC/1a/Scot and, where used, Agreement NSC/2a/Scot Where the person who will issue the nomination instruction is entitled to the use of the name 'Architect' the expression 'Contract Administrator' shall be deemed to have been deleted through out this Tender NSC/1a/Scot and, where used, in Agreement NSC/2a/Scot

*Delete as applicable

Names and Addresses of:

Employer: Tel No:

(h) Architect*/Contract Administrator: Tel No:

Quantity Surveyor: Tel No:

Main Contractor: Tel No:

1 Form of Main Contract:

Scottish Building Contract with Quantities*/Without Quantities*/With Approximate Quantities*/Sectional Completion*/Contractors Design Portion (1980 Edition, Revised January 1988) with Scottish Supplement to the Conditions of the Standard Form of Building Contract Private*/Local Authorities 1980 Edition, incorporating Amendments ....

2 Main Contract: alternative provisions not referred to in the Main Contract Appendix (see item 6, pages 5 and 6)

Scottish Building Contract Clause 3: Architect*/Contract Administrator
Works Insurance: Clause 22A*/22B*/22C.2 to .4
Insurance: Clause 21.2.1 Insurance may be*/is not required.
Clause 19.1.2 applies*/does not apply
Amount of indemnity for any one occurrence or series of occurrences arising out of one event
£..............
Master programme: Clause 5.3.1.2 Deleted*/not deleted

3 Main Contract Conditions – insert here any amendments or additions to Form of Main Contract referred to in item 5

4 Execution of Main Contract

This item which indicates whether the Main Contract is or is not executed under Seal is not applicable to Scotland but it is retained to maintain the same numerical sequence as in NSC/1a:Section 1 published by the J.C.T. for use in England.

5 Inspection of Main Contract

The unpriced Bills of Quantities*/Bills of Approximate Quantities*/Contract Specification*/Schedules of Work (which incorporate the general conditions and preliminaries of the Main Contract) and the Contract Drawings may be inspected at

*Delete as applicable
(j) When in item 1 it is stated that Sectional Completion of the Main Contract Works is to apply Appendix No. II of the Scottish Building Contract Sectional Completion Edition must be substituted as item 6

		Clause	
(j) 6 Main Contract: Appendix No. II and entries therein	Statutory tax deduction scheme – Finance (No: 2) Act 1975	31	Employer at Base Date is a 'contractor'*/is not a 'contractor' for the purposes of the Act and the Regulations
	Base Date	1.3	
	Defects Liability Period	17.2	
	Assignation by Employer of benefits after Practical Completion	19.2	Clause 19.1.2 applies*/does not apply

Particulars of the Main Contract continued

	Clause	
Insurance cover for any one occurrence or series of occurrences arising out of one event	21.1.1	£
Insurance – Liability of Employer	21.2.1	Insurance may be*/is not required. Amount of indemnity for any one occurrence or series of occurrences arising out of one event £
Insurance of the Works – Alternative clauses	22.1	Clause 22A*/22B*/22C applies
Percentage to cover Professional fees	22A*/22B*/ 22C.2	%
Annual renewal date of insurance as supplied by the Contractor	22A.3.1	
Insurance for Employer's loss of liquidate and ascertained damages – Clause 25.4.3	22D	Insurance may be*/is not required
	22D.2	Period of time
Date of Possession	23.1.1	
Date for Completion	1.3	
Deferment of Date of Possession	23.1.2 25.4.13	Clause 23.1.2 applies*/does not apply
	26.1	Period of deferment if it is to be less than 6 weeks is
Liquidate and Ascertained Damages	24.2	At the rate of £ .... per ....

*Delete as applicable

	Clause	
Period of delay	*Clause* 28.1.3	
Period of delay	28A.1.1 28A.1.3	
Period of delay	28A.1.2	
Period of Interim Certificates (if none stated is one month)	30.1.3	
Retention Percentage (if less than five per cent)	30.4.1.1	%
Work reserved for Nominated Sub-Contractors for which the Contractor desires to tender	35.2	
Fluctuations	37	Clause 38*/Clause 39*/Clause 40
Percentage addition	38.7 or 39.8	%
Formula Rules (December 1987) Rule 3	40.1.1.1	Base month .... 19 ......
Rule 3		*Non-Adjustable Element .... % (Local Authorities Edition only)
Rule 10 and 30(i)		Part I*/Part II of Section 2 of the Formula Rules is to apply
Settlement of disputes – Arbitration	41	The Chairman or Vice-Chairman of the Scottish Building Contract Committee*/The Dean of the Faculty of Advocates*/The Sheriff of the Sheriffdom in which the Works are situated

(k) This information unless included in the Sub Contract Numbered Documents should be given e.g. by repeating here or by attaching a copy of the relevant section of the Preliminaries Bill of the Main Contract Bills (or of the Main Contract Specification/Schedules of Works)

(k) 7 Obligations or restrictions which are or will be imposed by the Employer not covered by Main Contract Conditions (e.g. those in Preliminaries in the Contract Bills or Specification or Schedules of Works or in a Variation instruction):

8 Order of Works: Employer's requirements affecting the order of the Main Contract Works (if any).

9 Location and type of access:

10 New Date for Completion where this has been altered from the original date stated in the Main Contract Appendix reproduced at item 6:

11 Other relevant information (if any) relating to the Main Contract:

Sub-Contract Information

*Delete as applicable

12 Sub-Contract Conditions: Under Clause 35.12 of the Main Contract the Contractor is required to proceed so as to execute a sub-contract with you on Sub-Contract NSC/4a/Scot unamended (appropriate to the Building Contract identified in item 1 above) within 14 days of the nomination instruction under Clause 35.11. The Contractor has a right of reasonable objection to the nomination (see Clause 35.4.1 of the Main Contract).

Retention: The Retention Percentage to be the same as in the Main Contract: see item 6 – Main Contract, Appendix and entries therein, reference Clause 30.4.1.1.

(l) See item 6 and side note (j)

(l) 13 Main Contract Appendix and entries therein: These entries will, where relevant, apply to the Sub-Contract unless otherwise specifically stated here:

(m) This item as completed by the Architect/Contract Administrator, will be considered by the Sub-Contractor when completing Section 2, item 1, and by the Contractor and Sub-Contractor when completing the Appendix to NSC/4a/Scot, part 4.

Sub-Contract NSC/4a states in Clause 11.1 'The Sub-Contractor shall carry out and complete the Sub-Contract Works in accordance with the agreed programme details in the Appendix, part 4, and reasonably in accordance with the progress of the Main Contract Works but subject to receipt of the notice to commence work on site as detailed in the Appendix, part 4, and to the operation of Clause 11.2.' (extension of Sub-Contract time)

(m) 14 Any indication as to the period/periods when the Sub-Contract Works are to be carried out on site:

to be between __________

and __________

Period required by the Architect/the Contract Administrator to examine drawings after submission to him:

__________ weeks

15 *This item which indicates whether the Employer/Sub-Contractor Agreement is or is not executed under Seal is not applicable to Scotland but it is retained to maintain the same numerical sequence as in NSC/1a: Section 1 published by the J.C.T. for use in England.*

(n) Can only be completed if identity of Contractor is known at the date of this invitation to tender

(n) 16 Finance (No. 2) Act 1975 – Statutory Tax Deduction Scheme: The Contractor is*/is not entitled to be paid by the Employer without the statutory deduction referred to in the Act or such other deductions as may be in force.

*Delete as applicable

17 Fluctuations

(o) The Architect/Contract Administrator, by deleting three of the alternatives, should specify the fluctuation clause applicable or state that it is to be that chosen by the Sub-Contractor.

(o) The clause of Sub-Contract NSC/4a which shall apply is:

*Clause 35 – Contribution, levy and tax fluctuations
*Clause 36 – Labour and materials cost and tax fluctuations
*Clause 37 – Formula adjustment
*that chosen from clauses 35, 36 and 37 by the Sub-Contractor and stated by him in Section 2 page 12.

(p) The clause stated above shall be operated in accordance with the relevant items below together with those in Section 2 pages 12, 13 and 14.

(p) Where the Architect/Contract Administrator has specified the clause applicable he should complete only the items relevant to the clause specified. Where the applicable clause is to be that chosen by the Sub-Contractor the Architect/Contract Administrator should complete the items for all three clauses.

Clause 35 Contributions, levy tax and fluctuations

(q) 35.2.1 Fuels included*/excluded

35.6.1 Base Date __________

35.7 Percentage addition to fluctuation payments or allowances _____ %

Clause 36 Labour and materials cost and tax fluctuations

(q) 36.3.1 Fuels included*/excluded

36.7 Base Date __________

36.8 Percentage addition to fluctuation payments or allowances _____ %

(q) 'included' to be deleted by the Architect/Contract Administrator if fuels not to be included. See Sub-Contract NSC/4a clause 35.2.1 and Clause 36.3.1

Clause 37 Formula Adjustment

37.1 Nominated Sub-Contract/Works Contract Formula Rules are those dated

__________ 19 _____

(r) 37.3.3 and 3.4 Non-Adjustable Element _____ % (not to exceed 10%)

(r) Only applicable where the Main Contract is let on the Standard Form of Building Contract, Local Authorities edition: see 'Main Contract Information' item 1

Formula Rules

rule 3 Definition of Balance of Adjustable Work – any measured work not allocated to a Work Category

*as in the Schedule included in the Numbered Documents

*as in the Schedule completed by the Sub-Contractor and attached to Section 2: see Section 2 page 12.

rule 3 Base Month __________
(unless a Month is stated, the Base Month will be the calendar month prior to that in which this Tender is due to be returned)

(s) If not completed by the Architect/Contract Administrator to be completed by the Sub-Contractor: see Section 2 pages 12 and 13

rule 3 Base Date __________

(s) rule 8 Method of dealing with 'Fix-only' work

rule 8(i)*/rule 8(ii)*/rule 8(iii)

*Delete as applicable

(s) If not completed by the Architect/Contract Administrator to be completed by the Sub-Contractor: see Section 2 pages 12 and 13

(t) The weightings for sprinkler installations shall be inserted where weightings different from those for heating, ventilating and air conditioning apply. See rule 55

(u) The 'other items of attendance' which are, or will be, included in the Main Contract Bills or Specification or Schedules of Work should be set out here or on an attached sheet and may relate to the following:

rule 11a Work Categories applicable to the Sub-Contract Works and classification of items under the heads in rule 11a

*as in the Schedule included in the Numbered Documents

*as in the Schedule completed by the Sub-Contractor and attached to Section 2: see Section 2 page 12

rule 43 Weightings of labour and materials – Electrical Installations or Heating, Ventilating and Air Conditioning Installations

		Labour	Materials
(s)	Electrical	_____ %	_____ %
(s)	Heating, Ventilating & Air Conditioning	_____ %	_____ %

Sub-Contract Information continued

(1) Special scaffolding or scaffolding additional to the Contractor's standing scaffolding
(2) The provision of temporary access roads and hard standings in connection with structural steelwork, precast concrete components, piling, heavy items of plant and the like
(3) Unloading, distributing, hoisting and placing in position giving in the case of significant items the weight and/or size
(4) The provision of covered storage and accommodation including lighting and power thereto
(5) Power supplies giving the maximum load
(6) Maintenance of specific temperature or humidity levels
(7) Any other attendance not included under (1)-(6) or as general attendance

(v) The 'other items of attendance' set out here or on an attached sheet may be altered if the Sub-Contractor requires any change by insertion in the Tender, Section 2 on page 13 and if the Architect/Contract Administrator gives a nomination instruction accompanied by the Tender NSC/1a/Scot containing such an alteration, such alteration may give rise to an adjustment of the Main Contract Sum under clause 2.2.2 of the Main Contract Conditions

			Labour	Materials
(s)(t)		Sprinkler Installations	_____ %	_____ %

(s) rule 55a The separate materials index for sprinkler installations will*/will not apply

(s) rule 61a Lift installations: Adjustment shall be effected

*upon completion of manufacture of all fabricated components

*upon delivery to site of all fabricated components

18 Attendance items Sub-Contract NSC/4a – Clause 27

General attendance: Sub-Contract NSC/4a defines 'general attendance' in Clause 27.1.1 as follows: '*General attendance shall be provided by the Contractor free of charge to the Sub-Contractor and shall be deemed to include only use of the Contractor's temporary roads, pavings and paths, standing scaffolding, standing power operated hoisting plant, the provision of temporary lighting and water supplies, clearing away rubbish, provision of space for the Sub-Contractor's own offices and for the storage of his plant and materials and the use of messrooms, sanitary accommodation and welfare facilities.*'

(u)(v) Other items of attendance which the Contractor shall provide free of charge to the Sub-Contractor: In addition to the requirements for general attendance by the Contractor, Sub-Contract NSC/4a states in Clause 27.2: '*The Contractor shall provide, free of charge to the Sub-Contractor, the other items of attendance detailed in the Appendix, part 7.*'

Section 2 – Tender by Sub-Contractor

*Delete as applicable

(w) Sub-Contractor to complete this section and sign on page 17

(w) To the **Employer** and **Main Contractor**

In response to the invitation in Section 1

We __________

of __________

____

Tel No: __________

having duly noted the information therein contained or referred to now OFFER, upon and subject to the Stipulations on page 15:

to carry out and complete, as a Nominated Sub-Contractor, as part of the Main Contract Works referred to in Section 1, the Sub-Contract Works identified in the Numbered Documents listed in Section 1 which are*/will be signed by ourselves and by the Architect/the Contract Administrator and **in accordance with the entries we have made in items 1-6 of Section 2 (subject to agreement thereon with the Main Contractor)**:

to execute a sub-contract on Scottish Building Sub-Contract NSC/4a/Scot with the Contractor within 14 days of the Nomination instruction under Clause 35.11 of the Main Contract;

to enter into **Agreement between an Employer and a Sub-Contractor NSC/2a/Scot** with the Employer where in Section 1, page 1 it is stated that such Agreement is required

for the VAT-exclusive Sub-Contract Sum*/VAT-exclusive Tender Sum (whichever is required by the invitation to Tender, Section 1, page 1) of (*words*) __________

__________ (£ __________)

AND with the **daywork percentages** and **fluctuation provisions set out hereafter; and with the attendance items in Section 1 item 18 (including any changes set out in Section 2, page 13) to be provided by the Contractor free of charge to us.**

The **daywork percentages** (Sub-Contract NSC/4a Clause 16.3.4 or Clause 17.4.3) are:

(x) Where more than one Definition will be relevant set out percentage additions applicable to each such Definition. The three Definitions which are identified are: those agreed between the Royal Institution of Chartered Surveyors and the National Federation of Building Trades Employers (now BEC); the Royal Institution and the Electrical Contractors Association and the Electrical Contractors Association of Scotland; and the Royal Institution and the Heating and Ventilating Contractors Association

(x)

Definition	Labour %	Materials %	Plant %
RICS/NFBTE (now BEC)			
RICS/ECA/ECA of Scot			
RICS/HVCA			

The **Sub-Contract Sum/Tender Sum** and **daywork percentages** take into account the 2½% cash discount allowable to the Main Contractor under Sub-Contract NSC/4a/Scot

*Delete as applicable

Fluctuations: The clause of Sub-Contract NSC/4a which is to apply is that stated in Section 1 item 17; if that item states that the applicable clause shall be chosen by the Sub-Contractor from Clauses 35, 36 or 37 the clause to apply shall be:

*Clause 35 – Contribution, levy and tax fluctuations
*Clause 36 – Labour and materials cost and tax fluctuations
*Clause 37 – Formula adjustment

and the applicable clause shall be operated in accordance with the relevant items below together with those in Section 1, item 17

Clause 35: the list of materials, goods, electricity and fuels (where fuels are to be included: see Section 1, item 17) is set out in column 1 on page 14

Clause 36: the list of basic prices of materials, goods, electricity and fuels (where fuels are to be included: see Section 1, item 17) are set out on page 14

Clause 37: 37.4 Fluctuations – articles manufactured outside the United Kingdom. List of market prices of such articles which the Sub-Contractor is required by the Sub-Contract Documents to purchase and import (see JCT Nominated Sub-Contract/Works Contract Formula Rules, rule 4(ii)) – **attached.**

Section 2 – Tender by Sub-Contractor continued

Formula Rules

Clause 37 continued

	rule 3	Definition of Balance of Adjustable Work. Where not set out in the Schedule included in the Numbered Documents any measured work not allocated to a Work Category is as set out in the Schedule **attached**.

(y) To be completed but only to the extent that the Architect/Contract Administrator has not completed these items in Section 1, item 17

(y) rule 8 Method of dealing with 'Fix-only' work

rule 8(i) * /rule 8(ii) * /rule 8 (iii)

rule 11a Work Categories applicable to the Sub-Contract Works. Where not set out in the Schedule included in the Numbered Documents the classification of each item of the Sub-Contract Works under one of the heads set out in rule 11a together with the portion of the Sub-Contract Sum/Tender Sum attributable to each item is set out in the Schedule **attached**.

rule 43 Weightings of labour and materials – Electrical Installations or Heating, Ventilating and Air Conditioning Installations

	Labour	Materials
(y) Electrical	_____ %	_____ %
(y) Heating, Ventilating & Air Conditioning	_____ %	_____ %
(y)(z) Sprinkler Installations	_____ %	_____ %

(z) The weightings for sprinkler installations shall be inserted where weightings different from those for heating, ventilating and air conditioning are required. See rule 55

(y) rule 55a The separate materials index for sprinkler installations will * /will not apply.

* Delete as applicable

(y) To be completed but only to the extent that the Architect the Contract Administrator has not completed these items in Section 1, item 17

(y) rule 61a Lift Installations. Adjustment shall be effected

* upon completion of manufacture of all fabricated components

* upon delivery to site of all fabricated components

rule 64 Structural Steelwork Installations:

(i) Average price per tonne of steel delivered to fabricator's works

£ _____

(ii) Average price per tonne for erection of steelwork

£ _____

rule 70a Catering Equipment Installations:

apportionment of the value of each item between

(i) materials and shop fabrication
(ii) supply of factor items
(iii) site installations

is as set out in the **list attached**.

Attendance items Sub-Contract NSC/4a – Clause 27

General attendance: Sub-Contract NSC/4a defines 'general attendance' in Clause 27.1.1 as follows: 'General attendance shall be provided by the Contractor free of charge to the Sub-Contractor and shall be deemed to include only use of the Contractor's temporary roads, pavings and paths, standing scaffolding, standing power operated hoisting plant, the provision of temporary lighting and water supplies, clearing away rubbish, provision of space for the Sub-Contractor's own offices and for the storage of his plant and materials and the use of messrooms, sanitary accommodation and welfare facilities.'

(aa) See notes (u) and (v) in Section 1, item 18

(aa) **Other items of attendance** which the Contractor shall provide free of charge to us: Changes, if any, from the other items of attendance set out in Section 1, item 18 and/or any further attendances which the Sub-Contractor requires the Contractor to provide free of charge:

Fluctuations

Notes: Complete column (1) where Sub-Contract NSC/4a, Clause 35 applies. Complete columns (1)-(4) where Sub-Contract NSC/4a Clause 36 applies.

The 'Base Date' for the purposes of Sub-Contract NSC/4a, Clauses 35/36 is as stated in Section 1, item 17.

(bb) See Section 1, item 17 under Clause 35 or Clause 36, as to whether fuels are to be included or excluded

	(1)	(2)	(3)	(4)
(bb)	Materials, goods, electricity and fuels	Rate (or appropriate standard price list description)	Discount	Unit to which rate applies

Section 2 – Tender by Sub-Contractor continued

Stipulations

(cc) Stipulation 1 is only applicable where in Section 1 on page 17 is stated that Agreement NSC 2a Scot will be required

(cc) 1 Only when this Tender is signed by or on behalf of the Employer as 'approved' and the Employer has signed the Agreement NSC/2a/Scot do we agree to be bound by that Agreement as signed by or on behalf of ourselves.

2 If the identity of the Main Contractor is not known at the date of our signature on page 17 we reserve the right within 14 days of written notification by the Employer of such identity to withdraw this Tender and the Agreement NSC/2a/Scot notwithstanding any approval of this Tender by signature on page 17 by or on behalf of the Employer.

3 We reserve the right to withdraw this Tender if, after the nomination instruction under the Main Contract Clause 35.11 has been issued, we are unable to agree with the Main Contractor the terms of those parts of Scottish Building Sub-Contract NSC/4a/Scot which are required to be completed by us in agreement with the Main Contractor.

(dd) Sub-Contractor to insert acceptance period if not previously completed by Architect/Contract Administrator

(dd) 4 Without prejudice to 2 and 3 above, this Tender shall be deemed to be withdrawn if the nomination instruction is not issued by the Architect/the Contract Administrator (with a copy to ourselves) under the Main Contract Conditions Clause 35.11 within_____ of the date of our signature on page 17 or such other later date as may be notified in writing by ourselves to the Architect/the Contract Administrator.

5 Any withdrawal under 2, 3 and 4 above shall be at no charge to the Employer except for any amounts that may be due to us in accordance with the Agreement NSC/2a/Scot referred to in 1 above.

(ee) Items to be completed by the Sub-Contractor (and which are subject to agreement with the Main Contractor after the instruction nominating the Sub-Contractor has been issued)

* Delete as applicable

(ee) Items 1-7 below are to be completed by the Sub-Contractor when preparing his Tender; they are then to be agreed with the Main Contractor after the Architect/Contract Administrator has issued his instruction under JCT Standard Form, 1980 Edition Clause 35.11 nominating the Sub-Contractor and then, as so agreed, recorded in the relevant parts of Appendix No. III to Sub-Contract NSC/4a/Scot

(ff) Section 1, item 14 must be taken into account by the Sub-Contractor when completing this item; and by the Contractor and Sub-Contractor when completing Appendix No. III to NSC/4a/Scot part 4. Sub-Contract NSC/4a/Scot states in Clause 11.1: 'The Sub-Contractor shall carry out and complete the Sub-Contract Works in accordance with the agreed programme details in Appendix No. III, part 4, and reasonably in accordance with the progress of the Main Contract Works but subject to receipt of the notice to commence work on site as detailed in Appendix No. III, part 4, and to the operation of Clause 11.2 (extension of Sub-Contract time)

(ff) 1 The period/periods when Sub-Contract Works can be carried out on site:

to be between_____ and _____

Period required by the Architect/Contract Administrator to examine drawings after submission to be the same as that set out in Section 1, item 14.

Periods required:

(1) for submission of all further Sub-Contractor's drawings etc. (co-ordination, installation, shop or builder's work or other as appropriate) _____

(2) for execution of Sub-Contract Works:

off site _____

on site _____

(3) Notice required to commence work on site _____ weeks

2 Sub-Contract NSC/4a/Scot Clause 7.2

Insurance cover for any one occurrence or series of occurrences arising out of one event £_____

3 *This item which deals with the appointment of an Adjudicator and Trustee Stakeholder is not applicable to Scotland but it is retained to maintain the same numerical sequence as in NSC/1a: Section 2 published by the J.C.T. for use in England.*

4 Value Added Tax – alternative VAT provisions

Clause 19A * /19B to apply

5 Any other matters (e.g. special conditions or agreements on employment of labour, limitation on working hours) to be set out here or on an attached sheet.

* Delete as applicable

(gg) See footnote (c) in Sub-Contract NSC/4a/Scot Clause 20A on 'self-vouchering'

(gg) 6 Finance (No. 2) Act 1975 – Statutory Tax Deduction Scheme

We are * /are not the users of a current Sub-Contractor's Tax Certificate

The evidence to be produced by us to the Contractor for the verification of our Tax Certificate whose expiry date is

_____ 19 _____

will be:

7 Settlement of disputes – Arbitration – if no appointor is selected the appointor shall be the Chairman or Vice-Chairman, the Scottish Building Contract Committee

The Chairman or Vice-Chairman of the Scottish Building Contract Committee * / The Dean of the Faculty of Advocates * / The Sheriff of the Sheriffdom in which the Works are situated

Signed by or on behalf of the Sub-Contractor _____

Date _____ 19 _____

Approved by or on behalf of the Employer _____

Date _____ 19 _____

Agreement NSC/2A/Scot

7.03 This document is similar in many respects to Agreement NSC/2/Scot, the comments on which should be read in conjunction with this document, particularly those concerning clause 2 of the latter, which is clause 1 of Agreement NSC/2a/Scot. However, Agreement NSC/2A/Scot contains two fewer clauses than Agreement NSC/2/Scot, both of which refer to the formal tender which is not used when the alternative procedure is being employed – but see above: when Tender NGC/1a/Scot is used clause 12 of NSC/2/Scot should be added.

Nomination NSC/3a/Scot

7.04 This document, which, as has already been noted, has no counterpart in England, corresponds to Nomination NSC/3/Scot and requires no comment.

Sub-contract NSC/4a/Scot

7.05 Apart from the opening narrative of the Building Sub-contract which now makes a reference to Tender NSC/1a/Scot this document is identical to NSC/4/Scot and also makes provision in italics for sectional completion. When Tender NSC/1a/Scot *has* been completed it is not necessary to complete the complicated provisions of the lengthy Appendix No. II (because this information is already included in the Tender) but three items of Appendix No. III require completion giving (a) the amount of insurance cover required; (b) the period when the sub-contract works can be carried out; and (c) any other special conditions.

8 Scottish Minor Works Contract

8.01 This form is not a supplement to a JCT form but a separate form of contract altogether, intended for use when the works are of a simple straightforward content and of a duration which does not require full labour and material fluctuations. Unlike its English equivalent it does contain provisions for the use of Bills of Quantities and the employment of sub-contractors. Clause 4.01 states that if the contract documents provide that certain works are to be carried out by a sub-contractor taken from a list of not less than three, the selection is to be at the sole discretion of the contractor. This is similar to the provisions of clause 19.3 of JCT 80.

The SBCC has also published the Scottish Minor Works Sub-contract for use by sub-contractors selected as above.

9 Sub-contracts for Domestic Sub-contractors

9.01 There are two editions of this form of sub-contract:

1. DOM/1/Scot where a sub-contractor is selected under the provisions of 19.2 and 19.3 of JCT 80.
2. DOM/2/Scot where the main contract is under the Scottish Building Contract With Contractor's Design and the sub-contractor is appointed under clause 18.2 of that contract.

Both forms comprise the traditional format of a formal building sub-contract followed by an appendix containing the amendments required to DOM/1 and DOM/2 respectively.

10 Scottish Management Contract

10.01 Mention should also be made of the above form of contract issued to meet the growing demand in Scotland for management contracts where the main contractor accepts responsibility for wide management duties set out in clauses 1.4 to 1.8 of the contract and enters into a series of works contracts with individual contractors who actually carry out the construction of the works.

It is not possible within the confines of this article to do more than draw the reader's attention to the existence of this form of contract when its use is intended in Scotland.

11 Scottish Measured Term Contract

At the time of going to press the SBCC has just issued this form of contract intended for use by an employer (e.g. a local authority) who needs regular maintenance and minor works including improvements to be carried out in respect of their properties within a defined area and who wants also to engage one contractor to carry out such work for a specified period on receipt of individual orders for those works.

11

Arbitration

ANDREW FOYLE* (England)
GEORGE BURNET† (Scotland)

1 Nature of arbitration

1.01 The settlement of disputes by reference to arbitration, originally governed by the rules of common law, was a practice adopted by merchants and traders many years before it first received Parliamentary recognition under the Arbitration Act of 1697. Common law arbitrations of this kind are today regulated by the Arbitration Acts of 1950–1979, which provide a general code for all written arbitration agreements between disputing or potentially disputing parties. Of more recent origin is the introduction of statutory legislation in a very wide variety of fields with special provisions which often exclude wholly or in part those Acts and substitute their own codes of procedure and practice.

1.02 Arbitrations, to use the term in its broadest sense, include not only those of the kind with which architects are most familiar, and which arise under the standard building contracts, but also the various forms of land tribunals, which have become so common a feature of the present time. Except in the quasi-judicial role he plays in the administration of every building contract, not every architect has either the interest or the capacity to arbitrate on the disputes of others. However, he may never know when he is likely to be called upon to do so: or whether he should be involved, on behalf of his clients, in such a dispute. It is more likely that he may be concerned directly as an expert witness in public or private hearings, or on planning inquiries and similar tribunals where the rules of evidence and procedure differ only marginally from an arbitration hearing.

What is arbitration?

1.03 Arbitration has been defined as 'a method of settling disputes and differences between two or more parties by which such disputes are referred to one or more persons nominated for the purpose. These disputes are determined after a hearing in a quasi-judicial manner, either instead of having recourse to an action at law or, by order of the court after such an action has been commenced.' The features to note in this definition are:

1. There must be a real dispute, and not a mere difference of opinion.
2. There must be an agreement between the parties to refer the dispute to one or more specially nominated persons for hearing and settlement.

*Solicitor and partner of Lovell White Durrant.
†In the first edition, this chapter was written by William Gill. In other editions the section on Arbitration in England was revised by Evelyn Freeth and His Honour Judge Michael Parker QC.

3. The parties must intend to settle their differences in this way rather than in a court of law.

This last proposition does not mean that the parties to a domestic arbitration agreement can oust the jurisdiction of the courts to review the conduct of the arbitrator or the arbitration award itself, although the 1979 Act does enable the parties to agree that the court's power of review shall be limited in a number of respects (see para 3.07). Any provision in an arbitration agreement that the parties may not in any circumstances have recourse at all to a court of law is void as being contrary to public policy (*Doleman & Sons* v *Ossett Corporation* [1912] 3 KB 257 as explained in *Lloyd & Others* v *Wright* [1938] 2 All ER 969. But see para 1.13).

Reference to arbitration

1.04 A 'reference' to arbitration may originate in one of the following ways:

1. By agreement between the parties – voluntarily.
2. By requirements of a statute – legal mandate.
3. By order of the court – compulsorily.

1.05 A voluntary agreement will be made by the mutual consent of the parties to refer disputes when they arise, or in anticipation of the possibility of dispute at a future time. Agreements of this nature, as with any other form of contract, are open to variation and determination by the parties themselves (see Chapter 3). They may be made orally and informally, but as the Arbitration Act excludes all but written agreements, oral agreements are unenforceable by the courts, and enjoy none of the advantages and safeguards of the Arbitration Act. They must consequently rely upon the rules of common law, and not upon the provisions of a statute, with the initial handicap that they lack evidence of precise terms. In practice, therefore, it is usual for the parties either to subscribe to a separate agreement concerning the mode of settling any differences – actual or possible – or to arrange for the inclusion of an arbitration clause in their main contract, as is done in the JCT Standard Form of Building Contract. Either method ensures the statutory support of the Arbitration Act 1950 with its code governing procedures, and the powers and duties of nominated arbitrators.

Although the parties' mutual consent to refer disputes to arbitration is an essential ingredient of a valid arbitration clause, a clause providing that either party may elect to have a dispute referred to arbitration has been held to be valid. Although there was no agreement to arbitrate until an election was made, once the election was made and the option to arbitrate exercised, a binding arbitration agreement came into existence. (*The Messiniaki Bergen* [1983] 1 All ER

382). This principle has been further extended by the Court of Appeal in *Pittalis & Others* v *Sherefettin* [1986] 2 All ER 227, where it was held that an agreement which gave one party alone the right to refer a dispute to arbitration could be a valid arbitration agreement because the right to refer, although unilateral in effect, was a right which had been mutually agreed. Arbitrations may either be conducted on an ad hoc basis in accordance with the provisions of the Arbitration Acts 1950–1979, or in accordance with the rules of an arbitral body, such as the JCT Arbitration Rules, or those of the International Chamber of Commerce (ICC). This chapter focuses on ad hoc arbitrations, where the Arbitration Acts provide a very general code for the resolution of disputes by arbitration and leave the determination of the procedure to be adopted to resolve the dispute largely in the hands of the parties and the arbitrator. By contrast, arbitration in accordance with the rules of an arbitral body is more structured and the rules of the institution generally make provision for the appointment of arbitrators and for the procedural conduct of the early stages of the arbitration, providing, for example, a timetable for the exchange of the parties' written statements of their claims and defences.

1.06 By requirements of statutes. Provision for settlement of disputes by arbitration, or indeed by any other means, may be made by statute or statutory instruments. Some statutes often accept, with or without exceptions or variation, the general application of the Arbitration Act 1950. Others totally exclude the operation of the Act by special provisions in the statute itself, as, for instance, does the Agricultural Holdings Act 1986 (see section 84(1)). In circumstances where a dispute is referred to arbitration under a statute which embodies a special procedure, the general rule is that the arbitration clauses in the statute may override the Arbitration Act, but only to the extent that there is any inconsistency between them (Arbitration Act 1950, section 31 (1)).

1.07 By order of the court. Under powers derived from the Administration of Justice Act 1956, at any stage of an action commenced in the High Court, that Court may refer the action to an Official Referee for trial or for inquiry and report. (See Order 36, rule 5 of *The Supreme Court Practice 1988*). An Official Referee is a circuit judge experienced in disputes involving detailed technical evidence such as arises under building contracts. If the action is referred to him for trial the judgement that he delivers is that of the High Court and can be enforced as such or appealed to the Court of Appeal. If the action is referred to him for inquiry and report, his report is considered by the High Court judge who referred the matter to him, who may adopt it in whole or in part or remit it to the same Official Referee or to another for further consideration. If an action has been commenced in the County Court it can be referred to arbitration with the consent of the parties (see Order 19, County Court Rules).

Enforcement of arbitration agreement

1.08 Refusal to settle a dispute by arbitration, when there is an agreement to do so, is a breach of contract at common law and gives rise to an action for damages. That remedy may be an ineffective one, however, particularly in cases where arbitration has not actually been entered upon; it would be difficult to prove what damage the aggrieved party had suffered, for he could always sue in the courts in respect of the breach of contract to which the arbitration agreement refers. No action lies by way of injunction or specific performance to compel a party to appoint an arbitrator, and the court has no inherent jurisdiction or power to appoint one if a party to the agreement refuses to do so. On the other hand, if a party to an arbitration agreement seeks to sue in the courts rather than go to arbitration, the court will on application by the other party, under section 4 of the Arbitration Act 1950, generally stay the proceedings until the

arbitration has taken place, provided that the applicant has taken no step in the proceedings and that he is ready and willing to arbitrate. An exception to this general rule arises where there is a dispute between more than two parties to separate contracts containing arbitration clauses, where there is no provision for tripartite arbitration. Should the aggrieved party commence High Court proceedings against the other parties the court is likely to refuse to stay the proceedings because of the undesirability of there being two sets of proceedings before different tribunals, with the attendant risk of inconsistent decisions (*Taunton–Collins* v *Cromie & Anor* [1964] 2 All ER CA).

Arbitration, conciliation, and valuation

1.09 It is necessary to distinguish arbitration from conciliation and valuation. Arbitration is always a judicial process which must have regard to the fundamental rules laid down by the courts, particularly those relating to evidence. In arbitration there must first be a dispute. The parties have agreed that the arbitrator shall determine all matters of fact and law referred to him and are bound by the final decision made in his award. Should the parties not comply with his decision, it may be enforced in the same manner as a judgement of the court, i.e. refusal to conform becomes contempt of court.

Conciliation

1.10 In conciliation, the role of the conciliator is simply to bring the parties together in an endeavour to promote the settlement of a complaint or dispute without the necessity of reference to a court or tribunal. Unlike the arbitrator, he makes no decision on his own but merely assists the parties themselves to agree, and has no statutory powers of enforcement. By section 2 of the Employment Protection Act 1975, the Advisory Conciliation and Arbitration Service (ACAS) is empowered to appoint Conciliation Officers. These officers have been given statutory powers to effect the conciliation of parties in industrial dispute. These powers do not apply to simple contracts where the dispute does not involve industrial action.

Valuation

1.11 The difference between arbitration and valuation rests upon the distinction between the quasi-judicial nature of the former in the consideration of the facts presented and, in the case of valuation, where the person appointed to make a decision does so as the result of his own skill and experience, usually without hearing any evidence. A valuation arises from an agreement by two parties to be bound by the decision of a third party with the object of *preventing a dispute* arising. On the other hand, an arbitration depends entirely upon the *existence of a dispute* which must be settled by this form of judicial inquiry. The basic effect of the distinction is that the Arbitration Act 1950 does not apply to valuation. An arbitrator's award may be enforced by the courts, and he himself may not be sued for negligence; whereas the valuer has no such statutory protection, and could be liable in an action for negligence.

When is arbitration available?

1.12 It is not always easy to decide whether a dispute or a difference between the parties is one that can be settled by arbitration, as not every dispute is necessarily subject to a reference to arbitration. Article 5 of the JCT 1980 Standard Form and clause 41 of the Conditions of Contract are particularly comprehensive. Architects should however note clause 30.9, which provides that, save in cases of fraud or where proceedings have been commenced by either party before or within 28 days of issue of the Final Certificate, the

Final Certificate shall be conclusive evidence in any proceedings arising out of or in connection with the contract:

1. that where the quality of materials or standard of workmanship are to be to the reasonable satisfaction of the architect, they are to his satisfaction;
2. that any necessary effect has been given to the terms of the contract which require an adjustment to be made to the contract sum, save in certain specified circumstances;
3. that all and any such extensions of time as are due under clause 25 have been given; and
4. that the reimbursement of direct loss and/or expense to the contractor pursuant to clause 26.1 is in final settlement of any such claims.

In general, where a contract provides for arbitration in disputes arising 'under', 'in respect of', or 'with regard to' the contract, the arbitrator has jurisdiction. However, if the dispute is whether the contract which contains the clause has ever been entered into at all, that issue cannot go to arbitration under the clause, for the party who denies that he has ever entered into the contract is thereby denying that he has ever joined in the submission. Similarly, if one party to the alleged contract is contending that it is void *ab initio* (because, for example, the making of the contract is illegal), the arbitration clause cannot operate, for on this view the clause itself is also void (*Heyman* v *Darwins Ltd* [1942] AC 356).

1.13 Certain matters are not suitable for arbitration even under article 5. Where a party to a contract refuses to complete, the proper remedy is for the aggrieved party to sue for damages in the courts, or to ask the court for an order for the specific performance of the contract, an order which is rarely made in building contract cases. Similarly, failure to pay a sum due under a certificate is a matter for action in the courts. Although it will rarely rise in arbitrations with which an architect is concerned, an issue as to whether a party to the dispute has been guilty of fraud is not suitable for determination by arbitration unless express words in the agreement provide that it should be, and that issue should be determined by the court (section 24 (2) of the 1950 Act). See, however, the recent case of *Cunningham-Reid & Another* v *Buchanan Jardine* [1988] 2 All ER 438, where the party accused of fraud wished to proceed to arbitration and the court exercised its discretion in his favour, on the basis that the parties had agreed without reservation that disputes between them should be decided by arbitration and the plaintiffs' wish to proceed with their action was not sufficient reason to justify refusing a stay.) However, if one of the parties to the arbitration is a foreign national or is habitually resident abroad, or is a foreign corporation or a corporation whose central management or control is exercise abroad, and the arbitration agreement has been drafted so as to exclude the intervention of the courts, the High Court will have no power to order that the issue of fraud is determined in the High Court (section 3 (3) of the 1979 Act).

Parties to arbitration

1.14 Only the parties to a contract containing an arbitration clause are normally allowed to go to arbitration. Certainly no other person can be compelled to submit to an arbitration, but there is no reason why third or more parties cannot submit to arbitration if everyone agrees. In order to avoid a series of eliminating arbitrations or actions in the courts among employer, contractors, and sub-contractors, article 3 of the JCT Standard Form of Sub-contract (1980 edition) provides that if a dispute raises issues between the contractor and the sub-contractor 'either during the execution or after the completion or abandonment of the Sub-Contract Works', as to the agreement or in connection with it, then such dispute shall be referred to arbitration, and if such dispute raises

issues which are substantially the same as or connected with issues raised in a related dispute between:

1. the employer and the contractor under the Main Contract, or
2. the sub-contractor and the employer, or
3. the contractor and any other nominated sub-contractor, or
4. the contractor and any nominated supplier

and that related dispute has already been referred to arbitration, then the contractor and the sub-contractor agree that this dispute shall be referred to the same arbitrator, unless the contractor and the sub-contractor or either of them reasonably considers that the arbitrator appointed to determine the related dispute is not properly qualified to determine the dispute. Each of the JCT Standard Forms varies slightly in the scope of the arbitration clause and its wording, and the particular agreement should be studied carefully.

Capacity of arbitrators

1.15 Although the parties to a contract are free to choose their own arbitrator, where there is a written agreement section 6 of the Arbitration Act 1950 applies, and such agreement, in the absence of contrary intentions, is deemed to include reference to a sole arbitrator. The principal categories of people who may not act as arbitrators are bankrupts, minors, persons of unsound mind and those who are deaf, dumb or blind, persons convicted of perjury, and any person who has an interest in, or a bias against the parties, or any part of the proceedings.

1.16 It is often difficult to decide what is or is not included in the last category. The test, which was laid down by the Court of Appeal in *Bremer Handelsgesellschaft mbH* v *ETS Soules et Cie and Scott* [1985] 2 Lloyds' Rep 199, is whether a reasonable man would apprehend that there was a risk of the Arbitrator, either consciously or unconsciously, being influenced by a desire to favour one party in such a manner as to cause him to fail to assess the evidence on its merits. The objective test has recently been upheld by the Supreme Court of Hong Kong in *Asian Construction Company* v *Crown Pacific Ltd* [1989] 44 BLR 135. In that case, the court held that when deciding whether or not there existed grounds on which a reasonable person would think that there was a real likelihood that the arbitrator could not or would not fairly decide the issue, it was appropriate to take into account things which took place after the facts complained of, including the arbitrator's conduct.

Jurisdiction of arbitrators

1.17 Every architect appointed as an arbitrator should ensure that he is competent to adjudicate the facts in dispute, and in this sense 'competent' means that such matters are within his jurisdiction. An arbitration, being a private tribunal, is not open to members of the public as is a court of law, and the arbitrator must see that all procedure, evidence, and everything relating to the hearing before him is carried out correctly.

Arbitration and architects

1.18 It is not possible to make any accurate assessment of how many arbitrations are held, mainly because a good feature of arbitration is the privacy under which it takes place. However, it may be observed that the arbitration work which goes on is much greater than is realized, and also that it is on the increase. It is equally clear that architects are frequently in demand for this type of work, especially where the reference involves a Standard Form of Building Contract where their expert knowledge and experience is an obvious advantage. Expertise is seldom enough. The successful

arbitrator rests his authority not so much on his technical knowledge as on his judicial capacity to control the proceedings before him, to deal fairly, and to exclude from his mind all considerations which affect the case except those derived from the evidence. The RIBA have published an invaluable booklet *The Architect as Arbitrator* which is of equal interest to all arbitrators, summarizing most of the main points. The Appendices print in full the Arbitration Act 1950, and three Forms of Application for Appointment of an arbitrator.

Power of arbitrator to open up, review and revise architects' certificates

1.19 The respective powers of arbitrators and judges to open up, review and revise architects' certificates were considered by the Court of Appeal in the case of *Northern Regional Health Authority* v *Derek Crouch Construction Co Ltd* [1984] 2All ER 175. The case concerned a contract in the standard JCT form, which provided for the arbitration of disputes between the building owner and the main contractor and entitled the arbitrator 'to open up, review and revise any certificate, opinion, decision, requirement or notice' given by the building owner's architect.

1.20 In its judgement, the Court of Appeal held that the High Court, and thus an Official Referee, did not have the arbitrator's power to open up and review the exercise of the architect's discretion, since the court's jurisdiction was limited to determining and enforcing the contractual rights of the parties. It did not extend to substituting its own discretion simply because it would have reached a different conclusion, since to do so would interfere with the agreement of the parties. The arbitrator, on the other hand, was entitled to modify the parties' contractual rights by substituting his own discretion for that of the architect, if he disagreed with the architect's certificates and opinions. Accordingly, if the parties chose to litigate rather than arbitrate, the court would not have the same powers as an arbitrator to open up and revise the architect's opinions and certificates. The *Crouch* decision has since been approved and applied in other cases, notably *Oram Builders* v *Pemberton (MJ) and Pemberton (C)* [1985] CILL 169, and *Reed* v *Van Der Vorm* [1985] 5 Con Lr III.

1.21 The *Crouch* decision may well give rise to an increased use of arbitration as a method of resolving disputes in building contracts. It was suggested in the *Pemberton* case that a way round *Crouch* would be for the parties to agree to invoke section 11 of the Arbitration Act 1950, thereby appointing the Official Referee to act as an arbitrator,

1.22 A proposed limitation on the impact of the *Crouch* decision is contained in clause 69 of the Courts and Legal Services Bill, which provides that in any action in the High Court in connection with any contract incorporating an arbitration clause which confers specific powers upon the arbitrator, the High Court may, if all the parties to the proceedings agree, exercise any such powers.

Disputes between architects and clients

1.23 Rather special problems arise when architects and their clients are in dispute, possibly over fees and other matters.

Partnership disputes

1.24 Cases occur on the construction of the articles of a partnership. The law of partnership is an intricate subject (Chapter 19), and the architect-arbitrator is not advised to deal with such cases without legal assistance. Most articles of partnership contain an arbitration clause, for it would be injurious for everyone to know that partners are at odds; and

partners usually prefer to place their disputes before a private tribunal rather than before the public courts.

2 Procedure

Appointment of arbitrators

2.01 In arbitration agreements which generally concern architects, there is either an express clause for the parties to appoint an arbitrator, or the method of his appointment may be prescribed in the agreement. This mode of appointment is similar to the procedure laid down in clause 41 of the JCT 1980 Standard Form Conditions of Contract, as amended by amendment 6 of July 1988. Where there is no provision at all in the agreement on the number and appointment of arbitrators, the parties are bound by section 6 of the Arbitration Act 1950. If the parties cannot agree on the appointment of a single arbitrator under section 6, the court will make the appointment on the application of one of the parties (section 10 of the Act).

2.02 In most cases, therefore, architects are appointed as sole arbitrators. The arbitration agreement should also make provision for events such as the death, incapacity, refusal to act, or incapability to act of the appointed arbitrator. The parties who appoint the original arbitrator should also nominate his successor, or apply to the RIBA president to fill the vacancy. In the event of a complete deadlock the court may be asked to make a fresh appointment. An arbitrator should not be appointed verbally. The procedure adopted by the RIBA when the president is asked by the parties to an arbitration agreement (or under the provisions of article 5) to appoint an arbitrator is as follows. The RIBA asks the parties to supply brief details of the dispute and to complete an application form. This form contains an undertaking which protects the proposed arbitrator, because it asks for a guarantee of payment of his fees, or for the security to be provided for them. The guarantee in the RIBA form does not, of course, cover a defaulting party who refuses to pay any fees at all. But in any action brought in the courts the RIBA application form would be strong evidence against a defaulting party. When the parties have completed the RIBA application form (it is always preferable that both parties to the contract should sign but not always possible) it is returned to the RIBA, and either a senior member or the legal officer suggests the names of three competent architects to the president. If he approves these, they are approached in the suggested order. The first nominee to accept is formally appointed and sent the application form, which also contains his appointment and space for him to sign acceptance.

Sometimes the parties may request an arbitrator with special qualifications, and the RIBA maintains lists of solicitors, barristers, quantity surveyors, engineers, and accountants who are appointed in such circumstances. They can also be appointed when it appears to the president that a person with such qualifications would be most appropriate having regard to the nature of the dispute disclosed by the applicants.

Preparing for arbitration

2.03 As soon as an architect has accepted his nomination as an arbitrator (i.e. as soon as he signs the acceptance form sent him by the RIBA), the procedure of arbitration is set into action. A prudent arbitrator should write to the parties at once, to confirm his appointment. He should at the same time state the scale of fees he intends to charge and, if appropriate, seek and obtain the parties' agreement to his submitting interim accounts. The level of the arbitrator's fees may have a decisive effect on whether or not the parties wish to proceed further, so it is important to deal with this at the outset. Similarly, if the arbitrator anticipates that he may need to instruct a legal assessor to advise him on the legal aspects of the claims, he should obtain the parties' agreement to this course of action as soon as possible.

2.04 Once an arbitrator has been appointed he should call on the parties to deposit the arbitration agreement with him and, if there are no procedural rules for the conduct of the proceedings, he should order them (except in the clearest of disputes) to lodge Points of Claim and Points of Defence. These are the parties' written submissions as to the rights and wrongs of the dispute. The parties sometimes provide for their disputes to be conducted in accordance with recognized procedural rules, for example, the JCT Arbitration Rules. In those circumstances, the arbitrator rules will apply the relevant procedural rules relating to exchange of written submissions, discovery of documents, etc.

2.05 If no procedural rules apply, the next stage is for the arbitrator to make a full and searching study of the terms of the agreement and of the written submissions of the parties. Except in the simplest of cases it will then be prudent for the arbitrator to order the parties to 'disclose' to each other all relevant documents (for example, time-sheets, invoices, bills of quantities, and correspondence) relating to the dispute. In many cases it will be wise to then order that the parties prepare a document in the form of a 'Scott's Schedule', which sets out in tabular form all relevant allegations as to defects in the work done and cost of rectifying them, together with the answers to the complaints or admissions as to their validity and any comment as to their relevance or significance. If properly and skilfully drawn up, a 'Scott's Schedule' will save a great deal of time at the arbitration by eliminating the need to refer to many documents when considering any single point of detail. It may have the further advantage of making it clear that there is so little difference between the parties on some points that it is not worth spending the time and money arguing about them. Should a party fail to comply with an arbitrator's order that he should take some step in the arbitration (e.g. deliver his Points of Defence, disclose the documents that support his case), then the other party or the arbitrator can apply to the High Court for an order that he can go ahead with the arbitration without that step having been taken, subject to any conditions that the Court considers its right to impose (section 5 of the 1979 Act). It is more common for the application to be made by the other party than by the arbitrator, as he is generally already legally represented for the purpose of the arbitration proceedings.

2.06 The arbitrator should be careful not to exceed his authority when he studies the arbitration agreement, for it was held in *Walford Baker & Co* v *Macfie & Sons* (1915) 84 LJKB 2221, that any consideration of a contract other than the contract referred to the arbitrator by the parties constitutes misconduct. If the matters in dispute, or the arbitration itself, have arisen under an Act of Parliament, that Act governs everything, including the duties and powers of the contractor (see, for example, the provisions of the London Building Acts). It was held in *Crawford* v *Prowting* [1972] 2 WLR 749, that in the absence of a specific order by an arbitrator, there is no duty on a claimant to proceed with his claim expeditiously. Moreover, a court has no jurisdiction to dismiss a claim in an arbitration for want of prosecution or to grant an injunction restraining a claimant from proceeding with the arbitration even if he has been guilty of inordinate and inexcusable delay (*Bremer Vulkan* v *South Indian Shipping Corporation* [1981] 1 All ER 289, a decision of the House of Lords where the delay was eight years). The courts have, however, recently found a way around the decision in the *Bremer Vulkan*. In the first instance decision of the *Multitank Holsatia* [1988] Lloyds' Rep 486, it was held that an arbitration was consensually abandoned where neither party took any step in the proceedings for some six and a half years because the clear inference to be drawn was that the defendants did not wish to proceed with the arbitration

provided that the plaintiffs consented to its abandonment and that the plaintiffs, by their inactivity, did so consent.

2.07 If an arbitrator has obtained the leave of the High Court to proceed with an arbitration, notwithstanding that a party has failed to take some step in the arbitration that he had ordered, he could fix a date for the hearing and make an award in favour of the respondent if the claimant failed to appear, or debar the claimant from raising a claim of which he had failed to give adequate notice to the respondent in breach of any direction he had given (see para 2.05). The arbitrator should, however, ensure that the party in default is given every opportunity to comply with his order and to appear at any hearing, so as to minimize the possibility of the party in default subsequently contesting the validity of the arbitrator's award on the ground of his misconduct.

3 The award

Basic rules for an award

3.01 There are ten basic rules which are essential for an award to be valid, irrespective of the provisions of the Arbitration Act 1950:

1. The award should comply with the conditions of the arbitration agreement.
2. Unless the parties wish otherwise, the award should be in writing.
3. The arbitrator's decision must be certain, and not ambiguous. For example, the parties' performance of the award must be certain: the amount of money to be paid must be specified; specific explanation must be given on the performance of directions; the time of performance of the award must be set out. An award is uncertain if it is not in the form as required by section 26 of the Act (*Marguilies Brothers Ltd* v *Dafnis Thomaides & Co (UK) Ltd* [1958] 1 WLR 398).
4. The award must not be ambiguous in any of its parts.
5. The award must be within the scope of the arbitration agreement. For example, if an arbitrator has been asked to define boundaries of land, he need not investigate questions of title (*Doe d Lord Carlisle* v *Bailiff of Morpeth* (1810) 3 Taunt 378).
6. The award must contain all matters referred to in the agreement, but must not go outside it (*Duke of Beaufort and Swansea Harbour Trustees* (1869) 29 LJCP 582). For example, when there is a claim for several sums, and the arbitrator awards one lump sum, this is valid, unless the agreement deems otherwise. In a leading case, an arbitrator was asked to decide on certain defects in a building, and what was required to restore it, and to settle claims for extras on such restoration. The arbitrator awarded a fixed sum to settle all matters, and did not give any reason for the cause of the defects. It was held that his award was bad, because all matters in the dispute had not been decided (*Re Rider and Fisher* 1837).
7. The award must finally settle the dispute between the parties. It must deal with all matters referred to the arbitrator by the parties as set out in the agreement. The award will be bad should be arbitrator delegate his judicial authority to a second person, such as a legal adviser. And it will be bad when an arbitrator reserves his decision to take a counsel's opinion until a certain event has come about (*Thinne* v *Rigby* 1612).
8. The award should contain directions for its performance, but if such directions are illegal the award is bad.
9. The award must be legal and must be physically possible to carry out. An exception to this rule is where an award directs a bankrupt to pay a sum of money beyond his means.
10. The award must be properly executed, that is, it must be properly signed and witnessed, or must be under seal in a few instances.

Points to bear in mind on the award

3.02 The arbitrator should always state in his award his findings on the facts. Whilst an award which gives the arbitrator's findings without giving reasons is wholly effective, it is becoming increasingly common for reasoned awards to be requested. The award should contain reasons in the following circumstances:

1. If the arbitration agreement expressly provides for reasons to be given.
2. Where the arbitration is conducted under institutional rules or codes which state that the award should give reasons.
3. Where it is the practice in arbitrations of the kind in question to give reasoned awards.
4. Where a reasoned award has been requested by both parties. And
5. Where a reasoned award has been requested by one party and the arbitrator can see no injustice to the opposing party in giving reasons.

Note that if it appears to the High Court that an award does not set out its reasons in sufficient detail to enable the court to consider any question of law arising out of it, the court has power to order the arbitrator to give further reasons (see para 3.06).

The arbitrator should not include any extraneous matters in his award, such as his personal opinion about the behaviour of the parties, and he should not adjudicate on the rights and wrongs in any earlier proceedings or negotiations.

Clerical mistakes in award

3.03 By the provisions of section 17 of the Arbitration Act 1950, an arbitrator has powers to correct clerical errors or mistakes in his award arising from accidental slips or omissions. This power is strictly confined to such mistakes, and the arbitrator cannot alter the nature of his award, or amend a radical defect by pretending to correct a clerical error.

Judicial review

3.04 Unless a contrary intention is expressed in the arbitration agreement, every such agreement is deemed to contain a provision that the award shall be final and binding on the parties (see section 16 of the Arbitration Act 1950). The Arbitration Act 1979 has made important changes in the manner in which and the extent to which an arbitrator's award can be challenged in the courts. It should be noted first that once an arbitrator has been appointed and before the arbitration has been concluded, any of the parties to the arbitration may apply to the High Court for the determination of any question of law that has arisen (1) if all parties consent or (2) if the arbitrator consents, and the High Court will determine the question providing that it is satisfied that a substantial saving in costs will result from doing so, and that the determination of the question of law could substantially affect the rights of one or more of the parties (see section 2 of the 1979 Act).

3.05 After an award has been made by the arbitrator, an appeal lies from it to the High Court providing:

1. The appeal is on a point of law.
2. The point of law must arise out of an award made on an arbitration agreement.
3. Either all parties agree to the appeal being pursued or the High Court has granted leave to appeal.

Leave to appeal will not be granted (1) if the arbitration agreement expressly excludes the right of appeal, or (2) if the High Court does not consider that the question of law could substantially affect the rights of one or more of the parties. At

the hearing of the appeal, the High Court may confirm or vary the award aside, or remit the award to the arbitrator together with the court's opinion on the question of law. If the latter course is adopted, the arbitrator must make his new award within three months. There is a right of appeal from the High Court to the Court of Appeal in certain limited circumstances (see section 1 (7) of the 1979 Act).

3.06 An arbitrator must state the reasons for his award in sufficient detail for the High Court to consider any question of law arising out of the award, and, if not, he will be ordered to do so providing (1) before the award was made one of the parties gave notice to the arbitrator that a reasoned award would be required or there was a special reason why such notice was not given, and (2) both parties agree that the arbitrator should give his reasons in greater detail, or the court considers it right that he should.

3.07 The parties to an arbitration agreement can seek to limit the powers of the High Court in reviewing an arbitration. Such agreements (known as exclusion agreements) must be carefully drafted, however, and except in the case of arbitration agreements with a foreign element (para 1.13) cannot exclude its right to intervene where allegations of fraud are made, prohibit or restrict the duty on an arbitrator to make a reasoned award, or diminish the power of the courts to use this common law right to prevent abuse of power or position by the arbitrator.

3.08 Both at common law and by section 23 of the 1950 Act, an arbitrator may be removed and his award set aside if he had misconducted himself or if the proceedings or the award has been improperly procured. 'Misconduct' is a word to be used in its widest context; it includes irregular conduct (such as private site visits and hearing representations from one side in the absence of the other) as well as corrupt conduct (such as having a secret interest in the outcome of the proceedings).

3.09 The procedures for stating a Special Case for the opinion of the High Court, and for setting aside an award on the ground of errors of fact or law on the face of the award have been abolished (see section 1 (1) of the 1970 Act).

Enforcing awards

3.10 When the 1950 Act applies to an award, there are two methods by which the award may be enforced:

1. By section 26 of the Act, in the form of a judgement.
2. By action on the award.

Method 1 is cheaper and less difficult, and is generally used. It is made by originating summons before a Master in chambers. The effect is like any other judgement, and may be enforced by a writ which empowers one party to seize the property of the other if he defaults. Note that section 26 of the Act does not generally apply to disputes connected with Concession Agreements within the Channel Tunnel Act 1987. Method 2 is to begin an ordinary action in the courts such as to obtain specific performance of a contract, or an injunction to prevent a party carrying out a contract. It is the only method available when there has been an oral arbitration or if it has been alleged that the arbitrator has exceeded his powers. An award expressed in a foreign currency may be enforced on being converted into sterling at the rate of exchange prevailing on the date of the award.

Costs

3.11 Costs are governed by the terms of the arbitration agreement and the provisions of section 18 of the 1950 Act. It must be noted that the word 'costs' is used in two senses – costs of the reference, and costs of the award; the latter includes only the arbitrator's charges and expenses. When there are no qualifying words, 'costs' means costs of the reference. In the absence of any request to the contrary by the parties, the arbitrator should ensure that some direction as to costs is included in his award. If he fails to do so, section 18(4) of the Act empowers the parties to apply to the arbitrator for an order directing by and to whom the costs of the reference and of the award should be paid.

3.12 There are four conditions which may occur over costs:

1. The agreement does not mention costs.
2. The agreement may direct how costs are to be paid.
3. The agreement may direct the arbitrator to assess costs.
4. The agreement may give directions as to parties' liabilities as to costs.

Under condition 1, section 18 of the Act applies (as long as the agreement is in writing), and the arbitrator has absolute discretion as to costs, which is very wide but must be exercised judicially. Generally, the successful party is entitled to costs, but if the arbitrator departs from this rule, he need not give reason. The arbitrator should, however, ensure that his award makes it clear that he has considered the point and has exercised his discretion against the successful party in the arbitration. The court is then unlikely to overrule the arbitrator's ruling on costs (*The Evmar* [1984] 2 Lloyd's Rep 581). In his award, the arbitrator may either direct that the whole or part of specified costs be paid by a particular party, without fixing an actual sum, or he may name an actual figure in the form of a lump sum, and order such party or parties to pay accordingly.

3.13 When the arbitrator fixes the costs as a lump sum, this must be settled in the award, for such costs cannot be assessed after the award has been made. Under condition 2 the principle is the same as under condition 1. Under condition 3 the arbitrator himself must assess a lump sum or 'tax' (assess in detail) costs. Under condition 4 the general rule is that costs follow the event, which means that the losing party is liable for costs. There cannot be a provision in an award that one party in any event shall pay their own costs.

Occasionally, the parties may ask the arbitrator to issue an award dealing with all aspects of the claims save for the costs, reserving the right to request a second award dealing with the costs aspect, should they fail to reach agreement. Where such a request is made, one party has generally made a sealed offer, or an offer to settle the proceedings at a certain figure, on a without prejudice save as to costs basis. This is the arbitral equivalent of a payment into court and its effect may be to alter the general rule that the successful party is entitled to its costs.

If the amount of the arbitrator's award is less than the amount of the sealed offer and the parties cannot reach agreement over the costs, the losing party will put the letter before the arbitrator and request the arbitrator to exercise his discretion in his award on costs to award the losing party its costs from the date of the offer to the date of the award.

Arbitrator's fees

3.14 Arbitrators should fix their fees at the outset of the reference. They should be reasonable, and in accordance with some professional scale of charges. When an arbitrator is a specialist, and the dispute is on matters on which he specialises, his fees may be outside such a scale, but they should always be agreed to by the parties at the start of the proceedings.

An arbitrator has a lien* on his award and on documents directly concerned in the arbitration and may retain such documents until his fees have been paid. The usual practice is for the arbitrator to notify the parties that his award is available for collection, subject to payment in full of his fees

*Lien: right to retain possession of property until a debt is satisfied

by either or both of the parties. The lien does not include documentary evidence given at the hearing. The arbitrator should also include the amount of his fees in his award. The award should direct that if the unsuccessful party does not pay the arbitrator's fees, then the successful party must do so, and bring a claim against the party who is directly liable for costs. An arbitrator cannot sue for his fees unless there is an express or implied promise to pay them by either party or both (*Hoggins* v *Gordon* (1842) 11 LJQB 286).

4 Professional witnesses in arbitration

4.01 The principal duty of the professional witness is to assist in speedy and efficient conduct of the hearing to which he has been called. Expert witnesses should realize that they have a duty to the arbitrator as well as to their clients. Sometimes a witness might experience some difficulty in combining these functions. When an expert witness is in doubt whether or not to disclose a fact because he considers it irrelevant to the case, he should in all fairness disclose it, and at the same time explain his difficulty to the arbitrator, for all courts of law and arbitration distrust witnesses who are not frank in their statements. If a witness in cross-examination thinks he has made a mistake in his evidence it is more sensible to admit this openly rather than prevaricate or dodge the issue to justify his position.

Witnesses

4.02 In arbitration proceedings there may be two kinds of witness or, more correctly, two kinds of oral evidence; those relating to facts and those of expert opinion. Generally speaking, evidence of facts can be given by any person having 'legal capacity' and be able and willing to testify on oath or by affirmation. The expert witness, if he is to be of any advantage to the side he speaks for, or to the arbitrator, should be a person with the relevant technical knowledge and experience and seen to be of some standing in the profession or trade in which he sets himself out as being an expert.

The expert witness

4.03 One of the most important considerations in preparing a case for arbitration is the selection of the most suitable expert witnesses and the manner in which their particular expertise is to be presented and exploited at the hearing. Expert evidence is common in arbitration and is as admissible there as in the courts, when knowledge of a fact depends upon special training and experience. There are, however, some restrictions in respect of expert witnesses in the courts which need not concern us here. Anyone called upon to act in this capacity must first fully acquaint himself of the nature of the case he is being asked to support and try to assess his own ability to do so without fear or favour and having regard to his technical knowledge and experience. A witness who has been professionally involved directly or indirectly in any dispute before reference is made to arbitration is less likely to carry conviction as being in a position to offer unbiased opinions as one who is completely independent.

4.04 In an arbitration hearing a witness has usually complete freedom of choice to refuse or accept his appointment. However, if necessary in special circumstances, witnesses whom the parties desire to call may be compelled to attend the proceedings by a *subpoena ad testificandum* (the normal writ ordering witnesses to attend court), and to provide documents by *subpoena duces tecum* (a summons to attend and 'bring with you' various specified documents). An arbitrator is entitled himself to call the parties to the dispute to give evidence, but he has no right (of his own initiative) to call other witnesses unless one or both of the parties wishes it. He has power to postpone examination of witnesses.

4.05 If approached to act as witness the first steps to be taken before accepting are to find out what the dispute is about and between whom, to arrange for the solicitors to provide, if possible, copies of the Points of Claim and Points of Defence, and to outline the general nature of the evidence the witness is being asked to contribute.

Proof of evidence

4.06 When the potential expert witness has satisfied himself on all these matters and has visited the site, it is usual for him to be called upon by his legal adviser to prepare his 'proof of evidence'. This document is a statement of the evidence he proposes to give at the hearing. Its contents and the manner in which they are assembled is vital, as it may form an important part of the solicitor's instructions to counsel who may be briefed to appear at the hearing; and it may be used by counsel not only in the examination of his own witness, but also in the cross-examination of an expert witness who appears for his opponent. Accordingly, a proof of evidence should be set out so that learned counsel can bring forward the principal matters in issue without any difficulty for the parties at the hearing. For much the same reasons, the expert witness should have direct discussion with learned counsel on technical points, although such a meeting is generally arranged through the solicitor who briefs counsel.

4.07 It may be feasible and, if so, convenient for copies of the proof of evidence to be distributed and, subject always to the arbitrator's approval, be read by the witness at the hearing. Alternatively they may be used as notes from which counsel will direct his questions to the witnesses and which they will answer accordingly. Documentary evidence is based upon well-known rules of procedure. It opens with a statement of the witness's name, address, and qualifications, with reference to any special matters which suggest why he should be suitably qualified to represent his side. Thereafter, it proceeds to give an interpretation of the subject matter with any facts relevant to his witness, e.g. a day or time when he visited the site or property. Nothing discredits a witness and his testimony more easily than an admission that he has not seen the site! The expert witness should try to impress on the arbitrators his own process of reasoning and persuade the tribunal to listen to his own words before he leads up to his answer. His 'proof of evidence' must be clear, concise, and precise; he must avoid technical detail of any kind except where it is absolutely essential. In its drafting, he must always bear in mind that he will be subjected to searching examination and cross-examination on its contents, and particularly on the professional opinions he has put forward in his evidence.

Rules of evidence

4.08 In every court of law the rules of evidence, i.e. procedures in examination, re-examination, and cross-examination, are well known and must always be applied. In principle, these procedures and rules apply in nearly every form of legal tribunal including arbitration hearings (unless the parties to the 'reference' have otherwise agreed). They must be observe in arbitration hearings as in other legal tribunals whether at a public or private hearing – or at the discretion exercised by the person in charge of the proceedings. In consequence, it is possible for the rules of evidence to be less formal and complicated in arbitration than in the public courts. thus, subject to the accepted rules as to what questions may or may not be asked, and as to what documents may be produced, the admissibility of any question is for the decision of a judge in a court of record and therefore for an arbitrator at an arbitration hearing.

4.09 The law of evidence is too complicated for consideration at any length in this chapter. All that can be attempted is to

outline the general principles and to emphasize that no professional person or layman should contemplate the task of accepting the post of an arbitrator unless he knows fairly well the rules of evidence. His conduct of the proceedings and validity of his ultimate award may depend upon it. Full details are to be found in Wiliam H Gill's *The Law of Arbitration*. This work was originally published in 1965 under the title *Evidence and Procedure in Arbitration.**

4.10 There are two main categories of evidence: primary and secondary. Primary evidence denotes the best evidence available as being that of persons who have directly observed facts or heard statements, and it includes original documents. Where the best evidence is not procurable, secondary evidence will be allowed, e.g. certified copies of statements or documents, etc. Evidence may be rejected which cannot be adequately proved. The principle in regard to acceptance of secondary evidence generally is to allow it only if the original document is in possession of an oponent, or a stranger to the case, because it has been lost, damaged, or cannot be brought to the hearing because it is physically impossible to do so.

*The Evidence Act 1938, the Civil Evidence Act 1968, and the Civil Evidence Act 1972, all apply to arbitrations and their procedure.

Hearsay evidence

4.11 At common law hearsay evidence was not admissible. However, under the Civil Evidence Act 1968 both oral and documentary hearsay statements are generally admissible in civil proceedings subject to certain procedural safeguards.

Leading questions

4.12 Every party, or his counsel, when he examines his own witnesses (i.e. examination-in-chief) must be careful to avoid putting a leading question; that is to say questions which by their form suggest the answer desired. In practice, there is little for the arbitrator to query because if leading questions are constantly asked counsel for the other side will soon rise to put in an objection! Only in cross-examination are leading questions allowed; and there are, in fact, certain exceptions to the rule that they must not be put in examination-in-chief or in re-examination, namely:

1. On introductory matters such as the name, occupation, and address of the witness.
2. On matters not in dispute.
3. To identify persons or things, and
4. To assist the memory of the witness.

Note that in re-examination questions must usually be confined to matters raised in cross-examination, though the arbitrator may consent to fresh issues being raised by either party if the other is agreeable; but he must be careful in that in doing so he does not in any way extend the terms of his 'reference'. In the courts questions may not be asked which introduce wholly new matter. In cross-examination the rules on leading questions are somewhat relaxed and may be freely asked as long as they do not wilfully mislead by misstatement or false assumption. Vexatious questions must not be asked or any that are irrelevant to the case. Questions as to opinion and belief are not generally admissible.

5 Arbitration in Scotland

5.01 Generally the parties to a contract in Scotland are always entitled, but not compelled, to refer their disputes to the courts for a decision. In cases where they decide to have their disputes resolved outside the courts they are referred to a decision of an arbiter under a process known as arbitration. In modern practice many commercial contracts contain an arbitration clause, and almost invariably a building contract contains one.

5.02 The process of arbitration in England is clearly defined by the English Arbitration Act, but that Act does not apply to Scotland, apart from clause 4 (2). Because of the protocol set out in the first schedule to the Act this clause entitles a party to an arbitration to apply to the court to sist (stop) proceedings if the other party starts legal proceedings in court against him during the process of the arbitration. The court is bound to do this unless the judge feels that the arbitration cannot proceed, or there is no dispute.

5.03 For many years the only statute dealing with arbitrations in Scotland was the Arbitration (Scotland) Act 1894, which is still in force. This Act consists of seven sections dealing only with the appointment of an arbiter and an oversman in differing circumstances. More recently, however, two Acts have been passed which affect either directly or indirectly arbitration proceedings in this country, namely the Administration of Justice (Scotland) Act 1972 and the Prescription and Limitations (Scotland) Act 1973.

5.04 The 1972 Act in effect gave statutory authority to a clause in the Scottish supplement to the 1963 edition of the Standard Form of Building Contract, namely clause 35 (5), which gave the parties to an arbitration in Scotland the right in certain circumstances to request the arbiter to prepare a Special Case for the Opinion and Judgement of the Court of Session on any question or questions of law. With the passing of the 1972 Act, clause 35 (5) was amended to read as follows:

> 'The Law of Scotland shall apply to all arbitrations under these presents and the award of the Arbiter shall be final and binding on the parties subject always to the provisions of section 3 of the Administration of Justice (Scotland) Act 1972.'

A similar clause 41.4 is included in the January 1988 revision of the Scottish Building Contract.

Section 3 of the Act is in the following terms:

> 'Subject to express provision to the contrary in an agreement to refer to arbitration, the Arbiter or Oversman may, on the application of a party to the arbitration, and shall, if the Court of Session on such an application so directs, at any stage in the arbitration state a Case for the Opinion of that Court on any question of law arising in the arbitration.
>
> This Section shall not apply to an arbitration under any enactment which confers a power to appeal to or state a Case for the Opinion of a Court or Tribunal in relation to that arbitration.
>
> This Section shall not apply to any form of arbitration relating to a trade dispute within the meaning of the Industrial Courts Act 1919 or relating to an industrial dispute within the meaning of the Industrial Relations Act 1971: to any other arbitration arising from a collective agreement within the meaning of the said Act 1971: or to proceedings before the Industrial Arbitration Board described in Section 124 of that Act.
>
> This Section shall not apply in relation to an agreement to refer to arbitration made before the commencement of this Act.'

5.05 It should be noted that both under the former clause 35 (5) and under the 1972 Act it is only on questions of law that a Special Case may be presented, but in practice it can often be extremely difficult to distinguish between a question of fact and a true question of law. The procedure for initiating such appeals is enshrined in Rules of Court no. 277.

5.06 Many arbiters view this development in arbitrations in Scotland with concern, because the time involved in the preparation of the Special Case, even with the help of a legally qualified clerk, can be considerable, and it is not unknown for an arbiter to insist that the parties opt out of this procedure (as they can do in terms of the Act) as a condition of his acceptance of the arbitration.

5.07 The Prescription and Limitations (Scotland) Act 1973 indirectly affects arbitration proceedings through Part I of the Act, which came into force on 26 July 1976. This Act, and particularly Part I, which is extremely technical and difficult to interpret, provides in general that an obligation which has existed for a continuous period of five years without any claim being made, will be extinguished as from the expiry of that period, and this includes obligations arising from breach of contract or from any rule of law requiring reparation for loss or injury. There are extremely complicated rules for ascertaining the commencement date of the five-year period, which are outwith the terms of this article, and for which reference to the Act itself should be made.

5.08 These three Acts, therefore, are the only statutory enactments covering arbitrations in Scotland, and therefore such law as exists on commercial arbitrations is based on case law and what might loosely be described as 'use and wont'. There has recently been considerable growth in statutory arbitrations under specific Acts of Parliament such as the Workman's Compensation Acts and the Agricultural Holdings (Scotland) Act, but this article is concerned only with commercial arbitrations in general and building contract arbitrations in particular to which these latter statutes do not apply.

However, it might be relevant to add that in 1986 the Lord Advocate set up a Scottish Advisory Committee on arbitration law, charged among other things with advising whether or not Scotland should adopt in whole or in part the draft Model Law issued by the United Nations Commission on International Trade Law and generally to consider what changes might be made to improve arbitration procedure in Scotland. As much of the present law and practice of arbitration in Scotland is based on common law, it seems distinctly possible that this committee will be taking a close look at the English Arbitration Act 1950 and we may therefore expect substantial changes to the Scottish law of arbitration in the not too distant future.

5.09 Early editions of this book contained a commentary on the arbitration clauses included in the Scottish Supplement to the 1963 Edition of the Standard Form and readers requiring information on this earlier clause are referred to these editions. This commentary is confined to the arbitration

clause found in the January 1988 Revision of the Scottish Building Contract.

5.10 In this Revision the arbitration clause appears in Part 4 of the Scottish Supplement, in which clause 41 of JCT 80 is deleted and an amended clause applicable to Scotland is substituted. It should also be noted that under clause 4 of the Building Contract the employer and the contractor agree to submit any dispute or differences to arbitration in accordance with clause 41.

5.11 The opening paragraph of the clause contains new provisions for appointment of an arbiter failing agreement by the employer and the contractor on who it should be. The entry in Appendix no. 2 must be completed to show that the appointing authority is either the Chairman or Vice-Chairman of the SBCC, the Dean of the Faculty of Advocates or the Sheriff of the Sheriffdom in which the works are situated, but if inadvertently left uncompleted the Appendix states that the arbiter will be appointed by the Chairman or Vice-Chairman of the SBCC.

5.12 Clause 41.1 provides that no arbitration is to commence without mutual written agreement until after determination or alleged determination of the contractor's employment or until after practical completion or abandonment of the work except where it relates (1) to the appointment of a new architect or a new quantity surveyor; (2) to a question whether an instruction given by the architect comes within the terms of the contract; (3) to a question whether a certiicate has been improperly withheld or is not in accordance with the contract; (4) to whether or not a contractor is entitled to withhold consent to the employer taking partial possession of the works or to using the works for storage; and (5) to whether or not a contractor is required to comply with an architect's decision on the rectification of work not in accordance with the contract or regarding an extension of time or a question arising out of the outbreak of hostilities or war damage.

5.13 Clause 41.2 recognizes that in many instances an arbitration can readily involve sub-contractors as well as a main contractor and employer. It states that when there is a dispute between an employer and a contractor, which is substantially the same as one between an employer and a nominated sub-contractor under NSC/2/Scot or NSC/2a/Scot, or between a contractor and a nominated sub-contractor or between an employer/contractor and a nominated supplier, then in these cases such dispute shall be referred to the arbiter appointed to determine the related dispute – although if either party considers that arbiter unsuitable a different arbiter can be appointed.

5.14 The procedure for the conduct of a tripartite arbitration is necessarily complicated and it is in this type of arbitration in particular that an arbiter is well advised to appoint a legally qualified clerk to guide and advise him on procedural matters (see para 5.22).

5.15 Clause 41.3 contains a summary of the powers to be given to an arbiter and these are self-explanatory. Clause 41.3.5 gives the arbiter power to award compensation or damages and expenses which is necessary because in Scots Law, although an arbiter probably has implied power to award expenses, he does not – unless expressly given the power to do so – have the right to find either party liable in damages (cf *McKay* v *Leven Commissioners* 1893 2 LR 1093).

5.16 Clause 41.4 states that the law of Scotland shall apply to all arbitrations in terms of this clause and incorporates the provisions of section 3 of the Administration of Justice (Scotland) Act 1972 which allows appeals to the Court of Session on questions of law.

5.17 Clause 41.5 is new to the January 1988 Revision and specifically entitles an arbiter: (1) to appoint a clerk to make part and final awards and to issue proposed findings – all of which are normal procedure in Scotish arbitrations; (2) to receive remuneration and reimbursement of his outlays, which is necessary because at common law in Scotland an arbiter has no right to remuneration for his services unless he stipulated his fee before accepting office. At one time this rule was absolute, but it has been modified somewhat by the decision in the case of *McIntyre Brothers* v *Smith* 1913 50 SC 261, which states 'in accordance with general practice the rule must now be assumed that a professional man undertaking the duties of an arbiter is entitled in the absence of any agreement to the contrary to be remunerated for his services as arbiter in the same way as he is entitled to receive remuneration for his services in any other professional employment'. In the majority of building arbitrations where the arbiter is a professional person, his right to a fee is safeguarded by this decision, but this is only a modification of the common law and a specific right to payment of a fee is desirable particularly where the arbiter might be a non-professional person; (3) to find the parties jointly and severally liable; (4) to decern (this is a technical term which strictly speaking is required in any judgement before it can be enforced by the courts if the losing party refuses voluntarily to comply with it); (5) to dispense with a Deed of Submission.

Importance of using Scottish Supplement

5.18 The version of clause 41 which is included in JCT 80 provides, in clause 41.7, that the law of England will be the proper law of the contract and that the provisions of the Arbitration Acts 1950–1979 shall apply to any arbitration wherever it is conducted and whatever the nationality, residence or domicile of the employer, contractor or arbitrator. This clause was added after the well-known decision by the House of Lords in 1970 in the case of *James Miller & Partners Ltd* v *Whitworth Street Estates (Manchester) Ltd*. This case concerned the refusal of the arbiter, who was a Scottish architect, to state a case for the decision of the English High Court in accordance with the English Arbitration Act and the House of Lords eventually decided that the arbiter was right in declining to do so. A footnote to clause 41.7 originally stated that if the parties did not wish the law of England to apply 'appropriate amendments to clause 41.7 should be made' but in Amendment no. 6 to JCT 80 issued in July 1988, this footnote has been altered to state that if the works are situated in Scotland then the forms issued by the Scottish Building Contract Committee, which contain Scots proper law and arbitration provisions, are the appropriate documents.

At this stage reference should also be made to the JCT Arbitration Rules issued in July 1987 which are obligatory on all arbitrations conducted under JCT 80. These Rules, however, do not apply to Scotland, but instead the SBCC has established an arbitration appointment scheme in connection with which it has published a set of documents to facilitate the appointment of an arbiter if the parties fail to agree on this.

Selection of arbiter

5.19 In Scotland, as an arbiter is in effect a private judge selected by the parties themselves, virtually anybody can be appointed, and there are few personal disqualifications that cannot be waived by the parties. It has even been decided that a minor can act as an arbiter. If an arbiter shows himself committed to a certain point of view before taking up the reference, he is disqualified, and similarly if he accepts office with a promise to one party that he will do his best for him. In some building contracts, there is an arbitration clause in which the architect himself is appointed as arbiter on all disputes arising under the contract. One would think in such a case that the architect could not approach the question with

the completely open mind of an outside person, and moreover although he himself does not have a direct financial interest, he is incidentally involved in the financial outcome. But it has been held repeatedly by the courts in Scotland that employment by one of the parties to the arbitration is no bar to an arbiter acting.

5.20 As noted above (para 5.03) the Arbitration (Scotland) Act deals with the appointment of an arbiter. Prior to the Act, a submission to an un-named arbiter was not competent in Scotland, though this was altered by section 1 of the Act, which permits reference to un-named people or holders of a specific office. Where the parties have failed to agree on the nomination of a single arbiter, section II of the act provides that the arbiter may be appointed by the court on the application of either party to the arbitration. Section III provides that where two arbiters are envisaged and one of the parties refuses to nominate one, the court may make the appointment. Section IV of the Act gives two arbiters the power to appoint an oversman which, prior to the Act, had not been allowed, and section V states that the terms of the Act shall apply to all references before or after the passing of the Act.

5.21 The remaining two sections of the Act state that applications to the court under the Act can be either to the Sheriff Court or to the Court of Session and that the Act shall apply only to Scotland.

Appointment of clerk

5.22 It is not necessary to have a clerk, and many arbitrations are conducted perfectly satisfactorily without one; but in any arbitration where the procedure is in the least formal, it is common for an arbiter to appoint a clerk, who is responsible for organizing the arbitration and all its documentation. Although not necessarily so, the clerk is usually a solicitor, and in addition to his duties as clerk to the submission, he frequently advises the arbiter on legal points of procedure which occur during the process off the arbitration; he is not in any way responsible for decisions which the arbiter makes on the strength of his advice, however. The clerk is responsible for keeping arbitration papers, and all communications from the arbiter to the parties should be channelled through the clerk, who is also responsible for making the decisions of the arbiter known to the parties. If the arbiter proposes to appoint a clerk, it is usual for him to do so simultaneously with his acceptance of the office of arbiter.

Submissions

5.23 In Scotland, a reference to an arbiter is begun by a document known as a submission. This is the contract by which the parties to the arbitration confer jurisdiction on the arbiter. The length of time during which they wish to submit themselves to his jurisdiction is a matter for the parties to determine by the terms of the contract. A clause in the submission frequently gives an arbiter power to decide a dispute between two specified dates, and where the endurance of the arbitration is left blank the period is a year and a day from the date of the submission.

Form

5.24 There is no technical style for a submission, so long as the words used make the dispute clear to the arbiter; a special submission is one which refers a single specified dispute to the decision of the arbiter, and a general submission is one where all disputes arising between two parties are referred to the decision of an arbiter (although this does not cover disputes which were not in existence at the date of the submission). It is important to note that the death of one of the parties, or of the arbiter himself, ends the arbitration; similarly, if the contract is terminated for any reason, so also is the arbitration.

Procedure and hearing in an arbitration

5.25 Having had the submission, in all but the most informal types of arbitration, it is usual for an arbiter to accept the office by minute annexed to the submission. If an oversman (para 5.20) is required, this is the appropriate stage for his nomination.

5.26 While an arbiter is master of the procedure of his own arbitration, he must conform to the requirements of the parties as laid down in the submission. He is, however, entitled to take all steps to inform himself about the matter upon which he has been called upon to decide. He is therefore bound to make sure that he is properly informed as to the precise nature of the question, and that he investigates such facts as he considers relevant to the issue. He must hear both sides to the dispute as may be necessary to enable him to decide the case unbiasedly. He must not grant to one side what he refuses to the other.

5.27 In the ordinary course, in a formal submission, the clerk is responsible for the preparation of what is known as an interlocutor sheet (an interlocutor is the name given to the orders or instructions issued by the arbiter in the course of the hearing). The first interlocutor is an order from the arbiter requiring the pursuers (or claimants) to lodge their claim within a specified number of days and thereafter giving the respondents (or defenders) a further period of time within which to lodge their answers to the claim. Having lodged their original claim and answers, the parties almost always wish to adjust their pleadings, and an arbiter normally issues a further interlocutor giving the parties a specified time to do this. This process can be repeated at the arbiter's discretion until the parties have finalized their pleadings, when the arbiter makes an interlocutor closing the record, as it is known.

5.28 The closing of the record marks the end of the period within which the parties are entitled to adjust their pleadings. The closed record is the name given to the document which contains the adjusted claim of the pursuer and the adjusted answer of the defender. It is to be contrasted with the open record, which contains the claim and answers as originally lodged before adjustment. Prior to the formal hearing, the arbiter may, if he so wishes, decide to visit the object of the parties' dispute.

Hearing

5.29 A hearing is then convened at a place and time to be selected by the arbiter, bearing in mind the convenience of the parties. At the hearing, and at any stage of the arbitration, the parties may be represented by counsel, and the normal rules of evidence are followed during the hearing. The arbiter normally takes advice from his clerk (if the latter is a lawyer) on what may or may not be admitted in evidence if there is any dispute on this point. At the conclusion of the hearing, the arbiter may issue a verbal decision, but often he indicates to the parties that he wishes to defer his decision until he has had time to consider the evidence laid before him (known as '*avizandum*'), when he issues his decision as proposed findings.

Proposed findings

5.30 In a Scottish arbitration an arbiter usually issues proposed findings in the first instance and gives the parties time to lodge representations against these. If representations are received, a further hearing is held by the arbiter to

consider them. But after this, or if there are no representations lodged within the time specified, the arbiter issues his final interlocutor containing his findings. In the final interlocutor he may, if he has been asked to do so, deal with the question of expenses and damages, but if he has not been asked to award damages, he should not make any reference to this in the interlocutor. In the final interlocutor the arbiter should state that, as the terms of his remit have now been exhausted, the arbitration has been concluded.

Challenge of the award

5.31 Until clause 35 (5) of the 1963 Scottish supplement was introduced and more recently until the 1972 Act was enacted there was no appeal in Scotland against an arbiter's decision unless the arbiter had during the process of the arbitration misconducted himself in such a way as to make the award obviously biased, i.e. if he had accepted a bribe from one or other of the parties, or if the award dealt with a subject which was not the matter of the submission to the arbiter. But arbiters are now becoming used to the fact that on questions of law they may be appealed either under contract or under statute to the Court of Session or subsequently to the House of Lords.

5.32 There is an important difference between the former clause 35 (5) and the provisions of the Administration of Justice (Scotland) Act 1972. Under the former the arbiter is entitled to state a case to the Court of Session on a question of law should he wish to do so, and if requested by either of the parties he must do so. Under the Act again he may do so if he wishes to, but he is not obliged to do so simply because he is asked to state a case by one of the parties; if in the face of a request he refuses to do so, the complaining party must then petition the courts, and only if the courts so instruct him is the arbiter obliged to do so. It is also important to note that under both provisions it is only on a question of law that the arbiter can be appealed; on questions of fact his decision is binding. It may at first glance seem obvious whether a question is one of fact or law, but in practice it can be very difficult to differentiate between the two, and if there is a difference of opinion between the parties as to whether an appeal is required or not, an arbiter can easily find himself in a very difficult situation.

5.33 An arbiter who either at the request of the parties or on the instructions of the Court of Session finds himself with having to prepare a Stated Case should immediately take legal advice on how this is to be done, either from his clerk, if he has appointed one and he is legally qualified, or from some other source. A Stated Case is the name given to the legal process employed, and its preparation is a technical matter which would normally be outwith the skills of a lay arbiter. Briefly, in it the arbiter sets out the facts which he has found proven from the evidence submitted to him by the parties, and then lists the questions of law on which he requires the court's ruling. Normally the Case would be debated in court by counsel for the two parties, and while the arbiter would wish to be present in court while the debate is taking place it is highly unlikely that he would be required to take part.

5.34 Once the Court of Session has given its decision on the questions set out in the Stated Case (subject to an overriding right of appeal to the House of Lords) these decisions are binding on the parties and can be incorporated by the arbiter in his final interlocutor. If one of the parties to an arbitration refuses to comply with the terms of the award (whether or not this follows on the decision of the Court of Session after a Stated Case) the other party can take action in the courts to have it enforced.

12

Statutory Authorities in England and Wales

PROFESSOR J. F. GARNER
DR A. R. MOWBRAY

1 Introductory

1.01 Local government in England and Wales, outside London, was completely reorganized on 1 April 1974, when the Local Government Act 1972 came into force. The pattern of local authorities is now simpler than it was before 1974, but Greater London* (reorganized in 1965 by the London Government Act 1963) is administered differently, and there are also less important differences between England and Wales. These three parts of the country should therefore now be considered separately.

1.02 In London, the Local Government Act 1985 abolished the Greater London Council and redistributed its functions between the 32 London boroughs, the City of London and new specialized representative bodies (e.g. the London Fire and Civil Defence Authority). Housing is now the responsibility of the boroughs and the City.

1.03 In *England* outside the London area, the country is divided between 6 metropolitan areas (West Midlands, Merseyside, Greater Manchester, West Yorkshire, South Yorkshire, and Tyne and Wear) and 38 'ordinary' counties. Between 1974 and 1985 in the metropolitan areas there was a metropolitan county for each area, and a varying number of metropolitan districts, each with a council, within each county. Since 1985 the metropolitan counties have been abolished and their functions redistributed to the metropolitan districts and specialized representative bodies. Outside those areas there are 38 counties, each with a county council and a number of districts (approximately 390 in total) each again with a council. In addition, rural parishes which existed before 1974 have been allowed to continue. Further, some of the pre-1974 district councils have been re-formed with parish council status. As an additional complication, district councils have been allowed to apply for a charter giving themselves the status of a borough, although this is solely a ceremonial matter. Some parishes have been allowed to call themselves 'towns' and have appointed 'town mayors', again with no real legal significance.

1.04 In *Wales* there are no metropolitan areas. There are eight counties, each divided into districts with councils at each level. Also each district is divided into a number of 'communities' which have the functions of the English parishes.

1.05 Outside London county councils are responsible everywhere for the preparation of development plans and are concerned with development control involving (only) the mining and working of minerals.† They are also responsible for fire services, main and district highways, refuse disposal, and a few other functions. Outside the metropolitan areas county councils are also responsible for education and welfare services, which in the metropolitan areas are the responsibility of the district councils. All district councils are responsible for housing, refuse collection, drainage, clean air and public health generally (but *not* sewerage and water supply), development control, parks and open spaces, and building controls, etc. A district council may also (by arrangement with the county council) undertake the maintenance of urban roads (other than trunk roads), bridleways, and footpaths within its district. The parishes (communities in Wales) have very few substantial functions, but may provide and maintain recreation grounds, bus shelters, and roadside seats. Part 1 of the Local Government Act 1988 now states that if local authorities wish to provide certain designated services themselves (notably the collection of refuse) they must first subject the service to tender from private contractors.

1.06 From 1974–1989, the provision and maintenance of sewers and sewerage disposal, together with water supply and distribution and the prevention of river pollution, was the responsibility of special authorities, the ten regional water authorities (nine in England, one in Wales). Under the Water Act 1989 the water industry was privatized and as a consequence the sewerage functions of the former water authorities have passed to successor companies, which are in most instances also responsible for water supply, except in those areas where this was formerly the responsibility of statutory water companies which remain in existence. Water and sewerage undertakers are forbidden from causing river pollution, the prevention of which is the responsibility of a new authority (the National Rivers Authority) which operates under the supervision of the Director General of Water Services and the Secretary of State. The successor companies are constituted under the regime of the Companies Acts and are appointed by the Secretary of State to act as water and/or sewage undertakers. Customers can make complaints to a specially constituted Customer Services Committee who must investigate the matter and may make representations to the Director General, who in turn may issue an order, or suggest that the Secretary of State do so, requiring appropriate action to be taken by the relevant undertaker (Water Act 1989, sections 27 and 20).

---

*An extensive area including the whole of the former county of Middlesex and the boroughs of Croydon and East and West Ham.

†Under anticipated legislation (probably coming into force in 1990) the preparation of development plans will become the responsibility of district councils.

General characteristics of local authorities

1.07 The essential characteristics of every local authority under this complicated system is that it is governed by a council elected on a wide franchise at four-year intervals. In districts, one-third of the councillors retire on three out of four years every year; but a non-metropolitan district may resolve that all their members shall retire together. In counties all members retire together every fourth year. Since 1974 there have been no aldermen elected by the councillors.

1.08 Local authorities are legal persons, capable of suing and being sued in the courts, entrusted by Parliament with a range of functions over a precisely limited geographical area. Each local authority is subject to the doctrine of *ultra vires*; i.e. it can perform only those functions conferred on it by Parliament, and only in such a manner as Parliament may have laid down. On the other hand, within the powers defined by Parliament, each local authority is its own master. In the two-tier or three-tier system there is no question of an appeal from the lower rank authorities (the district or the parish) to the higher rank (the county council) or from the parish to the district. If the individual authority has acted within its statutory powers, its decision is final, except in cases precisely laid down by Parliament, where (as in many planning situations) there may be a right of appeal to a minister of the central Government (Chapter 14). If, however, a local authority has overstepped the limits of its legal powers, a private citizen who has been aggrieved in consequence may apply to the courts for an order requiring the errant local authority to keep within its powers. Thus, a ratepayer at Fulham successfully obtained an order against the borough council, requiring the council to stop spending ratepayers' money on the provision of a service for washing clothes for members of the public, when the council had statutory powers to provide a service for washing only the bodies of members of the public (*Attorney General* v *Fulham BC* [1921] 1 Ch 440).

Officers

1.09 All local authorities are alike in that they employ officers and workmen to carry out their instructions, while the elected members assembled in council make decisions as to what is to be done. Officers of the authority – chief executive, solicitor, treasurer, surveyor, architect, planning officer, and many others – play a large part in the decision-making process: they advise the council on the courses of action open to them, and also on the consequences of taking such actions. When a decision has been taken, it is then the duty of appropriate officers of the council to implement it: to notify persons concerned and to take any executive decisions or other action necessary to give effect to the main decision. It is sometimes said that the officers give advice and take action, while the council decides all matters of policy; although basically true (for statutes almost invariably confer the power to exercise discretion on the authority itself) this does not clarify what happens in practice. 'Policy' is incapable of precise definition, for what is policy to some local authorities and in some circumstances may be regarded as routine administration by other authorities or in different circumstances. Thus, every local authority approves its development plan in the final form. Some local authorities like to settle the details of each improvement or standard grant approved under the Housing Act 1985 (para 4.02), though most authorities would be content to leave details of such matters to their officers, trusting them to bring before the council (or a committee) particulars of any difficult case.

Committees

1.10 In practice, all local authorities conduct their affairs by the committee system. Committees, consisting of named

LAST SITTING of the OLD COURT of SESSION 11 of JULY 1808

councillors, are usually considerably smaller in membership than the council as a whole* and are entrusted with specified functions of the council. Thus, every county council has a planning committee and a finance committee, and most district councils will have a parks committee and a housing committee, although details vary from authority to authority. Since 1974, committees have tended to be wider in scope, and policy or 'general resources' committees are common. Every matter requiring a council decision within the terms of reference of a particular committee is first brought before the committee. The committee then considers the matter and either recommends a certain decision to the council or may itself make the decision. Whether the committee decides on behalf of the council depends on whether the council has delegated to the committee power to take the decision on its behalf, either in that particular matter, or in matters of that kind or falling within a particular class. Section 101 of the Local Government Act 1972 confers on all local authorities power to arrange for any of its functions (except levying a charge or raising a loan) to be discharged by a committee, a sub-committee, or an officer.

1.11 Proceedings in committee are normally held in public and tend to be informal. Officers attend, and volunteer advice and often take part in the discussion, although any decision is taken on the vote or assent of the councillors present. Council meetings and meetings of specified committees such as the education committee are more formal; the press and members of the public are entitled to be present unless they have been excluded by special resolution of the council passed because of the intention to discuss exempted information, such as facts regarding individual council employees (Local Government (Access to Information) Act 1985), and proceedings are conducted in accordance with the council's standing orders. Officers do not speak at a council meeting unless their advice is expressly requested, and as much business consists of receipt of reports from committees, discussion tends to be confined to more controversial topics. Because of the presence of the press and public, party politics tend to be more obvious at council meetings; often in committee, members from opposing political parties will agree, and members of a single party may disagree with one another. In recent years, however, there has been a tendency for authorities to be more closely organized on party political lines. When this occurs, 'group' meetings may be held preceding the committee meetings. Thus on important matters, decisions at committee meetings tend to be 'rubber stamps' of decisions already taken at the group meeting of the political party in power on the council.

1.12 The law requires that councils must meet at least four times a year. Most councils arrange committee meetings in a cycle, monthly or perhaps every six weeks, so that each committee will normally meet at least once between council meetings. The system whereby committees are given delegated powers (as is now customary) provides for a reasonably expeditious dispatch of business, but there may be long delays where the council meets less often than once a month, and there is no adequate provision for delegation to committees and/or to officers.

Officers' powers

1.13 All discretionary powers are in the first instance conferred on a local authority, but under section 101 of the Local Government Act 1972, every local authority has wide powers to delegate any of its discretionary decisions to any of its officers; a power which is often used, especially in

planning. But there must in every instance be a clear delegation before an officer can decide on behalf of his authority. Therefore, when an officer of a council who was asked for information as to the planning position in respect of a particular piece of land carelessly gave the wrong information, saying that planning permission was not required, it was held by the courts that the council were not bound by this statement. It could not be taken as the decision of the council, as the officer had in that case no power to act on their behalf (*Southend-on-Sea Corporation v Hodgson (Wickford) Ltd* [1961] 2 All ER 46). Similarly, when a public health inspector served a notice on the owner of property requiring certain work to be undertaken, it was declared that the notice was void and of no effect, because the statute required that the local authority should themselves decide to serve such a notice, and under the then existing law they could not delegate such a duty to one of their officers (*Firth v Staines* [1897] 2 QB 70). These decisions are still good law in circumstances where powers have not been expressly delegated to the officer concerned (see *Western Fish Products Ltd v Penwith DC* (1979) 77 LGR 185). As a consequence of local government reorganization there are many more large authorities than there were before 1974. They are also frequently differently organized. In place of the town or county clerk, the principal officer is often known as the 'Chief Executive', and often he has no departmental responsibilities. He may be assisted by a small management team of chief officers such as the Director of Technical Services, the Director of Welfare Services etc., each having broad

Table 12.1 Responsibilities of local authority officers

Subject matter	Officer	Local authority
Planning	Planning officer or surveyor	DC
Building regulations	Building inspector or surveyor	DC
Development in a private street	Surveyor	CC
Surface water sewerage	Engineer	SU
Sewer connections	Engineer	SU
Blocked sewers	Engineer	SU
Housing grants; housing generally	Environmental health officer or (sometimes) surveyor	DC
Height of chimneys or other clean air matters	Environmental health officer	DC
Petroleum licensing; most other licensing	Petroleum inspector (often environmental health officer or surveyor)	CC or DC
Music and dancing licences	Local magistrate's clerk	
Liquor licences	Local magistrate's clerk	

Key: CC, county council; DC, district council; SU, sewerage undertaker

Notes
A company operating under the Water Act 1989, whose functions may be exercised by the district council under an arrangement with the sewerage undertaker.
London In Greater London, in all cases (except for liquor licences) the responsible authority is the London borough council or the Common Council of the City.
Planning In planning the authority given above should be contacted in the first instance, although the county council may ultimately make the decision.
Roads In the counties highway functions are commonly administered by district or divisional surveyors, responsible to the county surveyor but stationed locally often at district council offices. In the case of trunk and special roads (motorways) the highway authority is the Secretary of State for Transport, but the local county surveyor acts as his agent at local level. Maintenance of urban roads may be claimed by the DC.
  Under the Local Government (Miscellaneous Provisions) Act 1982, several activities are made subject to licensing (e.g. acupuncture, tattooing, take-away food shops, etc.). These provisions are administered by the district council.

*There are no general rules, but a council of, say, 48 members may place about 12 councillors on each of its committees. Recently there has been a tendency to streamline committee organization, leaving more routine matters to the discretion of officers.

responsibilities and a number of departments subordinate to him. The committee structure also may be different from the pre-1974 system, being organized rather on a functional basis than one based upon departments.

A local authority does not stand outside the common law in respect of acts of negligence by its officers and employees. The decision in the case of *Anns* v *London Borough of Merton* [1977] 2 All ER 492, in the House of Lords, has strongly emphasized the extent of the legal liability of local authorities for the actions of their officers. (See Chapter 1.)

Finding the right officer

1.14 Architects in the course of their professional business are obliged to have dealings with numerous local authority officials. Table 12.1 shows the purposes for which a permission, licence, or certificate may have to be obtained from the local authority, giving the officers initially responsible (see Chapters 14 and 15). First, however, it is essential to ascertain the authority in whose area the site lies.

2 Connections to services – statutory undertakers

2.01 When starting to design a building for a client, any architect is obliged at an early stage to consider the availability of mains services and the rights of his client as landowner regarding the various statutory undertakers: sewer and highway authorities, water, gas, and electricity supply undertakings, and possibly the water undertaker if it is proposed to use a water course as a means of disposing of effluent from the building. The legal provisions regulating these matters are discussed below.

Sewers

2.02 Sewers are conduits (artificial or natural) used for conveying effluent (i.e. waste liquids – clear water, surface water from covered surfaces, land or buildings, foul water, or trade effluent) from two or more buildings not within the same curtilage*. A conduit which take effluent from one building only or from a number of buildings all within the same curtilage is in law a 'drain'. This distinction is important, as a landowner never has any legal right to let his effluent flow into a drain belonging to another person (even if that other person is a local authority) unless he has acquired such a right by at least 20 years' use or as the result of an agreement with the other person (Chapter 3). The same rule applies to a private sewer; but if the conduit to which he proposes to drain his effluent is a *public* sewer, he will have certain valuable rights to use it. All public sewers are vested in (owned by) the sewerage undertakers, and a sewer is a public sewer if it existed as a sewer (regardless of who constructed it) before 1 October 1937, if it was constructed by a local authority after 1 October 1937 and before 1 April 1974, or by a water authority before 1 November 1989, or by a sewerage undertaker after 1 November 1989 and was not designed to serve *only* property belonging to a local authority (e.g. a council housing estate), or if it has been adopted as a public sewer since 1 October 1937.

Rights to connection

2.03 If there is within any distance a public sewer capable of serving his property, any landowner has by section 34 of the Public Health Act 1936 a right to cause his own drains or private sewer to communicate with it and to discharge foul

*Curtilage: in non-technical terms, the natural boundaries of a particular building; thus the curtilage of an ordinary dwelling house would include the garage, the garden and its appurtenances, and any outbuildings.

and surface water from his premises to it. Connecting sewers or drains from the premises to the public sewer must be constructed at the expense of the landowner concerned. Sometimes – but not often – the sewerage undertaker may itself construct 'laterals', or connecting drains leading from the main sewer to the boundary of the street to which house drains may be connected.

2.04 There are a few exceptions to this general rule:

1. No substance likely to injure the sewer or to interfere with the free flow of its contents, no chemical refuse or steam, or any petroleum spirit or calcium carbide, may be caused to flow into a public sewer (Public Health Act 1936, section 27).
2. The general rule does not apply to trade effluents.
3. The general rule does not permit a communication directly with a storm-water overflow sewer (section 34 (1) (c) of the Act).
4. Where separate public sewers are provided for foul and for surface water, foul water may not be discharged into a sewer provided for surface water, and surface water may not, without the consent of the sewerage undertaker, be discharged into a sewer provided for foul water (section 34 (1) (b) of the Act). It is particularly important that an architect should know whether the undertaker's sewerage network is designed on the separate system, as he may in turn have to provide a separate drainage for the building he is designing.

Procedure

2.05 A person wishing to connect his sewer or drain to a public sewer must give the sewerage undertaker written notice of his proposal, and the undertaker may within 21 days of notice refuse to permit him to make the communication if the mode of construction or condition of the drain or sewer is such that the making of the communication would be prejudicial to their sewerage system (section 34 (3) of the Act), but they may not so refuse for any other reason. Further, within 14 days of the proposals so served on the undertaker they may give notice that they intend to make the communication to the public sewer (section 36 (1) of the Act). The private landowner is then obliged to permit the undertaker to do the work of making the house drains or sewer connect with the public sewer, and he has to bear the sewerage undertaker's reasonable expenses so incurred. This may include a reasonable sum extra on the actual cost by way of establishment expenses. When making the communication, the undertaker (or the private owner if he is allowed to do the work himself) has power as necessary to break open any street (sections 36 (4) of the 1936 Public Health Act read with the Water Act 1989, Schedule 19).

2.06 Any dispute with the undertaker under these provisions may be settled by way of an appeal to the local magistrates, or in some cases by a reference to arbitration. The landowner has a right to this redress if, for example, he is refused permission to make a communication with a public sewer.

Approval

2.07 The arrangements proposed to be made for the 'satisfactory provision' for drainage of a building must be approved by the district council or London borough council at the time when the building plans are considered under the Building Regulations (Building Act 1984, section 21 and Chapter 15). Disposal of the effluent may be to a public sewer, or to a cesspool or private septic tank, and in the case of surface water to a highway drain or a watercourse or to the sea. In this instance note that the powers remain with the district council and have not been transferred to the sewerage undertaker.

2.08 It remains to deal with discharges to highway drains, to watercourses, and to the sea, and with the special case of trade effluent. If it is desired to drain to a septic tank or similar receptacle on another person's land, this is a matter for private negotiation for an express easement (Chapter 3) with such other landowner.

2.09 If there is no existing main sewer into which the property could be drained, the owner or occupier (usually with the owners, etc., of other premises) may requisition the sewerage undertaker to provide a public sewer, under section 71 of the Water Act 1989. They must then satisfy conditions specified by the undertaker the most important of which is likely to be that those requisitioning the sewer shall undertake to meet any 'relevant deficit' of the undertaker in consequence of constructing the sewer. But this section applies only to sewers to be used for domestic purposes.

Highway drains

2.10 A landowner has no legal right to cause his drains (or sewers) to be connected with a highway drain, and this applies equally to surface water drains taking effluent from roads and paved surfaces on a private housing estate. Such drains may, in accordance with the statutory provisions outlined above, be connected with a public sewer, but if it is desired to connect with a drain or sewer provided for the drainage of a highway and vested in the highway authority, the consent of the highway authority must first be obtained: the highway authority will normally be the county council. A public sewer may be used to take surface water from a highway, but that does not affect its status as a public sewer, nor does the fact that house drains may in the past have been connected (probably unlawfully) with a highway drain convert such highway drain into a public sewer (*Rickarby* v *New Forest RDC* (1910) 26 TLR 586). It is only to public sewers that drains or sewers may be connected as of right.

Rivers

2.11 If it is desired to discharge effluent into a watercourse the consent of the National Rivers Authority must be obtained for making of a new or altered discharge of trade or sewage effluent under section 108 of the Water Act 1989. Consents may be granted subject to conditions. If the applicant objects to the conditions or has his application refused he can appeal to the Secretary of State (Water Act 1989, Schedule 12). If a person causes or knowingly permits the discharge of effluent into a watercourse without the permission of the NRA he commits an offence under section 107 of the 1989 Act.

The sea

2.12 A private landowner has at common law no legal right to discharge his sewage or other polluting matter to the sea; indeed, as the Crown originally owned the foreshore between high and low tides, he might not have any legal right to take his drain or sewer as far as the water. However, even if such a right can be acquired, and at the present day the Crown's rights have in many cases been sold or leased to local authorities or private landowners, it seems that the discharge of sewage by means of a pipe into the sea is subject to the same control of the NRA (Water Act 1989; see definition of 'controlled waters' in section 103 thereof). There must also be no nuisance caused as a consequence, and no breach of a local bye-law made by a sea fisheries committee prohibiting the discharge of matter detrimental to sea fish or sea fishing (Sea Fisheries Regulations Act 1966, section 5). If effluent discharging into the sea does cause a nuisance, any person harmed thereby can take proceedings for an injunction and/or damages, as in *Foster* v *Warblington UDC* [1906] 1 KB 648, where guests at a banquet were poisoned from oysters taken from a bed which had been affected by sewage.

Trade effluents

2.13 In the case of a proposed discharge of 'trade effluent', the special controls of the Public Health (Drainage of Trade Premises) Act 1937, as amended by the Control of Pollution Act 1974 and the Water Act 1989, Schedule 8 apply. 'Trade effluent' is defined in the Act of 1937 as meaning 'any liquid, either with or without particles of matter in suspension therein, which is wholly or in part produced by the course of any trade or industry carried on at trade premises, and, in relation to any trade premises, means any such liquid as aforesaid which is so produced in the course of any trade or industry carried on at those premises, but does not include domestic sewage' (1937 Act, section 14(1)).

Liquid produced 'solely in the course of laundering articles' is not normally trade effluent within this definition, being excluded expressly by section 4(4) of the Act, but the Secretary of State for the Environment may by order direct that this exemption shall not apply to laundry premises specified in the order. 'Trade premises' are not defined in the Act, but the term means any premises used or intended to be used for carrying on any trade or industry; under section 63 of the Public Health Act 1961 it is clear that effluent from premises used for agricultural or horticultural purposes, or for scientific research or experiment, are to be treated as trade premises for these purposes.

2.14 Where it is intended to discharge trade effluent as defined above into a public sewer, consent has first to be obtained from the sewerage undertaker. This is done by the owner or occupier of the premises serving on the undertaker a 'trade effluent notice'. This must specify (in writing) the nature or composition of the proposed effluent, the maximum quantity to be discharge in any one day, and the highest proposed rate of discharge of the effluent. This notice (for which there is no standard form) is then treated by the undertaker as an application for their consent to the proposed discharge. No effluent may then be discharged for a period of two months (or such less time as may be agreed by the undertaker). A decision, when given by the undertaker, may be a refusal to permit the discharge or a consent thereto, and in the latter case a consent may be given subject to conditions as to a number of matters 'including a payment by the occupier of the trade premises of charges for the reception and disposal of the effluent', as specified in section 59 of the Public Health Act 1961. These conditions may be varied (not more frequently than once every two years) by direction given by the sewerage undertaker. The owner or occupier of trade premises has a right of appeal to the Director General of Water Services against a refusal of consent to a discharge, against the conditions imposed in such a consent, or against a direction subsequently given varying the conditions (1937 Act, section 3, 1961 Act, section 66, Water Act 1989, Schedule 8), and such a direction may now be given varying the conditions relating to any discharge (even one made before the passing of the 1937 Act; 1974 Act, sections 43 and 44).

2.15 In practice, however, it is frequently desirable for an industrialist's professional advisers to discuss disposal of trade effluent with the officers of the sewerage undertaker, with a view to an agreement being entered into between the owner of the premises and the undertaker under section 7 of the 1937 Act. This will avoid the need to serve a trade effluent notice, and better terms can often be obtained by negotiation than by the more formal procedure of the trade effluent notice. The contents of any such agreement becomes public property, as a copy has to be kept at the sewerage undertaker's offices and made available for inspection and copying by any person (1989 Act, Schedule 8).

Water supply

2.16 The water supply authority will be the local water undertaker*, but where before 1989 supply was made by a statutory water company this will remain in existence (Water Act 1989, Chapter VI). The statutory water companies may have their own private Acts of Parliament regulating their affairs. Readers dealing in practice with a particular water undertaking should ascertain whether there are any local statutory variations.

Rights to connection

2.17 If the owner or occupier of premises within the area served by a water undertaker wishes to have a supply for *domestic purposes,* he must give at least 14 days' notice to the undertaker and lay a supply pipe (i.e. a pipe leading from the 'communication pipe' to his premises) at his own expense; if the supply pipe passes through any property belonging to another owner, his consent must be obtained in the form of an express easement or a licence (Chapter 3). The 'communication pipe' (i.e. that part of the pipe serving the premises which leads from the main to the boundary of the street in which the main is laid or to the stopcock) must then be laid by the undertaker, and they must connect the supply pipe with the communication pipe (Water Act 1989, Chapter II), and thereupon provide a supply of water (*ibid*, section 45). However, the owner will not be entitled to a supply from a trunk main if his fittings do not comply with the undertaker's bye-laws. The undertaker will also have an excuse for not providing a supply if such failure is due to the carrying out of necessary works' (*ibid*, section 51). Any breaking up of streets must be effected by the undertakers and not by the owner requiring the supply.

2.18 This assumes of course that the water main in the nearest street is within a reasonable distance from the house or other premises to be served. Where the main is not readily available, the owner of the premises may serve a requisition on the undertaker requiring them to extend their mains. (Water Act 1989, section 40). Where such a notice is served the water undertaker may require the owner to undertake to pay an annual sum not exceeding the amount (if any) by which the water charges payable for the use during that year of that main are exceeded by the annual borrowing costs of a loan of the amount required for the provision of that main. Such payments may be levied for a maximum of 12 years following the provision of the main (1989 Act, section 41). Provided those conditions have been satisfied, the water undertaker must extend their main within a period of 3 months (1989 Act, section 40).

Non-domestic premises

2.19 Owners or occupiers of premises requiring a supply of water for industrial or other (non-domestic) purposes must come to terms for a supply with the undertakers or failing agreement according to terms determined by the Director General of Water Services (1989 Act, section 46).

Gas supply

2.20 The gas industry was privatized in 1986 and gas is now supplied by a single company (British Gas plc).

2.21 If the owner or occupier of premises requires a supply of gas for any purpose (not necessarily domestic), he must serve a notice on British Gas at one of their local offices specifying the premises, and the day on which it is desired the service shall begin – and a reasonable time must be given (Gas Act

1986, section 10). The owner or occupier has to pay the cost of any pipe that may be laid upon the property of the owner or in the possession of the occupier, and for so much of any pipe as may be laid for a greater distribution distance than 30ft (9.144m*) from any of the company's pipes. The company must comply with such a request, but only if the premises are within 25yd (22.680m) of any of their mains not being a main used for a separate supply for industrial purposes or for conveying gas in bulk.

2.22 Once premises have been so connected to a gas main, the company must give a supply of gas (on the usual charges), unless the failure was due to circumstances not within their control. The company is not obliged to give a supply of gas for any purpose other than lighting or domestic use in any case where the capacity of the main is insufficient for the purpose, unless a special agreement has been entered into (Gas Act 1986, section 10(7).

Electricity supply

2.23 The Electricity Act 1989† provides for the privatizing of the generation and supply of electricity. The Secretary of State is authorized to license persons to generate, transmit and supply electricity in designated areas (1989 Act, section 6).

2.24 Under section 16 of the 1989 Act, the licensed public electricity supplier for an area is under a duty to give a supply to premises where requested by the owner or occupier (who must serve a notice specifying the premises, the date supply should commence, the maximum power which may be required and the minimum period for which the supply is required). Where such a request necessitates the provision of electrical lines or plant by the public electricity supplier they may require any expenses reasonably incurred in providing the supply to be paid by the consumer requesting the supply (1989 Act, section 19). Any dispute arising out of the above obligations may be referred by either the consumer or supplier to the Director General of Electricity Supply for resolution (1989 Act, section 23).

Telephones

2.25 The Telecommunications Act 1984 provided for the privatization of British Telecommunications. Today consumers can obtain telecommunication services from British Telecommunications plc or other licensed operators (e.g. Mercury Communications) (Telecommunications Act 1984, section 7). No statutory provisions regulate the provision of connections to telephone lines and each consumer must make his own contractual arrangements with the telecommunications operator he selects.

Construction of mains

2.26 All the utility undertakings have inherent powers to negotiate on terms with private landowners for the grant of easements or 'wayleaves' (Chapter 3) to enable them to place mains, cables, wires, apparatus, and so on over or under privately owned land. They also have powers to break open public streets for the purpose of constructing mains. Water and sewerage undertakers (Water Act 1989, Schedule 19), British Gas plc (Gas Act 1986, Schedule 3), electricity suppliers (Electricity Act 1989, Schedule 16) and licensed telecommunications operators (Telecommunications Act 1984, Schedule 2) all have statutory powers enabling them to place such mains and apparatus in private land, without the

---

*A company appointed for a designated area of England and Wales by the Secretary of State (Water Act 1989, section 11).

*The Act says 30ft exactly. All conversions in this article are therefore to the nearest millimetre.

†This Act is on the statute book, but at the time of preparing this edition (October 1989) the Act had not been brought into operation.

consent of the landowner or occupier concerned, on payment of proper compensation. Private persons have no such compulsory rights, although rights may be compulsorily acquired for an oil or other pipeline under the Pipelines Act 1962.

2.27 All the utility undertakers can also be authorized, without the consent of the landowner, to place their mains, apparatus, etc., on 'controlled land' (land forming part of a street or highway maintainable or prospectively maintainable at public expense – paras 3.01 ff) or in land between the boundary of such a highway and any improvement line prescribed for the street (Public Utilities Street Works Act 1950).

3 Private streets

3.01 It is not within the scope of this study to describe the whole law governing the making up of a private street by county councils at the expense of the frontagers to such a street, but the special rules that regulate the construction of a building in a 'private street' can be outlined.

Definition

3.02 A private street may or may not be a highway (i.e. any way, footpath, bridlepath, or carriageway over which members of the public have rights to pass and repass), but the word 'private' means, not that it is necessarily closed to the public (although it may be), but that the street has not been adopted by a highway authority, and therefore it is not maintainable by them on behalf of the public. It must also be a 'street', an expresion which has not been precisely defined, but which includes a cul-de-sac, lane, or passage (Highways Act 1980, section 331(1)). This does not mean, however, that every country road is a street; in a leading case, it was said by Pollock, Master of the Rolls, that

> 'it appears to me that what one has to find before one can determine that the highway in question is a street, is that the highway has become a street in the ordinary acceptation of that word, because by reason of the number of houses, their continuity and their proximity to one another, what would be a road or highway has been converted into a street' (*Attorney General* v *Laird* [1925] 1 Ch 318 at p 329).

Advance payments code

3.03 As a general principle, before a new building may be erected in a new street as explained above, the developer must either pay to the local authority or secure to their satisfaction (by means of a bond or mortgage etc.) a sum equivalent to the estimated cost, apportioned to the extent of the frontage of the proposed building to the private street, of carrying out street works to such an extent that the street would be adopted by the highway authority (the advance payments code – Highways Act 1980 section 221). 'Street works' means sewering, levelling, paving, metalling, flagging, channelling, making good, and lighting. The standards required are not specified in the legislation, but clearly they must not be unreasonably stringent. In general, the standard prevailing for similar streets in the authority's district is required.

Section 38 of Highways Act 1980

3.04 However, the necessity to pay or give security in advance of the building work being started can be avoided if an agreement has been entered into with the local authority under section 38 of the Highways Act 1980, pursuant to an

exception from the general principle contained in section 221 (4)(a) of the Act.

3.05 Under section 38, the local authority may enter into an agreement with the developer of land on either side or both sides of a private street; the authority can agree to adopt the street as a highway maintainable at public expense when all the street works have been carried out to their satisfaction, and the developer agrees to carry them out within a stated time. If the works are not so carried out, the local authority can still use their statutory powers to carry out the works (or to complete them), at the expense of the frontagers; it is therefore customary for the developer to enter into a bond for his performance with a bank or an insurance company.

3.06 Such an agreement takes the street, or the part of the street to which the agreement relates, outside the operation of the above general principle. The developer can then sell building plots or completed houses 'free of road charges' to purchasers. Though the street may not have been made up at the time of purchase, the purchaser is protected, as the developer has agreed to make up the street; if he fails to carry out his promise, the local authority will be able to sue on the bond and recover sufficient* to pay for street works expenses without having to charge them to the frontagers. If the authority should proceed against the frontagers, they in turn normally have a remedy against the developer and on the bond, but this may depend on the terms of their purchase.

3.07 The architect is not necessarily professionally concerned in such matters,but it is suggested that it is his duty to be aware of the potential expense to his client of building in an unmade private street, and he should advise his client to consult his solicitor in any difficult case, or where the exact legal position is not clear.

4 Grants

4.01 Below are considered circumstances in which a building owner is able to obtain a grant from the local authority (in this case, the district council) for some alteration or extension of his dwelling. All statutory provisions considered here concern dwelling-houses (or flats and so on), but it may be possible in development areas and enterprise zones (Local Government, Planning and Land Act 1980) to obtain grants for industrial development.

Grants under the Housing Act 1985†

4.02 There are now three basic kinds of grant under this statute: an *improvement grant* for provision of new dwellings by conversion of existing houses and other buildings, an *intermediate grant* for bringing existing dwellings up to a standard of amenity, and a *repairs grant*. A *special grant* also may be obtained for houses in multiple occupation. Similar grants were payable under earlier Housing Acts, but these are now replaced by the 1985 Act.

Improvement grants

4.03 An improvement grant is discretionary; it cannot be claimed from the local authority (the district council) as of right. A claim may be made by any person who is the owner

---

*Provided the bond was for a sufficient amount; inflation may cause problems here.

†Currently (October 1989) the Government has before Parliament a new Local Government and Housing Bill. The Bill, *inter alia*, proposes a new system of grants to enable elderly people to remain in their homes. Additionally, new arrangements for grants to repair and improve the external fabric of whole blocks of accommodation are proposed.

in fee simple (Chapter 1) or of a leasehold interest (of which at least five years remain unexpired), or by a tenant holding under a Rent Act protected tenancy, or even by a council house 'secure' tenant. The claim is for financial assistance from the local authority for improvement* of an existing dwelling, or for the conversion of a house or other building into two or more dwellings, or for the conversion of an 'other' building into a single dwelling. In each case the dwelling so improved or provided by conversion must, when the work has been completed, measure up to the minister's *standard* (DOE Circular 21/80). This means that the dwelling must:

1. Be substantially free from damp.
2. Have adequate natural lighting and ventilation in each habitable room.
3. Have adequate and safe provision throughout for artificial lighting, and have sufficient electric socket outlets for the safe and proper functioning of domestic appliances.
4. Be provided with adequate drainage facilities.
5. Be in a stable structural condition.
6. Have satisfactory internal arrangement.
7. Have satisfactory facilities for preparing and cooking food.
8. Be provided with adequate facilities for heating.
9. Have proper facilities for the storage of fuel (where necessary) and for the storage of refuse.
10. Have in the roof space thermal insulation sufficient to give, for the relevant structure, a U value of $0.4\,W/m^2\,°C$.

In addition the 1985 Act states (section 468) that the dwelling must provide satisfactory housing accommodation for at least 30 years (unless the local authority agree to a shorter period), it must be provided with all the standard amenities (see para 4.09), and it must be in reasonable repair (ignoring internal decorative repair).

4.04 Further, it is provided in section 469 that no application for an improvement grant (and a similar provision applies to intermediate grants) may be entertained if the rateable value of the dwelling before *improvement* exceeds £400 in Greater London or £225 elsewhere. If the works proposed are for a conversion the maximum rateable values are £600 in Greater London or £350 elsewhere (SI 1977/1213). These limits do not apply to dwellings in housing action areas (1980 Act, Schedule 12).

4.05 Satisfactory accommodation to this standard must be provided as the result of the improvement. In a particular case the local authority may waive any of the requirements of the *standard*, if it appears to them that the applicant for grant would have insufficient resources to carry out the improvement if he were not to receive a grant.

4.06 Normally the grant should be applied for (on the approved form) and a decision on it obtained before the improvement work starts, but the local authority may consider an application even after work has begun if they are satisfied 'that there were good reasons for beginning the works before the application was approved' (1985 Act, Section 465).

Amount

4.07 The exact amount of the grant is at the local authority's discretion, but they may pay not more than a prescribed limit

(1985 Act, section 471). This prescribed limit is calculated by reference to the following factors:

1. First the 'estimated expense' must be calculated; this means the proper actual expenditure required for the execution of the works, including professional fees, but not including the applicant's own time, etc., on a 'do-it-yourself' job. Not more than 50% of this expenditure may be incurred on repairs or replacements.
2. Second, the estimated expense may not exceed the 'eligible expense'. Unless special conditions† apply, this will normally be £2400 for each dwelling improved or provided.
3. The actual grant will then be an 'appropriate percentage' of the estimated expense or the eligible expense (whichever is the *less*). This percentage is 50% in most cases, but it is 60% if the premises are in an area declared by the local authority to be a general improvement area and 75% if the premises are within a housing action area (see 1985 Act, section 509).

4.08 The grant will not normally be paid until the work has been completed, but it may be paid by instalments as the work proceeds (1985 Act, section 511). There are now elaborate provisions requiring the deposit of certificates of owner occupation or availability for letting before an application can be approved, and also conditions applicable to the use of a building, or to the rent at which it may be let, wherever a grant has been made.

Intermediate grants

4.09 Intermediate grants (formerly known as standard grants) are in many ways similar to improvement grants, but they can be demanded as of right; if the statutory provisions are met, the local authority cannot refuse to pay a grant (1985 Act, section 479). They are claimed in the same manner as improvement grants, but they apply only to specified improvements made to a dwelling existing *before* 3 October 1961. These works are the provision of one or more of the following standard amenities, in so far as the dwelling in question does not have them. The maximum grant for each amenity is shown below, but the actual amount of the grant payable is calculated by reference to the actual expense, limited to an 'eligible expense' of the cost of the various items specified below, *plus* not more than £2000 for repairs and replacements. The grant is then the appropriate percentage of that total eligible expense (see para 4.07).

1. Fixed bath or shower £340.
2. Hot and cold water supply at a fixed bath or shower £430.
3. Wash-hand basin £130.
4. Hot and cold water supply at a wash-hand basin £230.
5. Sink £340.
6. Hot and cold water supply at a sink £290.
7. Water closet £515.

In some cases a grant may be made for the provision of some of the amenities, and special rules apply to provision for registered disabled persons. Higher amounts are acceptable for London (1985 Act, section 508).

4.10 When an intermediate grant is claimed, the authority must be satisfied that when the work has been carried out the dwelling will be fit for human habitation, unless it seems reasonable in all the circumstances to make a grant, although the dwelling will not reach that standard (1985 Act, section 476).

---

*An expression which is defined (Housing Act 1985, sections 467 and 525) to include alteration and enlargement and such works of repair or replacement as are needed for the purpose of enabling the dwelling to attain the relevant standard as to the amenities available, and in relation to a dwelling for a disabled person includes the doing of works required for making it suitable for his accommodation, welfare, or employment.

†In special cases this may be increased to 70%: SI 1982/1205. This will be a higher amount in certain circumstances, see the Grants by Local Authority (Eligible Expense Limits) Order 1983, SI 1983/613.

Repairs grants

4.11 The decision to make a grant towards *repairs* is normally at the discretion of the local authority. But a repairs grant will be mandatory on the local authority in so far as the repairs are required in order to comply with a notice served under section 189 of the Housing Act 1985 (requiring a house to be made fit for human habitation). The authority must be satisfied that the works proposed are of a substantial and structural character (1985 Act, section 491). The amount of the grant will be the appropriate percentage (para 4.07) of the eligible expense, which latter figure may not exceed £800.

Special grants

4.12 Special housing grants, limited to the estimated expense but computed on the intermediate grant scales, are paid for provision of the standard amenities or means of escape in case of fire, for houses in multiple occupation (1985 Act, section 483), i.e. any house which 'is occupied by persons who do not form a single household' (Housing Act 1985, section 525). These grants are normally discretionary, but are mandatory on the local authority in so far as the works are required to meet a notice served under section 352 of the 1985 Act (requiring certain facilities to be provided).

Agriculture

4.13 Under the Hill Farming and Livestock Rearing Acts 1946 and 1959, a grant may be obtained from the Minister of Agriculture, Fisheries and Food towards the cost of improving a dwelling as part of a scheme prepared with 'a view to the rehabilitation of livestock rearing land'.

Conversion of closets

4.14 A grant not exceeding half the cost may be claimed towards the expenditure incurred by the owners of a dwelling in converting an earth or pail closet to a WC, either pursuant to a notice served by the authority, or where it is proposed to undertake the work voluntarily. In the latter case the grant is payable at the local authority's discretion (Building Act 1984, section 66).

Clean air

4.15 Where a private dwelling (an expression which includes part of a house) is situated within a smoke control area, a grant may be claimed from the local authority amounting to 70% of the expenditure reasonably incurred in adapting any fireplace or fireplaces in the dwelling to enable them to burn only 'authorized fuels' such as gas, electricity, coke, or specially prepared solid fuels (Clean Air Act 1956, section 12, an amended by the Local Government, Planning and Land Act 1980). A similar grant may be obtainable for certain religious buildings (ibid, section 15).

Historic buildings

4.16 In the case of a building of special historic or architectural interest, whether or not it is 'listed' as such (under section 54 of the Town and Country planning Act 1971), a grant towards the cost of repair, restoration, or maintenance may be obtained from the local authority under the Local Authorities (Historic Buildings) Act 1962, but such grants are entirely discretionary and no amounts are specified in the legislation. Grants under the Housing Act (above) also may be payable; the maxima for improvement grants are higher in such cases.

Airport noise

4.17 Under the Civil Aviation Act 1982, section 79, a grant may be obtained from the manager of the aerodrome (a subsidiary company of BAA plc) for a building 'near' an aerodrome towards the cost of insulating it, or any part of it, against noise attributable to the use of the aerodrome. The details of such grants are specified in schemes approved by the Secretary of State for Transport, and further particulars are obtainable from the Secretary of State or BAA plc (130 Wilton Road, London SW1V 1LQ)*.

Water supply

4.18 Where a local authority has required a house to be connected to a piped water supply and the expense is likely to exceed £60, the owner would be best advised not to carry out the work himself, as the authority would then be empowered to do the work itself in default. It would be able to recover from the owner no more than £60 towards it expenses (Public Health Act 1936, section 138, as amended by section 30 of the Water Act 1945 and section 78 of the Public Health Act 1961). The local authority also has discretionary powers to make a grant towards all or any part of the expenses incurred in the provision of a separate service pipe for the supply of water for any house which has a piped supply from a main, but which does not have a separate service pipe (Housing Act 1985, section 523).

Home insulation

4.19 Under the Housing Act 1985, section 521, a grant not exceeding £69 or 66⅔% of the cost† (whichever is the *less*) may be claimed from the local authority by the occupier of a dwelling towards the cost of (1) insulating the roof space, (2) insulating the cold water tank and pipes in the roof space, *and* (3) providing a jacket for the hot water tank. A grant will be paid only by a local authority which has been put in funds by the central Government, so an applicant may find he is put on a waiting list.

5 Housing associations and societies

5.01 A housing association may be formed on a charitable basis for provision of houses for those in need, or for special groups of persons, such as elderly or handicapped, in a specified area. Such an association may also be constituted by an industrial firm for housing its employees, or by a group of persons proposing to build its own homes by voluntary (or part voluntary) and co-operative labour. Frequently such associations are strictly housing societies‡ having acquired corporate personality by registration with the Registrar of Friendly Societies. However, a housing association (which may be incorporated as a company under the Companies Acts, or by other means) which complies with the provisions of the Housing Acts (see definition in section 1 of the Housing Associations Act 1985) and, in particular, does not trade for profit, is entitled to be considered for certain benefits under the Housing Acts. Tenants of a housing association who have occupied their homes for at least five years will have a right to purchase the dwelling under Part V of the Housing Act 1985.

---

*The only aerodromes to which this provision applies at present are Heathrow and Gatwick (SI 1989/247 and SI 1989/248).
†These amounts are increased to £90 and 90% in the case of occupiers 'in special need'.
‡The term 'housing association' is the wider one including a housing society which is a special kind of housing association.

Benefits

5.02 First, the association may be able to obtain 'assistance' from the local housing authority in whose area they propose to build. This may mean making arrangements so that the association can improve existing council-owned houses, or acquisition of land by the local authority, which can then be sold or leased to the association for building houses; or, with the consent of the Secretary of State for the Environment, the authority may make grants or loans on mortgage (at favourable rates of interest – usually 0.25% above the ruling rate charged to local authorities by the Public Works Loan Board) to the association to enable them to build houses. They may be able to obtain a grant from the Housing Corporation (or in Wales a separate organization called Housing for Wales, Part II of the Housing Act 1988) towards the expenses of forming and running the association (Housing Act 1988, section 50). Registered housing associations may also be able to obtain grants from the Secretary of State where the associations' activities have incurred a liability for income or corporation tax (Housing Act 1988, section 54).

5.03 When the local authority has agreed to make arrangements of one of these kinds, houses provided as a result will attract annual subsidies from the central Government; these are payable to the local authority in the first instance, but the authority must pass on an equivalent amount to the housing association.

Housing Corporation loans

5.04 These provisions depend on the goodwill of the local authority; a housing association cannot insist on being given assistance. As an alternative, an association may be able to get help by ways of loans for obtaining land and general advice from the Housing Corporation, a public body set up under the Housing Act 1964.

5.05 A loan of money to an association from the Housing Corporation has an additional advantage in that the mortgage given by the association to secure such a loan may be deferred to a mortgage granted by a building society, thereby enabling the association to obtain better terms from the building society (Housing Associations Act 1985, section 63). However, houses provided by an association with the co-operation in one form or another of the Housing Corporation do not attract government subsidies.

Setting up a housing association

5.06 In practice people proposing to form a housing society would be well advised to obtain advice from the Housing Corporation (Maple House, 149 Tottenham Court Rd, London W1P 0BN), and those proposing to set up an association should get in touch with the National Federation of Housing Associations (175 Gray's Inn Road, London WC1X 8UP).

6 Special premises

6.01 If an architect is designing any kind of building, he must take into account the controls exercised under town and country planning legislation (Chapter 14) and under the Building Regulations (Chapter 15); and he must consider the question of sewerage and mains services and the other matters discussed in this chapter. But if his building is of a specialized kind, or is to be used for some specialized purpose, additional controls may have to be considered; the more usual types of special control are outlined below.

Factories

6.02 The Factories Act 1961 imposes an *a posteriori* control over certain constructional matters in a factory (Factories Act 1961, section 175, as amended by SI 1983/978); there is no special control over plans (other than normal controls of the planning legislation and the Building Regulations), but if the requirements of the Act are not met in a particular factory, the occupier or (in a tenement factory) the owner will be liable to be prosecuted for an offence.* Many of these requirements relate to the use and fencing of machinery, keeping walls and floors clean, and so on, and as such they are not of direct concern to the architect.

6.03 A fire certificate† will have to be obtained if more than 20 persons are employed or more than 10 persons are employed above (or below) the ground floor (Fire Precautions (Factories, Offices, Shops and Railway Premises) Order 1976, SI 1976/2009). If a certificate is not required, certain less stringent fire precautions must be observed (Fire Precautions (Non-Certified Factories, Offices, Shops and Railway Premises) Regulations 1976, SI 1976/2010).

6.04 The effluent from a factory's sewers or drains may well be 'trade effluent' and will then be subject to the special control of the Public Health (Drainage of Trade Premises) Act 1937, amended by the Water Act 1989, Schedule 8 (para 2.13).

6.05 Under the Clean Air Acts 1956 and 1968, factories are subject to several constructional controls operating quite independently of the Building Regulations, but administered by the same local authorities (district councils). Thus any furnace installed in a building which will be used to burn pulverized fuel, or to burn any other solid matter at a rate of 100 lb (45.36 kg) per hour or more, or any liquid or gaseous matter at a rate of 1 250 000 Btu/h (366.38 kW) or more, must be provided with plant for arresting emissions of grit and dust which has been approved by the local authority or has been installed with plans and specifications submitted to and approved by the local authority (Clean Air Act 1968, section 6). Limits are set by regulations for the rates of emission of grit and dust, and there are certain exemptions from the provisions of section 3 (see sections 2 and 4 of the 1968 Act and the Clean Air (Emissions of Grit and Dust from Furnaces) Regulations 1971).‡ In addition, a furnace of a type to which the section applies (see 1968 Act, section 6(10), as amended by the Energy Act 1983) may not be used in a building unless the height of the chimney serving the furnace has been approved by the local authority (1968 Act, section 6).

Public houses and restaurants

6.06 A public house or other premises used for the sale of intoxicating liquor either on or off the premises must be licensed by the local magistrates under the Licensing Act 1953. A new 'on-licence' may not be granted unless the premises are in the opinion of the magistrates 'structurally' adapted to the class of licence required (Licensing Act 1964, section 4(2)). The magistrates themselves are the final judges of what is or is not structurally adapted. In the case of a licence for a restaurant or guest house or the like, an application may be refused by the magistrates on the grounds that the premises are not 'suitable or convenient' for the use contemplated (ibid, section 98). A restaurant licence may be

*Sometimes by the district council, but more frequently (according to the section under which the proceedings are brought) by HM Inspector of Factories, who is now subject to the supervision of the Health and Safety Executive.
†See further under 'Hotels', para 6.10.
‡SI 1971/162.

granted only for premises structurally adapted and bona fide used or intended to be used for the provision of 'the customary main meal for the accommodation of persons frequenting the premises' (ibid, section 94). Other alterations to licensed premises, e.g. where there will be increased facilities for drinking, must be the subject of a formal consent obtained from the magistrates (ibid, section 20).

6.07 These controls are operated at the discretion of the magistrates. In practice they will normally not approve an application until they have received a report on the premises (or the proposed premises) from suitably qualified persons, such as an officer of the local firebrigade, an environmental health officer, and often a senior police officer. But such requirements are at their discretion, and details vary among different benches.

6.08 Under section 20 of the Local Government (Miscellaneous Provisions) Act 1976, as amended by section 4 of the Disabled Persons Act 1981, the local authority may by notice require the owner or occupier of any premises used for public entertainment or exhibitions or as a betting office to provide and maintain in suitable positions a specified reasonable number of sanitary appliances for the use of persons frequenting the premises. When complying with such a notice, provision must be made, as far as is practicable and reasonable in the circumstances, for the needs of disabled people (Chronically Sick and Disabled Persons Act 1970, section 6). If a 'refreshment house' is to be kept open late at night, a special licence will be required from the district council under the Refreshment Houses Acts 1860 to 1967.

Music and dancing

6.09 If a public entertainment is provided at any place there must be a licence issued by the local district council. 'Place' is not defined in the Act but it does not apply to music in the course of religious worship or to any entertainment provided at a pleasure fair or which takes place wholly or mainly in the open air. Public entertainment for this purpose includes 'public dancing or music or any other public entertaining of a like kind'. This was introduced by the Local Government (Miscellaneous Provisions) Act 1982; formerly music and dancing licences were issued by the magistrates.

Hotels

6.10 A fire certificate under the Fire Precautions Act 1971 is required for hotels (see SI 1972/236 and 238). An application for a certificate must be made to the fire authority in respect of any new or existing hotel, and this application must be made on the prescribed form (copies of which will be obtainable from the fire authority, i.e. the county council). The authority may ask for plans of the building in support of the application, and they will carry out an inspection. They may then require steps to be taken as to the provision and availability of means of escape in case of fire and as to the means for fighting fire and giving warning in case of fire. If and when they are satisfied as to these matters, a fire certificate will be issued, which may itself impose requirements as to these and related matters. A right of appeal to the local magistrates lies against requirements so imposed by the fire authority. It is a criminal offence under the Act to put premises to a 'designated use' (this includes a hotel) unless there is a valid fire certificate in force or an application is pending, and it is similarly an offence to fail to comply with any requirement imposed by a certificate.

Hotels will, of course, also have to comply with the legal provisions about intoxicating liquor (para 6.06), and possibly in relation to music and dancing (para 6.09).

Petroleum

6.11 Any premises used for keeping petroleum spirit must be licensed by the county council; otherwise the occupier is guilty of an offence (Petroleum Consolidation Act 1928, section 1). The only exception is when the spirit is kept in separate vessels containing not more than 1 pint (0.57 litre), with the total quantity not exceeding 3 gals (13.64 litres). Detailed conditions are usually imposed when such a licence is granted, and these normally follow the model conditions recommended by the Home Office. Petroleum licences are usually renewable each year at a fee (ibid, section 2).

Theatres and cinemas

6.12 Theatres are subject to control under the Theatres Act 1968. No premises may be used for the public performance of a play except in accordance with the terms of a licence granted by the local authority,* and in granting such a licence, conditions may be imposed as to structure, exits, safety curtains, and so on, but not so as to impose any censorship on the plays given in the theatre.

6.13 Similarly, showing cinematograph films at an exhibition of moving pictures (Cinemas Act 1985, section 21) must be licensed by the local authority, and structural matters will normally be provided for in the licence (Cinemas Act 1985, section 1). The local authority is the district council.

Shops and offices

6.14 Shops, offices, and railway premises where persons other than close relatives of the employer (1963 Act, sections 1 and 2) are employed to work are subject to control by the district council, under the Offices, Shops and Railway Premises Act 1963, provided the time worked at the premises exceeds 21 hours a week (ibid, section 3). This Act provides for such matters as cleanliness, temperature within rooms, ventilation, lighting, and the provision of WCs (if necessary for both sexes), washing accommodation, and so on. The standards specified are detailed, and the Act and regulations made thereunder should be referred to by architects designing such a building. See, in particular, the Sanitary Conveniences Regulations 1964† and the Washing Facilities Regulations 1964.‡ A fire certificate or special fire precautions are required for shops, offices, railway premises, and factories (para 6.03).

Food premises

6.15 In addition, if any part of the premises is used for a business involving food, the more stringent provisions of the Food Hygiene (General) Regulations 1970§ made under the Food Act 1984 must be observed. Premises used as a slaughterhouse or a knacker's yard for the slaughter of animals need to be licensed under the Slaughterhouses Act 1974.

Miscellaneous

6.16 Licences from the district council are also required for the storage or manufacture of rag flock (Rag Flock and Other Filling Materials Act 1951), for the use of premises as a shop for the sale of pet animals (Pet Animals Act 1951), for storage or sale of scrap metal (Scrap Metal Dealers Act 1964), for boarding cats and dogs (Animal Boarding Establishments Act

---

*Theatres Act 1968, section 12 and Schedule 1. The local authorities responsible for administering these provisions are the county councils and in London the city/borough councils (see section 18).
†SI 1964/966, as amended by SI 1982/827.
‡SI 1964/965, as amended by SI 1982/827.
§SI 1970/1172.

1963) or for guard dog kennels (Guard Dogs Act 1975), and for keeping a riding establishment (Riding Establishment Acts 1964 and 1970). Nursing homes must now be registered by the Secretary of State (Registered Homes Act 1984, Part II). In all these cases the suitability or otherwise of the premises for the particular purpose may be an issue in the grant or refusal of the licence. Caravan sites used for human habitation also need a licence in addition to planning permission (Caravan Sites and Control of Development Act 1960, Part 1), and detailed conditions as to hygiene and sanitary requirements are customarily imposed. In many districts it will also be necessary to obtain a licence from the council if premises are to be used as a sex shop or for the practice of tattooing or acupuncture or electrolysis or ear-piercing (Local Government (Miscellaneous Provisions) Act 1982). Closing orders may be made restricting the hours for the opening of take-away food shops and late night refreshment houses (1982 Act, sections 4 and 7).

13

Statutory Authorities in Scotland

ANGUS STEWART QC*

1 Introduction: Local government in Scotland

1.01 Local government in Scotland was reorganized by the Local Government (Scotland) Act 1973. Mainland Scotland has a two-tier administrative structure with 9 regions making up the top tier and 53 districts on the lower tier. The Western Isles, Orkney, and Shetland each have all-purpose islands councils exercising all functions which, on the mainland, are allocated between regional and district councils. The Act also provides for the creation, within each district and islands area, of community councils. Their role is mainly representative, and they have no statutory functions in the administration of local government.

1.02 All councils – regional, district, and islands – are directly elected. Members of all councils hold office for a four-year term. Elections are staggered so that district councillors are voted in mid-way through the regional term of office.

1.03 As in England local authorities are separate legal persons which perform certain functions laid down by statute, and the doctrine of ultra vires also applies in Scotland (Chapter 12, para 1.08) so that no authority may act outwith its statutory powers.

Officials and committees

1.04 Again, as in England, local authorities appoint officials and staff to enable them to carry out their statutory functions. The 1973 Act requires a regional authority to appoint a director of education, a director of social work and certain other officers. Otherwise it allows authorities a wide discretion in the matter of their internal organization. But in practice all authorities on the same level tend to be organized on broadly similar patterns of departmental responsibility. Each department comes under the jurisdiction of the appropriate committee of the authority. The top official, responsible for co-ordinating the various branches of an authority's activity, is generally styled 'Chief Executive'. 'Director of Finance' is the official in charge of overall financial management. There may be a Director of Administration or Director of Legal Services to supervise internal administration and act as legal adviser to the council in place of the old-style 'town clerk' or 'county clerk'. At district level, from the architect's point of view, the key official will be called something like 'Director of Planning and Building Control', the exact designation of the official and his department being a matter of choice for individual authorities. Certain officials, such as the assessor/poll tax registration officer and electoral registration officer, have specific statutory duties which they must perform regardless of any instructions from the authority.

Committees

1.05 Much of the work of the authority is, as in England, delegated to various committees. The implementation of policy is left to the appropriate service committee, such as the planning committee, the highways committee, and the education committee, which have delegated powers in the areas of their responsibility. In addition to standing committees such as these, the authority may also set up special committees from time to time to deal with particular problems as they arise.

1.06 In general all committees are composed of council members only. Officials are present at committee meetings to give advice when required, but without the right to vote.

Functions of local authorities

1.07 The major functions are now allocated by statute between regional and district authorities as follows:

Regional	District
Structure plans	Local plans
Highways	Housing (including improvement grants)
Transport, harbours, etc.	Planning permission
Water	Building control
Sewerage	Listed building consent and tree preservation

Lawyers going the Circuit

*In the first edition, this chapter was written by Andrew Grotrian.

Valuation	Designation of conservation
Poll tax	areas
Police	Improvement grants
Fire	Licensing
Social work	Environmental health
Education	Libraries
Parks	Allotments

There are certain exceptions to this scheme. The Borders and Lothian regions combine to form joint fire and police authorities. In the Borders, Highland, and Dumfries and Galloway areas, the regional council is responsible for planning and building control. The same regions are also responsible for all library services in their area. Certain water authorities have jurisdiction over areas which fall within the boundaries of adjoining regions. As has already been mentioned, islands councils exercise *all* local authority functions within their area. Certain areas have been designated as enterprise zones in terms of the Local Government Planning and Land Act 1980.

2   Connection to services

2.01 The 1973 Act is primarily concerned with the structure of local government and does not re-enact or spell out in detail the powers and functions which have been transferred from the old to the new authorities. The main local authority functions for present purposes are to be found in the Building (Scotland) Acts 1959–70, the Sewerage (Scotland) Act 1968, the Town and Country Planning (Scotland) Acts 1972–77. The Water (Scotland) Act 1980, the Civic Government (Scotland) Act 1982 and the Roads (Scotland) Act 1984. Under the Act of 1982 the Sheriff can authorize connections to services through other parts of a building in multiple ownership.

Sewers

2.02 The 1973 Act makes sewerage the responsibility of the regional authorities. The Sewerage (Scotland) Act 1968 details the powers and functions of those authorities in this area. The Act consolidates and simplifies all previous legislation, and introduces a statutory definition of 'drains' and 'sewers' which is the same as that used in England (Chapter 12, para 2.02).

2.03 The Act provides that all public sewers will continue to be vested in local authorities, as will various new sewers. Junctions to public sewers are also vested in local authorities. Thus if a private drain is joined to a sewer, it will be the local authority's responsibility to maintain the junction.

2.04 Sewerage authorities are obliged to provide public sewers as may be necessary for draining their area of domestic sewage, surface water, and trade effluent. The authority has to take public sewers to such a point as will enable owners of premises to connect their drains at reasonable cost. This is subject to the proviso that the authority need itself do nothing which is not practicable at a reasonable cost. Nevertheless, the responsibility for providing sewers is clearly that of the local authority, while the responsibility for installing drains in individual premises is that of the proprietor.

2.05 Local authorities have powers to construct, close, or alter sewers or sewage treatment works. Where they are not under an obligation to provide public sewers (i.e. where they cannot do so at reasonable cost), they may enter into an agreement on construction and taking over of sewers and treatment with any person they are satisfied is about to construct premises in their area. Where authorities are under an obligation to provide sewers, they may not enter into such agreements.

Drains

2.06 Any owner of premises is entitled to connect his drains or private sewer to a public sewer and to allow his drains to empty into a public sewer on giving the authority 28 days' notice. However, the authority may refuse permission or grant it subject to conditions. A proprietor may connect his drains to a sewer in a different local authority area, but he must first service notice on both authorities. The Secretary of State has powers to require the authority in whose area the premises are situated to pay for the service which the other authority is providing. Previously it was the proprietor who had to make any payment required.

2.07 Where a notice regarding connection of a drain or sewer to a public sewer is served on an authority, the authority has powers to direct the manner in which the junction is to be constructed and to supervise construction. The authority has the same powers in relation to any new drain or private sewer if it appears likely that the drain or sewer will be wanted by it to form part of the general system. Authorities are bound to meet the extra cost arising from implementation of their instructions. To allow supervision, three days' notice of the start of work must be given to the authority.

2.08 A local authority can also require defects in private drains and sewers to be remedied and may itself carry out the work if the proprietor fails to do so. Where the defect represents a health hazard, the authority is empowered to carry out emergency repairs on the basis of a 48-hour notice. The cost of repairs carried out by the authority can be recovered from proprietors.

2.09 Provisions relating to trade effluent, trade effluent notices and agreements, and so on, broadly similar to those contained in English legislation (Chapter 12, para 2.12), are also included in the Act.

2.10 Sewage discharged into a public sewer must not be of such a nature as to cause damage to the sewer or, through mixture with other sewage, to cause a nuisance.

2.11 Where a new development is proposed the responsibility for providing sewers rests with the sewerage authority, although this does not apply in the case of an individual house where all that is necessary is a drain or private sewer to connect with the public system. The situation may arise where a delay by the authority in fulfilling its duty holds up development. If a developer chooses to install sewers at his own expense, he will be able to recover from the authority only if, from the start, he adopts the correct procedure (*Lawrence Building Co* v *Lanarkshire County Council* [1977] SLT 110).

2.12 River Purification Boards have functions in relation to approving discharges of sewage and other effluent, the provision of septic tanks, etc.

Water supply

2.13 Legislation on water supply is consolidated in the Water (Scotland) Act 1980. Regional and islands councils are the authorities responsible for water supply. District councils have functions in connection with the supply of water to buildings. In terms of the 1980 Act persons erecting new buildings of any type are obliged to make adequate provisions to the satisfaction of the district authority for a supply of clean water for the domestic purposes of persons occupying or using the building. Local authorities may also require house owners to provide water supplies in, or if that is impracticable, immediately outside their houses.

2.14 Water authorities are under an obligation to provide supplies of wholesome water to every part of their regions

where a supply is required for domestic purposes and can be provided at reasonable cost. They are obliged to lay main water pipes so that buildings where domestic supplies are required can be connected at a reasonable cost. When a question arises as to whether water can be supplied in this manner to any area at a reasonable cost, the Secretary of State for Scotland must decide, if requested to do so by ten or more local electors.

2.15 The authorities are also obliged to supply water at reasonable terms for other than domestic purposes, provided that to do so would not prejudice their ability to supply water for domestic purposes.

2.16 The procedure for obtaining a water supply for domestic purposes in Scotland is regulated by the third schedule to the Water (Scotland) Act 1980, and is usually similar to that in England (Chapter 12, para 2.17). A period of 14 days' notice must be given to the authority of the intention to lay a supply pipe. The supply pipe is laid by the proprietor and then attached to the communication pipe by the authority.

Gas, electricity, and telephones

2.17 On these topics, reference should be made to Chapter 12, para 2.20 ff as what is said there applies also to Scotland. The Gas Act 1972 applies with minor modifications in Scotland as in England. Likewise the Electricity Act 1947 applies with small modifications. The North of Scotland Hydro-Electric Board (now Scottish Hydro) has particular functions in relation to economic development of rural areas. The costs of connection may be generously subsidized. Building control covers tanker-supplied gas storage tanks and pipes.

Construction of mains

2.18 Again the remarks on this topic in Chapter 12 (para 2.26) should be referred to. The term for a 'way-leave' in Scotland is 'servitude' (Chapter 8, para 3.08).

3 Private streets and footpaths

3.01 The law on roads, streets and footpaths is consolidated in the Roads (Scotland) Act 1984.

3.02 The Act defines roads as ways over which there is a public right of passage by any means, i.e. roads includes footpaths subject to a public sight of passage. Public roads are roads entered by regional and islands councils in their 'lists of public roads' and are roads which those authorities are bound to maintain. Private roads are roads which the authorities are not bound to maintain. The authorities can require frontagers to make up and maintain a private road. When a road has been properly made up, the council is bound to take it over and add it to the list of public roads if application is made by the requisite number of frontagers.

Footpaths

3.03 The above provisions apply to footpaths as well as vehicular routes. The authorities are also empowered to take over footpaths in new developments.

4 Grants

4.01 As in England various grants are obtainable by a proprietor in Scotland to assist him in alterations or improvements to his property. Discretionary improvement grants and standard grants are payable in Scotland under the Housing (Scotland) Act 1987. Although made under different legislation, these grants are payable on the same basis as in England, details of which are found in Chapter 12, para 4.01.

4.02 Various grants are available for improvement or rebuilding of agricultural workers' cottages. It is not proposed to examine these in detail, but it should be noted that special grants are available for the Highlands, islands, and crofting areas.

4.03 Many other grants are payable by various authorities, but it should be noted that the Public Health Act 1936 does not apply in Scotland. Grants for installation of WCs are available in the form of standard grants. The Local Authorities (Historic Buildings) Act does not apply in Scotland. The Clean Air Acts and the Airport Authority Act apply, and grants may be obtained under them where appropriate (Chapter 12, paras 4.15 and 4.17). A grant may be obtained as a standard grant for bringing a supply of piped water into a house for the first time. Assistance may be available to instal separate service pipes to houses sharing the same supply under section 233 of the Housing (Scotland) Act 1987.

5 Housing associations

5.01 As in England (Chapter 12, para 5.01 ff) housing associations in Scotland are entitled to various benefits under the Scottish Housing Act. The Secretary of State for Scotland may make advances to them, and they may also borrow money from the Public Works Loan Commissioners. The Scottish Special Housing Association has been reconstituted by the Housing (Scotland) Act 1988 under the name Scottish Homes.

6 Special considerations

6.01 In Scotland as well as in England (Chapter 12, para 6.01 ff) special considerations apply to certain types of building. The Factories Acts, the Offices, Shops and Railway Premises Act, and the Clean Air Acts all apply. Liquor licensing is operated under a separate statutory code, and the structural suitability of any premises is a question which may be considered by the Licensing Board for the district or islands area in which the premises are situated.

6.02 Scottish readers are advised to check all new legislation for applications and/or amendments to Scots law. For example, the Health and Safety at Work Act 1974 applies to Scotland, amending the Building (Scotland) Act 1959. Similarly the Control of Pollution Act 1974 has general application to Scotland (see section 106) and amends much other Scottish legislation of this kind. (See Chapters 12, 15 and 16.)

14

Planning Law

SIR DESMOND HEAP

Note

Throughout this chapter the following abbreviations are used:
TP = The Town and Country Planning Act 1990;
'The 1990 Act' = The Town and Country Planning Act 1990, except in Section 5 of this chapter where it means the Planning (Listed Buildings and Conservation Areas) Act 1990.

1 Introduction

1.01 Town and country planning control over the development of all land (including buildings) in England and Wales* is an administrative process deriving from the Town and Country Planning Act 1947. It has operated since 1 July 1948 and was brought about (to mention no other matter) for the simple reason that in England and Wales there is a limited amount of land for an increasing number of people who wish to live and work upon it and who, increasingly, call for more space both for working and for leisure. Thus the pressure on a limited acreage of land is great and is getting greater.

1.02 Today the principal Act on the subject is the Town and Country Planning Act 1990. It is 316 pages long and contains 337 sections and 17 schedules. It came into operation on 24 August 1990.

Associated with the principal Act are three further Acts related to planning, namely, the Planning (Listed Buildings and Conservation Areas) Act 1990, the Planning (Hazardous Substances) Act 1990 and the Planning (Consequential Provisions) Act 1990. These four Acts are defined (TP s. 336) as 'the Planning Acts'.

Planning control process

1.03 The planning control process is a bifurcated process involving, on the one hand, the making of development plans (that is to say, blueprints for the future) that seek to show what the state of affairs will be when all foreseeable development (or non-development) in the area covered by the plan has been achieved. On the other prong of the bifurcated process there is the day-to-day control over the carrying out of development through the medium of grants or refusals of planning permission for development. All this is a highly simplified, not to say over-simplified, statement of the entire complicated and sophisticated process of town planning control as it functions today.

*There is similar, but separate, statutory Code for Scotland.

1.04 In the ultimate analysis, all this control is done by the minister for town and country planning by whatever name he may be known. At the moment he is known as the Secretary of State for the Environment, but this does not alter the fact that, under the Secretary of State for the Environment Order 1970 (S1 1970 1681), one minister of the Crown is, by law, rendered responsible ultimately for the way in which all town planning control is carried out in England and Wales. For his actions he is answerable to the Sovereign Parliament. Thus the control is exercised, in the ultimate analysis, in accordance with the town and country planning policies of the central government for the time being functioning at Westminster.

1.05 In this chapter no attention is given to the first prong of this bifurcated process, namely, the making, approving, and bringing into operation of development plans comprising 'structure plans', 'local plans' and unitary development plans. It is assumed for the purpose of this article that all the requisite development plans are in operation. Accordingly, attention in succeeding paragraphs is given to the day-to-day process of development control through the medium of grants or refusals of planning permission for development.

1.06 Moreover, it should be made clear at the start that this chapter is written primarily for the guidance of architects: it is deliberately slanted in the direction of architects. An effort has been made to pick out from the surging cauldron of town planning controls some of the more important controls, and particularly those that would affect an architect seeking to organize development on behalf of a client. Thus the chapter does not purport to deal with control over advertisements, caravans, minerals working or hazardous substances.

1.07 Accordingly, there will be found in succeeding paragraphs a brief statement on local planning authorities (para 2.01 ff) and what they can do when faced with an application for planning permission for development (para 4.01 ff). Development itself is treated in some detail (para 3.01 ff) though, maybe, not in all the detail into which the expression breaks up once it is investigated. The method of making planning applications is dealt with, as are the consequences of a refusal or a grant of permission subject to conditions (para 4.01 ff). Special reference is made to buildings of special architectural or historic interest (para 5.01 ff) because these are matters which, although standing outside the main stream of town planning control, are nevertheless highly important matters to a developer and to any architect advising him.

There is a brief reference (para 6.01 ff) to the three new concepts in the planning field of urban development areas and corporations, of enterprise zones, and of simplified planning zones.

There is reference to the enforcement of planning control over the development of land (para 7.01 ff) or, in other words, there is a statement on what happens, or does not happen, if a person does indeed carry out development without getting the appropriate planning permission in advance. Finally, a few personal thoughts of the writer appear in para 8.01 ff.

1.08 The length of this article has been limited. This means that it has not been possible in every instance to put in all the qualifications, exceptions, reservations, and so forth which, in a more categorical statement, would necessarily be appended to the general statements set out in the paragraphs which follow.

Accordingly, it is emphasized that this article is in the nature of a guide – a guide for architects. It is hoped that it will be helpful to them, but in the limited space available it cannot be an exhaustive statement on everything on which the article touches. Further information can be obtained from the author's *An Outline of Planning Law* (9th edn, Sweet & Maxwell, London).

2 Local planning authorities; or who is to deal with planning applications?

2.01 The first thing an architect seeking to carry out development must do is to inspect the site of the proposed development. It is most important nowadays to discover:

1. whether it is a cleared site; or
2. whether it contains a building and, if it does, whether that building is a building of special architectural or historic interest (see para 5.01 ff).

2.02 Second, the architect must consider carefully the definition of 'development' in the 1990 Act (section 55) with the Town and Country Planning (Use Classes) Order 1987. Many building operations and changes of use do not constitute development by virtue of the definitions and provisions of this section and the 1987 Order. If they do not, then nothing in the town planning Acts applies to them. 'Development' is defined in para 3.01 ff.

2.03 Third, the architect must examine closely the type of development which is sought to be carried out. Is it development which can be dealt with in the normal run of planning control, or will it be subject to some additional control over and above the normal run? It certainly will be if it happens to be development land occupied by a building of special architectural or historic interest (para 5.01 ff) which has been listed by the Secretary of State.

2.04 Fourth, the architect must satisfy himself whether the site for the development does, or does not :

1. Comprise 'Article 1(5) land' (as defined in the Town and Country Planning General Development Order 1988, Schedule 1, Part 1) which land includes:
   (a) a national park declared under the National Parks and Access to the Countryside Act 1949;
   (b) an area of outstanding natural beauty (AONB) declared under the same Act of 1949;
   (c) an area designated as a conservation area under section 69 of the Planning (Listed Buildings in Conservation Areas) Act 1990;
   (d) an area specified for the purposes of the Wildlife and Countryside Act 1981, section 41(3); and
   (e) the Broads as defined in the Norfolk and Suffolk Broads Act 1988.
2. Comprise 'Article 1(6) land' (as defined in the GDO 1988, Schedule 1, Part 2) (Extracts follow at the end of this chapter) which land includes:

(a) the Norfolk and Suffolk Broads (as defined above); and
(b) land outside a national park but within an area (specified in article 1(6)) as set out in Schedule 1, Part 2, of the GDO 1988.

If the development site is on 'Article 1(5) land' or 'Article 1(6) land', then the amount of 'permitted development' (see para 2.05) allowed on the site is constricted by the GDO 1988.

2.05 Fifth, the architect must investigate the Town and Country Planning General Development Order 1988. It will be necessary to do this sort of investigation in order to ascertain whether the development is 'permitted development' under the Order because, if it is, it gets automatic planning permission and there is no need to make any application at all to a local planning authority (see para 4.02 and Extract 4). But it is to be remembered that the important widening of the field of 'permitted development' brought about by the General Development (Amendment) Order 1981 does *not* apply to 'Article 1(5) land' nor to 'Article 1(6) land' each as above described. Any such land falls within what are nowadays called 'sensitive areas' and the relaxation of development control brought about by the General Development (Amendment) Order 1981 was denied to them – and is still denied to them by the Town and Country Planning General Development Order 1988.

2.06 Sixth, the architect must ascertain whether the development site is in an Urban Development Area (see para 6.01 ff); in an Enterprise Zone (see para 6.09 ff); or in a Simplified Planning Zone (see para 6.12 ff). If the site is in any one of these areas or zones, then the normal constraints of development control (e.g. the need to obtain, from a local planning authority, planning permission for development (see para 2.10)) are relaxed (see paras 6.01 ff, 6.09 ff and 6.12 ff).

2.07 All these are preliminary matters about which the architect should become fully informed at the outset. In this article it will be assumed, for the moment, that the architect is dealing with a cleared site (or, at least, a site *not* containing anything in the nature of a special building), and that the development he wishes to carry out is development that can be dealt with under the general run of town planning control and does *not* attract any additional, i.e. special, control. The *special* control over development which is going to occupy the site of an existing building of archtectural or historic interest is dealt with separately later. For the moment it is assumed that the development which the architect is considering is straightforward building development not subject to any special form of control, but only to *general* town planning control under the Town and Country Planning Act 1990.

Which authority?

2.08 This being the case, the next thing which the architect must consider is the local government authority to whom the application for planning permission is to be made. It must be made to the local planning authority.

2.09 The local government system in England and Wales was completely reorganized as from 1 April 1974 under the provision of the Local Government Act 1972. (For further information on authorities, see Chapter 9.) It was further reorganized as from the 1 April 1986 by the Local Government Act 1985 which abolished the Greater London Council and the 6 metropolitan county councils (but not the metropolitan counties themselves) of Greater Manchester, Merseyside, South Yorkshire, Tyne and Wear, West Midlands, and West Yorkshire respectively.

2.10 The current system (outside Greater London) provides for local government to be discharged at three separate tiers, namely:

1. By 47 non-metropolitan county councils popularly called 'shire' county councils;
2. By 369 district councils (36 metropolitan district councils if they happen to be in a metropolitan county and 333 'shire' district councils if they happen to be in a 'shire' county) some of which have borough status; and
3. By parish councils
4. In Greater London local government is carried out by each of the 32 London borough councils plus the Corporation of the City of London.

2.11 The county councils and the district councils are now all local planning authorities, and thus current nomenclature speaks of the 'county planning authority' and the 'district planning authority'. Broadly speaking, the county planning authority is responsible for 'structure plans' and the district planning authority for 'local plans'. However, when it comes to the day-to-day control of development by the grant or refusal of planning permission in the 47 *shire* counties, this is the responsibility (except in the case of county matters, see para 2(12)) of the district council (but only after consultation with the appropriate county council) to whom application for planning permission must, in the first place, be made (TP Schedule 1, para 3 (1) (2) (3)). In the 6 *metropolitan* counties (where there are now no metropolitan county councils) the day-to-day control of development by the grant or refusal of planning permission is the responsibility of the metropolitan district council in respect of all development (TP Schedule (2) and Schedule 1, para 3 (1) (2) (3)).

2.12 The instances of 'county matters' when, in a *shire* county, the application for planning permission goes in the first place not to the district planning authority but to the county planning authority are (TP Schedule 1, para 1):

1. applications relating to mineral mining, working, and development (including the construction of cement works) (TP Schedule 1, para 1 (1) (a)–(h) inclusive);
2. applications relating to development straddling the boundary of a national park (TP Schedule 1, para 1 (1) (i)); and
3. applications in England relating to waste disposal matters (TP Schedule 1, para 1 (1) (j) and Town and Country Planning (Prescription of County Matters) Regulations 1980 (which does not apply to Greater London).

2.13 As indicated in para 2.11 all applications for planning permission will now go to the district planning authority (except in those instances set out in para 2.12). When an application is made to the district council, it is to be remembered that there are seven specified categories of development in which the interests of the county council receive special protection and in which consultation *by* the district council *with* the county council *must* take place. These refer to:

1. Development, the carrying out of which would 'materially conflict with or prejudice the implementation'
   (a) of any policy or general proposal in a structure plan (whether approved or merely proposed);
   (b) of any proposal to include in a structure plan any matter publicized by the county council;
   (c) of any 'fundamental provision' in an approved development plan;
   (d) of any proposal in a local plan prepared by the county council (whether or not it has yet been adopted);
   (e) of any publicized proposal by the county council for inclusion in a local plan being prepared by them;
   (f) of any publicized proposal by the county council for alterations to a local plan;
2. Any development which by reason of its scale, nature, or location would be of 'major importance' for the implementation of an approved structure plan;
3. Any development likely to affect, or be affected by, mineral workings 'other than coal';
4. Any development of land the county council wishes to develop themselves;
5. Any development which would prejudice development proposed by the county council;
6. Any development of land in England which is land the county council propose shall be used for waste disposal;
7. Any development which would prejudice a proposed use of land for waste disposal.

2.14 In each of the foregoing cases (the details of which are to be found in paragraph 7 of Schedule 1 to the Town and Country Planning Act 1990), where special protection is given to the interests of the county council, the district council *must* consult with the county council and take into account any representations made by the county council before they (the district council) determine the planning application. How long must these complicated consultations continue? That period has been fixed by the Town and Country Planning General Development Order 1988, article 19, as 14 days after notification to the county council.

2.15 Parish councils are not local planning authorities but, even so, have the right (if they have claimed it) to be consulted by the district council about planning applications for development falling within the area of the parish council (TP Schedule 1, para 8).

2.16 In Greater London the 32 London boroughs (each for its own borough) with the Common Council (for the City of London) are all local planning authorities (1990 Act, s. 1 (2)).

2.17 Although the application for planning permission will formally be made to a local planning authority it will often be

the case that a good deal of 'negotiation' relating to the application will take place between the applicant's architect and officers of the local planning authority for all of which a charge may be made by the local planning authority under the Local Government Act 1972 section 111 (1) – *R* v *London Borough of Richmond on Thames* (1990) *'Daily Telegraph'* Law Reports, 5 March. The power of a planning officer, acting within the scope of his duties as such to bind the planning authority in whose service he functions, is well illustrated in the highly important case of *Lever (Finance) Ltd* v *Westminster (City) London Borough Council* [1970] 3 All ER 496.

2.18 In this case certain developers, who proposed developing a piece of land by building 14 houses on it, applied for planning permission to the local planning authority, attaching to the application a detailed plan of the development showing one of the houses, house G, as sited 40ft away from all existing houses. Permission for the development in accordance with the detailed plan was given by the planning authority on 24 March 1969. A month later the developers' architect made some variations to the detailed plan submitted to the authority. The variations included altering the site of house G so that it was sited only 23ft away from existing houses. A further site plan showing this variation was sent to the planning authority.

2.19 The authority's planning officer had lost the file containing the original plan approved by the planning authority. Because of this he had made a mistake and told the architect over the telephone that the variation was not material and that no further planning consent was required. The telephone conversation took place in May 1969, and the developers acted on this representation and went ahead with the development, including the erection of house G, which was started in September 1969.

2.20 The residents of the existing houses made representations to the planning authority about the variation of the site of house G. The planning authority suggested to the developers that they should apply for planning permission for the variation. On 17 March 1970 the developers did so apply, the application being supported by the authority's planning officer, but the planning authority refused the application. It also refused a further application, made in April 1970, to sanction a variation in the structure of house G, and resolved that an enforcement notice should be issued to take down the house. By this time house G had been erected but not glazed.

2.21 The developers brought an action against the planning authority, claiming a declaration that they were entitled to complete the house on the site where it was, and an injunction restraining the authority from serving an enforcement notice.

2.22 It was the practice of many planning authorities, after detailed planning permission had been given, to allow their planning officers to decide whether any proposed minor modifications to the detailed plan were material or not, and where the planning officer said that a variation was not material, for the developer to proceed with the work as varied without applying for any further permission.

2.23 On the foregoing facts the Court of Appeal held that there was a valid planning permission for the erection of house G on the site as varied and that an enforcement notice should not be served. The court came to that conclusion because (per Lord Denning, Master of the Rolls, and Lord Justice Megaw) a planning permission covered work specified in the detailed plans and any immaterial variation therein; and, having regard to the practice of planning authorities allowing their officers to decide on the materiality of minor alterations to an approved plan (a practice which should be

affirmed), the planning officer's decision that the variation of the site of house G was not a material variation was a representation *within the officer's ostensible authority*; and, having been acted on by the developers, it was binding on the planning authority.

2.24 As already stated, this case is an important one. It warrants the closest reading and consideration because it illustrates how easily, in these days, a planning officer can bind the local planning authority in whose service he functions. It should be added that throughout the case mention is made of section 64 of the Town and Country Planning Act 1968, which later became section 4 of the Town and Country Planning Act 1971. That section 4 (relating to the delegation of functions of officers of local authorities) was repealed by the Local Government Act 1972, but this does not detract from the general principles enunciated in the *Lever* case. (See section 101 of the Local Government Act 1972.)

2.25 It is becoming more and more the custom for developers to engage, through their architects, in repeated interchanges with the planning staff of local planning authorities as to how, in detail, a piece of development shall be carried out. Do these interchanges bind the local planning authority? That is the question. There is no entirely clear answer. The position today, as a result of the case discussed above, is that such interchanges are *more prone* to bind the local authority than ever before. Even so, the ancient doctrine of *caveat emptor* may still be quoted as a warning to the developer and his architect. The purpose of negotiations with the planning staff of local planning authorities should be made clear; are negotiations intended to be binding or not? The architect (if he is the one doing the talking) owes to his client the duty of getting this important point made quite clear.

2.26 Fees are payable since 1 April 1981 to local planning authorities in respect of applications for planning permission, for approval of matters reserved in an outline planning permission, or for consent to display advertisements. The amount of the fees is set out in Schedule 1, Part II and Schedule 2 to the Town and Country Planning (Fees for Applications and Deemed Applications) Regulations 1989. The fees are shown in Extract 5 of this chapter.

2.27 A reduced planning fee is payable, in certain circumstances, where more than one application for planning permission is made for the same development or for approval of the same reserved matters provided all the applications are made by the same applicant within a period of 28 days.

2.28 Certain applications are exempt from liability to a fee. These are

1. certain applications on behalf of a disabled person;
2. applications to renew a temporary permission;
3. certain revised applications; and
4. applications relating to 'permitted development' prevented by a direction under article 4 of the General Development Order 1988.

There are no exceptions in respect of applications to display advertisements.

3 The meaning of development

3.01 The question as to whether that which the architect seeks to carry out is or is not development is a considerable one. The meaning of 'development' is amply defined in the Town and Country Planning Act 1990, section 55, and it is a question of taking the relevant provisions of this Act, working carefully through them, and then applying the appropriate parts of these provisions to the matter in hand to ascertain if

that which it is sought to do is, *in law* as well as in fact, development.

3.02 Putting the matter quite briefly, development consists of:

1. the carrying out of *operations* (that is to say, building, mining, engineering or other operations), or
2. the making of any *material change in the use* of land (including buildings on land).

It will be seen that the big cleavage in the definition is between the carrying out of *operations*, on the one hand, and the making of a *material change of use*, on the other.

What is an operation?

3.03 If the definition of what constitutes development is important, it may be said that the definition of what does *not* constitute development is equally important. Section 55 of the 1990 Act contains quite a list of operations (Extract 1 at the end of the chapter) and uses which do *not* amount to development. If that which the architect seeks to do falls within this particular list, then he need worry no more about the 1990 Act or any part of it.

What is a change of use?

3.04 This list of exceptions in section 55 of the 1990 Act must be read with the Town and Country Planning (Use Classes) Order 1987, which contains 16 classes of use (Extract 2 at the end of the chapter). If that which the architect seeks to do is, in fact, a material change of use, then if the existing use is any one of those specified in the 1987 Order, and if the change of use will still leave the use within the same use-class as specified in the Order, then the proposed change of use will *not*, in law, constitute development. In short, a use may switch around without planning permission, provided its total manoeuvring does not take it out of its use-class as set out in the 1987 Order.

3.05 However, since the case of *City of London Corporation v Secretary of State for the Environment and Watling Street Properties Ltd* (1971) 23 P. and C.R. 169, it is clear that, on granting planning permission, a local planning authority may impose such conditions as would prevent any future change of use, notwithstanding that any such change would *not* constitute development of land by virtue of the provisions of the Use Classes Order 1987 and section 55 (2) (f) of the 1990 Act. This decision, in respect of which no appeal was made, would seem to be a memorable decision when it is remembered that the whole object of the Town and Country Planning Act 1990 is to exercise control over things which constitute *development* and not over things which do not.

3.06 For the purpose of removing all doubt, section 55 (3) of the 1990 Act specifically states that merely using a single dwelling house as two or more separate dwelling houses *does* involve making a material change of use and it is 'development' needing planning permission before it can take place. Thus the architect may carry out, at ground level or above, *internal* building operations (not affecting the exterior elevations) on a single house in order to adapt it for use as two houses. Such building operations will *not* need planning permission. However, when it comes to inaugurating the *use* of the former single house as two houses, this change of use *will* call for planning permission which may or may not be granted.

3.07 If the architect has any doubts as to whether that which he seeks to do is or is not 'development', he can apply (1990 Act, section 64) to the local planning authority to determine the point for him. There is a right of appeal to the Secretary of State for the Environment (hereinafter referred to as 'the

Secretary of State') against the decision of the authority. Alternatively, an application may be made to the High Court to determine the point. The jurisdiction of the court is not ousted by section 64 of the 1990 Act, as is shown by the case of *Pyx Granite Co Ltd* v *Ministry of Housing and Local Government* [1958] 1 QB 554, CA.

Compensation for refusal of permission

3.08 In addition, section 55 (6) of the 1990 Act gives a specialized definition of the expression 'new development' which means any development (as discussed in para 3.02) *other than* development of the kind specified in Schedule 3 to the 1990 Act (Extract 3 at the end of the chapter). This (sometimes called 'existing use development') is development which falls within the existing use of land. 'New development' is development which goes outside the bounds of existing use. While *all* development, new or otherwise, needs planning permission, certain classes of existing use development, i.e. those six classes set out in Part II of Schedule 3 to the 1990 Act, have always carried a right to compensation for refusal of planning permission (see Extract 3).

4   Control of development in general

4.01 Once the architect is satisfied that that which he seeks to do is indeed *development* he must next ascertain whether it falls within the privileged category of 'permitted development'. For this he will have to investigate the Town and Country Planning General Development Order 1988 (see Extract 4 at the end of the chapter), as amended by the Town and Country Planning General Development (Amendment) Order 1989.

Permitted development

4.02 The 1988 Order, as amended, carries no less than 76 separate classes of development which are categorized as *permitted* development, that is to say, they comprise development for which a grant of planning permission is automatically given by virtue of the General Development Order 1988 itself (TP sections 58, 59, 60). If development falls within any one of these 76 classes of permitted development there is no need to make any application to any local planning authority for planning permission for the development. If the development is *not* permitted development, then a formal application must be made (TP sections 58, 62).

4.03 It is to be stressed that the General Development Order of 1988 is a most important document. The 76 classes of permitted development are spread across 28 Parts – Part 1 to Part 28 respectively – as set out in Schedule 2 to the Order as follows:

G.D.O. 1988
Sched. 2

PART	CLASS	PERMITTED DEVELOPMENT
1	A	The enlargement, improvement or other alteration of a dwelling-house
1	B	The enlargement of a dwelling-house consisting of an addition or alteration to its roof
1	C	Any other addition to the roof of a dwellinghouse
1	D	The erection or construction of a porch outside any external door of a dwellinghouse

G.D.O. 1988
Sched. 2

PART	CLASS	PERMITTED DEVELOPMENT
1	E	The provision within the curtilage of a dwellinghouse, of any building or enclosure, swimming or other pool required for a purpose incidental to the enjoyment of the dwellinghouse, or the maintenance, improvement or other alteration of such a building or enclosure
1	F	The provision within the curtilage of a dwellinghouse of a hard surface for any purpose incidental to the enjoyment of the dwellinghouse
1	G	The erection or provision within the curtilage of a dwellinghouse of a container for the storage of oil for domestic heating
1	H	The installation, alteration or replacement of a satellite antenna on a dwellinghouse or within the curtilage of a dwellinghouse
2	A to C	Minor operations
3	A to E	Changes of use
4	A to B	Temporary buildings and uses
5	A to B	Caravan sites
6	A to C	Agricultural buildings and operations
7	A	Forestry buildings and operations
8	A to D	Industrial and warehouse development
9	A	Repairs to unadopted streets and private ways
10	A	Repairs to services
11	A	Development under local or private Acts or Orders
12	A to B	Development by local authorities
13	A	Development by local highway authorities
14	A	Development by drainage bodies
15	A	Development by the National Rivers Authority
16	A	Development by or on behalf of sewerage undertakers
17	A to J	Development by statutory undertakers
18	A to J	Aviation development
19	A to C	Development ancillary to mining operations
20	A to E	British Coal mining development
21	A to B	Waste tipping at a mine
22	A to B	Mineral exploration
23	A to C	Removal of material from mineral-working deposits
24	A	Development by telecommunications code system operators
25	A	Other telecommunications development
26	A	Development by the Historic Buildings and Monuments Commission for England
27	A	Use by members of certain recreational associations
28	A	Development at amusement parks

Other than permitted development

4.04 If the proposed development does *not* fall within any of the 76 classes of 'permitted development' above mentioned, then a formal application for planning permission will need to be made TP s. 57: Sections 58 and 62 of the Town and Country Planning Act 1990 require an application for planning permission for development to be made in accordance with provisions 'prescribed by regulations' which today (1990) means the Town and County Planning (Applications) Regulations 1988 and the Town and Country Planning General Development Order 1988 to each of which reference must be made.

4.05 The requisite form on which the application is lodged can be obtained from the district planning authority and, in the making of the application, it is well worth paying attention to Part III of the memorandum to accompany Ministry Circular 48/59, Town and Country Planning Act 1959, and to the 'Notes for Applicants' set out in the Appendix to that Circular. These notes provide guidance not only to local authorities, but also to developers seeking to obtain planning permission for development.

4.06 When making an application for planning permission for development reference must further be made to the Town and Country Planning (Assessment of Environmental Effects) Regulations 1988.

4.07 As to what should be the attitude of a local planning authority when faced with an application for planning permission, attention should be paid to Circular 22/80 by the Secretary of State entitled 'Development Control – Policy and Practice'. The opening three paragraphs of this circular may be quoted here. They are as follows:

1. The planning system balances the protection of the natural and the built environment with the pressures of economic and social change. The need for the planning system is unquestioned, and its workings have brought great and lasting benefits. In each of the countless decisions many compromises are struck.
2. But the system has a price, and when it works slowly or badly, the price can be very high and out of all proportion to the benefits. Many cases could be dealt with more quickly than they are at present. The evidence from the statistical monitoring of the development control system and from case histories suggests that there is room for substantial improvments in efficiency in handling cases in both central and local government. Proposals are made elsewhere for streamlining the planning appeal system. This circular is concerned with planning applications. It has two aims – the first is to secure a general speeding up of the system. The second is to ensure that development is only prevented or restricted when this serves a clear planning purpose and the economic effects have been taken into account. This does not mean a lowering of the quality of decision but it does mean a greater awareness of the economic costs of planning control.
3. The planning system should play a helpful part in rebuilding the economy. Development control must avoid placing unjustified obstacles in the way of any development especially if it is for industry, commerce, housing or any other purpose relevant to the economic regeneration of the country. It is, and should be seen to be, part of the process of making things happen in the right place at the right time. Local planning authorities are asked therefore to pay greater regard to time and efficiency; to adopt a more positive attitude to planning applications; to facilitate development; and always to grant planning permission, having regard to all material considerations, unless there are sound and clear-cut means for refusal.'

4.08 Aesthetic matters (currently the subject of much disputation between traditionalists and *avant garde* architects) associated with planning control are referred to in paragraphs 18 to 21 of Circular 22/80 to which any applicant

for planning permission (or his architect) should make reference. They should also refer to the government's views on planning control as set out in DOE Circular 14/85, now replaced.

4.09 Under regulations made under section 303 of the Town and Country Planning Act 1990, fees are payable to the local planning authority in respect of any application for a grant of planning permission or for any consent, approval, determination, or certificate granted in respect of any such application. (See Extract 5 at the end of the chapter).

4.10 If the application for planning permission is refused, or is granted subject to conditions unacceptable to the applicant for planning permission, there is a right of appeal to the Secretary of State within six months of the authority's decision (TP sections 78 and 79). Before deciding the appeal the Secretary of State *must*, if either the applicant for planning permission or the local planning authority so requests, afford each of them an opportunity of being heard by a person appointed by the Secretary of State – an inspector. If the request is granted the hearing will be private to the two parties. Neither party can demand a public local enquiry although the Secretary of State (it is entirely a matter for him) frequently decides to hold such an inquiry. Procedure at such an inquiry is dealt with in the Town and Country Planning (Inquiries Procedure) Rules 1988. The decision of the Secretary of State is final (subject to appeal to the courts within six weeks on matters of law only), the procedure being regarded by the law as an adminstrative and not a justiciable procedure.

4.11 Even so, the increasing propensity of the judicature to interfere with an administrative decision if it is thought that the Secretary of State has come to a conclusion upon wrong evidence, or upon no evidence at all, is well illustrated in the case of *Coleen Properties Ltd* v *Minister of Housing and Local Government and Another* [1971] 1 All ER 1049.

4.12 Under section 79 and Schedule 6 of the 1990 Act, it is open to the Secretary of State to empower his inspector holding a local enquiry not only to hold the inquiry but to determine the appeal. The Secretary of State has exercised this power by making the Town and Country Planning (Determination of Appeals by Appointed Persons) (Prescribed Classes) Regulations 1981, whereby *all* planning appeals and *all* enforcement appeals (except when affecting a statutory undertaker) are now heard *and determined* by an inspector appointed by the Secretary of State. The procedure at such appeals is found in the Town and Country Planning Appeals (Determination by Inspectors) (Inquiries Procedure) Rules 1988.

4.13 In addition to appeals to the Secretary of State by private hearing or by public local enquiry (as above described), there is a third method of appeal by what is known as the 'Written Representation Process'. This is dealt with in DOE Circular 18/86 and in the Town and Country Planning (Appeals) (Written Representations Procedure) Regulations 1987.

4.14 In any planning appeal the Secretary of State *may* (if he can be persuaded) award costs to the appellant against the local planning authority.

4.15 Figures for planning appeals for England for the quarter ended June 1989 show the overall success rate for planning appeals in the quarter to be 40%, 1% lower than in the previous three quarters.

Outline permission

4.16 If the architect knows exactly what he wants to do by way of building operations he will be able to put in a complete detailed application for planning permission. But it may be that he wants in the first place to 'test the temperature of the water', that is to say, to see what are his chances of getting planning permission at all for, say, a block of offices 20 storeys high. If he wishes to do this, then he can save time, trouble, and expense by putting in an application for *outline* planning permission so that the principle of having a block of offices 20 storeys high may be tested. If it is approved, then it will be necessary for the architect later on, within the period (if any) specified in the grant of outline planning permission and *before he begins any development*, to put in detailed plans and specifications for the approval of the local planning authority, these being what are called 'reserved matters', that is to say, matters reserved, at the stage when the local authority is granting the planning application in outline, for later and further consideration.

4.17 An outline application should make it clear that it *is* an application in outline and nothing more. Thus any plans and drawings which accompany it should be clearly marked as being by way of illustration only. At the stage of applying for outline permission, the architect should not fetter himself as to the *styling* of development. All he wants at the outline stage is to know whether or not he can, under any circumstances at all, have planning permission to do the *sort* of thing he wishes to do. If he gets that permission, then he must return, in due course, to the local planning authority with detailed plans and specifications so that the authority may consider these detailed matters.

4.18 If the outline application for planning permission is refused, there is a right of appeal (as explained in para 4.10) against that refusal to the Secretary of State within six months. Similarly, if the outline application is granted but, later on, the local authority refuses to approve reserved matters, that is to say, refuses approval of detailed plans and specifications, then again there is an appeal against such refusal to the Secretary of State (see para 4.10).

4.19 It will be seen that for an applicant who does not own land and who wonders how much he ought to pay for it, the making of an outline application to test the position *vis-à-vis* the local planning authority is a useful arrangement. It is not necessary for the applicant to go into details and incur the expense thereby involved. All he wants to know before he makes his bid for the land is whether, if he is able to buy the land, he will then be able to develop it in anything like the manner he has in mind. To get to know this, all that he need do is make an outline planning application.

Certificates

4.20 Any application for planning permission must now be accompanied by a certificate (in one or other of four different forms called A, B, C, and D respectively) indicating the giving of notice to certain owners and agricultural tenants. If the appropriate certificate is not included with the planning application, then the local planning authority 'shall not entertain' the application. Which of the four forms of certificate is used depends on the circumstances of the case, but section 66 of the 1990 Act indicates which form is to be used, while article 12 and Part I of Schedule 5 to the General Development Order 1988 sets out each of the four forms of certificate from which the selection of one is to be made.

General publicity

4.21 In addition to the foregoing personal or private publicity deriving from the notices referred to in the previous paragraph, there must be what can be called *general* publicity (TP section 65) by newspaper advertisement for certain planning applications. These relate to the nine classes of 'bad neighbour' development (as it is called) set out in article 11 of

the General Development Order 1988. This bad neighbour development includes *any* building over 20 metres in height; buildings for use as a public convenience; for the disposal of refuse and waste material; for sewage disposal; for use as a slaughterhouse or knacker's yard or for killing or plucking poultry; for use as a casino, fun fair or bingo-hall, theatre, cinema, music hall, dance hall, skating rink, sports hall, swimming bath or gymnasium (not forming part of a school, college, or university), Turkish or other vapour or foam bath; or for the construction of buildings or the use of land as a zoo or for the business of boarding or breeding cats and dogs, or for motor car or motor cycle racing (including trials of speed); the construction of a stadium; the use of land as a cemetery or crematorium. All these matters are calculated to create noise or stench or to cause people to congregate in large numbers and hence are regarded as 'bad neighbour' development. Thus the owners and occupiers of neighbouring land must be informed of any application to carry out such development so that they may give their views and opinions to the local planning authority before a decision is arrived at.

Site notices

4.22 Moreover, in the case of 'bad neighbour' development a site notice, exhibited on the site where the development is to take place, must be given. The notice must be posted for not less than seven days during the month immediately preceding the making of the application for planning permission. It must be firmly fixed and displayed so as to be easily visible by the public, and it must state that the application is to be made and name a place *within the locality* where a copy of the application and of all plans and other documents related to it will be open to public inspection. It is the responsibility of *the applicant* and not the local planning authority to post the notice and make the plans and other documents open for public inspection at some place within the locality of the site.

4.23 If the development is within a conservation area a site notice must again be posted, but in this instance it is the responsibility of the local planning authority to post the notice.

4.24 Those instances in which a site notice must be posted are referred to (so far as concerns 'bad neighbour' development) in the 1990 Act, section 65 and article 11 and Schedule 4, Part I of the General Development Order 1988 and (so far as listed buildings and conservation areas are concerned) in the Planning (Listed Buildings and Conservation Areas) Act 1990 sections 67 and 73.

Local authority procedure

4.25 On receipt of an application for planning permission, the local planning authority (the district council) must consider the matter and, generally speaking, give a decision within eight weeks unless an extension of time is agreed. The district council will probably need to consult the appropriate county council and may also have to consult any parish council within whose area the proposed development is going to take place (see paras 2.10, 4.03, and 4.04). The district council may grant the application, may refuse it, or may grant it subject to conditions. If the answer is a refusal or conditions are attached to the grant, the reasons for such action must be given. This is to enable the applicant to challenge the decision of the local planning authority if the applicant decides to appeal to the Secretary of State, as he may do within a period of six months. If no decision is given within the appropriate period, the applicant may appeal (again, within six months) to the Secretary of State as if he had been faced with a refusal.

Conservation areas

4.26 If the site of the development is within a conservation area designated under the Planning (Listed Buildings and

Conservation Areas) Act 1990 sections 69 and 70, then the local planning authority, in considering the application, will have to pay attention to sections 71, 72, 74 and 75 of that Act and to any directions given to them by the Secretary of State as to the manner in which they should consider applications for development within areas of special architectural or historic interest, the character or appearance of which ought to be preserved or enhanced. In other words, the local planning authority has less of a free hand in connection with development in a conservation area than it has elsewhere.

Conditions

4.27 The local planning authority in granting planning permission may attach such conditions as it thinks fit, but this does not mean that it can attach any conditions it likes; not at all. The conditions must be fit, that is to say, fit, meet, and proper from a town planning point of view, because the legislation under which all this control functions is town planning legislation.

4.28 A local planning authority in attaching conditions must ensure that the conditions fairly and reasonably relate to the development. The authority is not at liberty to use its powers for an ulterior object, however desirable that object may seem to be in the public interest. If it mistakes or misuses its power, however bona fide, the court can interfere by declaration an injunction – per Lord Denning in *Pyx Granite Co Ltd* v *Minstry of Housing and Local Government* [1958] 1 QB 554, CA.

4.29 Suppose one of the conditions attached to a grant is improper and thereby unlawful; does this invalidate the entire planning permission or can the unlawful condition be severed from the rest, leaving the planning permission intact but shorn of the improper condition? There have been several cases on this particularly difficult point, and the last word was spoken in the decision in *Kent County Council* v *Kingsway Investments (Kent) Ltd* [1970] 1 All ER 70. It would appear from the decisions of the courts that the question of whether or not a planning permission is to be held wholly bad and of no effect, by reason of the invalidity of some condition attached to it, is a matter which could be decided on the basis of common sense and with particular inquiry as to whether the valid condition is fundamental or trivial.

4.30 The views of the Secretary of State on attaching conditions to a grant of planning permission are set out at length in the interesting and instructive DOE Circular 1/85 to which reference can be made with advantage (see the Bibliography at the end of the book).

4.31 Local planning authorities seem to be increasingly intent on attaching to a grant of planning permission conditions which seek to recover for the authority something in the nature of a planning gain or benefit which the carrying out of the proposed development itself will bring to the authority in the nature, for example, of increased rateable value for the area of the authority. Some of these conditions are of doubtful validity,* and on certain of these the Secretary of State has made a formal pronouncement. It is dated 1 November 1979 and was made in a decision letter on a planning appeal relating to the proposed creation of 800 houses (DOE reference APP/5231/A/74/6905 and APP/5231/78/06933). The Secretary of State declared that he agreed with the inspector that the local planning authority's only objection of substance related to their wish to obtain a substantial contribution towards the cost of social infrastructure. The Secretary of State went on to say that he 'is of the opinion that, in the absence of any statutory requirement for

---

*See the article 'Planning Bargaining – the Pros and the Cons' (1980) JPL 631.

the developer to contribute financially towards social infrastructure, such payments cannot properly be demanded of the developer even though the need for the infrastructure may have arisen in part from his proposed development. Nor, in the Secretary of State's view, would it be lawful to grant planning permission subject to a requirement that the developer shall enter into an agreement under section 106 of the Town and Country Planning Act 1990 and other statutory provisions; any such agreement must be entirely voluntary and a matter for negotiation between the relevant parties.'

4.32 The Annex to DOE Circular 1/85 (above mentioned) also refers to this matter of the imposition of planning conditions the object of which is to secure some sort of a planning gain for the local planning authority (see paras 11–15 of the Annex). The Annex sets out six tests to ascertain whether a planning condition is (as it should be) 'fair, reasonable and practical'. The six tests are:

1. necessity for the condition;
2. relevance of the condition to planning;
3. relevance of the condition to the development to be permitted;
4. enforceability of the condition;
5. precision of the condition; and
6. reasonableness of the condition in all other respects.

The Annex puts each of these six tests to close scrutiny which should certainly be read in full in the Annex itself. To take but one example (relating to test (1) about the necessity for a planning condition being imposed at all), the Annex, para 12, declares:

'Test of need
12. In considering whether a particular condition is necessary, authorities should ask themselves whether planning permission would have to be refused if that condition were not to be imposed. If it would not, then the condition needs special and precise justification. The argument that a condition will do no harm is no justification for its imposition: as a matter of policy, a condition ought not to be imposed unless there is a definite need for it.'

4.33 It should be remembered that obtaining planning permission for development may not necessarily be the end of the matter. Certain specialized forms of development, e.g. development relating to the display of advertisements or to the creation of caravan sites, are subject to additional control over and above the general run of town planning control.

4.34 Moreover, the architect must never forget that town planning control is a control which functions entirely without prejudice to the long-established control of building operations through the medium of building byelaws created under a code of law relating to public health and dating back to the Public Health Act 1875 and even before. Irrespective of town planning control, such detailed matters as the thickness of walls, the opening of exit doors in public places in an outward and not an inward direction, the provision of means of escape in case of fire – all these are matters which are entirely separate from the sort of control over development which is discussed in this chapter. (For such matters see Chapter 15.)

Duration of permission

4.35 Nowadays, any developer obtaining planning permission must remember that, unless the permission itself specifies otherwise, permission will last for only five years. This is to prevent, among other things, an accumulation in the records of local planning authorities of quantities of planning permissions granted from time to time over a long period of years and never acted upon. This sort of thing had been going on for a long time, but was brought to an end by provisions in the Town and Country Planning Act 1968, now sections 91 to 96 of the 1990 Act.

4.36 Anybody in possession of a planning permission granted before 1 April 1969 must remember that if he did not begin his development before the beginning of 1968, then he must have begun it not later than five years from 1 April 1969, that is to say, not later than 1 April 1974, after which date the planning permission dissolves.

4.37 In the case of a planning permission granted on or since 1 April 1969, or granted in the future, the limitation is again five years from the date of the grant unless the grant otherwise provides.

4.38 If that which is obtained is an outline planning permission (as discussed in para 4.13) granted on or since 1 April 1969, then it must be remembered that the submission of detailed plans and specifications under the aegis of that outline planning permission must be done not later than *three* years from the grant, while the development itself must be begun within five years of the grant or within two years of the final approval of any reserved matter, whichever of these two periods happens to be the longer. In the case of an outline planning permission granted before the 1 April 1969, then the aforementioned periods of three and five years respectively run from the 1 April 1969.

Starting development

4.39 When is a project of development to be regarded as having been begun? This is an important question. The 1990 Act provides the complete answer in section 56 by providing that a project of development is begun on the earliest date on which a material operation in connection with the development is started. A 'material operation' will include, among other things, the digging of a trench which is to contain the foundations of a building. Thus, only a trivial amount of labour needs to be spent in order to ensure that development has been begun and that a town planning permission has been embarked upon.

Abandoning development

4.40 A ticklish question has always been: can a planning permission be lost through non-use? Can it be abandoned? In *Pioneer Aggregates (UK) Ltd v Secretary of State for the Environment* (1985) AC 132) a decision of the House of Lords, it was held that there was no legal principle that a planning permission could be abandoned by the act of a party entitled to the benefit of the permission.

Completion notices

4.41 Having begun his development, a developer must remember not to rest unduly upon his oars. If he is dilatory it is open to the local planning authority to serve him with 'a completion notice' requiring the completion of his development within a certain period. A completion notice will declare that the relevant planning permission will cease to have effect on such date as may be specified in the notice but this date may not be earlier than twelve months from the date of the notice. A completion notice will not take effect unless and until it is confirmed by the Secretary of State, who may substitute a longer period for completion. Any person served with a completion notice may demand to be given an opportunity of being heard by an inspector appointed by the Secretary of State. Of course, a local planning authority, having served a completion notice, may for good and sufficient reason be prevailed upon to withdraw it; the law authorizes such withdrawal.

Revoking or modifying planning permission

4.42 It should be remembered that a planning permission once given ensures a right to develop for the benefit of all persons for the time being interested in the land, subject to any limitation of time contained in the grant of planning permission itself or imported into the matter by the 1990 Act, as mentioned in para 4.32. This, however, is subject to the right of a local planning authority to revoke or modify a planning permission by means of an order made by the authority and confirmed by the Secretary of State. Before confirming the order the Secretary of State must afford the owner and the occupier of the land affected by the order an opportunity of being heard by the Secretary of State's inspector. There are certain revoking or modifying orders which, being unopposed and unlikely to give rise to claims for compensation, can be made by the local planning authority without need for confirmation by the Secretary of State.

4.43 If the local planning authority wish to make a revocation or modifying order they must remember to do so before buildings authorized by the planning permission in question have been started. If they fail to do so, the revocation or modification may not affect so much of the building operations as have already been carried out. Compensation may become payable on the revocation or modification of a previously granted planning permission.

5 Buildings of special architectural or historic interest – listed buildings

Note: In Section 5 of this Chapter all references to 'the 1990 Act' refer to the Planning (Listed Buildings and Conservation Areas) Act 1990.

5.01 The British public has tardily come to realize that the quality of life in this country is still worth preserving, but if it is not exceptionally careful, the ambience of the physical environment in which it lives is going to slip away before its very eyes. There is an outcry against pollution of all kinds. We are reminded of our heritage and of the things that interest visitors when they come to this country, and, for sure, they are far more interested in the Cotswolds than nuclear power stations, helpful on a dark night though the latter may be.

5.02 Buildings of special architectural or historic interest are great tourist attractions in this country, and at the moment tourism is one of the biggest growth industries in our land. Accordingly, the Planning (Listed Buildings and Conservation Areas) Act 1990 (hereafter in this Section 5 referred to as 'the 1990 Act') sets out to give further, better, and more decisive protection to buildings of the sort which are here called 'special buildings'.

Listing

5.03 Lists of special buildings are compiled under section 1 of the 1990 Act by the Secretary of State or the Historic Buildings and Monuments Commission for England (established under the National Heritage Act 1983). Once a building is listed it is no longer possible for a local authority to make (as hitherto) a building preservation order for it; in lieu the 1990 Act provides a different kind of protection (see further paras 5.09 and 5.10).

5.04 The owner of such a special building need not be consulted before it is listed; he is merely told what has occurred. However, the statutory list of special buildings must be kept open by the Secretary of State for free public inspection. Similarly, a local authority must also keep open for free public inspection any portion of the list which relates to their area.

5.05 To damage a listed building is to commit a criminal offence punishable with a fine of £400 and a daily penalty of £40 (see further para 5.13).

5.06 A local authority may carry out works urgently necessary for the preservation of an *unoccupied* listed building after giving the owner seven days' notice. The Secretary of State may make loans as well as grants (Chapter 9) under the Historic Buildings and Ancient Monuments Act 1953, section 4, for the preservation of historic buildings not situated in England and the Historic Buildings and Monuments Commission for England may do the like for buildings in England (1953 Act, section 3A).

5.07 In deciding whether to list a building or not, the Secretary of State may now take into account not only the building itself, but also its relationship to other buildings and the desirability of preserving features associated with the building but not actually forming part of the building. Thus, it is not solely the building which is to be considered but the entire background to the building.

5.08 When speaking of a building it must be remembered that the law is so framed as to give protection to any object or structure fixed to a building or forming part of the land on which the building stands and comprised within the curtilage of the building.

Listed building consent

5.09 There is no provision for the owner of a special building to appeal against the listing of his building. Once the building is listed, the whole of the protective provisions of Part I of the 1990 Act automatically swing into operation. The consequence of this is that while (as already explained in para 3.08) it is necessary to get planning permission for any kind of development, if the site of the development happens to be occupied in whole or in part by a listed building, then the development simply cannot take place unless an additional form of consent, known as 'listed building consent', is first obtained.

5.10 Listed building consent must be obtained in order to demolish, alter, or extend a listed building. It may be granted (like a planning permission) with or without conditions. The application for listed building consent is made to the district planning authority, and the procedure is given in sections 10–16 of the 1990 Act and in the Town and Country Planning (Listed Buildings in Conservation Areas) Regulations 1987. A grant of listed building consent will, last for only five years. If planning permission for development has been granted, or if an application for planning permission has been duly made, and if there is a building (unlisted) on the site, the developer may, since 13 November 1980, apply to the Secretary of State for the Environment for a certificate that the Secretary will not list any such building for at least five years. This is a most useful new provision in the case where the architect feels that a building standing on the development site is potentially a 'listable' building.

5.11 In deciding whether or not to grant planning permission or to grant listed building consent with respect to a special building, the district planning authority must pay special regard to the desirability of preserving the building or its setting and of preserving any features of special architectural or historic interest which the building possesses. Notwithstanding this, the writer takes the view that the grant of planning permission is one thing and the grant of listed building consent is another. Merely because planning permission is granted for development, it does not follow that listed building consent will be given to remove some obstructive listed building to allow development, persuant to the planning permission, to go forward. The planning

permission, once granted, will (as explained in para 4.35) last, generally speaking, for five years. During that time views and opinions about a listed building may change; views and opinions about architecture do tend to fluctuate. During the first years of the planning permission it may be impossible to get the requisite listed building consent to demolish some obstructive listed building. Later on different opinions about preservation may prevail or pressure to carry out development may become stronger. Thus, different considerations in the view of this writer apply when a local planning authority is considering whether it should grant planning permission for development and when it is considering whether it should grant listed building consent for the demolition of a listed building in order to allow planned development to go forward.

5.12 If listed building consent is refused, there is a right of appeal to the Secretary of State after the style of the appeal against refusal of planning permission.

5.13 It is an offence to demolish, alter, or extend a listed building *so as to affect its character* as a building of special architecural or historic interest, without first getting listed building consent. It is also an offence to fail to comply with any conditions attached to such consent. The penalty for each of these offences is (on summary conviction) a fine of £2 000 or imprisonment for three months or both, and on conviction on indictment, a fine of unlimited amount or imprisonment for twelve months or both. It is, however, a defence to prove that any works carried out on a listed building were urgently necessary in the interests of safety or health, or for the preservation of the building and that notice in writing of the need for the works was given to the district planning authority as soon as was reasonably practicable.

5.14 If the owner is faced with a refusal of listed building consent and can demonstrate that in its present state his listed building has become incapable of reasonable beneficial use, then he may serve a listed building purchase notice on the district planning authority requiring the authority to purchase the building.

Listed building enforcement notice

5.15 If unauthorized works to a listed building are carried out, then the district planning authority, in addition to taking proceeding for the commission of a criminal offence, may serve a 'listed building enforcement notice' upon the owner, requiring full reinstatement of the listed building. There is a right of appeal against the notice to the Secretary of State. Penalties are provided in the case of non-compliance with the terms of the listed building enforcement notice. The guilty person is liable to a fine of £2000 on summary conviction and of unlimited amount on conviction on indictment. There is a daily penalty of £200. These penalties are recoverable from the person 'in default', and it should be remembered that this might include a subsequent owner. So the purchaser of a listed building must be careful to ascertain before he buys whether there are any listed building enforcement notices outstanding in respect of the building.

5.16 A local authority is authorized to acquire compulsorily any listed building which is not properly preserved. This power may not be exercised until at least two months after the service on the owner of the building of a repairs notice specifying the work considered necessary for the proper preservation of the building. An owner faced with the possibility of having his listed building compulsorily acquired from him cannot appeal to the Secretary of State, but curiously enough, he can, within 28 days, appeal to the local magistrates' court to stay the proceedings under the compulsory purchase order. If the court is satisfied that reasonable steps have been taken for properly preserving the building then the court may order accordingly. Against the order of the magistrates there is a further appeal to the Crown Court.

5.17 If a listed building is compulsorily acquired, then the compensation to be paid to the owner will, in general, disregard the depressive effect of the fact that the building has been listed. On the other hand, if it is established that the building has been allowed deliberately to fall into disrepair for the purpose of justifying the redevelopment of the site, then the 1990 Act provides for the payment of what is called 'minimum compensation'. This means that the compensation will be assessed at a price which disregards any profit which might have accrued to the owner from the redevelopment of the site. Against any direction in a compulsory purchase order providing for the payment of this minimum compensation there is a right of appeal and, again, this is to the local magistrates' court, with a further appeal to the Crown Court.

Building preservation notices

5.18 Are there any means today of protecting a building which is *not* a listed building, but which appears to the local planning authority to be of special architectural or historic interest? The answer is yes. Although the district planning authority can no longer make a building preservation order, it can serve on the owner of the building a building preservation notice which gives temporary protection for six months, during which time the building is protected just as if it were listed. The object of this is to give time for consideration by the district planning authority and the Secretary of State, or indeed by anybody else, as to whether the building should in fact be listed. If, at the end of six months, the Secretary of State will not make any such listing, then the building preservation notice automatically ceases, and the district planning authority may not serve a further building preservation notice within the next twelve months. Moreover, compensation may become payable to the owner of the building for loss or damage caused by the service of the building preservation notice which failed to be followed by the listing of the building.

5.19 Certain buildings of undoubted architectural and historic interest do not come within the protection of listing at all. These are:

1. Ecclesiastical buildings in use for church purposes (but not the parsonage house, which *is* capable of being listed).
2. A building included in the Schedule of monuments compiled and maintained by the Secretary of State under ancient monuments legislation.

Buildings in conservation areas

5.20 In addition to the special protection given to listed buildings as described above, the 1990 Act section 74 gives protection to *all* buildings if they happen to be in a conservation area designated under section 69 of the 1990 Act.

6 Urban Development Corporations; Enterprise Zones; Simplified Planning Zones

Urban Development Areas and Corporations

6.01 The Local Government, Planning and Land Act 1980 Part XVI and Part XVIII break new ground in the sphere of land development and planning control over such development by providing, respectively, for the establishment of Urban Development Corporations and Enterprise Zones. Each of these is briefly dealt with in the following paragraphs.

6.02 The Secretary of State is now empowered to designate an area of land as an 'urban development area' and to establish an Urban Development Corporation to regenerate the area. All is done by means of an order made by the Secretary of State and approved by affirmative resolution of each House of Parliament. On 14 November 1980 the Minister for Local Government and Environmental Services, Mr Tom King, MP, declared: 'We shall shortly be bringing forward Orders under powers in the [Local Government, Planning and Land] Act to set up Urban Development Corporations as single-minded agencies to spearhead the regeneration of the London and Merseyside docklands and to introduce the bold new experiment of enterprise zones, where business can be freed from such detailed planning control and from rates.'

The requisite orders for the London and Merseyside docklands were made in 1981. Further areas have since been made (in 1987) establishing Urban Development Corporations for:

1. Trafford (Manchester)
2. the Black Country
3. Teeside
4. Tyne and Wear
5. Cardiff Bay

and (in 1988) for:

6. Leeds
7. Bristol
8. Sheffield
9. Wolverhampton.

6.03 An Urban Development Corporation (like a New Town Development Corporation) is not an elected body. It is *appointed* by the Secretary of State and comprises a chairman, a deputy chairman, together with not less that five, nor more than eleven, other members as the Secretary of State may see fit to appoint. In making these appointments the Secretary of State must consult such local government authorities as appear to him to be concerned with the regeneration of the urban development area, and he must have regard to the desirability of appointing persons having special knowledge of the locality where the area is situated.

6.04 The Urban Development Corporations will have the duty of regenerating their respective areas by:

1. bringing land and buildings into effective use;
2. encouraging development of industry and commerce;
3. generating an attractive environment; and
4. ensuring that housing and social facilities are available.

The Urban Development Corporations will have powers similar to those of the New Town Development Corporations. They will be empowered to deal with matters of land assembly and disposal, planning, housing, and industrial promotion. They will be able to submit for approval by the Secretary of State their own proposals for the regeneration of their urban development areas. Before approving these proposals, the Secretary of State will need to consult any local planning authority within whose area the urban development area (or any part of it) falls.

6.05 An Urban Development Corporation may by order made by the Secretary of State (and subject to annulment by either House of Parliament) become the local planning authority for its own area (TP section 7), thereby taking over all the planning control duties of any local government planning authority functioning within the urban development area. If this occurs, a developer of land within an urban development area will find himself more in contact with the appropriate urban development corporation than with the district planning authority when it comes to the matter of obtaining planning permission for development.

6.06 An Urban Development Corporation, once established, must prepare within twelve months a code of practise as to consultation with the relevant local government authorities relating to the manner in which the Corporation proposes to exercise its regeneration powers. This code of practice *must* be prepared (and *may* be revised from time to time) by the Urban Development Corporation acting in consultation with the relevant local government authorities.

6.07 An Urban Development Corporation may, by agreement approved by the Secretary of State with the concurrence of the Treasury, transfer the whole or any part of its undertaking to a local government authority. When all the property and undertakings of an Urban Development Corporation have been transferred, the Corporation may be dissolved by order made by the Secretary of State after consultation with each local authority in whose area all or part of the urban development area is situated.

6.08 It will be observed that, each time an Urban Development Corporation is established, there is bound to be a consequential diminution of the planning control powers of any local government planning authority functioning within the urban development area over whose regeneration it is the responsibility of the Urban Development Corporation to preside. Accordingly, it will not be surprising to find that the establishment of any Urban Development Corporation, and the demarcation of the boundaries of any urban development area, are matters which will be eyed critically by any local government authority out of whose area the urban development area is to be carved. On this it may be mentioned that the London borough of Southwark petitioned the House of Lords to have the boundaries of the London Dockland Development Corporation redrawn. The petition failed.

Enterprise Zones

6.09 Part XVIII of, and Schedule 32 to, the Local Government, Planning and Land Act 1980 deals with the designation of Enterprise Zones within which special provisions relating to planning and rating will apply.

6.10 The following bodies may be invited by the Secretary of State to prepare a scheme with a view to the designation as an Enterprise Zone of the particular area of land for which the scheme was prepared. Such a scheme may be prepared by a district council, a London borough, a New Town Corporation, or an Urban Development Corporation. If any such scheme is formally adopted by the scheme-making body, then the Secretary of State, if he thinks it expedient to do so, may designate the area to which the scheme relates as an Enterprise Zone. The important point about all this is that any order designating an Enterprise Zone is *of itself* to have the effect of granting planning permission for such development as may be specified in the scheme.

6.11 In the words of the Minister of Local Government and Environment Services (quoted above – para 6.02), 'the bold new experiment of Enterprise Zones will so arrange things that business can be freed from detailed planning control and from rates'. As to freedom from rates, this is to last for ten years. The financial memorandum to the Bill for the 1980 Act declared:

'The establishment of enterprise zones will entail a loss of rate revenue for which local authorites will be fully compensated by specific Exchequer grant. The cost will depend on the number of zones, where they are sited, their area and the extent to which they attract new industrial and commercial development. On the basis of the Government's current plans the immediate cost will be £5–10 millions per annum; this will rise as development occurs and the final figure will depend on the amount and value of development.'

Simplified Planning Zones

6.12 In the White Paper (Cmnd 9571) dated July 1985 and entitled 'Lifting the Burden' – the Burden being that of various forms of government control (including planning and development control) over enterprise in all its manifestations – the Government declared (para 3.5):

'There is therefore always a presumption in favour of development, unless that development would cause demonstrable harm to interests of acknowledged importance.'

The White Paper went on (para 3.6) to declare that:

'3.6 In line with this approach to the control of development, and in support of the general aim of deregulation, a number of other measures are being taken to simplify the planning system and reduce the burden of control:

(i) It is proposed to introduce new legislation to permit the setting up of *Simplified Planning Zones* (SPZ) which will extend to other areas the type of planning regime already established in Enterprise Zones. This will enable the local planning authority to specify the types of development allowed in an area, so that developers can then carry out development that conforms to the scheme without the need for a planning application and the related fee. Planning permission for other types of development can be applied for in the normal way. This type of planning scheme has proved to be effective and successful in Enterprise Zones and can provide a real stimulus to the redevelopment of derelict or unused land and buildings in areas that are badly in need of regeneration. In addition to providing local planning authorities with powers to introduce SPZs, they will also require to consider proposals for the establishment of SPZs initiated by private developers. The Secretaries of State would have reserve powers to direct the preparation of proposals for an SPZ, similar to those that they already have to direct the preparation of alterations to development plans.'

6.13 The Government fulfilled the forgoing promise by the enactment of the Housing and Planning Act 1986, Part II of which related to Simplified Planning Zones. Simplified Planning Zones are now dealt with in the Town and Country Planning Act 1990 sections 82–87, 94 and Schedule 1, para 9 and Schedule 7, and in the Town and Country Planning (Simplified Planning Zones) Regulations 1987. Simplified Planning Zones will be established by local planning authorities by means of a new system of Simplified Planning Zone Schemes (it is the word 'Scheme' which is the really important part of this expression) each of which will specify types of development permitted in a zone. A developer will be able to carry out such development without making an application for planning permission and paying the requisite fee.

6.14 The following land may *not* be included in a simplified planning zone:

1. land in a national park;
2. land in a conservation area;
3. land within the Norfolk and Suffolk Broads;
4. land in an area of outstanding natural beauty;
5. land in a greenbelt identified in a development plan; and
6. land notified under the Wildlife and Countryside Act 1981, sections 28 or 29 as an area of special scientific interest.

If, however, land in a simplified planning zone *becomes* land in any one of the above descriptions, it does not thereby become excluded from the zone.

The Secretary of State may by order provide that no simplified planning zone scheme shall grant automatic planning permission for development:

1. in any area or areas specified in the order; or
2. of any development specified in the order.

But development already begun when the order of the Secretary of State comes into force is not affected.

6.15 Clearly the making of a Simplified Planning Zone Scheme is going to be no simple matter and is going to take time – months rather than weeks (or is it years rather than months?). The local planning authority will need to consider very closely the details of their proposals because the wider or more liberal the development automatically granted by the scheme, the less will the authority, on an *ad hoc*, individual basis, be able to exercise their own policies relating to development control. Control by planning authorities of details about development permitted by the scheme (e.g. the siting of buildings, the materials to be used in their construction, and the dimensions, design and external appearance of buildings) will be beyond control by the local planning authority unless they have been spelt out deliberately and in detail in the scheme itself. Yet if too much detail is put into a scheme there is a chance that more objections to it will be lodged and, accordingly, the more protracted will be any public local inquiry relating to such objections.

On the other hand, a developer will wish to know (by his reading and examination of the scheme) with some certainty whether he may safely go ahead with his development without making any formal application for planning permission and paying the fees currently applicable in such a case, relying on the provisions of the scheme to support his action. After all, if he goes beyond the scope of the scheme (including its conditions, limitations and exceptions) he is in danger of being faced with an enforcement notice on the basis that he has carried out development without planning permission. The developer may decide to take this risk or (if he has time on his hands) he may apply under section 64 of the 1990 Act for a determination by the local planning authority as to whether or not his development falls within the scope of the scheme.

In short, the drafting of a Simplified Planning Zone Scheme may well be as big a headache to the local planning authority as the construing of the meaning and scope of the scheme will be to a developer eager to press on with development which happens to be of an expensive and substantial nature. In such a case, and in order to be absolutely sure of his ground, will the developer seek an *ad hoc* grant of planning permission from the local planning authority? Will he think it better to be slow but sure rather than rapid and wrong? But if he *does* apply to the local planning authority for an *ad hoc* grant of planning permission, will the authority accept his application and deal with it in the ordinary way or will they refer the developer to the contents of their simplified planning zone scheme? We shall see.

7 Enforcement of planning control

7.01 The enforcement of planning control is dealt with in sections 172–196 of the Town and Country Planning Act 1990.

7.02 The Town and Country Planning Act 1968 made two important alterations to the law relating to enforcement of planning control wherever development is carried out without planning permission. One of these was the abolition of what is commonly called 'the four-year rule' in the case of development comprising a change of use of land (but not a building operation); and the other was the introduction of the 'stop notice' in the case of development comprising a building operation (but not a change of use of land). Today the stop notice procedure applies (since 22 August 1977) also to development involving not operations but only a material change of use (see para 7.12).

7.03 Architects, being associated more with the sort of development that amounts to a building operation rather than a mere change of use, will be affected more by the new stop notice procedure than by the abolition of the four-year rule. Accordingly, the latter is mentioned only briefly here.

Four-year rule

7.04 The four-year rule derives from the fact that, under the form of town planning control introduced in 1948, if development is carried out without planning permission and if the authorities allow four years to elapse without doing anything about the matter (i.e. without taking action by issuing an enforcement notice), then such development becomes validated automatically for town planning purposes and no enforcement action can be taken thereafter. It may be said at once that nothing in the 1990 Act interferes with this state of affairs so far as building development is concerned.

7.05 However, so far as development involving only a change of use of land is concerned, the four-year rule is abolished, and nowadays it is open to a local planning authority to serve an enforcement notice in respect of a change of use of land which did not carry the appropriate planning permission even though the change of use took place more than four years previously. Indeed, in such circumstances there is now no period of limitation at all. There is one important exception; i.e. the change of use of a building into use as a single dwelling house, in which case the four-year rule still applies.

Certificates of established use

7.06 In the case of a use of land which was instituted before 1 January 1964 (i.e. four years before the Town and Country Planning Act 1968) provision is made in the 1990 Act sections 191–196 for obtaining a certificate, namely, a 'certificate of established use'. This is obtained from the local planning authority, and there is a right of appeal to the Secretary of State if one is refused. The certificate makes it clear that the use in question, though originally instituted without planning permission, is now immune from enforcement action.

Enforcement notices

7.07 Enforcement action is by way of enforcement notice served by the local planning authority upon the owner and occupier of the land to which it relates. Briefly, the notice requires the doing of all things necessary to amend the breach of planning control which, it is alleged in the notice, has occurred. There is an appeal to the Secretary of State against the notice, and the appeal must now state not only the grounds of the appeal but the facts on which it is based. The penalty for non-compliance with an enforcement notice is, on summary conviction, a fine of £2 000 or on conviction on indictment, a fine of unlimited amount. Further penalties of £200 per day on summary conviction or of unlimited amount on conviction on indictment, are recoverable for any continuing infringement of the enforcement notice.

7.08 Architects should note that a local planning authority is *never obliged* to serve an enforcement notice whenever there has been a breach of planning control. The authority always has a discretion which it must be expected to exercise reasonably, as must any public authority holding discretionary powers. What the authority have to consider is whether, notwithstanding the breach of planning control, it is *expedient* to take enforcement action, and on this the authority must have regard not only to the provisions of the relevant development plan but also to 'any other material considerations'.

7.09 Without doubt, enforcement notices are very trickey things indeed, and the law reports are full of decisions of the courts in which the validity of such notices has been challenged successfully on the ground of some legal flaw in the drafting or the service of the notice. However, all these things are problems for the local authority rather than for the developer and his architect.

Stop notices

7.10 The legal pitfalls associated with an enforcement notice have, in the past, sometimes led a developer to spin out the appeal procedure while getting on in the meantime with his building development. There is an appeal to the High Court on a point of law from the Secretary of State's decision in an enforcement notice appeal, and there are further appeals (on points of law) to the Court of Appeal and to the House of Lords. This is still the position, but the 1990 Act prevents a building developer from continuing his building operations while the protracted appeals procedure is working itself out. There is no longer the possibility of (quite lawfully) finishing the building before the appeal to, and in, the House of Lords in concluded. The stop notice procedure prevents this from happening.

7.11 Once an enforcement notice has been served, the local authority may follow it with a stop notice which brings all building operations or changes of use to a halt under a penalty, for breach of the notice, of £2000 on summary conviction or of a fine of unlimited amount on conviction on indictment. Further penalties of £200 per day on summary conviction or of unlimited amount on conviction on indictment are recoverable for any continuing infringement of the stop notice.

7.12 Since 22 August 1977 (when the Town and Country Planning (Amendment) Act 1977 came into operation), a stop notice may also be served following an enforcement notice which relates, not to building or other operations, but to any material change in the use of land. If a stop notice is so served, it must be served within twelve months of the change of use occurring. But a stop notice on a change of use can never be served when the change of use is change of use of a building into use as a dwelling house.

7.13 There is no appeal against a stop notice. Such a notice is dependent entirely on the enforcement notice with which it is associated. If, on appeal, the enforcement notice fails, so does the stop notice. In this instance, compensation is payable under the 1990 Act in certain (but not all) cases for loss or damage arising from the stop notice. Thus a local authority will be inclined to think twice before serving a stop notice.

8 L'envoi

8.01 The proof of the pudding is in its eating; the proof of planning control may be said to be in its administration. Heaven knows, there is enough planning *law* these days, as the size of the planning Acts of 1990 show. After statutory pronouncement on the subject there come voluminous quantities of subordinate legislation in the form of rules and regulations. Then, all this legislation must be read in association with vast quantities of circulars, pronouncements and so forth emanating from the Department of the Environment.

8.02 Notwithstanding all these powers and legal authority, it is said, from time to time, that planning control fails. If it does fail, the failure will have little to do with the powers but with the way they are used or (and this is often the case) *not* used.

202

8.03 Planning control is not a finite science but an artistic process in which there is, and always will be, room for more than one point of view. Architectural design comes prominently into the arena of planning control, and architectural design, like other types of design, is a matter of taste; e.g. one planning authority will like buildings built one way and another authority will like buildings built another way.

8.04 The important thing about buildings, one would have thought, is to get variety, that is to say, a state of affairs in which the buildings are different but not stridently in opposition to one another. Nobody wants bad manners in civic architecture. Thus, one would not regard it the responsibility of the local planning authority, as a matter of administration, always to turn down an application for planning permission purely because they do not entirely like the design of the building. The authority may not like it but,

without doubt, somebody else will. It is not the job of the planning authority constantly to be redesigning buildings so that they conform with some overall corporate taste (established, no doubt, through the processes of a democratic vote) on the part of the authority. If this were to happen, it would lead to a progressive spread of something in the nature of a local government school of architecture. (If one wants to know what this could mean, one need look no further than the rash of metropolitan borough town halls which sprouted across London after the boroughs had been created in 1899.)

Importance of preliminary discussion

8.05 Because town planning control is so much a matter of taste, it is felt that a highly useful purpose can always be served by the developer, through the medium of his architect, discussing with the appropriate planning officer the design and styling of the development which is to be undertaken. There is always room for more than one point of view, but if some form of agreement can be reached between the developer and the planning officer as a result of informal discussion and negotiation, all this is to the good. Later on it may lead to the developer getting a good deal of what he wants out of the planning authority. In addition he will be able to get all of this far more speedily than he would if he chose to stand on strict legal rights and formally appeal to the Secretary of State against a decision of the planning authority which did not entirely please him.

8.06 With today's rapidly rising costs there has never been an age when it could more truly be said that time is money. The planning control process can be a long one, but informal discussions with the planning authority (or their representative) can often achieve perfectly proper and entirely legal short-cuts to a decision which gives the developer a good deal of what he wants. For time spent on these discussions by their officers, local planning authorities are entitled (but not obliged) to make a charge – see para 2.17).

8.07 It is to be emphasized that, in any discussions with the local planning officer about a proposed development, the potential applicant for planning permission should carefully bear in mind what is said earlier in this Chapter (see paragraphs 2.17–2.25). A local planning authority can formally delegate to its planning officer power to discharge the planning functions of the authority. The paramount question is: Has the authority done so? If so, what are the terms of the delegation?

Extract 1 Operations and uses which do not constitute development – Town and Country Planning Act 1990, section 55

GENERAL PLANNING CONTROL

Meaning of development and requirement of planning permission

Meaning of "development" and "new development".

55.—(1) Subject to the following provisions of this section, in this Act, except where the context otherwise requires, "development" means the carrying out of building, engineering, mining or other operations in, on, over or under land, or the making of any material change in the use of any buildings or other land.

(2) The following operations or uses of land shall not be taken for the purposes of this Act to involve development of the land—

(*a*) the carrying out for the maintenance, improvement or other alteration of any building of works which affect only the interior of the building or which do not materially affect the external appearance of the building and are not works for making good war damage or works begun after 5th December 1968 for the alteration of a building by providing additional space in it underground;

(*b*) the carrying out on land within the boundaries of a road by a local highway authority of any works required for the maintenance or improvement of the road;

(*c*) the carrying out by a local authority or statutory undertakers of any works for the purpose of inspecting, repairing or renewing any sewers, mains, pipes, cables or other apparatus, including the breaking open of any street or other land for that purpose;

(*d*) the use of any buildings or other land within the curtilage of a dwellinghouse for any purpose incidental to the enjoyment of the dwellinghouse as such;

(*e*) the use of any land for the purposes of agriculture or forestry (including afforestation) and the use for any of those purposes of any building occupied together with land so used;

(*f*) in the case of buildings or other land which are used for a purpose of any class specified in an order made by the Secretary of State under this section, the use of the buildings or other land or, subject to the provisions of the order, of any part thereof for any other purpose of the same class.

(3) For the avoidance of doubt it is hereby declared that for the purposes of this section—

(*a*) the use as two or more separate dwellinghouses of any building previously used as a single dwellinghouse involves a material change in the use of the building and of each part thereof which is so used;

(*b*) the deposit of refuse or waste materials on land involves a material change in the use thereof, notwithstanding that the land is comprised in a site already used for that purpose, if (i) the superficial area of the deposit is thereby extended, or (ii) the height of the deposit is thereby extended and exceeds the level of the land adjoining the site.

(4) For the purposes of this Act mining operations include—

(*a*) the removal of material of any description—
  (i) from a mineral-working deposit;
  (ii) from a deposit of pulverised fuel ash or other furnace ash or clinker; or
  (iii) from a deposit of iron, steel or other metallic slags; and

(*b*) the extraction of minerals from a disused railway embankment.

(5) Without prejudice to any regulations made under the provisions of this Act relating to the control of advertisements, the use for the display of advertisements of any external part of a building which is not normally used for that purpose shall be treated for the purposes of this section as involving a material change in the use of that part of the building.

(6) In this Act "new development" means any development other than development of a class specified in Part I or Part II of Schedule 3; and Part III of that Schedule has effect for the purposes of Parts I and II.

Extract 2 Uses classes – Town and Country Planning (Use classes) Order 1987

SCHEDULE

PART A

Class A1. Shops

Use for all or any of the following purposes–

(a) for the retail sale of goods other than hot food,
(b) as a post office,
(c) for the sale of tickets or as a travel agency,
(d) for the sale of sandwiches or other cold food for consumption off the premises,
(e) for hairdressing,
(f) for the direction of funerals,
(g) for the display of goods for sale,
(h) for the hiring out of domestic or personal goods or articles,
(i) for the reception of goods to be washed, cleaned or repaired,

where the sale, display or service is to visiting members of the public.

Class A2. Financial and professional services

Use for the provision of –

(a) financial services, or
(b) professional services (other than health or medical services), or
(c) any other services (including use as a betting office) which it is appropriate to provide in a shopping area,

where the services are provided principally to visiting members of the public.

Class A3. Food and drink

Use for the sale of food or drink for consumption on the premises or of hot food for consumption off the premises.

PART B

Class B1. Business

Use for all or any of the following purposes–

(a) as an office other than a use within class A2 (financial and professional services),
(b) for research and development of products or processes, or
(c) for any industrial process,

being a use which can be carried out in any residential area without detriment to the amenity of that area by reason of noise, vibration, smell, fumes, smoke, soot, ash, dust or grit.

Class B2. General industrial

Use for the carrying on of an industrial process other than one falling within class B1 above or within classes B3 to B7 below.

Class B3. Special Industrial Group A

Use for any work registrable under the Alkali, etc. Works Regulation Act 1906(a) and which is not included in any of classes B4 to B7 below.

Class B4. Special Industrial Group B

Use for any of the following processes, except where the process is ancillary to the getting, dressing or treatment of minerals and is carried on in or adjacent to a quarry or mine:–

(a) smelting, calcining, sintering or reducing ores, minerals, concentrates or mattes;
(b) converting, refining, re-heating, annealing, hardening, melting, carburising, forging or casting metals or alloys other than pressure die-casting;
(c) recovering metal from scrap or drosses or ashes;
(d) galvanizing;
(e) pickling or treating metal in acid;
(f) chromium plating

Class B5. Special Industrial Group C

Use for any of the following processes, except where the process is ancillary to the getting, dressing or treatment of minerals and is carried on in or adjacent to a quarry or mine:–

(a) burning bricks or pipes;
(b) burning lime or dolomite;
(c) producing zinc oxide, cement or alumina;
(d) foaming, crushing, screening or heating minerals or slag;
(e) processing pulverized fuel ash by heat;
(f) producing carbonate of lime or hydrated lime;
(g) producing inorganic pigments by calcining, roasting or grinding.

Class B6. Special Industrial Group D

Use for any of the following processes:–

(a) distilling, refining or blending oils (other than petroleum or petroleum products);
(b) producing or using cellulose or using other pressure sprayed metal finishes (other than in vehicle repair workshops in connection with minor repairs, or the application of plastic powder by the use of fluidised bed and electrostatic spray techniques);
(c) boiling linseed oil or running gum;
(d) processes involving the use of hot pitch or bitumen (except the use of bitumen in the manufacture of roofing felt at temperatures not exceeding 220°C and also the manufacture of coated roadstone);
(e) stoving enamelled ware;
(f) producing aliphatic esters of the lower fatty acids, butyric acid, caramel, hexamine, iodoform, napthols, resin products (excluding plastic moulding or extrusion operations and producing plastic sheets, rods, tubes, filaments, fibres or optical components produced by casting, calendering, moulding, shaping or extrusion), salicylic acid or sulphonated organic compounds;
(g) producing rubber from scrap;
(h) chemical processes in which chlorphenols or chlorcresols are used as intermediates;
(i) manufacturing acetylene from calcium carbide;
(j) manufacturing, recovering or using pyridine or picolines, any methyl or ethyl amine or acrylates.

Class B7. Special Industrial Group E

Use for carrying on any of the following industries, businesses or trades:–

Boiling blood, chitterlings, nettlings or soap.
Boiling, burning, grinding or steaming bones.
Boiling or cleaning tripe.
Breeding maggots from putrescible animal matter.
Cleaning, adapting or treating animal hair.
Curing fish.
Dealing in rags and bones (including receiving, storing, sorting or manipulating rags in, or likely to become in, an offensive condition, or any bones, rabbit skins, fat or putrescible animal products of a similar nature).
Dressing or scraping fish skins.
Drying skins.
Making manure from bones, fish, offal, blood, spent hops, beans or other putrescible animal or vegetable matter.
Making or scraping guts.
Manufacturing animal charcoal, blood albumen, candles, catgut, glue, fish oil, size or feeding stuff for animals or poultry from meat, fish, blood, bone, feathers, fat or animal offal either in an offensive condition or subjected to any process causing noxious or injurious effluvia.
Melting, refining or extracting fat or tallow.
Preparing skins for working.

Class B8. Storage or distribution

Use for storage or as a distribution centre.

PART C

Class C1. Hotels and hostels

Use as a hotel, boarding or guest house or as a hostel where, in each case, no significant element of care is provided.

Class C2. Residential institutions

Use for the provision of residential accommodation and care to people in need of care (other than a use within class C3 (dwelling houses)).

Use as a hospital or nursing home.

Use as a residential school, college or training centre.

Class C3. Dwellinghouses

Use as a dwellinghouse (whether or not as a sole or main residence) –

  (a) by a single person or by people living together as a family, or
  (b) by not more than 6 residents living together as a single household (including a household where care is provided for residents).

PART D

Class D1. Non-residential institutions

Any use not including a residential use –

  (a) for the provision of any medical or health services except the use of premises attached to the residence of the consultant or practitioner.
  (b) as a crèche, day nursery or day centre.
  (c) for the provision of education.
  (d) for the display of works of art (otherwise than for sale or hire).
  (e) as a museum.
  (f) as a public library or public reading room.
  (g) as a public hall or exhibition hall.
  (h) for, or in connection with, public worship or religious instruction.

Class D2. Assembly and leisure

Use as –

  (a) a cinema.
  (b) a concert hall.
  (c) a bingo hall or casino.
  (d) a dance hall.
  (e) a swimming bath, skating rink, gymnasium or area for other indoor or outdoor sports or recreations, not involving motorised vehicles or firearms.

Extract 3 Existing use development – Town and Country Planning Act 1990, Schedule 3

DEVELOPMENT NOT CONSTITUTING NEW DEVELOPMENT

Part I

DEVELOPMENT NOT RANKING FOR COMPENSATION UNDER S. 114

1. The carrying out of any of the following works, that is to say—
  (a) the rebuilding, as often as occasion may require, of any building which was in existence on 1st July 1948, or of any building which was in existence before that date but was destroyed or demolished after 7th January 1937, including the making good of war damage sustained by any such building;
  (b) the rebuilding, as often as occasion may require, of any building erected after 1st July 1948 which was in existence at a material date;
  (c) the carrying out for the maintenance, improvement or other alteration of any building, of works which affect only the interior of the building, or do not materially affect the external appearance of the building and are works for making good war damage,

so long as the cubic content of the original building is not substantially exceeded—

2. The use as two or more separate dwellinghouses of any building which at a material date was used as a single dwellinghouse.

Part II

DEVELOPMENT RANKING FOR COMPENSATION UNDER S. 114

Sch. 8

3. The enlargement, improvement or other alteration, as often as occasion may require, of any such building as is mentioned in paragraph 1(a) or (b), or any building substituted for such a building by the carrying out of any such operations as are mentioned in that paragraph, so long as the cubic content of the original building is not substantially increased or exceeded.

4.—(1) The carrying out, on land which was used for the purposes of agriculture or forestry at a material date, of any building or other operations required for the purposes of that use. (2) Sub-paragraph (1) does not apply to operations for the erection, enlargement, improvement or alteration of dwellinghouses or of buildings used for the purposes of market gardens, nursery grounds or timber yards or for other purposes not connected with general farming operations or with the cultivation or felling of trees.

5. The winning and working, on land held or occupied with land used for the purposes of agriculture, of any minerals reasonably required for the purposes of that use, including the fertilisation of the land so used and the maintenance, improvement or alteration of buildings or works on the land which are occupied or used for those purposes.

6. In the case of a building or other land which, at a material date, was used for a purpose falling within any general class specified in the Town and Country Planning (Use Classes for Third Schedule Purposes) Order 1948, or having been unoccupied on and at all times since 1st July 1948 was last used (otherwise than before 7th January 1937) for any such purpose, the use of that building or land for any other purpose falling within the same general class.

7. In the case of any building or other land which at a material date was in the occupation of a person by whom part only of it was used for a particular purpose, the use for that purpose of any additional part of the building or land not exceeding one-tenth of the cubic content of the part of the building used for that purpose on 1st July 1948 or, if later, the date when the building began to be so used, or, as the case may be, one-tenth of the area of the land so used on that date as the case may be.

8. The deposit of waste materials or refuse in connection with the working of minerals, on any land comprised in a site which at a material date was being used for that purpose, so far as may be reasonably required in connection with the working of those minerals.

Part III

SUPPLEMENTARY PROVISIONS

9. Where after 1st July 1948—
  (a) any buildings or works have been erected or constructed, or any use of land has been instituted, and
  (b) any condition imposed under Part III of this Act, limiting the period for which those buildings or works may be retained, or that use may be continued, has effect in relation to those buildings or works or that use,
this Schedule shall not operate except as respects the period specified in that condition.

10.—(1) Any reference in this Schedule to the cubic content of a building shall be construed as a reference to that content as ascertained by external measurement.

(2) For the purposes of paragraphs 1 and 3 the cubic content of a building is substantially increased or exceeded—
  (a) in the case of a dwellinghouse, if it is increased or exceeded by more than one-tenth or 1,750 cubic feet, whichever is the greater; and
  (b) in any other case, if it is increased or exceeded by more than one-tenth.

11. For the purposes of paragraph 3—
  (a) the erection, on land within the curtilage of any such building as is mentioned in that paragraph, of an additional building to be used in connection with the original building shall be treated as the enlargement of the original building; and
  (b) where any two or more buildings comprised in the same curtilage are used as one unit for the purposes of any institution or undertaking, the reference in that paragraph to the cubic content of the original building shall be construed as a reference to the aggregate cubic content of those buildings.

12.—(1) In this schedule "at a material date" means at either—
  (a) 1st July 1948; or
  (b) the date by reference to which this Schedule falls to be applied in the particular case in question:

(2) Sub-paragraph (1) (b) of this paragraph shall not apply in relation to any buildings, works or use of land in respect of which, whether before or after the date mentioned in that sub-paragraph, an enforcement notice served before that date has become or becomes effective.

13.—(1) In relation to a building erected after 1st July 1948, which results from the carrying out of any such works as are described in paragraph 1, any reference in this Schedule to the original building is a reference to the building in relation to which those works were carried out and not to the building resulting from the carrying out of those works.

(2) This paragraph has effect subject to section 326(3).

14.—(1) In the application of this Schedule for the purposes of any determination under section 138(1)—
  (a) paragraph 3 shall be construed as not extending to works involving any increase in the cubic content of a building erected after 1st July 1948 (including any building resulting from the carrying out of such works as are described in paragraph 1); and
  (b) paragraph 7 shall not apply to any such building.

(2) Sub-paragraph (1) applies also to the application of this Schedule for the purposes of any determination to which section 326(1) applies and for the purposes of that sub-paragraph, so far as applicable by virtue of this sub-paragraph to any determination of existing use value as defined in section 144(6)—
  (a) references to this Schedule and to paragraphs 3 and 7 shall be construed as references to Schedule 3 to the 1947 Act and to the corresponding paragraphs of that Schedule; and
  (b) that Schedule shall have effect as if it contained a paragraph corresponding to paragraph 13 of this Schedule.

Extract 4 Permitted development in general – Town and Country Planning General Development Order 1988, Schedule 2 (as amended by Town and Country Planning General Development Order 1989)

SCHEDULE 2

PART 1

DEVELOPMENT WITHIN THE CURTILAGE OF A DWELLINGHOUSE

Class A

Permitted development

A. The enlargement, improvement or other alteration of a dwellinghouse.

Development not permitted

A.1 Development is not permitted by Class A if–
(a) the cubic content of the resulting building would exceed the cubic content of the original dwellinghouse–
   (i) in the case of a terrace house or in the case of a dwellinghouse on article 1(5) land, by more than 50 cubic metres or 10%, whichever is the greater;
   (ii) in any other case, by more than 70 cubic metres or 15%, whichever is the greater;
   (iii) in any case, by more than 115 cubic metres;
(b) the height of the building enlarged, improved or altered would exceed in height the highest part of the roof of the original dwellinghouse.
(c) any part of the building enlarged, improved or altered would be nearer to any highway which bounds the curtilage of the dwellinghouse than–
   (i) the part of the original dwellinghouse nearest to that highway; or
   (ii) 20 metres,
   whichever is nearest to the highway;
(d) the part of the building enlarged, improved or altered would be within 2 metres of the boundary of the curtilage of the dwellinghouse and would exceed 4 metres in height;
(e) the total area of ground covered by buildings within the curtilage (other than the original dwellinghouse) would exceed 50% of the total area of the curtilage (excluding the ground area of the original dwellinghouse);
(f) it would consist of or include the installation, alteration or replacement of a satellite antenna;
(g) it would consist of or include the erection of a building within the curtilage of a listed building; or
(h) it would consist of or include an alteration to any part of the roof.

*Paras. (b) (c) and (d) were substituted by the Town and Country Planning General Development (Admendment) Order 1989.

A.2 In the case of a dwellinghouse on any article 1(5) land, development is not permitted by Class A if it would consist of or include the cladding of any part of the exterior with stone, artificial stone, timber, plastic or tiles.

Interpretation of Class A

A.3 For the purposes of Class A–
(a) the erection within the curtilage of a dwellinghouse of any building with a cubic content greater than 10 cubic metres shall be treated as the enlargement of the dwellinghouse for all purposes including calculating cubic content where–
   (i) the dwellinghouse is on article 1(5) land, or
   (ii) in any other case, any part of that building is within 5 metres of any part of the dwellinghouse;
(b) where any part of the dwellinghouse would be within 5 metres of an existing building within the same curtilage, that building shall be treated as forming part of the resulting building for the purpose of calculating the cubic content.

Class B

Permitted development

B. The enlargement of a dwellinghouse consisting of an addition or alteration to its roof.

Development not permitted

B.1 Development is not permitted by Class B if–
(a) any part of the dwellinghouse would as a result of the works, exceed the height of the highest part of the existing roof;
(b) any part of the dwellinghouse would, as a result of the works, extend beyond the plane of any existing roof slope which fronts any highway;
(c) it would increase the cubic content of the dwellinghouse by more than 40 cubic metres, in the case of a terrace house, or 50 cubic metres in any other case;
(d) the cubic content of the resulting building would exceed the cubic content of the original dwellinghouse–
   (i) in the case of a terrace house by more than 50 cubic metres or 10%, whichever is the greater,
   (ii) in any other case, by more than 70 metres or 15%, whichever is the greater, or
   (iii) in any case, by more than 115 cubic metres; or
(e) the dwellinghouse is on article 1(5) land.

Class C

Permitted development

C. Any other alteration to the roof of a dwellinghouse.

Development not permitted

C.1 Development is not permitted by Class C if it would result in a material alteration to the shape of the dwellinghouse.

Class D

Permitted development

D. The erection or construction of a porch outside any external door of a dwellinghouse.

Development not permitted

D.1 Development is not permitted by Class D if–
(a) the ground area (measured externally) of the structure would exceed 3 square metres;
(b) any part of the structure would be more than 3 metres above ground level; or
(c) any part of the structure would be within 2 metres of any boundary of the curtilage of the dwellinghouse with a highway.

Class E

Permitted development

E. The provision within the curtilage of a dwellinghouse of any building or enclosure, swimming or other pool required for a purpose incidental to the enjoyment of the dwellinghouse, or the maintenance, improvement or other alteration of such a building or enclosure.

Development not permitted

E.1 Development is not permitted by Class E if–
(a) it relates to a dwelling or a satellite antenna;
(b) any part of the building or enclosure to be constructed or provided would be nearer to any highway which bounds the curtilage than–
   (i) the part of the original dwellinghouse nearest to that highway, or
   (ii) 20 metres,
   whichever is nearer to the highway;
(c) where the building to be constructed or provided would have a cubic content greater than 10 cubic metres, any part of it would be within 5 metres of any part of the dwellinghouse;
(d) the height of that building or enclosure would exceed–
   (i) 4 metres, in the case of a building with a ridged roof; or
   (ii) 3 metres, in any other case;
(e) the total area of ground covered by buildings or enclosures within the curtilage (other than the original dwellinghouse) would exceed 50% of the total area of the curtilage (excluding the ground area of the original dwellinghouse); or
(f) in the case of any article 1(5) land or land within the curtilage of a listed building, it would consist of the provision, alteration or improvement of a building with a cubic content greater than 10 cubic metres.

Interpretation of Class E

E.2 For the purposes of Class E "purpose incidental to the enjoyment of the dwellinghouse" includes the keeping of poultry, bees, pet animals, birds or other livestock for the domestic needs or personal enjoyment of the occupants of the dwellinghouse.

Class F

Permitted development

F. The provision within the curtilage of a dwellinghouse of a hard surface for any purpose incidental to the enjoyment of the dwellinghouse.

Class G

Permitted development

G. The erection or provision within the curtilage of a dwellinghouse of a container for the storage of oil for domestic heating.

Development not permitted

G.1 Development is not permitted by Class G if–
(a) the capacity of the container would exceed 3500 litres;
(b) any part of the container would be more than 3 metres above ground level; or
(c) any part of the container would be nearer to any highway which bounds the curtilage than–
   (i) the part of the original building nearest to that highway, or
   (ii) 20 metres,
   whichever is nearer to the highway.

Class H

Permitted development

H. The installation, alteration or replacement of a satellite antenna on a dwellinghouse or within the curtilage of a dwellinghouse.

Development not permitted

H.1 Development is not permitted by Class H if–
(a) the size of the antenna (excluding any projecting feed element) when measured in any dimension would exceed 90 centimetres;
(b) there is any other satellite antenna on the dwellinghouse or within its curtilage;
(c) the highest part of the antenna to be installed on a dwellinghouse would be higher than the highest part of the roof on which it would be installed.

Interpretation of Part I

I. For the purposes of Part 1–
"resulting building" means the dwellinghouse as enlarged, improved or altered, taking into account any enlargement, improvement or alteration to the original dwellinghouse, whether permitted by this Part or not.

PART 2

MINOR OPERATIONS

Class A

Permitted development

A. The erection, construction, maintenance, improvement or alteration of a gate, fence, wall or other means of enclosure.

Development not permitted

A.1 Development is not permitted by Class A if–
(a) the height of any gate, fence, wall or means of enclosure erected or constructed adjacent to a highway used by vehicular traffic would, after the carrying out of the development, exceed one metre above ground level;
(b) the height of any other gate, fence, wall or means of enclosure erected or constructed would exceed two metres above ground level;
(c) the height of any gate, fence, wall or other means of enclosure maintained, improved or altered would, as a result of the development, exceed its former height or the height referred to in sub-paragraph (a) or (b) as the height appropriate to it if erected or constructed, whichever is the greater; or
(d) it would involve development within the curtilage of, or to a gate, fence, wall or other means of enclosure surrounding, a listed building.

Class B

Permitted development

B. The formation, laying out and construction of a means of access to a highway which is not a trunk road or a classified road, where that access is required in connection with development permitted by any class in this Schedule (other than by Class A of this Part).

Class C

Permitted development

C. The painting of the exterior of any building or work.

Development not permitted

C.1 Development is not permitted by Class C where the painting is for the purpose of advertisement, announcement or direction.

Interpretation

C.2 In Class C "painting" includes any application of colour.

PART 3
CHANGES OF USE

Class A

Permitted development

A. Development consisting of a change of the use of a building to a use falling within Class A1 (shops) of the Schedule to the Use Classes Order from a use falling within Class A3 (food and drink) of that Schedule or from a use for the sale, or display for sale, of motor vehicles.

Class B

Permitted development

B. Development consisting of a change of the use of a building–
(a) to a use for any purpose falling within Class B1 (business) of the Schedule to the Use Classes Order from any use falling within Class B2 (general industrial) or B8 (storage and distribution) of that Schedule;
(b) to a use for any purpose falling within Class B8 (storage and distribution) of that Schedule from any use falling within Class B1 (business) or B2 (general industrial).

Development not permitted

B.1 Development is not permitted by Class B where the change is to or from a use falling within Class B8 of that Schedule, if the change of use relates to more than 235 square metres of floorspace in the building.

Class C

Permitted development

C. Development consisting of a change of use to a use falling within Class A2 (financial and professional services) of the Schedule to the Use Classes Order from a use falling within Class A3 (food and drink) of that Schedule.

Class D

Permitted development

D. Development consisting of a change of use of any premises with a display window at ground floor level to a use falling within Class A1 (shops) of the Schedule to the Use Classes Order from a use falling within Class A2 (financial and professional services) of that Schedule.

Class E

Permitted development

E. Development consisting of change in the use of any building or other land from a use permitted by a planning permission granted on an application, to another use which that permission would have specifically authorised when it was granted.

Development not permitted

E.1 Development is not permitted by Class E if–
(a) the application for planning permission referred to was made before the date of coming into force of this order;
(b) it would be carried out more than ten years after the grant of planning permission; or
(c) it would result in the breach of any condition, limitation or specification contained in that planning permission in relation to the use in question.

PART 4
TEMPORARY BUILDINGS AND USES

Class A

Permitted development

A. The provision on land of buildings, moveable structures, works, plant or machinery required temporarily in connection with and for the duration of operations being or to be carried out on, in, under or over that land or on land adjoining that land.

Development not permitted

A.1 Development is not permitted by Class A if–
(a) the operations referred to are mining operations, or
(b) planning permission is required for those operations but is not granted or deemed to be granted.

Conditions

A.2 Development is permitted by Class A subject to the conditions that, when the operations have been carried out–
(a) any building, structure, works, plant or machinery permitted by this Class shall be removed, and
(b) any adjoining land on which development permitted by this Class has been carried out shall as soon as reasonably practicable, be reinstated to its condition before that development was carried out.

Class B

Permitted development

B. The use of any land for any purpose for not more than 28 days in total in any calendar year, of which not more than 14 days in total may be for the purposes referred to in paragraph B.2, and the provision on the land of any moveable structure for the purposes of the permitted use.

Development not permitted

B.1 Development is not permitted by Class B if–
(a) the land in question is a building or is within the curtilage of a building, or
(b) the use of the land is for a caravan site.

Interpretation of Class B

B.2 The purposes mentioned in Class B above are–
(a) the holding of a market;
(b) motor car and motorcycle racing including trials of speed, and practising for these activities;
(c) clay pigeon shooting.

PART 5
CARAVAN SITES

Class A

Permitted development

A. The use of land, other than a building, as a caravan site in the circumstances referred to in paragraph A.2.

Condition

A.1 Development is permitted by Class A subject to the condition that the use shall be discontinued when the circumstances specified in paragraph A.2 cease to exist, and all caravans on the site shall be removed as soon as reasonably practicable,

Interpretation of Class A

A.2 The circumstances mentioned in Class A are those specified in paragraphs 2 to 10 of Schedule 1 to the 1960 Act, but in relation to those mentioned in paragraph 10 do not include use for winter quarters.

Class B

Permitted development

B. Development required by the conditions of a site licence for the time being in force under the 1960 Act.

PART 6
AGRICULTURAL BUILDINGS AND OPERATIONS

Class A

Permitted development

A. The carrying out on agricultural land comprised in an agricultural unit of–
(a) works for the erection, extension or alteration of a building, or
(b) any excavation or engineering operations,
reasonably necessary for the purposes of agriculture within that unit.

Development not permitted

A.1 Development is not permitted by Class A if–
(a) the development would be carried out on agricultural land less than 0.4 hectare in area;
(b) it would consist of or include the erection, extension or alteration of a dwelling;
(c) a building, structure or works not designed for the purposes of agriculture would be provided on the land;
(d) the ground area to be covered by–
(i) any works or structure (other than a fence) for the purposes of accommodating livestock or any plant or machinery arising from engineering operations; or
(ii) any building erected or any building as extended or altered by virtue of this Class,
would exceed 465 square metres, calculated as described in paragraph A.3.;
(e) the height of any part of the building, structure or works within 3 kilometres of the perimeter of an aerodrome would exceed 3 metres;
(f) the height of any part of the building, structure or works not within 3 kilometres of the perimeter of an aerodrome would exceed 12 metres;
(g) any part of the development would be within 25 metres of the metalled portion of a trunk or classified road;
(h) it would consist of engineering operations of a kind described in Class C below; or
(j) it would consist of or include the erection or construction of, or the carrying out of any works to, a building, structure or excavation used or to be used for the accommodation of livestock or for the storage of slurry or sewage sludge, and the building, structure or works is or would be within 400 metres of the curtilage of any protected building.

Conditions

A.2(1) Development is permitted by Class A subject to the following conditions–
(a) where development is carried out within 400 metres of the curtilage of a protected building, any building, structure, excavation or works resulting from the development shall not be used for the accommodation of livestock or the storage of slurry or sewage sludge within a period of five years from the carrying out of those operations;
(b) where the development involves–
(i) the extraction of any mineral from the land or from any disused railway embankment on the land, or
(ii) the removal of any mineral from a mineral-working deposit on the land,
the mineral shall not be moved off the land, unless planning permission for the winning and working of that mineral has been granted on an application made under Part III of the Act;
(c) in the case of development which involves the deposit of waste materials on or under the land, no waste materials shall be brought onto the land from elsewhere except for development of the kind described in Class A(a) or the creation of a hard surface, where the materials are incorporated into the building or works forthwith.

(2) In the case of any article 1(6) land, development consisting of the erection, extension or alteration of a building is permitted by Class A subject to the following conditions–
(a) the developer shall, before beginning the development give the local planning authority a written description of the proposed development, the materials to be used and a plan indicating the site, and shall not begin the development until a period of 28 days has elapsed from their receipt by the authority;
(b) if within 28 days of receiving that description and plan the local planning authority give the developer notice in writing to that effect, the development shall not be begun without the prior approval of that authority to the siting, design and external appearance of the building;
(c) the development shall, except to the extent that the local planning authority have agreed otherwise in writing, be carried out in accordance with–
(i) any details approved by that authority in accordance with subparagraph (b) above, or
(ii) the description and indication of siting given to them under subparagraph (a) above;
(d) the development shall be carried out–
(i) where approval has been given by the local planning authority, within a period of five years from the date on which approval was given;
(ii) in any other case, within a period of five years from the date on which the local planning authority were given the information referred to in subparagraph (a).

Interpretation of Class A

A.3(1) For the purposes of Class A–
(a) the area of 0.4 hectares shall be calculated without taking into account any separate parcels of land;
(b) the ground area referred to in paragraph A.1(d) is the ground area which would be covered by the proposed development, together with the ground area of any building (other than a dwelling), or any structure, works, plant or machinery within the same unit which is being provided or has been provided within the preceding two years and any part of which would be within 90 metres of the proposed development;
(c) 400 metres is to be measured along the ground.

(2) For the purposes of this class–
"agricultural unit" means agricultural land which is occupied as a unit for the purposes of agriculture, including–
(a) any dwelling or other building on that land occupied for the purpose of farming the land by the person who occupies the unit, or
(b) any dwelling on that land occupied by a farmworker;
"building" does not include anything resulting from engineering operations;

"protected building" means any permanent building which is normally occupied by people or would be so occupied, if it were in use for purposes for which it is apt; but does not include–
  (i) a building within the agricultural unit,
  (ii) a building used for a purpose referred to in classes B3 to B7 (special industrial uses) of the Schedule to the Use Classes Order, or
  (iii) a dwelling or other building on another agricultural unit which is used for or in connection with agriculture.

Class B

Permitted development

B. The winning and working on land held or occupied with land used for the purposes of agriculture of any minerals reasonably necessary for agricultural purposes within the agricultural unit of which it forms part.

Development not permitted

B.1 Development is not permitted by Class B if any excavation would be made within 25 metres of the metalled portion of a trunk or classified road.

Condition

B.2 Development is permitted by Class B subject to the condition that no mineral extracted during the course of the operation shall be moved to any place outside the land from which it was extracted, except to land which is held or occupied with that land and is used for the purposes of agriculture.

Interpretation of Class B

B.3 For the purposes of Class B the expression "the purposes of agriculture" includes fertilising land used for the purposes of agriculture, and the maintenance, improvement or alteration of any buildings, structures or works occupied or used for such purposes on land so used.

Class C

Permitted development

C. The carrying out on agricultural land used for the purposes of any registered business of fish farming or of shellfish farming of–
  (a) operations for the construction of fishponds, or
  (b) other engineering operations for the purposes of that business.

Development not permitted

C.1 Development is not permitted by Class C if–
  (a) the area of the site within which the operations would be carried out exceeds 2 hectares;
  (b) any part of the operation would be carried out within 25 metres of the metalled portion of a trunk or classified road;
  (c) in a case where the operations would involve the winning or workings of minerals–
    (i) any excavation would exceed a depth of 2.5 metres; or
    (ii) the area of any excavation, taken together with any other excavations carried out on the land within the preceding two years, would exceed 0.2 hectares.

Interpretation of Class C

C.2 For the purposes of Class C–
  "construction of fishponds" includes the excavation of land and the winning and working of minerals for that purpose;
  "fishpond" means a pond, tank, reservoir, stew or other structure used for the keeping of live fish or the cultivation or propagation of shellfish;
  "registered business of fish farming or shellfish farming" means such a business registered in a register kept by the Minister of Agriculture Fisheries and Food or the Secretary of State (as the case may be) for the purposes of an order made under section 7 of the Diseases of Fish Act 1983(a).

Interpretation of Part 6

D. For the purposes of Part 6,
  "agricultural land" means land which, before development permitted by this Part is carried out, is land in use for agriculture and which is so used for the purposes of a trade or business, and excludes any dwellinghouse or garden.

PART 7

FORESTRY BUILDINGS AND OPERATIONS

Class A

Permitted development

A. The carrying out on land used for the purposes of forestry, including afforestation, of development reasonably necessary for those purposes consisting of–
  (a) works for the erection, extension or alteration of a building;
  (b) the formation, alteration or maintenance of private ways;
  (c) operations on that land, or on land held or occupied with that land, to obtain the materials required for the formation, alteration or maintenance of such ways,
  (d) other operations (not including engineering or mining operations).

Development not permitted

A.1 Development is not permitted by this Class if–
  (a) it would consist of or include the provision or alteration of a dwelling;
  (b) the height of any building or works within 3 kilometres of the perimeter of an aerodrome would exceed 3 metres in height, or
  (c) any part of the development would be within 25 metres of the metalled portion of a trunk or classified road.

Conditions

A.2 In the case of any article 1(6) land, development consisting of the erection, extension or alteration of a building or the formation or alteration of a private way is permitted by this class subject to the following conditions–
  (a) the developer shall before beginning the development, give the local planning authority a written description of the proposed development and the materials to be used and a plan indicating the site, and shall not begin the development until a period of 28 days has elapsed from their receipt by the authority;
  (b) if within 28 days of receiving that description and plan the local authority give the developer notice in writing to that effect, the development shall not be begun without the prior approval of that authority to the siting, design and external appearance of the building and the siting and means of construction of the private way;

(a) 1983 c.30.

  (c) the development shall, except to the extent that the local planning authority have agreed otherwise in writing, be carried out in accordance with–
    (i) any details approved by that authority in accordance with subparagraph (b), or
    (ii) the description and indication of siting given to them under subparagraph (a);
  (d) the development shall be carried out–
    (i) where approval has been given by the local planning authority, within a period of five years from the date on which approval was given,
    (ii) in any other case, within a period of five years from the date on which the local planning authority were given the information referred to in subparagraph (a).

PART 8

INDUSTRIAL AND WAREHOUSE DEVELOPMENT

Class A

Permitted development

A. The extension or alteration of an industrial building or a warehouse.

Development not permitted

A.1 Development is not permitted by Class A if–
  (a) the building as extended or altered is to be used for purposes other than those of the undertaking concerned;
  (b) the building is to be used for a purpose other than the carrying out of an industrial process, or, in the case of a warehouse, other than storage or distribution;
  (c) the height of the building as extended or altered would exceed the height of the original building;
  (d) the cubic content of the original building would be exceeded by more than–
    (i) 10%, in respect of development on any article 1(5) land, or
    (ii) 25%, in any other case;
  (e) the floorspace of the original building would be exceeded by more than–
    (i) 500 square metres in respect of development on any article 1(5) land, or
    (ii) 1,000 square metres in any other case;
  (f) the external appearance of the premises of the undertaking concerned would be materially affected;
  (g) any part of the development would be carried out within 5 metres of any boundary of the curtilage of the premises; or
  (h) the development would lead to a reduction in the space available for the parking or turning of vehicles.

Interpretation of Class A

A.2(1) For the purposes of Class A–
  (a) the erection of any additional building within the curtilage of another building (whether by virtue of this class or otherwise) and used in connection with it is to be treated as the extension of that building, and the additional building is not to be treated as an original building;
  (b) where two or more original buildings are within the same curtilage and are used for the same undertaking, they are to be treated as a single original building in making any measurement.

Class B

Permitted development

B. Development carried out on industrial land for the purposes of an industrial process consisting of–
  (a) the installation of additional or replacement plant or machinery,
  (b) the provision, rearrangement or replacement of a sewer, main, pipe, cable or other apparatus, or
  (c) the provision, rearrangement or replacement of a private way, private railway, siding or conveyor.

Development not permitted

B.1 Development described in Class B(a) is not permitted if–
  (a) it would materially affect the external appearance of the premises of the undertaking, or
  (b) any plant or machinery would exceed a height of 15 metres above ground level or the height of anything replaced, whichever is the greater.

Interpretation of Class B

B.2 In Class B "industrial land" means land used for the carrying out of an industrial process, including land used for the purposes of an industrial undertaking as a dock, harbour or quay, but does not include land in or adjacent to and occupied together with a mine.

Class C

Permitted development

C. The creation of a hard surface within the curtilage of an industrial building or warehouse to be used for the purpose of the undertaking concerned.

Class D

Permitted development

D. The deposit of waste material resulting from an industrial process on any land comprised in a site which was used for that purpose on 1st July 1948 whether or not the superficial area or the height of the deposit is extended as a result.

Development not permitted

D.1 Development is not permitted by Class D if–
  (a) the waste material is or includes material resulting from the winning and working of minerals, or
  (b) the use on 1st July 1948 was for the deposit of material resulting from the winning and working of minerals.

Interpretation of Part 8

E. For the purposes of Part 8,
  In Classes A and C of this Part,
  "industrial building" means a building used for the carrying out of an industrial process and includes a building used for the carrying out of such a process on land used as a dock, harbour or quay for the purposes of an industrial undertaking but does not include a building on land in or adjacent to and occupied together with a mine;
  "warehouse" does not include a building on land in or adjacent to and occupied together with a mine.

PART 9

REPAIRS TO UNADOPTED STREETS AND PRIVATE WAYS

Class A

Permitted
development

The carrying out on land within the boundaries of an unadopted street or private way of works required for the maintenance or improvement of the street or way.

PART 10

REPAIRS TO SERVICES

Class A

Permitted
development

The carrying out of any works for the purposes of inspecting, repairing or renewing any sewer, main, pipe, cable or other apparatus, including breaking open any land for that purpose.

PART 11

DEVELOPMENT UNDER LOCAL OR PRIVATE ACTS OR ORDERS

Class A

Permitted
development

A. Development authorised by—
  (a) **a local or private Act of Parliament,**
  (b) **an order approved by both Houses of Parliament, or**
  (c) **any order made under section 14 or 16 of the Harbours Act 1964(a)**
which designates specifically the nature of the development authorised and the land upon which it may be carried out.

Condition

A.1 Development is not permitted by Class A if it consists of or includes—
  (a) the erection, construction, alteration or extension of any building, bridge, aqueduct, pier or dam, or
  (b) the formation, laying out or alteration of a means of access to any highway used by vehicular traffic,
unless the prior approval of the detailed plans and specifications of the appropriate authority is first obtained.

Prior
Approvals

A.2 The prior approval referred to in paragraph A.1 is not to be refused by the appropriate authority nor are conditions to be imposed unless they are satisfied that—
  (a) the development (other than the provision of or works carried out to a dam) ought to be and could reasonably be carried out elsewhere on the land; or
  (b) the design or external appearance of any building, bridge, aqueduct, pier or dam would injure the amenity of the neighbourhood and is reasonably capable of modification to avoid such injury.

Interpreta-
tion of Class
A

A.3 In this class "appropriate authority" means—
  (a) in Greater London or a metropolitan county, the local planning authority,
  (b) in a National Park, outside a metropolitan county, the county planning authority,
  (c) in any other case, the district planning authority.

PART 12

DEVELOPMENT BY LOCAL AUTHORITIES

Class A

Permitted
development

A. The erection or construction and the maintenance, improvement or other alteration by a local authority or by an urban development corporation of—
  (a) **any small ancillary building, works or equipment on land belonging to or maintained by them required for the purposes of any function exercised by them on that land otherwise than as statutory undertakers;**
  (b) **lamp standards, information kiosks, passenger shelters, public shelters and seats, telephone boxes, fire alarms, public drinking fountains, horse-troughs, refuse bins or baskets, barriers for the control of people waiting to enter public service vehicles, and similar structures or works required in connection with the operation of any public service administered by them.**

Interpreta-
tion of Class
A

A.1 The reference in Class A to any small building, works or equipment is a reference to building, works or equipment not exceeding 4 metres in height or 200 cubic metres in capacity.

Class B

Permitted
development

B. The deposit by a local authority of waste material on any land comprised in a site which was used for that purpose on 1st July 1948 whether or not the superficial area or the height of the deposit is extended as a result.

Develop-
ment not
permitted

B.1 Development is not permitted by Class B if the waste material is or includes material resulting from the winning and working of minerals.

PART 13

DEVELOPMENT BY LOCAL HIGHWAY AUTHORITIES

Class A

Permitted
development

The carrying out by a local highway authority on land outside but adjoining the boundary of an existing highway of works required for or incidental to the maintenance or improvement of the highway.

PART 14

DEVELOPMENT BY DRAINAGE BODIES

Class A

Permitted
development

A. Development by a drainage body in, on or under a watercourse or land drainage works in connection with the improvement, maintenance or repair of the watercourse or works.

Interpreta-
tion of Class
A

A.1 For the purposes of Class A "drainage body" means a drainage body within the meaning of the Land Drainage Act 1976(b) which is not a water authority.

(a)   1964 c.40.
(b)   1976 c. 70.

PART 15

DEVELOPMENT BY THE NATIONAL RIVERS AUTHORITY

Class A

Permitted
development

A. Development by the National Rivers Authority for the purposes of their functions consisting of—
  (a) **(revoked),**
  (b) **development not above ground level required in connection with conserving, redistributing or augmenting water resources,**
  (c) **development in, on or under any watercourse or land drainage works and required in connection with the improvement or maintenance or repair of that watercourse or those land drainage works,**
  (d) **the provision of a building, plant or machinery or apparatus in, on, over or under land for the purpose of survey or investigation,**
  (e) **the maintenance, improvement or repair of works for measuring the flow in any watercourse or channel,**
  (f) **(revoked),**
  (g) **any works authorised by or required in connection with an order made under section 1 or 2 of the Drought Act 1976(a),**
  (h) **any other development in, on, over or under their operational land, other than the provision of a building but including the extension or alteration of a building.**

Develop-
ment not
permitted

A.1 Development is not permitted by Class A if—
  (a) in the case of any Class A(b) development, it would include the construction of a reservoir,
  (b) in the case of any Class A(f) development involving the installation of a station or house exceeding 29 cubic metres in capacity, that installation would be carried out at or above ground level or under a highway used by vehicular traffic,
  (c) in the case of any Class A(h) development, it would consist of or include the extension or alteration of a building so that—
    (i) its design or external appearance would be materially affected, or
    (ii) the height of the original building would be exceeded, or the content of the original building would be exceeded by more than 25%, or
    (iii) the floorspace of the original building would be exceeded by more than 1,000 square metres, or
  (d) in the case of any Class A(h) development, it would consist of the installation or erection of any plant or machinery exceeding 15 metres in height or the height of anything it replaces, whichever is the greater.

Condition

A.2 Development is permitted by Class A(d) subject to the condition that, on completion of the survey or investigation, or at the expiration of 6 months from the commencement of the development concerned, whichever is the sooner, all such operations shall cease and all such buildings, plant or apparatus shall be removed and the land restored as soon as reasonably practicable to its former condition (or to any other condition which may be agreed with the local planning authority).

PART 16

DEVELOPMENT BY OR ON BEHALF OF SEWERAGE UNDERTAKERS

Permitted
development

A. Any development not above ground level by or on behalf of a sewerage undertaker required in connection with the provision, improvement, maintenance or repair of a sewer, outfall pipe or sludge main or associated apparatus.

Interpreta-
tion of Class
A

A.1 (Revoked).

PART 17

DEVELOPMENT BY STATUTORY UNDERTAKERS

Class A   Railway or light railway undertakings

Permitted
development

A. Development by railway undertakers on their operational land, required in connection with the movement of traffic by rail.

Develop-
ment not
permitted

A.1 Development is not permitted by Class A if it consists of or includes—
  (a) the construction of a railway,
  (b) the constructions or erection of a hotel, railway station or bridge, or
  (c) the construction or erection otherwise than wholly within a railway station of—
    (i) an office, residential or educational building, or a building used for an industrial process,
    (ii) a car park, shop, restaurant, garage, petrol filling station or other building or structure provided under transport legislation.

Interpreta-
tion of Class
A

A.2 For the purposes of Class A references to the construction or erection of any building or structure include references to the reconstruction or alteration of a building or structure where its design or external appearance would be materially affected.

Class B   Dock, pier, harbour, water transport, canal or inland navigation undertakings

Permitted
development

B. Development on operational land by statutory undertakers or their lessees in respect of dock, pier, harbour, water transport, or canal or inland navigation undertakings, required—
  (a) **for the purposes of shipping, or**
  (b) **in connection with the embarking, disembarking, loading, discharging or transport of passengers, livestock or goods at a dock, pier or harbour, or with the movement of traffic by canal or inland navigation or by any railway forming part of the undertaking.**

(a)   1976 c.44.

Development not permitted	B.1 Development is not permitted by Class B if it consists of or includes– (a) the construction or erection of a hotel, or of a bridge or other building not required in connection with the handling of traffic, (b) the construction or erection otherwise then wholly within the limits of a dock, pier or harbour of– (i) an educational building, or (ii) a car park, shop, restaurant, garage, petrol filling station or other building provided under transport legislation.
Interpretation of Class B	B.2 For the purposes of Class B references to the construction or erection of any building or structure include references to the reconstruction or alteration of a building or structure where its design or external appearance would be materially affected.

Class C Works to inland waterways

Permitted development	C. The improvement, maintenance or repair of an inland waterway (other than a commercial waterway or cruising waterway) to which section 104 of the Transport Act 1968(a) applies, and the repair or maintenance of a culvert, weir, lock, aqueduct, sluice, reservoir, let-off valve or other work used in connection with the control and operation of such a waterway.

Class D Dredgings

Permitted development	D. The use of any land by statutory undertakers in respect of dock, pier, harbour, water transport, canal or inland navigation undertaking for the spreading of any dredged material.

Class E Water or hydraulic power undertakings

Permitted development	E. Development for the purposes of their undertaking by statutory undertakers for the supply of water or hydraulic power consisting of— (a) development not above ground level required in connection with the supply of water or for conserving, redistributing or augmenting water resources, or for the conveyance of water treatment sludge, (b) development in, on or under any watercourse and required in connection with the improvement or maintenance of that watercourse, (c) the provision of a building, plant, machinery or apparatus in, on, over or under land for the purpose of survey or investigation, (d) the maintenance, improvement or repair of works for measuring the flow in any watercourse or channel, (e) the installation in a water distribution system of a booster station, valve house, meter or switch-gear house, (f) any works authorized by or required in connection with an order made under section 1 or 2 of the Drought Act 1976(b), (g) any other development in, on, over or under operational land other than the provision of a building but including the extension or alteration of a building.
Development not permitted	E.1 Development is not permitted by Class E if– (a) in the case of any Class E(a) development, it would include the construction of a reservoir, (b) in the case of any Class E(e) development involving the installation of a station or house exceeding 29 cubic metres in capacity, that installation is carried out at or above ground level or under a highway used by vehicular traffic, (c) in the case of any Class E(g) development, it would consist of or include the extension or alteration of a building so that– (i) its design or external appearance would be materially affected; (ii) the height of the original building would be exceeded, or the cubic content of the original building would be exceeded by more than 25%, or (iii) the floor space of the original building would be exceeded by more than 1,000 square metres, or (d) in the case of any Class E(g) development, it would consist of the installation or erection of any plant or machinery exceeding 15 metres in height or the height of anything it replaces, whichever is the greater.
Condition	E.2 Development is permitted by Class E(c) subject to the condition that, on completion of the survey or investigation, or at the expiration of 6 months from the commencement of the development, whichever is the sooner, all such operations shall cease and all such buildings, plant or apparatus shall be removed and the land restored as soon as reasonably practicable to its former condition (or to any other condition which may be agreed with the local planning authority).

Class F Gas Suppliers

Permitted development	F. Development by a public gas supplier required for the purposes of its undertaking consisting of– (a) the laying underground of mains, pipes or other apparatus; (b) the installation in a gas distribution system of apparatus for measuring, recording, controlling or varying the pressure, flow or volume of gas, and structures for housing such apparatus; (c) the construction in any storage area or protective area specified in an order made under section 4 of the Gas Act 1965(c), of boreholes, and the erection or construction in any such area of any plant or machinery required in connection with the construction of such boreholes; (d) the placing and storage on land of pipes and other apparatus to be included in a main or pipe which is being or is about to be laid or constructed in pursuance of planning permission granted or deemed to be granted under Part III of the Act; (e) the erection on operational land of the public gas supplier of a building solely for the protection of plant or machinery; (f) any other development carried out in, on, over or under the operational land of the public gas supplier.
Development not permitted	F.1 Development is not permitted by Class F if– (a) in the case of any Class F(b) development involving the installation of a structure for housing apparatus exceeding 29 cubic metres in capacity, that installation would be carried out at or above ground level, or under a highway used by vehicular traffic,

	(b) in the case of any Class F(c) development (i) the borehole is shown in an order approved by the Secretary of State for Energy for the purpose of section 4(6) of the Gas Act 1965; or (ii) any plant or machinery would exceed 6 metres in height, (c) in the case of any Class F(e) development, the building would exceed 15 metres in height, or (d) in the case of any Class F(f) development– (i) it would consist of or include the erection of a building, or the reconstruction or alteration of a building where its design or external appearance would be materially affected; (ii) it would involve the installation of plant or machinery exceeding 15 metres in height, or capable without the carrying out of additional works of being extended to a height exceeding 15 metres; or (iii) it would consist of or include the replacement of any plant or machinery, by plant or machinery exceeding 15 metres in height or exceeding the height of the plant or machinery replaced, whichever is the greater.
Conditions	F.2 Development is permitted by Class F subject to the following conditions– (a) in the case of any Class F(a) development, not less than 8 weeks before the beginning of operations to lay a notifiable pipeline, the public gas supplier shall give notice in writing to the local planning authority of its intention to carry out that development, identifying the land under which the pipeline is to be laid, (b) in the case of any Class F(d) development, on completion of the laying or construction of the main or pipe, or at the expiry of a period of 9 months from the beginning of the development, whichever is the sooner, the pipe or apparatus shall be removed and the land restored as soon as reasonably practicable to its condition before the development took place (or to any other condition which may be agreed with the local planning authority), (c) in the case of any Class F(e) development, approval of the details of the design and external appearance of the building shall be obtained, before the development is begun, from– (i) in Greater London or a metropolitan county, the local planning authority, (ii) in a National Park, outside a metropolitan county, the county planning authority, (iii) in any other case, the district planning authority.

Class G Electricity Undertakings

Permitted development	G. Development by statutory undertakers for the supply of electricity for the purposes of their undertaking consisting of– (a) the laying underground of pipes, cables or any other apparatus, and the construction of shafts and tunnels reasonably necessary in connection with such pipes, cables or apparatus; (b) the installation in an electric line of feeder or service pillars or transforming or switching stations or chambers; (c) the installation of service lines to individual consumers from an electric line; (d) the sinking of boreholes to ascertain the nature of the subsoil and the installation of any plant or machinery reasonably necessary in connection with such boreholes; (e) the extension or alteration of buildings on operational land; (f) the erection on operational land of the undertaking of a building solely for the protection of plant or machinery; (g) any other development carried out in, on, over or under the operational land of the undertaking.
Development not permitted	G.1 Development is not permitted by Class G if– (a) in the case of any Class G(b) development involving the installation of a chamber for housing apparatus exceeding 29 cubic metres in capacity, that installation would be carried out at or above ground level, or under a highway used by vehicular traffic; (b) in the case of any Class G(e) development– (i) the height of the original building would be exceeded, (ii) the cubic content of the original building would be exceeded by more than 25% (or 10% in the case of any building on article 1(5) land), or (iii) the floorspace of the original building would be exceeded by more than 1000 square metres (or 500 square metres in the case of any building on article 1(5) land); (c) in the case of any Class G(f) development, the building would exceed 15 metres in height, or (d) in the case of any Class G(g) development, it would consist of or include– (i) the erection of a building, or the reconstruction or alteration of a building where its design or external appearance would be materially affected, or (ii) the installation or erection by way of addition or replacement of any plant or machinery exceeding 15 metres in height or the height of any plant or machinery replaced, whichever is the greater.
Conditions	G.2 Development is permitted by Class G subject to the following conditions– (a) in the case of any Class G(d) development, on the completion of that development, or at the end of a period of six months from the beginning of that development (whichever is the sooner) any such plant or machinery shall be removed and the land shall be restored as soon as reasonably practicable to its condition before the development took place, (b) in the case of any Class G(f) development, approval of details of the design and external appearance of the buildings shall be obtained, before development is begun, from– (i) in Greater London or a metropolitan county, the local planning authority, (ii) in a National Park, outside a metropolitan county, the county planning authority, (iii) in any other case, the district planning authority.

Class H Tramway or road transport undertakings

Permitted development	H. Development required for the purposes of the carrying on of any tramway or road transport undertaking consisting of– (a) the installation of posts, overhead wires, underground cables, feeder pillars or transformer boxes in, on, over or adjacent to a highway for the purpose of supplying current to public service vehicles;

(a) 1968 c.73.
(b) 1976 c.44.
(c) 1965 c.36.

(b) the installation of tramway tracks, and conduits, drains and pipes in connection with such tracks for the working of tramways;

(c) the installation of telephone cables and apparatus, huts, stop posts and signs required in connection with the operation of public service vehicles;

(d) the erection or construction and the maintenance, improvement or other alteration of passenger shelters and barriers for the control of people waiting to enter public service vehicles;

(e) any other development on operational land of the undertaking.

Development not permitted

H.1 Development is not permitted by Class H, if it would consist of–

(a) in the case of any Class H(a) development, the installation of a structure exceeding 17 cubic metres in capacity,

(b) in the case of any Class H(e) development–

(i) the erection of a building or the reconstruction or alteration of a building where the design or external appearance would be materially affected,

(ii) the installation or erection by way of addition or replacement of any plant or machinery which would exceed 15 metres in height or the height of any plant or machinery it replaces, whichever is the greater,

(iii) development, not wholly within an omnibus or tramway station, in pursuance of powers contained in transport legislation.

Class I Lighthouse undertakings

Permitted development

I. Development required for the purposes of the functions of a general or local lighthouse authority under the Merchant Shipping Act 1894(a) and any other statutory provision made with respect to a local lighthouse authority, or in the exercise by a local lighthouse authority of rights, powers or duties acquired by usage prior to the Act of 1894.

Development not permitted

I.1 Development is not permitted by Class I if it consists of or includes the erection of offices, or the reconstruction or alteration of offices where their design or external appearance would be materially affected.

Class J Post Office

Permitted development

J. Development required for the purposes of the Post Office consisting of–

(a) the installation of posting boxes or self-service machines,

(b) any other development carried out in, on, over or under the operational land of the undertaking.

Development not permitted

J.1 Development is not permitted by Class J if–

(a) it would consist of or include the erection of a building, or the reconstruction or alteration of a building where its design or external appearance would be materially affected, or

(b) it would consist of or include the installation or erection by way of addition or replacement of any plant or machinery which would exceed 15 metres in height or the height of any existing plant or machinery, whichever is the greater.

PART 18

AVIATION DEVELOPMENT

Class A—Development at an airport

Permitted development

A. The carrying out on operational land by a relevant airport operator or its agent of development (including the erection or alteration of an operational building) in connection with the provision of services and facilities at a relevant airport.

Development not permitted

A.1 Development is not permitted by Class A if it would consist of or include–

(a) the construction or extension of a runway;

(b) the construction of a passenger terminal the floorspace of which would exceed 500 square metres;

(c) the extension or alteration of a passenger terminal, where the floorspace of the building as existing at the date of coming into force of this order or, if built after that date, of the building as built, would be exceeded by more than 15%;

(d) the erection of a building other than an operational building;

(e) the alteration or reconstruction of a building other than an operational building, where its design or external appearance would be materially affected.

Condition

A.2 Development is permitted by Class A subject to the condition that the relevant airport operator consults the local planning authority before carrying out any development, unless that development falls within the description in paragraph A.3(2).

Interpretation of Class A

A.3 (1) For the purposes of paragraph A.1 floorspace shall be calculated by external measurement and without taking account of the floorspace in any pier or satellite.

(2) Development falls within this paragraph if–

(a) it is urgently required for the efficient running of the airport, and

(b) it consists of the carrying out of works, or the erection or construction of a structure or of an ancillary building, or the placing on land of equipment, and the works, structure, building, or equipment do not exceed 4 metres in height or 200 cubic metres in capacity.

Class B—Air navigation development at an airport

Permitted development

B. The carrying out on operational land within the perimeter of a relevant airport by a relevant airport operator or its agent of development in connection with–

(a) the provision of air traffic control services,

(b) the navigation of aircraft using the airport, or

(c) the monitoring of the movement of aircraft using the airport.

Class C—Air navigation development near an airport

Permitted development

C. The carrying out on operational land outside but within 8 kilometres of the perimeter of a relevant airport, by a relevant airport operator or its agent, of development in connection with–

(a) the provision of air traffic control services,

(b) the navigation of aircraft using the airport, or

(c) the monitoring of the movement of aircraft using the airport.

Development not permitted

C.1 Development is not permitted by Class C if–

(a) any building erected would be used for a purpose other than housing equipment used in connection with the provision of air traffic control services, with assisting the navigation of aircraft, or with monitoring the movement of aircraft using the airport;

(b) any building erected would exceed a height of 4 metres;

(c) it would consist of the installation or erection of any radar or radio mast, antenna or other apparatus which would exceed 15 metres in height, or, where an existing mast, antenna or apparatus is replaced, the height of that mast, antenna or apparatus, if greater.

Class D Development by the Civil Aviation Authority within an airport

Permitted development

D. The carrying out by the Civil Aviation Authority or its agents, within the perimeter of an airport at which the Authority provides air traffic control services, of development in connection with–

(a) the provision of air traffic control services,

(b) the navigation of aircraft using the airport, or

(c) the monitoring of the movement of aircraft using the airport.

Class E Development by the Civil Aviation Authority for air traffic control and navigation

Permitted development

E. The carrying out on operational land of the Civil Aviation Authority by the authority or its agents of development in connection with–

(a) the provision of air traffic control services,

(b) the navigation of aircraft, or

(c) monitoring the movement of aircraft.

Development not permitted

E.1 Development is not permitted by Class E if–

(a) any building erected would be used for a purpose other than housing equipment used in connection with the provision of air traffic control services, assisting the navigation of aircraft or monitoring the movement of aircraft;

(b) any building erected would exceed a height of 4 metres; or

(c) it would consist of the installation or erection of any radar or radio mast, antenna or other apparatus which would exceed 15 metres in height, or, where an existing mast, antenna or apparatus is replaced, the height of that mast, antenna or apparatus, if greater.

Class F Development by the Civil Aviation Authority in an emergency

Permitted development

F. The use of land by or on behalf of the Civil Aviation Authority in an emergency to station moveable apparatus replacing unserviceable apparatus.

Condition

F.1 Development is permitted by Class F subject to the condition that on or before the expiry of a period of 6 months beginning with the date on which the use began, the use shall cease, and any apparatus shall be removed, and the land shall be restored to its condition before the development took place, or to any other condition as may be agreed in writing between the local planning authority and the developer.

Class G Development by the Civil Aviation Authority for air traffic control etc.

Permitted development

G. The use of land by or on behalf of the Civil Aviation Authority to provide services and facilities in connection with–

(a) the provision of air traffic control services,

(b) the navigation of aircraft, or

(c) the monitoring of aircraft,

and the erection or placing of moveable structures on the land for the purpose of that use.

Condition

G.1 Development is permitted by Class G subject to the condition that, on or before the expiry of the period of 6 months beginning with the date on which the use began, the use shall cease, and any structure shall be removed, and the land shall be restored to its condition before the development took place, or to any other condition as may be agreed in writing between the local planning authority and the developer.

Class H Development by the Civil Aviation Authority for surveys etc.

Permitted development

H. The use of land by or on behalf of the Civil Aviation Authority for the stationing and operation of apparatus in connection with the carrying out of surveys or investigations.

Condition

H.1 Development is permitted by Class H subject to the condition that on or before the expiry of the period of 6 months beginning with the date on which the use began, the use shall cease, and any apparatus shall be removed, and the land shall be restored to its condition before the development took place, or to any other condition as may be agreed in writing between the local planning authority and the developer.

Class J Use of airport buildings managed by relevant airport operators

Permitted development

J. The use of buildings within the perimeter of an airport managed by a relevant airport operator for purposes connected with air transport services or other flying activities at that airport.

Interpretation of Part 18

K. For the purposes of Part 18–

"operational building" means a building, other than a hotel, required in connection with the movement or maintenance of aircraft, or with the embarking, disembarking, loading, discharge or transport of passengers, livestock or goods at a relevant airport;

"relevant airport" means an airport to which Part V of the Airports Act 1986(a) applies;

"relevant airport operator" means a relevant airport operator within the meaning of section 57 of the Airports Act 1986.

(a) 1894 c.60.

(a) 1986 c.31.

PART 19

DEVELOPMENT ANCILLARY TO MINING OPERATIONS

Class A

Permitted development

A. The carrying out of operations for the erection, extension, installation, rearrangement, replacement, repair or other alteration of any—

    (a) plant or machinery,

    (b) buildings,

    (c) private ways or private railways or sidings, or

    (d) sewers, mains, pipes, cables or other similar apparatus,

on land used as a mine.

Development not permitted

A.1. Development is not permitted by Class A—

    (a) in relation to land at an underground mine—

        (i) otherwise than on an approved site; or

        (ii) from a date 6 months after the coming into force of this order, on land within the definition in paragraph D.1(b), unless a plan of that land has before that date been deposited with the mineral planning authority;

    (b) if the principal purpose of the development would be any purpose other than—

        (i) purposes in connection with the winning and working of minerals at that mine or of minerals brought to the surface at that mine; or

        (ii) the treatment, storage or removal from the mine of such minerals or waste materials derived from them;

    (c) if the external appearance of the mine would be materially affected;

    (d) if any building, plant or machinery which is not in an excavation would exceed a height of—

        (i) 15 metres above ground level;

        (ii) the building, plant or machinery, if any, which is being rearranged, repaired or replaced,

    whichever is the greater;

    (e) if any building, plant or machinery in an excavation would exceed a height of—

        (i) 15 metres above the excavated ground level; or

        (ii) 15 metres above the lowest point of the unexcavated ground immediately adjacent to the excavation; or

        (iii) the building, plant or machinery, if any, which is being rearranged, repaired or replaced,

    whichever is the greatest;

    (f) if any building erected (other than a replacement building) would have a floor space exceeding 1000 square metres; or

    (g) if the cubic content of any replaced, extended or altered building would exceed by more than 25% the cubic content of the building replaced, extended or altered or the floor space would exceed by more than 1000 square metres the floor space of that building.

Condition

A.2. Development is permitted by Class A subject to the condition that before the end of the period of 24 months from the date when the mining operations have permanently ceased, or any longer period which the mineral planning authority agree in writing—

    (a) all buildings, plant or machinery permitted by this Class shall be removed from the land unless the mineral planning authority have otherwise agreed in writing; and

    (b) the land shall be restored, so far as is practicable, to its condition before the development took place, or restored to such condition as may have been agreed in writing between the mineral planning authority and the developer.

Class B

Permitted development

B. The carrying out, on land used as a mine or on ancillary mining land, with the prior approval of the mineral planning authority, of operations for the erection, installation, extension, rearrangement, replacement, repair or other alteration of any—

    (a) plant or machinery,

    (b) buildings, or

    (c) structures or erections.

Development not permitted

B.1. Development is not permitted by Class B—

    (a) in relation to land at an underground mine—

        (i) otherwise than on an approved site; or

        (ii) from a date 6 months after the coming into operation of this order, on land within the definition in paragraph D.1(b), unless a plan of that land has, before that date, been deposited with the mineral planning authority; or

    (b) if the principal purpose of the development would be any purpose other than—

        (i) purposes in connection with the operation of the mine,

        (ii) the treatment, preparation for sale, consumption or utilization of minerals won or brought to the surface at that mine, or

        (iii) the storage or removal from the mine of such minerals, their products or waste materials derived from them.

B.2. The prior approval referred to in Class B shall not be refused or granted subject to conditions unless the authority are satisfied that it is expedient to do so because—

    (a) the proposed development would injure the amenity of the neighbourhood and modifications can reasonably be made or conditions reasonably imposed in order to avoid or reduce that injury, or

    (b) the proposed development ought to be, and could reasonably be, sited elsewhere.

Condition.

B.3. Development is permitted by Class B subject to the condition that before the end of the period of 24 months from the date when the mining operations have permanently ceased, or any longer period which the mineral planning authority agree in writing—

    (a) all buildings, plant, machinery, structures or erections permitted by this Class shall be removed from the land unless the mineral planning authority have otherwise agreed in writing; and

    (b) the land shall be restored, so far as is practicable, to its condition before the development took place or restored to such condition as may have been agreed in writing between the mineral planning authority and the developer.

Class C

Permitted development

C. The carrying out with the prior approval of the mineral planning authority of development required for the maintenance or safety of a mine or a disused mine or for the purposes of ensuring the safety of the surface of the land at or adjacent to a mine or a disused mine.

Development not permitted

C.1. Development is not permitted by Class C if it is carried out by the British Coal Corporation, or any lessee or licensee of theirs.

Prior approvals

C.2—(1) The prior approval of the mineral planning authority to development permitted by Class C is not required if—

    (a) the external appearance of the mine or disused mine at or adjacent to which the development is to be carried out would not be materially affected;

    (b) no building, plant, machinery, structure or erection—

        (i) would exceed a height of 15 metres above ground level, or

        (ii) where a building, plant or machinery is rearranged, replaced or repaired, would exceed a height of 15 metres above ground level or the height of what was replaced, rearranged or repaired, whichever is the greater; and

    (c) the development consists of the extension, alteration or replacement of an existing building, within the limits set out in paragraph (3) below.

(2) The approval referred to in Class C shall not be refused or granted subject to conditions unless the authority are satisfied that it is expedient to do so because—

    (a) the proposed development would injure the amenity of the neighbourhood and modifications could reasonably be made or conditions reasonably imposed in order to avoid or reduce that injury, or

    (b) the proposed development ought to be, and could reasonably be, sited elsewhere.

(3) The limits referred to in paragraph C.2(1)(c) are—

    (a) that the cubic content of the building as extended, altered or replaced does not exceed that of the existing building by more than 25%, and

    (b) that the floor area of the building as extended, altered or replaced does not exceed that of the existing building by more than 1,000 square metres.

Interpretation of Part 19

D.1 An area of land is an approved site for the purposes of Part 19 if—

    (a) it is identified in a grant of planning permission or any instrument by virtue of which planning permission is deemed to be granted, as land which may be used for development described in this Part; or

    (b) in any other case, it is land immediately adjoining an active access to an underground mine which, on the date of coming into force of this order, was in use for the purposes of that mine, in connection with the purposes described in paragraph A.1(b)(i) or (ii) or paragraph B.1(b)(i) to (iii) above.

D.2. For the purposes of Part 19—

"active access" means a surface access to underground workings which is in normal and regular use for the transportation of minerals, materials, spoil or men;

"ancillary mining land" means land adjacent to and occupied together with a mine at which the winning and working of minerals is carried out in pursuance of planning permission granted or deemed to be granted under Part III of the Act;

"minerals" includes coal won or worked by virtue of section 36(1) of the Coal Industry Nationalisation Act 1946**(a)**, but not any other coal;

"the prior approval of the mineral planning authority" means prior written approval of that authority of detailed proposals for the siting, design and external appearance of the proposed building, plant or machinery as erected, installed, extended or altered;

"underground mine" is a mine at which minerals are worked principally by underground methods.

PART 20

BRITISH COAL MINING DEVELOPMENT

Class A

Permitted development

A. The winning and working underground by the British Coal Corporation, their lessees or licensees, in a mine started before 1st July 1948, of coal or coal-related minerals, and any underground development incidental to such winning and working.

Interpretation of Class A

A.1. For the purposes of this class "coal-related minerals" means minerals other than coal referred to in paragraph 1(2) of Schedule 1 to the Coal Industry Nationalisation Act 1946.

Class B

Permitted development

B. Any development required for the purposes of a mine which is carried out on an authorised site at that mine by the British Coal Corporation, their lessees or licensees, in connection with coal industry activities.

Development not permitted

B.1. Development is not permitted by Class B if—

    (a) the external appearance of the mine would be materially affected;

    (b) any building, plant or machinery structure or erection or any deposit of minerals or waste—

        (i) would exceed a height of 15 metres above ground level, or

        (ii) where a building, plant or machinery would be rearranged, replaced or repaired, the resulting development would exceed a height of 15 metres above ground level or the height of what was replaced, rearranged or repaired, whichever is the greater;

    (c) any building erected (other than a replacement building) would have a floor space exceeding 1000 square metres;

    (d) the cubic content of any replaced, extended or altered building would exceed by more than 25% the cubic content of the building replaced, extended or altered or the floor space would exceed by more than 1000 square metres, the floor space of that building;

(a) 1946 c.59.

(e) it would be for the purpose of creating a new surface access to underground workings or of improving an existing access (which is not an active access) to underground workings; or

(f) from a date 6 months after the coming into force of this order, it would be carried out on land within the definition in paragraph F.2(1)(b), and a plan of that land has not, before that date, been deposited with the mineral planning authority.

Conditions

B.2. Development is permitted by Class B subject to the condition that before the end of the period of 24 months from the date when the mining operations have permanently ceased, or any longer period which the mineral planning authority agree in writing–

(a) all buildings, plant and machinery, structures or erections or deposits of minerals or waste permitted by this class shall be removed from the land unless the mineral planning authority have otherwise agreed in writing; and

(b) the land shall, so far as is practicable, be restored to its condition before the development took place or to such condition as may have been agreed in writing between the mineral planning authority and the developer.

Class C

Permitted development

C. Any development required for the purposes of a mine which is carried out on an authorised site at that mine by the British Coal Corporation, their lessees or licensees in connection with coal industry activities and with the prior approval of the mineral planning authority.

Development not permitted

C.1. Development is not permitted by Class C if–

(a) it would be for the purpose of creating a new surface access or improving an existing access (which is not an active access) to underground workings; or

(b) from a date 6 months after the coming into force of this order, it would be carried out on land within the definition in paragraph F.2(1)(b), and a plan of that land has not before that date, been deposited with the mineral planning authority.

Condition

C.2. Development is permitted by Class C subject to the condition that before the end of the period of 24 months from the date when the mining operations have permanently ceased, or any longer period which the mineral planning authority agree in writing–

(a) all buildings, plant and machinery, structures or erections or deposits of minerals or waste permitted by this class shall be removed from the land, unless the mineral planning authority have otherwise agreed in writing; and

(b) the land shall, so far as is practicable, be restored to its condition before the development took place or to such condition as may have been agreed in writing between the mineral planning authority and the developer.

Interpretation

C.3. The prior approval referred to in Class C shall not be refused or granted subject to conditions unless the authority are satisfied that it is expedient to do so because–

(a) the proposed development would injure the amenity of the neighbourhood and modifications could reasonably be made or conditions reasonably imposed in order to avoid or reduce that injury, or

(b) the proposed development ought to be, and could reasonably be, sited elsewhere.

Class D

Permitted development

D. The carrying out of operations by the British Coal Corporation for the purpose of prospecting for coal workable by opencast methods and the use of land for that purpose while such operations are being carried out.

Conditions

D.1. Development is permitted by Class D subject to the following conditions–

(a) at least 42 days before the development is begun, notice in writing has been served on the mineral planning authority, indicating the nature, extent and probable duration of the development;

(b) as soon as possible after the end of the period of the carrying out of the prospecting operations–

(i) any buildings, plant, machinery or waste materials shall be removed; and

(ii) any boreholes shall be sealed and any other excavations filled in and levelled, any topsoil removed being replaced as the uppermost layer.

Class E

Permitted development

E. The carrying out by the British Coal Corporation, their lessees or licensees, with the prior approval of the mineral planning authority, of development required for the maintenance or safety of a mine or a disused mine or for the purposes of ensuring the safety of the surface of the land at or adjacent to a mine or a disused mine.

Prior approvals

E.1.—(1) The prior approval of the mineral planning authority to development permitted by Class E is not required if–

(a) the external appearance of the mine or disused mine at or adjacent to which the development is to be carried out would not be materially affected;

(b) no building, plant or machinery, structure or erection–

(i) would exceed a height of 15 metres above ground level, or

(ii) where any building, plant or machinery, structure or erection is rearranged, replaced or repaired, would exceed a height of 15 metres above ground level or the height of what was replaced, rearranged or repaired, whichever is the greater; and

(c) the development consists of the extension, alteration or replacement of an existing building, within the limits set out in paragraph (3).

(2) The approval referred to in Class E shall not be refused or granted subject to conditions unless the authority are satisfied that it is expedient to do so because–

(a) the proposed development would injure the amenity of the neighbourhood and modifications could reasonably be made or conditions reasonably imposed in order to avoid or reduce that injury, or

(b) the proposed development ought to be, and could reasonably be, sited elsewhere.

(3) The limits referred to in paragraph E.1(c) are–

(i) that the cubic content of the building as extended, altered or replaced does not exceed that of the existing building by more than 25%; and

(ii) that the floor area of the building as extended, altered or replaced does not exceed that of the existing building by more than 1,000 square metres.

Interpretation of Part 20

F.1. For the purposes of Part 20–

"active access" is a surface access to underground workings which is in normal and regular use for the transportation of coal, materials, spoil or men;

"coal industry activities" means such activities as defined in section 63 of the Coal Industry Nationalisation Act 1946;

"normal and regular use" is use other than intermittent visits to inspect and maintain the fabric of the mine or any plant or machinery;

"prior approval of the mineral planning authority" means prior written approval of that authority of detailed proposals for the siting, design and external appearance of the proposed building, plant or machinery or structure or erection as erected, installed, extended or altered.

F.2.—(1) Subject to sub-paragraph (2), land is an authorised site for the purposes of Part 20 if–

(a) it is identified in a grant of planning permission or any instrument by virtue of which planning permission is deemed to be granted as land which may be used for development described in this Part; or

(b) in any other case, it is land immediately adjoining an active access which, on the date of coming into force of this order, was in use for the purposes of that mine in connection with coal industry activities.

(2) For the purposes of sub-paragraph (1), land is not to be regarded as in use in connection with coal industry activities if–

(a) it is used for the permanent deposit of waste derived from the winning and working of minerals; or

(b) there is on, over or under it a railway, conveyor, aerial ropeway, roadway, overhead power line or pipeline which is not itself surrounded by other land used for those purposes.

PART 21

WASTE TIPPING AT A MINE

Class A

Permitted development

A. The deposit, on premises used as a mine or on ancillary mining land already used for the purpose, of waste derived from the winning and working of minerals at that mine or from minerals brought to the surface at that mine, or from the treatment or the preparation for sale, consumption or utilization of minerals from the mine.

Development not permitted

A.1. Development is not permitted by Class A if–

(a) in the case of waste deposited in an excavation, waste would be deposited at a height above the level of the land adjoining the excavation, unless that is provided for in a waste management scheme or a relevant scheme;

(b) in any other case, the superficial area or height of the deposit (measured as at the date of the making of this order) would be increased by more than 10%, unless such an increase is provided for in a waste management scheme or in a relevant scheme.

Conditions

A.2. Development is permitted by Class A subject to the following conditions–

(a) except in a case where a relevant scheme or a waste management scheme has already been approved by the mineral planning authority, the developer shall, if the mineral planning authority so require, within three months or such longer period as the authority may specify, submit a waste management scheme for that authority's approval;

(b) where a waste management scheme or a relevant scheme has been approved, the depositing of waste and all other activities in relation to that deposit shall be carried out in accordance with the scheme as approved.

Interpretation

A.3. For the purposes of Class A–

"ancillary mining land" means land adjacent to and occupied together with a mine at which the winning and working of minerals is carried out in pursuance of planning permission granted or deemed to be granted under Part III of the Act;

"waste management scheme" means a scheme required by the mineral planning authority to be submitted for their approval in accordance with the condition in paragraph A.2(a) which makes provision for–

(a) the manner in which the depositing of waste (other than waste deposited on a site for use for filling any mineral excavation in the mine or on ancillary mining land in order to comply with the terms of any planning permission granted on an application or deemed to be granted under Part III of that Act) is to be carried out after the date of the approval of that scheme,

(b) where appropriate, the stripping and storage of the subsoil and topsoil,

(c) the restoration and aftercare of the site.

Class B

Permitted development

B. The deposit on land comprised in a site used for the deposit of waste materials or refuse on 1st July 1948 of waste resulting from colliery production activities.

Development not permitted

B.1. Development is not permitted by Class B on or after a date 3 months after the coming into force of this order unless–

(a) it is in accordance with a relevant scheme which has been approved by the mineral planning authority before the date of coming into force of this order; or

(b) an application for planning permission has been made–

(i) the development is in terms of the permission sought; and

(ii) the application has not been determined by the mineral planning authority, or, if an appeal is made, the Secretary of State.

Interpretation of Class B

B.2. For the purposes of Class B–
"colliery production activities" has the meaning it is given in paragraph 2 of Schedule 1 to the Coal Industry Nationalisation Act 1946(**a**).

Interpretation of Part 21

C. For the purposes of Part 21–
"relevant scheme" means a scheme, other than a waste management scheme, requiring approval by the mineral planning authority in accordance with a condition or limitation on any planning permission granted or deemed to be granted under Part III of the Act, for making provision for the manner in which the deposit of waste is to be carried out and for the carrying out of other activities in relation to that deposit.

PART 22

MINERAL EXPLORATION

Class A

Permitted development

A. Development on any land during a period not exceeding 28 consecutive days consisting of–
(a) the drilling of boreholes,
(b) the carrying out of seismic surveys, or
(c) the making of other excavations,
for the purpose of mineral exploration, and the provision or assembly on that land or adjoining land of any structure required in connection with any of those operations.

Development not permitted

A.1. Development is not permitted by Class A if–
(a) it consists of the drilling of boreholes for petroleum exploration;
(b) any operation would be carried out within 50 metres of any part of an occupied residential building or a building occupied as a hospital or school;
(c) any operation would be carried out within a National Park, an area of outstanding natural beauty or a site of archaeological or special scientific interest;
(d) any explosive charge of more than 1 kilogram would be used;
(e) any excavation referred to in paragraph A(c) would exceed 10 metres in depth or 12 square metres in surface area;
(f) in the case described in paragraph A(c) more than 10 excavations would, as a result, be made within any area of 1 hectare within the land during any period of 24 months; or
(g) any structure assembled or provided would exceed 12 metres in height, or, where the structure would be within 3 kilometres of the perimeter of an aerodrome, 3 metres in height.

Conditions

A.2. Development is permitted by this class subject to the following conditions–
(a) no operations shall be carried out between 6pm and 7am;
(b) no trees on the land shall be removed, felled, lopped or topped and no other thing shall be done on the land likely to harm or damage any trees, unless the mineral planning authority have so agreed in writing;
(c) before any excavation (other than a borehole) is made, any topsoil and any subsoil shall be separately removed from the land to be excavated and stored separately from other excavated material and from each other;
(d) within a period of 28 days from the cessation of operations unless the mineral planning authority have, in a particular case, agreed otherwise in writing–
(i) any structure permitted by Class A and any waste material arising from development permitted by Class A shall be removed from the land,
(ii) any borehole shall be adequately sealed,
(iii) any other excavation shall be filled with material from the site,
(iv) the surface of the land on which any operations have been carried out shall be levelled and any topsoil replaced as the uppermost layer, and
(v) the land shall, so far as is practicable, be restored to its condition before the development took place, including the carrying out of any necessary seeding and replanting.

Interpretation of Class A

A.3. For the purposes of Class A–
"mineral exploration" means ascertaining the presence, extent or quality of any deposit of a mineral with a view to exploiting that mineral;
"structure" means a building, plant or machinery or other structure.

Class B

Permitted development

B. Development on any land during a period not exceeding 4 months consisting of–
(a) the drilling of boreholes,
(b) the carrying out of seismic surveys, or
(c) the making of other excavations,
for the purposes of mineral exploration, and the provision or assembly on that land or on adjoining land of any structure required in connection with any of those operations.

Development not permitted

B.1. Development is not permitted by Class B if–
(a) it consists of the drilling of boreholes for petroleum exploration;
(b) the developer has not previously notified the mineral planning authority in writing of his intention to carry out the development (specifying the nature and location of the development);
(c) the relevant period has not elapsed;
(d) any explosive charge of more than 2 kilograms would be used;
(e) any excavation referred to in paragraph B(c) would exceed 10 metres in depth or 12 square metres in surface area; or
(f) any structure assembled or provided would exceed 12 metres in height.

Conditions

B.2. Development is permitted by Class B subject to the following conditions–
(a) the development shall be carried out in accordance with the details in the notification referred to in paragraph B.1(b), unless the mineral planning authority have otherwise agreed in writing;
(b) no trees on the land shall be removed, felled, lopped or topped and no other thing shall be done on the land likely to harm or damage any trees, unless the mineral planning authority have otherwise agreed in writing;

(c) before any excavation other than a borehole is made, any topsoil and any subsoil shall be separately removed from the land to be excavated and stored separately from other excavated material and from each other;
(d) within a period of 28 days from operations ceasing, unless the mineral planning authority have, in a particular case, agreed otherwise in writing–
(i) any structure permitted by Class B and any waste material arising from development so permitted shall be removed from the land,
(ii) any borehole shall be adequately sealed,
(iii) any other excavation shall be filled with material from the site,
(iv) the surface of the land shall be levelled and any topsoil replaced as the uppermost layer, and
(v) the land shall, so far as is practicable, be restored to its condition before the development took place, including the carrying out of any necessary seeding and replanting.

Interpretation of Class B

B.3. For the purposes of Class B–
"mineral exploration" means ascertaining the presence, extent or quality of any deposit of a mineral with a view to exploiting that mineral;
"relevant period" means the period elapsing–
(a) where a direction is not issued under article 6, 28 days after the notification referred to in paragraph B.1(b) or, if earlier, on the date on which the mineral planning authority notify the developer in writing that they will not issue such a direction, or
(b) where a direction is issued under article 6, 28 days from the date on which notice of that decision is sent to the Secretary of State, or, if earlier, the date on which the mineral planning authority notify the developer that the Secretary of State has disallowed the direction;
"structure" means a building, plant or machinery or other structure.

PART 23

REMOVAL OF MATERIAL FROM MINERAL-WORKING DEPOSITS

Class A

Permitted development

A. The removal of material of any description from a mineral-working deposit from which material was removed at any time during the period of 12 months before 19th May 1986.

Development not permitted

A.1. Development is not permitted by Class A–
(a) if no application was made before 19th November 1986 for planning permission to continue to remove material from the deposit;
(b) where such an application has been made, except in the terms of the planning permission sought;
(c) if the application has been determined by the mineral planning authority, or, if an appeal has been made, finally determined by the Secretary of State; or
(d) if the removal of material from the deposit during the 12 month period was in breach of planning control.

Class B

Permitted development

B. The removal of material of any description from a stockpile.

Class C

Permitted development

C. The removal of material of any description from a mineral-working deposit other than a stockpile.

Development not permitted

C.1. Development is not permitted by Class C if–
(a) the developer has not previously notified the mineral planning authority in writing of his intention to carry out development together with the appropriate details;
(b) the deposit covers a ground area exceeding 2 hectares, unless the deposit contains any mineral or other material deposited on the land at a date 5 years or less before the date on which it would be removed; or
(c) the deposit derives from the carrying out of any operations permitted under Part 6 of this Schedule or any class in a previous development order which it replaces.

Conditions

C.2. Development is permitted by Class C subject to the following conditions–
(a) it shall be carried out in accordance with the details given in the notice sent to the mineral planning authority referred to in paragraph C.1(a) above, unless that authority have agreed otherwise in writing;
(b) if the mineral planning authority so require, the developer shall within a period of 3 months from the date of the requirement (or such other longer period as that authority may provide) submit to them for approval a scheme providing for the restoration and aftercare of the site;
(c) where such a scheme is required, the site shall be restored and aftercare shall be carried out in accordance with the provisions of the approved scheme;
(d) development shall not be commenced until the relevant period has elapsed.

Interpretation of Class C

C.3. In Class C–
"appropriate details" means the nature of the development, the exact location of the mineral-working deposit from which the material would be removed, the proposed means of vehicular access to the site at which the development is to be carried out, and the earliest date at which any mineral presently contained in the deposit was deposited on the land;
"relevant period" means the period elapsing–
(a) where a direction is not issued under article 6, 28 days after the notification referred to in paragraph C.1(a) or, if earlier, on the date on which the mineral planning authority notify the developer in writing that they will not issue such a direction; or
(b) where a direction is issued under article 6, 28 days from the date on which notice of that direction is sent to the Secretary of State, or, if earlier, the date on which the mineral planning authority notify the developer that the Secretary of State has disallowed the direction.

Interpretation of Part 23

D. In Classes B and C of this Part–
"stockpile" means a mineral-working deposit consisting primarily of minerals which have been deposited for the purposes of their processing or sale.

(**a**) 1946 c.59.

PART 24

DEVELOPMENT BY TELECOMMUNICATIONS CODE SYSTEM OPERATORS

Class A

Permitted development

A. Development by or on behalf of a telecommunications code system operator for the purpose of the operator's telecommunication system in, on, over or under land controlled by that operator or in accordance with his licence, consisting of—

  (a) the installation, alteration or replacement of any telecommunication apparatus, or

  (b) the use of land in an emergency for a period not exceeding 6 months to station and operate moveable telecommunication apparatus required for the replacement of unserviceable telecommunication apparatus, including the provision of moveable structures on the land for the purposes of that use.

Development not permitted

A.1. Development is not permitted by Class A(a) if—

  (a) in the case of the installation of apparatus (other than on a building or other structure) the apparatus would exceed a height of 15 metres above ground level;

  (b) in the case of the alteration or replacement of apparatus already installed (other than on a building or other structure), the apparatus would when altered or replaced exceed the height of the existing apparatus or a height of 15 metres above ground level, whichever is the greater;

  (c) in the case of the installation, alteration or replacement of apparatus on a building or other structure, the height of the apparatus (taken by itself) would exceed—

    (i) 15 metres, where it is installed, or is to be installed, on a building or other structure which is 30 metres or more in height; or

    (ii) 10 metres in any other case;

  (d) in the case of the installation, alteration or replacement of apparatus on a building or other structure, the highest part of the apparatus when installed, altered or replaced would exceed the height of the highest part of the building or structure by more than—

    (i) 10 metres, in the case of a building or structure which is 30 metres or more in height;

    (ii) 8 metres, in the case of a building or structure which is more than 15 metres but less than 30 metres in height;

    (iii) 6 metres in any other case;

  (e) in the case of the installation or replacement of any apparatus other than—

    (i) a mast,

    (ii) any kind of antenna,

    (iii) a public call box, or

    (iv) any apparatus which does not project above the level of the surface of the ground,

  the ground or base area of the structure would exceed 1.5 square metres;

  (f) in the case of the installation, alteration or replacement on a building or structure of a microwave antenna or apparatus which includes or is intended for the support of such an antenna—

    (i) the building or other structure on which the antenna is to be installed is less than 15 metres in height;

    (ii) the size of the antenna when measured in any dimension would exceed 1.3 metres (excluding any projecting feed element); or

    (iii) the development would result in the presence on the building or structure of more than two microwave antennas; or

  (g) in the case of development on any article 1(5) land, it would consist of—

    (i) the installation or alteration of a microwave antenna or of any apparatus which includes or is intended for the support of such an antenna; or

    (ii) the replacement of such an antenna or such apparatus by an antenna or apparatus which differs from that which is being replaced,

  unless the development is carried out in any emergency.

Conditions

A.2.—(1) Class A(a) development is permitted subject to the condition that any antenna or supporting apparatus installed, altered or replaced on a building in accordance with that permission shall, so far as is practicable, be sited so as to minimise its effect on the external appearance of the building.

  (2) Class A(b) development is permitted subject to the condition that any apparatus or structure provided in accordance with that permission shall at the expiry of the relevant period be removed from the land and the land restored to its condition before the development took place.

  (3) Development on any article 1(5) land is permitted by Class A subject to the condition that in the case of the installation of apparatus on or over land controlled by the operator, he shall—

    (a) except in a case of emergency, give notice in writing to the local planning authority not less than eight weeks before development is begun of his intention to carry out such development; or

    (b) in a case of emergency, give written notice of such installation as soon as possible after the emergency begins.

Interpretation

A.3. For the purposes of this class—

  "1984 Act" means the Telecommunications Act 1984(a);

  "land controlled by an operator" means land occupied by the operator in right of a freehold interest or a leasehold interest under a lease granted for a term of not less than 10 years;

  "development in accordance with a licence" means development carried out by an operator in pursuance of a right conferred on that operator under the telecommunications code, and in accordance with any conditions relating to the application of that code imposed by the terms of his licence;

  "relevant period" means a period which expires either six months from the commencement of the use permitted by this paragraph or when the need for that use ceases, whichever occurs first;

  "telecommunications apparatus" means any apparatus falling within the definition of that term in paragraph 1 of Schedule 2 to the 1984 Act;

  "the telecommunications code" means the code contained in Schedule 2 to the 1984 Act;

  "telecommunications code system operator" means a person who has been granted a licence under section 7 of the 1984 Act which applies the telecommunications code to him in pursuance of section 10 of that Act;

  "telecommunication system" has the meaning assigned to that term by section 4(1) of the 1984 Act.

(a) 1984 c.12.

PART 25

OTHER TELECOMMUNICATIONS DEVELOPMENT

Class A

Permitted development

A. The installation, alteration or replacement on any building or other structure of a microwave antenna and any structure intended for the support of a microwave antenna.

Development not permitted

A.1. Development is not permitted by Class A if—

  (a) the building is a dwellinghouse;

  (b) the development is permitted by Part 24;

  (c) the building or structure is less than 15 metres in height;

  (d) the development would result in the presence on the building or structure of more than two microwave antennas;

  (e) in the case of a satellite antenna, the size of the antenna, including its supporting structure but excluding any projecting feed element, would exceed 90 centimetres;

  (f) in the case of a terrestrial microwave antenna—

    (i) the size of the antenna, when measured in any dimension but excluding any projecting feed element, would exceed 1.3 metres; and

    (ii) the highest part of the antenna or its supporting structure would be more than 3 metres higher than the highest part of the building or structure on which it is installed or is to be installed; or

  (g) it is on article 1(5) land.

Conditions

A.2. Development is permitted by Class A subject to the following conditions—

  (a) the antenna shall, so far as is practicable, be sited so as to minimise its effect on the external appearance of the building or structure on which it is installed;

  (b) an antenna no longer needed for the reception or transmission of microwave radio energy shall be removed from the building or structure as soon as reasonably practicable.

PART 26

DEVELOPMENT BY THE HISTORIC BUILDINGS AND MONUMENTS COMMISSION FOR ENGLAND

Class A

Permitted development

A. Development by or on behalf of the Historic Buildings and Monuments Commission for England, consisting of—

  (a) the maintenance, repair or restoration of any building or monument;

  (b) the erection of screens, fences or covers designed or intended to protect or safeguard any building or monument; or

  (c) the carrying out of works to stabilise ground conditions by any cliff, water-course or the coastline;

where such works are required for the purposes of securing the preservation of any building or monument.

Development not permitted

A.1. Development is not permitted by Class A(a) if the works involve the extension of the building or monument.

Condition

A.2. Except for development also falling within Class A(a), Class A(b) development is permitted subject to the condition that any structure erected in accordance with that permission shall be removed at the expiry of a period of 6 months (or such longer period as the local planning authority may agree in writing) from the date on which work to erect the structure was begun.

Interpretation of Class A

A.3. For the purposes of Class A, "building or monument" means any building or monument in the guardianship of the Historic Buildings and Monuments Commission for England or owned, controlled or managed by them.

PART 27

USE BY MEMBERS OF CERTAIN RECREATIONAL ORGANISATIONS

Class A

Permitted development

A. The use of land by members of a recreational organisation for the purposes of recreation or instruction, and the erection or placing of tents on the land for the purposes of the use.

Development not permitted

A.1. Development is not permitted by Class A if the land is a building or is within the curtilage of a dwellinghouse.

Interpretation

A.2. For the purposes of Class A, a "recreational organisation" is an organisation holding a certificate of exemption under section 269 of the Public Health Act 1936(a).

PART 28

DEVELOPMENT AT AMUSEMENT PARKS

Class A

Permitted development

A. Development on land used as an amusement park consisting of—

  (a) the erection of booths or stalls or the installation of plant or machinery to be used for or in connection with the entertainment of the public within the amusement park; or

  (b) the extension, alteration or replacement of any existing booths or stalls, plant or machinery so used.

Development not permitted

A.1. Development is not permitted by Class A if—

  (a) in the case of any plant or machinery installed, extended, altered or replaced pursuant to this permission, that plant or machinery—

    (i) would, if the land or pier is within 3 kilometres of the perimeter of an aerodrome, exceed a height of 25 metres or the height of the highest existing structure (whichever is the lesser), or

    (ii) would in any other case exceed a height of 25 metres;

  (b) in the case of an extension to an existing building or structure, that building or structure would as a result exceed 5 metres above ground level or the height of the roof of the existing building or structure, whichever is the greater; or

---

(a) 1936 c.49.

(c) in any other case, the height of the building or structure erected, extended, altered or replaced would exceed 5 metres above ground level.

Interpreta-tion of Class A	A.2. For the purposes of Class A– "amusement park" means an enclosed area of open land, or any part of a seaside pier, which is principally used (other than by way of a temporary use) as a funfair or otherwise for the purposes of providing public entertainment by means of mechanical amusements and side-shows; but, where part only of an enclosed area is commonly so used as a funfair or for such public entertainment, only the part so used shall be regarded as an amusement park; and "booths or stalls" includes buildings or structures similar to booths or stalls.

Extract 5 Fees payable under the Town and Country Planning (Fees for Applications and Deemed Applications) Regulations 1989, Schedule 1

PART II
SCALE OF FEES

Category of development	Fee payable
I. Operations	
1. The erection of dwellinghouses (other than development within category 6 below).	(a) Where the application is for outline planning permission, £76 for each 0.1 hectare of the site area, subject to a maximum of £1,900; (b) in other cases, £76 for each dwellinghouse to be created by the development, subject to a maximum of £3,800.
2. The erection of buildings (other than buildings coming within categories 1, 3, 4, 5 or 7).	(a) Where the application is for outline planning permission, £76 for each 0.1 hectare of the site area, subject to a maximum of £1,900; (b) in other cases– (i) where no floor space is to be created by the development, £38; (ii) where the area of gross floor space to be created by the development does not exceed 40 sq metres, £38; (iii) where the area of gross floor space to be created by the development exceeds 40 sq metres but does not exceed 75 sq metres, £76; and (iv) where the area of gross floor space to be created by the development exceeds 75 sq metres, £76 for each 75 sq metres, subject to a maximum of £3,800.
3. The erection, on land used for the purposes of agriculture, of buildings to be used for agricultural purposes (other than buildings coming within category 4).	(a) Where the application is for outline planning permission, £76 for each 0.1 hectare of the site area, subject to a maximum of £1,900; (b) in other cases– (i) where the area of gross floor space to be created by the development does not exceed 465 sq metres, nil; (ii) where the area of gross floor space to be created by the development exceeds 465 sq metres but does not exceed 540 sq metres, £76; (iii) where the area of gross floor space to be created by the development exceeds 540 sq metres, £76 for the first 540 sq metres and £76 for each 75 sq metres in excess of that figure, subject to a maximum of £3,800.
4. The erection of glasshouses on land used for the purposes of agriculture.	(a) Where the area of gross floor space to be created by the development does not exceed 465 sq metres, nil; (b) where the area of gross floor space to be created by the development exceeds 465 sq metres, £450.
5. The erection, alteration or replacement of plant or machinery.	£76 for each 0.1 hectare of the site area, subject to a maximum of £3,800.
6. The enlargement, improvement or other alteration of existing dwellinghouses.	(a) Where the application relates to one dwellinghouse, £38; (b) where the application relates to 2 or more dwellinghouses, £76.

SCHEDULE 1: Part II—*continued*

Category of development	Fee payable
7. (a) The carrying out of operations (including the erection of a building) within the curtilage of an existing dwellinghouse, for purposes ancillary to the enjoyment of the dwellinghouse as such, or the erection or construction of gates, fences, walls or other means of enclosure along a boundary of the curtilage of an existing dwellinghouse; or (b) the construction of car parks, service roads and other means of access on land used for the purposes of a single undertaking, where the development is required for a purpose incidental to the existing use of the land.	£38.
8. The carrying out of any operations connected with exploratory drilling for oil or natural gas.	£76 for each 0.1 hectare of the site area, subject to a maximum of £5,700.
9. The carrying out of any operations not coming within any of the above categories.	£38 for each 0.1 hectare of the site area, subject to a maximum of– (a) in the case of operations for the winning and working of minerals, £5,700; (b) in other cases, £380.
II. Uses of Land	
10. The change of use of a building to use as one or more separate dwellinghouses.	(a) Where the change is from a previous use as a single dwellinghouse to use as two or more single dwellinghouses, £76 for each additional dwellinghouse to be created by the development, subject to a maximum of £3,800; (b) in other cases, £76 for each dwellinghouse to be created by the development, subject to a maximum of £3,800.
11. (a) The use of land for the disposal of refuse or waste materials or for the deposit of material remaining after minerals have been extracted from land; or (b) the use of land for the storage of minerals in the open.	£38 for each 0.1 hectare of the site area, subject to a maximum of £5,700.
12. The making of a material change in the use of a building or land (other than a material change of use coming within any of the above categories).	£76.
13. The continuance of a use of land, or the retention of buildings or works on land, without compliance with a condition subject to which a previous planning permission has been granted (including a condition requiring the discontinuance of the use or the removal of the building or works at the end of a specified period).	£38.

SCHEDULE 2

SCALE OF FEES IN RESPECT OF APPLICATIONS FOR CONSENT TO DISPLAY ADVERTISEMENTS

Category of advertisement	Fee Payable
1. Advertisements displayed on business premises, on the forecourt of business premises or on other land within the curtilage of business premises, wholly with reference to all or any of the following matters– (a) the nature of the business or other activity carried on on the premises; (b) the goods sold or the services provided on the premises; or (c) the name and qualifications of the person carrying on such business or activity or supplying such goods or services.	£21
2. Advertisements for the purpose of directing members of the public to, or otherwise drawing attention to the existence of, business premises which are in the same locality as the site on which the advertisement is to be displayed but which are not visible from that site.	£21
3. All other advertisements.	£76.

15

Construction Regulations in England and Wales

VINCENT POWELL-SMITH

1 Building Acts and Regulations

1.01 Planning legislation is largely concerned with policy and, in relation to the external appearance of a building, with safeguarding of amenity (Chapter 14). But obtaining planning permission is only the first legal hurdle. The architect is then faced with controls over the construction and design of buildings.

In England and Wales the basic framework of control is found in the Building Act 1984 and in the Regulations made under it. An important feature of the present system of building control is that there are two alternative means of control – one by local authorities operating under the Building Regulations 1985, and the other a system of private certification which relies on 'approved inspectors' operating under the Building (Approved Inspectors, etc.) Regulations 1985.

In practice, most building work will be subject to control by the local authority because at present there is only one approved inspector, namely the National House Building Council (NHBC): see para 3.03.

Not all the provisions of the 1984 Act are yet in force, and building control remains in a state of flux, since further consultations are taking place and further changes tending to more flexibility are promised.

Checklist 15.1 sets out the provisions of the 1984 Act.

The Building Act 1984 is a consolidating statute and draws together most, but not all, of the statutory requirements previously found elsewhere, but notably in the Public Health Acts 1936 and 1961, as amended. The position is complicated by the fact that in more than thirty English counties and boroughs there are local Acts containing additional building control provisions and these must also be compiled with. A comprehensive treatment of these controls will be found in *Guide to Building Control by Local Acts 1987* by P. H. Pitt.

Checklist 15.2 sets out the local Acts with building control provisions.

Although the Building Regulations have applied to Inner London since 1986, the London Building Acts 1930 to 1978 remain in force with modifications and the position in Inner London is considered later in this chapter.

Approved Documents

1.02 The Building Regulations 1985 contain no technical detail but are supported by a series of thirteen Approved Documents whose status and use is laid down in sections 6 and 7 of the Building Act 1984. Section 6 provides for documents giving 'practical guidance with respect to the requirements of any provision of building regulations' to be approved by the Secretary of State or some other body designated by him.

Checklist 15.1 continued

Checklist 15.1 continued

Compensation, and recovery of sums
106. Compensation for damage.
107. Recovery of expenses etc.
108. Payments by instalments.
109. Inclusion of several sums in one complaint.
110. Liability of agent or trustee.
111. Arbitration.

Obstruction
112. Obstruction.

Prosecutions
113. Prosecution of offences.
114. Continuing offences.

Protection of members etc. of authorities
115. Protection of members etc. of authorities.

Default powers
116. Default powers of Secretary of State.
117. Expenses of Secretary of State.
118. Variation or revocation of order transferring powers.

Local inquiries
119. Local inquiries.

Orders
120. Orders.

Interpretation
121. Meaning of 'building'.
122. Meaning of 'building regulations'.
123. Meaning of 'construct' and 'erect'.
124. Meaning of deposit of plans.
125. Construction and availability of sewers.
126. General interpretation.
127. Construction of certain references concerning Temples.

Savings
128. Protection for dock and railway undertakings.
129. Savings for Local Land Charges Act 1975.
130. Savings for other laws.
131. Definition of application of Part IV to Schedule 3.

Part V
Supplementary
132. Transitional provisions.
*133. *Consequential amendments and repeals.*
134. Commencement.
135. Short title and extent.

Schedules:
  Schedule 1 – Building regulations.
  Schedule 2 – Relaxation of building regulations.
  Schedule 3 – Inner London.
  Schedule 4 – Provisions consequential upon public body's notice.
  Schedule 5 – Transitional provisions.
  Schedule 6 – Consequential amendments.
  * *Schedule 7 – Repeals.*

The current approved documents all refer to other non-statutory material, including British Standards. The approved documents are intended to give designers a greater degree of flexibility than was available under the previous regulations. Their use is not mandatory except in the case of the one entitled 'Mandatory Rules for Means of Escape in case of fire'.

1.03 Section 7 of the 1984 Act specifies the legal effect of the approved documents. Failure to comply with their recom-

Checklist 15.2: Principal local Acts with building control provisions

Act	Year	Act	Year
Avon	1982	Kent	1981
Berkshire	1986	Lancashire	1984
Bournemouth	1985	Leicestershire	1985
Cheshire	1980	Merseyside	1980
Cleveland	1987	Mid Glamorgan	1987
Clwyd	1985	Nottinghamshire	1985
Cornwall	1984	Poole	1986
Cumbria	1982	South Glamorgan	1976
Derbyshire	1981	South Yorkshire	1980
Dyfed	1987	Staffordshire	1983
East Sussex	1981	Surrey	1985
Essex	1987	Tyne & Wear	1980
Greater Manchester	1981	West Glamorgan	1987
Hampshire	1983	West Midlands	1980
Humberside	1982	West Yorkshire	1980
Isle of Wight	1980	York City Council	1987

Note: The London Building Acts 1930–1978 apply to Inner London.

mendations does not involve civil or criminal liability, but they can be relied on by either party to any proceedings for alleged contravention of the regulation requirements. Thus, if an architect proves that he has complied with the requirements of an approved document in any proceedings which are brought against him, he can rely on this 'as tending to negative liability'. Conversely, his failure to so comply may be relied on by the local authority 'as tending to establish liability' and the onus will be on the architect to establish that he has met the functional requirement in some other way.

In *Rickards* v *Kerrier District Council* (1987) CILL 345, in enforcement proceedings under section 36 of the 1984 Act, the High Court had to consider the application of section 6. The judge held that the burden of proving non-compliance with the Regulations was on the local authority, but if they established that the works did not comply with an approved document, then the burden shifted. The appellant against a section 36 notice would then have to show compliance with the Regulations in some other way.

1.04 Space does not permit a detailed analysis of the technical content of the approved documents, and readers should refer to *The Building Regulations Explained and Illustrated* (8th edn, 1990) which is a narrative explanation dealing with all types of buildings, and to the *Guide to the Building Regulations* (1986), both of which are definitive treatments of the topic.

2 The Building Regulations 1985

Local authority control

2.01 The Building Regulations 1985 contain the detailed rules and procedures governing building control by local authorities and came into force on 11 November 1985. They are shorter than the previous regulations because the technical requirements have mostly been recast in a functional form. Each functional requirement is supported by an approved document (see para 1.02). The requirements are mostly expressed in very general terms. For example, regulation 7 provides that 'any building work shall be carried out with proper materials and in a workmanlike manner'.

Checklist 15.3 sets out the content of the Regulations.

Schedule 1 of the Building Regulations 1985 sets out the requirements to be met in respect of structure, fire protection and means of escape, site preparation and resistance to moisture, toxic substances, sound, ventilation, hygiene, drainage and waste disposal, heat-producing appliances, stairways, ramps and guards, energy conservation and

Checklist 15.3: Content of the Building Regulations 1985

Part I General
1. Title, commencement and application.
2. Interpretation.

Part II Control of building work
3. Meaning of building work.
4. Requirements relating to building work.
5. Meaning of material change of use.
6. Requirements relating to material change of use.
7. Materials and workmanship.
8. Limitation on requirements.
9. Exempt buildings and work.

Part III Relaxation of requirements
10. Power to dispense with or relax requirements.

Part IV Notices and plans
11. Giving of a building notice or deposit of plans.
12. Particulars and plans where a building notice is given.
13. Full plans.
14. Notice of commencement and completion of certain stages of work.

Part V Miscellaneous
15. Testing of drains and private sewers.
16. Sampling of material.
17. Supervision of building work otherwise than by local authorities.
18. Repeals.
19. Revocations.
20. Transitional provisions.

Schedules
1 Requirements
2 Repealed
3 Exempt buildings and work
4 Revocations

facilities for the disabled, together with the limits on application of the requirements. This is set out in tabular form:

Part A: Structure – covers loading, ground movement and disproportionate collapse.
Part B: Fire – covers means of escape, and internal and external fire spread.
Part C: Site Preparation and Resistance to Moisture – covers preparation of site, dangerous and offensive substances, subsoil drainage, and resistance to weather and ground moisture.
Part D: Toxic Substances – deals with cavity insulation.
Part E: Resistance to the passage of sound – covers airborne and impact sound.
Part F: Ventilation – covers means of ventilation and condensation.
Part G: Hygiene – deals with food storage, bathrooms, hot water storage and sanitary conveniences.
Part H: Drainage and waste disposal – deals with sanitary pipework and drainage, cesspools, septic tanks and settlement tanks, rainwater drainage and solid waste storage.
Part J: Heat-producing appliances – covers air supply, discharge of combustion products and protection of the building.
Part K: Stairways, ramps and guards – covers stairways and ramps, protection from falling and barriers.
Part L: Conservation of fuel and power – covers resistance to the passage of heat in buildings, heating system controls and insulation of heating services.
Part M: Facilities for disabled people – deals with the provision of reasonable facilities for disabled people.

Subject to specified exemptions (see para 4.02) *all* building work (as defined in the regulations) in England and Wales must be carried out in compliance with Schedule 1.
Checklist 15.4 sets out the requirements of Schedlue 1.

Checklist 15.4: Technical requirements in functional form in Schedule 1 of the Building Regulations 1985

SCHEDULE 1 – REQUIREMENTS   Regulations 4 and 6

	Requirement	Limits on application

PART A STRUCTURE

Loading

Structure.
A1. – (1) The building shall be so constructed that the combined dead, imposed and wind loads are sustained and transmitted to the ground—

(*a*) safely, and

(*b*) without causing such deflection or deformation of any part of the building, or such movement of the ground, as will impair the stability of any part of another building.

(2) In assessing whether a building complies with sub-paragraph (1) regard shall be had to the imposed and wind loads to which it is likely to be subjected in the ordinary course of its use for the purpose for which it is intended.

Ground movement

Structure.
A2. The building shall be so constructed that movements of the subsoil caused by swelling, shrinkage or freezing will not impair the stability of any part of the building.

Disproportionate collapse

Structure.
A3. The building shall be so constructed that in the event of an accident the structure will not be damaged to an extent disproportionate to the cause of the damage.

This requirement applies only to—

(*a*) a building having five or more storeys (each basement level being counted as one storey); and

(*b*) a public building the structure of which incorporates a clear span exceeding nine metres between supports.

PART B FIRE

Means of escape

B1. – (1) There shall be means of escape in case of fire from the building to a place of safety outside the building capable of being safely and effectively used at all material times.

(2) This requirement may be met only by complying with the relevant requirements of the publication entitled "The Building Regulations 1985 — Mandatory rules for means of escape in case of fire" published by HMSO (1985 edition).

1. This requirement applies only to—

(*a*) a building which is erected and which—

(i) is or contains a dwelling-house of three or more storeys,

(ii) contains a flat and is of three or more storeys,

(iii) is or contains an office, or

(iv) is or contains a shop;

(*b*) a dwelling-house which is extended or materially altered and will have three or more storeys, and

(*c*) a building of three or more storeys, the use of which is materially changed to use as a dwelling-house.

2. The means of escape provided need only, in the case of a dwelling-house or a building containing a flat, afford escape for people from the third storey and above and, in the case of a building containing an office or a shop, afford escape for people from the office or shop.

Internal fire spread (surfaces)

Internal walls; ceilings.
B2. In order to inhibit the spread of fire within the building, surfaces of materials used on walls and ceilings—

(*a*) shall offer adequate resistance to the spread of flame over their surfaces; and

(*b*) shall have, if ignited, a rate of heat release which is reasonable in the circumstances.

Internal fire spread (structure)

Structure.
B3. – (1) The building shall be so constructed that, in the event of

Checklist 15.4 continued

fire, its stability will be maintained for a reasonable period.

(2) The building, or the building as extended, shall be sub-divided into compartments where this is necessary to inhibit the spread of fire within the building.

(3) Concealed spaces in the structure or fabric of the building, or the building as extended, shall be sealed and sub-divided where this is necessary to inhibit the unseen spread of fire and smoke.

(4) A wall common to two or more buildings shall offer adequate resistance to the spread of fire and smoke.

(5) For the purposes of sub-paragraph (4) a house in a terrace and a semi-detached house are each to be treated as being a separate building.

External fire spread

External walls; roofs.
B4. – (1) The external walls of the building shall offer adequate resistance to the spread of fire over the walls and from one building to another, having regard to the height, use and position of the building.

(2) The roof of the building shall offer adequate resistance to the spread of fire over the roof and from one building to another, having regard to the use and position of the building.

PART C SITE PREPARATION AND RESISTANCE TO MOISTURE.

Preparation of site

Site.
C1. The ground to be covered by the building shall be reasonably free from vegetable matter.

Dangerous and offensive substances

Site.
C2. Precautions shall be taken to avoid danger to health caused by substances found on or in the ground to be covered by the building.

Subsoil drainage

C3. Subsoil drainage shall be provided if it is needed to avoid—

(a) the passage of ground moisture to the interior of the building; or

(b) damage to the fabric of the building.

Resistance to weather and ground moisture

Walls; roofs; floors.
C4. The walls, floors and roof of the building shall adequately resist the passage of moisture to the inside of the building.

PART D TOXIC SUBSTANCES

Cavity insulation

Walls.
D1. If insulating material is inserted into a cavity in a cavity wall reasonable precautions shall be taken to prevent the subsequent permeation of any toxic fumes from that material into any part of the building occupied by people.

PART E RESISTANCE TO THE PASSAGE OF SOUND.

Airborne sound (walls)

Walls.
E1. – (1) A wall which—

(a) separates a dwelling from another building or from another dwelling, or

(b) separates a habitable room within a dwelling from another part of the same building which is not used exclusively with the dwelling,

shall have reasonable resistance to airborne sound.

(2) In this paragraph "habitable room" means a room used for dwelling purposes but not a kitchen or scullery.

This requirement does not apply to a wall falling within the description in paragraph (b) which separates a habitable room within a dwelling from another part of the same building if that part is used only for the inspection, maintenance or repair of the building, its services or fixed plant or machinery.

Airborne sound (floors)

Floors.
E2. A floor which separates a dwelling from another dwelling, or from another part of the same building which is not used exclusively with the dwelling, shall have reasonable resistance to airborne sound.

This requirement does not apply to a floor which separates a dwelling from another part of the same building if that part is used only for the inspection, maintenance or repair of the building, its services or fixed plant or machinery.

Impact sound (floors)

Floors.
E3. A floor above a dwelling which separates it from another dwelling, or from another part of the same building which is not used exclusively with the dwelling, shall have reasonable resistance to impact sound.

This requirement does not apply to a floor which separates a dwelling from another part of the same building if that part is used only for the inspection, maintenance or repair of the building, its services or fixed plant or machinery.

PART F VENTILATION

Means of ventilation

Walls; roofs.
F1. There shall be means of ventilation so that an adequate supply of air may be provided for people in the building.

This requirement applies only to—

(a) dwellings;

(b) buildings containing dwellings;

(c) rooms containing sanitary conveniences; and

(d) bathrooms.

Condensation

Roof voids.
F2. Reasonable provision shall be made to prevent excessive condensation in a roof void above an insulated ceiling.

This requirement applies only to dwellings.

PART G HYGIENE.

Food storage

G1. There shall be adequate accommodation for the storage of food or adequate space for the provision of such accommodation by the occupier.

This requirement applies only to dwellings.

Bathrooms

Bathrooms.
G2. A bathroom shall be provided containing either a fixed bath or a shower bath, and there shall be a suitable installation for the provision of hot and cold water to the bath or shower bath.

This requirement applies only to dwellings.

Hot water storage

Hot water supply systems.
G3. If hot water is stored and the storage system does not incorporate a vent pipe to the atmosphere, there shall be adequate precautions to—

(a) prevent the temperature of the stored water at any time exceeding 100°C; and

(b) ensure that the hot water discharged from safety devices is safely conveyed to where it is visible but will cause no danger to persons in or about the building.

This requirement does not apply to—

(a) a system having a storage capacity of 15 litres or less;

(b) a space heating system;

(c) a system which heats or stores water for the purposes of an industrial process.

Sanitary conveniences

Sanitary accommodation.
G4. Sufficient sanitary conveniences shall be provided which shall be—

(a) in rooms separated from places where food is stored or prepared; and

(b) designed and installed so as to allow effective cleaning.

PART H DRAINAGE AND WASTE DISPOSAL.

Sanitary pipework and drainage

Discharge pipes; drains; private sewers.
H1. – (1) Any system which carries foul water from appliances within the building to a foul water outfall shall be adequate.

(2) "Foul water" in sub-paragraph (1) means waste from a sanitary convenience or other soil appliance, and water which has been used for cooking or washing, but does not include waste containing any trade effluent.

Checklist 15.4 continued

Cesspools, septic tanks and settlement tanks

Cesspools; septic tanks; settlement tanks.

H2. Cesspools, septic tanks and settlement tanks shall be sited and constructed so as to—

(a) permit access for emptying; and

(b) avoid contamination of water supplies by leakage or spilling over of the contents.

Rainwater drainage

Roofs.

H3. Any system which carries rainwater from the roof of the building to a rainwater outfall shall be adequate.

Solid waste storage

—

H4. There shall be—

(a) satisfactory means of storing solid waste; and

(b) adequate means of access to a street from the building for the removal of solid waste.

PART J   HEAT PRODUCING APPLIANCES

Air supply

Walls; roofs.

J1. Heat producing appliances shall be so installed that there is an adequate supply of air to them for combustion and for the efficient working of any flue-pipe or chimney.

The requirements in this Part apply only to fixed heat producing appliances which—

(a) are designed to burn solid fuel, oil or gas; or

(b) are incinerators.

Discharge of products of combustion

Chimneys; flue-pipes.

J2. Heat producing appliances shall have adequate provision for the discharge of the products of combustion to the outside air.

Protection of building

J3. Heat producing appliances and flue-pipes shall be so installed, and fire-places and chimneys shall be so constructed, as to reduce to a reasonable level the risk of the building catching fire in consequence of their use.

PART K   STAIRWAYS, RAMPS AND GUARDS.

Stairways and ramps

Stairways; ramps.

K1. Stairways and ramps shall be such as to afford safe passage for the users of the building.

The requirements of this Part apply to stairways and ramps which form part of the structure of the building.

Protection from falling

K2. Stairways, ramps, floors and balconies, and any roof to which people normally have access, shall be guarded with barriers where they are necessary to protect users from the risk of falling.

Vehicle barriers

Vehicle ramps; floors; roofs.

K3. Vehicle ramps, and any floor and roof to which vehicles have access, shall be guarded with barriers where they are necessary to provide protection for people in or about the building.

PART L   CONSERVATION OF FUEL AND POWER.

Interpretation of Part L

L1. In this Part—

"element" means a wall, floor or roof;

"exposed", in the case of a dwelling, means—

(a) exposed to the outside air, or

(b) separating the dwelling from a part of the building ventilated by means of an opening or duct to the outside air which allows the passage of air at all times and has an aggregate area exceeding 5% of the area of the walls enclosing that part of the building,

and, in the case of a building not consisting of a dwelling, means—

(a) exposed to the outside air, or

(b) separating a part of the building which is heated from a part which is not and which is exposed to the outside air;

"industrial building" means a factory within the meaning of section

175 of the Factories Act 1961 (**a**) (but does not include slaughter-houses and other premises referred to in paragraphs (*d*) and (*e*) of subsection (1) of that section);

"residential building" means a building used for residential purposes and includes a hotel or institution, but any part of such a building which consists of a dwelling shall not be regarded as part of a residential building;

"solid parts", in relation to an exposed element, means those parts of it which are not doors, meter-cupboards, roof-lights, windows or other openings;

"U value" means the thermal transmittance coefficient in watts per square metre of fabric per kelvin;

"wall" includes a roof or part of a roof which has a pitch of 70° or more; and

"window" includes a door which contains more than two square metres of glass; and a lintel, jamb or sill may be regarded either as part of the window or as part of the surrounding element at the option of the person carrying out the work.

Resistance to the passage of heat (dwellings)

Exposed fabric.

L2. – (1) Subject to sub-paragraph (3), the calculated rate of heat loss (W/K) through any windows and roof-lights shall be no greater than it would be if—

(a) the aggregate of the areas of windows and roof-lights were 12% of the area of the walls bounding the dwelling, and

(b) the windows and roof-lights had a U value of 5.7.

(2) The calculated rate of heat loss through the solid parts of the exposed elements shall be no greater than it would be if—

(a) the exposed walls and exposed floors had a U value of 0.6, and

(b) the roof had a U value of 0.35.

(3) To the extent that the calculated rate of heat loss through the solid parts of the exposed elements is less than the maximum permitted under sub-paragraph (2), the calculated rate of heat loss through the windows and roof-lights may be greater than the maximum permitted under sub-paragraph (1).

This requirement applies only to dwellings.

Resistance to the passage of heat (buildings other than dwellings)

Exposed fabric.

L3. – (1) Subject to sub-paragraphs (3) to (5), the calculated rate of heat loss (W/K) through any windows and roof-lights shall be no greater than it would be if—

(a) the aggregate area of the roof-lights were 20% of the roof area,

(b) the aggregate area of the windows were—

(i) in the case of a residential building, 25%,

(ii) in the case of a shop, office or assembly building, 35%,

(iii) in the case of an industrial or any other building, 15%,

of the exposed wall area; and

(c) the windows and roof-lights had a U value of 5.7.

(2) Subject to sub-paragraphs (4) and (5), the calculated rate of heat loss through the solid parts of the exposed elements shall be no greater than it would be if those parts had a U value—

(a) in the case of a residential building, shop, office or assembly building, of 0.6, and

(b) in the case of an industrial or any other building, of 0.7.

(3) Where the building consists of a shop with a display window, the storey in which the window is situated shall be disregarded in considering compliance with the requirements in sub-paragraph (1).

This requirement applies only to a building having a floor area greater than 30 m² which is—

(a) a residential building,

(b) a shop,

(c) an office,

(d) a building, whether public or private, in which people assemble for recreational, educational, business or other activities ("an assembly building"),

and which is likely to be heated by a space heating system having an output exceeding 25 watts per square metre of floor area, or which is—

(e) an industrial building, or

(f) a building used for a purpose not referred to above, ("any other building"),

and which is likely to be heated by a space heating system having an output exceeding 50 watts per square metre of floor area.

Checklist 15.4 continued

(4) An alternative requirement to those specified in sub-paragraphs (1) and (2) is that the calculated heat loss from the building in the conditions in which it is likely to be used, taking account of any useful gain, shall be no greater than it would be if those requirements were met.

(5) Where the building is divided into parts used for different purposes, separate calculations shall be made for each part falling within a description in *(a)* to *(f)* in the limits an application to this requirement, but a building not so divided which is used for more than one purpose shall be regarded as used for its main purpose and not for any ancillary purpose.

Heating system controls

Space heating and hot water systems.	L4. Space heating or hot water systems in buildings shall be provided with automatic controls capable of controlling the operation and output of space heating systems and the temperature of stored water.	This requirement does not apply to— *(a)* systems in dwellings; *(b)* systems which heat or store water for the purpose of an industrial process; *(c)* systems provided to serve a building with a floor area which does not exceed 125m²; or *(d)* individual appliances with an output rating of 10 kilowatts or less.

Insulation of heating services

Hot water pipes and warm air ducts.	L5. – (1) Hot water pipes and warm air ducts shall have adequate thermal insulation unless— *(a)* they are intended to contribute to the heating of a part of the building which is insulated, or *(b)* they give rise to no significant heat loss.	This requirement does not apply to systems which heat or store any water for the purpose of an industrial process.
Hot water storage vessels.	(2) Hot water storage vessels shall have adequate thermal insulation.	

2.02 Subject to a number of exemptions which are dealt with later (see para 4.01 ff), the procedural requirements of Part IV of the Building Regulations must be observed where a person proposes to undertake building work covered by the regulations and subject to the control of the local authority. The local authority for this purpose is the district council, a London borough council, the Common Council of the City of London, the Sub-Treasurer of the Inner Temple, the Under Treasurer of the Middle Temple, and the Council of the Isles of Scilly (1984 Act, section 126(1)).

Regulation 3 defines 'building work' as meaning the erection or extension of a building, the material alteration of a building, the provision of controlled services or fittings, i.e. bathrooms, hot water supply systems, sanitary conveniences, drainage and waste disposal, certain fixed heat-producing appliances and heating systems, as well as work required as a consequence of a material change of use of a building.

Two main options are available under the local authority control system, namely the service of a building notice and the deposit and submission of full plans. Either option brings into operation a number of other controls vested in the local authority and commonly called 'the linked powers' (see paras 5.01–5.05).

2.03 The Building Regulations 1985 are not a self-sufficient code and other legislation (and non-statutory documents) must be referred to. For example, sanitary accommodation is dealt with in the Regulations. This leads back by inference to the Building Act 1984, section 26, which provides that plans for new buildings or extensions deposited with the local authority shall be rejected unless they 'show that sufficient and satisfactory closet accomodation . . . will be provided, or . . . the authority are satisfied that in the case of the particular building they may properly dispense with' the requirement.

Nature of approval

2.04 Before considering the procedural requirements in detail, three important matters must be emphasized: discretion of local authorities, building without approval, and dispensation and relaxation of requirements.

Discretion of local authority

2.05 Local authorities have no discretion when considering a building notice or plans deposited under the Regulations. The wording of section 16 of the Building Act 1984 is mandatory. It states that the authority must pass the plans of any proposed work deposited with it under the Regulations unless they are defective or show that the proposed work would contravene any of the regulations or unless some other provision of the Act expressly requires or authorizes them to reject the plans.

Where the plans are defective or show contravention of the Regulations, the local authority does have a discretion since in that case they may either reject the plans or pass them subject to conditions as to modification of the deposited plans and/or that further plans be deposited.

Building control authorities do have a discretion in deciding whether to inspect building work in progress. Section 91(2) of the 1984 Act provides that 'it is the function of local authorities to enforce building regulations in their areas' and it is a matter for their discretion as to whether they inspect or not. They must, of course, give proper consideration to the question of whether they should inspect or not.

'It is for the local authority, a public and elected body, to decide upon the scale of resources which it can make available to carry out its functions . . . – how many inspectors, with what expert qualifications, it should recruit, how often inspections are to be made, what tests are to be carried out – must be for its decision' (per Lord Wilberforce in *Anns* v *London Borough of Merton* [1978] AC 728).

Building without approval

2.06 If a building owner fails to serve a building notice or deposit plans or use the option of the approved inspector, he is guilty of an offence, just as he is when work is done contrary to the Regulations: Building Act 1984, section 35. In *Sunley Homes Ltd* v *Borg* [1969] All ER 332, one of the main points at issue was whether an offence against the Regulations could be complete even though work on the buildings concerned had not been finished, as the buildings were in the course of construction at the time the prosecution was brought.

The builders argued that no offence was committed under section 4 of the Public Health Act 1961 until the building in question was completed or, alternatively, until the time when the builder could no longer say that he would have remedied the offending work before completion. Lord Parker (then Lord Chief Justice) summarized the problem in this way:

'No one has been able to satisfy me at what stage it might properly be said that a building is complete. If all the workmen have left but the Building Regulations have not been complied with, I should have thought one could say that the building is not complete. However it seems to me that this argument becomes untenable when one looks: (a) at the Regulations; and (b) at the powers given to local authorities to deal with contraventions. . . . [The] general tenor of the Regulations is clearly against [the developer's] contentions. They deal throughout with the erection of a building, and while erection might mean the completed building, it might also mean the operation of erecting the building. . . . (It) seems to me clear that the erection of a building refers to the operation of erecting and not the completed erection.'

The position appears to be the same under current regulations.

2.07 A related matter is whether breach of any duty imposed by the Building Regulations can give rise to liability in damages. Although section 38 of the Building Act 1984 provides that, except where regulations otherwise provide, 'breach of a duty imposed by building regulations, so far as it causes damage, is actionable' it has not yet been brought into force. The section goes on to provide that it does not affect the extent (if any) to which a breach of duty imposed by or arising under Part I of the Act or other relevant legislation or of duties imposed by the regulations generally is actionable at civil law, nor does it 'prejudice a right of action that exists apart from the enactments relating to the building regulations'.

Until section 38 is activated, the position appears to be that breach of building regulations does not of itself give rise to liability in damages for breach of statutory duty. There are conflicting judicial dicta on the point, but the relevant authorities were fully considered in *Perry* v *Tendring District Council* (1985) 3 Con LR 74 where Judge John Newey QC, a judge of great experience in this field, held that breach of duty of the former building byelaws did not give rise to liability in damages. The liability imposed on the local authority was not an absolute one. His Honour's reasoning was applied by the late Judge David Smout QC in *Kimbell* v *Hart District Council* (1987) 9 ConLR 118 who held that a breach of statutory duty, as set out in section 64 of the Public Health Act 1936, such as a failure to reject plans, did not of itself give rise to a claim in damages. The statutory duty was not an absolute one, and the plaintiff could only succeed on proof of negligence.

Perry v *Tendring District Council* was also followed in *Kijowski* v *New Capital Properties Ltd* (1988) 15 Con LR 1, where Judge Esyr Lewis QC expressly held that breach of the Building Regulations 1965 did not of itself give rise to liability in damages. It is submitted that this is also the position under the Building Regulations 1985 and that unless and until section 38 of the 1984 Act is brought into effect, and breach of the Regulations without proof of negligence does not of itself give rise to a claim for damages.

2.08 Under the enforcement provisions, the local authority may require the removal or alteration of offending work and/or they may initiate criminal proceedings: Building Act 1984, sections 35 and 36. Notice to remove, alter, or pull down contravening work may not be given after the expiry of twelve months from the date of completion of the work in question, nor where the local authority have passed the plans and the work has been carried out in accordance with them. The wording of the provision is important; time begins to run against the local authority from the moment when the particular contravention is complete, and not from the date when the building as a whole is completed. However, in a case where the twelve months' time limit had expired, the local authority could apply to the High Court for an injunction, but only with the consent and in the name of the Attorney-General.

Experts' reports

2.09 The person on whom a section 36 notice is served has a right of appeal to the magistrates' court and an important procedure is provided by section 37 of the 1984 Act. Under section 37, the recipient of a section 36 notice may notify the local authority of his attention to obtain from a 'suitably qualified person' a written report about the matter to which the section 36 notice relates. The expert's report is then submitted to the local authority and in light of that report the authority may withdraw the notice and pay the expenses reasonably incurred in obtaining the report which will relate to technical matters. If the local authority rejects the report,

it can then be used as evidence in any appeal under section 40 of the Act, and if the appeal is successful the appellant would normally recover the costs of obtaining the report as well as his other costs: 1984 Act, section 40(6).

Dispensations and relaxations

2.10 An important dispensing power is conferred on the Secretary of State by section 8 of the Building Act 1984. This enables him to dispense with or relax any regulation requirement 'if he considers that the operation of [that] requirement would be unreasonable in relation to the particular case'. This power has been delegated to local authorities who may grant a relaxation if, because of special circumstances, the terms of a requirement cannot be fully met: see regulation 9.

In practice the majority of the requirements of the regulations cannot be relaxed because they require that something is provided at an 'adequate', 'satisfactory', or 'reasonable' level. The regulation can therefore effectively be relaxed in two cases only:

– Means of escape in case of fire: Schedule 1, B1.
– Resistance to the passage of heat: Schedule 1, L2 and L3.

2.11 Sections 9 and 10 of the 1984 Act lay down the procedure for application; there is no prescribed form. The application must be advertised in a local newspaper. There is a right of appeal to the Secretary of State against a local authority's refusal to dispense or relax with Regulation requirements : 1984 Act, section 39. If the local authority fails to give a decision on an application for relaxation within two months, it is deemed to be refused and the application may appeal forthwith.

2.12 This power of dispensation or relaxation must be distinguished from that of the Secretary of State to grant a *type relaxation* under section 11 of the 1984 Act, i.e. his power to dispense with a requirement of the Regulations generally. However, no type applications have been granted under the current legislation.

Application procedure

2.13 Unless the developer wishes to employ an approved inspector (see para 3) the general rule is that anyone wishing to erect, extend or structurally alter buildings, to install services or fittings, or to make material changes in the use of buildings, must apply to the local authority for approval under the Building Regulations 1985. All building work must also be carried out so that it complies with the requirements of Schedule 1 of the Regulations. The work must also be carried out so that, after completion, an existing building, controlled service or fitting, to which work has been done is not 'adversely affected' as regards compliance with Schedule 1 requirements. The procedure on application is governed by Part IV of the Regulations and there are two main procedures. Prescribed fees are payable.

Building notice procedure

2.14 The first procedure is based on the service of a building notice and is governed by regulations 11 and 12. This procedure can be used unless the building concerned is one for which a means of escape is required and is specified in regulation B1 and which is designated under the Fire Precautions Act 1971, i.e. the bigger factories, offices, shops and railway premises.

There is no prescribed form of building notice, but it must be signed by or on behalf of the person intending to carry out the work. It must contain or be accompanied by the information set out in *Checklist 15.5*.

- Name and address of person intending to carry out work.
- Statement that notice is given in accordance with regulation 11(1) (a).
- Description of the building's location and its use or intended use.
- If it relates to the erection or extension of a building it must be supported by a plan to a scale of not less than 1:1250, showing size and position in relation to streets and adjoining buildings on the same site, number of storeys, drainage details.
- If local legislation applicable, how it will be complied with.
- If it relates to erecting a new building or extending an existing building covered by section 24 of the 1984 Act (provision of exits), details of entrances and exits must be given.
- If cavity wall insulation is involved, information must be given about the proposed insulating material, Agreement Certificate (if appropriate) or conforms to BS and whether or not the installer has a BSI Certificate of Registration or has been approved by the Agreement Board.
- If work includes provision of a hot water storage system with a storage capacity of 16 litres or more (Schedule 1, G1) details of the system and its installer are required.

The local authority are not required to approve or reject the notice and have no power to do so. They may ask for any plans necessary to enable them to discharge their building control functions and may specify a time limit for their provision. They may also require information in connection with their linked powers under sections 18 to 21 of the 1984 Act (see para 7). If the work involves building over a sewer they can insist on an access agreement. Work can be commenced once a building notice has been given, although there is a further requirement (regulation 14(1)(a)) that the local authority be notified at least 48 hours before work commences.

Deposit of plans

2.15 Where the building notice procedure is inapplicable, or the developer wishes to adopt this course, full plans may be deposited in accordance with section 16 of the Building Act 1984 and regulation 13. The advantage of the full deposit of plans method of control is that if the work is carried out exactly in conformity with the plans as approved by the local authority, they cannot take any action under section 36 of the Building Act 1984, and the work involved is supervised by the local authority's building control officer.

Under this system, the local authority must give notice of approval or rejection of the plans within five weeks from the date of the deposit of plans. This period does not, however, begin to run unless the applicant submits a 'reasonable estimate' of the cost of the works and pays the prescribed fees at the same time as the plans are deposited. The five week period may be extended by written agreement. The extended period cannot be later than two months from the deposit of plans, and any extension must be agreed before the expiry of the five week period.

2.16 If the local authority gives formal notice to that effect, the approval lapses if work is not commenced within three years from the date of deposit of plans: 1984 Act, section 32. The local authority must pass the plans unless they are defective, or show that the proposed work would contravene the regulations or some other statutory requirement. If the plans are rejected, the notice must specify the alleged defects or contraventions. The applicant then has a right of appeal to the Secretary of State (1984 Act, section 16). The local authority may pass plans by stages. In giving stage approval local authorities can impose a condition that certain work is not to commence until further information is received from the applicant.

Subject to giving the local authority 48 hours notice of commencement of work (regulation 14(1)(a)), work may start as soon as plans have been deposited.

2.17 There is a further important power contained in section 30 of the 1984 Act. If there is a dispute as to whether the Regulations apply in any particular case, or the drawings are in conformity with the Regulations, or the work has been executed in accordance with the drawings as passed, it may be referred by joint application to the Secretary of State for determination. His decision is final, although he may 'at any stage in the proceedings on the reference and shall, if so directed by the High Court, state in the form of a special case for the opinion of the High Court any question of law arising'.

3 Private certification

Approved inspectors

3.01 Part II of the Building Act 1984 deals with 'supervision of building work etc. otherwise than by local authorities', i.e. an alternative system of building control based on private certification. In broad terms, sections 47 to 58 of the 1984 Act provide that responsibility for ensuring compliance with the Building Regulations may, at the option of the person intending to carry out the work, be given to an approved inspector instead of to the local authority. It also enables approved public bodies to approve their own work. The detailed rules and procedures relating to certification are to be found in the Building (Approved Inspector, etc.) Regulations 1985, which also contain prescribed forms which must be used.

3.02 Section 49 of the 1984 Act defines an 'approved inspector' as being a person approved by the Secretary of State or a body designated by him for that prupose. Part II of the 1985 Regulations contains the procedures for the grant and withdrawal of approval. Approved inspectors may be corporate bodies, who must be approved by the Secretary of State, or individuals (not firms) approved by a designated body. The designated bodies are eight professional institutions, including the RIBA.

3.03 At the time of writing, the only approved inspector is the National House Building Council (NHBC) which is an approved inspector for dwellings. No other bodies or individuals are likely to be approved in the foreseeable future because of difficulties in obtaining adequate insurance cover, and full private certification is very much a long-term aim.

3.04 Details of the NHBC scheme are to be found in the NHBC booklet *At Your Service* (obtainable from NHBC, 58 Portland Place, London W1N 4BU). This building control service is available to registered house builders, and the fees charged by NHBC compare favourably with those charged by local authorities.

4 Exemptions from control

4.01 Section 121 of the Building Act 1984 defines the word 'building' in the widest possible terms, and its strict application would bring within the orbit of the regulations all kinds of structures which were never intended to be so included. One purpose of the 1985 Regulations was to eliminate controls over the erection of certain small buildings and some alterations and changes of use. Consequently, regulation 9 and Schedule III list seven classes of exempted buildings and work: see *Checklist 15.6*.

Checklist 15.6: Exempted buildings

SCHEDULE 3 — EXEMPT BUILDINGS AND WORK   Regulation 9

CLASS I

Buildings controlled under other legislation

1. Any building the construction of which is subject to the Explosives Acts 1875 and 1923 (a) .

2. Any building (other than a building containing a dwelling or a building used for office or canteen accommodation) erected on a site in respect of which a licence under the Nuclear Installations Act 1965 (b) is for the time being in force.

3. A building included in the schedule of monuments maintained under section 1 of the Ancient Monuments and Archaeological Areas Act 1979 (c) .

CLASS II

Buildings not frequented by people

1. A detached building into which people cannot or do not normally go.

2. A detached building housing fixed plant or machinery, the only normal visits to which are intermittent visits to inspect or maintain the plant or machinery.

CLASS III

Greenhouses and agricultural buildings

1. A building used as a greenhouse unless the main purpose for which it is used is for retailing, packing or exhibiting.

2.—(1) A building used for agriculture which is—

    (a) sited at a distance not less than one and a half times its own height from any building containing sleeping accommodation, and

    (b) provided with an exit which may be used in case of fire which is not more than 30 metres from any point within the building,

unless the main purpose for which the building is used is retailing, packing or exhibiting.

(2) In this paragraph, "agriculture" includes horticulture, fruit growing, seed growing, dairy farming, fish farming and the breeding and keeping of livestock (including any creature kept for the production of food, wool, skins or fur or for the purpose of its use in the farming of land).

CLASS IV

Temporary buildings and mobile homes

1. A building intended to remain where it is erected for less than 28 days.

2. A mobile home within the meaning of the Mobile Homes Act 1983 (d) .

CLASS V

Ancillary buildings

1. A building on an estate which is intended to be used only in connection with the disposal of buildings or building plots on that estate.

2. A building used only by people engaged in the construction, alteration, extension or repair of a building during the course of that work.

3. A building, other than a building containing a dwelling or used as an office or showroom, erected in connection with a mine or quarry.

CLASS VI

Small detached buildings

1. A detached building having a floor area which does not exceed 30 m² which contains no sleeping accommodation and is either—

    (a) situated more than one metre from the boundary of its curtilage, or

    (b) a single storey building constructed wholly of non-combustible material.

2. A detached building designed and intended to shelter people from the effects of nuclear, chemical or conventional weapons, and not used for any other purpose, if—

    (a) its floor area does not exceed 30 m², and

    (b) the excavation for the building is no closer to any exposed part of another building or structure than a distance equal to the depth of the excavation plus one metre.

CLASS VII

Extensions

The extension of a building by the addition at ground level of—

    (a) a greenhouse, conservatory, porch, covered yard or covered way; or

    (b) a carport open on at least two sides,

where the floor area of that extension does not exceed 30 m².

4.02 Section 4(1) of the Building Act 1984 itself exempts specified buildings from the scope of the regulations. These are:

1. Buildings required for the purposes of any educational establishment erected according to plans which have been approved by the Secretary of State for Education and Science.
2. Buildings of statutory undertakers held and used by them for the purpose of their undertaking, subject to minor exceptions.

4.03 Also exempted from control by regulation 11(3), is building work which consists only of the installation of a heat-producing gas appliance which is to be installed by, or under the supervision of, the British Gas Corporation. This exemption covers various sorts of gas-fire heaters but does not apply if any other building work is involved. No building notice or deposit of plans is required.

5 Other controls under the Building Act

5.01 Local authorities exercise a number of statutory public health functions in conjunction with the process of building control. These provisions are commonly called 'the linked powers' because their operation is linked with the authority's building functions, both in checking deposited plans or considering a building notice, and under the private certification scheme. The most important of these linked powers are described below.

Building over sewers and drains

5.02 Section 32 of the Public Health Act 1936 states that local authorities must keep a map showing the location of all public sewers in their districts. The map distinguishes among public sewers, those with respect to which a vesting declaration has been made but which has not yet taken effect, and those subject to an agreement as to future declaration (see Chapter 9, paras 2.02 ff). Where separate sewers are reserved for foul and surface water, this must be clearly shown. These four groups of sewers and drains are shown on the map.

5.03 Section 18 of the Building Act 1984 prohibits building over any sewer or drain shown on the map except with the local authority's consent. It provides, where the plans show that the building will be constructed over any sewer or drain, that the authority shall reject the plans unless they are satisfied that in the circumstances of the particular case they may properly consent to its erection.

5.04 The rejection of drawings showing an intended contravention of the Building Regulations, as described in para 2.05, is obligatory because of the wording of section 16. Section 18 is a provision which expressly authorizes rejection. Any dispute between the applicant and the local authority as to whether the proposed building will be over a sewer and as to the granting of consent can be determined by the magistrates' court.

5.05 What is the position if a local authority simply passes the drawing and says nothing about the sewer or drain over which the building is erected? The point is undecided, but Lumley's *Public Health* suggests that in such circumstances the local authority must 'be taken to have been "satisfied" and to have consented unconditionally and cannot afterwards be heard to say that they had overlooked what was shown on the map'. The editors cite *Attorney General* v *Denby* [1925] Ch 596, in support of this statement, and a reading of the case certainly gives strength to the contention.

New buildings and drains

5.06 Under section 21 of the 1984 Act new buildings must be provided with drains. This section states that unless the drawings show satisfactory provision for the drainage of the building, or the local authority is satisfied that it may dispense with any provisions for drainage in the particular case, the plans shall be rejected. 'Drainage' in this connection includes roof drainage. The local authority *must* reject plans deposited if no satisfactory provision for drainage is shown on them. Where the local authority is not satisfied with the provision for drainage shown on the drawings, its decision can be challenged by reference to the magistrates' court. In

Chesterton RDC v Ralph Thompson, Ltd [1947] KB 300, the High Court held that the local authority is not entitled to reject plans on the ground that the sewerage system, into which the drains lead, is unsatisfactory. What the local authority must consider is the drainage of the particular building only.

5.07 This statutory provision is badly phrased, particularly in the wording of subsection (3), which does not make it clear whether the authority can pass the drawings subject to conditions instead of rejecting them. The best view is that it may impose any conditions or requirements that can be shown on a drawing, but not other conditions.

5.08 As a result of this provision, the local authority can insist on a separate drain being provided for each building, although in practice, plans showing combined drainage are invariably approved. Moreover, under the next section (section 22) it may require buildings to be drained in combination into an existing sewer 'where the drains of the building are first laid'. It cannot insist on drainage in combination where it has previously passed the plans, except with the agreement of the owners concerned.

Closet accommodation

5.09 Section 26 of the 1984 Act imposes a mandatory obligation to reject drawings of a building or extension unless they show that sufficient and satisfactory closet accommodations is provided, or the local authority is satisfied that it may properly dispense with the requirement in the particular case.

5.10 'Water closets and earth closets' are referred to in section 26, and it is for the local authority to decide which type is to be provided. It cannot reject the plans merely because an earth closet is shown 'unless a sufficient water supply and sewer are available'. This phraseology has an antiquated ring today, and is of little practical importance. Of more importance is the grant which can be claimed under section 66 of the Act when converting any kind of old-fashioned closet (including chemical closets) to a water closet (see Chapter 12 para 4.14).

Water supply

5.11 The effect of section 25 of the 1984 Act is that drawings of a house deposited with the local authority are to be rejected, unless 'there is put before (the local authority) a proposal which appears to it to be satisfactory for providing the occupants with a supply of wholesome water sufficient for their domestic purposes', and if possible the water is to be from a piped supply.

Building constructed of materials unsuitable for permanent buildings

5.12 Section 20 of the Building Act 1984 contains special provisions as to materials, etc., unsuitable for permanent buildings. It provides a wide power of control over the use in buildings of materials, components, fittings, etc., which are short-lived or for some other reason require special measures. Where plans show that it is proposed to construct a building of materials which are unsuitable for permanent buildings, the local authority may reject the plans, even though they are generally in accordance with the Regulations. Alternatively, the local authority may set a period at the end of which the building must be removed, unless an extension is granted. The local authority may impose conditions which are relevant to the use of these materials. There is a right of appeal to the Secretary of State against the local authority's decision.

Continuing requirements

5.13 Section 2 of the 1984 Act provides for imposing continuing requirements on owners and occupiers of buildings which were not subject regulations when erected. In the event of contravention of requirements so imposed, the local authority may execute the work and then charge for it.

Erection of buildings on ground filled with offensive matter

5.14 29 of the 1984 Act confers on the local authority power to reject drawings where the site of the building is ground which has been filled up with any material impregnated with faecal or offensive animal or vegetable matter or upon which such material has been deposited. The rejection of plans is obligatory, for unless the council is satisfied that the offensive material has been removed or has become or been rendered innocuous, it has no discretion entitling it to pass the drawings.

5.15 Rejection of the drawings under section 29 does not give rise to any right of appeal, but the applicant may apply to the magistrates' court to determine 'whether the local authority ought to approve the erection of the building . . . on the site in question'. No time limit is imposed.

Removal of refuse

5.16 Section 23 of the 1984 Act requires the local authority to reject drawings for erection or entension of a house unless satisfactory means of access from the house to the street is provided for the removal of refuse. 'House' is defined in section 126 of the Act as meaning a dwelling house, whether a private dwelling house or not. Thus, the power to reject drawings does not extend to other buildings such as commercial premises, albeit there is an equal need in such cases for the satisfactory removal of refuse. The provision is couched in imperative terms, and there is a right of appeal to the magistrates' court.

Exits and entrances of public buildings

5.17 Section 71 of the 1984 Act allows local authorities to control entrances and exits of certain buildings, but it applies only to the kinds of buildings listed in subsection (5) (see *checklist 15.7*). The local authority must reject the plans for such a building unless they show that the building 'will be provided with such means of ingress and egress and passages or gangways as the authority deems satisfactory, regard being had . . . to the purpose for which the building is intended to

---

Checklist 15.7: Types of building subject to special control over entrances and exits (Building Act 1984, section 71)

This section applies to the following:

1. Any theatre, and any hall or other building which is used as a place of public resort.
2. Any restaurant, shop, store, or warehouse to which members of the public are admitted and in which more than 20 persons are employed.
3. Any licensed club required to be registered.
4. Any school not exempted from the operation of Building Regulations.
5. A church, chapel or other place of public worship, except that this section does not apply to a private house to which members of the public are admitted occasionally or exceptionally, or to a building which was used as a church, chapel, or other place of worship immediately before the date when section 36 of the Public Health Acts Amendment Act 1890, or a corresponding provision in a local Act, came into operation in the district, or which was so used immediately before October 1937: Building Act 1984, section 24.

be, or is, used, and the number of persons likely to resort thereto at any one time'.

In practice this may necessitate installation of fire-escapes, and is really a matter for liaison among the architect, the local authority, and the local fire authority.

Other matter subject to control

5.18 The preceding eight cases are examples of the controls which come into play as the result of a deposit of plans or the giving of a building notice under the Building Regulations or the service of an intial notice when using the approved inspector. There are others, e.g. the height of chimneys controlled under section 10 of the Clean Air Act 1956 (dealt with in para 6.12), but the ones discussed serve to emphasize the importance of the Building Regulations procedure and the local authority's powers.

6 Other national legislation

6.01 More than 200 general statutes contain further provisions affecting the construction of buildings, although this is not apparent from the titles of the Acts concerned. There are also numerous statutory instruments made under powers conferred by many of these Acts. In this section some statutory rules which affect the bulk of building developments will be considered. This list does not claim to be exhaustive, nor does it cover all the relevant sections. (Some provisions of statutes not discussed here are covered in Chapter 12.)

6.02 Certain requirements are dealt with automatically on the deposit of drawings under the Building Regulations or, in some cases, at the same time as the application for planning permission. The following are some of the more important provisions which are relevant at that stage.

The Fire Precautions Act 1971

6.03 The object of this Act is to meet the criticisms that the law relating to fire precautions in certain kinds of residential accommodation and places of public entertainment was inadequate.

6.04 At the time of writing, the Act applies to the following categories of premises:

1. Hotels and boarding houses where sleeping accommodation is provided for six or more guests or staff or any number of guests or staff above the first floor or below the ground floor.
2. Factories, offices, shops and railway premises where more than 20 people are employed, or more than 10 people are employed elsewhere than on the ground floor, or (in factories only) explosive or highly inflammable materials are stored or used in or under the premises.

These are the 'designated' uses under the Act. Places of public religious worship, and single private dwellings are specifically excluded from control.

It should be noted that there is an obligation to provide *reasonable* means of escape in *all* offices, shops and railway premises. Regulations have been made under the 1971 Act which apply to factories, offices, shops and railway premises which do not require a fire certificate relating to the availability of exits and the provision and maintenance of fire appliances.

6.05 Fire certificates issued by the local fire authority are the main form of control under the Act. The occupier of affected premises must obtain a certificate to the effect that the premises are provided with such means of escape in case of fire as may reasonably be required.

6.06 Under section 3 the fire authority (in consultation with the local authority) has power to serve a notice which makes a fire certificate compulsory for certain kinds of dwellings, mainly blocks of flats, but this provision is not activated yet.

6.07 If premises fall within the Act, an application for a fire certificate must be made to the fire authority under section 5. The authority must then inspect the premises and, if they are satisfied as to the means of escape in case of fire and other relevant fire precautions, they must issue the certificate, or inform the applicant of what must be done to bring the premises up to standard.

6.08 It must be noted that the Secretary of State is empowered by section 11 to make building regulations regarding means of escape in new buildings. Once these regulations have been made in relation to fire-escapes in new buildings, the architect will know what requirements will satisfy the authority by way of fire-escapes in any new building. There is a safeguard for the building owner: section 13 provides that except in specially defined circumstances, the fire authority cannot require alterations to a building or an extension, if it has already been subject to Building Regulations approval relating to means of escape. The various authorities concerned are also under a duty to consult each other in appropriate circumstances, e.g. under section 15, the local authority must consult the fire authority before passing plans under the Building Regulations if the premises are likely to require a certificate.

6.09 This measure extends fire precautions to further categories of premises and aims to provide a comprehensive and flexible system of control. The greater part of the Act is now in force.

The Clean Air Acts 1965 to 1968

6.10 Among other things, these Acts control the height of chimneys on industrial premises, types of installation, and the treatment of offensive fumes from appliances.

6.11 Section 6 of the 1968 Act requires the approval of the local authority for the height of a chimney serving a furnace, and approval may be granted subject to conditions as to the rate and/or quality of emissions from the chimney. There is a right of appeal to the minster.

6.12 Similarly section 10 of the 1956 Act provides that in other cases the local authority must reject plans of residences, shops, or offices unless the height of the chimney as shown on the drawings will be sufficient to prevent fumes from being a nuisance or a health hazard. The factors to be considered are the purpose of the chimney, the position and description of nearby buildings, level of neighbouring ground, and other relevant matters. These provisions represent an important negative control. See further Chapter 12, para 6.05.

Highways Act 1980

6.13 The Highways Act 1980 consolidates, with amendments, earlier legislation and contains many provisions affecting building work. For example, sections 73 and 74 deal with improvment and building lines respectively. An improvement line is designed to prevent the erection of buildings on land that may later be required for road widening. Where an improvement line has been prescribed, no new building may be erected nor may a permanent excavation be made nearer to the centre line of the street than the improvement line, except with the highway authority's consent. This may be granted subject to conditions. There is a right of appeal to the Crown Court against the refusal of consent or its grant subject to conditions.

6.14 A building line is a frontage line beyond which a building may not project, irrespective of road widening. A building line may be prescribed by the highway authority under section 74, and, where it is prescribed, no new building (other than the boundary wall) may be erected in front of the prescribed line except with the authority's consent. This may be granted subject to conditions, or for a limited time. In both cases, a new building includes an addition or extension to an existing building, and hence both provisions are always relevant at the design stage.

6.15 The Highways Act 1980 contains many other prohibitions and rules which affect the architect's work, including Part X (sections 186 to 196) dealing with new streets. Where new street byelaws have been made, the proposed work must not contravene them, and plans showing any contravention will be rejected (section 191). Where a new street order has been made under section 188 and new street byelaws are in force, these will prescribe the centre line of the new street and lines defining its minimum width. Effectively, new buildings will have to be set back in order to leave sufficient land for a street of the necessary width to be formed at that point. Another relevant provision is section 206, which enables the authority to make a street designation order.

6.16 Even minor works of alteration and extension will not necessarily escape the net of the 1980 Act. For instance, if a building owner wishes to have a garage erected, it will be necessary in many cases for a carriage crossing to be constructed, thus bringing into play the provisions of section 184. The building owner who wishes to provide new means of access to his premises to be constructed at his expense may initiate proposals for a carriage crossing. In addition, the local authority may, in certain circumstances, construct a crossing on their own initiative, again at the building owner's expense.

6.17 Section 124 of the 1980 Act gives power for a highway authority to be authorized by order of the Secretary of State for the Environment to stop up private access to highways from any premises, if it considers that the access is likely to cause danger to, or interfere unnecessarily with, traffic on the highway. Such an order can be made only where no access to the premises from the highway is reasonably required, or where other reasonably convenient means of access is available or will be provided. There is an objections procedure, and compensation may be payable (1980 Act, section 126(2)).

6.18 Attention is also drawn to section 168 of the Act which provides that if, in the course of carrying out building work in or near a street, an accident occurs which gives rise to the risk of serious bodily injury to a person in the street, the owner of the land or building where the work is being carried out is guilty of an offence punishable by a maximum fine of £500.

6.19 Again, section 177 places restrictions on construction (and subsequent alteration) of buildings over highways maintainable at the public expense, without the licence of the highway authority. Licences may be granted subject to conditions and are registrable as a local land charge (Chapter 7 para 1.08).

6.20 Section 174 prescribes that precautions against accidents must be taken where a person is executing works in a street.

These safety measures include, where appropriate, the shoring up of any building adjoining the street. Stringent safety precautions must be observed in relation to builders' skips which may not be deposited on the highway without the highway authority's consent. This may be granted subject to conditions. The provisions relating to skips are found in sections 139 to 140.

The Factories Act 1961

6.21 The provisions of this complex measure and of the many regulations made under it affect building construction in two ways: provision of sanitary accommodation; health and welfare provisions generally.

Means of escape in case of fire are now dealt with under the Fire Precautions Act 1971 as discussed in para 6.03 to 6.09.

Sanitary accommodation

6.22 Section 7, read in conjunction with the Sanitary Accommodation Regulations 1938, requires the provision of adequate sanitary accommodation for employees of both sexes. Where women are employed, there must be at least one sanitary convenience for every 25 females. There must be one suitable sanitary convenience (not simply a urinal) for every 25 men employed. However, where more than 100 men are employed and there is adequate urinal accommodation, one water closet for the first 25 employees and one for every 40 after that number are sufficient. Reference should be made to the text of the Regulations for exemptions and for other contingencies. The preceding section (section 6) requires the provision of adequate floor drainage, e.g. by gulleys, where the factory process is likely to make the floor wet.

6.23 Other rules of the Factories Act concern architects. For example, sections 57 to 79 which, among other things, require the provision of cloakroom and clothes-drying accommodation, washing facilities, and so on.

The Offices, Shops and Railway Premises Act 1963

6.24 Similar rules to those in the Factories Act 1961 are applied by this Act to offices, shops, and railway premises (see further Chapter 12 and Chapter 19).

Special classes of building

6.25 The legislation dealt with so far is, in one sense, of general application. The architect dealing with the design and construction of specialized types of building may find that special controls apply.

All these specialized provisions are extremely complex, and space does not permit any detailed examination of them. As examples, we may refer to the special controls applicable to cinemas and to the keeping and use of radioactive substances.

7 Building control in Inner London

7.01 Inner London consists of the City of London and the twelve London Boroughs of Camden, Greenwich, Hackney, Hammersmith, Islington, Kensington and Chelsea, Lambeth, Lewisham, Southwark, Tower Hamlets, Wandsworth, and Westminister: London Government Act 1963, section 43.

7.02 Until 1986, the design, construction and use of buildings in this area were regulated by the London Building Acts and Byelaws, which formed a code of control different from that which operated elsewhere. The Building (Inner London) Regulations 1985 came into effect on 6 January 1986 and repealed the London Building Byelaws, brought most of the national regulations into force in Inner London, and made some amendments to the London Building Acts. The remaining building regulations were applied to Inner London by the Building (Inner London) Regulations 1987, which came into effect on 1 June 1987.

7.03 Nonetheless, Inner London is still subject to many additional controls under the remaining provisions of the London Building Acts 1930 to 1978, and so building control in the area is subject to many special features. The function of building control there is undertaken by 14 District Surveyors/ Chief Building Regulaton Officers whose former special statutory powers have been emasculated. They supervise the work of approving plans and construction to secure compliance with the regulations, but they also have power to serve Notices of Objection and Notices of Irregularity where the requirements of the London Building Acts are being contravened.

Powers of entry

7.04 The district surveyor and other authorized officers have wide powers of entry, inspection and examination to enable then to carry out their functions: e.g., section 142 of the London Building Acts (Amendment) Act 1939.

Appeals tribunals

7.05 Provision exists in the London Building Acts for special Tribunals of Appeal (one for each of the building control authorities) which hear appeals referred to them under the London Building Acts: 1939 Act, section 109. The Tribunals have power to award costs and wide powers to order the production of documents, plans, specifications, and so on. A further appeal lies, by way of case stated, to the High Court: 1939 Act, section 116.

7.06 Where a notice is given or plans deposited in respect of a building affected by the provisions of the Acts, and it discloses a contravention of the provisions, the district surveyor must serve Notice of Objection on the builder or owner or other person causing or directing the work. In effect this provides a *locus poenitentiae* (an opportunity for repentence).

However, an appeal may be made to the magistrates' court within 14 days after service of the notice: 1939 Act, section 39.

Notice of irregularity

7.07 The district surveyor also has power to serve a Notice of Irregularity under section 88 of the 1939 Act. This can be served after the builder has completed the work. It was decided in *Coggin* v *Duff* (1907) 96 LT 670, that failure to give Notice of Objection is not a bar to proceedings under Notice of Irregularity. This notice will be served where work has been done and it is found that some contravention exists or that the work is so far advanced that the district surveyor cannot ascertain whether anything has been done in contravention. Its effect is to require the builder within 48 hours to amend any contravention or to open up as much of the work as may be necessary for the district surveyor to ascertain whether or not a contravention exists. The opening-up and rectification is done at the builder's or owner's expense. The notice cannot be served on the builder when he has completed the building, but there is power to serve notice on the owner, occupier, or other person directing the work.

7.08 The sanction behind a Notice of Irregularity is a fine. However, the district surveyor may apply to the magistrates' court for an order requiring the builder to comply within a

stated time. Failure to obey an order of the court renders the builder liable to a daily fine: 1939 Act, section 148.

Specific provisions

7.09 Space does not permit a detailed examination of the provisions of the London Building Acts, but consideration will be given to a number of points of practical importance. For a full treatment of this complex legislation reference should be made to *Guide to Building Control in Inner London 1987*, by P. H. Pitt., which is both up-to-date and authoritative.

Large and high buildings

7.10 Section 20 of the London Building Acts (Amendments) Act 1939, as amended, is important, and gives the borough councils wide control over the following buildings, so far as relates to precautions against fire:

1. Buildings of excess height over 30 metres, or over 25 metres high if the area of the building exceeds 930 square metres.
2. Certain trade buildings of additional cubical extent, i.e. buildings over 7100 cubic metres in extent used for trade (including warehouses and department stores) or manufacture.

Except where a trade building is properly subdivided into fire divisions of less than 7100 cubic metres each, all buildings coming within the scope of section 20 require special consent from the borough council, which will send a copy of the plans, etc., to the London Fire and Civil Defence Authority for comment. When these are received, a consent will be issued, but this is usually conditional upon compliance with a schedule of requirements, e.g. higher standards of fire resistance, automatic sprinklers, hose reels, dry risers, firemen's lifts, emergency lighting on stairs and escape routes.

Full details are required and approval must be obtained of all electrical installations, heating and ventilation systems, sprinkler installations, etc. Additional precautions can be required in 'special fire risk areas' (defined in section 20(2D)), e.g. where any storey of a garage is located in a basement or is not adequately ventilated.

Readers are advised to obtain the 'Code of Practice for Buildings of Excess Height or Cubical Extent' (Ref 7168 0316X) published by the former GLC, which is essential for those dealing with the design of section 20 buildings.

Means of escape in case of fire

7.11 Part V of the London Building Acts (Amendment) Act 1939 deals with means of escape in case of fire. An application, accompanied by drawings, must be submitted to the council for approval as to the proposed means of escape for every 'new building' (broadly, those built after 1939)to which section 34 applies. The notice and drawings must be deposited before or at the same time as any notice is given or plans are deposited in respect of the building. The buildings concerned are:

1. Public buildings.
2. Places of worship or assembly.
3. Every other new building which:
   (a) if single storey, exceeds 600 square feet in area.
   (b) If more than one storey, exceeds 1000 square feet (excluding basements used only for storage).

The section does not, however, apply to licensed places of entertainment (which have their means of escape dealt with under the licensing procedure) or to a private house in single family occupation which does not have a floor at a height of more than 20 feet or to houses or flats of three or more storeys.

The local authority have two months from the deposit of the plans (or such longer period as may be agreed in writing) in which to approve the proposed means of escape or to refuse it. Approval may be given subject to conditions.

The approved means of escape arrangements from buildings to which Part V of the 1939 Act applies are required by section 133 to be maintained and fines for contravention are prescribed in section 148.

Dwelling houses on low-lying land

Part XII of the London Building Act 1930 prohibits the erection or rebuilding of dwelling houses on low-lying land without the consent of the appropriate Inner London borough council.

Party structures

7.12 Part VI of the 1939 Act contains a special statutory code governing party structures and rights of adjoining owners. It does not abrogate common law rules but they are excluded to the extent of these statutory provisions which do not affect the legal title to the structure or any easements or rights in connection with them (section 54). Negotiations about right of light are separate from awards under Part VI.

Party wall

7.13 Section 44 gives a special definition of 'party wall':

1. A wall which forms part of a building and stands on lands of different owners. Projection of any artificially formed support on which the wall rests on to land of any adjoining owner does not make the wall a party wall.
2. Any part of any other wall as separates buildings belonging to different owners.

Party structure

7.14 Party structure is a party wall, floor, partition, or other structure separating buildings or parts of buildings approached only by separate staircases or entrances from outside the building (section 4). Tenancy separations in blocks of flats and maisonettes are therefore normally excluded.

Party fence wall

7.15 The legislation also refers to a 'party fence wall'. This is a wall that is not part of a building, but which stands on the lands of different owners and is used or constructed for separating such lands. It does not include a wall constructed on one owner's land, of which only artificially formed supports project on to the adjoining land. Thus rights of adjoining owners do not arise where only the foundations project on to the adjoining land if the wall concerned is a boundary wall, not being part of a building, but they do arise if such a wall separates buildings belonging to different owners.

Procedure

7.16 A special procedure has to be followed if the building owner wishes to invoke his rights under the Act. These are more extensive than the limited rights he has at common law, and as regards existing structures, may be summarized:

1. Where a structure is defective, he may repair, make good, thicken or underpin it, or demolish and rebuild it.
2. If he wishes to build against it and it is of insufficient height or strength, he may rebuild it subject to making good all damage to adjoining property, and raising the height as necessary of chimney and flues.

3. He may carry out all necessary incidental works to connect with the adjoining premises.

A full list of the authorized works is given in section 46 (*Checklist 15.8*).

Section 50 deals with the underpinning of independent buildings and confers valuable rights on both adjoining owners.

Checklist 15.8: Authorized works to party structures (London Building Acts (Amendment) Act 1939, section 46)

Where lands of different owners adjoin and at the line of junction the said lands are built on, or a boundary wall being a party fence wall or the external wall of a building has been erected, the building owner shall have the following rights:

1. To make good, underpin, thicken or repair, or demolish and rebuild a party structure or party fence wall in any case where such work is necessary on account of defect or want of repair of the party structure or party fence wall.
2. To demolish a timber or other partition which separates buildings belonging to different owners but is not in conformity with the London Building Acts or any byelaws made in pursuance of those Acts and to build instead a party wall in conformity therewith.
3. In relation to a building having rooms or storeys belonging to different owners intermixed to demolish such of those rooms or storeys or any part thereof as are not in conformity with the London Building Acts or any byelaws made in pursuance of those Acts and to rebuild them in conformity therewith.
4. Where buildings are connected by arches or structures over public ways or over passages belonging to other persons to demolish such of those buildings arches or structures or such parts thereof as are not in conformity with the London Building Acts or any byelaws made in pursuance of those Acts and to rebuild them in conformity therewith.
5. To underpin, thicken, or raise any party structure or party fence wall permitted by this Act to be underpinned thickened or raised or any external wall built against such a party structure or party fence wall subject to:
   (a) making good all damage occasioned thereby to the adjoining premises or to the internal finishings and decorations thereof;
   (b) carrying up to such height and in such materials as may be agreed between the building owner and the adjoining owner or in the event of difference determined in the manner provided in this part of this Act all flues and chimney stacks belonging to the adjoining owner on or against the party structure or external wall.
6. To demolish a party structure which is of insufficient strength or height for the purposes of any intended building of the building owner and to rebuilt it of sufficient strength or height for the said purposes subject to:
   (a) making good all damage occasioned thereby to the adjoining premises or to the internal finishings and decorations thereof;
   (b) carrying up to such height and in such materials as may be agreed between the building owner and the adjoining owner or in the event of difference determined in the manner provided in this part of this Act all flues and chimney stacks belonging to the adjoining owner on or against the party structure or external wall.
7. To cut into a party structure subject to making good all damage occasioned thereby to the adjoining premises or to the internal finishings and decorations thereof.
8. To cut away any footing or any projecting chimney-breast, jamb or flue, or other projection on or over the land of the building owner from a party wall, party fence wall, external wall, or boundary wall in order to erect, raise, or underpin an external wall against such party wall, party fence wall, external wall, or boundary wall or for any other purpose subject to making good all damage occasioned thereby to the adjoining premises or to the internal finishings and decorations thereof.
9. To cut away or demolish such parts of any wall or building of an adjoining owner overhanging the land of the building owner as may be necessary to enable a vertical wall to be erected against that wall or building subject to making good any damage occasioned thereby to the wall or building or to the internal finishings and decorations of the adjoining premises.

Checklist 15.8 continued

10. To execute any other necessary works incidental to the connection of a party structure with the premises adjoining it.
11. To raise a party fence wall to raise and use as a party wall, a party fence wall, or to demolish a party fence wall and rebuild it as a party fence wall or as a party wall.

For the purposes of this section a building or structure which was erected before the commencement of this Act shall be deemed to be in conformity with the London Building Acts and any byelaws made in pursuance of those Acts if it is in conformity with the Acts and any byelaws made in pursuance of the Acts which regulated buildings or structures in London at the date at which it was erected.

Nothing in this section shall authorize the building owner to place special foundations on land of the adjoining owner without his previous consent in writing.

7.17 The first step in the process is for the building owner to serve a *party structure notice* upon adjoining owners, except where their prior written consent has been given or the work is necessary as a result of a dangerous structure notice. The notice contains particulars of the proposed works and is normally accompanied by a party-wall drawing, although drawing need only be served where it is proposed to use 'special foundations', i.e. foundations in which steel beams or rods are used to spread the load. The notice must be served at least two months before the work is to be commenced in the case of a party structure or one month in the case of special foundations or a party fence wall (section 47 (2)). The adjoining owner has the right to serve counter-notice requiring carrying out of additional works for his protection. Most party wall surveyors hold that the full 'particulars' of the proposed work (as required by section 47) must include *plans*. These are also required by section 48 (2)(c) – counter-notice. The RICS publish a set of Party Structure Notice forms.

7.18 The adjoining owner may, in fact, consent to the proposed works under section 49. If an owner does not so express his consent in writing to a counter-notice or a notice within 14 days of service, a 'difference' is deemed to have arisen between the parties (section 49). The special procedure for settlement of differences is in effect an arbitration (Chapter 11) and is contained in section 55. This enables the parties to agree to the appointment of an agreed surveyor who will make an award upon the difference. This is not usual. In practice, each party appoints his own surveyor, and normally the difference is settled by negotiation between them and they make a joint award. There is provision for the two nominated surveyors to call in a third surveyor who acts as intermediary, but this is very rare.

7.19 When the party wall award has been agreed, it is engrossed (expressed in legal form) and executed in duplicate, each copy being signed and witnessed by the two surveyors. The award will deal with the supervision of the works and the costs. Normally, costs will be borne by the building owner, but this is not necessarily the case. The award can be challenged by an appeal to the County Court within 14 days of issue, or, in certain circumstances, by appeal to the High Court.

7.20 Expenses in respect of party structures are dealt with by section 56. Where works are for the benefit of both owners (normally when a party structure is in disrepair) the costs are to be shared proportionately. The adjoining owner may also be liable to contribute towards the costs when he makes any use of the works as compared with the use when the works were begun. Such a right of contribution does not exist at common law. Section 56 is not clear as to what can be included in the 'expenses incurred', for which the building and adjoining owners may be severally or jointly liable, and these have been held to include district surveyors',

surveyors', and architects' fees in connection with design (see *Fifoot* v *Applerley* (1905) reported only in *Building News*, 18 September 1905). The costs of the party wall itself are not included, as these will be dealt with specifically in the award itself.

7.21 Any works which are carried out by a building owner under the provisions of the Act are subject to four general conditions under section 51:

1. The work is not to be carried out in such a way or at such a time as to cause unnecessary inconvenience to the adjoining owner or occupier. It is submitted that building work carried out at normal times and in a normal manner and taking reasonable precautions to reduce noise and dust to a minimum cannot be said to cause 'unnecessary inconvenience', just as it would not constitute a nuisance at common law (*Andreae* v *Selfridge & Co* [1938] 1 Ch 9).
2. Where any part of the adjoining land or building is laid open, the building owner must erect and maintain at his own expense proper protective hoardings and so on for protection and security of the adjoining occupier.
3. The works must comply with the London Building Acts and Byelaws.
4. The works must be in accordance with any plans, sections, and particulars agreed between the owners or approved by their surveyors in the party-wall award.

7.22 The works which are authorized by the Act are set out in section 46 (*Checklist 15.1*). However, it must be be remembered that special foundations cannot be placed under adjoining land without the adjoining owner's written consent.

7.23 Section 53 confers on the building owner, his servants, agents, and workmen a power of entry upon premises, and if the building is closed, he may break open doors to enter, provided he is accompanied by a police officer. Fourteen days must be given, except in emergency.

7.24 In *Gyle-Thompson* v *Wall Street Properties Ltd* [1974] 1 All ER 295, the High Court considered what Mr Justice Brightman described as 'important points of law' arising out of the operation of the 1939 Act. His lordship held that, in the absence of any express right to lower a party fence wall, sections 46(a) and (k) of the Act (which give a building owner the right to demolish and rebuild) require reconstruction of the wall to its original height. The defendants also contended that under section 55 the award was conclusive against the plaintiff and could be challenged only by an appeal to the county court. The judge rejected this submission, saying that it is not correct 'in relation to an award which is ultra vires and therefore not a valid award'. 'This case also emphasizes that the steps laid down by the Act as to procedure 'should be scrupulously followed throughout, and short cuts are not desirable'.

8 Local legislation outside London

8.01 Although the Building Act 1984 and Regulations made under it were intended to provide a national code of building control, there are many provisions in local Acts which impose additional controls on the construction of buildings. They supplement the national code, and many of them were enacted quite recently: see *Checklist 15.2*.

8.02 These local Acts have a special significance in the context of private certification. Regulation 10 of the Building (Approved Inspectors, etc.) Regulations 1985 provide that an approved inspector must ensure that the building regulations are complied with and, inter alia, where a local Act so requires, must consult with the Fire Authority. A local authority can reject an approved inspector's initial notice where the work proposed would 'contravene any local enactment which authorises them to reject plans submitted in accordance with building regulations': 1984 Act, Schedule 3, para 11. However, under private certification the local authority remains responsible for ensuring that the work complies with the requirements of any local Act.

8.03 The provisions of section 90 of the 1984 Act should be noted. This provides that (outside Inner London) where there is any local Act in force imposing obligations or restrictions as to the construction, nature or situation of buildings, they 'shall keep a copy of those provisions at their offices for inspection by the public at all reasonable times free of charge'.

The following is not an exhaustive list, but indicates some common local provisions, the content of many local Acts being similar. Reference should be made to *Guide to Building Control by Local Acts 1987* by P. H. Pitt which is a comprehensive coverage of this local legislation.

Fire precautions for underground parking places

8.04 This is a common provision in many local Acts and applies only to basement garages for more than three vehicles or garages for more than 20 vehicles not belonging to one dwelling. The local authority or approved inspector must consult with the Fire Authority and can impose conditions on the approval of plans, e.g. means of access for the fire brigade, fire-fighting equipment, etc.

Access for the fire brigade

8.05 Another common requirement. Plans deposited with the local authority must show adequate access for the fire brigade. In some cases, fire tenders must be provided and special fire-fighting stairs and firemens' lifts may be required. The local authority can reject the plans where, after consulting with the Fire Authority, it is satisfied that access is inadequate. An approved inspector must also consult with the Fire Authority.

Multi-storey car parks

8.06 Stringent requirements must be met where there are three or more cars below ground level or more than 20 above. Requirements can include means of escape, cross-ventilation, fire fighting equipment and so on.

External stacks of flammable materials

8.07 A not uncommon provision where flammable material is to be stored. Special fire precautions and fire-fighting requirements can be insisted upon.

Separate drainage system

8.08 In some areas, e.g. Lancashire, Leicestershire, South Yorkshire, Staffordshire, West Glamorgan and West Yorkshire, local legislation requires that each building must have a separate system of drainage for soil and surface water.

High buildings

8.09 Buildings over six storeys may be required to have fire alarms, fire-fighting equipment, sprinklers, etc., with approved internal and external access for the fire brigade. Consultation with the Fire Authority is required.

Large storage buildings

8.10 Where this provision applies, storage buildings exceeding $7000 \, m^3$ may be required by the local authority to have fire alarms, access for the fire brigade, etc. The Fire Authority must be consulted.

Means of escape in case of fire

8.11 Where this provision is in force, it is additional to the requirements of Schedule 1, B1 of the Building Regulations 1985, and section 72 of the 1984 Act (means of escape) is not applicable. After consultation with the Fire Authority, the council may require means of escape and requirements can be made for buildings other than those listed in Schedule 1, G1 of the regulations, e.g. flats, hostels, stores, warehouses, etc.

Other provisions

8.12 This is not an exhaustive catalogue of local legislation. Many other provisions are encountered in different local authority areas. These authorities concerned are of the opinion that they form an essential part of the machinery of control. Indeed, many of these local provisions could well be made applicable to all urban conurbations.

16

Construction Regulations in Scotland

PETER FRANKLIN

1 Introduction

1.01 Building control in Scotland is based on Building Acts. To understand Scottish practice, a knowledge of the Acts is required, as well as of the Regulations made under them. The Building Standards (Scotland) Regulations 1981 are only one part of the whole scene, although admittedly a very important part. Anyone trying to compare Scottish and English building control must bear the above in mind, so that there is a comparison of like with like wherever possible.

1.02 This study is intended to describe the main provisions of the Act and procedures laid down under it, as well as the various Statutory Instruments associated with it. In regard to the Building Standards Regulations themselves, it is obviously impossible to go into minute detail regarding interpretations, etc. The object of each part of the Regulations has, therefore, been stated and reference made to the more important provisions and, where thought applicable, to individual regulations.

Historical background

1.03 Building control is not new, and records of building law go back to the pre-Christian era. The first known are those found in the Mosaic Law of King Hammurabi of Persia c.2000 BC. Fire precautions which have always formed a major part of building codes were an accepted factor of Roman law and of English law from the twelfth century.

Dean of Guild Courts

1.04 In Scotland building control in royal burghs was exercised by Dean of Guild Courts where these existed. Originally, the Dean of Guild was the president of the merchants' guild, which was composed of traders who had acquired the freedom of a royal burgh. The post is an ancient one, e.g. in 1403 one Simon de Schele was appointed Dean of Guild and Keeper of the Kirk Work by Edinburgh Town Council. The Dean of Guild Court's original mercantile jurisdiction fell gradually into disuse to be replaced by a jurisdiction over such areas as markets, streets, and buildings. 'Questions of neighbourhood' were dealt with by Edinburgh Dean of Guild as early as 1584. Gradually the scope and nature of the powers of the Dean of Guild Courts became more precise until during the last 150 years they were subjected to a process of statutory modification.

1.05 Not all burghs had Dean of Guild Courts, and it was not until 1947 that the Local Government (Scotland) Act required burghs without Dean of Guild Courts to appoint one. In other burghs, the functions of the Dean of Guild

Courts were either carried out by magistrates or the town council itself. In counties, plans were usually approved by a sub-committee of the public health committee. There was no warrant procedure as in burghs.

Byelaws

1.06 During the last 150 years, statutory requirements laid the foundation of specific and more widely applicable standards. The Burgh Police Act 1833 empowered burghs to adopt powers of paving, lighting, cleansing, watching, and supplying water. However, the building legislation content of the nineteenth century Acts was not large and was related mainly to ruinous property and drainage, attention to the latter being attracted by the large-scale outbreaks of cholera at that time. In 1892 the Burgh Police Act introduced a detailed set of building rules which were repealed by the 1903 Burgh Police Act. This Act gave powers to burghs to make byelaws in respect of building and public health matters. Meanwhile in the counties, the Public Health (Scotland) Act 1897 had already given them the power to make similar byelaws.

1.07 Byelaws made under these Acts, although limited in scope, remained the main form of building control until 1932 when the Department of Health for Scotland published model building byelaws for both burghs and countries. Local authorities could, if they wished, adopt these byelaws for application in their own area. However, many did not. The model byelaws were revised in 1934 and 1937, but, apart from a widening of scope, later editions did not differ much from the original 1932 version. A much more comprehensive review was carried out in 1954. Although many local authorities adopted the 1954 model byelaws, adoption was at the discretion of the local authority and many did not. (By 1957, 26 of the 33 counties, 127 of the 173 small burghs, 13 of the 20 large burghs, and none of the cities had adopted model byelaws.) However, Edinburgh, Aberdeen, and Glasgow had local Acts which combined many of the requirements of old statutes and byelaws with local features.

1.08 The then existing legislation fell short of the requirements of a modern building code able to cope with the rapidly expanding building of post-war Scotland where new techniques and materials were rapidly being introduced. It was decided that the whole concept of building control should be reviewed, and to this end a committee under the chairmanship of C. W. G. Guest QC, later Lord Guest, was appointed by the Secretary of State.

1.09 The committee's terms of reference required that it examine the existing law pertaining to building and jurisdic-

tion of the Dean of Guild Courts and make recommendations on the future form of a building control system for counties and burghs, which was to be flexible enough to take account of new techniques and materials.

1.10 The committee published its report in October 1957. Its main recommendation was that legislation was essential to enable a comprehensive building code to be set up in the form of national regulations to achieve uniformity throughout the country. The basic purpose of building control should be the protection of the public interest as regards health and safety. The law must ensure that occupants, neighbours, and passers-by are protected by preventing the erection of buildings that are liable to collapse or lead to unhealthy or insanitary conditions. It must also prevent individual and collective fire hazards.

1.11 The recommendations were accepted and led to the existing form of control now established in Scotland.

Review of the building control system

1.12 During the period from its introduction until the late 1970s the building control system was kept under constant review. Some of the principles in the original legislation were expanded, and amendments, additions and deletions were made, where necessary to the regulations. This is a continuous process necessary to keep abreast of developments in building practice, technology and materials.

1.13 It is a principle of good management, however, that every so often a detailed analysis and examination be carried out on any system and building control is no exception. It was with this view in mind, together with Government's determination to remove unnecessary restrictions on individual freedoms and minimize the involvement of central Government, that the Secretary of State decided in 1980 that the Scottish Development Department should undertake a comprehensive review of building control.

1.14 In July 1980, in order to gauge the climate of opinion, a wide field of Scottish Interests were invited to give views on the following:

1. the structure and operation of the present system in Scotland with relevance to any major deficiencies and areas of difficulty;
2. changes which might be introduced to make the system more efficient without undermining the protection of public health and safety.

1.15 These consultations revealed that there was wide agreement that the basic framework of building control works satisfactorily, but with scope for improvement. The first priority was seen as rationalizing over-complex building standards regulations. Other areas of concern involved inconsistent interpretation of regulations by enforcing authorities, differences of technical detail within the UK, the effect of liability for latent danger and the scope for private sector involvement. The Secretary of State announced in May 1981 that as a result of the comments received and the parallel review being undertaken in England and Wales proposals for change would be further developed.

Consultative Paper – The Future of Building Control in Scotland

1.16 In 1983, the Scottish Development Department issued for comment a Consultative Paper – The Future of Building Control in Scotland – and invited comment from interested bodies.

The paper was the outcome of the Secretary of State's statement of May 1981 (para 1.15) and the object of the review was stated as:

1. upholding the prime purposes of building control as laid down in the Building Acts;
2. securing simplicity in operation;
3. promoting consistency in interpretation and enforcement;
4. minimizing central Government involvement;
5. providing for increased participation by the private sector within a system of control which continued to be based on enforcement by *local authorities*;
6. making the system self-financing.

1.17 The paper was divided into various headings under which proposals were described in general terms. These headings were as follows:

Simplification of the Building Standards Regulations
Liaison and Co-operation between Building Control Authorities
Certification and Type Approvals
Appeals
Liability for Latent Damage
Relaxation of Building Standards Regulations
Exempted Works
Fees for Building Warrants
Other Procedural Refinements.

The paper concluded that earlier consultations endorsed the views that the Scottish building control system was founded on sound principles, but was in need of alterations and improvements rather than demolition and replacement. Many of the proposals could be implemented under existing powers given in the Building Acts with priority being given to the preparation of a more compact and rational set of Building Standards Regulations.

1.18 As a result of the Consultative Paper, a large number of those consulted submitted many and varied comments to the Department. After these comments had been given serious consideration, a statement of intent was issued by the Secretary of State on 29 November 1985.
The statement sums up the results of the consultations and the actions to be followed as a result of the exercise.

Statement of Intent by Secretary of State, 29 November 1985

1.19 The statement by the Secretary of State put forward a series of proposals based on the headings in paragraph 1.15. These can be summarized as follows:

1. *Building Standards Regulations* Particular attention would be focused upon matters of health, safety and conservation of energy while taking account of welfare and convenience. The revised Regulations would take the form of a functional statement coupled with a qualifying standard and backed up by supporting technical documents. The standards will be prescribed by Statutory Instrument. A revision of the technical content would be carried out at the same time.
2. *Certification* Powers would be legislated for to give local authorities, within clearly defined limits, the right to accept at their discretion certificates from suitably qualified persons responsible for designing a building.
3. *Liaison/co-ordination between building control authorities* After listening to various views put forward, the Government proposed to build on its previous liaison meetings with the Scottish Association of Chief Building Control Offices. It will set up a committee chaired and serviced by the Scottish Development Department which will meet at regular intervals to:
(a) foster common interpretation and administration of the Building Regulations;

(b) pool and disseminate information for use and reference;

(c) provide a collective liaison channel between building control authorities and the Scottish Development Department;

(d) furnish an advisory service for building control authorities on interpretive and other issues.

4. *Appeals*   The present system of appeals to the Sheriff would be retained.

5. *Relaxation of the regulations*   Delegation of the power to relax regulations for all buildings would be delegated in stages to local authorities. The Secretary of State would retain the responsibility for all Class Relaxations and in respect of buildings owned by the local authority in its own area.

6. *Exempted works*   There would be much wider exemption from the Regulations in respect of small buildings including additions to existing buildings. Limited requirements would be retained in certain cases in respect of drainage and structure.

7. *Other procedural matters*   Fees would be kept under constant review.

The possibility of removing Crown exemption was proposed and this was still under discussion with the interests involved. Immunity from the technical requirements of the Regulations is expected to be removed by June 1991.

Progress arising from the Statement of Intent

Simplification of the building standards regulations

1.20   Draft regulations in the form envisaged in the Statement were drawn up and circulated for comment. In the light of these comments a second draft was issued to consultative bodies. As a result a new set of regulations has been drafted along with a set of technical standards which have the status of *legally acceptable* methods of meeting the functional requirements laid down in the regulations.

Liaison on harmonizing technical content within the UK has formed an important part of the exercise and joint meetings with DOE and NI form a regular feature of the consultation.

In completely revising and repackaging Building Standards in a new form a great amount of time and effort has to be expended and delays are to be expected. In addition the final package has to be sent to the European Commission for approval before laying before Parliament. This submission was made in March 1990. The Commission has a time limit of three months in which objections to the proposals may be raised.

Liaison with local authorities

1.21   A Building Control Forum as envisaged in the Statement of Intent has been set up and met for the first time on 12 September 1985. Its terms of reference were those set out in the Secretary of State's statement and to fulfil these terms the Forum will be required to:

1. identify inconsistencies of interpretation and administration of the regulations;
2. ensure authoritative consideration of ways to eliminate such difficulties;
3. ensure effective communication of the Forum's advice and recommendations to all parties involved with building control (these would include existing professional bodies, trade interests, developers, etc.) and allow then to raise problems, subject to suitable arrangements being worked out, with the Forum.

The Forum will meet quarterly and SDD would be responsible for issue of any relevant information.

It should be stressed, however, that the Forum is *not* an alternative to the courts and will not consider the content of the Regulations. The latter is the province of the Building Standards Advisory Committee (BSAC). The Forum will take a collective look at the *system* in operation.

Exempted works

1.22   Powers have been taken to extend the scope of exemption from the Regulations to parts of a building. The present powers are restricted to complete buildings being exempted.

New powers

1.23   New powers have been taken in the Housing (Scotland) Act 1986 with regard to certification and class warrants. These powers when they are introduced into the system will considerable speed up the process of work starting on site once designs are completed.

The Department will seek an independent assessment from designated bodies as to the building or part of the building's compliance with regulations – thus involving the private sector in the decision-making process.

The class warrant will be binding on all local authority building control departments.

Relaxations

1.24 A further delegation of powers to relax the regulations in respect of building standards regulations was made under the Building Standards (Relaxation by Local Authorities) (Scotland) Regulations 1985, which came into force on 7 October 1985. These regulations considerably widen the scope of local authority powers to deal with relaxation in respect of buildings erected or the date a warrant for erection was granted not less than five years before the relaxation application.

The Secretary of State still retains relaxation powers in respect of certain large extensions and enclosed shopping centres as well as new buildings.

Further delegation will be considered once the new form has been introduced and local authorities are familiar with its implementation.

2 Building (Scotland) Acts 1959 and 1970

2.01 As a direct result of the deliberations of the Guest Committee, the Building (Scotland) Act 1959 was passed. The aim of the Act was to introduce a system which while utilizing some of the then current practice in a more modern form, produced new procedures and standards which were flexible enough to meet rapidly changing building processes. The Act itself was unique in UK legislation and gave Scotland the lead in the field of national building control.

2.02 Certain sections of the Act came into effect on the day the Act was passed, 30 April 1959, but the main provisions did not come into effect until 15 June 1964, a day appointed by the Secretary of State.

2.03 In common with much of our legislation, the Building Acts have in their short history been subject to amendment because of changes in other spheres of Government and in particular the effect of the Local Government (Scotland) Act 1973, the Health and Safety at Work etc. Act 1974 and the Housing (Scotland) Act 1986. While the basic philosophy of the original Building Act and that of 1970 has not changed, details in the enforcement of the requirements and indeed the scope of the Act have been altered. These have been incorporated in the text.

The Act is laid out in four parts, and a brief summary of the content of each is given below.

Local authorities

2.04 The requirement in the 1959 Act for local authorities to appoint building authorities was amended by the Local Government (Scotland) Act 1973, which vested building control in authorities as follows: in the Highland, Borders, and Dumfries and Galloway regions, the regional councils and in other cases, the district councils or island authorities. The Act gave the authorities power to set up their own means of building control, and this has varied from large independent building control departments with directors in charge to combined departments under either planning, environmental health, architectural services, or technical services. It means that powers to deal directly with warrant applications vary with the amount of delegation given to officials. In some instances the chief building control officer deals with and signs warrants for all unopposed applications, in others all applications are put before the appropriate committee, and in others delegation to officials is based on whether or not the application is for work valued above or below a certain financial limit. While the principle of the Local Government Act was to give autonomy to authorities, the lack of central Government guidance or suggested model for a building control department has, therefore, led in turn to anomalies which were not so apparent under the specific legislation of the 1959 Act. The intention of the Act in placing building control in the hands of regional councils – i.e. Highland, Borders, and Dumfries and Galloway – has been neatly sidestepped in the Highland region. The power of delegation given to local authorities has been used to delegate building control back to the district councils making up the region. This would appear directly against the purpose of the Act itself in specifying responsibility to the specific regional councils.

Building Standards

2.05 Part II of the Building (Scotland) Act 1959, as amended by section 75 and Schedule 7 of the Health and Safety at Work Act 1974, deals with building standards and building operations. Section 3 of the Act gives the Secretary of State power to prescribe Building Standards Regulations and details the necessary procedure to be carried out before making regulations (described below in para 2.15). The basis of the Building Standards Regulations is stated as follows: 'they shall be such as in the opinion of the Secretary of State can reasonably be expected to be attained in buildings of the classes to which they relate, having regard to the need for securing the health, safety, welfare and convenience of the persons who inhabit or frequent such buildings and the safety of the public generally and for furthering the conservation of fuel and power'. The standards may make reference to any document published by the Secretary of State or other persons. This means in practice that the Secretary of State can deem-to-satisfy any document he thinks fit. It is worth noting the fact that the power to make regulations contains two qualifying phrases, i.e. 'in the opinion of' and 'can reasonably', and may well explain the compromise situations which sometimes affect a final regulation as compared with original proposals and indeed technical advice. Certain buildings are exempted from regulations, e.g. Crown buildings and some Atomic Energy Authority Buildings (but see para 1.19 above). The Secretary of State has also been given the power to repeal or modify any enactment in force before or passed in the same session as the Health and Safety at Work Act 1974 if he considers it inconsistent with or unnecessary or requires alteration in consequence of any provision of the Building Standards Regulations.

2.06 The Secretary of State may also make regulations for the conduct of building operations as he thinks necessary to secure the safety of the general public.

2.07 Only the Secretary of State is given power to relax Building Standards Regulations. However, section 2 of the 1970 Act gives the Secretary of State power to make regulations delegating the power to give relaxation to the local authority.

Class warrants (formerly known as type approvals)

2.08 Under the Health and Safety at Work etc. Act 1974 powers were taken to issue type approvals. The system of type approvals required a designating order to bring it into place. The designating order was never made. When new powers were being taken under the Housing (Scotland) Act 1986 it was decided to redefine the type approval system at the same time. This was done and the term 'type approval' was changed to 'class warrant'.

The basis of a class warrant system is that the Secretary of State would have the power to issue such warrants in respect of buildings which are of a repetitious nature which comply with the relevant building standards. For example, a standard house plan which is built in various areas all over the country might be given a class warrant in respect of its design above damp proof course. The class warrant which is binding on all local authority building control authorities will alleviate the need for separate sets of plans to be prepared for each

authority and avoid differences of interpretation. It will speed up the process of commencement of building once plans are completed.

The Scottish Development Department will seek an independent assessment from designated bodies as to the building's compliance with building standards before making a decision on an application for class warrant. This involves the private sector in the decision-making process.

It might also be useful to compare the term 'class warrant' with the term 'class relaxation' in order to avoid confusion. The former would apply where a building, component, etc., met the regulations. The latter would apply where building, etc., does not meet the regulations but is given a waiver of a regulation or regulations either conditionally or unconditionally.

Warrants for construction and demolition

2.09 A warrant for construction is issued subject to the conditions that the building is built in accordance with the description in the warrant, drawings, and specification. The building must also conform to the Building Standards Regulations and any direction from the Secretary of State relaxing any of the Regulations. The local authority cannot impose any other constructional conditions. The warrant is not subject to any requirements for planning permission. The attention of local authorities, regarding the issue of warrants and attempts to impose conditions, was drawn to the relevant statutory instruments by a Building Note* 6/77 issued by the Scottish Development Department.

Local authorities have the power, however, to grant warrant for work to be carried out in stages. This is a discretionary power. Warrant for the demolition of a building must state the length of time the works will take.

2.10 Section 6(8) as amended by the 1970 Act gives provisions where it would be competent for a buildings authority to refuse warrant. This important section is worthy of careful study, as incorrect interpretation could cause inconvenience and delay. Local authorities can refuse warrant if:

1. The application has not been made in the prescribed manner.
2. The authority considers that application for alterations or extensions to a building would result in either of the following:
   (a) where a building conforms to the Regulations at the time of application, but would fail to conform as a direct result of the proposed works or;
   (b) where a building fails to conform to the Regulations at the time of application and would fail to conform to an even greater degree as a direct result of the proposed works.

2.11 The phrase 'as a direct result' is the important point. The following examples may help to elucidate it:

1. An existing cottage, built pre-Regulation, has a roof which is nearer its boundary than would be permitted by current Regulations. Should an extension to the cottage be built, the roof of which meets the current Regulations, then the existing roof is still acceptable. In other words the new works are not making the existing roof part of the Regulations to any greater degree.
2. An extension to a factory resulted in the travel distance within the building as a whole being made worse; therefore the travel distance of the whole building, new and existing, was subject to the building standards for a new building.

*Building Note 6/77 issued by Scottish Development Department, December 1977.

Travel distance in relation to means of escape from fire is measured from a point on a storey to a protected doorway in accordance with rules laid down in the Regulations.

In regard to the term 'change of use', which plays an important part in determining this area of building control law, particular attention must be paid to the definition of 'change of use'. The meaning is different to that used in England and Wales and failure to appreciate that fact in its context could involve unnecessary extra work. Change of use applies to a component or element of structure as much as to the whole building.

2.12 Section 8 of the Act which allowed the local authority power to issue permission to occupy portions of roads for the deposit of materials was amended by the Road Traffic Act 1984 which transfers the power to the highway authority.

Certificates of completion

2.13 Section 9 relates to the issue of completion certificates by the buildings authority. Where electrical installations are concerned, another certificate is required from the installer certifying that the installations meet the necessary requirements of the Building Standards Regulations. No person may occupy a building erected under warrant unless a certificate of completion has been issued. However, temporary certificates may be issued at the discretion of the buildings authority. The Secretary of State has powers to extend the provision for certification to other than electrical installations, e.g. gas installations.

It should be noted that under an amendment introduced by the Health and Safety at Work Act 1974 and activated by Commencement Order No. 2 under that Act, the wording of section 9 in respect of completion certificates was modified. The granting of the certificate is now qualified in respect of the building authority's inspection of the building by the words 'so far as they are able to ascertain after taking all reasonable steps in that behalf'.

This phrase recognizes that it is impossible for a building control officer to be continually on site inspecting the construction of a building at all times – indeed, that is not his job. Local authorities were worried that the previous phrasing of the certificate, with its blanket statement that 'the building met both regulations and plans completely', placed an unacceptable and unreasonable liability on their shoulders and represented for the rewording of the certificate in the new terms.

2.14 Powers are given in section 9 to deal with buildings erected without warrant or in contravention of warrant, and procedures are described. Section 11 of the 1959 Act empowers the authority to enforce certain provisions of the Building Standards Regulations on existing buildings.

2.15 Self certification of design

Following upon the Secretary of State's statement of Intent of November 1984, powers were taken in the Housing (Scotland) Act 1986, section 19 to introduce a new section to the Building (Scotland) Act 1959 in respect of self certification of design only. The local authority retains final control over the assessment of compliance of a building through its powers to grant or refuse a certificate of Completion Under section 9 of the 1959 Act.

Benefits of self certification of design are:

.1. The speeding up of the processing of applications for warrants by allowing local authorities to accept without further checking certificates of compliance for certain requirements of regulations.
2. The promoting of a degree of self-regulation by the private sector within the framework of local authority building control.

3. The reduction of the workload of local authority building control departments.
4. Recognizing existing good practice by the acceptance of design certificates from, for example, qualified structural and civil engineers.

The introduction of the powers will be by designating order. The parts of the Regulations and who will be entitled to certify have yet to be specified.

New Regulations

2.16 Section 12 requires the Secretary of State to appoint a Building Standards Advisory Committee, the main purposes of which are to advise him on the making of Building Standards Regulations and keeping the operation of the Regulations under review. The members of the committee are selected as individuals and not as representatives of particular interests. It should be noted, however, that various professional, commercial, research bodies, etc., do nominate representatives for consideration as members. The committee is usually reconstituted at three-year intervals. The present committee consists of a chairman who is both a chartered engineer with representatives from building control, architecture, engineering, law, fire services, building, material producers and local government administration.

2.17 The procedure for making regulations is as follows: the Secretary of State consults the Building Standards Advisory Committee and other such bodies which are representative of the interests concerned. In practice, over 200 bodies are asked for their comments regarding proposed amendments to the Building Regulations. 'This is usually done by issuing a document which details the proposals and invites comments and representations.'

Dangerous buildings

2.18 Part III deals with dangerous buildings and goes into detail regarding action to be taken to make them safe, the powers of local authorities with regard to purchasing buildings where owners cannot be found, and the selling of materials from buildings demolished by the local authority.

Civil liability

2.19 New section 19A lays down breaches of regulations which may be actionable so far as damage is concerned. Damage includes death or injury of persons.
  This section has not yet been brought into operation.

Crown rights

2.20 The Secretary of State has made it clear that Crown buildings should conform to the Building Standards Regulations regarding new buildings and extensions and alterations to other buildings. While Crown buildings do not have to follow the warrant application procedure, other 'rules' apply and a procedure for relaxations has been evolved. See also comments in para 1.19 above.

Enforcement officers

2.21 Section 21 of the 1959 Act, which laid down a requirement for the appointment of masters of works, was repealed by the Local Government (Scotland) Act 1973 and the enforcement of building control left in the hands of local authorities. There are at present, therefore, no specific qualifications laid down for building officers.

Schedules

2.22 These relate to matters in regard of which regulations may be made, recovery of expenses, evacuation of dangerous buildings, minor and consequential amendments of enactments.

Commencement Orders

2.23 It should be noted that the extra powers contained in the Health and Safety at Work Act and the Housing (Scotland) Act 1986 have to be activated by Commencement Order, and the first of these was issued as Commencement No. 2 Order 1975 and came into force on 27 March 1975. A further order – Commencement No. 6 Order 1980 – came into force on 17 March 1980 and deals with increased penalties for contravention under certain provisions of the Building (Scotland) Act 1959.

Other provisions

2.24 Part IV is concerned with supplementary provisions and deals with appeals, references to other enactments such as Ancient Monuments Acts, building preservation orders and so on, inspection and tests, penalties, fees, transitional provisions, and general interpretation.

Building (Scotland) Act 1970

2.25 The main purpose of the Building (Scotland) Act 1970 was to amend the 1959 Act as regards making Building Standards Regulations, depositing building materials on roads, and application for warrants. These points have already been mentioned.

2.26 The following additional powers were granted under the Act:
  Section 2 gives the Secretary of State powers to delegate to local authorities the power of relaxation, and a new form of relaxation power in respect of certain classes of buildings. This power, which might be described as an 'omnibus relaxation', permits him to direct that a building which may not meet the exact requirements of the Regulations can nevertheless be accepted by local authorities when warrant applications are made. It should be remembered that the term 'building' is defined in both the Act and Standards Regulations and covers both a whole building and its constituent parts. Class relaxations have been issued, e.g. for air supported structures, framed structures, various components in chimney and fire protection. These are situations where individual relaxations would be required in each case.
  Section 4 permits the Secretary of State to call in any application for warrant received by a local authority and enables him to determine whether the building concerned will conform to the Building Standards Regulations, to give relaxations, and to impose, after consulting the Building Standards Advisory Committee, requirements additional to or more onerous than those in the Building Standards Regulations. This power is most useful in very large and complex developments where, for instance, the traditional means of protection from fire have to be supplemented by automatic detection systems and sophisticated ventilation schemes.

Building (Procedure) (Scotland) Regulations 1981 and 1987

2.27 The Procedure Regulations were laid before Parliament on 9 November 1981 and came into force on 30 November 1981. They replaced the previous Procedure Regulations, which had been in force since 1975. The Regulations prescribe in detail the procedures to be followed by local authorities. They amend in detail areas of procedure relating

to notification of adjoining proprietors and relaxation of regulations by local authorities. The Regulations consolidate amendments since 1975 in the scale of fees, for warrant. The Building (Procedure) (Scotland) Amendment Regulations 1987 amended regulation 7 of the principal Procedure Regulations in respect of fees. These are not to be charged in respect of building operations consisting solely of the alteration or extension of a building to provide facilities (including in particular means of access to and within the building) for disabled persons who frequent or in the case of dwellings who inhabit or are about to inhabit the building. At the time of writing new revised Procedure Regulations have been issued for consultation.

For note on Building (Procedure) (Scotland) Amendment Regulations 1990, see the end of this chapter.

Interpretation

2.28 Part I of the Regulations deals with interpretation, citation and revocation, definitions, powers of local authorities to charge fees, to issue warrant for the construction of a building in specified stages, and details of certificates of completion. Attention is drawn specifically to the following points:

1. Duration of warrant. A warrant is valid for three years only. This does not mean that a building must be completed within three years of the issue of warrant; it means that construction must be commenced within three years. A warrant is only a permission to construct and is required before the commencement of work to ensure that the building will comply with the Regulations. (See also section 6 of the 1959 Act.) The interpretation of this section has led to some confusion in the past and draft regulations include a proposal to include both a starting and completion date to clarify the position.
2. Local authorities must either grant or refuse an application for a completion certificate within 14 days, and in the event of a refusal must notify the applicant as to that refusal.
3. The description of the prescribed stages of construction, where work is permitted, under a warrant issued by stages.

Applications for warrant

2.29 Part II of the Regulations deals with applications for warrant. The 1981 Regulations considerably simplify the previous process, particularly in the light of neighbour notification requirements introduced in August 1981 under planning procedures. The following is a précis of the new arrangements. The applicant must lodge his application with the local authority in writing on the appropriate forms. It can be signed by the applicant or by his agent. The application should be accompanied by the principal plan and a duly certified copy. If a direction relaxing any regulation has already been given by the Secretary of State, this should accompany the application. The local authority may ask for additional plans and information and, if necessary, up to two extra copies of the application and plans lodged with it. The form and scale of the plans required are described in Schedule 1, section H of the Regulations.

2.30 When the application is received, the local authority shall 'forthwith' – the regulation term – consider and determine the application. The local authority shall not refuse an application without giving the applicant notification of the proposed grounds of refusal and an opportunity of being heard and making written representations. Any such oral or written representations must be taken account of in finally determining the application.

Calling in warrants

2.31 Part III deals with the procedure to be followed where the Secretary of State 'calls in' an application for warrant to deal with it partly or wholly by himself. Where the Secretary of State calls in an application for warrant, the local authority must send him the plans, confirmation that the application has been properly made, copies of any previous warrants dealing with temporary buildings and which relate to the application under consideration, and any comments the local authority may wish to make. If on consideration the Secretary of State decides to impose more onerous requirements additional to or more serious than those in the Building Regulations at present, he must consult the applicant, the local authority, the Building Standards Advisory Committee, and any other person he thinks might have an interest. If the Secretary of State thinks fit, he may convene a hearing for the interested parties. It should be stressed that this procedure may also apply only in respect of individual parts of Regulations and in such a case the Secretary of State would then return the application, along with his requirements, for the local authority to process in the normal way. It is for the local authority to notify the applicant of the Secretary of State's decisions and his reasons for those decisions.

Local authority relaxation

2.32 Part IV gives the procedures to be followed by local authorities when dealing with applications for relaxation. These have been considerably simplified from the previous Regulations and give the local authority discretion in relation to who is to be notified as an affected proprietor.

2.33 Part V gives the procedure for appealing to the Secretary of State against the refusal of a local authority to grant relaxation or against a condition of relaxation.

Relaxation by Secretary of State

2.34 Part VI gives the procedure for application to the Secretary of State for a relaxation. The new procedures in Part IV are, in effect, now very closely allied to those which have applied under this part for some years. The applicant must lodge a copy of his plans and application with the local authority when he makes his application to the Secretary of State. The Secretary of State may consult by means of a draft direction with the applicant and other persons he considers to have an interest, and in his final determination shall take into consideration any comments made. The Secretary of State can, however, issue a final direction without consultation, and this has, in fact, been done in certain cases.

Class relaxations

2.35 These are the province of the Secretary of State and relate to a general relaxation, binding on all local authorities, in respect of either a building type or a component of a building. Class relaxations usually refer to individual regulations and parts of the Regulations and may be conditional. Over 50 class relaxations are in force. Examples of such relaxations include:

2.1 Various forms of fire resisting collars and sleeves for use with internal pipe and duct work.
2.2 Various designs of air admittance valves for drainage systems.
2.3 Low level discharge oil appliances.
2.4 Approved unvented hot water systems.
2.5 Specially designed emergency escape windows for pitched roofs.

The Secretary of State must consult the Building Standards Advisory Committee and such other bodies as he deems have an interest before making his determination of an application. The relaxations are only granted after a detailed investigation including results of research and testing. The possession of an Agreement Certificate is also a contributing factor and in some cases the conditions of relaxation will specifically refer

to the appropriate BBA Certificate in whole or in part. It must be stressed that a class relaxation must *not* be confused with a class warrant. With the coming into force of the projected new Regulations, the very nature of the latter should dispense with the need for many of the existing class relaxations although there will be the occasional need for the procedures to be used.

Orders made by local authorities

2.36 Part IX deals with orders relating to buildings constructed without or in contravention of warrant and in respect of dangerous buildings. The part goes into detail regarding notices, appeals, and, where necessary, the convening of hearings.

General

2.38 Part X deals with procedure to be followed at hearings, appointment of assessors (if deemed necessary), maintenance of records, and inspection of records and applications (which must be available for inspection by the public at all reasonable hours). Decisions of the local authority must follow laid-down rules and must be made in writing. Where an application is refused or, for example, where a relaxation is given despite objections, the local authority must state the reasons for their decision.

2.39 Persons carrying out building operations under warrant must give notice to the local authority:

1. of the date on which work commenced within seven days of that date;
2. when a drain has been laid and is ready for inspection and test;
3. when a drain has been infilled and is ready for the second inspection or test;
4. of the date on which operations are completed.

Items (1) and (4) shall be in writing, except in the case of (4) where an application for a certificate of completion has been made in the prescribed form.

Plans to be submitted

2.40 Schedule 1 goes into detail of the particulars of plans required and the minimum scales to which they have to be drawn. The Schedule is divided into sections relating to whether the application for warrant deals with erection, alteration, extension, change of use, or demolition of a building.

2.41 Schedule 2 gives the table of fees applicable for a warrant. The fee scale is based on the estimated cost of the operations and ranges from £5 for small works to figures in excess of £1000. The fees are a once-only charge – there are no extra fees for inspection, etc. The figures are regularly upgraded to take account of inflation.

Building Operations (Scotland) Regulations 1975

2.42 The Secretary of State had powers conferred on him by section 5 of the Building (Scotland) Act 1959 to make regulations for the conduct of operations for the construction, repair, maintenance, or demolition of buildings, as he thinks expedient for securing the safety of the public while building operations are in progress.

2.43 The Building Operations (Scotland) Regulations 1975, which came into operation on 16 May 1975, revoke the previous Regulations made in 1963. They lay down requirements for the safety of passers-by and deal with such matters as the erection of hoardings, barricades and fences, footpaths with safe platforms, handrails, steps or ramps, overhead coverings, and so on. In addition, protective works are to be properly lit to the satisfaction of the local authority.

2.44 There are also provisions for clearing footpaths and the securing of partly constructed or demolished buildings. A special regulation deals with additional requirements for demolition operations.

These Regulations are administered by the local authority. At the time of writing these are being revised.

Building (Forms) (Scotland) Regulations 1975 as read with Building (Forms) (Scotland) Amendment Regulations 1981

2.45 Section 24 of the Building (Scotland) Act 1959 gave the Secretary of State power to make Regulations prescribing the type of form to be used in the various procedures under the Act.

2.46 The amending Regulations were laid before Parliament on 9 November 1981 and came into force on 30 November 1981. The Regulations prescribe the forms in which applications for warrants, notices, orders, and other documents should be made under the Act. The Regulations are the latest in a series which have been updated in the light of changes to principal legislation and to related regulations. The Regulations provide a common system of forms applicable throughout Scotland for building control purposes.

Building Standards (Relaxation by Local Authorities), (Scotland) Regulations 1985

2.47 These Regulations are made under section 4(2) of the Building (Scotland) Act 1959 (as amended). The main provisions of these Regulations are to delegate certain powers of relaxation of the Building Standards Regulations to local authorities in respect of existing buildings. The latter are defined as having been erected or warrant to build was granted, five years before the application for relaxation was made. The Regulations apply to buildings not ancillary to houses. In the case of ancillary building to houses, unconditional powers to relax are given to local authorities. All other applications for relaxation for new and existing buildings are made to the Secretary of State. The 1985 Regulations came into force on 7 October 1985 and revoke all previous delegation Regulations.

2.48 The Building Standards Regulations are relaxable by a building control authority in relation to alterations, extensions and change of use of existing buildings. The delegated powers are restricted and do not apply to:

1 enclosed shopping centres as defined in regulation 3 of the delegating Regulations;
2 applications from a local authority in respect of its own buildings;
3 a case involving an application for warrant referred to the Secretary of State under powers contained in the Building Acts;
4 an extension in the case of a house which results in an *increase* of cubic capacity of more than 30%;
5 an extension in any case, other than a house, which results in an increase in cubic capacity of more than 5000 cubic metres or 30% whichever is *the less*.

In cases 1–5 above, such applications would be made to the Secretary of State. In calculating 4 and 5 above, the mode of measurement in Schedule 3 of the Building Standards Regulations applies.

2.49 The delegation is in respect of individual buildings and must not be confused with class relaxations (para 2.34).

The procedure to be followed both in applying for relaxation and in appealing against a decision of a local authority, should this be sought, is detailed under the Building (Procedure) (Scotland) Regulations 1981 and the Building (Forms) (Scotland) Regulations 1981.

3 Building Standards (Scotland) Regulations 1981 to 1987

3.01 The original Regulations were laid before Parliament on 11 December 1963 and came into force on 15 June 1964. They had been issued for comment in 1961, and the final document took into account the many hundreds of representations made to the Department. Over the years, the Regulations have been subject to amendment, consolidation, and metrication. The latest Regulations, which are both amending and consolidating, were laid before Parliament on 16 December 1981 and came into force on 17 March 1982. The Regulations were subject to amendment by the Building Standards (Scotland) Regulations 1982, 1984, 1986 and 1987. **Note:** these Regulations are being completely rewritten and will be brought into operation in late 1990. The new forms of Regulations will be based on a short statutory instrument written in functional requirement terms with a legally acceptable technical memorandum acting as a form of deemed to satisfy.

3.02 The Regulations are laid out in the form of 16 Parts and 15 Schedules. Originally the Parts were numbered consecutively throughout, but after consolidation in 1970 a system of lettered parts and numbered regulations and schedules was adopted. It is important to note that where an asterisk appears beside a regulation number, this denotes a deemed to satisfy specification which is included in Schedule 13 to the Regulations.

The Regulations contain three indices, situated at the rear of the book; these are, of course, not part of the statutory Regulations.

3.03 The interpretation of the Regulations is the province of the local authorities that have building control functions. If any dispute arises regarding interpretation, the final decision rests with the Sheriff Court.

3.04 Wherever possible throughout the book, an attempt has been made to tabulate technical data, and these tables appear as part of the regulations to which they apply. Definitions have been grouped together in Part A, but a list of defined terms is included at the beginning of each part. It should also be noted that the application and interpretation of each part appears at the beginning of each part.

Part A: General

3.05 This Part is now divided into five sections.

1. Section 1 deals with citation and commencement.
2. Section 2 deals with revocation and transitional provisions. Being a consolidating document, the 1981 Regulations revoke all previous Regulations. However, in relation to an application for warrant made before the 1981 Regulations came into force, the Regulations in force at the time shall be taken as applying to the warrant or to any future extension or amendment to warrant.
3. Section 3 deals with general interpretation and is an extremely important section. Regulation A4 describes in detail the classification of building by occupancy and the situation regarding multi-use buildings and buildings having uses ancillary to the main use. This regulation refers to Schedule 1, which gives an occupancy letter to occupancy groups and a number to occupancy sub-groups, e.g. A1 occupancy sub-group refers to houses of up to two storeys, and wherever A1 appears in a regulation, the reader knows to which group of buildings it applies. It is essential to establish the occupancy group at the outset of any project, as a mistake here could affect the application of the subsequent Regulations and lead either to a costly amendment of plans or to the wastefulness of trying to meet regulations which do not apply. This regulation, which must be read with regulation A8 – occupant capacity (i.e. the number of persons a room or storey is deemed to accommodate for Regulations purposes) – controls ventilation, means of escape, and sanitary requirements. Regulation A5 now includes in alphabetical order all the defined terms used in the Regulations. While all such terms are important, attention is drawn to the following definitions: 'building', 'change of use', 'element of structure', 'escape route', 'land in different occupation', 'protected doorway', 'room', 'site', 'storey' (which differs from that in the English and Welsh Regulations), and 'thermal transmittance co-efficient'.

4. Section 4 deals with application. The most important point to note is that regulation A10 gives total exemption from the need to apply for warrant to build to the list of buildings given in Schedule 4 and to a list of fixtures contained in Schedule 5. A designer should check carefully whether his building comes within either category.

5. Section 5 deals with general points and refers to temporary buildings. These are specified as those which have an intended life of not more than five years. Regulation A13 should be carefully studied in its references to deemed to satisfy specifications. It specifically states that while compliance with a deemed to satisfy specification will be deemed to meet the requirements of the relevant regulation, nothing shall prevent the use of any other material, component, design, method of construction or operation, or combination of these, provided that the alternative satisfies the functional requirement of the Regulations.

Part B: Materials and durability

3.06 This part is in broad functional terms along the lines previously used in the model byelaws. However, a proviso allows the use of relatively short-lived but otherwise suitable materials in circumstances where protection can be given or periodic maintenance readily and easily carried out. The proviso does not seem to appear in the English and Welsh Regulations.

The 1981 Regulations updated the BS documents which are deemed to satisfy this part, to 30 April 1981.

Part C: Structural strength and stability

3.07 This Part states the requirements for structural strength and stability in a functional way with reference to loading criteria in BS Codes of Practice. The regulations in the part are backed up by an extensive number of deemed to satisfy specifications.

3.08 Regulation C2 deals with foundation and structure above the foundation. It requires that calculations of dead and imposed loads shall be in accordance with the recommendations of BS Code of Practice CP 3: Chapter V, Part 1: 1967, as amended, and wind loads in accordance with BS Code of Practice CP 3: Chapter V, Part 2: 1972, as amended. Regulation C3, which owes its existence to the aftermath of Ronan Point, applies only to buildings of five storeys and over and is intended to give safeguards against progressive collapse. It requires either the provision of 'alternative paths' to carry the load of the building should part of a structural member be damaged or removed, or the strengthening of critical members. The criteria to be used in calculations are included in the regulation.

Part D: Structural fire precautions

3.09 The theory of fire resistance embodied in the byelaws which the Regulations replaced was intended to ensure that each individual building would contain its own fire as far as possible and would be protected against fire from outside. This applied as much to buildings on a plot of land in one occupation as to buildings on separate plots. Two changes were made by the regulation.

1. It was considered unnecessary that buildings should resist fire from outside if they are capable of containing any fire starting within them.
2. Control has been restricted to safeguarding public interest by preventing general conflagration.

3.10 The Part attempts to achieve its purposes by laying down requirements for the fire resistance of the structure. It controls the type of materials used and specifies when non-combustible materials have to be used, as well as the surface finishes of lining materials. The criteria on which the requirements are based are those to be found in BS fire tests, notably BS 476 and its constituent parts. Roofs do not require fire resistance and are not classified as an element of structure under regulation A5. They are, however, given a classification in regulation A9 for the purposes of Part D. This classification is based on the roof's ability to resist penetration by and the surface spread of flame.

3.11 The Part requires that large buildings be divided into compartments by means of compartment walls and separating floors, and similarly buildings in different occupation be divided by separating walls and floors. Concessions are given to certain buildings of a lower fire load and risk, in respect of non-combustibility requirements of certain elements, e.g. houses up to three storeys in height only require separating walls of the requisite fire resistance and do not attract the non-combustibility requirement.* The part lays down strong criteria to prevent the passage of fire via pipes and ducts which penetrate separating and compartment walls and floors. Additionally, the 1981 Regulations require the introduction of fire stops and cavity barriers to prevent the rapid spread of flame and smoke along cavities such as suspended ceilings, roof voids, etc. (regulation D14).

3.14 The Part does, however, accept the principle that as long as a building is far enough away from its boundary, it will not spread fire to buildings or adjoining land in different occupation. Regulation D18 as read with Schedule 8 gives the required distances from boundaries, these being related to the openings in the side of the building facing the boundary. Schedule 9 has a similar effect in respect of roofs designations and their distance to the boundary.

3.13 Regulations D22 and D23 refer to small buildings which may be attached to or within the curtilage of houses in A1 or A2 occupancy sub-groups. These requirements are in the nature of a relaxation of the standards applied to other buildings, as they are not considered to be of a high fire risk. It should be noted, however, that with respect to detached small buildings, such as garages, greenhouses and garden huts, meeting certain conditions exemption is given in Schedule 4.

3.14 Part D also contains a regulation dealing with fuel oil storage tanks which serve appliances used primarily for space and water heating and cooking facilities within buildings. The fire-resistance requirements are based on the size of the tank and its siting in relation to the building and the boundary of land in different occupation. Larger tanks require a catchpit under certain conditions. Tanks also require to be fitted with such safety devices as are necessary to enable them to operate safely and efficiently, as well as a lockable drainage valve or outlet cock. The latter is an anti-vandal device.

A new regulation dealing with the bulk storage of liquid petroleum gas in certain residential buildings was introduced by the Building Standards (Scotland) Amendment Regulations 1986. This regulation lays down requirements as to size of tank and siting. The latter is subject to either distance to boundary or building, or protective barriers.

Part E: Means of escape from fire and assistance to the fire service

3.15 This part was extensively revised by the 1981 Regulations. It applies to all buildings, but the extent of the coverage to certain occupancy groups is given in the table to regulation E1. A1 (houses up to two storeys) only require to meet the lining requirements; A2 (flats up to two storeys) are given a slightly wider coverage, and small chalets likewise.

Because of the extensive revision and the difficulties which some designers find in dealing with this subject, the following is a breakdown of the requirements regulation by regulation.

Regulation E2

3.16 Attention is drawn to new definitions. The old description of 'exit' has been replaced by 'escape route', with 'exit' now referring to the point of egress from a room or storey. The term 'circulation space' replaces the term 'passage' and should give more flexibility in interpretation. Other new definitions include 'protected circuit' to replace 'independent circuit' and 'dry and wet rising mains'. This regulation contains two important tables. Table 1 is particularly interesting in that it lists every reference in the part which requires an element of structure or component (e.g. door) to have fire resistance and then states the exact fire resistance required. Table 2 classifies various plastic materials into types.

Regulation E3

3.17 This regulation requires escape routes from rooms and storeys and gives the specific references to requirements for separate building types.

Regulation E4

3.18 This regulation brings together general requirements applicable for escape routes in all buildings. It makes clear, for example, that once a person has entered a circulation area, the route shall not pass back through a room, but must lead to a protected doorway.

Regulation E5

3.19 Additional requirements for escape routes relating to specific cases or designs are grouped in this regulation. Attention should be paid to the new provisions for dividing extra long corridors into sections for smoke-stopping purposes. Centre cored blocks are also included in this provision. Rooms and auditoriums with closely seated audiences must have at least one exit situated in the rear third of the room, and where more than eleven seats are provided in a seatway, there must be a gangway at each end.

Regulation E6

3.20 This regulation lays down the minimum number of escape routes related to occupancy load. A table attached to this regulation gives the minimum number of escape routes required based on the building occupancy group. Attention is drawn to the new entries relating to children's residential school hostels and the hostels for handicapped persons.

---

*This concession has been extended by class relaxation no. 75 to certain flatted accommodation: see para 3.66.

Additionally, concessions are granted for areas containing basements and plant and tank rooms at roof level.

Regulation E7

3.21 This regulation, which deals with travel distance, is of great importance to designers. While regulation E6 lays down the minimum number of escape routes depending on the design and layout of a building, extra escape routes might be required to meet this regulation. The travel distances – which include differential travel distances – are given in tabular form related to occupancy group or sub-group, special areas in buildings, e.g. lecture theatre in an office block, and areas which attract concessions. It is made clear that under certain circumstances, travel distance can be measured to a protected doorway in a compartment wall. Attention is drawn to the rules for determining if two escape routes are available from a point on a storey. This basically requires that from the point, if the directions of escape are at 45° or more to each other, the requirement is satisfied. To cater for the odd-shape room or the dead end, an alternative method may be used. This permits travel in one direction, up to a maximum of the single direction travel distance, to the point where two directions become available. The angle at that point must meet the criteria of 45° and 2½° for every metre travelled.

Regulation E8

3.22 This regulation deals with width of escape routes. These use a unit width of 530 mm to calculate the escape route width. For the 1981 Regulations, the scope is extended to cover certain areas within a room or an auditorium. Special escape route widths in respect of gangways, seatways, fixed storage areas, and stairways to fixed storage areas in certain occupancy groups are tabulated. The situation where a doorway placed across an escape route slightly restricts that route is also clarified. The calculations in regard to stairways have been simplified, and where all the stairways in a building are lobby approach, certain concessions as to calculation of widths are given.

Regulation E9

3.23 The 1981 Regulations introduced new requirements in respect of places of special fire risk in relation to escape routes.

Regulation E10

3.24 The requirement that all escape stairways be enclosed has been a bone of contention, particularly in respect of existing buildings. The 1981 Regulations now introduce a concession for external escape stairways and do not require enclosure if certain conditions relating to adjacent openings are met. The concession applies to stairways where the upper landing is not more than 6 m above ground level.

Regulation E11

3.25 This is a new entry introduced by the 1981 Regulations and covers stairways and escalators other than those specifically designed for escape purposes. The requirements, which relate to enclosure and which are extensive, give wide scope for design solutions via a series of provisos.

Regulation E12

3.26 Lobby approach stairs are now required for buildings over 18 m instead of 24 m, as previously. Requirements for fire brigade access are included, and the area of the lobby for such purposes is now 5.5 sq m.

Regulation E14

3.27 This regulation refers to doors in escape routes. It covers such items as direction of swing and devices for opening doors in an emergency. It also requires that no door to a stairway enclosure shall be fitted with a device to hold it open other than electro-magnetic or electro-mechanical device susceptible to smoke.

Regulation E16

3.28 This is a new regulation and requires emergency lighting for means of escape purposes only in designated buildings or in parts of a building. These are tabulated. The regulation is deemed to satisfy by BS 5266: Part 1: 1975 and CP 1007: 1955.

Regulation E17

3.29 This covers the spread of flame characteristics for linings in rooms, and it relates the classification to the occupants' use of the building. The main requirements are in tabular form, and it is important to check carefully the various concessions which are given for certain building types.

Regulations E18 and E19

3.30 These are extensions of the requirements of regulation E17 and deal with surfaces which cannot be classified under that regulation, such as plastic ceilings. Additionally, requirements as to rooflights and panels and their spacing in roofs are dealt with.

Regulation E20

3.31 This regulation recognizes that window escape in case of fire is important. It requires that in low-rise residential buildings having only one escape route, certain windows are suitable in size and position to enable occupants to escape from them. The required size also permits firefighters wearing breathing apparatus to climb through the window opening. The requirements for the construction and siting of the windows are common up to four storeys, but only above two storeys do the access requirements for firefighters' equipment apply. Considerable flexibility has been given in the type and position of both windows and access, including the acceptance of certain dormer windows for escape purposes.

Regulation E21

3.32 The requirements for access for firefighters have been totally rewritten by the 1981 Regulations. The regulation is now in a functional form, backed up by a schedule which has a status fimilar to that of deemed to satisfy. The regulation does allow a designer of a special or unusual design to negotiate with the local authority the form of his fire service access, rather than at present be forced to seek relaxation of the regulation.

Regulations E22 and E23

3.33 These cover requirements for fire mains and hydrant provision. It should be noted that wet rising mains are required for very high buildings. In respect of hydrant provision, the 1981 Regulations have recognized the difficulties faced by buildings in remote areas, and accept, for firefighting purposes, water other than through water mains. Examples are lochs, rivers, static water tanks, etc., provided access for a pumping appliance is available.

Regulation E24

3.34 The requirements for fire lifts include car sizes, electrical devices, and the requirement for such a lift in buildings over 18 m in height.

Regulation E25

3.35 This is a new regulation under the 1981 Regulations and brings together the requirements for flats and maisonettes. The regulation is in two parts. The first part gives definitions, general exclusions, and general requirements. The second is in the form of a series of tables. These relate to the design of the internal layout of the flat or maisonette, and to the design of the building between the flat or maisonette and the escape stairway. Depending on the layout, the number and type of escape route is then detailed.

Regulation E26

3.36 This is also a new regulation and deals with houses of three storeys and over. The requirements are mainly stated in tabular form.

Part F: Chimneys, flues, hearths and installation of heat-producing appliances

3.37 This part is divided into five sections. These sections deal with

1. Application and interpretation.
2. Solid-fuel appliances and certain gas appliances and incinerators. The appliances are those having an output rating of not more than 44 kW.
3. Oil-burning appliances having an output rating of not more than 44 kW.
4. Gas-burning appliances having an input rating of not more than 60 kW as well as certain incinerators.
5. General. This includes high-rated appliances and incinerators, large electric warm-air heaters, general requirements for efficiency and safety of appliances, and permissible fuels for appliances.

3.38 The object of the Part is to prevent the risk of ignition of any part of a building or danger to persons using the building from appliances and their chimneys and flues. The Part, therefore, goes into detail regarding the construction of chimneys, flue-pipes, lining of flues, thickness of materials around fireplace openings, hearths, and the fitting of fireguard fittings in certain classes of buildings with open fires, e.g. domestic dwelling houses. The 1981 Regulations also introduce a general requirement for combustion air for all appliances, including those which operate without a flue. The Part is backed up by extensive deemed to satisfy specifications, see also para 5.03, Building Notes.

Part G: Resistance of sites and resistance to passage of moisture

3.39 Generally, the Part is written in functional terms to allow the most flexible possible requirement to safeguard the users of a building and its fabric. It contains requirements regarding the protection of a site and the grounds in its vicinity, which must be drained or treated to prevent harmful effects of ground and flood water in the building. Certain requirements of this Part do not apply to temporary building of any occupancy group other than A1 and A2.

3.40 Safeguarding existing drains and removal of harmful matter from a site as well as removal of surface soil and vegetable matter are dealt with in this part. It is required that the solum* be treated to prevent any harmful effects in the

*The area within the containing walls of a building after removal of surface soil and vegetable matter.

building or to the health of its occupants, and suitable damp proof coursing is necessary. Every building must be constructed in such a way as to resist moisture from rain or snow.

Part H: Resistance to the transmission of sound

3.41 This Part refers only to dwellings and lays down functional requirements only. The Part was completely rewritten and amended by the Building Standards (Scotland) Amendment Regulations 1987. The functional requirements are deemed to be met by the appropriate specification in Schedule 17, Part II or by obtaining the appropriate performance standard set out in Schedule 17, Part III. The Schedule is unusual in that it contained in great detail various wall and floor constructions together with diagrams of sections and plans.

Part J: Thermal insulation

3.42 This Part was extensively amended by the 1982 amendment Regulations. It is divided into three sections:

I Resistance to the transmission of heat from buildings
II Thermal insulation of pipes, ducts and storage vessels
III Heating controls in buildings other than houses.

3.43 The scope of this Part was considerably expanded when powers to make Building Regulations for the conservation of energy were added to those of public health, safety, and convenience. The requirements of the regulation are based on stated standards of average 'U' value being achieved by the construction of walls, roofs and floors (the latter being important when a floor is exposed: e.g. over a pend). In general the requirements are fairly uniform for the main elements of roof and external walls in all buildings, but slight differences may be found between industrial buildings and the rest. The other main difference is in housing and chalets where a 'U' value of 0.35 is required as opposed to 0.6 in all buildings other than industrials which require a 0.7 minimum value. The section is well tabulated with a comprehensive set of deemed to satisfy specifications. Attention is drawn specifically however to regulation JI (1) which lists those buildings which are exempted from the requirements.

Section 2 of the Part contains new requirements for the thermal insulation of pipes, ducts and storage vessels and was introduced in order to give effect to article 2 of the EEC Council Directive 78/170 which provides that 'Member states shall take all necessary measures to ensure that economically justifiable insulation of the distribution and storage system is made compulsory in new non-industrial buildings, both as regards heating fluid and domestic hot water'.

Part K: Ventilation of buildings

3.44 This Part is divided into four main sections and is quite comprehensive in its requirements. It does not, however, apply to buildings subject to the Factories Act 1961, to schools under the School Premises (General Requirements and Standards) (Scotland) Regulations 1967 to 1979, or to a theatre or cinema. The Regulations recognize the unsuitability of permanent ventilation as the only alternative to mechanical ventilation in houses, offices, etc. There is a tendency to block up such ventilation due to excessive draught caused by a variety of bad design features. The Part accepts controllable ventilation, which allows fine adjustment to suit the individual comforts of the user.

3.45 Section I of the Part goes into detail regarding the ventilation of houses. The rates for natural ventilation are still based on empirical formula relating ventilator size to floor area and cubic size of the room. Those for mechanical ventilation are more precise, and the air changes for different rooms or uses are given in Schedule II.

3.46 Section II deals with the requirements for garages. These are divided into small garages and other garages, including basement garages.

3.47 Section III deals with all other buildings.

3.48 Section IV deals with general requirements and covers such items as enclosed accesses to houses and other buildings, lift machine rooms, courts, and passages. Additional requirements for sleeping rooms in buildings other than houses – e.g. hotels – lay down not only ventilation rates, but also minimum cubic capacity and ceiling heights.

Part L: Daylighting and space about houses

3.49 This part was deleted from the Regulations in 1980, but it is important to note that its requirements regarding the size of windows is now included in Part Q, regulation Q5 (1986 amendment regulations).

Part M: Drainage and sanitary appliances

3.50 The whole of this Part is based mainly on functional requirements backed up by deemed to satisfy specifications. The latter are mostly based on BS Codes of Practice and Specifications. Every building is required to have a drainage system connected to a public sewer or to a private sewage treatment works. The latter are usually septic tanks in rural areas. The wording of the Regulations precludes any other form of drainage, and designers must note that cesspools are not permitted. Drainage requirements are very flexible so as to permit the use of a wide variety of materials, e.g. clay pipes, UPVC pipes, pitch fibre, etc. Detailed deemed to satisfy specifications have recently been added to the Regulations to cover the materials and methods of installation of pipes under buildings. The flexibility of materials approach is also applied to pipework above ground. Ducts containing pipework in flats and in houses over four storeys must be situated within the building and be provided with suitable access points.

3.51 Provision is also made for suitable and sufficient sanitary accommodation to be required in occupancy sub-groups A3 and A4 and in occupancy groups B and C. The scale of provision is based on Offices and Shops Regulations (Sanitary Conveniences) (Regulations) 1964 and on recommendations in BS Code of Practice 305: Part 1: 1974. The attention of designers is drawn to the requirements of the Sewerage (Scotland) Act 1968, which may overlap those of the Building Regulations. Examples of excessive demands of materials and design have been reported under that Act, and care should be taken that such demands are in accordance with the powers under the Act. Attention is drawn to the circulars sent out to local authorities in 1975 and to Building Note 2/76 issued by the Scottish Development Department.

Part N: Electrical installations

3.52 The Building Standards (Scotland) Amendment Regulations 1986 replaced the existing Part N with a new and shortened version. The requirements are basically written in functional terms with the 15th edition of the *Regulations for Electrical Installations* published by the Institute of Electrical Engineers as a deemed to satisfy specification.

Part P: Prevention of danger and obstruction

3.53 This refers to projections or fixtures which might be dangerous, requiring them to be secured so as not to cause danger or obstruction. There is a regulation dealing with pipes discharging steam, smoke, hot water, and so on. The Regulations contain requirements for the safe cleaning of windows any part of which is more than 4 m above ground

level. There are differing conditions for housing and for other classifications of buildings. A new regulation introduced in 1973 covers safety requirements in escalators and passenger conveyors, including emergency stop switches and notices to be displayed.

The 1981 Regulations transferred to this Part, regulations dealing with access to roofs for maintenance purposes and the requirement to display notices giving the maximum imposed floorload under certain conditions and a similar notice in respect of roofs which cannot carry a concentrated load of 0.9 Kilonewtons or more per 130 sq mm).

The Building Standards (Scotland) Amendment Regulations 1986 contained an addition to Part P dealing with the use of unventilated hot water storage systems. Any system exceeding 15 litres in capacity and which is not an industrial use or space heating appliance is not permitted. The effect of this regulation is that all such systems have to receive relaxation before being permitted to be used. It allows only those approved by SDD to be used and class relaxation has been given detailing the conditions of installation and construction.

Part Q: Housing standards

3.54 Housing standards were covered previously in various enactments, e.g. Housing Acts, Burgh Police, Public Health Acts. The Guest Committee recommended that the requirements should all be brought together under the Building Regulations. It should be stressed that all the new requirements are minimum requirements. In this Part are detailed regulations dealing with access to houses, and within a house a requirement that a house should have a stairway. Lift requirements and details of the scale of lifts are given.

3.55 Until 1986 Part Q gave detailed requirements for standards to be achieved within a house. The Building Standards (Scotland) Amendment Regulations 1986 amended the requirements to the provision of basic amenities only. Many standards included in building control legislation for many years were removed, e.g. the need for a minimum ceiling height. The introduction of amenity spaces with a clear height above, say, a bath or above and around a cooker were substituted. The amendment caused very considerable consternation and objection from local authority sources and others.

3.56 While Part Q requires a water supply to the fittings, etc., in the house, public water supplies are the responsibility of the regional councils, and designers should liaise with them at an early stage. There are parts of the country, however, which are not served by such a supply, and recourse has to be made to private supplies. It is recommended that any such supplies should be tested at an early stage for adequacy and potency. In respect of the latter, it should be tested chemically and bacteriologically.

Part R: Refuse storage and disposal

3.57 This Part, which formerly dealt with ashpits and dungsteads, has been completely rewritten. Requirements for ashpits have been deleted. The new Part is divided into three sections, dealing with general interpretation, houses and flats, and dungsteads and farm effluent tanks. The Part has not included requirements for buildings other than houses in respect of refuse storage because there was no fully comprehensive code on the subject at the time.

3.58 The new Part is detailed in its requirements for refuse storage and introduces a concept of carry disease, designed to avoid anyone having to carry refuse, from his front door to a designated storage point, a distance of more than 30 m. Requirements to prevent fire and health hazards are the basis of the regulations dealing with the construction of refuse-

storage areas. Access for vehicles to collect the refuse are also described in detail. The type of vehicle depends on the requirements for storage containers, chutes, etc.

Part S: Construction of stairways, landings and balconies

3.59 This new Part to the Regulations came into force on 1 January 1972 and brought together all the requirements for stairways, landings, and balconies previously located in various other parts of the Regulations. The new Part takes account of metric changes and dimensional co-ordination, and, by the use of tables, wherever possible simplifies the interpretation of the specific requirements.

3.60 Regulation S2 defines the four types of stairway to be found in the Regulations and lays down a mode of measurement of the minimum required widths. These are different for different types of stairs and are based on the use of the stairs; e.g. an exit stair should be as unobstructed as possible, and its width is a calculated one depending on the number of persons likely to use it for escape purposes, whereas a stair in a house will have very intermittent use and is unlikely to be heavily loaded with persons. *Note* that where a stair falls into more than one category, the most onerous requirements apply, except in the special circumstances of three-storey houses.

Regulation S2 also gives definitions used throughout the Part and attention is drawn to those of 'balustrade' and 'handrail' particularly. Those two components are often taken in error to be synonymous. The definition of 'balustrade. is couched in such terms as to allow flexibility in interpretation depending on the case in question. For example, a balustrate of horizontal railings, which are an open invitation to children to climb them, would not be permitted, say, in a school!

Regulation S3 gives general requirements for all stairs. A point to note is that it only requires one value, that of vertical headroom, instead of the traditional method of measurements vertically from and at right angles to the pitch line. Requirements are also stated for open riser stairways, provision of handrails and balustrades, protection of external stair wells where a stair descends below ground level, and protection of glazed areas in stairways.

Regulation S4 is in tabular form and allows ready reference and comparisons to be made among the four types of stair.

Regulation S5 deals with landings. Particular note should be made of the minimum balustrade heights required where a landing is open to the external air and is part of a house or building primarily used by children.

Regulation S6 deals with balconies and is similar in its requirements to those for landings, but does include balconies which are not necessarily part of a stairway.

Part T: Facilities for disabled persons

3.61 The Building Standards (Scotland) Amendment Regulations 1984 introduced a new Part dealing with requirements in respect of disabled persons.

Disabled persons are defined in regulation A5(1).

The Part requires that in certain buildings in occupancy sub-groups A1, A2, A3 and A4 and in occupancy groups B, C and D, any building to which there is access at *ground* level shall include suitable access for disabled persons including suitable access within the storey. Within stadia and auditoria there is a further requirement relating to a minimum number of seats for disabled persons.

Where sanitary conveniences are provided on any floor subject to the regulation a reasonable number shall be suitable for the disabled.

BS 5810:1979 is deemed to satisfy subject to certain limitations.

Schedules

3.62 The Regulations contain 15 Schedules. These cover a variety of subjects from mode of measurement to drainage tests. The Schedules are, in general, laid out in a form which directly relates to the part of the Regulations to which they are applicable. Attention is especially drawn to Schedule 6, which gives notional periods of fire resistance for a wide variety of constructions and which was extensively revised by the 1981 Regulations; to Schedule 13, which gives deemed to satisfy specifications for all regulations which are written in a functional form; and to Schedule 15, which gives constructions which can be used to meet the requirements of Part J.

Extract 16.1 Building Standards (Scotland) Regulations 1981 – Schedule 1

SCHEDULE 1
Regulation A4

Classification of buildings by occupancy

Occupancy group (1)	Occupancy sub-group (2)	Description of occupancy use (3)
A (Residential)	1	Houses of not more than 2 storeys, other than flats or maisonettes– including any surgeries, consulting rooms, offices and other accommodation not exceeding an aggregate of 46 square metres, forming part of the house of any person providing professional or scientific services and used in his professional or scientific capacity.
	2	Houses of more than 2 storeys, and flats and maisonettes– including any surgeries, consulting rooms, offices and other accommodation not exceeding an aggregate of 46 square metres, forming part of the house of any person providing professional or scientific services and used in his professional or scientific capacity.
	3	Residential clubs Residential colleges and schools Residential ecclesiastical buildings Hotels Motels Hostels Lodging houses Boarding houses Bothies and chaumers Chalets Fire stations with sleeping or residential accommodation attached Police stations with sleeping or residential accommodation attached.
	4	Children's homes Old people's homes Special schools for handicapped children Hospitals Private nursing homes Sanatoria.
B (Commercial)	1	Office premises (including Post Office sorting offices and telephone exchanges).
	2	Shop premises (including sub-post offices attached thereto but excluding shop premises to which other occupancy sub-groups apply) Licensed betting offices Beauty parlours Hairdressers Television, radio, recording and film studios Laboratories Launderettes (self-service) Dry cleaning (self-service).

Classification of buildings by occupancy – continued

Occupancy group (1)	Occupancy sub-group (2)	Description of occupancy use (3)
C (Assembly)	1	Bus passenger roadside shelters Passenger stations Public conveniences Grandstands Stadia Sports pavilions Gymnasia Indoor bowling alleys Indoor games courts Riding schools Skating rinks Swimming baths (including any swimming pool, changing rooms, slipper baths, turkish baths or similar facilities pertaining thereto) Funfairs Menageries and zoos Amusement arcades.
	2	Non-residential clubs Non-residential colleges and schools Clinics, surgeries, consulting rooms and related accommodation (other than those covered in occupancy sub-groups A1 and A2) Ecclesiastical buildings, meeting houses Court rooms Museums, art galleries Libraries to which persons other than employees have access Public houses Fire stations (other than those covered in occupancy sub-group A3) Police stations (other than those covered in occupancy sub-group A3).
	3	Theatres, cinemas, radio and television studios to which the public are admitted Casinos and bingo halls Concert halls Restaurants, cafes, canteens Exhibition halls Dance halls, dancing schools.
D (Industrial)	1	Mining and quarrying other than coal and shale mining Manufacture, process or repair of any of the following– tobacco; steel tubes; aluminium and aluminium alloys; mechanical handling equipment; mechanical equipment or parts not elsewhere specified; photographic and document copying equipment; watches and clocks; surgical instruments and appliances; scientific and industrial instruments and systems; electrical machinery; insulated wires and cables; telegraph and telephone apparatus and equipment; radio and electronic components; broadcast receiving and sound reproducing equipment; electronic computers; radio, radar and electronic capital goods; electric appliances primarily for domestic use; other electrical goods; aerospace equipment; locomotives and railway track equipment; railway carriages, wagons and trams; cutlery; bolts, nuts, screws, rivets, etc; wire and wire products; cans and metal boxes; metal goods not elsewhere specified; hosiery and other knitted goods; glass; cement; abrasives and building materials not elsewhere specified; plaster cast, image and models.
	2	Agriculture and horticulture Coal mining Exploration (including boring) for and extracting petroleum Oil shale mining

Classification of buildings by occupancy – continued

Occupancy group (1)	Occupancy sub-group (2)	Description of occupancy use (3)
D (Industrial)- continued	2—continued	Shipbuilding and marine engineering Paper, printing and publishing Laundries and dry cleaners Slaughterhouses and abattoirs Motor repairers, distributors, garages and filling stations Manufacture, process or repair of any of the following– food and drink; chemicals and allied industries; metal; engineering and electrical goods; vehicles; tools and implements; jewellery and precious metals; textiles; fur; clothing and footwear; bricks, fire clay and refractory goods; pottery; rubber; brushes and brooms; stationers' goods; gas, electricity and water Any other industry not separately classified in occupancy sub-groups D1 or D3.
	3	Manufacture, process or repair of any of the following– animal and poultry foods; vegetable and animal oils and fats; soap and detergents; rope, twine and net; narrow fabrics; made-up textiles; leather (tanning and dressing); sheepskin wool (fellmongery); leather goods; hats, caps and millinery; timber; furniture and upholstery; bedding and similar goods; shop and office fittings; wooden containers and baskets; miscellaneous wood and cork goods; linoleum, plastic floor covering; leather cloth and similar material; toys, games and sports equipment; plastic products not elsewhere specified; musical instruments.
E (Storage)	1	(a) Storage of goods and materials not specified as hazardous in occupancy sub-group E2 (b) Garages used solely for the storage or parking of motor vehicles, multi-storey car parks, transit sheds and transport services other than any used for the storage of vehicles loaded with hazardous materials or for the storage of hazardous materials in transit (c) Libraries (other than those covered in occupancy sub-group C2).
	2	(a) Storage of hazardous materials including– (i) any compressed, liquified or dissolved gas; (ii) any substance which becomes dangerous by interaction with either water or air; (iii) any liquid substance with a flash point below 65° Celsius including whisky or other spirituous liquor; (iv) any corrosive substance; (v) any substance that emits poisonous fumes when heated; (vi) any oxidising agent; (vii) any substance liable to spontaneous combustion; (viii) any substance that changes or decomposes readily giving out heat when doing so; (ix) any combustible solid substance with a flash point less than 121° Celsius;

Classification of buildings by occupancy – continued		
Occupancy group (1)	Occupancy sub-group (2)	Description of occupancy use (3)
E (Storage)-continued	2 – continued	(x) any substance likely to spread fire by flowing from one part of a building to another (b) Transit sheds and transport services used for the storage of hazardous materials or vehicles loaded with hazardous materials.

Conclusion

3.63 The Regulations are subject to regular scrutiny and subsequent alteration by amendment in order to take cognizance of new building processes and materials and to bring references to British Standards Codes of Practice and Specifications up to date. The form and presentation of the Regulations are also under review, in order to improve their interpretation by both designer and enforcement officer alike. It must, however, be remembered that the Regulations are a legal document, and revision is subject to that discipline.

It may be useful to mention here the main areas of difference between the Scottish and the English and Welsh Regulations. Scottish Regulations include the following Parts not included in those other Regulations:

1. Means of escape from fire. The requirements in the English Regulations are at present couched in functional terms and limited in application to certain categories of buildings using Codes of Practice as deemed to satisfy conditions.
2. Assistance to fire fighters.
3. Electrical installations.
4. Housing standards.
5. Obstruction and prevention of danger.

3.64 In addition the Scottish Regulations are more detailed in their requirements for ventilation, fire precautions for small buildings such as garages, huts, etc., and give a wide range of total exemptions (in Schedule 4) from the Regulations. There are considerable differences in the contents of schedules.

Extract 16.2 Building Standards (Scotland) Regulations 1981 – Schedule 4

SCHEDULE 4

Regulation A10(1)

Exempted classes of buildings

Class (1)	Description (2)	Limitations (3)
1.	A building erected on agricultural land having an area of more than 0.4 hectare and comprised in an agricultural unit, being a building required for the use of that land for the purposes of agriculture and of which every part falls within one or more of the following descriptions– (a) building for housing cattle (other than milking dairy cattle), horses, sheep or dogs; (b) barn, shed or other building for storage purposes in which no feeding stuffs for livestock are prepared; (c) gate, fence, wall or other means of enclosure not exceeding 2.1 metres in height.	(i) In the case of a building falling under head (a) or (b)– (A) the cubic capacity does not exceed 1130 cubic metres; (B) no part thereof is nearer to the boundary of the agricultural unit than 13 metres. (ii) In the case of a wall falling under head (c), no part of the wall which is over 1.2 metres in height adjoins any road or other place to which the public have access as of right. (iii) There shall not be included in this Class any building to which regulation R11 or R12 applies.

Exempted classes of buildings – continued		
Class (1)	Description (2)	Limitations (3)
2.	A building erected on land used for the purposes of forestry (including afforestation), being a building required for the use of the land for such purposes and of which every part falls within one or more of the following descriptions– (a) building for housing animals; (b) shed or other building for storage purposes; (c) gate, fence, wall or other means of enclosure not exceeding 2.1 metres in height.	(i) In the case of a building falling under head (a) or (b)– (A) the cubic capacity does not exceed 1130 cubic metres; (B) no part thereof is nearer to the boundary than 13 metres; (ii) In the case of a wall falling under head (c), no part of the wall which is over 1.2 metres in height adjoins any road or other place to which the public have access as of right.
3.	A building consisting only of plant or machinery or of a structure or erection of the nature of plant or machinery.	No part of the building is nearer to any point on the boundary than– (A) 13 metres; or (B) the height of the building, whichever is the less, unless at that point the boundary is a boundary with agricultural land on which there is no building nearer to the point than 13 metres.
4.	An electricity transformer not exceeding 1000 kVA capacity and switchgear and control pillars associated therewith.	No part of the apparatus is nearer to the boundary of the site than 1 metre.
5.	A building used only to house fixed plant or machinery in which there is no human occupation or no human occupation other than intermittent occupation for the purposes of maintenance.	As for Class 3.
6.	A building essential for the operation of a railway and comprising or erected within– (a) a locomotive depot; (b) a carriage depot; (c) a goods yard; (d) a marshalling yard; (e) a signal box: Provided that a building shall not be excluded from this class by reason only that a part thereof of a cubic capacity not exceeding one-tenth of the total cubic capacity of the building does not conform to this description.	There shall not be included in this Class any building of occupancy sub-group D1.
7.	A bus passenger roadside shelter providing no facilities other than a waiting room.	(i) The building does not exceed 9 square metres in area. (ii) The building is constructed of non-combustible materials, or if constructed of combustible materials, is sited not less than 6 metres from any other building.
8.	A building essential for the operation of a dock, harbour or pier and erected within the area of the dock, harbour or pier undertaking.	There shall not be included in this Class any building in respect of the construction of which the approval or consent of the local authority would have been required under a local act in force immediately before 15th June 1964.
9.	A work of civil engineering construction including dock, wharf, harbour, pier, quay, sea defence work, lighthouse, embankment, river work, dam, bridge, tunnel, filter station (including filter bed), inland navigation, water works, viaduct, aqueduct, reservoir, pipe line, sewerage work, sewage treatment works, gas holder, gas main, electric supply line and supports.	
10.	A building in respect of which there is constructional control by virtue of the powers under the Explosives Acts 1875 and 1923(a).	
11.	A detached hut or other building ancillary to a house including one used for the keeping of poultry, bees, birds or other animals for the domestic needs or personal enjoyment of the occupants of the house.	(i) There shall not be included in this Class any garage, carport, covered way or greenhouse. (ii) The building is erected on land in the same occupation as a building of occupancy sub-group A1 or A2 not being a block of flats or maisonettes. (iii) The height of the building does not exceed 3 metres. (iv) The floor area of the building does not exceed 5 square metres and where any part of an external wall is less than 500 millimetres from the boundary– (A) such part is constructed of non-combustible materials (other than internal framing) and has no openings therein; and (B) the roof of the building is so constructed as to be designated AA, AB or AC or is of glass or rigid polyvinylchloride sheeting.

Exempted classes of buildings – continued

Class (1)	Description (2)	Limitations (3)
	A detached hut or other building ancillary to a house including one used for the keeping of poultry, bees, birds or other animals for the domestic needs or personal enjoyment of the occupants of the house.–continued	(v) The floor area of the building exceeds 5 square metres but does not exceed 10 square metres and the building is either– (A) constructed of non-combustible materials (other than internal framing) and the roof is so constructed as to be designated AA, AB or AC or is of glass or rigid polyvinylchloride sheeting; or (B) situated not less than 2 metres from the house and not less than 2 metres from the boundary; or (C) situated not less than 2 metres from the house and where any part of an external wall is less than 500 millimetres from the boundary such part is constructed of non-combustible materials (other than internal framing) and has no openings therein and the roof of the building is so constructed as to be designated AA, AB or AC or is of glass or rigid polyvinylchloride sheeting.
12.	A detached carport or covered way ancillary to a house.	(i) The building is erected on land in the same occupation as a building of occupancy sub-group A1 or A2 not being a block of flats or maisonettes. (ii) The floor area of the building does not exceed 30 square metres. (iii) The roof of the building is so constructed as to be designated AA, AB or AC or is of glass or rigid polyvinylchloride sheeting.
13.	A detached greenhouse ancillary to a house.	(i) The building is erected on land in the same occupation as a building of occupancy sub-group A1 or A2 not being a block of flats or maisonettes. (ii) The height of the building does not exceed 3 metres. (iii) The floor area of the building does not exceed 20 square metres. (iv) Not less than three-quarters of the total external surface area of the building is of glass (including glazing bars) or polythene or rigid polyvinylchloride sheeting.
14.	A detached garage ancillary to a house.	(i) The building is erected on land in the same occupation as a building of occupancy sub-group A1 or A2 not being a block of flats or maisonettes. (ii) The floor area of the building does not exceed 30 square metres. (iii) The building is either– (A) constructed of non-combustible materials (other than internal framing) and the roof is so constructed as to be designated AA, AB or AC or is of glass or rigid polyvinylchloride sheeting; or (B) situated not less than 2 metres from the house and not less than 2 metres from the boundary; or (C) situated not less than 2 metres from the house and not less than 500 millimetres from the boundary and any part of an external wall less than 2 metres from the boundary contains no openings.
15.	A building constructed to be used only in connection with and during the construction, alteration, demolition or repair of any building or other work.	The building is neither used nor intended to be used for human habitation.
16.	A moveable dwelling including a tent, caravan, shed or similar structure used for human habitation.	
17.	A building erected on a site during a period of not more than 28 days in any period of 12 months.	
18.	(a) A gate or fence not exceeding 2.1 metres in height; (b) a wall or other means of enclosure not exceeding 1.2 metres in height.	In the case of a building falling under head (a), the gate or fence does not adjoin any road or other place to which the public have access as of right.
19.	A pipe, cable or other apparatus laid underground or a sewage treatment works (not being a sewage treatment works falling into Class 9) which is the subject of a direction under section 14(1) of the Sewerage (Scotland) Act 1968.	There shall not be included in this Class– (a) a drain provided so as to comply with Part M; (b) a conductor or apparatus provided so as to comply with Part N.
	(a) 1875 c. 17; 1923 c. 17.	

3.65 The Scottish Development Department issues a detailed set of explanatory memoranda in A4 size, to help with understanding the basic principles and technical detail of the Regulations. These are related to the specific parts of the Regulations, and contain sketches and diagrams to help in interpretation. It must, however, be understood, when using the memoranda, that they are an aid to interpretation and carry no statutory value whatsoever. Another point to bear in mind is that a check should always be made to ensure that a Regulation has not been amended, the date of publication of the memoranda, and the date of reference. Revised editions of explanatory memoranda have been published since 1972 and deal with individual parts or groups of parts of the Regulations.

3.66 The Regulations in metric from came into force on 7 February 1972 and use the SI system of measurement.

Proposed amendments

3.67 Proposals are about to be laid before Parliament to revise totally the form and presentation of the Regulations.

4 Other national legislation affecting building

4.01 The following list of legislation (although not completely exhaustive) applies in Scotland, and the comments under each heading may give guidance regarding the Scottish scene.

Offices, Shops and Railway Premises Act 1963

4.02 Precise standards for ventilation, means of escape from fire, and occupant load factors are laid down in the Building Standards Regulations. The requirements in the Offices, Shops and Railway Premises Act 1963 are in general framed so that standards of the Building Regulations are *usually* taken by the enforcing authority to meet the requirements of the Act. However, the Building Standards Regulations accept the Sanitary Convenience Regulations 1964 made under the Act (regulation D24 (2) proviso (1) – provision of sanitary accommodation).

Section 29 of the Offices, Shops and Railway Premises Act previously covered fire and certification, but has been repealed and responsibility passed to the Fire Precautions Act from 1 January 1977. Check also the amendments contained in the Health and Safety at Work etc. Act 1974.

Clean Air Acts 1956 to 1968

4.03 Section 6 of the 1968 Act provides a new control for the heights of chimneys serving furnaces. The situation, therefore, is that special application must be made to the local authority for chimney height approval for furnace chimneys. The height of non-furnace chimneys is dealt with under the Building Regulations without need for special application. Constructional details of all chimneys are of course subject to local authority approval. See further Chapter 12, para 6.05 and Chapter 15, para 6.10.

Thermal Insulation Act 1957
Thermal Insulation (Industrial Buildings) Regulations 1972

4.04 The requirements of this Act and Regulations which formerly applied to Scotland in an amended form were repealed by the Thermal Insulation (Insulation Buildings) Act 1958, Repeal (Scotland) Order 1979 (SI 1979/S94) with effect from 1 June 1979.

Factories Act 1961

4.05 Provisions of Part K (ventilation) do not apply to premises subject to the Factories Act 1961, and it is advised that particular ventilation requirements should be discussed with the factory inspectorate at an early stage. However, means of escape for fire requirements are subject to Part F of the Building Standards Regulations. Fire certification previously under this Act is now the responsibility of the Fire Precautions Act as from 1 January 1977 – see the Fire Precautions (Factories, Offices, Shops and Railway Premises) Order 1976. In Scotland, fire authorities are area authorities, eight in number, with their boundaries roughly equivalent to the local authority regional boundaries, but with one brigade covering the Lothian and Borders area. Check carefully the implications of amendment contained in Health and Safety at Work etc. Act 1974.

Fire Precautions Act 1971

4.06 Under this Act, certain premises must obtain a fire certificate from the fire authority as to the suitability of their means of escape. The premises are designated by order, and on 31 January 1972 the Secretary of State designated hotels and boarding houses above a certain size as the first class of premises requiring certificates. The order came into force on 1 June 1972. As the Building Standards Regulations contain requirements for the provision of means of escape, certain sections of the Fire Precautions Act are disapplied to Scotland and certain others apply only to Scotland. Section 14 contains a stautory bar in that where the means of escape meet the Building Regulations requirements, then they must be accepted for fire certificate purposes. This does not mean that all *existing* premises necessarily have to meet Building Regulations standards for new buildings, and many will have reasonable means of escape at present (although not quite up to new building standards). The fire officer has scope to use his judgment in existing premises as far as the statutory bar allows. Attention is also drawn to the definition of 'owner' which differs from that in England. See Chapter 15, para 6.03 ff.

Fire Certificates (Special Premises) Regulations 1976

4.07 These provide that a certificate issued by the Health and Safety Executive shall be required for premises of a kind specified in Schedule 1 of these Regulations and lay down the conditions which may be imposed. The statutory bar for building regulations does not apply to these buildings, but they are of such a specialized nature that close consultation would take place with the relevant authorities at an early stage of design. The Regulations came into force on 1 January 1977.

Sewerage (Scotland) Act 1968

4.08 This Act, which came into force on 1 May 1973, has a bearing on the requirements of the drainage section (Part M) of the Building Standards Regulations. The main effect is to limit the range of the Building Standards Regulations, as many parts of what were termed common drainage will in future become 'public sewer' and will be vested in a local authority.* The term 'drain' is defined as that within the curtilage of a building and for its sole use. Attention is drawn to the definitions in section 59.

The Act under section 12 and subject to the conditions of that section gives an owner a right to connect to a local authority sewer or sewage treatment works. The owner of any premises who proposes to connect his drains or sewers to a public sewer or works of a local authority, or who is altering his drain or sewer in such a way as to interfere with those of a local authority, must, however, give 28 days' notice to the *local* authority, who may or may not give permission for the work to proceed. The authority can give conditional approval, and the owner has right of appeal against any decision.

Powers are given in the Act to require defects in drains or sewage treatment works to be remedied. Local authorities have the powers to take over private sewage treatment works, including septic tanks. Other powers include rights to discharge trade effluents into public sewers, emptying of septic tanks, provision of temporary sanitary conveniences, etc.

Health and Safety at Work etc Act 1974

4.09 The most important effect of this Act is contained in section 75 as read with Schedule 10. These clauses introduce amendments to the principal Building Acts and extend and alter the powers contained in them. It should be noted that in Part III of the Act only section 75 is applicable to Scotland. The powers under this section come into force only when the Secretary of State issues a designating order. To date, two such orders have been made: the Health and Safety at Work etc. Act 1974 (Commencement No. 2) Order 1975, and the Health and Safety at Work etc. Act 1974 (Commencement No. 6) Order 1980.

The Act also includes important changes in transferring fire certification carried out under other legislation, e.g. Offices, Shops and Railway Premises Act and Factories Act to the Fire Precautions Act.

Safety of Sports Ground Act 1975

4.10 This Act contains references to buildings authorities in sections 3 (3), 4 (7), 5 (5), 10 (5), and 11. Work carried out which requires structural attention is subject to Building Regulations and Procedures. It should also be noted that the only public enquiry in the UK under this Act took place in 1979 in Dundee, with the Secretary of State's decision being issued in 1980.

Fire Safety and Safety of Places of Sport Act 1987

4.11 As well as introducing a number of new requirements, the above Act contains amendments to the Factories Act, and the Offices, Shops and Railway Premises Act 1963. In addition it changes the term stadium in the Safety of Sports Ground Act 1975 to 'sports ground' which has a wider meaning.

In terms of Scots law, attention is drawn to section 7. Note that the references to building regulations in section 7(3), (4) and (5) relate to England and Wales only and that section 48 amends the Civic Government (Scotland) Act 1982, section 98. This section at the moment gives the Secretary of State powers to make regulations for the safe operation of electrical luminous signs exceeding 650 volts. The reference to a limiting size has been replaced by a more functional description.

Licensing (Scotland) Act 1976

4.12 The Act contains references to building control in section 23(3). Again, structural alterations and change of use are subject to building regulations and procedures.

Local acts

4.13 A few local Acts exist, for instance in Edinburgh and Glasgow. While the Building Standards (Scotland) Regulations must be complied with, there may be fringe areas outside that control where slight differences may arise.

NB Advice should be sought from the authority concerned.

---

*The local authority is usually the regional council.

Civic Government (Scotland) Act 1982

4.14 This Act covers a wide range of activities and functions controlled by local authorities. It gives power to make and enforce byelaws. Mention should be made of the powers to license various forms of businesses or functions: e.g. places of public entertainment.

Special attention is drawn to part VIII, Buildings etc. This covers various requirements as to maintenance and repair of buildings, installation of lighting, fire precautions in common stairs. Of particular interest is section 88 regarding the installation of pipes through a neighbouring property and the procedure to be followed where consent of the neighbouring owner has been withheld or refused.

5 General

5.01 The following points may be useful to persons wishing to design and build in Scotland for the first time:

1. Scots law differs from that of the rest of the UK (see Scottish articles in this handbook).
2. Building control is exercised by local authorities.
3. Warrant must be obtained from the local authority before any building (including alterations and extensions) can begin, and it is separate from planning permission. A fee related to the total cost of the job is usually payable in accordance with the scale laid down in the table of fees (Schedule 2 of the Procedure Regulations).
4. Ensure that the latest amendments to the Building Standards Regulations are available as well as a copy of the Regulations themselves, the Procedure Regulations, and the correct forms (paras 2.26 and 2.40).
5. Relaxation of the Regulations (except for certain existing buildings) is the responsibility of the Secretary of State for Scotland.
6. If problems occur, consult the building control officer of the appropriate authority, but remember that although he will normally give advice, he is not there to design or redesign, draw or redraw plans.
7. Check carefully the requirements of the sewerage authority where appropriate.
8. Check carefully whether a class relaxation has been issued in respect of a new building product.

EEC

5.02 Legislation produced by the EEC is already having an effect on Building Regulations. The Construction Products Directive of 12/12/88 lays down requirements for all member countries and is very wide in its scope.

Directive 78/170/EEC covers the performance of heat generators and production of hot water in new industrial buildings and insulation of its distribution in new industrial building.

New Health and Safety directives being prepared will also affect Building Regulations.

Building Notes

5.03 The Scottish Development Department has issued Building Notes to local authorities giving guidance on Building Regulation matters.

As an example, Building Note 6/77 gave advice regarding a number of cases in respect of building control which had come to its notice. The note dealt with technical problems encountered in the actual installation of certain warm air heaters and with procedural aspects under the Building Acts and Procedures Regulations. The latter is particularly interesting to warrant applicants and have been summarized below:

1. A number of cases have been reported where Building Regulations have been wrongly applied to features of existing buildings. The attention of building control authorites is drawn to the extent to which they can apply Regulations to existing buildings, and the appropriate legal references are given. It would appear that some authorities may have erroneously used the application for warrant by a developer to demand that features of a building, not directly involved with the works to be carried out, and which may because they were built pre-Regulations, be brought up to Regulations standard. The Building (Scotland) Act 1959, as amended by the Building (Scotland) Act 1970, is quite specific in its guidelines with regard to existing buildings. If authorities wish to upgrade buildings to current Regulations standard, section 11 of the 1959 Act lays down the procedure and limitations which have to be followed and cannot be used in relation to warrant procedures.
2. Reports of authorities attaching conditions to warrants have come to the Department's notice, as well as the practice of withholding warrants until planning permission had been granted. The Department point out that no conditions may be attached to a warrant other than those specified in the Building Act (e.g. in relation to demolition) and that if a warrant is in accordance with the relevant requirements of the Regulations and made in the approved manner, it must be granted.
3. Two Building Notes were issued in the early part of 1984. In one, local authorities are reminded that they must accept the deemed to satisfy requirements in athe Regulations for resistance to sound transmission and in the other, information is given regarding the fitting of balanced flues and their separation from combustible materials in timber-framed houses.

Late addition to para 2.27

The Building (Procedure) (Scotland) Amendment Regulations 1990 have introduced a revised scale of fees. The new scale is designed to raise the recovery rate through fees of local authority costs in administering building control responsibilities to approximately 80 per cent. Fees for demolition warrants are now included in the main sliding scale instead of the previous fixed minimum rate. Applications for an extension of warrant will now also be charged a fee. These Regulations came into force from 1st September 1990.

17

Copyright

MICHAEL FLINT*

1 The basic rules of copyright

1.01 The copyright law of the United Kingdom is contained in the Copyright, Designs and Patents Act 1988 and the subsidiary legislation made under that Act. Copyright exists only in material which comes within one of the categories prescribed as being capable of having copyright protection. These are as follows:

1. Literary works
2. Dramatic works.
3. Musical works.
4. Artistic works.
5. Sound recordings.
6. Films.
7. Broadcasts.
8. Cable programmes.
9. Typographical arrangements of copyright designs of patents; published editions.

The Act describes all these categories of material as 'works'.

Material which does not fall within one of the categories will have no copyright protection; it will not be copyright material.

1.02 Copyright subsists for defined periods which differ according to the category of work.

The duration of copyright in each category of work can be summarized as follows:

1. Literary, dramatic, musical and artistic works: 50 years from the end of the calender year in which the author died.
2. Sound recordings and films: 50 years from the end of the year in which they were made, or if released before the end of that period, 50 years from the end of the calendar year in which released.
3. Broadcasts and cable programmes: 50 years from the end of the year in which the broadcast was made or cable programme included in a cable programme service.
4. Typographical arrangements: 25 years from the end of the calendar year in which the edition was first published.

1.03 If material is entitled to copyright, the right vested in the copyright owner is that of preventing others from doing certain specified acts, called 'the restricted acts' (para 2.02).

The restricted acts are specified by the Copyright Act in relation to each category of work and differ for each category.

If something is done in relation to copyright material which is not one of the restricted acts specified for that type of work

or an act which constitutes 'secondary infringement' and was done by a person who knew, or had reason to believe that the act would be an infringement of copyright, there is no breach of copyright.

1.04 There are certain circumstances in which doing restricted acts without the authority of the copyright owner does not constitute breach of copyright.

The most important of these general exceptions are:

1. Fair dealing (e.g. for purposes of research, private study, criticism, or review).
2. Use of less than a substantial part of a work.
3. Use for certain educational purposes.
4. Use for certain library and archival purposes.
5. Use in parliamentary and judicial proceedings.

There are other important exceptions, differing according to the types of works or subject matters (paras 1.05 to 1.10).

1.05 In most cases the author of a work is its first owner. But there are special rules which can override this general provision.

1.06 There is no copyright in ideas – only in the manner of their expression.

1.07 To acquire copyright protection, works must be reduced to a material form.

1.08 Literary, dramatic, musical and artistic works must be original in order to be entitled to copyright.

1.09 The work must have involved the use of skill and labour by the author.

1.10 The work does not have to be published, nor does it have to be registered, for it to have copyright protection.

1.11 The author or maker of the work must be a 'qualified person': basically a citizen or resident of the United Kingdom or of one of the countries which is a signatory to the Berne Copyright Convention or the Universal Copyright Convention (UCC). Alternatively, the work must have been made or published in a qualifying country, which generally speaking although there are important exceptions for sound recordings, films, broadcasts and cable programmes, are the same countries. There are no significant countries in the copyright context which are not parties to one or the other of these conventions, except China.

---

* In the first edition, this chapter was written by George Stringer. In the second edition, it was revised by Evelyn Freeth. George Burnet has advised as to the law of copyright in Scotland.

The nature of copyright

1.12

'Copyright is a right given to or derived from works, and is not a right in novelty of ideas. It is based on the right of an author, artist or composer to prevent another person copying an original work, whether it be a book, picture or tune, which he himself has created. There is nothing in the notion of copyright to prevent a second person from producing an identical result (and himself enjoying a copyright in that work) provided it is arrived at by an independent process.'

That quotation is from the report of the Gregory Committee on Copyright Law (1952), whose recommendations formed the basis of the Copyright Act 1956.

'A writer writes an article about the making of bread. He puts words on paper. He is not entitled to a monopoly in the writing of articles about the making of bread, but the law has long recognised that he has an interest not merely in the manuscript, the words on paper which he produces, but in the skill and labour involved in the choice of words and the exact way in which he expresses his ideas by the words he chooses. If the author sells copies of his article then again a purchaser of a copy can make such use of that copy as he pleases. He can read it or sell it second-hand, if he can find anyone who will buy it. If a reader of the original article is stimulated into writing another article about bread the original author has no reason to complain. It has long been recognised that only the original author ought to have the right to reproduce the original article and sell the copies thus reproduced. If other people were free to do this they would be making a profit out of the skill and labour of the original author. It is for this reason that the law has long given to authors, for a specified term, certain exclusive rights in relation to so-called literary works. Such rights were recognised at common law at least as early as the fifteenth century.'

The latter quotation is from the report of the Whitford Committee on Copyright and Design Law (1977), upon whose recommendations the Copyright, Designs and Patents Act 1988 is largely based. These two quotations contain as clear an exposé of the nature of copyright as can be found anywhere.

As the word itself implies, 'copyright' is literally a right to prevent other people copying an original work. It should be noted that it must be an original work, *not* an original idea.

Intellectual property and copyright

1.13 The main difficulty in comprehending copyright seems to be the association that is made among copyright, patents, and trade marks. These diverse creatures are, for convenience, usually grouped under the headings of 'industrial property' or 'intellectual property'. It is certainly appropriate to include design copyright – which is registrable, unlike any other form of copyright – under these generic headings, but whilst copyright certainly is a form of property, it is arguable that it would be preferable to group copyright with passing off, breach of confidence, and invasion of privacy.

The sources of copyright law

1.14 Statute copyright law is now entirely contained in the Copyright, Designs and Patents Act 1988 ('the Act').

There are a number of rules and regulations contained in statutory instruments made under the above legislation. In addition, certain Orders in Council extend the provisions of the Act to works originating outside the United Kingdom.

The United Kingdom is party to a number of conventions dealing with international copyright recognition and other matters of an international nature concerning copyright, of which the most important are the Berne Copyright Convention and the Universal Copyright Convention.

There is a body of case law contained in the law reports consisting of the judgements of copyright cases. Decisions on earlier legislation, the Copyright Acts of 1911 and 1956, are frequently still relevant. They are of particular importance, for example, when determining what constitutes plagiarism and where judgments on matters of degree, rather than pure construction of legislation, must be made.

The history of copyright law

1.15 Copyright effectively came into existence with the invention of printing. The first indications of copyright were the granting of licences by the Crown to printers giving them the right to print (i.e. copy) against the payment of fees to the Crown. In 1662 the Licensing Act was passed, which prohibited the printing of any book which was not licensed and registered at the Stationers Company.

The first Copyright Act was passed in 1709. This Act gave protection for printed works for only 21 years from the date of printing and unprinted works for 14 years. Again, books had to be registered at the Stationers Company.

The Copyright Act 1842 was the next important piece of legislation relating to copyright. Although it accorded copyright protection only to literary works, it laid down as the period of copyright the life of the author plus 7 years after his death, or 42 years from the date of publication, whichever should be the longer.

Architects' plans, provided they had artistic quality, first became entitled to copyright protection as artistic works under the Fine Arts Copyright Act 1862.

The Copyright Act 1911 repealed all previous copyright legislation. This Act extended copyright protection to 'architectural works of art', with the result that, as the courts held in *Meikle* v *Maufe* [1941] 3 All ER 144, both buildings and the plans upon which they were based were entitled to copyright protection. Plans and sketches were protected as 'literary works' and drawings as 'artistic works'. The Copyright Act 1911 was repealed by the Copyright Act 1956.

Protection for works of architecture under the 1956 Act was similar to that accorded by the 1911 Act.

The 1988 Act repealed the 1956 Act. It came into force on 1 August 1989.

2 Protection under the Copyright Designs and Patents Act 1988

2.01 Works of architecture are included with 'artistic works' for copyright purposes. Section 4 of the Act defines an 'artistic work'. In view of its importance in considering architectural copyright it is worth quoting in full:

S.4 (1) In this Part 'artistic work' means—
   (*a*) a graphic work, photograph, sculpture or collage, irrespective of artistic quality,
   (*b*) a work of architecture being a building or a model for a building, or
   (*c*) a work of artistic craftmanship.
   (2) In this part—
   'building' includes any fixed structure, and a part of a building or fixed structure;
   'graphic work' includes—
      (*a*) any painting, drawing, diagram, map, chart or plan, and
      (*b*) any engraving, etching, lithograph, woodcut or similar work;
   'photograph' means a recording of light or other radiation on any medium on which an image is produced or from which an image may by any means be produced, and which is not part of a film;
   'sculpture' includes a cast or model made for purposes of sculpture.

Works of architecture include both buildings and models for buildings. The plans, sketches, and drawings upon which works of architecture are based are also artistic works which have their own separate copyright. So also do the notes prepared by the architect, but these are protected not as artistic works but as literary works.

There is no definition of 'fixed structure' although a decision under the 1956 Act held that a garden, in that case a somewhat elaborately laid out garden, was a 'structure' and therefore a work of architecture.

A 'drawing' is not defined by the Act. The definitions of 'artistic work' and 'literary work' are so wide that they cover all the typical output of an architect's office: design sketches, blueprints, descriptive diagrams, working drawings, final drawings, artistic presentations, notes, both alphabetical and numerical and reports.

Restricted acts

2.02 As mentioned in para 1.03 above, there are separate restricted acts specified in the Act in relation to each category of work. The restricted acts applicable to works of architecture are the same as those applicable to artistic works, although there are certain special exceptions (paras 4.03 to 4.06) from these restricted acts in relation to works of architecture.

The acts restricted by the copyright in artistic work are:

1. Copying the work.
2. Issuing copies of the work to the public.
3. Making an adaptation of the work or doing either of the above in relation to an adaptation.

Originality and artistic content

2.03 Buildings and models require in theory to have an artistic character or design, but in the few reported cases, it would appear that no architect has failed to prove an infringement even though the original building was so ordinary that it might be thought inevitable that someone else would design something substantially similar. In the case of *University of London Press Ltd* v *University Tutorial Press Ltd*, which concerned the copying of examination papers, the judge stated that 'the word "original" does not in this connection mean that the work must be the expression of original or inventive thought . . . but that it should originate from the author'.

2.04 For architectural works, the inclusion of some distinctive design detail will make the architect's task of proving infringement much easier. In the case of *Stovin-Bradford* v *Volpoint Properties Ltd* [1971] Ch 1007, the courts were influenced by the fact that although many details of the architect's drawings were not reproduced in the constructed buildings, 'a distinctive diamond-shaped feature which gave a pleasing appearance to the whole' was reproduced. In *Meikle* v *Maufe* the judge dismissed them as not being of artistic merit.

2.05 Some distinctive design feature may also be important when it could otherwise be proved that the person sued was without any knowledge of the plaintiff's prior design, and that he produced identical solutions because of a similarity in circumstances. In *Muller* v *Triborough Bridge Authority* the United States Supreme Court held that a copyright of the drawing showing a novel bridge approach designed to disentangle traffic congestion was not infringed by copying, because the system of relieving traffic congestion shown embodied an idea which cannot be copyright and was the only obvious solution to the problem.

Duration of copyright

2.07 The protection of copyright in an artistic work extends for the lifetime of the author and a further period of 50 years from the end of the calendar year in which he died. In the case of architectural works, this period is not affected by the fact that the work was not published during the architect's lifetime.

In the case of joint works, the 50 years begins to run from the end of the calendar year in which the last of the joint authors dies. A joint work is one in which the work is produced by the collaboration of two or more authors in which the contribution of each author is not distinct from that of the other author or authors. Thus if a building is designed by two architects, but one is exclusively responsible only for the design of the doors and windows, so that it is possible to distinguish between the contributions of the two archtiects it will not be a joint work.

3 Qualification

3.01 In order to qualify for copyright protection in the United Kingdom, the qualification requirements of the Act must be satisfied either as regards the author or the country in which the work was first published.

3.02 As regards authors, in the case of unpublished works, copyright will subsist only if the author was a 'qualified person' at the time when the work was made, or, if it was being made over a period, for a substantial part of that period. In the case of a published work, the author must have been qualified at the time when the work was published, or immediately before his death (if earlier).

3.03 For copyright purposes, the expression 'qualified person' does not refer to a professional qualification, but to any British citizen, British Dependent Territories citizen, a British National (overseas), a British Overseas citizen, a British subject, or a British protected person within the meaning of the British Nationality Act 1981, or a person domiciled or resident in the UK or in another country to which the Act extends or is applied, or a body incorporated under the laws of the UK or such another country. The countries to which the Act extends or has been applied are the signatories to the Berne Copyright Convention and the Universal Copyright Convention, which (apart from the People's Republic of China and some Muslim countries) includes all the major and most of the developing countries in the world.

The provision relating to corporations is not important to architects because a corporation cannot be the author of an artistic work.

3.04 As regards the country of publication, the work must have been published first in either the United Kingdom or another country to which the Act extends or has been applied.

Publication in one country shall not be regarded as other than first publication by reason of the simultaneous publication elsewhere. Publication elsewhere within 30 days shall be regarded as simultaneous.

3.05 The Act now provides that the territorial waters of the UK shall be treated as part of the UK for copyright purposes. In addition, oil rigs and other structures which are present on the UK continental shelf for purposes directly connected with the exploration of the sea bed or the exploration of their natural resources are subject to UK copyright law as if they were in the UK.

4 Publication

4.01 The meaning of the word 'publication' is important as it is relevant to qualification for copyright protection and the duration of copyright.

'Publication' is defined in the Act as meaning the issue of copies to the public. In the case of literary, dramatic, musical and artistic works it includes making it available to the public by means of an electronic retrieval system.

There is a special provision in relation to architectural works. In the case of works of architecture in the form of a building or an artistic work incorporated in a building, construction of the building shall be treated as equivalent to publication of the work.

4.02 However, the issue to the public of copies of a graphic work representing, or of photographs of, a work of architecture in the form of a building, or a model for a building, a sculpture or a work of artistic craftsmanship, does not constitute publication for the purposes of the Act. Nor does the exhibition, issue to the public of copies of a film including the work, or the broadcasting of an artistic work constitute publication. Thus, the inclusion of a model of a building in a public exhibition such as the Royal Academy Summer Exhibition, would not amount to publication, nor would the inclusion of photographs of the model in a book.

5 Ownership

5.01 Subject to the exception set out in the following paragraph, ownership of copyright resides with the architect who actually drews the plan, drawing, sketch, or diagram, and, being personal property in law, passes to its owner's personal representatives after his death, and thence as directed in his will, or, in the event of intestacy, to his next of kin.

Employees

5.02 There is, however, an important exception to this provision: the copyright in architects' drawings, buildings, or models produced by an employee in the course of his employment automatically vests in his employer, whether the latter is an architect in partnership, a limited company, or a public authority. The copyright in work done by employees in their time and not in the course of employment vests in them. But an employer can discourage employees from accepting private commissions by providing in the contract of service – and a simple letter agreement is a contract of service – that all the copyright in the employee's work, whether produced in the course of employment or not, will vest in the employer. Section 178 of the Act provides that the words 'employed', 'employee', 'employer' and 'employment' refer to employment under a 'contract of service or apprenticeship'. Frequently architects employ independent architects and artists to carry out parts of the drawing service; increasingly persons who would appear to be employees are for a variety of reasons (not unconnected with tax and Social Security payments) engaged as self-employed sub-contractors. Such persons are rarely employed under 'a contract of service' as distinct from 'a contract for services', which is not the same thing (Chapter 3). Employer architects would be well advised to make it an express term of such a sub-contractor's appointment that any copyright arising out of his work should vest in the employing architect.

The old provisions regarding Crown copyright have been changed in the 1988 Act. The position now is that where a work is made by an officer or servant of the Crown in the course of his duties, the Crown will be the first owner of the copyright in the work.

Partners

5.03 Unless the partnership deed (Chapter 19) states anything to the contrary, the copyright in all work produced during the currency of a partnership is a partnership asset, and like other assets is owned and passes in accordance with the general provisions of the partnership deed concerning assets. To avoid dissemination of shares in copyright, it is usually desirable to provide that, upon the death or retirement of a partner, his share in the copyright should vest in the surviving partners. Alternatively, partners could in their wills, leave their shares in the copyright to their surviving partners.

Ownership of drawings

5.04 Ownership of copyright in drawings should be distinguished from ownership of the actual pieces of paper upon which they are drawn. It is settled law that upon payment of the architect's fees the client is entitled to physical possession of all the drawings prepared at his expense. In the absence of agreement to the contrary, copyright remains with the architect who also has a lien on (right to withhold) the drawings until his fees are paid. If all copyright *is* assigned to the client he may make such use of it as he wishes. Architects should note that even if they have assigned the copyright by virtue of the provisions of section 64 of the Act, they may reproduce in a subsequent work part of their own original design provided that they do not repeat or imitate the main design. This provision enables architects to repeat standard details which would otherwise pass to the client upon prior assignment of copyright.

6 Exceptions from infringement of architects' copyright

Photographs, graphic works

6.01 Frequently photographs of buildings designed by architects appear as part of advertisements by the contractors who constructed the buildings. As a matter of courtesy, the contractor usually makes some acknowledgment of the design, but he is not required to do so. By section 62 of the Act, the copyright in a work of architecture is not infringed by making a graphic work representing it, making a photograph or film of it, or broadcasting or including a visual representation of it in a cable programme service a visual of it. Copies of such graphic works, photographs and films can be issued to the public without infringing the copyright in the building and models of it. Making a graphic work in this sense refers to a perspective or even detailed survey of the building as built. it would remain an infringement to copy the drawing or plan from which the building was constructed.

Reconstruction

6.02 Section 65 provides that where copyright exists in a building, it is not infringed by any reconstruction of the building. There will be no infringement of the drawings or plans in accordance with which the building was, by or with the licence of the copyright owner, constructed if subsequent reconstruction of the building or part thereof is carried out by reference to original drawings or plans. This point is of particular importance in connection with the now established 'implied licence' considered in paras 8.05–8.12 below.

Fair dealing

6.03 A general defence to any alleged infringement of copyright in an artistic work is 'fair dealing' for the purpose of criticism or review, provided that there is sufficient acknowledgment. As reproduction by photograph is the most

likely method of illustrating a review and as a photograph of a building is specifically exempt from infringement, this defence of 'fair dealing' would appear to be needed only in the case of drawings of buildings. A sufficient acknowledgment is an acknowledgment identifying the building by its name and location, which also identifies the name of the architect who designed it. The name of the copyright owner need not be given if he has previously required that no acknowledgment of his name should be made. As certain self-appointed groups have now taken to awarding prizes for ugliness in design, some architects might find themselves in the unusual position of wishing to have no acknowledgment made of their connection with a design, although perhaps such publicity would hardly be 'fair dealing'.

Fair dealing with an artistic work for the purposes of research and private study, without any acknowledgment, is also a defence to an alleged copyright infringement. However, there are limits on how, and how many copies may be made.

6.04 Special exceptions are contained in the Act for copying for educational purposes and copying by libraries and archives and by public administration. These provisions are too detailed to be included here, and if necessary they should be specifically referred to or professional advice should be obtained.

7 Infringement

7.01 To prove infringement, a plaintiff must show:

1. Copyright subsists in his work.
2. The copyright is vested in him.
3. The alleged infringement is identical to his work in material particulars.
4. The alleged infringement was copied from his work.

7.02 No action for infringement of copyright can succeed if the person who is claimed to have infringed had no knowledge of the existence of the work of the owner. In this respect it differs from patents, which must be registered but which give an absolute protection even if the person infringing a patent had no knowledge of its existence. Copyright restricts the right to copy, which presupposes some knowledge of the original by the copier. Ignorance of the fact that the work copied was the copyright owner's is not, however, a defence. It is in the nature of architects' copyright that the person allegedly infringing must have had access directly or indirectly to the drawings. Infringement can therefore take three forms, as detailed below.

Copying in the form of drawings

7.03 It is rare for drawings to be copied in every detail, and many would-be infringers of an architect's copyright believe that if details are altered, infringement is avoided. This is not so, and section 16 of the Act makes it clear that references to reproduction include reproduction of a 'substantial part'. The word 'substantial' refers to quality rather than to quantity. Reference has already been made to the distinctive diamond-shaped detail in the *Stovin-Bradford* case. It does not matter that the size of the copy may have been increased or reduced or that only a small detail of an original drawing has been copied.

Copying the drawing in the form of a building

7.04 The leading case on this form of infringement is *Chabot v Davies* [1936] 3 All ER. Mr Chabot, who was not an architect but 'a designer and fixer of shop fronts and the like' prepared a drawing for the defendant, who 'was just about to open what is known as a fish and chip shop'. Mr Chabot was lucky enough to be able to prove that the contractor had actually been handed his drawing by the defendant and had made a tracing from it, but the defendant argued that a plan cannot be reproduced by a shop front but only by something in the nature of another plan. The judge held, however, that 'reproduce . . . in any material form whatsoever' must include reproduction of a drawing by the construction of an actual building based on that drawing.

Copying a building by another building

7.05 The leading case on this type of infringement and until recently on architects' copyright generally is *Meikle v Maufe* [1941] 3 All ER 144. Most architects have heard of this case, but the facts and argument bear repetition. In 1912 Heal & Son Ltd employed Smith & Brewer as architects for the building of premises on the northern part of the present site of Heal's store in Tottenham Court Road. At that time there were vague discussions about a future extension on the southern part of the site, but because of difficulties over land acquisition nothing could be done. In 1935 Heal's employed Maufe as their architect for the extension of the building. Meikle was by this time the successor in title to Smith & Brewer's copyright, and he claimed that both the extension as erected and the plans for its erection infringed the original copyright. Maufe admitted that he thought it necessary to reproduce in the southern section of the facade the features which appeared in the original northern section. His object was 'to make the new look like the old throughout nearly the whole of the Tottenham Court Road frontage'. The layout of the interiors was also substantially reproduced. The defendants put forward three arguments:

1. There could not be a separate copyright in a building as distinct from copyright in the plans on which it was based.
2. If there were a separate copyright in a building it would belong to the building contractor.
3. It was an implied term of Smith & Brewer's original engagement that Heal's should have the right to reproduce the design of the original in the extension.

7.06 The first argument failed following *Chabot v Davies*. The second argument failed because copyright protection in a building is limited to the original character or design, and in the making of such character or design the contractor plays no part. The third argument failed in this particular case as the Copyright Act 1911, under which this case was tried, provided that copyright remained with its original author, unless he had agreed to pass the right to another. Heal's contended that Smith & Brewer had impliedly consented to the reproduction of their design because they had known of the possibility of extension. The judge having heard the facts concerning the discussion about land acquisition held that he could not reasonably imply such a term in this case.

Copying a building in the form of drawings

7.07 As mentioned in para 6.01, copyright in a work of architecture is not infringed by two-dimensional reproductions.

8 Licences

Express licence

8.01 Clause 3.15 of the RIBA Architect's Appointment states that copyright in all documents and drawings and in the work executed from them remains the property of the architect unless otherwise agreed. Section 91 of the Act permits prior assignment of future copyright so that client and architect can agree at the beginning of an engagement to vary the Conditions of Engagement so that the copyright which will come into existence during the commission will vest in the client.

8.02 Clause 3.16 of the RIBA Architect's Appointment provides for an express licence for the client to execute the project if the architect has completed stage D (Scheme Design) or provides detailed designs in stages E, F, G. However, this licence is subject to the client paying or tendering any fees due to the architect and is limited to the site to which the design relates. If the architect has not completed stage D or when the architect and the client have agreed that clause 3.16 is not to apply, then the client may not reproduce the design by proceeding to execute the design without the architect's consent (which must not be unreasonably withheld (clause 3.18)) and payment of any additional fee that may be agreed in exchange for the architect's consent (clause 3.17). If the architect's engagement was limited to making and negotiating planning applications, he can withhold consent at his absolute discretion unless otherwise determined by an arbitrator (clause 3.18).

8.03 Copyright may also be expressly assigned to the client at some later stage, but it is usual to grant a licence authorizing use of copyright subject to conditions rather than an outright assignment of all the architect's rights. An increasing number of public and commercial clients make it a condition of the architect's appointment that all copyright shall vest in the client, but the architect should not consent to this without careful thought. Following *Meikle* v *Maufe* it would seem reasonable that a client should not be prevented from extending a building and incorporating distinctive design features of the original building so that the two together should form one architectural unit. If the time between the original building and the extension were 23 years, as in that case, it would be restrictive to make use of copyright to force the client into employing the original architect or his successor in title. Less scrupulous clients could, however, make use of an architect's design for a small and inexpensive original building with the undisclosed intention of greatly extending the building using the same design but at no extra cost in terms of architect's fees.

8.04 So far as drawings are concerned, it must be remembered that they are the subject of copyright 'irrespective of artistic quality' so that a prior express assignment of copyright to the client could theoretically grant him copyright in respect of even the most simple standard detail contained in the drawings (but see para 5.04).

Implied licence

8.05 Whilst the RIBA Architect's Appointment contains an express licence of the architect's copyright, situations may arise where the RIBA Architect's Appointment does not form part of the contract between the architect and the client or where the terms of the RIBA Architect's Appointment do not cover particular circumstances. Problems may then arise as to what rights the client has to use the architect's drawings. As long ago as 1938, the RIBA took counsel's opinion on the theory that an architect impliedly licenses his client to make use of the architect's drawings for the purposes of construction even when the client does not employ the architect to supervise the building contract. Such an implied consent can be understood when from the beginning of the engagement the client made it clear that all he required of the architect was drawings; for if the client received the drawings and paid for them, they would be valueless unless he could use them for the purpose of construction. The courts would not allow an architect to use his copyright to prevent construction in such circumstances. Counsel advised further that even if it had originally been assumed that the architect would perform the full service and supervise construction but the client subsequently decided that he did not require supervision, an implied licence to use the copyright in the drawings would arise in the client's favour when working drawings had been completed. Counsel did not then believe that an implied

licence could arise at an earlier stage, but since 1938 the extent of architects' work and its stages have increased greatly. Cumulatively detailed drawings required for outline planning consent, detailed planning consent, and Building Regulations consent all create different stages, and an implied licence can now arise earlier than was contemplated in 1938.

8.06 Before any term can be implied into a contract, the courts must consider what the parties would have decided if they had considered the question at the time they negotiated other terms of the engagement. The courts are reluctant to imply a term unless it is necessary to give efficacy to the intention of the parties. Application of these rules to an architect's engagement would suggest that it is reasonable to infer that the architect impliedly consents to the client making use of his drawings for the purpose for which they were intended. If, therefore, the nature of the engagement is not full RIBA service but, for example, obtaining outline planning permission and no more, the architect impliedly consents to the client making use of his copyright to apply for such permission. Again, if an architect is instructed to prepare drawings of a proposed alteration for submission to the client's landlord, the client may use the drawings to obtain a consent under the terms of his lease but not for any other purpose, and certainly not for the purpose of instructing a contractor to carry out the alteration work.

8.07 The whole question of implied licence has been considered by the Court of Appeal in the cases of *Blair* and *Stovin-Bradford*, both of which have been fully reported. The facts in these cases were as follows.

Blair v *Osborne & Tompkins*

8.08 Blair was asked by his clients whether it would be possible to obtain planning consent for development at the end of his clients' garden. Having made inquiries, Blair advised that it should be possible to obtain consent for erection of two semi-detached houses. The clients instructed Blair to proceed to detailed planning consent stage and agreed to pay on the RIBA scale. The application was successful, and Blair sent the planning consent to his clients, with his account for £70 for 'taking instructions, making survey, preparing scheme and obtaining full planning consent'. As was well known to the architect, the clients did not at that stage know whether they were going to develop the land or sell it.

They paid Blair's account which he acknowledged adding 'wishing you all the best on his project' but did not employ him to do any further work because they sold the plot to a contractor/developer. They also handed over Blair's drawings to the contractor, who used his own surveyors to add the detail necessary to obtain Building Regulations consent, and this consent having been obtained the contractor erected the houses. When the architect discovered that his plans were being used he claimed that this was an infringement of his copyright. The Master of the Rolls pointed out that although the RIBA Conditions of Engagement stated that copyright remained with the architect, it was open to him to give a licence for the drawings to be used for a particular site. His Lordship was influenced by the provision in the RIBA Conditions which entitled both architect and client to terminate the engagement 'upon reasonable notice'. To his Lordship it seemd inconceivable that upon the architect withdrawing he could stop any use of the plans on the ground of infringement of copyright. It seemed equally inconceivable that he could stop their use at an earlier stage when he had done his work up to a particular point and had been paid according to the RIBA scale. Lord Justice Widgery approved the defendant's submission that the implied licence was 'to use whatever plans had been prepared at the appropriate

stage for all purposes for which they would normally be used, namely, all purposes connected with the erection of the building to which they related'. If this was not right 'the architect' could hold a client to ransom and that would be quite inconsistent with the term that the engagement could be 'put an end to at any time'. In the writer's opinion this was an unfortunate decision and went much further than was required. But it must be lived with.

Stovin-Bradford v Volpoint Properties Ltd and Another

8.09 The defendant companies, which had their own drawing office, acquired an old factory which they considered had considerable development potential, and applied for planning consent for the erection of seven large warehouses. Permission was refused, and the defendants approached Stovin-Bradford, whose work they had previously admired, explaining that they needed a plan and drawing that 'showed something which was more attractive looking than the existing building'. What they wanted was 'a pretty picture', but because they had their own drawing office, they did not need the full services of an architect. It was accepted by the court that although the then Conditions of Engagement were not incorporated in their contract, both architect and defendants were fully aware that they existed. It was also accepted that both parties were concerned only with obtaining planning permission. As the trial judge held, the agreement reached between the parties was very simple and amounted to this: 'that Stovin-Bradford would suggest architectural improvements to the defendant's existing plan for the modification and extension of the existing building for

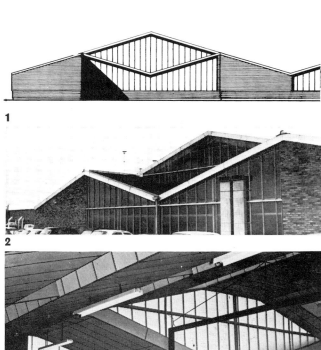

1

2

3

1 Stovin-Bradford's original design, and warehouses as built **2, 3**

the purpose of trying to obtain planning permission and that he would receive for this plan the sum of 100 guineas and his out-of-pocket expenses'. The drawing was produced showing an 'effect quite striking to the eye: a unification of two original structures into one with, in particular, a diamond feature in the left hand building caused by the arrangement of the roof line and the windows placed in the top part of the old portal frame building'. The plan was passed to the defendants, who made certain amendments and obtained planning permission. Stovin-Bradford had presented his account for the agreed 'nominal' 100 guineas, headed it 'Statement no. 1' and confirmed that the payment was 'for preparing sketch plans and design drawings in sufficient detail to obtain or apply for planning permission'. With commendable foresight, at the foot of the bill was typed a note saying: 'The copyright of the design remains with the architect and may not be reproduced in any form without his prior written consent'. The defendants proceeded to erect the buildings, and although many details were changed, the result incorporated the particular features of the Stovin-Bradford design to which the trial judge drew notice **1, 2, 3**. At first instance, the trial judge held that there was an infringement and awarded £500 damages as the amount which would have been reasonably chargeable for a licence to make use of the copyright.

8.10 The Court of Appeal judgment in the *Blair* case having been published shortly afterwards, the defendants appealed on the ground that the *Blair* case was decisive authority for the view that whenever an architect prepared plans for obtaining planning permission, the client could use them for the building as he liked without further payment. This time Lord Denning, the Master of the Rolls, referred to the stages of normal service in the RIBA Conditions (now replaced by Architect's Appointment), which he defined as being: (1) plans up to an application for outline planning permission; (2) plans up to an application for detailed planning permission; (3) working drawings and specification for contractor to tender; (4) all an architect's work to completion of the building. (The author has often thought that this would be the most sensible division of the RIBA stages of normal service, but in fact the stages were not so defined in the then existing Conditions – though the stages in the current Architect's Appointment roughly correspond to this division.) Again the judges referred to the provision for termination upon reasonable notice and commented that the scale charges for 'partial services' seemed to be so fixed that they contained an in-built compensation for the use of designs and drawings right through to completion of the work. Lord Denning pointed out that in the *Blair* case charges had been in accordance with the RIBA scale, i.e. ⅙ of the full fee. But in this case the architect had charged on 'agreed nominal fee' basis, and his fee was far less than the percentage fee (which would have been, at ⅙, some £900). The Court of Appeal confirmed that there was an infringement, that an implied licence had not arisen, and that damages of £500 were reasonable.

Conclusions

8.11 From these two decisions it would appear that charging by the RIBA scales for partial services (whether originally contemplated or brought about by a termination) will give rise to an implied licence, while charging a nominal fee will not. The RIBA Architect's Appointment provides that the client will have an express licence to use the drawings only for the specific purpose for which they were prepared, and in particular that the preparation of drawings for obtaining planning permission does not carry with it the right to use them for construction of the building without the architect's express consent (which ought not to be unreasonably withheld).

8.12 The implied licence probably includes a right to modify the plans, although the law is not settled on this point (*Hunter v Fitzroy Robinson* [1978] FSR 167). If the Architect's Appointment does not apply, the probability is that the implied licence will not be revocable by the architect even if his fees have not been paid (this point is not settled law, but see Laddie, Prescott and Vitoria *The Modern Law of Copyright*).

Alterations to architect's drawings and works of architecture

8.13 If the client alters the plans or the completed building, the probability is that he will not thereby be in breach of the architect's copyright (*Hunter v Fitzroy Robinson*). However, the client may not 'sell or hire' buildings or plans as the unaltered work of the architect (see paragraph 11 below dealing with moral rights).

9   Remedies for infringement

Injunction

9.01 An injunction can be obtained to prevent the construction of a building that would infringe the copyright in another building, even if that building is part-built. Section 17 of the 1956 Act, provided that no injunction could be granted after the construction of a building had started, nor could an injunction be granted to require the building (so far as it has been constructed) to be demolished. This provision was repealed by the 1988 Act and is not re-enacted in any form.

However, there is a general principle of law that an injunction will not be granted if damages are an adequate relief. It is probable that a court would, in most cases, apply this rule in the case of an injunction to prevent the construction of a building when the construction has substantially commenced. The decision of the court will depend upon all the facts and circumstances of the case.

Damages

9.02 In *Chabot v Davies* the court held that the measure of damages for infringement of the designer's copyright was the amount which he might reasonably have charged for granting a licence to make use of his copyright. In *Meikle v Maufe* the court rejected an argument that the architect might reasonably claim the profit which he would have made if he had been employed to carry out the work which infringed his copyright. 'Such profits do not provide either a mathematical measure for damages or a basis upon which to estimate damages. Copyright is not the sickle which reaps an architect's profit.'

Mr Justice Graham in the *Stovin-Bradford* case confirmed the licence fee basis of the two earlier cases and awarded £500 against the plaintiff's request for £1000 and the defendant's suggestion of between £10 and £20. Although this point has not been decided with reference to architect's copyright, it would appear that on general principles, exemplary damages could be awarded in addition to the licence fee where the breach was particularly flagrant.

In the case of *Potton Limited v Yorkelose Ltd* (17 FSR [1990]), the defendants admitted that they had constructed 14 houses, in infringement of the plantiffs' copyright, on a style of house named 'Grandsen'. The defendants' houses were substantial reproductions of the plantiffs' Grandsen drawings and they had copied the drawings for obtaining outline planning permission and detailed planning permission. It was held that the plantiffs were entitled to the profits realised on the sale of the houses, apportioned to include profits attributable to (i) the purchase, landscaping and sale of the land on which the houses were built; (ii) any increase in value of the houses during the interval between the completion of

the houses and their sale; and (iii) the advertising, marketing and selling of the houses.

In the case of *Charles Church Development plc v Cronin* (17 FSR [1990]) the defendants admitted that they had had a house built based on plans which were the copyright of the plaintiff. The distinction between this case and *Potton Ltd v Yorkelose Ltd* is that in the former case the houses were built for sale and had been sold, whereas in this case the house had not been sold and the plaintiffs had obtained an injunction to prevent its sale. In the former case the plaintiff sued for an account of profits. In the latter case the claim was for compensatory damages for the loss caused by the infringement. The Judge held that the measure of damages was a fair fee for a licence to use the drawings, based on what an architect would have charged for the preparation of drawings. The architect's fee should be calculated on the basis that the architect would have provided the whole of the basic services – in that case 8.5% of the building costs.

10   Industrial designs

10.01 The law on this subject is complicated and extremely technical. It is not proposed to deal with this matter at length, but merely to warn architects, who may be commissioned to design articles or components capable of mass reproduction, to seek professional advice before entering into any agreement commissioning the design of such articles or components or assigning or licensing the rights therein.

Moreover, any architect who does design such articles or components should seek professional advice as to what steps should be taken to protect them. Industrial design falls mid-way between copyright (not registrable in the UK), which is concerned with 'artistic quality', and patents, which must be registered and are not concerned with artistic quality but with function and method of manufacture. The law on industrial designs was considerably changed by the 1988 Act. The present law is thus contained in the Registered Designs Act 1949 (as amended by the 1988 Act) and the 1988 Act.

Design registration

10.02 Certain designs which are intended for industrial application and which possess an element of eye appeal may be registered at the Patent Office, under the provisions of the Registered Designs Act 1949.

'In this Act, the expression "design" means features of shape, configuration, pattern of ornament applied to an article by any industrial process or means, being features which in the finished article appeal to and are judged by the eye, but does not include; a method or principle of construction, or features of shape or configuration which are dictated solely by the function which the article has to perform, or are dependent upon the appearance of another article of which the article is intended by the author of the design to form an integral part.' (Registered Designs Act 1949, section 1(1).)

10.03 Unlike copyright, which is negative and entitles the owner to restrain infringements, registration of design is positive and grants to the registered owner the exclusive right to make, sell, hire, etc., any article in respect of which the design is registered. Design registration protects a person who has independently evolved an identical design. For this reason design copyright can subsist, and a registration be valid, only if the design has not previously been used or published in the UK.

Copyright Act 1956

10.04 The Copyright Act 1956 established two sets of rules in respect of artistic designs created before or after 1 June 1957.

The basic principle concerning works created *before* this date is that copyright in the original artistic design may be lost if at the time it was created it was capable of being registered as a design under the Design Acts and the author had intended that his design should be used as a model for multiplication by industrial process. After this date, artistic copyright was lost only in respect of designs actually used for industrial reproduction and only in so far as so used. Copyright protection continued for any form of user, and as the date of actual use is what mattered, previous publication of the artistic work did not prevent a subsequent registration of the design for industrial application.

Design Copyright Act 1968

10.05 The policy behind the 1968 Act was simple: the Copyright Acts were concerned with articles of artistic craftsmanship, not mass-productions. The Registered Designs Act 1949 provided all the protection necessary for industrial designs, and those who did not avail themselves of it had only themselves to blame – there was no need for two hammers to hit one nail. Unhappily, design pirates often proved to be so much quicker than the Registrar that they frequently pinched the nail before the hammer fell. This led to the passing of the Design Copyright Act 1968, which amended the relevant section of the 1956 Act so that industrial designs which were also artistic works (and these include design and production drawings) enjoyed artistic copyright for a period of 15 years. Purely functional designs, incapable of registration, enjoyed copyright protection for 50 years plus life.

Protection by registration

10.06 Registered design protection lasts for 5 years, on payment of fees, and is renewable up to 25 years. The owner of the registered design would normally be the original author, and therefore the copyright owner as well, but frequently manufacturers who commission a component insist upon the design being registered in their names.

Definition of industrial use

10.07 Design is taken to have been used industrially for the purposes of the Registered Designs Act if it is applied to more than 50 articles.

Copyright, Designs and Patents Act 1988

10.08 The Act largely abolished copyright protection for most industrial designs and instead introduced a new unregistered right described as 'design right'. 'Design' means the design of any aspect of the shape or configuration (whether internal or external) or the whole or part of an article.

It should be noted that design right does not subsist in a method or principle of construction, nor does it subsist in surface decoration. Moreover, it does not subsist in features of shape or configuration of an article which enables the article to be connected to, or placed in, around or against, another article so that either article may perform its function; nor must it be dependent upon the appearance of another article of which the article is intended by the designer to be an integral part. This means that designs of spare parts are normally excluded from design right protection. Because design right subsists additionally to and does not replace artistic copyright, the exclusions from design right protection do not remove artistic copyright protection from, for example, surface decoration.

Design right does not subsist unless and until the design has been recorded in a design document or an article has been made to the design.

Design right expires 15 years from the end of the calendar year in which the design was first recorded in a design document or an article was made to the design. Alternatively, if articles made to the design are made available for sale or hire within five years from the end of that calendar year, the design right will expire 10 years from the end of the calendar year in which that first occurred.

To qualify for design right protection the requirements set out in sections 217 to 221 of the Act must be met: these are too detailed to be set out here but have similarity to the qualification requirements described in para 3 above. However, the differences are such that reference must be made to the actual sections.

Conclusion

10.09 Any architect who designs something which he can foresee might have an industrial application is advised to consult a solicitor or a chartered patent agent before he publishes the design in any way. If he does reveal the design to a manufacturer before registration, his only remaining legal weapon may be an action for misuse of confidential information.

11 Moral rights

11.01 Moral rights of authors have existed in all continental European legal systems for many years, but the 1988 Act introduced them to UK law for the first time.

11.02 There are four basic categories of moral rights contained in the Act:

1. the right to be identified as author;
2. the right to object to derogatory treatment of work;
3. false attribution of work;
4. the right of privacy of certain photographs and films.

11.03 Under section 77(4)(c) of the Act the author of a work of architecture in the form of a building or a model for a building, has the right to be identified whenever copies of a graphic work representing it, or of a photograph of it, are issued to the public.

Section 77(5) also provides that the author of a work of architecture in the form of a building also has the right to be identified on the building as constructed, or, where more than one building is constructed to the design, on the first to be constructed.

The right must be asserted by the author on any assignment of copyright in the work or by instrument in writing signed by the author. In the case of the public exhibition as an artistic work (for example, the inclusion of a model of a building in an exhibition), the right can be asserted by identifying the author on the original or copy of the work, or on a frame, mount or other thing to which the work is attached. If the author grants a licence to make copies of the work, then the right can be asserted for exhibitions by providing in the licence that the author must be identified on copies which are publicly exhibited.

There are certain exceptions to the right of which the most important is that it does not apply to works originally vested in the author's employer (see para 5.02).

11.04 The author of a literary, dramatic, musical or autistic work has the right to object to his work being subjected to derogatory treatment.

'Treatment' means any addition to, deletion from or alteration to or adaptation of the work. The treatment is derogatory if it amounts to distortion or mutilation of the work or is otherwise prejudicial to the honour or reputation of the author.

The right in an artistic work is infringed by the commercial publication or exhibition in public of a derogatory treatment of the work, or a broadcast or the inclusion in a cable programme service of a visual image of a derogatory treatment of the work.

In the case of a work of architecture in the form of a model of a building the right is infringed by issuing copies of a graphic work representing or of a photograph of a derogatory treatment of the work.

However, and most importantly, the right is not infringed in the case of a work of architecture in the form of a building. But if a building is the subject of a derogatory treatment, the architect is entitled to have his identification on the building as its architect removed.

In the case of works which vested originally in the author's employer the right does not apply.

11.05 In the case of a literary, dramatic, musical or artistic work, a person has the right not to have its authorship falsely attributed to him. Thus an architect can prevent a building which he has not designed being attributed to him as its architect.

11.06 The right to privacy of certain films and photographs applies only to films and photographs commissioned for private and domestic purposes and accordingly is hardly relevant here.

11.07 The rights to be identified as an author of a work and to object to derogatory treatment of a work subsist as long as copyright subsists in the work. The right to prevent false attribution continues to subsist until 20 years after a person's death.

11.08 Moral rights can be waived by an instrument in writing signed by the person entitled to the right. However, moral rights may not be assigned to a third party although they pass on death as part of the author's estate and can be disposed of by his will.

12 Law of copyright in Scotland

12.01 There is no difference between the law of copyright in Scotland and England and the new Copyright Designs and Patents Act 1988 applies equally to both countries with the exception of sections 287 and 292, which deal with Patents County Courts and section 301 which grants the Great Ormond Street Hospital permanent copyright in Peter Pan, all of which apply only to England.

18

Architects and the Law of Employment

PATRICK ELIAS QC
NICHOLAS VINEALL

1 Sources and institutions

1.01 The law of employment is a mixture of rules developed at common law (see Chapter 1) and those laid down by Parliament. The latter are playing an increasingly important part, sometimes modifying and sometimes supplementing the common law rules.

1.02 A useful basic division can be drawn between individual employment law, which is concerned with the relationship between employers and workers, and collective labour relations law, which regulates the relationship between employers and trade unions.

Individual employment law

1.03 The basic relationship between the employer and the individual worker is defined by the contract of employment. This is the starting point for determining the rights and liabilities of parties. But as we shall see below, the last 20 years have seen the emergence of a whole range of statutory rights relating to such matters as unfair dismissal, redundancy, and maternity rights. Furthermore, it is a fundamental principle that, save in certain very exceptional cases, it is not open to the parties to contract out of these rights. They provide what is sometimes called a 'floor of rights', below which the rights of employees cannot sink. Although these rights originated in different statutes, they are now found consolidated in the Employment Protection (Consolidation) Act 1978, though further amendments have been introduced by the Employment Act 1980.

1.04 An important feature of these rights is that they are not enforced in the courts in the usual way. Contractual rights arising directly out of the contract of employment are, but these new statutory rights are enforced in industrial tribunals. These tribunals consist of a lawyer-chairman and two other persons, one drawn from a panel nominated by the TUC, and the other from a panel nominated by the CBI and other employers' organizations. All three members of the tribunal should be impartial, and indeed decisions are generally unanimous. The purpose behind the creation of the tribunals is to establish a system for hearing employment disputes which will be cheaper, quicker, more accessible, and generally more informal than the courts. The intention is to enable the worker to represent himself if necessary (and this frequently happens, since there is no legal aid available for cases before tribunals). Furthermore, it does not cost the employee anything to take a case (unless he pays lawyers to represent him) and whichever party loses he will not have to pay costs to the other side unless he was frivolous, vexatious, or otherwise unreasonable in bringing or defending the case.

1.05 Two further points about these tribunal hearings are worth noting. First, in most cases which go to the tribunals (notably unfair dismissals and those where sex or race discrimination is alleged) a conciliation officer seeks to bring about a settlement of the case before it is heard by the tribunal. These officers are employed by the Advisory, Conciliation and Arbitration Service (ACAS), and, like the tribunals themselves, they are to be found throughout the country. They have no power to compel anyone to discuss the case with them. But it is often advisable to do so, because a settlement can save both publicity and the costs of the action. There is another reason, too, why co-operation is advisable. If employer and employee agree that for a certain sum the employee will not pursue his claim for unfair dismissal, this is not binding upon the employee. He cannot be required to sign away his statutory rights. Consequently, he can change his mind and make a claim (though if the employee is successful, any payment made by the employer will be taken into account when assessing compensation). However, if the agreement is made under the auspices of the conciliation officer – even if it is in fact drawn up by the parties themselves – it is binding upon the employee. This is one of the exceptions to the principle that the employee cannot sign away his rights.

The second point to note about the tribunals system is that there is an appeal from the industrial tribunal, but only on a point of law, to the Employment Appeal Tribunal (EAT). This is technically a branch of the High Court (see Chapter 1) but is differently constituted, consisting of a judge and two others with experience in industrial relations, rather than a single judge alone. Appeals from the EAT then go to the Court of Appeal, and any final appeal is to the House of Lords.

Collective labour relations law

1.06 The law regulating collective labour relations is still significantly the law of the jungle, being a power relationship. However, the law does regulate this relationship in various ways. First, it sets limits to the industrial sanctions which can lawfully be used by the parties. This area of the law is highly complex, and it is not considered further in this chapter. Second, the state provides conciliation and arbitration services (ACAS) to help promote the peaceful settlement of disputes. Finally, various rights are given to recognized trade unions, i.e. those which have been recognized by employers, and also to the officials and members of recognized trade unions (see para 4).

2 The contract of employment

2.01 Every worker has a contract with his employer. But a distinction is drawn in law between employees and independent contractors. The former are integrated into the organization of the business, and work under what is termed a contract of service. In contrast, the latter perform a specific function and are usually in business on their own account – e.g. the plumber or window cleaner – and work under a contract for services. In borderline cases the distinction is often very difficult to draw. And the description of the parties as to their status is not decisive, though it will be a factor to consider in a marginal case. The main importance of the distinction in the field of employment law is that only employees working under a contract of service are eligible to benefit from most of the statutory rights, e.g. unfair dismissal, redundancy, and maternity. In addition, an employer may be vicariously liable for the torts committed by his employees, but only rarely for those of independent contractors (see Chapter 4).

Creating the contract: control of recruitment

2.02 The basic principle is that the contract of employment is a voluntary agreement. This means that the employer can choose both with whom he will contract and the terms on which he is willing to contract. However, statute law has curbed this freedom in a number of ways. In relation to recruitment, the employer can choose to employ whomsoever he like, save that under the Sex Discrimination Act 1975 he cannot discriminate against a person because of his or her sex or marital status, and under the Race Relations Act 1976 he cannot discriminate on grounds of race, colour, ethnic or national origins, or nationality. But other forms of discrimination, such as against trade unionists or non-unionists, or on grounds of age, disability, religion, or politics, are not directly made unlawful.

The anti-discrimination laws

2.03 The scope of sex and race discrimination legislation is quite significant. It covers not merely recruitment to employment but also promotion and any other non-contractual aspects of employment. For example, if the employer gives certain benefits, e.g. cheap loans or mortgages, or training opportunities, he cannot grant these on a discriminatory basis. Also, it is not only direct discrimination that is covered, but also indirect discrimination. This arises where the employer stipulates criteria for a job with which ostensibly both men and women can comply, but in reality a considerably smaller proportion of one sex than the other can meet the criteria, and the complainant has suffered as a result. Unless the employer can justify the criteria, he will be acting unlawfully. A simple example would be an employer who requires applicants for employment to be 6 feet tall and 15 stones. Unless the nature of the job justifies these criteria, it will be discrimination, since obviously a considerably smaller proportion of women than men can meet these conditions. Under this indirect form of discrimination, age discrimination has been held to constitute an indirect form of sex discrimination. The civil service would not accept persons over the age of 28. A woman complained that this in practice operated as a form of discrimination against women because, although in theory both men and women could meet the criteria of being 28 or under, in reality a considerably smaller proportion of women could do so whilst remaining on the labour market because of the responsibility of having and rearing children. The EAT upheld her claim (*Price* v *Civil Service Commission* [1978] 1 All ER 1228).

2.04 Exceptionally, sex discrimination is permitted where it is a genuine occupational qualification, for example on the grounds of physiology or decency. The most relevant permissible discrimination for architects is where a job is given in the UK, but it requires duties to be performed in a country whose laws and customs are such that a woman could not effectively carry out the task. Even then, it must be *necessary* for the employer to discriminate for this reason. So if he already employs a sufficient number of male architects to cater adequately for that particular foreign connection, this exception will not apply. Advertisements for job vacancies also need careful drafting to avoid any suggestion of unlawful discrimination.

2.05 Those who consider they have been discriminated against may complain to an industrial tribunal. If the complaint is successful, the tribunal may award a declaration of the rights of the parties, an order requiring the employer to take such action as is necessary to obviate the adverse effects of the discrimination, or compensation. The maximum at present is £8,925, and may include compensation for injured feelings. The legal employer is normally liable, but if the employer has taken all reasonably practical steps to eliminate the discrimination, e.g. has a clear policy and monitors it, then he can escape liability. In that case, the particular managers who discriminate will be personally liable.

The interview

2.06 An employee being interviewed is under no obligation gratuitously to disclose details of his past. However, he must not misrepresent it, save that in certain exceptional cases he may lawfully be able to deny that he has committed any criminal offences if his convictions are 'spent convictions' within the meaning of the Rehabilitation of Offenders Act 1974. Whether or not a conviction is spent depends upon the nature of the offence and the period since the conviction.

The terms of the contract

2.07 The basic position, consistent with the notion of freedom of contract, is that it is up to the parties to agree to the terms which will bind them. Exceptionally, terms of the agreement may be struck out as being contrary to public policy, e.g. a term in unreasonable restraint or trade (see para 3.34). But generally the parties will be held to their bargain. From an employer's point of view it is sensible for all the important terms of the contract to be committed to paper and for the job to be conditional on their acceptance. This may eliminate later confusion and disagreements.

2.08 However, in the sphere of employment law the contract is not always expressly stipulated in this way. A number of points need to be noted. First, in many situations there is no real bargaining between individuals at all. The terms of employment are agreed between the employer and a recognized trade union negotiating collective agreements, and variations in those terms occur as the collective agreements are amended from time to time. So the collective agreement operates as the source of the terms of the individual contract of employment.

Secondly, even where terms are expressly agreed between the parties to the contract, they will rarely cover all the matters that will arise in the course of the employment relationship. So the express terms will have to be supplemented by implied terms. These implied terms may be usefully divided into two categories. Some will arise because of the particular relationship between the employer and the employee, and will often depend upon the customs and practices of a particular firm. For example, it may have become the practice of overtime to be worked in certain circumstances, or for employees to be more flexible in the range of tasks they perform than their specific job obligations would suggest. Once practices of this kind become reasonable, well-known, and certain, they will become contractual

duties. Other implied terms depend not so much on the particular employment relationship but are imposed as an incident of the general relationship between employers and employees. The judges have said that certain duties will be implied into all employment relationships, e.g. a duty on the employee not to disclose confidential information to third parties, to take reasonable care in the exercise of his duties, and to show good faith in his dealings with the employer. Likewise there are some implied duties imposed on the employer, e.g. a duty to treat the employee with respect, and to take reasonable care for his health and safety.

Equal Pay Act 1970

2.09 Thirdly, it is unlawful for the employer to treat women less favourably because of their sex. This is regulated by the Equal Pay Act 1970, which came into force at the end of 1975. Strictly it is a misnomer, for it covers not merely pay but also all contractual terms and conditions of employment. Broadly it states that if a woman is employed on like work with a man (and this involves looking at what they actually do, and not what they might be required to do under their contracts) or on work which is rated as equivalent on a job evaluation scheme, then she is entitled to have the same terms and conditions applied to her as apply to him. An 'Equality Clause' automatically becomes part of her contract of employment. The main exception to this is where there are differences which stem from a material difference, other than sex, between the situations of the man and the woman. For example, men and women may both be employed doing the same work, but the man may be employed on the night shift and the woman on the day. Here the man could be paid an extra premium for night work, but the basic rates would have to be the same (*Dugdale* v *Kraft Foods Ltd* [1977] 1 All ER 454). Again, if an employee is demoted because of illness, but retains his old wage, this will usually be justified.

2.10 However, if the woman is not employed on like work, she cannot complain under the Act because she considers that the differential between the respective rates of pay is too great. Indeed, in one case a woman who was a leader of a group of adventure playground workers was paid less than one of the men in the group. But the EAT held that since her job was more responsible than the man's, this meant that it was not like work, and consequently she could not claim the same pay (*Waddington* v *Leicester Council for Voluntary Services* [1977] 2 All ER 633)!

2.11 A woman who claims that her employer is infringing the Equal Pay Act may take a case to an industrial tribunal. She may be awarded arrears of pay, but not for a period exceeding two years prior to the date on which the proceedings were instituted.

Race Relations Act 1970

2.12 It is also unlawful, under the Race Relations Act 1976, to discriminate on grounds of race, colour, ethnic or national origins, or nationality in respect of the terms of employment.

Statement of the main terms of the contract

2.13 The sources of the contract of employment are so diverse that Parliament in 1963 thought it desirable that the employer should give to the employee a written statement of the principal terms. Subsequent legislation has added to these terms. They should be given to all employees working 16 hours or more a week, within 13 weeks of their starting work. Alternatively, the employer can refer the employee to some document, e.g. a collective agreement, which is readily available and wherein all the relevant information can be found. But the written statement is not itself the contract of employment; it is merely the employer's version of the contract and can be challenged by the employee.

2.14 However, if the employer does in fact draw up a proper written contract, this will be binding upon the employee, provided he accepts it as such. If the contract contains all the information that would have to be put in the written particulars, the latter can be dispensed with.

Maternity rights

2.15 In addition to the protections afforded by the Sex Discrimination and Equal Pay Acts, women are given three separate rights relating to maternity. First, a woman cannot be fairly dismissed because of her pregnancy or a reason connected with it, unless she is incapable of doing her normal job as a result. Even then she must be offered any other available job which is suitable for her to do in her pregnant state, though she is not obliged to accept the job offered. Second, in certain circumstances she is entitled to maternity pay when absent. This arises where she works until at least the eleventh week before the date of confinement, has two years continuous employment by that time, and gives three weeks notice or, if this is not possible, as much notice as is reasonably practicable, that she will be leaving. She is then entitled to pay for up to six weeks. The amount is $9/10$ of a week's pay, minus any state maternity benefit, whether she actually receives it or not. Initially the employer pays the woman concerned, but he can recover the whole amount from the Maternity Fund, which is financed by a levy on all employers.

2.16 Finally, provided the conditions outlined above in relation to maternity pay are met, a woman will generally be entitled to resume her old job after the baby is born. She can claim her job back any time up to 29 weeks after the date of confinement. If this is refused, she is treated in law as having been dismissed for the reason for which she was refused her job back. Although an employer might very exceptionally be able to show that there is a good reason and that the dismissal is fair – e.g. where she holds a vital post, and it was impossible to employ a temporary replacement or divide her work among other employees – this will be very rare indeed. Usually a refusal to take her back will constitute an unfair dismissal. However, an exception is provided in circumstances where the employer can show that it is simply not reasonably practicable to give her the job back. In this case, if the employer employs fewer than five employees, he need offer her no alternative employment at all; but if he employs more than five, he must offer her suitable alternative employment, which must not be on substantially less favourable terms than those applying to the original job.

3 Dismissal

Wrongful dismissal at common law

3.01 The most significant intervention of statute law in the area of individual rights has been in relation to dismissal. At common law, provided the employer terminates the contract in accordance with its terms, the employee will have no redress. Generally this means that the employer must give the employee that notice to which he is entitled under his contract of employment. The relevant period of notice will often be specified in the contract, but if it is not, then it will be a reasonable period. However, statute law now lays down a minimum period of notice which must be given, whatever the contract says. This is 1 week's notice for each year of employment up to 12 years, i.e. if 2 years' employment, 2 weeks' notice; 6 years', 6 weeks'; 10 years', 10 weeks'; 14 years', 12 weeks', because this is the maximum minimum period! The contract may stipulate more than this, but not less. Note that this is the notice that the employer must give

to the employee. It does not operate the other way. An employee with over 4 weeks' service must give 1 week's notice, but that is the only minimum requirement. Again, though, the contract might specify a longer period.

3.02 If the employer dismisses with no notice or with inadequate notice, then this is termed a 'wrongful dismissal', and the employee will have a remedy in the ordinary courts for breach of contract. The only exception is where the employee has committed an act of gross misconduct; then he may be lawfully summarily dismissed. But the courts do not readily find that misconduct is gross. Such conduct might include dishonesty or physical violence.

Unfair dismissal

3.03 The common law, then, sees a man's job essentially in contractual terms. Provided the contract is complied with, the employee has no grounds of complaint. This means that the reason for a dismissal can rarely be questioned at common law. As long as the employer has given the required notice, it matters not whether it is because the employee is dishonest, or smokes cigarettes, or has blond hair. Managerial prerogative is left untouched. But unfair dismissal does question management's reasons in a much more fundamental way. It requires the employer to have a fair reason for the dismissal, and to be acting reasonably in relying upon it.

The basic law of unfair dismissal can be considered under the following heads.

Eligibility

3.04 The employee must be eligible to take his complaint. This means he must be working at least 16 hours a week (or 8 hours after 5 years); he must have 2 years' continuous employment, he must be below the normal retiring age for the job or, if there is none, 65 if a man or 60 if a woman; he cannot claim if he ordinarily works abroad (though if he works in various countries but his base is in Britain, he will not fall into this category); and he must present his claim within 3 months of the dismissal.

Dismissal

3.05 The employee must show that he has been dismissed. Sometimes what in form appears to be a resignation will in law constitute a dismissal (known as constructive dismissal). For example, if the employer unilaterally reduces the wages or alters the hours of work, the employee may leave and claim that he has been dismissed (though the dismissal is not inevitably unfair). Moreover, if the employer takes action which involves destroying the trust and confidence in the employment relationship, this will likewise entitle the employee to leave and claim that he has been dismissed. For instance, such conduct as falsely and without justification accusing an employee of theft, failing to support a supervisor, upbraiding a supervisor in the presence of her subordinates, and a director using intemperate language and criticizing his personal secretary in front of a third party, have all been held to amount to conduct which justifies the employee leaving and claiming that he has been dismissed. In one case a judge even suggested that unwanted amorous advances to a female employee would fall into that category! Technically all these matters constitute a breach of contract, though, of course, it is hardly likely that they would be expressly dealt with in any written document. In addition, a refusal to renew a fixed term contract will amount to a dismissal (see para 3.27).

A fair reason

3.06 Once a dismissal is established, the employer must show that he has a fair reason for the dismissal. A number of reasons are specifically stated to be fair – misconduct,

capability, redundancy, the fact that a statutory provision prohibits a person from working, and any other substantial reason.

Capability covers both inherent incompetence and incapability arising from ill health. The latter may include a prolonged absence or perhaps a series of short, intermittent absences. Some other substantial reason is a residual category covering a potentially wide range of reasons. Perhaps the most important is that it may justify dismissals where the employer takes steps to protect his business interests. For example, an employer who was concerned about his employees leaving and setting up in competition decided to require them to enter into a restraint of trade agreement (see para 3.34). Some employees refused to sign the agreement and were dismissed. They claimed that the dismissal was unfair. They had merely kept to the terms of their contract; it was the employer who was seeking to change them. Nevertheless, the dismissal was considered to be fair. The employer was entitled to require this change, under threat of ultimate dismissal, in order to protect his interests (*R S Components Ltd* v *Irwin* [1973] ICR 535). Again, employees who are dismissed because they refuse to accept new hours of work introduced by the employer may well be found to have been fairly dismissed if the changes had been made in order to improve efficiency.

The employer must be acting reasonably

3.07 But it is not enough simply for the employer to have a fair reason. In addition, the tribunal must be satisfied that he is acting reasonably in relying upon that fair reason. Many factors may have to be considered in determining this question. The length of service of the employee, the need for the employer to act consistently, the size and resources of the company or firm will all be relevant factors. For example, a small firm cannot as readily accommodate the lengthy illness of an employee as a large organization.

Procedural factors are often important in these cases. ACAS has produced a code of practice on disciplinary matters – Disciplinary Practice and Procedures in Employment. Like other codes, it is not directly legally binding but should be taken into account in any legal proceedings before a tribunal.

3.08 The code emphasizes the need for warnings, a chance to state a case, and a right of appeal. Usually two warnings will be necessary before the dismissal is carried out. But the code is not sacred: it is advisable for the employer to follow its guidelines in most cases, but a failure to do so will not make a dismissal automatically unfair. For example, there are a number of situations in which the warning procedure can be dispensed with, e.g. where the employee commits gross misconduct, or is negligent in circumstances where the employer cannot afford a repeat performance (e.g. the airline pilot who crashed his plane on landing), or makes it plain that he is at odds with the system of work developed by the employer and intends to do things his own way.

3.09 Employers have got to be especially careful to ensure that the procedure they adopt when deciding to dismiss somebody is fair in itself. The employer cannot say 'I know the procedure I used was unfair, but as it turns out it would not have made any difference to the result even if I had operated a fair procedure'. The view of the courts is that an employee dismissed under an unfair procedure has (in almost all cases) been unfairly dismissed. (See the important case of *Polkey* v *Dayton Services Limited* 1988 ICR 142). Such an employee will probably not recover much compensation if the only thing that made his dismissal unfair was the procedure, but in some circumstances a procedural flaw can make the difference between a large award and no award at all.

3.10 Strictly the ACAS code of practice and procedure applies only to disciplinary cases, but analogous requirements have been required in other dismissals. For example, in illness cases it is hardly apt to talk of warning the employee that he will be dismissed if he does not return. 'Counselling' is a more appropriate term. The employer should consult with the employee and his doctor about the illness, its likely duration, and the chances of the employee being able to do the same work on his return. In the light of this evidence, together with the need of the employer to have the work done and the extent to which he might be expected to be able to cover the absence, the employer must decide at what point it is reasonable to dismiss the employee. Consultation in redundancy cases is also important.

3.11 One general point in these cases is that it is not open to the tribunal to find a dismissal unfair merely because it disagrees with the employer. To put it colloquially, it must not 'second guess' the employer. For example, in a disciplinary case a tribunal might conclude that it would probably have given a further, final warning before dismissing. But that does not necessarily make the dismissal unfair. It is often perfectly possible for there to be a number of reasonable responses to a particular situation. One employer might dismiss, another might give a final warning, yet both may be acting within the range of reasonable responses to particular conduct. Provided the employer acts in a way in which a reasonable employer might have acted, the tribunal should not find the dismissal to be unfair.

Remedies

3.12 There are three remedies envisaged: reinstatement, which means the employee being given the old job back and treated in all respects as though he had never been dismissed; re-engagement, which may involve being taken back in a different job, or perhaps in the same job but without back-pay, or on slightly different terms; and compensation. A tribunal must consider the three remedies in the order just given. In deciding whether to order reinstatement or re-engagement, the tribunal must consider three factors: (1) whether the employee wants his job back – if not, the tribunal must go straight on to consider compensation; (2) whether it is practicable to take the employee back – and in regard to a small firm it is likely that a tribunal will find that it is not because of personality conflicts involved; and (3) whether the employee has caused or contributed to his own dismissal – if he has, at least to any significant degree, he is unlikely to be awarded his job back.

3.13 Usually employees do not want reinstatement or re-engagement, so the tribunal simply assesses compensation. However, even if reinstatement or re-engagement is ordered, the employer is not finally compelled to obey the order, though he will have to pay additional compensation if he refuses to do so.

3.14 The usual compensation is made up of two elements. One is the basic award, which is calculated in essentially the same way as a redundancy payment (see para 3.22). The other is the compensatory award, which is designed to take account of the actual loss suffered by the employee following from the dismissal. This will depend on such factors as when he is likely to obtain new employment, and what he will then earn. Obviously the assessment is very approximate. Furthermore, the amount will be reduced if the employee has caused or contributed to his own dismissal, the tribunal deciding what reduction would be just and equitable in all the circumstances, e.g. the tribunal may find that the employee is 50 per cent to blame and reduce his compensation by half. The compensatory award is subject to a final maximum level of £8,925.

Redundancy

3.15 Sometimes jobs come to an end because there is no more work for the firm or for particular employees employed by it. Usually a dismissal for these reasons will constitute a dismissal for redundancy as defined by the Employment Protection (consolidation) Act 1978, though since the concept of redundancy as defined in that Act is a rather technical one, it should not be assumed that every case where the employee is dismissed for business efficiency reasons and through no fault of his own will be a redundancy.

3.16 The three main situations in which a redundancy arises are (1) where the employer closes down altogether; (2) where the employer moves the place of work (though it should be noted that the place of work is where the employee can be required to work under his contract and not where he normally works, e.g. if the contract stipulates that he can be required to work anywhere in Great Britain and the firm moves from London to Glasgow, but his job is still available in Glasgow, this is not a redundancy); and (3) where the need for employees to do a particular kind of work has ceased or diminished.

Establishing a redundancy claim

3.17 As with unfair dismissal the employee must jump a number of hurdles before he can successfully claim for redundancy.

Eligibility

3.18 He must be eligible to present the claim. In order to do this he must be working normally at least 16 hours a week (or 8 hours after 5 years' service), have 2 years' employment over the age of 18, be below 65, and normally work in Great Britain. (Exceptionally, even if he normally works abroad he will be entitled to claim, this being where he is in Great Britain at the employer's instructions at the time of dismissal.)

Dismissal

3.19 This is defined in the same way as for unfair dismissal. So constructive dismissal applies here also. One point to note, though, is that an advanced warning of redundancy at some time in the future, with no specific date of dismissal being given, is not in law a dismissal. Consequently, an employee who leaves in response to this warning may well be disentitled from claiming under the Act.

Redundancy

3.20 There must be a redundancy situation as outlined above.

Offers of alternative employment

3.21 Once these three hurdles are crossed, the employee is *prima facie* entitled to redundancy pay. But he loses that entitlement if the employer offers him suitable alternative employment which he unreasonably refuses. The job is unlikely to be considered suitable if it means a significant loss of status or pay. Whether any refusal is reasonable will depend upon the employee's personal circumstances. However, the employee does have a trial period of up to four weeks to decide whether a job is suitable, and within that period he is working without prejudice to his redundancy claim. But, of course, if he refuses the job after the trial period, it will still be open to the employer to claim that it was suitable employment and has been unreasonably refused.

Amount

3.22 The employee's compensation depends on his age, wages at the time he was dismissed, and years of service. Broadly speaking it is ½ a week's pay for a complete year of service between the ages of 18 and 22, 1 week's pay for each year of service between 24 and 41, and 1½ weeks' pay for each complete year of service between 41 and 65. The maximum number of years that can be taken into account is 20. The week's pay is calculated from the gross figure, but is subject to a maximum (at present) of £184 per week. So the most that can be recovered under the statute is for someone with 20 years' service, all over the age of 41, who on dismissal was earning at least £184 per week gross. He will receive £184 × 20 × 1½ = £5,520. Of course, employers may voluntarily pay more than the law requires, or they may be bound to pay more than the law requires by a term in the contract of employment.

3.23 Employees in their 64th year when they are dismissed have their redundancy payment reduced by 1/12 for each month of their 64th year, so that by the time they reach 65 their redundancy payment has reduced to nil. Of course this makes good sense: employees who retire do not get redundancy payments.

3.24 The redundancy fund, which used to help employers meet redundancy payments, has been abolished.

Redundancy and unfair dismissal

3.25 Generally a redundancy is a fair reason for dismissal. But it might occasionally constitute an unfair dismissal, e.g. if the employer selects trade unionists first, or selects on a wholly unreasonable basis, or perhaps fails to consult with the employees affected. In calculating the unfair dismissal compensation, any redundancy payment already made will be taken into account.

Consultation with recognized trade unions and the D of E

3.26 This is discussed in paras 4.04 to 4.06.

Fixed term contracts

3.27 Special rules apply to fixed term contracts. First, if a fixed term contract is not renewed, this in law amounts to a dismissal. But it is not necessarily unfair. In particular, if the employee is taken on for a fixed period and knows in advance that his contract is likely to be temporary and will not be renewed when the fixed term expires, a refusal to renew the contract is likely to be justified. The employer will still have to show that he is acting reasonably in not renewing the contract, but that should not be too difficult in most situations.

3.28 Second, where a fixed term contract is for a year or more, an employee may sign away his rights to unfair dismissal, i.e. he may agree in writing that he will not claim for unfair dismissal if his contract is not renewed once the fixed term ends. This is one of the exceptional cases where an agreement to sign away statutory rights is binding. But such an agreement is not binding as regards dismissals which take effect during the fixed term, e.g. for misconduct. It applies only to the dismissal arising from the non-renewal of the fixed term. Similarly, rights to redundancy may also be signed away, but curiously only where the fixed term is for two years or more.

3.29 This leaves the crucial question: What is a fixed term contract? The answer is one with an ascertainable date of termination (though it is still fixed term even if the parties can terminate it earlier by giving notice). So if the contract is to last for a particular task, and it is impossible to predict how long the job will last, this is not a fixed term contract. When it comes to an end, it terminates because the task is completed. But this in law will not constitute a dismissal. Consequently, even if the employer is acting unreasonably in not continuing to employ the employee, the latter will have no claim for unfair dismissal.

Reference

3.30 An employer is under no legal duty to provide a reference. If he does so, there are certain legal pitfalls he must take care to avoid. If the statement is untrue, it may be libellous and he could be liable in defamation. However, he will be able to rely upon the defence of qualified privilege, which means that he will not be liable unless it can be shown that the statement was inspired by malice, i.e. was deliberately false and intended to injure the employee.

3.31 An employer who hires and employee on the basis of an untrue reference may bring a legal action against the employer issuing the reference. If it is deliberately false, the liability will be for deceit. If it is negligently written, e.g. claims are made which he could have discovered were false with some inquiries, liability will probably exist for negligence mis-statement under the doctrine of *Hedley Byrne* v *Heller* [1964] AC 465 (see Chapter 4, para 7).

3.32 Finally, if the employer dismisses an employee for misconduct or incompetence, but then proceeds to write him a glowing reference, he may find difficulty in convincing the tribunal that the reason for which he dismissed was, in fact, the true reason.

Duties on ex-employees

3.33 Once the contract is terminated, this does not mean that there are no further duties imposed on the ex-employee. In particular, the employee is not free to divulge confidential information or trade secrets to rivals. However, he can use his own individual skill and experience, e.g. organizational ability, even though that was gained as a result of working for the former employer. But the distinction between the knowledge which can and cannot be imparted is vague.

Restricting competition: restraint of trade

3.34 In addition, the employee may be prevented from setting up in competition with his former employer. But this will be so only if he entered into an express clause in his contract of employment which prohibited such competition. Even then, such clauses will be binding only if they are reasonable and not contrary to the public interest. They must not be drawn wider than is necessary to protect the employer's interests; otherwise they will be considered to be in unreasonable restraint of trade and therefore void. Reasonable restrictions might prevent an architect from soliciting the clients of his former employer, and they may even encompass restrictions on the employee's right to compete within a certain area for a particular time. But if the area is drawn too widely, or the duration too long, the clause will be void and unenforceable.

4 Collective labour relations law

4.01 As mentioned above, the main provisions in the area of collective labour relations law are concerned with giving certain rights to unions and their officials. However, these are in practice given only to *recognized* trade unions, i.e. those with which the employer is willing to negotiate. There is no

The Court of Session Second Division March 1812 312

legal procedure by which a union can compel an employer to recognize it. The ultimate sanctions for non-recognition are industrial, not legal.

The consequences of recognition

4.02 Once a union is recognized by an employer, the following consequences follow.

Disclosure of information

4.03 The unions have a right to receive information from the employer without which they would be impeded in collective bargaining and which it is good industrial relations practice to disclose. However, there is a wide range of exceptions, e.g. information received in confidence, or information which would damage the employer's undertakings (such as how tender prices are calculated). Some guidance can be given by the Code of Practice on Disclosure of Information produced by ACAS. It should be emphasized, though, that no information need be divulged until the recognized union asks for it.

Consultation over redundancies

4.04 As soon as the decision to dismiss even a single employee for redundancy has crystallized, the employer should consult with any recognized trade union which negotiates for the group from which the redundancy or redundancies are to be made. This consultation is required even if the persons whom it is proposed to make redundant are not union members. The union should be given such information as the numbers to be made redundant, how they have been selected, and how the dismissals will be effected. The union may make representations upon these proposals, and the employer must in turn reply to their points, though he is not obliged to accept them.

4.05 In the case of collective redundancies, certain minimum time limits are specified. Where the employer is proposing to dismiss over 10 workers in a 30-day period he must give at least 30 days' notice, and where over 100 workers in a 90-day period, at least 90 days'. But these periods will not apply if

there are special circumstances making it impossible for him to comply with them, e.g. a sudden and unforseen loss of work.

4.06 In the case of these collective redundancies, it is also necessary to notify the Department of Employment.

Reasonable time off for union officials and members

4.07 Union officials have a right to reasonable time off with pay for industrial relations activities involving the employer, e.g. negotiating, handling grievances, and attending training courses connected with these matters. What is reasonable will depend upon such factors as the size of the firm, the job of the employee, and the number of other officials. Some guidance can be found in the ACAS Code of Practice on Time Off.

4.08 Union members also have a right to reasonable time off, but without pay, for trade union matters, e.g. attending union conferences. Again the ACAS Code of Practice gives some guidance, though its principal message is that it is for employers and unions themselves to negotiate what is reasonable in all circumstances.

Health and safety representatives

4.09 Recognized unions are entitled to appoint safety representatives, who have an important role to play in helping to maintain health and safety standards. This is further discussed in para 5.04.

Dismissal for union membership or non-membership

4.10 Under the Employment Act 1988 it is automatically unfair to dismiss an employee because he does not belong to a particular trade union, or because he has been refused membership of any particular trade union. The closed shop – and the complicated law relating to it – are now both things of the past.

4.11 The other side of the coin is the same. It is also automatically unfair to dismiss an employee because he does belong to a union.

5 Health and safety

5.01 Two major statutes concerned with health and safety apply to offices in which architects are employed. One is the Health and Safety at Work Act 1974, which is concerned with the general responsibility of employers, employees, and the self-employed, with respect to both each other and third parties. The other is the Offices, Shops and Railway Premises Act 1963, and the regulations made thereunder. This establishes in more detail the obligations of the employer in relation to health and safety. (Technically the duties imposed by the 1963 Act rest on the occupier rather than on the employer, but they will usually be the same person.) The infringement of the provisions of either Act involves the commission of a criminal offence. Offences may be committed by the legal employer, individual managers, and employees, for all have duties imposed upon them by the legislation.

The Health and Safety at Work Act 1974

5.02 This Act imposes a general duty on employers to ensure, so far as is reasonably practicable, the safety, health, and welfare of his employees. More specifically, he must provide and maintain safe plant and equipment, ensure that systems of work are safe, that entrances and exits from the working area are safe, and that such information, training, instruction, and supervision is given as will ensure the health and safety of employees at work. In addition, the general public coming onto the premises must not be exposed to health and safety risks.

5.03 If the employer employs more than five employees, he should draw up a health and safety policy and bring it to the attention of employees. This should include a statement of the employer's organizational arrangements for dealing with health and safety.

Employees are under a duty to take reasonable care of their own health and safety and that of fellow employees, to co-operate with the employer in health and safety matters, and not to misuse safety equipment.

Safety representatives and committees

5.04 Where the employer recognizes a trade union, that union is entitled to appoint safety representatives, who must then be consulted by the employer on health and safety matters. In addition, the safety representatives have a right to formally inspect at least once every three months those parts of the premises for which they are responsible; to investigate any reportable accidents, i.e. those that result in the employee being absent for three days or more; and to examine any documents relating to health and safety, save those for which there are specific exemptions, e.g. personal medical records. Furthermore, provided at least two safety representatives request this, the employer must set up a safety committee within three months of the request. This committee may keep under review health and safety policies and performance.

The Offices, Shops and Railway Premises Act 1963

5.05 This Act applies only to premises where the employer employs someone, other than immediate relatives, for more than 21 hours a week. It covers a very wide range of matters which cannot be considered in detail here. They include the need for adequate heating, lighting, ventilation, sanitary conveniences, washing facilities, and drinking water. In addition, the safety requirements include an obligation to maintain all floors, passages, and stairs properly, and to ensure that they are, so far as is reasonably practicable, free from obstruction and slippery surfaces. Details of the provisions are found in an abstract of the Act, published by HMSO (OSR9), which should, by law, be placed in every office, in a prominent position, for the information of employees.

Enforcement of the legislation

5.06 Inspectors are appointed to enforce legislation. Usually offices belonging to local authorities are inspected by inspectors from the Health and Safety Executive, whilst private offices come under the control of environmental health officers employed by the local authority.

5.07 The powers of inspectors are quite wide, having been extended significantly by the Health and Safety at Work Act. They can enter premises uninvited at any reasonable time, require the production of records or documents which the law requires to be kept, and oblige persons to answer questions. They may prosecute in the criminal courts if they find the laws infringed. But, in addition, they can now take effective action without the need to have recourse to the courts. They may issue 'improvement' or 'prohibition' orders. The former oblige the employer to bring his place or premises up to scratch within a certain specified period. The latter actually compel him to stop using the place or premises until the necessary improvements have been made. But prohibition orders can be issued only if the inspector considers that there is a risk of serious personal injury. The employer can appeal to an industrial tribunal against these orders. An appeal suspends the operation of an improvement order until the appeal is heard, but a prohibition order continues in force pending the appeal unless the employer obtains permission to the contrary from a tribunal. Breach of either order is automatically a criminal offence. Indeed, individual managers who are knowingly parties to a breach of the prohibition order may even be sent to prison.

Reporting accidents

5.08 Every employer should keep a record of accidents at the work place. In addition, some accidents may have to be reported to the enforcing authorities. These include fatalities and accidents involving serious personal injury, including those resulting in hospital in-patient treatment. These accidents have to be reported to the authorities by the quickest practicable means, and a written report must be sent within seven days. For other accidents, involving absences from work of three days or more, notification to the authorities is not necessary provided the employer has reasonable grounds to believe that the employee will claim industrial injury benefit. In this case the relevant information will, in any event, be sent to the Department of Health and Social Security, and they will transfer it to the enforcing authorities.

Compensation for accidents at work

5.09 The legislation discussed above is designed to prevent accidents. It establishes standards that can be enforced irrespective of whether an accident has been caused or not. Where accidents have occurred, though, it is not sufficient for the injured worker to know that criminal proceedings may be instituted. He will wish to recover compensation for the loss he has suffered arising from the accident. This may be claimed in one or more of the following ways:

1. Every employer owes a common law duty to take reasonable care to ensure the safety of his employees. More specifically this requires that he should provide safe plant and appliances, adopt safe systems of work, and employ competent employees. If an accident occurs because of a breach of this duty, the employer will be liable.

2. If an accident arises from a breach of the Offices, Shops and Railway Premises Act, then in some circumstances the employee may be able to claim compensation because of the employer's breach of statutory duty. However, no such claim can be made arising out of breach of the Health and Safety at Work Act.

3. The employer may be liable under the Occupiers Liability Act 1954. This imposes a duty of care on occupiers of premises to all those lawfully entering his premises. The standard of the duty is to take all reasonable practicable steps to make the premises safe. A claim under this Act may be made by someone not employed by the occupier.

4. Where a person, whether a worker or a third party, is injured as a result of the negligence of an employee acting in the course of his employment, the employer will be vicariously liable for the injury caused. Even if he is not personally liable under items 1–3, he may still be held responsible.

19

Legal Organization of Architects' Offices

GEORGE YOUNG
SUSANNA FISCHER*

1 Running an architectural business

1.01 The manager of an architectural business, as opposed to the manager of an architectural project, faces a wide variety of legal problems of which the two most important and universal arise from the choice of formal organization he adopts and from his status as employer in a labour-intensive operation. A manager will be concerned with three levels of relationship. First, with relationships between the owners of the business and those with whom they contract, second with relationships between employer and employee, and third with relationships between the several owners of the business.

The first type of relationship is dealt with in Chapter 9. The second type of relationship is dealt with in Chapter 23. This chapter is concerned with the third type of relationship.

1.02 There are no longer any formal restrictions in the professional codes to the structures under which architects carry on their practices. ARCUK advised that the 1931 Registration Act permits architects to practise as partnerships or companies, whether limited or unlimited, provided that the business is under the control and management of a registered architect. The September 1988 RIBA Code states in its preface that 'A member is at liberty to engage in any activity, whether as proprietor, director, principal, partner manager, superintendent, controller or salaried employee or consultant to, any body corporate or unincorporate, or in any other capacity, provided that his conduct complies with the Principles of this Code and the Rules applying to his circumstances'.

1.03 While architects may choose to practise as sole traders, form companies or create larger amalgamations as group practices or consortia, the most common form of association found in architectural businesses is still the partnership. The main choice for architects setting up business is between partnerships and companies. A partnership provides the breadth of expertise a sole trader cannot provide without the formality of incorporating a registered company. The advantages and disadvantages of each will be considered. (See *Checklist 19.4* for a basic outline of the differences between partnerships and companies.)

2 Partnership

2.01 The law of partnership is governed by the Partnership Act 1890. (References to section numbers in the text which follows are references to the Partnership Act 1890.) No one should consider partnership without first having had the

provisions of this Act explained to them, since, unless specified in a partnership agreement, the provisions of the Partnership Act will apply. It may be reassuring to note that this Act is short, more straightforward and more easily understood than most legislation. Partnership is defined in section 1 as 'the relation which subsists between persons carrying on a business in common with a view to profit'. 'Business' will include the practice of architecture. A single act, such as designing a house for an aunt, may not make a business, but if there is a series of such acts, a business exists. 'A view to profit' requires only the intention to make a profit even if the architects fail lamentably in this objective. The requirement of acting in common is important. It may be contrasted with barristers, who are in business with a view to a profit but do not act in common, merely sharing facilities. Unlike a company, a partnership, or firm, has no legal personality. Is is nothing more than the sum total of individuals comprising it.

Formation of partnership

2.02 A partnership is a form of contract (see Chapter 3). Although many architects set up practice in partnership quite casually it is prudent to create the business formally and expressly by a deed of partnership executed under a seal or written articles of partnership. However, the existence of a partnership can sometimes be inferred in law from the behaviour of the parties even if no deed of partnership exists, and despite both parties' vigorous denials that there is indeed a partnership.

Importance of clarity

2.03 Considerable importance may be attached to the existence of a partnership. For example, if two architects work together occasionally over several years and then a case of negligence arises, both can be sued if a partnership exists. If there is no partnership, however, one of them may be out of trouble. It can be vital to a client or supplier of a practice to establish whether he is dealing with a partnership or one man. Architects are recommended on all possible occasions to make the point clear, particularly when they work as group practices and consortia (see Section 4, below).

Sharing facilities and profits

2.04 If two or more architects do not intend to practise in partnership, but merely share facilities, they must take great care to avoid the possibility of third persons with whom any of them has dealings being led to assume that they practise together as partners. Normally, shared ownership of property, even if accompanied by sharing of net profits, is not itself

*George Burnet has advised as to legal organization of offices in Scotland.

evidence of the existence of a partnership. However, profit sharing is prima facie evidence of a partnership, but if it is just one piece of evidence will be weighed equally with all other available evidence. This may be particularly important to architectural practices, since profit-sharing in the form of profit-related bonus payments is quite a common means of remunerating staff. However, payment by profit-sharing will not of itself make an employee a partner in the business, nor will sharing in gross returns if not accompanied by sharing of property from which those returns are derived of itself create a partnership. It is important to draft any contract of employment including any profit-sharing provision very carefully.

Deed of partnership

2.05 Even though there are ways of determining whether a partnership exists, and the 1890 Act sets out terms which apply if partners have nothing written down, it is more satisfactory if intending partners agree they are going into a business together and set out the terms of their relationship in a deed of partnership. The deed should cover the points set out in *Checklist 19.1*.

Name of practice

2.06 In naming a firm, there are various things which must be considered.

First, permission to use the term 'architect' is restricted by the Architects Registration Act 1931 and the Architects Registration (Amendment) Act 1938. Only those who are on the register of the Architects Registration Council of the United Kingdom (ARCUK) and have paid the requisite fee are permitted to describe themselves as 'architect'. It is only the use of the noun 'architect' which is restricted; the adjective 'architectural' may be used by anyone. Moreover, the acts do not prohibit anyone from *practising* as an architect. 'Landscape architects' and 'naval architects' are also outside the scope of the Acts. It is advisable for any architect wishing to use the term 'architect' in a firm name to check with ARCUK.

Secondly, the provisions of the Business Names Act 1985 must be complied with if the partnership does not consist of the names of the partners or an addition indicating that the business is carried on in succession to the former owner of the business. Certain names which are set out in statutory regulations or give the impression that the business is connected with HM's Government or a local authority must gain the approval of the Secretary of State for Trade and Industry. The use in the firm's name of a retired, former or deceased distinguished partner may be permissible provided there is no intent to mislead; but caution is necessary to avoid the implication that such a person is still involved in the practice. The Act requires businesses to disclose certain information. The names and addresses of each partner must be prominently displayed at the business premises where the public have access. It is important to comply with the provisions of this Act. Failure to do so is a criminal offence or may render void contracts entered into by the firm. The Business Names Act requires that business documentation must contain the names of each partner. However, if there are more than 20 partners the names of all partners can be omitted from business documents if they state the address of the principal place of business and also state that a full list of partners' names and relevant addresses may be inspected there.

(See further Notes for Guidance on Business Names and Business Ownership available from the Registrar of Companies, Companies House, Crown Way, Maindy, Cardiff CF4 3UZ (telephone 0222 388588). Businesses with offices in Scotland should address enquiries to the Registrar of Companies for Scotland, Companies Registration Office,

Checklist 19.1: Items to be considered when drawing up deed of partnership

Note: The terms of a partnership agreement, like any other contract, may be widely varied by mutual consent of the parties. Where no provision is made those of the Partnership Act 1890 will apply. The figures in brackets ( ) in Checklists 19.1–3 refer to relevant clauses in that Act.

Name of firm

Place of business

Commencement

Duration

Provision of capital
Amount.
Proportion to be contributed by each partner.
Distinctions between what is:

1. not partnership capital – a premium, and
2. capital which is partnership property – contribution to working capital.

Capital should be expressed in money terms.
Any special agreement for interest on capital (24(3), (4)).
Valuation and repayments on death etc. (42 and 43).
Rules for settlement for accounts after dissolution (44).

Property
What (if any) partners bring to the firm including contracts (20, 22, 24).
What

1. belongs to firm as a whole (21);
2. co-owners but not partnership property;
3. individual ownership for use in the partnership business (24).

Mutual rights and duties
If these are to be differentiated then specify them – e.g. holiday times, sabbaticals, work brought into firm etc.

Miscellaneous earnings
For example, lectures, journalistic work, various honoraria . . . whether to be paid into firm.

Profits and losses
Basis for division among partners: if not equally then specify (24(1)).
Any reservations, e.g. about guaranteed minimum share of profits in any individual case.

Banking and accountants
Arrangements for signing cheques, presentation of audited accounts, etc.

Employment of 'locum tenens'
Authority for, circumstances, and terms.

Constitution of firm
Provisions for changes (36).

Retirement at will
Age, fixed term or partnership for life, notice of retirement, etc.
Arrangements for consultants and for payment during retirement.
Repayment of capital and current accounts on death or retirement.

Dissolution
Any special circumstances (see *Checklist 19.3*).

Restrictions on practice
Any covenant in respect of restraining competition (must be reasonable to interests of parties and public). Areas of operation.

Insurances
Various, including liability of surviving partners for dead partners share in firm.

Arbitration
method, number of arbitrators, etc.

100-102 George Street, Edinburgh, EH2 3DJ (telephone 031 225 5777).)

Size of practice

2.07 There are still restrictions on the size of some partnerships. In the case of architects these have been removed by the Partnerships (Unrestricted Size) No. 4 Regulations 1970 so long as not less than three-quarters are registered under the Architects (Registration) Act 1931.

Types of partner

2.08 The law is not concerned with distinctions between senior and junior partners. It is up to the partners to decide how to share profits, but they will be shared equally unless special provision is made. There is an RIBA Practice Note dated May 1974 to the effect that all those persons who are held out to be partners shall be described as such without further distinction. In particular the term 'salaried partner' is to be avoided. The purpose of this is to ensure that all persons described as partners share in the decision-making of the business and have access to appropriate information. They are also fully responsible for the professional conduct of their practice and for keeping themselves and their partners properly informed of partnership matters.

Associates

2.09 It is common in architects' firms to recognize the status and contribution of senior staff by calling them 'associates'. The device is often used to retain important staff members while preventing them having any real responsibility or appreciable share of the profits. The title 'associate' is not referred to in the Partnership Act; it has no meaning in law, and, if it is not intended that associates be partners and share in the liabilities of the partnership, it is extremely unwise to use the term 'associate partner', and would also probably contravene professional codes. If people were misled into thinking associates were partners, associates might find themselves liable as though they were partners, having all the liabilities without much profit. A man or woman should be either partner or associate and the distinction should be clear.

Rights and liabilities of partners

2.10 Every partner will have the following rights unless there is a contrary agreement:

1. The right to take full part in management of the business (section 24 (5)).
2. The right to have an equal share in profits and capital of the business (section 24 (1)).
3. The right not to have new partners added without his consent (section 24 (7)).
4. The right not to have the fundamental nature of the partnership business altered without his consent. The consent of a majority of partners will suffice for changes in all other ordinary matters connected with the business.
5. By section 24 (2) a firm must indemnify every partner in respect of payments made and personal liabilities incurred by him in doing necessary acts or acts in the ordinary and proper conduct of the business of the firm.
6. There is a right to inspect the partnership books, which must be kept at the principal place of business of each firm (section 24 (9)).
7. There is a right not to be expelled without express agreement (section 25).
8. Any partner has the right to dissolve the partnership at any time by giving notice to the other partners (section 26 (1)).

Assignment

2.11 Assignment will not transfer right to management, accounts, or inspection of partnership books. It will only entitle the assignee to receive a share in the profits. (section 31(1)).

Rights to which partners are not entitled

2.12 By section 24(4) there is no right to interest on capital subscribed by a partner although by section 24(3) there is a right to interest on capital subscribed beyond that which was agreed to be subscribed.

2.13 There is no right to renumeration for acting in the partnership business by section 24(6).

Liabilities

2.14 In English law a partnership is a collection of individuals and not a corporate body. In addition to all his normal individual liabilities, each partner has added responsibilities as a member of a partnership.

2.15 If a partnership is sued, a partner may be proceeded against jointly, or jointly and severally (see *Checklist 19.2*). By sections 9 and 10 of the Partnership Act every partner in a

---

Checklist 19.2: Liability for civil cases under Partnership Act 1890

Debts and obligations to firm
Jointly in absence of agreement to the contrary (5–13 inclusive).

Torts, including negligence
Jointly and severally.

Contract
Jointly and severally – if partners have expressly agreed to be so liable. Note: A deceased partner's estate may be severally liable to the prior payments of his private debts.

---

firm is personally liable jointly with the other partners for all debts and obligations incurred by the firm when he is a partner as well as jointly and severally for wrongs done by other partners who are acting in the ordinary course of the business of the firm or for wrongs done with the authority of co-partners. If a partnership is sued jointly, one or more partners may be sued at the same time; when judgement is given, even if it is not satisfied, no further action can be taken against any of the other partners. If the action is brought against a firm jointly and severally, the partners may be sued singly or together. When judgement is given against one, further action may be brought against the others one by one or together until the full amount is paid. If only some of the partners are sued, they may apply to the courts to have their other partners joined with them as co-defendants.

2.16 Under the Limitation Act 1980, liability runs from the date for twelve years from the breach of a contract under seal but six years for simple contracts. For negligence, the limitation period was traditionally six years from the date of the cause of action. This was unsatisfactory because it did not elucidate whether the cause of action arose when the tort was committed, when the plaintiff suffered damage, or when the plaintiff knew he had suffered damage. In 1982 in a case decided by the House of Lords (*Pirelli General Cable Works Ltd* v *Oscar Faber and Partners* [1983] AC1) it was held that the cause of action arose when damage occurred. The matter is now governed by the Latent Damage Act 1986. This Act introduced a 'long-stop' period of 15 years from the date of a negligent act beyond which an action could not be brought.

Otherwise the limitation period is six years from the date when damage was sustained or, if later, three years from the time when the plaintiff knew of the damage or could with reasonable diligence have discovered it.

2.17 Partners are not liable for the criminal actions of other partners, unless they contributed to them or have knowledge of them. But the RIBA has always considered an architect liable for breaches of the Code of Professional Conduct by his fellow partners (see Chapter 23).

2.18 Some (though not all) partners may have their liability limited by agreement with the other members of the partnership. The other partners agree to indemnify such partners for liability above a certain figure. Such partners may draw a smaller share of the profits than the others, and they rely for income mainly on a guaranteed remuneration. This device is often used to encourage talented members of staff to remain with a firm and to share in its management while ensuring that they do not have to outlay capital to join the partnership.

2.19 A new partner entering the firm does not normally become liable for debts, obligations, or wrongs incurred or committed before his entry (section 17(1)). However, the position is different for a partner leaving the firm, whether by retirement or death. If a partner retires he will still be liable for debts or obligations incurred before his retirement (section 17(2)). If he dies his estate will be liable for such debts or obligations (Proceedings Against Estates Act 1970). Moreover, a partner will continue to be treated as a member of the firm, attracting the usual liability, until he gives notice of the change by advertising in the London Gazette section 36).

2.20 Every partner will be an agent of the firm. Any act done by him for carrying out the firm's business will bind the firm unless it is outside his authority to act for the firm in that particular matter, and the person with whom he is dealing knows that he has no authority or does not believe him to be a partner (section 5).

2.21 Partners must render true accounts and full information on anything affecting the partnership or the partners (section 28).

2.22 Partners are accountable to the partnership for any private profits they have received from any partnership transaction or from using the partnership property, names, or connection (section 29(1)).

2.23 If a partner competes with the business without the consent of the firm he must pay the firm all profits made from this business (section 30).

The relationship of partners to one another

2.24 A firm of any size may not discriminate against women partnerships with regard to the provision of benefits, facilities or services or by expelling her or subjecting her to detriment (Sex Discrimination Act 1976, section 11(1) as amended by the Sex Discrimination Act 1986, section 59). Firms larger than six members may not discriminate in such matters on racial grounds (Race Relations Act 1976, section 10).

Dissolution of partnerships

2.25 A partnership comes to an end:

1. At the end of a fixed term if it has been so set up.
2. At the end of a single specific commission, if it was set up for the commission alone.

3. On the death or bankruptcy of any partner unless partnership agreements make provision for continuity of the partnership.
4. If any partner gives notice.

2.26 Prior to the Finance Act 1985 there were tax benefits in cessation and re-formation of a partnership, but those have now been ended.

2.27 If a partner wishes to end the firm but is prevented by his fellow partners, he may apply to the court for a dissolution on one of the grounds shown in *Checklist 19.3*.

Checklist 19.3: Grounds for dissolution of partnerhip

---

1 By agreement of parties

a. Agreement per deed

End of fixed term or of single project.

b. By expiration, or notice (32)

If for undefined time – any partner giving notice of intention (32(c)).

c. Illness

Special provisions in deed (to avoid need to apply to courts (35)).

Note: Expulsion. No majority of partners can expel unless express agreement in deed (25). There can be no implied consent to expel.

2 By operation of law and courts

Death and bankruptcy

Subject to express agreement, partnership is dissolved as regards *all* by death or bankruptcy of *any* partner (33).

Illegality

Any event making it illegal to carry on business of firm:

> If partner insane.
> If partner incapable of carrying on their part of agreement.
> If partner guilty of conduct prejudicial to the interests of the firm.
> If partner wilfully and persistently breaches the agreement or if their conduct is such that the others can no longer carry on business with them.
> If firm can only carry on at a loss.
> If, in the opinion of the courts, it is just and equitable that the firm should be dissolved.

---

3 Limited partnerships

3.01 Limited partnerships are governed by the Limited Partnership Act 1907. At first glance these might appear to be an advantageous form of association for architects concerned with protecting themselves from liability. However, there are so many disadvantages in limited partnerships that these are rarely used:

1. At least one partner must retain unlimited liability.
2. Limited partners' capital must be paid up immediately. They are liable for debts or obligations up to but not beyond the amount contributed (LPA, section 4(2)).
3. The limited partners may have no role in the management of the business and have no power to bind the firm. If a limited partner takes a management role he will be fully liable as if he were a general partner. Any difference arising as to ordinary matters connected with the partnership business may be decided by a majority of the general partners.
   A person may be introduced as a partner without the consent of the other limited partners.

4. Limited partners can only dispose of their share in the partnership with the consent of the partner(s) with unlimited liability.
5. Limited partnerships of architects are limited to 20 persons.
6. A limited partnership is not dissolved by the death or bankruptcy of a limited partner and a limited partner has no right to dissolve the partnership by notice.

4 Companies

The view of the professional organizations

4.01 For the purposes of the application of Byelaw 5 and the September 1988 RIBA Code the Royal Institute may hold a member acting through a body corporate or unincorporate responsible for the acts of that body. This means that for the purposes of suspension or expulsion from the RIBA an architect who is a director of a company may be held personally liable for the acts of the company, but it does not mean that he will be personally liable under the general law for the acts of the company.

A separate legal persona

4.02 The most fundamental principle of company law is that a company is a distinct and separate entity in law from its members or directors. As a separate legal person a company can own and alienate property, sue and be sued, and enter into contracts in its own right. Although the company is owned by its members, or shareholders, and governed by its directors, or managing director, with the supervision of its shareholders, it is distinct in law from all of these. In relation to third parties it is the company which will be primarily liable, and not the shareholders or directors. This is so however large the percentage of shares or debentures held by one shareholder. A company may be liable in contract, tort, crime and for matters of property. The 'corporate veil' can only be pierced in very rare cases such as fraud and the directors or shareholders made liable for debts and obligations of the company.

Types of company

4.03 A company may either be limited (by shares or guarantee) or unlimited. A company limited by shares will be one in which the shareholders' liability to contribute to the company's assets is stated in the Memorandum to be limited, that is, is limited to the amount unpaid on their shares. A company limited by guarantee is one where the shareholders are liable as guarantors for an amount set out in the Memorandum (see para 4.04) in the event of the company being wound up. In an unlimited company the members will be fully liable for debts incurred by the company and effectively function as guarantors for the debts and obligations of the company.

Formation of companies

4.04 Companies are formed in three ways: by Royal Charter, by special Act of Parliament, and by registration under the Companies Act 1985. The first two methods are archaic and little used, so this chapter will only describe the procedure for registration. Any two people can register a company. The following must be sent to the Company Registrar:

1. A Memorandum of Association setting out the objects of the company. A company may only pursue the objects conferred expressly or impliedly by the Memorandum. All other activity is *ultra vires* and void. For example, a company will not be able to borrow money unless provision for this is set out in the Articles. Thus the drafting of a Memorandum of Association requires special care; the drafter must take care

to comply with the professional Codes as well. The Memorandum should normally always contain provision for its alteration as it can only be altered in certain circumstances limited by the Companies Act 1985 (see section 2(7), 4).

2. Articles of Association containing the regulations of the company (subject to the Memorandum). Companies limited by shares need not register Articles but these will then be in the form of Table A in the Companies (Tables A-F) Regulations 1985 (SI 1985/805). The Articles may be altered by special resolution (a majority of at least three-quarters vote of members). The Articles may be altered to an almost unlimited extent by special resolution.

3. A statement of initial nominal capital.

4. Particulars of the director(s) and secretary. There must be at least two directors and one secretary. Any change in the directors or secretary must be notified to the Registrar of Companies or the company may not rely on the change. Sometimes directors will be required by the Articles to have qualification shares. Anyone, even a corporation, may be a company director unless he is an undischarged bankrupt (though the court may give him leave to act) or is disqualified by the court under the Company Directors Disqualification Act 1986 or the Articles. The company may remove a director by ordinary resolution before the end of his term (Companies Act 1986, section 303(2)). Under the Articles, directors nomally retire in rotation (one-third each year). A director may resign by giving such notice as is required in the Articles. Section 285 of the Companies Act 1985 provides that the acts of a director are valid despite any defect that may subsequently be discovered in a director's appointment or qualification, though this section has been narrowly constructed by the courts. Directors only are entitled to such remuneration as is stated in the Articles. Companies may not loan to directors or connected persons except in certain stated exceptions (Companies Act 1985, section 330) (see para 4.15 for powers and duties of directors).

5. Intended location of the registered office of the company.

6. The prescribed fee.

4.05 The Registrar of Companies will issue a Certificate of Incorporation, being evidence that the company is legally registered, and give the company a registered number. Without a Certificate of Incorporation a company does not exist in law and cannot do business.

Public and private companies

4.06 Companies, whether limited or unlimited, may be either public or private. A public company is the only sort of company permitted to offer its shares to the public. Only companies with a nominal share capital of £50 000 may be public limited companies. The Memorandum of Association must state that the company is a public company. Before registering, it is advisable to consider whether the company is to be public or private. It is possible to re-register, but this requires a special resolution. It is also normally possible, though difficult, to re-register as a limited or unlimited company except in the case of a public company which wishes to re-register as an unlimited company. Otherwise it requires a special resolution for an unlimited company to re-register as a limited company and the unanimous approval of members to change from a limited to an unlimited company (see Companies Act 1985, sections 43–52). In general an architect's practice, in which a decision to incorporate is taken, will form a private company: probably the individuals who would otherwise be partners will be the directors and also the shareholders.

Profits

4.07 Profits are distributed among shareholders in accordance with the rights attached to their shares. Although there

is a presumption that all shares confer equal rights and equal liabilities, that is normally rebutted by a power in the company's articles to issue different classes of shares. An example of a class of share is a preference share. Holders of preference shares will be entitled to dividends before ordinary shareholders will be paid theirs. If there are insufficient funds, preference shareholders will be the only shareholders to receive dividends. Shares are also classed according to whether they have voting rights or not. Directors and employees are paid salaries out of the profits of the companies. (These payments will be tax-deductible which will not be the case for partners' salaries, which are just their share of the profits.) In practice, in most architectural companies profits and dividends will be small, since the directors will be remunerated under their service contracts with the company.

Name of company

4.08 Like partnerships, the name of a company will be restricted by the Architects Registration Act 1931, the Architects Registration (Amendment) Act 1938, and the Business Names Act 1985. (see para 2.06). Public limited companies must use the word 'limited' after their name. It is an offence for public companies to choose names giving the impression that they are private companies, and vice versa. The use of a name similar to that of another company with the same type of business may constitute the tort of passing off.

4.09 A company must state its corporate name on all business documents and on its seal. It must display this name legibly on the outside of its business premises. Other particulars including the place of registration, the registration number and the address of the registered office must be on company business documents.

Size of company

4.10 The number of shareholders which a company may have is unlimited.

Rights and liabilities of shareholders

Rights

4.11 A shareholder holding shares with voting rights (see para 4.07) has the right to supervise the management of the company by voting in the annual general meeting, which meetings must be held each year at no greater than a fifteen-month interval, or such extraordinary general meetings as may be called.

4.12 A shareholder will be paid dividends out of the profits of the company, in accordance with the rights belonging to the shares he holds.

Liabilities

4.13 As we have seen above, a partnership is bound by contracts made by one of its partners and is liable for torts committed by each member. By contrast, no shareholder can make contracts binding on the company. Nor will a shareholder be liable personally for torts or obligations incurred by other shareholders. A shareholder will only be liable for torts and obligations of the company to the amount unpaid on his shares, if the company is limited. He will however, as noted above, be fully liable for such torts or obligations if the company is unlimited.

4.14 When a company is dissolved by winding-up (see para 4.18), both members and past members (those who have been members within 12 months of the winding-up) will be liable to contribute towards the assets of the company so that it can meet its liabilities (subject to limited liability, if that exists). Thus, the liabilities of past company members are not so wide-reaching as those of partners. This is one great advantage of companies.

Rights and liabilities of directors

4.15 Under the Articles, the directors normally are given the power to manage the company under the ultimate supervision of shareholders. They may often delegate the management to a managing director. In an architect's practice company, generally only those who would otherwise have been partners should be directors.

4.16 A director is not a servant or agent of the company and can only bind it if some organ of the company has conferred appropriate authority upon him. The authority depends on what has been given by the Articles or shareholders by special resolution. A director may be held to have had usual authority or to have been held out as having authority and thus will bind the company. The third party need not be familiar with the Articles in either of these two latter cases. However, a managing director will normally have such authority to bind the company.

4.17 There are many statutory duties and criminal offences created for directors by the Companies Act 1985. This work does not have space to discuss all of these in depth but will only briefly list the main duties. Every prudent director should obtain a copy of the Companies Act and peruse it with care.

1. By section 221 of the Companies Act 1985 company directors must prepare and disclose company accounts in a specified form stating the financial position of the company. They must keep the books at the registered office of the company and they must be available for inspection by the company officers at any time.

2. The directors must prepare an annual report reviewing the business of the company and recommending the amount of dividends to be paid.

3. The company must be audited yearly.

4. The report, audit, and accounts must be filed with the Registrar of Companies at specified times and will be available for inspecton by the public.

5. All companies must hold an annual general meeting of shareholders in each calendar year at no greater intervals than once every 15 months. Two persons can constitute a quorum. Extraordinary general meetings may be convened if there is some business the directors consider to be of special importance.

6. A company must keep a register of directors at its registered office disclosing certain information about directors and their interest in the shares or debentures of the company. These particulars must be notified to the Registrar, who must be informed of any change. A register of members containing similar information must also be kept by the company.

7. Directors have no right to remuneration except that specified in the Articles. Normally remuneration of directors is voted on by the shareholders at their general meetings.

8. Directors owe the company a fiduciary duty of loyalty and good faith. They are considered trustees of company assets under their control. They must account to the company for any profits they make by virtue of their position as directors and generally cannot use their powers as directors except to benefit the company, not themselves or third parties. They must always devote themselves to promoting the company's interests and act in its best interest. Their duty of loyalty means they cannot enter into engagements where their personal interests might conflict with the company's interest and they must disclose their personal interests in such engagements to the shareholders. This duty can continue even after a director leaves the company.

9. A director has a duty of care to the company to exercise reasonable care in the conduct of the business. Such duties are not unduly onerous. Courts are reluctant to intervene in areas involving business judgment. In some circumstances directors will be expected to seek specialist advice and will be liable if they do not. Directors will not be liable for anything they have been authorized to do by shareholders. This duty is not owed to shareholders, contractors or creditors (though a director can be liable to the creditor for fraudulent or wrongful trading). Since the duty is owed to the company, the company itself can sue a director who has been negligent or in breach of its fiduciary duties or negligent. Or a shareholder can bring a derivative action on behalf of other shareholders. In a derivative action all funds must, however, go into the company funds.

Dissolution

4.18 A company may be dissolved in two ways:

1. By winding-up (see sections 84–205 of the Insolvency Act 1986). This may be voluntary or compulsory. Once a company has been wound up no judgment may be enforced against it.
2. By being struck off the Register under section 652 of the Companies Act 1985. This will happen when the Registrar of Companies acquires the belief that the company is no longer carrying on business. Companies may seek this form of dissolution themselves. They may do this to save the costs of a formal liquidation.

Advantages and disadvantages of companies and partnerships

4.19 A list of the differences is set out in *Checklist 19.4*. The relative advantages and disadvantages will obviously differ for individual businesses. An architect principal will need to assess the priorities of the business in making a decision between a company and a partnership. The size of the business may be very relevant to the decision as smaller businesses may find the paperwork and administration required for a company too arduous. On the other hand, companies certainly appear to protect architects from liability, although in practice many companies are financed by personal guarantees on the part of their members. Taxation is another possibly crucial factor in the decision. This is regrettably a topic beyond the scope of this chapter. Architects should seek professional advice from an accountant or from a local tax office.

Service companies

4.20 Service companies are companies formed to provide services to a partnership whilst siphoning off profits which would otherwise go to the partnership. The company may employ staff and hold the premises. It will also normally provide things such as office equipment, stationery, cars and accountancy services to the firm. The partnership will pay a fee which is a margin over costs. So long as the margin is not too high, this can be treated for tax purposes as a partnership expense. A service company will be advantageous when income tax is high relative to corporation tax, which is not the case at the time of writing.

Checklist 19.4: The differences between companies and partnerships

Partnerships	Companies
1. No separate legal personality (except in Scotland)	Has separate legal personality from its shareholders
2. Partners have unlimited liability	Shareholders are liable only to the amount unpaid on their shares but may be liable on personal guarantees for some liabilities, e.g. borrowing.
3. Interest of a partner is his partnership which may be difficult to transfer	Interest of a shareholder is his shares which are usually easy to transfer unless subject to limitations in Articles
4. It may be difficult for a young architect to join a partnership as he will have to amass capital sufficient to buy a share in the partnership or take over a retiring partner's interest	It will be easier to join the company as it will not necessarily involve buying in.
5. The only promotion is to become a partner, so career prospects may be limited	There are more possible kinds of promotion
6. Management through meetings of partners	Management through Board of Directors supervised by shareholders, who meet annually
7. Partners will share profits equally unless there is an agreement to the contrary	Company profits are divided according to rights attached to the shares.
8. Can be formed informally by just starting up business with another person	Must be registered to come into existence. It costs money to register a company (£80–£200) and it will require time unless an 'off the peg' company is purchased
9. No restrictions on the powers of a partnership	A company only has the powers in the objects clause of its Memorandum. Other powers will be ultra vires and void
10. Each partner can bind the partnership	No shareholder can bind the company.
11. There is no place where partnership details may be inspected by members of the public	Matters filed with the Registrar of Companies are open to public inspection. Such matters include the Memorandum, Articles, details of directors, secretary, and registered office
12. Partnerships need not publicize their accounts	Companies must file their accounts with the Registrar of Companies
13. No audit required	Annual audit required.
14. A partnership does not require much paperwork or administration.	A company requires more paperwork and administration.
15. A partnership cannot borrow money unless a trading firm	A company can more easily raise money (if allowed by its Memorandum), e.g. by debentures and fixed and floating charges.
16. Death or departure of a partner causes dissolution of the partnership	Transfer of shares will not end the company's existence
17. There are many ways to dissolve a partnership. It can be dissolved instantly by agreement	A company is dissolved only by liquidation in accordance with the Companies Act 1985 and the Insolvency Act 1986.

Group practices and consortia

4.21 Architects' businesses may come together to work in several forms of association, whether for a single project or on a more permanent basis. This section is not concerned with the operational and management factors for and behind the choice of form, but only with the legal issues. Further guidance is given in the RIBA *Handbook of Architectural Practice and Management* (1973 edn) and in the *Guide to Group Practice and Consortia* (RIBA, 1965). The RIBA *Handbook* is presently being completely remodelled. It should begin to appear in parts in 1990. One part will replace the old *Guide to Group Practice and Consortia*. The creation of any association needs to be carefully checked with the professional indemnity insurers of each party.

Loose groups

4.22 These are associations in which firms or individuals group to pool knowledge and experience. Such a group does not need to be registered, but some short constitution is desirable which clearly distinguishes it from a partnership. In company law a more formal 'Memorandum and Articles of Association' is necessary and is of far greater significance because it must set out the most important provisions of the company's constitution, including the activities which the company may carry on, and is accordingly of special concern to persons who deal with it.

Group practices

4.23 Individual private firms may be grouped for their mutual benefit and to give better service while each retains some independence:

1. *Association of individual firms* The degree of association may vary considerably from simply sharing office accommodation and facilities and expense, or extending to a fully comprehensive system of mutual help. Beyond agreeing to a division of overhead expenses they retain the profits of the individual firms and their normal responsibility to their respective clients.
2. *Co-ordinated groups* For large jobs or extensive development projects it is not unusual for the work to be undertaken by two or more architectural firms with one of them appointed to co-ordinate the activities of the others.

The co-firms are nevertheless liable to the coordinating firm for torts committed in their areas of activity. The arrangement may also be constructed under head and sub-consultancy agreements.

Single project partnerships and group partnerships may be entered into on terms which are entirely a matter for individual agreements between the parties and are similar in law to any ordinary partnership.

Consortia

4.24 In law, consortia are little different from group practices. The term normally implies the association of firms of different professional skills acting as one for carrying out projects jointly yet retaining their separate identities and each with their own responsibility to the building owner. A consortium may be formed for the duration of a single contract or on a more regular and permanent basis.

Difficulties

4.25 Clearly, any association of practices, whether permanent or temporary, must be very carefully planned. If firms are to merge completely, assets should be carefully assessed (including work in progress), and specific agreement is necessary on debts, including liabilities relating to previous contractors. These could be significant if a pre-merger job became the subject of a claim for professional negligence.

Agreements

4.26 If the constituent firms are to preserve their identities and to continue to practise in their own right as well as on common projects, the form of agreement becomes more critical and more complex. A new firm (group or consortium, partnership or company) should be created to contract with clients for common projects. The agreement which sets up the new firm must resolve how far member firms' assets are brought in, to what extent member firms are liable for liabilities of the group, and the degree of independence retained by each member to carry on its own activities. The RIBA's guide gives draft articles of association for various types of grouping, but a solicitor should always be consulted.

5 Premises and persons

5.01 There is a general common law duty of care on employers to protect employees against personal injury in the course of their work. Employers have a statutory obligation to provide employees with safe and decent working conditions. For office workers these are set out in the Offices, Shops and Railway Premises Act 1963 and the Health and Safety at Work Act 1974 together with regulations made under the two Acts. Since the coming into force of the Offices, Shops and Railway Premises Act in 1964, the office employer, including the architect, has had statutory responsibilities to provide a minimally satisfactory working environment for his employees. The Health and Safety at Work Act 1974 shifted the focus from premises to people. This Act has many implications for architects as professional designers of buildings. Here we are only concerned with its impact on an architect as employer, employee, or occupier of premises. The Health and Safety at Work Act is designed eventually to phase out, *inter alia*, the Offices, Shops and Railway Premises Act 1963 by means of Regulations.

The Offices, Shops and Railway Premises Act 1963

5.02 Under the Offices, Shops and Railway Premises Act 1963, architects' offices and the activities normally associated with them count as office premises. Some activities such as

modelmaking (if they are carried on in distinct parts of the premises and to sufficient extent) might be within the scope of the Factories Act; factory inspectors should be consulted.

Application of Act

5.03 Office premises are outside the Act if they are occupied only by self-employed people, or if the only employees are immediate relatives of the occupier, or if all employees work less than 21 hours on the premises. Thus an architect in practice by himself with a part-time typist coming in a couple of hours a day is not affected, but if he employs a full-time assistant, even if he works at home, the part of his house used as an office is governed by the Act. If the premises are used only temporarily (for less than six weeks) they are not affected.

5.04 The Act and the regulations made under it cover a wide variety of conditions which cannot be dealt with here in detail. They include the maintenance and construction of floors, passages, and stairs, the safety of lifts, the provision of first aid, the amount of space to be provided for each person on the premises, cleanliness, heating, ventilation and lighting, provision of washing, sanitary, and eating facilities, drinking water, facilities for storing outdoor clothing and seating.

Accidents

5.05 Employers are required to notify the enforcing authority of accidents on the premises which cause the death, or the disablement for more than three days, of a person employed to work on the premises. A record must be kept of all accidents as they occur. In any case this is useful as a check against the possibility of persons making claims for accidents which did not happen on office premises.

Employees' right to information

5.06 Because the Act is primarily for the benefit of employees and because some employers are forgetful or unscrupulous, the occupier is obliged to give employees information about the Act either by posting up an abstract in a sufficiently prominent place or by giving them an explanatory booklet (see SI 1982/827 amended by SI 1989/682).

Division of responsibility

5.07 One of the potentially confusing aspects of the Act is the division of responsibility between owner and occupier, particularly in multi-occupied buildings. The employer, if not the occupier (e.g. a window cleaner's boss), is responsible for notifying the occupier of accidents to his employees and for notifying his own employees of the provision of the Act.

Single occupation

5.08 An employer who occupies a whole building is responsible for ensuring that all provisions of the Act are met.

Multi-occupation

5.09 When a building is in multi-occupation responsibility is divided. The owner is responsible for cleaning, lighting and safety of the common parts, washing and sanitary facilities, fire alarms and signposting, and keeping free from obstruction all exits and means of escape in the building as a whole. Occupiers are responsible for all other provisions of the Act within the parts of the building that they occupy.

Occupiers' liability

5.10 An occupier owes a duty of care to all entrants on his premises. If the entrants are lawful visitors, he must take all reasonably practicable steps to make his premises safe for them and to protect all hazards, or give sufficient notice of them, although visiting workpeople such as window cleaners or chimney sweeps are responsible for their own safe working methods. If it is foreseeable that persons unlikely to be able to read warnings may be likely to get into hazardous areas (e.g. children, the blind), then protection must be adequate to keep them out. A duty of care is even owed to trespassers, although this duty of care is to take such care as is reasonable in all the circumstances of the case to see that they do not suffer injury on the premises by reason of the danger concerned. Sufficient warnings or discouragements will discharge the duty.

5.11 Responsibility for injury or damage arising from defects caused by improper maintenance, or indeed construction, is not avoided by the disposal of the premises to another party. This clearly concerns architects both as designers and as owners or occupiers of premises (see the Defective Premises Act 1972, section 5).

5.12 If a landlord has tenants to whom he has a repairing obligation, and this can obviously include architects who sub-let part of their office, then it is the landlord who has a responsibility to anyone who could be affected by his failure to keep the premises properly maintained.

Health and Safety at Work Act 1974

5.13 The Health and Safety of Work Act is directed at people who work, whether employer, employee, or self-employed persons, and their responsibilities to each other and to third parties who may be affected by the work process or its results. The Health and Safety (Training for Employment) Regulations 1988 apply the provisions of this Act to certain training schemes, e.g. YTS. Under the Act an employer must now maintain safe systems of work and keep his plant and premises in safe condition. He must give adequate instruction, training, and supervision for the purposes of safety to those who work for him. This may extend to guidance or instruction to employees visiting buildings or construction sites in the course of their employment particularly at times when the premises or site may be otherwise unoccupied. Unless he employs fewer than five people he must prepare a written statement of his business's safety policies, organization and arrangements and make this known to his employees. In step with the trend to greater consultation at work he may be required to set up means whereby his safety measures may be explained and discussed.

5.14 It is suggested that the safety policy should deal with the safety responsibilities of all levels of management, inspection procedures, supervision, training, research and consultative arrangements regarding safety, fire drill procedure, reminders on keeping stairways and corridors free of obstructions, the marking and guarding of temporary hazards, use of machinery, accidents and first aid. An employer can seek advice from the Health and Safety Commission and Health and Safety Executive. Both are contactable at the following addresses: Baynard's House, 1 Chepstow Place, London W2 4TC, telephone 071-221 0870, or St Hugh's House, Stanley Precinct, Bootle, Merseyside L20 3QY, telephone 051-951 4223. However, the employer should ensure that the safety policy is specially tailored to meet the individual needs of the business.

5.15 By regulations made under the Act, the Health and Safety (First Aid) Regulations 1981, which came into operation on 1 July 1982, employers have a duty to provide first-aid equipment and facilities, to provide suitable persons with some training in first aid, and to inform employees of the arrangements they have made. A Code of Practice (Approved Code of Practice, Health and Safety (First Aid) Regulations 1981, published by the British Safety Council, 62–64 Chancellor's Row, London W6 9RS) has been approved by the Health and Safety Commission to provide practical guidance in respect of the regulations. Although failure to comply with this Code is not itself an offence, it will be both prudent and practical to follow it.

5.16 The employee in his turn has a duty to exercise reasonable care to himself and his fellow employees, to cooperate with his employer in carrying out statutory requirements and not to interfere with safety provisions.

Enforcement

5.17 To ensure that the law on health and safety is respected, inspectors appointed by the enforcing authority have the power to enter premises to which the Act applies. They may inspect the premises, question anyone, or ask to see relevant certificates or notices. They should have evidence of their authority, and it is good practice to ask to see this before taking anyone round.

5.18 Under the Health and Safety at Work Act, after an inspection, inspectors have the power to make 'improvement' notices under which the offending practice must cease or the deficiency must be remedied within a certain period. More fearsomely, they also have a power to issue a 'prohibition' notice under which the practice must cease or the premises must not be used until their requirements have been met. An appeal against the notice may be made to an Industrial Tribunal. Offences under the Health and Safety at Work Act are criminal offences, although breaches or the regulations made thereunder can result in civil liability. It is an offence to contravene requirements imposed by a notice. The offender may be liable to a fine even though no one has suffered damage. It should be borne in mind that, although insurance may be taken out against the possibility of damages being awarded, insurance may not be used to protect against the results, e.g. fines, of criminal acts.

Fire certificate

5.19 The Fire Precautions Act 1971 took over the fire provisions of the Offices, Shops and Railway Premises Act 1963 in January 1977. The Fire Precautions Act has itself been amended by the Fire Safety and Safety of Places of Sport Act 1987 and by various regulations.

5.20 Section 1 of the Fire Precautions Act makes a fire certificate compulsory in the case of use as a place of work (amended by the Health and Safety at Work Act 1974) and a use for teaching, training or research, or use for any purpose involving access to the premises by members of the public unless no more than 20 people work in the relevant building at one time (no more than 10 above the ground floor) (see Fire Precautions (Factories Offices Shops and Railway Premises) Order 1989, SI 1989/76). A fire certificate must be obtained from the enforcing authority. For private practices this is normally the local fire authority and for premises owned or occupied by the Crown, HM Inspectors of Fire Services. However, the fire authority may exempt premises from the need to have a fire certificate if they think fit or in certain cases specified in the above Order. Even if exemption is granted, the premises will still have to be provided with fire fighting equipment and means of escape as are reasonable. If this duty is contravened, the fire authority will serve an improvement notice which must be complied with or it constitutes an offence. If the fire authority believes that the use of the premises involves a serious fire risk they may serve

a prohibition notice prohibiting or restricting use of the premises until remedied.

5.21 For a certificate to be granted, fire authority requirements on means of escape, keeping them clear and signposted, firefighting equipment, fire alarm systems and arrangements for fire drills must be satisfied. Failure to have a fire certificate if not exempted will amount to an offence.

5.22 Fire alarms should be tested at intervals and occupiers are required to take effective steps to ensure that all occupants are familiar with the action to be taken in the case of fire and with the means of escape. Fire drills are the most effective way of doing this.

5.23 If after a certificate has been issued or an exemption has been made, alterations are made to the premises which may significantly affect the requirements of that certificate or exemption, the issuing authority should be advised. The authority has continuing powers of inspection to see whether the premises are being kept in the original standard and whether changes have been made which render those standards inadequate.

6 Insurance

6.01 A practice protects itself by insurance against financial risks. Some of these are ordinary risks such as fire, some are eventualities which a firm is not obliged to cover but which, as a good employer, it may wish to provide for, such as prolonged sickness of a member of staff. But there are cases when a firm is obliged in law to cover damage caused to other persons. Varieties of insurance which cover all these risks are covered below:

Public liability

6.02 An owner or a lessee of premises, or someone carrying on a business in premises, may be legally liable for personal injury or damage to property of third parties caused by his negligence or that of his staff (see Chapter 4).

6.03 Since several people may be involved in a single incident and the level of damages may be very high, it is important for cover to be:

1. Appropriate to status – owner, lessee, or occupier.
2. Extended to cover principals' and employees' actions, not only on the premises, but anywhere while on business.
3. Extended to cover abroad if principals or employees are liable to be abroad on business.

Employers' liability

6.04 An employer is legally liable for personal injury caused to an employee in the course of his employment by the employer's negligence or that of another member of staff. It is important to provide cover:

1. For injuries during employment whether occasioned on or off the employer's premises.
2. For injuries overseas if employees are liable to be abroad on business.

Employer's Liability Act 1969

6.05 An employer is required by law to take out specific insurance so that he is able to meet his obligations. The Employer's Liability (Compulsory Insurance) Act 1969 and the Statutory Instrument (1971/1117) making General Regulations which came into operation on 1 January 1972 (amended by SI 1974/208 and SI 1975/194), requires that every employer who carries on business in Great Britain shall maintain insurance under approved policies with authorized insurers against liability for bodily injury or disease sustained by employees and arising out of and in the course of their employment in that business. Cover must extend to an amount of £2 million for any one occurrence. Employers' liability policies are contracts of indemnity. The premium is often based on the amount of wages paid by the insured to his employees during the year of insurance. The size of the business is immaterial – a single clerical or technical assistant qualifies, whether full-time or only part-time. The Act also provides for employees not ordinarily resident but who may be temporarily in Great Britain in the course of employment for a continuous period of not less than 14 days in the same way as it applies to all employees normally resident. The Act does not apply to Northern Ireland. The maximum penalty for non-compliance is a fine of up to level 4 on the standard scale for any day on which the employer is not insured. As from 1 January 1973, under sections 6 and 7 of the General Regulations 1971, there are further obligations upon the employer to display copies of the insurance certificate at the place or places of business for the information of his employees.

Motor vehicles

6.06 There are two points to note about car insurance:

First carrying third party cover is a legal requirement (by section 143 of the Road Traffic Act 1972) in respect of death or personal injury to third parties. From 31 December 1988 this sort of cover has become compulsory in respect of damage to a third party's property. Cover may be invalidated if a car is used for purposes not covered by the policy. Thus it is important to establish that cars owned and operated by a firm are covered for business use and for carrying normal professional impedimenta and that cars owned by employees and used by them in their duties are covered for occasional business use.

Secondly, if staff use their own cars on the firm's business their cover must be adequate, particularly in respect of cover for fellow employees. Their policies should also be checked to ensure that they include a third party indemnity in favour of the employer, otherwise if a claim results from an incident while the car is used on the firm's business, insurers may repudiate liability.

Professional indemnity

6.07 This is the insurance necessary to cover professional people for negligence in the course of their professions. Normally such policies will only cover liabilities to third parties, not loss caused to a person's own business by reason of their negligence. Nor will it cover fraud, whether by the employee or the professional.

6.08 Every architect in every form of practice should consider taking out such insurance in light of the high damages which can be awarded by courts in negligence actions. The appropriate scope of the policy, amount of the premium and other details are a matter which must be worked out on an individual basis by the architect and an experienced insurance broker. Further information is available from RIBA Insurance Agency, Room 201, Ibex House, The Minories, London, EC3N 1DY, telephone 071-283 2000. See also *Your Professional Liability and Risk Avoidance* published by RIBA Indemnity Research Limited (RIBAIR) at the same address.

6.09 In view of its importance for architects today, professional indemnity insurance is separately dealt with in Chapter 20. It cannot be over-emphasized that a practice which incorporates still requires professional indemnity insurance.

7 Differences between English and Scots law partnerships

7.01 The Partnership Act 1890, with the Registration of Business Names Act 1985 and the Limited Partnership Act 1907, all of which are referred to earlier, apply equally to Scottish partnerships. It should be noted, however, that the provisions of the second named Act are now contained, with minor amendments, in section 28 of the Companies Act 1981: in the case of architectural practice consisting of more than twenty partners their names need not appear on the firm's letterhead so long as a list of the partners' names is on public display at the address of the firm.

7.02 There is, however, an important difference between English and Scottish law regarding the meaning of the word 'firm'. As explained in para 2.14, in England a partnership is a collection of individuals and not a corporate body, but in Scotland a partnership is a legal persona, distinct in its own right from the partners of which it is composed. In the event of bankruptcy, therefore, the creditors of individual partners do not have a claim on the estate of the firm, although the creditors of the firm qualify for dividends from the estate of individual partners. In England, however, the firm's creditors have a claim only on the firm's estate and the partners' creditors on their private estates, each to the exclusion of the other.

7.03 The difference between the laws of Scotland and of England result in the following features in Scotland:

1. A partnership itself owns the funds of the partnership, and the parters are not joint owners of partnership funds (though the tax position of a Scottish partnership is exactly the same as for an English one).
2. A firm is the principal debtor in debts owed by the partnership, although the debts must in the first place be constituted against the firm.
3. A partner may sue or be sued by a firm and a firm may be either a debtor or creditor to any of its partners.
4. A firm can be sequestrated* without any of the partners themselves being sequestrated.

5. When a partner retires or when a partner joins the firm, the existing partnership comes to an end and a new one is created unless the partnership agreement itself provides to the contrary. The result is that a new partner is not liable for the debts of the firm incurred before his admission, and a retiring partner is on the other hand liable for the debts of the firm up to the date of his retirement.

7.04 The Statute of Limitations referred to in para 2.16 does not apply to Scotland, where the distinction between a contract executed under seal and one under hand is not known. The relevant Act is the Prescription and Limitation (Scotland) Act 1973.

7.05 Mention has been of the practice of creating 'Associates' from senior staff. In recent years this has become widespread in Scotland, where it originally was confined in the main to architectural firms, and is now common practice in all professions. Associates are usually appointed either as a 'reward' to long serving senior employees who may be shortly retiring or from young employees who are being 'groomed' for full partnership. While the additional status thus afforded to the persons concerned is important great care must be taken to define the authority of an associate and on the firm's notepaper to distinguish clearly between partners and associates so as to avoid any question of an associate being 'held out' as a partner.

At the time of this article in the first edition of this book, architects were only permitted to practise on their own or in partnership with others. However, this rule has now been relaxed and an increasing number of architectural practices are in business as either limited liability companies or as unlimited companies.

Other branches of law

7.06 Para 4 discusses the effect of the Offices, Shops and Railway Premises Act 1963 and the Health and Safety at Work Act 1974. The remarks apply equally to architects practising in Scotland, to which the statutes mentioned also apply.

---

*Sequestration: appropriation of income of a property (or firm) to satisfy claims against the owners.

20

Architects' Professional Indemnity Insurance

PETER MADGE

1 Some basic insurance principles

1.01 The subject matter of an insurance policy may be the property owned by the insured against which he wishes to insure, i.e. the contract works, or the creation of a legal liability against him for which he wants insurance protection, i.e. professional liability.

Good faith

1.02 Like other forms of contract, insurance is subject to the normal contractual rules of offer and acceptance, consideration (the premium), legality, agreement of the parties, contractual capacity of the parties and the intention to create a legal relationship. Insurance contracts, however, differ fundamentally from other commercial contracts in the sense that they are bound by the principle of utmost good faith. There is a duty on the insured to disclose to the insurer all material facts bearing on the risk.

Disclosure of material facts

1.03 A material fact is something which would influence the judgment of a prudent insurer in agreeing to accept the risk or not and in deciding the amount of premium he would charge. The test of whether a fact is material or not is whether it would have influenced the judgment of a prudent insurer, not the particular insurer issuing the policy. Whether or not the insured considered the fact to be material is not relevant. It is the test of the prudent insurer, not the prudent insured.

The insured has a duty to disclose all material facts which have a bearing on the risk proposed and must make no misrepresentation about those facts or the risk. The onus of proving that there has been a non-disclosure of information or fact is upon the insurers. The insured must disclose all those material facts which are within his knowledge, whether actual or presumed. He must disclose all those facts which he knows, or ought in the ordinary course of business affairs to know or have known about.

1.04 This represents the common law position. Insurers often insist upon a proposal form being completed before insurance is offered. This asks a number of relevant questions which are material to the risk but the important point to note is that even though a question is not asked, if there is something material to the risk then the insured must disclose it. Moreover, most proposal forms contain a declaration and warranty at the foot of the form saying the insured has answered all questions accurately and not withheld material information. The insured has to sign this. The effect of signing this declaration and warranty is that the insured warrants the accuracy of all the answers on the proposal form and further warrants that he has not withheld or failed to disclose all material facts. A warranty in insurance law has a strict interpretation. Thus, any inaccuracy on the proposal form or non-disclosure of material information gives the insurers the right, if they so wish, to treat the policy as void. Hence the importance of making sure that all answers to questions and information shown on proposal forms are correct.

1.05 Over the years many technical and legal rules have been established in relation to non-disclosure. Generally the following will be held to be material and must, therefore, be disclosed:

1. Facts indicating that the subject matter of the insurance is exposed to more than the ordinary degree of risk.
2. Facts indicating that the insured is activated by some special motive as, for example, where he greatly over-insures.
3. Facts showing that the liability of the insurer is greater than he would normally have expected it to be.
4. Facts showing that there is a moral hazard attaching to the insured suggesting that he is not a fit person to whom insurance can be granted, for example a person with a bad criminal history.
5. Facts which to the insured's knowledge are regarded by the insurers as material.

1.06 On the other hand there are facts which, although material, may become immaterial in certain circumstances

and there is, therefore, no obligation upon the insured to disclose them. For example:

1. Facts which are already known to the insurers or which they may be reasonably presumed to know.
2. Facts which the insurers could have discovered themselves by making some enquiries.
3. Facts where the insurer has waived further information.
4. Facts tending to lessen the risk – for obvious reasons, since anything that lessens the risk is beneficial to the underwriter.

2 Professional indemnity insurance policy

Purpose

2.01 To protect the insured against his legal liability for claims made against him for breach of professional duty.

The policy

2.02 Policies vary from insurer to insurer. All, however, will make the proposal form, completed by the insured, the basis of the contract. Any inaccuracies on that form or any non-disclosure of material fact may make the policy void.

Most policies agree:

1. To indemnify the insured (the firm or practice including past directors, principals or partners)
2. against any claim made against him during the period of insurance
3. for which he shall become legally liable to pay compensation, together with claimants' costs, fees and expenses
4. in accordance with any judgment, award or settlement made in the United Kingdom (or any order made anywhere in the world to enforce such judgment, award or settlement in whole or in part) in consequence of
5. any breach of professional duty of care by the assured to any claimant or
6. any libel, slander or slander of title, slander of goods or injurious falsehood.

The policy covers *legal* liability not moral liability.

Limit of indemnity

2.03 There is a limit up to which insurers will pay claims but not beyond. It is the insured's responsibility to select an adequate limit. The limit may be an *aggregate* limit covering all claims in every policy year or a limit in respect of each and every *claim* (or series of claims from the same originating cause).

Legal costs

2.04 In addition to the limit of indemnity, insurers will normally pay defence costs incurred with their consent in the investigation, defence or settlement of any claim. However, if a payment is made which is greater than the limit of indemnity insurers' agreement to pay the legal costs is scaled down, e.g. if the limit of indemnity is £1 million and the claim is settled for £2 million then the insurer will only pay 50% of legal costs.

Claims made cover

2.05 It is important to note that the policy is a *claims made* policy. In other words it pays only for claims made against the insured during the period of insurance. It is not a negligence committed policy. *Once the policy lapses so does the cover.* Retired partners should make sure the firm's policy covers them. Sole practitioners need 'run off' cover. Liability continues into retirement.

Exclusions

2.06 These should be read very carefully. Normally the policy will *not* pay for:

1. Any excess or deductible, i.e. the first amount of each and every claim.
2. Any claim arising out of participation in any consortium or joint venture, of which the insured forms part (because the liability of the insured in any consortium or joint venture agreement can be varied or increased by the terms of the joint venture or consortium agreement).
3. Any claim arising out of any circumstance or event which has been disclosed by the insured on the proposal form or renewal declaration form (the previous policy should cover the eventuality – make sure it does by telling the insurers before the policy expires).
4. Claims caused by a dishonest, fraudulent, criminal or malicious act or omission of any partner, director or principal of the insured (but such conduct on the part of *employees* may be covered to the extent it gives rise to legal liability). Where it is the insured's own money or property which has been stolen, it is a fidelity guarantee policy which will apply, not a professional liability policy.
5. Any claim arising out of performance warranties, collateral warranties, penalty clauses or liquidated damages clauses unless the liability of the insured to the claimant would have existed in the absence of such warranties or clauses. Performance warranties or fitness for purpose clauses often extend the insured's duty which is to exercise reasonable care and skill so as to almost guarantee the work performed. Most underwriters take the view that they are only prepared to indemnify the insured against accidental or fortuitous mistakes and not to 'guarantee' the work performed. Collateral warranties may extend the insured's duty to third parties, e.g. subsequent owners of the building or tenants.

Surveys

2.07 Where the insured engages in surveys or valuation reports, there will be a policy condition regulating how such reports should be carried out. Normally such work will only be covered if carried out by a qualified architect or surveyor or ones who have had some years experience. In addition the survey or valuation report must contain a disclaimer to the effect that woodwork or other parts of the structure which are covered, unexposed or inaccessible have not been inspected and the report therefore is unable to comment on whether such property is free from defect.

Where the insured considers that high alumina cement may be present in the building a similar clause must be included in the report to the effect that no detailed investigations have been carried out to determine whether high alumina cement was used during the construction of the building and the report therefore is enabled to say whether the building is free from risk in this respect.

Contract terms must be communicated to the client at the outset and become part of the conditions of engagement. They cannot be introduced after the contract has been concluded.

Territorial limits

2.08 The policy normally covers work performed in the United Kingdom which means England, Wales, Scotland, Northern Ireland, the Isle of Man or the Channel Islands. If work outside these limits is to be performed or you have offices abroad then the insurers must be told and cover agreed.

Fees recovery extension

2.09 Often the insured has to sue his client to recover his fees. The result normally is a counter-claim for breach of

professional duty. It may be possible to extend the policy to protect the insured against costs which are necessarily incurred on his behalf in recovering or attempting to recover professional fees.

Policy conditions

2.10 These stipulate certain things that must be done or complied with before insurers pay. They must be read with care since any breach or non-observance of them may result in the insurers refusing to deal with any claim.

1. Once a claim is made against the insured then the insurers must be notified immediately. If the insured becomes aware from any third party that there is an intention to make a claim against him then again the insurers must be notified immediately.
2. If the insured becomes aware of any circumstance or event *which has not yet resulted in a claim* but which is likely to do so, the insured must give full details of that circumstance or event to the insured. Once he has done so then any claim which subsequently arises from that circumstance or event will be covered under the policy in force at the date the circumstance or event *was notified*, notwithstanding that that policy may not be in force at the time of the claim. Make sure *full details* of the circumstance or event are given. Remember your new or renewal policy will exclude the claim and you will be relying upon your old policy for protection.
3. The insured must not admit liability and make no admission, arrangement, offer, promise or payment without the insurers' written consent.
4. The insured must give all such assistance to the insurers as is necessary for them to handle any claim. However, in the event of a dispute the insured will not be required to contest any legal proceedings unless a Queen's Counsel (or by mutual agreement between the insured and the insurers a similar authority) shall advise that such proceedings could be contested with the probability of success.
5. Insurers will not exercise any right of subrogation against any employee or former employee of the insured unless there is any dishonest, fraudulent, criminal or malicious conduct on the part of that employee.
6. If any claim which is made under the policy for indemnity is false or fraudulent then the policy becomes void.
7. The policy is normally governed by the laws of England and any dispute or difference arising between the insured and his insurers will be referred to a Queen's Counsel to be mutually agreed between the insured and the insurers.

Alleviation of non-disclosure rule

2.11 The non-disclosure rule in insurance law is harsh. Any failure to disclose a material fact or any mistake on the proposal form may make the policy void. Breach of the policy conditions may also invalidate a claim. Some policies contain a clause to the effect that the insurers will not exercise their rights to void the policy or to refuse indemnity to the insured for any breach of non-disclosure of material facts or breach of policy conditions provided always that *the insured* shall establish to the satisfaction of insurers that such non-disclosure or breach was innocent and free of any fraudulent conduct or intent to deceive. *The onus of proof is on the insured*. The words used differ amongst insurers.

3 Risk management

3.01 A sensible approach to the risks that may affect an architect can eliminate some of them and mitigate the effects of others. It is logical to identify and control risk at the outset, rather than to argue about who is responsible for injury, loss or damage after it has taken place.

3.02 Risk management entails a sensible overview of risks and falls into four stages:

1. the identification of those risks which can arise;
2. an analysis and measurement of those risks to see what is involved;
3. treatment of those risks so as to eliminate them or reduce their impact;
4. controlling those risks or transferring them to another party, either by means of clauses in the contract conditions or by insurance.

Some risk management suggestions which may help to prevent claims or put you in better position to defend

3.03

1. Read conditions of *engagement* carefully.
   Be clear what you have agreed – Confirm in writing any variations – Be clear what the *fee* is – Disputes trigger off *claims*.
2. Control/supervise the work carefully.
3. Review all office procedures – Control incoming/outgoing post.
4. Have you the experience or knowledge required?
5. Does the fee justify the exposure?
6. Risk/insurance to be put on board meeting agenda.
7. Check agreements with consultants – are they insured?
8. Consider any assignment carefully if it has a US exposure or overseas exposure – take advice. Which law applies?
9. Don't destroy important documents. Have an agreed policy on document retention.
10. Know the work which has problems.
11. Keep an eye on staff with problems (work/domestic/personal).
12. Read collateral agreements, warranties and duty of care agreements carefully. Take advice before signing them.

21

European Community Law affecting Architects

ANDREW GEDDES

1 The European Community and its institutions

Introduction

1.01 The opening up of the Single European Market which it is intended should be completed by 1992, will have a profound effect on every sector of the UK construction industry. Building material producers will have easier access to some 320 million people living in the Community (a market which is a third larger than the US, and double the Japanese). Building products and practices will be standardized, building contractors will have greater opportunities to tender for public sector projects throughout the Community and architects, surveyors and other professionals will be able to practise with greater ease in the EEC. In addition, the growing tendency of the community to insist on higher standards of protection for the consumer and for the environment will place greater burdens on those working in the building industry who are affected by these matters.

1.02 The Single European Market provides an opportunity for the UK construction industry but it also poses a threat. UK suppliers, contractors and professionals will be exposed to increased competition in the UK from their competitors in the rest of the EC and it is anticipated that this threat will be at its most formidable in respect of the largest and most profitable contracts where economies of scale justify the effort involved in competing away from the home market.

1.03 If the UK construction industry is to compete successfully in this new environment it must have an understanding of those EC measures which affect it and ensure that its interests are taken into account when legislation is being drafted and standards are being agreed. A basic knowledge of the Community institutions and how they work is essential if this is to be achieved.

2 The treaties

2.01 The European Community is founded on three treaties. The European Coal and Steel Community was set up by the treaty of Paris in 1951. The two other European Communities were established by the Treaties of Rome signed on 25 March 1952. The first of these established the European Atomic Energy Community (Euratom), and the second, and by far the most important, is the founding treaty of the European Economic Community (EEC).

2.02 The initial objectives of the EEC were the establishment of a customs union with free movement of goods between member states, the dismantling of quotas and barriers to trade of all kind and the free movement of people, services and capital. The EEC Treaty also provided for the adoption of common policies on agriculture, transport and competition. It looked forward to the harmonization of laws and technical standards to facilitate its fundamental objectives and to the creation of a social fund and an Investment Bank.

The Single European Act (SEA)

2.03 By 1982 it was recognized that the progress towards the completion of a European Market without physical technical or fiscal barriers had been unacceptably slow and the European Council in that year pledged itself to the completion of this internal market as a high priority. In 1985 the Commission published its White Paper entitled 'Completing the Internal Market' in which it set out proposals for some 300 legislative measures which it considered would have to be adopted in order to achieve this aim. At the same time the member states agreed to amend parts of the Treaty of Rome so as to extend their scope and to facilitate the implementation of the legislative programme. The result was the Single European Act which came into force on 1 July 1987. The principal objective of the SEA is the removal by 31 December 1992 of all the remaining barriers within the EEC to the free movement of goods, services, persons and capital. It introduces for the first time a system of qualified majority voting in the Council so that proposed legislation cannot so easily be blocked. The Act also provides for further technological development, the strengthening of economic and social ties and the improvment of the environment and working conditions throughout the Community.

The member states

2.04 The founding member states were Belgium, France, West Germany, Italy, Luxembourg and the Netherlands. Denmark, Ireland and the UK became members in 1973. Greece entered the Community in 1981 and Portugal and Spain in 1986.

The Community institutions and legislation

2.05 Each of the Treaties provides that the tasks entrusted to the ECSC, EEC and Euratom should be carried out by four institutions: the Council, the Commission, the European Parliament and the Court of Justice. The Parliament and the Court of Justice have always been common to all three communities and since 1967 this has also been true of the Council and the Commission. Because the three Communities are now managed by common institutions they are

increasingly referred to as the European Community (EC). The Council is assisted by a Committee of Permanent Representatives (COREPER) made up of representatives of the various member states and for EEC and Euratom matters the Council and the Commission are assisted by an Economic and Social Committee acting in an advisory capacity.

The Commission

2.06 The Commission, whose headquarters is in Brussels, is composed of at least one representative from each member state and at November 1989 consisted of 17 members. Members of the Commission are appointed for four years by mutual agreement of EC governments.

The Commission is supported by a staff of some 12 000 officials, a quarter of whom are involved in translation made necessary by the use of three official languages. The staff are mainly divided between a number of directorates-general, each with a separate share of responsibility. Commission decisions, however, are made on a corporate basis. The Commission is the official guardian of the Treaties and ensures that the EC rules and principles it contains are respected. It is responsible for proposing to the Council measures likely to advance the development of EC policies. Once a measure has been adopted it is the Commission's task to ensure that it is implemented throughout the Community. It has wide investigative powers which it may initiate itself or which it may set into motion as a result of a complaint by a third party. It can impose fines on individuals or companies found to be in breach of EC Rules and these frequently run into millions of pounds. An appeal against a Commission decision lies to the European Court of Justice. In addition the Commission can take a member state before the Court if they fail to respect their obligations.

The members of the Commission act only in the interest of the EC. During their term of office they must remain independent of the governments of the member states and of the Council. They are subject to the supervision of the European Parliament which is the only body that can force them to resign collectively.

The Council

2.07 The Council is made up of representatives of the governments of the member states. Each government normally sends one of its ministers. Its membership thus varies with the subjects proposed for discussion. The Foreign Minister is regarded as his country's main representative in the Council but the other ministers meet frequently for more specialized Council meetings. The Presidency of the Council is held for a term of six months by each member in turn. The Council is the EC's principal legislative body and makes all the main policy decisions. It can act only on a proposal from the Commission.

For some issues (such as taxation, and certain social and environmental matters) the Council must act unanimously if it wishes to alter the text of a proposal from the Commission. Since the passing of the SEA, however, the Council may now act in a wide range of matters by qualified majority. Under this system France, West Germany, Italy and the UK have ten votes each, Spain eight votes, Belgium, Greece, the Netherlands and Portugal five, Denmark and Ireland three and Luxembourg two votes. Out of the total of 76 votes, 54 are needed to approve a Commission proposal. The groundwork for the Council's response to Commission proposals is carried out by officials of the member states, coordinated by COREPER.

EC legislation

2.08 Measures adopted by Council and by the Commission where it has decision-making powers have the force of law, which take precedence over the national laws of the member states. In some cases these measures have direct effect throughout the EC. In others the member states must first implement them by way of national legislation.

These measures may be:

1. Regulations in which case they apply directly.
2. Directives which lay down compulsory objectives to be achieved by a certain date but leave to member states how they are to be implemented into national law. In certain

defined circumstances when a member state has failed to implement a directive in due time a citizen can rely directly on the directive as against the state.

3. Decisions, which are binding only on the member states, companies or individuals to whom they are addressed.

The Council also from time to time adopts resolutions which are declarations of intent and do not have legal force.

The European Court of Justice

2.09 The Court, which sits in Luxembourg, consists of thirteen judges assisted by six advocates-general. They are appointed for a period of six years by mutual consent of the member states and are entirely independent. The Court is entrusted with the interpretation of the Treaties and can quash any measures adopted by the Council, the Commission or national governments which are incompatible with it. An application for this purpose may be made by an EC institution government or individual. The Court also gives judgment when requested to do so by a national court on any question of EC law.

Judments of the Court in the field of EC law are binding on all national courts.

As from September 1989, a Court of First Instance has sat to hear cases principally relating to competition matters. An appeal on a point of law only lies from that court to the ECJ.

The European Parliament

2.10 The Parliament which meets in plenary session in Strasbourg currently consists of 518 members elected from the member states broadly in proportion to their size. Elections take place every five years. Although the Parliament does not have legislative powers like those of national parliaments, it has an important part to play in three areas:

1. *It adopts and controls the EC budget.*
2. *It considers proposals for EC legislation.* In many cases (including those relating to completion of the internal market and the improvment of the working environment), Parliament must be consulted before the Council can take a decision. In practice Parliament is consulted on all issues of any importance and can and does influence the Council's final decision.
3. *It supervises activities of the EC institutions.* It has the power to question and criticize the Commission's proposals and activities in debate. It can exert influence through its budgetary power and has the power to dismiss the Commission by a two-thirds majority.

3 Public procurement

Introduction

3.01 It has been recognized by the member states that the opening up of government procurement to EC-wide competition is a key component in the creation of a single European market. This huge sector of the economy is estimated by the Commission as representing some 15% (592 billion Ecu at 1989 prices) of Community GDP of which some 7%–10% (260–380 billion Ecu) takes the form of contracts subject to formal purchasing procedures. Of that total, building and construction represents 28.6% (Public Procurement Regional and Social Aspects COM (89) 400 final). In order to further this aim the EC has adopted two principal measures: a Public Works Directive (71/305/EEC) and a Public Supplies Directive (77/62/EEC) which have been in force in the UK since 1973 and 1978 respectively. The 'Works' Directive has now been substantially amended by

Directive (89/440/EEC) (Extract 21.2) which is required to be implemented by all the member states (except for Greece, Portugal and Spain) by not later than 19 July 1990 and will be implemented by the UK on that date. Greece, Portugal and Spain must implement the Directive by 1 March 1992. The 'Supplies' Directive has been amended principally by Directive 88/295 EC which came into force on 1 January 1989. These directives are intended to harmonize tendering and award procedures in the EC in respect of contracts awarded by public bodies over a certain estimated value, and to ensure that such contracts are properly advertised and that there is no discrimination against suppliers and contractors from other member states. The Supplies Directive, covering as it does the public procurement of products is of, perhaps, marginal interest to architects and it is not proposed to deal with it in detail in this work.

The Commission have been dissatisfied with the degree to which member states have complied with these directives (it is estimated, for example, that only about 20% of public contracts falling within the provisions of the directives are properly advertised) and have therefore proposed a number of measures that they intend will overcome this problem while at the same time extending the scope of the current legislation (see Guide to Community Rules on Open Government Procurement OJ 1987 C358 P2). The amendments to the Works Directive and the Supplies Directive have already been mentioned. In addition, a directive has been prepared which will extend the scope of the current directives into sectors hitherto excluded, namely public energy, water, transport, and telecommunications (COM (89) 380 Final). It is anticipated that this directive will be implemented in the UK on 1 January 1992. A 'common position' has been reached in the Council in regard to a proposed directive on enforcing the provisions of the Works and Supplies Directives and a parallel directive is proposed in relation to the 'excluded sectors' directive. It is estimated that these will come into force in about 1992. Finally, the Commission have prepared a draft directive (November 1989) setting out similar rules to those contained in the Works and Supplies Directives in relation to public contracts awarded in the services sector. The services covered will include architectural engineering and other technical consultancy services.

Although the Works Directive and the Supplies Directive (and the amendments thereto) have been implemented by way of a circular letter from the DTI to the bodies concerned, it is expected that the proposed directives, which will apply at least in part to the private sector, will have to be implemented by way of national legislation. As it is anticipated that many, if not all, of these proposed measures will be in force in the near future, it is necessary to consider both these and the existing measures in some detail. In respect of the Works Directive it has been thought appropriate to refer to the law as it will be from 19 July 1990. The DTI take the view that in the absence of any transitional provisions being provided in the amending directive, the old provisions will continue to apply to any contract which has been advertised in accordance with the unamended directive prior to 19 July 1990. It is submitted that that view is probably correct. It will continue to be necessary therefore to refer to the old legislation for the provisions applicable to such contracts.

The Works Directive

3.02 The Directive has three principal aims in respect of the contracts to which it applies:

1. EC-wide advertising of contracts so that firms in every member state have an opportunity of tendering for them.
2. The prohibition of technical specifications liable to discriminate against foreign tenderers.
3. The application of objective criteria in tendering and award procedures.

The public works contracts to which the Works Directive applies

3.03 These are defined in article 1 of the Directive as:

'Contracts for pecuniary interest concluded in writing between a contractor and a contracting authority as defined in (b) which have as their object either the execution, or both the execution and design, of works related to one of the activities referred to in Annex II or a work defined in (c) below, or the execution by whatever means of a work corresponding to the requirements specified by the contracting authority.'

Meaning of 'contractor'

3.04 Contractors may be companies, firms or individuals, or groups (consortia) of such. Groups may not be required to assume any particular legal form in order to bid for a contract but may be required to do so if they are awarded the contract.

Meaning of 'Contracting authorities'

3.05 'Contracting authorities' are defined in article 1(b) as:

'the State, regional or local authorities, bodies governed by public law, associations formed by one or several of such authorities or bodies governed by public law'.

A body governed by public law is defined as:

'any body
– established for the specific purpose of meeting needs in the general interest, not having an industrial or commercial character, and
– having legal personality, and
– financed, for the most part, by the State or regional or local authorities, or other bodies governed by public law, or subject to management supervision by those bodies or having an administrative, managerial or supervisory board more than half of whose members are appointed by the State regional or local authorities or by other bodies governed by public law.'

It is perhaps fortunate therefore that lists of bodies or categories of such bodies which fall within that definition are set out in Annex I to the Directive. These lists are intended to be as 'exhaustive as possible' and will be amended from time to time.

Meaning of 'Works'

3.06 The works must either:

1. 'relate' to one of the activities listed in Annex II, or
2. they must be a 'work' as defined in article 1(c), or
3. they must 'correspond to the requirements specified by the contracting authority, however these works are executed.

1. The activities listed in Annex II broadly cover building and civil engineering works. It is not essential that the contract should be for one of the works listed for it to fall within the Directive. It is sufficient if it is for works that are 'related' to such activity.
2. Article 1(c) defines 'a work' as 'the outcome of building or civil engineering works taken as a whole that is sufficient of itself to fulfil an economic and technical function'. Although the wording is somewhat obscure it is submitted that the purpose of this limb is to include within the provisions of the Directive contracts for part of a public works contract which fall below the qualifying threshold where the project as a whole is over that threshold. For example, a contract to provide scaffolding worth 400 000 Ecu for a hospital estimated to cost 10 million Ecu would fall within the provisions of the Directive. However, certain part contracts may be exempted under the provisions of article 4(a)(3) (see below).

3. The wording of the third limb is also, it is submitted, unclear. What seems to be intended is that what are termed 'management contracts' should be covered by the Directive. These are contracts which are made with a management contractor who actually runs the project and then sub-contracts the work to other contractors. Under this provision both the management contract and the sub-contract would be covered by the provisions of the Directive if the project value exceeded the threshold and it was not otherwise exempted.

Additional contracts covered by the Directive

3.07 The Directive also applies to certain civil engineering works where the 'contracting authority' subsidizes directly by more than 50% a 'works' contract awarded by an entity other than themselves (section 1a). These works are listed under sub-heading 502 in Annex II of the Directive (broadly relating to roads, bridges, railways, etc.). In addition, contracts relating to building works for hospitals, sports facilities, educational establishments and buildings used for administrative purposes are also covered.

Special conditions apply to 'public works concession contracts' of not less than 5 million Ecu (section 1b). A 'public works concession contract' is 'a public works contract' where the consideration for the works to be carried out consists either solely in the right to exploit the construction or in that right together with payment (section 1d).

Form of contracts

3.08 The Directive requires merely that the contract be for 'pecuniary interest' and be drawn up in writing. Contracts for other than a pecuniary consideration (e.g. a construction contract where the contractor receives a grant of building land) are therefore excluded. There being no express restriction on the terms of the contract, the Directive covers the widest possible range of contracts a public authority can make with a private contractor for construction works. Thus it includes, for example, contracts covering the planning and/or financing of a project as well as its execution.

Excluded contracts

3.09 The following types of contract are excluded from the scope of the Directive:

1. Works contracts falling below an estimated value net of VAT of 5 million Ecu (article 4(a)(1)).
2. Works contracts awarded by carriers by land, air, sea or inland waterways (article 3(4)(a)).
3. Works contracts awarded by contracting authorities in so far as those contracts concern the production, transport and distribution of drinking water or those contracting authorities whose principal activity lies in the production and distribution of energy (article 3(4)(b)).
4. Works contracts which are secret or which involve state security (as defined) (article 3(4)(c)).
5. Certain contracts awarded in pursuance of international agreement (article 4).

1. *Value threshold.* The threshold value from which a public works contract becomes subject to the provisions of the Directive is 5 million Ecu (or approximately £3.3 million at January 1990). The value of this threshold in national currencies will normally be revised every two years with effect from 1 January 1993 and published in the Official Journal of the European Communities.

When calculating the estimated value of a works contract there must be included the value of the supplies made available to the contractor by the contracting authorities (article 4(a)(5)). When a work is sub-divided into several lots, each one the subject of a contract, the value of all the lots must be aggregated and if the total

exceeds 5 million Ecu, the Directive will apply to each lot. This provision does not apply to lots of less than 1 million Ecu in value where the aggregate estimated value of such lots does not exceed 20% of the total estimated value of all lots. It is prohibited to split up contracts with the intention of evading the rules of the Directive.

2. *Works contracts awarded by transport authorities.* This exemption is limited to organizations actually undertaking the carriage of passengers or goods as common carriers. Authorities operating facilities such as ports or airports are subject to the directive.

3. *Works contracts awarded by authorities providing certain public services.* In the public services sector only services whose specific function is the production, transport or distribution of water or energy are excepted. As far as water services are concerned the exception only applies to services undertaking the collection, supply and distribution of drinking water, i.e. generally water that has been purified for residentual or industrial use. River management, irrigation drainage and sewage services are covered by the directive. When an organization provides several services at once, for example, a local authority combining the functions of sewage treatment and drinking water supply, only contracts relating to the latter are excepted.

Public procurement by entities operating in the water, energy, transport and telecommunications sectors will be covered as from 1 January 1992 by the proposed directive already referred to. The proposed directive should, however, be looked at with caution as the details of its provisions may well be altered before final adoption.

Borderline cases with 'supplies' contracts

3.10 Where both goods and services are required under one contract and it is in consequence difficult to decide which directive applies, the general rule is that if the value of the goods to be supplied exceeds that of the services to be performed then it is a supply contract. If on the other hand the value of the works falling within the directive exceeds that of the goods, it is a public works contract (see Guide to Community Rules on Open Government Procurement, page 16).

The rules applying to 'works' contracts

Tendering procedures

3.11 Tendering procedures under the Directive must be 'open', 'restricted', 'negotiated' or 'special' (see articles 5 and 6).

1. *Open procedures* Open procedures are defined in article 1(e) as 'those national procedures whereby all interested contractors may submit tenders'.
2. *Restricted procedures* Restricted procedures are defined in article 1(f) as 'those national procedures whereby only those contractors invited by the contracting authorities may submit tenders'.
3. *Negotiated procedures* Negotiated procedures are defined by article 1(g), as 'those national procedures whereby contracting authorities consult contractors of their choice and negotiate the terms of the contract with one or more of them'.
4. *Special procedures relating to public housing schemes* 'Special procedures' are not defined in the Directive but by article 6 it is provided that:

> 'In the case of contracts relating to the design and construction of a public housing scheme whose size and complexity, and the estimated duration of the work involved require the planning to be based from the outset on close collaboration within a team comprising representatives of the authorities awarding contracts experts and the contractor to be responsible for carrying

out the works, a special procedure may be adopted for selecting the contractor most suitable for integration into the team.'

However, even where such a special procedure is justified certain rules must be complied with:

1. Contract notices must include an accurate description of the works to be carried out so as to enable interested contractors to form a valid idea of the project.
2. Contract notices must set out in accordance with the directive the personal, technical and financial conditions to be fulfilled by candidates.
3. When the special procedure is adopted, the authority awarding the contract must apply the common advertising rules relating to the 'restricted procedure' and to the criteria for qualitative selection (see below).

The circumstances in which tendering procedures may be 'negotiated'

3.12 The circumstances in which the 'negotiated' tendering procedure may be used are exhaustively set out in article 5. These are:

1. In the event of irregular tenders in response to an open or restricted procedure.
2. Where the works involved are carried out purely for the purpose of research experiment or development.
3. In exceptional cases when the nature of the works or the risks attaching thereto do not permit overall pricing.

In each of the above circumstances there must be prior publication of a tender notice and the candidates must be selected according to 'qualitative public criteria'.

4. In the absence of, or of appropriate, tenders in response to an open or restricted procedure.
5. Where for technical or artistic reasons or for reasons connected with the protection of exclusive rights the works may only be carried out by a particular contractor.
6. In certain situations or 'extreme urgency', where such urgency is not attributable to the contracting authorities.
7. In certain circumstances where unforseen additional works not included in the original project are required and these do not exceed 50% by value of the main contract.
8. In certain cases where new works are required consisting of the repetition of similar works entrusted to the undertaking to which the same contracting authorities awarded an earlier contract. This procedure may only be applied during the three years following the conclusion of the original contract.

In cases of 4–8 above the contracting authorities may award the contract without prior publication of a tender notice.

In all other circumstances contracting authorities must award their public works contracts by the open procedure or the restricted procedure (article 5(4)).

Advertising rules in relation to 'works' contracts

3.13

1. The essential characteristics of a works contract covered by the Directive must be advertised in a tender notice together with the proposed tendering procedure in relation to it (article 12(1)(4)).
2. Contracting authorities who have awarded a contract must, save in specified circumstances, advertise the result by means of a notice (article 12(5)).
3. Such notices must be sent 'as rapidly as possible and by the most appropriate channels' to the office for official publications of the EC. In the case of the 'accelerated procedure' (see below), the notice must be sent by telex, telegram or telefax. The notices must be published in the Official Journal not later than twelve days (in the case of

accelerated procedure, five days) after despatch. The notice must not be published in the country of the contracting authority before the above-mentioned date of despatch and it must mention that date. It must not contain information other than that published in the Official Journal.

4. The notice in (1) must be sent as soon as possible after the decision approving the planning of the works contract in question and the notice in (2) must be sent not later than 48 days after the award of the contract.

5. All the notices referred to must be drawn up in accordance with the models given in Annexes IV to VI and must specify the information requested in those annexes.

6. No conditions may be required other than those specified in articles 25 and 26 when requesting information covering the economic and technical standards which the contracting authorities require of contractors for their selection.

Technical specifications contained in contractual documents

3.14 Detailed rules as to permitted technical specifications (as defined in Annex III) are set out in article 10 to which reference should be made. These rules apply to all works contracts irrespective of the tendering procedure. The purpose behind these rules is to avoid any discrimination against foreign contractors who might be disadvantaged if technical specifications were required which could only be met or more easily met by a national contractor. Broadly, the rules require that without prejudice to legally binding national technical rules where these exist, and where these are compatible with Community law, technical specifications must be defined by reference to 'national standards implementing European standards or by reference to European technical approvals or by reference to common technical specifications' (each of these terms is defined in Annex II) (article 10(2)). Certain exceptions to this requirement are permitted but where those exceptions are relied upon the reasons for doing so must be recorded 'wherever possible' in the published tender notice or in the contract documents and in every case must be recorded in the contracting authority's internal documents which must be open to inspection.

In the absence of any European standard or European technical approval or common technical specification, the technical specifications must be defined by reference 'to the national technical specifications recognized as complying with the basic requirements listed in the Community directives on technical harmonization in accordance with the procedures laid down in those directives' and in particular with the Construction Products Directive 89/106EEC (see Section 4, below).

Technical specifications are prohibited which mention products of a specific make or source or of a particular process 'and which therefore favour or eliminate certain undertakings'. In particular, the indication of trade marks, patent types or of a specific origin or production are forbidden. However, if such indication is accompanied by the words 'or equivalent', it is permissible in cases where the contracting authority is unable to use a specification which is sufficiently precise and intelligible to all parties concerned (article 10(6)).

Time limits

3.15 Time limits for submitting tenders or for requesting to participate must be clearly specified in the notices so that it is not more difficult for contractors from other countries to determine closing dates than it is for contractors from the awarding authority's country. Where the open tendering procedure is used the normal minimum time limit for the receipt of tenders is 52 days from the date of sending the notice although this may be reduced to 36 days in the

circumstances specified in article 13(2). Time limits are also prescribed for the sending of supporting documentation by the contracting authorities. When the restricted procedure is employed, the time limit for receipt of requests to participate must be not less than 37 days from the date of sending the notice (article 14(a)). The contracting authority must then simultaneously and in writing invite the candidates to submit their tenders. The letter must contain the information specified in article 14(2). In restricted procedures the time limit for receipt of tenders must not be less than 40 days from the date of despatch of the written invitation, although this can be reduced to 36 days in the circumstances set out in article 14(4). In cases where urgency renders impracticable the time limits laid down in article 14, reduced time limits as provided in article 15 may be imposed. Special time limits apply to works concession contracts (see article 15(a) and (b)).

Criteria for qualitative selection of contractors

3.16 Detailed rules are laid down in the Directive as to the only criteria on which applicants to bid or bidders may be disqualified or eliminated as well as the only permitted criteria on which selection of candidates permitted to tender may be based. The grounds on which a contractor may be excluded from participation in the contract are set out in article 23. These relate broadly to disqualification based on ethical, professional or financial grounds.

The grounds on which a contractor may be eliminated as unsuitable are set out in articles 25 to 28 and broadly cover economic and financial standing and technical knowledge or ability. Strict rules are set out in those articles of how proof of such financial standing and technical competence may be furnished, the purpose of such rules being to ensure that foreign contractors should in no way be at a disadvantage. No tenderer may be required to furnish proof of his good standing or reputation by any other means than those set out in the Directive (*SA Transporoute et Travaux* v *Minister of Public Works* 1982 ECR 417). Provision is also made in article 28 for the situation where contractors are established in member states which have official lists of approved contractors. The criteria for acceptance on such a list must be consistent with those laid down in the Directive and registration on such a list constitutes a presumption of suitability for works corresponding to the contractor's classification, although the contractor may be required to furnish fresh proof of certain matters such as his financial standing. In restricted and negotiated procedures the contracting authorities, once they have excluded or eliminated candidates on the basis of the criteria set out in articles 23 to 28, must select those candidates whom they intend to invite to tender or negotiate solely on the basis of the information obtained regarding the contractor's personal position and his economic and technical standing. There must be no discrimination on other than objective criteria. In particular, there must be no discrimination on grounds of nationality.

In the case of negotiated procedures the contracting authorities may prescribe the range within which the number of undertakings which they intend to invite will fall. The number invited must not be less than 5 nor more than 20 (article 22(2)) but in any event the number must be sufficient to ensure genuine competition.

Where the negotiated procedure is employed the number of candidates admitted to negotiate must be not less than three provided there is a sufficient number of suitable candidates.

Criteria for the award of 'works' contracts

3.17 The criteria on which the award of contracts must be based must be either (1) the lowest price only, or (2) the economically most advantageous tender overall (article 29).

So far as the second criterion is concerned, the contracting authority may take into consideration when determining which is the best offer various matters according to the nature of the contract, e.g. price, period of completion, running costs, profitability and technical merit. The list is not exhaustive but it is clear from the examples given that only objective criteria may be used which are strictly relevant to the particular project and uniformly applicable to all bidders.

All the criteria the contracting authority intends to apply in determining the most economically advantageous offer must be stated in the tender notice or tender documents, preferably in descending order of importance. No criteria not mentioned in the notice or tender documents may be used.

A distinction, however, must be made between a contractual condition requiring the successful contractor to cooperate with some policy objective of the contracting authority on the one hand, and the criteria for the selection of firms or for the award of a contract on the other. In a recent case (Case 31/87 *Gebreeders Beentjes BV* v *The Netherlands*) the Court of Justice was requested to rule on the compatibility with Community law of a condition attached to the award of a public works contract under which the contractor was required to engage a given number of long-term unemployed registered with the regional employment office. The Court held that such a condition was compatible with the Works Directive in that it was not relevant to an assessment of the bidder's economic, financial or technical capacity to carry out the work, nor did it form part of the criteria applied by the contracting authority to decide to whom to award the contract. It was simply an obligation which the firm securing the contract would have to accept. Nevertheless, such conditions must be compatible with the Treaty, particularly with those provisions on freedom to provide services, freedom of establishment and non-discrimination on the grounds of nationality. Thus it would breach the Treaty if it appeared on the facts that the condition could only be fulfilled by national firms or if it would be more difficult for bidders coming from other member states to fulfil that condition. It is submitted that other policy objectives might equally be included in the contract on the same principles. Thus, for example, a condition might legitimately be included that the successful candidate must undertake that a specific proportion of its workforce would be drawn from the ethnic minority or that it would agree to employ a certain number of trainees. It would not, however, be legitimate if it were further specified that those employees or trainees should be from a specific area or even from a specific member state as this would amount to unlawful discrimination (see Case 243/89 *The Danish Great Belt Bridge*).

Even a request for information from tenderers (as opposed to the insertion of a contractual term) can in certain circumstances be in breach of the rules if such request would reasonably lead the tenderer to believe that discrimination on local or national grounds is likely to occur. In this context, the UK Department of Environment has published a circular to assist local authorities in complying with the rules governing public procurement (Circular 21/89 Department of Environment 14.9.89). The Circular clarifies the Commission's view that requiring the tenderer to give information on whether local labour and local experience will be used may imply that a tenderer using local labour would be more likely to win the contract. Local authorities are advised therefore not to put such requirements into future contract notices.

Abnormally low tenders

3.18 If a bid appears to be abnormally low given the contract specification, the authority awarding the contract must, before rejecting that tender, request in writing an explanation of those parts of the tender which it considers suspect and take those explanations into account (see *SA Transporoute et Travaux* v *Minister of Public Works*, above). In cases where the criterion for awarding the contract is the lowest price, the contracting authority must inform the Commission where it rejects a tender which it considers too low.

However, until the end of 1992, this procedure need not be followed where:

1. national law so permits, and
2. where the number of tenders is so high that implementation of this procedure would lead to delay and jeopardize the public interest, and
3. there is no discrimination on grounds of nationality.

3.19 The only exception from the rule set out in para 3.17 is where national legislation in force on 26 July 1971 (when the Directive was adopted) provides for certain bidders to be given preference. However, this legislation must be compatible with the Treaty and in particular the rules in respect of state aid contained in articles 92 ff (article 29(4)).

In addition, until 31 December 1992, the Directive does not prevent the application of national provisions on the award of public works contracts which have regional aid as their objective so long as those provisions are compatible with the Treaty, in particular with the principles of non-discrimination on the grounds of nationality, freedom of establishment and freedom to provide services.

Obligations to inform with regard to the outcome of the contract procedure

3.20 Within 15 days of the date on which a request is received the contracting authorities must inform any eliminated candidate or tenderer who so requests of the reasons for rejection of his application or tender and, in the case of a tender, the name of the successful tenderer (article 5(a)). In addition, the result of the award procedure must be advertised in the Official Journal (article 12) and a report prepared for the purposes of the Commission setting out specified information (article 5(a) (3)).

Remedies for breach of the Community rules governing public procurement

3.21 Where a supplier or contractor believes his interests have been damaged by the failure of a public authority (or a member state) to observe the EC tendering rules relevant to public procurement and construction there are at present (November 1989) principally two avenues by which he may seek redress:

1. he may make a complaint to the Commission, or
2. he may bring an action against the authority concerned in the national court.

Complaint to the Commission

3.22 Complaint may be lodged direct with the Directorate-General for the Internal Market and Industrial Affairs at the Commission headquarters in Brussels. If the complainant so wishes, the Commission will keep their identity secret when it takes the matter up with the national authorities.

If the complaint is found to be justified the Commission commences infringement proceedings against the member state responsible for the authority. These proceedings may ultimately lead to the Commission bringing a case before the ECJ and in an appropriate case they may apply to the Court for an injunction to suspend award of the contract pending judgement on the merits of the case.

It is not, however, yet certain whether the Court will go so far as to suspend the works after a contract has been awarded in breach of the public procurement rules.

In the *Danish Great Belt Bridge case* (above) the Danish Government had invited tenders for the construction of a major infrastructure project to link the main islands in the Danish Baltic. The project documentation incorporated

obligations to use Danish labour and materials. Following Commission intervention, these clauses were removed and the Commission requested a reopening of the tender procedure. However, the award went ahead without renewed tendering and the Commission applied to the Court for interim measures to have the works suspended pending appropriate retendering. The Court was reluctant to go that far and encouraged the parties to reach a settlement which was achieved by the Commission withdrawing its application in return for a declaration by Denmark that it was in breach of the Treaty and that it recognized that the unsuccessful candidates for the project would recover their tender costs.

It is submitted that a similar course is likely to be followed in other similar cases which come before the ECJ pending the introduction of the directive introducing a common enforcement procedure (see para 3.23). In the draft of that directive, it is to be noted that the Commission's powers of intervention are limited to the period before a contract is concluded (article 3).

Action in the national court

3.23 The public procurement directives having been implemented by administrative action in the UK, it is not possible to bring an action for breach of their provisions. Further, since there is no contract between a disappointed tenderer and the procuring authority, no action lies in English law. The only remedy open to a complainant is to bring an action for judicial review of the award of the contract. The complainant must have the leave of the court to make such an application and he must show 'a sufficient interest in the matter to which the application relates' (Supreme Court Act 1981, section 31(3)). The court may refuse leave to apply (or a remedy) if it considers that the grant of the relief sought would be likely 'to cause substantial hardship to, or substantially prejudice the rights of any person, or would be detrimental to good administration' (ibid, section 31(6)). Damages may be awarded on an application for judicial review if claimed in the original application, but such awards are very rare. The usual remedy is an injunction or a declaration. Relief may, in addition, be available under the provisions of section 17 of the Local Government Act 1988 where this applies.

Proposed legislation in relation to enforcement procedure

3.24 The lack of any common enforcement procedure in the EC in relation to public procurement, and indeed the absence in some member states of any effective procedure at all, resulted in a Commission proposal for a directive designed to remedy this situation. The member states have on 22 December 1989 adopted this directive and its provision must be implemented into national law by 1 January 1992 (see Extract 21.1).

Under this directive national review procedures will have to be implemented which will enable a disappointed tenderer to obtain interlocutory relief, including measures to suspend the procedure for the award of a public contract on the implementation of any decision taken by the contracting authority (article 2(a)).

The review body must be given the power to 'set aside or ensure the setting aside of decisions taken unlawfully, including the removal of discriminatory technical economic or financial specifications in the invitation to tender, the contract documents or in any other document relating to the contract award procedure' (article 2(6)). In addition, the review body must have power to award damages to persons harmed by the infringement (article 2(c)).

The enforcement procedure may in addition be initiated by the commission where 'prior to a contract being concluded, it considers that a clear and manifest infringement of Community provisions in the field of public procurement has been committed during a contract award procedure falling within

the scope of [the Works Directive or the Supplies Directive]. It is anticipated that the Directive will be implemented in the UK some time during the course of 1992.

Extract 21.1

COUNCIL DIRECTIVE

of 21 December 1989

on the coordination of the laws, regulations and administrative provisions relating to the application of review procedures to the award of public supply and public works contracts

(89/665/EEC)

THE COUNCIL OF THE EUROPEAN COMMUNITIES,

Having regard to the Treaty establishing the European Economic Community, and in particular Article 100a thereof,

Having regard to the proposal from the Commission (¹),

In cooperation with the European Parliament (²),

Having regard to the opinion of the Economic and Social Committee (³),

Whereas Community Directives on public procurement, in particular Council Directive 71/305/EEC of 26 July 1971 concerning the coordination of procedures for the award of public works contracts (⁴), as last amended by Directive 89/440/EEC (⁵), and Council Directive 77/62/EEC of 21 December 1976 coordinating procedures for the award of public supply contracts (⁶), as last amended by Directive 88/295/EEC (⁷), do not contain any specific provisions ensuring their effective application;

Whereas the existing arrangements at both national and Community levels for ensuring their application are not always adequate to ensure compliance with the relevant Community provisions particularly at a stage when infringements can be corrected;

Whereas the opening-up of public procurement to Community competition necessitates a substantial increase in the guarantees of transparency and non-discrimination; whereas, for it to have tangible effects, effective and rapid remedies must be available in the case of infringements of Community law in the field of public procurement or national rules implementing that law;

Whereas in certain Member States the absence of effective remedies or inadequacy of existing remedies deter Community undertakings from submitting tenders in the Member State in which the contracting authority is established; whereas, therefore, the Member States concerned must remedy this situation;

Whereas, since procedures for the award of public contracts are of such short duration, competent review bodies must, among other things, be authorized to take interim measures aimed at suspending such a procedure or the implementation of any decisions which may be taken by the contracting authority; whereas the short duration of the procedures means that the aforementioned infringements need to be dealt with urgently;

Whereas it is necessary to ensure that adequate procedures exist in all the Member States to permit the setting aside of decisions taken unlawfully and compensation of persons harmed by an infringement;

Whereas, when undertakings do not seek review, certain infringements may not be corrected unless a specific mechanism is put in place;

Whereas, accordingly, the Commission, when it considers that a clear and manifest infringement has been committed during a contract award procedure, should be able to bring it to the attention of the competent authorities of the Member State and of the contracting authority concerned so that appropriate steps are taken for the rapid correction of any alleged infringement;

Whereas the application in practice of the provisions of this Directive should be re-examined within a period of four years of its implementation on the basis of information to be supplied by the Member States concerning the functioning of the national review procedures,

HAD ADOPTED THIS DIRECTIVE:

Article 1

1.   The Member States shall take the measures necessary to ensure that, as regards contract award procedures falling withing the scope of Directives 71/305/EEC and 77/62/EEC, decisions taken by the contracting authorities may be reviewed effectively and, in particular, as rapidly as possible in accordance with the conditions set out in the following Articles, and, in particular, Article 2 (7) on the grounds that such decisions have infringed Community law in the field of public procurement or national rules implementing that law.

2.   Member States shall ensure that there is no discrimination between undertakings claiming injury in the context of a procedure for the award of a contract as a result of the distinction made by this Directive between national rules implementing Community law and other national rules.

3.   The Member States shall ensure that the review procedures are available, under detailed rules which the Member States may establish, at least to any person having or having had an interest in obtaining a particular public supply or public works contract and who has been or risks being harmed by an alleged infringement. In particular, the Member States may require that the person seeking the review must have previously notified the contracting authority of the alleged infringement and of his intention to seek review.

Article 2

1.   The Member States shall ensure that the measures taken concerning the review procedures specified in Article 1 include provision for the powers to:

(a)   take, at the earliest opportunity and by way of interlocutory procedures, interim measures with the aim of correcting the alleged infringement or preventing further damage to the interests concerned, including measures to suspend or to ensure the suspension of the procedure for the award of a public contract or the implementation of any decision taken by the contracting authority;

(b)   either set aside or ensure the setting aside of decisions taken unlawfully, including the removal of discriminatory technical, economic or financial specifications in the invitation to tender, the contract documents or in any other document relating to the contract award procedure;

(c)   award damages to persons harmed by an infringement.

2.   The powers specified in paragraph 1 may be conferred on separate bodies responsible for different aspects of the review procedure.

3.   Review procedures need not in themselves have an automatic suspensive effect on the contract award procedures to which they relate.

4.   The Member States may provide that when considering whether to order interim measures the body responsible may take into account the probable consequences of the measures for all interests likely to be harmed, as well as the public interest, and may decide not to grant such measures where their negative consequences could exceed their benefits. A decision not to grant interim measures shall not prejudice any other claim of the person seeking these measures.

5.   The Member States may provide that where damages are claimed on the grounds that a decision was taken unlawfully, the contested decision must first be set aside by a body having the necessary powers.

6.   The effects of the exercise of the powers referred to in paragraph 1 on a contract concluded subsequent to its award shall be determined by national law.

Furthermore, except where a decision must be set aside prior to the award of damages, a Member State may provide that, after the conclusion of a contract following its award, the powers of the body responsible for the review procedures shall be limited to awarding damages to any person harmed by an infringement.

7.   The Member States shall ensure that decisions taken by bodies responsible for review procedures can be effectively enforced.

8.   Where bodies responsible for review procedures are not judicial in character, written reasons for their decisions shall always be given. Furthermore, in such a case, provision must be made to guarantee procedures whereby any allegedly illegal measure taken by the review body or any alleged defect in the exercise of the powers conferred on it can be the subject of judicial review or review by another body which is a court or tribunal within the meaning of Article 177 of the EEC Treaty and independent of both the contracting authority and the review body.

The members of such an independent body shall be appointed and leave office under the same conditions as members of the judiciary as regards the authority responsible for their appointment, their period of office, and their removal. At least the President of this independent body shall have the same legal and professional qualifications as members of the judiciary. The independent body shall take its decisions following a procedure in which both sides are heard, and these decisions shall, by means determined by each Member State, be legally binding.

(¹) OJ No C 230, 28. 8. 1987, p. 6 and OJ No C 15, 19. 1. 1989, p. 8.
(²) OJ No C 167, 27. 6. 1988, p. 77 and OJ No C 323, 27. 12. 1989.
(³) OJ No C 347, 22. 12. 1987, p. 23.
(⁴) OJ No L 185, 16. 8. 1971, p. 5.
(⁵) OJ No L 210, 21. 7. 1989, p. 1.
(⁶) OJ No L 13, 15. 1. 1977, p. 1.
(⁷) OJ No L 127, 20. 5. 1988, p. 1.

Extract 21.1 contd

Article 3

1. The Commission may invoke the procedure for which this Article provides when, prior to a contract being concluded, it considers that a clear and manifest infringement of Community provisions in the field of public procurement has been committed during a contract award procedure falling within the scope of Directives 71/305/EEC and 77/62/EEC.

2. The Commission shall notify the Member State and the contracting authority concerned of the reasons which have led it to conclude that a clear and manifest infringement has been committed and request its correction.

3. Within 21 days of receipt of the notification referred to in paragraph 2, the Member State concerned shall communicate to the Commission:

(a) its confirmation that the infringement has been corrected; or

(b) a reasoned submission as to why no correction has been made; or

(c) a notice to the effect that the contract award procedure has been suspended either by the contracting authority on its own initiative or on the basis of the powers specified in Article 2 (1) (a).

4. A reasoned submission in accordance with paragraph 3 (b) may rely among other matters on the fact that the alleged infringement is already the subject of judicial or other review proceedings or of a review as referred to in Article 2 (8). In such a case, the Member State shall inform the Commission of the result of those proceedings as soon as it becomes known.

5. Where notice has been given that a contract award procedure has been suspended in accordance with paragraph 3 (c), the Member State shall notify the Commission when the suspension is lifted or another contract procedure relating in whole or in part to the same subject matter is begun. That notification shall confirm that the alleged infringement has been corrected or include a reasoned submission as to why no correction has been made.

Article 4

1. Not later than four years after the implementation of this Directive, the Commission, in consultation with the Advisory Committee for Public Contracts, shall review the manner in which the provisions of this Directive have been implemented and, if necessary, make proposals for amendments.

2. By 1 March each year the Member States shall communicate to the Commission information on the operation of their national review procedures during the preceding calendar year. The nature of the information shall be determined by the Commission in consultation with the Advisory Committee for Public Contracts.

Article 5

Member States shall bring into force, before 1 December 1991, the measures necessary to comply with this Directive. They shall communicate to the Commission the texts of the main national laws, regulations and administrative provisions which they adopt in the field governed by this Directive.

Article 6

This Directive is addressed to the Member States.

Done at Brussels, 21 December 1989.

For the Council
The President
É. CRESSON

The role of the architect in relation to the Works Directive

3.25 It is to be noted that the obligations imposed by the Works Directive are placed on the 'contracting authority' concerned. However, the architect employed by that contracting authority may be under a contractual duty to carry out those obligations as the authority's agent and liable to indemnify the authority where a breach of that duty results in loss to the authority. This could occur, for example, where the contract award is delayed or where the authority is compelled to pay damages, as a result of an infringement.

Extract 21.2

COUNCIL DIRECTIVE

of 26 July 1971

concerning the co-ordination of procedures for the award of public works contracts

(71/305/EEC)

as amended by

COUNCIL DIRECTIVE

of 18 July 1989

amending Directive 71/305/EEC concerning coordination of procedures for the award of public works contracts

(89/440/EEC)

Title I

General Provisions

'*Article 1*

For the purpose of this Directive:

(a) "public works contracts" are contracts for pecuniary interest concluded in writing between a contractor and a contracting authority as defined in (b), which have as their object either the execution, or both the execution and design, of works related to one of the activities referred to in Annex II or a work defined in (c) below, or the execution by whatever means of a work corresponding to the requirements specified by the contracting authority;

(b) "contracting authorities" shall be the State, regional or local authorities, bodies governed by public law, associations formed by one or several of such authorities or bodies governed by public law.

A body governed by public law means any body:

— established for the specific purpose of meeting needs in the general interest, not having an industrial or commercial character, and

— having legal personality, and

— financed, for the most part, by the State, or regional or local authorities, or other bodies governed by public law; or subject to management supervision by those bodies; or having an administrative, managerial or supervisory board, more than half of whose members are appointed by the State, regional or local authorities or by other bodies governed by public law.

The lists of bodies or of categories of such bodies governed by public law which fulfil the criteria referred to in the second subparagraph are set out in Annex I. These lists shall be as exhaustive as possible and may be reviewed in accordance with the procedure laid down in Article 30b. To this end, Member States shall periodically notify the Commission of any changes to their lists of bodies and categories of bodies;

(c) a "work" means the outcome of building or civil engineering works taken as a whole that is sufficient of itself to fulfil an economic and technical function;

Extract 21.2 contd

(d) "public works concession" is a contract of the same type as that indicated in (a) except for the fact that the consideration for the works to be carried out consists either solely in the right to exploit the construction or in this right together with payment;

(e) "open procedures" are those national procedures whereby all interested contractors may submit tenders;

(f) "restricted procedures" are those national procedures whereby only those contractors invited by the contracting authority may submit tenders;

(g) "negotiated procedures" are those national procedures whereby contracting authorities consult contractors of their choice and negotiate the terms of the contract with one or more of them;

(h) a contractor who submits a tender shall be designated by the term "tenderer" and one who has sought an invitation to take part in a restricted and negotiated procedure by the term "candidate".'

'*Article 1a*

1. Member States shall take the necessary measures to ensure that the contracting authorities comply or ensure compliance with this Directive where they subsidize directly by more than 50% a works contract awarded by an entity other than themselves.

2. Paragraph 1 shall concern only contracts covered by Class 50, Group 502, of the NACE nomenclature and to contracts relating to building work for hospitals, facilities intended for sports, recreation and leisure, school and university buildings and buildings used for administrative purposes.

Article 1b

1. Should contracting authorities conclude a public works concession contract as defined in Article 1 (d), the advertising rules as described in Article 12 (3), (6), (7) and (9) to (13), and in Article 15a, shall apply to that contract when its value is not less than ECU 5 000 000.

2. The contracting authority may:

— either require the concessionaire to award contracts representing a minimum of 30% of the total value of the work for which the concession contract is to be awarded, to third parties, at the same time providing the option for candidates to increase this percentage. This minimum percentage shall be specified in the concession contract,

— or request the candidates for concession contracts to specify in their tenders the percentage, if any, of the total value of the work for which the concession contract is to be awarded which they intend to assign to third parties.

3. When the concessionaire is himself one of the authorities awarding contracts within the meaning of Article 1 (b), he shall comply with the provisions of this Directive in the case of works to be carried out by third parties.

4. Member States shall take the necessary steps to ensure that a concessionaire other than an authority awarding contracts shall apply the advertising rules listed in Article 12 (4), (6), (7), and (9) to (13), and in Article 15b, in respect of the contracts which it awards to third parties when the value of the contracts is not less than ECU 5 000 000. Advertising rules shall not be applied where works contracts meet the conditions laid down in Article 5 (3).

Undertakings which have formed a group in order to obtain the concession contract, or undertakings affiliated to them, shall not be regarded as third parties.

An "affiliated undertaking" means any undertaking over which the concessionaire may exercise, directly or indirectly, a dominant influence or which may exercise a dominant influence over the concessionaire or which, in common with the concessionaire, is subject to the dominant influence of another undertaking by virtue of ownership, financial participation or the rules which govern it. A dominant influence on the part of an undertaking shall be presumed when, directly or indirectly in relation to another undertaking, it:

— holds the major part of the undertaking's subscribed capital, or

— controls the majority of the votes attaching to shares issued by the undertakings, or

— can appoint more than half of the members of the undertaking's administrative, managerial or supervisory body.

A comprehensive list of these undertakings shall be enclosed with the candidature for the concession. This list shall be brought up to date following any subsequent changes in the relationship between the undertaking.'

(Article 2 is repealed)

Article 3 (1), (2) and (3) is hereby repealed and paragraphs 4 and 5 thereof are replaced by the following:

'4. This Directive shall not apply to:

(a) works contracts awarded by carriers by land, air, sea or inland waterway;

(b) works contracts awarded by contracting authorities, in so far as those contracts concern the production, transport and distribution of drinking water, or those contracting authorities whose principal activity lies in the production and distribution of energy;

(c) works contracts which are declared secret or the execution of which must be accompanied by special security measures in accordance with the laws, regulations or administrative provisions in force in the Member State concerned or when the protection of the basic interests of that State's security so requires.'

'*Article 4*

This Directive shall not apply to public contracts governed by different procedural rules and awarded:

(a) in pursuance of an international agreement, concluded in conformity with the EEC Treaty, between a Member State and one or more non-member countries and covering works intended for the joint implementation or exploitation of a project by the signatory States; all agreements shall be communicated to the Commission which may consult the Advisory Committee for Public Contracts set up by Decision 71/306/EEC ([1]), as amended by Decision 77/63/EEC ([2]);

(b) to undertakings in a Member State or a non-member country in pursuance of an international agreement relating to the stationing of troops;

(c) pursuant to the particular procedure of an international organization.

([1]) OJ No L 185, 16. 8. 1971, p. 15.
([2]) OJ No L 13, 15. 1. 1977, p. 15.'

'*Article 4a*

1. The provisions of this Directive shall apply to public works contracts whose estimated value net of VAT is not less than ECU 5 000 000.

2. The value of the threshold in national currencies shall normally be revised every two years with effect from 1 January 1993. The calculation of this value shall be based on the average daily values of these currencies in terms of the ecu over the 24 months terminating on the last day of October immediately preceding the 1 January revision. The values shall be published in the *Official Journal of the European Communities* at the beginning of November.

3. Where a work is subdivided into several lots, each one the subject of a contract, the value of each lot must be taken into account for the purpose of calculating the amounts referred to in paragraph 1. Where the aggregate value of the lots is not less than the amount referred to in paragraph 1, the provisions of that paragraph shall apply to all lots. Contracting authorities shall be permitted to depart from this provision for lots whose estimated value net of VAT is less than ECU 1 000 000, provided that the total estimated value of all the lots exempted does not, in consequence, exceed 20% of the total estimated value of all lots.

4. No work or contract may be split up with the intention of avoiding the application of the preceding paragraphs.

5. When calculating the amounts referred to in paragraph 1 and in Article 5, account shall be taken not only of the amount of the public works contracts but also of the estimated value of the supplies needed to carry out the works which are made available to the contractor by the contracting authorities.'

'*Article 5*

1. In awarding public works contracts the contracting authorities shall apply the procedures defined in Article 1 (e), (f) and (g), adapted to this Directive.

2. The contracting authorities may award their public works contracts by negotiated procedure, with prior publication of a tender notice and after having selected the candidates according to qualitative public criteria, in the following cases:

(a) in the event of irregular tenders in response to an open or restricted procedure or in the event of tenders which are unacceptable under national provisions that are in accordance with the provisions of Title IV, in so far as the original terms of the contract are not substantially altered. The contracting authorities shall not, in these cases, publish a tender notice where they include in such negotiated procedure all the enterprises satisfying the criteria of Articles 23 to 28 which, during the prior open or restricted procedure, have submitted offers in accordance with the formal requirements of the tendering procedure;

(b) when the works involved are carried out purely for the purpose of research, experiment or development, and not to establish commercial viability or to recover research and development costs;

(c) in exceptional cases, when the nature of the works or the risks attaching thereto do not permit prior overall pricing.

Extract 21.2 contd

3. The contracting authorities may award their public works contracts by negotiated procedure without prior publication of a tender notice, in the following cases:

(a) in the absence of tenders or of appropriate tenders in response to an open or restricted procedure in so far as the original terms of the contract are not substantially altered and provided that a report is communicated to the Commission at its request;

(b) when, for technical or artistic reasons or for reasons connected with the protection of exclusive rights, the works may only be carried out by a particular contractor;

(c) in so far as is strictly necessary when, for reasons of extreme urgency brought about by events unforeseen by the contracting authorities in question, the time limit laid down for the open, restricted or negotiated procedures referred to in paragraph 2 above cannot be kept. The circumstances invoked to justify extreme urgency must not in any event be attributable for the contracting authorities;

(d) for additional works not included in the project initially considered or in the contract first concluded but which have, through unforeseen circumstances, become necessary for the carrying out of the work described therein, on condition that the award is made to the contractor carrying out such work:

— when such works cannot be technically or economically separated from the main contract without great inconvenience to the contracting authorities, or

— when such works, although separable from the execution of the original contract, are strictly necessary to its later stages,

however, the aggregate value of contracts awarded for additional works may not exceed 50% of the amount of the main contract;

(e) for new works consisting of the repetition of similar works entrusted to the undertaking to which the same contracting authorities awarded an earlier contract, provided that such works conform to a basic project for which a first contract was awarded according to the procedures referred to in paragraph 4.

As soon as the first project is put up for tender, notice must be given that this procedure might be adopted and the total estimated cost of subsequent works shall be taken into consideration by the contracting authorities when they apply the provisions of Article 4a. This procedure may only be applied during the three years following the conclusion of the original contract.

4. In all other cases, the contracting authorities shall award their public works contracts by the open procedure or by the restricted procedure.'

'Article 5a

1. The contracting authority shall, within 15 days of the date on which the request is received, inform any eliminated candidate or tenderer who so requests of the reasons for rejection of his application or his tender, and, in the case of a tender, the name of the sucessful tenderer.

2. The contracting authority shall inform candidates or tenderers who so request of the grounds on which it decided not to award a contract in respect of which a prior call for competition was made, or to recommence the procedure. It shall also inform the Office for Official Publications of the European Communities of that decision.

3. For each contract awarded the contracting authorities shall draw up a written report which shall include at least the following:

— the name and address of the contracting authority, the subject and value of the contract,

— the names of the candidates or tenderers admitted and the reasons for their selection,

— the names of the candidates or tenderers rejected and the reasons for their rejection,

— the name of the successful tenderer and the reasons for his tender having been selected and, if known, any share of the contract the successful tenderer may intend to subcontract to a third party,

— for negotiated procedures, the circumstances referred to in Article 5 which justify the use of these procedures.

This report, or the main features of it, shall be communicated to the Community at its request.'

Article 6

In the case of contracts relating to the design and construction of a public housing scheme whose size and complexity, and the estimated duration of the work involved, require that planning be based from the outset on close collaboration within a team comprising representatives of the authorities awarding contracts, experts and the contractor to be responsible for carrying out the works, a special award procedure may be adopted for selecting the contractor most suitable for integration into the team.

In particular, authorities awarding contracts shall include in the contract notice as accurate as possible a description of the works to be carried out so as to enable interested contractors to form a valid idea of the project. Furthermore, authorities awarding contracts shall, in accordance with the provisions of Articles 23 to 28, set out in such contract notice the personal, technical and financial conditions to be fulfilled by candidates.

Where such procedure is adopted, authorities awarding contracts shall apply the common advertising rules relating to restricted procedure and to the criteria for qualitative selection.

Title II

Common rules in the technical field

'Article 10

1. The technical specifications defined in Annex III shall be given in the general or contractual documents relating to each contract.

2. Without prejudice to the legally binding national technical rules and in so far as these are compatible with Community law, such technical specifications shall be defined by the contracting authorities by reference to national standards implementing European standards, or by reference to European technical approvals or by reference to common technical specifications.

3. A contracting authority may depart from paragraph 2 if:

(a) the standards, European technical approvals or common technical specifications do not include any provision for establishing conformity, or technical means do not exist for establishing satisfactorily the conformity of a product to these standards, European technical approvals or common technical specifications;

(b) use of these standards, European technical approvals or common technical specifications would oblige the contracting authority to acquire products or materials incompatible with equipment already in use or would entail disproportionate costs or disproportionate technical difficulties, but only as part of a clearly defined and recorded strategy with a view to change-over, within a given period, to European standards, European technical approvals or common technical specifications;

(c) the project concerned is of a genuinely innovative nature for which use of existing European standards, European technical approvals or common technical specifications would not be appropriate.

4. Contracting authorities invoking paragraph 3 shall record, wherever possible, the reasons for doing so in the tender notice published in the *Official Journal of the European Communities* or in the contract documents and in all cases shall record these reasons in their internal documentation and shall supply such information on request to Member States and to the Commission.

5. In the absence of European standards or European technical approvals or common technical specifications, the technical specifications:

(a) shall be defined by reference to the national technical specifications recognized as complying with the basic requirements listed in the Community directives on technical harmonization, in accordance with the procedures laid down in those directives, and in particular in accordance with the procedures laid down in Council Directive 89/106/EEC of 21 December 1988 on construction products (¹);

(b) may be defined by reference to national technical specifications relating to design and method of calculation and execution of works and use of materials;

(c) may be defined by reference to other documents.

In this case, it is appropriate to make reference in order of preference to:

(i) national standards implementing international standards accepted by the country of the contracting authority;

(ii) other national standards and national technical approvals of the country of the contracting authority;

(iii) any other standard.

6. Unless such specifications are justified by the subject of the contract, Member States shall prohibit the introduction into the contractual clauses relating to a given contract of technical specifications which mention products of a specific make or source or of a particular process and which therefore favour or eliminate certain undertakings. In particular, the indication of trade marks, patents, types, or of a specific origin or production shall be prohibited. However, if such indication is accompanied by the words "or equivalent", it shall be authorized in cases where the authorities awarding contracts are unable to give a description of the subject of the contract using specifications which are sufficiently precise and intelligible to all parties concerned.

(¹) OJ No L 40, 11. 2. 1989, p. 12.'

Title III

Common advertising rules

'Article 12

1. Contracting authorities shall make known, by means of an indicative notice, the essential characteristics of the works contracts which they intend to award and the estimated value of which is not less than the threshold laid down in Article 4a (1).

2. Contracting authorities who wish to award a public works contract by open, restricted or negotiated procedure referred to in Article 5 (2), shall make known their intention by means of a notice.

3. Contracting authorities who wish to award a works concession contract shall make known their intention by means of a notice.

4. Works concessionaires, other than a contracting authority, who wish to award a work contract to be carried out by third parties as defined in Article 1b (4), shall make known their intention by means of a notice.

5. Contracting authorities who have awarded a contract shall make known the result by means of a notice. However, certain information on contract award may, in certain cases, not be published where release of such information would impede law enforcement or otherwise be contrary to the public interest, would prejudice the legitimate commercial interests of particular enterprises, public or private, or might prejudice fair competition between contractors.

6. The contracting authorities shall send the notices referred to in the preceding paragraphs as rapidly as possible and by the most appropriate channels to the Office for Official Publications of the European Communities. In the case of the accelerated procedure referred to in Article 15, the notice shall be sent by telex, telegram or telefax.

(a) The notice referred to in paragraph 1 shall be sent as soon as possible after the decision approving the planning of the works contracts that the contracting authorities intend to award;

(b) the notice referred to in paragraph 5 shall be sent at the latest 48 days after the award of the contract in question.

7. The notices referred to in paragraphs 1, 2, 3, 4 and 5 shall be drawn up in accordance with the models given in Annexes IV, V and VI, and shall specify the information requested in those Annexes.

In open, restricted and negotiated procedures, the contracting authorities may not require any conditions but those specified in Articles 25 and 26 when requesting information concerning the economic and technical standards which they require of contractors for their selection (point 11 of Annex IV B, point 10 of Annex IV C and point 9 of Annex IV D).

8. The notices referred to in paragraphs 1 and 5 above shall be published in full in the *Official Journal of the European Communities* and in the TED data bank in the official languages of the Communities, the original text alone being authentic.

9. The notices referred to in paragraphs 2, 3 and 4 shall be published in full in the *Official Journal of the European Communities* and in the TED data bank in their original language. A summary of the important elements of each notice shall be published in the other official languages of the Community, the original text alone being authentic.

10. The Office for Official Publications of the European Communities shall publish the notices not later than 12 days after their dispatch. In the case of the accelerated procedure referred to in Article 15, this period shall be reduced to five days.

11. The notice shall not be published in the official journals or in the press of the country of the contracting authority before the abovementioned date of dispatch, and it shall mention this date. It shall not contain information other than that published in the *Official Journal of the European Communities*.

12. The contracting authorities must be able to supply proof of the date of dispatch.

13. The cost of publication of the notices in the *Official Journal of the European Communities* shall be borne by the Communities. The length of the notice shall not be greater than one page of the Journal, or approximately 650 words. Each edition of the Journal containing one or more notices shall reproduce the model notice or notices on which the published notice or notices are based.

Article 13

1. In open procedures the time limit for the receipt of tenders shall be fixed by the contracting authorities at not less than 52 days from the date of sending the notice.

2. The time limit for the receipt of tenders provided for in paragraph 1 may be reduced to 36 days where the contracting authorities have published a tender notice, drafted in accordance with the specimen in Annex IV A provided for in Article 12 (1), in the *Official Journal of the European Communities*.

3. Provided they have been requested in good time, the contract documents and supporting documents must be sent to the contractors by the contracting authorities or competent departments within six days of receiving their application.

4. Provided it has been requested in good time, additional information relating to the contract documents shall be supplied by the contracting authorities not later than six days before the final date fixed for receipt of tenders.

5. Where the contract documents, supporting documents or additional information are too bulky to be supplied within the time limits laid down in paragraph 3 or 4 or where tenders can only be made after a visit to the site or after on-the-spot inspection of the documents supporting the contract documents, the time limits laid down in paragraphs 1 and 2 shall be extended accordingly.

Article 14

1. In restricted procedures and negotiated procedures as described in Article 5 (2), the time limit for receipt of requests to participate fixed by the contracting authorities shall be not less than 37 days from the date of dispatch of the notice.

2. The contracting authorities shall simultaneously and in writing invite the selected candidates to submit their tenders. The letter of invitation shall be accompanied by the contract documents and supporting documents. It shall include at least the following information:

(a) where appropriate, the address of the service from which the contract documents and supporting documents can be requested and the final date for making such a request; also the amount and terms of payment of any sum to be paid for such documents;

(b) the final date for receipt of tenders, the address to which they must be sent and the language or languages in which they must be drawn up:

(c) a reference to the contract notice published;

(d) an indication of any documents to be annexed, either to support the verifiable statements furnished by the candidate in accordance with Article 12 (7), or to supplement the information provided for in that Article under the same conditions as those laid down in Article 25 and 26;

(e) the criteria for the award of the contract if these are not given in the notice.

3. In restricted procedures, the time limit for receipt of tenders fixed by the contracting authorities may not be less than 40 days from the date of dispatch of the written invitation.

4. The time limit for receipt of tenders laid down in paragraph 3 may be reduced to 26 days where the contracting authorities have published the tender notice, drafted according to the specimen in Annex IV A provided for in Article 12 (1), in the *Official Journal of the European Communities*.

5. Requests to participate in procedures for the award of contracts may be made by letter, by telegram, telex, telefax or by telephone. If by one of the last four, they must be confirmed by letter dispatched before the end of the period laid down in paragraph 1.

6. Provided it has been requested in good time, additional information relating to the contract documents must be supplied by the contracting authorities not later than six days before the final date fixed for the receipt of tenders.

Extract 21.2 contd

7. Where tenders can only be made after a visit to the site or after on-the-spot inspection of the documents supporting the contract documents, the time limit laid down in paragraphs 3 and 4 shall be extended accordingly.

Article 15

1. In cases where urgency renders impracticable the time limits laid down in Article 14, the contracting authorities may fix the following time limits:

(a) a time limit for receipt of requests to participate which shall be not less than 15 days from the date of dispatch of the notice;

(b) a time limit for the receipt of tenders which shall be not less than 10 days from the date of the invitation to tender.

2. Provided it has been requested in good time, additional information relating to the contract documents must be supplied by the contracting authorities not later than four days before the final date fixed for the receipt of tenders.

3. Requests for participation in contracts and invitations to tender must be made by the most rapid means of communication possible. When requests to participate are made by telegram, telex, telefax or telephone, they must be confirmed by letter dispatched before the expiry of the time limit referred to in paragraph 1.'

'Article 15a

Contracting authorities who wish to award a works concession contract as defined in Article 1 (d) shall fix a time limit for receipt of candidatures for the concession, which shall not be less than 52 days from the date of dispatch of the notice.

Article 15b

In works contracts awarded by a concessionaire of works other than an authority awarding contracts, the time limit for the receipt of requests to participate shall be fixed by the concessionaire at not less than 37 days from the date of dispatch of the notice, and the time limit for the receipt of tenders at not less than 40 days from the date of dispatch of the notice or the invitation to tender.'

(Articles 16, 17 and 18 are repealed)

'Article 19

Contracting authorities may arrange for the publication in the *Official Journal of the European Communities* of notices announcing public works contracts which are not subject to the publication requirement laid down in this Directive.

Title IV

Common rules on participation

Article 20

Contracts shall be awarded on the basis of the criteria laid down in Chapter 2 of this Title, taking into account Article 20a, after the suitability of the contractors not excluded under Article 23 has been checked by the contracting authorities in accordance with the criteria of economic and financial standing and of technical knowledge or ability referred to in Articles 25 to 28.'

'Article 20a

Where the criterion for the award of the contract is that of the most economically advantageous tender, contracting authorities may take account of variants which are submitted by a tenderer and meet the minimum specifications required by the contracting authorities.

The contracting authorities shall state in the contract documents the minimum specifications to be respected by the variants and any specific requirements for their presentation. They shall indicate in the tender notice whether variants will be considered.

Contracting authorities may not reject the submission of a variant on the sole grounds that it has been drawn up with technical specifications defined by reference to national standards transposing European standards, to European technical approvals or to common technical specifications referred to in Article 10 (2) or again by reference to national technical specifications referred to in Article 10 (5) (a) and (b).

Article 20b

In the contract documents, the contracting authority may ask the tenderer to indicate in his tender any share of the contract he may intend to subcontract to third parties.

This indication shall be without prejudice to the question of the principal contractor's responsibility.'

Article 21

Tenders may be submitted by groups of contractors. These groups may not be required to assume a specific legal form in order to submit the tender; however, the group selected may be required to do so when it has been awarded the contract.

'Article 22

1. In restricted and negotiated procedures the contracting authorities shall, on the basis of information given relating to the contractor's personal position as well as to the information and formalities necessary for the evaluation of the minimum conditions of an economic and technical nature to be fulfilled by him, select from among the candidates with the qualifications required by Articles 23 and 28 those whom they will invite to submit a tender or to negotiate.

2. Where the contracting authorities award a contract by restricted procedure, they may prescribe the range within which the number of undertakings which they intend to invite will fall. In this case the range shall be indicated in the contract notice. The range shall be determined in the light of the nature of the work to be carried out. The range must number at least 5 undertakings and may be up to 20.

In any event, the number of candidates invited to tender shall be sufficient to ensure genuine competition.

3. Where the contracting authorities award a contract by negotiated procedure as referred to in Article 5 (2), the number of candidates admitted to negotiate may not be less than three provided that there is a sufficient number of suitable candidates.

4. Each Member State shall ensure that contracting authorities issue invitations without discrimination to those nationals of other Member States who satisfy the necessary requirements and under the same conditions as to its own nationals.'

'Article 22a

1. The contracting authority may state in the contract documents, or be obliged by a Member State so to do, the authority or authorities from which a tenderer may obtain the appropriate information on the obligations relating to the employment protection provisions and the working conditions which are in force in the Member State, region or locality in which the works are to be executed and which shall be applicable to the works carried out on site during the performance of the contract.

2. The contracting authority which supplies the information referred to in paragraph 1 shall request the tenderers or those participating in the contract procedure to indicate that they have taken account, when drawing up their tender, of the obligations relating to employment protection provisions and the working conditions which are in force in the place where the work is to be carried out. This shall be without prejudice to the application of the provisions of Article 29 (5) concerning the examination of abnormally low tenders.'

Chapter I

Criteria for qualitative selection

Article 23

Any contractor may be excluded from participation in the contract who:

(a) is bankrupt or is being wound up, whose affairs are being administered by the court, who has entered into an arrangement with creditors, who has suspended business activities or who is in any analogous situation arising from a similar procedure under national laws and regulations;

(b) is the subject of proceedings for a declaration of bankruptcy, for an order for compulsory winding up or administration by the court or for an arrangement with creditors or of any other similar proceedings under national laws or regulations;

(c) has been convicted of an offence concerning his professional conduct by a judgement which has the force of *res judicata*;

(d) who has been guilty of grave professional misconduct proven by any means which the authorities awarding contracts can justify;

(e) has not fulfilled obligations relating to the payment of social security contributions in accordance with the legal provisions of the country in which he is established or with those of the country of the authority awarding contracts;

(f) has not fulfilled obligations relating to the payment of taxes in accordance with the legal provisions of the country of the authority awarding contracts;

(g) is guilty of serious misrepresentation in supplying the information required under this Chapter.

Where the authority awarding contracts requires of the contractor proof that none of the cases quoted in (a), (b), (c), (e) or (f) applies to him, it shall accept as sufficient evidence:

— (for (a), (b) or (c), the production of an extract from the 'judicial record' or failing this, of an equivalent document issued by a competent judicial or administrative authority in the country of origin or in the country whence that person comes showing that these requirements have been met;

— for (e) or (f); a certificate issued by the competent authority in the Member State concerned.

Where the country concerned does not issue such documents or certificates, they may be replaced by a declaration on oath made by the person concerned before a judicial or administrative authority, a notary or a competent professional or trade body, in the country of origin or in the country whence that person comes.

Member States shall, within the time limit laid down in Article 32, designate the authorities and bodies competent to issue these documents and shall forthwith inform the other Member States and the Commission thereof.

'Article 24

Any contractor wishing to take part in a public works contract may be requested to prove his enrolment in the professional or trade register under the conditions laid down by the laws of the Member State in which he is established:

— in Belgium, the registre du commerce — Handelsregister,

— in Denmark, the Erhvervs- og Selskabsstyrelsen,

— in Germany, the Handelsregister and the Handwerksrolle,

— in Greece, a declaration on the exercise of the profession of public works contractor made on oath before a notary may be required,

— in Spain, the Registro Oficial de Contratistas del Ministerio de Industria y Energia,

— in France, the registre du commerce and the répertoir des métiers,

— in Italy, the Registro della Camera di commercio, industria, agricoltura e artigianato,

— in Luxembourg, the registre aux firmes and the rôle de la Chambre des métiers,

— in the Netherlands, the Handelsregister,

— in Portugal, the Commissão de Alvarás de Empresas de Obras Públicas e Particulares (CAEOPP),

— in the United Kingdom and Ireland, the contractor may be requested to provide a certificate from the Registrar of Companies or the Registrar of Friendly Societies or, if this is not the case, a certificate stating that the person concerned has declared on oath that he is engaged in the profession in question in the country in which he is established, in a specific place and under a given business name.'

Article 25

Proof of the contractor's financial and economic standing may, as a general rule, be furnished by one or more of the following references:

(a) appropriate statements from bankers;

(b) the presentation of the firm's balance sheets or extracts from the balance sheets, where publication of the balance sheet is required under company law in the country in which the contractor is established;

(c) a statement of the firm's overall turnover and the turnover on construction works for the three previous financial years.

The authorities awarding contracts shall specify in the notice or in the invitation to tender which reference or references they have chosen and what references other than those mentioned under (a), (b) or (c) are to be produced.

If, for any valid reason, the contractor is unable to supply the references requested by the authorities awarding contracts, he may prove his economic and financial standing by any other document which the authorities awarding contracts consider appropriate.

Article 26

Proof of the contractor's technical knowledge or ability may be furnished by:

(a) the contractor's educational and professional qualifications and/or those of the firm's managerial staff, and, in particular, those of the person or persons responsible for carrying out the works;

(b) a list of the works carried out over the past five years, accompanied by certificates of satisfactory execution for the most important works, These certificates shall indicate the value, date and site of the works and shall specify whether they were carried out according to the rules of the trade and properly completed. Where necessary, the competent authority shall submit these certificates to the authority awarding contracts direct;

(c) a statement of the tools, plant and technical equipment available to the contractor for carrying out the work;

(d) a statement of the firm's average annual manpower and the number of managerial staff for the last three years;

(e) a statement of the technicians or technical divisions which the contractor can call upon for carrying out the work, whether or not they belong to the firm.

The authorities awarding contracts shall specify in the notice or in the invitation to tender which of these references are to be produced.

Article 27

The authority awarding contracts may, within the limits of Articles 23 to 26, invite the contractor to supplement the certificates and documents submitted or to clarify them.

Article 28

1. Member States who have official lists of recognised contractors must, when this Directive enters into force, adapt them to the provisions of Article 23 (a) to (d) and (g) and of Articles 24 to 26.

2. Contractors registered in these lists may, for each contract, submit to the authority awarding contracts a certificate of registration issued by the competent authority. This certificate shall state the references which enabled them to be registered in the list and the classification given in this list.

3. Certified registration in such lists by the competent bodies shall, for the authorities of other Member States awarding contracts, constitute a presumption of suitability for works corresponding to the contractor's classification only as regards Articles 23 (a) to (d) and (g), 24, 25 (b) and (c) and 26 (b) and (d) and not as regards Articles 25 (a) and 26 (a), (c) and (e).

Information which can be deduced from registration in official lists may not be questioned. However, with regard to the payment of social security contributions, an additional certificate may be required of any registered contractor whenever a contract is offered.

The authorities of other Member States awarding contracts shall apply the above provisions only in favour of contractors who are established in the country holding the official list.

4. For the registration of contractors of other Member States in such a list, no further proofs and statements may be required other than those requested of nationals and, in any event, only those provided for under Articles 23 to 26.

5. Member States holding an official list shall communicate to other Member States the address of the body to which requests for registration may be made.

Chapter II

Criteria for the award of contracts

1. The criteria on which the authorities awarding contracts shall base the award of contracts shall be:

— either the lowest price only;

— or, when the award is made to the most economically advantageous tender, various criteria according to the contract: e.g. price, period for completion, running costs, profitability, technical merit.

2. In the latter instance, the authorities awarding contracts shall state in the contract documents or in the contract notice all the criteria they intend to apply to the award, where possible in descending order of importance.

Article 29 (3) is hereby repealed and Article 29 (4) and (5) replaced by the following:

4. Paragraph 1 shall not apply when a Member State bases the award of contracts on other criteria, within the framework of rules in force at the time of the adoption of this Directive whose aim is to give preference to certain tenderers, on condition that the rules invoked are compatible with the Treaty.

5. If, for a given contract, tenders appear to be abnormally low in relation to the transaction, before it may reject those tenders the contracting authority shall request, in writing, details of the constituent elements of the tender which it considers relevant and shall verify those constituent elements taking account of the explanations received.

The contracting authority may take into consideration explanations which are justified on objective grounds including the economy of the construction method, or the technical solutions chosen, or the exceptionally favourable conditions available to the tenderer for the execution of the work, or the originality of the work proposed by the tenderer.

If the documents relating to the contract provide for its award at the lowest price tendered, the contracting authority must communicate to the Commission the rejection of tenders which it considers to be too low.

Extract 21.2 contd

However, until the end of 1992, if current national law so permits, the contracting authority may exceptionally, without any discrimination on grounds of nationality, reject tenders which are abnormally low in relation to the transaction, without being obliged to comply with the procedure provided for in the first subparagraph if the number of such tenders for a particular contract is so high that implementation of this procedure would lead to a considerable delay and jeopardize the public interest attaching to the execution of the contract in question. Recourse to this exceptional procedure shall be mentioned in the notice referred to in Article 12 (5).'

Title V

Final provisions

'*Article 29a*

1. Until 31 December 1992, this Directive shall not prevent the application of existing national provisions on the award of public works contracts which have as their objective the reduction of regional disparities and the promotion of job creation in regions whose development is lagging behind and in declining industrial regions, on condition that the provisions concerned are compatible with the Treaty, in particular with the principles of non-discrimination on grounds of nationality, freedom of establishment and freedom to provide services, and with the Community's international obligations.

2. Paragraph 1 shall be without prejudice to Article 29 (4).

Article 29b

1. Member States shall inform the Commission of national provisions covered by Article 29 (4) and Article 29a and of the rules for applying them.

2. Member States concerned shall forward to the Commission, every year, a report describing the implementation of these provisions. The reports shall be submitted to the Advisory Committee for Public Works Contracts.'

Article 30

The calculation of the time limit for receipt of tenders or requests to participate shall be made in accordance with Council Regulation (EEC, Euratom) No 1182/71 of 3 June 1971 determining the rules applicable to periods, dates and time limits[2].

'*Article 30a*

1. In order to permit assessment of the results of applying the Directive, Member States shall forward to the Commission a statistical report on the contracts awarded by contracting authorities by 31 October 1993 at the latest for the preceding year and thereafter by 31 October of every second year.

Nevertheless, for the Hellenic Republic, the Kingdom of Spain and the Portuguese Republic, the date of 31 October 1993 shall be replaced by 31 October 1995.

2. This report shall detail at least the number and value of contracts awarded by each contracting authority or category of contracting authority above the threshold, subdivided as far as possible by procedure, category of work and the nationality of the contractor to whom the contract has been awarded, and in the case of negotiated procedures, subdivided in accordance with Article 5, listing the number and value of the contracts awarded to each Member State and to third countries.

3. The Commission shall determine the nature of any additional statistical information, which is requested in accordance with the Directive, in consultation with the Advisory Committee for Public Works Contracts.

Article 30b

1. Annex I to this Directive shall be amended by the Commission when, in particular on the basis of the notifications from the Member States, it is necessary:

(a) to remove from Annex I bodies governed by public law which no longer fulfil the criteria laid down in Article 1(b);

(b) to include in that Annex bodies governed by public law which meet those criteria.

2. Amendments to Annex I shall be made by the Commission after consulting the Advisory Committee for Public Works Contracts.

The chairman of the committee shall submit to the committee a draft of any measures to be taken. The committee shall deliver its opinion on the draft, if necessary by taking a vote, within a time limit to be fixed by the chairman in the light of the urgency of the matter.

The opinion shall be recorded in the minutes. In addition, each Member State shall have the right to request that its position be recorded in the minutes.

The Commission shall take the fullest account of the opinion delivered by the committee. It shall inform the committee of the manner in which its opinion has been taken into account.

3. Amended versions of Annex I shall be published in the *Official Journal of the European Communities*.'

Article 32

Member States shall adopt the measures necessary to comply with this Directive within twelve months of its notification and shall forthwith inform the Commission thereof.

Article 33

Member states shall ensure that the text of the main provisions of national law which they adopt in the field covered by this Directive is communicated to the Commission.

Article 34

This Directive is addressed to the Member States.

ANNEX I

LISTS OF BODIES AND CATEGORIES OF BODIES GOVERNED BY PUBLIC LAW REFERRED TO IN ARTICLE 1 (b)

XII. In THE UNITED KINGDOM:

— education authorities,
— fire authorities,
— National Health Service authorities,
— police authorities,
— Commission for the New Towns,
— new towns corporations,
— Scottish Special Housing Association,
— Northern Ireland Housing Executive.

The proposed extension of the public Procurement Directive to the service sectors including architectural services

3.26 This proposed directive is still only at the draft stage and therefore is not authoritative but is probably a good indication of what the final legislation is likely to contain.

It is modelled closely on the provisions of the Works Directive and the Supplies Directive. Of particular importance to architects are the following provisions:

– *Article 8* 'Thresholds' which proposes inter alia that contracts for architectural services in relation to a public works contract should be subject to the Directive where the estimated value of those services exceeds 400 000 Ecu (£290 394 at November 1989).

– *Article 14* 'Design contests' which lays down rules for the holding of design contests for the preparation of a project with an estimated value exceeding 5 million Ecu.

It is not yet known when this proposed directive will be implemented but it is likely to be in force throughout the Community in 1992 or 1993.

Public works contracts and article 30 EEC

3.27 Even where a public works contract falls outside the provisions of the Directive, architects will still have to take care that they do not specify in such a manner as will render any public authority employer in breach of article 30 EEC.

Article 30 provides that:

'Quantitative restrictions on imports and all measures having equivalent effect shall, without prejudice to the following provisions be prohibited between Member States.'

In Case 45/87 *Commission* v *Ireland*, the Dundalk Urban District Council (a public body for whose acts the Irish Government are responsible), permitted the inclusion in the contract specification for a drinking water supply scheme of a clause providing that certain pipes should be certified as complying with an Irish standard and consequently refusing to consider without adequate justification a tender providing for such pipes manufactured to an alternative standard providing equivalent guarantees of safety, performance and reliability. The contract fell outside the provisions of the Works Directive because it concerned the distribution of drinking water (see article 3(4)). Nevertheless, the Court held that Ireland had acted in breach of article 30. Only one undertaking was capable of producing pipes to the required standard and that undertaking was situated in Ireland. Consequently, the inclusion of that specification had the effect of restricting the supply of the pipes needed to Irish manufacturers alone and was a quantitive restriction on imports or a measure having equivalent effect. The breach of article 30 could have been avoided if the specifier had added the words 'or equivalent' after the specification concerned (see para 22 of the judgment).

4 Technical harmonization and standards

The Construction Products Directive 89/106 EEC

4.01 A major barrier to the free movement of construction products within the Community has been the differing national requirements relating to such matters as building safety, health, durability, energy economy and protection of the environment, which in turn directly influence national product standards, technical approvals and other technical specifications and provisions.

In order to overcome this problem, the Community has adopted the Construction Products Directive whose aim is to provide for the free movement, sale and use of construction products which are fit for their intended use and have such characteristics that structures in which they are incorporated meet certain essential requirements. Products, in so far as these essential requirements relate to them, which do not meet the appropriate standard may not be placed on the market (article 2).

4.02 These essential requirements are similar in style to the functional requirements of the Building Regulations in force in England and Wales, but rather wider in scope. They relate to mechanical resistance and stability, safety in case of fire,

hygiene, health and the environment, safety in use, protection against noise, and energy economy and heat retention. These requirements must, subject to normal maintenance, be satisfied for an economically reasonable working life and generally provide protection against events which are foreseeable.

The performance levels of products complying with these essential requirements may, however, vary according to geographical or climatic conditions or in ways of life, as well as different levels of protection that may prevail at national regional or local level and member states may decide which class of performance level they require to be observed within their territory.

4.03 Products will be presumed to be fit for their intended use if they bear an EC conformity mark showing that they comply with a European standard or a European technical approval or (when documents of this sort do not exist) relevant national standards or agreements recognized at Community level as meeting the essential requirements. If a manufacturer chooses to make a product which is not in conformity with these specifications, he has to prove that his product conforms to the essential requirements before he will be permitted to put it on the market. Conformity may be verified by third party certification.

4.04 European standards which will ensure that the essential requirements are met will be drawn up by a European standards body usually CEN or CENELEC. These will be published in the UK as identically worded British standards. European technical approvals will be issued by approvals bodies designated for this purpose by the member states in accordance with guidelines prepared by the European body comprising the approval bodies from all the member states.

4.05 Member states are prohibited from interfering with the free movement of goods which satisfy the provisions of the Directive and are to ensure that the use of such products is not impeded by any national rule or condition imposed by a public body, or private bodies acting as a public undertaking or acting as a public body on the basis of a monopoly position (article 6). This would appear to include such bodies as the NHBC in their standard setting role.

4.06 Measures to implement the provisions of the Directive in UK law are currently under consideration but the Directive provides that it must be implemented into national law not later than 27 June 1991. The implementation of this measure throughout the Community should greatly ease the task of the architect who is designing buildings in more than one member state as it will mean that in future he can be sure that the products he specifies, so long as they comply with the Directive, will comply with the regulations and requirements of every member state, without his having to carry out a detailed check for that purpose.

5 Right of establishment and freedom to provide services – the Architects Directive 85/384 EEC

The background

5.01 Three of the fundamental principles underlying the Treaty of Rome are the free movement of workers, the freedom to set up business in any member state and the freedom to provide services in a member state, other than that in which the provider of these services is based. In order to ensure that those principles are met so far as architects are concerned the Community had adopted Directive 85/384 EEC which has been implemented into UK law by Order in Council.

Mutual recognition of architectural qualifications

5.02 The Directive allows architects with appropriate UK qualifications to practise anywhere in the EC and architects from other member states to have the equivalent right to practise in this country. The Directive sets out in detail what are the minimum qualifications required for such mutual recognition and how these are to be proved.

Right of establishment and freedom to provide services

5.03 The Directive similarly lays down rules for the mutual recognition of an architect's rights to set up in practice in a host member state or to provide architectural services in another member state.

The fundamental principle contained in the Directive is that there must be no discrimination against foreign nationals which would make it more difficult for them to establish themselves or provide services in the host state than it would be for nationals of that state.

6 The Product Liability Directive 85/374 and the Consumer Protection Act 1987

6.01 The Product Liability Directive 85/374 which was adopted on 25 July 1985 is required to be implemented throughout the EC by 30 July 1988. It has been implemented into UK law by the Consumer Protection Act 1987, Part I.

6.02 The Directive introduces into every member state a system of strict liability (i.e. without the need to prove negligence) for death, personal injury and damage to private property resulting from defective products put into circulation after the date when the national law came into force (in the UK this is 1 March 1988). A 'product' is very widely defined under the Act (section 1(2)) as:

'any goods or electricity and . . . includes a product which is comprised in another product, whether by virtue of being a component part or raw material or otherwise'.

Goods are defined (section 45) as:

'substances, growing crops and things comprised in land by virtue of being attached to it . . .'

It is clear therefore, that building products are covered by the Act and at first sight it might appear that buildings themselves and/or parts of buildings such as roofs or foundations are also covered.

6.03 However, by section 46(3) of the Act it is provided that:

'subject to subsection (4) below the performance of any contract by the erection of any building or structure on any land or by carrying out of any other building works shall be treated for the purpose of the Act as a supply of goods in so far as it involves the provision of any goods to any person by means of their incorporation into the building, structure or works'.

6.04 Subsection 4 provides in so far as is relevant:

'References in this Act to supplying goods shall not include references to supplying goods comprised in land where the supply is affected by the creation or disposal of an interest in land.'

In the case, therefore, of a builder building under a contract and who does not own the land on which he builds he may be liable as 'supplier' or 'producer' (see below) in respect of defective products supplied or produced by him and incorporated into the building whether by way of construction, alteration or repair and will not be liable as producer of

the defective building itself or of its immovable parts such as foundations.

In the case of a speculative builder however, who builds on his own land and then effects the supply of that building by the creation or disposal of an interest in land (e.g. by sale of the freehold or lease) the Act appears to leave him liable as *producer* of the defective building while exempting him from any liability as supplier of any defective product comprised within the building. It is submitted that that is not the case.

6.05 By section 1(1) of the Act it is provided that the Act must be construed to give effect to the Directive.

It is clear from the Recitals and from article 2 that the Directive does not apply to 'immovables' and that buildings and probably parts of buildings fall within that term. It is submitted therefore that when the Act is properly construed to give effect to the Directive it must follow that a speculative builder cannot be liable under it as producer of a defective house.

Similarly, neither in article 3(6) (which renders a supplier of a defective product liable if he fails to identify its producer within a reasonable time) nor anywhere else in the Directive is any exemption from liability accorded *to the supplier* where the supply is affected by the creation or disposal of an interest in land. It is submitted therefore that no distinction should be made between the liability of a speculative builder and a contract builder under the Act and indeed it is difficult to see in logic why there should be any.

6.06 The Act places primary liability on the 'producer' of the product who will normally be the manufacturer but may also be the product's importer into the EC where it has been manufactured outside the EC. Secondary liability is placed on the supplier of the goods in question where that supplier fails to identify within a reasonable time the person who sold the goods to him.

It may be a matter of importance therefore to know who in a given case is the 'producer' or 'supplier' of a building product for the purpose of the Act. There is as yet no authority on the matter but the following is put forward as a tentative answer:

1. *Where the building is erected by a speculative builder.* The builder alone will be the 'supplier' in the first instance of the products incorporated into the building and may therefore be liable as such under the Act (i.e. where he fails to identify his supplier within a reasonable time). He may also be liable as 'producer' of a product where he has given that product its 'essential characteristics' (see section 1(2)), an example of such a product would be concrete where this is mixed by the contractor, or where he has imported that product into the EC.
2. *When the building is erected under a contract with the building owner.* The contract builder's liability as 'producer' and 'supplier' of the building products he incorporates into the building he erects will normally be no different from that of the speculative builder. However, circumstances may arise, whether by express agreement or otherwise, where the contractor acts as agent for the building owner or his architect in the 'production' or 'supply' of the product in question. In that case the building owner or the architect would be liable as 'producer' or 'supplier' under the Act in the same way as the contractor would have been. Such cases outside express contract are, however, likely to be rare. In *Young & Marten Ltd* v *McManuschilds ([1986] AC 454, HL)*, it

was held that even where a product was specified that could only be purchased from one source, the contractor purchasing it was liable to the building owner for breach of implied warranty of merchantable quality where the product proved to be defective. It was implicit in that decision that the contractor was not acting as the building owner's agent in making the purchase.

6.07 Even where the builder is not acting as the building owner's agent, he may well wish in future to seek an indemnity from the building owner in respect of any liability he may incur under the Act, particularly in respect of any latent defects in products specified by the architect. Similarly, the building owner will no doubt seek an indemnity in respect of such liability from his architect.

6.08 Where the builder has no choice in the product he purchases and where the exercise of reasonable skill and care on his part in the selection of that product is ineffective in ensuring that the product is of merchantable quality (as might well be the case where there is a design defect) it would seem reasonable that ultimate liability under the Act (when this cannot be passed on the others) should fall on the architect who has chosen the product and who has had the best chance of assessing that product's quality. Such indemnity provisions may well become a common feature of building and architectural service contracts in the future.

7 Safety and Health Requirements of Workplaces Directive 89/391/EEC

7.01 On 12 June 1989 the Council adopted a directive entitled 'On the Introduction of Measures to Encourage Improvements in the Safety and Health of Workers'. It must be implemented by member states by 31 December 1992. The Directive applies *inter alia* to the building industry. The general duties to ensure safety and health of workers are placed on the employer and he cannot discharge the responsibility by employing an independent contractor for this purpose (article 5(2)).

In addition, specific duties are placed upon the employer, including the prevention of occupational risks, the provision of information and training, as well as the provision of the necessary organization and means for achieving these aims.

8 Other proposals

8.01 Further legislative proposals relevant to the building industry are in the pipeline. These are likely to cover such areas as liability and guarantee arrangements, quality control, indemnity insurance, model clauses for contract documents and research and development with a view to achieving the Single European Market. These subjects are being examined by member states' officials and by major professional and trade associations under the auspices of the Group on Regulations, Information and Management (GRIM). They have already produced a proposal for a European Foundation on construction, industry led and financed, which would examine industry problems in a European context. The proposal has been met with some scepticism by the UK construction industry.

22

International Work by Architects

RICHARD DYTON

1 Introduction

1.01 Any international work undertaken by architects is subject to legal complications over and above those in Britain because of the different legal systems involved. This is not to say that such work should be avoided since, after 1992, there will be greater opportunities for British architects to undertake work within the Single European market, but they should be aware of the problems which arise; consequently they should seek appropriate advice before entering into their appointments.

1.02 The summary below is taken, primarily, from the RIBA document, *1992 – An Information Pack for Architects* which provides a useful starting point for architects who will become involved in international work. The RIBA intends to commission a series of more detailed reports on each EEC country to stand beside the CIRIA reports and detailing the market opportunities and the practicalities, including the legal aspects, of practising in each country. The RIBA anticipates that these will be available before 1992.

France

1.03 France is perhaps the most attractive location due to its proximity and language. In France the architect's profession has traditionally been regarded as artistic rather than technical. By contrast, engineers are highly trained technically and tend to perform the type of technical duties undertaken in Britain by an architect. The architects and engineers in France are assumed to be jointly responsible with the contractor for the completed development.

In the event of a claim arising from a defect in the building, all the parties are normally joined in the action and responsibilities will be apportioned between them. The contractual period of liability in France against architects is two years from 'Reception' (approximately equivalent to Practical Completion) for minor repairs and ten years for structural defects.

West Germany

1.04 The position is rather different. Architects and engineers supervise the construction of a project and the architect's responsibility does not, therefore, end with the design. There is more management and administration work in their job than is the case in many of the other EEC member countries. The demarcation between engineers and architects is less clear-cut than in the UK. Both professionals have four to six years' technical training, then an additional two years' training for each gives them their qualification to practise. For contractual claims the limitation period against an architect can be as long as thirty years but in tort it is three years.

Italy

1.05 The roles of the architect and engineer overlap considerably. Clients may appoint an architect or an engineer to a project, or alternatively a director of works who takes responsibility not only for the design, but also manages and supervises the construction. Design-and-build contracts have also been popular there since the mid-seventies. As for France, the contractual limitation period for actions against architects is ten years.

Spain

1.06 The architect is in a unique position. He has a monopoly over certain types of work relating to the design and construction of buildings and, therefore, every building must have an architect who must be a member of the 'Collegio'. A local architect must sign drawings and supervise the building work. Claims against architects must be made within ten years of the commencement of the project, but this is extended to fifteen years where there has been a breach of contract.

Belgium

1.07 Architects are divided into three categories: principals, civil servants and salaried architects. Despite being required to supervise the building work, the architect acts only as adviser to the client and not generally as agent. He provides designs, costings and qualities, technical drawings and supervision. Contractors and architects in Belgium are jointly responsible for major defects in buildings for a period of ten years. Following changes in the law in 1984, insurance is now obligatory for Belgian architects and the insurance companies have established a Technical Inspectorate to reduce the risk of major defects. Approval of a building is usually accepted by insurance companies as evidence of satisfactory construction. The contractual liability of the architect is ten years following the completion of a building but in tort the normal period of limitation is thirty years.

Netherlands

1.08 Liability, once again, in contract extends for ten years for major defects. However, one important difference in the Netherlands is that the damages awarded to a plaintiff may only amount to half the designer's fees and it is possible to opt out of liability as part of the contract of engagement.

Portugal

1.09 The role of an architect in Portugal is unfortunately ill-defined, but a significant difference is that, for contractors, liability extends only for five years after the commissioning of a building.

Greece

1.10 Contractual liability of architects usually extends ten years.

Ireland

1.11 The duties of an architect in Ireland are similar to those in the rest of the UK so that his terms of engagement will exclude him from liability in respect of work or advice provided by other professional advisers but will make him liable for errors, patent or latent, in the design for which he is responsible. Whereas in England and Wales the position of an architect's liability in negligence towards third parties has been restricted by recent case law, this is not so for Ireland, where anyone affected by the careless act of another, whose interests that other person ought reasonably to have taken into account, would be entitled to recover compensation for negligence unless there was some public policy reason why this should not be permitted.

Denmark

1.12 The contractual limitation period is twenty years.

USA

1.13 Apart from Europe, one potential but as yet largely unrealized market for British architects is the USA.

Whereas in the UK the client normally engages the architect by an appointment separate from those of other consultants, in the USA it is far more common for the architect to be appointed by the client and then for the architect to sub-contract to other consultants the performance of the engineering and mechanical services. Thus the architect will assume vicarious liability for the actions of the consultants employed by him, something which the British architect is best advised to avoid.

In contrast to the UK position, there is much wider use of standard forms produced by the American Institute of Architects (AIA). The AIA produce a whole series of agreements from the 'Owner and Architect' agreement to the main form of building contract, together with sub-contracts. These are widely accepted within the USA, although there may be slight amendments from State to State.

Although ARCUK is responsible for registration of architects in the UK, in the USA architects *must* be licensed and individual States and Territories regulate entry into, and practice of, the professions within their jurisdiction. State statutes and regulations are based on the principle that practice by one who is not of proven technical and professional competence endangers 'the public's health, safety and welfare'. Licensing laws and regulations often restrict the use of the title 'architect', as well as outlining qualifications and procedures for registration as an architect, addressing any issues of reciprocity of registration with other States and defining the unlawful practice of architecture.

In a similar way, and unlike the UK, each State has its own Building Codes and these are the primary regulatory instruments for the design of buildings and structures on the site. Since local jurisdictions are authorized to adopt and enforce building regulations, Building Codes vary among States and even among cities within the same State. There are an estimated 13 000 Building Codes in the United States. The Codes cover, *inter alia*, specific design and construction requirements, permissible construction types, and egress requirements.

Another important contrast with the UK is that there are no quantity surveyors in the USA. The architect is therefore responsible for preparation of the contract documents for approval by the client. However, as mentioned above, the standard forms produced by the AIA usually do not require modification since they are widely accepted.

It is the contractor's responsibility to quantify and estimate once the architect has produced plans and specificatons. Once again, the AIA produces a guide to tendering or 'bidding' which the client and architect can use to determine to whom the contract is let. The architect's role in producing designs and plans is not greatly different from that in the UK although in the USA, 'shop drawings' are produced and a contractor is given somewhat greater scope to decide how to implement those plans.

On the question of liability in general architects tend to be sued slightly more in the USA than in the UK. This may be partly because the nature of US society is more litigious and partly because up to approximately 20% of all claims against the architect are personal injury claims. This latter characteristic is because building workers tend to sue the architect as a way of increasing the amount of compensation received for physical injury (the State-run basis being a no-fault compensation scheme, known as 'Workers' Compensation Insurance'). By accepting the state-run compensation, the worker cannot pursue his employer and may look to the architect to top up his damages.

In relation to insurance, there are general differences between the UK and the USA. Usually, in the latter, there is only one annual aggregate of liability cover whereas in the UK it is usual for each and every claim to be covered (although this may contain a limit in aggregate and other conditions). Also, in the USA there are specific areas of exclusion from cover such as a claim relating to asbestos or pollution. UK insurers will not automatically extend cover for a UK architect to work in the USA and it may be necessary to obtain additional insurance in the USA itself.

1.14 The larger firms of architects in the UK have already been active in seeking appointments abroad and the type of involvement will depend very much on the role their client gives them. They may be appointed directly by the client as the main architect for the project; they may combine with a local firm of architects and form a kind of joint venture; they may establish a local office in that particular country, governed by local laws; or they may simply have an advisory role, either to the client or as the job architect from an otherwise uninvolved position.

Following the EEC Directive 85/384/EC21, which was implemented in this country on 10 June 1986, British architects have been able to practise in any other member country without restriction. In theory this sounds very simple but in practice there are still some restrictions as, for example, in West Germany, where foreign architects who wish to practise there must satisfy qualification requirements and show adequate knowledge of German regulations and the language. As 1992 approaches, in theory, these restrictions should become less and less as harmonization proceeds. This topic is more fully discussed in Chapter 21.

Although these opening paragraphs have concentrated mainly on Europe and the USA, the object of this chapter is to give architects a brief glimpse of some of the legal pitfalls in working abroad together with the areas where architects will need to seek specialist legal advice in relation to their employment worldwide.

The next section deals with the problem of conflicts between different jurisdictions and some examples of the different approaches used to deal with these problems.

2 Conflicts of laws

2.01 The legal problems which the architect encounters when working overseas always involve jurisdiction and proper law: Do the courts of the country in which the building is constructed have jurisdiction over him and which law will be applied to resolve a dispute arising from the design and construction of the building? In particular, it is important for the architect to know whether the terms of his appointment will be recognized in another country; whether he will be able to enforce his rights against a foreign party in a foreign jurisdiction; what law will govern the performance of the architect's services; and whether the architect's insurance will cover him for work done overseas.

Jurisdiction and proper law

2.02 It is of the utmost importance that the architect gives early consideration, before the employer has retained other consultants, the contractor or sub-contractors, to the question of jurisdiction and proper law. Even if the employer has in mind certain contractors/consultants, the architect should attempt to influence the employer in relation to the type of appointment/building contract/sub-contract to be used so that its terms are familiar to the architect and so that the jurisdiction and proper law clauses throughout the contract documents are consistent.

Clearly, the choice of jurisdiction is an important consideration and, in such a clause, consideration should be given to such matters as which law is to be applied, convenience, reliability of the different courts, speed, costs, the location of assets, and whether the resulting judgment will travel. It is possible to provide for *exclusive* jurisdiction clauses or alternatively, *non-exclusive* clauses which will allow the parties a choice of forum. In circumstances where there are restrictions on the parties' rights to choose jurisdiction, jurisdiction may be reserved to the local courts. For example, local statutes may prohibit choice of jurisdiction clauses in certain types of contract, or a party may have a constitutional right to be sued in the courts of his State. Furthermore, there may be treaty obligations which regulate the choice, or there may be relevant matters of local public policy. This underlines the importance of taking legal advice so that the position can be confirmed.

There should also be a 'proper' or 'governing' law clause which may be included in the jurisdiction clause but, more usually, is dealt with in a separate clause. Without such provision the English courts, if asked to adjudicate on a dispute between two French parties with the subject matter in France, would apply French law on the basis that this implements the reasonable and legitimate expectations of the parties to a transaction. Although this is the principle adopted by the English courts it is far better to provide expressly in the contract for the proper law. This is because first, local courts in another jurisdiction may adopt other principles and, secondly, it does not leave the parties' intentions open and uncertain to be decided by the court. Most countries with established legal systems will apply the law chosen expressly by the parties to the contract.

Brussels Convention

2.03 The above analysis helps to answer the question, whether the terms of the architect's appointment can be made subject to a familiar jurisdiction and law despite the fact that he is working in a foreign jurisdiction and being subject to foreign laws, provided that care is taken in the drafting of the jurisdiction clause. There is, however, an important qualification to these comments, brought about by the implementation of the Brussels Convention of 1968 (as amended by the Accession Convention and due to be further amended in respect of the accession of Portugal and Spain) which became law in the UK from 1 January 1987. Currently, the Brussels

Convention relates only to France, Germany, Italy, Belgium, the Netherlands, Luxembourg, Denmark, Ireland and the UK, although Greece, Spain and Portugal will accede to the Convention in due course.

Although the principles are to be extended to other countries, such as Austria, under the Lugano Covention, under the Brussels Convention the general rule is that persons domiciled in a particular member country must be sued in that country. Domicile is a complex concept but can be loosely equated to residence combined with a 'substantial connection' with a chosen country. For corporations domicile is associated with 'seat'. Article 17 of the Convention, however, provides that where parties agree to settle disputes under the jurisdiction of the court in a particular member country, 'that court, or those courts, shall have exclusive jurisdiction'. This over-rides any local law prohibiting jurisdiction clauses but it is important that the formalities are complied with in order to give effect to article 17. These are that the agreement confirming jurisdiction shall be in writing unless it relates to a matter involving international trade or commerce, where other rules apply. In addition, there must be evidence of consent by all the relevant parties and it is not sufficient for such clauses to be simply included in printed business forms, not expressly agreed to by the other relevant parties.

The question of the architect suing for his fees in the context of the rules of the Brussels Convention has been considered by the European Court of Justice in *Hassan Shenavai* v *Klaus Kreischer*. Here a German architect was suing a German national residing in the Netherlands for his fees. According to the Brussels Convention the general criterion for determining jurisdiction is the domicile of the defendant. However, the court held that in matters relating to a contract the defendant may also be sued in 'the courts for the place of performance of the obligation in question'. The obligation in question, when the proceedings were for the recovery of architects' fees, was held to be the specific contractual obligation for the defendant to pay out the fee, in the Netherlands, rather than the contractual relationship as a whole. Thus in this case the place of performance was not the place of the architect's practice nor the site of the planned building but the place where the fee was to be treated as being paid, and this was held to be the residence of the client in the Netherlands. Whether that position would apply if the proper law of the contract were English is doubtful. The architect could have safeguarded himself by a jurisdiction clause providing for bare jurisdiction.

2.04 Where there appears to be a conflict between, for example, the obligations of the architect as described in the appointment and governed by English law, and the obligations of the architect as described in the building contract (governed by another law), the appropriate law to be applied would be determined by the particular court having jurisdiction under its domestic law. Thus, for example, if the dispute were to be settled in an English court, that court would be obliged to enquire with which legal system the overall transaction had its closest and most real connection. This would determine the 'proper law' of the contract and the judges would consider a variety of circumstances, such as the nature of the contract, the customs of business, the place where the contract was made or was to be performed, the language and form of the contract, in order to determine which legal system should apply.

2.05 The second question which concerns an architect, once he has gone through the trauma and expense of pursuing, defending or counter-claiming in a dispute against a party from another jurisdiction, is whether he would be able to enforce his successful judgment against that party. Most EEC countries are parties to the Brussels Convention, but outside the EEC the recognition of foreign judgments depends on common law enforcement and/or whether the UK has a treaty with the particular country concerned, which provides for reciprocal enforcement of judgments. If such a treaty exists then, subject to various formalities, the court will enforce the judgment against the defendant's assets in that jurisdiction provided, normally, that the judgment is for money only. Where no mutual recognition treaty exists between the country of judgment and the desired country of execution, the process has to be started afresh in that country unless common law rights can assist. This matter should be dealt with by professional advisers when entering into the appointment.

For enforcement within the EEC, the Brussels Convention is not limited to money judgments nor to final judgments and the court in which enforcement is sought has very limited powers to investigate the jurisdiction of the court which gave the judgment. In other words, it is much easier to enforce a judgment in a country within the EEC than outside the EEC. Enforcement may only be refused on the grounds of public policy, lack of notice of proceedings, the irreconcilability of the judgment with judgments of the other State, and certain cases involving preliminary questions as to status. The foreign court may not question the findings of fact on which the original court based its judgment, nor can a judgment be reviewed as to its substance.

Insurance

2.06 The third question which the architect should always consider in relation to overseas work is the extent to which his insurance will cover him for breaches of duty in the particular country in which he is working. No general answer can be given to this, nor can any statement be guaranteed in the future, since insurers will take different views in relation to various countries and at different times. For example, the type of insurance available on any project carried out in France would be the decennial project insurance towards which all the construction team pay premiums. This would cover the architect for breaches of duty for up to ten years although it may not relieve the architect altogether because there may be subrogation rights to the insurers. However, architects who wish to practise in the USA may (due, perhaps, to the increased prevalence of claims brought against the architect there) have to seek separate professional indemnity insurance with local insurers since many insurers will not extend their cover to claims arising in the USA. In any event, before undertaking any overseas work the architect should check with his professional indemnity insurers whether or not he will be covered or can obtain cover from them in respect of that work.

Contractual duties

2.07 The standard of performance which local law may impose on architects clearly depends exclusively on the law at any particular time in the country concerned, and this can only be determined through personal experience of the architect of work in the jurisdiction and legal advice. As between the parties who are bound contractually, the architect's duties will normally be defined in the contract documents. If the local law provides that duties are owed by the architect to third parties in tort, or indeed to parties with whom he is already in contract, the standard and scope of such duties can only be determined by reference to local lawyers. The architect will normally have to ensure that there is compliance with the local building regulations, etc., although it will first be necessary to check the architect's role under the building contract to determine if it is simply to check or to ensure compliance.

Copyright

2.08 One important aspect of international work that should be considered by architects is the protection of their copyright

in relation to the designs, plans and drawings which they have prepared for the overseas work. Although it may be possible to include provision in the appointment for protection of copyright vis-à-vis the client, the drawings may be used by a number of parties who may be tempted to infringe the copyright of the architect and use the designs elsewhere, without permission. The position in the majority of developed countries roughly approximates to the provisions of the Berne Convention drawn up in 1886 with the most recent revisions in Paris in 1971. The UK has acceded to these provisions in the Copyright Act 1988 which came into force on 1 August 1989. The Berne Convention gives protection for a minimum of the life of the author, and a post-mortem period of fifty years, and requires countries bound by it to abandon any rules of deposit or registration as a condition of copyright protection. The Berne Convention also provides for the protection of the author's moral rights, which protects the author's right to have the work attributed to his name and the right to object to derogatory treatment of the work (once the moral right has been asserted). Clearly, if the architect is dealing in a country which is a signatory to the Berne Convention he is fully protected. In other countries there may be a lesser form of protection, as under the Universal Copyright Convention, which gives protection for the life of the author plus twenty-five years and provides for any condition of registration or deposit to be satisfied when copies bear the symbol © accompanied by the name of the copyright owner and the year of first publication of the document. Significantly, the USA has recently ratified the Berne Convention but there are a significant number of countries which belong only to the lesser of the two Conventions, i.e. the UCC (this includes the USSR). In many developing countries no international treaty obligations subsist whatsoever and the architect will have to rely on local copyright law, if any. Local legal advice should be sought as to the means of protecting copyright and to comply with those local laws.

Commercial consideratons

2.09 Finally, the architect should consider practical commercial matters, such as failure of the employer to pay fees, the country's available resource of hard currency, and exchange rate fluctuations, taking advice from persons experienced in international work who may be able to recommend suitable insurance to cover these risks, together with ECGD cover and political credit risk insurance and possibly a performance bond. In addition, if the advice of local lawyers is to be obtained, this might best be channelled through British lawyers since many foreign lawyers, such as those in West Germany, are not obliged to advise on the most cost-efficient procedure in any situation.

3 FIDIC

3.01 Although, quite clearly, the FIDIC Conditions of Contract embodied in the 'Conditions of Contract (International) for Works of Civil Engineering Construction' (3rd edn, 1977) applies to duties of the engineer, the role of architect and engineer, particularly in many European countries, becomes indistinguishable, unlike the system in the UK where roles are more clearly defined. It may be helpful to look at some of the problems which British engineers have faced when working with the FIDIC contracts and compare them with corresponding problems which may arise for the British architect if he is appointed under a normal form of RIBA Appointment for a development governed by the FIDIC terms, appropriately amended. At the last count, in 1986, 49 separate national Contractors' Federations have given their stamp of approval to the FIDIC Conditions and the Conditions are used extensively in building and in industrial and process engineering as well as civil engineering. It is not unreasonable to suppose, therefore, that a British

architect may, if he is working aroad, be administering the project under the terms of FIDIC.

3.02 Some of the clauses which require the architect's attention are the following:

Clause 2(1): Duties and powers of the engineer Where the architect is acting in the role of an engineer, he must check whether this clause is in the contract since it refers to duties for which specific approval is required from the client, and these duties are listed in part 2 of the Conditions. The items that require approval will generally accord with the legal code of certain countries in which the Conditions are used.

Clause 5(1): Governing language and law Clearly this clause is of major significance since the contract provisions will be construed in accordance with the specified law. The language in which the contract is written is also significant, not only from the point of view of everyday administration but also from the point of view of interpretation. Very often an international contract is written in two languages, one the local tongue and one the language of the engineering consultants who drafted the contract in the first place. In these cases it can be useful to include an express clause which will state which version shall prevail in the event of conflict or ambiguity between the two versions.

Once the law of the contract has been established, legal advice should be sought from lawyers experienced in international jurisdictional points and the local law. In addition, a translation of the contract is helpful (if not already in two versions).

Clause 5(2): Ambiguities and discrepancies The architect should check whether this clause is included since it provides for the conditions of contract to prevail over any other document forming part of the contract. There may be an interpretation problem existing between the general conditions and the conditions of particular application (these are the conditions which would be included in Part 2 of the Conditions) and if the relevant law reflects the position in English law, the conditions of particular application would take precedence over any standard printed condition since those would be the ones considered by the parties as particular to the contract.

Clause 8: Responsibility for construction and design This clause is of importance because it sets out very clearly the division of responsibility between the contractor and the engineer or architect. As presently drafted, the engineer or architect has responsibility for the adequacy of the design of permanent works, unless specified works have been nominated to be designed by the contractor.

Clause 11: Inspection of the site This is not usually a function of the architect although, under the RIBA appointment, the architect can be employed to advise on the suitability of sites and to make surveys and various other investigations. Under clause 11 of the FIDIC Conditions there are certain items upon which the contractor is deemed to have obtained information by his own enquiries. Therefore it is important to determine whether such a clause has been amended in any way to require the engineer or architect to provide more information than usual.

There are other clauses of importance in FIDIC but to consider such would be to go beyond the scope of this brief. The above details some of the main areas for consideration.

4 The future

4.01 As can be seen in other chapters in this book, the liability of architects is not clear-cut and is a point of constant discussion and negotiation, particularly in relation to the architect's appointment and the problems encountered by architects striving to stay within the terms of their insurance cover. In the UK this is due to the change of direction in the

law relating to architects' duties. Clearly, when there is such uncertainty in our own country, that confusion can only be compounded when dealing with other jurisdictions, some based on the common law system (which is the basis of our own system) and some based on civil law systems as in many of the European countries. An answer to both of these problems, i.e. clarification of the duty and extent of insurance cover, may be found in proposals currently being considered and recommended by the EEC Consultant (Claude Mathurin) looking into these matters in the run-up to 1992. A single contract which would limit architects' responsibilities to a specific 'duty of care' and prevent them from being sued for sums greater than the level of their fees is currently being discussed and would prevent developers and financial institutions using collateral warranties to impose onerous liabilities on architects such as guaranteeing a building's fitness for purpose (further discussed in Chapter 5). Although such a contract has not yet been formulated, the idea is to have one standard contract which can be adapted from country to country, providing for the developer to take full contractual responsibility for the whole project whilst the architect would be defined as the building's 'author'.

4.02 It would be hard to see such a system being effectively implemented or achieving widespread commercial acceptability without making the contract mandatory. However, the creeping power of the EEC may mean that this is a possibility by 1992. Thereafter such a standard contract could possibly become a standard for adoption worldwide depending on the success or not of its use within the EEC. Such a system with a 'single contract' would be particularly useful if linked with the French system of 'single project' or decennial insurance. In the move towards harmonization in Europe, which should, in theory, be complete by 1992, the EEC is promoting the French system which British architects would favour, as a contrast to the somewhat uncertain and expensive professional indemnity arrangements. The scheme would limit professionals' liability and provide for new organizations monitoring insurance to provide certainty, although from the architect's point of view the effectiveness of such single project insurance would depend entirely upon the scope of cover available (i.e. whether limited to structural defects or applicable to all defects of design and workmanship), and the extent to which the single project insurer would be willing to waive rights of subrogation within the scope of the policy.

4.03 The difficult task of drawing up a single contract and a single insurance scheme would fall, in practice, on the European Commission, who have also drawn up directives relating to public procurement. In the meantime, whilst awaiting the result of the various discussions taking place and the final outcome, the architect can only take care in taking on overseas commissions, and obtaining legal advice as appropriate.

23

Professional Conduct in England

A. RODERICK MALES*

1 The nature of professionalism in architecture

1.01 The concept of a professional person and an institutional profession has been continually evolving since the eighteenth century. Numerous studies of the subject have been made; the most concise appeared in 1970 as the report of the Monopolies Commission (Part 1: *The Report* A report on the general effect on the public interest of certain restrictive practices so far as they prevail in relation to the supply of professional services (Cmnd 4463). Part 2: *The Appendices* (Cmnd 4463–1)). Appendix 5 of the report provides a range of definitions and descriptions which vary considerably. There is general agreement, however, that a professional person offers competence and integrity of service based upon a skilled intellectual technique.

1.02 The history and development of the architectural profession in Britain may be studied in Barrington Kaye, *The Development of the Architectural Profession in Britain* and in Frank Jenkins, *Architect and Patron*.

1.03 The relationship of a professional person and his client is that of mutual trust. It is unique in the world of business and requires considerable dedication on the part of practitioners and protection from society if it is to survive. Although there has been a general widening of the scope of both professional and business activities in society over the last decade, the distinction between professional and commercial attitudes remains.

1.04 The professional relationship becomes most meaningful when contrasted with commercial relationships. Traditionally, the latter are involved with growing, manufacturing, or buying goods, and selling at a profit. Only recently has the concept of service developed in commercial relationships. An essential characteristic of trade has been that buyer and seller are free to drive a hard bargain, each at his own risk (*caveat emptor*). Apart from fair dealing, neither party is expected to look to the other's interests. In contrast, professionalism has evolved to reduce the risks which would otherwise be much greater for individuals seeking personal services on a commercial basis. The client must have faith in those from whom he seeks advice (*credat emptor*).

The principles and values of professionalism are probably now of greater significance at a time of commercial pressures than at any time since the middle of the nineteenth century. The architect's role in community affairs, environmental issues and energy conservation demands and depends upon the total commitment of impartial professionalism.

1.05 A common misconception about professionalism is that it is concerned mainly with technical skill. Hence the resentment of some architects that they should be deprived of the professional title for which they have qualified by examination, merely because they choose to practice in a particular way. Professional people are experts; where no specialist knowledge and skill is required, there is no need for professional advice. But they have no monopoly of expertise. Traditionally it has been available only from those whose lives have been devoted to a particular calling; from this stems the common use of the word to distinguish the man who earns his living at some activity from the amateur. But suitably qualified amateurs may, in fact, offer their services professionally and be judged accordingly, while the necessity of earning a living may create interests that conflict with the disinterested nature of professional service. Therefore, professional institutions developed with two-fold objectives. On the one hand, they provide additional protection to the public by reinforcing the law of contract with an assurance of special competence and a code of ethics. On the other, they have sought to protect the professional man by creating a climate in which relationships of mutual trust with clients may flourish, free from the need to advertise, to drive hard bargains over fees, and the fear of unfair competition during a job. Debate about the role and nature of professionalism in a changing society continues.

2 Codes of professional conduct

2.01 The codes of conduct of a professional body are devised to protect the interests of the clients of the profession and to

*In the first edition, this chapter was written by David Keate. In the second edition, it was revised by Evelyn Freeth.

maintain the status of the profession in the eyes of society. The requirements of the codes develop with changing circumstances and the needs of society. They reflect the attitudes of the membership of the profession and the requirements of statute and public opinion.

2.02 The codes of the architectural profession have been the subject of increasing discussion and negotiation. In particular, the fee scale and the involvement of architects as directors of associated businesses in the construction industry have been subject to heated debate.

2.03 Two codes apply to the profession. The first is that of the Architects' Registration Council of the United Kingdom (ARCUK), to which all architects must subscribe. The second is that of the Royal Institute of British Architects (RIBA), which applies to its members alone. For a period, these two Codes were virtually identical but are now different in concept and content.

2.04 Failure to comply with the ARCUK code could result in the removal of the architect's name from the Register. The person would no longer be entitled to use the title Architect. Failure to comply with the code of the RIBA could result in the suspension of the person from membership of the RIBA but he/she would be entitled to retain the title Architect as long as his/her name remained on the Register of the ARCUK.

3 ARCUK guidelines

```
The Standard of Conduct for Architects

A registered person who intends to maintain his integrity
so as to deserve the respect and confidence of all those
for whom or with whom he may work in his capacity as
an architect

Will assure himself that information given in connection
with his services is in substance and presentation factual
and relevant to the occasion and neither misleading nor
unfair to others nor intended to oust another architect
from an engagement

Will before making an engagement whether by an agree-
ment for professional services by a contract of employ-
ment or by a contract for the supply of services or goods
have defined beyond reasonable doubt the terms of the
engagement including
        the scope of the service
        the allocation of responsibilities and any limitation of
            liability
        the method of calculation of remuneration
        the provision for termination

Will have declared to the other parties to the engagement
any business interest which might be or appear to be
prejudicial to the proper performance of the engagement
which he will carry out faithfully and conscientiously
        with proper regard for the interests of those who
            may be expected to use or enjoy the product of
            his work
        with fairness in administering the conditions of a
            building contract
        and without inducements to show favour

Will if at any time he finds that his interests whether
professional or personal conflict so as to put his integrity
in question inform without delay those who may be
concerned and if agreement is not reached to the
continuance of any engagement will withdraw from it.
```

3.01 For many years the code of professional conduct of the ARCUK had been very similar to that of the RIBA. The differences have varied from time to time, but until December 1980 the only difference between the codes was a matter of technical definition. For practical purposes a person registered as an architect was subject to the same restrictions and conditions as a member of the RIBA.

3.02 The code of conduct now takes the form of a simple statement, the *Standard of Conduct for Architects*, based upon an interpretation of the expression 'conduct disgraceful to him in his capacity as an architect' which appears in section 7 of the Architects Registration Act of 1931. It promulgates the standard of conduct which architects are expected to maintain. The Architects Registration Council reserves to itself the right to deal with specific cases of complaint or comment on merit. The *Standard of Conduct for Architects* is supported by an explanatory memorandum which is revised from time to time in the light of the Council's findings.

```
Explanatory Memorandum

The Architects Registration Council of the United Kingdom is
empowered under Section 7 of the Architects (Registration) Act
1931 to remove the name of an architect from the Register if after
enquiry he has been found to be guilty of conduct disgraceful to
him in his capacity as an architect.

"This power is not limited by any formal definition of disgraceful
conduct and a registered person whose conduct in any circum-
stances appears to be disgraceful may be called to account for it
under the Disciplinary Procedures (See Appendix 2).

Without prejudice to the generality of this power the Standard of
Conduct for Architects draws attention in general terms to the
more common circumstances of the activities of registered persons.
It is published as a guide towards good conduct for the benefit of
architects, the Discipline Committee of ARCUK and the public".

Every architect is expected to guard his integrity irrespective of his
field of activity or contract of employment or membership of any
association whether acting independently or through a corporate
body or through any other person.

Subject to this and to Section 17 of the 1931 Act no specific
occupation is proscribed nor is any restraint of trade imposed.

Any person who is uncertain about a particular course of action in
the context of the Standard may seek advice from the Registrar
who will if necessary refer the matter to the Professional Purposes
Committee or through that Committee to the Council. Advice
given will be within the disciplinary powers of ARCUK.

Where disgraceful conduct is alleged, the Discipline Committee
may take into account whether or not the person arraigned sought
such advice before carrying out the activity which is the subject of
complaint.

Decisions of the Discipline Committee and any advice given during
the course of the year will be reviewed by the Professional
Purposes Committee and may be published in the Annual Report.
```

3.03 The standard does not prohibit any specific occupation or activity and it contains no 'rules'. It is devised as a positive guide to good conduct.

3.04 The statement of the ARCUK should be read in conjunction with the Code of Conduct of the RIBA. Certain activities which are permissible under the ARCUK guide Conduct and Discipline are prohibited by the RIBA Code of Conduct. It is important that RIBA members should be aware of the differences between the two Codes.

3.05 The Standard of Conduct for Architects lays down four requirements to which a registered person is subject. The first concerns information being given by the architect concerning his services; the second concerns the engagement of the architect; the third concerns the declaration of interest; and the fourth concerns conflict of interest.

3.06 In addition to the *Standard of Conduct for Architects*, and the *Explanatory Memorandum*, the ARCUK also issues

an occasional notice *Advice to Architects*, which offers practical advice on the interpretation of its principles and rules.

4 The RIBA Code of Conduct

4.01 The RIBA Code of Conduct which came into effect in January 1981 made fundamental changes in the Institute's traditional attitude towards professional conduct. It removed the restrictions on carrying on the business of trading in land or buildings, or as property developers, auctioneers, estate agents or contractors, sub-contractors, manufacturers or suppliers in or to the construction industry. It permitted members to negotiate fees with potential clients and abandoned the mandatory minimum fee system. It removed the ban on practising in the form of a limited liability company, it extended the permitted means by which an architect might bring himself to the notice of potential clients and this was further broadened in subsequent revisions. The Rules and Notes concerning the application of the Principles have been frequently amended since the introduction of the Code, most recently: September 1989.

Principle One

The Principle 1.0
A member shall faithfully carry out the duties which he undertakes. He shall also have a proper regard for the interests both of those who commission and those who may be expected to use or enjoy the product of his work.

Note 1.0.1
A member is advised before undertaking or continuing with any work to arrange that his resources are adequate and properly directed to carry it out.

Note 1.0.2
A student member who undertakes a commission is advised to seek guidance from an architect.

Rule 1.1
A member shall when making an engagement, whether by an agreement for professional services by a contract of employment or by a contract for the supply of services of goods, have defined beyond reasonable doubt and recorded the terms of the engagement including the scope of the service, the allocation of responsibilities and any limitation of liability, the method of calculation of remuneration and the provision for termination.

Note 1.1.1
A member proposing or making an agreement for an engagement as an independent consulting architect should make use of the RIBA Architect's Appointment to define the terms of engagement.

Rule 1.2
A member shall arrange that the work of his office and any branch office insofar as it relates to architecture is under the control of an architect.

Rule 1.3
A member shall not sub-commission or sub-let work without the prior agreement of his client nor without defining the changes in the responsibilities of those concerned.

Rule 1.4
A member shall act impartially in all cases in which he is acting between parties. Where he has responsibilities as architect under a building contract, or is similarly acting between the parties, he shall interpret the conditions of such contract with fairness and impartiality.

Principle Two

The Principle 2.0
A member shall avoid actions and situations inconsistent with his professional obligations or likely to raise doubts about his integrity.

Rule 2.1
A member shall declare to any prospective client any business interest the existence of which, if not so declared, would or might be likely to raise doubts about his integrity by reason of an actual or apparent connection with or effect upon his engagement.

Note 2.1.1
This Rule requires the prior disclosure of relevant business interests which could not be inferred from the description of the services offered. If such interests arise during the currency of the engagement Rule 2.8 applies.

Rule 2.2
A member shall not simultaneously practise as, or purport to be, an independent consulting architect and engage in or have as a partner or co-director a person who, whether or not in a separate firm, engages in any of the following:

the business of trading in land or buildings; or of property developers, auctioneers, or house or estate agents; or of contractors, sub-contractors, manufacturers or suppliers in or to the building industry

unless he is able to demonstrate that the combination would not prevent his compliance with the Principles of this Code and the Rules that apply to his circumstances.

Rule 2.3
A member shall not and shall not purport to carry out the independent functions of an architect or any similar independent functions in relation to a contract in which he or his employer is the contractor.

Note 2.3.1
Where the client of a member providing a contracting service requires independent advice on quality and budgetary control the member should inform the client of his right to appoint another architect to act as his professional adviser and agent.

Rule 2.4
A member shall ensure that whenever he offers or takes part in offering a service combining consulting services with contracting services the consulting component is not represented as independent of the combined service.

Rule 2.5
A member shall not have or take as a partner or co-director in his firm any person who is disqualified for registration by reason of the fact that his name has been removed from the Register under Section 7 of the Architects (Registration) Act 1931; any person disqualified for membership of the RIBA by reason of expulsion under Byelaw 5.1; any person disqualified for membership of another professional institution by reason of expulsion under the relevant disciplinary regulations, unless the RIBA otherwise allows.

Rule 2.6
A member shall not take discounts, commissions or gifts as an inducement to show favour to any person or body; nor shall he recommend or allow his name to be used as recommending any service or product in advertisements.

Note 2.6.1
This Rule does not prevent a member who is a contractor from accepting the trade and cash discounts customarily allowed by manufacturers or suppliers.

Rule 2.7
A member shall not improperly influence the granting of planning consents or statutory approvals.

Rule 2.8
A member who in circumstances not specifically covered in these Rules finds that his interests whether professional or personal conflict so as to risk a breach of this Principle shall, as the circumstances may require, either withdraw from the situation or remove the source of conflict or declare it and obtain the agreement of the parties concerned to the continuance of his engagement.

Note 2.8.1
An example of the application of this Rule is that a member who has been appointed assessor for any competition shall not subsequently act in any other capacity for the work except that he may act as arbitrator in any dispute between the promoters and the selected architect or as consultant where that appointment was arranged before his appointment as assessor.

Note 2.8.2
A member appointed to give expert advice shall not subsequently allow his terms of reference to be extended into those of an arbitrator.

Note 2.8.3
It should be noted that the RIBA may, depending on the circumstances, be one of the 'parties concerned'. For example, where in any case a member is under pressure to act in a way which would bring him into non-compliance with the Code, in addition to any other declarations which it may be appropriate to make, he should declare the facts to the RIBA.

Rule 2.9
A member shall have a proper regard for the professional obligations and qualifications of those from whom he receives or to whom he gives authority, responsibility or employment, or with whom he is professionally associated. A member who employs architects shall define their conditions of employment*, authority, responsibility and liability.

Note 2.9.1†
Upholding this Rule requires that:

(a) a member enables the architects he employs to exercise their professional skills and provides them with opportunities to accept progressively greater delegated authority and responsibility in accordance with their ability and experience;

(b) a member acknowledges the contribution and responsibilities of the architects he employs by giving them credit in any publications, exhibitions, etc;

(c) a member permits the architects he employs to engage in sparetime practice and to enter architectural competitions and that the employee does not do so without the knowledge of his employer, and that he acts in accordance with Rule 2.8;

---

* The RIBA publishes a Guide to Employment Practice which may be of use to employers and to those who are employed.

† Salaried Practice Advisory and Conciliation Panel: responsible to the RIBA Council, exercises advisory and conciliatory functions in relation to any question of employer/employee relations brought to its attention which appears to be in conflict with this Note.

(d) a member encourages the architects he employs to maintain and advance their competence by participating in continuing professional development and allows them to have reasonable time off to participate in the affairs of the profession;

(e) a member who employs students cooperates with the RIBA and schools of architecture in the practical training scheme; provides as varied experience as possible compatible with his professional responsibilities; and allows student employees to take reasonable time off for academic purposes leading to the qualifying examinations.

Rule 2.10
A member shall conform with the Members' Rules for Clients' Accounts from time-to-time in force.

Note 2.10.1
The Members' Rules for Clients' Accounts are reproduced on pages 13 and 14 hereof.

Principle Three

The Principle 3.0
A member shall rely only on ability and achievement as the basis for his advancement.

Note 3.0.1
Members are encouraged to participate by means of RIBA regional and branch activities, amenity societies and other bodies concerned with the quality of the environment, in local and national affairs concerning the environment and to criticize what they believe to be harmful, shoddy or inappropriate provided that criticism is not malicious or contrary to any Rule under this Principle.

Rule 3.1
A member shall not give discounts, commissions, gifts or other inducements for the introduction of clients or of work.

Note 3.1.1
This Rule does not prevent a member who is a contractor from giving the trade and cash discounts customarily allowed by manufacturers or suppliers.

Rule 3.2
A member who is offering services as an independent consulting architect shall not quote a fee without having received from the prospective client an invitation to do so and sufficient information to enable the member to know the nature and scope of the project and the services required.

Rule 3.3
A member who is offering services as an independent consulting architect shall not revise a fee quotation to take account of the fee quoted by another architect for the same service.

Rule 3.4
A member shall not attempt to oust another architect from an engagement.

Note 3.4.1
(a) Subject to these Rules a member may enter into negotiation with a prospective client on the fee basis for that member's services provided that, in compliance with Rule 1.1 the other terms of engagement are properly defined.

(b) Any member who, in the course of such negotiation, having regard to the objects of the RIBA and Principle 1 of this Code, is unwilling or unable to accept a fee basis proposed by a prospective client, should comply with Rule 2.8 by withdrawing from the negotiation, and declare the facts to the RIBA.

(c) A member who is concerned with the appointment of another as an independent consulting architect should respect the obligations of that member under these Rules.

Rule 3.5
A member on being approached to undertake work upon which he knows, or can ascertain by reasonable inquiry, that another architect has an engagement with the same client shall notify the fact to such architect.

Note 3.5.1
A member who is engaged to give an opinion on the work of another architect should notify the fact to that architect unless it can be shown to be prejudicial to prospective litigation to do so.

Rule 3.6
A member may make his availability and experience known by any means provided that the information given is in substance and in presentation factual, relevant and – neither misleading nor unfair to others – nor otherwise discreditable to the profession.

Note 3.6.1
A member may commission an external public relations consultant or similarly designated person to carry out all or any aspect of his public relations policy provided that he furnishes the RIBA with a written declaration signed by the appointed person that he has received and read Byelaw 5, this Code and the Practice Note entitled 'Members and public relations'. In the declaration the appointed person must acknowledge that he will be in breach of contract with his client if any action of his brings the latter into breach of the Byelaws or any Rule of this Code at any time.

Rule 3.7
A member shall not enter any architectural competition which the RIBA has declared to be unacceptable.

Members' Rules for Clients' Accounts

Introduction

Members will see that these Rules require them (a) to keep full books of account recording all money received from and spent for clients, and, (b) in addition to keep clients money in a separate Clients bank account, from which no more may be drawn on the account of a particular client than is held on his behalf.

Handling clients money is an extra service, and consideration should be given to making the agreement in respect of handling and making payments of interest.

The Rules

1.　Members shall keep properly written up books of Account.

(a) When a member makes any disbursement on behalf of a client he shall maintain a sufficient record thereof to be able to produce clear and understandable particulars of all disbursements for any client.

(b) When a member receives money belonging to any client the following rules shall also apply.

2.　In the event that a member receives any money belonging to any client he shall open a ledger account in the name of each such client showing office and client receipts and payments; in the event of a member's having more than one commission from any client it is open to him to deal with each commission on a separate ledger account according with the requirements of these rules.

3.　A member receiving money belonging to clients must open a client's account or clients' accounts at a branch of any bank in the United Kingdom in his name or in the name of the relevant practice. The title of such an account must contain the word "client" or "clients". Such accounts may be either current accounts or deposit accounts.

4.　Members shall pay any money they receive (in whatever form) which belongs to any client into a clients account or clients accounts as soon as is practicable, save that this rule shall not apply:

(a) to money being paid without delay to a third party in the ordinary course of business,

(b) when the client has authorised the member in writing not to pay the money into the Clients Account, provided that it is dealt with in accordance with the client's instructions.

Money received and paid under 4. must be recorded in the member's books of account in conformity with 1.

No money other than that specified by this Rule or paid into the account under Rule 8 or 9 below shall be paid into any clients account.

5.　Money may be withdrawn from a client's account:

(a) if required for a payment to or on behalf of a client

(b) to make a payment of or to account of a debt due to the member by a client and/or to reimburse a member for money spent on behalf of a client. In the event that money is withdrawn in respect of the member's fees and/or value added tax payable in respect of these fees the member must notify the client in writing of the amount claimed before transferring relevant money from the clients account.

(c) to make a payment on the client's written authority.

Provided that in no case shall more money be withdrawn under this rule than is shown in the members' books of account to be held on behalf of the relevant client.

6.　Members keeping a clients account or clients accounts shall at intervals of not more than three calendar months (or alternatively on each quarter day) balance the Clients Cash Book and Clients Ledger with the relevant bank statements and shall retain the reconciliation statement prepared at the date of each balance for a period of not less than eighteen months.

7.　Any member may be required under the Disciplinary Procedures to produce audit certificates in respect of clients accounts forthwith at any time. Such certificates must be signed by a person who is a member of one of the following bodies:

(a) The Institute of Chartered Accountants in England and Wales

(b) The Institute of Chartered Accountants of Scotland

(c) The Association of Certified and Corporate Accountants

(d) The Institute of Chartered Accountants in Ireland

8.　If any money is paid into or withdrawn from a clients account erroneously the member shall forthwith withdraw or pay in (as the case may be) such money as is necessary to restore the account to its proper condition and shall make a record in the Journal (i.e. a book of account) stating the date the mistake was made, the accounts to which the mistake relates and the amount of money involved. An example of an erroneous payment in is a cheque in settlement of a members fees, which belong to the member. An example of an erroneous withdrawal is making a payment from the clients account against a cheque which is not paid by bankers.

9.　In the event that a member receives money which in part belongs to a client and which in part does not belong to a client and which he wishes to pay into a single account, he shall pay the money into a clients account and shall immediately thereafter withdraw such part as does not belong to the client from the clients account and pay it into an appropriate account.

Additional Points

Members are reminded that in some circumstances there are statutory requirements which relate to the keeping of accounts, for example under *Estate Agents Act 1979*.

Members are reminded that there may be a requirement to pay interest on money held as an agent under the rule in *Brown v The Commissioners of Inland Revenue* (1965) AC 244 or otherwise. In these circumstances if they are holding money for any length of time or are holding a substantial amount of money even for a short time, members should consider placing it in a clients deposit account. The accounting implications of the *Brown* case should also be borne in mind, i.e. that interest earned on a single account may have to be apportioned between several clients.

Approved by the Council, March 1986

4.02 The Code of Conduct recognizes the needs of current practice and changing circumstances. It establishes three principles as the core of professionalism and a series of rules for their interpretation, supported by a number of guidance notes.

4.03 Principle 1 concerns the work of the architect in relation to both the client and the users of the buildings. It requires an agreement of service of fees to be made before commencement; it requires the work to be carried out under the control of an architect; it prevents the sub-letting of work without agreement; and it maintains the traditional impartiality of the architect in the carrying out of his work.

4.04 Principle 2 is directed towards the avoidance of inconsistencies or doubts of integrity in the work of the architect. It requires the architect to declare the existence of anything likely to raise doubts about his integrity; it prohibits simultaneous practice as an independent consultant and engagement in one of the previously restricted businesses, unless it can be shown that the two are compatible and that this is so declared. It prohibits simultaneous functions of contracting and the independent practice of architecture; it prohibits partnership with a disqualified person; it prohibits the taking of bribes; it prohibits the improper influencing of statutory approvals; it requires the architect to notify the client of anything likely to breach this principle and if so to either withdraw from the engagement or to obtain the agreement of the client for the continuation of the commission; it requires the member to have proper regard for the status of the architect to whom he gives, or from whom he receives, authority.

4.05 Principle 3 endeavours to ensure that advancement of a member is on the basis of ability and achievement alone. It prohibits the giving of discounts for the introduction of work; it requires fees to be quoted only when the nature of the work is known; it prohibits fee auctions; it prohibits the supplanting of another architect; it requires a member to notify any other architect who may have previously been engaged upon the project; it allows most forms of advertising of services provided that it is not misleading, unfair, or discreditable to the profession; and it restricts competition entries to those approved by RIBA regulations.

24

Professional Conduct in Scotland

GEORGE BURNET

1 Introduction

1.01 An architect practising in Scotland can find himself subject to three Codes of Conduct – the RIAS Code, the RIBA Code, and the Code issued by ARCUK – and hopefully a 'super' Code will be published in due course combining the best features of all three. Unfortunately, this has not been found possible so far, but at least there has been some slight improvement inasmuch as, although there are still three Codes, they all now reflect modern attitudes and thinking, and generally speaking permit or forbid the same course of conduct. In particular the RIAS and the RIBA Codes both reflect the abolition, at government insistence, of fee Scales – mandatory or otherwise – and recognize the existence of fee competition which is becoming more and more the norm.

1.02 In method of presentation the RIAS and the RIBA Codes are still widely different, and this must tend to confuse the layman and possibly also, at times, members of the architectural profession. It should still be possible for the RIAS and the RIBA to have identical Codes of Conduct, and both bodies must surely work towards this goal. The existence of a separate RIAS Code stems from the fact that the RIAS is rightly proud of the fact that it is a body with its own Royal Charter formed in 1916, at a time when the voice of the RIBA was seldom heard in Scotland and when many architects practising in that country belonged only to the RIAS and not to the RIBA. Times have changed, and although the RIBA has delegated practically all its functions in Scotland to the RIAS, it has tended to retain under its own control the procedure for disciplining its members: this has meant that contrary to the hopes and aspirations voiced in earlier editions, occasions do arise when an architect can be 'tried' twice for the same offence – once under the RIBA disciplinary proceedings and again under the RIAS procedure.

1.03 While at first glance this may well seem contrary to the basic principle of natural justice, it must be pointed out that if an architect chooses to belong to both the RIBA and the RIAS (to neither of which he need belong to practise as an architect), he must be assumed to be agreeing to subject himself to the Codes of both organizations, and if transgressing these Codes, must run the risk of being disciplined separately by both. It must always be remembered that the RIAS can discipline only its own members and cannot, therefore, take action against a member of the RIBA practising in Scotland, unless such a member also belongs to the RIAS; nor, of course, can it proceed against a member under any provision of the RIBA Code. At the present time the majority of architects practising in Scotland belong to
308

both organizations, although there is a growing tendency among newly qualified architects to seek membership of the RIAS.

2 The RIAS Code

2.01 The current RIAS Code of Conduct was approved by the members of the Royal Incorporation at a general meeting held in March 1982, and took effect on 1 July 1982. It is, in effect, not so much a Code as a Statement of Professional Conduct that consists solely of one paragraph: 'A Member shall be mindful of the Declaration signed by him upon his election, and in particular of his responsibility for upholding the repute of the Royal Incorporation as a professional body and of his fellow Members as individuals. Dishonouring of the Declaration shall be held to constitute unprofessional conduct, and as such will be dealt with by Council.'

2.02 The Declaration referred to in the Statement is in the following terms: 'I declare that I have read the Charter and Bye-Law of the said Incorporation and the Bye-Laws of my Chapter, and will be governed and bound thereby, and will submit myself to every part thereof and to any alterations thereof which may hereafter be made until I have ceased to be a member; and that by every lawful means in my power I will advance the interests and objects of the said Incorporation.'

2.03 The preamble to the Statement makes it clear that an architect who contravenes the declaration renders himself liable in terms of the bye-laws to reprimand, suspension, or expulsion. The same bye-laws also authorize the Council of the RIAS to issue from time to time intimations defining action to be taken on current matters of professional conduct, and these intimations, in practical terms, point an architect in the direction in which he should be going.

3 Intimations

3.01 The following are the intimations published by the Council simultaneously with the adoption of the Statement of Professional Conduct:

1. 'A Member in practice shall observe the provisions for Conduct and Discipline adopted by ARCUK on 17 June 1981.'

While there is no similar Principle or Rule (as they are called) in the RIBA Code, it may be compared with rule 2.5 interpreting principle 2 of that Code. Membership of

ARCUK is one of the qualifications required for election to Associate or Fellowship of the RIAS.

2. 'If a Member engages in any activity concurrent or otherwise with that as architect, he shall at all times act in compliance with the spirit of the Declaration.'

This intimation may be compared with rule 2.2 of the RIBA Code. Although not specific in its terms, it is presumably intended to achieve the same result as the RIBA Rule – to ensure that if an architect is in fact acting as a house agent or a property developer, for example, this role is subordinate to his professions as an architect and in the spirit of the overriding Declaration.

3. 'A Member shall not in his capacity as an architect accept any trade or other discounts. However, this does not prohibit receipt by a member of the discounts which are customary and normal when engaged in commercial activities otherwise than as an architect.'

This is similar to rule 3.1 to principle 3 of the RIBA Code and recognizes the accepted custom in the contracting industry that trade and cash discounts are frequently allowed by manufacturers or suppliers.

4. 'If a Member wishes to make approaches to individuals and organizations or make public display of his work or advertise his services in any other way, he should have care to observe the spirit of the Declaration signed by each member upon election.'

This intimation corresponds to rule 3.6 of principle 3 of the RIBA Code and reflects the freedom to advertise now permitted to the profession. In the last few years all professions – not least the architectural profession – have begun to advertise their services and the boundary between an acceptable and an unacceptable advertisement is often difficult to define.

5. 'If a Member at any stage attempts to supplant another architect by any means, he may be found by Council to have contravened the Declaration.'

This intimation is directly comparable to rule 3.14 to principle 3 of the RIBA Code, and the prohibition against an attempt to supplant another architect remains as adamant as ever.

6. 'A Member having any matter of complaint or protest against another member of the profession must in the first instance bring the matter before the Council of the Incorporation through his own Chapter, and must on no account make any other protest.'

Strangely enough, there is no comparable principle to this intimation in the RIBA Code, although it has always found a place in Codes of Conduct issued by the RIAS. Its absence from the RIBA Code is surprising, as it provides a dignified way of resolving disputes between architects, and its value has been proved on many occasions in the history of the RIAS.

7. 'If a Member undertakes any architectural commission he shall arrange for the architectural work on that commission to be under the control of an architect.'

This intimation is the equivalent of rule 1.2 to principle 1 of the RIBA Code. It is, however, more widely expressed, although clearly covering the limited situations envisaged by the RIBA rule.

8. 'If a Member is invited or instructed to proceed with work upon which he knows or which he can ascertain by reasonable enquiry that another architect has been engaged by the same client, he shall notify the fact to such artefact.'

Rule 3.5 to principle 3 of the RIBA Code is identical to this intimation. Until recently it was fairly generally understood that an architect approached by a client who had previously employed another architect should not accept that client's instructions until satisfied that fees due to the first architect had been paid in full. It seems clear, in fact, that there is no such duty and that all the second architect is required to do is to send a simple notification to the original architect informing him of his appointment, and thereafter no further action is required.

9. 'A Member shall have regard to the RIAS Architect's Appointment.'

This intimation is similar to rule 1.1.1 to principle 1 of the RIBA Code.

10. 'A Member offering services as an independent consulting architect shall not quote a fee without having received from the prospective client an invitation to do so, and sufficient information to enable the member to know the nature and scope of the project and the services required.'

11. 'A Member offering services as an independent consulting architect shall not revise a fee quotation to take account of the fee quoted by another architect for the same service.'

These two intimations which can conveniently be considered together are in similar terms to rules 3.2 and 3.3 to principle 3 of the RIBA Code. They mark the end of the mandatory fee scales which were abolished by both the RIAS and the RIBA in 1982. Both organizations still publish *recommended* fee scales and while in practice these may be used as 'a bench mark' in many sectors fees are frequently negotiated down from these levels. The clear instruction contained in intimation 11 ensures that in no circumstances may any form of 'auction' take place after an architect has submitted his quotation to his potential client.

12. 'A Member handling money belonging to a client shall be required to comply with the Client Account Rules approved by the Council on 29 November 1989 and any amendments thereto which may be subsequently approved by the Council.'

This important intimation corresponds with rule 2.10 of principle 2 of the RIBA Code. Both the RIAS and the RIBA (whose Client Account Rules were issued in 1986) have now come to grips with the fact that there are occasions when architects have to handle clients' money (although both organizations advise members to avoid this if possible) and their failure to do this in a business-like and efficient way is undoubtedly a major source of complaint by clients. While the RIAS and the RIBA Client Account Rules are not identical they each lay down a clearly defined Code for dealing with clients' money which must be complied with. The RIBA Rules contain a statement making it clear that a member of the RIBA who is also obliged to follow the Client Account Rules of the RIAS, will be deemed to have satisfied the RIBA Rules if he complies with the Rules of the RIAS.

4 Conclusion

4.01 Whatever merits there may be in a single paragraph statement – and from the point of view of the RIAS Council they are considerable – it does place a firm duty on that Council to ensure that members of the RIAS are kept fully aware of how the Council interprets the Statement and the Declaration by issuing further intimations as and when they are necessary. The recent publication of intimation 12 and of the Client Account Rules is a clear indication of the Council's determination to do this.

Bibliography

General books on law and procedure affecting the construction industry

Burns, A. (1989) *Construction Disputes: Liability and the Expert Witness,* Butterworths, London

Fay, E. (1988) *Official Referee's Business* (2nd edn), Sweet and Maxwell, London

Fenwick-Elliot, R. J. (1988) *Building Contract Litigation* (3rd edn) Longman, London

Hudson: Building and Engineering Contracts (10th edn) (1970) Wallace, I. N. Duncan (ed.), also 1979 Supplement, Sweet and Maxwell, London

Ilff, J. (1985) *Construction Law* (4th edn), Sweet and Maxwell, London

Phillips, E. and Serjeantson, M. (1988) *Legal Reminders for Architects,* Butterworth Architecture, London

Liability generally

Burns, A. (1990) *The Architect: Liabilities,* Butterworths, London

Cecil, R. (1984) *Professional Liability,* Butterworth Architecture, London

Charlesworth and Percy on Negligence (7th edn) (1983) Percey, R. A. (ed.), also 1989 Supplement, Sweet and Maxwell, London

Chitty on Contracts (1989) Guest, A. G. (ed.), also 1990 Supplement, Sweet and Maxwell, London

Clerk and Lindsell on the Law of Torts (16th edn) (1989) Dias, R. W. M. (ed.), Sweet and Maxwell, London

Cornes, D. L. (1989) *Design Liability in the Construction Industry* (3rd edn) BSP Professional, Oxford

Jackson, R. and Powell, J. (1987) *Professional Negligence* (2nd edn) Sweet and Maxwell, London

A Legal Guide to the Professional Liability of Architects, RIBA Publications, London

Speaight, A. and Stone, G. (1982) *The Law of Defective Premises,* Pitman, London

Thomas, N. P. G. (1990) *Professional Indemnity Claims* (2nd edn), Butterworth Architecture, London

Treitel, G. H. (1989) *An Outline of the Law of Contract* (4th edn) Butterworths, London

Your Professional Liability, RIBA Publications, London

Arbitration

Bernstein, R. (1987) *Handbook of Arbitration Practice,* Sweet and Maxwell, London

Johnstone, R. J. M. (ed.) (1987) *The Architect as Arbitrator,* RIBA Publications, London

Grill: The Law of Arbitration (3rd edn) (1983) Marshall, Enid A. (ed.) Sweet and Maxwell, London

Mustill, Sir Michael and Boyd, S. (1989) *Commercial Arbitration* (2nd edn) Butterworths, London

Walton, A. (1982) *Russell on Arbitration* (20th edn) Sweet and Maxwell, London

Building Contracts

Architect's Appointment (1982) RIBA Publications, London

Chappell, D. and Powell-Smith, V. (1985) *JCT Intermediate Form of Contract,* Butterworth Architecture, London

Chappell, D. and Powell-Smith, V. (1986) *JCT Minor Works Form of Contract,* Butterworth Architecture, London

Cherry, I. S. (1985) *JCT 80 and the Design Team,* Butterworth Architecture, London

Code of Procedure for Fee Tendering, RIBA Publications, London

Code of Procedure for Selective Tendering for Design and Building, RIBA Publications, London

Emden's Building Contracts and Practice (8th edn) (1980) Bickford-Smith, S. and Freeth, E. (eds), Butterworths, London

Emden's Construction Law, Andsom, A. J. *et al.* (eds), Butterworths, London

Greenstreet, R. (1989) *Legal and Contractual Procedures for Architects* (3rd edn) Butterworth Architecture, London

Handbook of Architectural Practice (5th edn) (1990), RIBA Publications, London

JCT Guide to the Standard Form of Building Contract (1980), RIBA Publications, London

JCT Nominated Sub-contracts (1980) RIBA Publications, London

JCT Standard Form of Building Contract, Scottish Supplement (1988) , SBCC Publications

Keating, D. (1978) *Building Contracts* (4th edn), also 1984 Supplement, Sweet and Maxwell, London

Meopham, B. (1986) *FIDIC Conditions of Contract – a commercial manual*

Powell-Smith, V. and Chappell, D. (1985) *Building Contract Dictionary,* Butterworth Architecture, London

Copyright

Copinger and Skone James on Copyright (13th edn) (1990) Skone James, E. P., Mummery, J. F. and Rayner, J. E. (eds), Sweet and Maxwell, London

Flint, M. F. (1990) *A User's Guide to Copyright* (3rd edn), Butterworths, London

Laddie, H. L., Prescott, P. and Vitoria, M. (1991) *The Modern Law of Copyright* (2nd edn), Butterworths, London

Employment

Guide to Employment Practice, RIBA Publications, London

Guide to Group Practice and Consortia (1965), RIBA Publications, London

Harvey: Industrial Relations and Employment Law (Looseleaf Service) Elias, P. *et al.* (eds), Butterworths, London

European Community Law

1992 – An Information Pack for Architects (1989) RIBA Publications, London

Note: The RIBA will be publishing *Country Profiles* on architectural practice in Europe. The first of these will be published on France in September, closely followed by a Country Profile in relation to Iberia: Spain and Portugal.

Land Law

Burn, E. H. (1988) *Modern Law of Real Property* (14th edn), Butterworths, London

Gray, K. J. (1987) *Elements of Land Law,* Butterworths, London

Megarry (1982) *Manual of the Law of Real Property* (6th edn), Stevens and Sons, London

Megarry and Wade (1984) *Tha Law of Real Property* (5th edn) Stevens and Sons, London

Partnership and Company Law

Charlesworth's Company Law (13th edn) (1987) Morse, G., Marshall, E. and Morris R. (eds), Sweet and Maxwell, London

Gower's Principles of Modern Company Law (4th edn) (1979) Gower, L. C. B., *et al.* (eds), also 1988 Supplement, Sweet and Maxwell, London

Hardy Ivamy, E. R. (1985) *Dictionary of Company Law* (2nd edn), Butterworths, London

Lindley on Partnership (15th edn) (1984) Scannell, E. H. and l'Anson Banks, R. C. (eds), Sweet and Maxwell, London

Underhill:- Principles of the Law of Partnerships (20th edn) (1986) Hardy Ivamy, E. R. (ed.), Butterworths, London

Planning

Cross on Local Government Law (7th edn) (1986) Cross, C. and Bailey, S. (eds), Sweet and Maxwell, London

Elder, A. J. (1989) *Guide to the Building Regulations 1985* (2nd edn), Butterworth Architecture, London

Garner, J. F. (1990) *The Law of Sewers and Drains* (2nd edn), Shaw and Sons, London

Grant, M. (1982) *Urban Planning Law,* also 1990 Supplement, Sweet and Maxwell, London

Heap, Sir Desmond (1987) *An Outline of Planning Law* (9th edn), Sweet and Maxwell, London

Powell-Smith, V. and Billington, M. J. (1990) *The Building Regulations Explained and Illustrated* (8th edn), BSP Professional Books, London

Sauvain, S. (1989) *Highway Law and Practice,* Sweet and Maxwell, London

Miller, J. B. (1973) *Law of Partnership in Scotland* (2nd edn), Sweet and Maxwell, London

Professional Conduct for Architects

Code of Professional Conduct, RIBA Publications, London

Conduct and Discipline (1989), ARCUK Publications, London

The Functions of Architects (1987) ARCUK Publications, London

Statutory Authorities

Cross on Local Government Law (7th edn) (1986) Cross, C. and Bailey, S. (eds), Sweet and Maxwell, London

Lewis, J. R. (1976) *Administrative Law for the Construction Industry,* Macmillan, London

Pitt, P. H. (1987) *Guide to Building Control by Local Acts,* Butterworth Architecture, London

Pitt, P. H. (1987) *Guide to Building Control in Inner London,* Butterworth Architecture, London

Table of Statutes and Statutory Instruments

Table of Cases

Index